ABIOLA DEBORAH LENTILES STUDY BIBLE

ABIOLA DEBORAH LENTILES STUDY BIBLE

Book of Matthew : Volume I

Abiola Adaramola Ariyehun

ISBN:	Softcover	978-1-5035-6447-3
	eBook	978-1-5035-6446-6

Print information available on the last page.

Rev. date:01/21/2016

To order additional copies of this book, contact:
Xlibris
1-888-795-4274
www.Xlibris.com
Orders@Xlibris.com
710453

ACKNOWLEDGEMENTS AND REFERENCES

The 1600s King James Bible version used is the old king James free to publish and in public domain The bulk of the meanings of Bible names references are from: Hitchcock's Bible Names Dictionary published 1869, in public domain; and others from Williams Smith's Bible Dictionary published 1863, in public domain; and King James Bible Dictionary published in 1828.

Bible Measurements and Jewish calendar from the internet-www. biblestudio.com/weights_and_measures/

Mathematical Four figure tables; **Logarithm** is another word for **Power**

Logarithm in Greek language is a combination of **Logos** meaning **"word"** and **arithmos** meaning **"numbers"**

Logarithm is the mathematical raising of base number: the power to which a base must be raised to equal a given number. For example, the logarithm of 4 to the base 2 is 2, since $2^2 = 4$.

Laws of Logarithm

Log (MN) = LogM + LogN ; Log M/N = LogM - LogN ; Log (M^p) = pLog M

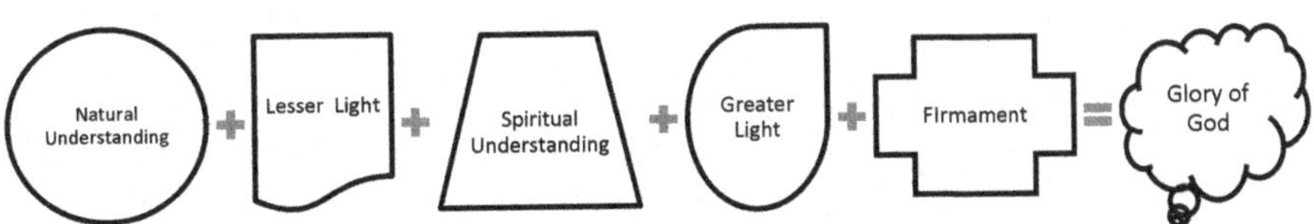

BROOKS OF THE BIBLE CHART

BROOK OF ARNON-----REJOICING, SUNLIGHT

BROOK OF GAASH----TEMPEST, COMMOTION

BROOK OF ESHCOL-----BUNCH OF GRAPES

BROOK OF ZERED----- DYER'S VAT

BROOK OF BEZOR-----GLAD NEWS; INCARNATION

BROOK KIDRON-----OBSCURE, MAKING BLACK OR SAD

BROOK CHERITH----- CUTTING; PIERCING; SLAYING

BROOK KISON----- HARD; SORE

BROOK CEDRON---------- BLACK; SAD

BROOK OF HONEY AND BUTTER--------- SEVEN SPIRITS OF GOD AND THE ANNOINTING

BROOK OF DEFENSE----------THE CHARACTER OF THE LORD

LENTILES BIBLICAL MEANING OF NUMBERS TABULATION

BIBLE MEANING	BIBLE NUMBERS	LEAST COMMON MULTIPLES LCM
Absolute Singleness in Purpose, Will, Mind And Emotion or Magnetized State; Unique, Sole, Single, Lone, Solitary, Exceptional, Exclusive, Rare, Inimitable, Distinctive, Matchless, Irreplaceable	1 (one)	1 x 1
Earliest, Initial, Original, Foremost, Opening, Primary, Former	1 (first)	1 x 1
Witness And Support	2	1 x 2
Completion Or Perfection And Unity	3	1 x 3
Balance Or Earth	4	2 x 2
Grace	5	1 x 5
Man	6	2 x 3
Divine Perfection Or Completeness	7	1 x 7
New Beginnings	8	2 x 2 x 2
Fullness Of Blessing	9	3 x 3

Human Governments And Law Or Commandment	10	2 x 5
Disperse or Disorder or Confusion	11	1 x 11
Divine Government Or Dominion	12	2 x 2 x 3
Rebellion and Divine Atonement	13	1 x 13
Mourning And Sorrow Or Maturity	30	2 x 3 x 5
Testing And Trials Or Enlighten	40	2 x 2 x 2 x 5
Feasts, Celebrations, And Ceremonies	50	2 x 5 x 5
Judgment And Human Delegations	70	2 x 5 x 7
Beast (Man - Man - Man)	666 (600 + 60 + 6)	(2 x 2 x 2 x 3 x 5 x 5) + (2 x 2 x 3 x 5) + (2 x 3)

LENTILES PARTS OF SPEECH CHART

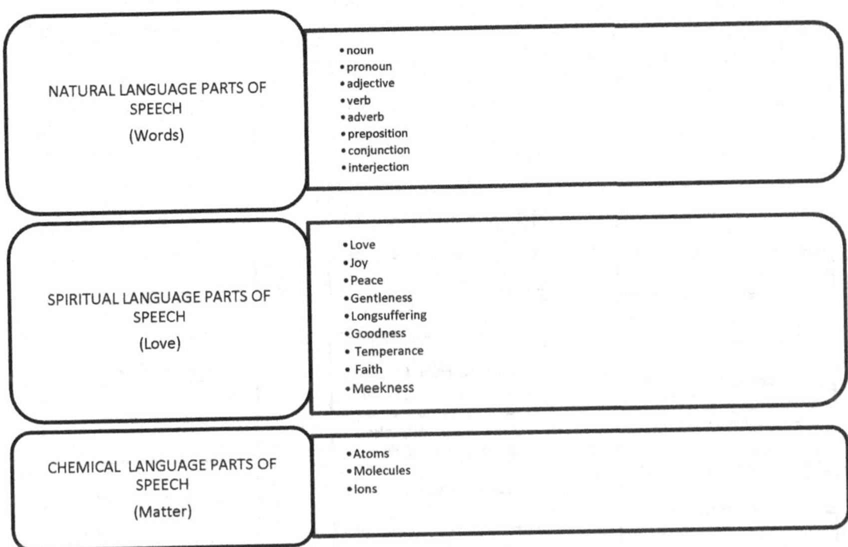

Rules of spiritual language: Jer.9:24- But let him that glorieth glory in this, that he understandeth and knoweth me, that I am the LORD which exercise **lovingkindness, judgement,** and **righteousness,** in the earth: for in these things I delight, saith the LORD.

Rules of natural language: the system of rules by which words are formed and put together to make sentences; the rules for speaking or writing a particular language; a systematic treatment of the elementary principles of a subject and their interrelationships.

Rules or Laws of Chemical Combination or Language: Atom can neither be created nor destroyed but change from one form to another;All pure samples of a particular chemical compound contain similar elements combined in the same proportion by mass; If two elements, A and B, combine to form more than one chemical compound, then the various masses of one element, A, which combine separately with a fixed mass of the other element, B, are in simple multiple ratio; The masses of several elements, A, B, C, which combine separately with a fixed mass of another element, D, are the same as, or simple multiples of, the masses in which A, B, C, themselves combine with one another.

LENTILES BOND CHART

NATURAL SPEECH BONDS

- comma ,
- colon :
- full stop .
- semi colon ;
- quotation marks ' ' " "
- hyphen -
- bracket ( )
- dash –
- question mark ?
- apostrophe '
- exclamation mark or point !

SPIRITUAL/LOVE SPEECH BONDS

- Charity suffereth long, and is kind
- charity envieth not
- charity vaunteth not itself, is not puffed up
- Doth not behave itself unseemly
- seeketh not her own
- is not easily provoked
- Rejoiceth not in iniquity, but in truth
- thinketh no evil
- Beareth all things
- believeth all things
- hopeth all things
- endureth all things

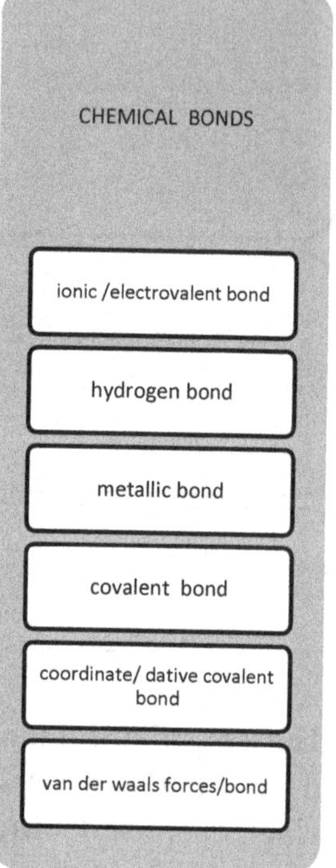

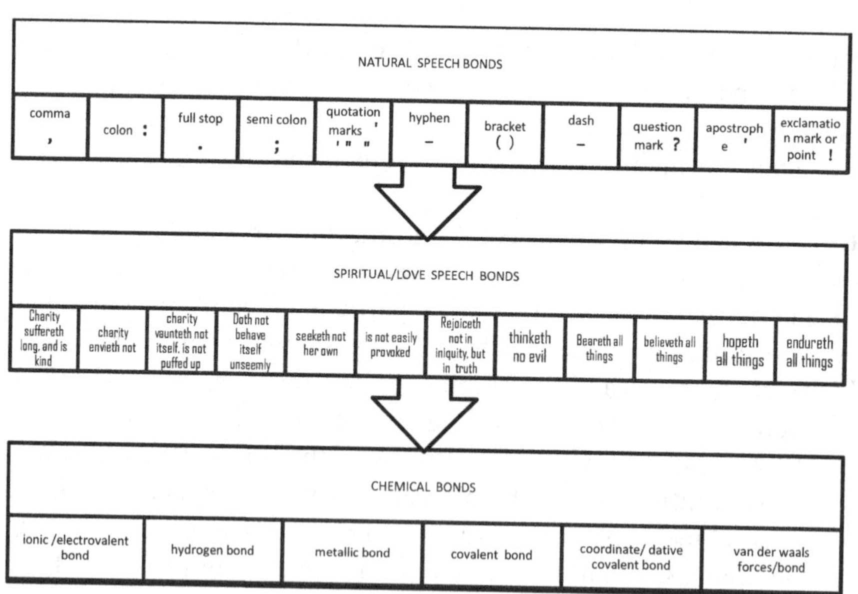

GRAPH OF PERFECTION

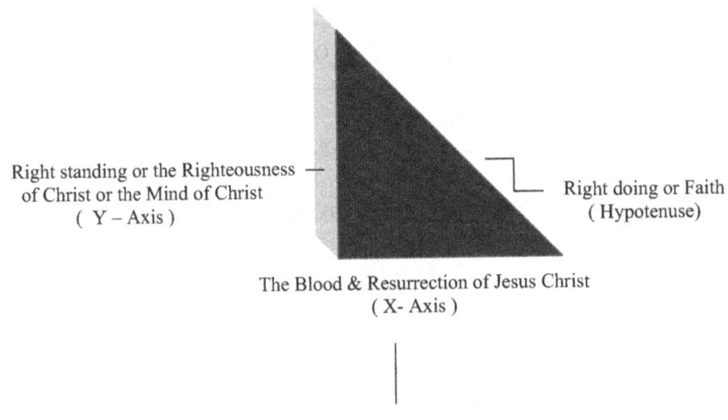

2 Sam 23:11

After him was Shammah fame; renown; eminence; distinction; legend; loss; desolation; astonishment **the son of Agee** fugitive; a valley; deepness **the Hararite** the mountaineer. **And the Philistines** immigrants; settler; migrant; refugee; those who dwell in villages **were gathered together into a troop, where was a piece of ground full of LENTILES: and the people fled from the Philistines** immigrant; colonizer; those who dwell in villages

10.9, 9:7 Bible Matrices

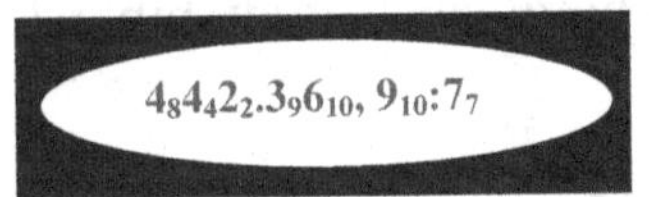

Pilled Poplar, Hazel, Chestnut bible rods 1

$\log_8 4 = y$	$\log_4 4 = y$	$\log_2 2 = y$	$\log_9 3 = y$	$\log_7 7 = y$	$\log_{10} 6 = 0.7782$	$\log_{10} 9 = 0.9542$
$8^y = 4^1$	$4^y = 4$	$2^y = 2$	$9^y = 3$	$7^y = 7^1$		
$2^{3y} = 2^2$	$2^{2y} = 2^2$	$y = 1$	$3^{2y} = 3^1$	$y = 1$		
$3y = 2$	$2y = 2$		$2y = 1$			
$y = 2/3$	$y = 1$		$y = 1/2$			

10.9, 9:7 Deep calls unto deep study bible 1

2/3 1 1 . ½ 0.7782, 0.9542 : 1 Deep calls to Deep study bible 2

X-axis	Y-axis
10	2.7
9	1.2782
9	0.9532
7	1

Water Spout *(lightning; combinatorics)* study bible 1

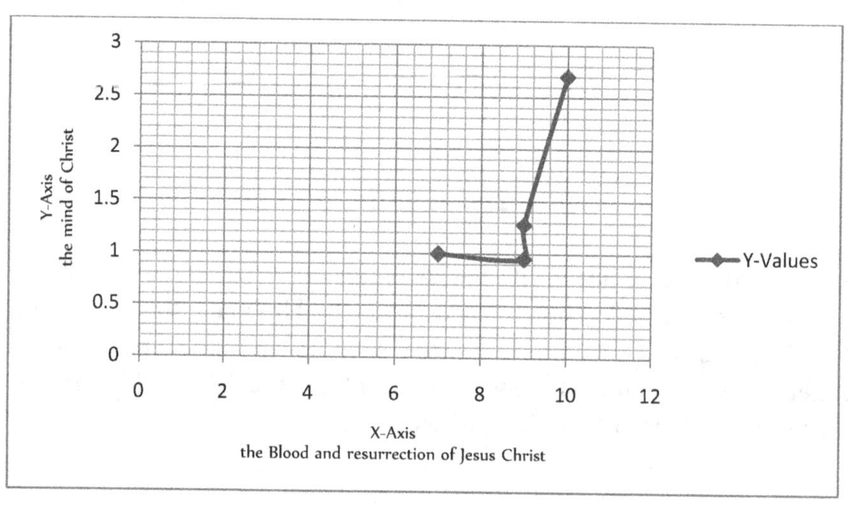

Water Spout *(lightning; combinatorics)* study bible 2

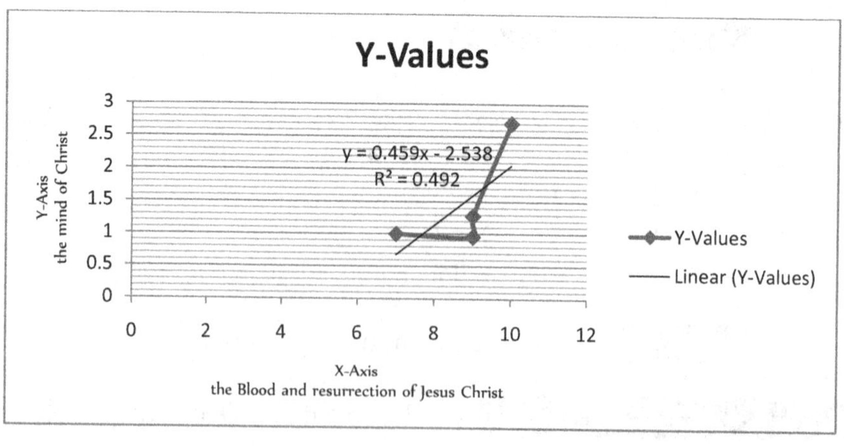

$8^{0.7}4^{1}\,2^{1}.\ 9^{0.5}\,10^{0.7782},\ 10^{0.9542}:7^{1}$

Pilled Poplar, Hazel, Chestnut bible rods 2

Applying the knowledge of bible matrices to a BOOK by Derek Prince titled **Life's bitter Pool**, we have the following scriptures references

Exodus 15 vs 19 – 26; Galatians 3 vs 13 – 14; 1 Peter 2 vs 24; Isaiah 53 vs 5;
Deuteronomy 21 vs 23; Malachi 3 vs 6; Hebrews 13 vs 8; Exodus 19 vs 4; Psalms 73 vs 26; Isaiah 12 vs 2; Matthew 11 vs 28; Hosea 2 vs 14 – 16; 2 Corinthians 1 vs 8-10; James 1 vs 2-4

This is a triangular matrix book with an order of 28 x 8 read as

Twenty eight by eight

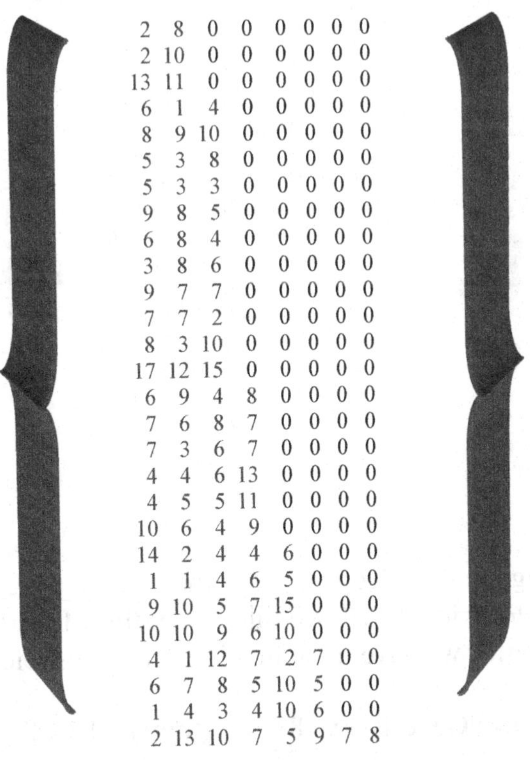

2	8	0	0	0	0	0	0
2	10	0	0	0	0	0	0
13	11	0	0	0	0	0	0
6	1	4	0	0	0	0	0
8	9	10	0	0	0	0	0
5	3	8	0	0	0	0	0
5	3	3	0	0	0	0	0
9	8	5	0	0	0	0	0
6	8	4	0	0	0	0	0
3	8	6	0	0	0	0	0
9	7	7	0	0	0	0	0
7	7	2	0	0	0	0	0
8	3	10	0	0	0	0	0
17	12	15	0	0	0	0	0
6	9	4	8	0	0	0	0
7	6	8	7	0	0	0	0
7	3	6	7	0	0	0	0
4	4	6	13	0	0	0	0
4	5	5	11	0	0	0	0
10	6	4	9	0	0	0	0
14	2	4	4	6	0	0	0
1	1	4	6	5	0	0	0
9	10	5	7	15	0	0	0
10	10	9	6	10	0	0	0
4	1	12	7	2	7	0	0
6	7	8	5	10	5	0	0
1	4	3	4	10	6	0	0
2	13	10	7	5	9	7	8

Applying the knowledge of bible matrices to a SERMON by Pastor Olubi Johnson titled **Praying with your Thoughts**, we have the following scriptures references

1 Thessalonians 5 vs 17 – 18; Luke 21 vs 36 – 37; Philippians 4 vs 5 – 8; 2 Corinthians 13 vs 14;
Proverbs 23 vs 7; John 20 vs 25; Psalm 116 vs 9 – 10; 2 Corinthians 4 vs 13; Deuteronomy 30 vs 14; 2 Corinthians 10 vs 5; 1 John 5 vs 16; 1 John 2 vs 12 – 14

This is a triangular matrix sermon with an order of 20 x 11 read as

twenty by eleven

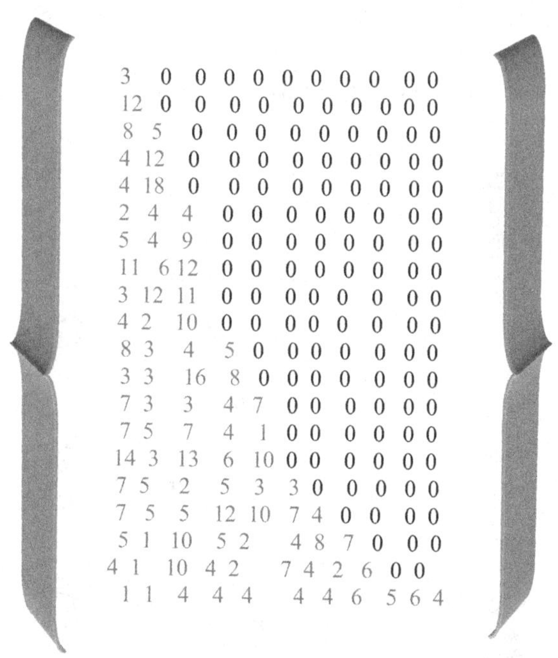

3	0	0	0	0	0	0	0	0	0	0
12	0	0	0	0	0	0	0	0	0	0
8	5	0	0	0	0	0	0	0	0	0
4	12	0	0	0	0	0	0	0	0	0
4	18	0	0	0	0	0	0	0	0	0
2	4	4	0	0	0	0	0	0	0	0
5	4	9	0	0	0	0	0	0	0	0
11	6	12	0	0	0	0	0	0	0	0
3	12	11	0	0	0	0	0	0	0	0
4	2	10	0	0	0	0	0	0	0	0
8	3	4	5	0	0	0	0	0	0	0
3	3	16	8	0	0	0	0	0	0	0
7	3	3	4	7	0	0	0	0	0	0
7	5	7	4	1	0	0	0	0	0	0
14	3	13	6	10	0	0	0	0	0	0
7	5	2	5	3	3	0	0	0	0	0
7	5	5	12	10	7	4	0	0	0	0
5	1	10	5	2	4	8	7	0	0	0
4	1	10	4	2	7	4	2	6	0	0
1	1	4	4	4	4	4	6	5	6	4

Applying the knowledge of bible matrices to a SERMON by Pastor Alex Adegboye titled **Location! Location!! Location!!!**, we have the following scriptures references

Hebrews 11 vs 6; Genesis 3 vs 8 – 10; Romans 1 vs 17; Galatians 3 vs 11;

Hebrews 10 vs 38; Habakukk 2 vs 4; Exodus 32 vs 26; 2 Chronicles 16 vs 9; Luke 8 vs 24-25; Luke 22 vs 31; 1 Timothy 5 vs 8; Romans 10 vs 6 – 11; Luke 13 vs 19; Hebrews 11 vs 13.

This is a triangular matrix sermon with an order of 22 x 11 read as

Twenty two by eleven

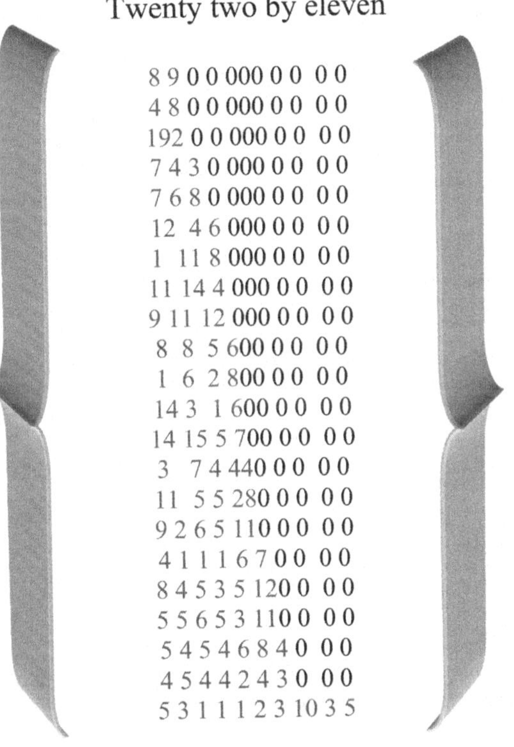

NEW TESTAMENT

MATTHEW

CHAPTER 1

1. The book of the generation of Jesus Christ anointed savior, **the son of David** beloved; dear, **the son of Abraham** father of great multitude.

8, 4, 4. Bible Matrices

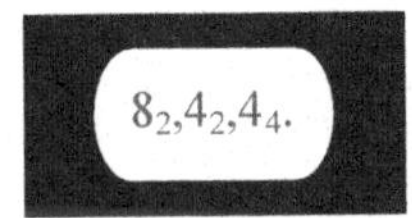

$8_2, 4_2, 4_4.$

Pilled Poplar, Hazel, Chestnut bible rods 1

$\log_2 8 = y,$

$2^y = 8 = 2^3$

$y = 3$

$\log_2 4 = y,$

$2^y = 2^2$

$y = 2$

$\log_4 4 = y$

Then $4^y = 4$

$2^{2y} = 2^2$

$2y = 2$

$y = 1$

8, 4, 4. Deep calls unto Deep study bible 1

3, 2, 1. Deep calls unto Deep study bible 2

X-Axis	Y-Axis
8	3
4	2
4	1

Water Spout *(lightning; combinatorics)* study bible 1

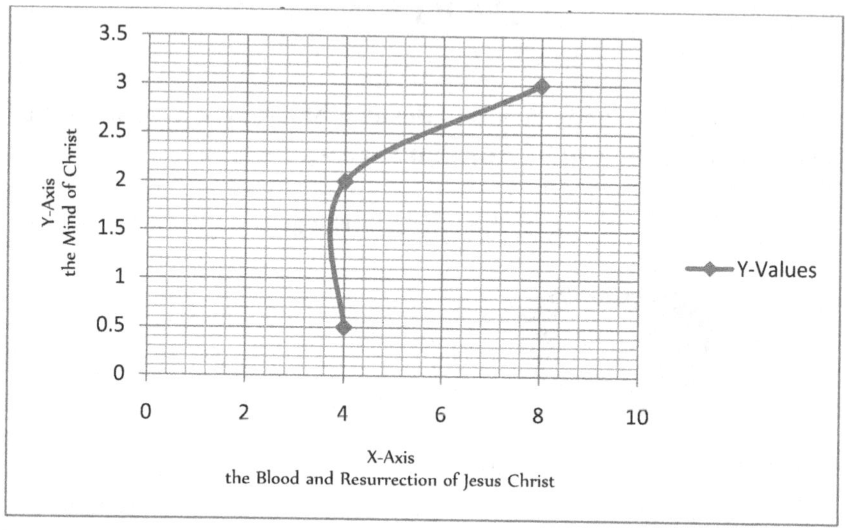

Water Spout *(lightning;combinatoric)* Study Bible 2

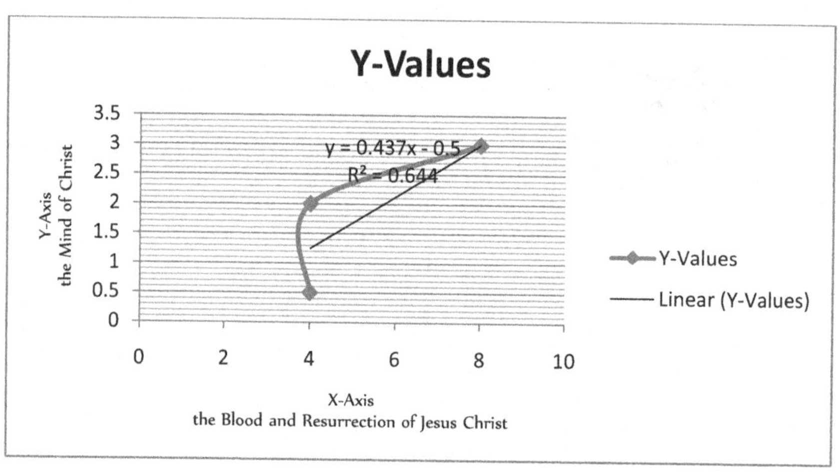

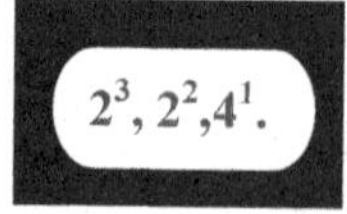

Pilled Poplar, Hazel, Chestnut bible rods 2

2. Abraham father of great multitudes **begat Isaac** laughter; sound; **and Isaac** laughter; sound **begat Jacob** supplanter, undermines; the heel; **and Jacob** supplanter, undermines; the heel **begat Judas** praise of the Lord; confession of the Lord **and his brethren;**

3;4;7; Bible Matrices

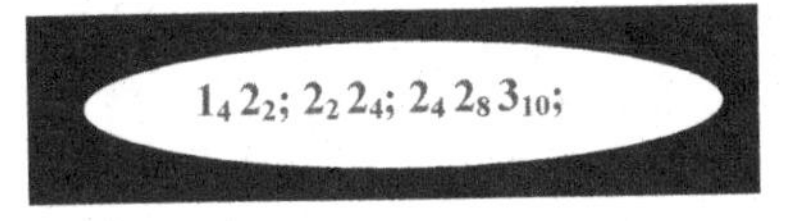

Pilled Poplar Hazel, Chestnut bible rods 1

$\text{Log}_4 1 = y$ $\text{Log}_2 2 = y$ $\log_2 2 = y$ $\log_4 2 = y$ $\log_4 2 = x$ $\log_8 2 = y$ $\log_{10} 3 = 0.4771$

$4^y = 4^0 = 0$ $2^y = 2^1, y = 1$ $2^y = 2^1, y = 1$ $4^y = 2, 2^{2y} = 2^1,$ $4^y = 2, 2^{2y} = 2^1,$ $8^y = 2^1, 2^{3y} = 2^1$

y =1/2 or 0.5. y =1/2 or 0.5. y = 1/3

3; 4; 7 ; Deep calls unto Deep study bible 1

0 1; 1 ½ ; ½ 1/3 0.4771 ; Deep calls unto Deep study bible 2

X-axis	Y-axis
3	1
4	1.5
7	1.3071

Water Spout *(lightning;combinatorics)* Study Bible 1

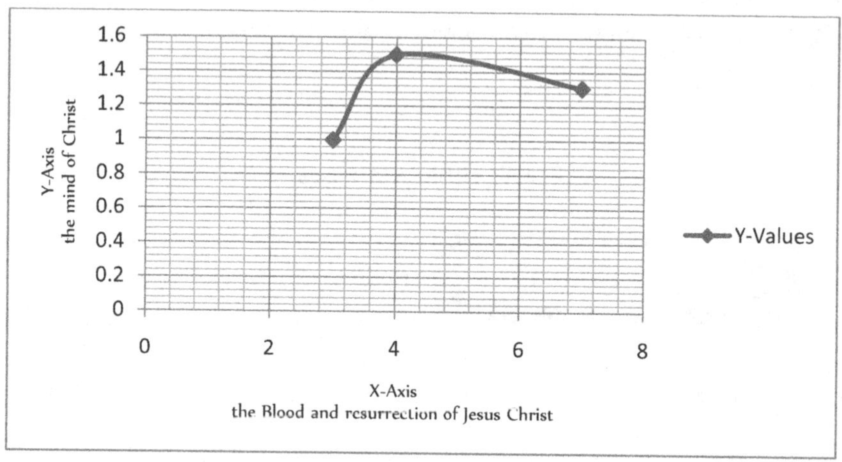

Water Spout *(lightning;combinatorics)* Study Bible 2

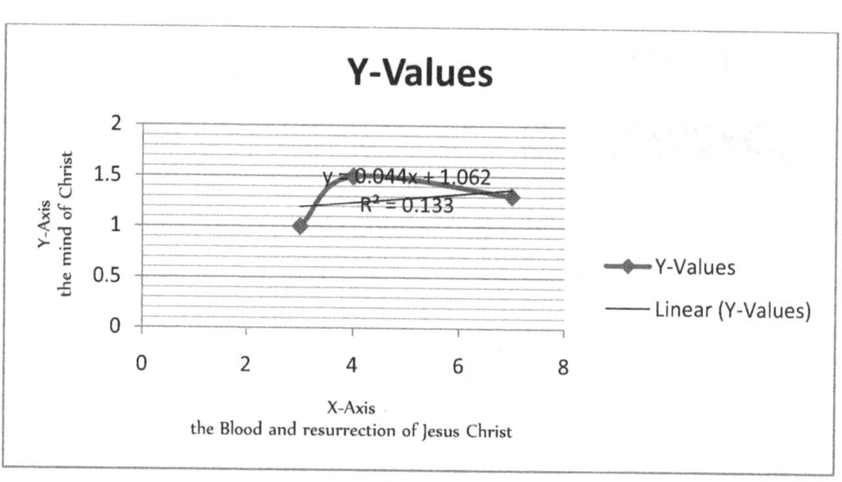

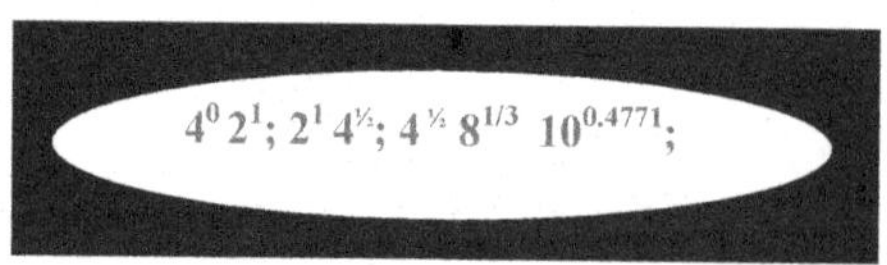

Pilled Poplar Hazel, Chestnut bible rods 2

3. And Judas praise of the Lord; confession of the Lord **begat Phares** divided; breach; rupture; split **and Zara** east; brightness; sunrise;dawn **of Thamar** palm; palm-tree; **and Phares** divided; breach; rupture; crack **begat Esrom**dart of joy; division of a song; enclosed; **and Esrom** dart of joy; division of a song; enclosed **begat Aram** highness; magnificence; deceives; curse;

8; 4; 4; Bible Matrices

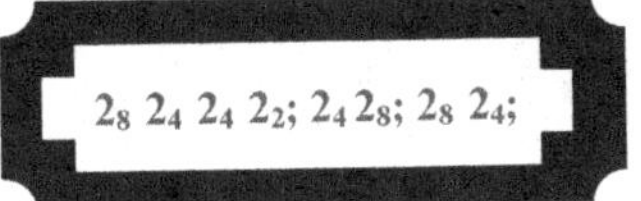

Pilled Poplar, Hazel, and Chesnut bible rods 1

$\text{Log}_8 2 = y$	$\text{Log}_4 2 = y$	$\log_4 2 = y$	$\log_2 2 = y$	$\log_4 2 = y$	$\log_8 2 = y$	$\log_8 2 = y$	$\log_4 2 = y$
$8^y = 2^1$	$4^y = 2$	$4^y = 2^1$	$2^y = 2^1$	$4^y = 2^1$	$8^y = 2^1$	$8^y = 2^1$	$4^y = 2^1$
$2^{3y} = 2^1$	$2^{2y} = 2^1$	$2^{2y} = 2^1$	$y = 1$	$2^{2y} = 2^1$	$2^{3y} = 2^1$	$2^{3y} = 2^1$	$2^{2y} = 2^1$
$3y = 1$	$2y = 1$	$2y = 1$	$2y = 1$	$3y = 1$	$3y = 1$	$2y = 1$	
$y = 1/3$	$y = ½$	$y = ½$	$y = ½$	$y = 1/3$	$y = 1/3$	$y = ½$	

8; 4; 4 Deep calls unto Deep study bible 1

1/3 ½ ½ 1; ½ 1/3 ; 1/3 ½ ; Deep calls unto Deep study bible 2

x-axis	y-axis
8	2.33
4	0.83
4	0.83

Water Spout *(lightning;combinatorics)* Study Bible 1

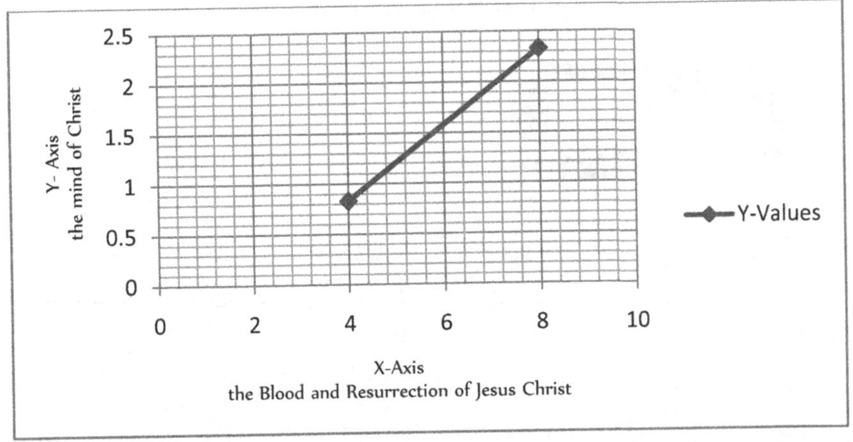

Water Spout *(lightning;combinatorics)* Study bible 2

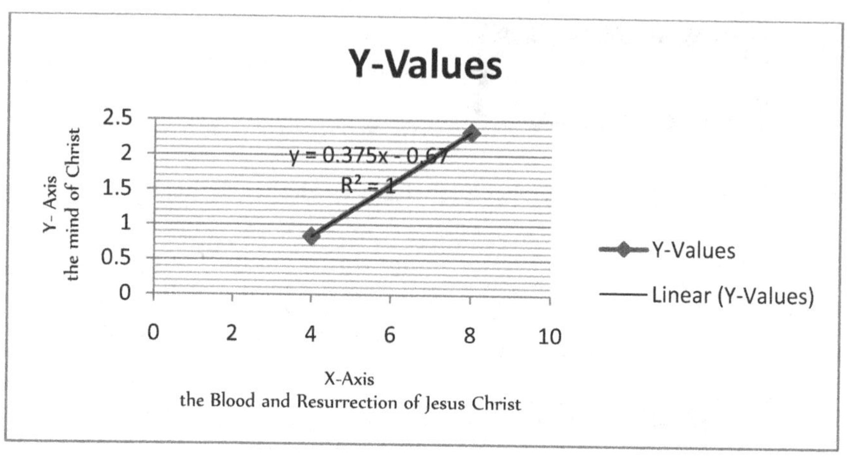

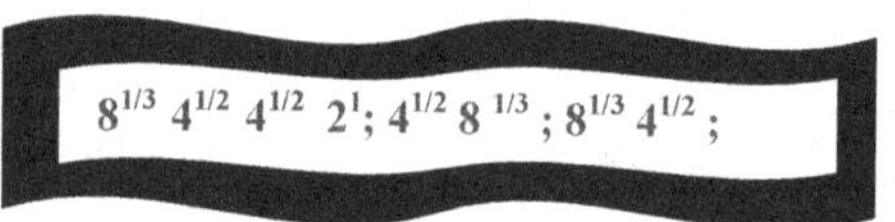

Pilled Poplar, Hazel, and Chesnut bible rods 2

4. And Aram highness; magnificence; deceives; curse **begat Aminadab**my people is liberal; kindred of the prince; **and Aminadab**my people is li beral; kindred of the prince**begat Naasson** enchanter; sorcerer; bewitch; charm; that foretells; that conjectures; **and Naasson** enchanter; sorcerer; beguile; hypnotize; that foretells; that conjectures **begat Salmon** hill; shady; garment; peaceable; perfect; he that rewards;

4;4;4; Bible Matrices

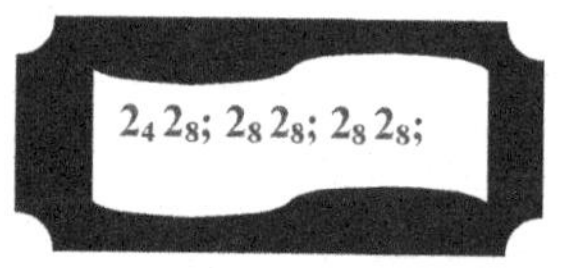

Pilled Poplar, Hazel, and Chesnut bible rods 1

$\text{Log}_4 2 = y$	$\log_8 2 = y$	$\log_8 2 = y$	$\log_8 2 = y$	$\log_8 2 = y$	$\log_8 2 = y$
$2^{2y} = 2^1$	$8^y = 2^1$	$8^y = 2^1$	$8^y = 2^1$	$8^y = 2^1$	$8^y = 2^1$
$2^{2y} = 2^1$	$2^{3y} = 2^1$	$2^{3y} = 2^1$	$2^{3y} = 2^1$	$2^{3y} = 2^1$	$2^{3y} = 2^1$
$2y = 1$	$3y = 1$	$3y = 1$	$3y = 1$	$3y = 1$	$3y = 1$
$y = 1/2$	$y = 1/3$	$y = 1/3$	$y = 1/3$	$y = 1/3$	$y = 1/3$

4;4;4; Deep calls unto deep study bible 1

½ 1/3; 1/3 1/3; 1/3 1/3 ; Deep calls unto Deep study bible 2

x-axis	y-axis
4	0.83
4	0.67
4	0.67

Water Spout *(lightning;combinatorics)* Study Bible 1

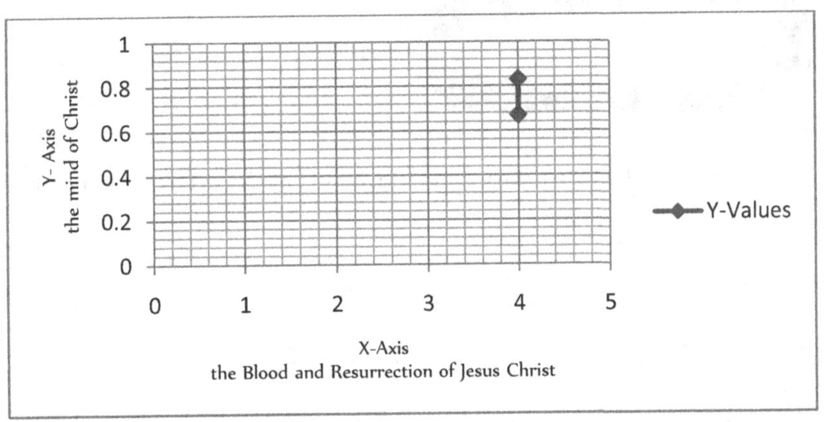

Water Spout *(lightning; combinatorics)* Study bible 2

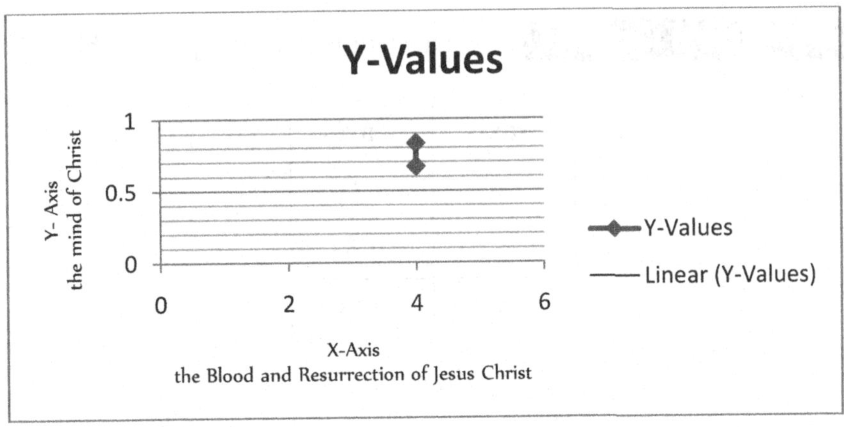

$4^{1/2}\, 8^{1/3}; 8^{1/3}\, 8^{1/3}; 8^{1/3}\, 8^{1/3};$

Pilled Poplar, Hazel, and Chesnut bible rods 2

5. And Salmon hill; shady; garment; peaceable; perfect; he that rewards **begat Booz** alacrity; in strength; fleetness **of Rachab**wide; large; extended; broad; **and Booz** alacrity; in strength; fleetness **begat Obed** servant; workman; serving; worshipping **of Ruth** a friend; drunk; satisfied; **and Obed** servant; workman; serving; worshipping **begat Jesse**firm; wealthy; gift; one who is; Jehovah exists;

6;6;4; Bible Matrices

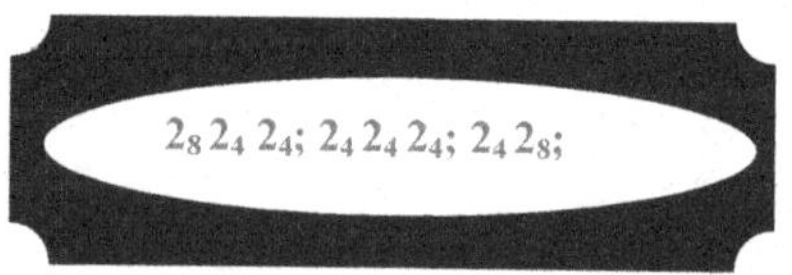

Pilled Poplar, Hazel, and Chesnut bible rods 1

$\log_8 2 = y$	$\log_4 2 = y$	$\log_4 2 = y$	$\log_4 2 = y$	$\log_4 2 = y$	$\log_4 2 = y$	$\log_4 2 = y$	$\log_8 2 = y$
$8^y = 2^1$	$2^{2y} = 2^1$	$2^{2y} = 2^1$	$2^{2y} = 2^1$	$2^{2y} = 2^1$	$2^{2y} = 2^1$	$2^{2y} = 2^1$	$8^y = 2^1$
$2^{3y} = 2^1$	$2^{2y} = 2^1$	$2^{2y} = 2^1$	$2^{2y} = 2^1$	$2^{2y} = 2^1$	$2^{2y} = 2^1$	$2^{2y} = 2^1$	$2^{3y} = 2^1$
$3y = 1$	$2y = 1$	$2y = 1$	$2y = 1$	$2y = 1$	$2y = 1$	$2y = 1$	$3y = 1$
$y = 1/3$	$y = ½$	$y = ½$	$y = ½$	$vy = ½$	$y = ½$	$y = ½$	$y = 1/3$

6;6;4; Deep calls unto deep study bible 1

1/3 ½ ½ ; ½ ½ ½ ; ½ 1/3 ; Deep calls unto Deep study bible 2

x-axis	y-axis
6	1.33
6	1.5
4	0.83

Water Spout *(lightning; combinatorics)* Study Bible 1

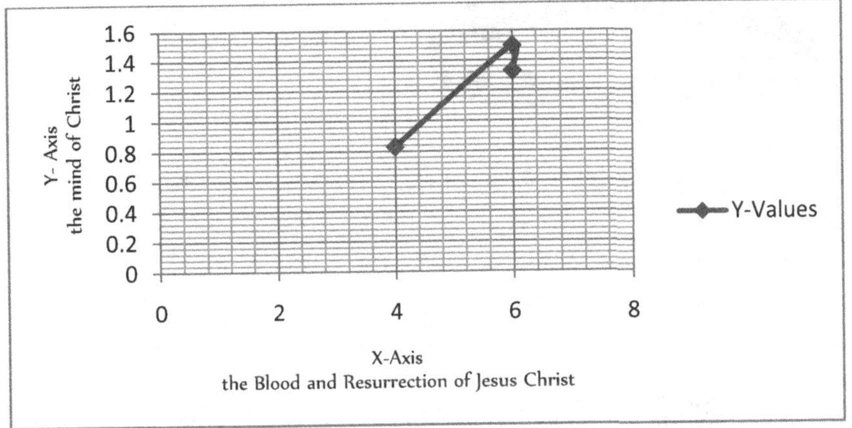

Water spout *(lightning;combinatorics)* study bible 2

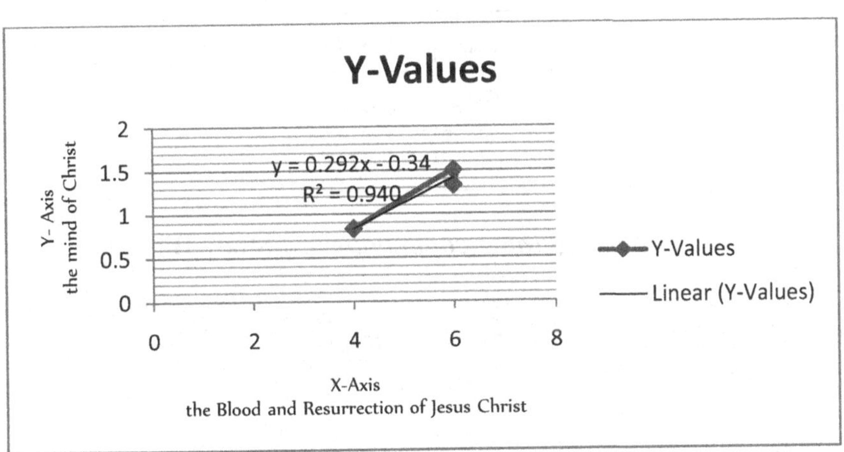

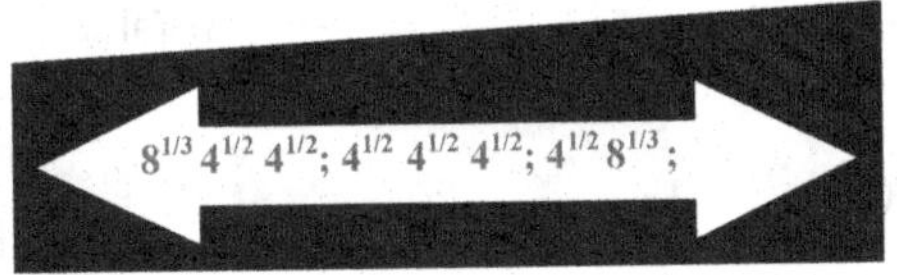

Pilled Poplar, Hazel, and Chesnut bible rods 2

6. And Jessefirm; wealthy; gift; Jehovah exists; one who is **begat David** beloved; dear **the king; and David**beloved;dear **the king begat Solomon**peaceable; peaceful; perfect; harmonious; ordered; one who recompenses**of her that had been the wife of Urias** the Lord is my light or fire; illumination; radiance;

6;15; Bible Matrices

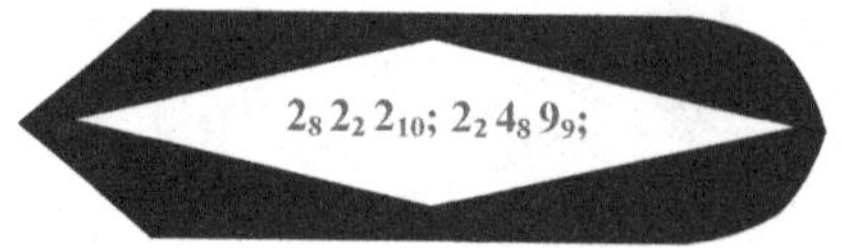

Pilled Poplar, Hazel, and Chesnut bible rods 1

$Log_8 2 = y$	$Log_2 2 = y$	$Log_2 2 = y$	$Log_8 4 = y$	$Log_9 9 = y$	$Log_{10} 2 = 0.3010$
$8^y = 2^1$	$2^y = 2^1$	$2^y = 2^1$	$8^y = 4^1$	$9^y = 9^1$	
$2^{3y} = 2^1$	$y = 1$	$y = 1$	$2^{3y} = 2^2$	$3^{2y} = 3^2$	
$3y = 1$	$3y = 2$	$2y = 2$			
$y = 1$	$y = 2/3$	$y = 1$			

6; 15 ; Deep calls unto Deep study bible 1

1 1 0.3010 ; 1 2/3 1 ; Deep calls unto Deep study bible 2

x-axis	y-axis
6	2.3010
15	2.67

Water Spout *(lightning;combinatorics)* Study Bible 1

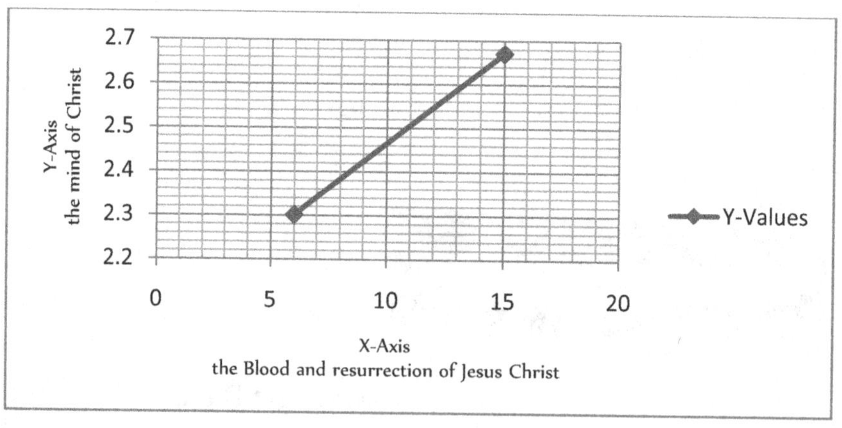

Water Spout *(lightning;combinatorics)* Study Bible 2

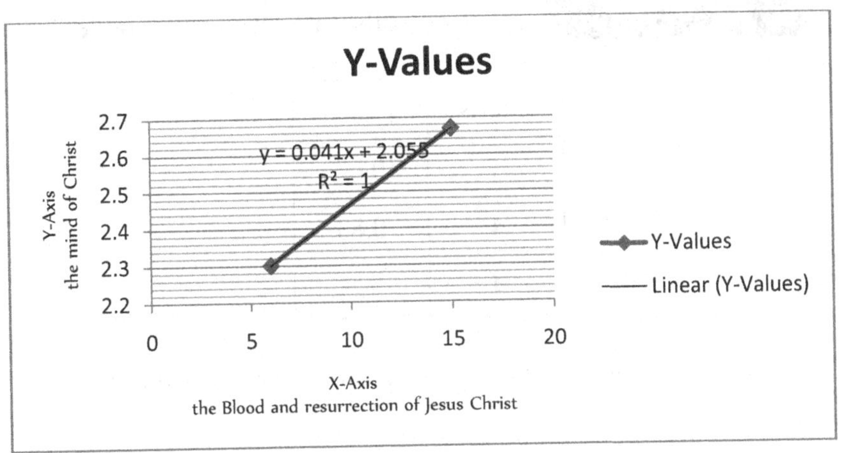

Pilled Poplar, Hazel, and Chesnut bible rods 2

7. And Solomon peaceable; peaceful; perfect; restful; tranquil; one who recompenses **begat Roboam** set's the people at liberty; enlarges the people; **and Roboam** set's the people at liberty; enlarges the people **begat Abia** the Lord' s my father; **and Abia** the Lord's my father **begat Asa** physician; cure;

4;4;4; Bible Matrices

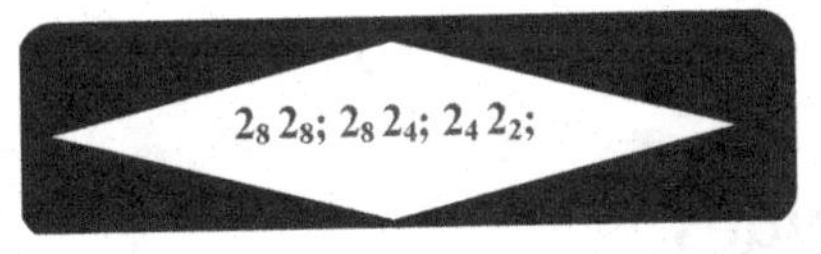

Pilled Poplar, Hazel, and Chesnut bible rods 1

$\text{Log}_8 2 = y$	$\text{Log}_8 2 = y$	$\text{Log}_8 2 = y$	$\text{Log}_4 2 = y$	$\text{Log}_4 2 = y$	$\text{Log}_2 2 = y$
$8^y = 2^1$	$8^y = 2^1$	$8^y = 2^1$	$2^{2y} = 2^1$	$2^{2y} = 2^1$	$2^y = 2^1$
$2^{3y} = 2^1$	$2^{3y} = 2^1$	$2^{3y} = 2^1$	$2^{2y} = 2^1$	$2^{2y} = 2^1$	$y = 1$
$3y = 1$	$3y = 1$	$3y = 1$	$2y = 1$	$2y = 1$	
$y = 1/3$	$y = 1/3$	$y = 1/3$	$y = ½$	$y = ½$	

4;4;4; Deep calls unto Deep study bible 1

1/3 1/3 ; 1/3 ½; ½ 1; Deep calls unto Deep study bible 2

x-axis	y-axis
4	0.67
4	0.83
4	1.5

Water Spout *(lightning; combinatorics)* Study bible 1

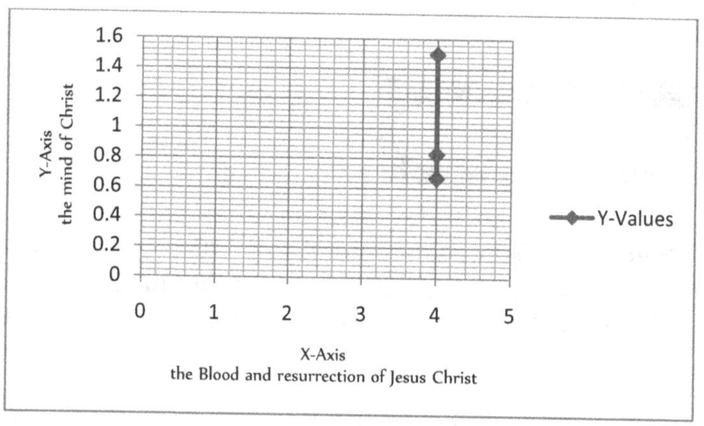

Water Spout *(lightning;combinatorics)* Study bible 2

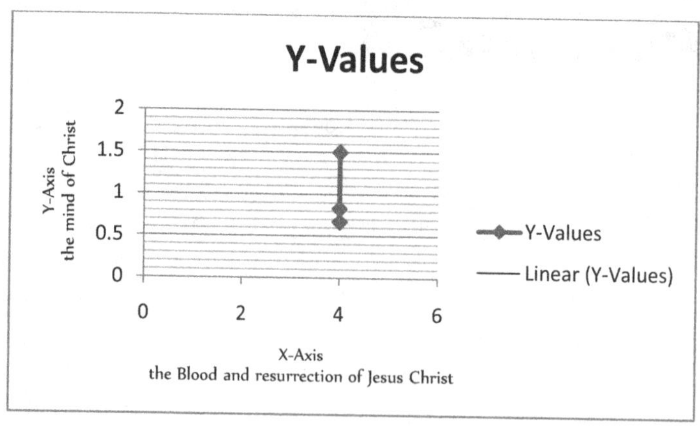

$8^{1/3} 8^{1/3}$; $8^{1/3}$ $4^{1/2}$; $4^{1/2}$ 2^{1} ;

Pilled Poplar, Hazel, and Chesnut bible rods 2

9. And Ozias strength from the Lord **begat Joatham** the perfection of the Lord; Jehovah is upright; **and Joatham** the perfection of the Lord; Jehovah is upright **begat Achaz** one that takes; possesses; **and Achaz** one that takes; possesses **begat Ezekias** the strength of God;

4;4;4; Bible Matrices

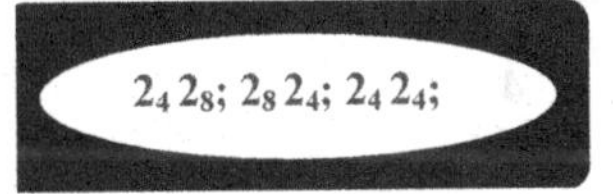

Pilled Poplar, Hazel, and Chesnut bible rods 1

$Log_4 2 = y$	$Log_8 2 = y$	$Log_8 2 = y$	$Log_4 2 = y$	$Log_4 2 = y$	$Log_4 2 = y$
$4^y = 2^1$	$8^y = 2^1$	$8^y = 2^1$	$4^y = 2^1$	$4^y = 2^1$	$4y = 2^1$
$2^{2y} = 2^1$	$2^{3y} = 2^1$	$2^{3y} = 2^1$	$2^{2y} = 2^1$	$2^{2y} = 2^1$	$2^{2y} = 2^1$
$2y = 1$	$3y = 1$	$3y = 1$	$2y = 1$	$2y = 1$	$2y = 1$
$y = ½$	$y = 1/3$	$y = 1/3$	$y = ½$	$y = ½$	$y = ½$

4;4;4; Deep calls unto Deep study bible 1

½ 1/3 ; 1/3 ½; ½ ½ ; Deep calls unto Deep study bible 2

x-axis	y-axis
4	0.83
4	0.83
4	1.0

Water Spout *(lightning;combinatorics)* Study bible 1

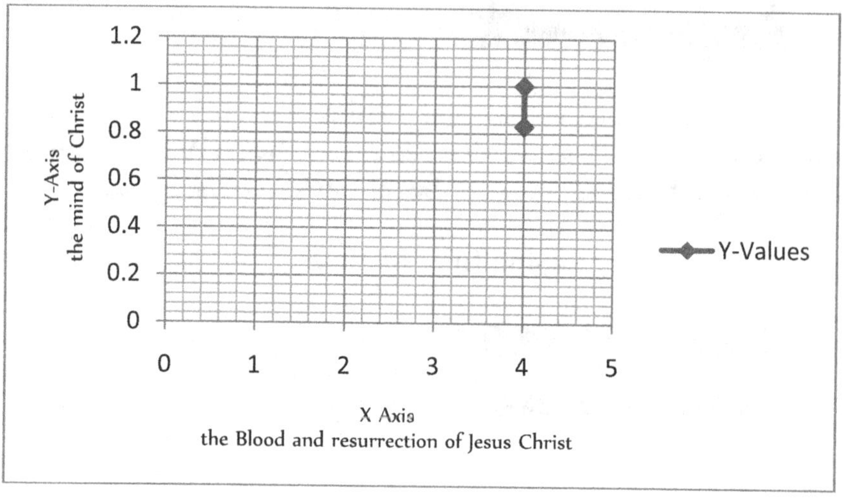

Water Spout *(lightning;combinatorics)* Study bible 2

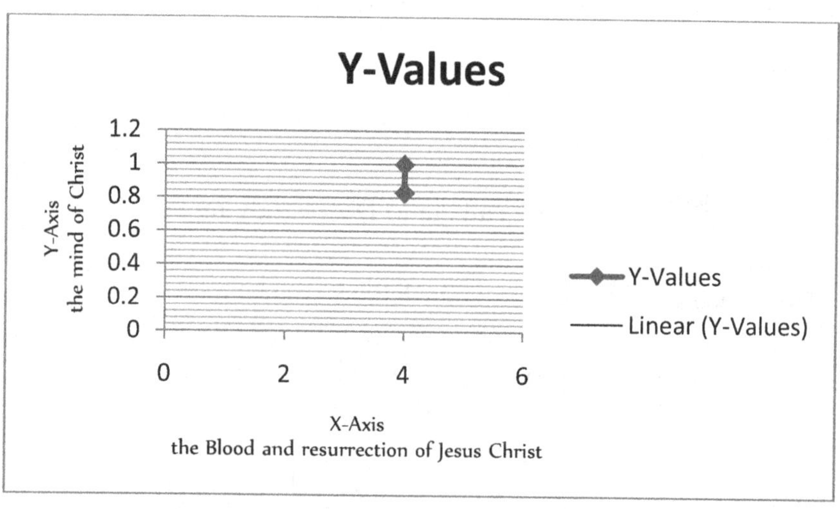

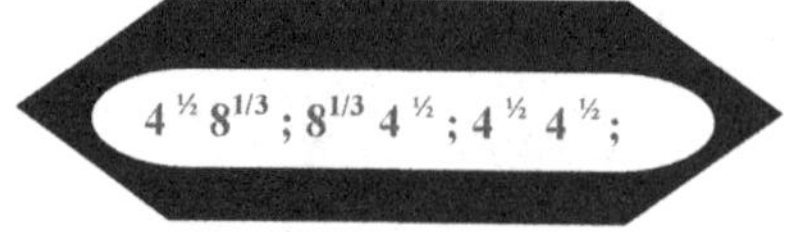

Pilled Poplar, Hazel, and Chesnut bible rods 2

10. And Ezekias the strength of God **begat Manasses**forgetfulness; forgetting; neglectful; careless; he that is forgotten; **and Manasses**forgetfulness; forgetting; scatterbrained; unfocused; he that is forgotten **begat Amon** faithful; true; devoted; builder; **and Amon** faithful; dedicated; true; builder **begat Josias** fire of the Lord burns; whom Jehovah heals;

4;4;4; Bible Matrices

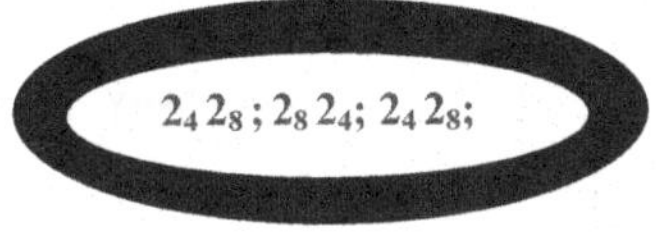

Pilled Poplar, Hazel, and Chesnut bible rods 1

$\text{Log}_4 2 = y$	$\text{Log}_8 2 = y$	$\text{Log}_8 2 = y$	$\text{Log}_4 2 = y$	$\text{Log}_4 2 = y$	$\text{Log}_8 2 = y$
$4^y = 2^1$	$8^y = 2^1$	$8^y = 2^1$	$4^y = 2^1$	$4^y = 2^1$	$8^y = 2^1$
$2^{2y} = 2^1$	$2^{3y} = 2^1$	$2^{3y} = 2^1$	$2^{2y} = 2^1$	$2^{2y} = 2^1$	$2^{3y} = 2^1$
$2y = 1$	$3y = 1$	$3y = 1$	$2y = 1$	$2y = 1$	$3y = 2^1$
$y = ½$	$y = 1/3$	$y = 1/3$	$y = ½$	$y = ½$	$y = 1/3$

4;4;4; Deep calls unto Deep study bible 1

½ 1/3 ; 1/3 ½; ½ 1/3 ; Deep calls unto Deep study bible 2

x-axis	y-axis
4	0.83
4	0.83
4	0.83

Water Spout *(lightning;combinatorics)* Study bible 1

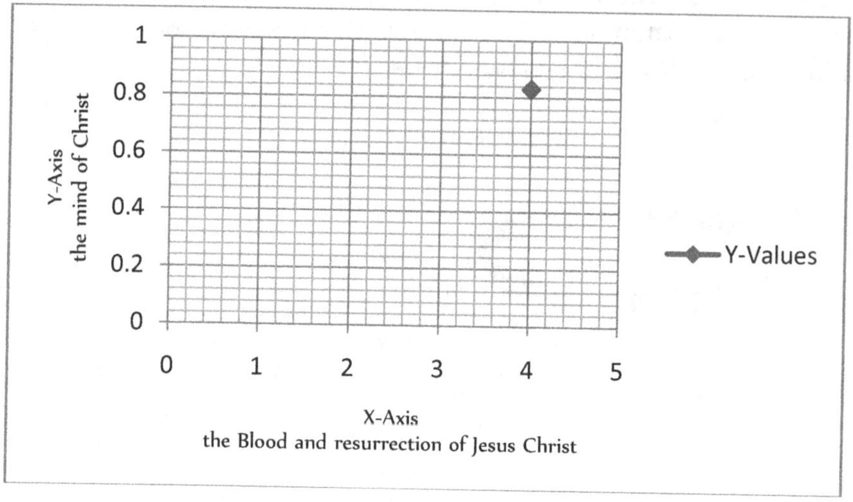

Water Spout *(lightning;combinatorics)* Study bible 2

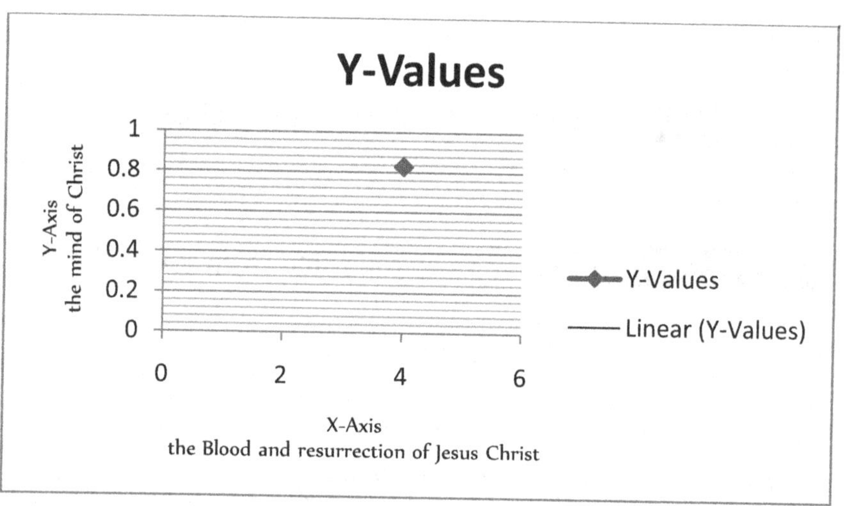

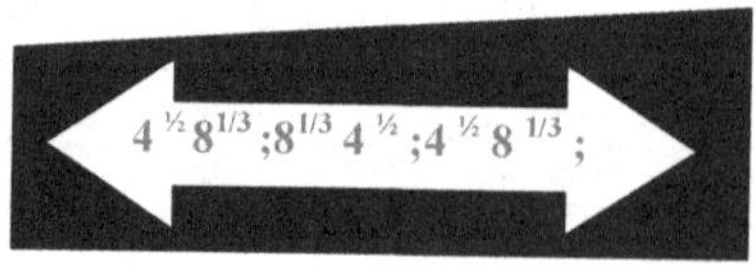

Pilled Poplar, Hazel, and Chesnut bible rods 2

11. And Josias fire of the Lord burns; whom Jehovah heals **begat Jechonias** Jehovah establishes; preparation, stability, **of the Lord and his brethren, about the time they were carried away to Babylon**mixture; confusion; babel:

4, 6, 9: Bible Matrices

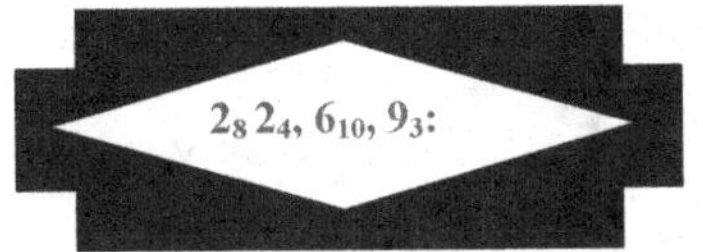

Pilled Poplar, Hazel, and Chesnut bible rods 1

$\log_8 2 = y$	$\log_4 2 = y$	$\log_3 9 = y$
$8^y = 2^1$	$4^y = 2^1$	$3^y = 9$
$2^{3y} = 2^1$	$2^{2y} = 2^1$	$3^y = 3^2$
$3y = 1$	$2y = 1$	$y = 2$
$y = 1/3$	$y = ½$	

4, 6, 9: Deep calls unto Deep study bible 1

1/3 ½, 0.7782, 2: Deep calls unto Deep study bible 2

x-axis	y-axis
4	0.83
6	0.7782
9	2

Water Spout *(lightning;combinatorics)* Study bible 1

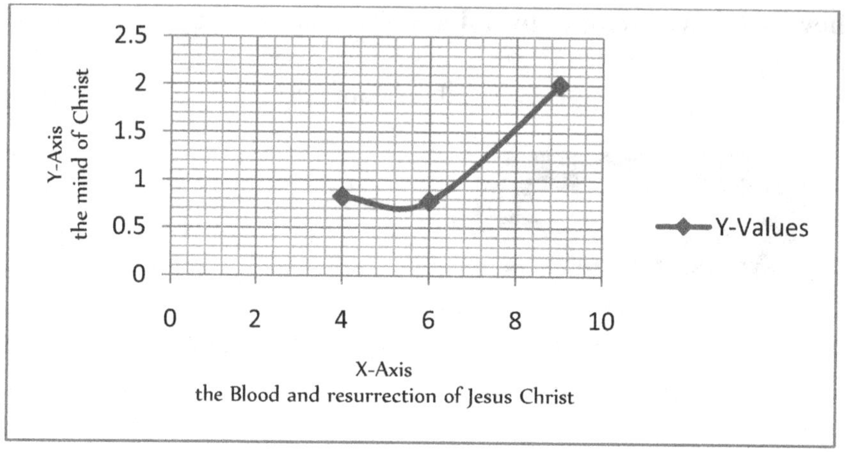

Water Spout *(lightning;combinatorics)* Study bible 2

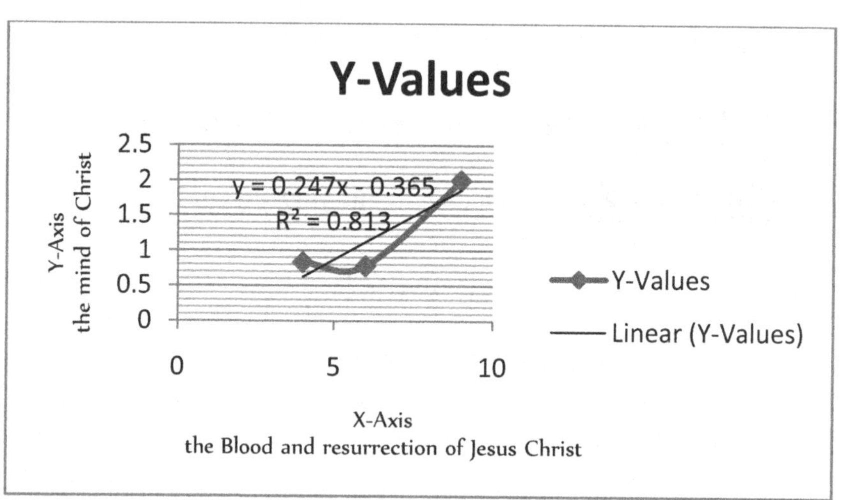

$8^{1/3}\ 4^{1/2},\ 10^{0.7782},\ 3^{2}$:

Pilled Poplar, Hazel, and Chesnut bible rods 2

12. And after they were brought to Babylon mixture; confusion; muddle; mix; misunderstanding; error; tangle, **Jechonias** Jehovah establishes; preparation, stability **begat Salathiel**asked ; lent of God; **and Salathiel** asked; lent of God **begat Zorobabel** a Stranger at Babylon, Babel; dispersion of confusion;

7, 3; 4; Bible Matrices

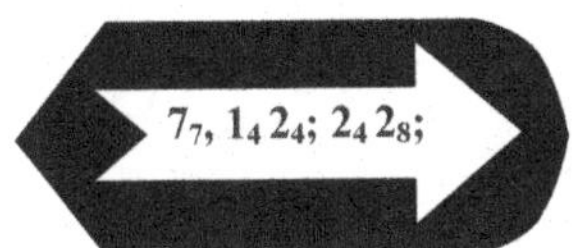

Pilled Poplar, Hazel, and Chesnut bible rods 1

$\text{Log}_7 7 = y$	$\text{Log}_4 1 = y$	$\text{Log}_4 2 = y$	$\text{Log}_4 2 = y$	$\text{Log}_8 2 = y$
$7^y = 7^1$	$4^y = 4^0$	$4^y = 2^1$	$4^y = 2^1$	$8^y = 2^1$
$y = 1$	$y = 0$	$2^{2y} = 2^1$	$2^{2y} = 2^1$	$2^{3y} = 2^1$
		$2y = 1$	$2y = 1$	$3y = 1$
		$y = ½$	$y = ½$	$y = 1/3$

7, 3 ; 4; Deep calls unto Deep study bible 1

1, 0 ½ ; ½ 1/3 ; Deep calls unto Deep study bible 2

x-axis	y-axis
7	1
3	0.5
4	0.83

Water Spout *(lightning;combinatorics)* Study bible 1

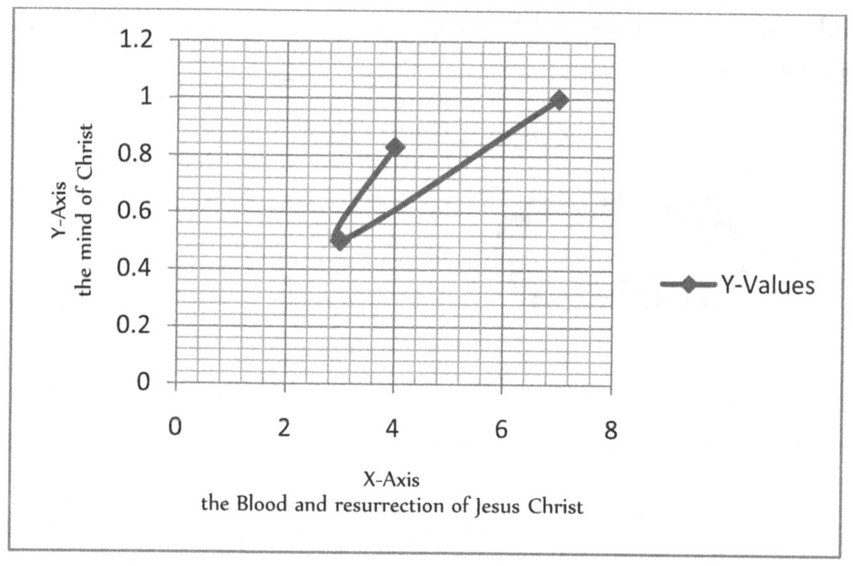

Water Spout *(lightning;combinatorics)* Study bible 2

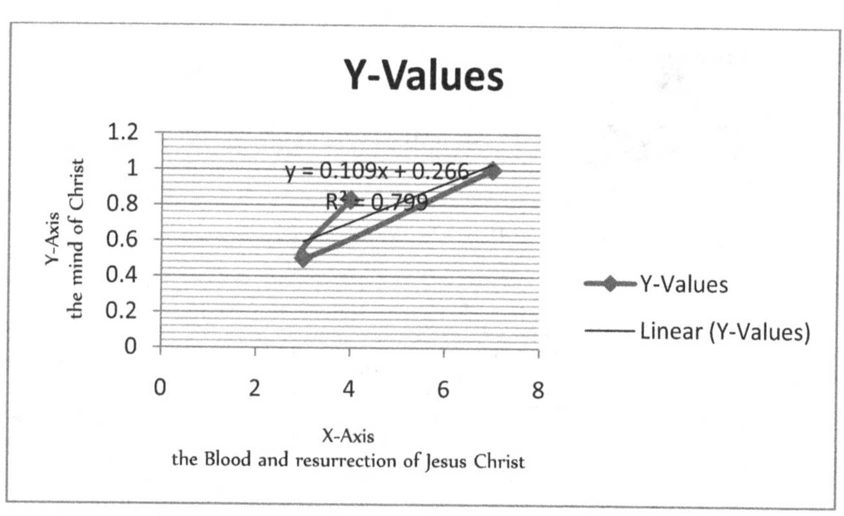

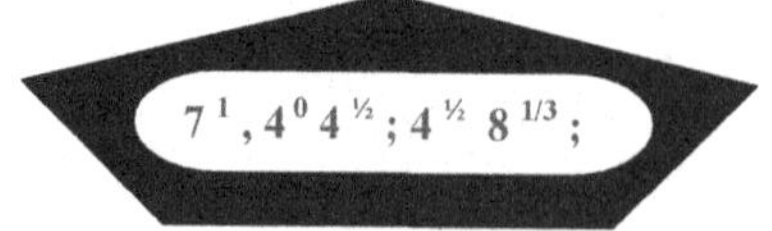

Pilled Poplar, Hazel, and Chesnut bible rods 2

13. And Zorobabel a Stranger at Babylon, Babel ; dispersion of confusion**begat Abiud** father of praise; possessor; holder; father of honor; **and Abiud**father of praise; possessor; owner; father of honor **begat Eliakim** resurrection of God; rebirth; raised up by God; **and Eliakim**resurrection of God; restoration; raised up by God**begat Azor**a helper; a court;

4;4;4; Bible Matrices

$2_8 2_8$; $2_8 2_8$; $2_8 2_4$;

Pilled Poplar, Hazel, and Chesnut bible rods 1

$\log_8 2 = y$	$\log_8 2 = y$	$\log_8 2 = y$	$\log_8 2 = y$	$\log_8 2 = y$	$\log_4 2 = y$
$8^y = 2^1$	$8^y = 2^1$	$8^y = 2^1$	$8^y = 2^1$	$8^y = 2^1$	$4^y = 2^1$
$2^{3y} = 2^1$	$2^{3y} = 2^1$	$2^{3y} = 2^1$	$2^{3y} = 2^1$	$2^{3y} =2^1$	$2^{2y} = 2^1$
$3y = 1$	$3y = 1$	$3y = 1$	$3y = 1$	$3y =2^1$	$2y = 1$
$y = 1/3$	$y = 1/3$	$y = 1/3$	$y = 1/3$	$y = 1/3$	$y = ½$

4;4;4; Deep calls unto Deep study bible 1

1/3 1/3 ; 1/3 1/3; 1/3 ½ ; Deep calls unto Deep study bible 2

x-axis	y-axis
4	0.67
4	0.67
4	0.83

Water Spout *(lightning;combinatorics)* Study bible 1

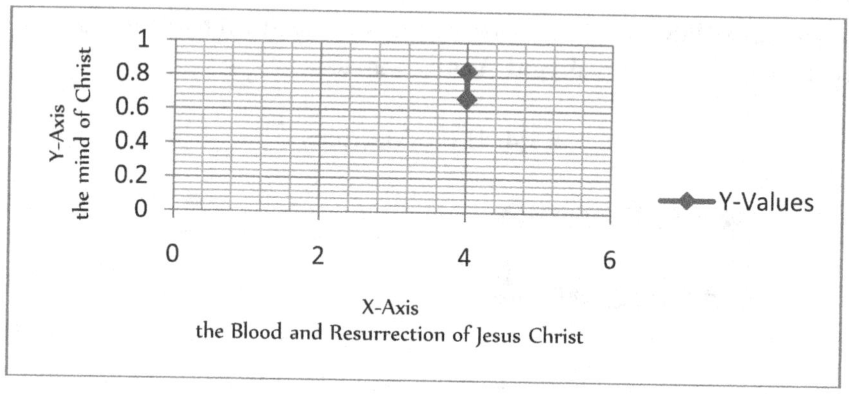

Water Spout *(lightning;combinatorics)* Study bible 2

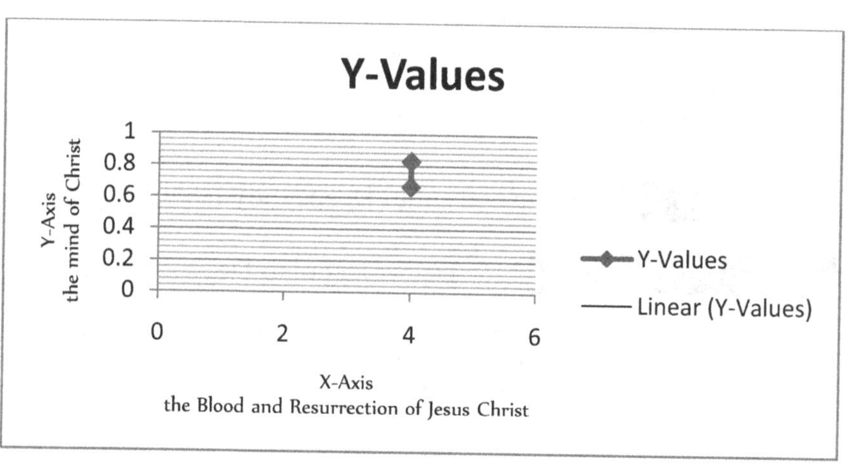

Pilled Poplar, Hazel, and Chesnut bible rods

14. And Azor helper; court **begat Sadoc** just; justified; right; righteous; **and Sadoc** just; justified; balanced; righteous **begat Achim**preparing; revenging; confirming;woes; **and Achim**preparing; revenging; confirming; woes **begat Eliud**God is my praise;

4;4;4; Bible Matrices

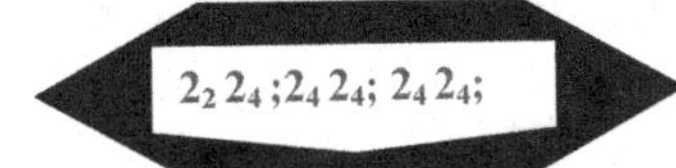

Pilled Poplar, Hazel, and Chesnut bible rods 1

$\text{Log}_2 2 = y$
$2^y = 2^1$
$y = 1$

$\text{Log}_4 2 = y$
$4^y = 2^1$
$2^{2y} = 2^1$
$2y = 1$
$y = ½$

$\text{Log}_4 2 = y$
$4^y = 2^1$
$2^{2y} = 2^1$
$2y = 1$
$y = ½$

$\text{Log}_4 2 = y$
$4^y = 2^1$
$2^{2y} = 2^1$
$2y = 1$
$y = ½$

$\text{Log}_4 2 = y$
$4^y = 2^1$
$2^{2y} = 2^1$
$2y = 1$
$y = ½$

$\text{Log}_4 2 = y$
$4^y = 2^1$
$2^{2y} = 2^1$
$2y = 1$
$y = ½$

4;4;4; Deep calls unto Deep study bible 1

1 ½ ; ½ ½ ; ½ ½ ; Deep calls unto Deep study bible 2

x-axis	y-axis
4	1.5
4	1
4	1

Water Spout *(lightning;combinatorics)* Study bible 1

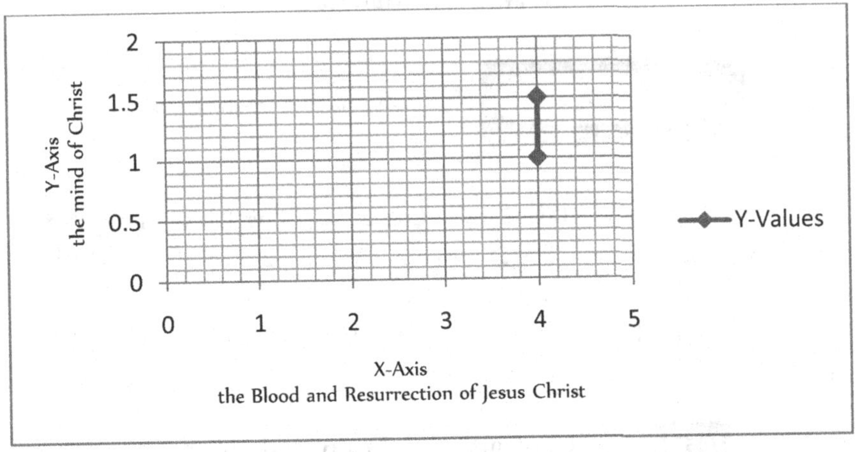

Water Spout *(lightning;combinatorics)* Study bible 2

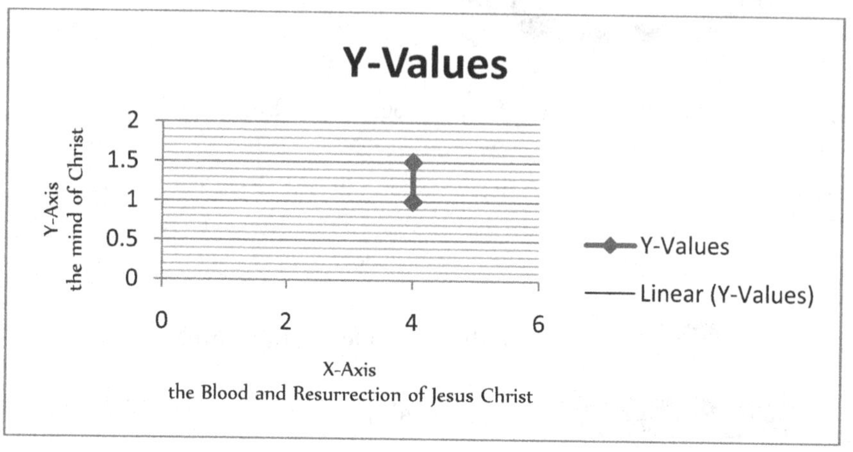

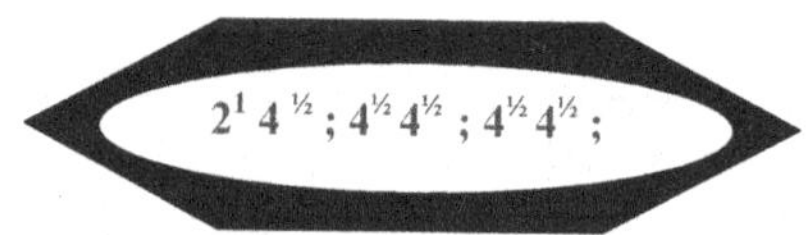

Pilled Poplar, Hazel, and Chesnut bible rods 2

15. And Eliud God is my praise**begat Eleazar** the court of God; God is my helper; **and Eleazar** the court of God; God is my helper **begat Matthan** gift; rains; **and Matthan** gift; rains **begat Jacob** supplanter, undermines; the heel;

4;4;4; Bible Matrices

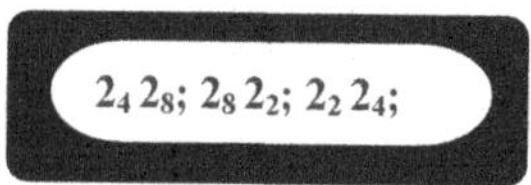

Pilled Poplar, Hazel, and Chesnut bible rods 1

$\text{Log}_4 2 = y$	$\text{Log}_8 2 = y$	$\text{Log}_8 2 = y$	$\text{Log}_2 2 = y$	$\text{Log}_2 2 = y$	$\text{Log}_4 2 = y$
$4^y = 2^1$	$8^y = 2^1$	$8^y = 2^1$	$2^y = 2^1$	$2^y = 2^1$	$4^y = 2^1$
$2^{2y} = 2^1$	$2^{3y} = 2^1$	$2^{3y} = 2^1$	$y = 1$	$y = 1$	$2^{2y} = 2^1$
$2y = 1$	$3y = 1$	$3y = 1$	$2y = 1$		$2y = 1$
$y = ½$	$y = 1/3$	$y = 1/3$	$y = ½$		$y = ½$

4;4;4; Deep calls unto Deep study bible 1

½ 1/3 ; 1/3 1 ; 1 ½ ; Deep calls unto Deep study bible 2

x-axis	y-axis
4	0.83
4	1.33
4	1.50

Water Spout *(lightning; combinatorics)* Study bible 1

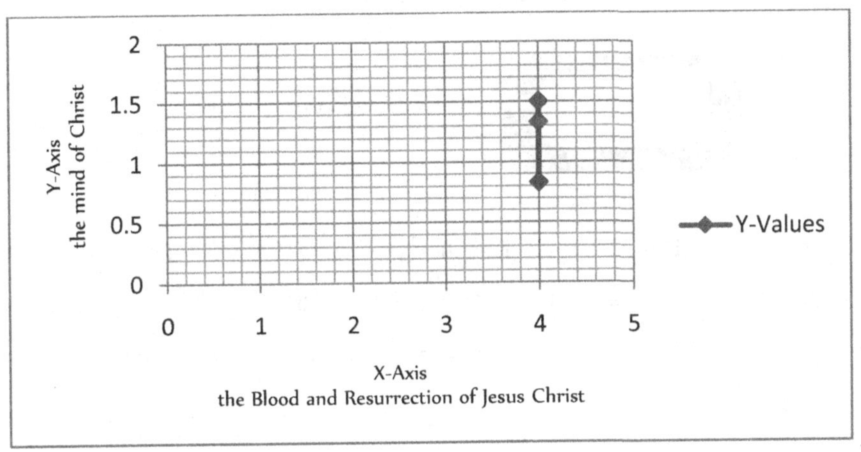

Water Spout *(lightning; combinatorics)* Study bible 2

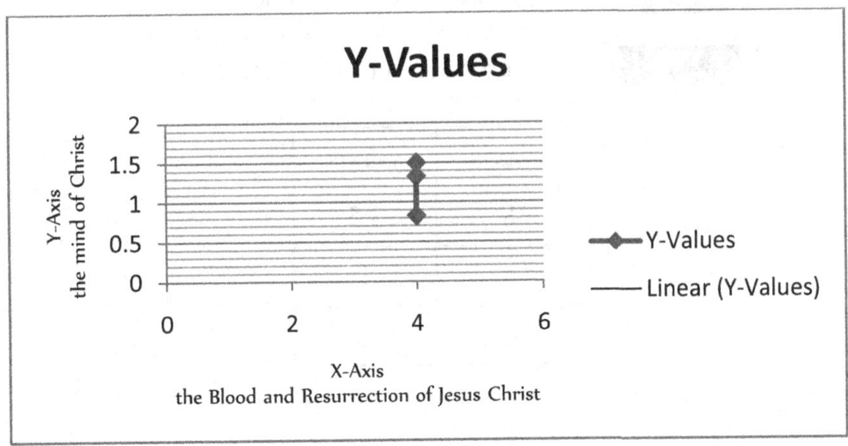

$4^{½} 8^{1/3}$; $8^{1/3} 2^{1}$; $2^{1} 4^{½}$;

Pilled Poplar, Hazel, and Chesnut bible rods 2

16. And Jacob supplanter, undermines; the heel**begat Joseph** increase; addition **the husband of Mary**a tear, **of whom was born Jesus**savior; deliverer; redeemer; liberator; rescuer,**who is called Christ**anointed; smear; oil; daub.

8, 5, 4. Bible Matrices

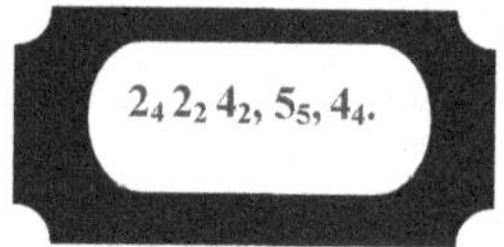

Pilled Poplar, Hazel, and Chesnut bible rods 1

$\text{Log}_4 2 = y$	$\text{Log}_2 2 = y$	$\text{Log}_2 4 = y$	$\text{Log}_5 5 = y$	$\text{Log}_4 4 = y$
$4^y = 2^1$	$2^y = 2^1$	$2^y = 4^1$	$5^y = 5^1$	$4^y = 4^1$
$\mathbf{2}^{2y} = 2^1$	$y = 1$	$\mathbf{2}^y = 2^2$	$\mathbf{y} = 1$	$\mathbf{2}^{2y} = 2^2$
$2y = 1$		$y = 2$		$2y = 2$
$y = ½$				$y = 1$

8, 5, 4. Deep calls unto Deep study bible 1

½ 1 2, 1, 1 . Deep calls unto Deep study bible 2

x-axis	y-axis
8	3.5
5	1
4	1

Water Spout *(lightning; combinatorics)* Study bible 1

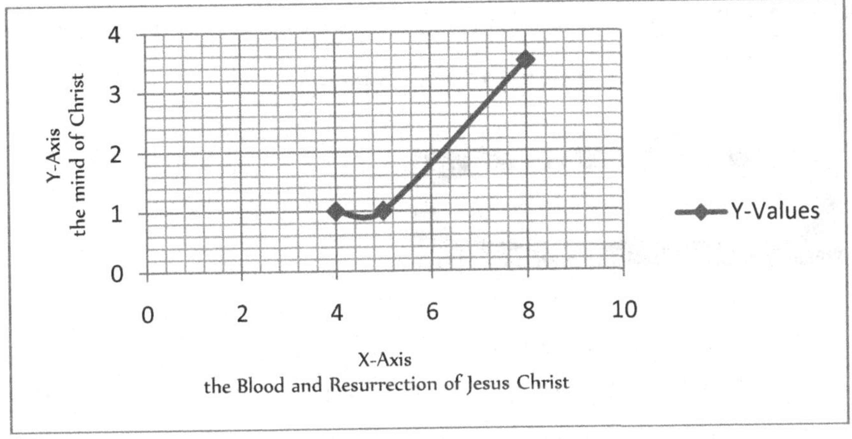

Water Spout *(lightning; combinatorics)* Study bible 2

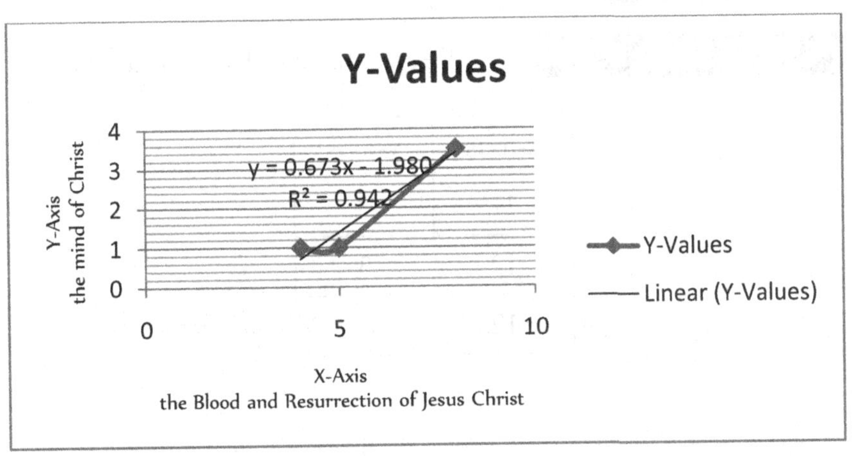

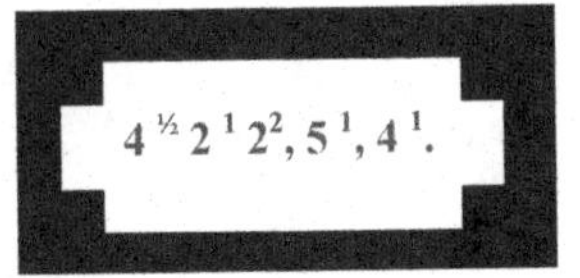

Pilled Poplar, Hazel, and Chesnut bible rods 2

17. So all the generations from Abraham father of a great multitude, assembly **to David** beloved;dear **are fourteen** $_{2} {}^{x} {}_{7}$ **generations; and from David** beloved; dear; cherished **until the carrying away into Babylon** mixture; confusion; babel; misunderstanding; muddle; mistake **are fourteen** $_{2} {}^{x} {}_{7}$ **generations; and from**

the carrying away into Babylon mixture; confusion; misunderstanding; muddle; error; miscalculation; misperception **unto Christ** anointed ;smear **are fourteen** 2 x 7 **generations.**

11;12;12. Bible Matrices

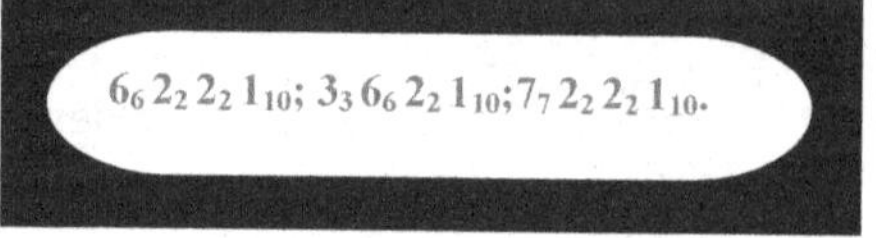

Pilled Poplar, Hazel, and Chesnut bible rods 1

$Log_6 6 = y$	$Log_2 2 = y$	$Log_2 2 = y$	$Log_3 3 = y$	$Log_6 6 = y$	$Log_2 2 = y$	$Log_7 7 = y$	$Log_2 2 = y$	$Log_2 2 = y$
$6^y = 6^1$	$2^y = 2^1$	$2^y = 2^1$	$3^y = 3^1$	$6^y = 6^1$	$2^y = 2^1$	$7^y - 7^1$	$2^y = 2^1$	$2^y = 2^1$
$y = 1$	$y = 1$	$y = 1$	$y = 1$	$y = 1$	$y = 1$	$y = 1$	$y = 1$	$y = 1$

11 ; 12 ; 12 . Deep calls unto Deep study bible 1

1 1 1 0 ; 1 1 1 0 ; 1 1 1 0. Deep calls unto Deep study bible 2

x-axis	y-axis
11	3
12	3
12	3

Water Spout *(lightning; combinatorics)* Study bible 1

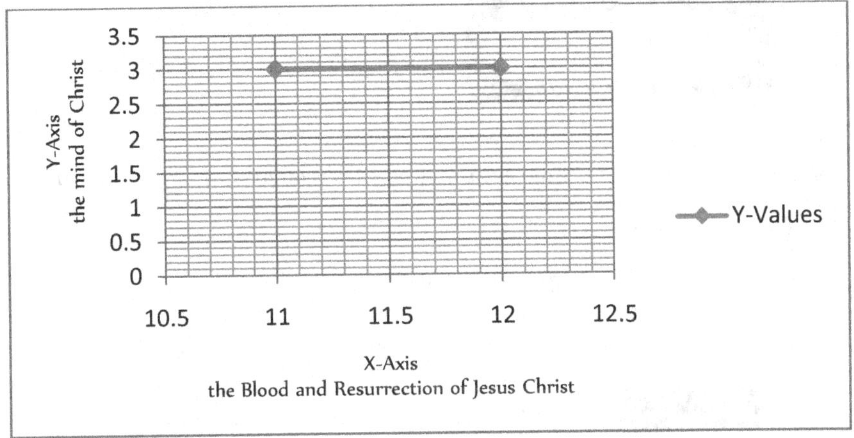

Water Spout *(lightning; combinatorics)* Study bible 2

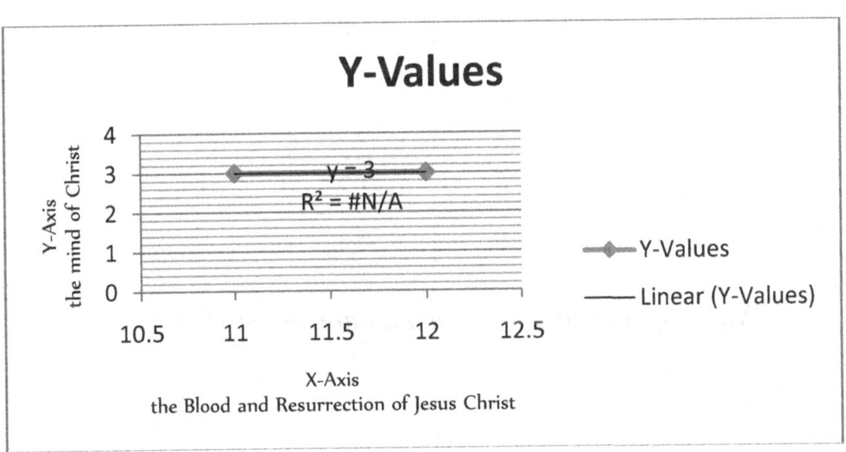

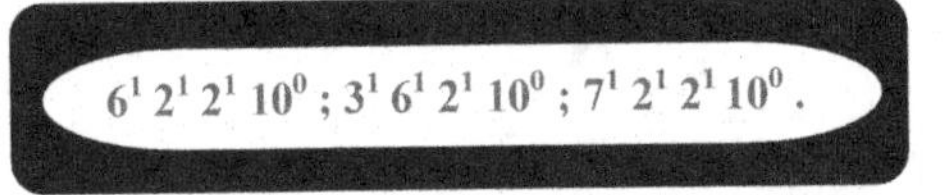

Pilled Poplar, Hazel, and Chesnut bible rods 2

18. Now the birth of Jesus Christannointed savior, deliverer, rescuer, redeemer, liberator **was on this wise: When as his mother Mary** a tear; hole; split; slit **was espoused to Joseph**increase; addition, **before they came together, she was found with child of the Holy Ghost.**

10:9, 4, 9. Bible Matrices

$6_6\ 4_{10}: 5_5\ 4_2, 4_{10}, 9_{10}.$ Pilled Poplar, Hazel, and Chesnut bible rods 1

$\text{Log}_6 6 = y$ $\text{Log}_5 5 = y$ $\text{Log}_2 4 = y$ $\text{Log}_{10} 4 = 0.6020$ $\text{Log}_{10} 9 = 0.9542$

$6^y = 6^1$ $5^y = 5^1$ $2^y = 4^1$

$y = 1$ $y = 1$ $2^y = 2^2$

$y = 2$

10 : 9, 4, 9. Deep calls unto Deep study bible 1

1 0.6020 : 1 2, 0.6020, 0.9542. Deep calls unto Deep study bible 2

x-axis	y-axis
10	1.6020
9	3
4	0.6020
9	0.9542

Water Spout *(lightning; combinatorics)* Study bible 1

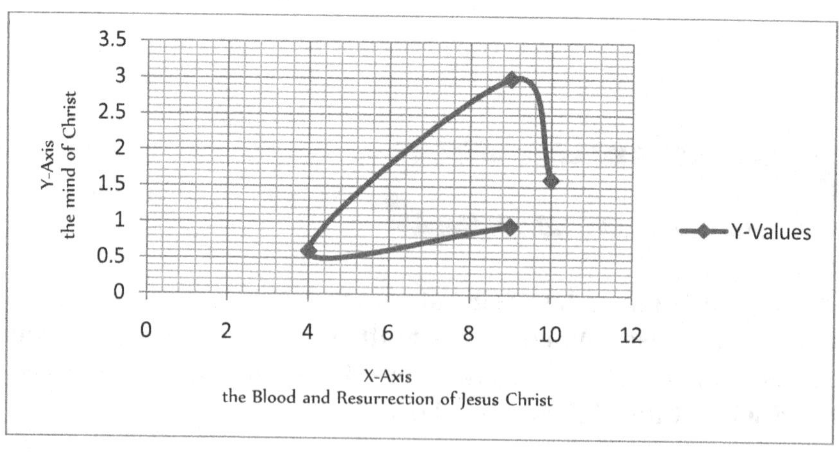

Water Spout *(lightning; combinatorics)* Study bible 2

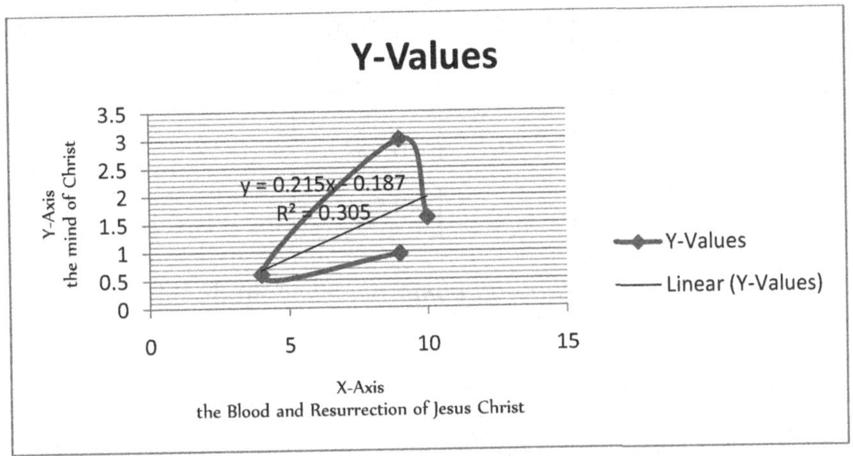

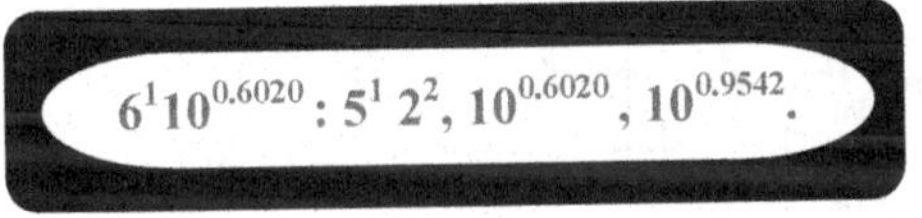

Pilled Poplar, Hazel, and Chesnut bible rods 2

19. Then Joseph increase; addition **her husband, being a just man, and not willing to make her a publick example, was minded to put her away privily.**

4, 4, 9, 7. Bible Matrices

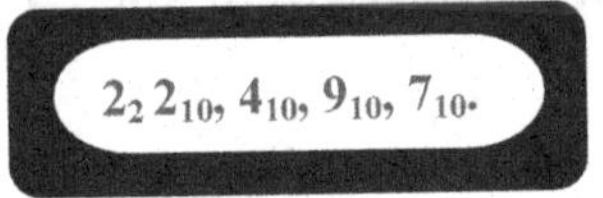

Pilled Poplar, Hazel, and Chesnut bible rods 1

$\log_2 2 = y$ $\log_{10} 2 = 0.3010$ $\log_{10} 4 = 0.6020$ $\log_{10} 9 = 0.9542$ $\log_{10} 7 = 0.8450$

$2^y = 2^1$

$y = 1$

4, 4, 9, 7. Deep calls unto Deep study bible 1

1 0.3010, 0.6020, 0.9542, 0.8450. Deep calls unto Deep study bible 2

x-axis	y-axis
4	1.3010
4	0.6020
9	0.9542
7	0.8450

Water Spout *(lightning; combinatorics)* Study bible 1

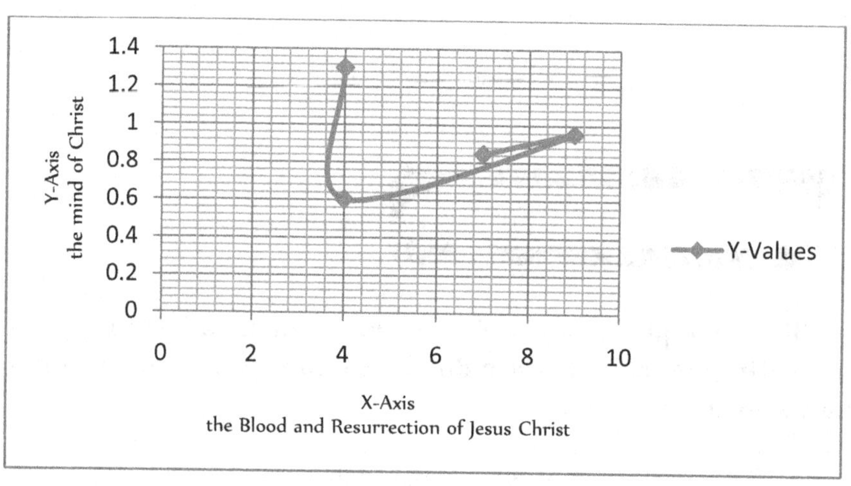

Water Spout *(lightning; combinatorics)* Study bible 2

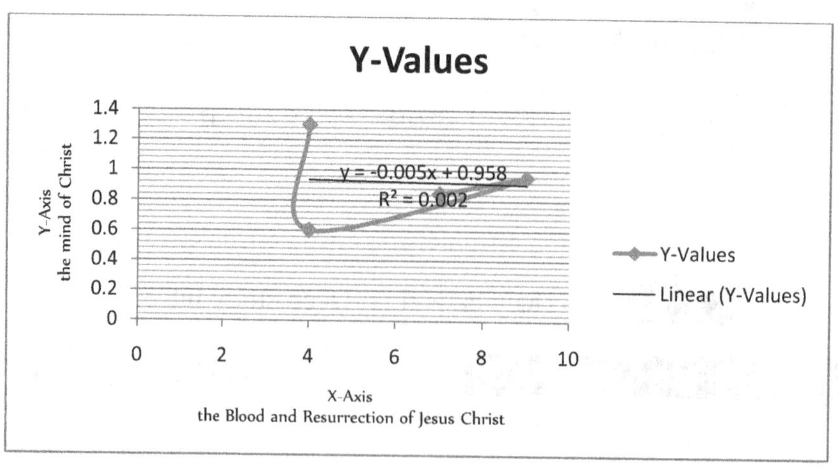

$2^1\ 10^{0.3010}, 10^{0.6020}, 10^{0.9542}, 10^{0.8450}.$

Pilled Poplar, Hazel, and Chesnut bible rods 2

20. But while he thought on these things, behold, the angel of the Lord appeared unto him in a dream, saying, Joseph increase; addition, **thou son of David**beloved; dear, **fear not to take unto thee Mary**a tear; hole; split; slit; rent; gash **thy wife: for that which is conceived in her is of the Holy Ghost.**

7, 1, 11, 1, 1, 4, 9: 12. Bible Matrices

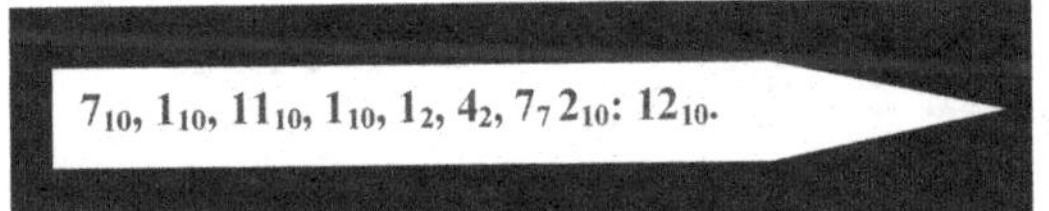

Pilled Poplar, Hazel, and Chesnut bible rods 1

$\text{Log}_2 1 = y$ $\text{Log}_2 4 = y$ $\text{Log}_7 7 = y$ $\text{Log}_{10} 7 = 0.8450$ $\text{Log}_{10} 2 = 0.3010$ $\text{Log}_{10} 12 = 1.0791$ $\text{Log}_{10} 1 = 0$ $\text{Log}_{10} 11 = 1.0413$

$2^y = 2^0$ $2^y = 4^1$ $7^y = 7^1$

$y = 0$ $2^y = 2^2$ $y = 1$

$y = 2$

7, 1, 11, 1, 1, 4, 9: 12. Deep calls unto Deep study bible 1

0.8450, 0, 1.0413, 0, 0, 2, 1 0.3010: 1.0791.

Deep calls unto Deep study bible 2

x-axis	y-axis
7	0.8450
1	0
11	1.0413
1	0
1	0
4	2
9	1.3010

12	1.0791

Water Spout*(lightning; combinatorics)* Study bible 1

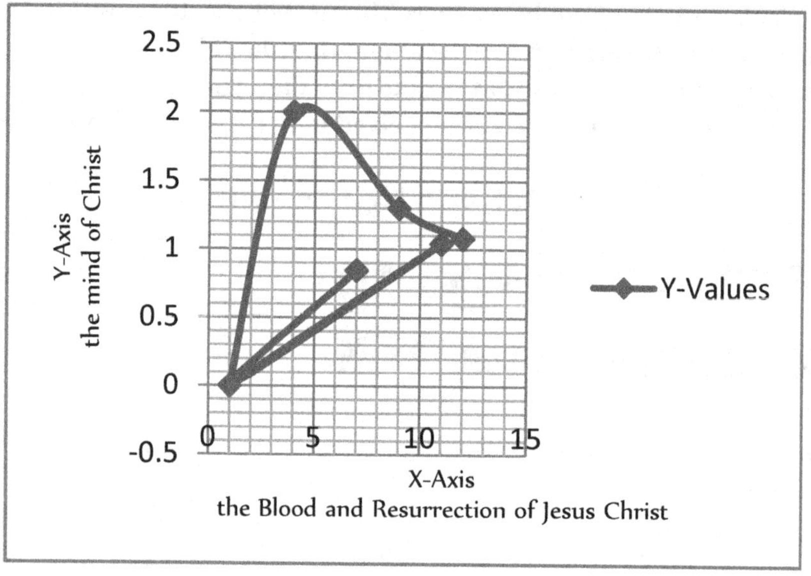

Water Spout *(lightning; combinatorics)* Study bible 2

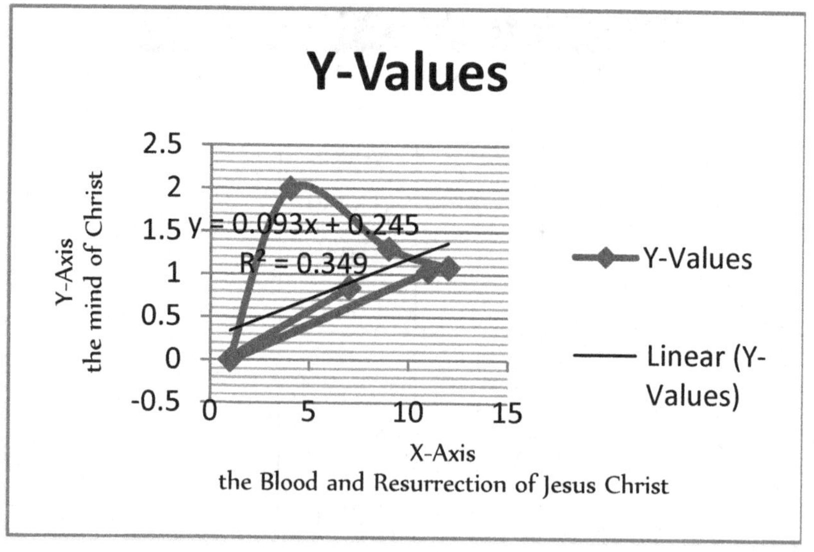

$10^{0.8450}, 10^{0}, 10^{1.0413}, 10^{0}, 2^{0}, 2^{2}, 7^{1}10^{0.3010}: 10^{1.0791}.$

Pilled Poplar, Hazel, and Chesnut bible rods 2

21. And she shall bring forth a son, and thou shalt call his name JESUSsavior; deliverer: **for he shall save his people from their sins.**

7, 7: 9. Bible Matrices

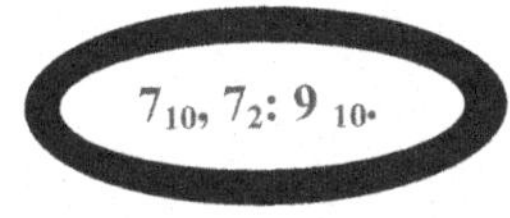

Pilled Poplar, Hazel, and Chesnut bible rods 1

$\text{Log}_2 7 = y$ $\qquad$ $\text{Log}_{10} 7 = 0.8450$ $\qquad$ $\text{Log}_{10} 9 = 0.9542$

$2^y = 7^1$

$\text{Log}_{10} 2^y = \log_{10} 7$

$y \log_{10} 2 = \log_{10} 7$

$y = \log_{10} 7/\log_{10} 2$

$y = 2.8073$

7, 7: 9. Deep calls unto Deep study bible 1

0.8450, 2.8073: 0.9542. Deep calls unto Deep study bible 2

x-axis	y-axis
7	0.8450
7	2.8073
9	0.9542

Water Spout *(lightning; combinatorics)* Study bible 1

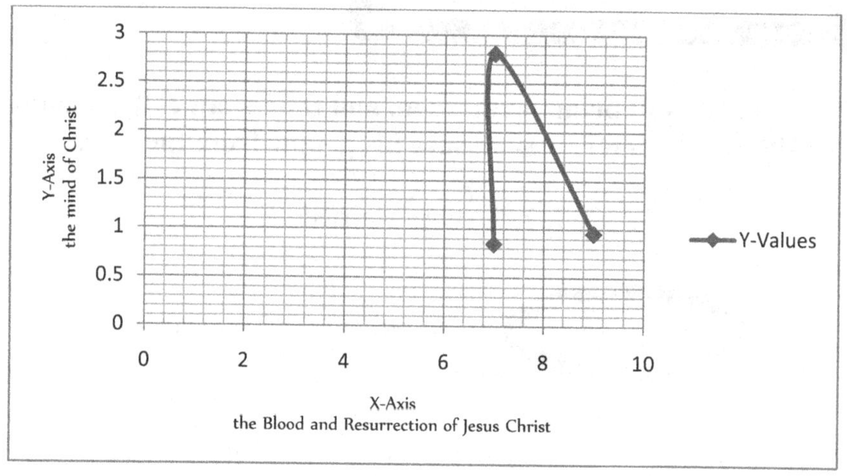

Water Spout *(lightning; combinatorics)* Study bible 2

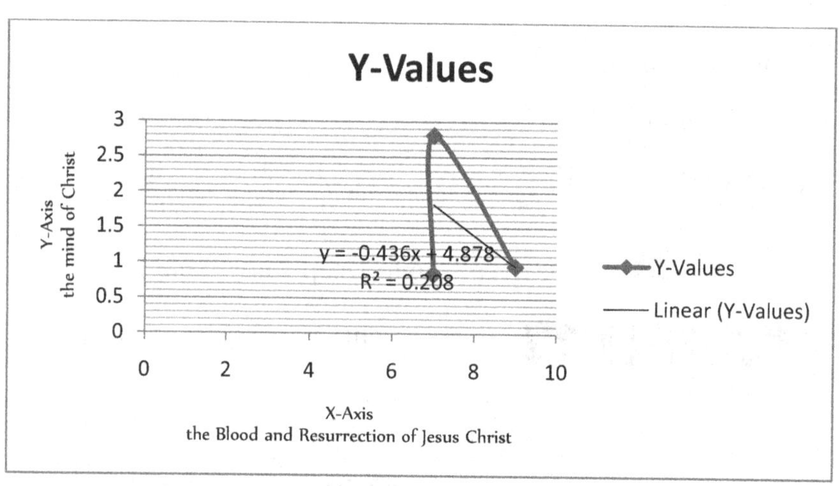

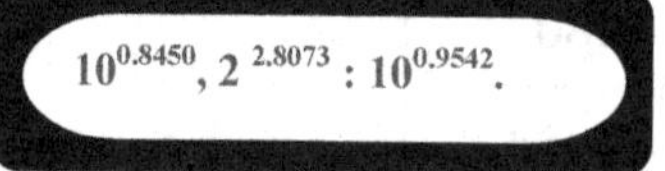

Pilled Poplar, Hazel, and Chesnut bible rods 2

22. Now all this was done, that it might be fulfilled which was spoken of the Lord by the prophet to bubble forth, as from a fountain; utter, **saying,**

5, 14, 1, Bible Matrices

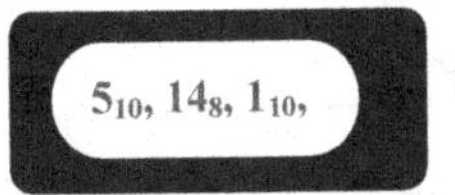

Pilled Poplar, Hazel, and Chesnut bible rods 1

$\text{Log}_8 14 = y$ $\text{Log}_{10} 1 = 0$ $\text{Log}_{10} 5 = 0.6989$

$8^y = 14$

$\text{Log}_{10} 8^y = \log_{10} 14$

$y \log_{10} 8 = \log_{10} 14$

$y = \log_{10} 14/\log_{10} 8$

$y = 1.1461/0.9030$

$y = 1.2692$

5, 14, 1, Deep calls unto Deep study bible 1

0.6989, 1.2692, 0, Deep calls unto Deep study bible 2

x-axis	y-axis
5	0.6989
14	1.2692
1	0

Water Spout *(lightning; combinatorics)* Study bible 1

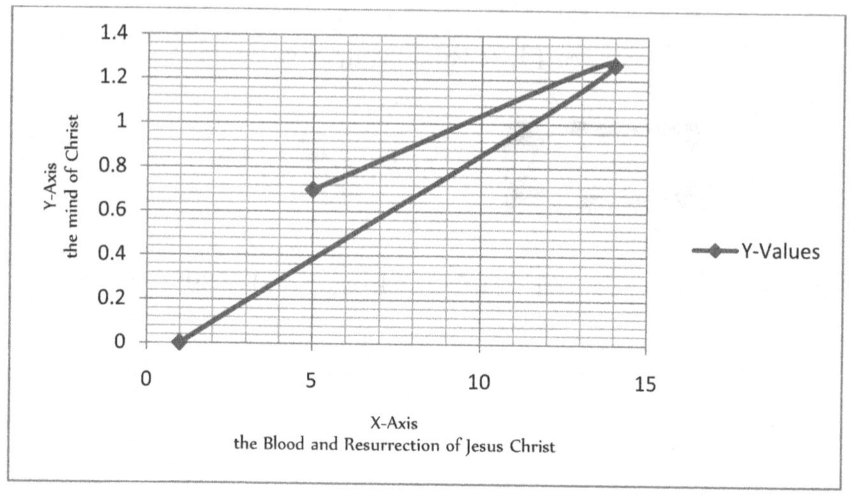

Water Spout *(lightning; combinatorics)*Study bible 2

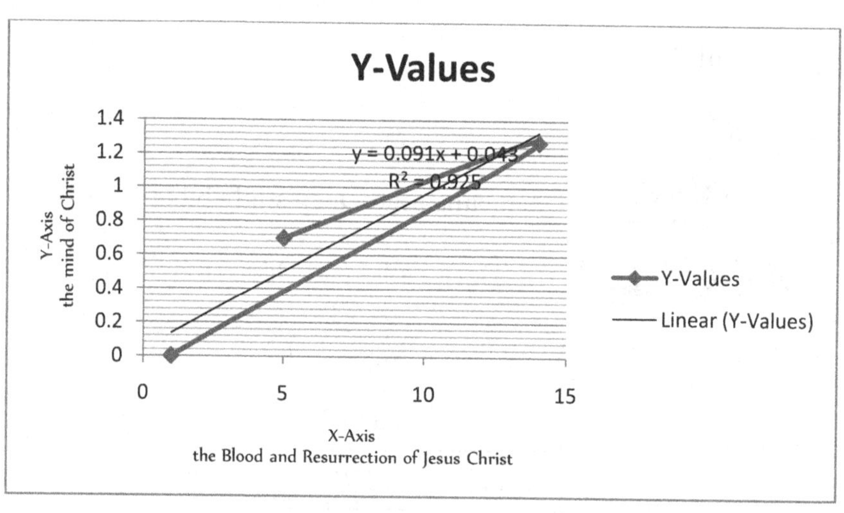

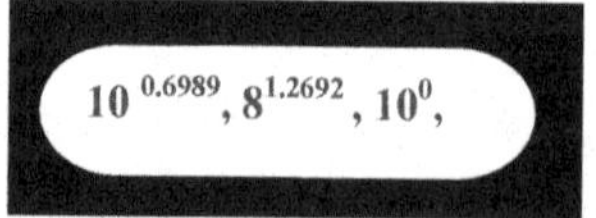

Pilled Poplar, Hazel, and Chesnut bible rods 2

23. Behold, a virgin shall be with child, and shall bring forth a son, and they shall call his name Emmanuel God with us,**which being interpreted is, God with us.**

1, 6, 6, 7, 4, 3. Bible Matrices

Pilled Poplar, Hazel, and Chesnut bible rods 1

$\text{Log}_{10} 1 = 0$ $\text{Log}_{10} 6 = 0.7781$ $\text{Log}_{10} 6 = 0.7781$ $\text{Log}_{10} 4 = 0.6020$ $\text{Log}_{10} 3 = 0.4771$

$\text{Log}_3 7 = y$

$3^y = 7$

$\text{Log}_{10} 3^y = \log_{10} 7$

$y \log_{10} 3 = \log_{10} 7$

$y = \log_{10} 7/\log_{10} 3$

$y = 0.8450/0.4771$

$y = 1.7711$

1, 6, 6, 7, 4, 3. Deep calls unto Deep study bible 1

0, 0.7781, 0.7781, 1.7711, 0.6020, 0.4771.
Deep calls unto Deep study bible 2

x-axis	y-axis
1	0
6	0.7781
6	0.7781
7	1.7711
4	0.6020
3	0.4771

Water Spout *(lightning; combinatorics)* Study bible 1

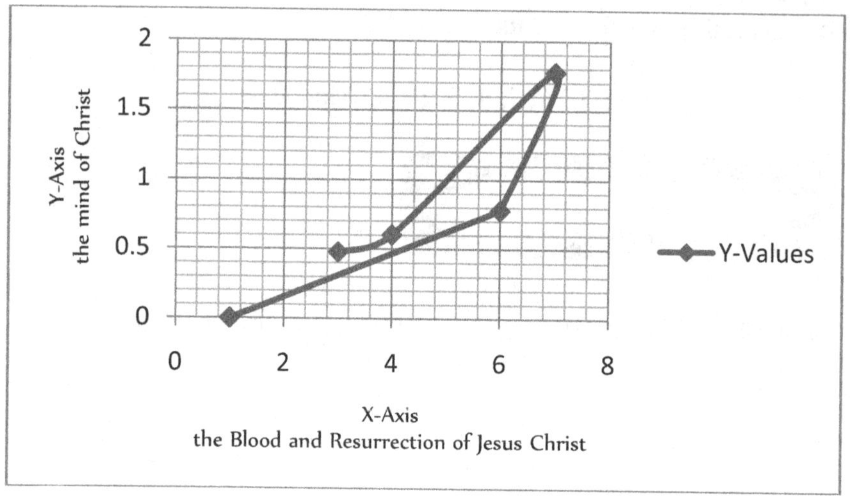

Water Spout *(lightning; combinatorics)*Study bible 2

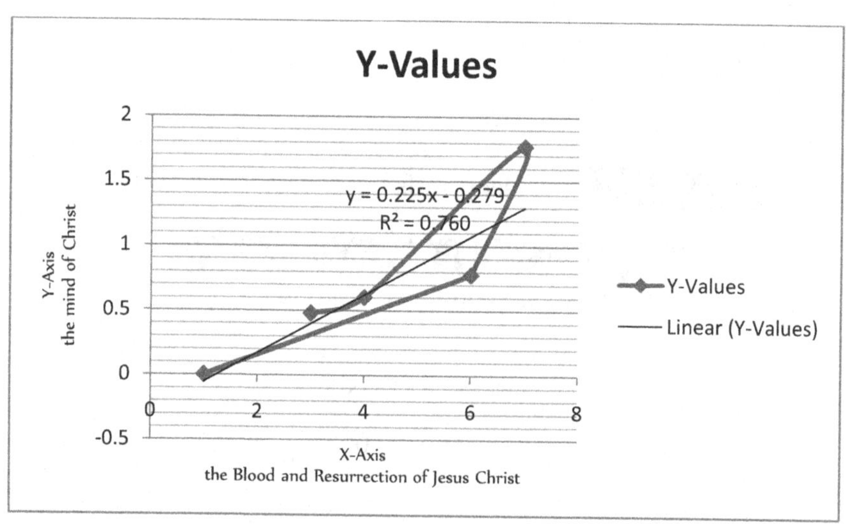

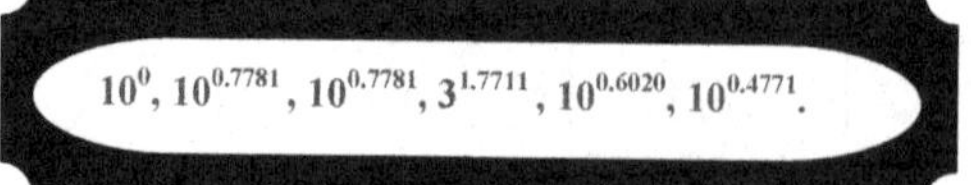

Pilled Poplar, Hazel, and Chesnut bible rods 2

24. Then Joseph increase; addition **being raised from sleep did as the angel of the Lord had bidden him, and took unto him his wife:**

16, 6: Bible Matrices

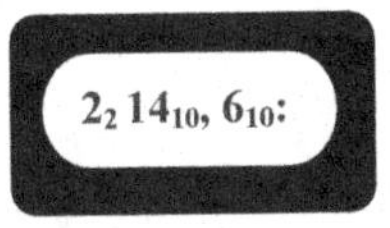

Pilled Poplar, Hazel, and Chesnut bible rods 1

$\text{Log}_2 2 = y$ $\text{Log}_{10} 14 = 1.1461$ $\text{Log}_{10} 6 = 0.7781$

$2^y = 2^1$

$y = 1$

16, 6: Deep calls unto Deep study bible 1

1, 1.1461, 0.7781: Deep calls unto Deep study bible 2

x-axis	y-axis
16	2.1461
6	0.7781

Water Spout *(lightning; combinatorics)*Study bible 1

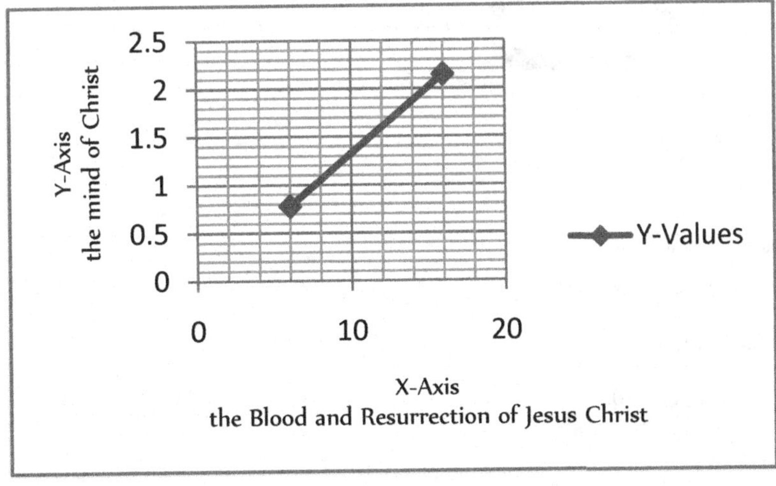

Water Spout *(lightning; combinatorics)*Study bible 2

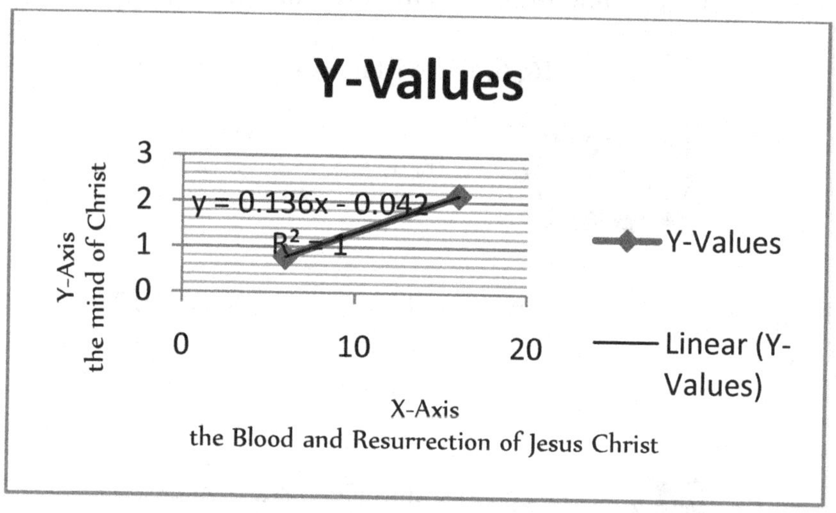

Pilled Poplar, Hazel, and Chesnut bible rods 2

25. And knew her not till she had brought forth her firstborn son: and he called his name JESUS savior; deliverer.

12: 6. Bible Matrices

Pilled Poplar, Hazel, and Chesnut bible rods 1

$\text{Log}_2 6 = y$

$2^y = 6$

$\text{Log}_{10} 2^y = \log_{10} 6$

$y \log_{10} 2 = \log_{10} 6$

$y = \log_{10} 6/\log_{10} 2$

$y = 0.7781/0.3010$

$y = 2.5850$

12: 6. Deep calls unto Deep study bible 1

1.0791: 2.5850. Deep calls unto Deep study bible 2

x-axis	y-axis
12	1.0791
6	2.5850

Water Spout *(lightning; combinatorics)* Study bible 1

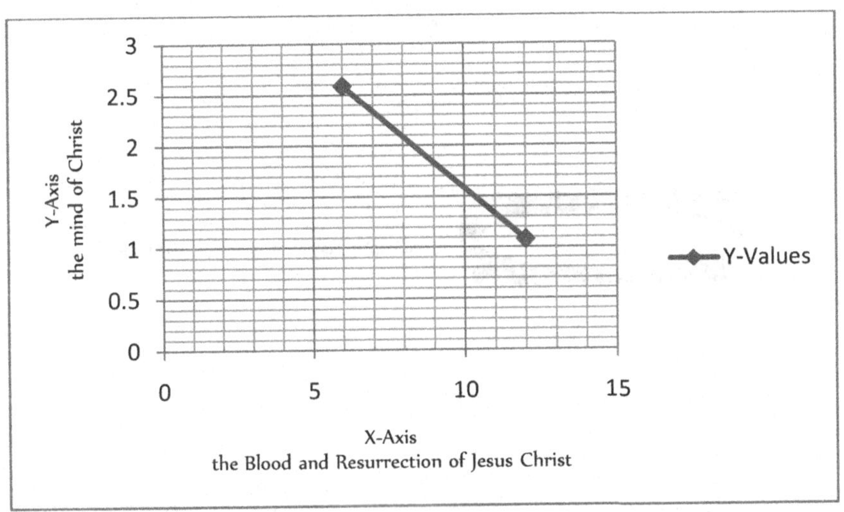

Water Spout *(lightning; combinatorics)* Study bible 2

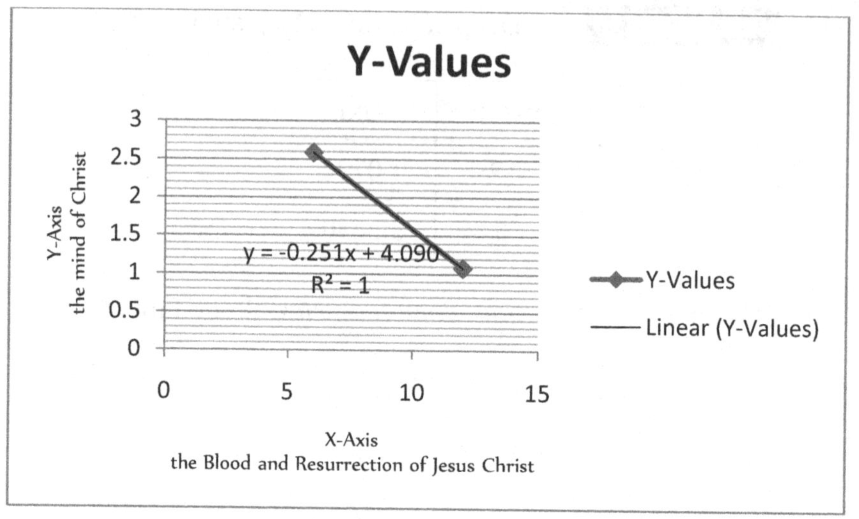

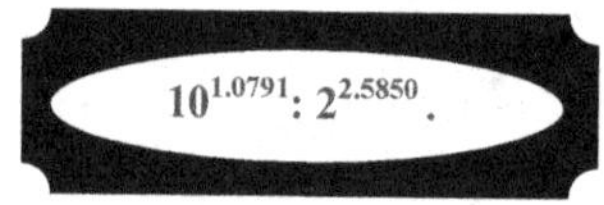

Pilled Poplar, Hazel, and Chesnut bible rods 2

CHAPTER 2

1. Now when Jesus savior; deliverer **was born in Bethlehem** house of bread; fruitfulness **of Judaea** praise of the Lord; confession of the Lord **in the days of Herod** son of a hero **the king, behold, there came wise men from the east to Jerusalem**possession of peace;habitation of peace; vision of peace,

16, 1, 9, Bible Matrices

$3_2\ 4_4\ 2_8\ 5_4\ 2_{10},\ 1_{10},\ 9_9,$ Pilled Poplar, Hazel, and Chestnut bible rods 1

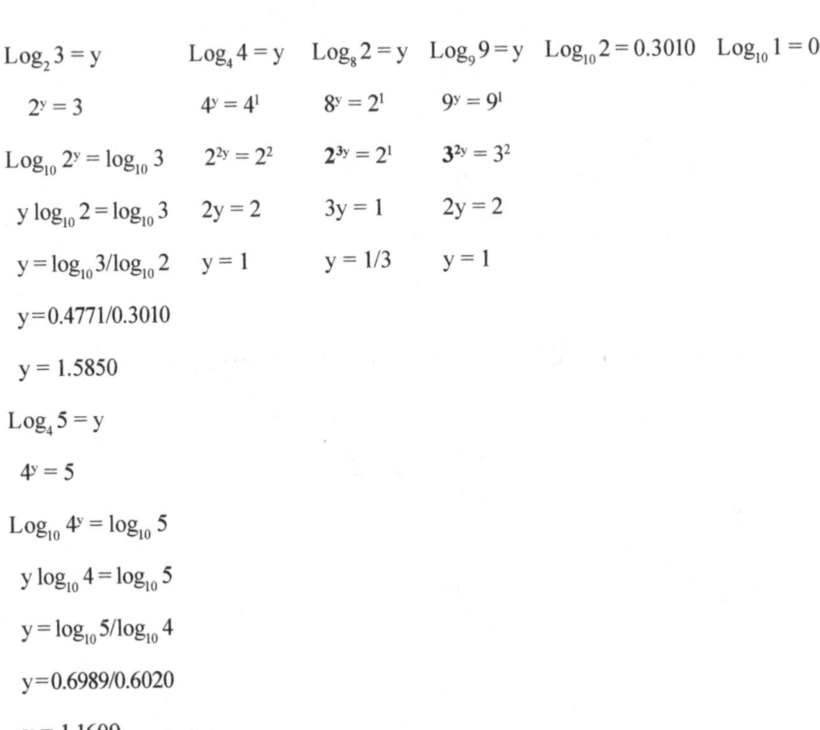

$\text{Log}_2 3 = y$

$2^y = 3$

$\text{Log}_{10} 2^y = \log_{10} 3$

$y \log_{10} 2 = \log_{10} 3$

$y = \log_{10} 3/\log_{10} 2$

$y = 0.4771/0.3010$

$y = 1.5850$

$\text{Log}_4 4 = y$

$4^y = 4^1$

$2^{2y} = 2^2$

$2y = 2$

$y = 1$

$\text{Log}_8 2 = y$

$8^y = 2^1$

$2^{3y} = 2^1$

$3y = 1$

$y = 1/3$

$\text{Log}_9 9 = y$

$9^y = 9^1$

$3^{2y} = 3^2$

$2y = 2$

$y = 1$

$\text{Log}_{10} 2 = 0.3010$

$\text{Log}_{10} 1 = 0$

$\text{Log}_4 5 = y$

$4^y = 5$

$\text{Log}_{10} 4^y = \log_{10} 5$

$y \log_{10} 4 = \log_{10} 5$

$y = \log_{10} 5/\log_{10} 4$

$y = 0.6989/0.6020$

$y = 1.1609$

16, 1, 9, Deep calls unto Deep study bible 1

1.5850 1 1/3 1.1609 0.3010, 0, 1,

Deep calls unto Deep study bible 2

x-axis	y-axis
16	4.3802
1	0
9	1

Water Spout *(lightning; combinatorics)* Study bible 1

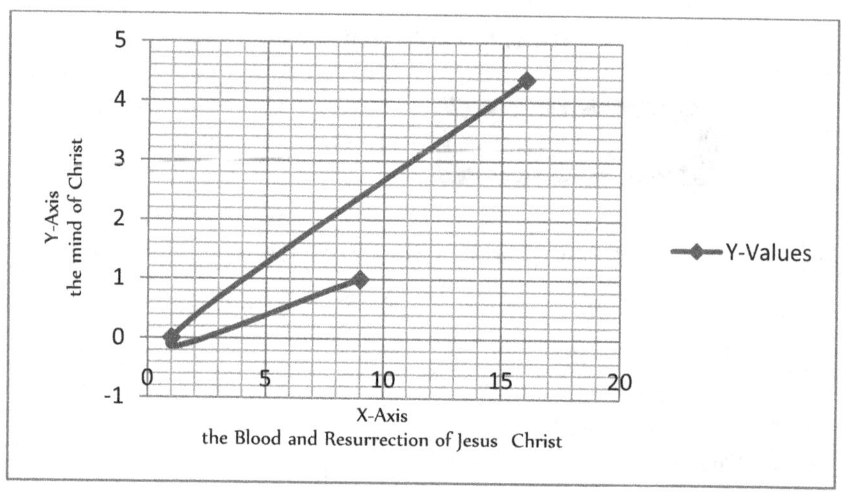

Water Spout *(lightning; combinatorics)* Study bible 2

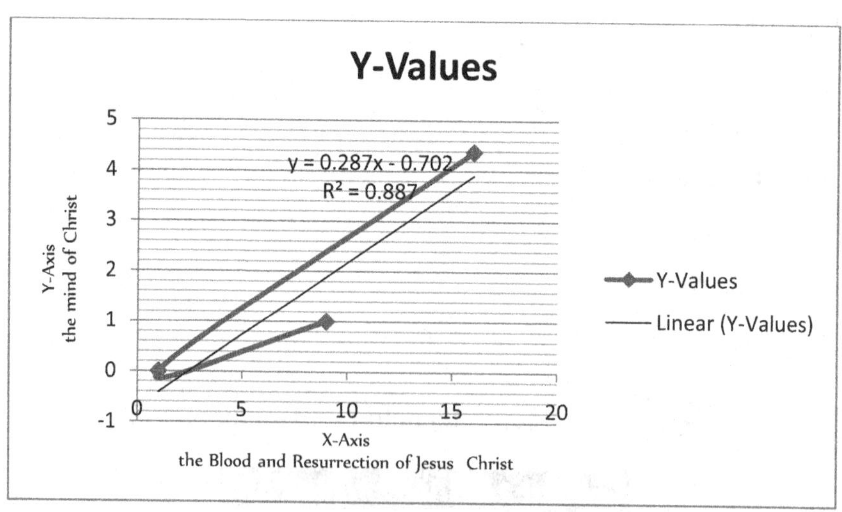

$3^{1.5850}$ 4^{1} $8^{1/3}$ $5^{1.1609}$ $2^{0.3010}$, 1^{0}, 9^{1},

Pilled Poplar, Hazel, and Chestnut bible rods 2

2. Saying, Where is he that is born King of the Jews the praise of the Lord; the confession of the Lord ? **for we have seen his star in the east, and are come to worship him.**

1, 10? 9, 6. Bible Matrices

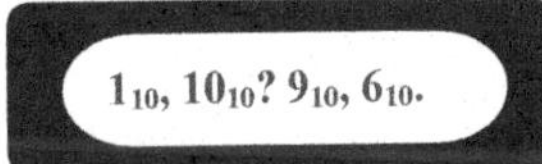

Pilled Poplar, Hazel, and Chestnut bible rods 1

$\text{Log}_{10} 10 = y$ $\quad$ $\text{Log}_{10} 1 = 0$ $\quad$ $\text{Log}_{10} 9 = 0.9542$ $\quad$ $\text{Log}_{10} 6 = 0.7781$

$10^{y} = 10^{1}$

$y = 1$

1, 10? 9, 6 . Deep calls unto Deep study bible 1

0, 1 ? 0.9542, 0.7781 . Deep calls unto Deep study bible 2

x-axis	y-axis
1	0
10	1
9	0.9542
6	0.7781

Water Spout*(lightning; combinatorics)* Study bible 1

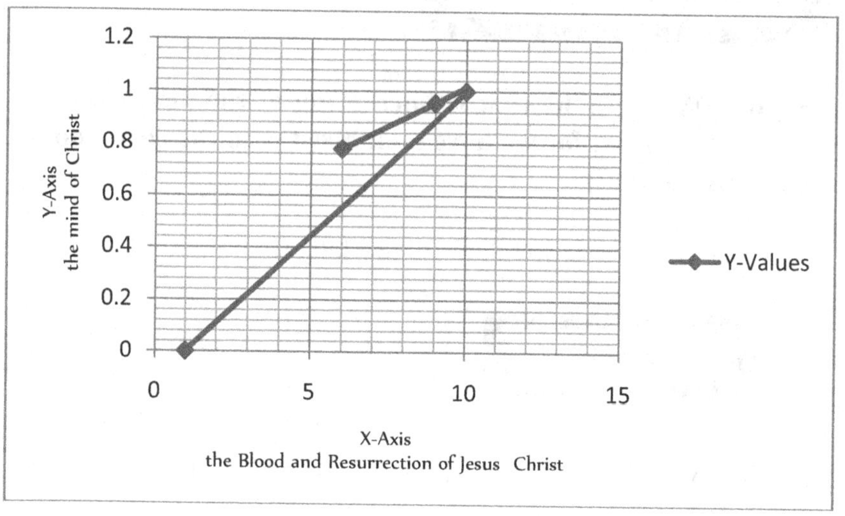

Water Spout *(lightning; combinatorics)* Study bible 2

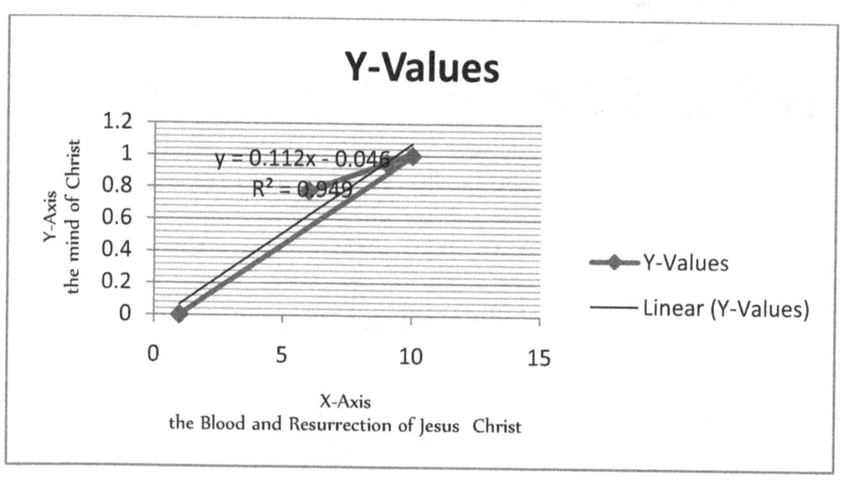

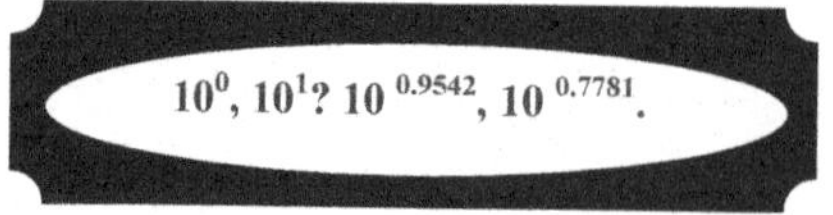

Pilled Poplar, Hazel, and Chestnut bible rods 2

3. When Herod son of a hero **the king had heard these things, he was troubled, and all Jerusalem**vision of peace; possession of peace; habitation of peace **with him.**

8, 3, 5. Bible Matrices

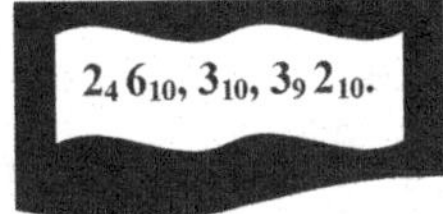

Pilled Poplar, Hazel, and Chestnut bible rods 1

$\text{Log}_4 2 = y$ $\text{Log}_9 3 = y$ $\text{Log}_{10} 6 = 0.7781$ $\text{Log}_{10} 3 = 0.4771$ $\text{Log}_{10} 2 = 0.3010$

$4^y = 2^1$ $9^y = 3^1$

$2^{2y} = 2^1$ $3^{2y} = 3^1$

$2y = 1$ $2y = 1$

$y = ½$ $y = ½$

8, 3, 5 . Deep calls unto Deep study bible 1

½ 0.7781, 0.4771, ½ 0.3010 . Deep calls unto Deep study bible 2

x-axis	y-axis
8	1.2781
3	0.4771
5	0.8010

Water Spout *(lightning; combinatorics)* Study bible 1

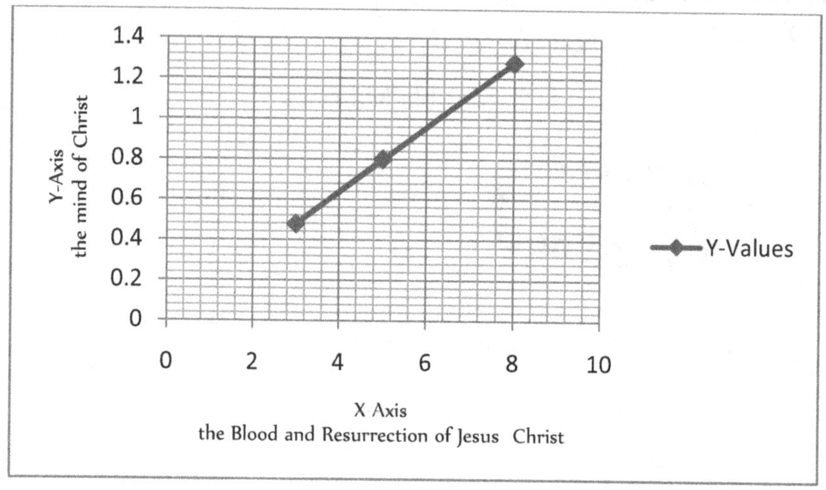

Water Spout *(lightning; combinatorics)* Study bible 2

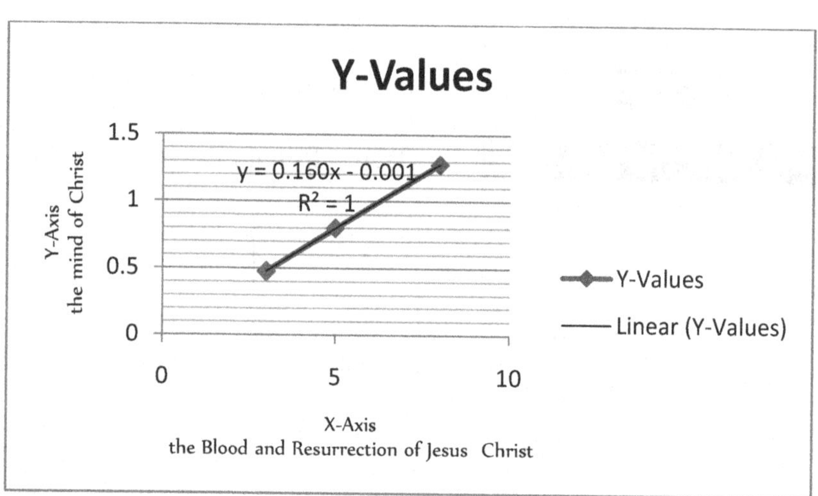

4 ½ $10^{0.7781}$, $10^{0.4771}$, 9 ½ $10^{0.3010}$.

Pilled Poplar, Hazel, and Chesnut bible rods 2

4. And when he had gathered all the chief priests and scribes lawyers, book copier, transcriber **of the people together, he demanded of them where Christ** anointed; smear **should be born.**

15, 9. Bible Matrices

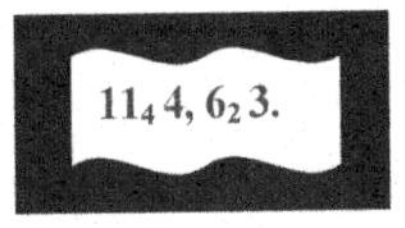
$11_4 4, 6_2 3.$

Pilled Poplar, Hazel, and Chestnut bible rods 1

$\text{Log}_4 11 = y$	$\text{Log}_2 6 = y$	$\text{Log}_{10} 4 = 0.6020$	$\text{Log}_{10} 3 = 0.4771$
$4^y = 11$	$2^y = 6$		
$\text{Log}_{10} 4^y = \log_{10} 11$	$\text{Log}_{10} 2^y = \log_{10} 6$		
$y \log_{10} 4 = \log_{10} 11$	$y \log_{10} 2 = \log_{10} 6$		
$y = \log_{10} 11/\log_{10} 4$	$y = \log_{10} 6/\log_{10} 2$		
$y = 1.0413/0.6020$	$y = 0.7781/0.3010$		
$y = 1.7297$	$y = 2.5850$		

15, 9. Deep calls unto Deep study bible 1

1.7297 0.6020, 2.5850 0.4771. Deep calls unto Deep study bible 2

x-axis	y-axis
15	2.3317
9	3.0621

Water Spout *(lightning; combinatorics)* Study bible 1

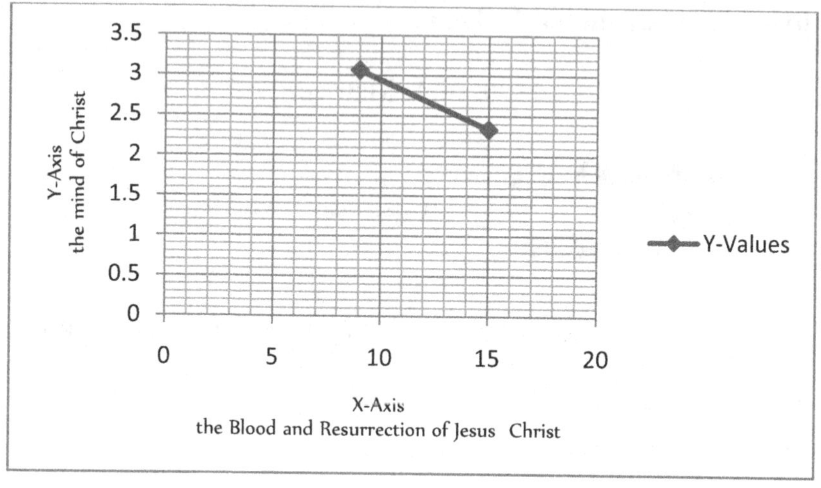

Water Spout *(lightning; combinatorics)* Study bible 2

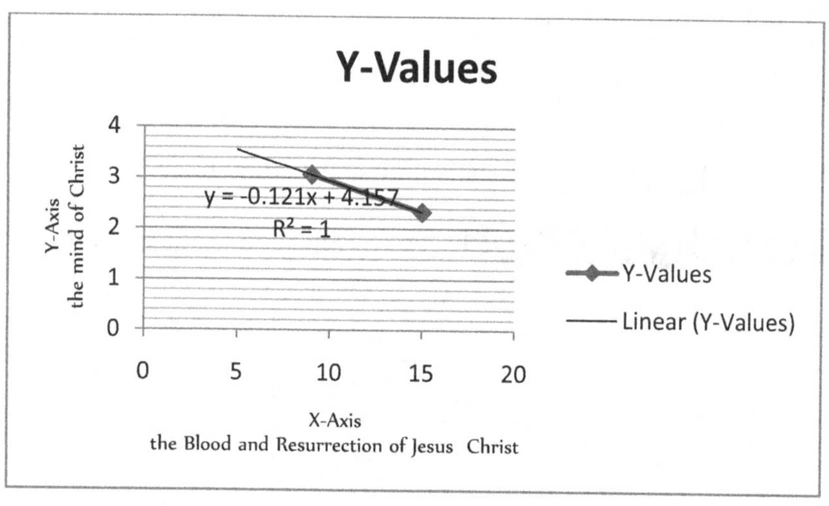

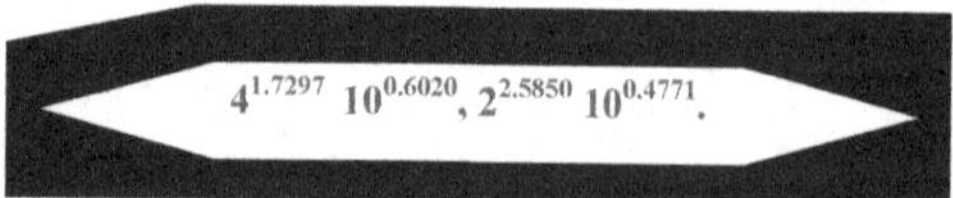

Pilled Poplar, Hazel, and Chestnut bible rods 2

5. And they said unto him, In Bethlehem house of bread; fruitfulness **of Judaea** praise of the Lord; confession of the Lord : **for thus it is written by the prophet** to bubble forth, as from a fountain; utter,

5, 4: 8, Bible Matrices

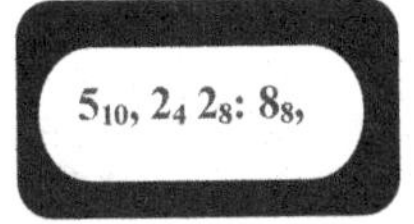

Pilled Poplar, Hazel, and Chestnut bible rods 1

$\log_4 2 = y$	$\log_8 2 = y$	$\log_8 8 = y$	$\log_{10} 5 = 0.6989$
$4^y = 2^1$	$8^y = 2^1$	$8^y = 8^1$	
$2^{2y} = 2^1$	$2^{3y} = 2^1$	$2^{3y} = 2^3$	
$2y = 1$	$3y = 1$	$3y = 3$	
$y = ½$	$y = 1/3$	$y = 1$	

5, 4 : 8, Deep calls unto Deep study bible 1

0.6989, ½ 1/3 : 1, Deep calls unto Deep study bible 2

x-axis	y-axis
5	0.6989
4	0.83
8	1

Water Spout *(lightning; combinatorics)* Study bible 1

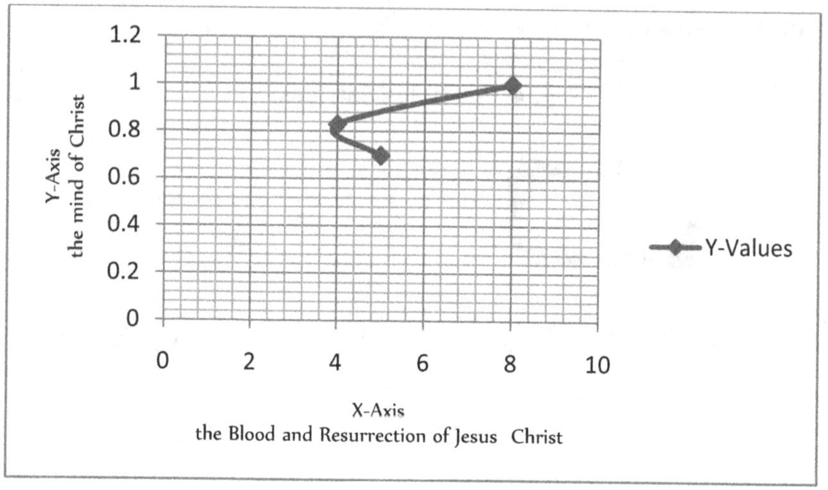

Water Spout *(lightning; combinatorics)* Study bible 2

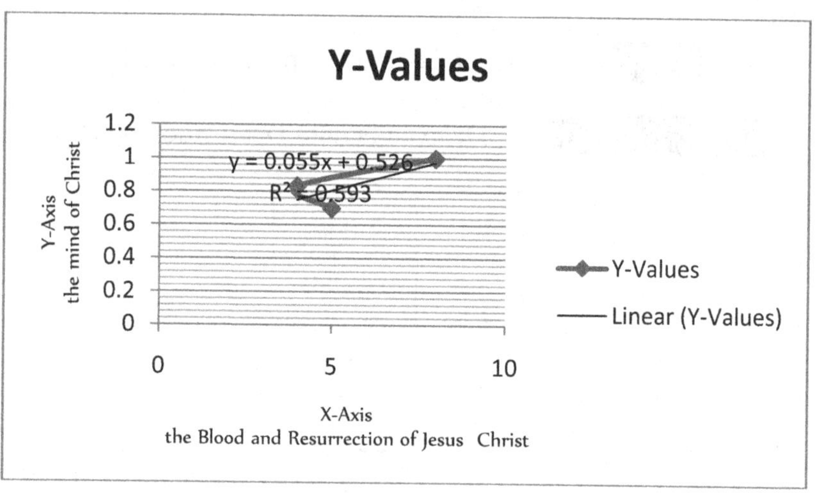

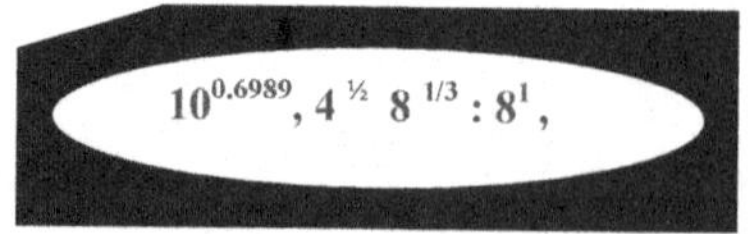

Pilled Poplar, Hazel, and Chestnut bible rods 2

6. And thou Bethlehem house of bread; fruitfulness, **in the land of Juda** praise of the Lord; confession, **art not the least among the princes of Juda** the praise of the Lord; confession of the Lord: **for out of thee shall come a Governor, that shall rule my people Israel** who prevails with God; God strives.

3, 5, 9: 8, 6. Bible Matrices

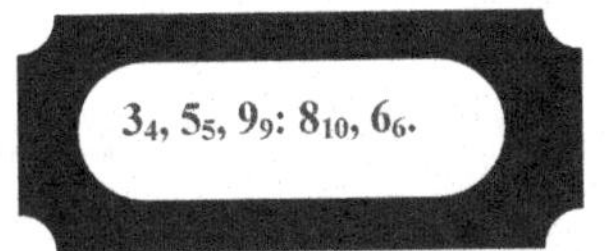

Pilled Poplar, Hazel, and Chestnut bible rods 1

$\text{Log}_5 5 = y$
$5^y = 5^1$
$y = 1$

$\text{Log}_9 9 = y$
$9^y = 9^1$
$y = 1$

$\text{Log}_6 6 = y$
$6^y = 6^1$
$y = 1$

$\text{Log}_{10} 8 = 0.9030$

$\text{Log}_4 3 = y$

$4^y = 3$

$\text{Log}_{10} 4^y = \log_{10} 3$

$y \log_{10} 4 = \log_{10} 3$

$y = \log_{10} 3/\log_{10} 4$

$y = 0.4771/0.6020$

$y = 0.7925$

3, 5, 9 : 8, 6. Deep calls unto Deep study bible 1

0.7925, 1, 1: 0.9030, 1 . Deep calls unto Deep study bible 2

x-axis	y-axis
3	0.7925
5	1
9	1
8	0.9030
6	1

Water Spout *(lightning; combinatorics)* Study bible 1

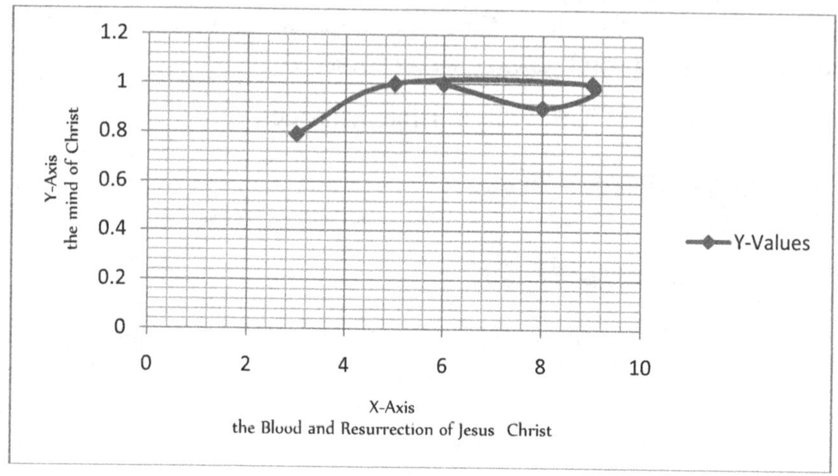

Water Spout *(lightning; combinatorics)* Study bible 2

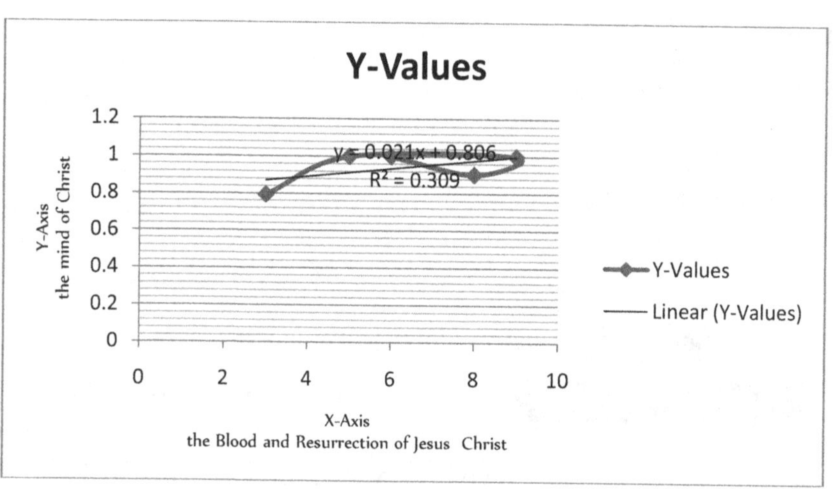

$4^{0.7925}, 5^{1}, 9^{1} : 10^{0.9030}, 6^{1}$.

Pilled Poplar, Hazel, and Chestnut bible rods 2

7. Then Herod son of a hero, **when he had privily called the wise men, enquired of them diligently what time the star appeared.**

2, 8, 9. Bible Matrices

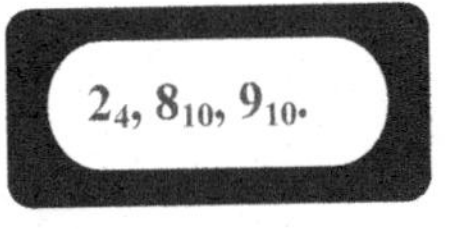

Pilled Poplar, Hazel, and Chestnut bible rods 1

$\text{Log}_4 2 = y$ $\text{Log}_{10} 8 = 0.9030$ $\text{Log}_{10} 9 = 0.9542$

$4^y = 2^1$

$2^{2y} = 2^1$

$2y = 1$

$y = ½$

2, 8, 9 . Deep calls unto Deep study bible 1

½, 0.9030, 0.9542. Deep calls unto Deep study bible 2

x-axis	y-axis
2	0.5
8	0.9030
9	0.9542

Water Spout *(lightning; combinatorics)* Study bible 1

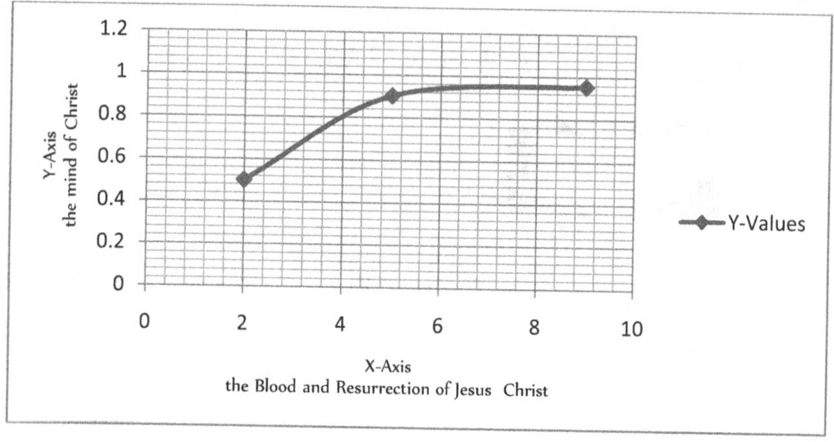

Water Spout*(lightning; combinatorics)* Study bible 2

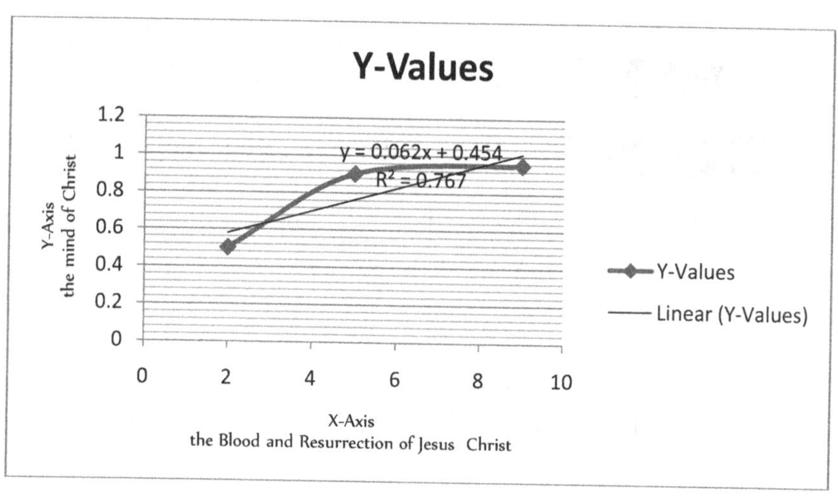

Pilled Poplar, Hazel, and Chestnut bible rods 2

8. And he sent them to Bethlehem house of bread; fruitfulness, **and said, Go and search diligently for the young child; and when ye have found him, bring me word again, that I may come and worship him also.**

6, 2, 8; 6, 4, 8. Bible Matrices

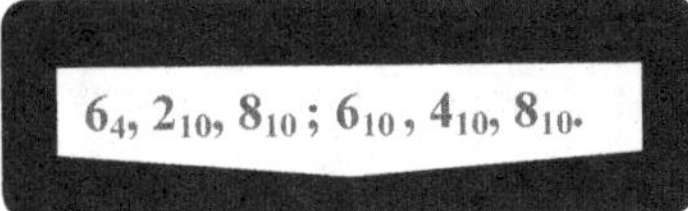

Pilled Poplar, Hazel, and Chestnut bible rods 1

$Log_4 6 = y$ $Log_{10} 4 = 0.6020$ $Log_{10} 6 = 0.7781$ $Log_{10} 8 = 0.9030$ $Log_{10} 2 = 0.3010$

$4^y = 6$

$Log_{10} 4^y = log_{10} 6$

$y \log_{10} 4 = \log_{10} 6$

$y = \log_{10} 6/\log_{10} 4$

$y = 0.7781/0.6020$

$y = 1.2925$

6, 2, 8; 6, 4, 8 . Deep calls unto Deep study bible 1

1.2925, 0.3010, 0.9030; 0.7781, 0.6020, 0.9030.
Deep calls unto Deep study bible 2

x-axis	y-axis
6	1.2925
2	0.3010
8	0.9030
6	0.7781
4	0.6020
8	0.9030

Water Spout *(lightning; combinatorics)* Study bible 1

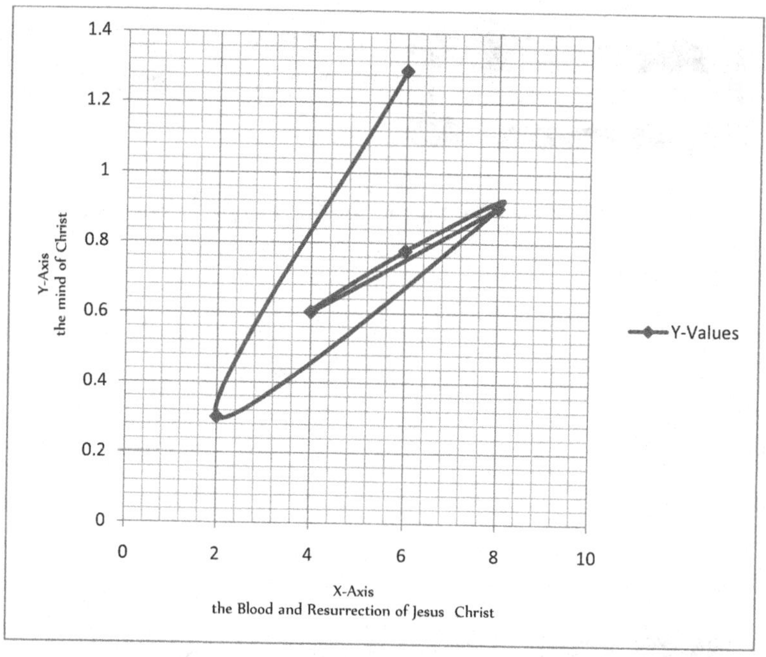

Water Spout *(lightning; combinatorics)* Study bible 2

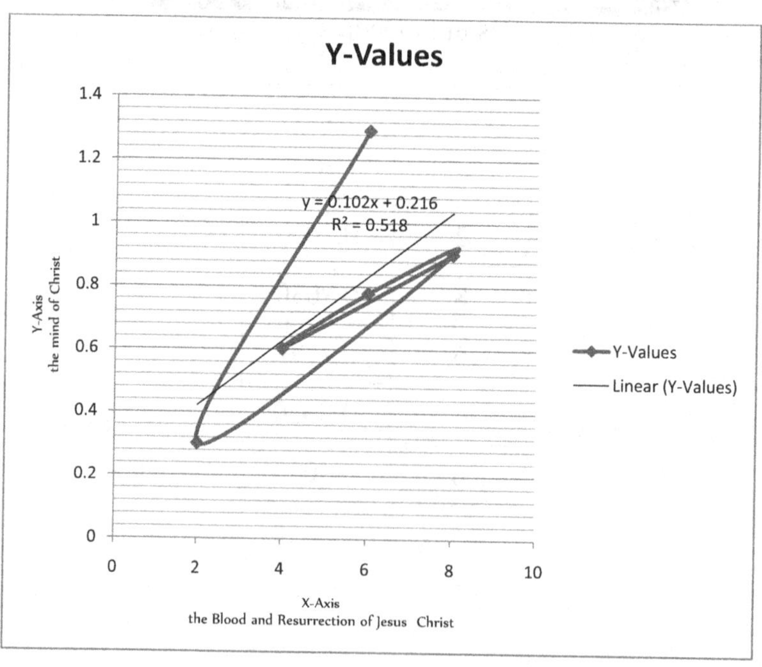

$4^{1.2925}, 10^{0.3010}, 10^{0.9030}; 10^{0.7781}, 10^{0.6020}, 10^{0.9030}.$

Pilled Poplar, Hazel, and Chestnut bible rods 2

9. When they had heard the king, they departed; and, lo, the star, which they saw in the east, went before them, till it came and stood over where the young child was.

6, 2; 1, 1, 2, 6, 3, 11. Bible Matrices

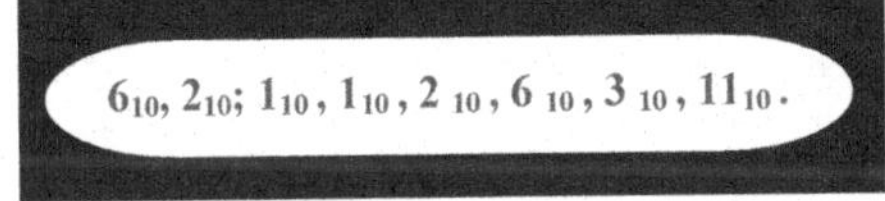

Pilled Poplar, Hazel, and Chestnut bible rods 1

$\text{Log}_{10} 6 = 0.7781$ $\text{Log}_{10} 2 = 0.3010$ $\text{Log}_{10} 1 = 0$ $\text{Log}_{10} 1 = 0$

$\text{Log}_{10} 2 = 0.3010$ $\text{Log}_{10} 6 = 0.7781$ $\text{Log}_{10} 3 = 0.4771$ $\text{Log}_{10} 11 = 1.0413$

6, 2; 1, 1, 2, 6, 3, 11. Deep calls unto Deep study bible 1

0.7781, 0.3010; 0, 0, 0.3010, 0.7781, 0.4771, 1.0413.

Deep calls unto Deep study bible 2

x-axis	y-axis
6	0.7781
2	0.3010
1	0
1	0
2	0.3010
6	0.7781
3	0.4771
11	1.0413

Water Spout *(lightning; combinatorics)* Study bible 1

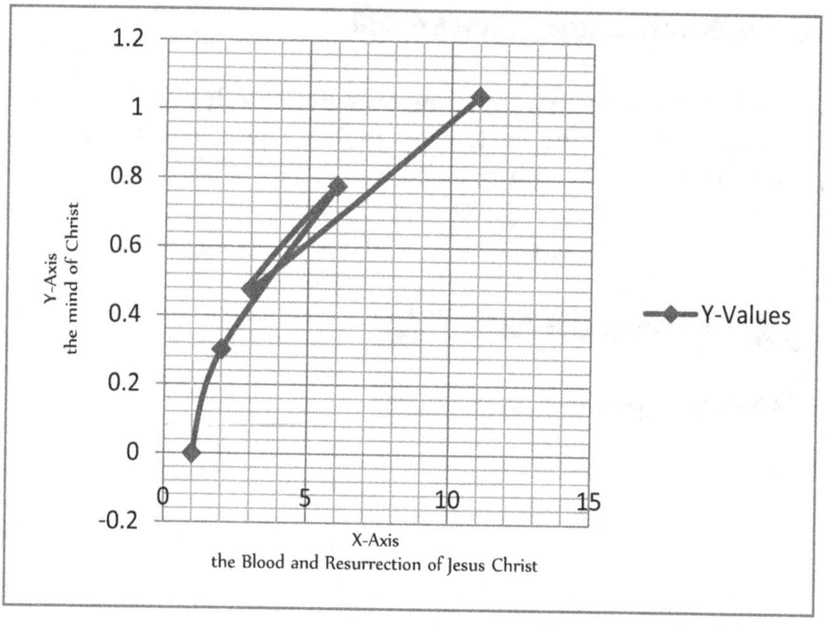

Water Spout *(lightning; combinatorics)* Study bible 2

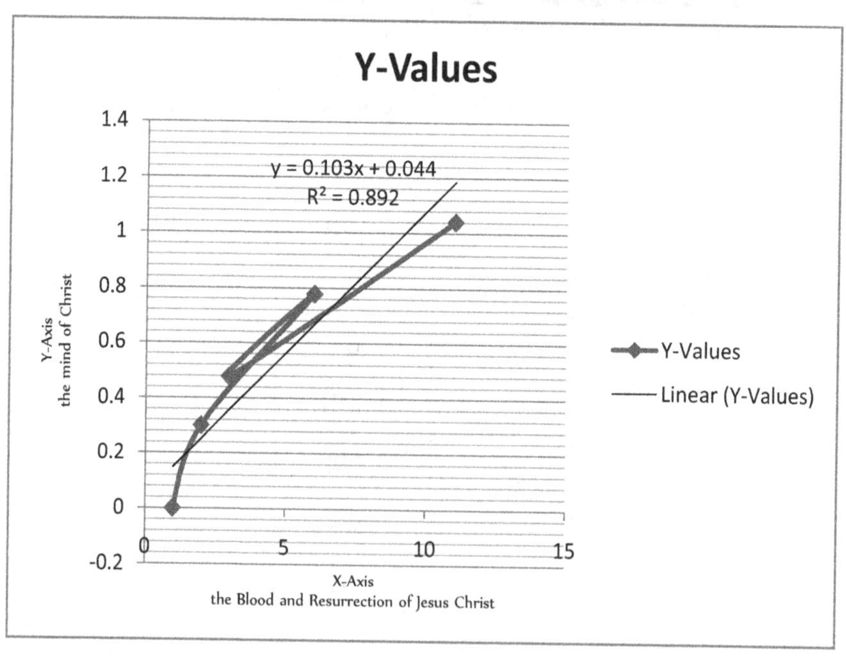

Pilled Poplar, Hazel, and Chestnut bible rods

10. When they saw the star, they rejoiced with exceeding great joy.

5, 6. Bible Matrices

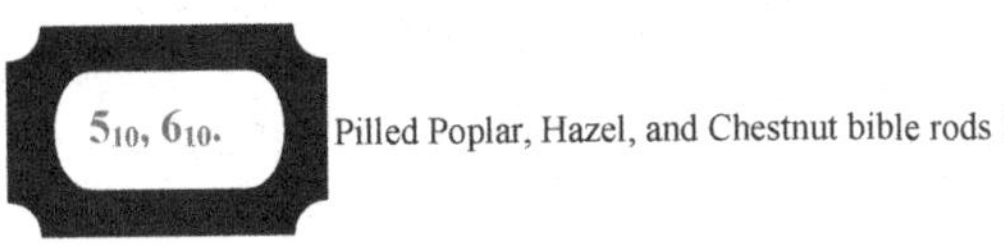

Pilled Poplar, Hazel, and Chestnut bible rods 1

$\text{Log}_{10} 5 = 0.6989$ $\text{Log}_{10} 6 = 0.7781$

5, 6. Deep calls unto Deep study bible 1

0.6989, 0, 7781. Deep calls unto Deep study bible 2

x-axis	y-axis
5	0.6989
6	0.7781

Water Spout *(lightning; combinatorics)* Study bible 1

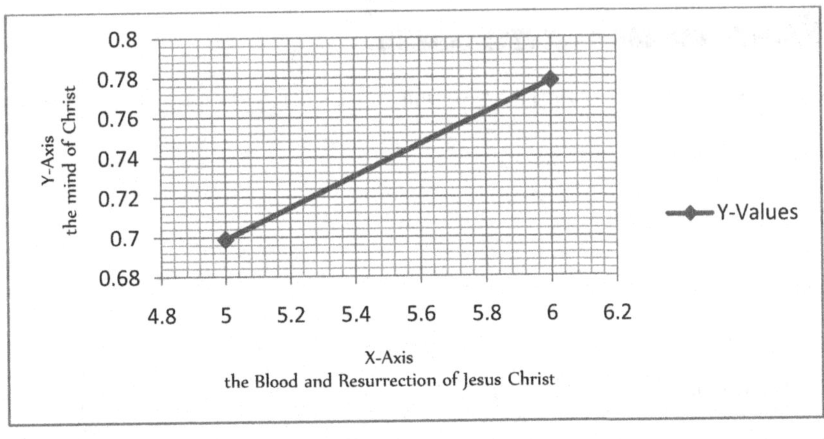

Water Spout *(lightning; combinatorics)* Study bible 2

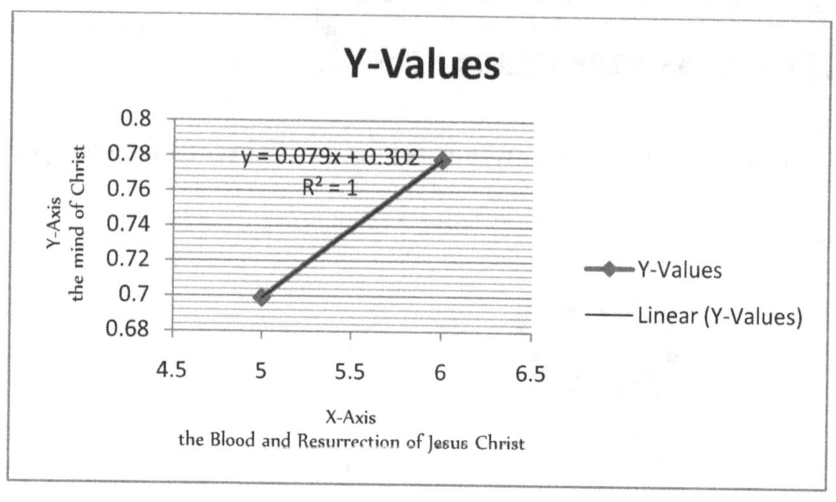

Pilled Poplar, Hazel, and Chestnut bible rods 2

11. And when they were come into the house, they saw the young child with Marya tear **his mother, and fell down, and worshipped him: and when they had opened their treasures, they presented unto him gifts; gold, and frankincense, and myrrh.**

8, 9, 3, 3: 7, 5; 1, 2, 2. Bible Matrices

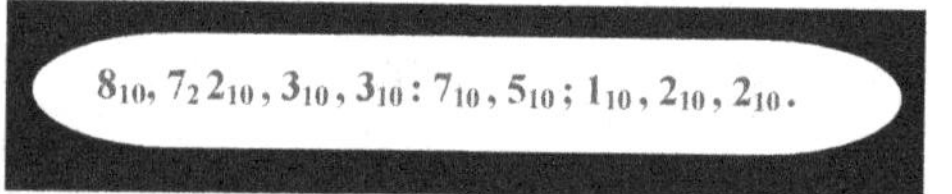

Pilled Poplar, Hazel, and Chestnut bible rods 1

$\text{Log}_{10} 8 = 0.9030$ $\text{Log}_{10} 7 = 0.8450$ $\text{Log}_{10} 2 = 0.3010$ $\text{Log}_{10} 1 = 0$ $\text{Log}_{10} 3 = 0.4771$ $\text{Log}_{10} 5 = 0.6989$

$\text{Log}_2 7 = y$

$2^y = 7$

$\text{Log}_{10} 2^y = \log_{10} 7$

$y \log_{10} 2 = \log_{10} 7$

$y = \log_{10} 7/\log_{10} 2$

$y = 0.8450/0.3010$

$y = 2.8073$

8, 9, 3, 3: 7, 5 ; 1, 2, 2. Deep calls unto Deep study bible 1

0.9030, 2.8073 0.3010, 0.4771, 0.4771: 0.8450, 0.6989 ; 0, 0.3010, 0.3010. Deep calls unto Deep study bible 2

x-axis	y-axis
8	0.9030
9	3.1083
3	0.4771
3	0.4771
7	0.8450
5	0.6989
1	0
2	0.3010
2	0.3010

Water Spout *(lightning; combinatorics)* Study bible 1

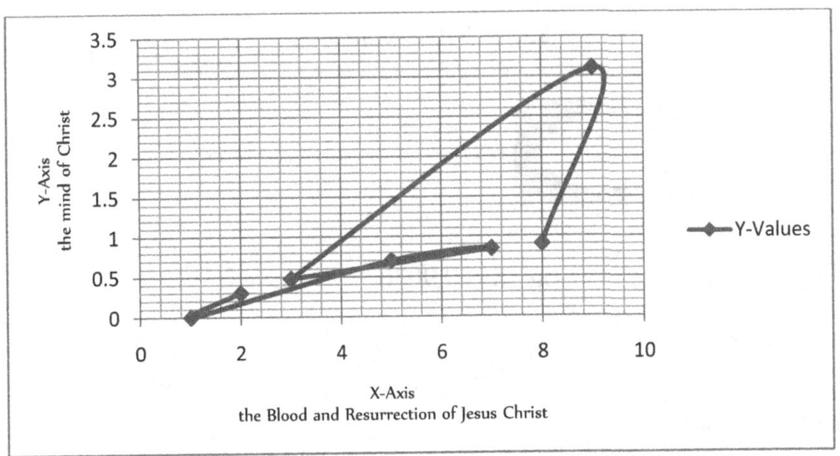

Water Spout *(lightning; combinatorics)* Study bible 2

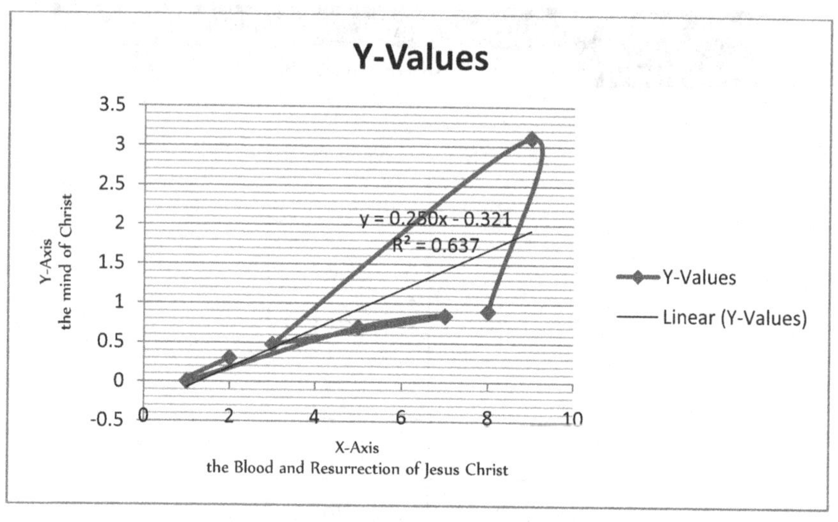

$10^{0.9030}$, $2^{2.8073}$ $10^{0.3010}$, $10^{0.4771}$, $10^{0.4771}$: $10^{0.8450}$, $10^{0.6989}$; 10^{0}, $10^{0.3010}$, $10^{0.3010}$.

Pilled Poplar, Hazel, and Chestnut bible rods 2

12. And being warned of God in a dream that they should not return to Herod son of a hero, **they departed into their own country another way.**

15, 8. Bible Matrices

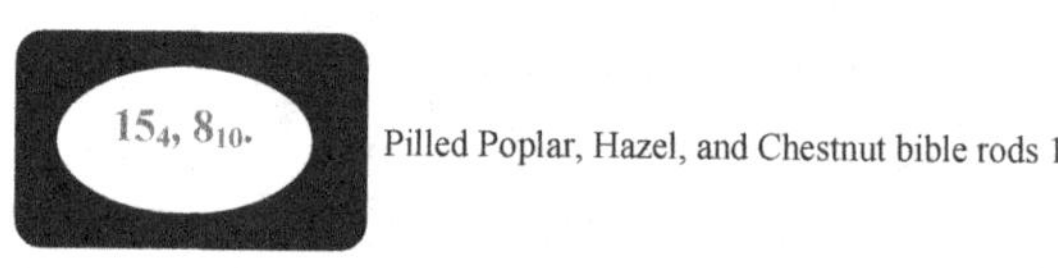
15_4, 8_{10}.

Pilled Poplar, Hazel, and Chestnut bible rods 1

$\text{Log}_4 15 = y$ $\text{Log}_{10} 8 = 0.9030$

$4^y = 15$

$\text{Log}_{10} 4^y = \log_{10} 15$

$y \log_{10} 4 = \log_{10} 15$

$y = \log_{10} 15/\log_{10} 4$

$y = 1.1760/0.6020$

$y = 1.9534$

15, 8. Deep calls unto Deep study bible 1

1.9534, 0.9030. Deep calls unto Deep study bible 2

x-axis	y-axis
15	1.9534
8	0.9030

Water Spout *(lightning; combinatorics)*Study bible 1

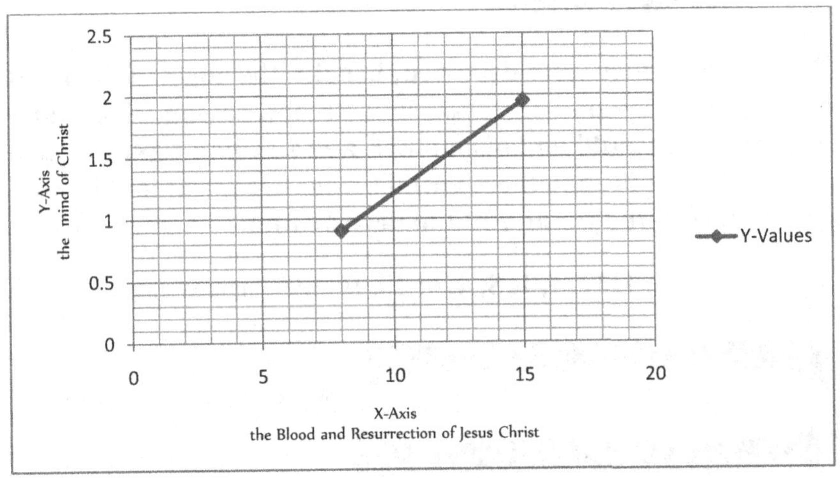

Water Spout *(lightning; combinatorics)* Study bible 2

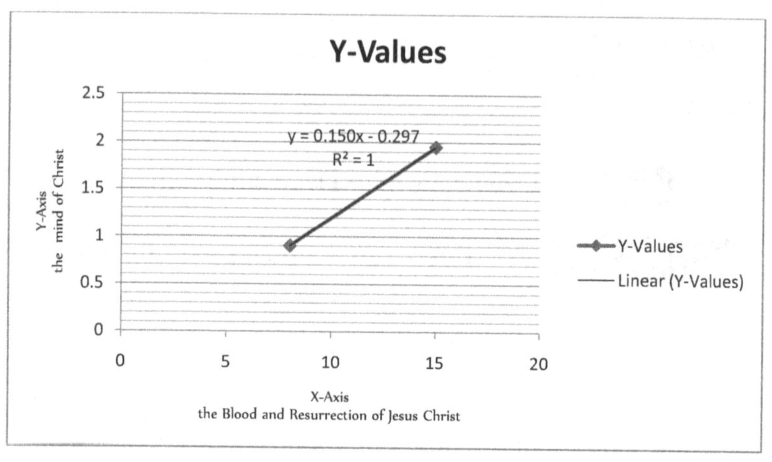

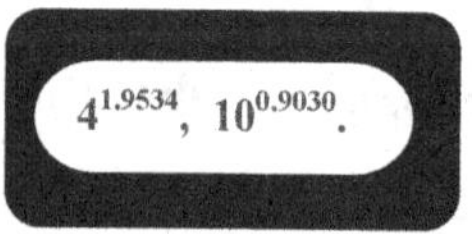

Pilled Poplar, Hazel, and Chestnut bible rods 2

13. And when they were departed, behold, the angel of the Lord appeareth to Joseph increase; addition **in a dream, saying, Arise, and take the young child and his mother, and flee into Egypt** that trouble; oppresses; anguish, **and be thou there until I bring thee word: for Herod** son of a hero **will seek the young child to destroy him.**

5, 1, 11, 1, 1, 8, 4, 9: 10. Bible Matrices

5_{10}, 1_{10}, $8_2 3_{10}$, 1_{10}, 1_{10}, 8_{10}, 4_4, 9_{10}: $2_4 8_{10}$.

Pilled Poplar, Hazel, and Chestnut bible rods 1

$\text{Log}_{10} 8 = 0.9030$ $\text{Log}_{10} 9 = 0.9542$ $\text{Log}_{10} 1 = 0$ $\text{Log}_{10} 3 = 0.4771$ $\text{Log}_{10} 5 = 0.6989$

$\text{Log}_2 8 = y$	$\text{Log}_4 2 = y$	$\text{Log}_4 4 = y$
$2^y = 8$	$4^y = 2$	$4^y = 4$
$2^y = 2^3$	$2^{2y} = 2^1$	$2^{2y} = 2^2$
$y = 3$	$2y = 1$	$2y = 2$
	$y = ½$	$y = 1$

5, 1, 11, 1, 1, 8, 4, 9: 10. Deep calls unto Deep study bible 1

0.6989, 0, 3 0.4771, 0, 0, 0.9030, 1, 0.9542: ½ 0.9030.

Deep calls unto Deep study bible 2

x-axis	y-axis
5	0.6989
1	0
11	3.4771
1	0
1	0
8	0.9030
4	1
9	0.9542
10	1.4030

Water Spout *(lightning; combinatorics)* Study bible 1

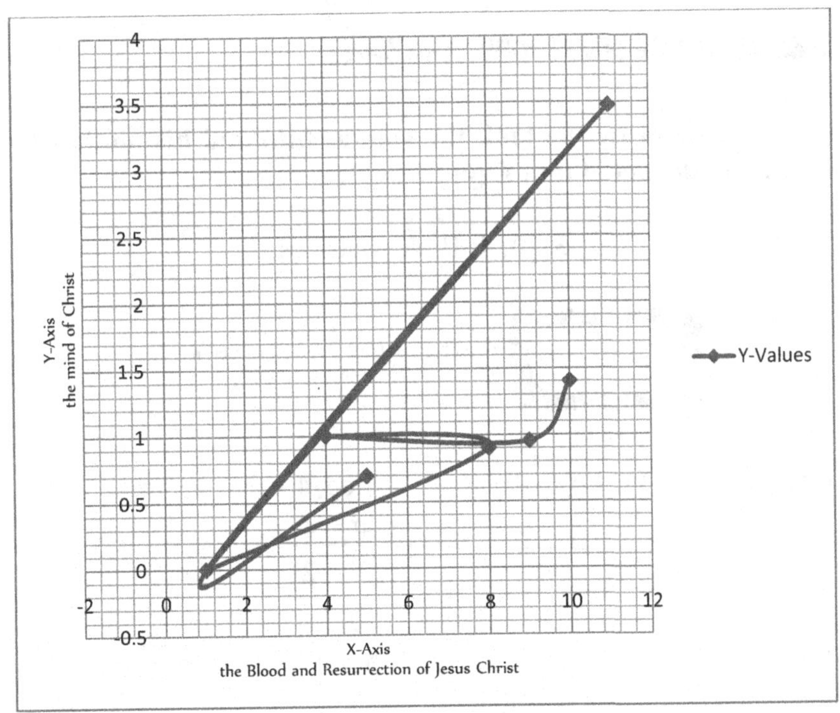

Water Spout *(lightning; combinatorics)* Study bible 2

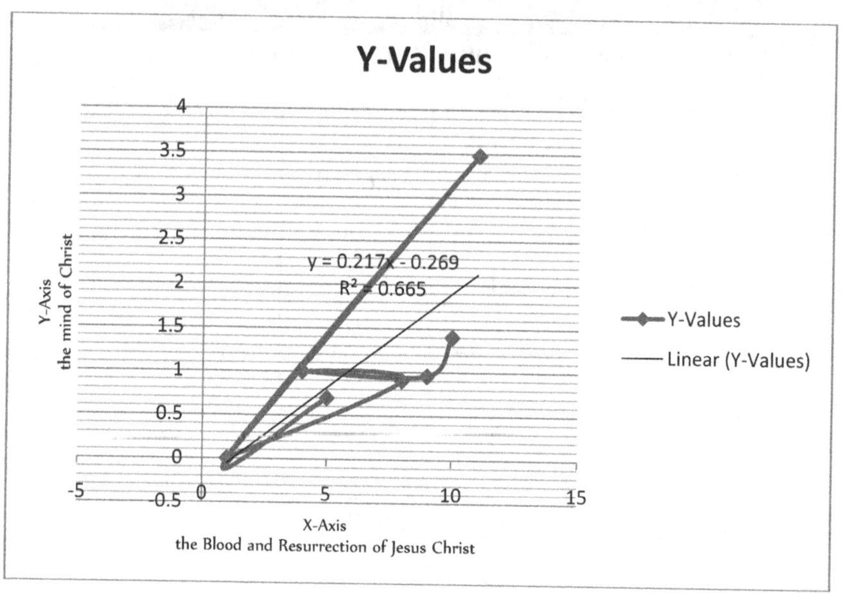

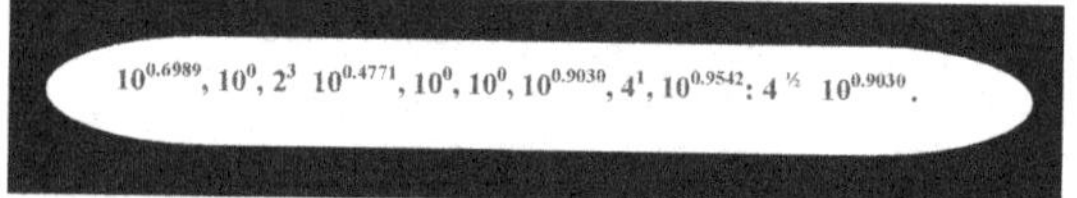

Pilled Poplar, Hazel, and Chestnut bible rods

14. When he arose, he took the young child and his mother by night, and departed into Egyptthat troubles, oppresses; anguish:

3, 10, 4: Bible Matrices

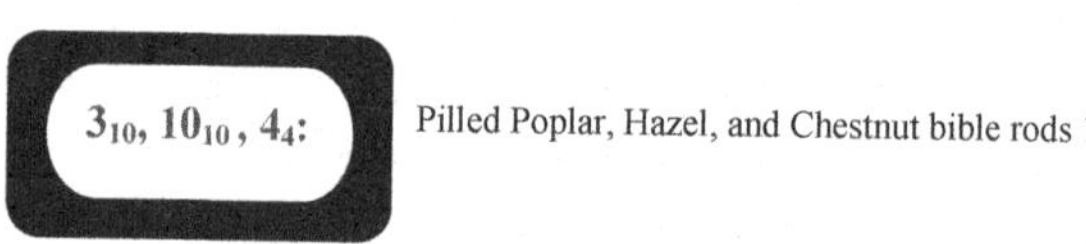

Pilled Poplar, Hazel, and Chestnut bible rods 1

$\text{Log}_{10} 3 = 0.4771$ $\text{Log}_{10} 10 = 1$

$$\text{Log}_4 4 = y$$
$$4^y = 4$$
$$2^{2y} = 2^2$$
$$2y = 2$$
$$y = 1$$

3, 10, 4: Deep calls unto Deep study bible 1

0.4771, 1, 1: Deep calls unto Deep study bible 2

x-axis	y-axis
3	0.4771
10	1
4	1

Water Spout *(lightning; combinatorics)* Study bible 1

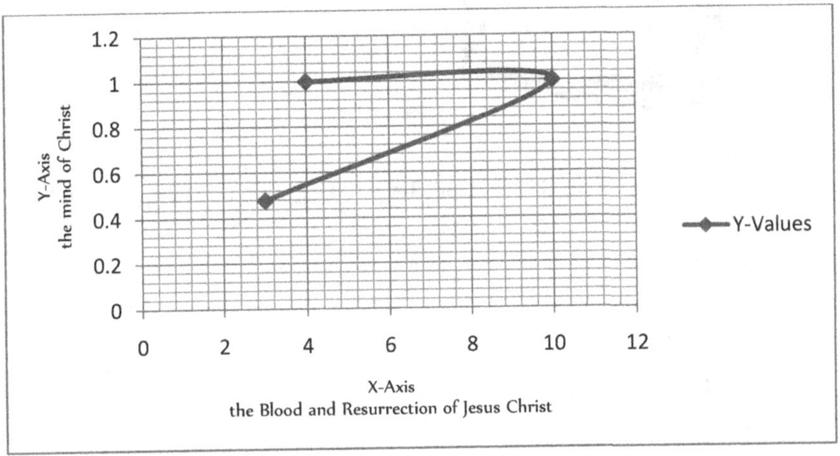

Water Spout *(lightning; combinatorics)* Study bible 2

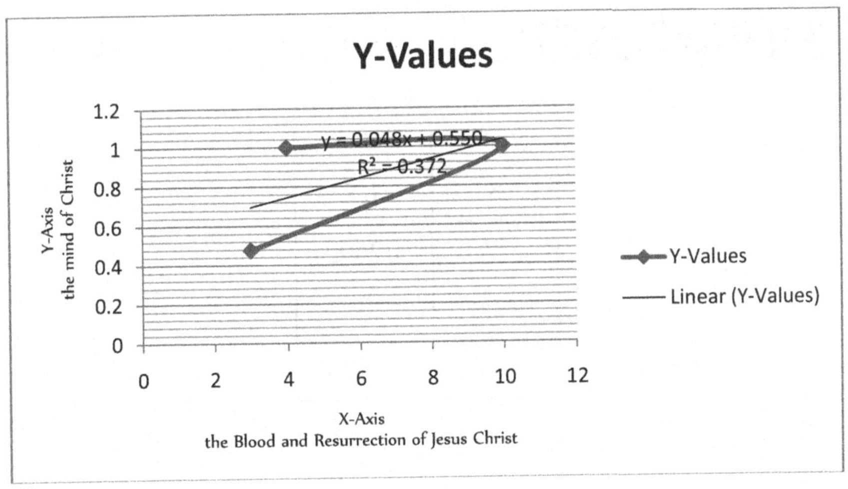

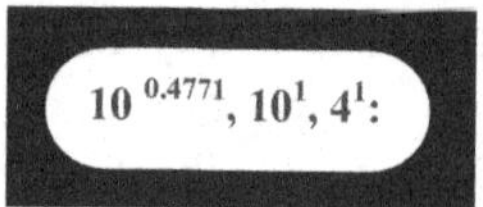

Pilled Poplar, Hazel, and Chestnut bible rods 2

15. And was there until the death of Herod son of a hero: **that it might be fulfilled which was spoken of the Lord by the prophet** to bubble forth, as from a fountain; utter, **saying, Out of Egypt** troubler, oppresses; anguish **have I called my son.**

8: 14, 1, 8. Bible Matrices

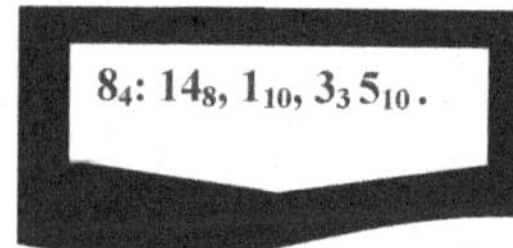

Pilled Poplar, Hazel, and Chestnut bible rods 1

$\text{Log}_8 14 = y$ $\quad$ $\text{Log}_4 8 = y$ $\quad$ $\text{Log}_3 3 = y$ $\quad$ $\text{Log}_{10} 1 = 0$ $\quad$ $\text{Log}_{10} 5 = 0.6989$

$8^y = 14$ $\quad$ $4^y = 8$ $\quad$ $3^y = 3^1$

$\log 8^y = \log 14$ $\quad$ $2^{2y} = 2^3$ $\quad$ $y = 1$

$y \log 8 = \log 14$ $\quad$ $2y = 3$

$y = \log 14/\log 8$ $\quad$ $y = 3/2$

$y = 1.1461/0.9030$ $\quad$ $y = 1.5$

$y = 1.2692$

8: 14, 1, 8 . Deep calls unto Deep study bible 1

1.5: 1.2692, 0, 1 0.6989. Deep calls unto Deep study bible 2

x-axis	y-axis
8	1.5
14	1.2692
1	0
8	1.6989

Water Spout *(lightning; combinatorics)* Study bible 1

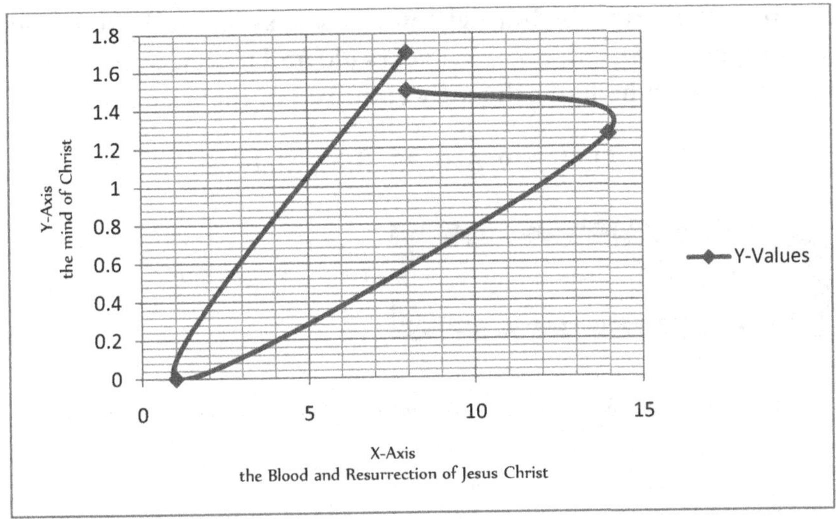

Water Spout *(lightning; combinatorics)* Study bible 2

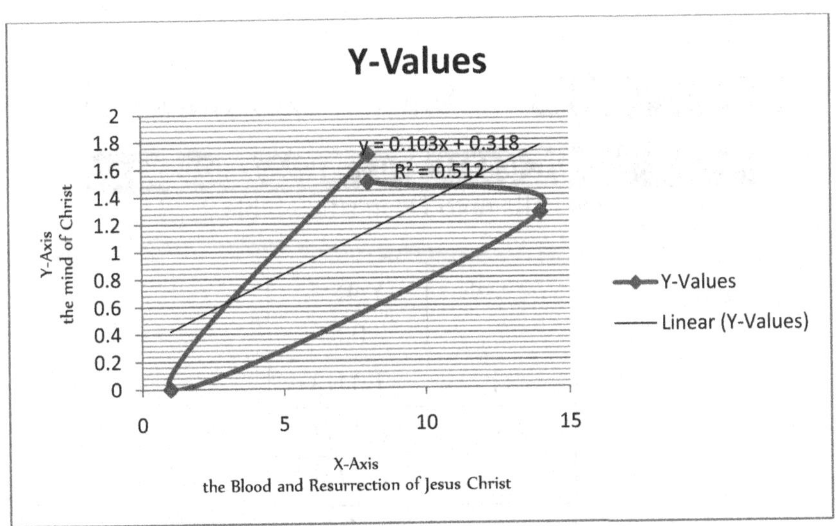

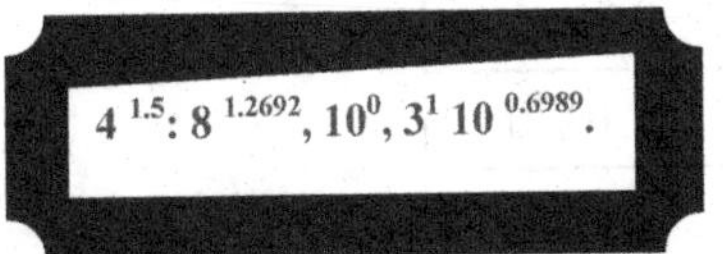
$4^{1.5}: 8^{1.2692}, 10^{0}, 3^{1}\ 10^{0.6989}.$

Pilled Poplar, Hazel, and Chestnut bible rods 2

16. Then Herodson of a hero, **when he saw that he was mocked of the wise men, was exceeding wroth, and sent forth, and slew all the children that were in Bethlehem**house of bread, **and in all the coasts thereof, from two** witness, support; 2 x 1 **years old and under, according to the time which he had diligently enquired of the wise men.**

2, 11, 3, 3, 9, 6, 6, 13. Bible Matrices

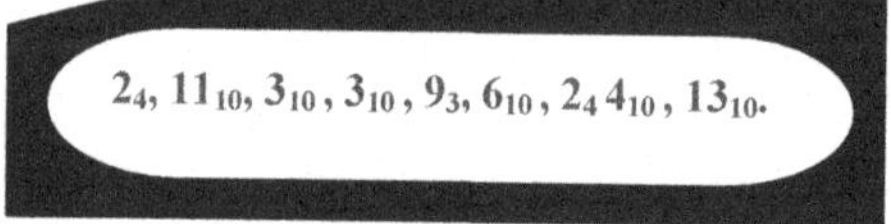

Pilled Poplar, Hazel, and Chestnut bible rods 1

$\text{Log}_{10} 11 = 1.0413$ $\text{Log}_{10} 3 = 0.4771$ $\text{Log}_{10} 6 = 0.7781$ $\text{Log}_{10} 4 = 0.6020$ $\text{Log}_{10} 13 = 1.1139$

$\text{Log}_4 2 = y$	$\text{Log}_4 2 = y$	$\text{Log}_3 9 = y$
$4^y = 2^1$	$4^y = 2$	$3^y = 9$
$2^{2y} = 2^1$	$2^{2y} = 2^1$	$3^y = 3^2$
$2y = 1$	$2y = 1$	$y = 2$
$y = ½$	$y = ½$	

2, 11, 3, 3, 9, 6, 6, 13. Deep calls unto Deep study bible 1

½, 1.0413, 0.4771, 0.4771, 2, 0.7781, ½ 0.6020, 1.1139
Deep calls unto Deep study bible 2

x-axis	y-axis
2	0.5
11	1.0413
3	0.4771
3	0.4771
9	2
6	0.7781
6	1.1020
13	1.1139

Water Spout *(lightning; combinatorics)* Study bible 1

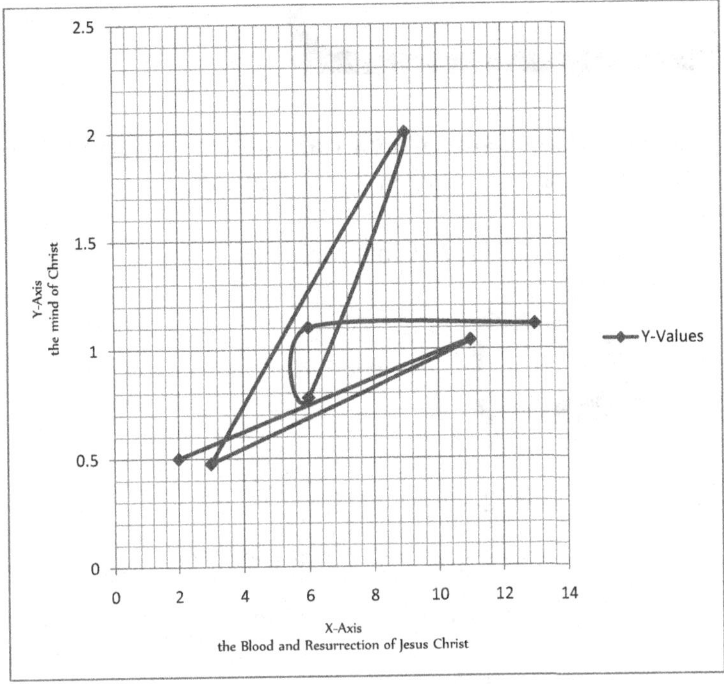

Water Spout *(lightning; combinatorics)* Study bible 2

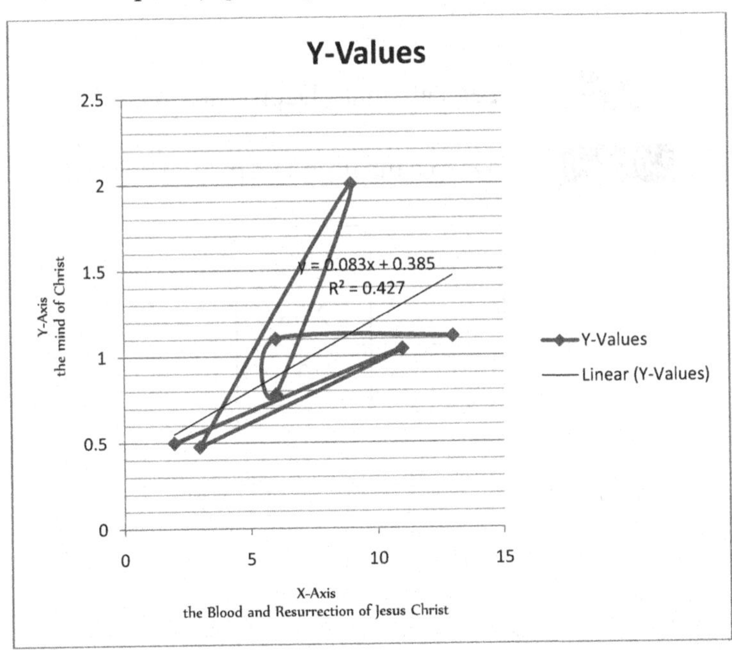

$4^{½}$, $10^{1.0413}$, $10^{0.4771}$, $10^{0.4771}$, 3^{2}, $10^{0.7781}$, $4^{½}$ $10^{0.6020}$, $10^{1.1139}$.

Pilled Poplar, Hazel, and Chestnut bible rods 2

17. Then was fulfilled that which was spoken by Jeremy exaltation of God **the prophet** to bubble forth, as from a fountain; utter, **saying,**

11, 1, Bible Matrices

Pilled Poplar, Hazel, and Chestnut bible rods 1

$\mathrm{Log}_{10} 1 = 0$

$\mathrm{Log}_{8} 2 = y$

$8^y = 2$

$2^{3y} = 2^1$

$3y = 1$

$y = 1/3$

$\mathrm{Log}_{3} 9 = y$

$3^y = 9$

$3^y = 3^2$

$y = 2$

11, 1, Deep calls unto Deep study bible 1

2 0.33, 0, Deep calls unto Deep study bible 2

x-axis	y-axis
11	2.33
1	0

Water Spout *(lightning; combinatorics)* Study bible 1

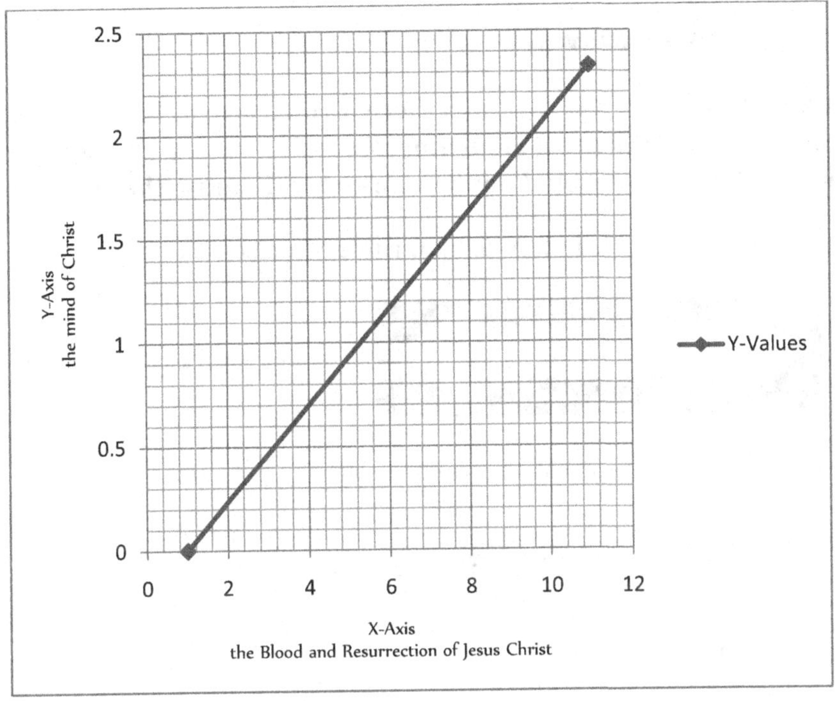

Water Spout *(lightning; combinatorics)* Study bible 2

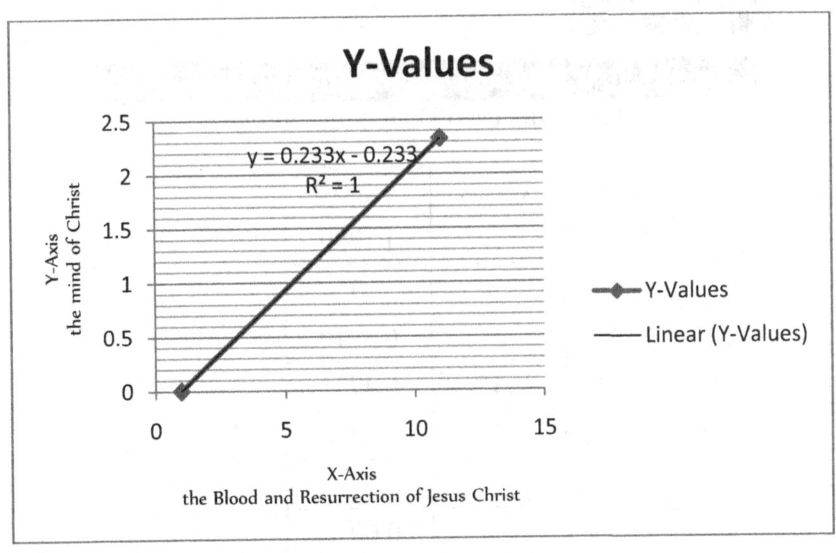

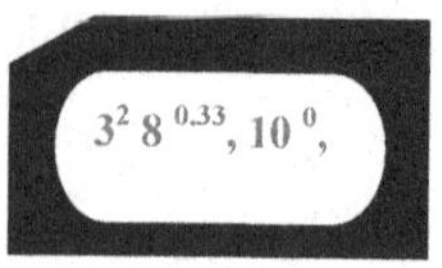

Pilled Poplar, Hazel, and Chestnut bible rods 2

18. In Rama a hill; elevated; sublime **was there a voice heard, lamentation, and weeping, and great mourning, Rachel** ewe; female sheep **weeping for her children, and would not be comforted, because they are not.**

7, 1, 2, 3, 5, 5, 4. Bible Matrices

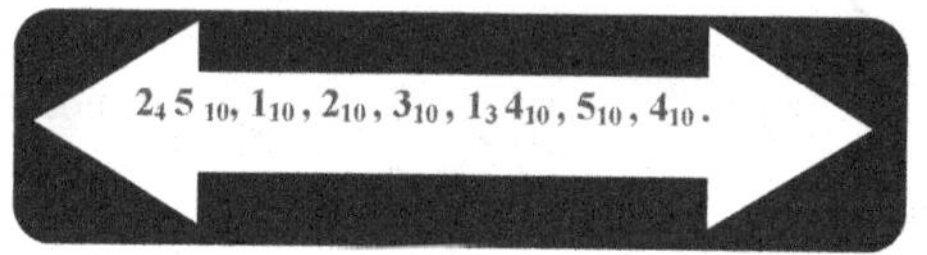

Pilled Poplar, Hazel, and Chestnut bible rods 1

$\text{Log}_{10} 5 = 0.6989$ $\text{Log}_{10} 3 = 0.4771$ $\text{Log}_{10} 2 = 0.3010$ $\text{Log}_{10} 4 = 0.6020$ $\text{Log}_{10} 1 = 0$

$\text{Log}_4 2 = y$

$4^y = 2^1$

$2^{2y} = 2^1$

$2y = 1$

$y = ½$

$\text{Log}_3 1 = y$

$3^y = 1$

$3^y = 3^0$

$y = 0$

7, 1, 2, 3, 5, 5, 4. Deep calls unto Deep study bible 1

½ 0.6989, 0, 0.3010, 0.4771, 0 0.6020, 0.6989, 0.6020

Deep calls unto Deep study bible 2

x-axis	y-axis
7	1.1989
1	0
2	0.3010
3	0.4771
5	0.6020
5	0.6989
4	0.6020

Water Spout *(lightning; combinatorics)* Study bible 1

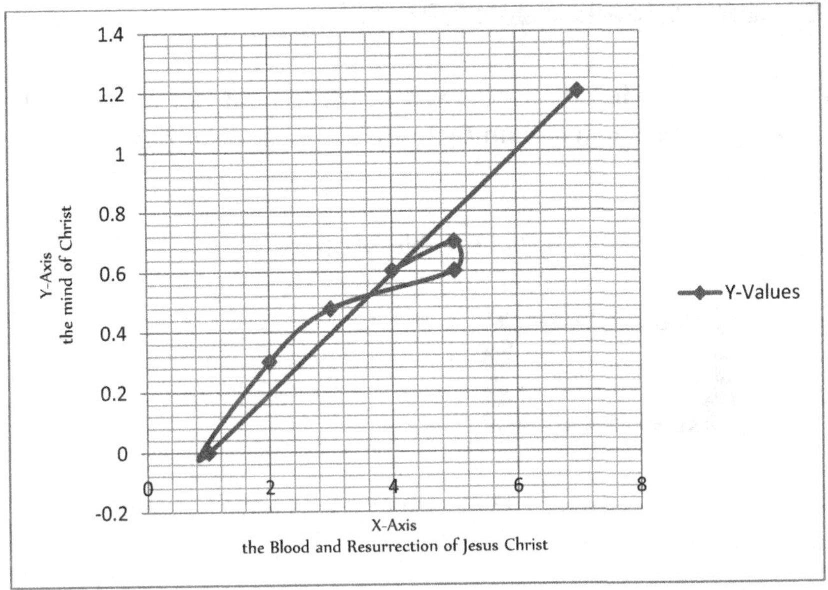

Water Spout *(lightning; combinatorics)* Study bible 2

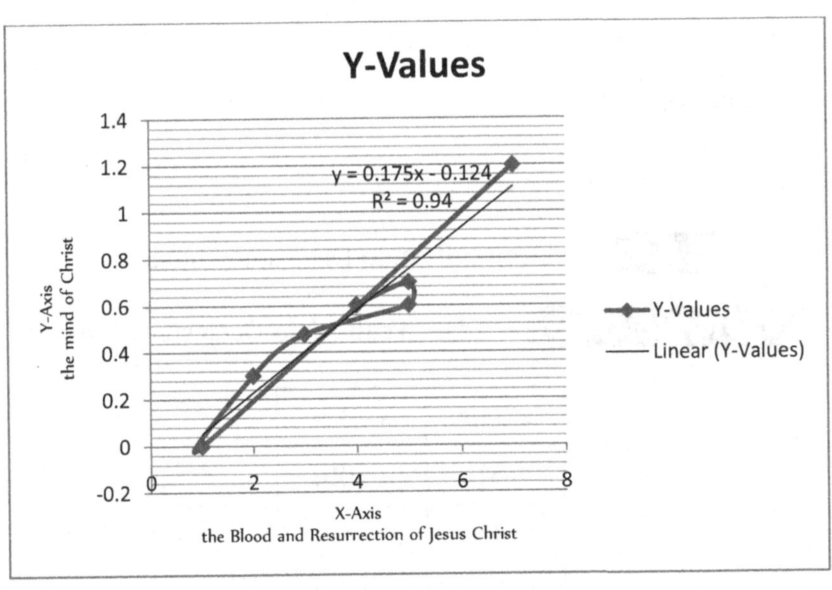

$4^{½} 10^{0.6989}, 10^{0}, 10^{0.3010}, 10^{0.4771}, 3^{0} 10^{0.6020}, 10^{0.6989}, 10^{0.6020}$.

Pilled Poplar, Hazel, and Chestnut bible rods 2

19. But when Herod son of hero **was dead, behold, an angel of the Lord appeareth in a dream to Joseph** increase; addition **in Egypt**that troubles, oppresses; anguish,

5, 1, 13, Bible Matrices

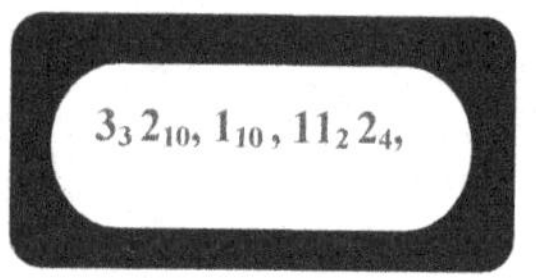

Pilled Poplar, Hazel, and Chestnut bible rods 1

$\text{Log}_2 11 = y$

$2^y = 11$

$\text{Log}_{10} 2^y = \log_{10} 11$

$y \log_{10} 2 = \log_{10} 11$

$y = \log_{10} 11/\log_{10} 2$

$y = 1.0413/0.3010$

$y = 3.4594$

$\text{Log}_{10} 2 = 0.3010$ $\text{Log}_{10} 1 = 0$

$\text{Log}_3 3 = y$

$3^y = 3^1$

$y = 1$

$\text{Log}_4 2 = y$

$4^y = 2$

$2^{2y} = 2^1$

$2y = 1$

$y = ½$

5, 1, 13, Deep calls unto Deep study bible 1

1 0.3010, 0, 3.4594 ½, Deep calls unto Deep study bible 2

x-axis	y-axis
5	1.3010
1	0
13	3.9594

Water Spout *(lightning; combinatorics)* Study bible 1

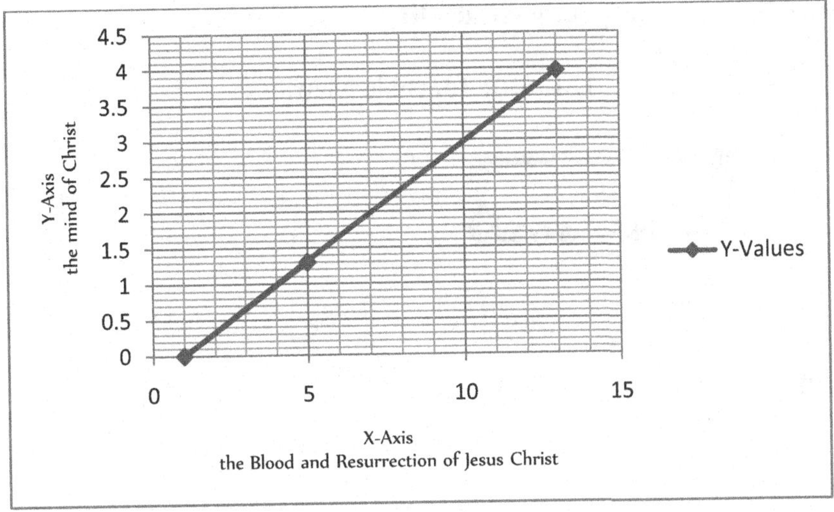

Water Spout *(lightning; combinatorics)* Study bible 2

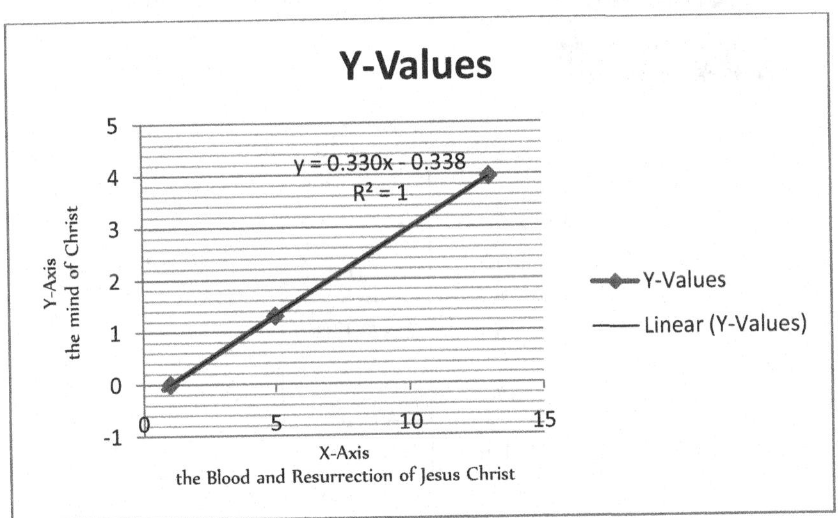

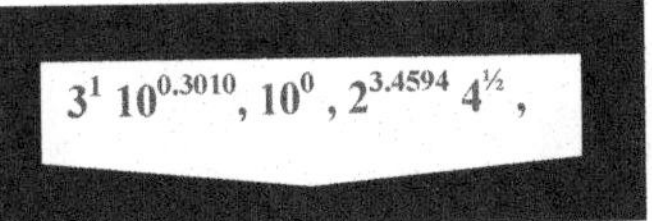
$3^1\ 10^{0.3010},\ 10^0,\ 2^{3.4594}\ 4^{½},$

Pilled Poplar, Hazel, and Chesnut bible rods 2

20. Saying, Arise, and take the young child and his mother, and go into the land of Israel one who prevails with God; God strives: **for they are dead which sought the young child's life.**

1, 1, 8, 7: 10. Bible Matrices

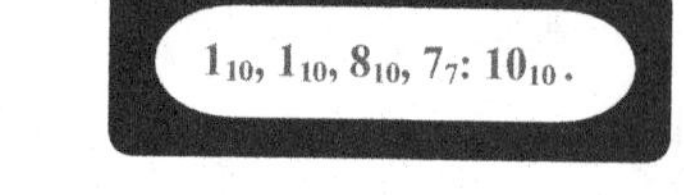

Pilled Poplar, Hazel, and Chestnut bible rods 1

$\text{Log}_{10} 8 = 0.9030$ $\text{Log}_{10} 10 = 1$ $\text{Log}_{10} 1 = 0$ $\text{Log}_{10} 1 = 0$

$\text{Log}_7 7 = y$

$7^y = 7^1$

$y = 1$

1, 1, 8, 7: 10. Deep calls unto Deep study bible 1

0, 0, 0.9030, 1: 1. Deep calls unto Deep study bible 2

x-axis	y-axis
1	0
1	0
8	0.9030
7	1
10	1

Water Spout *(lightning; combinatorics)* Study bible 1

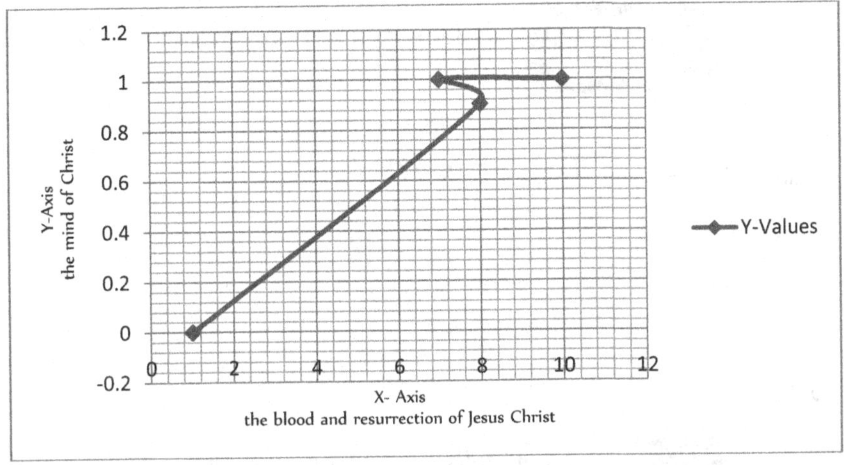

Water Spout *(lightning; combinatorics)* Study bible 2

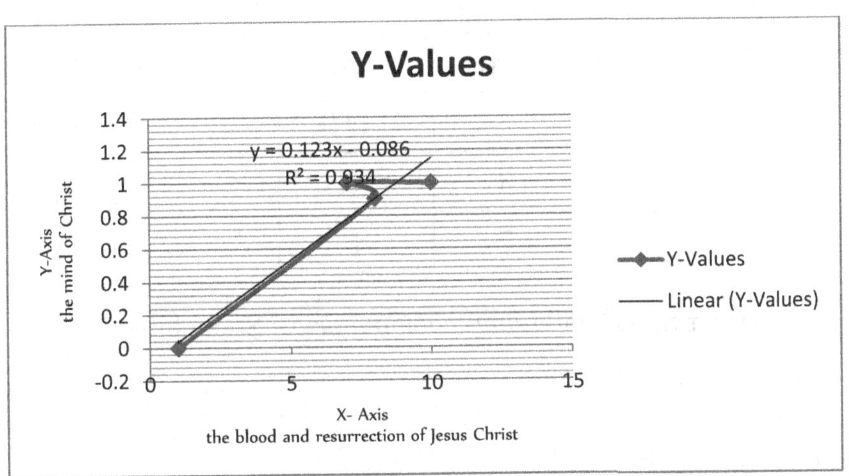

Pilled Poplar, Hazel, and Chestnut bible rods 2

21. And he arose, and took the young child and his mother, and came into the land of Israel one who prevails with God; God strives.

3, 8, 7. Bible Matrices

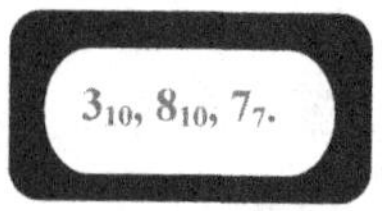

Pilled Poplar, Hazel, and Chestnut bible rods 1

$\text{Log}_{10} 8 = 0.9030$ $\text{Log}_{10} 3 = 0.4771$

$\text{Log}_7 7 = y$

$7^y = 7^1$

$y = 1$

3, 8, 7. Deep calls unto Deep study bible 1

0.4771, 0.9030, 1. Deep calls unto Deep study bible 2

x-axis	y-axis
3	0.4771
8	0.9030
7	1

Water Spout *(lightning; combinatorics)* Study bible 1

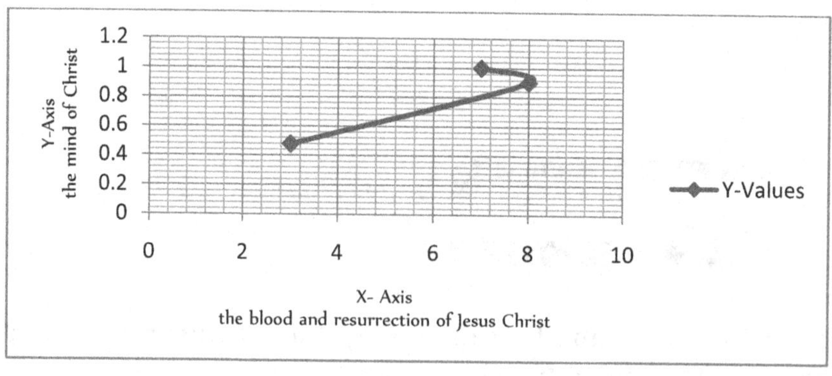

Water Spout *(lightning; combinatorics)* Study bible 2

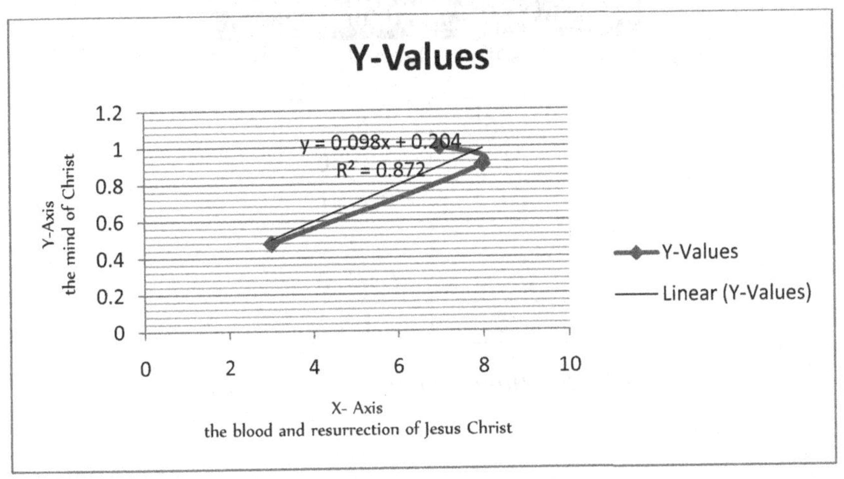

Pilled Poplar, Hazel, and Chestnut bible rods 2

22. But when he heard that Archelaus prince and ruler of the people **did reign in Judaea** praise, confession of God **in the room of his father Herod**son of a hero, **he was afraid to go thither: notwithstanding, being warned of God in a dream, he turned aside into the parts of Galilee**circuit;wheel; revolution;circle:

17, 6: 1, 7, 8: Bible Matrices

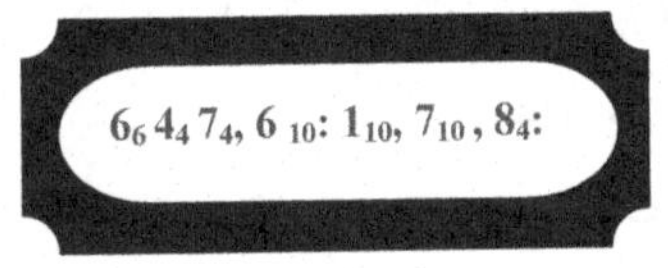

Pilled Poplar, Hazel, and Chestnut bible rods 1

$\mathrm{Log}_{10} 7 = 0.8450$

$\mathrm{Log}_6 6 = y$

$6^y = 6^1$

$y = 1$

$\mathrm{Log}_{10} 1 = 0$

$\mathrm{Log}_4 4 = y$

$4^y = 4^1$

$y = 1$

$\mathrm{Log}_{10} 6 = 0.7781$

$\mathrm{Log}_4 7 = y$

$4^y = 7$

$\log 4^y = \log 7$

$y \log 4 = \log 7$

$y = \log 7 / \log 4$

$y = 0.8450 / 0.6020$

$y = 1.4036$

$\mathrm{Log}_4 8 = y$

$4^y = 8$

$2^{2y} = 2^3$

$2y = 3$

$y = 3/2$

$y = 1.5$

17, 6: 1, 7, 8: Deep calls unto Deep study bible 1

1 1 1.4036, 0.7781, 0, 0.8450, 1.5 :
Deep calls unto Deep study bible 2

x-axis	y-axis
17	3.4036
6	0.7781
1	0
7	0.8450
8	1.5

Water Spout *(lightning; combinatorics)* Study bible 1

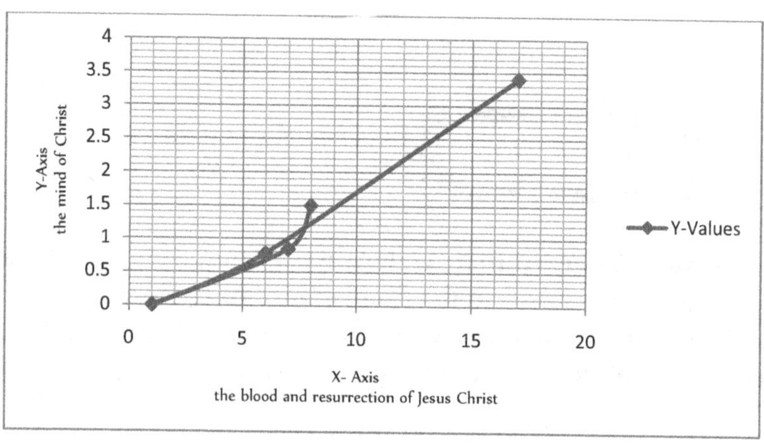

Water Spout *(lightning; combinatorics)* Study bible 2

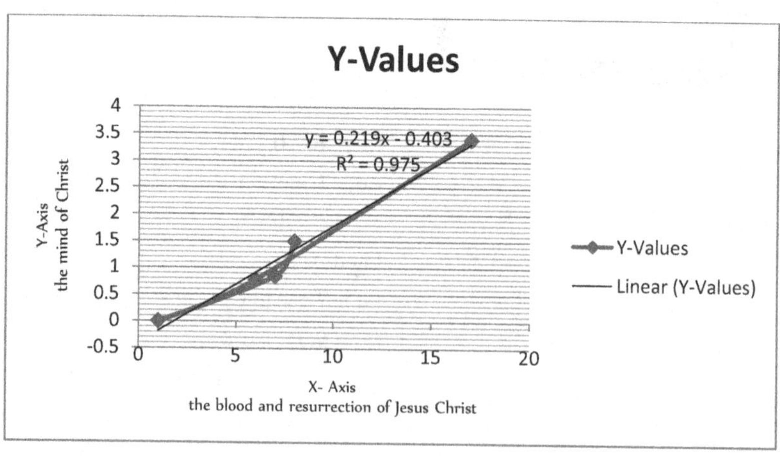

$6^1 4^1 4^{1.4036}, 10^{0.7781}: 10^0, 10^{0.8450}, 4^{1,5}:$

Pilled Poplar, Hazel, and Chestnut bible rods 2

23. And he came and dwelt in a city called Nazarethseparated; crowned; sanctified; the guarded one; a shoot; set apart: **that it might be fulfilled which was spoken by the prophets** to bubble forth, as from a fountain; utter, **He shall be called a Nazarene.**

10: 11, 6. Bible Matrices

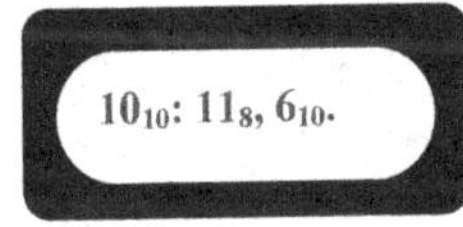

$10_{10}: 11_8, 6_{10}.$

Pilled Poplar, Hazel, and Chestnut bible rods 1

$\text{Log}_{10} 10 = 1$

$\text{Log}_{10} 6 = 0.7781$

$\text{Log}_8 11 = y$

$8^y = 11$

$\log 8^y = \log 11$

$y \log 8 = \log 11$

$y = \log 11 / \log 8$

$y = 1.0413 / 0.9030$

$y = 1.1531$

10: 11, 6. Deep calls unto Deep study bible 1

1 : 1.1531, 0.7781. Deep calls unto Deep study bible 2

x-axis	y-axis
10	1
11	1.1531
6	0.7781

Water Spout *(lightning; combinatorics)* Study bible 1

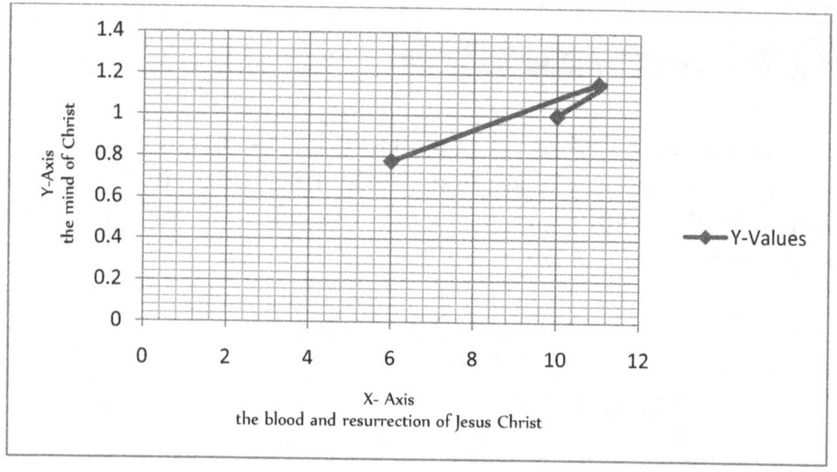

Water Spout *(lightning; combinatorics)* Study bible 2

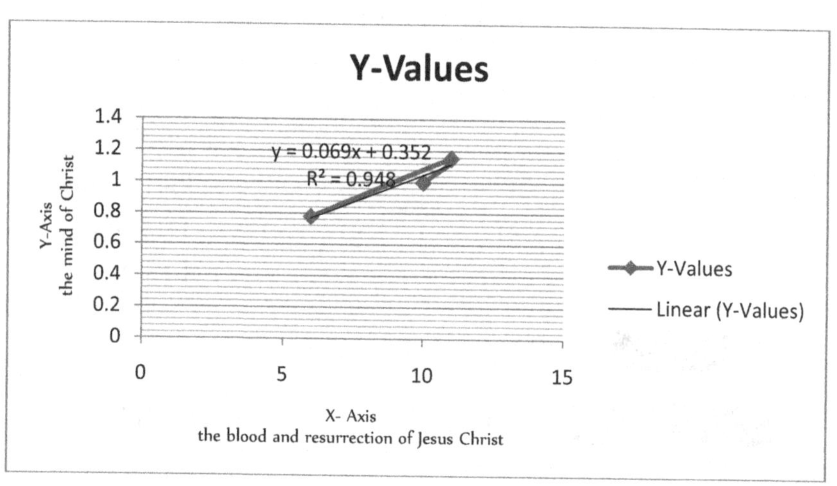

10^1: $8^{1.1531}$, $10^{0.7781}$.

Pilled Poplar, Hazel, and Chestnut bible rods 2

CHAPTER 3

1. In those days came John grace, mercy of the Lord **the Baptist, preaching in the wilderness of Judaea**the praise of theLord; confession of the Lord,

7, 6, Bible Matrices

Pilled Poplar, Hazel, and Chestnut bible rods 1

$\text{Log}_5 5 = y$

$5^y = 5^1$

$y = 1$

$\log_9 6 = y$

$\log 9^y = \log 6$

$y \log 9 = \log 6$

$y = \log 6 / \log 9$

$y = 0.7781 / 0.9542$

$y = 0.8154$

$\log_{10} 2 = 0.3010$

7, 6, Deep calls unto Deep study bible 1

1 0.3010, 1.2263, Deep calls unto Deep study bible 2

x-axis	y-axis
7	1.3010
6	0.8154

Water Spout *(lightning; combinatorics)* Study bible 1

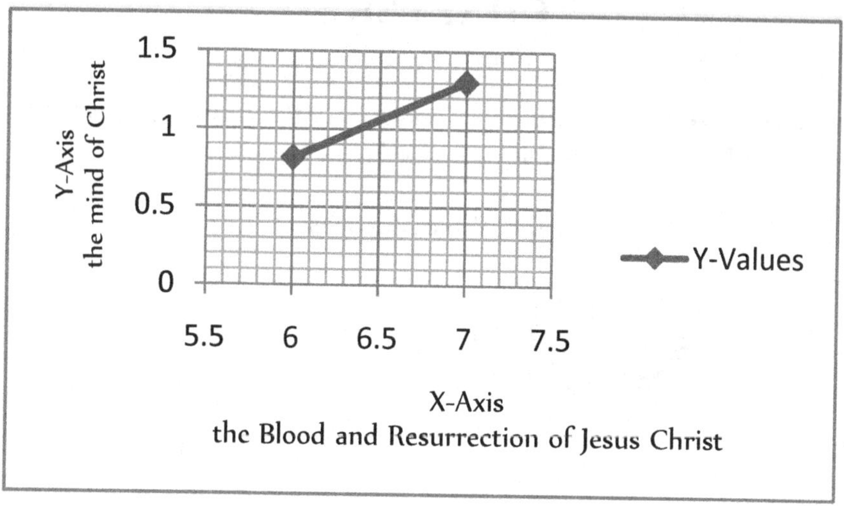

Water Spout *(lightning; combinatorics)* Study bible 2

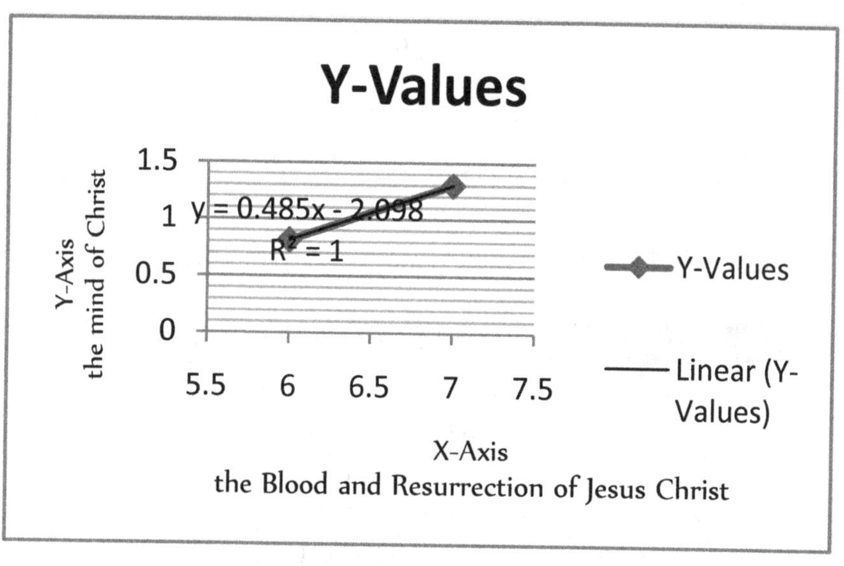

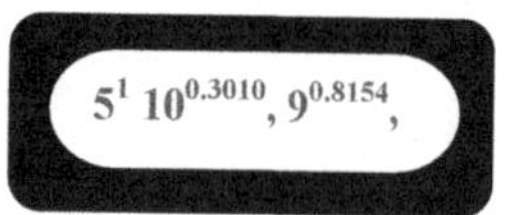

Pilled Poplar, Hazel, and Chestnut bible rods 2

2. And saying, Repent ye: for the kingdom of heaven is at hand.

2, 2: 8. Bible Matrices

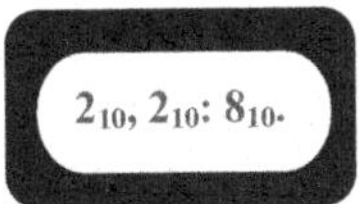

Pilled Poplar, Hazel, and Chestnut bible rods 1

$\log_{10} 2 = 0.3010$ $\log_{10} 2 = 0.3010$ $\log_{10} 8 = 0.9030$

2, 2: 8. Deep calls unto Deep study bible 1

0.3010, 0.3010: 0.9030. Deep calls unto Deep study bible 2

x-axis	y-axis
2	0.3010
2	0.3010
8	0.9030

Water Spout *(lightning; combinatorics)* Study bible 1

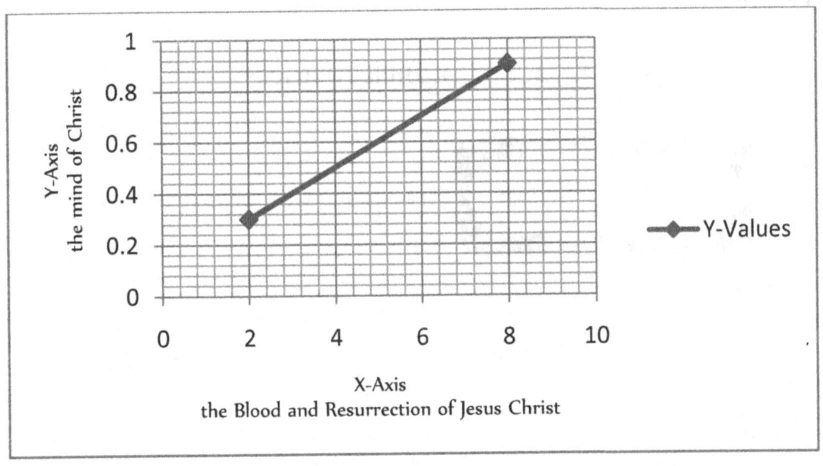

Water Spout *(lightning; combinatorics)* Study bible 2

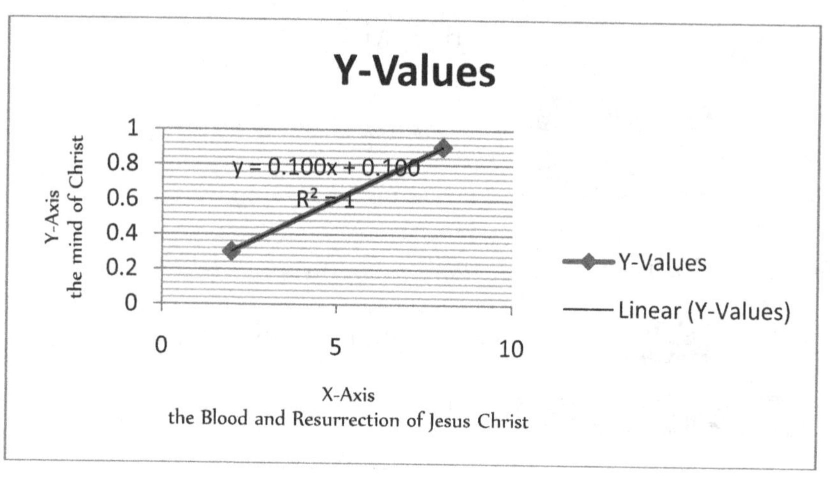

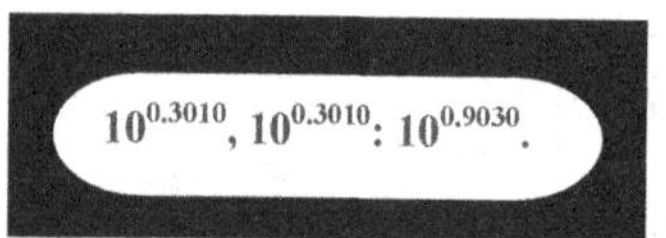

Pilled Poplar, Hazel, and Chestnut bible rods 2

3. For this is he that was spoken of by the prophet to bubble forth, as from a fountain; utter **Esaias**the salvation of the Lord, **saying, The voice of one crying in the wilderness, Prepare ye the way of the Lord, make his paths straight.**

12, 1, 8, 7, 4. Bible Matrices

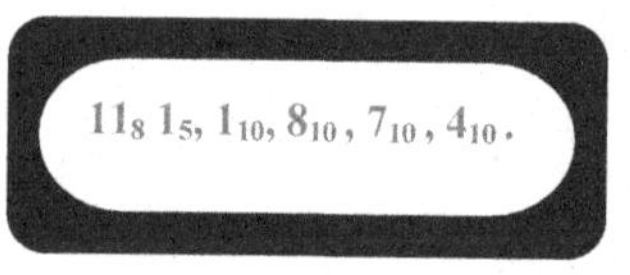

Pilled Poplar, Hazel, and Chestnut bible rods 1

$\text{Log}_5 1 = y$ $\text{Log}_{10} 1 = 0$ $\text{Log}_{10} 7 = 0.8450$ $\text{Log}_8 11 = y$ $\text{Log}_{10} 8 = 0.9030$ $\text{Log}_{10} 4 = 0.6020$

$5^y = 1$

$5^y = 5^0$

$y = 0$

$8^y = 11$

$\log 8^y = \log 11$

$y \log 8 = \log 11$

$y = \log 11 / \log 8$

$y = 1.0413 / 0.9030$

$y = 1.1531$

12, 1, 8, 7, 4. Deep calls unto Deep study bible 1

1.1531 0, 0, 0.9030, 0.8450, 0.6020.
Deep calls unto Deep study bible 2

x-axis	y-axis
12	1.1531
1	0
8	0.9030
7	0.8450
4	0.6020

Water Spout *(lightning; combinatorics)* Study bible 1

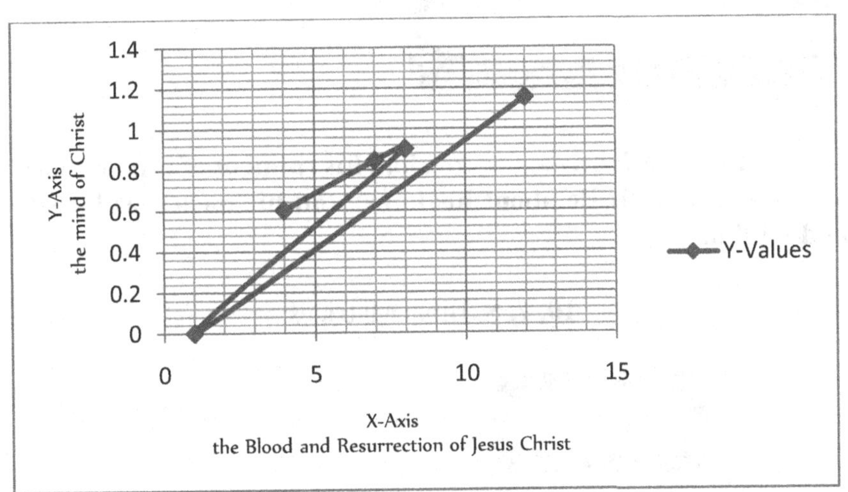

Water Spout *(lightning; combinatorics)* Study bible 2

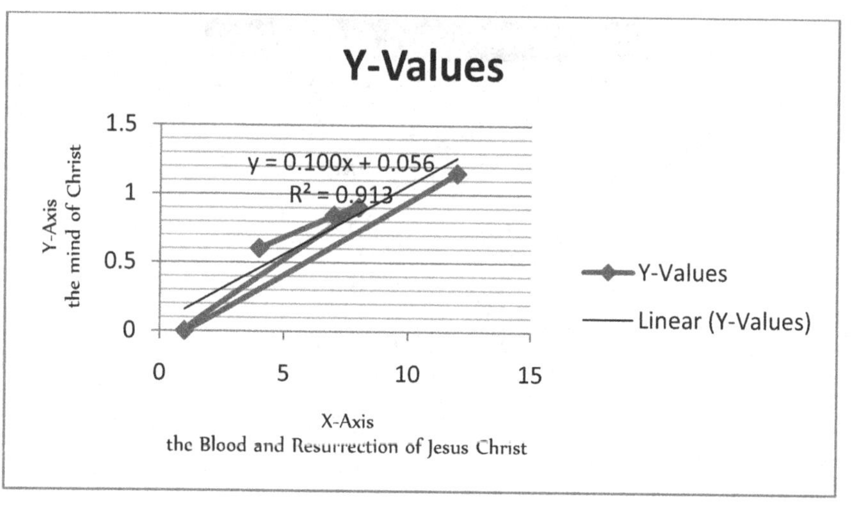

Pilled Poplar, Hazel, and Chestnut bible rods 2

4. And the same John grace, mercy of God **had his raiment of camel's hair, and a leathern girdle about his loins; and his meat was locusts and wild honey.**

10, 7; 8. Bible Matrices

$4_4 6_{10}, 7_{10}; 8_{10}$.

Pilled Poplar, Hazel, and Chestnut bible rods 1

$\log_{10} 6 = 0.7781$ $\log_{10} 7 = 0.8450$ $\log_{10} 8 = 0.9030$ $\log_4 4 = y$

$4^y = 4^1$

$y = 1$

10, 7; 8. Deep calls unto Deep study bible 1

1 0.7781, 0.8450; 0.9030. Deep calls unto Deep study bible 2

x-axis	y-axis
10	1.7781
7	0.8450
8	0.9030

Water Spout *(lightning; combinatorics)* Study bible 1

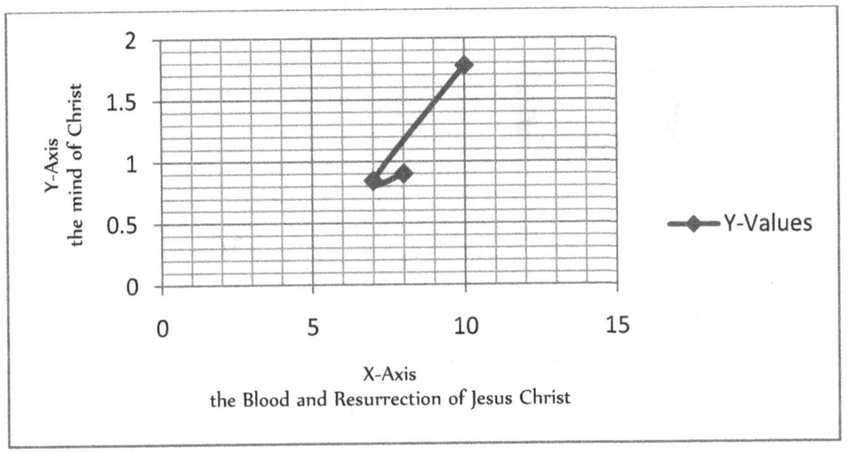

Water Spout *(lightning; combinatorics)* Study bible 2

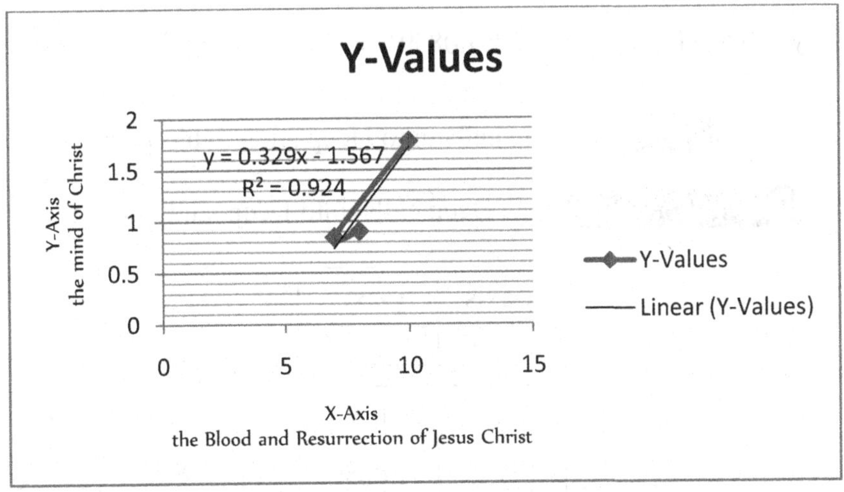

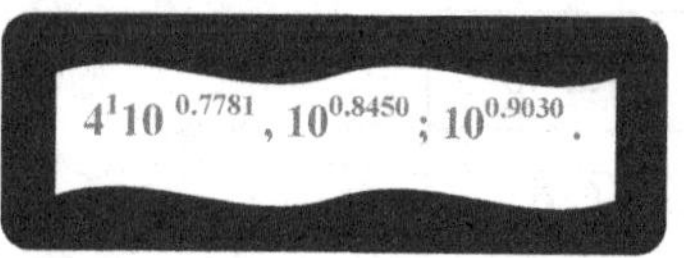

Pilled Poplar, Hazel, and Chestnut bible rods 2

5. Then went out to him Jerusalem habitation of peace, vision of peace; possession of peace, **and all Judaea**the praise of the Lord; confession of the Lord, **and all the region round about Jordan**the descender; the river of judgment,

6, 3, 7, Bible Matrices

$6_9, 3_9, 7_6,$ Pilled Poplar, Hazel, and Chestnut bible rods 1

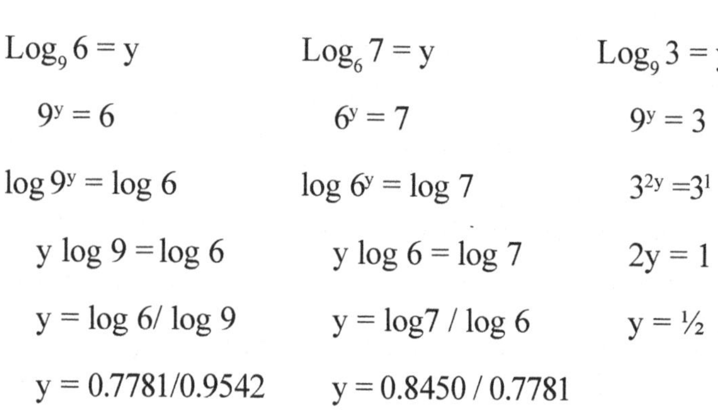

$\log_9 6 = y$	$\log_6 7 = y$	$\log_9 3 = y$
$9^y = 6$	$6^y = 7$	$9^y = 3$
$\log 9^y = \log 6$	$\log 6^y = \log 7$	$3^{2y} = 3^1$
$y \log 9 = \log 6$	$y \log 6 = \log 7$	$2y = 1$
$y = \log 6 / \log 9$	$y = \log 7 / \log 6$	$y = ½$
$y = 0.7781/0.9542$	$y = 0.8450 / 0.7781$	
$y = 0.8154$	$y = 1.0859$	

6, 3, 7, Deep calls unto Deep study bible 1

0.8154, 0.5, 1.0859, Deep calls unto Deep study bible 2

x-axis	y-axis
6	0.8154
3	0.5
7	1.0859

Water Spout *(lightning; combinatorics)* Study bible 1

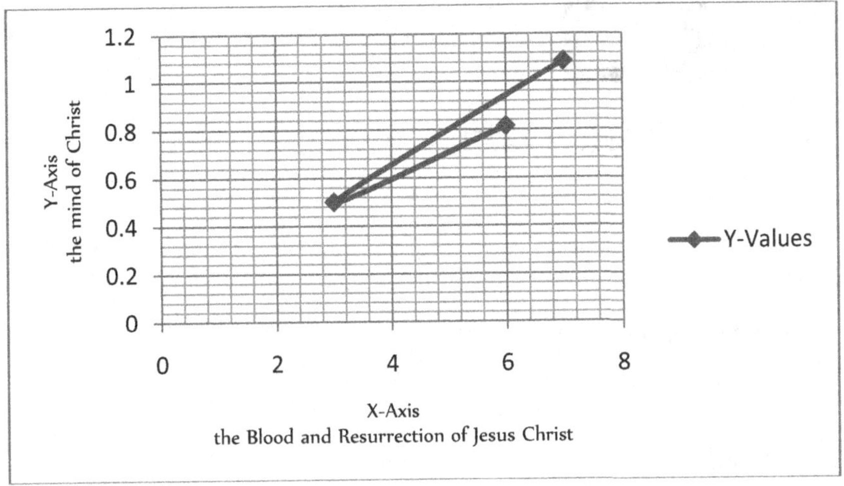

Water Spout *(lightning; combinatorics)* Study bible 2

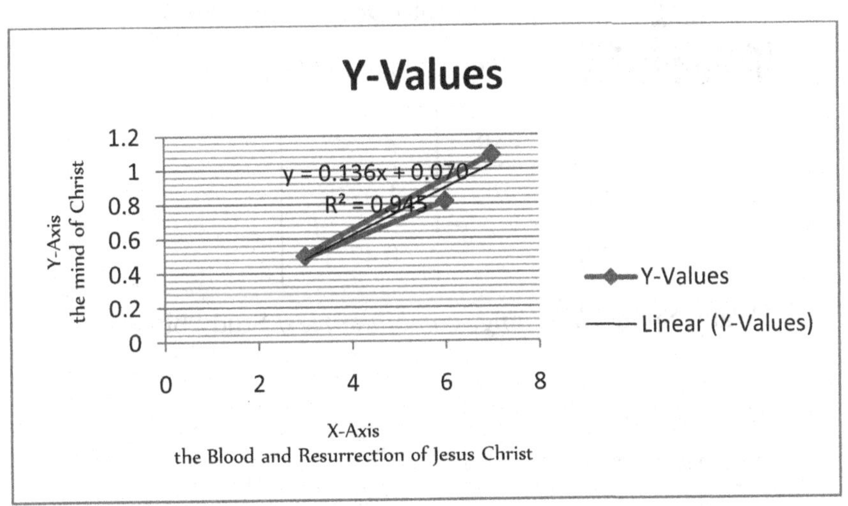

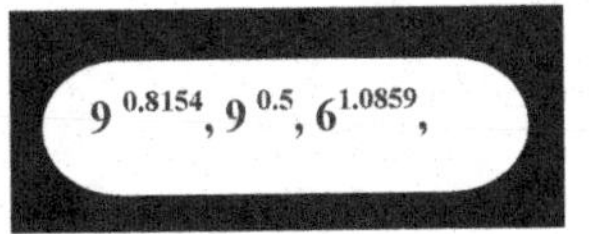

Pilled Poplar, Hazel, and Chestnut bible rods 2

6. And were baptized of him in Jordan the descender; the river of judgment, **confessing their sins.**

7, 3. Bible Matrices

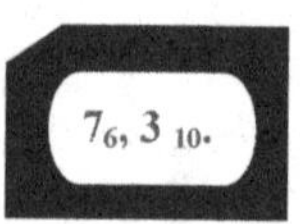

Pilled Poplar, Hazel, and Chestnut bible rods 1

$\text{Log}_6 7 = y$ $\quad$ $\text{Log}_{10} 3 = 0.4771$

$6^y = 7$

$\log 6^y = \log 7$

$y \log 6 = \log 7$

$y = \log 7 / \log 6$

$y = 0.8450 / 0.7781$

$y = 1.0859$

7, 3. Deep calls unto Deep study bible 1

1.0859, 0.4771. Deep calls unto Deep study bible 2

x-axis	y-axis
7	1.0859
3	0.4771

Water Spout *(lightning; combinatorics)* Study bible 1

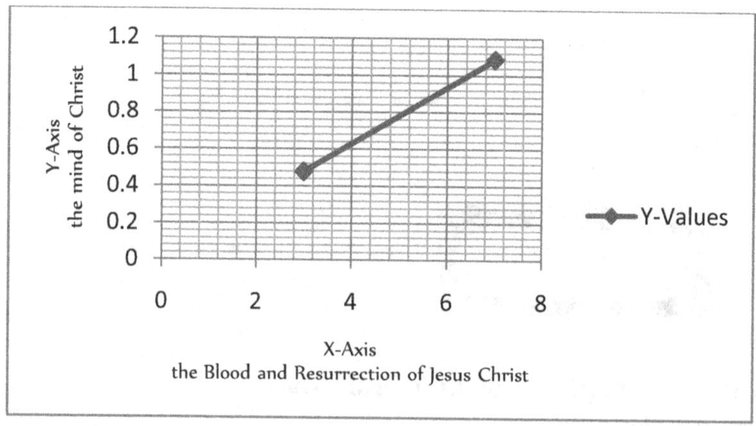

Water Spout *(lightning; combinatorics)* Study bible 2

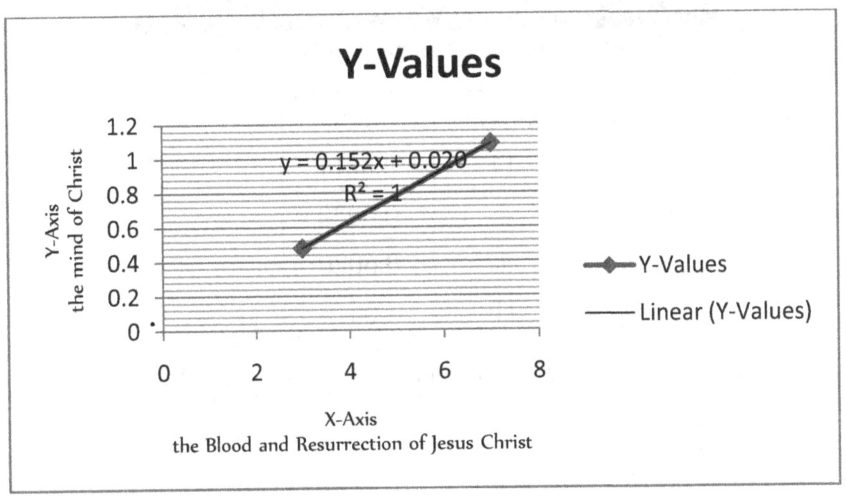

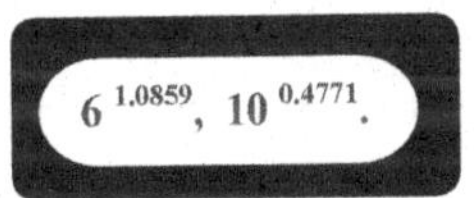

Pilled Poplar, Hazel, and Chestnut bible rods 2

7. But when he saw many of the Pharisees set apart; separatist **and Sadducees** followers of Zadok-just, justified, righteous **come to his baptism, he said unto them, O generation of vipers, who hath warned you to flee from the wrath to come?**

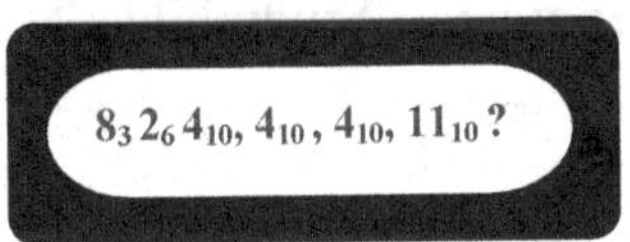

Pilled Poplar, Hazel, and Chestnut bible rods 1

$\text{Log}_3 8 = y$ $\text{Log}_6 2 = y$ $\text{Log}_{10} 11 = 1.0413$ $\text{Log}_{10} 4 = 0.6020$

$\text{Log}_3 8 = y$	$\text{Log}_6 2 = y$
$3^y = 8$	$6^y = 2$
$\log 3^y = \log 8$	$\log 6^y = \log 2$
$y \log 3 = \log 8$	$y \log 6 = \log 2$
$y = \log 8 / \log 3$	$y = \log 2 / \log 6$
$y = 0.9030/0.4771$	$y = 0.3010 / 0.7781$
$y = 1.8926$	$y = 0.3868$

14, 4, 4, 11? Deep calls unto Deep study bible 1

1.8926 0.3868 0.6020, 0.6020, 0.6020, 1.0413?
Deep calls unto Deep study bible 2

x-axis	y-axis
14	2.8814
4	0.6020
4	0.6020
11	1.0413

Water Spout *(lightning; combinatorics)* Study bible 1

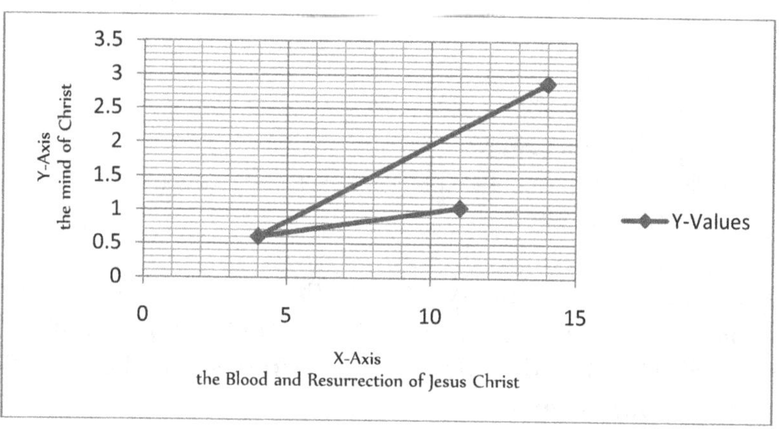

Water Spout *(lightning; combinatorics)* Study bible 2

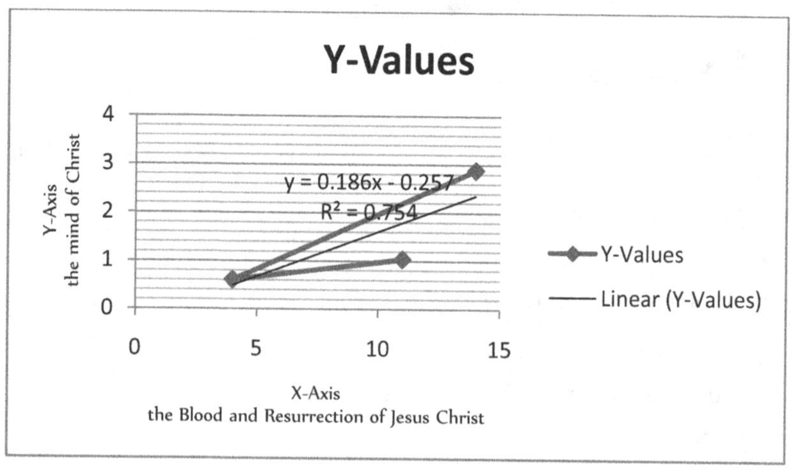

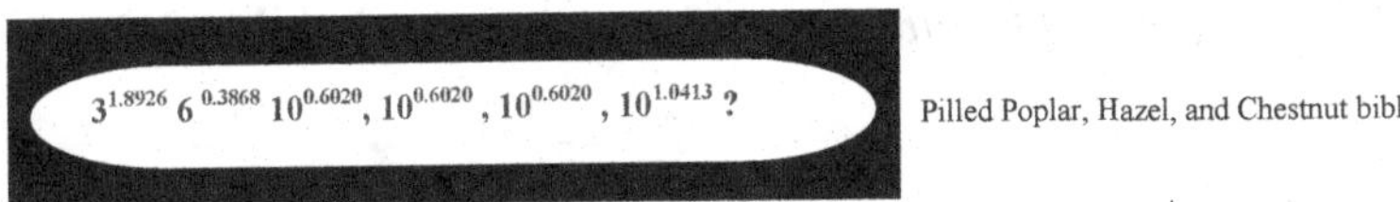

Pilled Poplar, Hazel, and Chestnut bible rods 2

8. Bring forth therefore fruits meet for repentance:

7: Bible Matrices

Pilled Poplar, Hazel, and Chestnut bible rods 1

$\text{Log}_{10} 7 = 0.8450$

7: Deep calls unto Deep study bible 1

0.8450: Deep calls unto Deep study bible 2

x-axis	y-axis
7	0.8450

Water Spout *(lightning; combinatorics)* Study bible 1

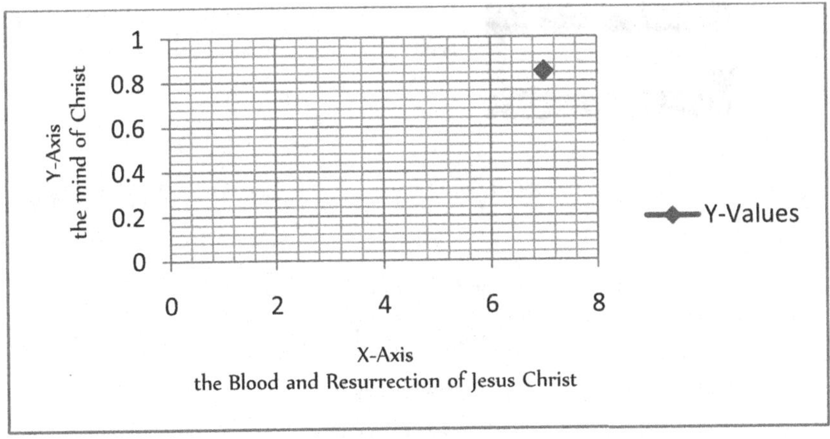

Water Spout *(lightning; combinatorics)* Study bible 2

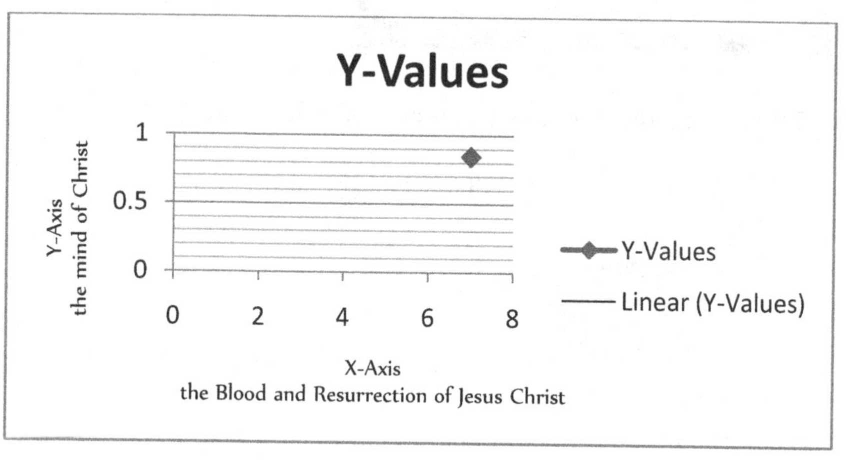

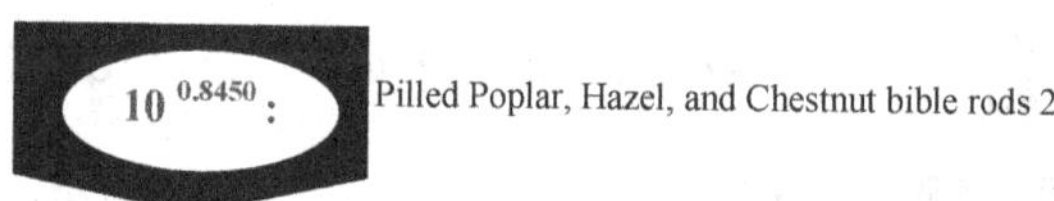

Pilled Poplar, Hazel, and Chestnut bible rods 2

9. And think not to say within yourselves, We have Abraham father of multitudes **to our father: for I say unto you, that God is able of these stones to raise up children unto Abraham** father of a great multitudes.

7, 6: 5, 13. Bible Matrices

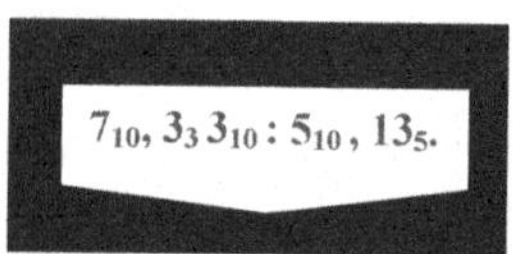

Pilled Poplar, Hazel, and Chestnut bible rods 1

$\text{Log}_{10} 3 = 0.4771$ $\text{Log}_{10} 5 = 0.6989$ $\text{Log}_5 13 = y$ $\text{Log}_3 3 = y$ $\text{Log}_{10} 7 = 0.8450$

$5^y = 13$

$\log 5^y = \log 13$

$y \log 5 = \log 13$

$y = \log 13 / \log 5$

$y = 1.1139 / 0.6989$

$y = 1.5937$

$3^y = 3^1$

$y = 1$

7, 6: 5, 13. Deep calls unto Deep study bible 1

0.8450, 1 0.4771: 0.6989, 1.5937.
Deep calls unto Deep study bible 2

x-axis	y-axis
7	0.8450
6	1.4771
5	0.6989
13	1.5937

Water Spout *(lightning; combinatorics)* Study bible 1

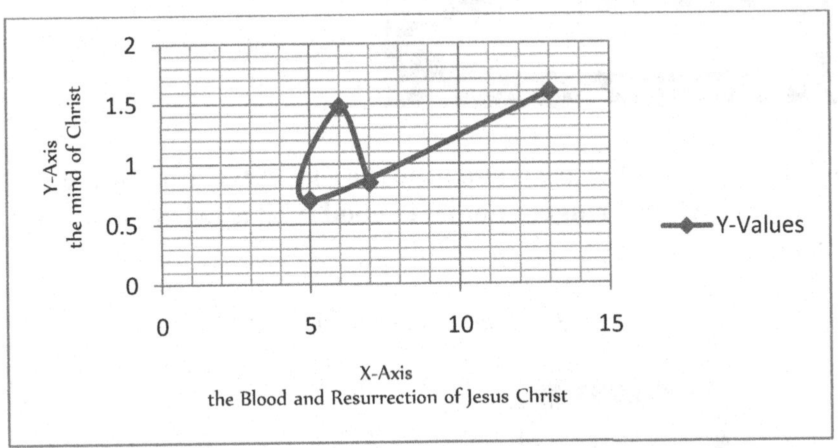

Water Spout *(lightning; combinatorics)* Study bible 2

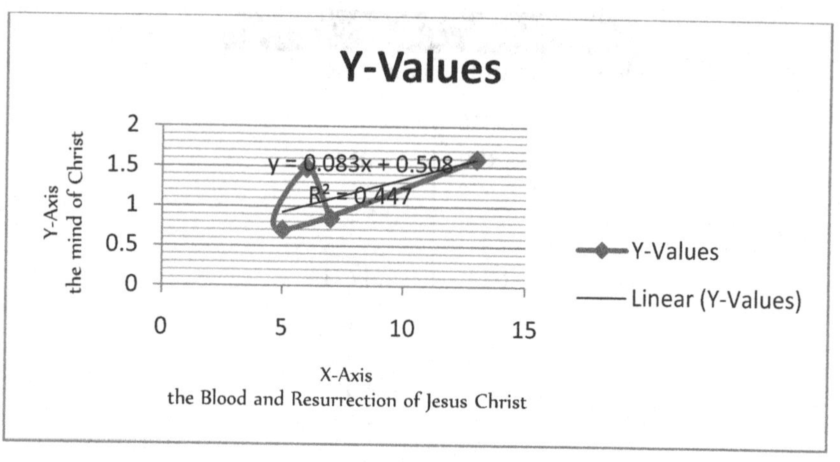

Pilled Poplar, Hazel, and Chestnut bible rods 2

10. And now also the axe is laid unto the root of the trees: therefore every tree which bringeth not forth good fruit is hewn down, and cast into the fire.

13: 12, 5. Bible Matrices

Pilled Poplar, Hazel, and Chestnut bible rods 1

$\text{Log}_{10}\, 13 = 1.1139$ $\text{Log}_{10}\, 12 = 1.0791$ $\text{Log}_{10}\, 5 = 0.6989$

13: 12, 5. Deep calls unto Deep study bible 1

1.1139: 1.0791, 0.6989. Deep calls unto Deep study bible 2

x-axis	y-axis
13	1.1139
12	1.0791
5	0.6989

Water Spout *(lightning; combinatorics)* Study bible 1

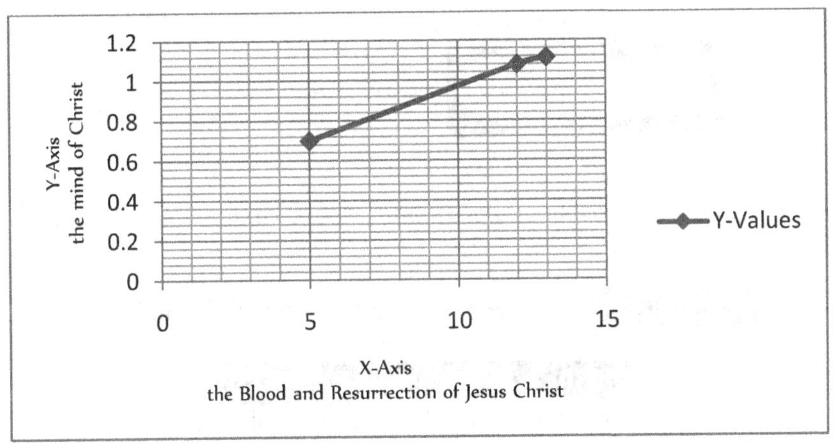

Water Spout *(lightning; combinatorics)* Study bible 2

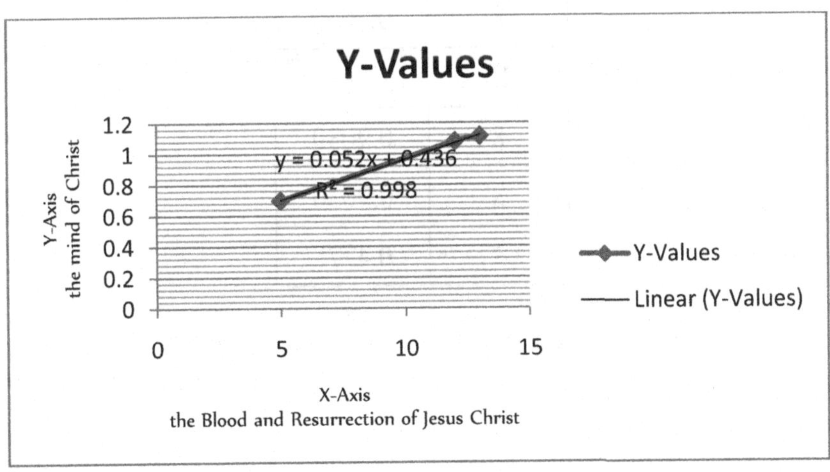

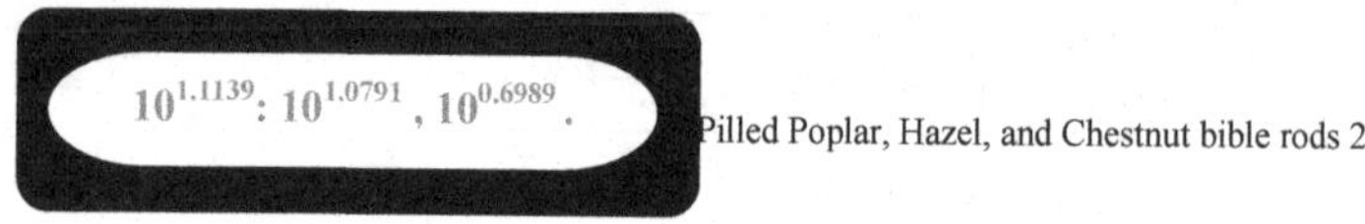

Pilled Poplar, Hazel, and Chestnut bible rods 2

11. I indeed baptize you with water unto repentance: but he that cometh after me is mightier than I, whose shoes I am not worthy to bear: he shall baptize you with the Holy Ghost, and with fire:

8: 10, 8: 8, 3: Bible Matrices

Pilled Poplar, Hazel, and Chestnut bible rods 1

$\log_{10} 3 = 0.4771$ $\log_{10} 10 = 1$ $\log_{10} 8 = 0.9030$ $\log_{10} 8 = 0.9030$ $\log_{10} 8 = 0.9030$

8: 10, 8: 8, 3: Deep calls unto Deep study bible 1

0.9030: 1, 0.9030: 0.9030, 0.4771:
Deep calls unto Deep study bible 2

x-axis	y-axis
8	0.9030
10	1
8	0.9030
8	0.9030
3	0.4771

Water Spout *(lightning; combinatorics)* Study bible 1

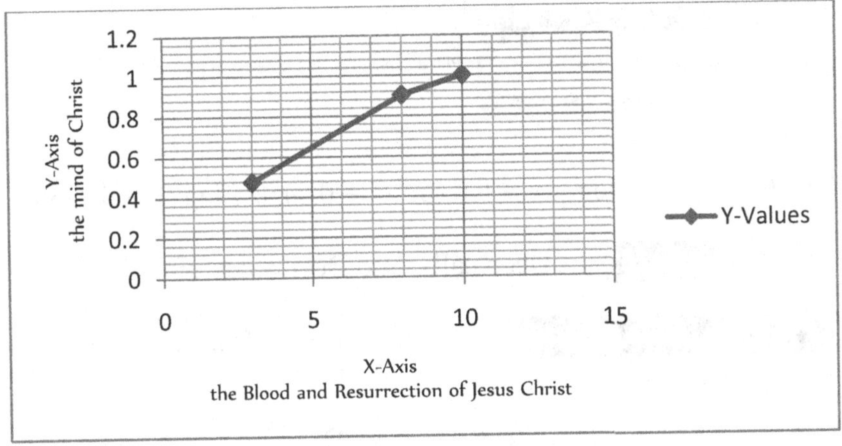

Water Spout *(lightning; combinatorics)* Study bible 2

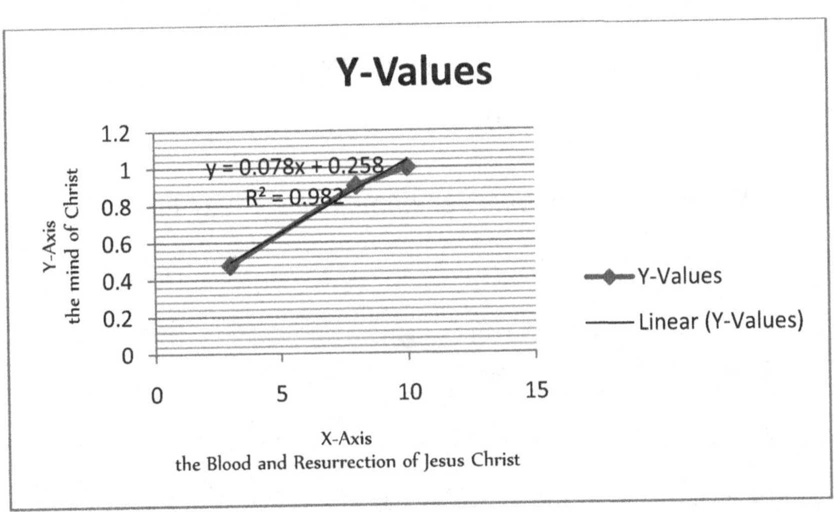

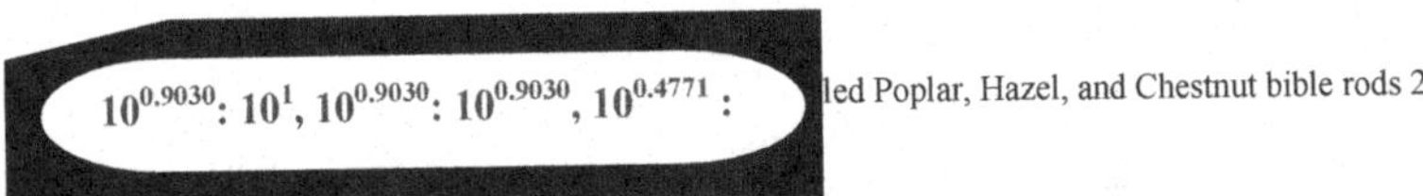

led Poplar, Hazel, and Chestnut bible rods 2

12. Whose fan is in his hand, and he will throughly purge his floor, and gather his wheat into the garner; but he will burn up the chaff with unquenchable fire.

6, 7, 7; 10. Bible Matrices

Pilled Poplar, Hazel, and Chestnut bible rods 1

$\log_{10} 6 = 0.7781$ $\log_{10} 10 = 1$ $\log_{10} 7 = 0.8450$ $\log_{10} 7 = 0.8450$

6, 7, 7; 10. Deep calls unto Deep study bible 1

0.7781, 0.8450, 0.8450; 1. Deep calls unto Deep study bible 2

x-axis	y-axis
6	0.7781
7	0.8450
7	0.8450
10	1

Water Spout *(lightning; combinatorics)* Study bible 1

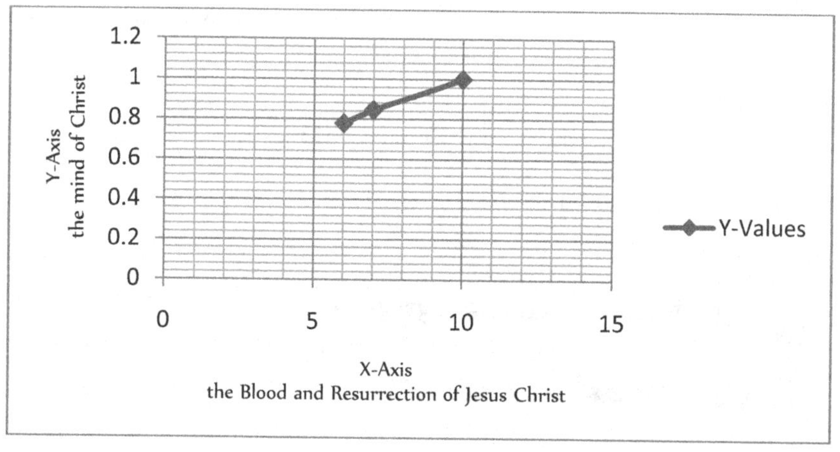

Water Spout *(lightning; combinatorics)* Study bible 2

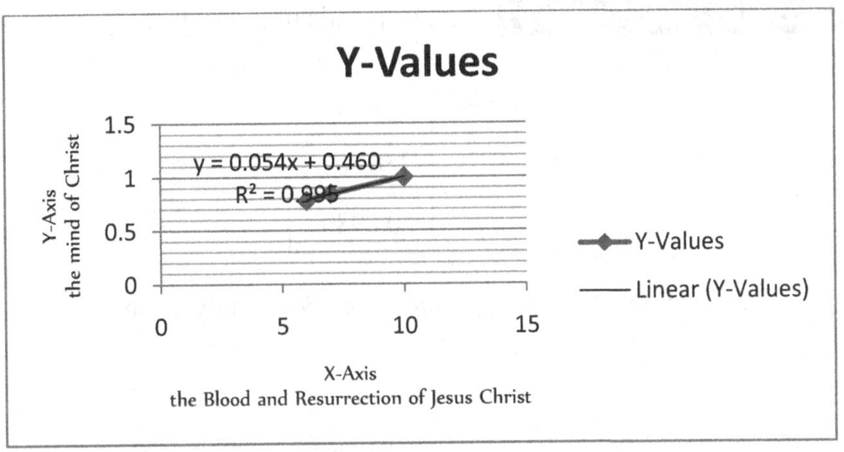

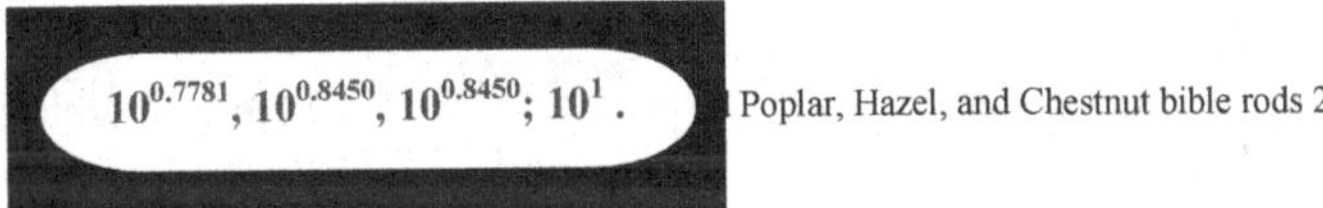

Poplar, Hazel, and Chestnut bible rods 2

13. Then cometh Jesussavior; deliverer **from Galilee** circuit; wheel; circle; revolution**to Jordan** descender; river of judgment **unto John** grace of the Lord, mercy of the Lord, **to be baptized of him.**

9, 5. Bible Matrices

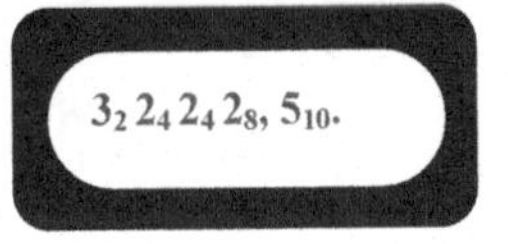

Pilled Poplar, Hazel, and Chestnut bible rods 1

$\text{Log}_2 3 = y$

$2^y = 3$

$\log 2^y = \log 3$

$y \log 2 = \log 3$

$y = \log 3/ \log 2$

$y = 0.4771/0.3010$

$y = 1.5850$

$\text{Log}_8 2 = y$

$8^y = 2^1$

$2^{3y} = 2^1$

$3y = 1$

$y = 1/3$

$\text{Log}_4 2 = y$

$2^{2y} = 2^1$

$2^{2y} = 2^1$

$2y = 1$

$y = ½$

$\text{Log}_4 2 = y$

$2^{2y} = 2^1$

$2^{2y} = 2^1$

$2y = 1$

$y = ½$

$\text{Log}_{10} 5 = 0.6989$

9, 5. Deep calls unto Deep study bible 1

1.5850 0.5 0.5 0.33, 0.6989. Deep calls unto Deep study bible 2

x-axis	y-axis
9	2.9150
5	0.6989

Water Spout *(lightning; combinatorics)* Study bible 1

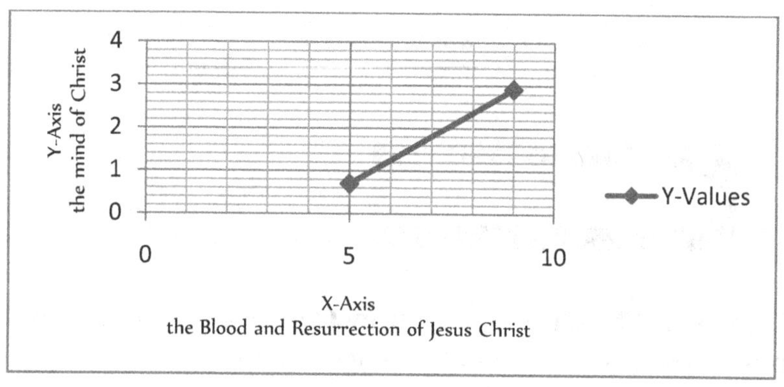

Water Spout *(lightning; combinatorics)* Study bible 2

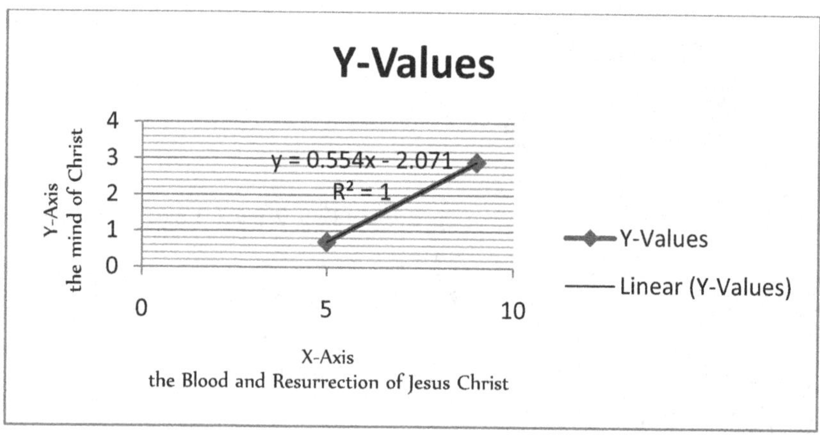

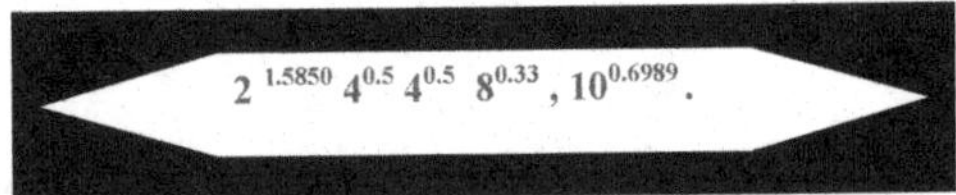

Pilled Poplar, Hazel, and Chestnut bible rods 2

14. But John grace of the Lord, mercy of the Lord **forbad him, saying, I have need to be baptized of thee, and comest thou to me?**

4, 1, 8, 5? Bible Matrices

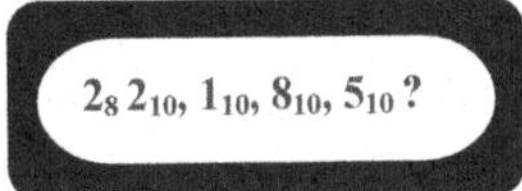

Pilled Poplar, Hazel, and Chestnut bible rods 1

$\text{Log}_8 2 = y \quad \text{Log}_{10} 2 = 0.3010 \quad \text{Log}_{10} 1 = 0 \quad \text{Log}_{10} 8 = 0.9030 \quad \text{Log}_{10} 5 = 0.6989$

$8^y = 2^1$

$2^{3y} = 2^1$

$3y = 1$

$y = 1/3$

4, 1, 8, 5? Deep calls unto Deep study bible 1

0.33 0.3010, 0, 0.9030, 0.6989?

Deep calls unto Deep study bible 2

x-axis	y-axis
4	0.6310
1	0
8	0.9030
5	0.6989

Water Spout *(lightning; combinatorics)* Study bible 1

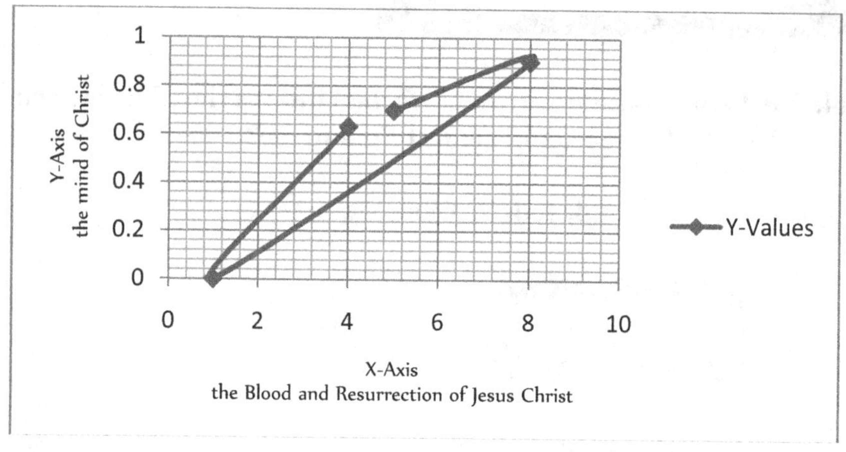

Water Spout *(lightning; combinatorics)* Study bible 2

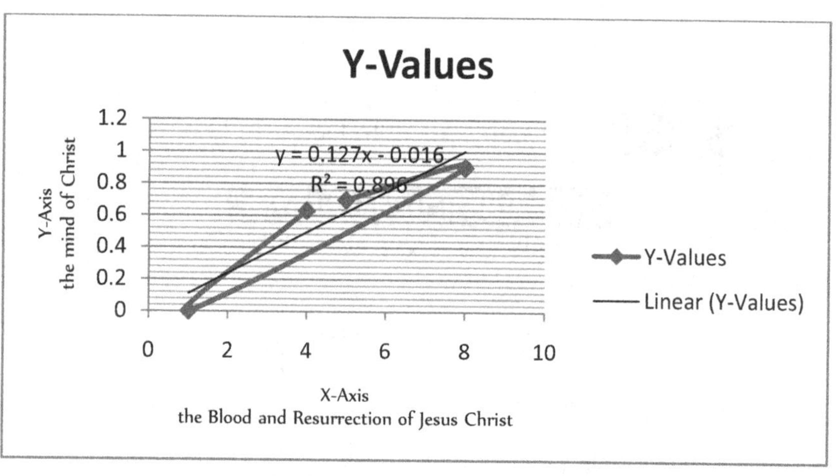

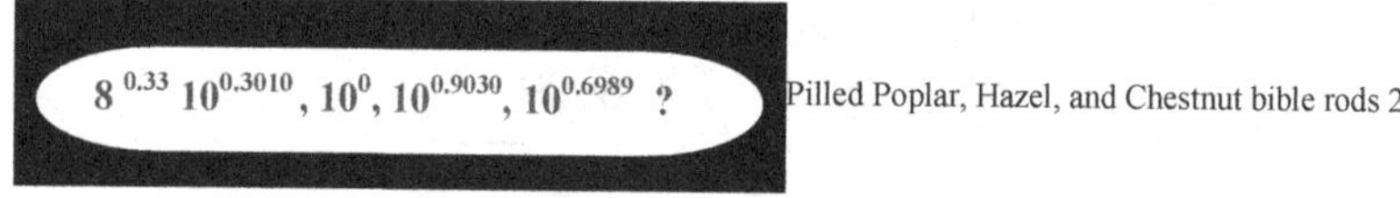

Pilled Poplar, Hazel, and Chestnut bible rods 2

15. And Jesussavior; deliverer**answering said unto him, Suffer it to be so now: for thus it becometh us to fulfil all righteousness. Then he suffered him.**

6, 6: 9. 4. Bible Matrices

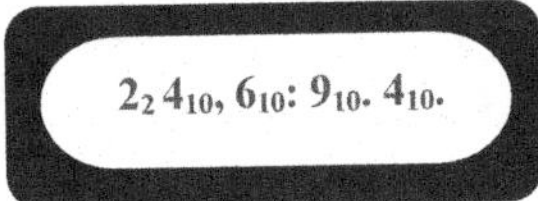

Pilled Poplar, Hazel, and Chestnut bible rods 1

$Log_2 2 = y$ $Log_{10} 4 = 0.6020$ $Log_{10} 6 = 0.7781$ $Log_{10} 9 = 0.9542$ $Log_{10} 4 = 0.6020$

$2^y = 2^1$

$y = 1$

6, 6: 9. 4. Deep calls unto Deep study bible 1

1 0.6020, 0.7781: 0.9542. 0.6020.

Deep calls unto Deep study bible 2

x-axis	y-axis
6	1.6020
6	0.7781
9	0.9542
4	0.6020

Water Spout *(lightning; combinatorics)* Study bible 1

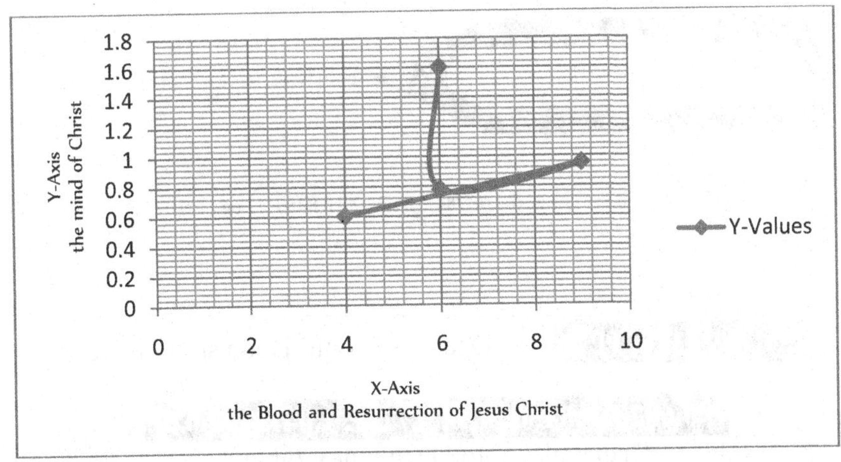

Water Spout *(lightning; combinatorics)* Study bible 2

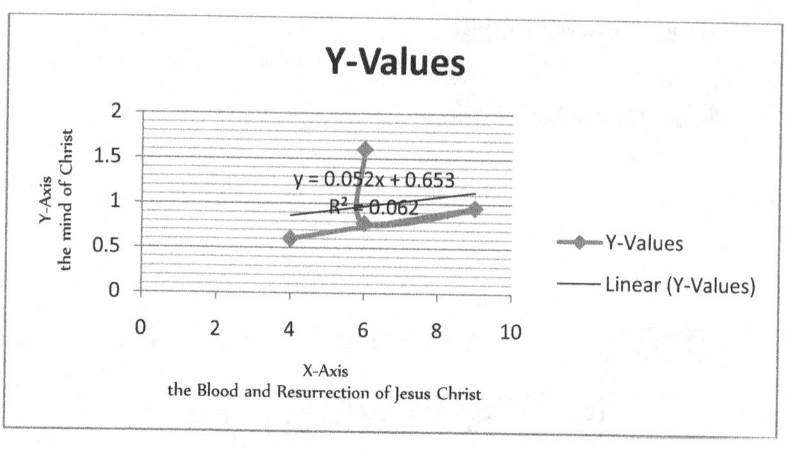

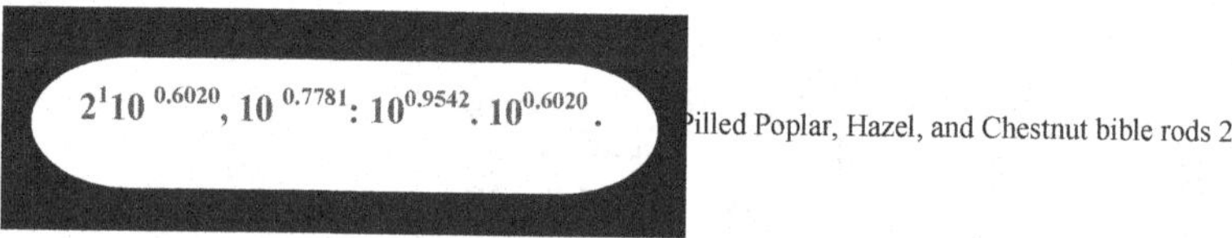

Pilled Poplar, Hazel, and Chestnut bible rods 2

16. And Jesussavior; deliverer, **when he was baptized, went up straightway out of the water: and, lo, the heavens were opened unto him, and he saw the Spirit of God descending like a dove, and lighting upon him:**

2, 4, 7: 1, 1, 6, 11, 4: Bible Matrices

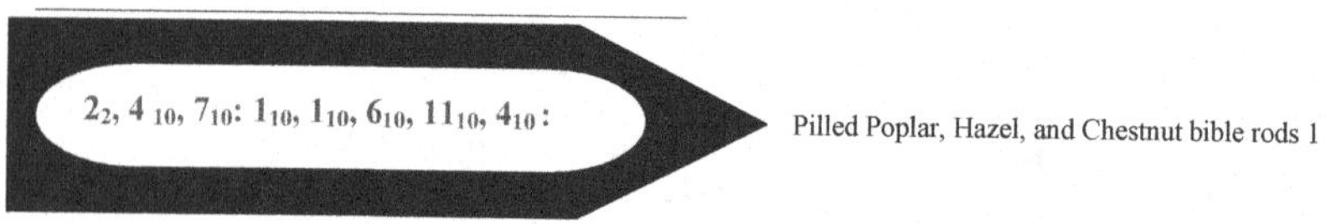

Pilled Poplar, Hazel, and Chestnut bible rods 1

$Log_2 2 = y$ $Log_{10} 4 = 0.6020$ $Log_{10} 6 = 0.7781$ $Log_{10} 7 = 0.8450$ $Log_{10} 1 = 0$ $Log_{10} 11 = 1.0413$

$2^y = 2^1$

$y = 1$

2, 4, 7: 1, 1, 6, 11, 4: Deep calls unto Deep study bible 1

1, 0.6020, 0.8450: 0, 0, 0.7781, 1.0413, 0.6020:

Deep calls unto Deep study bible 2

x-axis	y-axis
2	1
4	0.6020
7	0.8450
1	0
1	0
6	0.7781
11	1.0413
4	0.6020

Water Spout *(lightning; combinatorics)* Study bible 1

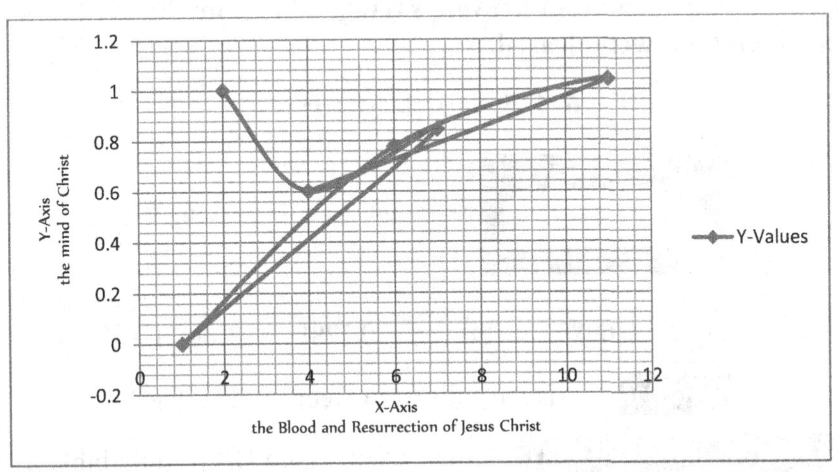

Water Spout *(lightning; combinatorics)* Study bible 2

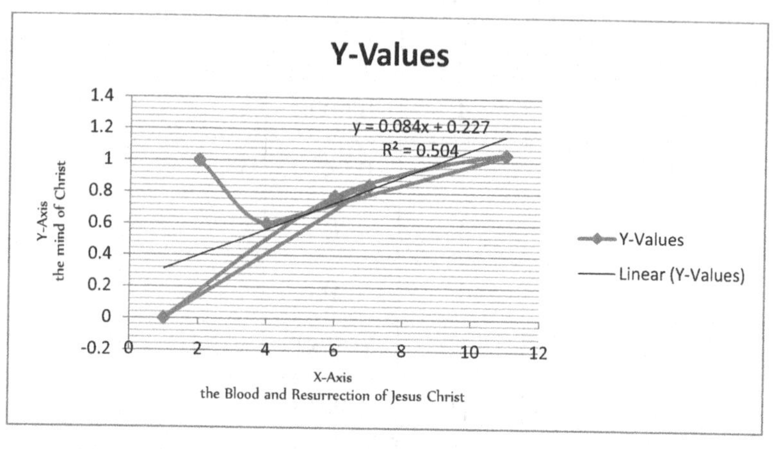

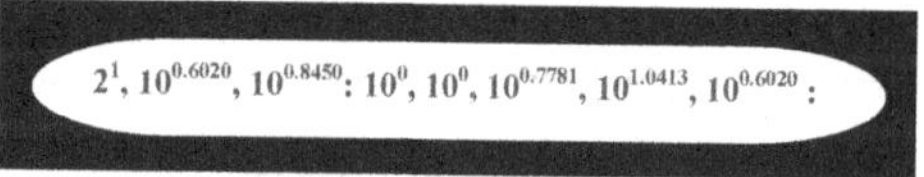

Pilled Poplar, Hazel, and Chestnut bible rods 2

17. And lo a voice from heaven, saying, This is my beloved Son, in whom I am well pleased.

6, 1, 5, 6. Bible Matrices

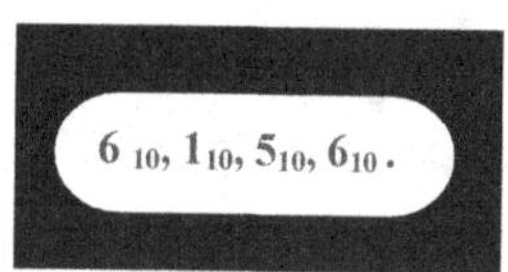

Pilled Poplar, Hazel, and Chestnut bible rods 1

$Log_{10} 5 = 0.6989$ $Log_{10} 6 = 0.7781$ $Log_{10} 1 = 0$

6, 1, 5, 6. Deep calls unto Deep study bible 1

0.7781, 0, 0.6989, 0.7781. Deep calls unto Deep study bible 2

x-axis	y-axis
6	0.7781
1	0
5	0.6989
6	0.7781

Water Spout *(lightning; combinatorics)* Study bible 1

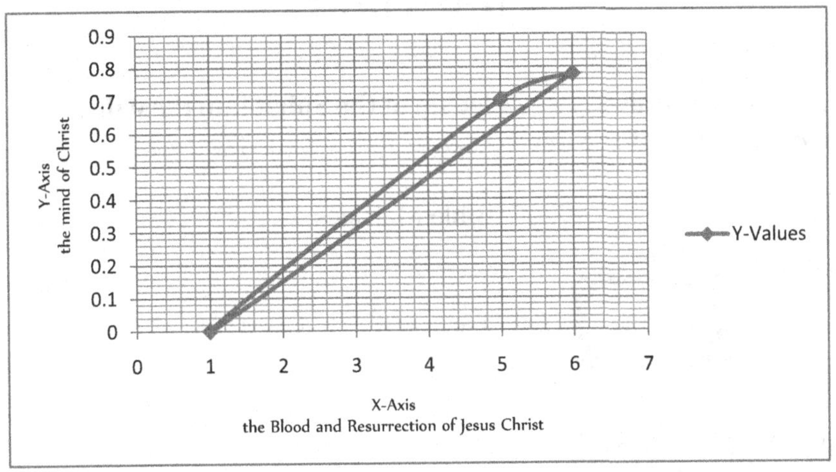

Water Spout *(lightning; combinatorics)* Study bible 2

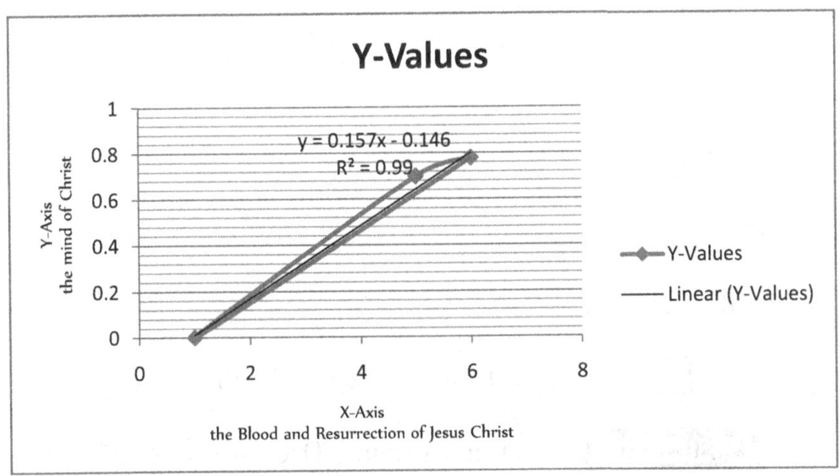

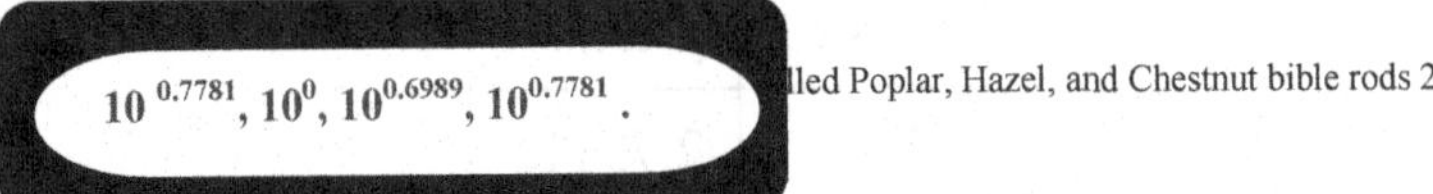

CHAPTER 4

1. Then was Jesus savior; deliverer **led up of the Spirit into the wilderness to be tempted of the devil** false accuser, slanderer, the arch-enemy of man's spiritual interest.

17. Bible Matrices

Pilled Poplar, Hazel, and Chestnut bible rods 1

$\text{Log}_2 3 = y \qquad \text{Log}_{10} 14 = 1.1461$

$2^y = 3$

$\log 2^y = \log 3$

$y \log 2 = \log 3$

$y = \log 3 / \log 2$

$y = 0.4771/0.3010$

$y = 1.5850$

17. Deep calls unto Deep study bible 1

1.5850 1.1461. Deep calls unto Deep study bible 2

x-axis	y-axis
17	2.7311

Water Spout *(lightning; combinatorics)* Study bible 1

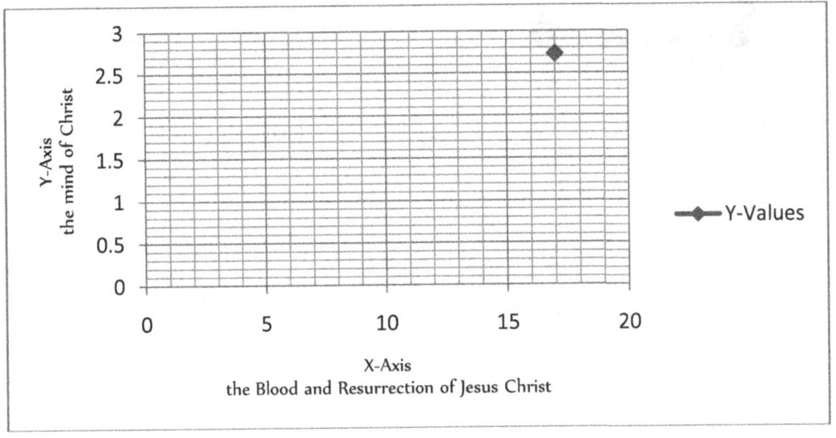

Water Spout *(lightning; combinatorics)* Study bible 2

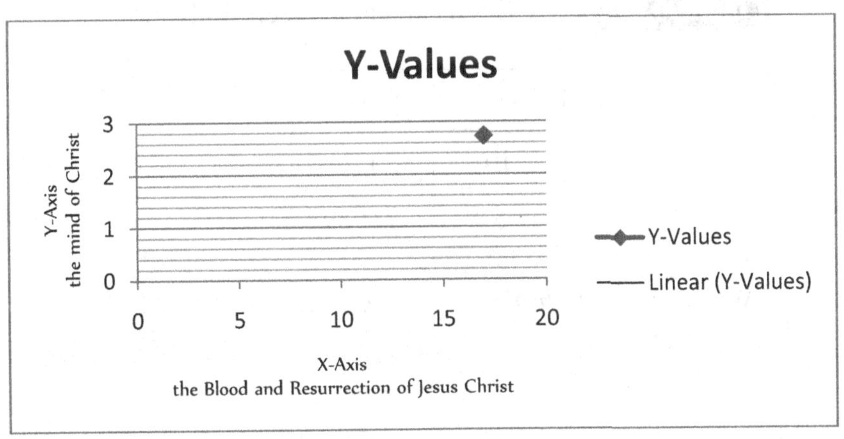

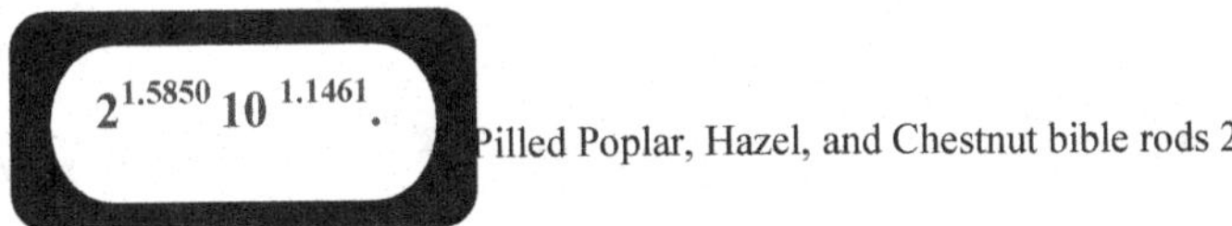

Pilled Poplar, Hazel, and Chestnut bible rods 2

2. And when he had fasted forty testings, trials; 2 x 2 x 2 x 5 **days and forty** testings and trials; and enlightenment; 2 x 2 x 2 x 5 **nights, he was afterward an hungred.**

10, 5. Bible Matrices

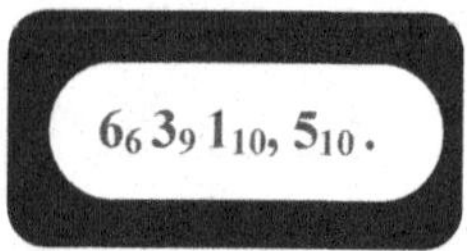

Pilled Poplar, Hazel, and Chestnut bible rods 1

$\log_6 6 = y$ $\log_9 3 = y$ $\log_{10} 1 = 0$ $\log_{10} 5 = 0.6989$

$6^y = 6^1$ $9^y = 3^1$

$y = 1$ $3^{2y} = 3^1$

$2y = 1$

$y = ½$

10, 5. Deep calls unto Deep study bible 1

1 0.5 0, 0.6989. Deep calls unto Deep study bible 2

x-axis	y-axis
10	1.5
5	0.6989

Water Spout *(lightning; combinatorics)* Study bible 1

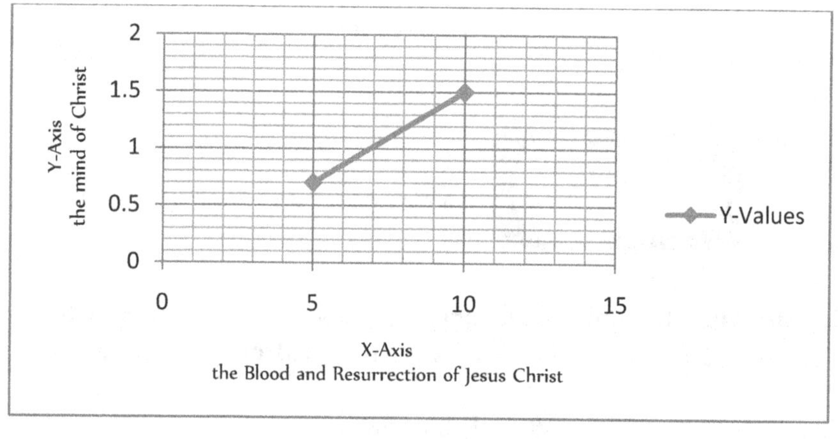

Water Spout *(lightning; combinatorics)* Study bible 2

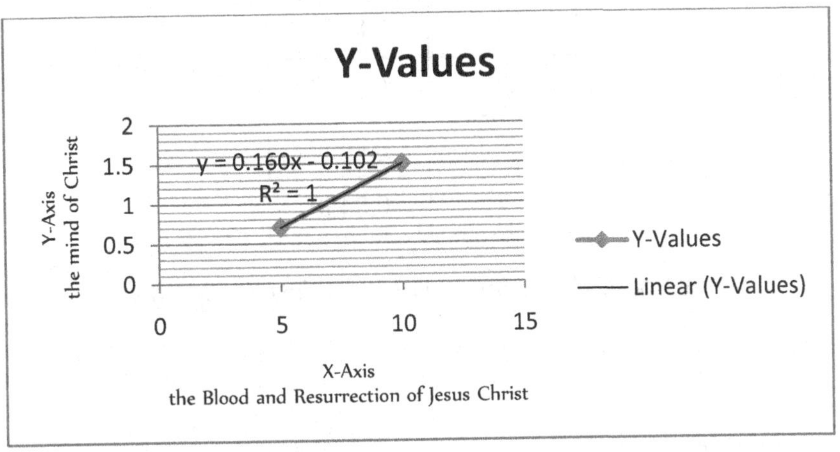

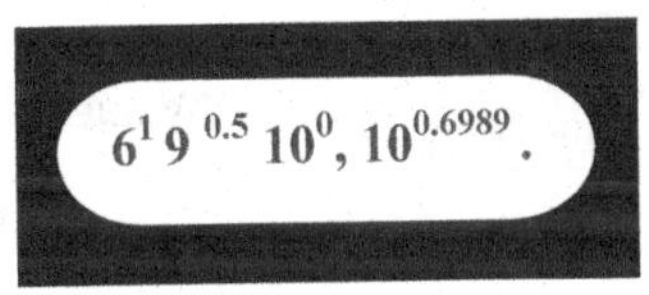

Pilled Poplar, Hazel, and Chestnut bible rods 2

3. And when the tempter came to him, he said, If thou be the Son of God, command that these stones be made bread.

7, 2, 7, 7. Bible Matrices

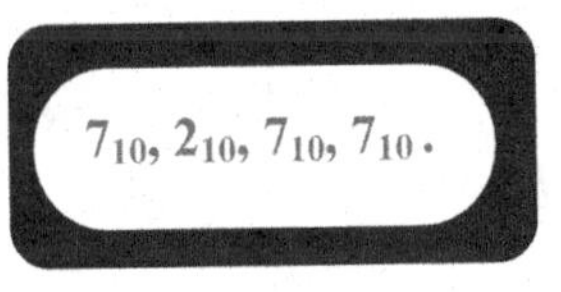

Pilled Poplar, Hazel, and Chestnut bible rods 1

$\text{Log}_{10} 7 = 0.8450$ $\text{Log}_{10} 2 = 0.3010$ $\text{Log}_{10} 7 = 0.8450$ $\text{Log}_{10} 7 = 0.8450$

7, 2, 7, 7. Deep calls unto Deep study bible 1

0.8450, 0.3010, 0.8450, 0.8450.

Deep calls unto Deep study bible 2

x-axis	y-axis
7	0.8450
2	0.3010
7	0.8450
7	0.8450

Water Spout *(lightning; combinatorics)* Study bible 1

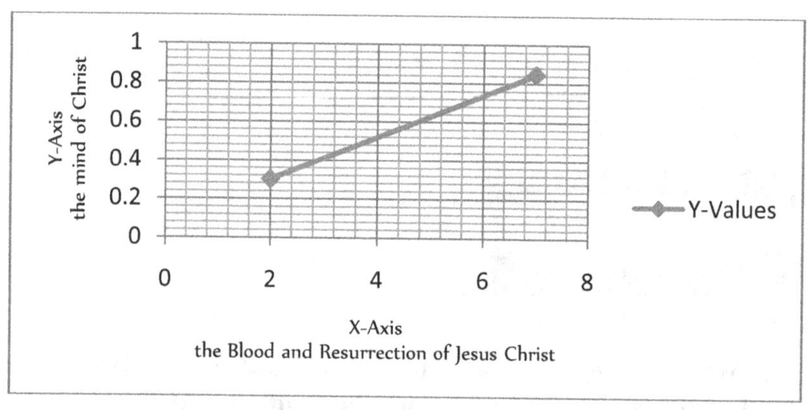

Water Spout *(lightning; combinatorics)* Study bible 2

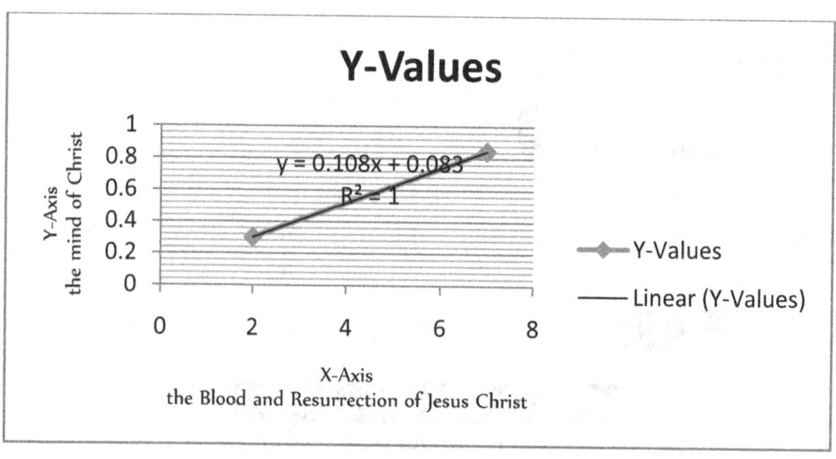

$10^{0.8450}, 10^{0.3010}, 10^{0.8450}, 10^{0.8450}$.

Pilled Poplar, Hazel, and Chestnut bible rods 2

4. But he answered and said, It is written, Man shall not live by bread alone, but by every word that proceedeth out of the mouth of God.

5, 3, 7, 12. Bible Matrices

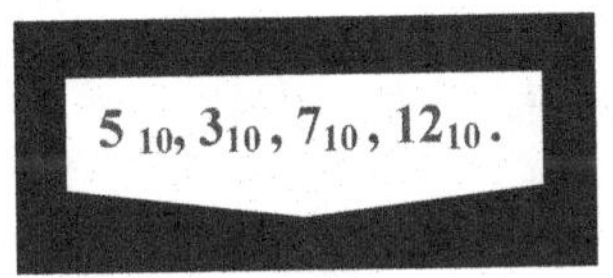

Pilled Poplar, Hazel, and Chestnut bible rods 1

$\text{Log}_{10} 7 = 0.8450$ $\text{Log}_{10} 3 = 0.4771$ $\text{Log}_{10} 5 = 0.6989$ $\text{Log}_{10} 12 = 1.0791$

5, 3, 7, 12. Deep calls unto Deep study bible 1

0.6989, 0.4771, 0.8450, 1.0791.
Deep calls unto Deep study bible 2

x-axis	y-axis
5	0.6989
3	0.4771
7	0.8450
12	1.0791

Water Spout *(lightning; combinatorics)* Study bible 1

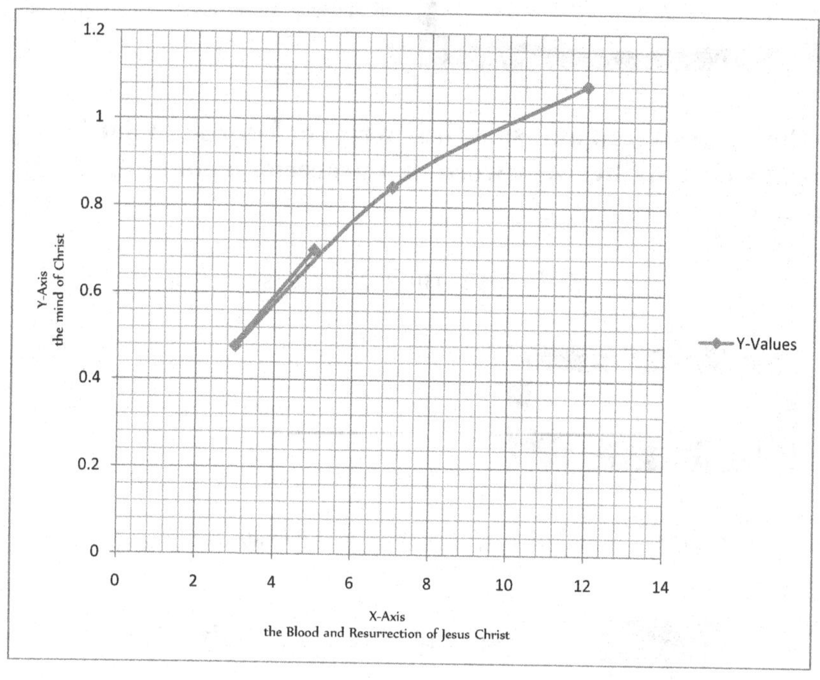

Water Spout *(lightning; combinatorics)* Study bible 2

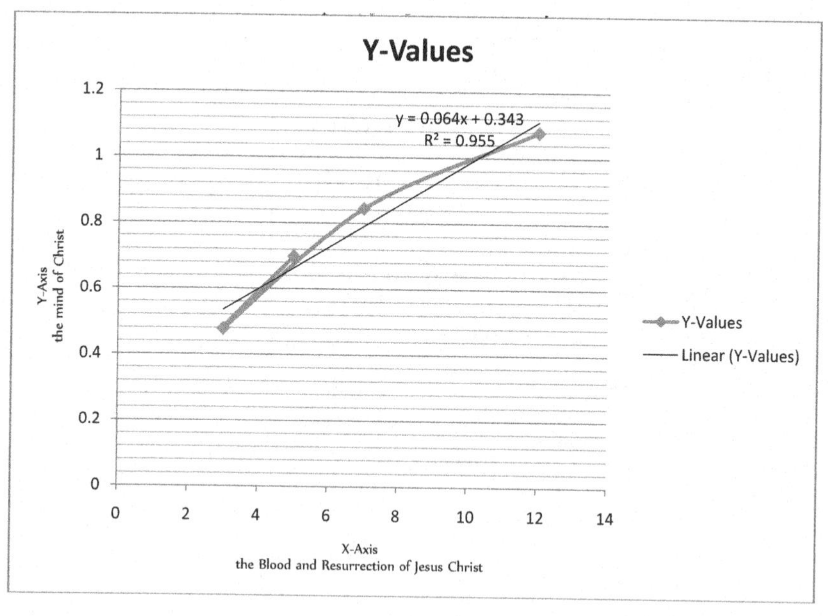

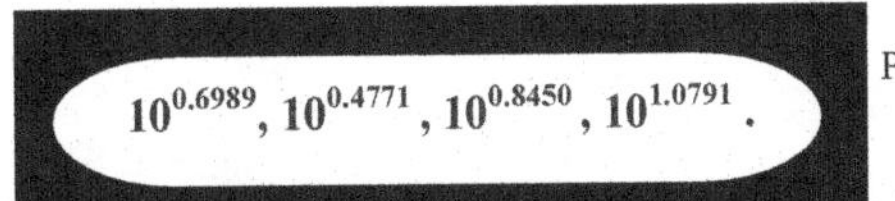

Pilled Poplar, Hazel, and Chestnut bible rods 2

5. Then the devil slanderer; false accuser **taketh him up into the holy city, and setteth him on a pinnacle of the temple,**

10, 9, Bible Matrices

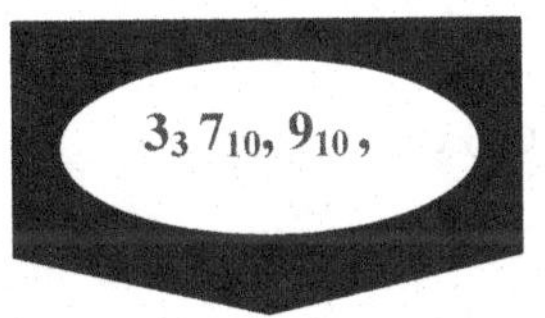

Pilled Poplar, Hazel, and Chestnut bible rods 1

$\text{Log}_{10} 7 = 0.8450$ $\text{Log}_{10} 9 = 0.9542$ $\text{Log}_3 3 = y$

$$3^y = 3^1$$

$$y = 1$$

10, 9, Deep calls unto Deep study bible 1

1 0.8450, 0.9542, Deep calls unto Deep study bible 2

x-axis	y-axis
10	1.8450
9	0.9542

Water Spout *(lightning; combinatorics)* Study bible 1

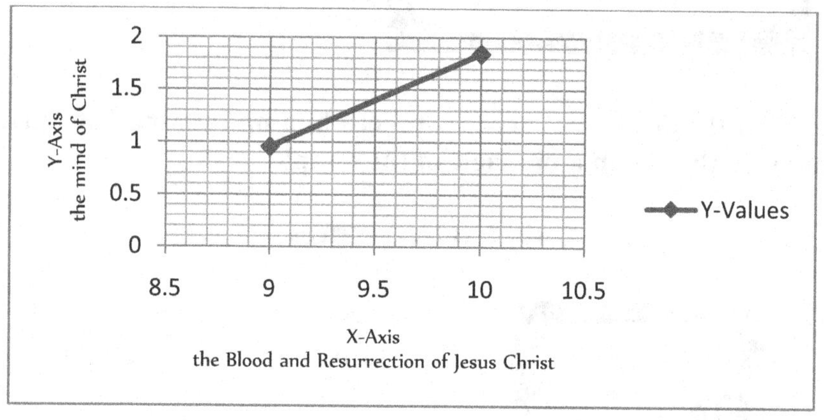

Water Spout *(lightning; combinatorics)* Study bible 2

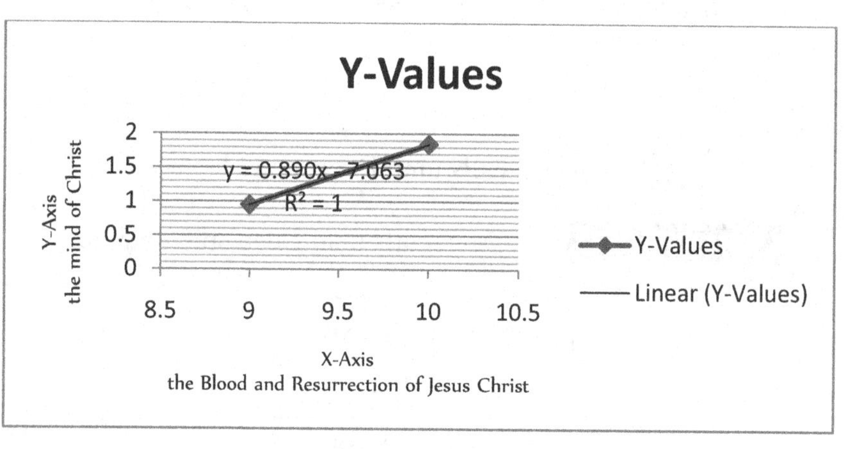

Pilled Poplar, Hazel, and Chestnut bible rods 2

6. And saith unto him, If thou be the Son of God, cast thyself down: for it is written, He shall give his angels charge concerning thee: and in their hands they shall bear thee up, lest at any time thou dash thy foot against a stone.

4, 7, 3: 4, 8: 9, 11. Bible Matrices

$4_{10}, 7_{10}, 3_{10} : 4_{10}, 8_{10} : 9_{10}, 11_{10}$. lled Poplar, Hazel, and Chestnut bible rods 1

$\text{Log}_{10} 7 = 0.8450$ $\text{Log}_{10} 3 = 0.4771$ $\text{Log}_{10} 4 = 0.6020$ $\text{Log}_{10} 8 = 0.9030$ $\text{Log}_{10} 9 = 0.9542$

$\text{Log}_{10} 11 = 1.0413$

4, 7, 3: 4, 8: 9, 11. Deep calls unto Deep study bible 1

0.6020, 0.8450, 0.4771: 0.6020, 0.9030: 0.9542, 1.0413 Deep calls unto Deep study bible 2

x-axis	y-axis
4	0.6020
7	0.8450
3	0.4771
4	0.6020
8	0.9030
9	0.9542
11	1.0413

Water Spout *(lightning; combinatorics)* Study bible 1

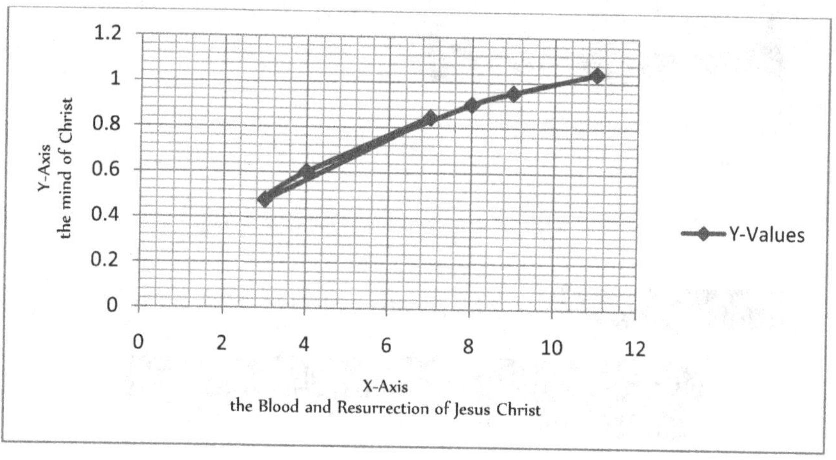

Water Spout *(lightning; combinatorics)* Study bible 2

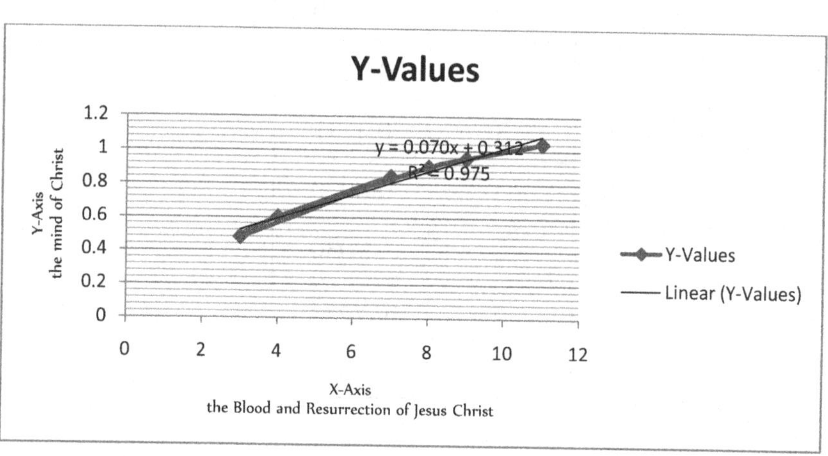

Pilled Poplar, Hazel, and Chestnut bible rods 2

7. Jesussavior; deliverer**said unto him, It is written again, Thou shalt not tempt the Lord thy God.**

4, 4, 8. Bible Matrices

$1_2\ 3_{10},\ 4_{10},\ 8_{10}.$ Pilled Poplar, Hazel, and Chestnut bible rods 1

$Log_{10}3 = 0.4771$ $Log_{10}4 = 0.6020$ $Log_{10}8 = 0.9030$ $Log_2 1 = y$

$2^y = 1$

$2^y = 2^0$

$y = 0$

4, 4, 8. Deep calls unto Deep study bible 1

0 0.4771, 0.6020, 0.9030, Deep calls unto Deep study bible 2

x-axis	y-axis
4	0.4771
4	0.6020
8	0.9030

Water Spout *(lightning; combinatorics)* Study bible 1

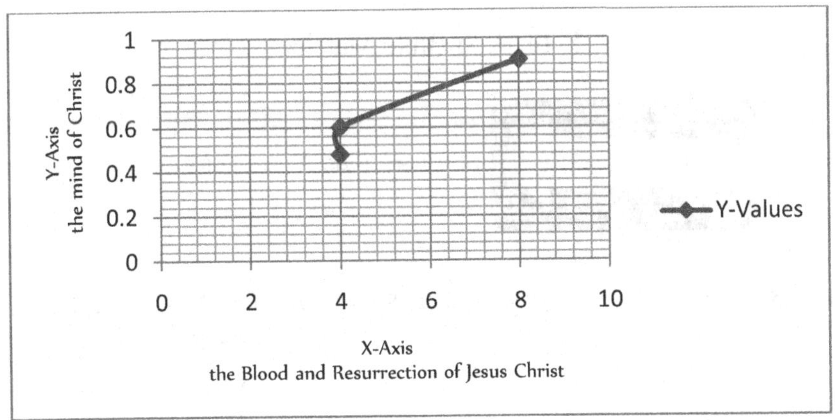

Water Spout *(lightning; combinatorics)* Study bible 2

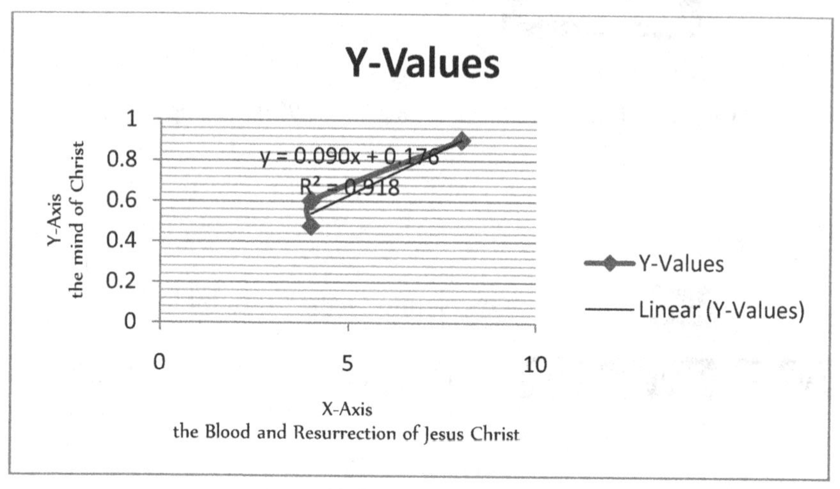

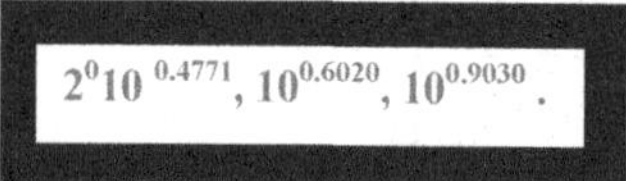

Pilled Poplar, Hazel, and Chestnut bible rods 2

8. Again, the devil slanderer; false accuser, attacker **taketh him up into an exceeding high mountain, and sheweth him all the kingdoms of the world, and the glory of them;**

1, 10, 9, 5; Bible Matrices

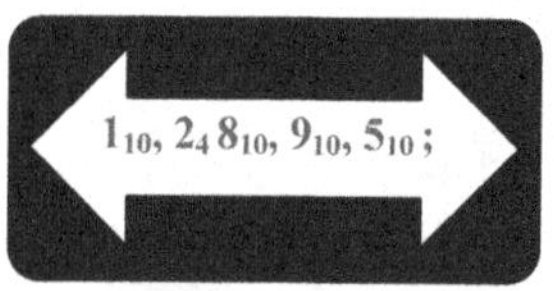

Pilled Poplar, Hazel, and Chestnut bible rods 1

$\text{Log}_{10} 5 = 0.6989$ $\text{Log}_{10} 9 = 0.9542$ $\text{Log}_{10} 8 = 0.9030$ $\text{Log}_4 2 = y$ $\text{Log}_{10} 1 = 0$

$4^y = 2$

$2^{2y} = 2^1$

$2y = 1$

$y = ½$

1, 10, 9, 5; Deep calls unto Deep study bible 1

0, 0.5 0.9030, 0.9542, 0.6989; Deep calls unto Deep study bible 2

x-axis	y-axis
1	0
10	1.4030
9	0.9542
5	0.6989

Water Spout *(lightning; combinatorics)* Study bible 1

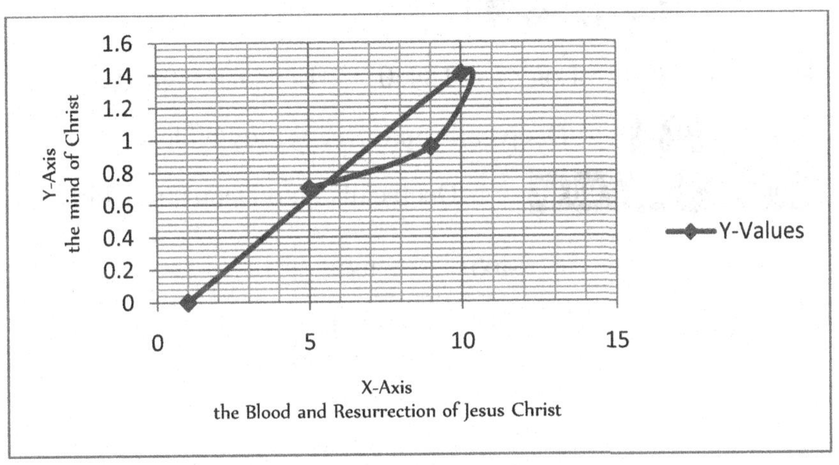

Water Spout *(lightning; combinatorics)* Study bible 2

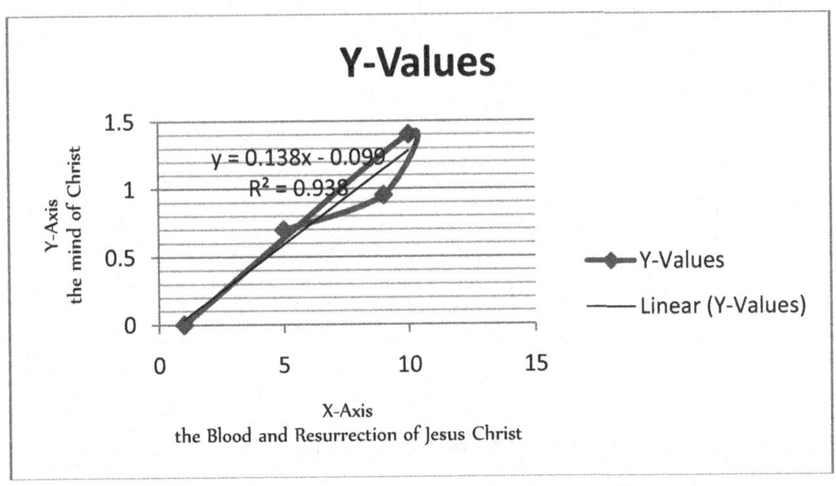

$10^0, 4^{½}\ 10^{0.9030}, 10^{0.9542}, 10^{0.6989}$; Pilled Poplar, Hazel, and Chestnut bible rods 2

9. And saith unto him, All these things will I give thee, if thou wilt fall down and worship me.

4, 7, 8. Bible Matrices

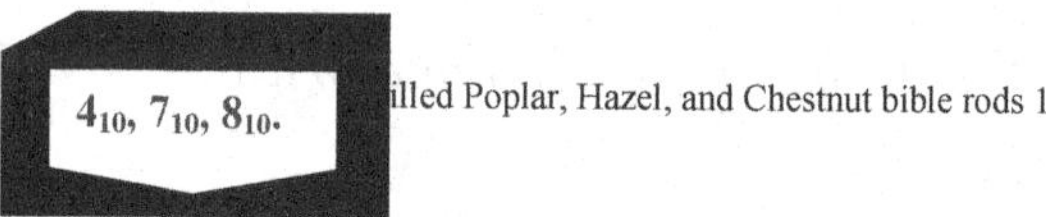

illed Poplar, Hazel, and Chestnut bible rods 1

$\text{Log}_{10} 4 = 0.6020$ $\text{Log}_{10} 7 = 0.8450$ $\text{Log}_{10} 8 = 0.9030$

4, 7, 8. Deep calls unto Deep study bible 1

0.6020, 0.8450, 0.9030. Deep calls unto Deep study bible 2

x-axis	y-axis
4	0.6020
7	0.8450
8	0.9030

Water Spout *(lightning; combinatorics)* Study bible 1

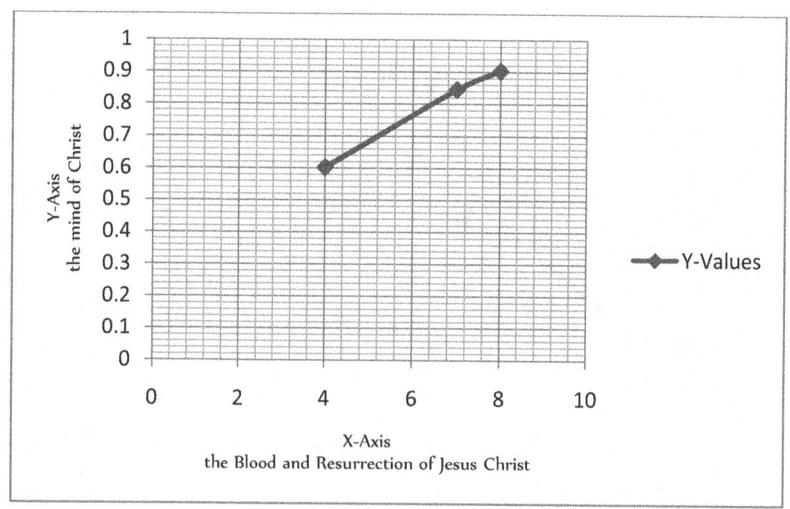

Water Spout *(lightning; combinatorics)* Study bible 2

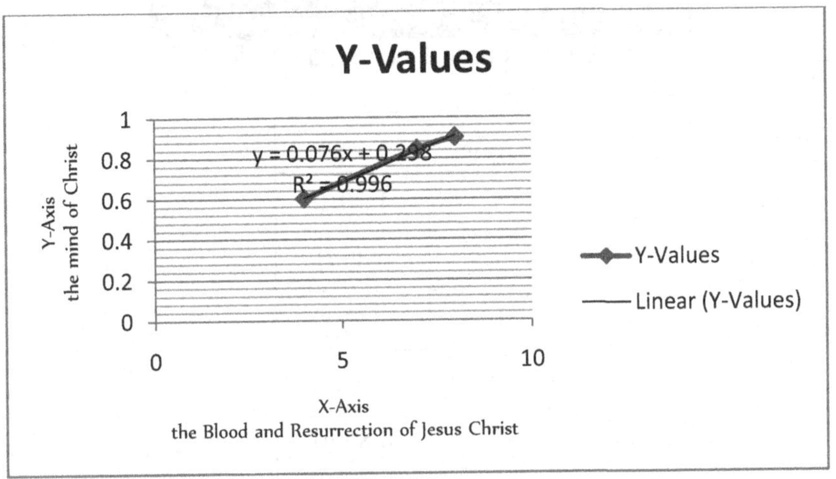

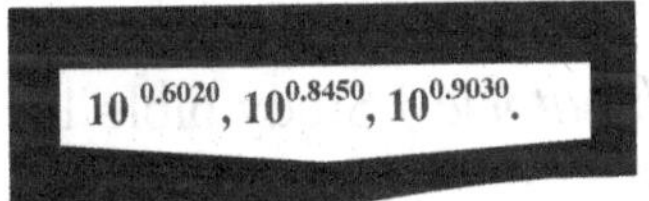

$10^{0.6020}, 10^{0.8450}, 10^{0.9030}.$

Pilled Poplar, Hazel, and Chestnut bible rods 2

10. Then saith Jesus savior; deliverer, redeemer **unto him, Get thee hence, Satan**contrary; adversary; enemy; accuser: **for it is written, Thou shalt worship the Lord thy God, and him only shalt thou serve.**

5, 3, 1: 4, 7, 6. Bible Matrices

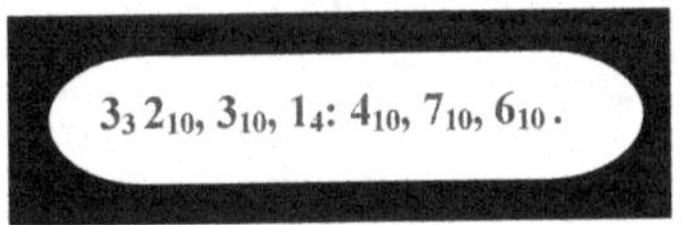

$3_3\, 2_{10}, 3_{10}, 1_4: 4_{10}, 7_{10}, 6_{10}.$

Pilled Poplar, Hazel, and Chestnut bible rods 1

$\log_{10} 4 = 0.6020$ $\log_{10} 7 = 0.8450$ $\log_{10} 6 = 0.7781$ $\log_3 3 = y$ $\log_4 1 = y$ $\log_{10} 3 = 0.4771$

$3^y = 3^1$ $4^y = 1$

$y = 1$ $4^y = 4^0$

$\log_{10} 2 = 0.3010$

5, 3, 1: 4, 7, 6. Deep calls unto Deep study bible 1

1 0.3010, 0.4771, 0, 0.6020, 0.8450, 0.7781.
Deep calls unto Deep study bible 2

x-axis	y-axis
5	1.3010
3	0.4771
1	0
4	0.6020
7	0.8450
6	0.7781

Water Spout *(lightning; combinatorics)* Study bible 1

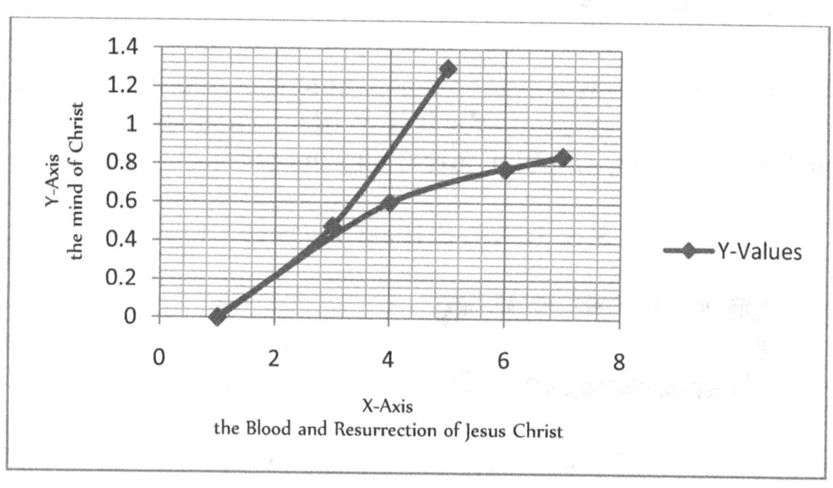

Water Spout *(lightning; combinatorics)* Study bible 2

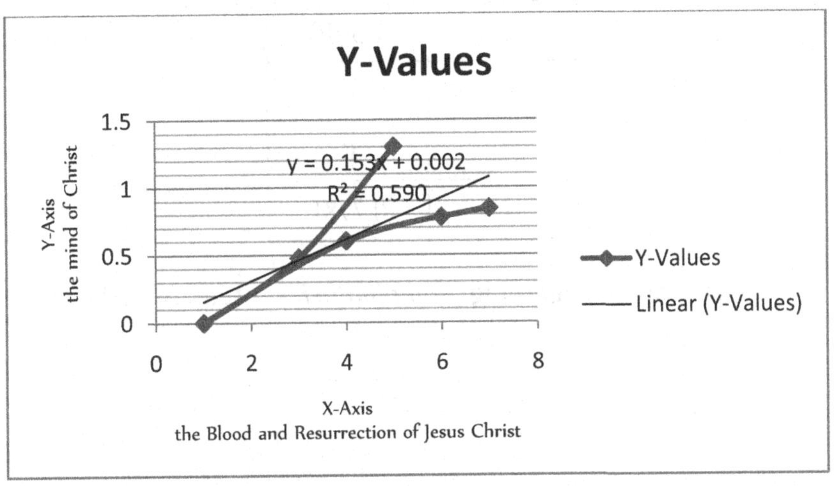

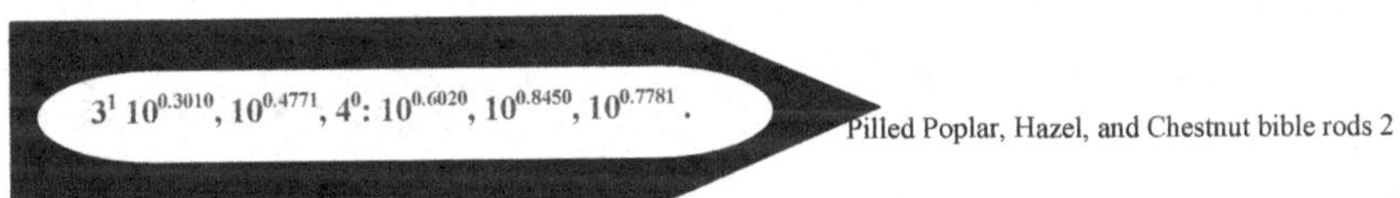

Pilled Poplar, Hazel, and Chestnut bible rods 2

11. Then the devil slanderer; false accuser **leaveth him, and, behold, angels came and ministered unto him.**

5, 1, 1, 6. Bible Matrices

3_3 2_{10}, 1_{10}, 1_{10}, 6_{10}.

Pilled Poplar, Hazel, and Chestnut bible rods 1

$\text{Log}_{10} 2 = 0.3010$ $\text{Log}_{10} 6 = 0.7781$ $\text{Log}_{10} 1 = 0$ $\text{Log}_3 3 = y$ $\text{Log}_{10} 1 = 0$

$3^y = 3$

$3^y = 3^1$

$y = 1$

5, 1, 1, 6. Deep calls unto Deep study bible 1

1 0.3010, 0, 0, 0.7781. Deep calls unto Deep study bible 2

x-axis	y-axis
5	1.3010
1	0
1	0
6	0.7781

Water Spout *(lightning; combinatorics)* Study bible 1

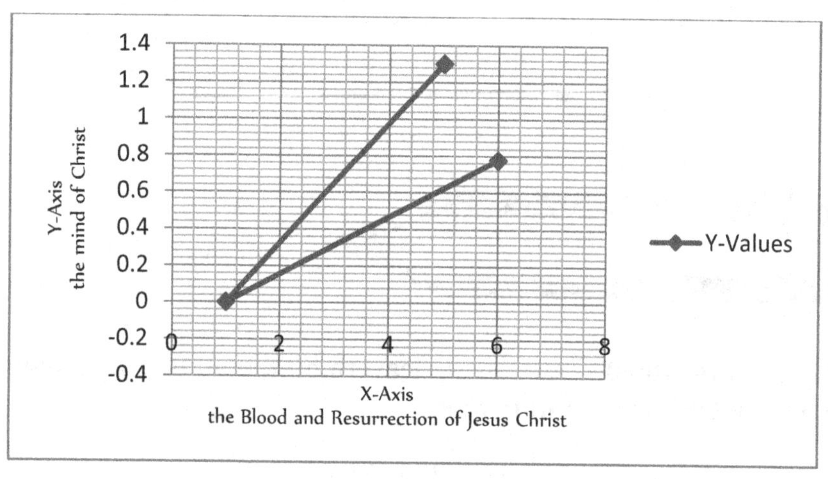

Water Spout *(lightning; combinatorics)* Study bible 2

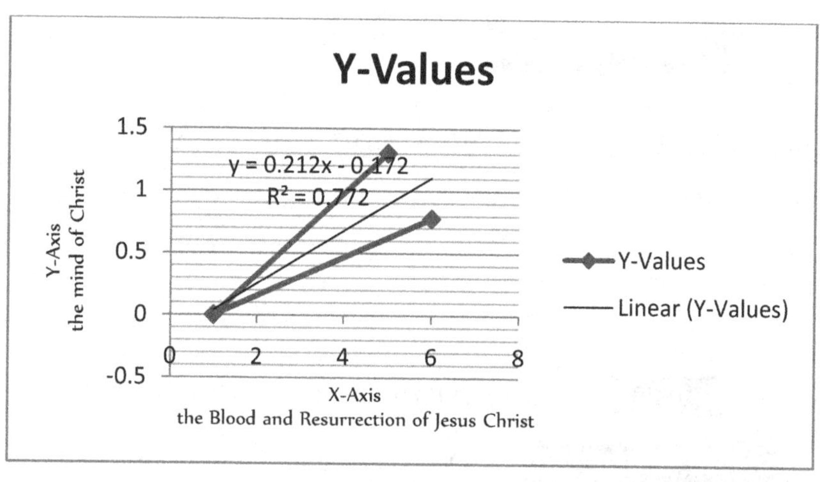

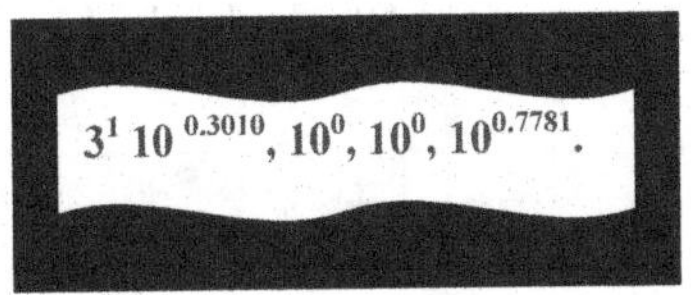

Pilled Poplar, Hazel, and Chestnut bible rods 2

12. Now when Jesussavior; deliverer, redeemer **had heard that John** grace mercy of
God **was cast into prison, he departed into Galilee**circuit; wheel; revolution; circle;

11, 4; Bible Matrices

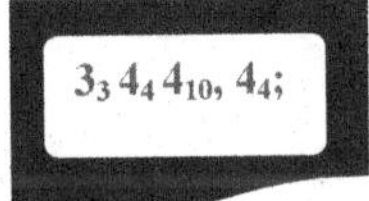

Pilled Poplar, Hazel, and Chestnut bible rods 1

$\text{Log}_3 3 = y$ $\quad$ $\text{Log}_4 4 = y$ $\quad$ $\text{Log}_4 4 = y$ $\quad$ $\text{Log}_{10} 4 = 0.6020$

$3^y = 3^1$ $\quad$ $4^y = 4$ $\quad$ $4^y = 4$

$y = 1$ $\quad$ $2^{2y} = 2^2$ $\quad$ $2^{2y} = 2^2$

$2y = 2$ $\quad$ $2y = 2$

$y = 1$ $\quad$ $y = 1$

11, 4; Deep calls unto Deep study bible 1

1 1 0.6020, 1 ; Deep calls unto Deep study bible 2

x-axis	y-axis
11	2.6020
4	1

Water Spout *(lightning; combinatorics)* Study bible 1

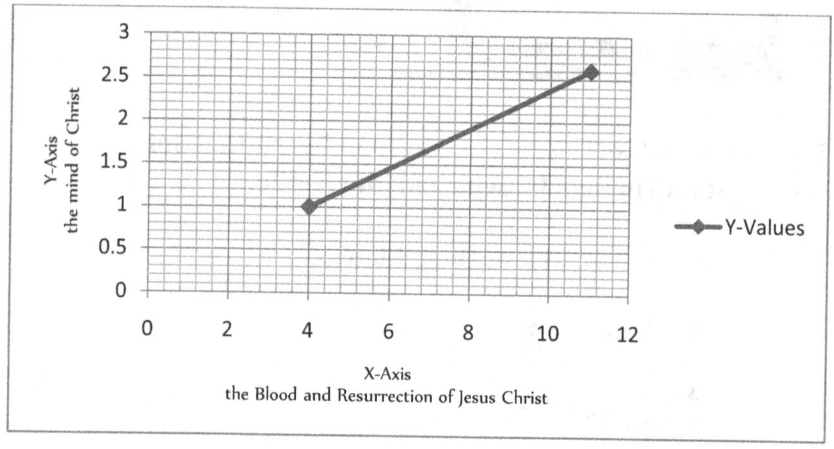

Water Spout *(lightning; combinatorics)* Study bible 2

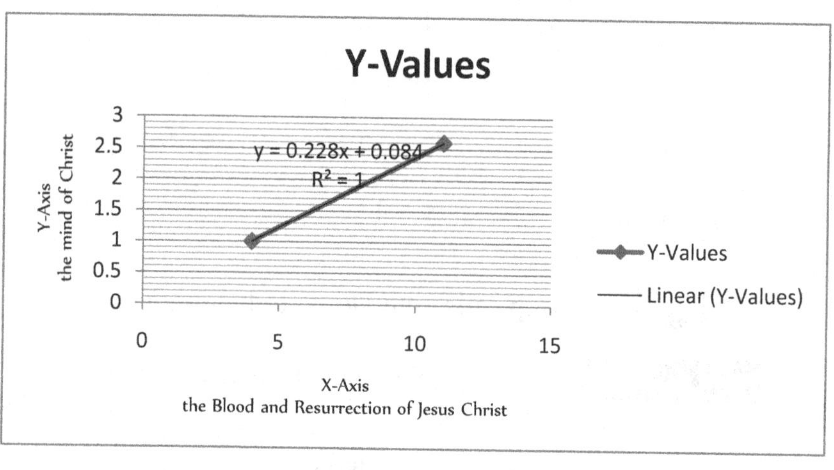

Pilled Poplar, Hazel, and Chestnut bible rods 2

13. And leaving Nazarethseparated; crowned; sanctified; the guarded one; a shoot; set-apart, **he came and dwelt in Capernaum** field of repentance; city of comfort, **which is upon the sea coast, in the borders of Zabulon**dwelling; habitation **and Nephthalim**wrestling; that struggles, fights:

3, 6, 6, 7: Bible Matrices

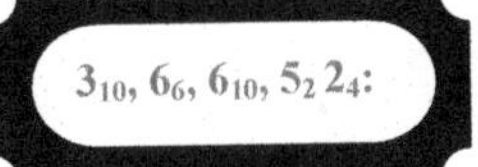

Pilled Poplar, Hazel, and Chestnut bible rods 1

$\text{Log}_6 6 = y$	$\text{Log}_4 2 = y$	$\text{Log}_2 5 = y$	$\text{Log}_{10} 3 = 0.4771 \quad \text{Log}_{10} 6 = 0.7781$
$6^y = 6^1$	$4^y = 2^1$	$2^y = 5$	
$\mathbf{y} = 1$	$2^{2y} = 2^1$	$\log \mathbf{2}^y = \log 5$	
	$2y = 1$	$y \log 2 = \log 5$	
	$y = ½$	$y = \log 5 / \log 2$	
		$y = 0.6989/0.3010$	
		$y = 2.3219$	

3, 6, 6, 7: Deep calls unto Deep study bible 1

0.4771, 1, 0.7781, 2.3219 0.5 Deep calls unto Deep study bible 2

x-axis	y-axis
3	0.4771
6	1
6	0.7781
7	2.8219

Water Spout *(lightning; combinatorics)* Study bible 1

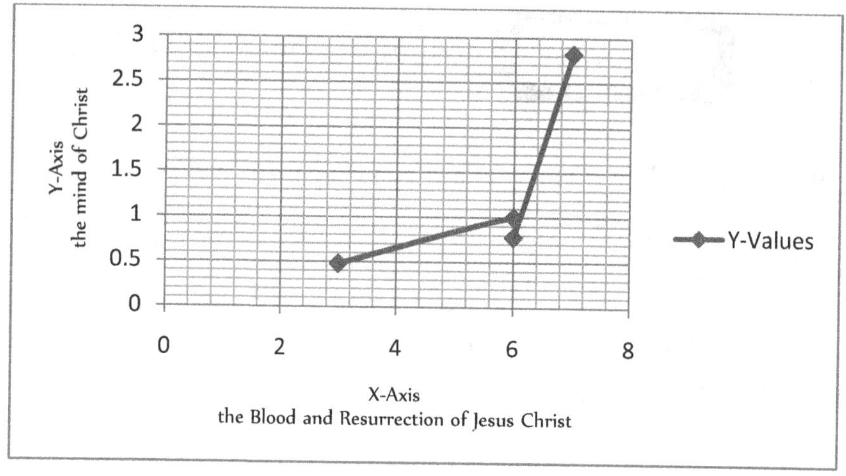

Water Spout *(lightning; combinatorics)* Study bible 2

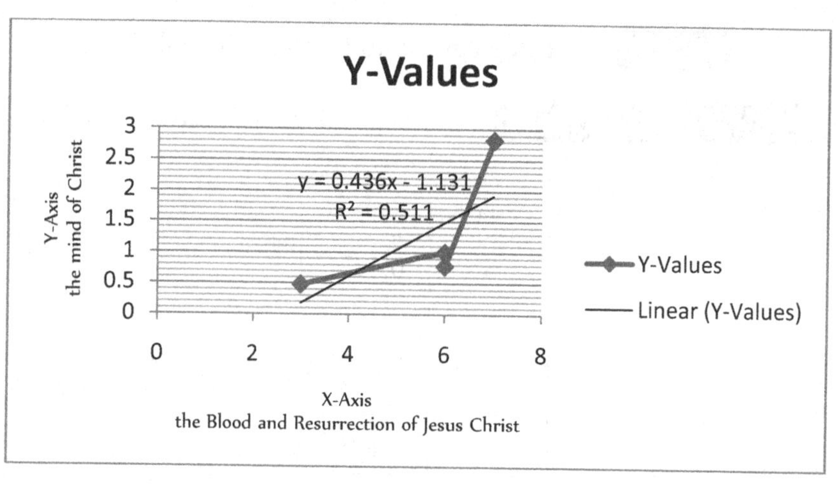

Pilled Poplar, Hazel, and Chestnut bible rods 2

14. That it might be fulfilled which was spoken by Esaias salvation of the Lord; God is savior; salvation of God **the prophet** to bubble forth, as from a fountain; utter, **saying,**

12, 1, Bible Matrices

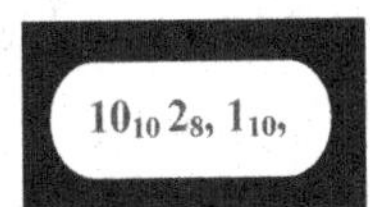

Pilled Poplar, Hazel, and Chestnut bible rods 1

$\text{Log}_8 2 = y$

$8^y = 2^1$

$2^{3y} = 2^1$

$3y = 1$

$y = 1/3$

$\text{Log}_{10} 10 = y$

$10^y = 10^1$

$y = 1$

$\text{Log}_{10} 1 = 0$

12, 1, Deep calls unto Deep study bible 1

1 1/3, 0, Deep calls unto Deep study bible 2

x-axis	y-axis
12	1.33
1	0

Water Spout *(lightning; combinatorics)* Study bible 1

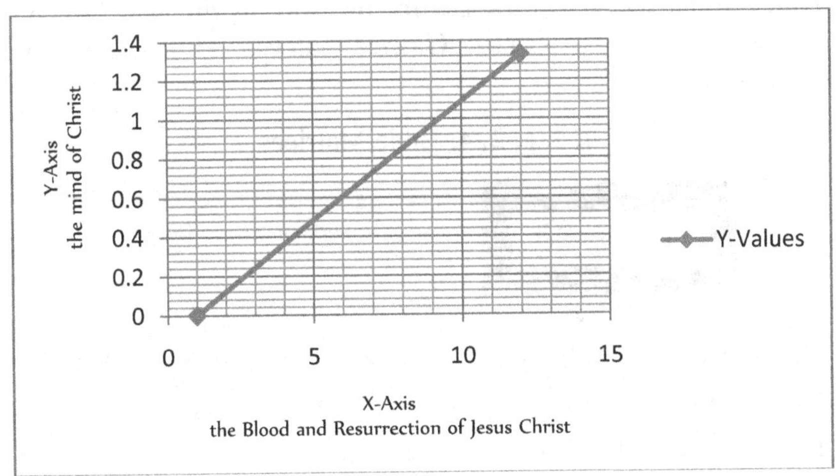

Water Spout *(lightning; combinatorics)* Study bible 2

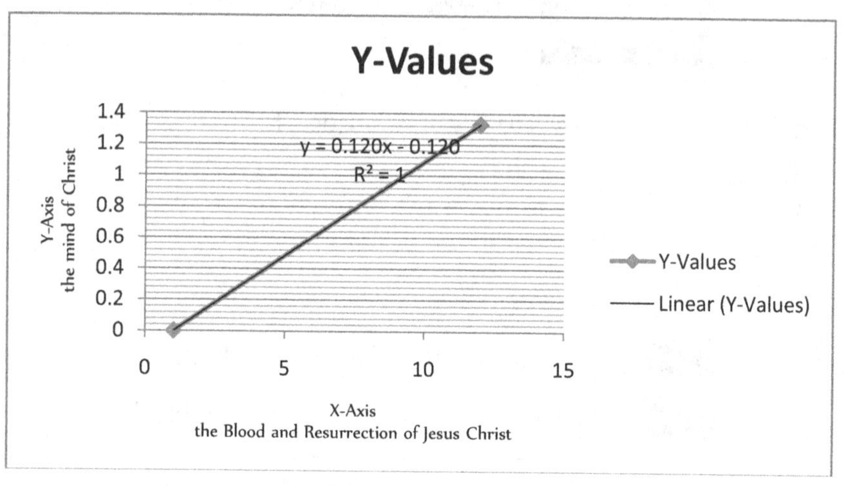

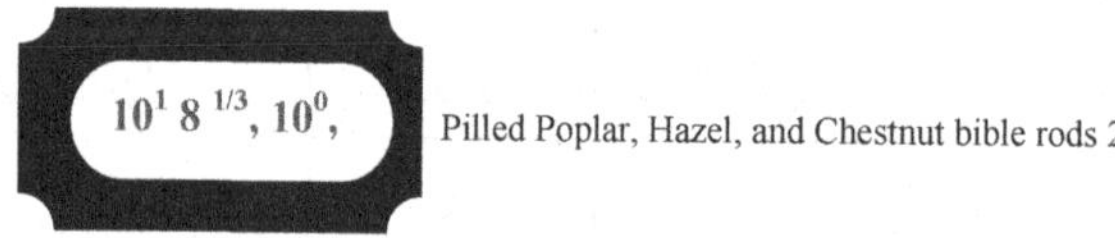

Pilled Poplar, Hazel, and Chestnut bible rods 2

15. The land of Zabulondwelling; habitation, **and the land of Nephthalim**wrestling;that struggles or fights, **by the way of the sea, beyond Jordan**the descender; the river of judgment, **Galilee** circuit;wheel; circle; revolution **of the Gentiles** non- jews ;

4, 5, 6, 2, 4; Bible Matrices

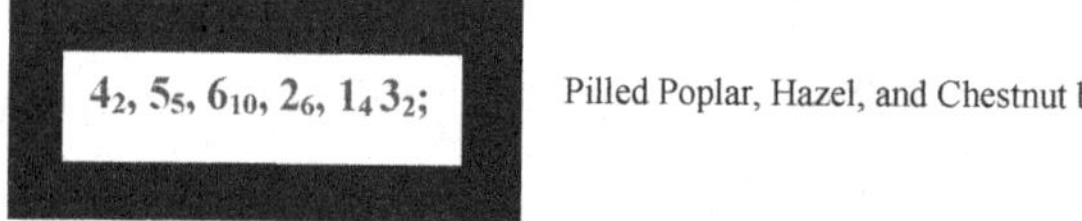

Pilled Poplar, Hazel, and Chestnut bible rods 1

$\text{Log}_2 4 = y$ $\quad 2^y = 4$ $\quad 2^y = 2^2$ $\quad y = 2$

$\text{Log}_5 5 = y$ $\quad 5^y = 5^1$ $\quad y = 1$

$\text{Log}_6 2 = y$ $\quad 6^y = 2$ $\quad \log 6^y = \log 2$ $\quad y \log 6 = \log 2$ $\quad y = \log 2 / \log 6$ $\quad y = 0.3010/0.7781$ $\quad y = 0.3868$

$\text{Log}_2 3 = y$ $\quad 2^y = 3$ $\quad \log 2^y = \log 3$ $\quad y \log 2 = \log 3$ $\quad y = \log 3 / \log 2$ $\quad y = 0.4771/0.3010$ $\quad y = 1.5850$

$\text{Log}_{10} 6 = 0.7781$

$\text{Log}_4 1 = y$ $\quad 4^y = 1$ $\quad 4^y = 4^0$ $\quad y = 0$

4, 5, 6, 2, 4; Deep calls unto Deep study bible 1

2, 1, 0.7781, 0.3868, 0 1.5850 ; Deep calls unto Deep study bible 2

x-axis	y-axis
4	2
5	1
6	0.7781
2	0.3868
4	1.5850

Water Spout *(lightning; combinatorics)* Study bible 1

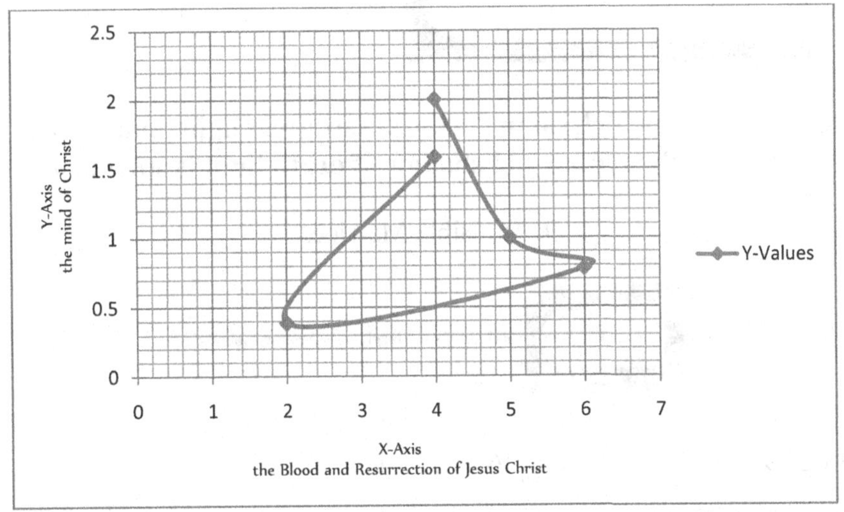

Water Spout *(lightning; combinatorics)* Study bible 2

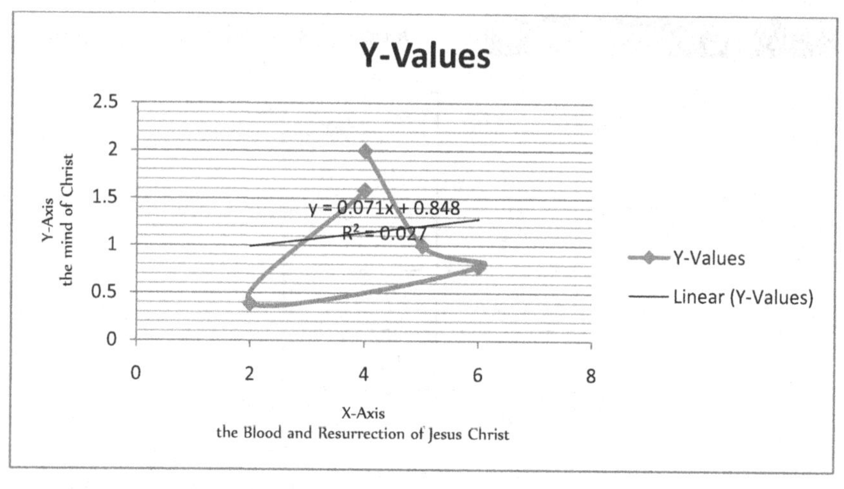

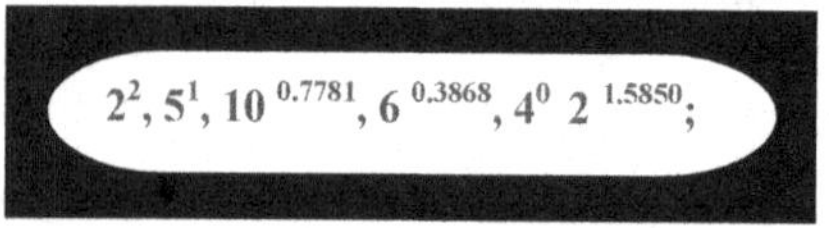

Pilled Poplar, Hazel, and Chestnut bible rods 2

16. The people which sat in darkness saw great light; and to them which sat in the region and shadow of death light is sprung up.

9; 16. Bible Matrices

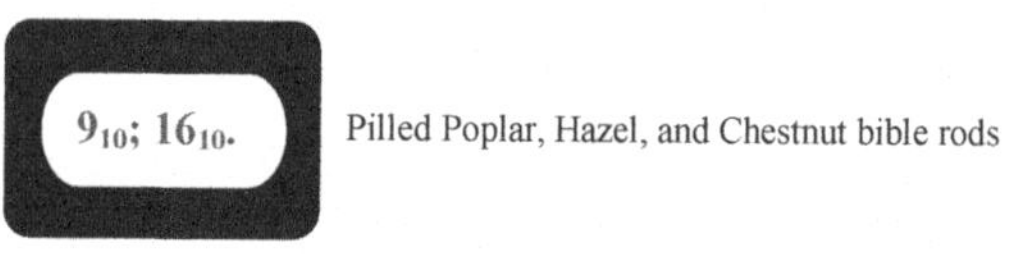

$\text{Log}_{10} 9 = 0.9542$ $\text{Log}_{10} 16 = 1.2041$

9; 16. Deep calls unto Deep study bible 1

0.9542 ; 1.2041. Deep calls unto Deep study bible 2

x-axis	y-axis
9	0.9542
16	1.2041

Water Spout *(lightning; combinatorics)* Study bible 1

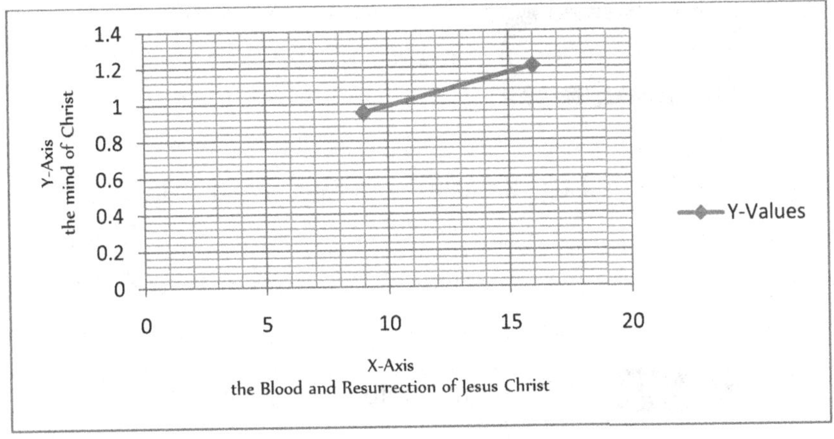

Water Spout *(lightning; combinatorics)* Study bible 2

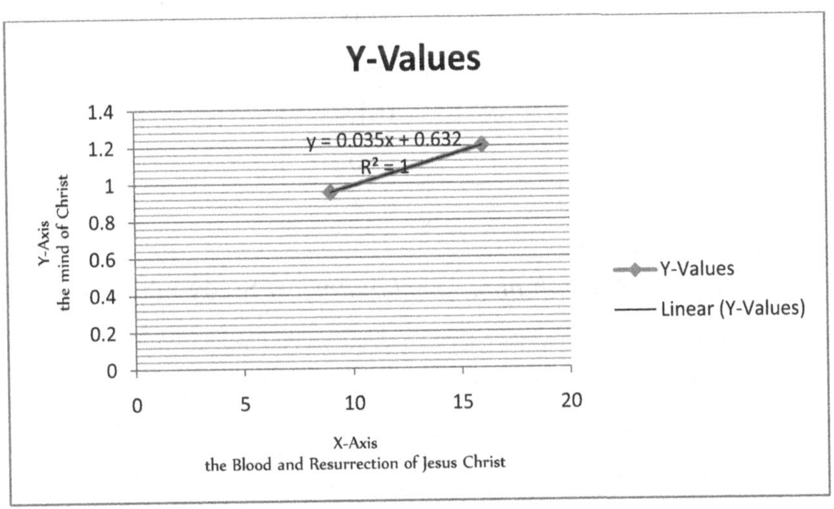

Pilled Poplar, Hazel, and Chestnut bible rods 2

17. From that time Jesussavior; deliverer**began to preach, and to say, Repent: for the kingdom of heaven is at hand.**

7, 3, 1: 8. Bible Matrices

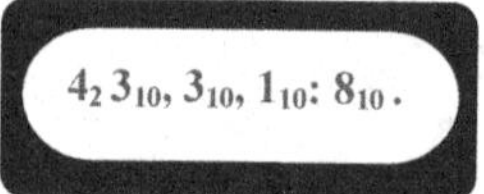

Pilled Poplar, Hazel, and Chestnut bible rods 1

$\text{Log}_{10} 3 = 0.4771$ $\text{Log}_{10} 8 = 0.9030$ $\text{Log}_{10} 1 = 0$ $\text{Log}_2 4 = y$

$2^y = 4$

$2^y = 2^2$

$y = 2$

7, 3, 1: 8. Deep calls unto Deep study bible 1

2 0.4771, 0.4771, 0, 0.9030. Deep calls unto Deep study bible 2

x-axis	y-axis
7	2.4771
3	0.4771
1	0
8	0.9030

Water Spout *(lightning; combinatorics)* Study bible 1

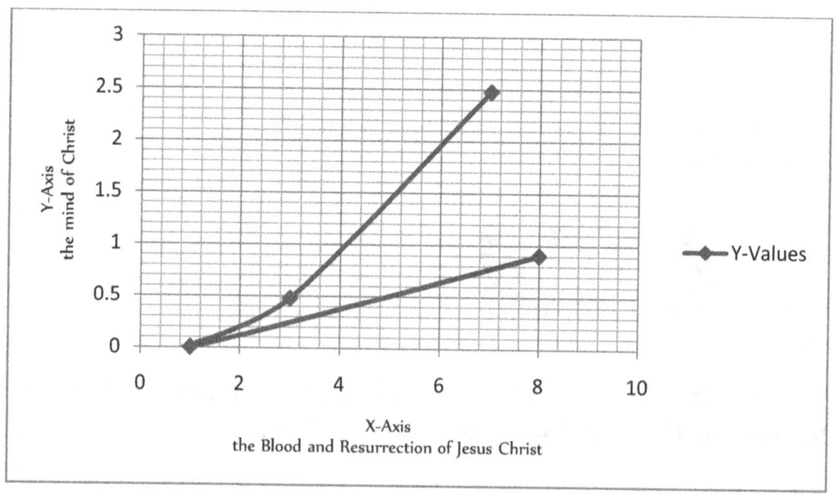

Water Spout *(lightning; combinatorics)* Study bible 2

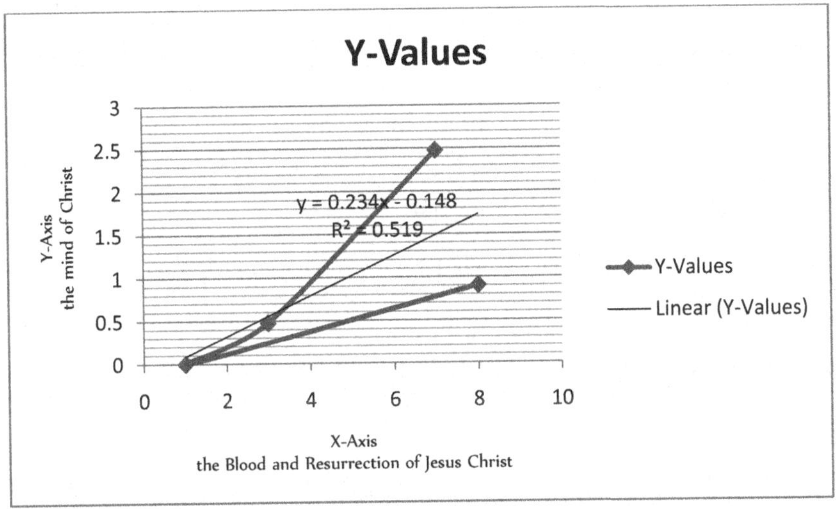

2^2 $10^{0.4771}$, $10^{0.4771}$, 10^0: $10^{0.9030}$.

Pilled Poplar, Hazel, and Chestnut bible rods 2

18. And Jesussavior; deliverer, **walking by the sea of Galilee**circuit; wheel; circle; revolution, **saw two** witness, support; 2 x 1 **brethren, Simon**a hearing; that hears; that obeys**called Peter**a rock, a stone, **and Andrew**manly; manliness; strong man **his brother, casting a net into the sea: for they were fishers.**

2, 6, 3, 3, 4, 6: 4. Bible Matrices

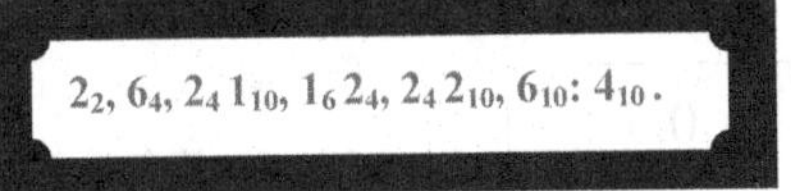

2_2, 6_4, 2_4 1_{10}, 1_6 2_4, 2_4 2_{10}, 6_{10}: 4_{10} .

Pilled Poplar, Hazel, and Chesnut bible rods 1

$\text{Log}_{10} 2 = 0.3010$ $\text{Log}_{10} 6 = 0.7781$ $\text{Log}_{10} 4 = 0.6020$ $\text{Log}_{10} 1 = 0$

$\text{Log}_2 2 = y$

$2^y = 2$

$2^y = 2^1$

$y = 1$

$\text{Log}_4 2 = y$

$4y = 2$

$2^{2y} = 2^1$

$2y = 1$

$y = ½$

$\text{Log}_4 6 = y$

$4^y = 6$

$\log_{10} 4y = \log_{10} 6$

$y \log_{10} 4 = \log_{10} 6$

$y = \log_{10} 6/ \log_{10} 4$

$y = 0.7781/0.6020$

$y = 1.2925$

$\text{Log}_6 1 = y$

$6y = 1$

$6^y = 6^0$

$y = 0$

2, 6, 3, 3, 4, 6: 4. Deep calls unto Deep study bible 1

1, 1.2925, 0.5 0, 0 0.5, 0.5 0.3010, 0.7781 : 0.6020.
Deep calls unto Deep study bible 2

x-axis	y-axis
2	1
6	1.2925
3	0.5
3	0.5
4	0.8010
6	0.7781
4	0.6020

Water Spout *(lightning; combinatorics)* Study bible 1

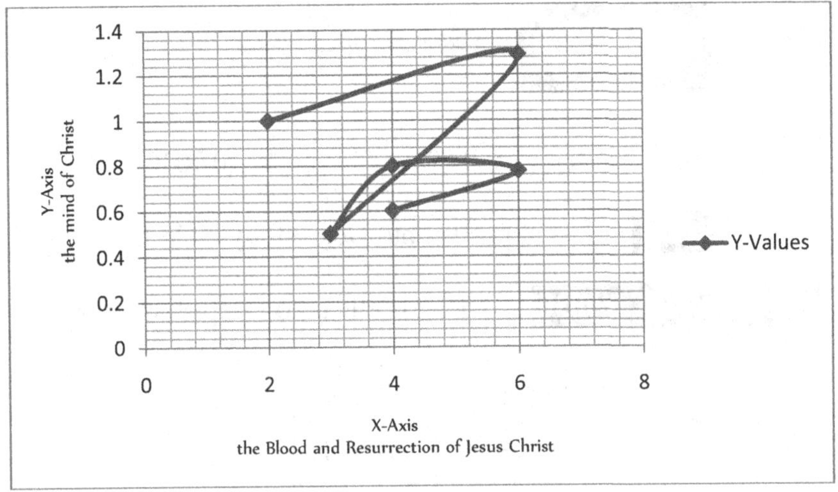

Water Spout *(lightning; combinatorics)* Study bible 2

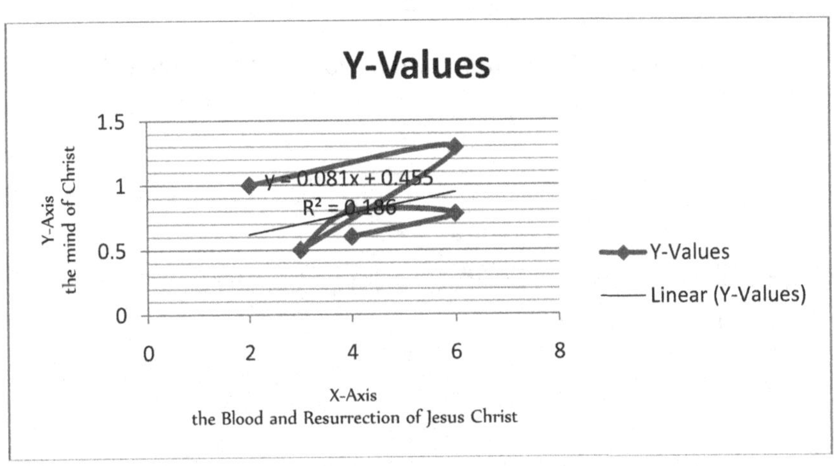

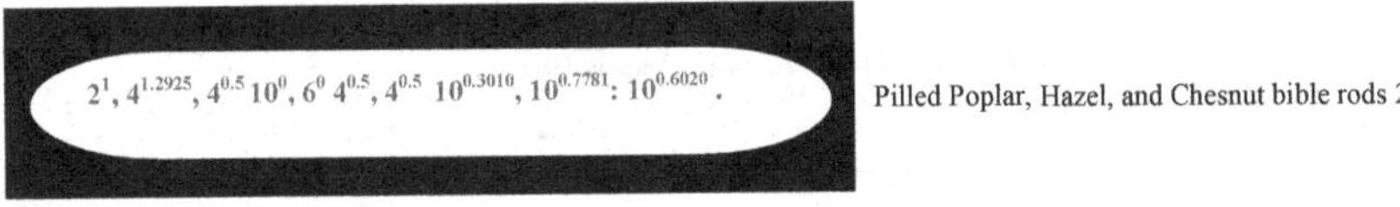

Pilled Poplar, Hazel, and Chesnut bible rods 2

19. And he saith unto them, Follow me, and I will make you fishers of men.

5, 2, 8. Bible Matrices

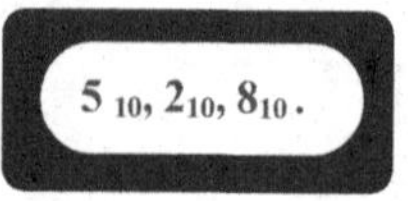

Pilled Poplar, Hazel, and Chesnut bible rods 1

$Log_{10} 2 = 0.3010$ $log_{10} 5 = 0.6989$ $log_{10} 8 = 0.9030$

5, 2, 8. Deep calls unto Deep study bible 1

0.6989, 0.3010, 0.9030. Deep calls unto Deep study bible 2

x-axis	y-axis
5	0.6989
2	0.3010
8	0.9030

Water Spout *(lightning; combinatorics)* Study bible 1

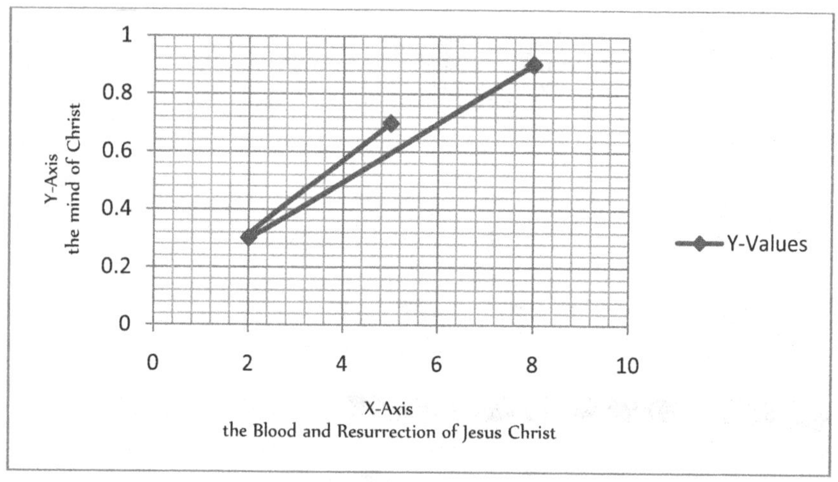

Water Spout *(lightning; combinatorics)* Study bible 2

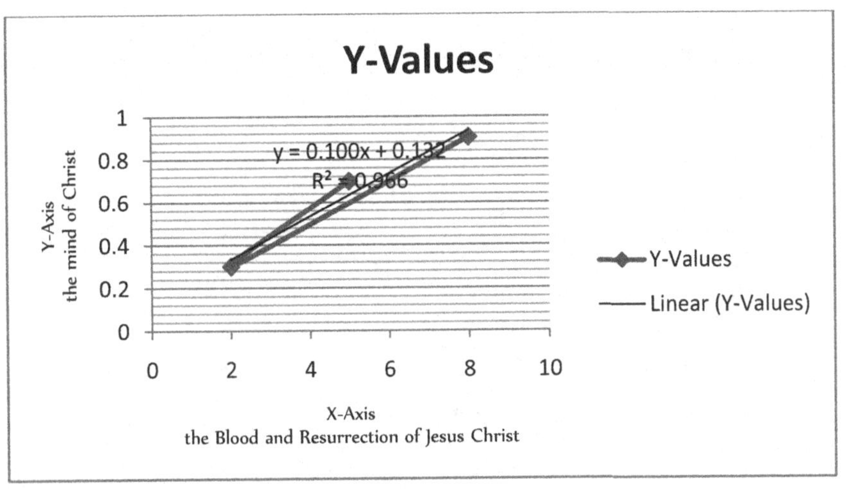

Pilled Poplar, Hazel, and Chestnut bible rods 2

20. And they straightway left their nets, and followed him.

6, 3. Bible Matrices

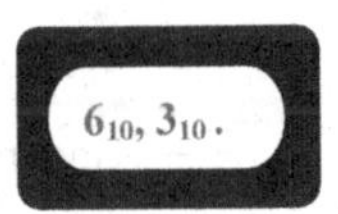

Pilled Poplar, Hazel, and Chestnut bible rods 1

$\text{Log}_{10} 6 = 0.7781$ $\log_{10} 3 = 0.4771$

6, 3. Deep calls unto Deep study bible 1

0.7781, 0.4771. Deep calls unto Deep study bible 2

x-axis	y-axis
6	0.7781
3	0.4771

Water Spout *(lightning; combinatorics)* Study bible 1

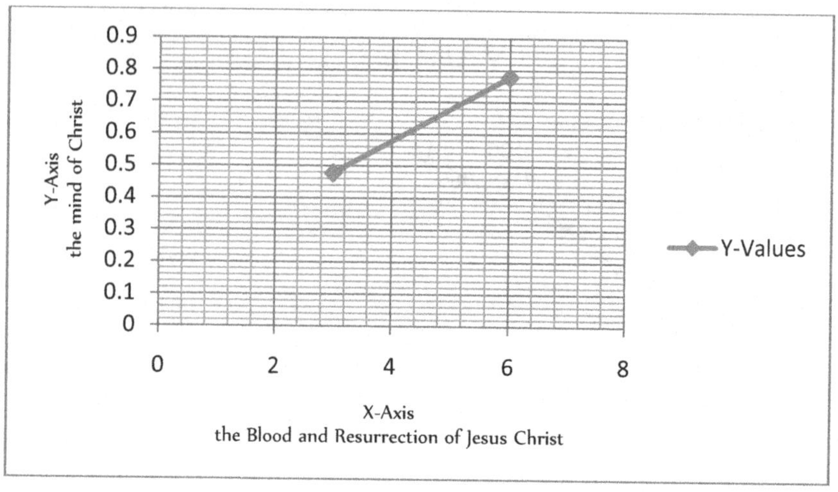

Water Spout *(lightning; combinatorics)* Study bible 2

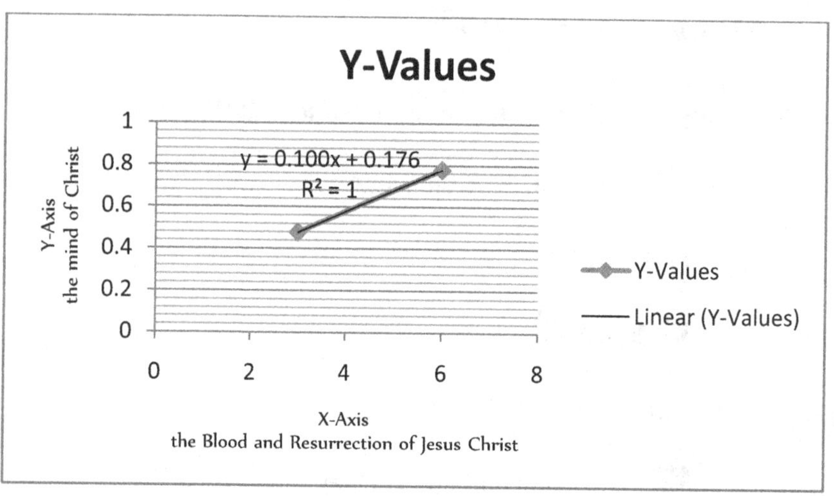

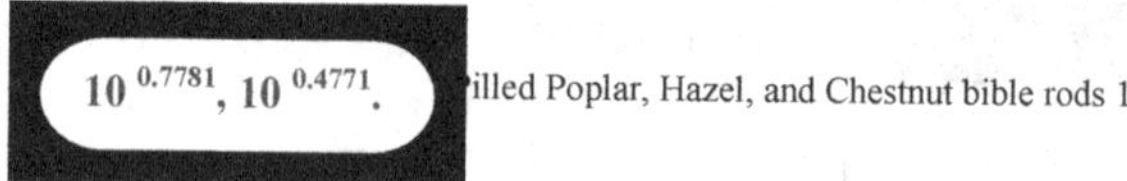

21. And going on from thence, he saw other two witness & support; 2 x 1 **brethren, James**that supplants, undermines; the heel **the son of Zebedee**my gift; abundant; portion, **and John** grace, mercy of God **his brother, in a ship with Zebedee**my gift; abundant; portion; lot **their father, mending their nets; and he called them.**

5, 5, 5, 4, 7, 3; 4. Bible Matrices

$5_{10}, 4_4\,1_{10}, 1_5\,4_4, 2_4\,2_{10}, 5_5\,2_{10}, 3_{10}; 4_{10}.$

Pilled Poplar, Hazel, and Chestnut bible rods 1

$\log_4 4 = y$	$\log_4 4 = y$	$\log_4 2 = y$	$\log_5 5 = y$	$\log_5 1 = y$	$\log_{10} 1 = 0$
$4^y = 4^1$	$4^y = 4^1$	$4^y = 2$	$5^y = 5^1$	$5^y = 1$	
$2^{2y} = 2^2$	$2^{2y} = 2^2$	$2^{2y} = 2^1$	$y = 1$	$5^y = 5^0$	
$2y = 2$	$2y = 2$	$2y = 1$		$y = 0$	
$y = 1$	$y = 1$	$y = ½$			

$\log_{10} 2 = 0.3010 \quad \log_{10} 3 = 0.4771 \quad \log_{10} 4 = 0.6020 \quad \log_{10} 5 = 0.6989$

5, 5, 5, 4, 7, 3; 4. Deep calls unto Deep study bible 1

0.6989, 1 0, 0 1, 0.5 0.3010, 1 0.3010, 0.4771; 0.6020.

Deep calls unto Deep study bible 2

x-axis	y-axis
5	0.6989
5	1
5	1
4	0.8010
7	1.3010
3	0.4771
4	0.6020

Water Spout *(lightning; combinatorics)* Study bible 1

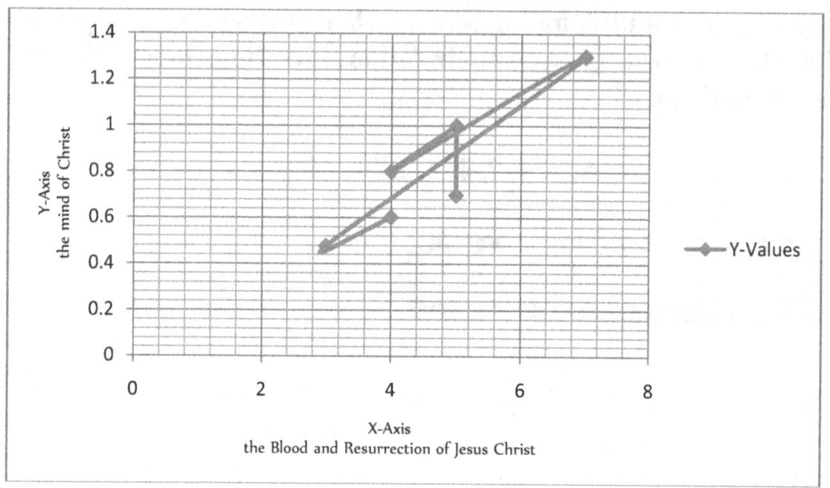

Water Spout *(lightning; combinatorics)* Study bible 2

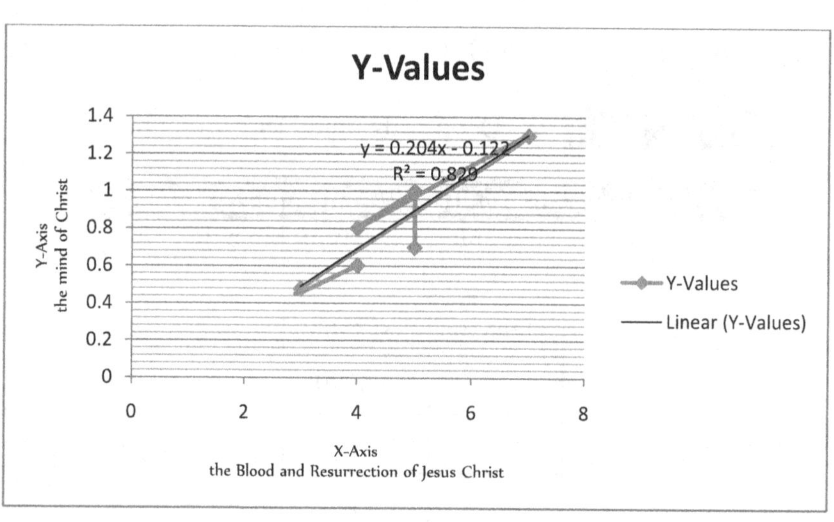

$10^{0.6989}$, 4^{1} 10^{0}, 5^{0} 4^{1}, $4^{0.5}$ $10^{0.3010}$, 5^{1} $10^{0.3010}$, $10^{0.4771}$; $10^{0.6020}$.

Pilled Poplar, Hazel, and Chestnut bible rods 2

22. And they immediately left the ship and their father, and followed him.

9, 3. Bible Matrices

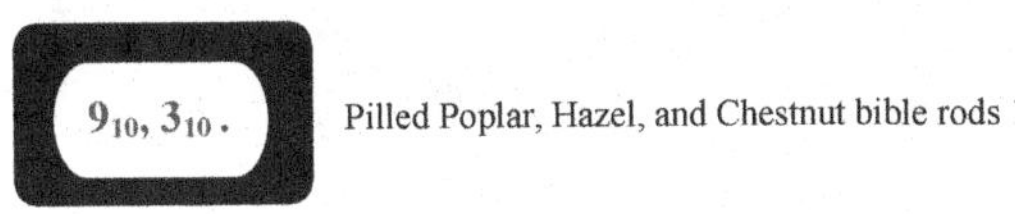

Pilled Poplar, Hazel, and Chestnut bible rods 1

$\text{Log}_{10} 9 = 0.9542$ $\log_{10} 3 = 0.4771$

9, 3. Deep calls unto Deep study bible 1

0.9542, 0.4771. Deep calls unto Deep study bible 2

x-axis	y-axis
9	0.9542
3	0.4771

Water Spout *(lightning; combinatorics)* Study bible 1

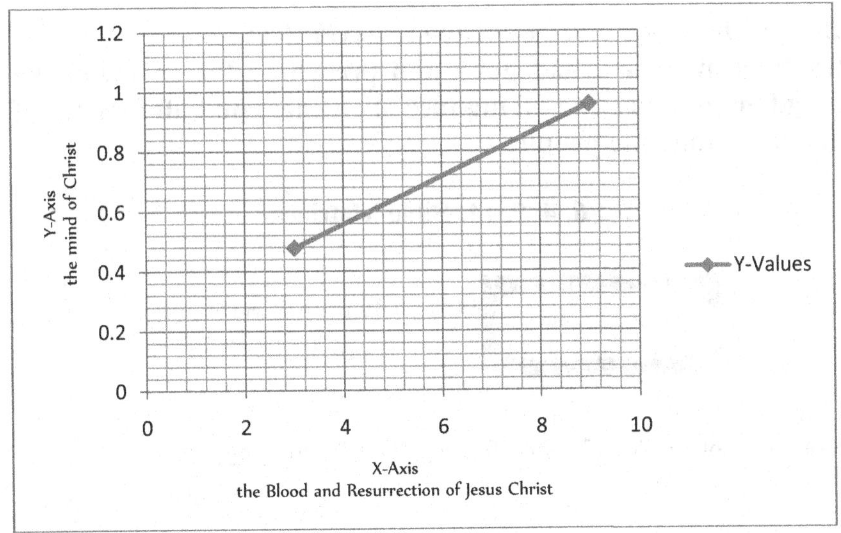

Water Spout *(lightning; combinatorics)* Study bible 2

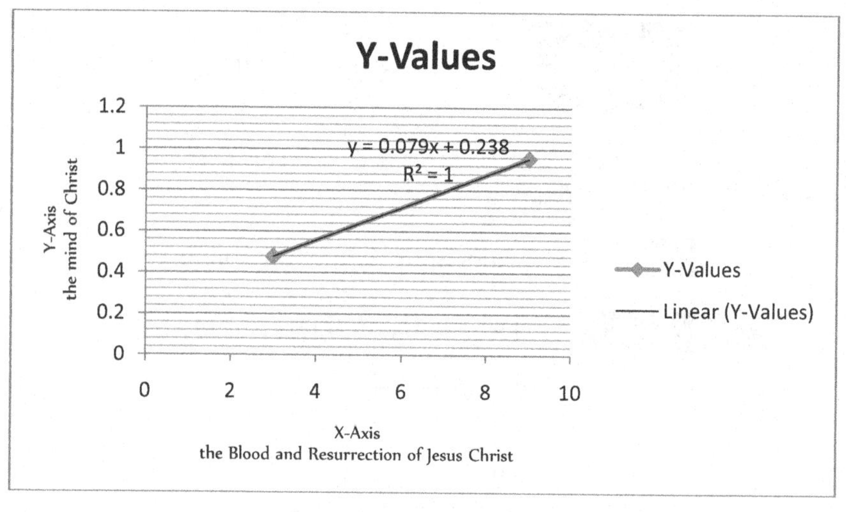

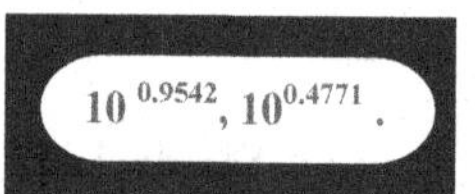

Pilled Poplar, Hazel, and Chestnut bible rods 2

23. And Jesus savior; deliverer **went about all Galilee** circuit; wheel; circle; revolution, **teaching in their synagogues, and preaching the gospel of the kingdom, and healing all manner of sickness and all manner of disease among the people.**

6, 4, 7, 14. Bible Matrices

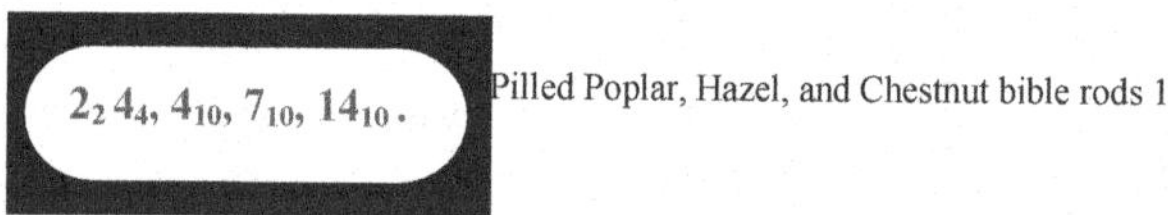

Pilled Poplar, Hazel, and Chestnut bible rods 1

$\log_{10} 4 = 0.6020$ $\log_{10} 7 = 0.8450$ $\log_{10} 14 = 1.1461$ $\log_4 4 = y$ $\log_2 2 = y$

$4^y = 4^1$ $2^y = 2^1$

$y = 1$ $y = 1$

6, 4, 7, 14. Deep calls unto Deep study bible 1

1 1, 0.6020, 0.8450, 1.1461. Deep calls unto Deep study bible 2

x-axis	y-axis
6	2
4	0.6020
7	0.8450
14	1.1461

Water Spout *(lightning; combinatorics)* Study bible 1

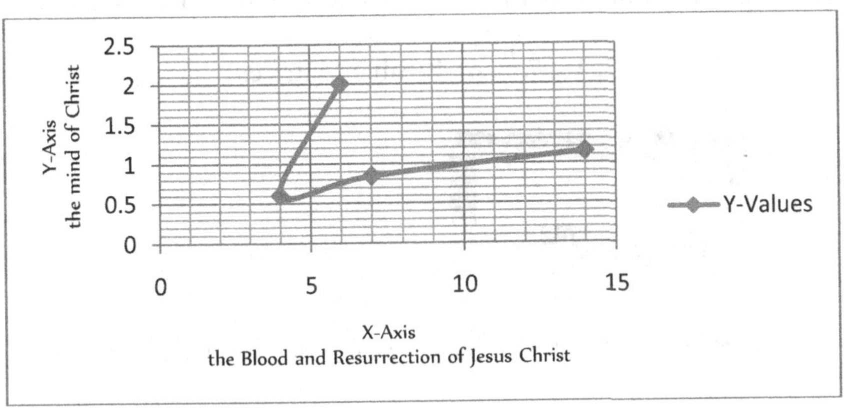

Water Spout *(lightning; combinatorics)* Study bible 2

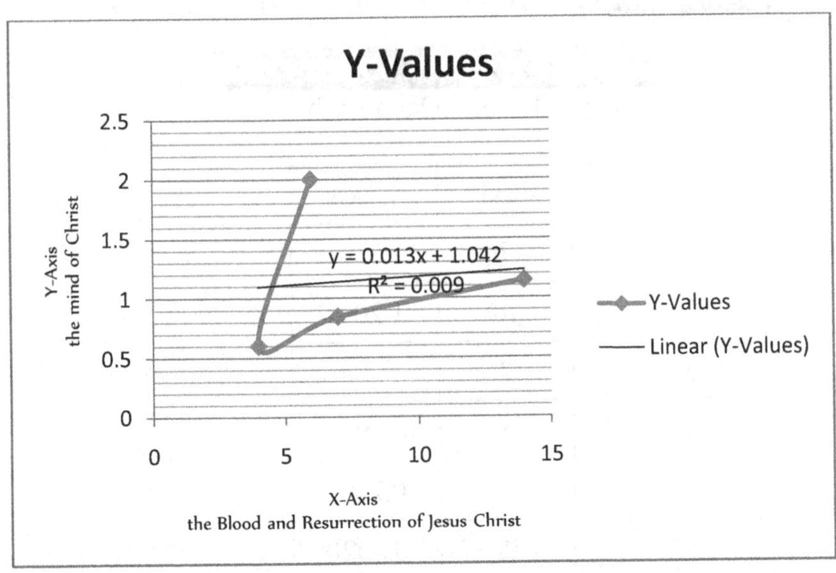

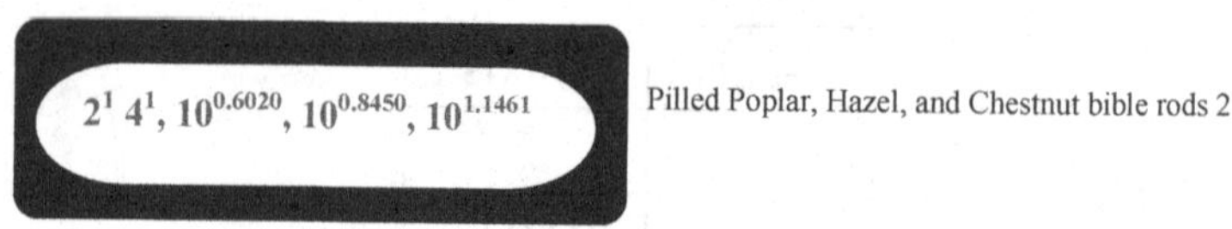
$2^1\ 4^1, 10^{0.6020}, 10^{0.8450}, 10^{1.1461}$

Pilled Poplar, Hazel, and Chestnut bible rods 2

24. And his fame went throughout all Syriahighness, magnificence, grandness, one that deceives; curse:**and they brought unto him all sick people that were taken with divers diseases and torments, and those which were possessed with devils** slanderer, the arch-enemy of man's spiritual interest, **and those which were lunatick, and those that had the palsy; and he healed them.**

7: 16, 7, 5, 6; 4. Bible Matrices

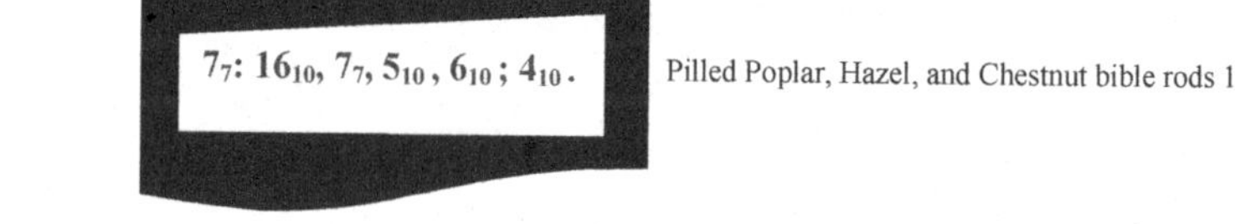
$7_7: 16_{10}, 7_7, 5_{10}, 6_{10}; 4_{10}.$

Pilled Poplar, Hazel, and Chestnut bible rods 1

$\log_{10} 4 = 0.6020$ $\log_{10} 5 = 0.6989$ $\log_{10} 6 = 0.7781$ $\log_{10} 16 = 1.2041$ $\log_7 7 = y$

$7^y = 7^1$

$y = 1$

7: 16, 7, 5, 6; 4. Deep calls unto Deep study bible 1

1: 1.2041, 1, 0.6989, 0.7781; 0.6020.

Deep calls unto Deep study bible 2

x-axis	y-axis
7	1
16	1.2041
7	1
5	0.6989
6	0.7781
4	0.6020

Water Spout *(lightning; combinatorics)* Study bible 1

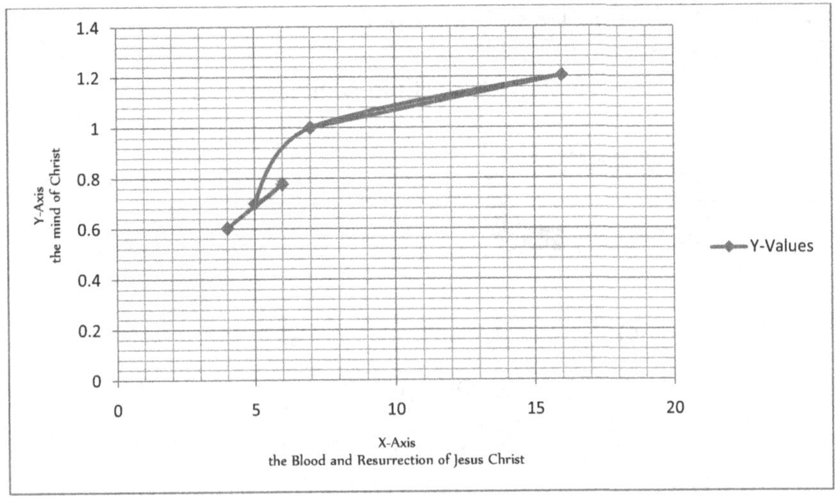

Water Spout *(lightning; combinatorics)* Study bible 2

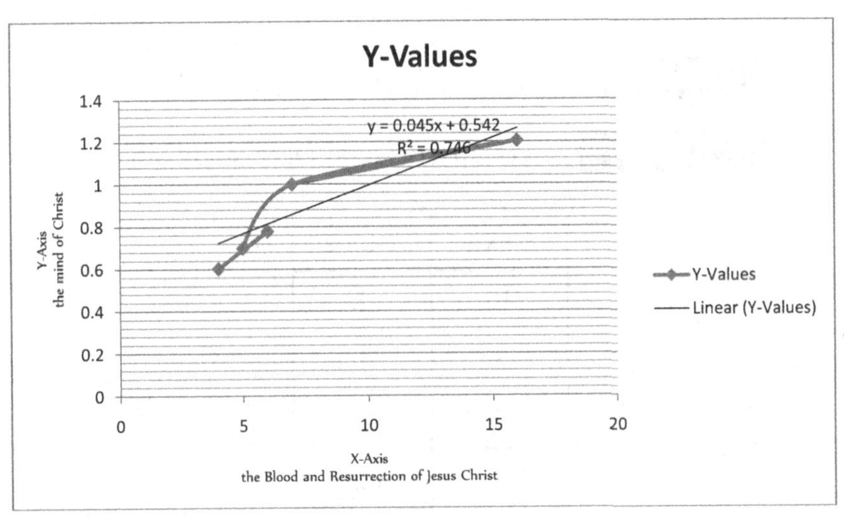

$7^1 : 10^{1.2041}, 7^1, 10^{0.6989}, 10^{0.7781}; 10^{0.6020}$. Pilled Poplar, Hazel, and Chestnut bible rods 2

25. And there followed him great multitudes of people from Galileecircuit, trail, path, track, route, wheel; revolution; circle, loop, ring, **and from**

Decapolis containing ten cities, **and from Jerusalem** habitation of peace; vision of peace;possession of peace, **and from Judaea** the praise of the Lord; confession of the Lord, **and from beyond Jordan** descender; river of judgment.

10, 3, 3, 3, 4. Bible Matrices

$10_{10}, 3_3, 3_9, 3_9, 4_4$. Pilled Poplar, Hazel, and Chestnut bible rods 1

$\text{Log}_3 3 = y$	$\text{Log}_9 3 = y$	$\text{Log}_9 3 = y$	$\text{Log}_4 4 = y$	$\text{Log}_{10} 10 = 1$
$3^y = 3^1$	$9^y = 3^1$	$9^y = 3^1$	$4^y = 4^1$	
$y = 1$	$3^{2y} = 3^1$	$3^{2y} = 3^1$	$2^{2y} = 2^2$	
	$2y = 1$	$2y = 1$	$2y = 2$	
	$y = \frac{1}{2}$	$y = \frac{1}{2}$	$y = 1$	

10, 3, 3, 3, 4. Deep calls unto Deep study bible 1

1, 1, 0.5, 0.5, 1. Deep calls unto Deep study bible 2

x-axis	y-axis
10	1
3	1
3	0.5
3	0.5
4	1

Water Spout *(lightning; combinatorics)* Study bible 1

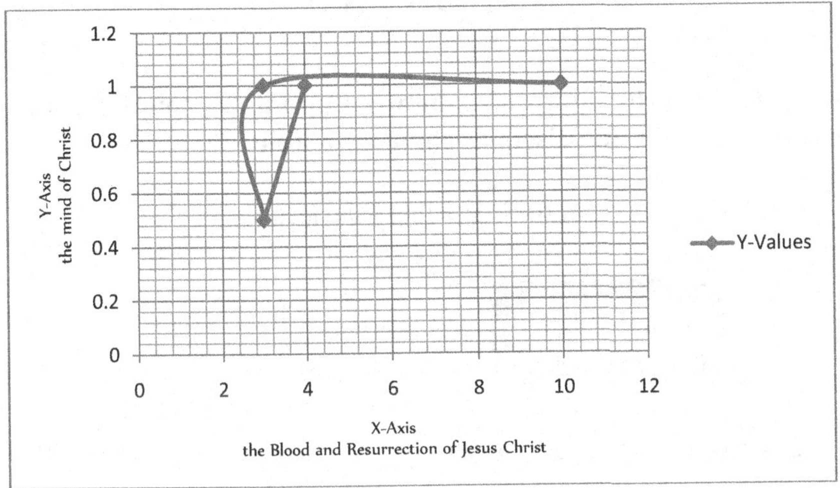

Water Spout *(lightning; combinatorics)* Study bible 2

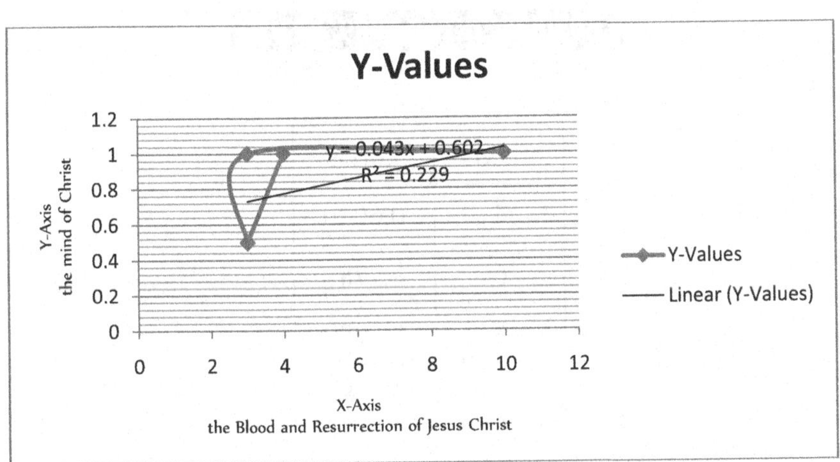

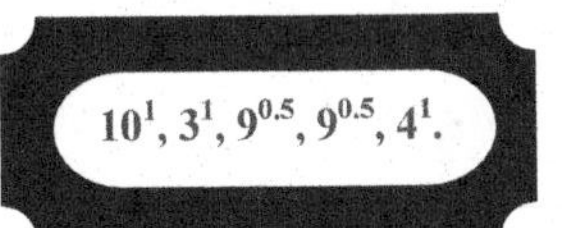

Pilled Poplar, Hazel, and Chestnut bible rods 2

CHAPTER 5

1. And seeing the multitudes, he went up into a mountain: and when he was set, his disciples came unto him:

4, 6: 5, 5: Bible Matrices

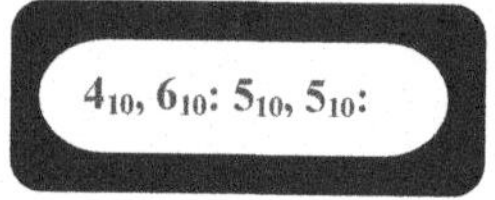

Pilled Poplar, Hazel, and Chestnut bible rods 1

$\text{Log}_{10} 4 = 0.6020$ $\log_{10} 5 = 0.6989$ $\log_{10} 5 = 0.6989$ $\log_{10} 6 = 0.7781$

4, 6: 5, 5: Deep calls unto Deep study bible 1

0.6020, 0.7781: 0.6989, 0.6989:
Deep calls unto Deep study bible 2

x-axis	y-axis
4	0.6020
6	0.7781
5	0.6989
5	0.6989

Water Spout *(lightning; combinatorics)* Study bible 1

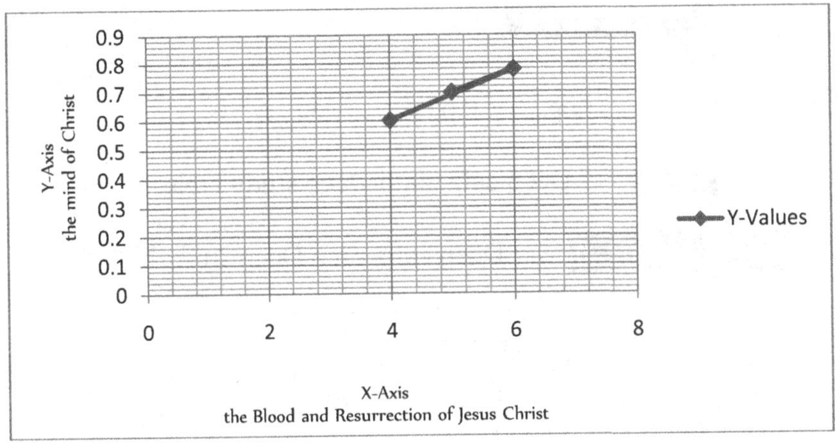

Water Spout *(lightning; combinatorics)* Study bible 2

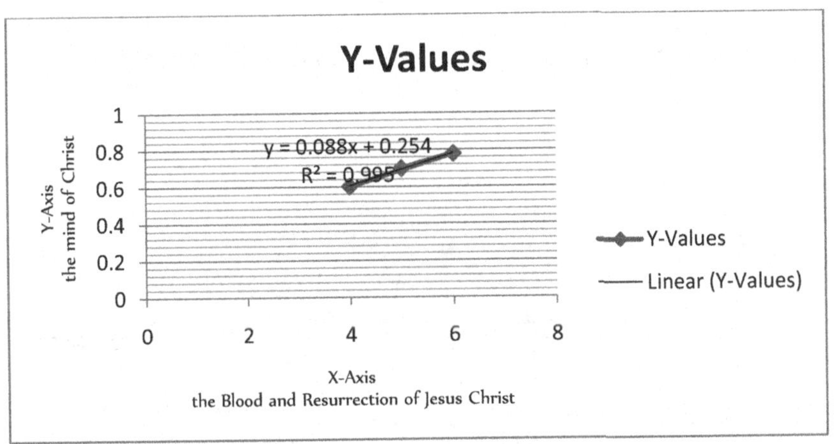

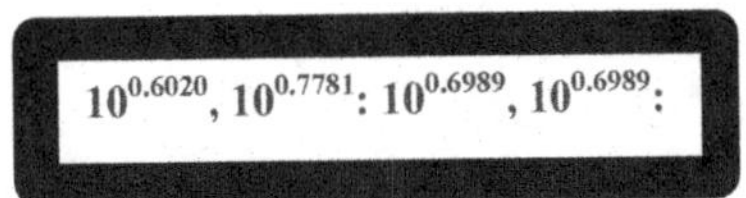

$10^{0.6020}$, $10^{0.7781}$: $10^{0.6989}$, $10^{0.6989}$:

2. And he opened his mouth, and taught them, saying,

5, 3, 1, Bible Matrices

$5_{10}, 3_{10}, 1_{10}$, Pilled Poplar, Hazel, and Chestnut bible rods 1

$\text{Log}_{10} 3 = 0.4771$ $\log_{10} 5 = 0.6989$ $\log_{10} 1 = 0$

5, 3, 1, Deep calls unto Deep study bible 1

0.6989, 0.4771, 0, Deep calls unto Deep study bible 2

x-axis	y-axis
5	0.6989
3	0.4771
1	0

Water Spout *(lightning; combinatorics)* Study bible 1

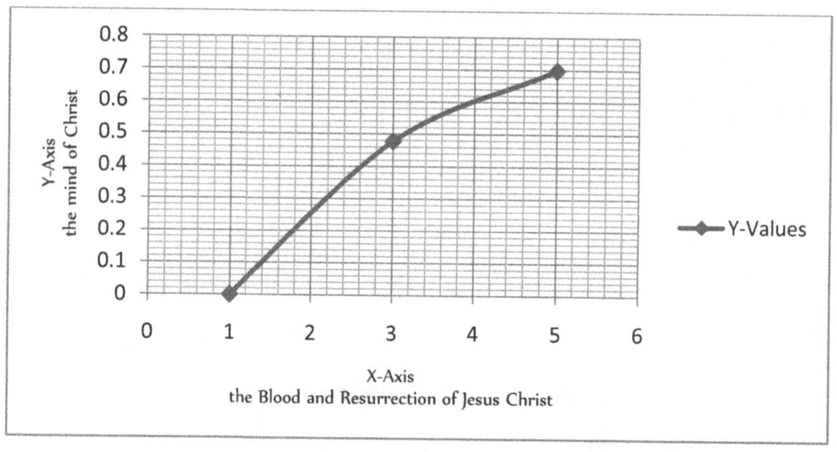

Water Spout *(lightning; combinatorics)* Study bible 2

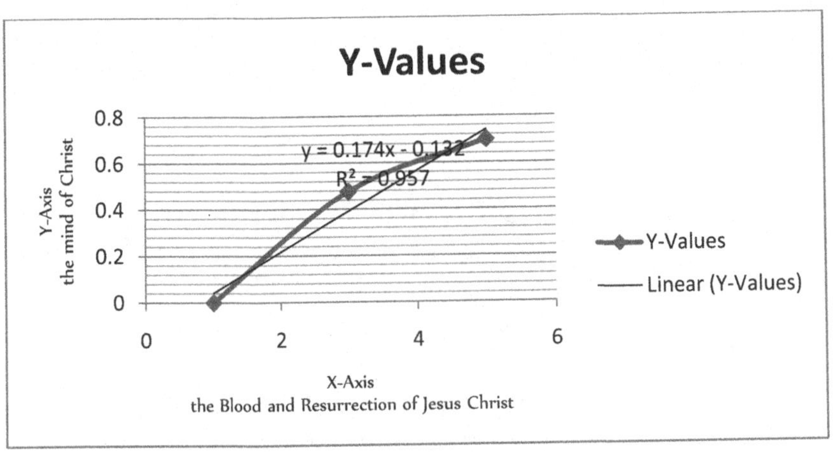

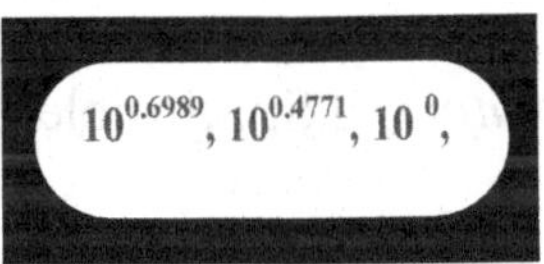

Pilled Poplar, Hazel, and Chestnut bible rods 2

3. Blessed are the poor in spirit: for theirs is the kingdom of heaven.

6: 7. Bible Matrices

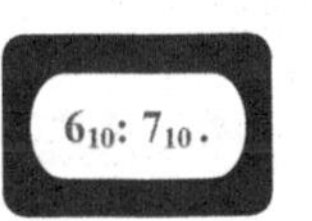

Pilled Poplar, Hazel, and Chestnut bible rods 1

$\mathrm{Log}_{10} 6 = 0.7781$ $\log_{10} 7 = 0.8450$

6: 7. Deep calls unto Deep study bible 1

0.7781: 0.8450. Deep calls unto Deep study bible 2

x-axis	y-axis
6	0.7781
7	0.8450

Water Spout *(lightning; combinatorics)* Study bible 1

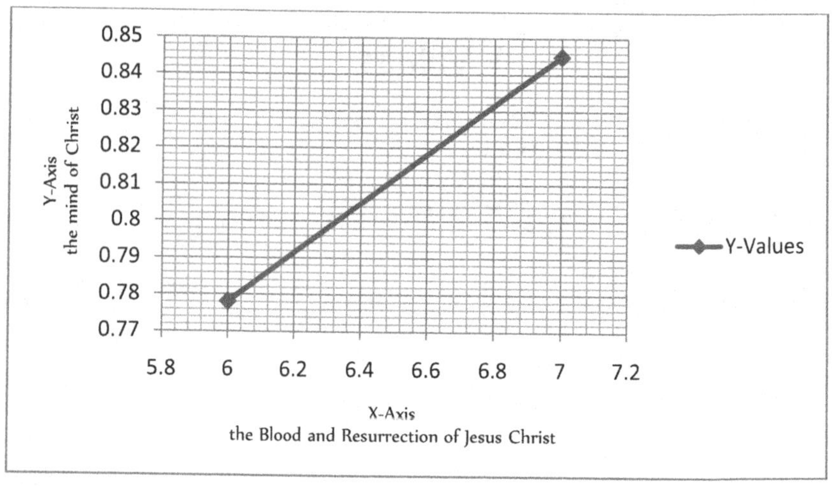

Water Spout *(lightning; combinatorics)* Study bible 2

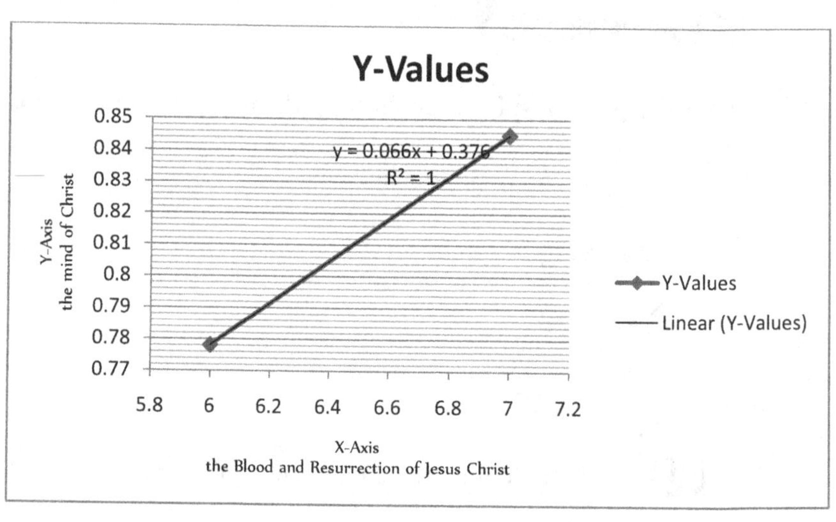

$10^{0.7781}$: $10^{0.8450}$. Pilled Poplar, Hazel, and Chestnut bible rods 2

4. Blessed are they that mourn: for they shall be comforted.

5: 5. Bible Matrices

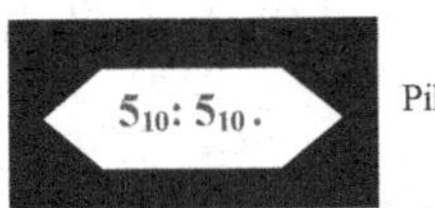

Pilled Poplar, Hazel, and Chestnut bible rods 1

$\text{Log}_{10} 5 = 0.6989$ $\log_{10} 5 = 0.6989$

5: 5. Deep calls unto Deep study bible 1

0.6989: 0.6989. Deep calls unto Deep study bible 2

x-axis	y-axis
5	0.6989
5	0.6989

Water Spout *(lightning; combinatorics)* Study bible 1

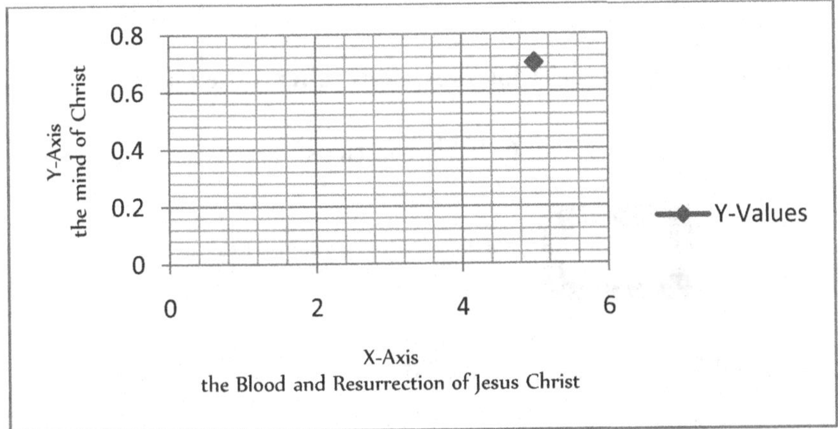

Water Spout *(lightning; combinatorics)* Study bible 2

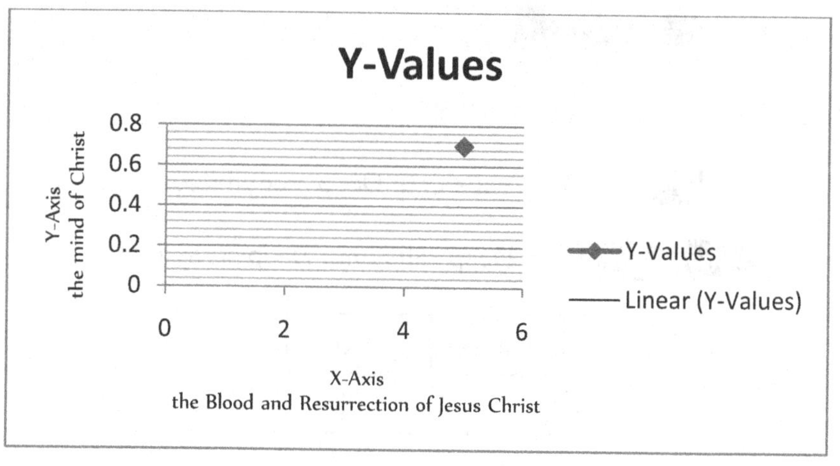

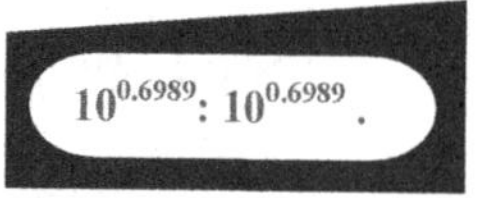

Pilled Poplar, Hazel, and Chestnut bible rods 2

5. Blessed are the meek: for they shall inherit the earth.

4: 6. Bible Matrices

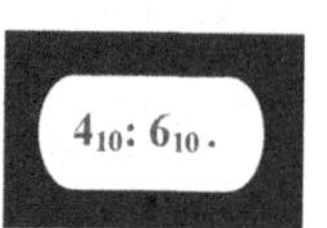

Pilled Poplar, Hazel, and Chestnut bible rods 1

$\text{Log}_{10} 4 = 0.6020$ $\log_{10} 6 = 0.7781$

4: 6. Deep calls unto Deep study bible 1

0.6020: 0.7781. Deep calls unto Deep study bible 2

x-axis	y-axis
4	0.6020
6	0.7781

Water Spout *(lightning; combinatorics)* Study bible 1

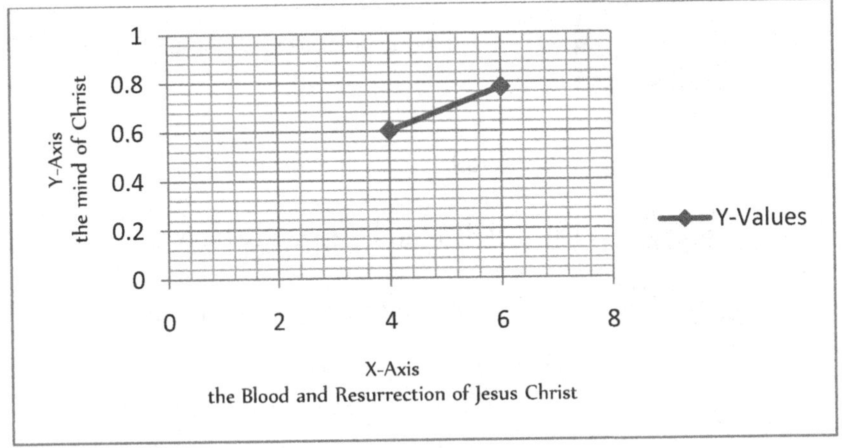

Water Spout *(lightning; combinatorics)* Study bible 2

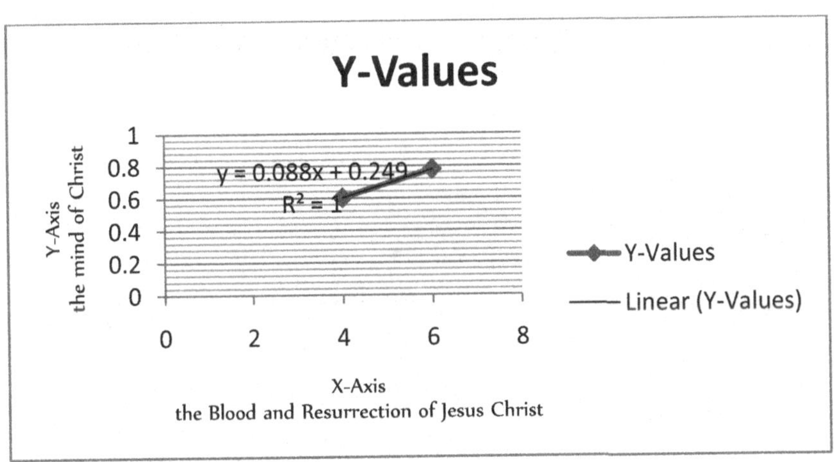

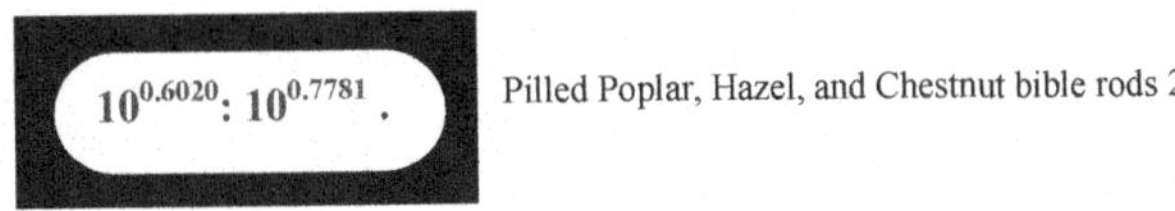

Pilled Poplar, Hazel, and Chestnut bible rods 2

6. Blessed are they which do hunger and thirst after righteousness: for they shall be filled.

10: 5. Bible Matrices

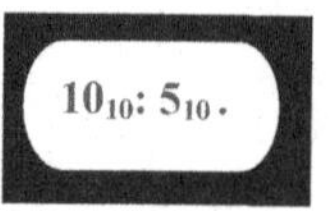

Pilled Poplar, Hazel, and Chestnut bible rods 1

$\text{Log}_{10}10 = 1$ $\log_{10}5 = 0.6989$

10: 5. Deep calls unto Deep study bible 1

1: 0.6989. Deep calls unto Deep study bible 2

x-axis	y-axis
10	1
5	0.6989

Water Spout *(lightning; combinatorics)* Study bible 1

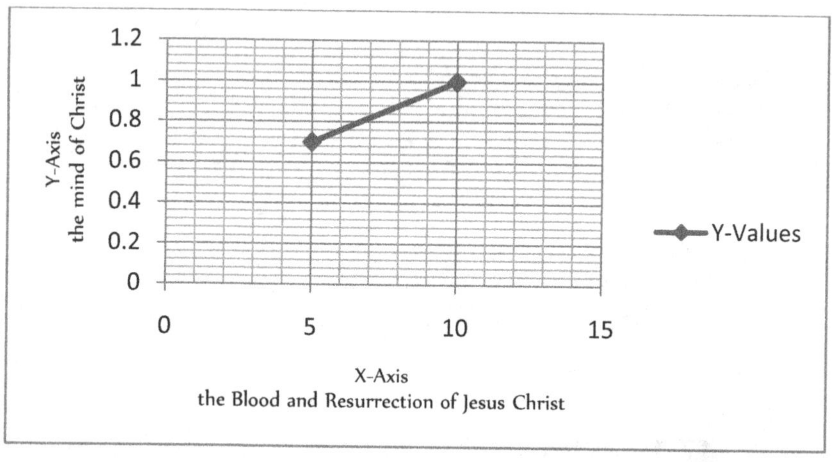

Water Spout *(lightning; combinatorics)* Study bible 2

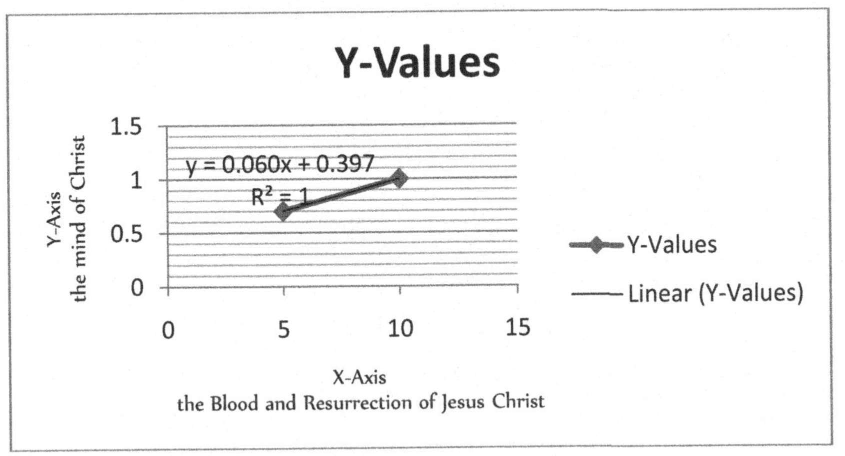

Pilled Poplar, Hazel, and Chestnut bible rods 2

7. Blessed are the merciful: for they shall obtain mercy.

4: 5. Bible Matrices

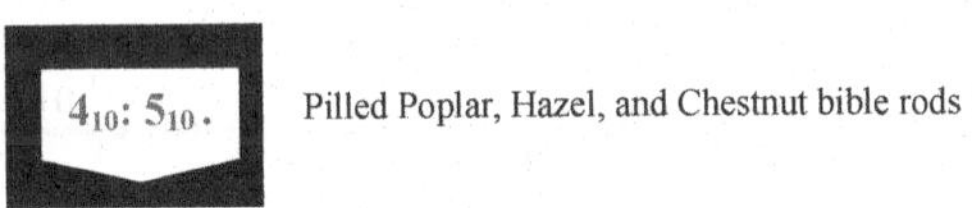

Pilled Poplar, Hazel, and Chestnut bible rods 1

$\text{Log}_{10} 4 = 0.6020$ $\log_{10} 5 = 0.6989$

4: 5. Deep calls unto Deep study bible 1

0.6020: 0.6989. Deep calls unto Deep study bible 2

x-axis	y-axis
4	0.6020
5	0.6989

Water Spout *(lightning; combinatorics)* Study bible 1

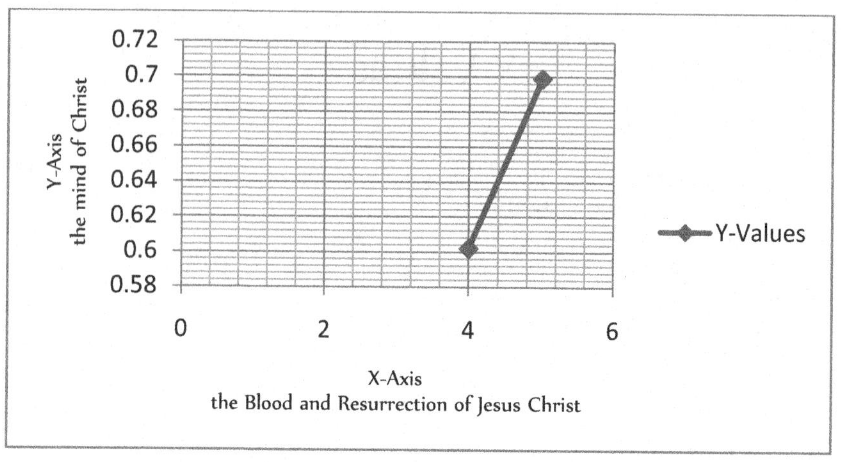

Water Spout *(lightning; combinatorics)* Study bible 2

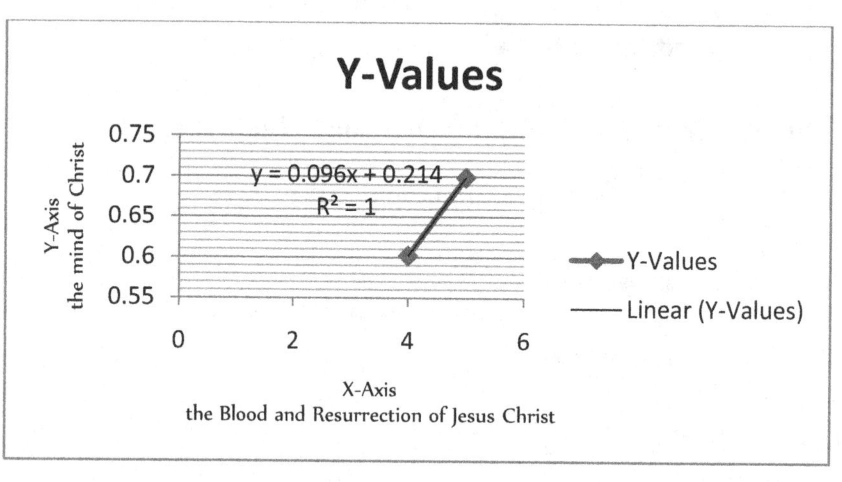

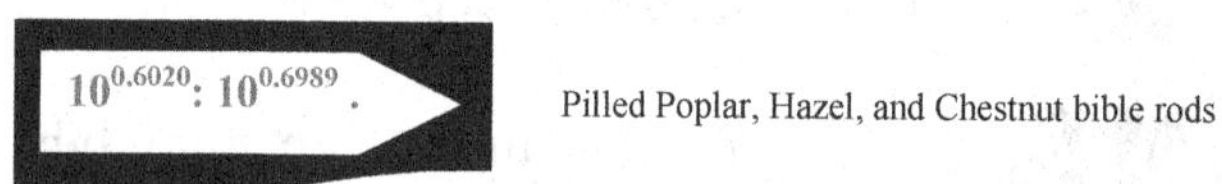

Pilled Poplar, Hazel, and Chestnut bible rods 2

8. Blessed are the pure in heart: for they shall see God.

6: 5. Bible Matrices

Pilled Poplar, Hazel, and Chestnut bible rods 1

$\text{Log}_{10} 6 = 0.7781$ $\log_{10} 5 = 0.6989$

6: 5. Deep calls unto Deep study bible 1

0.7781: 0.6989. Deep calls unto Deep study bible 2

x-axis	y-axis
6	0.7781
5	0.6989

Water Spout *(lightning; combinatorics)* Study bible 1

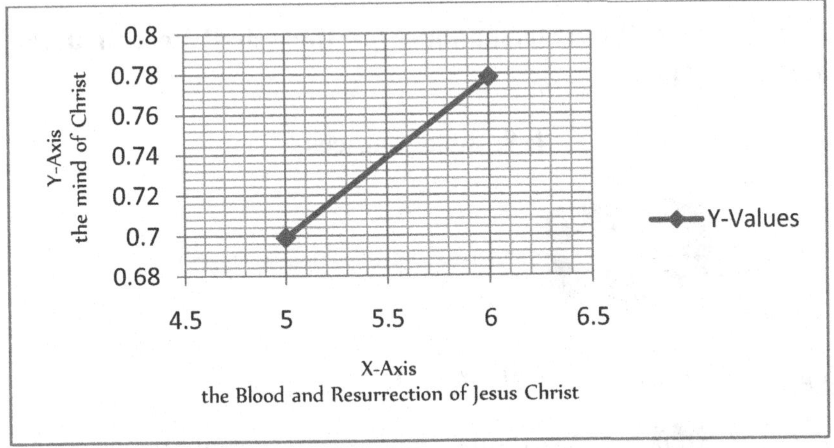

Water Spout *(lightning; combinatorics)* Study bible 2

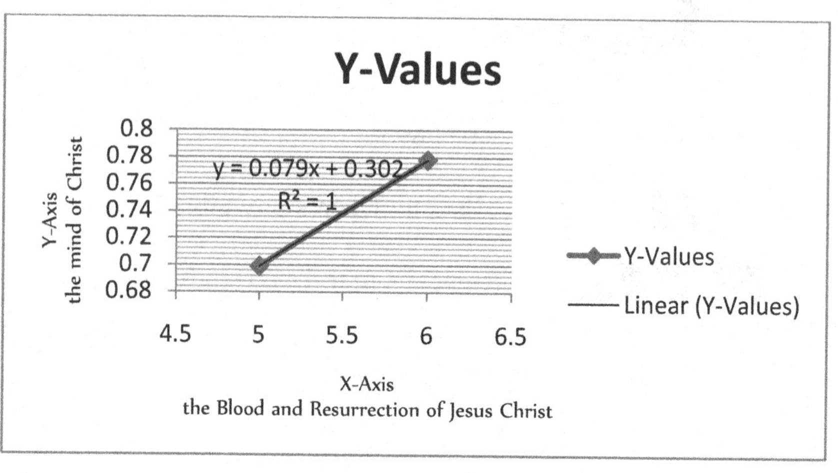

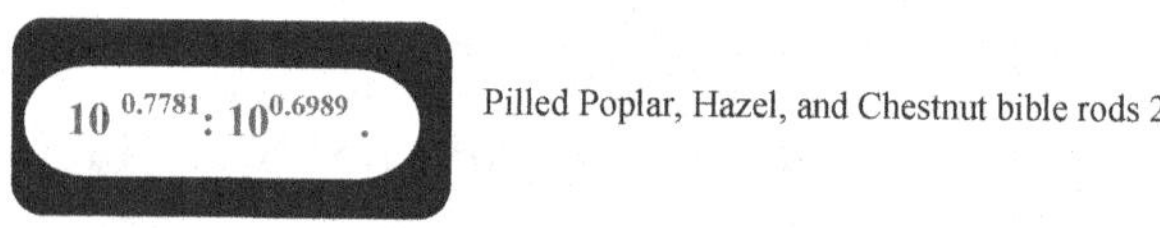

Pilled Poplar, Hazel, and Chestnut bible rods 2

9. Blessed are the peacemakers: for they shall be called the children of God.

4: 9. Bible Matrices

Pilled Poplar, Hazel, and Chestnut bible rods 1

$\text{Log}_{10} 4 = 0.6020$ $\log_{10} 9 = 0.9542$

4: 9. Deep calls unto Deep study bible 1

0.6020: 0.9542. Deep calls unto Deep study bible 2

x-axis	y-axis
4	0.6020
9	0.9542

Water Spout *(lightning; combinatorics)* Study bible 1

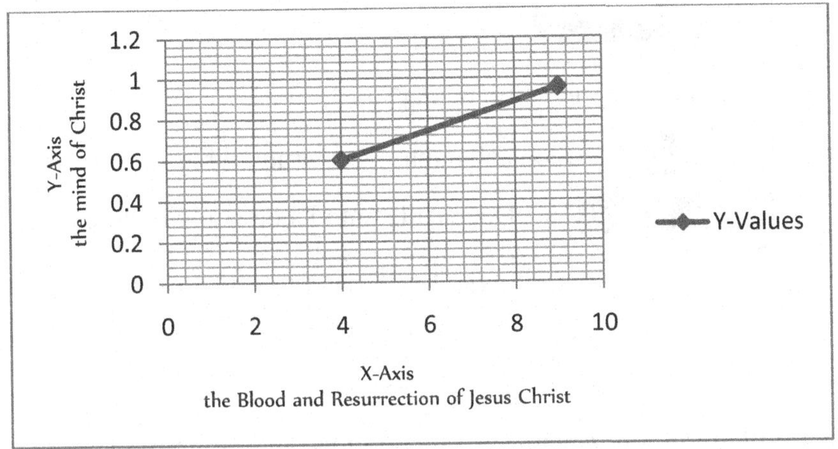

Water Spout *(lightning; combinatorics)* Study bible 2

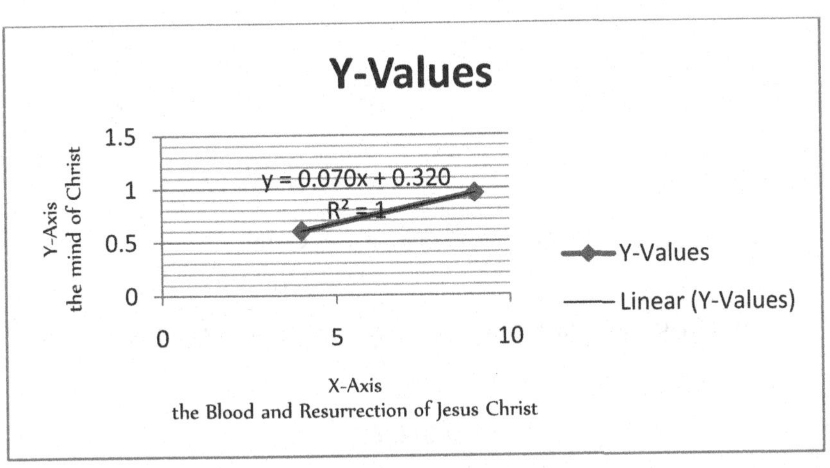

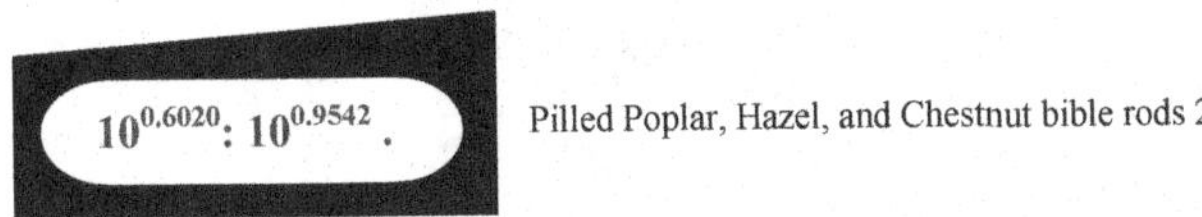

Pilled Poplar, Hazel, and Chestnut bible rods 2

10. Blessed are they which are persecuted for righteousness' sake: for theirs is the kingdom of heaven.

9: 7. Bible Matrices

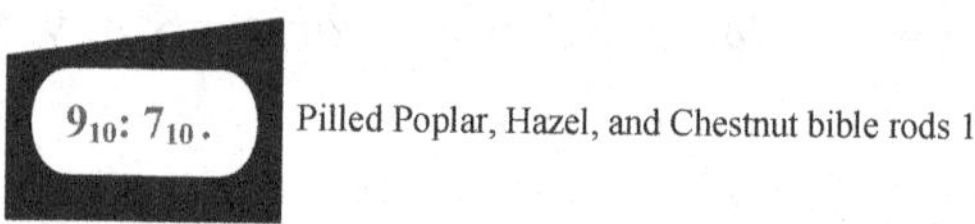

$Log_{10}7 = 0.8450$ $\quad log_{10}9 = 0.9542$

9: 7. Deep calls unto Deep study bible 1

0.9542: 0.8450. Deep calls unto Deep study bible 2

x-axis	y-axis
9	0.9542
7	0.8450

Water Spout *(lightning; combinatorics)* Study bible 1

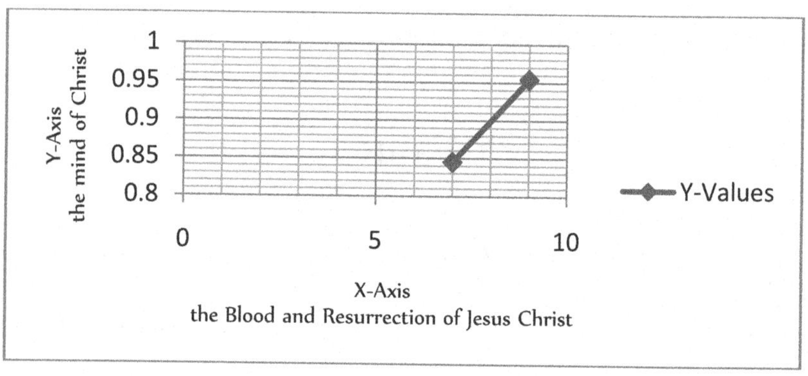

Water Spout *(lightning; combinatorics)* Study bible 2

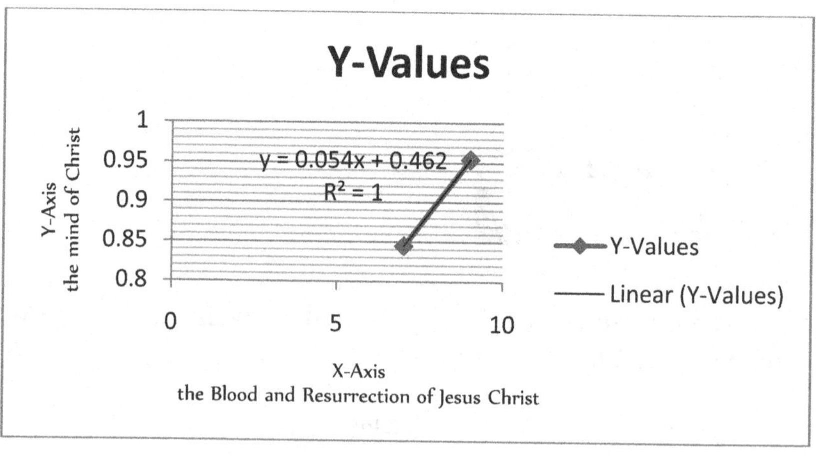

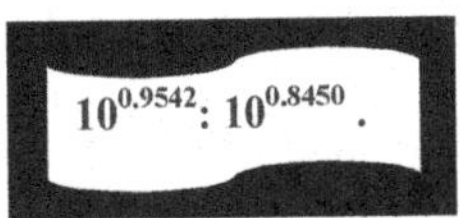
$10^{0.9542}$: $10^{0.8450}$.

Pilled Poplar, Hazel, and Chestnut bible rods 2

11. Blessed are ye, when men shall revile you, and persecute you, and shall say all manner of evil against you falsely, for my sake.

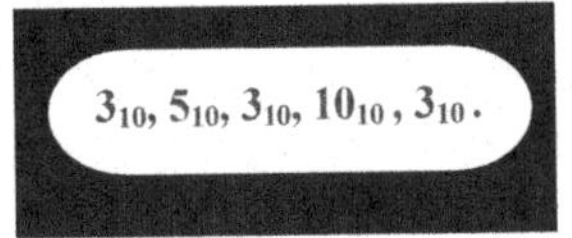
3_{10}, 5_{10}, 3_{10}, 10_{10}, 3_{10}.

Pilled Poplar, Hazel, and Chestnut bible rods 1

$\text{Log}_{10} 3 = 0.4771$ $\log_{10} 5 = 0.6989$ $\log_{10} 3 = 0.4771$ $\log_{10} 10 = 1$ $\log_{10} 3 = 0.4771$

3, 5, 3, 10, 3. Deep calls unto Deep study bible 1

0.4771, 0.6989, 0.4771, 1, 0.4771.

Deep calls unto Deep study bible 2

x-axis	y-axis
3	0.4771
5	0.6989
3	0.4771
10	1
3	0.4771

Water Spout *(lightning; combinatorics)* Study bible 1

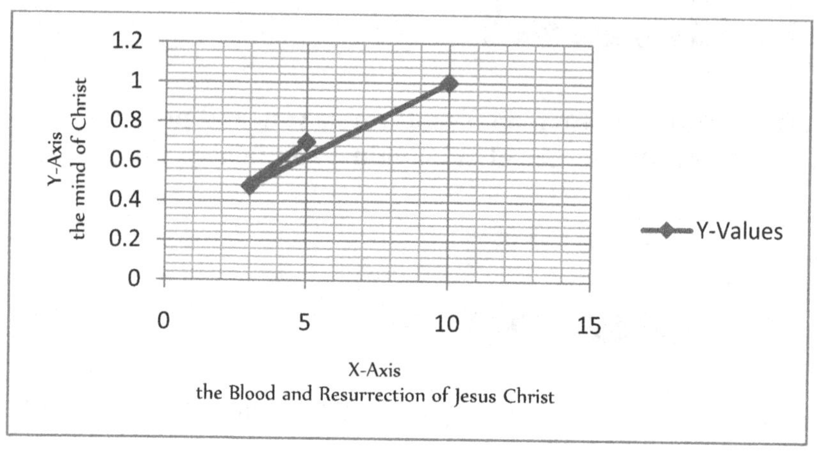

Water Spout *(lightning; combinatorics)* Study bible 2

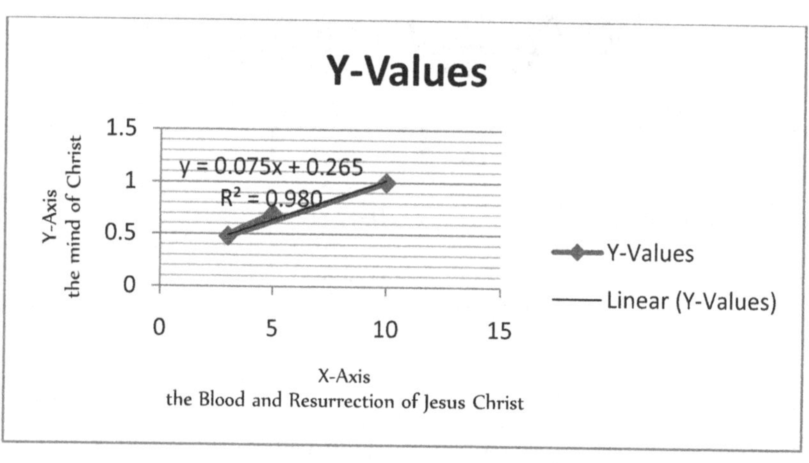

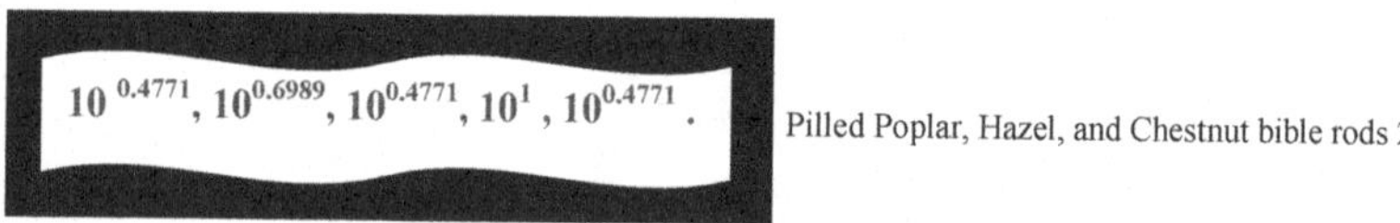

Pilled Poplar, Hazel, and Chestnut bible rods 2

12. Rejoice, and be exceeding glad: for great is your reward in heaven: for so persecuted they the prophets to bubble forth, as from a fountain; utter **which were before you.**

1, 4: 7: 10. Bible Matrices

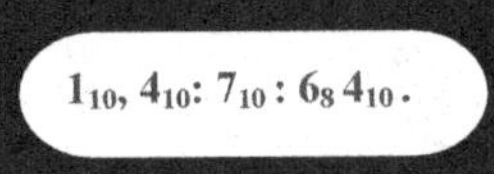

Pilled Poplar, Hazel, and Chestnut bible rods 1

$\text{Log}_8 6 = y$ $\text{Log}_{10} 1 = 0$ $\text{Log}_{10} 4 = 0.6020$ $\text{Log}_{10} 7 = 0.8450$ $\text{Log}_{10} 4 = 0.6020$

$8^y = 6$

$\text{Log}_{10} 8^y = \log_{10} 6$

$y \log_{10} 8 = \log_{10} 6$

$y = \log_{10} 6 / \log_{10} 8$

$y = 0.7781/0.9030$

$y = 0.8616$

1, 4: 7: 10. Deep calls unto Deep study bible 1

0, 0.6020: 0.8450: 0.8616 0.6020.
Deep calls unto Deep study bible 2

x-axis	y-axis
1	0
4	0.6020
7	0.8450
10	1.4636

Water Spout *(lightning; combinatorics)* Study bible 1

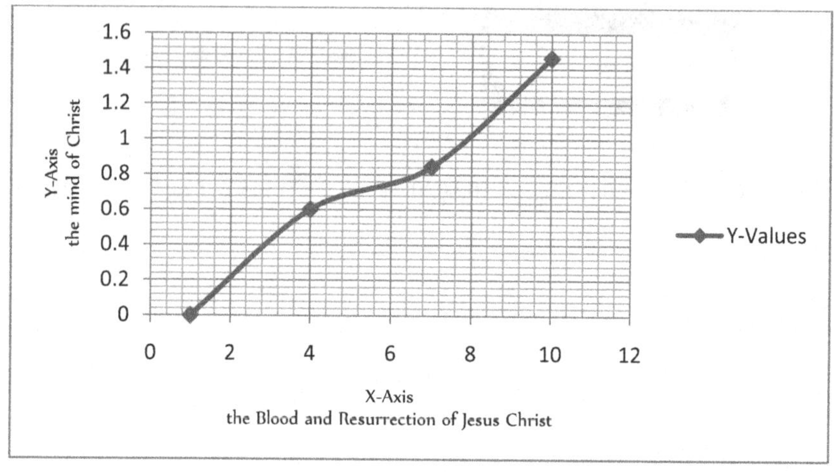

Water Spout *(lightning; combinatorics)* Study bible 2

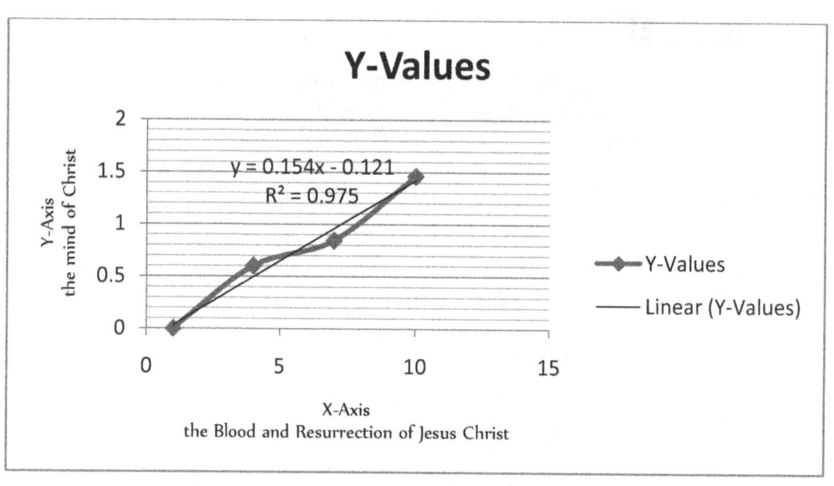

10^0, $10^{0.6020}$: $10^{0.8450}$: $8^{0.8616}$ $10^{0.6020}$.

Pilled Poplar, Hazel, and Chestnut bible rods 2

13. Ye are the salt of the earth: but if the salt have lost his savour, wherewith shall it be salted? it is thenceforth good for nothing, but to be cast out, and to be trodden under foot of men.

7: 8, 5? 6, 5, 8. Bible Matrices

7_{10}: 8_{10}, 5_{10}? 6_{10}, 5_{10}, 8_{10}. Pilled Poplar, Hazel, and Chestnut bible rods 1

$\text{Log}_{10} 7 = 0.8450$ $\text{Log}_{10} 8 = 0.9030$ $\text{Log}_{10} 5 = 0.6989$ $\text{Log}_{10} 6 = 0.7781$ $\text{Log}_{10} 5 = 0.6989$

$\text{Log}_{10} 8 = 0.9030$

7: 8, 5? 6, 5, 8. Deep calls unto Deep study bible 1

0.8450: 0.9030, 0.6989? 0.7781, 0.6989, 0.9030.
Deep calls unto Deep study bible 2

x-axis	y-axis
7	0.8450
8	0.9030
5	0.6989
6	0.7781
5	0.6989
8	0.9030

Water Spout *(lightning; combinatorics)* Study bible 1

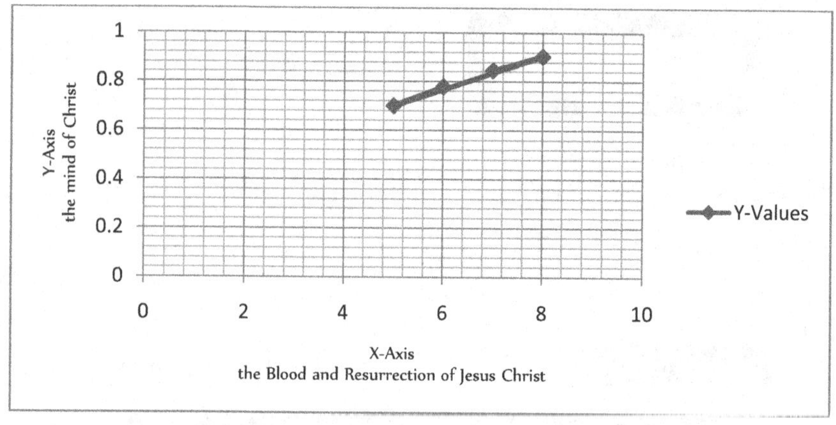

Water Spout *(lightning; combinatorics)* Study bible 2

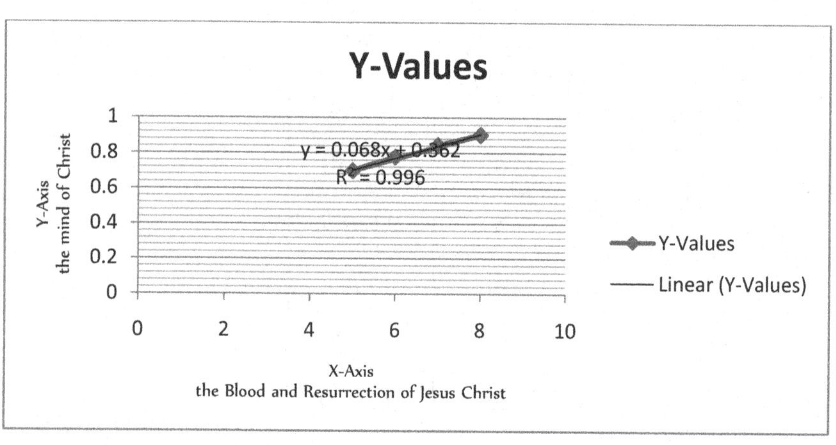

$10^{0.8450}: 10^{0.9030}, 10^{0.6989}? 10^{0.7781}, 10^{0.6989}, 10^{0.9030}.$

Pilled Poplar, Hazel, and Chestnut bible rods 2

14. Ye are the light of the world. A city that is set on an hill cannot be hid.

7. 11. Bible Matrices

$7_{10}.\ 11_{10}.$ Pilled Poplar, Hazel, and Chestnut bible rods 1

$\text{Log}_{10} 7 = 0.8450$ $\text{Log}_{10} 11 = 1.0413$

7. 11. Deep calls unto Deep study bible 1

0.8450. 1.0413. Deep calls unto Deep study bible 2

x-axis	y-axis
7	0.8450
11	1.0413

Water Spout *(lightning; combinatorics)* Study bible 1

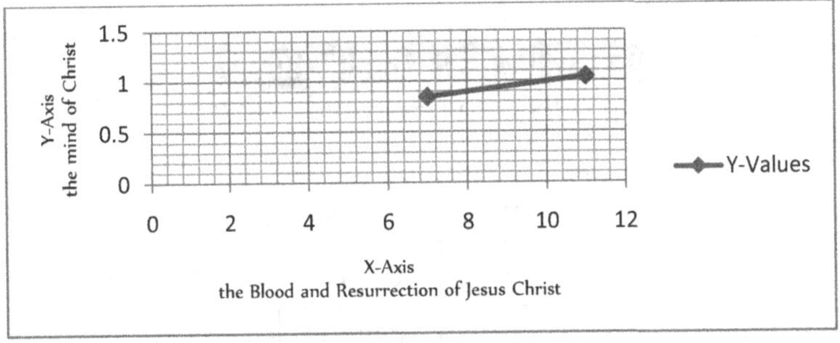

Water Spout *(lightning; combinatorics)* Study bible 2

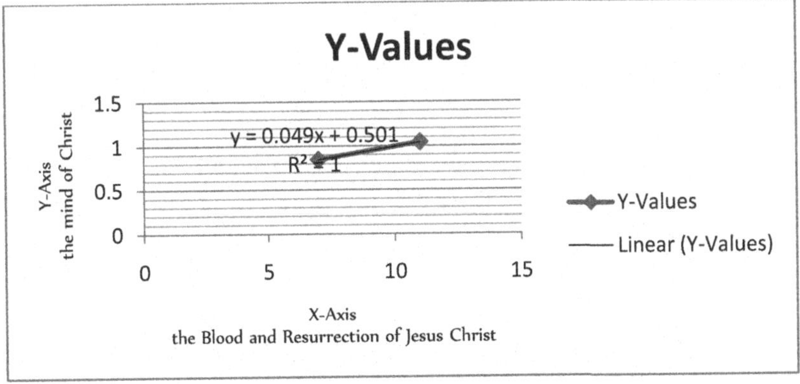

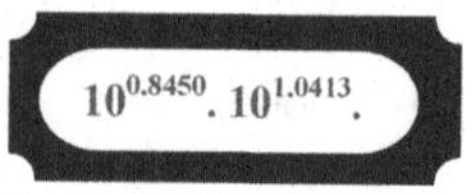
$10^{0.8450} . 10^{1.0413}$.

Pilled Poplar, Hazel, and Chestnut bible rods 2

15. Neither do men light a candle, and put it under a bushel, but on a candlestick; and it giveth light unto all that are in the house.

6, 6, 4; 11. Bible Matrices

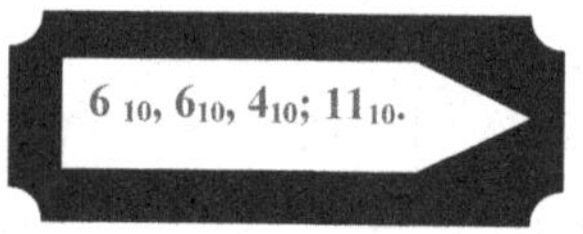
$6_{10}, 6_{10}, 4_{10}; 11_{10}$.

Pilled Poplar, Hazel, and Chestnut bible rods 1

$\log_{10} 4 = 0.6020$ $\log_{10} 6 = 0.7781$ $\log_{10} 6 = 0.7781$ $\log_{10} 11 = 1.0413$

6, 6, 4; 11. Deep calls unto Deep study bible 1

0.7781, 0.7781, 0.6020; 1.0413.
Deep calls unto Deep study bible 2

x-axis	y-axis
6	0.7781
6	0.7781
4	0.6020
11	1.0413

Water Spout *(lightning; combinatorics)* Study bible 1

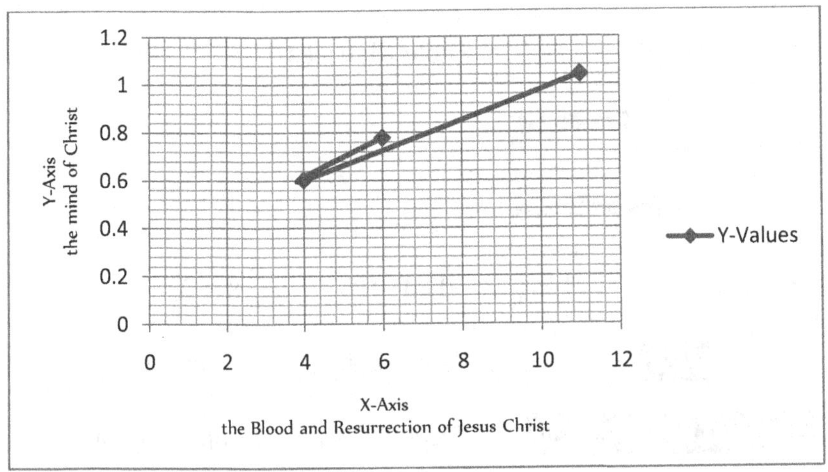

Water Spout *(lightning; combinatorics)* Study bible 2

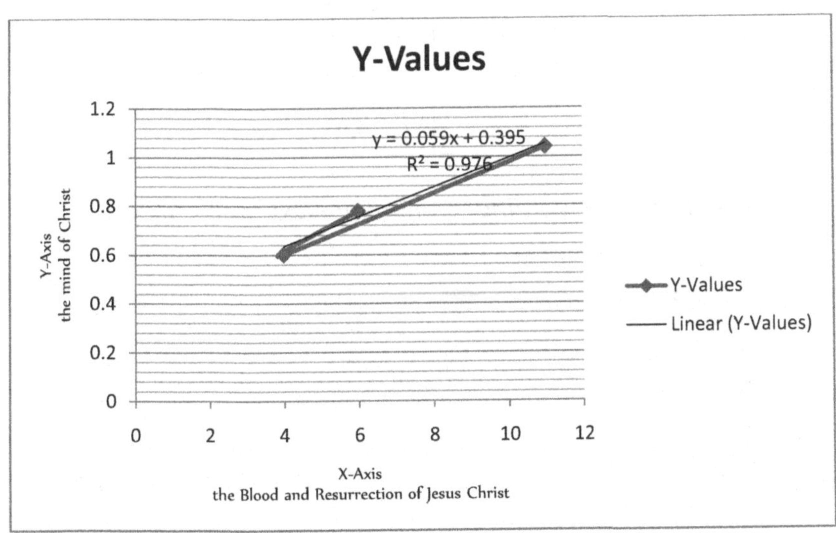

Pilled Poplar, Hazel, and Chestnut bible rods 2

16. Let your light so shine before men, that they may see your good works, and glorify your Father which is in heaven.

7, 7, 8. Bible Matrices

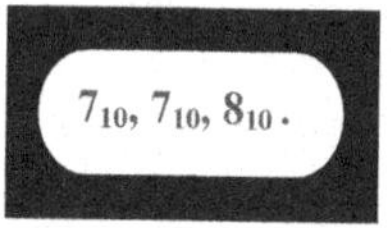

Pilled Poplar, Hazel, and Chestnut bible rods 1

$\text{Log}_{10} 7 = 0.8450$ $\text{Log}_{10} 7 = 0.8450$ $\text{Log}_{10} 8 = 0.9030$

7, 7, 8. Deep calls unto Deep study bible 1

0.8450, 0.8450, 0.9030. Deep calls unto Deep study bible 2

x-axis	y-axis
7	0.8450
7	0.8450
8	0.9030

Water Spout *(lightning; combinatorics)* Study bible 1

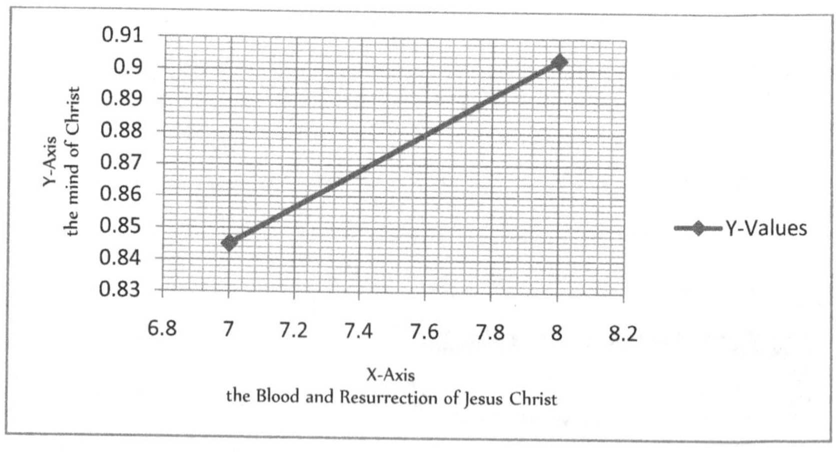

Water Spout *(lightning; combinatorics)* Study bible 2

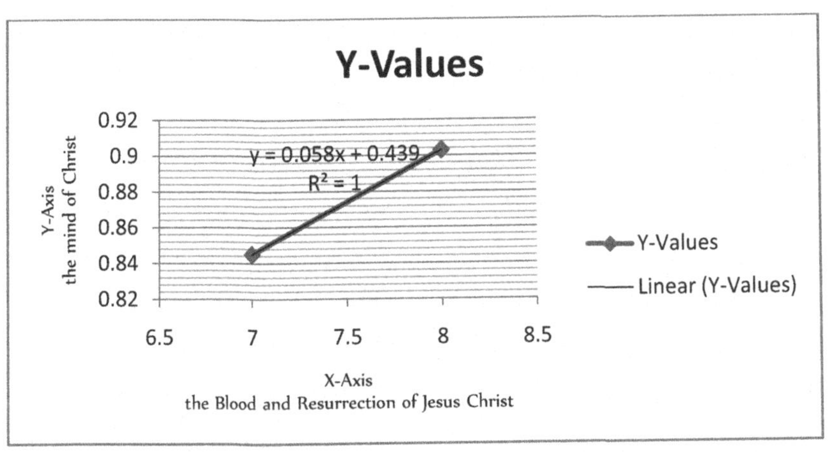

$10^{0.8450}$, $10^{0.8450}$, $10^{0.9030}$. Pilled Poplar, Hazel, and Chestnut bible rods 2

17. Think not that I am come to destroy the law, or the prophets: I am not come to destroy, but to fulfil.

10, 3: 6, 3. Bible Matrices

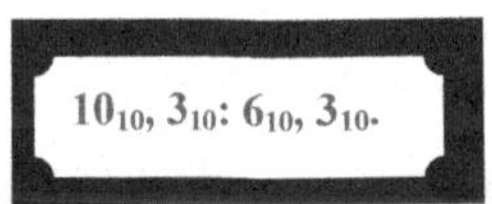

Pilled Poplar, Hazel, and Chestnut bible rods 1

$\text{Log}_{10} 10 = 1$ $\text{Log}_{10} 3 = 0.4771$ $\text{Log}_{10} 3 = 0.4771$ $\text{Log}_{10} 6 = 0.7781$

10, 3: 6, 3. Deep calls unto Deep study bible 1

1, 0.4771: 0.7781, 0.4771. Deep calls unto Deep study bible 2

x-axis	y-axis
10	1
3	0.4771
6	0.7781
3	0.4771

Water Spout *(lightning; combinatorics)* Study bible 1

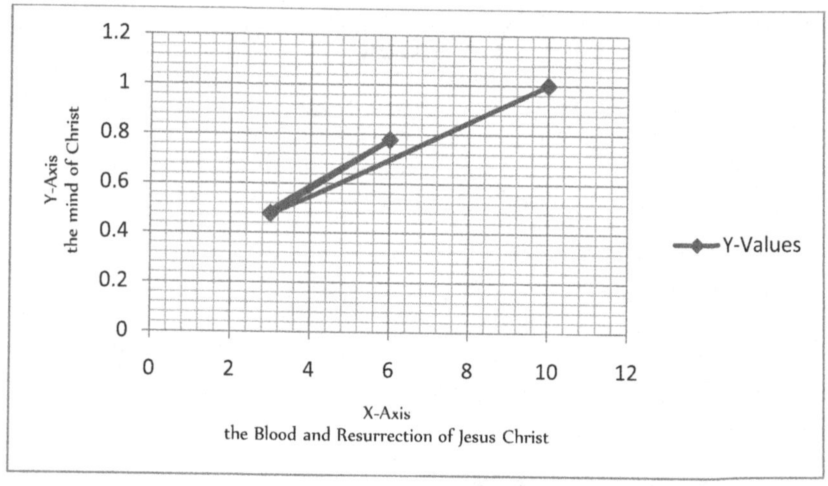

Water Spout *(lightning; combinatorics)* Study bible 2

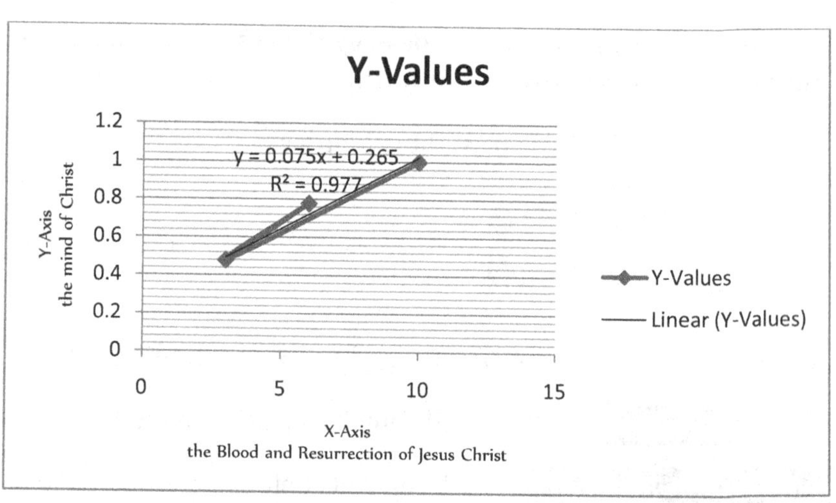

Pilled Poplar, Hazel, and Chestnut bible rods 2

18. For verily I say unto you, Till heaven and earth pass, one jot or one tittle shall in no wise pass from the law, till all be fulfilled.

6, 5, 13, 4. Bible Matrices

$6_{10}, 5_{10}, 13_{10}, 4_{10}$. Pilled Poplar, Hazel, and Chestnut bible rods 1

$Log_{10} 6 = 0.7781$ $Log_{10} 5 = 0.6989$ $Log_{10} 13 = 1.1139$ $Log_{10} 4 = 0.6020$

6, 5, 13, 4. Deep calls unto Deep study bible 1

0.7781, 0.6989, 1.1139, 0.6020. Deep calls unto Deep study bible 2

x-axis	y-axis
6	0.7781
5	0.6989
13	1.1139
4	0.6020

Water Spout *(lightning; combinatorics)* Study bible 1

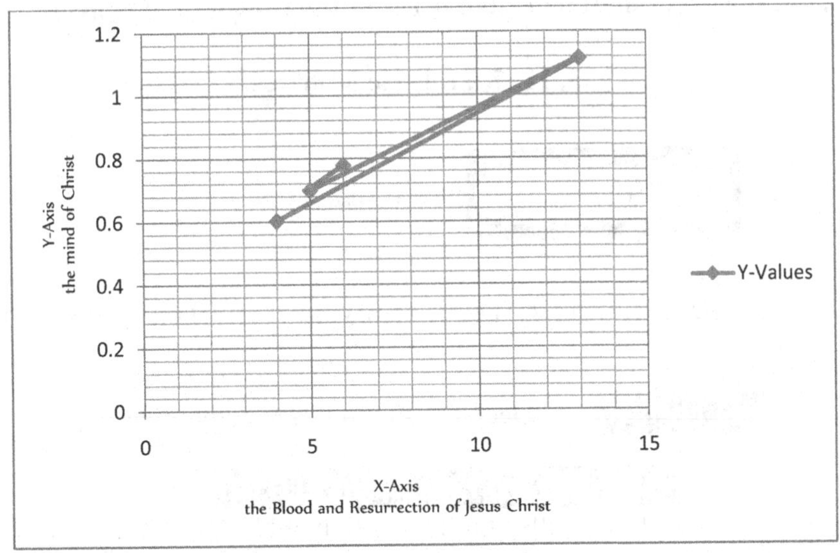

Water Spout *(lightning; combinatorics)* Study bible 2

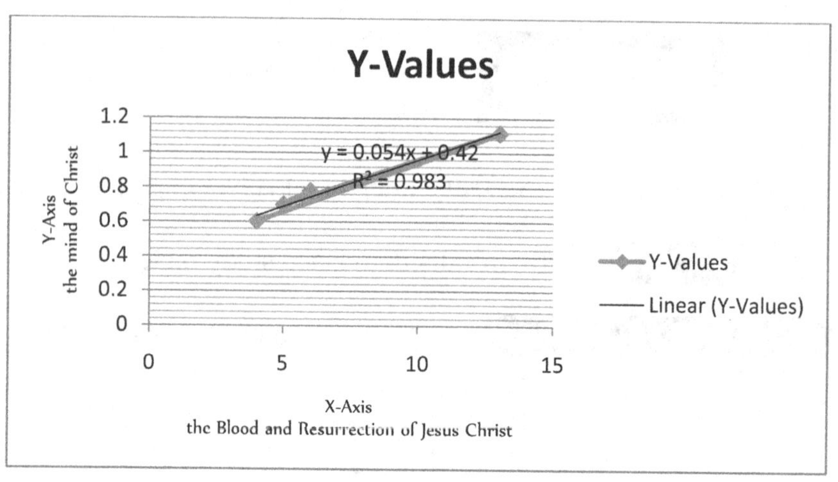

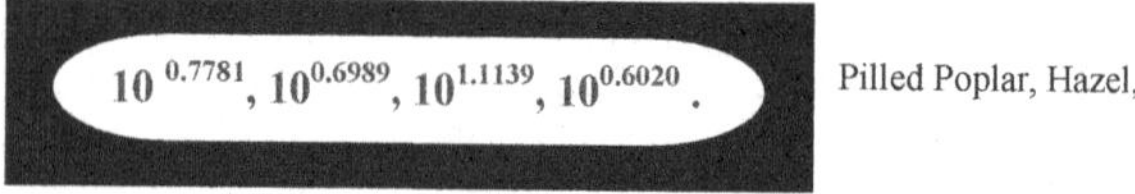
$10^{0.7781}, 10^{0.6989}, 10^{1.1139}, 10^{0.6020}$.

Pilled Poplar, Hazel, and Chestnut bible rods 2

19. Whosoever therefore shall break one of these least commandments, and shall teach men so, he shall be called the least in the kingdom of heaven: but whosoever shall do and teach them, the same shall be called great in the kingdom of heaven.

9, 5, 11: 7, 11. Bible Matrices

$9_{10}, 5_{10}, 11_{10}: 7_{10}, 11_{10}$.

Pilled Poplar, Hazel, and Chestnut bible rods 1

$\text{Log}_{10} 9 = 0.9542$ $\text{Log}_{10} 5 = 0.6989$ $\text{Log}_{10} 11 = 1.0413$ $\text{Log}_{10} 7 = 0.8450$ $\text{Log}_{10} 11 = 1.0413$

9, 5, 11: 7, 11. Deep calls unto Deep study bible 1

0.9542, 0.6989, 1.0413: 0.8450, 1.0413.
Deep calls unto Deep study bible 2

x-axis	y-axis
9	0.9542
5	0.6989
11	1.0413
7	0.8450
11	1.0413

Water Spout *(lightning; combinatorics)* Study bible 1

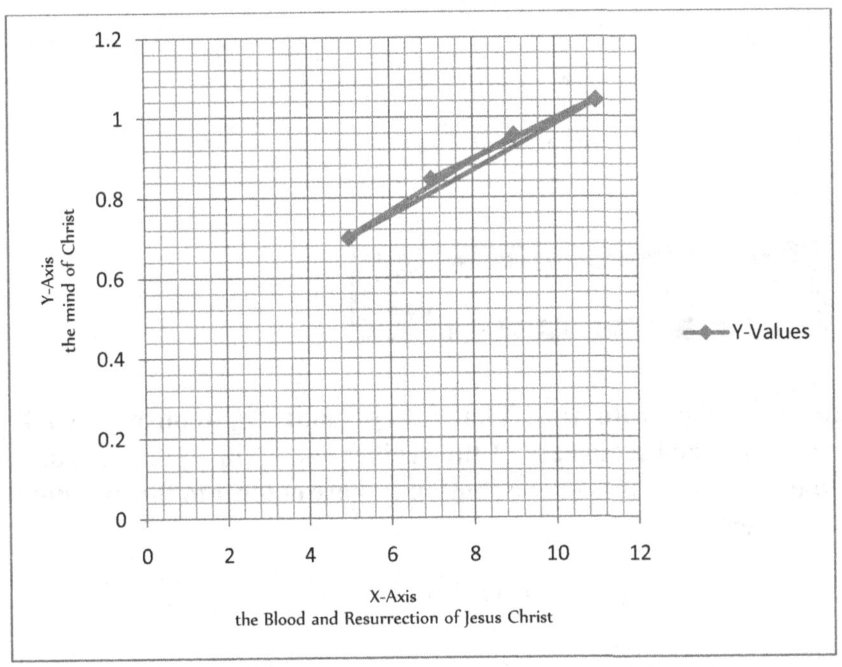

Water Spout *(lightning; combinatorics)* Study bible 2

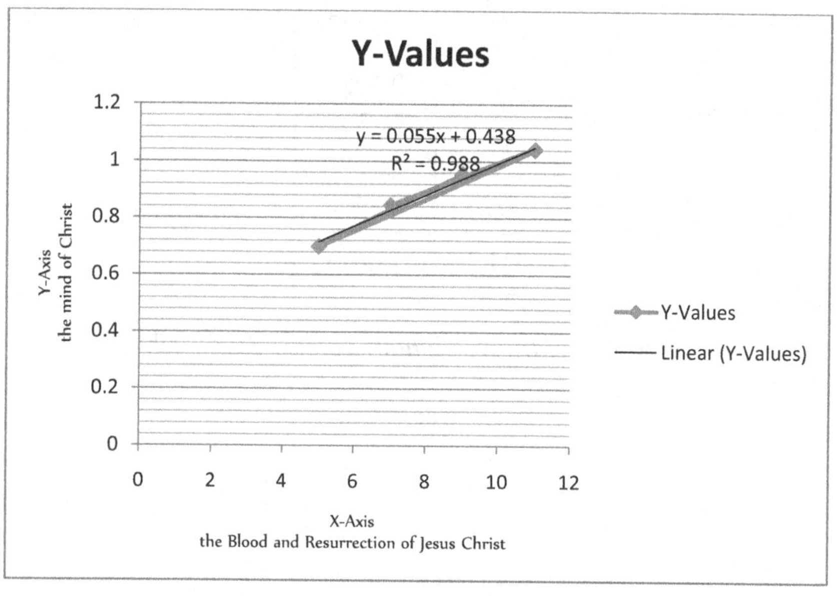

$10^{0.9542}$, $10^{0.6989}$, $10^{1.0413}$: $10^{0.8450}$, $10^{1.0413}$.

Pilled Poplar, Hazel, and Chestnut bible rods 2

20. For I say unto you, That except your righteousness shall exceed the righteousness of the scribes lawyers; an expert in legal matters, **and Pharisees**separated ones; set apart, **ye shall in no case enter into the kingdom of heaven.**

5, 13, 11. Bible Matrices

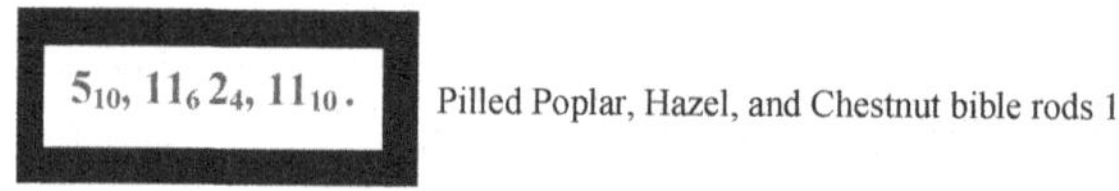
5_{10}, 11_6 2_4, 11_{10}.

Pilled Poplar, Hazel, and Chestnut bible rods 1

$\text{Log}_6 11 = y$ $\text{Log}_{10} 11 = 1.0413$ $\text{Log}_{10} 5 = 0.6989$ $\text{Log}_4 2 = y$

$6^y = 11$

$\text{Log}_{10} 6^y = \log_{10} 11$

$y \log_{10} 6 = \log_{10} 11$

$y = \log_{10} 11 / \log_{10} 6$

$y = 1.0413/0.7781$

$y = 1.3382$

$4^y = 2$

$2^{2y} = 2^1$

$2y = 1$

$y = ½$

5, 13, 11. Deep calls unto Deep study bible 1

0.6989, 1.3382 0.5, 1.0413. Deep calls unto Deep study bible 2

x-axis	y-axis
5	0.6989
13	1.8382
11	1.0413

Water Spout *(lightning; combinatorics)* Study bible 1

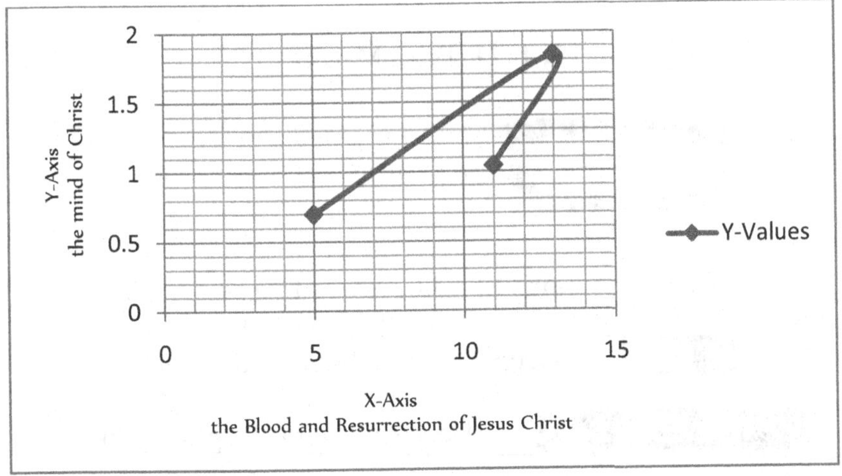

Water Spout *(lightning; combinatorics)* Study bible 2

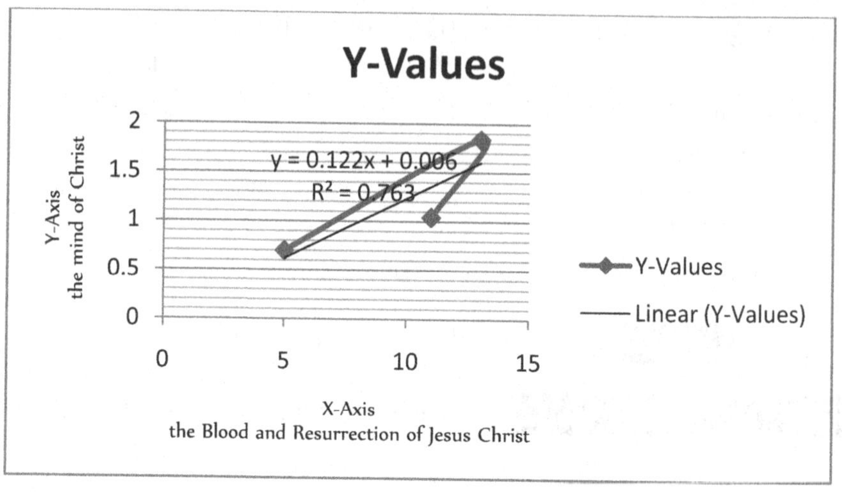

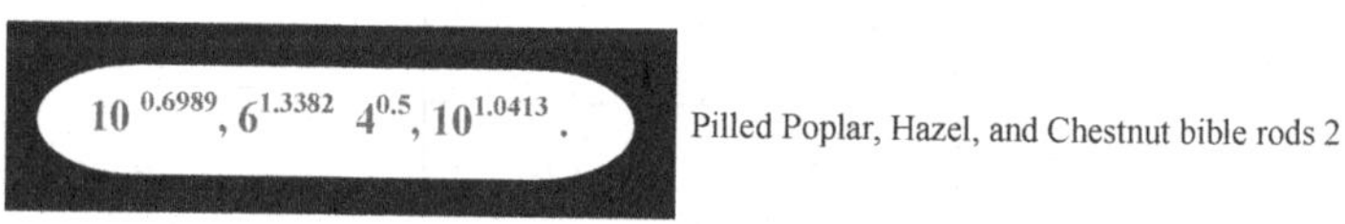

Pilled Poplar, Hazel, and Chestnut bible rods 2

21. Ye have heard that it was said by them of old time, Thou shalt not kill; and whosoever shall kill shall be in danger of the judgment:

12, 4; 11: Bible Matrices

Pilled Poplar, Hazel, and Chestnut bible rods 1

$\text{Log}_{10} 11 = 1.0413$ $\text{Log}_{10} 12 = 1.0791$ $\text{Log}_{10} 4 = 0.6020$

12, 4, 11. Deep calls unto Deep study bible 1

1.0791, 0.6020, 1.0413. Deep calls unto Deep study bible 2

x-axis	y-axis
12	1.0791
4	0.6020
11	1.0413

Water Spout *(lightning; combinatorics)* Study bible 1

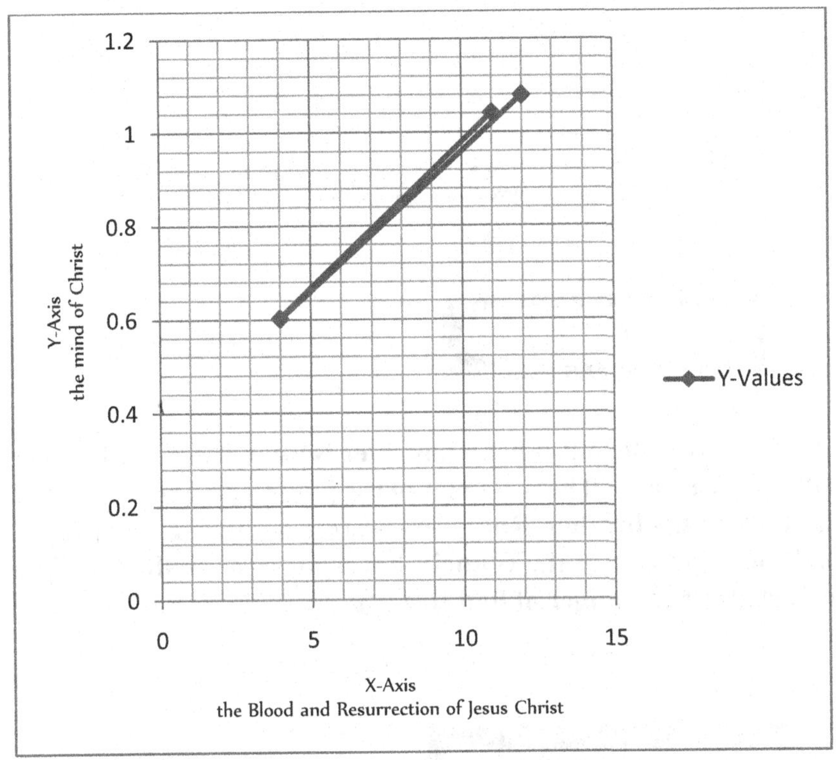

Water Spout *(lightning; combinatorics)* Study bible 2

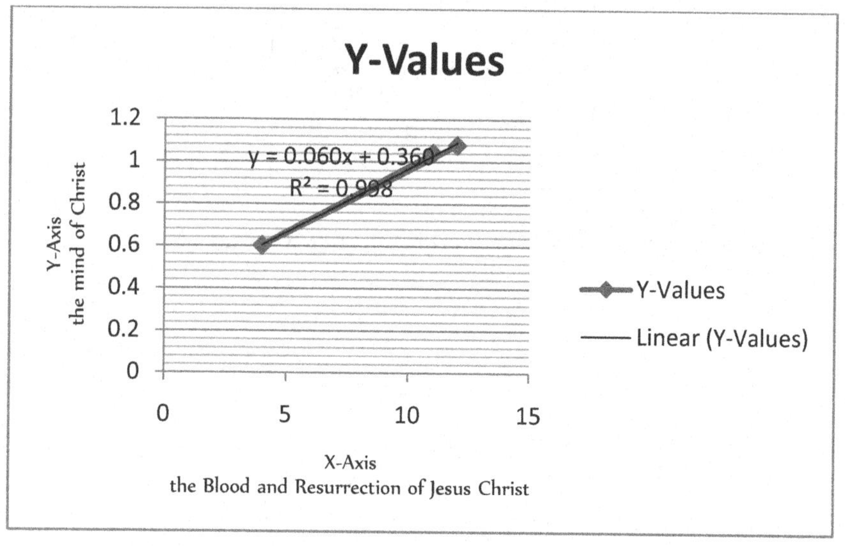

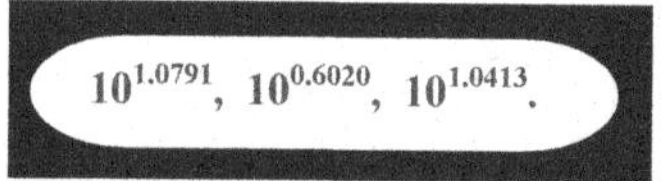

$10^{1.0791}$, $10^{0.6020}$, $10^{1.0413}$.

Pilled Poplar, Hazel, and Chestnut bible rods 2

22. But I say unto you, That whosoever is angry with his brother without a cause shall be in danger of the judgment: and whosoever shall say to his brother, Racaworthless; good-for-nothing; Senseless; vain; empty-headed, **shall be in danger of the council: but whosoever shall say, Thou fool, shall be in danger of hell fire.**

5, 17: 7, 1, 7: 4, 2, 7. Bible Matrices

$5_{10}, 17_{10}: 7_{10}, 1_8, 7_{10}: 4_{10}, 2_{10}, 7_{10}.$

Pilled Poplar, Hazel, and Chestnut bible rods 1

$\text{Log}_8 1 = y$ $\text{Log}_{10} 17 = 1.2304$ $\text{Log}_{10} 7 = 0.8450$ $\text{Log}_{10} 2 = 0.3010$ $\text{Log}_{10} 5 = 0.6989$ $\text{Log}_{10} 4 = 0.6020$

$8^y = 1$

$8^y = 8^0$

$y = 0$

5, 17: 7, 1, 7: 4, 2, 7. Deep calls unto Deep study bible 1

0.6989, 1.2304: 0.8450, 0, 0.8450: 0.6020, 0.3010, 0.8450.

Deep calls unto Deep study bible 2

x-axis	y-axis
5	0.6989
17	1.2304
7	0.8450
1	0
7	0.8450
4	0.6020
2	0.3010
7	0.8450

Water Spout *(lightning; combinatorics)* Study bible 1

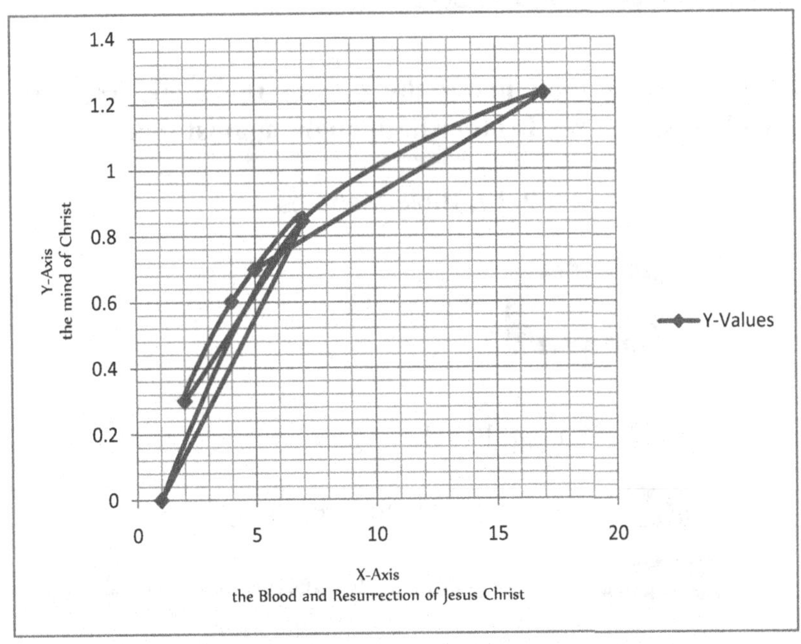

Water Spout *(lightning; combinatorics)* Study bible 2

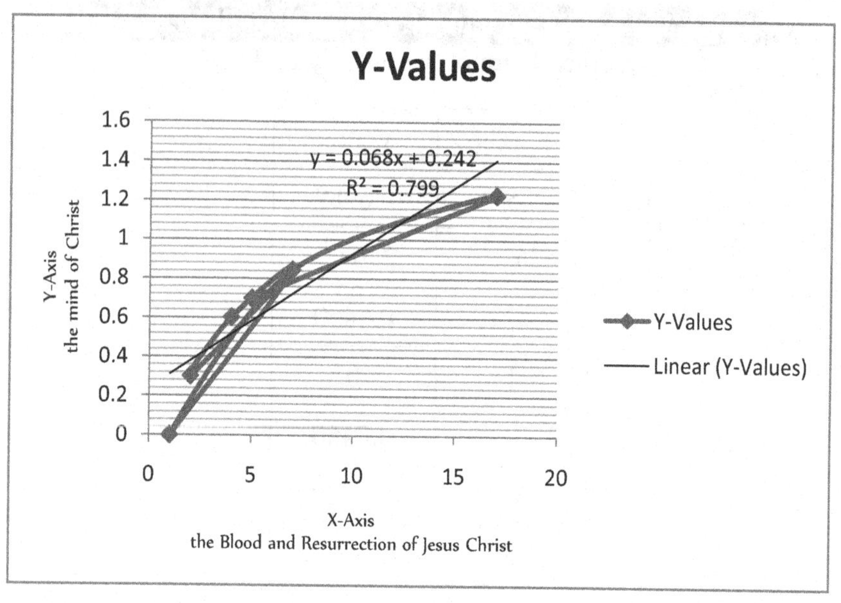

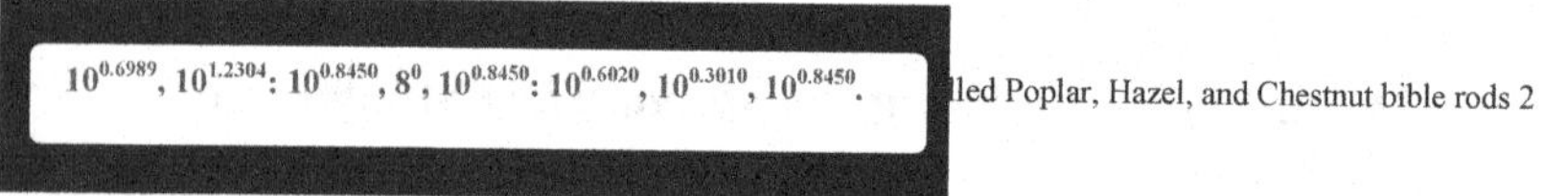
$10^{0.6989}$, $10^{1.2304}$: $10^{0.8450}$, 8^{0}, $10^{0.8450}$: $10^{0.6020}$, $10^{0.3010}$, $10^{0.8450}$.

lled Poplar, Hazel, and Chestnut bible rods 2

23. Therefore if thou bring thy gift to the altar, and there rememberest that thy brother hath ought against thee;

9, 10; Bible Matrices

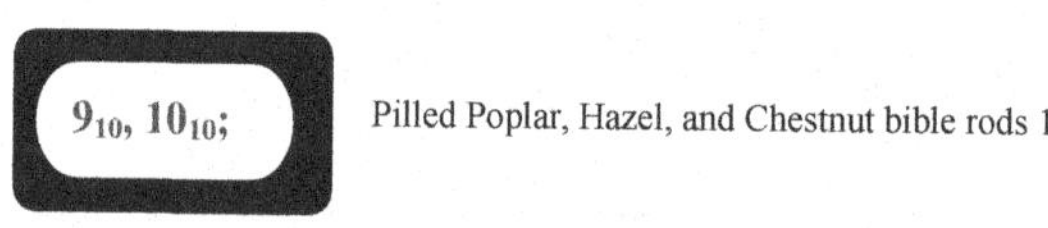
9_{10}, 10_{10};

Pilled Poplar, Hazel, and Chestnut bible rods 1

$\text{Log}_{10} 9 = 0.9542$ $\text{Log}_{10} 10 = 1$

9, 10; Deep calls unto Deep study bible 1

0.9542, 1; Deep calls unto Deep study bible 2

x-axis	y-axis
9	0.9542
10	1

Water Spout *(lightning; combinatorics)* Study bible 1

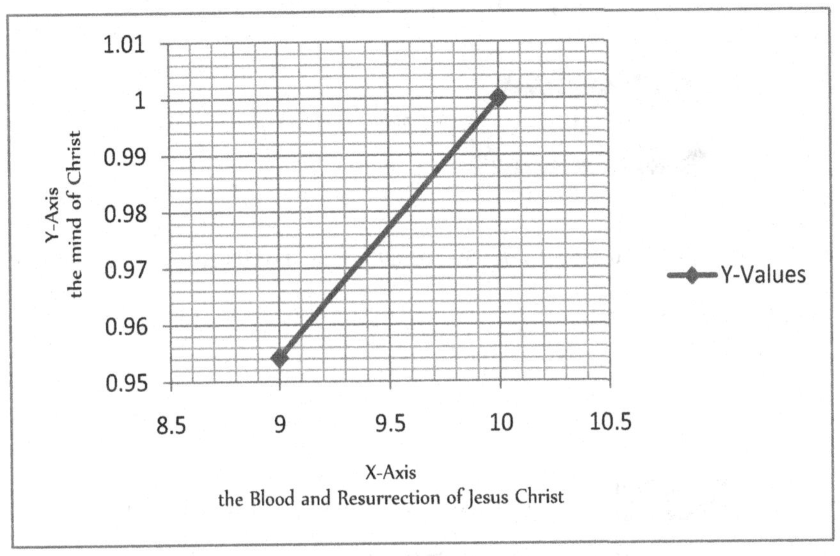

Water Spout *(lightning; combinatorics)* Study bible 2

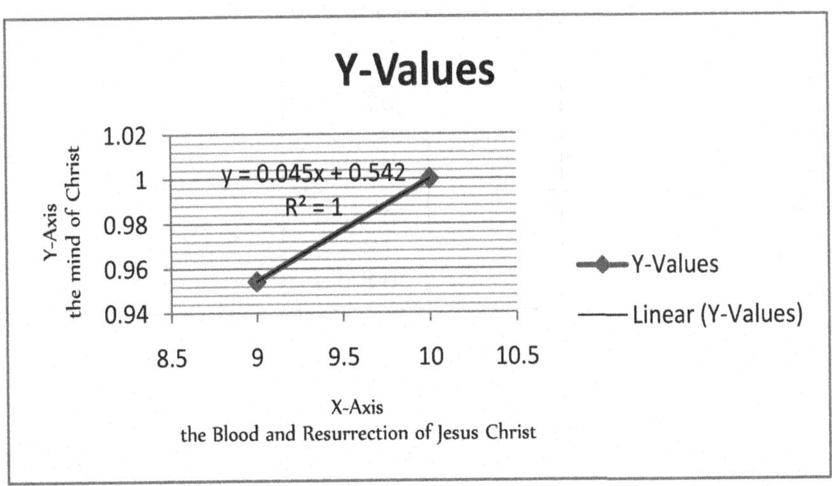

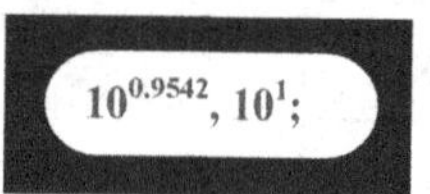

Pilled Poplar, Hazel, and Chestnut bible rods 2

24. Leave there thy gift before the altar, and go thy way; first 1 x
1 **be reconciled to thy brother, and then come and offer thy gift.**

7, 4; 6, 7. Bible Matrices

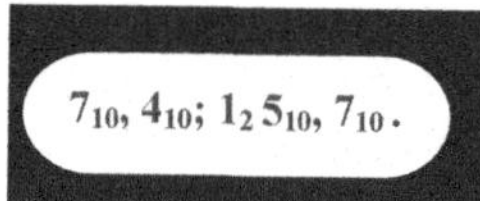

Pilled Poplar, Hazel, and Chesnut bible rods 1

$\text{Log}_2 1 = y$ $\text{Log}_{10} 7 = 0.8450$ $\text{Log}_{10} 5 = 0.6989$ $\text{Log}_{10} 4 = 0.6020$ $\text{Log}_{10} 7 = 0.8450$

$2^y = 1$

$2^y = 2^0$

$y = 0$

7, 4; 6, 7. Deep calls unto Deep study bible 1

0.8450, 0.6020; 0 0.6989, 0.8450.
Deep calls unto Deep study bible 2

x-axis	y-axis
7	0.8450
4	0.6020
6	0.6989
7	0.8450

Water Spout *(lightning; combinatorics)* Study bible 1

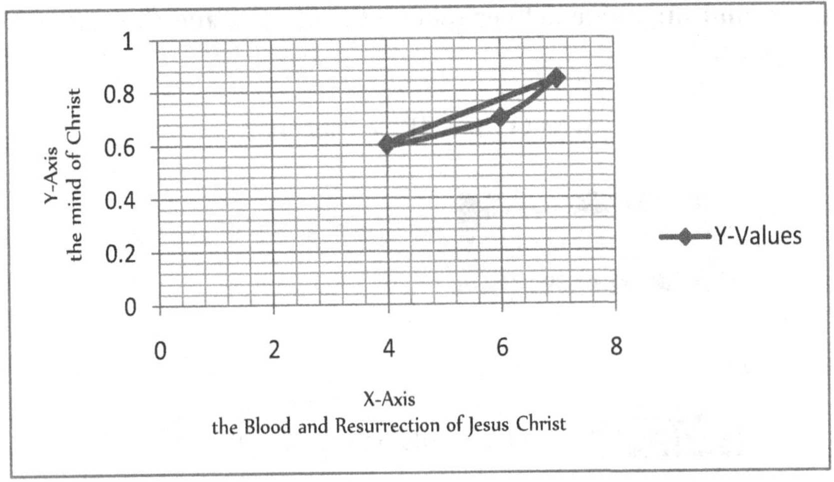

Water Spout *(lightning; combinatorics)* Study bible 2

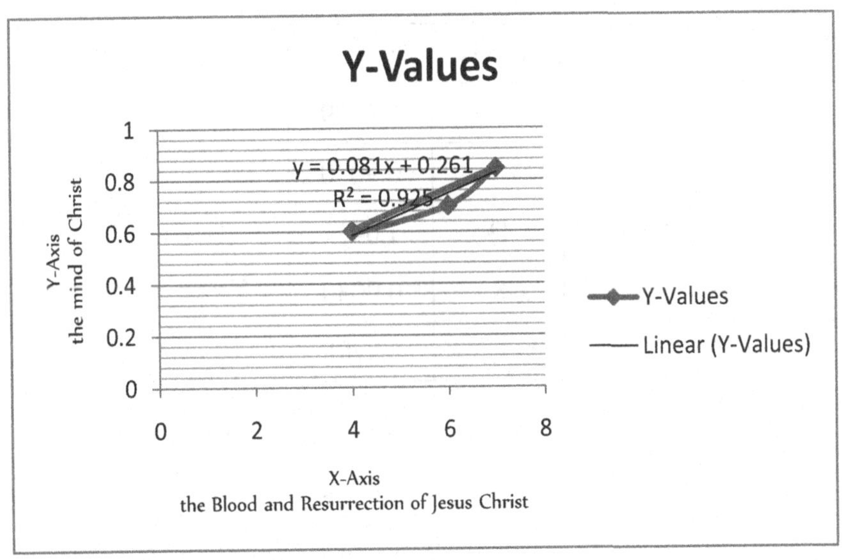

$10^{0.8450}$, $10^{0.6020}$; 2^{0} $10^{0.6989}$, $10^{0.8450}$

Pilled Poplar, Hazel, and Chestnut bible rods 2

25. Agree with thine adversary quickly, whiles thou art in the way with him; lest at any time the adversary deliver thee to the judge, and the judge deliver thee to the officer, and thou be cast into prison.

5, 8; 11, 8, 6. Bible Matrices

Pilled Poplar, Hazel, and Chestnut bible rods 1

$\text{Log}_{10} 8 = 0.9030$ $\text{Log}_{10} 5 = 0.6989$ $\text{Log}_{10} 11 = 1.0413$ $\text{Log}_{10} 6 = 0.7781$ $\text{Log}_{10} 8 = 0.9030$

5, 8; 11, 8, 6. Deep calls unto Deep study bible 1

0.6989, 0.9030; 1.0413, 0.9030, 0.7781.
Deep calls unto Deep study bible 2

x-axis	y-axis
5	0.6989
8	0.9030
11	1.0413
8	0.9030
6	0.7781

Water Spout *(lightning; combinatorics)* Study bible 1

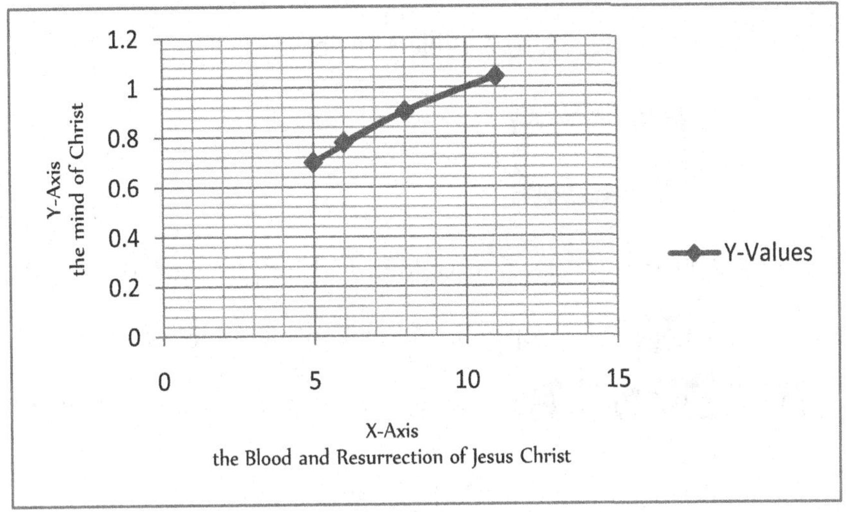

Water Spout *(lightning; combinatorics)* Study bible 2

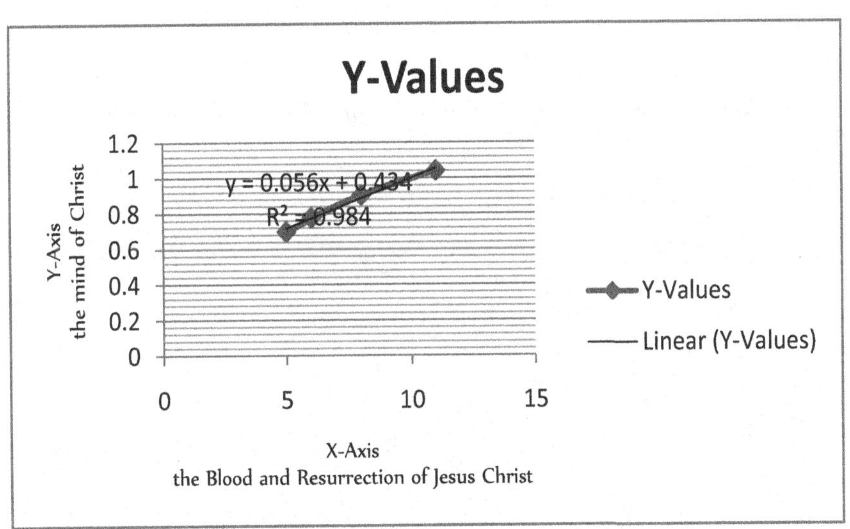

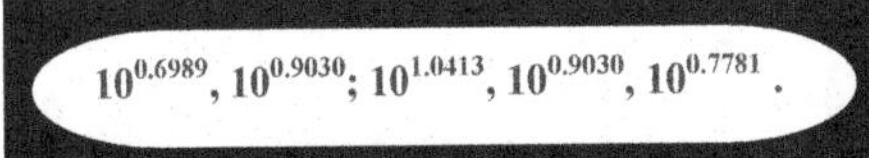

Pilled Poplar, Hazel, and Chestnut bible rods 2

26. Verily I say unto thee, Thou shalt by no means come out thence, till thou hast paid the uttermost farthing.

5, 8, 7. Bible Matrices

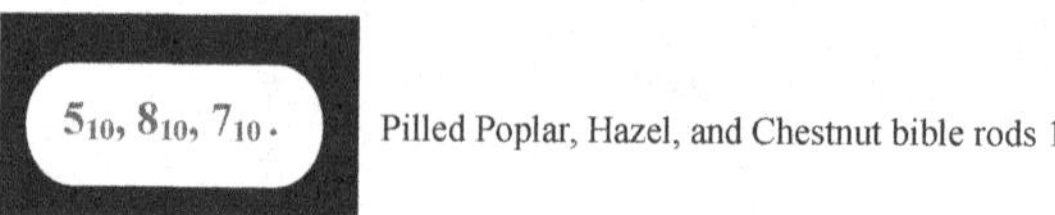

$\text{Log}_{10} 8 = 0.9030$ $\text{Log}_{10} 5 = 0.6989$ $\text{Log}_{10} 7 = 0.8450$

5, 8, 7. Deep calls unto Deep study bible 1

0.6989, 0.9030, 0.8450. Deep calls unto Deep study bible 2

x-axis	y-axis
5	0.6989
8	0.9030
7	0.8450

Water Spout *(lightning; combinatorics)* Study bible 1

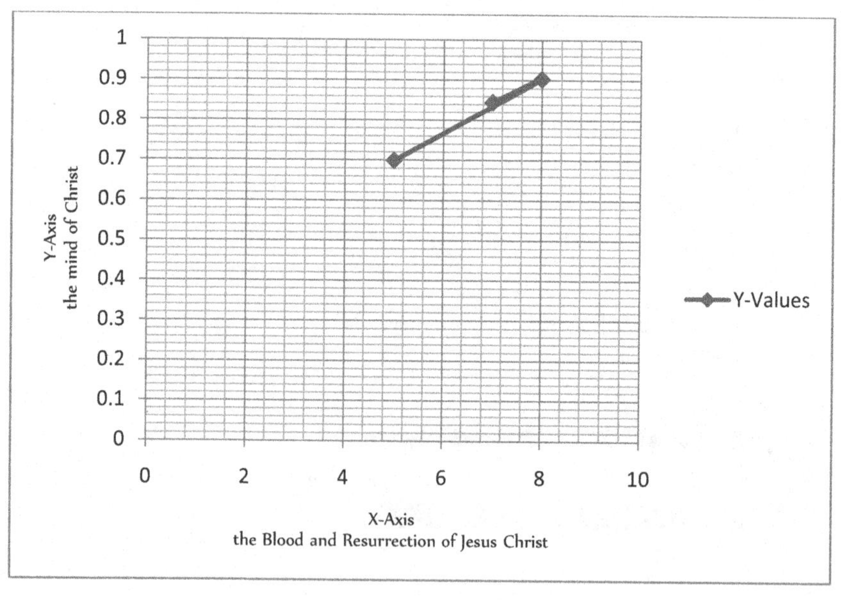

Water Spout *(lightning; combinatorics)* Study bible 2

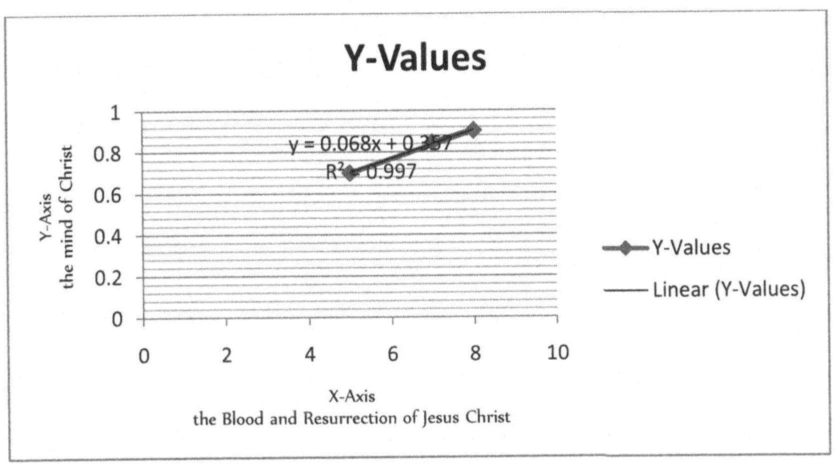

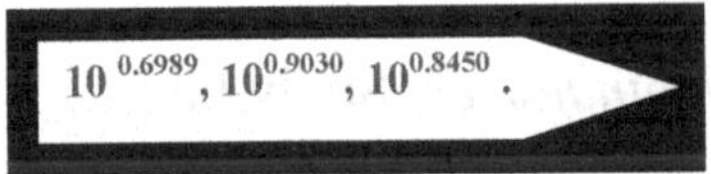

Pilled Poplar, Hazel, and Chestnut bible rods 2

27. Ye have heard that it was said by them of old time, Thou shalt not commit adultery:

12, 5: Bible Matrices

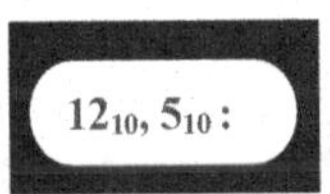

Pilled Poplar, Hazel, and Chestnut bible rods 1

$\text{Log}_{10} 12 = 1.0791$ $\text{Log}_{10} 5 = 0.6989$

12, 5: Deep calls unto Deep study bible 1

1.0791, 0.6989: Deep calls unto Deep study bible 2

x-axis	y-axis
12	1.0791
5	0.6989

Water Spout *(lightning; combinatorics)* Study bible 1

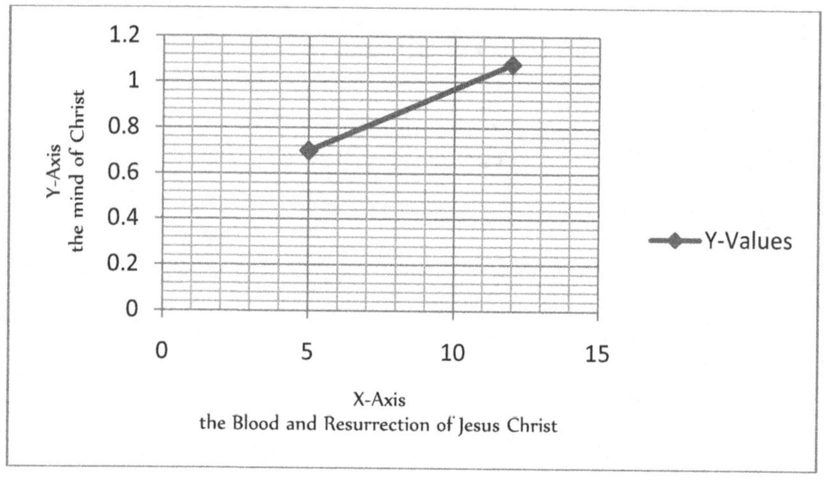

Water Spout *(lightning; combinatorics)* Study bible 2

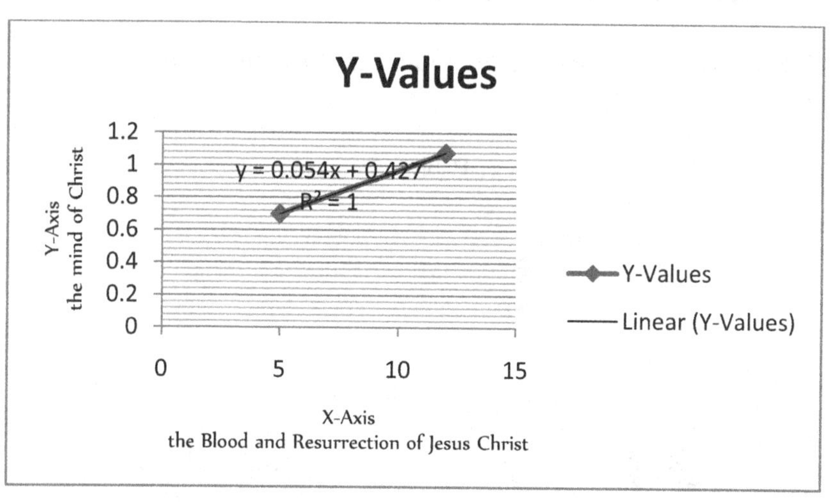

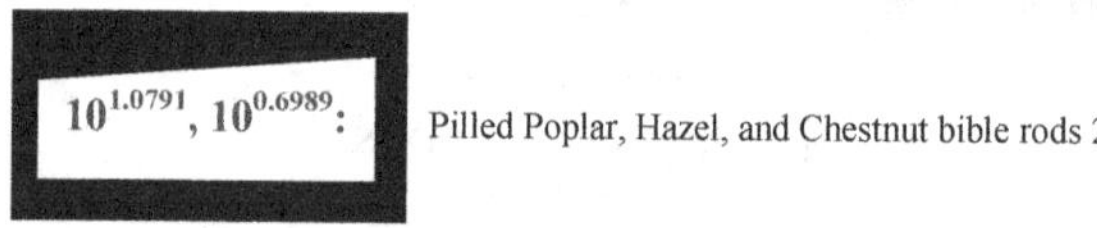

Pilled Poplar, Hazel, and Chestnut bible rods 2

28. But I say unto you, That whosoever looketh on a woman to lust after her hath committed adultery with her already in his heart.

5, 19. Bible Matrices

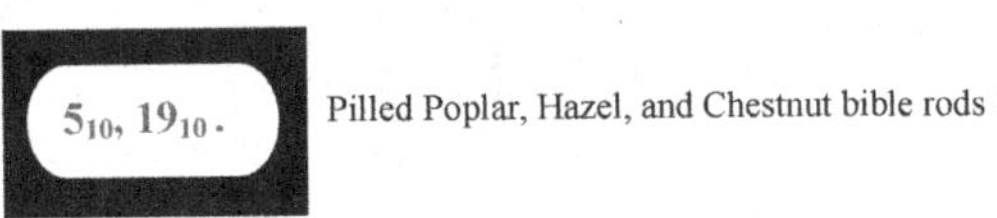

$\text{Log}_{10}\ 19 = 1.2787$ $\text{Log}_{10}\ 5 = 0.6989$

5, 19. Deep calls unto Deep study bible 1

0.6989, 1.2787. Deep calls unto Deep study bible 2

x-axis	y-axis
5	0.6989
19	1.2787

Water Spout *(lightning; combinatorics)* Study bible 1

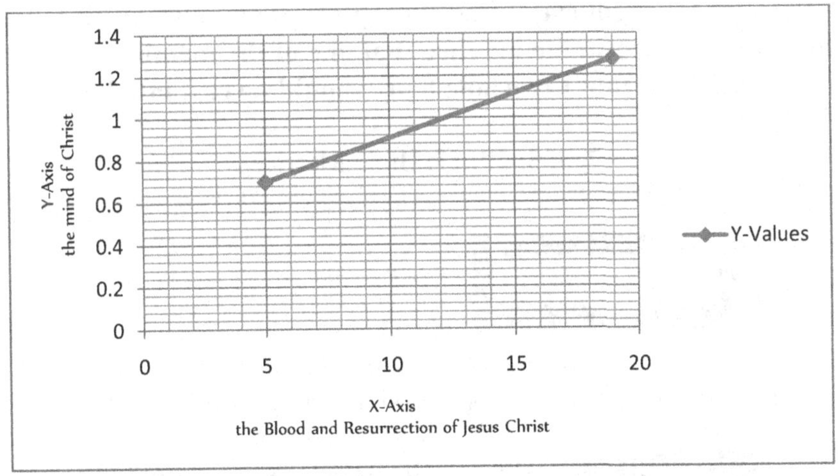

Water Spout *(lightning; combinatorics)* Study bible 2

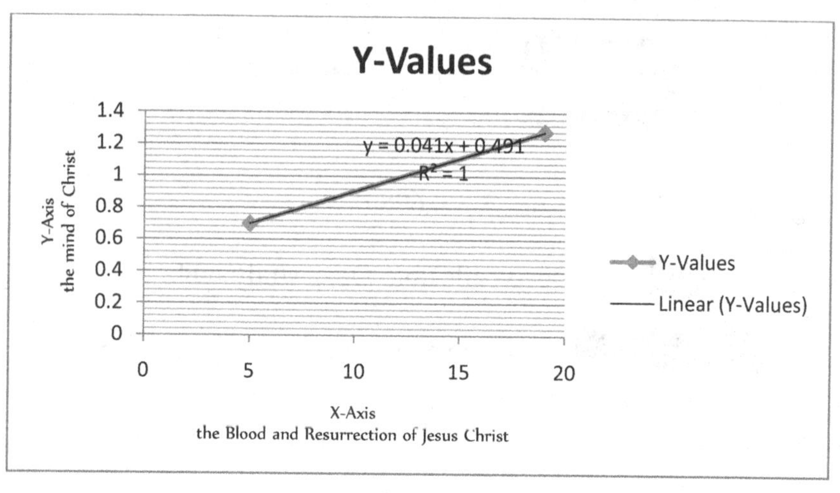

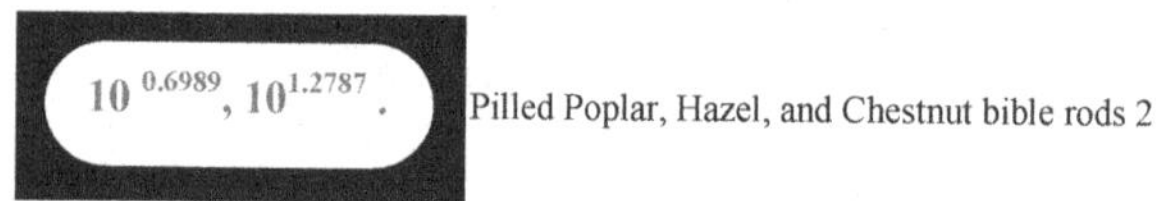

Pilled Poplar, Hazel, and Chestnut bible rods 2

29. And if thy right eye offend thee, pluck it out, and cast it from thee: for it is profitable for thee that one of thy members should perish, and not that thy whole body should be cast into hell.

7, 3, 5: 13, 11. Bible Matrices

Pilled Poplar, Hazel, and Chestnut bible rods 1

$\text{Log}_{10} 13 = 1.1139$ $\text{Log}_{10} 5 = 0.6989$ $\text{Log}_{10} 7 = 0.8450$ $\text{Log}_{10} 11 = 1.0413$ $\text{Log}_{10} 3 = 0.4771$

7, 3, 5: 13, 11. Deep calls unto Deep study bible 1

0.8450, 0.4771, 0.6989: 1.1139, 1.0413.
Deep calls unto Deep study bible 2

x-axis	y-axis
7	0.8450
3	0.4771
5	0.6989
13	1.1139
11	1.0413

Water Spout *(lightning; combinatorics)* Study bible 1

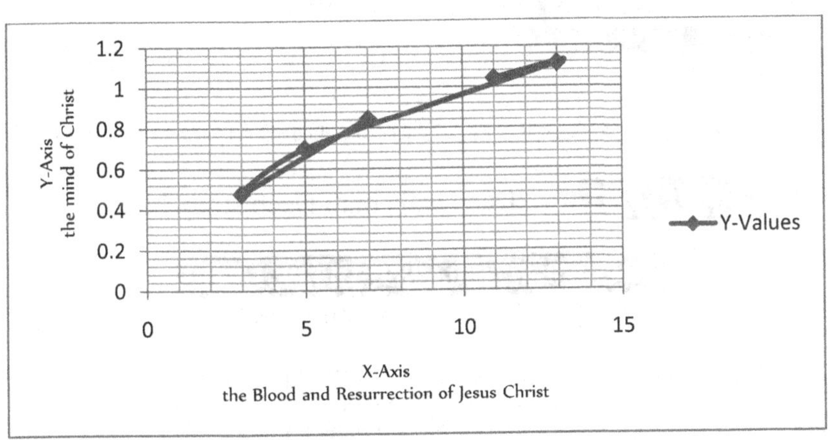

Water Spout *(lightning; combinatorics)* Study bible 2

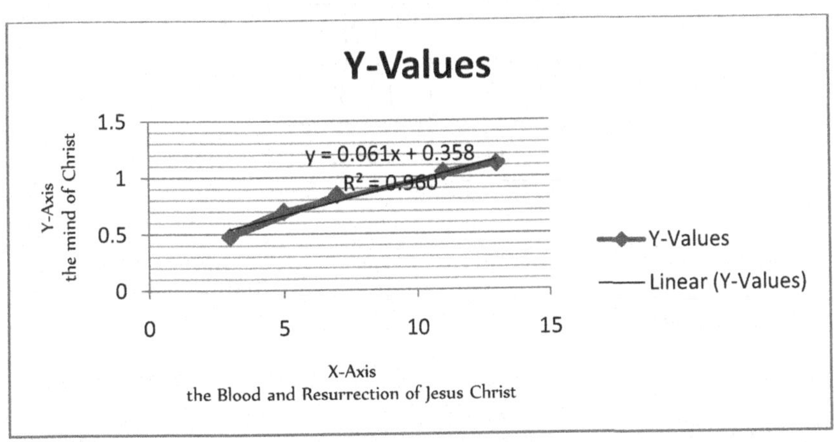

$10^{0.8450}, 10^{0.4771}, 10^{0.6989}: 10^{1.1139}, 10^{1.0413}.$ Pilled Poplar, Hazel, and Chestnut bible rods 2

30. And if thy right hand offend thee, cut it off, and cast it from thee: for it is profitable for thee that one of thy members should perish, and not that thy whole body should be cast into hell.

7, 3, 5: 13, 11. Bible Matrices

$7_{10}, 3_{10}, 5_{10}: 13_{10}, 11_{10}.$ Pilled Poplar, Hazel, and Chestnut bible rods 1

$\text{Log}_{10} 13 = 1.1139$ $\text{Log}_{10} 5 = 0.6989$ $\text{Log}_{10} 7 = 0.8450$ $\text{Log}_{10} 11 = 1.0413$ $\text{Log}_{10} 3 = 0.4771$

7, 3, 5: 13, 11. Deep calls unto Deep study bible 1

0.8450, 0.4771, 0.6989: 1.1139, 1.0413.
Deep calls unto Deep study bible 2

x-axis	y-axis
7	0.8450
3	0.4771
5	0.6989
13	1.1139
11	1.0413

Water Spout *(lightning; combinatorics)* Study bible 1

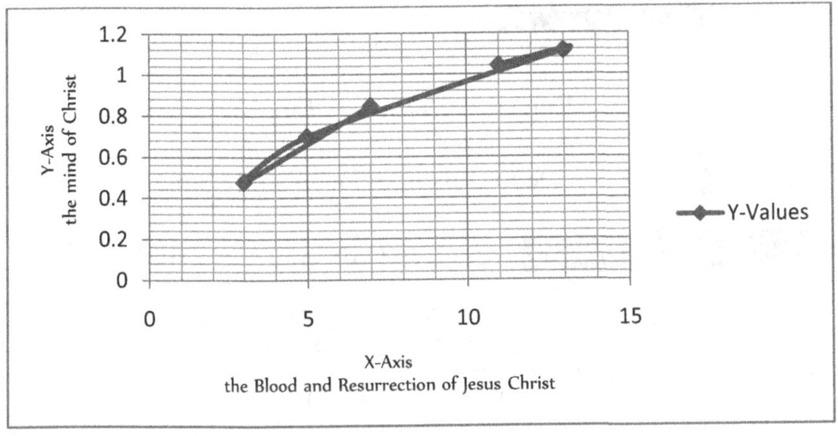

Water Spout *(lightning; combinatorics)* Study bible 2

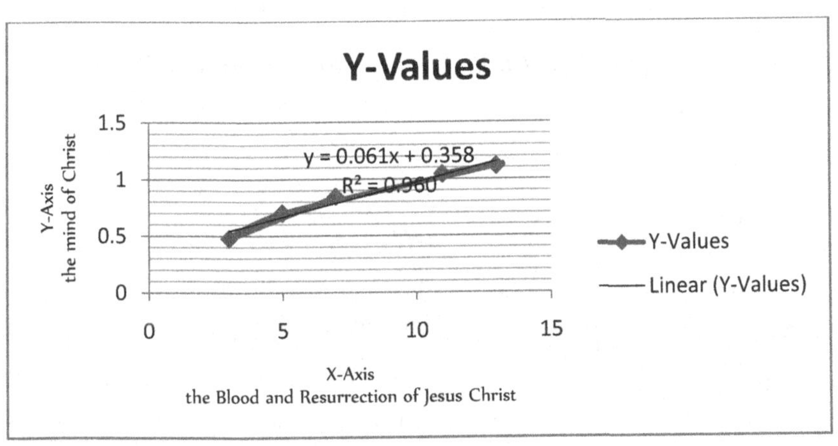

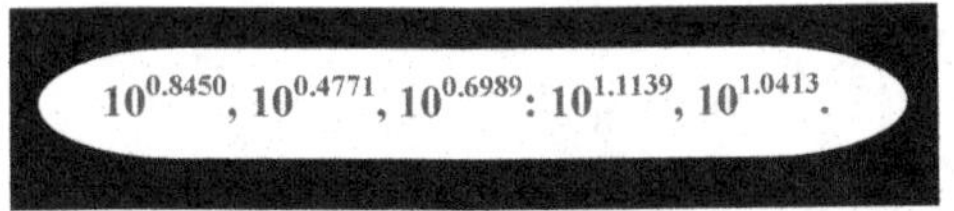

Pilled Poplar, Hazel, and Chestnut bible rods 2

31. It hath been said, Whosoever shall put away his wife, let him give her a writing of divorcement:

4, 6, 8: Bible Matrices

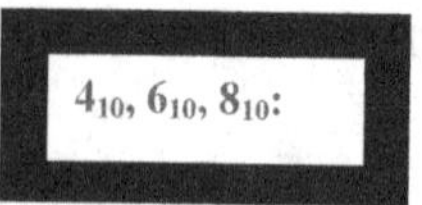

Pilled Poplar, Hazel, and Chestnut bible rods 1

$Log_{10} 4 = 0.6020$ $Log_{10} 6 = 0.7781$ $Log_{10} 8 = 0.9030$

4, 6, 8: Deep calls unto Deep study bible 1

0.6020, 0.7781, 0.9030: Deep calls unto Deep study bible 2

x-axis	y-axis
4	0.6020
6	0.7781
8	0.9030

Water Spout *(lightning; combinatorics)* Study bible 1

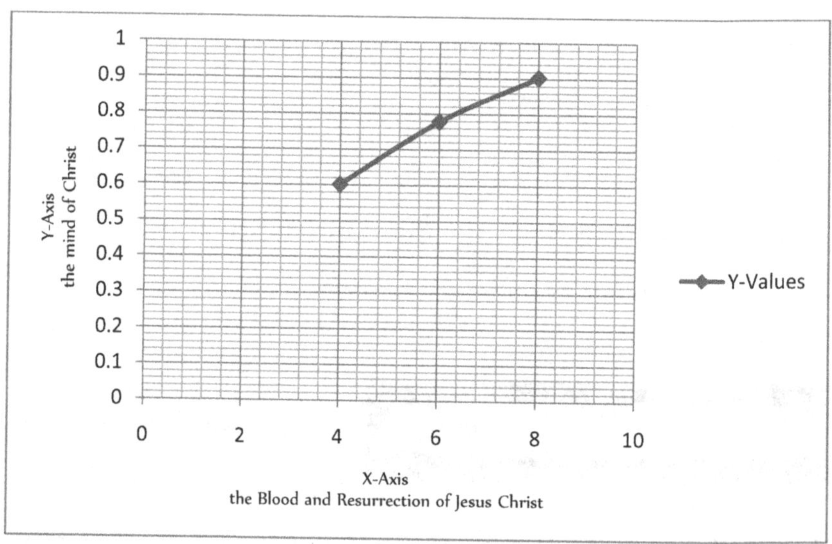

Water Spout *(lightning; combinatorics)* Study bible 2

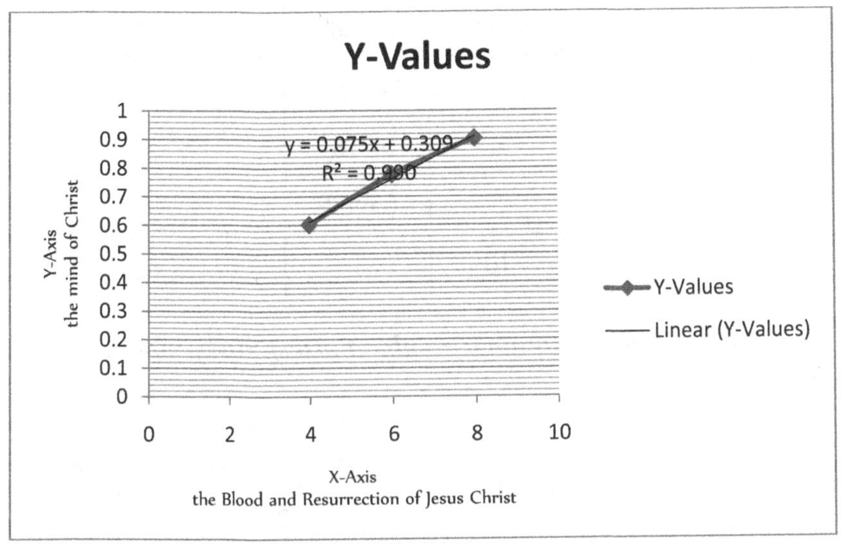

$10^{0.6020}$, $10^{0.7781}$, $10^{0.9030}$:

Pilled Poplar, Hazel, and Chestnut bible rods 2

32. But I say unto you, That whosoever shall put away his wife, saving for the cause of fornication, causeth her to commit adultery: and whosoever shall marry her that is divorced committeth adultery.

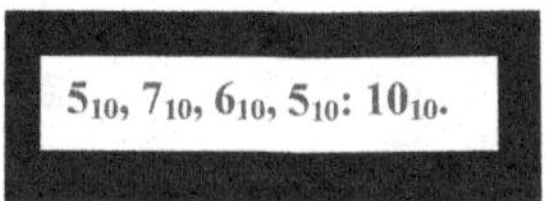
5_{10}, 7_{10}, 6_{10}, 5_{10}: 10_{10}.

Pilled Poplar, Hazel, and Chestnut bible rods 1

$\text{Log}_{10} 10 = 1$ $\text{Log}_{10} 5 = 0.6989$ $\text{Log}_{10} 7 = 0.8450$ $\text{Log}_{10} 6 = 0.7781$ $\text{Log}_{10} 5 = 0.6989$

5, 7, 6, 5: 10. Deep calls unto Deep study bible 1

0.6989, 0.8450, 0.7781, 0.6989: 1

Deep calls unto Deep study bible 2

x-axis	y-axis
5	0.6989
7	0.8450
6	0.7781
5	0.6989
10	1

Water Spout *(lightning; combinatorics)* Study bible 1

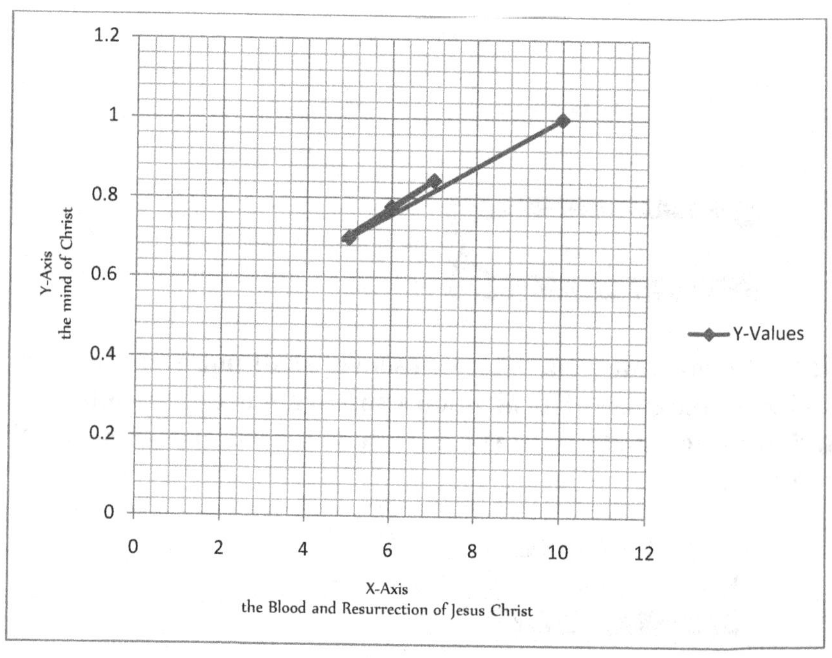

Water Spout *(lightning; combinatorics)* Study bible 2

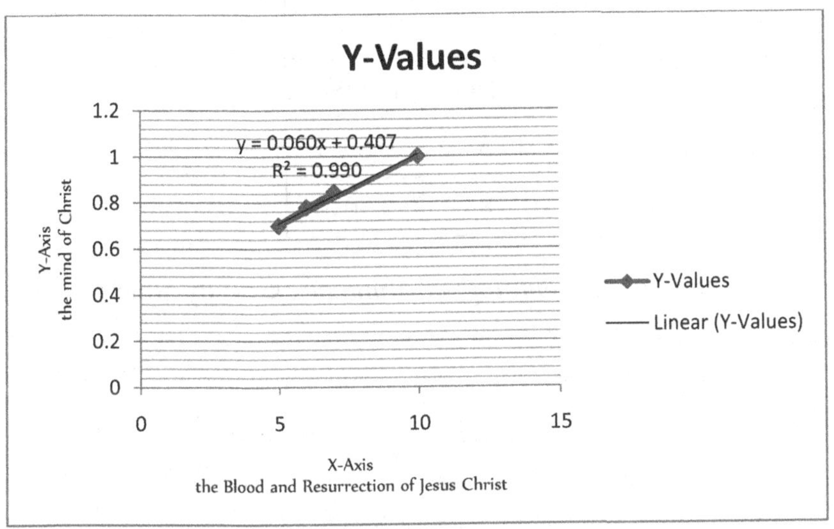

$10^{0.6989}, 10^{0.8450}, 10^{0.7781}, 10^{0.6989}: 10^1.$

Pilled Poplar, Hazel, and Chestnut bible rods 2

33. Again, ye have heard that it hath been said by them of old time, Thou shalt not forswear thyself, but shalt perform unto the Lord thine oaths:

1, 13, 5, 8: Bible Matrices

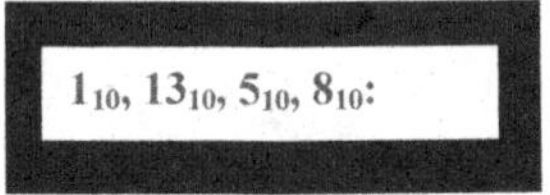
$1_{10}, 13_{10}, 5_{10}, 8_{10}:$

Pilled Poplar, Hazel, and Chestnut bible rods 1

$\text{Log}_{10} 1 = 0$ $\text{Log}_{10} 13 = 1.1139$ $\text{Log}_{10} 5 = 0.6989$ $\text{Log}_{10} 8 = 0.9030$

1, 13, 5, 8: Deep calls unto Deep study bible 1

0, 1.1139, 0.6989, 0.9030: Deep calls unto Deep study bible 2

x-axis	y-axis
1	0
13	1.1139
5	0.6989
8	0.9030

Water Spout *(lightning; combinatorics)* Study bible 1

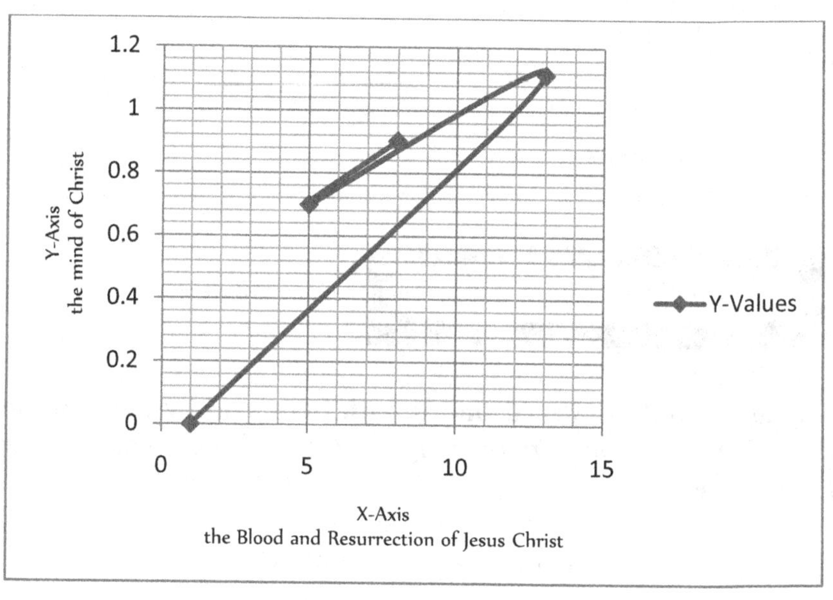

Water Spout *(lightning; combinatorics)* Study bible 2

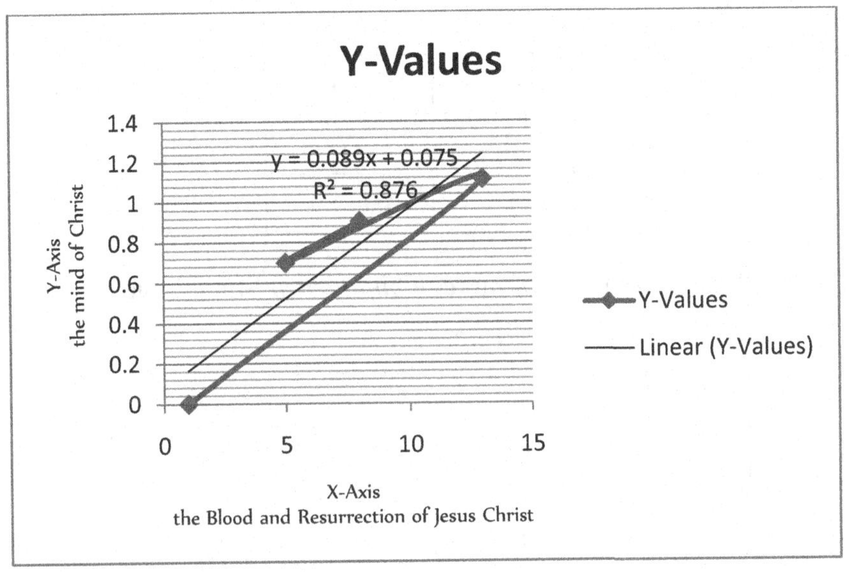

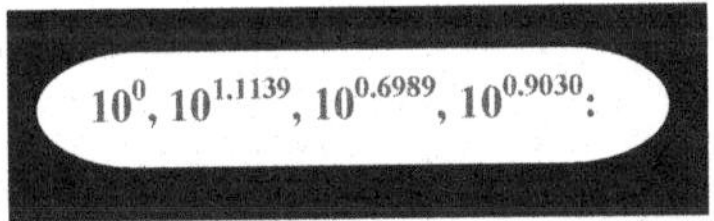

$10^{0}, 10^{1.1139}, 10^{0.6989}, 10^{0.9030}$:

Pilled Poplar, Hazel, and Chestnut bible rods 2

34. But I say unto you, Swear not at all; neither by heaven; for it is God's throne:

5, 4; 3; 5: Bible Matrices

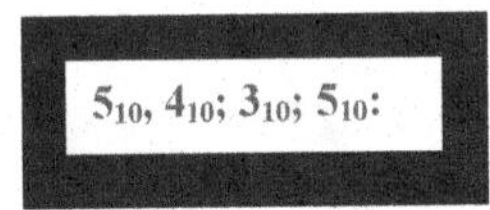

$5_{10}, 4_{10}; 3_{10}; 5_{10}$:

Pilled Poplar, Hazel, and Chestnut bible rods 1

$\text{Log}_{10} 5 = 0.6989$ $\text{Log}_{10} 4 = 0.6020$ $\text{Log}_{10} 3 = 0.4771$ $\text{Log}_{10} 5 = 0.6989$

5, 4; 3; 5: Deep calls unto Deep study bible 1

0.6989, 0.6020; 0.4771; 0.6989:

Deep calls unto Deep study bible 2

x-axis	y-axis
5	0.6989
4	0.6020
3	0.4771
5	0.6989

Water Spout *(lightning; combinatorics)* Study bible 1

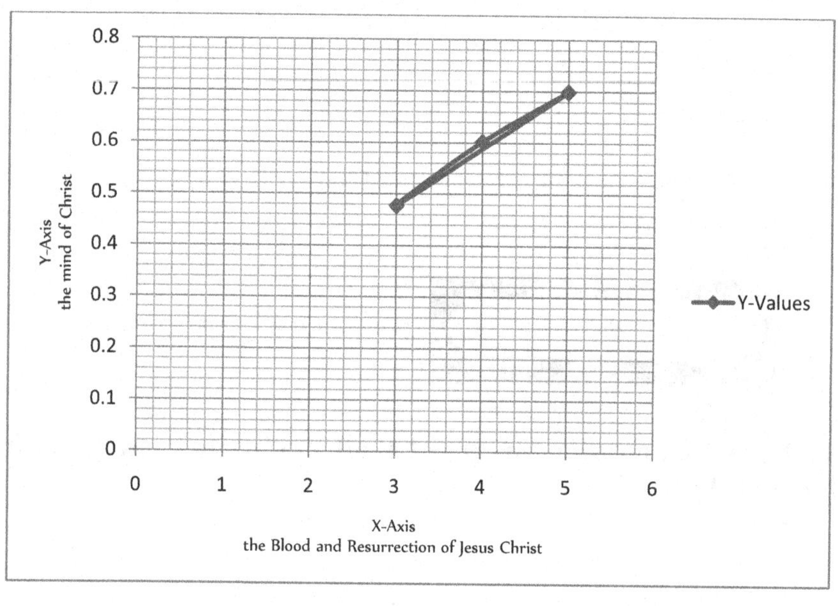

Water Spout *(lightning; combinatorics)* Study bible 2

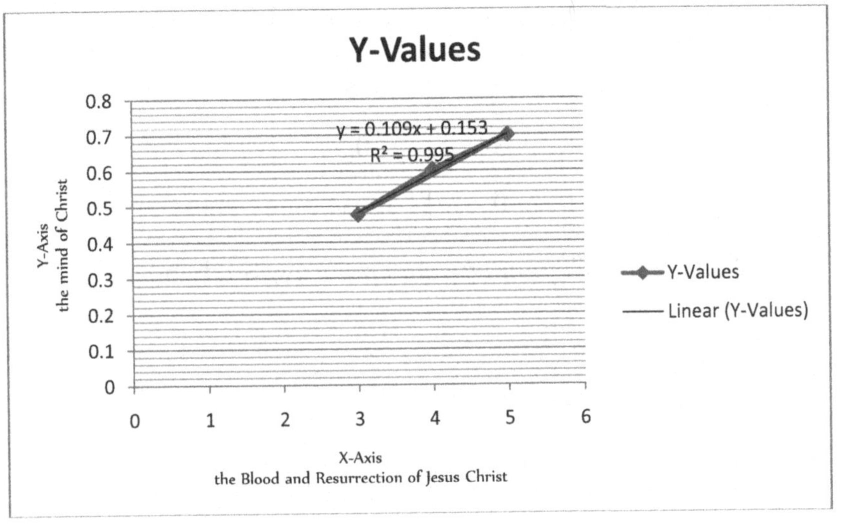

$10^{0.6989}$, $10^{0.6020}$; $10^{0.4771}$; $10^{0.6989}$:

Pilled Poplar, Hazel, and Chestnut bible rods 2

35. Nor by the earth; for it is his footstool: neither by Jerusalem habitation of peace; vision of peace;possession of peace; **for it is the city of the great King.**

4; 5: 3; 9. Bible Matrices

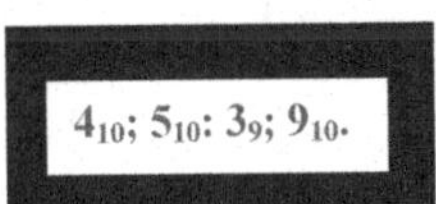
4_{10}; 5_{10}: 3_9; 9_{10}.

Pilled Poplar, Hazel, and Chestnut bible rods 1

$\text{Log}_{10} 4 = 0.6020$ $\text{Log}_{10} 5 = 0.6989$ $\text{Log}_{10} 9 = 0.9542$ $\text{Log}_9 3 = y$

$$9^y = 3$$
$$3^{2y} = 3^1$$
$$2y = 1$$
$$y = \tfrac{1}{2}$$

4; 5: 3; 9. Deep calls unto Deep study bible 1

0.6020; 0.6989: 0.5; 0.9542. Deep calls unto Deep study bible 2

x-axis	y-axis
4	0.6020
5	0.6989
3	0.5
9	0.9542

Water Spout *(lightning; combinatorics)* Study bible 1

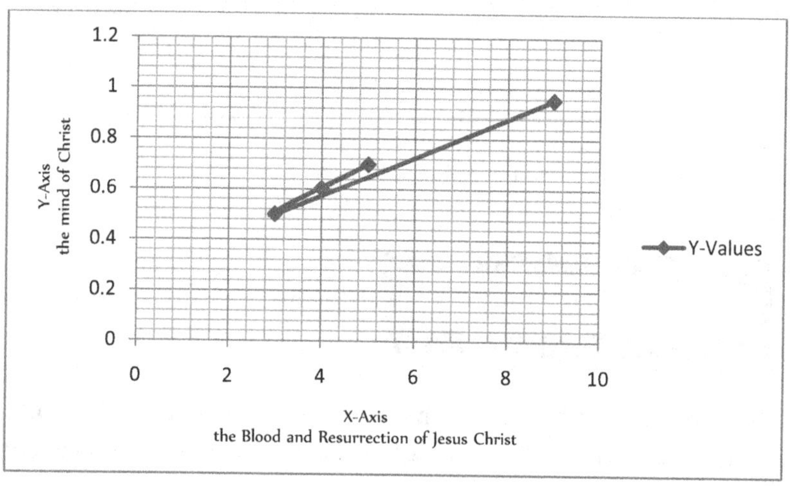

Water Spout *(lightning; combinatorics)* Study bible 2

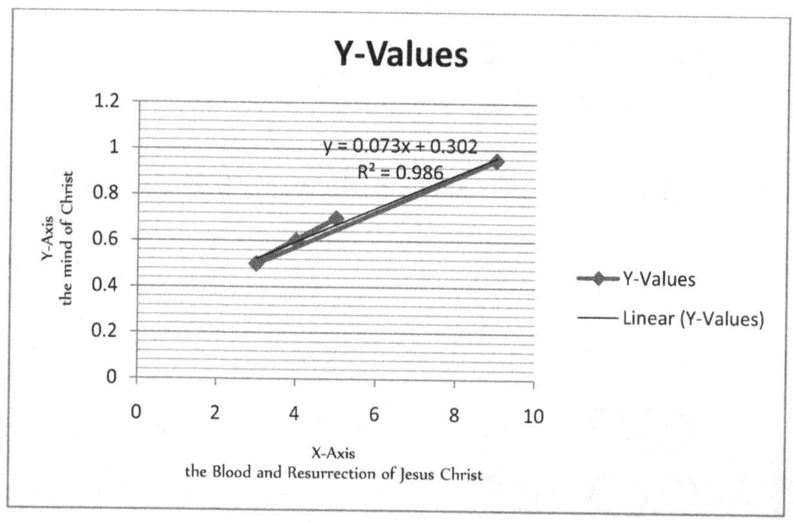

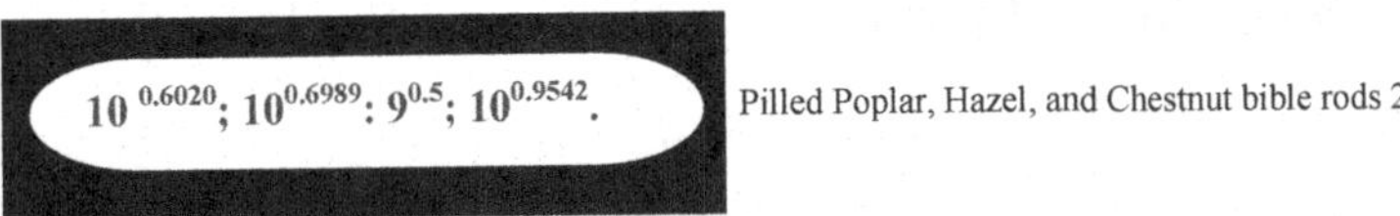

36. Neither shalt thou swear by thy head, because thou canst not make one hair white or black.

7, 10. Bible Matrices

$\text{Log}_{10} 10 = 1$ $\text{Log}_{10} 7 = 0.8450$

7, 10. Deep calls unto Deep study bible 1

0.8450, 1. Deep calls unto Deep study bible 2

x-axis	y-axis
7	0.8450
10	1

Water Spout *(lightning; combinatorics)* Study bible 1

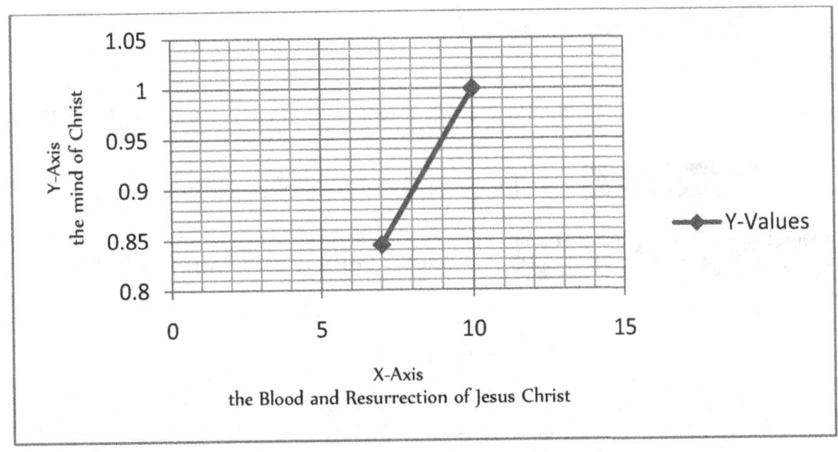

Water Spout *(lightning; combinatorics)* Study bible 2

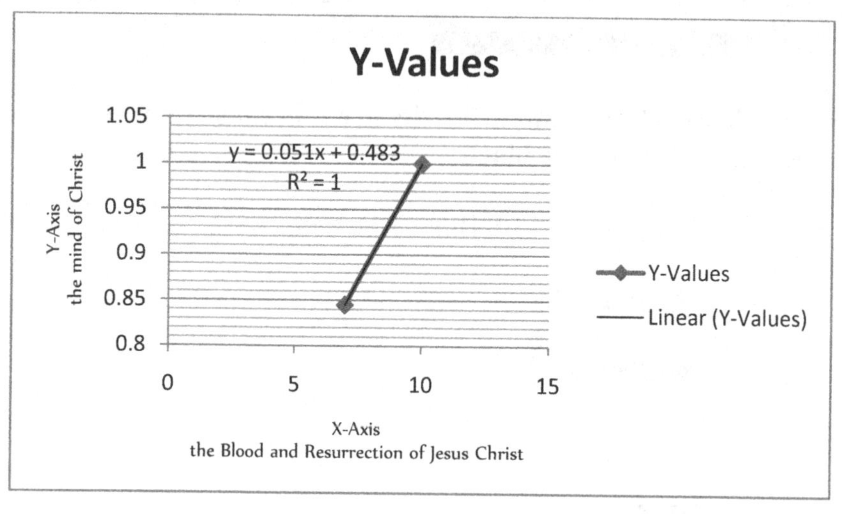

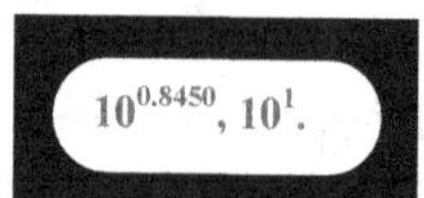

Pilled Poplar, Hazel, and Chestnut bible rods 2

37. But let your communication be, Yea, yea; Nay, nay: for whatsoever is more than these cometh of evil.

5, 1, 1; 1, 1: 9. Bible Matrices

$5_{10}, 1_{10}, 1_{10}; 1_{10}, 1_{10}: 9_{10}.$

Pilled Poplar, Hazel, and Chestnut bible rods 1

$\text{Log}_{10} 5 = 0.6989$ $\text{Log}_{10} 1 = 0$ $\text{Log}_{10} 1 = 0$ $\text{Log}_{10} 1 = 0$ $\text{Log}_{10} 1 = 0$ $\text{Log}_{10} 9 = 0.9542$

5, 1, 1; 1, 1: 9. Deep calls unto Deep study bible 1

0.6989, 0, 0; 0, 0: 0.9542. Deep calls unto Deep study bible 2

x-axis	y-axis
5	0.6989

1	0
1	0
1	0
1	0
9	0.9542

Water Spout *(lightning; combinatorics)* Study bible 1

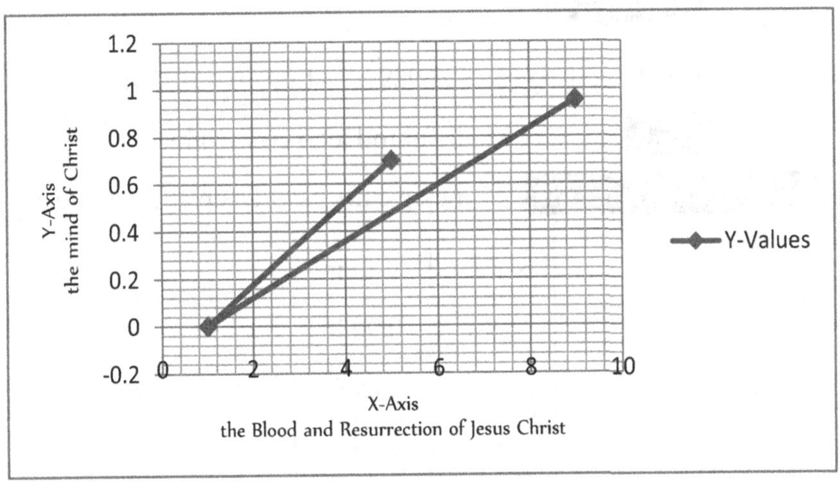

Water Spout *(lightning; combinatorics)* Study bible 2

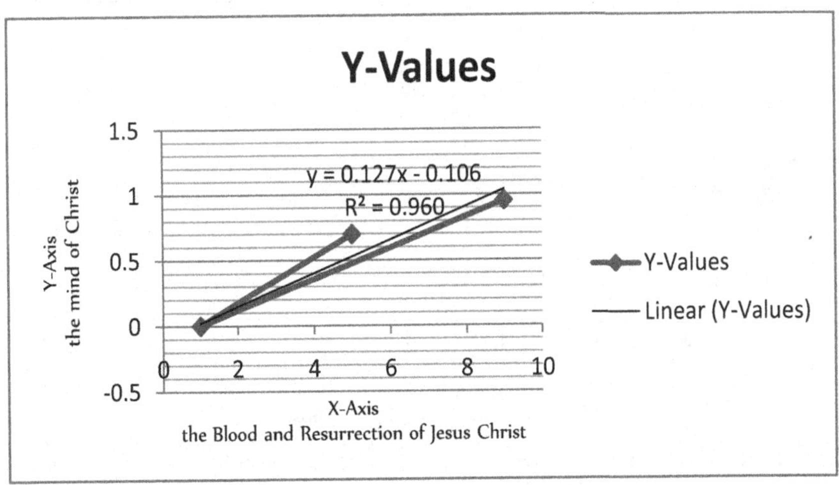

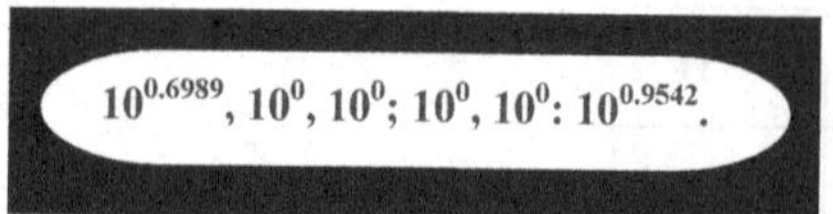

Pilled Poplar, Hazel, and Chestnut bible rods 2

38. Ye have heard that it hath been said, An eye for an eye, and a tooth for a tooth:

8, 5, 6: Bible Matrices

Pilled Poplar, Hazel, and Chestnut bible rods 1

$\text{Log}_{10} 8 = 0.9030$ $\text{Log}_{10} 5 = 0.6989$ $\text{Log}_{10} 6 = 0.7781$

8, 5, 6. Deep calls unto Deep study bible 1

0.9030, 0.6989, 0.7781: Deep calls unto Deep study bible 2

x-axis	y-axis
8	0.9030
5	0.6989
6	0.7781

Water Spout *(lightning; combinatorics)* Study bible 1

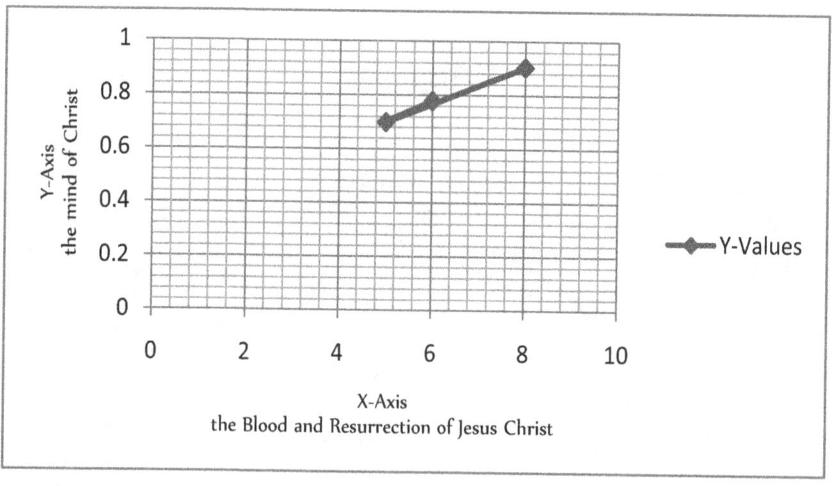

Water Spout *(lightning; combinatorics)* Study bible 2

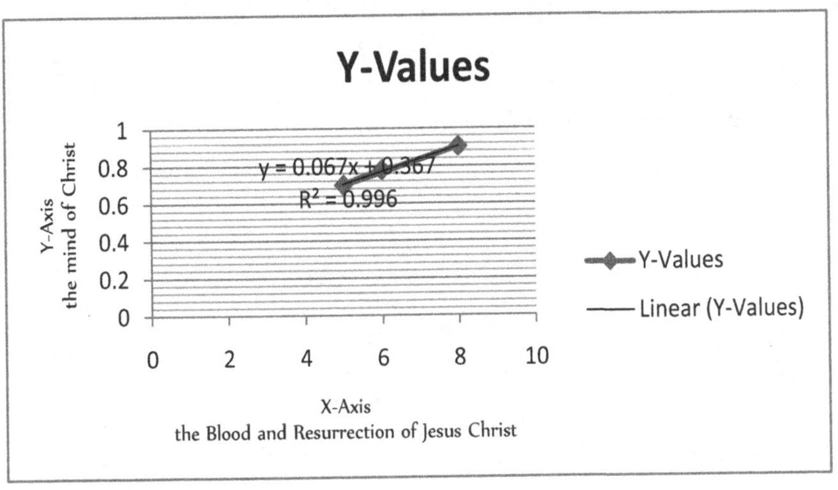

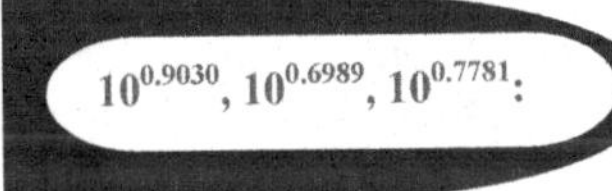

$10^{0.9030}, 10^{0.6989}, 10^{0.7781}$:

Pilled Poplar, Hazel, and Chestnut bible rods 2

39. But I say unto you, That ye resist not evil: but whosoever shall smite thee on thy right cheek, turn to him the other also.

5, 5: 9, 6. Bible Matrices

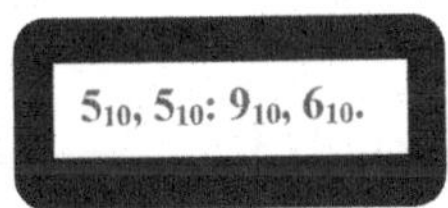

$5_{10}, 5_{10}: 9_{10}, 6_{10}$.

Pilled Poplar, Hazel, and Chestnut bible rods 1

$\text{Log}_{10} 5 = 0.6989$ $\text{Log}_{10} 6 = 0.7781$ $\text{Log}_{10} 5 = 0.6989$ $\text{Log}_{10} 9 = 0.9542$

5, 5: 9, 6. Deep calls unto Deep study bible 1

0.6989, 0.6989: 0.9542, 0.7781.

Deep calls unto Deep study bible 2

x-axis	y-axis
5	0.6989
5	0.6989

9	0.9542
6	0.7781

Water Spout *(lightning; combinatorics)* Study bible 1

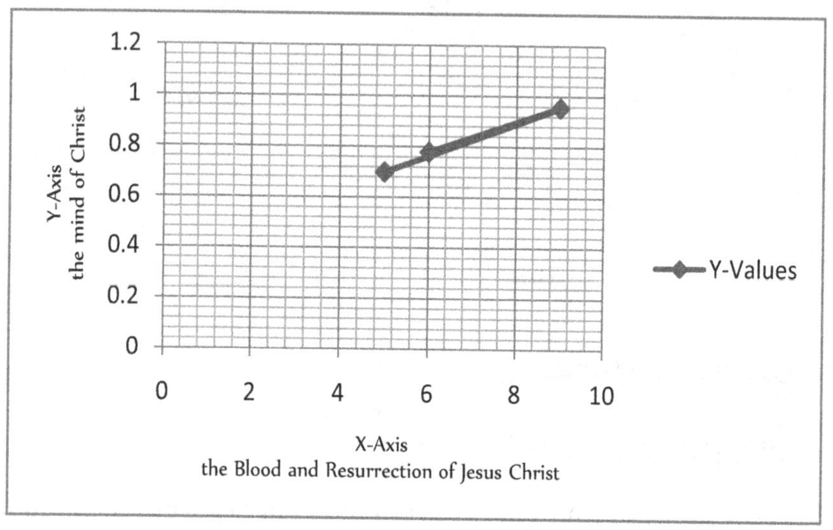

Water Spout *(lightning; combinatorics)* Study bible 2

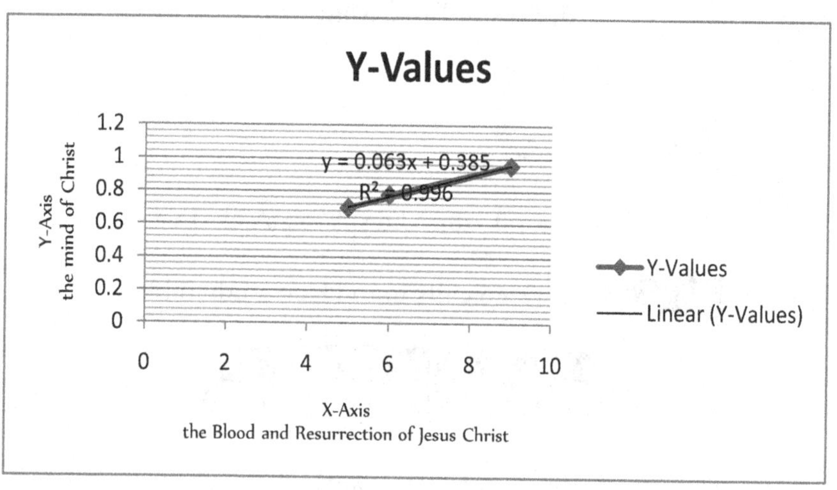

$10^{0.6989}$, $10^{0.6989}$: $10^{0.9542}$, $10^{0.7781}$. Pilled Poplar, Hazel, and Chestnut bible rods 2

40. And if any man will sue thee at the law, and take away thy coat, let him have thy cloke also.

10, 5, 6. Bible Matrices

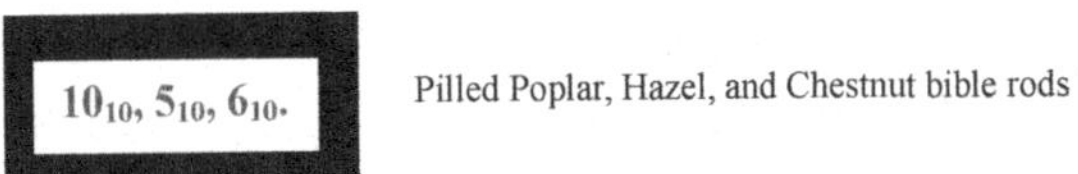

Pilled Poplar, Hazel, and Chestnut bible rods 1

$Log_{10} 10 = 1$ $Log_{10} 5 = 0.6989$ $Log_{10} 6 = 0.7781$

10, 5, 6. Deep calls unto Deep study bible 1

1, 0.6989, 0.7781. Deep calls unto Deep study bible 2

x-axis	y-axis
10	1
5	0.6989
6	0.7781

Water Spout *(lightning; combinatorics)* Study bible 1

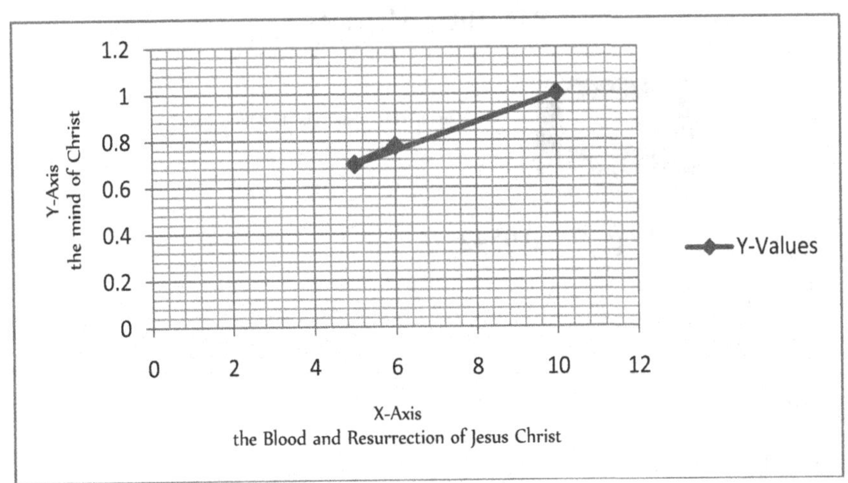

Water Spout *(lightning; combinatorics)* Study bible 2

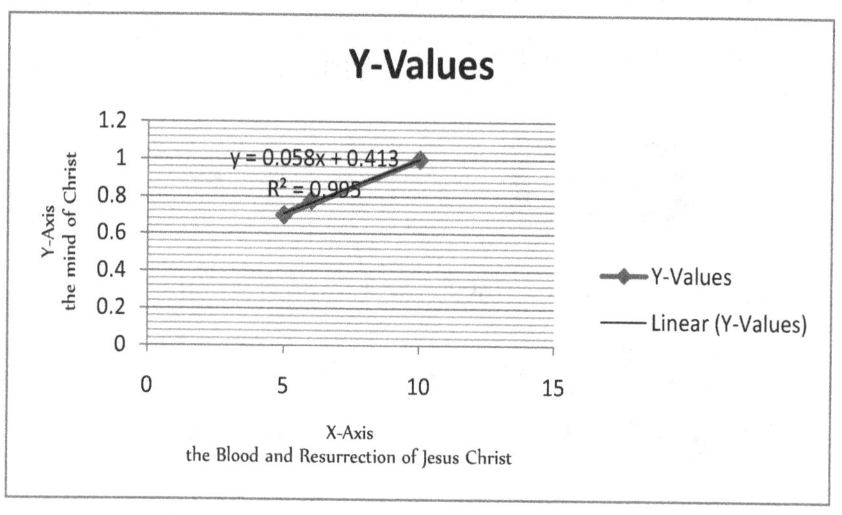

Pilled Poplar, Hazel, and Chestnut bible rods 2

41. And whosoever shall compel thee to go a mile, go with him twain witness, support; 2 x 1.

9, 4. Bible Matrices

Pilled Poplar, Hazel, and Chestnut bible rods 1

$\log_4 4 = y$ $\log_{10} 9 = 0.9542$

$4^y = 4$

$2^{2y} = 2^2$

$2y = 2$

$y = 1$

9, 4. Deep calls unto Deep study bible 1

0.9542, 1. Deep calls unto Deep study bible 2

x-axis	y-axis
9	0.9542
4	1

Water Spout *(lightning; combinatorics)* Study bible 1

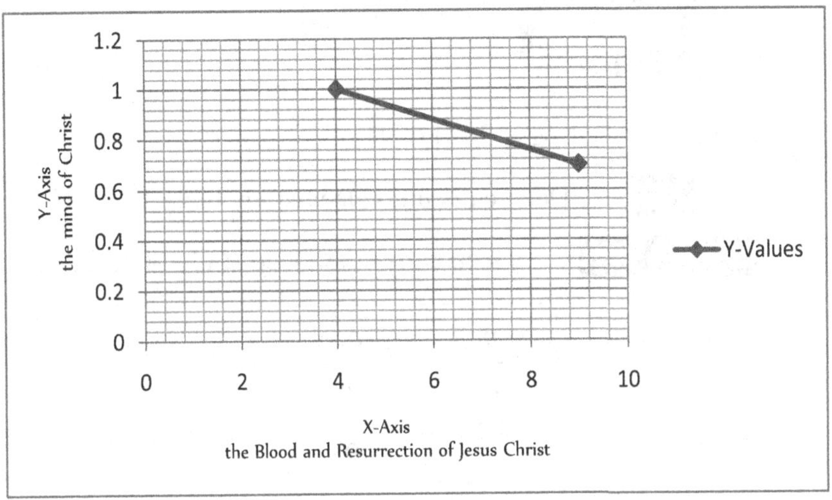

Water Spout *(lightning; combinatorics)* Study bible 2

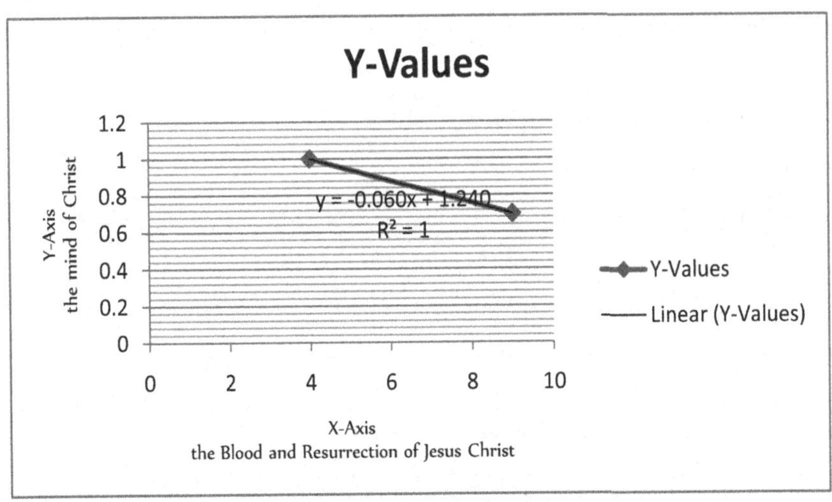

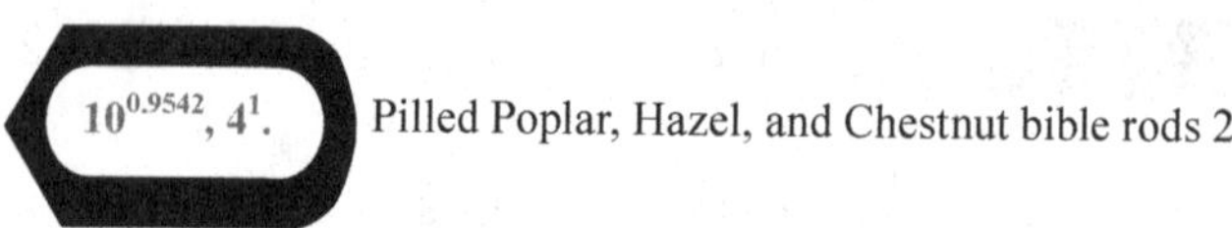

42. Give to him that asketh thee, and from him that would borrow of thee turn not thou away.

6, 12. Bible Matrices

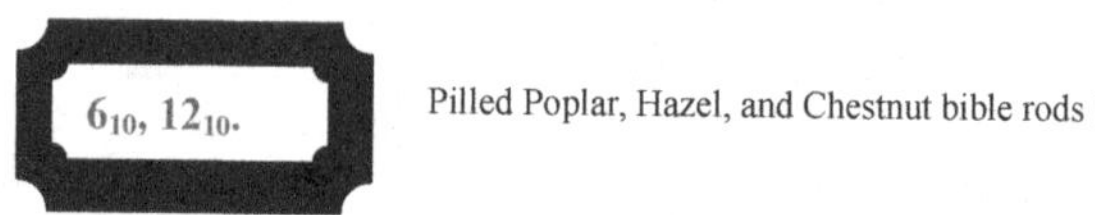

$\text{Log}_{10} 6 = 0.7781$ $\text{Log}_{10} 12 = 1.0791$

6, 12. Deep calls unto Deep study bible 1

0.7781, 1.0791 Deep calls unto Deep study bible 2

x-axis	y-axis
6	0.7781
12	1.0791

Water Spout *(lightning; combinatorics)* Study bible 1

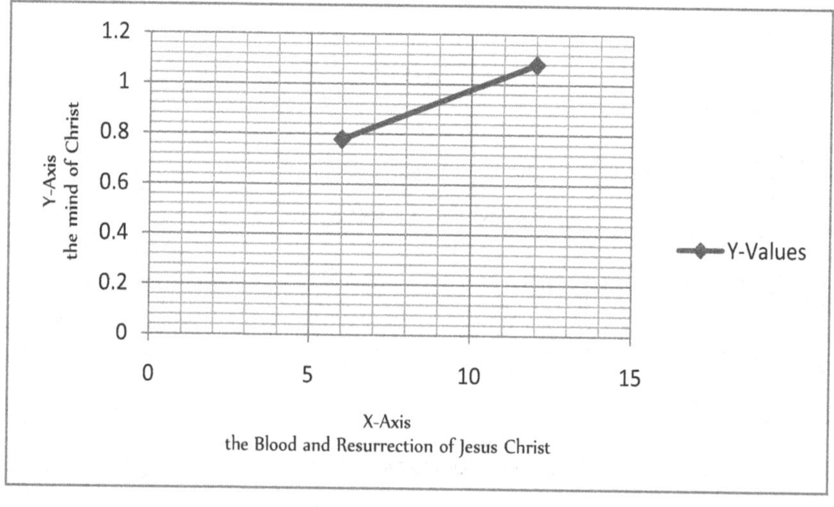

Water Spout *(lightning; combinatorics)* Study bible 2

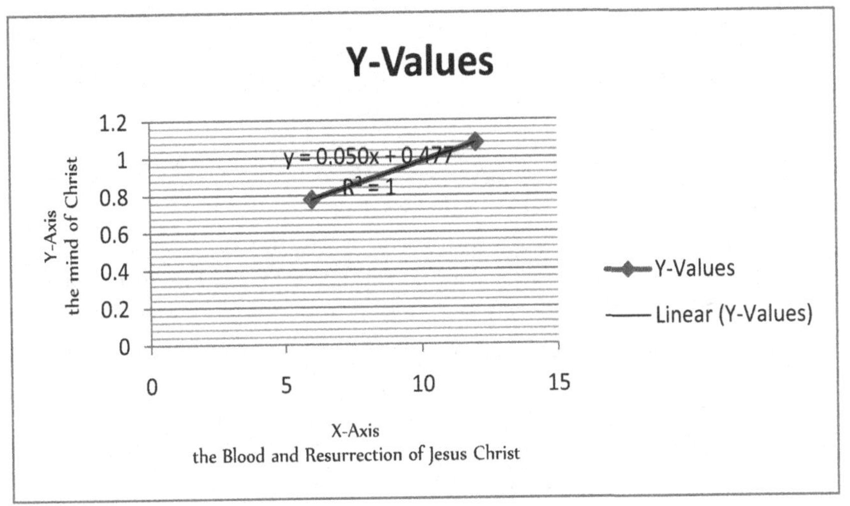

Pilled Poplar, Hazel, and Chestnut bible rods 2

43. Ye have heard that it hath been said, Thou shalt love thy neighbour, and hate thine enemy.

8, 5, 4. Bible Matrices

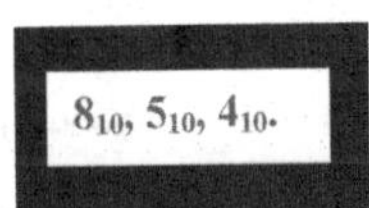

Pilled Poplar, Hazel, and Chestnut bible rods 1

$\text{Log}_{10} 8 = 0.9030$ $\text{Log}_{10} 5 = 0.6989$ $\text{Log}_{10} 4 = 0.6020$

8, 5, 4. Deep calls unto Deep study bible 1

0.9030, 0.6989, 0.6020. Deep calls unto Deep study bible 2

x-axis	y-axis
8	0.9030
5	0.6989
4	0.6020

Water Spout *(lightning; combinatorics)* Study bible 1

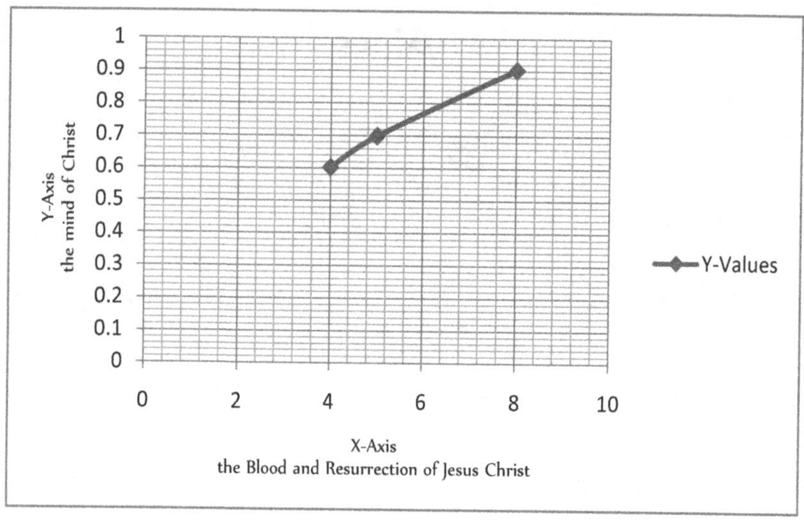

Water Spout *(lightning; combinatorics)* Study bible 2

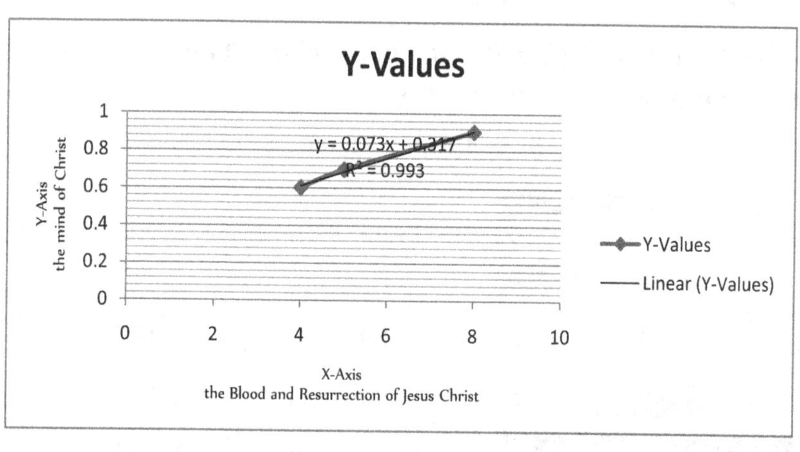

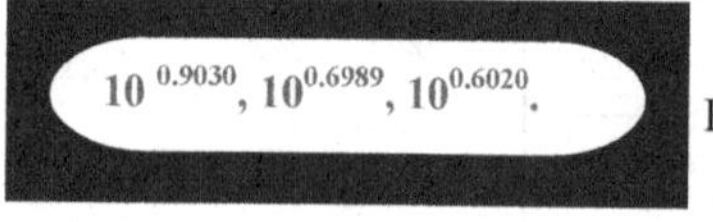

Pilled Poplar, Hazel, and Chestnut bible rods 2

44. But I say unto you, Love your enemies, bless them that curse you, do good to them that hate you, and pray for them which despitefully use you, and persecute you;

5, 3, 5, 7, 8, 3; Bible Matrices

$5_{10}, 3_{10}, 5_{10}, 7_{10}, 8_{10}, 3_{10}$; Pilled Poplar, Hazel, and Chestnut bible rods 1

$\text{Log}_{10}3 = 0.4771$ $\text{Log}_{10}5 = 0.6989$ $\text{Log}_{10}7 = 0.8450$ $\text{Log}_{10}8 = 0.9030$ $\text{Log}_{10}5 = 0.6989$

5, 3, 5, 7, 8, 3; Deep calls unto Deep study bible 1

0.6989, 0.4771, 0.6989, 0.8450, 0.9030, 0.4771;
Deep calls unto Deep study bible 2

x-axis	y-axis
5	0.6989
3	0.4771
5	0.6989
7	0.8450
8	0.9030
3	0.4771

Water Spout *(lightning; combinatorics)* Study bible 1

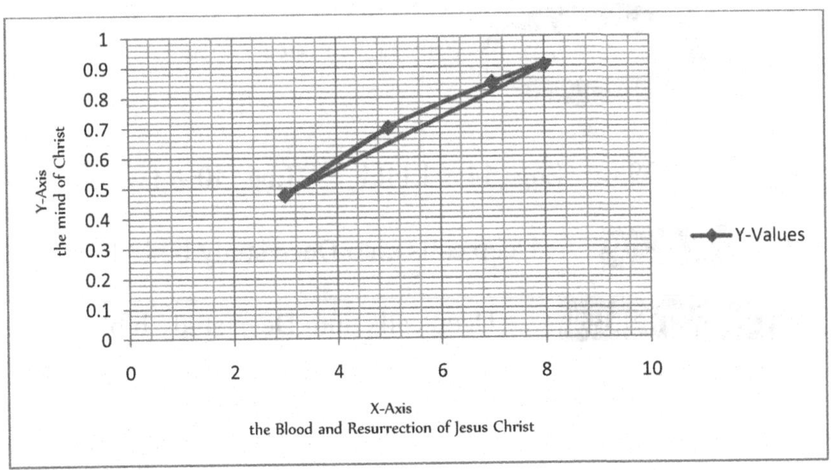

Water Spout *(lightning; combinatorics)* Study bible 2

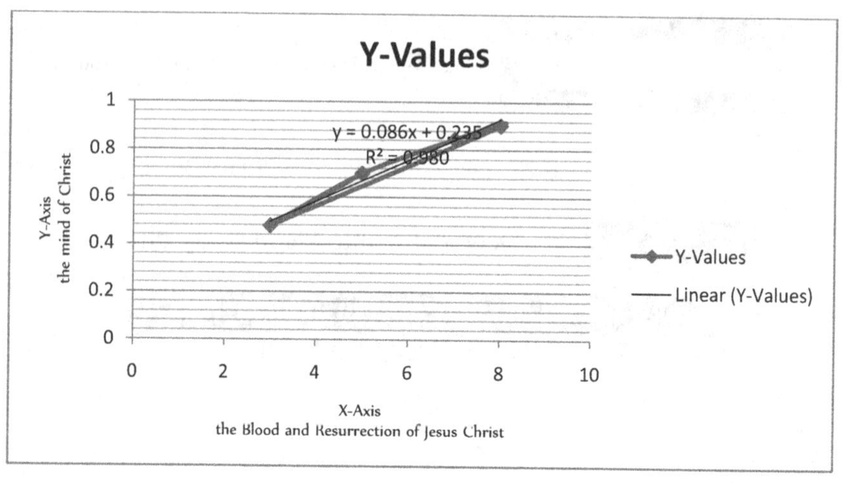

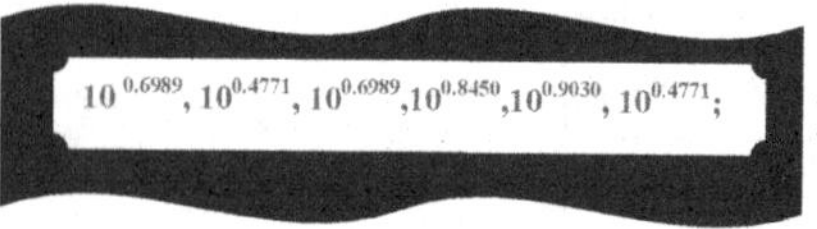

Pilled Poplar, Hazel, and Chestnut bible rods 2

45. That ye may be the children of your Father which is in heaven: for he maketh his sun to rise on the evil and on the good, and sendeth rain on the just and on the unjust.

13: 14, 10. Bible Matrices

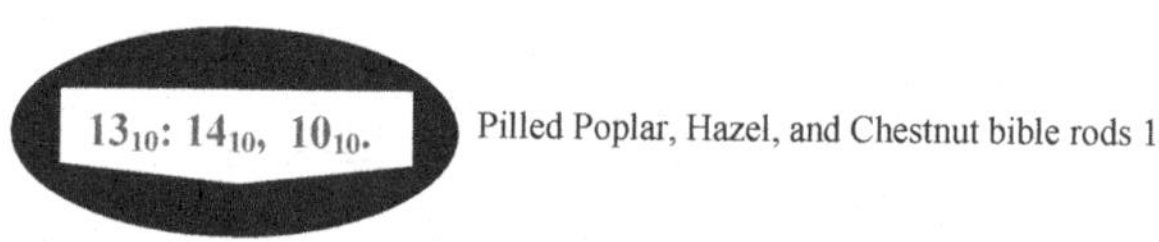

Pilled Poplar, Hazel, and Chestnut bible rods 1

$\text{Log}_{10} 13 = 1.1139$ $\text{Log}_{10} 14 = 1.1461$ $\text{Log}_{10} 10 = 1$

13: 14, 10. Deep calls unto Deep study bible 1

1.1139: 1.1461, 1. Deep calls unto Deep study bible 2

x-axis	y-axis
13	1.1139
14	1.1461
10	1

Water Spout *(lightning; combinatorics)* Study bible 1

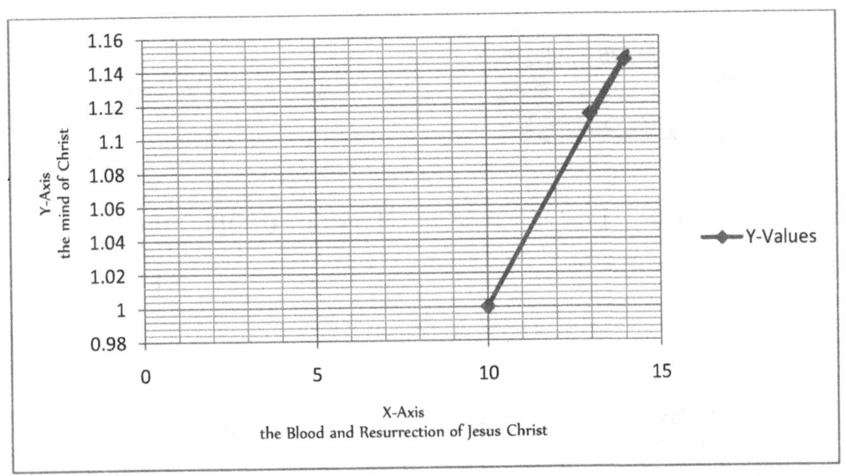

Water Spout *(lightning; combinatorics)* Study bible 2

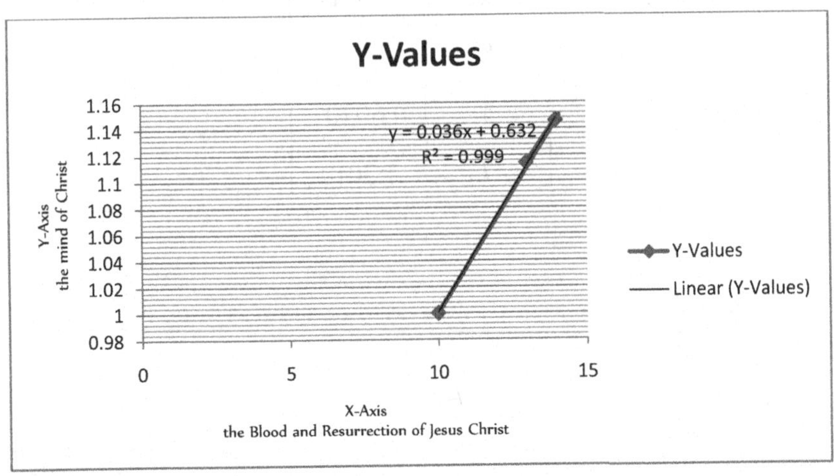

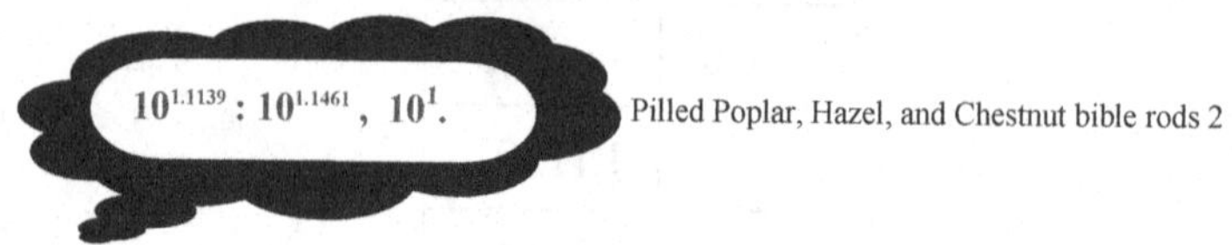

Pilled Poplar, Hazel, and Chestnut bible rods 2

46. For if ye love them which love you, what reward have ye? do not even the publicans one who farmed the taxes **the same?**

8, 4? 7? Bible Matrices

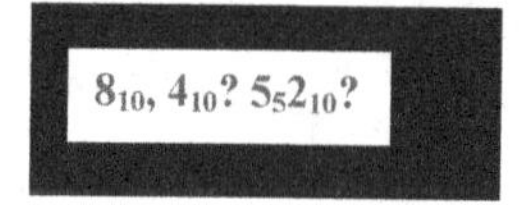

Pilled Poplar, Hazel, and Chestnut bible rods 1

$\mathrm{Log}_{10} 8 = 0.9030$ $\mathrm{Log}_{10} 4 = 0.6020$ $\mathrm{Log}_{10} 2 = 0.3010$ $\mathrm{Log}_5 5 = y$

$\mathrm{Log}\ 5^y = 5^1$

$y = 1$

8, 4? 7? Deep calls unto Deep study bible 1

0.9030, 0.6020? 1 0.3010? Deep calls unto Deep study bible 2

x-axis	y-axis
8	0.9030
4	0.6020
7	1.3010

Water Spout *(lightning; combinatorics)* Study bible 1

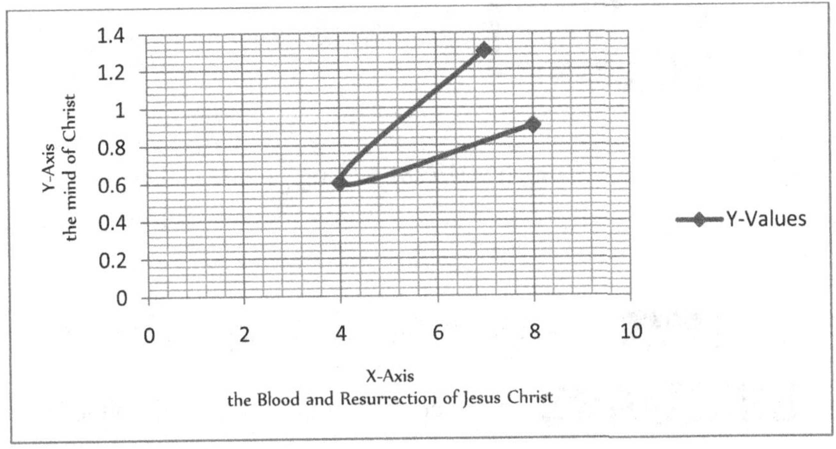

Water Spout *(lightning; combinatorics)* Study bible 2

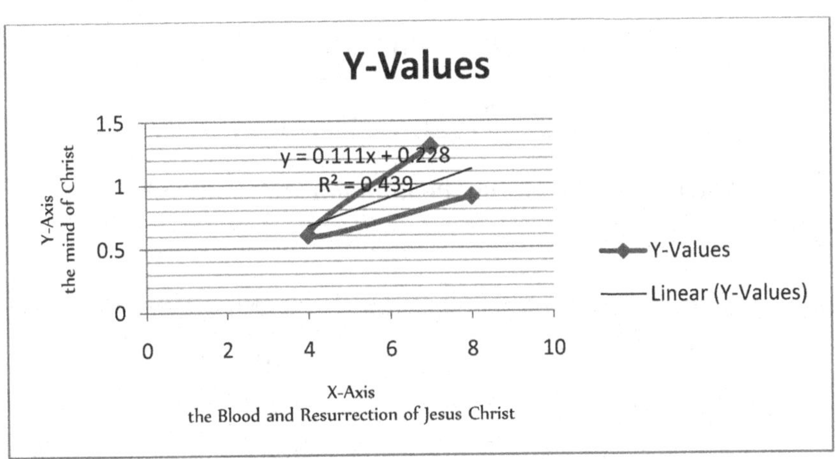

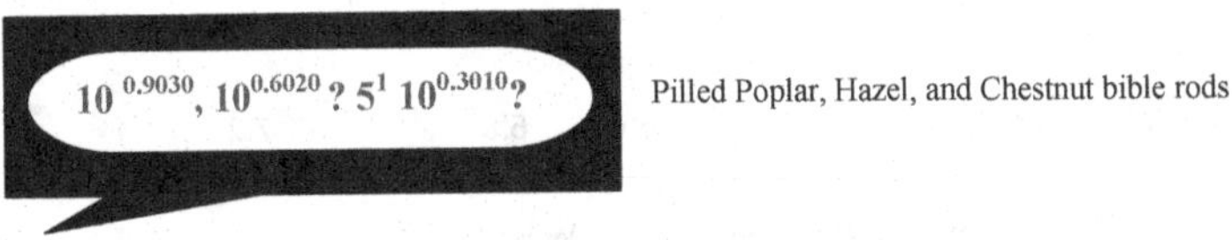

Pilled Poplar, Hazel, and Chestnut bible rods 2

47. And if ye salute your brethren only, what do ye more than others? do not even the publicansone who farmed the taxes **so?**

7, 6? 6? Bible Matrices

$7_{10}, 6_{10}? 5_5 1_{10}?$ Pilled Poplar, Hazel, and Chestnut bible rods 1

$\text{Log}_{10} 7 = 0.8450$ $\text{Log}_{10} 6 = 0.7781$ $\text{Log}_{10} 1 = 0$ $\text{Log}_5 5 = y$

$\text{Log } 5^y = 5^1$

$y = 1$

7, 6? 6? Deep calls unto Deep study bible 1

0.8450, 0.7781? 1 0? Deep calls unto Deep study bible 2

x-axis	y-axis
7	0.8450
6	0.7781
6	1

Water Spout *(lightning; combinatorics)* Study bible 1

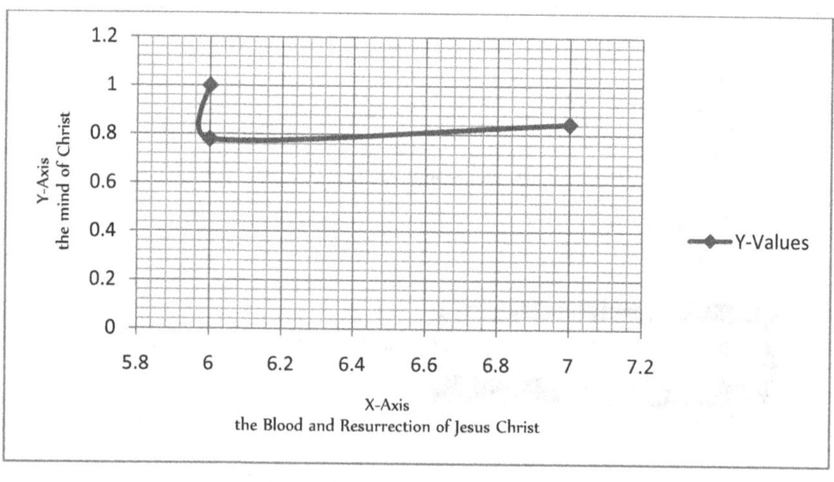

Water Spout *(lightning; combinatorics)* Study bible 2

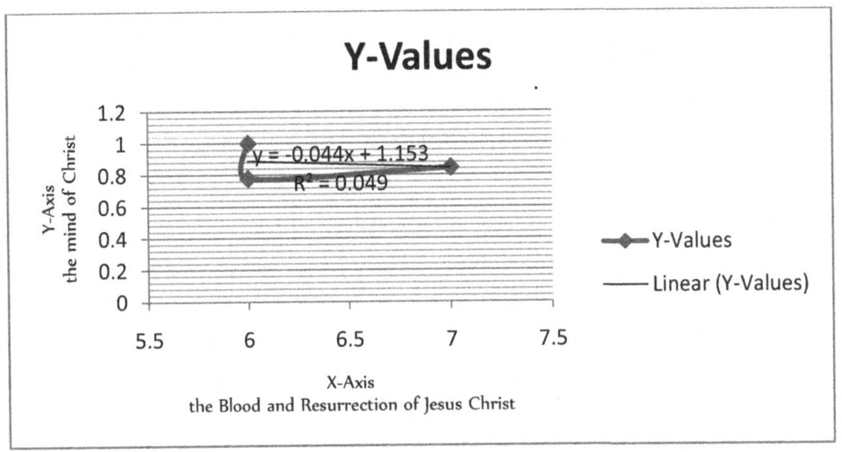

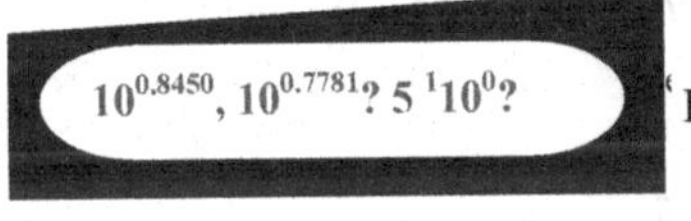
$10^{0.8450}$, $10^{0.7781}$? 5 '10^0?

Pilled Poplar, Hazel, and Chestnut bible rods 2

48. Be ye therefore perfect, even as your Father which is in heaven is perfect.

4, 10. Bible Matrices

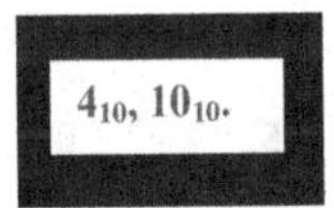
4_{10}, 10_{10}.

Pilled Poplar, Hazel, and Chestnut bible rods 1

$\text{Log}_{10} 10 = 1$ $\text{Log}_{10} 4 = 0.6020$

4, 10. Deep calls unto Deep study bible 1

0.6020, 1. Deep calls unto Deep study bible 2

x-axis	y-axis
4	0.6020
10	1

Water Spout *(lightning; combinatorics)* Study bible 1

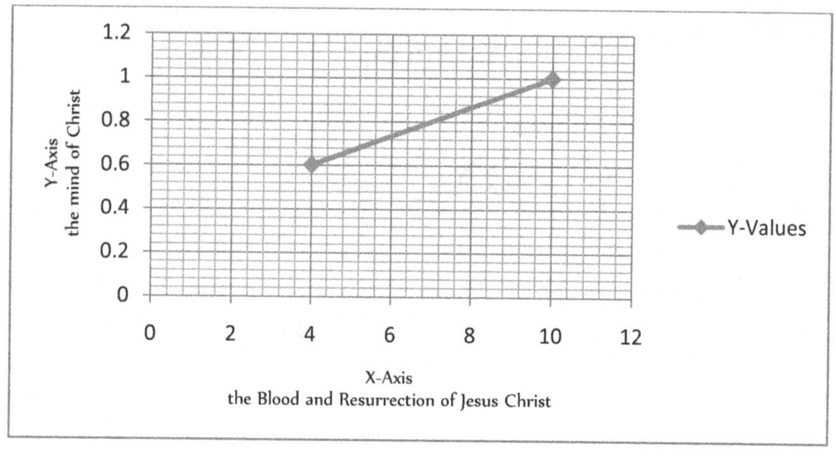

Water Spout *(lightning; combinatorics)* Study bible 2

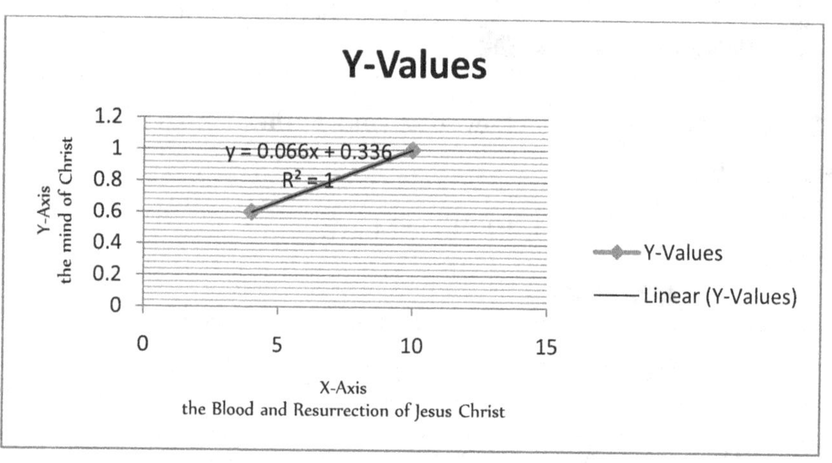

$10^{0.6020}$, 10^{1}. Pilled Poplar, Hazel, and Chestnut bible rods 2

CHAPTER 6

1. Take heed that ye do not your alms before men, to be seen of them: otherwise ye have no reward of your Father which is in heaven.

10, 5: 12. Bible Matrices

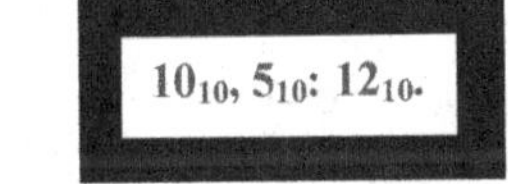
$10_{10}, 5_{10}: 12_{10}.$

Pilled Poplar, Hazel, and Chestnut bible rods 1

$Log_{10}\ 10 = 1$ $Log_{10}\ 5 = 0.6989$ $Log_{10}\ 12 = 1.0791$

10, 5: 12. Deep calls unto Deep study bible 1

1, 0.6989: 1.0791. Deep calls unto Deep study bible 2

x-axis	y-axis
10	1
5	0.6989
12	1.0791

Water Spout *(lightning; combinatorics)* Study bible 1

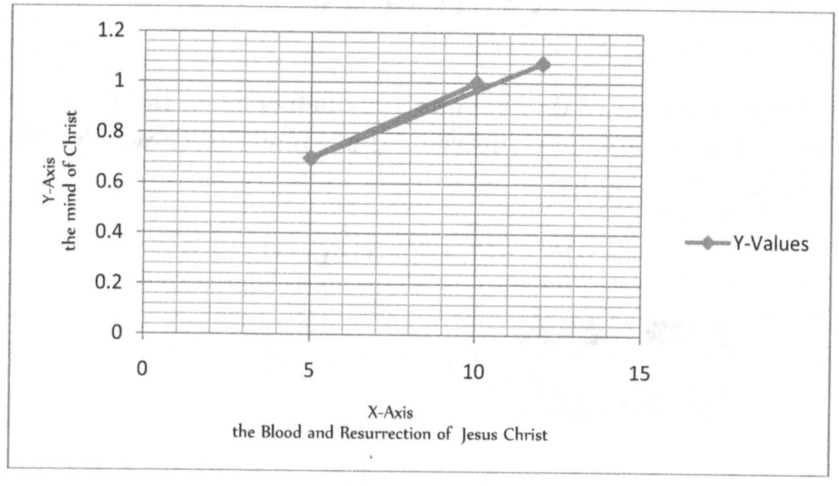

Water Spout *(lightning; combinatorics)* Study bible 2

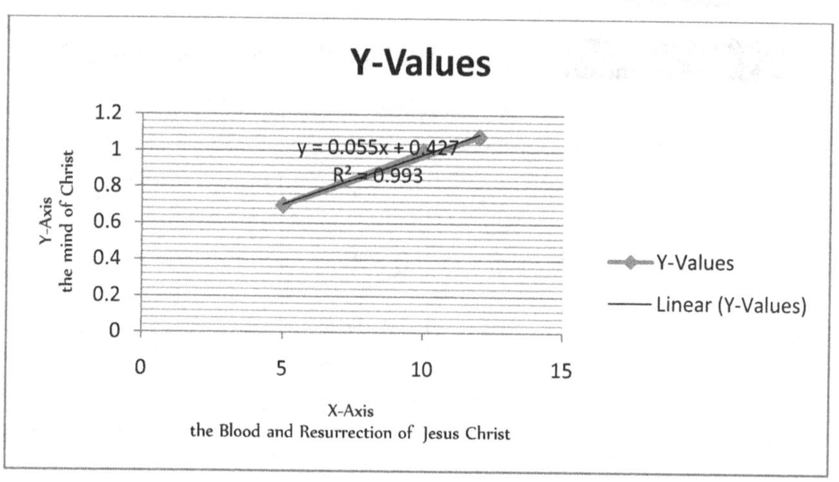

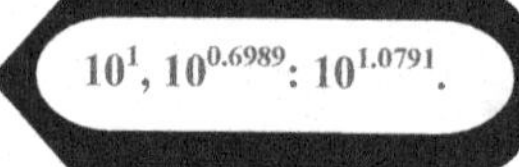

Pilled Poplar, Hazel, and Chestnut bible rods 2

2. Therefore when thou doest thine alms, do not sound a trumpet before thee, as the hypocrites do in the synagogues and in the streets, that they may have glory of men. Verily I say unto you, They have their reward.

6, 7, 11, 7. 5, 4. Bible Matrices

$6_{10}, 7_{10}, 11_{10}, 7_{10}. 5_{10}, 4_{10}.$ Pilled Poplar, Hazel, and Chestnut bible rods 1

$\text{Log}_{10} 11 = 1.0413$ $\text{Log}_{10} 5 = 0.6989$ $\text{Log}_{10} 7 = 0.8450$ $\text{Log}_{10} 6 = 0.7781$ $\text{Log}_{10} 4 = 0.6020$

6, 7, 11, 7. 5, 4. Deep calls unto Deep study bible 1

0.7781, 0.8450, 1.0413, 0.8450. 0.6989, 0.6020.
Deep calls unto Deep study bible 2

x-axis	y-axis
6	0.7781
7	0.8450
11	1.0413
7	0.8450
5	0.6989
4	0.6020

Water Spout *(lightning; combinatorics)* Study bible 1

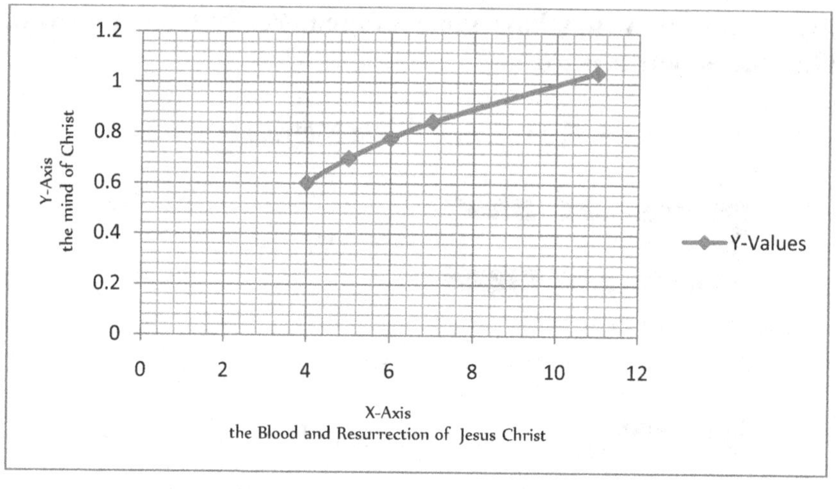

Water Spout *(lightning; combinatorics)* Study bible 2

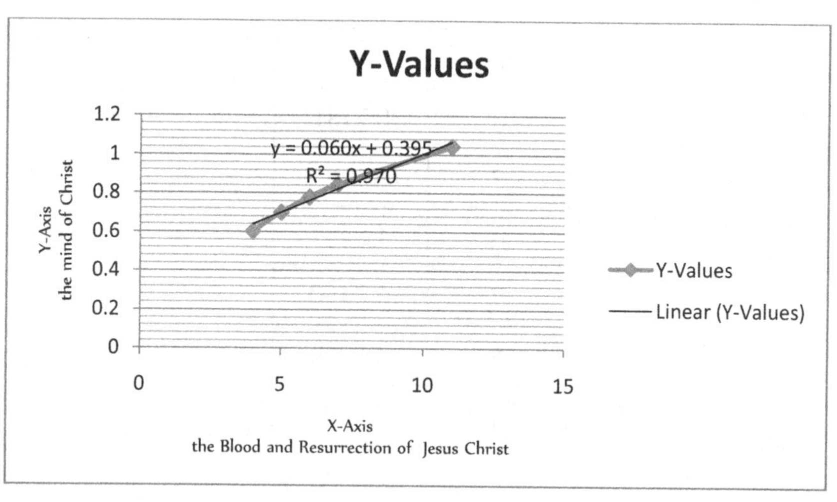

Pilled Poplar, Hazel, and Chestnut bible rods 2

3. But when thou doest alms, let not thy left hand know what thy right hand doeth:

5, 11: Bible Matrices

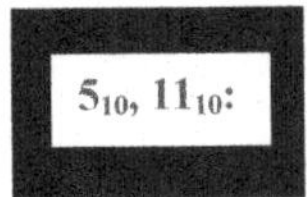

Pilled Poplar, Hazel, and Chestnut bible rods 1

$\text{Log}_{10} 5 = 0.6989$ $\text{Log}_{10} 11 = 1.0413$

5, 11: Deep calls unto Deep study bible 1

0.6989, 1.0413: Deep calls unto Deep study bible 2

x-axis	y-axis
5	0.6989
11	1.0413

Water Spout *(lightning; combinatorics)* Study bible 1

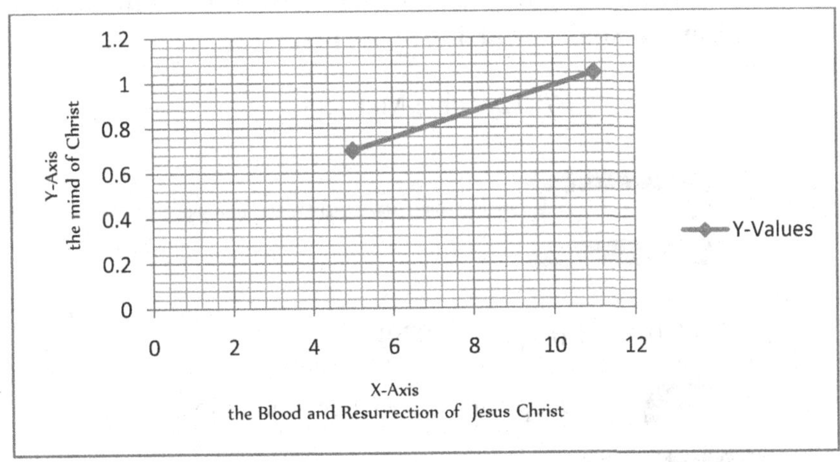

Water Spout *(lightning; combinatorics)* Study bible 2

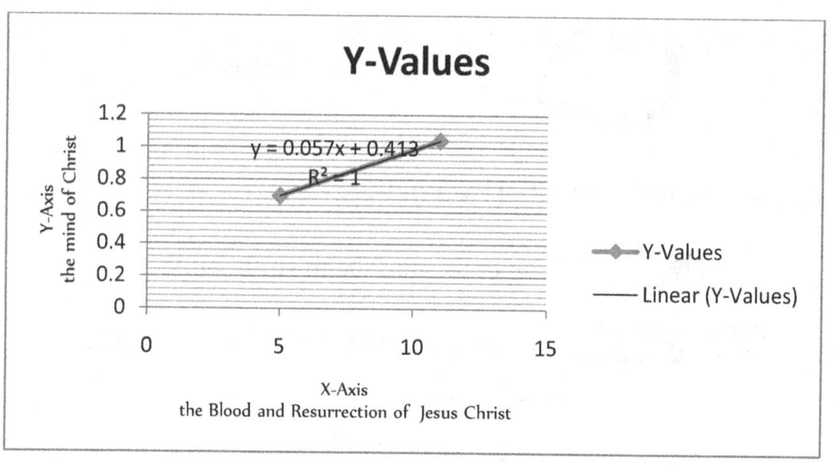

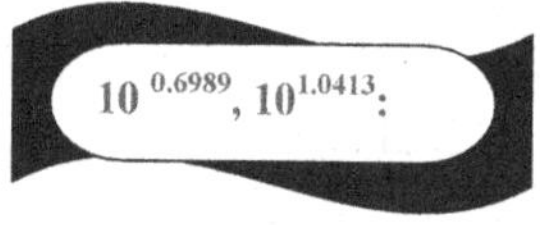

Pilled Poplar, Hazel, and Chestnut bible rods 2

4. That thine alms may be in secret: and thy Father which seeth in secret himself shall reward thee openly.

7: 12. Bible Matrices

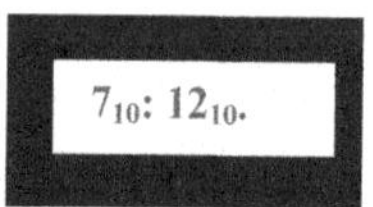

Pilled Poplar, Hazel, and Chestnut bible rods 1

$\text{Log}_{10} 7 = 0.8450$ $\text{Log}_{10} 12 = 1.0791$

7: 12. Deep calls unto Deep study bible 1

0.8450, 1.0791. Deep calls unto Deep study bible 2

x-axis	y-axis
7	0.8450

12	1.0791

Water Spout *(lightning; combinatorics)* Study bible 1

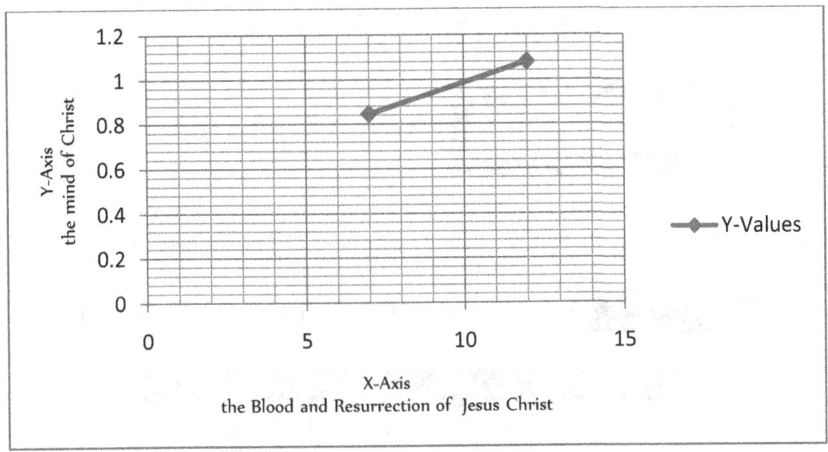

Water Spout *(lightning; combinatorics)* Study bible 2

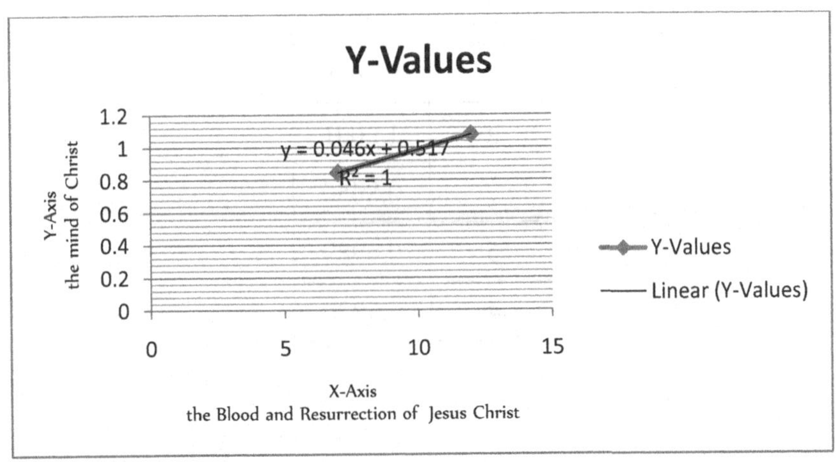

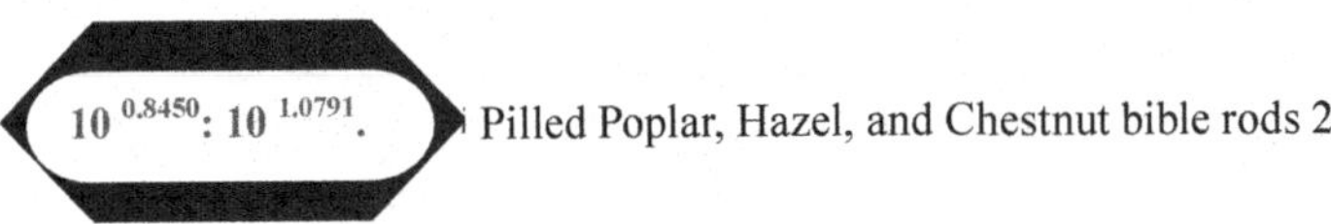

Pilled Poplar, Hazel, and Chestnut bible rods 2

5. And when thou prayest, thou shalt not be as the hypocrites are: for they love to pray standing in the synagogues and in the corners of the streets, that they may be seen of men. Verily I say unto you, They have their reward.

4, 8: 16, 7. 5, 4. Bible Matrices

$4_{10}, 8_{10}: 16_{10}, 7_{10}. 5_{10}, 4_{10}.$ Pilled Poplar, Hazel, and Chestnut bible rods 1

$\text{Log}_{10}4 = 0.6020$ $\text{Log}_{10}8 = 0.9030$ $\text{Log}_{10}7 = 0.8450$ $\text{Log}_{10}16 = 1.2041$ $\text{Log}_{10}5 = 0.6989$

4, 8: 16, 7. 5, 4. Deep calls unto Deep study bible 1

0.6020, 0.9030: 1.2041, 0.8450. 0.6989, 0.6020.
Deep calls unto Deep study bible 2

x-axis	y-axis
4	0.6020
8	0.9030
16	1.2041
7	0.8450
5	0.6989
4	0.6020

Water Spout *(lightning; combinatorics)* Study bible 1

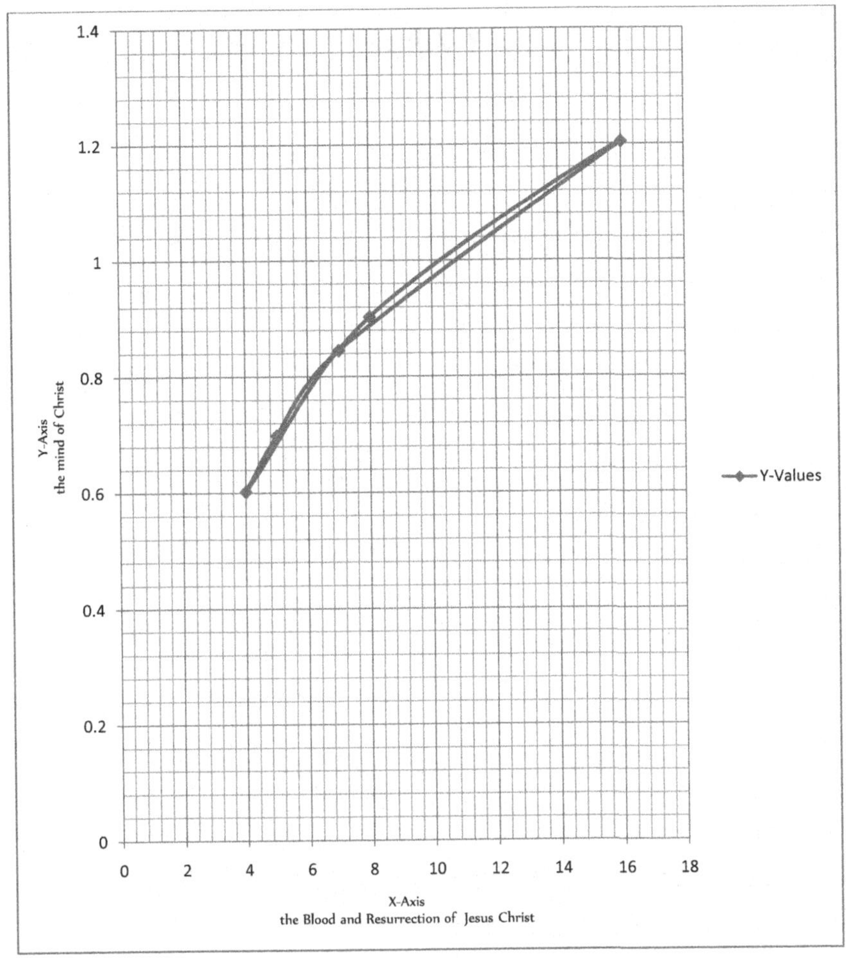

Water Spout *(lightning; combinatorics)* Study bible 2

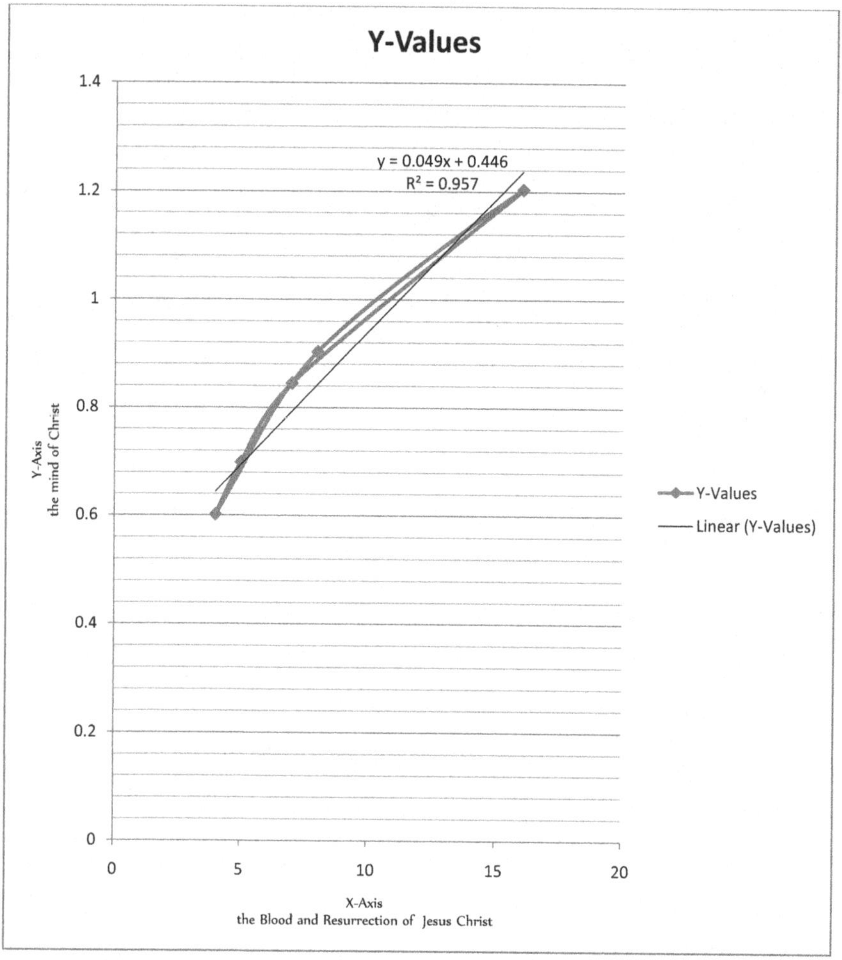

Y-Values

$y = 0.049x + 0.446$
$R^2 = 0.957$

Y-Axis
the mind of Christ

X-Axis
the Blood and Resurrection of Jesus Christ

Y-Values
Linear (Y-Values)

$10^{0.6020}, 10^{0.9030}: 10^{1.2041}, 10^{0.8450}. 10^{0.6989}, 10^{0.6020}.$

Pilled Poplar, Hazel, and Chestnut bible rods 2

6. But thou, when thou prayest, enter into thy closet, and when thou hast shut thy door, pray to thy Father which is in secret; and thy Father which seeth in secret shall reward thee openly.

2, 3, 4, 7, 8; 11. Bible Matrices

2_{10}, 3_{10}, 4_{10}, 7_{10}, 8_{10}; 11_{10}.

Pilled Poplar, Hazel, and Chestnut bible rods 1

$\text{Log}_{10} 2 = 0.3010$ $\text{Log}_{10} 7 = 0.8450$ $\text{Log}_{10} 3 = 0.4771$ $\text{Log}_{10} 8 = 0.9030$ $\text{Log}_{10} 4 = 0.6020$

$\text{Log}_{10} 11 = 1.0413$

2, 3, 4, 7, 8; 11. Deep calls unto Deep study bible 1

0.3010, 0.4771, 0.6020, 0.8450, 0.9030; 1.0413.

Deep calls unto Deep study bible 2

x-axis	y-axis
2	0.3010
3	0.4771
4	0.6020
7	0.8450
8	0.9030
11	1.0413

Water Spout *(lightning; combinatorics)* Study bible 1

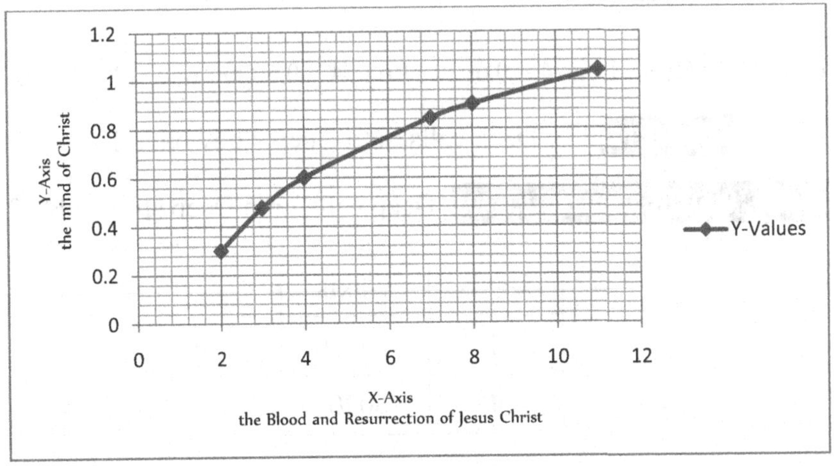

Water Spout *(lightning; combinatorics)* Study bible 2

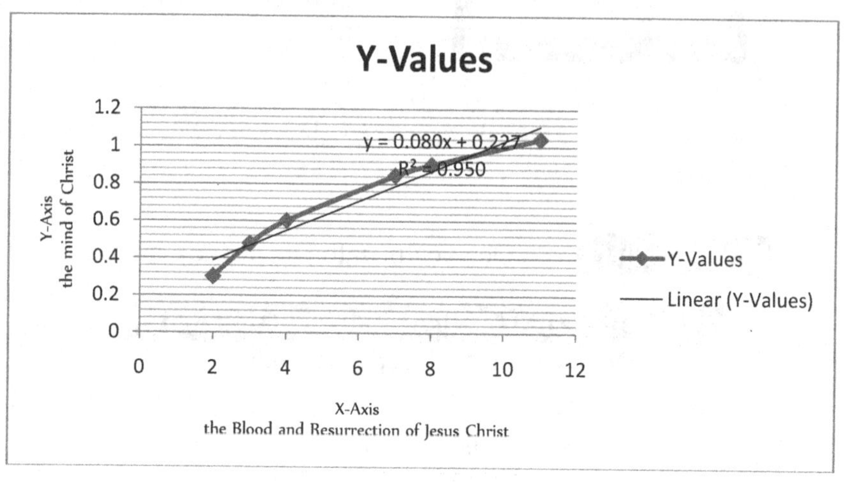

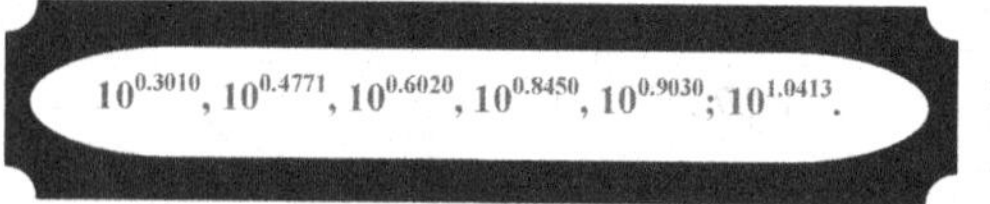

Pilled Poplar, Hazel, and Chestnut bible rods 2

7. But when ye pray, use not vain repetitions, as the heathen do: for they think that they shall be heard for their much speaking.

4, 4, 4: 12. Bible Matrices

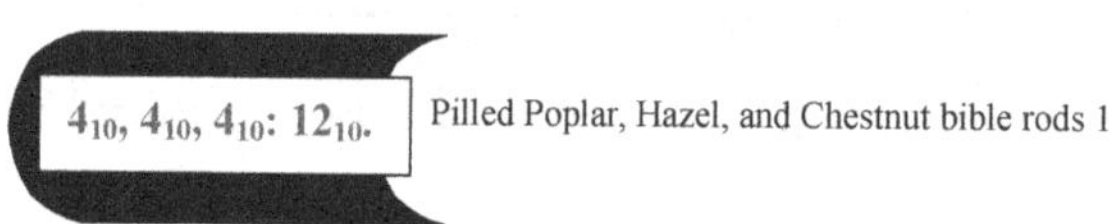

Pilled Poplar, Hazel, and Chestnut bible rods 1

$\text{Log}_{10} 4 = 0.6020$ $\text{Log}_{10} 4 = 0.6020$ $\text{Log}_{10} 4 = 0.6020$ $\text{Log}_{10} 12 = 1.0791$

4, 4, 4: 12. Deep calls unto Deep study bible 1

0.6020, 0.6020, 0.6020: 1.0791 Deep calls unto Deep study bible 2

x-axis	y-axis
4	0.6020
4	0.6020

4	0.6020
12	1.0791

Water Spout *(lightning; combinatorics)* Study bible 1

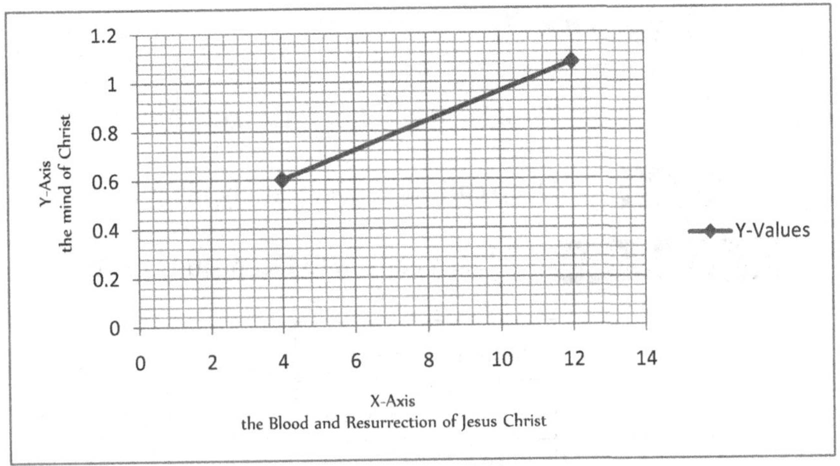

Water Spout *(lightning; combinatorics)* Study bible 2

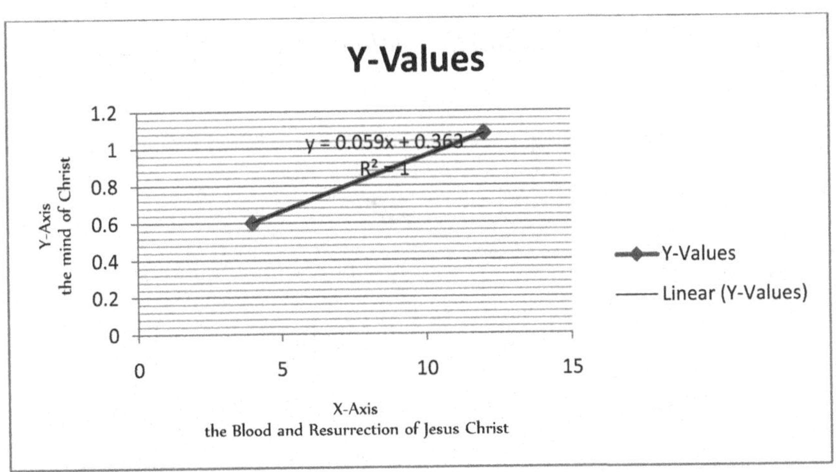

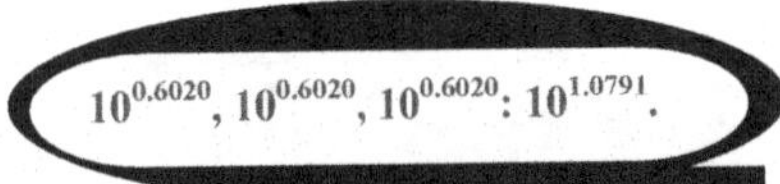

Pilled Poplar, Hazel, and Chestnut bible rods 2

8. Be not ye therefore like unto them: for your Father knoweth what things ye have need of, before ye ask him.

7: 10, 4. Bible Matrices

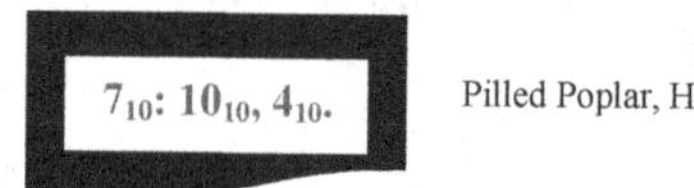

Pilled Poplar, Hazel, and Chestnut bible rods 1

$\text{Log}_{10} 10 = 1$ $\text{Log}_{10} 7 = 0.8450$ $\text{Log}_{10} 4 = 0.6020$

7: 10, 4. Deep calls unto Deep study bible 1

0.8450: 1, 0.6020. Deep calls unto Deep study bible 2

x-axis	y-axis
7	0.8450
10	1
4	0.6020

Water Spout *(lightning; combinatorics)* Study bible 1

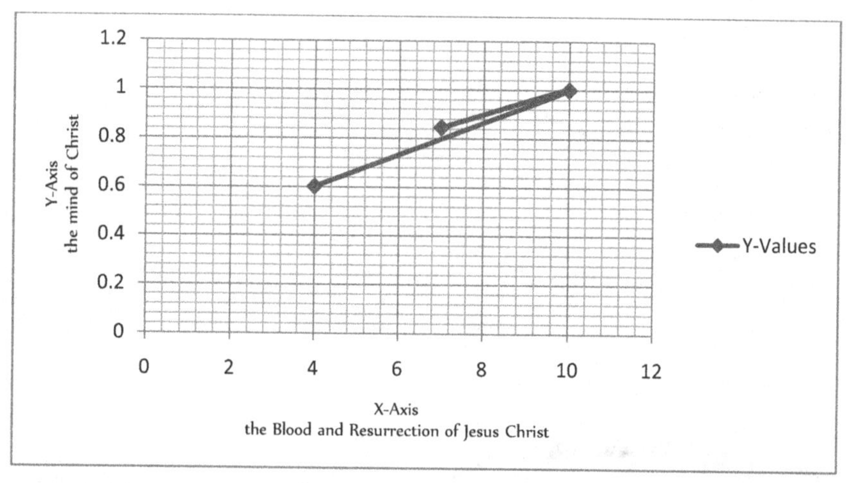

Water Spout *(lightning; combinatorics)* Study bible 2

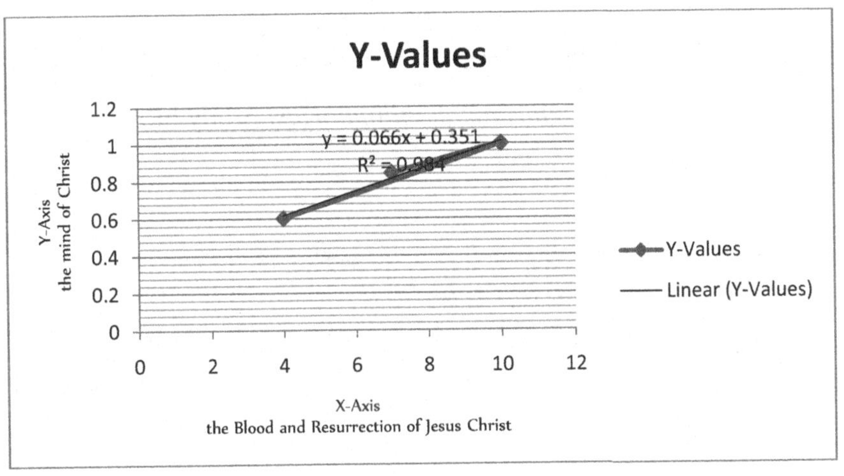

Pilled Poplar, Hazel, and Chestnut bible rods 2

9. After this manner therefore pray ye: Our Father which art in heaven, Hallowed be thy name.

6: 6, 4. Bible Matrices

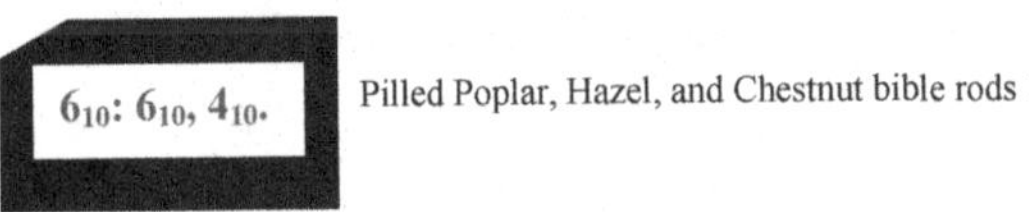

Pilled Poplar, Hazel, and Chestnut bible rods 1

$\text{Log}_{10} 6 = 0.7781$ $\text{Log}_{10} 6 = 0.7781$ $\text{Log}_{10} 4 = 0.6020$

6: 6, 4, Deep calls unto Deep study bible 1

0.7781: 0.7781, 0.6020. Deep calls unto Deep study bible 2

x-axis	y-axis
6	0.7781

6	0.7781
4	0.6020

Water Spout *(lightning; combinatorics)* Study bible 1

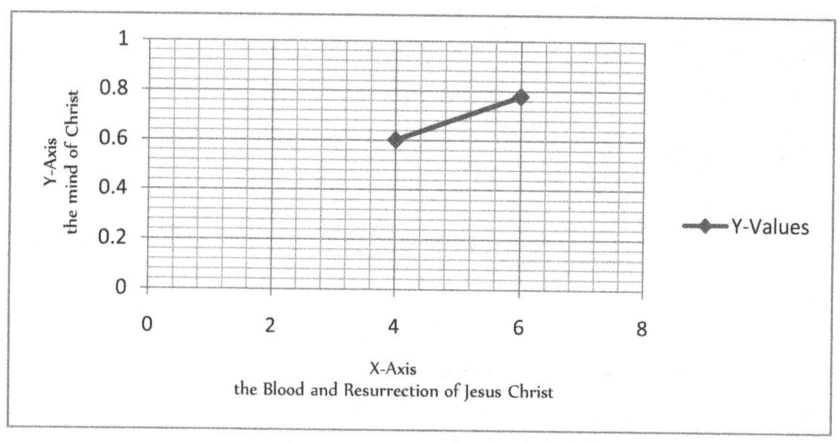

Water Spout *(lightning; combinatorics)* Study bible 2

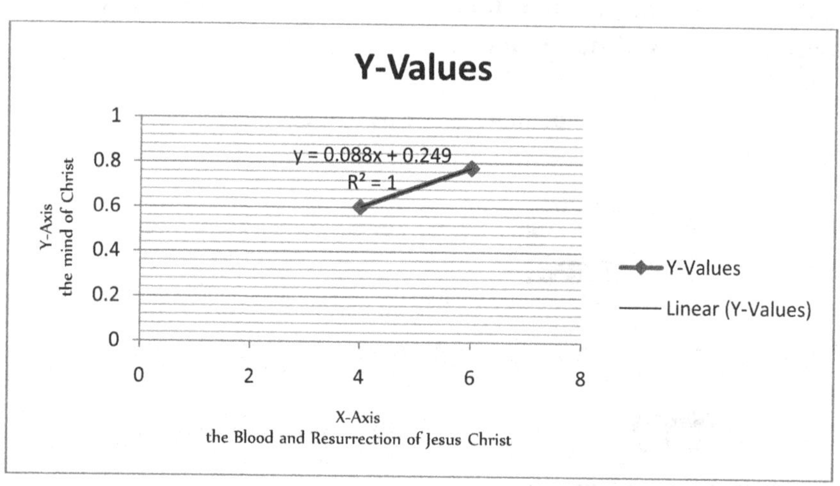

$10^{0.7781}$: $10^{0.7781}$, $10^{0.6020}$. Pilled Poplar, Hazel, and Chestnut bible rods 2

10. Thy kingdom come. Thy will be done in earth, as it is in heaven.

3. 6, 5. Bible Matrices

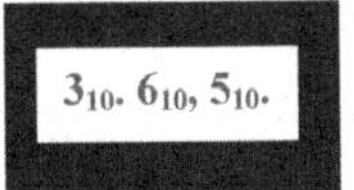

Pilled Poplar, Hazel, and Chestnut bible rods 1

$\text{Log}_{10} 3 = 0.4771$ $\text{Log}_{10} 6 = 0.7781$ $\text{Log}_{10} 5 = 0.6989$

3, 6, 5 Deep calls unto Deep study bible 1

0.4771, 0.7781, 0.6989. Deep calls unto Deep study bible 2

x-axis	y-axis
3	0.4771
6	0.7781
5	0.6989

Water Spout *(lightning; combinatorics)* Study bible 1

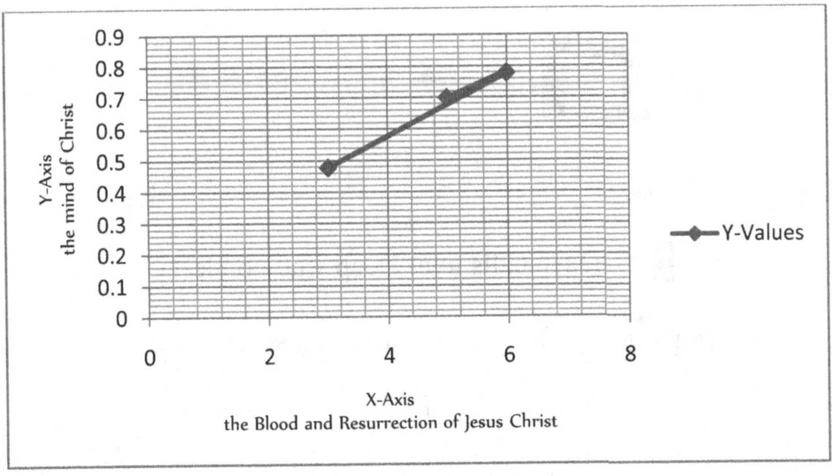

Water Spout *(lightning; combinatorics)* Study bible 2

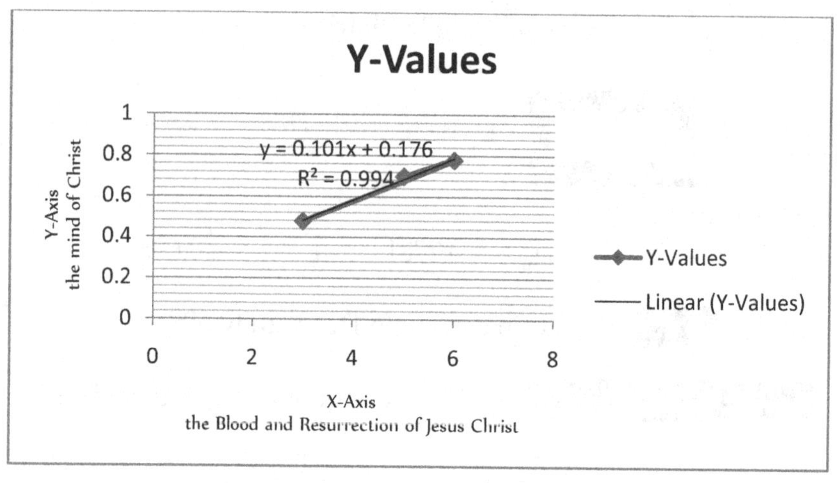

Pilled Poplar, Hazel, and Chestnut bible rods 2

11. Give us this day our daily bread.

7. Bible Matrices

Pilled Poplar, Hazel, and Chestnut bible rods 1

$\text{Log}_{10} 7 = 0.8450$

7. Deep calls unto Deep study bible 1

0.8450. Deep calls unto Deep study bible 2

x-axis	y-axis
7	0.8450

Water Spout *(lightning; combinatorics)* Study bible 1

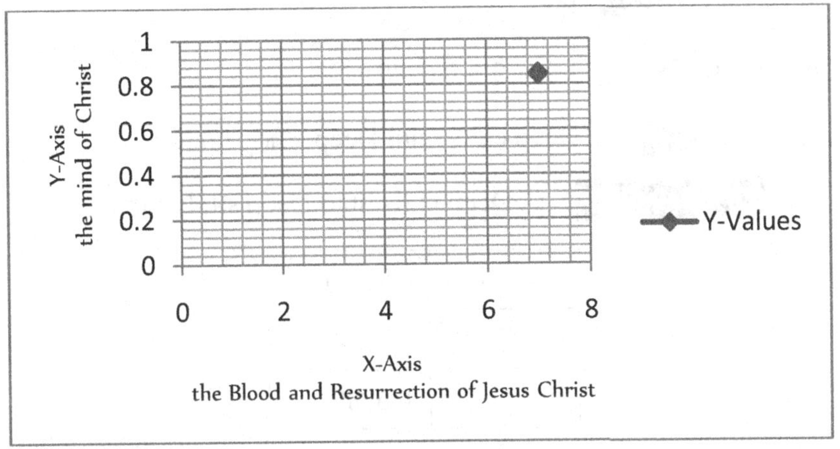

Water Spout *(lightning; combinatorics)* Study bible 2

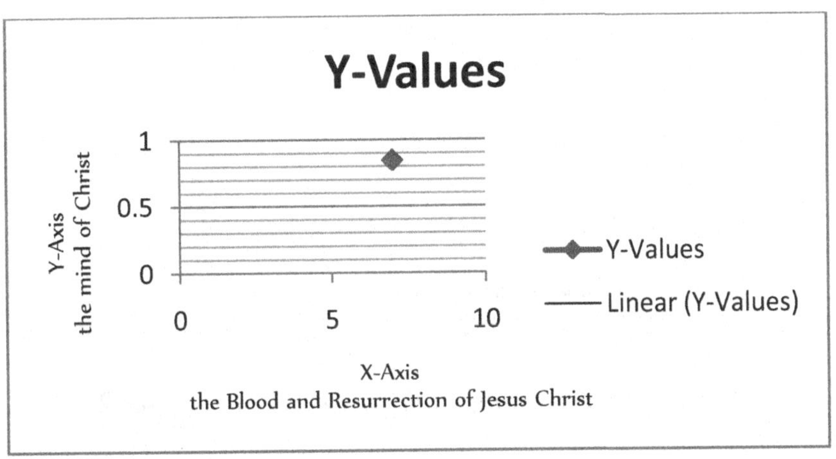

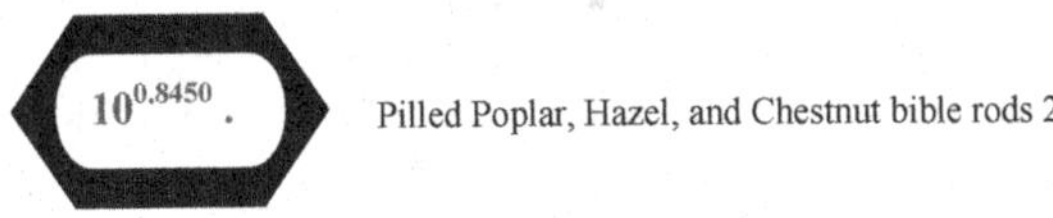

12. And forgive us our debts, as we forgive our debtors.

5, 5. Bible Matrices

$5_{10}, 5_{10}.$ Pilled Poplar, Hazel, and Chestnut bible rods 1

$\text{Log}_{10} 5 = 0.6989$ $\text{Log}_{10} 5 = 0.6989$

5, 5. Deep calls unto Deep study bible 1

0.6989, 0.6989. Deep calls unto Deep study bible 2

x-axis	y-axis
5	0.6989
5	0.6989

Water Spout *(lightning; combinatorics)* Study bible 1

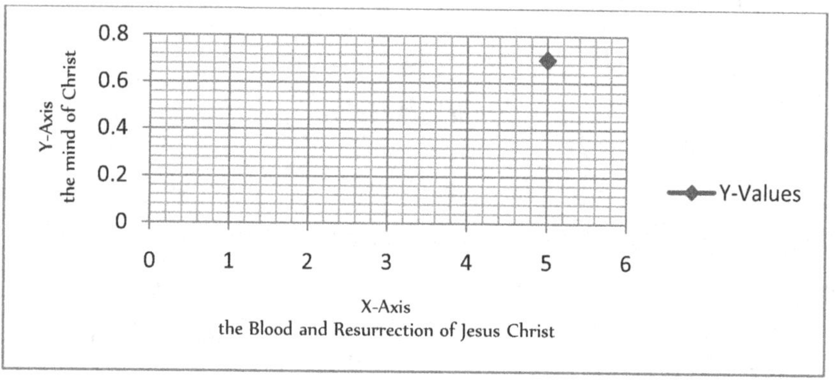

Water Spout *(lightning; combinatorics)* Study bible 2

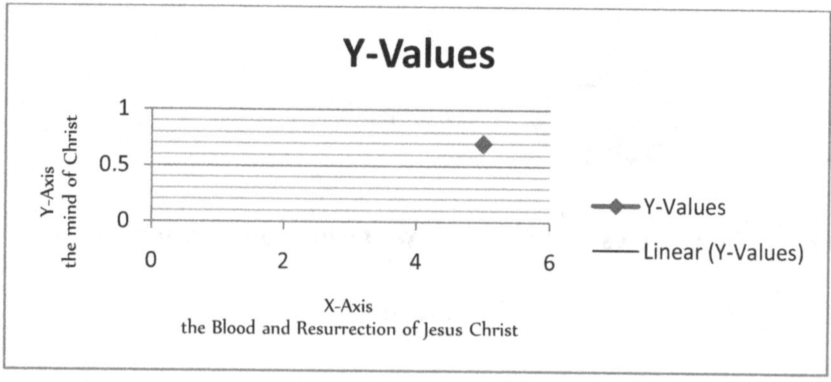

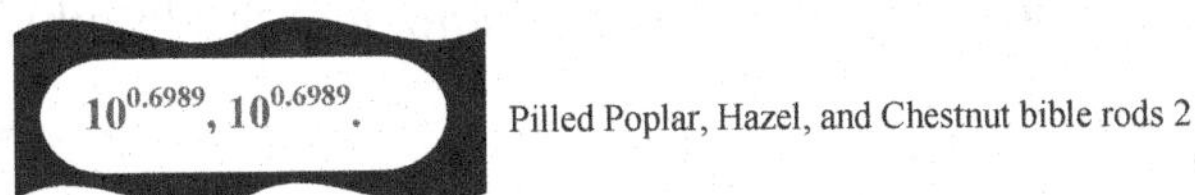

Pilled Poplar, Hazel, and Chestnut bible rods 2

13. And lead us not into temptation, but deliver us from evil: For thine is the kingdom, and the power, and the glory, for ever. Amen dependable; faithful; true; certain; firm

6, 5: 5, 3, 3, 2.1 Bible Matrices

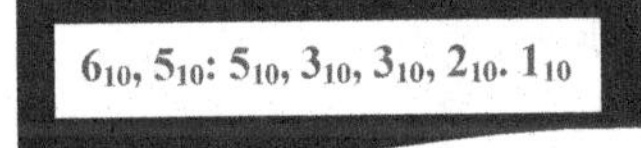

Pilled Poplar, Hazel, and Chestnut bible rods 1

$\text{Log}_{10}6 = 0.7781$ $\text{Log}_{10}5 = 0.6989$ $\text{Log}_{10}5 = 0.6989$ $\text{Log}_{10}3 = 0.4771$ $\text{Log}_{10}3 = 0.4771$

$\text{Log}_{10}2 = 0.3010$ $\text{Log}_{10}1 = 0$

6, 5: 5, 3, 3, 2. 1 Deep calls unto Deep study bible 1

0.7781, 0.6989: 0.6989, 0.4771, 0.4771, 0.3010. 0

Deep calls unto Deep study bible 2

x-axis	y-axis
6	0.7781
5	0.6989
5	0.6989
3	0.4771
3	0.4771
2	0.3010
1	0

Water Spout *(lightning; combinatorics)* Study bible 1

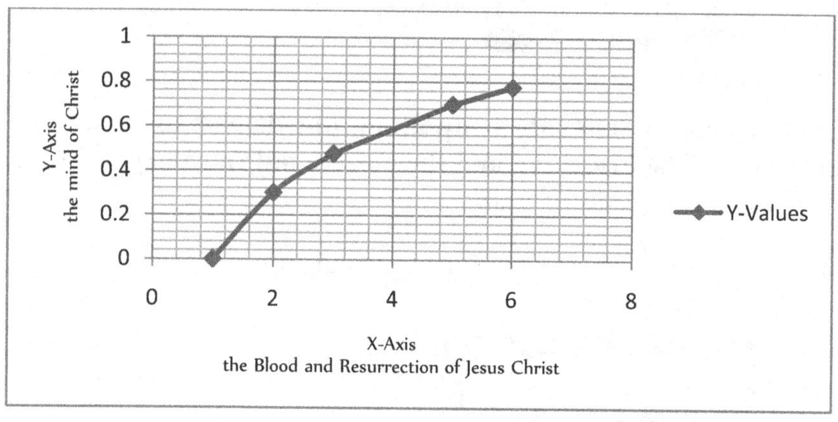

Water Spout *(lightning; combinatorics)* Study bible 2

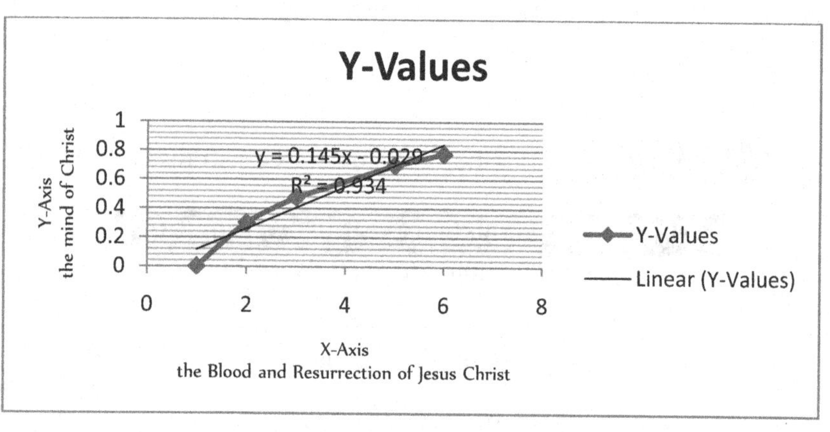

$10^{0.7781}$, $10^{0.6989}$: $10^{0.6989}$, $10^{0.4771}$, $10^{0.4771}$, $10^{0.3010}$. 10^{0}

Pilled Poplar, Hazel, and Chestnut bible rods 2

14. For if ye forgive men their trespasses, your heavenly Father will also forgive you:

7, 7: Bible Matrices

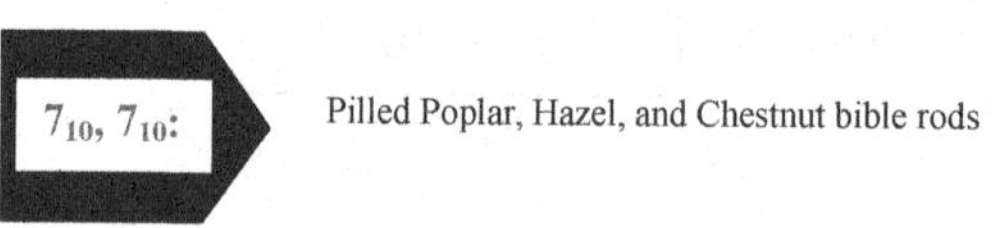

7_{10}, 7_{10}:

Pilled Poplar, Hazel, and Chestnut bible rods 1

$\text{Log}_{10} 7 = 0.8450$ $\text{Log}_{10} 7 = 0.8450$

7, 7: Deep calls unto Deep study bible 1

0.8450, 0.8450: Deep calls unto Deep study bible 2

x-axis	y-axis
7	0.8450
7	0.8450

Water Spout *(lightning; combinatorics)* Study bible 1

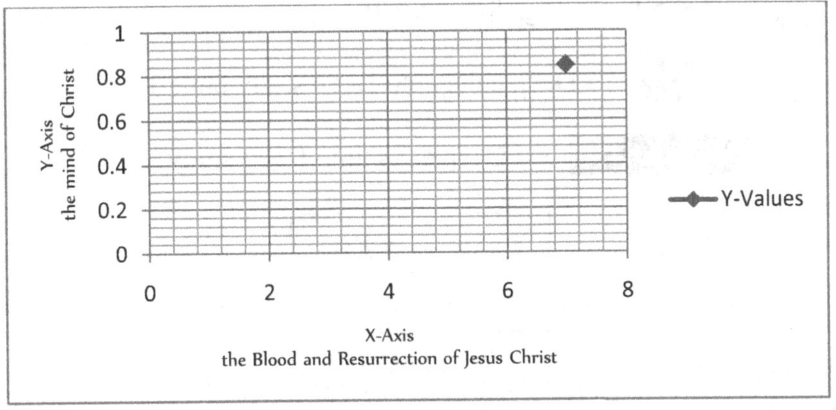

Water Spout *(lightning; combinatorics)* Study bible 2

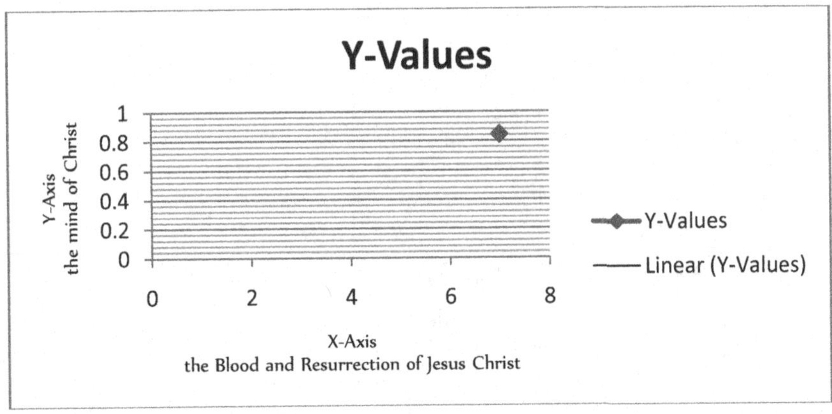

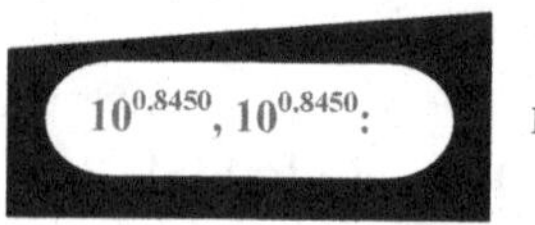

Pilled Poplar, Hazel, and Chestnut bible rods 2

15. But if ye forgive not men their trespasses, neither will your Father forgive your trespasses.

8, 7. Bible Matrices

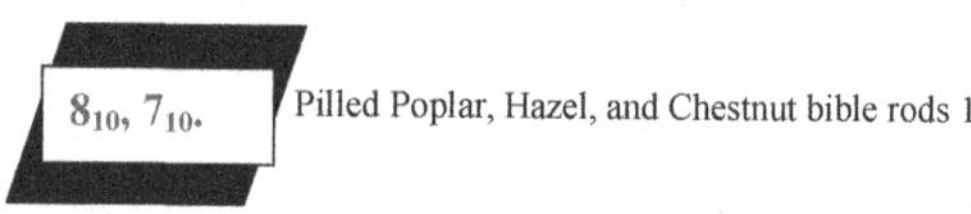

$\text{Log}_{10} 7 = 0.8450$ $\text{Log}_{10} 8 = 0.9030$

8, 7. Deep calls unto Deep study bible 1

0.9030, 0.8450. Deep calls unto Deep study bible 2

x-axis	y-axis
8	0.9030
7	0.8450

Water Spout *(lightning; combinatorics)* Study bible 1

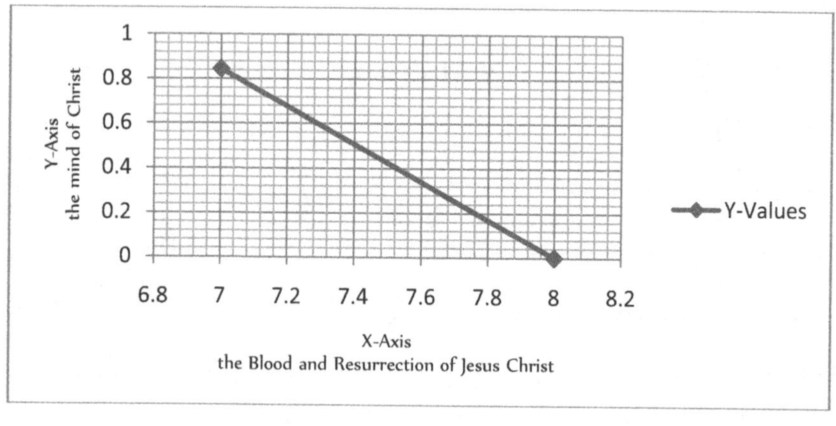

Water Spout *(lightning; combinatorics)* Study bible 2

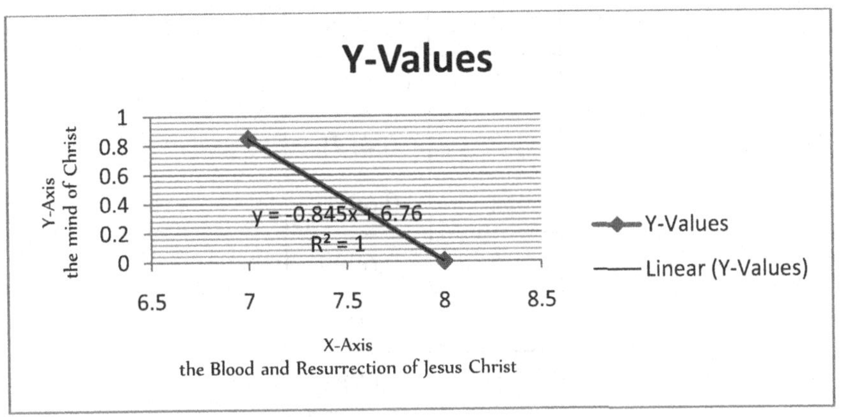

Pilled Poplar, Hazel, and Chestnut bible rods 2

16. Moreover when ye fast, be not, as the hypocrites, of a sad countenance: for they disfigure their faces, that they may appear unto men to fast. Verily I say unto you, They have their reward.

4, 2, 3, 4: 5, 8. 5, 4. Bible Matrices

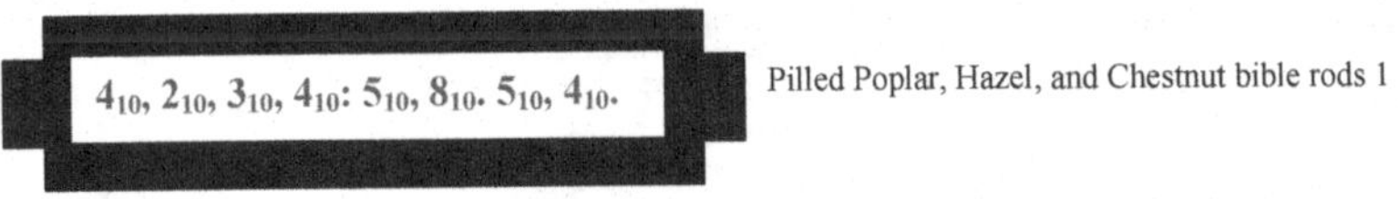

Pilled Poplar, Hazel, and Chestnut bible rods 1

$\text{Log}_{10} 4 = 0.6020$ $\text{Log}_{10} 2 = 0.3010$ $\text{Log}_{10} 3 = 0.4771$ $\text{Log}_{10} 4 = 0.6020$ $\text{Log}_{10} 5 = 0.6989$
$\text{Log}_{10} 8 = 0.9030$ $\text{Log}_{10} 5 = 0.6989$ $\text{Log}_{10} 4 = 0.6020$

4, 2, 3, 4: 5, 8. 5, 4. Deep calls unto Deep study bible 1

0.6020, 0.3010, 0.4771, 0.6020: 0.6989, 0.9030. 0.6989, 0.6020.

Deep calls unto Deep study bible 2

x-axis	y-axis
4	0.6020
2	0.3010
3	0.4771
4	0.6020
5	0.6989
8	0.9030
5	0.6989
4	0.6020

Water Spout *(lightning; combinatorics)* Study bible 1

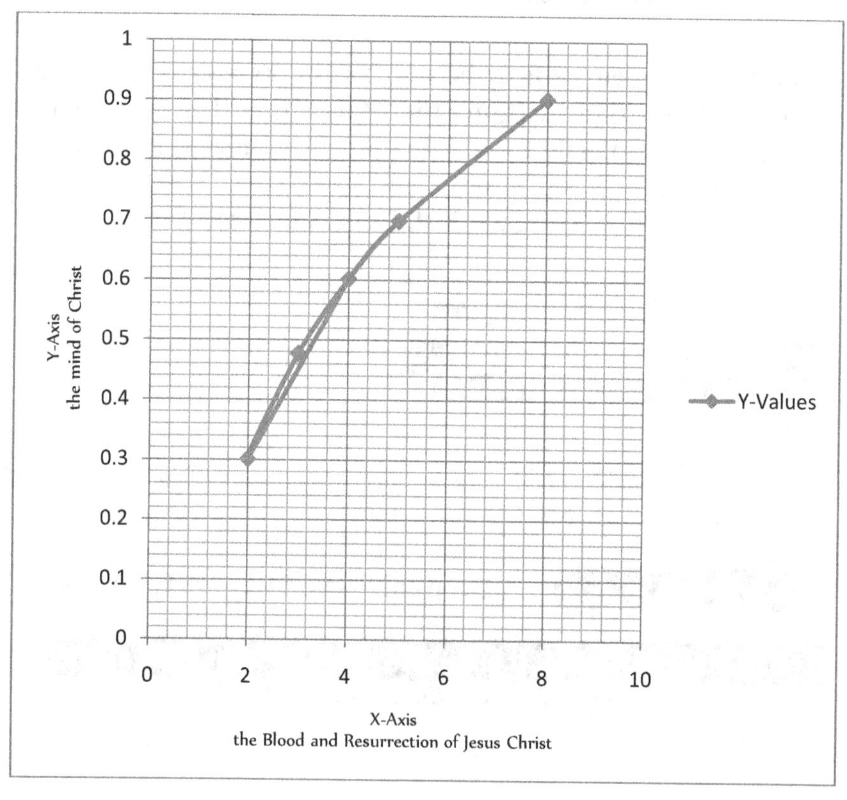

Water Spout *(lightning; combinatorics)* Study bible 2

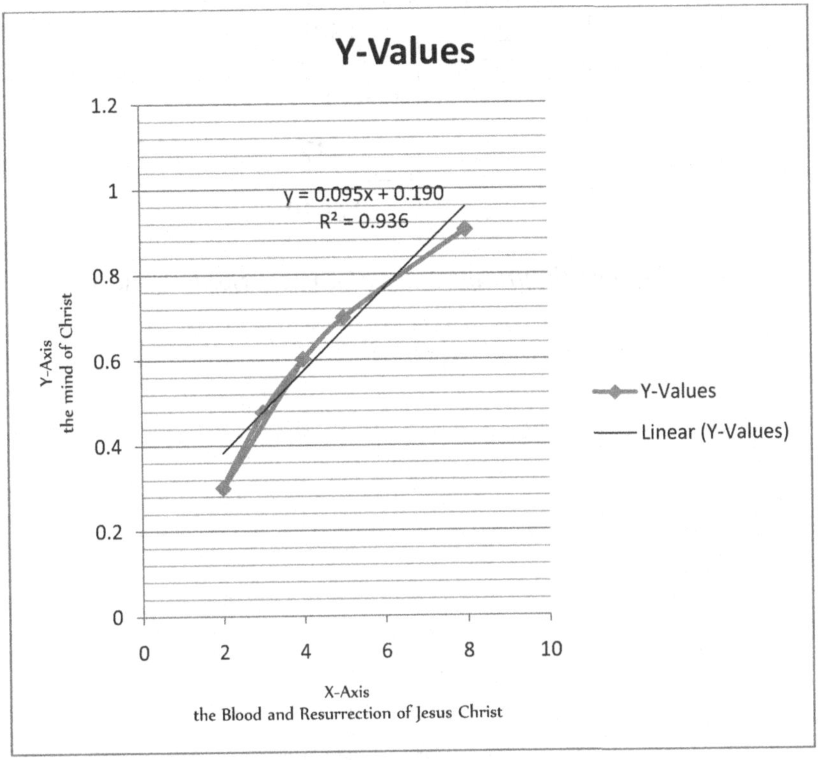

Y-Values

y = 0.095x + 0.190
R^2 = 0.936

Y-Axis
the mind of Christ

X-Axis
the Blood and Resurrection of Jesus Christ

Y-Values
Linear (Y-Values)

$10^{0.6020}, 10^{0.3010}, 10^{0.4771}, 10^{0.6020}: 10^{0.6989}, 10^{0.9030}. 10^{0.6989}, 10^{0.6020}.$

Pilled Poplar, Hazel, and Chestnut bible rods 2

17. But thou, when thou fastest, anoint thine head, and wash thy face;

2, 3, 3, 4; Bible Matrices

$2_{10}, 3_{10}, 3_{10}, 4_{10};$

Pilled Poplar, Hazel, and Chestnut bible rods 1

$\text{Log}_{10} 2 = 0.3010$ $\text{Log}_{10} 3 = 0.4771$ $\text{Log}_{10} 3 = 0.4771$ $\text{Log}_{10} 4 = 0.6020$

2, 3, 3, 4; Deep calls unto Deep study bible 1

0.3010, 0.4771, 0.4771, 0.6020;
Deep calls unto Deep study bible 2

x-axis	y-axis
2	0.3010
3	0.4771
3	0.4771
4	0.6020

Water Spout *(lightning; combinatorics)* Study bible 1

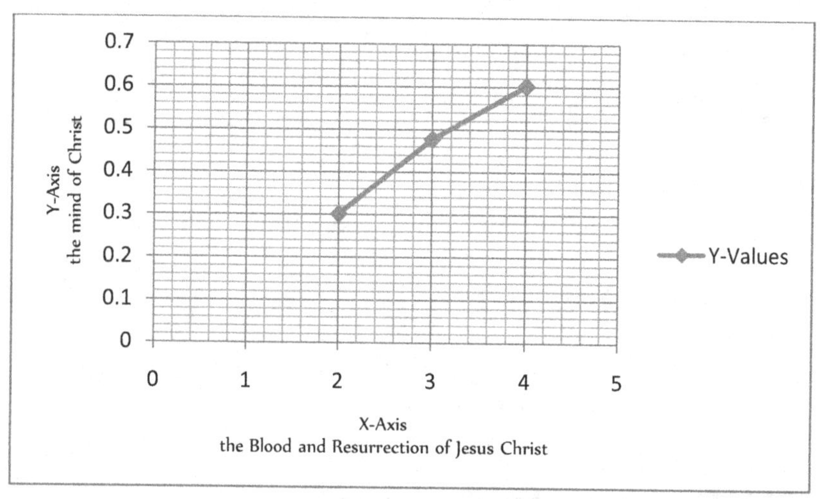

Water Spout *(lightning; combinatorics)* Study bible 2

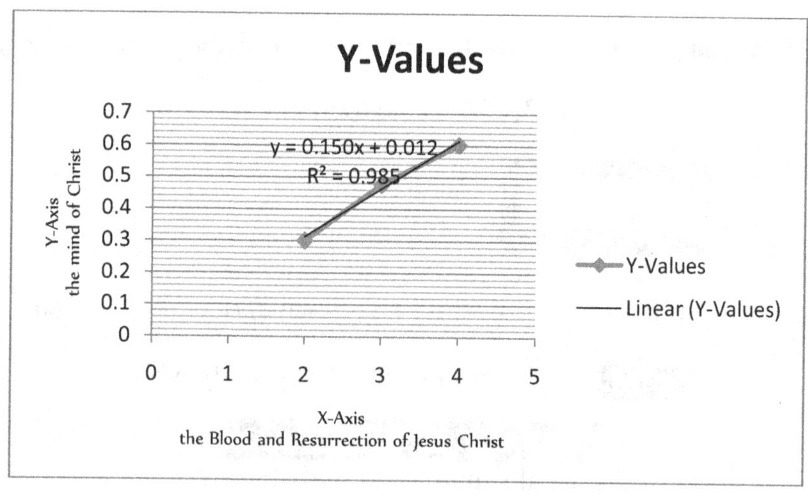

$10^{0.3010}, 10^{0.4771}, 10^{0.4771}, 10^{0.6020};$

Pilled Poplar, Hazel, and Chestnut bible rods 2

18. That thou appear not unto men to fast, but unto thy Father which is in secret: and thy Father, which seeth in secret, shall reward thee openly.

8, 8: 3, 4, 4. Bible Matrices

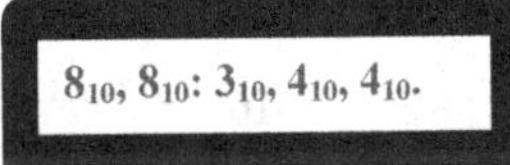
$8_{10}, 8_{10}: 3_{10}, 4_{10}, 4_{10}.$

Pilled Poplar, Hazel, and Chestnut bible rods 1

$\text{Log}_{10} 8 = 0.9030$ $\text{Log}_{10} 8 = 0.9030$ $\text{Log}_{10} 3 = 0.4771$ $\text{Log}_{10} 4 = 0.6020$ $\text{Log}_{10} 4 = 0.6020$

8, 8: 3, 4, 4. Deep calls unto Deep study bible 1

0.9030, 0.9030: 0.4771, 0.6020, 0.6020.
Deep calls unto Deep study bible 2

x-axis	y-axis
8	0.9030
8	0.9030
3	0.4771
4	0.6020
4	0.6020

Water Spout *(lightning; combinatorics)* Study bible 1

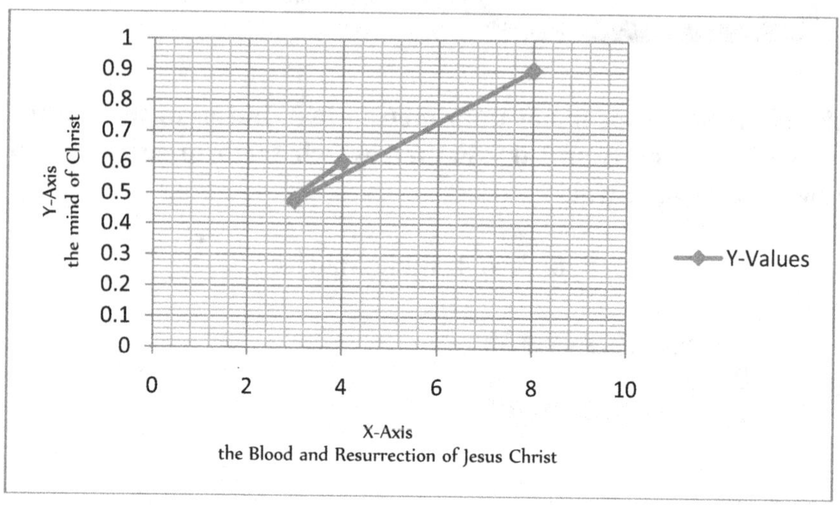

Water Spout *(lightning; combinatorics)* Study bible 2

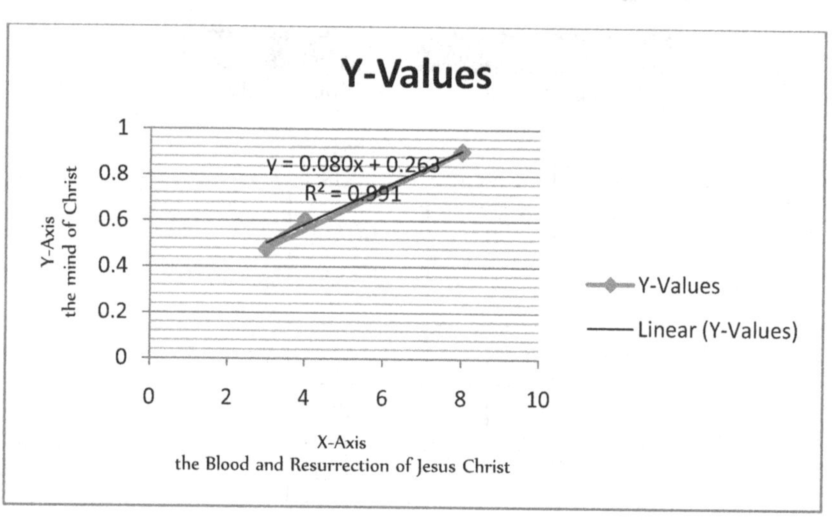

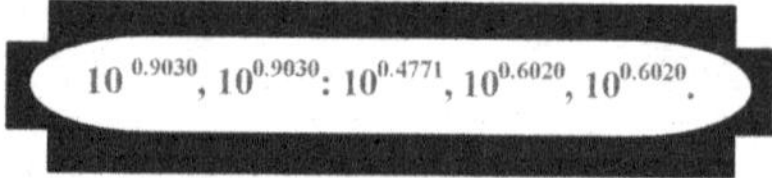

Pilled Poplar, Hazel, and Chestnut bible rods 2

19. Lay not up for yourselves treasures upon earth, where moth and rust doth corrupt, and where thieves break through and steal:

8, 6, 7: Bible Matrices

Pilled Poplar, Hazel, and Chestnut bible rods 1

$Log_{10} 8 = 0.9030$ $Log_{10} 7 = 0.8450$ $Log_{10} 6 = 0.7781$

8, 6, 7: Deep calls unto Deep study bible 1

0.9030, 0.7781, 0.8450: Deep calls unto Deep study bible 2

x-axis	y-axis
8	0.9030
6	0.7781
7	0.8450

Water Spout *(lightning; combinatorics)* Study bible 1

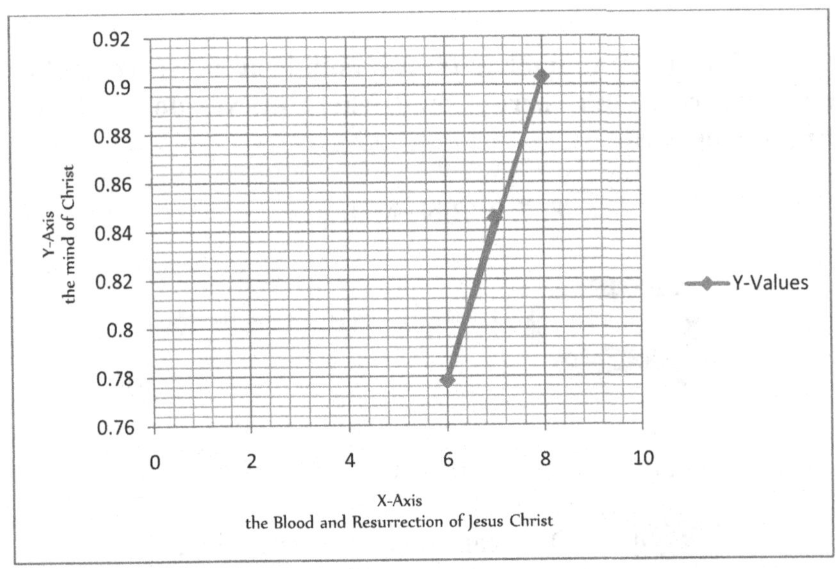

Water Spout *(lightning; combinatorics)* Study bible 2

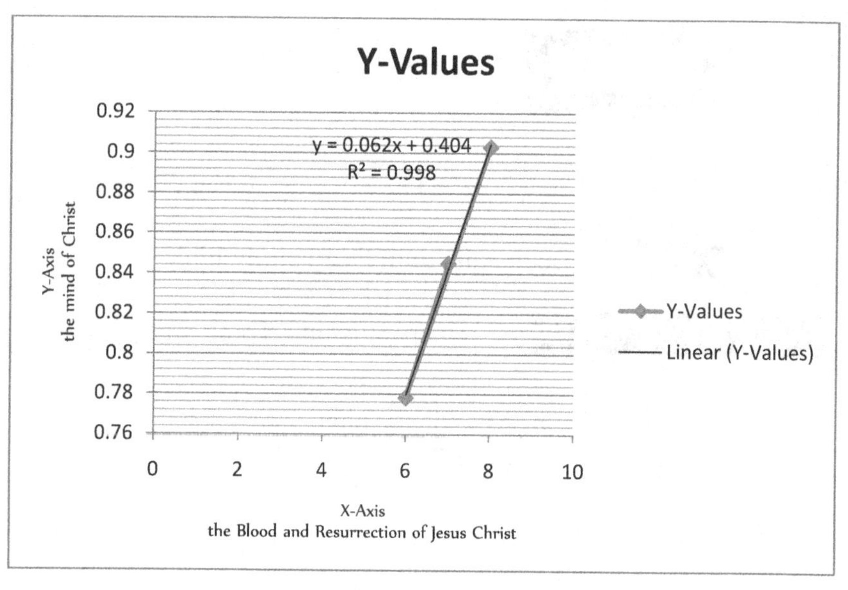

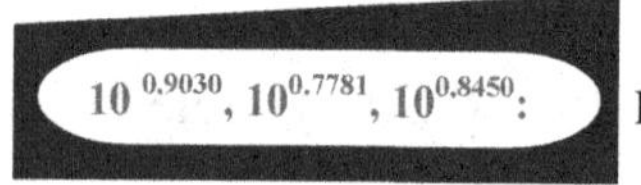

Pilled Poplar, Hazel, and Chestnut bible rods 2

20. But lay up for yourselves treasures in heaven, where neither moth nor rust doth corrupt, and where thieves do not break through nor steal:

8, 7, 9: Bible Matrices

$\text{Log}_{10} 8 = 0.9030$ $\text{Log}_{10} 7 = 0.8450$ $\text{Log}_{10} 9 = 0.9542$.

8, 7, 9: Deep calls unto Deep study bible 1

0.9030, 0.8450, 0.9542: Deep calls unto Deep study bible 2

x-axis	y-axis
8	0.9030
7	0.8450
9	0.9542

Water Spout *(lightning; combinatorics)* Study bible 1

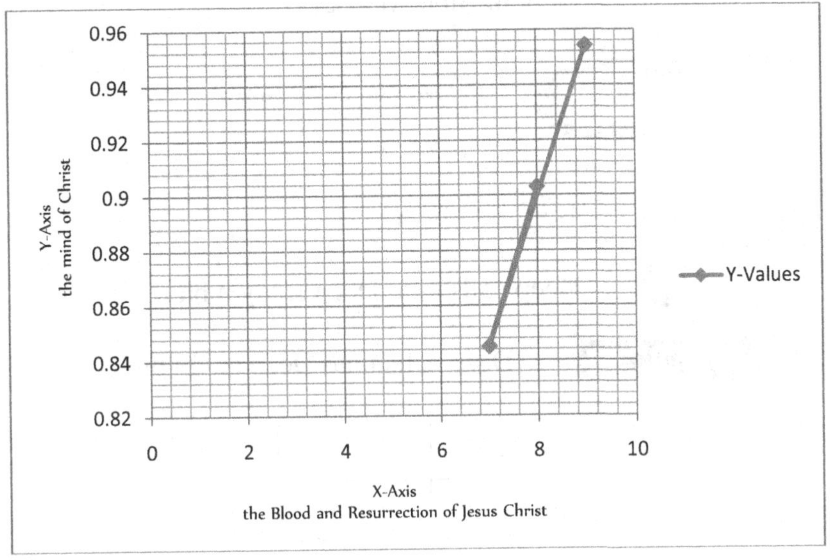

Water Spout *(lightning; combinatorics)* Study bible 2

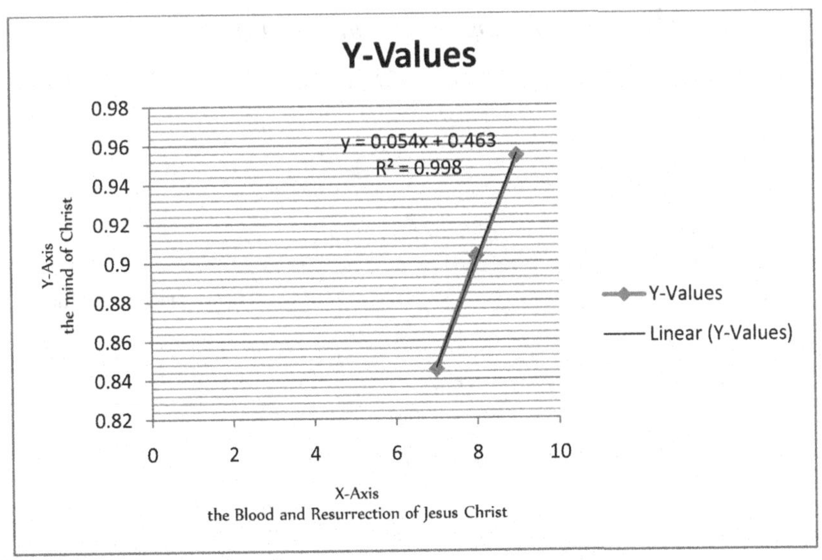

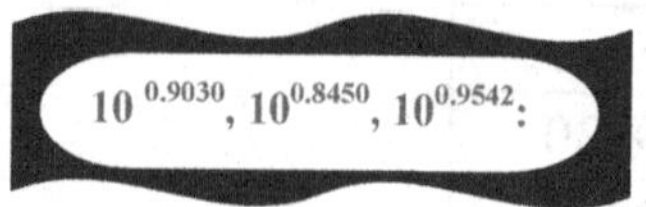

Pilled Poplar, Hazel, and Chestnut bible rods 2

21. For where your treasure is, there will your heart be also.

5, 6. Bible Matrices

Pilled Poplar, Hazel, and Chestnut bible rods 1

$\text{Log}_{10} 5 = 0.6989$ $\text{Log}_{10} 6 = 0.7781$

5, 6. Deep calls unto Deep study bible 1

0.6989, 0.7781. Deep calls unto Deep study bible 2

x-axis	y-axis
5	0.6989
6	0.7781

Water Spout *(lightning; combinatorics)* Study bible 1

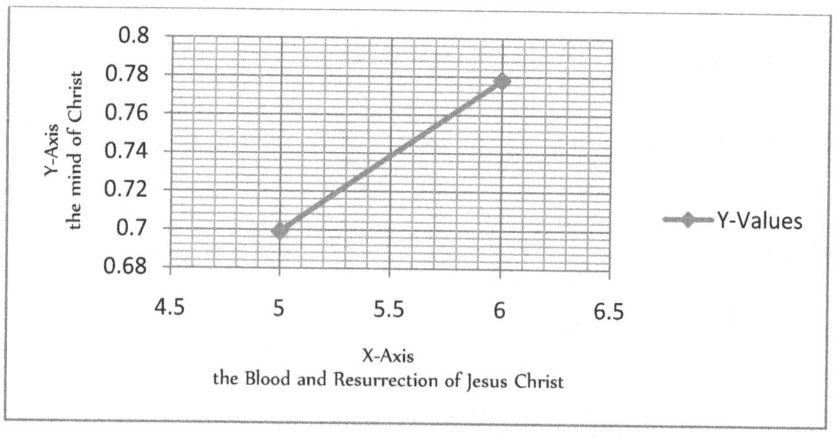

Water Spout *(lightning; combinatorics)* Study bible 2

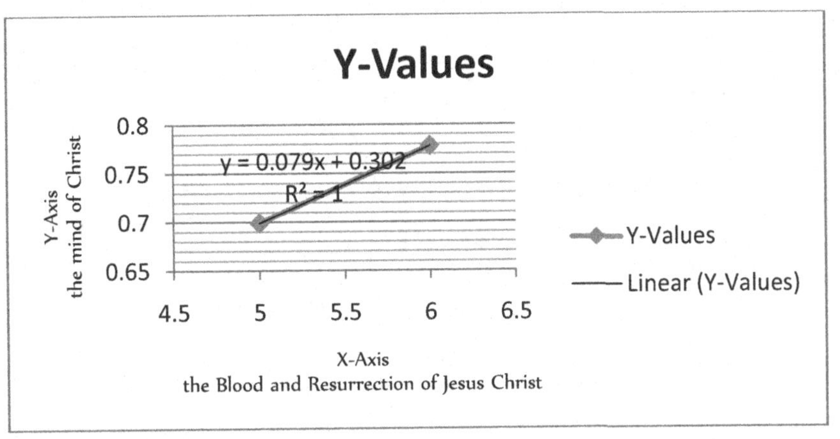

Pilled Poplar, Hazel, and Chestnut bible rods 2

22. The light of the body is the eye: if therefore thine eye be single, thy whole body shall be full of light.

8: 6, 8. Bible Matrices

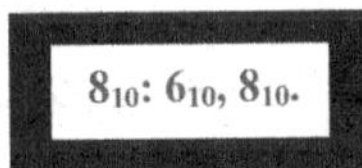

Pilled Poplar, Hazel, and Chestnut bible rods 1

$\text{Log}_{10} 8 = 0.9030$ $\text{Log}_{10} 6 = 0.7781$ $\text{Log}_{10} 8 = 0.9030$

8: 6, 8. Deep calls unto Deep study bible 1

0.9030: 0.7781, 0.9030. Deep calls unto Deep study bible 2

x-axis	y-axis
8	0.9030
6	0.7781
8	0.9030

Water Spout *(lightning; combinatorics)* Study bible 1

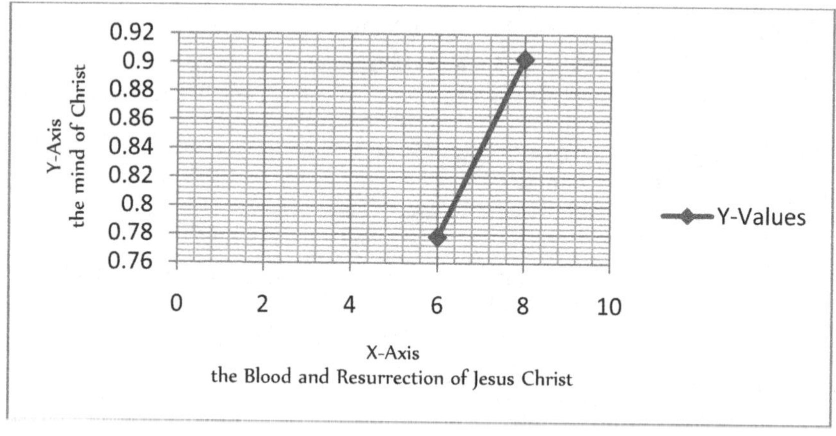

Water Spout *(lightning; combinatorics)* Study bible 2

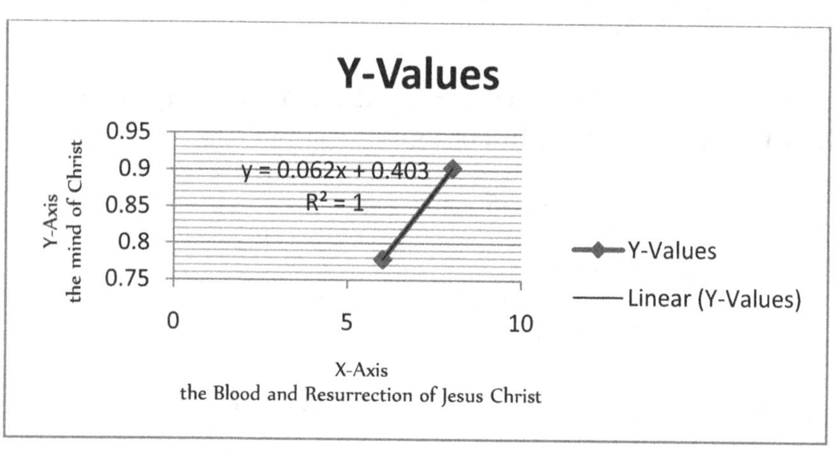

Pilled Poplar, Hazel, and Chestnut bible rods 2

23. But if thine eye be evil, thy whole body shall be full of darkness. If therefore the light that is in thee be darkness, how great is that darkness!

6, 8. 10, 5! Bible Matrices

$6_{10}, 8_{10}. 10_{10}, 5_{10}!$ Pilled Poplar, Hazel, and Chestnut bible rods 1

$\text{Log}_{10} 10 = 1$ $\text{Log}_{10} 8 = 0.9030$ $\text{Log}_{10} 6 = 0.7781$ $\text{Log}_{10} 5 = 0.6989$

6, 8. 10, 5! Deep calls unto Deep study bible 1

0.7781, 0.9030, 1, 0.6989! Deep calls unto Deep study bible 2

x-axis	y-axis
6	0.7781
8	0.9030
10	1
5	0.6989

Water Spout *(lightning; combinatorics)* Study bible 1

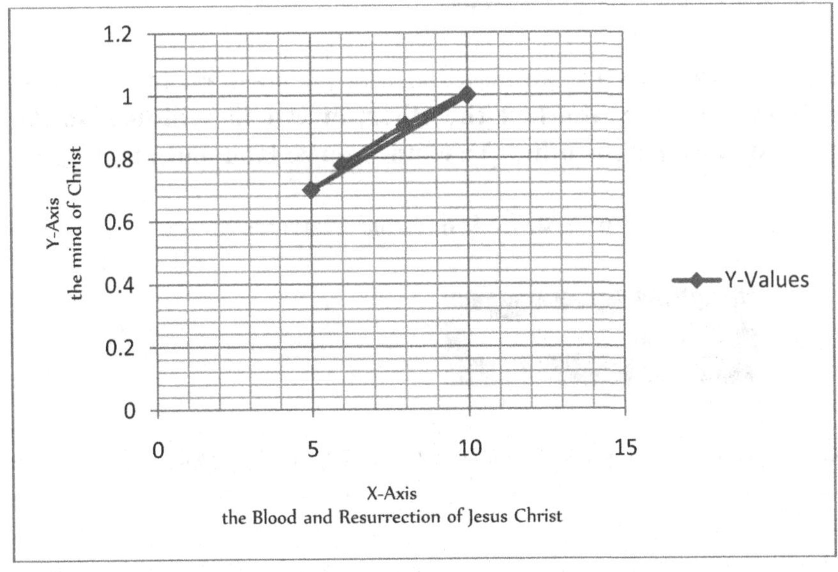

Water Spout *(lightning; combinatorics)* Study bible 2

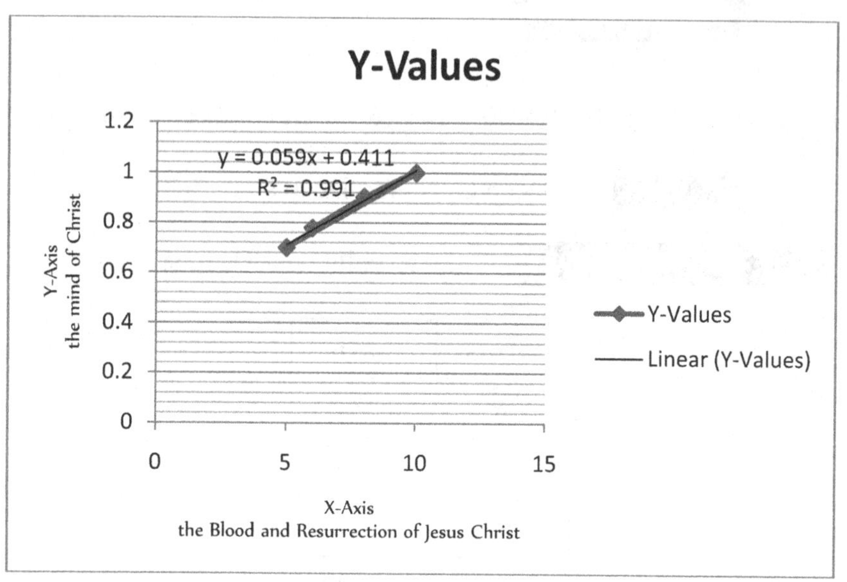

Pilled Poplar, Hazel, and Chestnut bible rods 2

24. No man can serve two witness and support$_{;\,2} \times {}_{1}$ **masters: for either he will hate the one, and love the other; or else he will hold to the one, and despise the other. Ye cannot serve God and mammon.**

6: 7, 4; 8, 4. 6. Bible Matrices

Pilled Poplar, Hazel, and Chestnut bible rods 1

$\text{Log}_{10} 1 = 0$ $\text{Log}_{10} 8 = 0.9030$ $\text{Log}_{10} 7 = 0.8450$ $\text{Log}_{10} 6 = 0.7781$ $\text{Log}_{10} 4 = 0.6020$ $\text{Log}_{10} 4 = 0.6020$

$\text{Log}_5 5 = y$

$5^y = 5^1$

$y = 1$

6: 7, 4; 8, 4. 6. Deep calls unto Deep study bible 1

1 0: 0.8450, 0.6020; 0.9030, 0.6020. 0.7781.
Deep calls unto Deep study bible 2

x-axis	y-axis
6	1
7	0.8450
4	0.6020
8	0.9030
4	0.6020
6	0.7781

Water Spout *(lightning; combinatorics)* Study bible 1

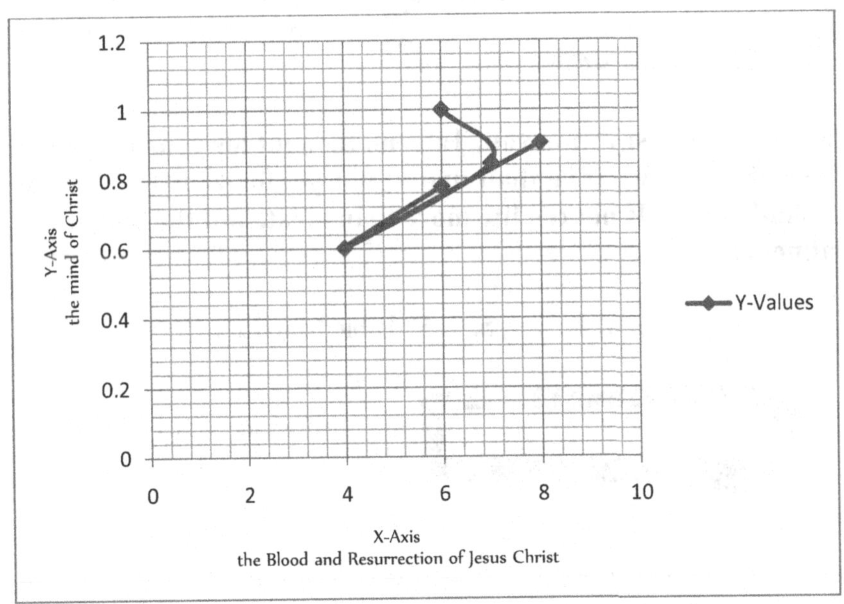

Water Spout *(lightning; combinatorics)* Study bible 2

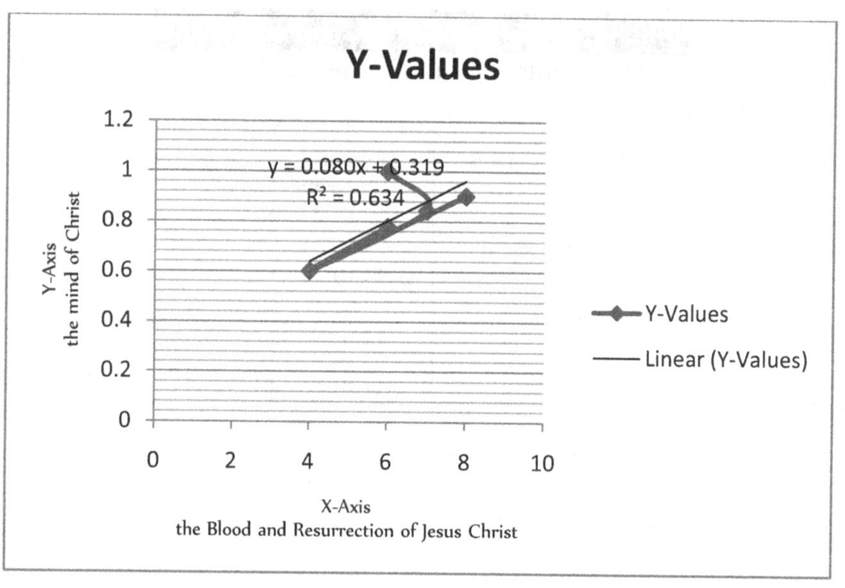

Pilled Poplar, Hazel, and Chestnut bible rods 2

25. Therefore I say unto you, Take no thought for your life, what ye shall eat, or what ye shall drink; nor yet for your body, what ye shall put on. Is not the life more than meat, and the body than raiment?

5, 6, 4, 5; 5, 5. 7, 5? Bible Matrices

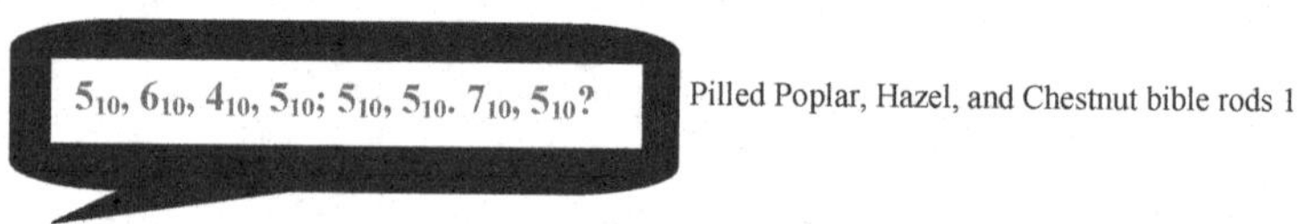

Pilled Poplar, Hazel, and Chestnut bible rods 1

$\text{Log}_{10} 4 = 0.6020$ $\text{Log}_{10} 5 = 0.6989$ $\text{Log}_{10} 7 = 0.8450$ $\text{Log}_{10} 6 = 0.7781$ $\text{Log}_{10} 5 = 0.6989$

$\text{Log}_{10} 5 = 0.6989$ $\text{Log}_{10} 5 = 0.6989$ $\text{Log}_{10} 5 = 0.6989$

5, 6, 4, 5; 5, 5. 7, 5? Deep calls unto Deep study bible 1

0.6989, 0.7781, 0.6020, 0.6989; 0.6989, 0.6989. 0.8450, 0.6989?

Deep calls unto Deep study bible 2

x-axis	y-axis
5	0.6989
6	0.7781
4	0.6020
5	0.6989
5	0.6989
5	0.6989
7	0.8450
5	0.6989

Water Spout *(lightning; combinatorics)* Study bible 1

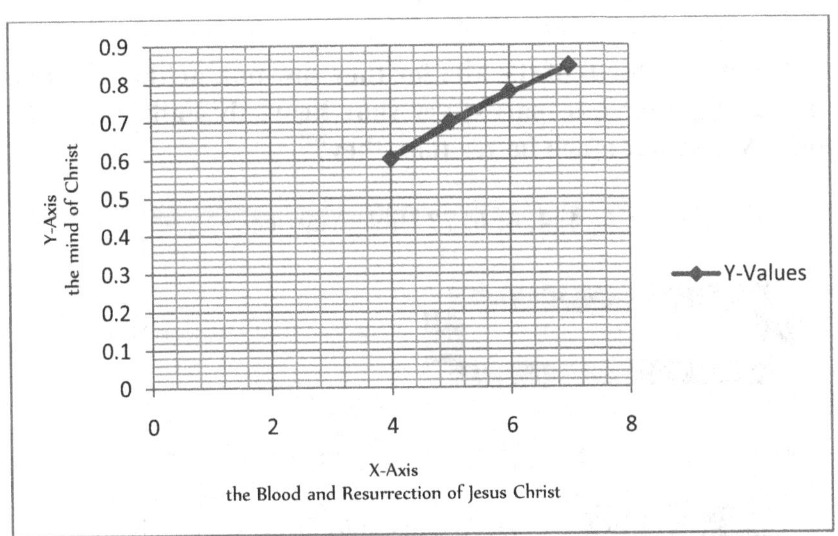

Water Spout *(lightning; combinatorics)* Study bible 2

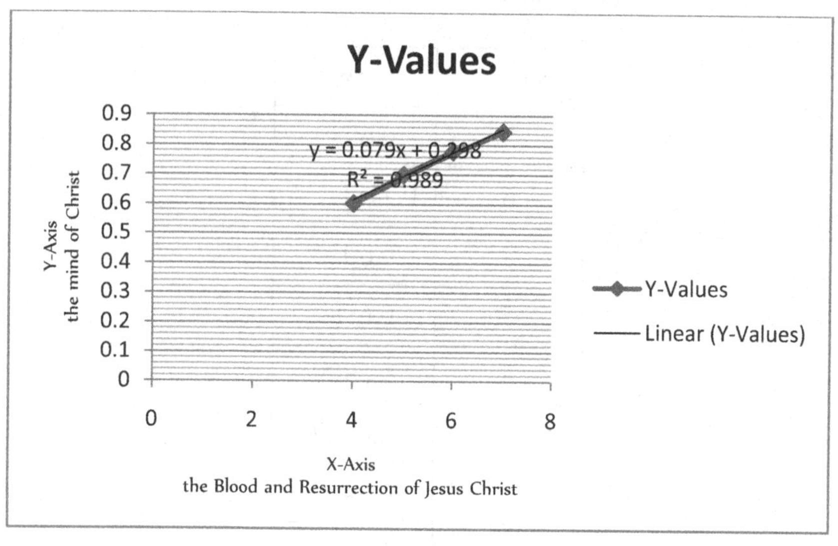

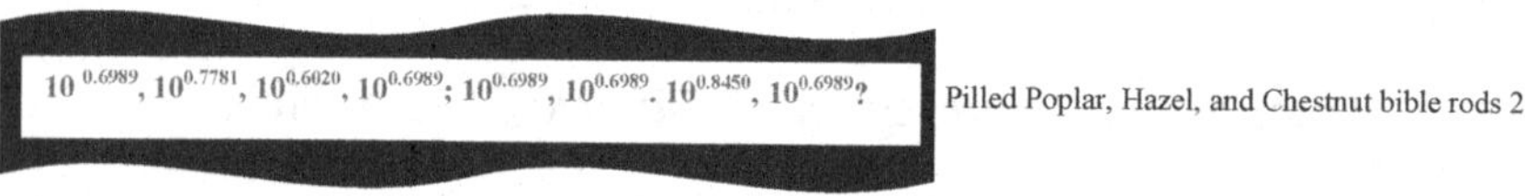
$10^{0.6989}, 10^{0.7781}, 10^{0.6020}, 10^{0.6989}; 10^{0.6989}, 10^{0.6989}. 10^{0.8450}, 10^{0.6989}?$

Pilled Poplar, Hazel, and Chestnut bible rods 2

26. Behold the fowls of the air: for they sow not, neither do they reap, nor gather into barns; yet your heavenly Father feedeth them. Are ye not much better than they?

6: 4, 4, 4; 6. 7? Bible Matrices

$6_{10}: 4_{10}, 4_{10}, 4_{10}; 6_{10}. 7_{10}?$

Pilled Poplar, Hazel, and Chestnut bible rods 1

$\text{Log}_{10}4 = 0.6020$ $\text{Log}_{10}4 = 0.6020$ $\text{Log}_{10}4 = 0.6020$ $\text{Log}_{10}7 = 0.8450$ $\text{Log}_{10}6 = 0.7781$ $\text{Log}_{10}6 = 0.7781$

6: 4, 4, 4; 6. 7? Deep calls unto Deep study bible 1

0.7781: 0.6020, 0.6020, 0.6020; 0.7781. 0.8450?

Deep calls unto Deep study bible 2

x-axis	y-axis
6	0.7781
4	0.6020
4	0.6020
4	0.6020
6	0.7781
7	0.8450

Water Spout *(lightning; combinatorics)* Study bible 1

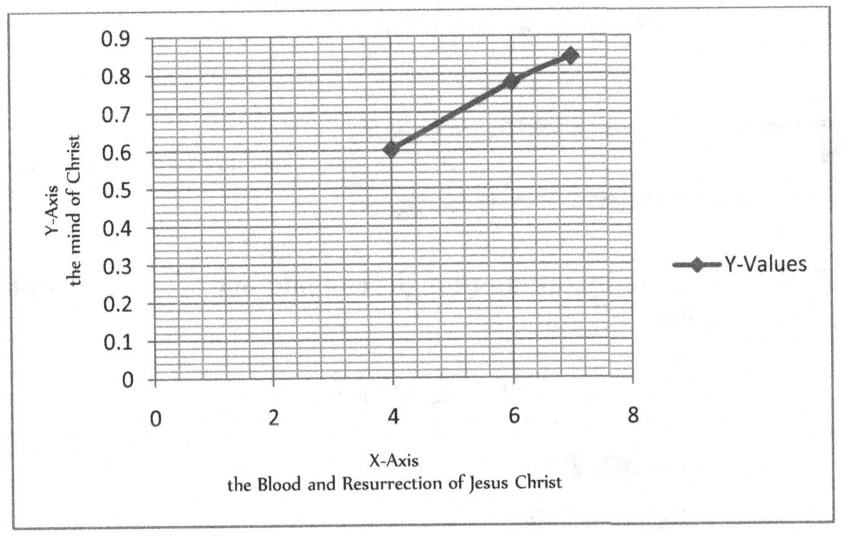

Water Spout *(lightning; combinatorics)* Study bible 2

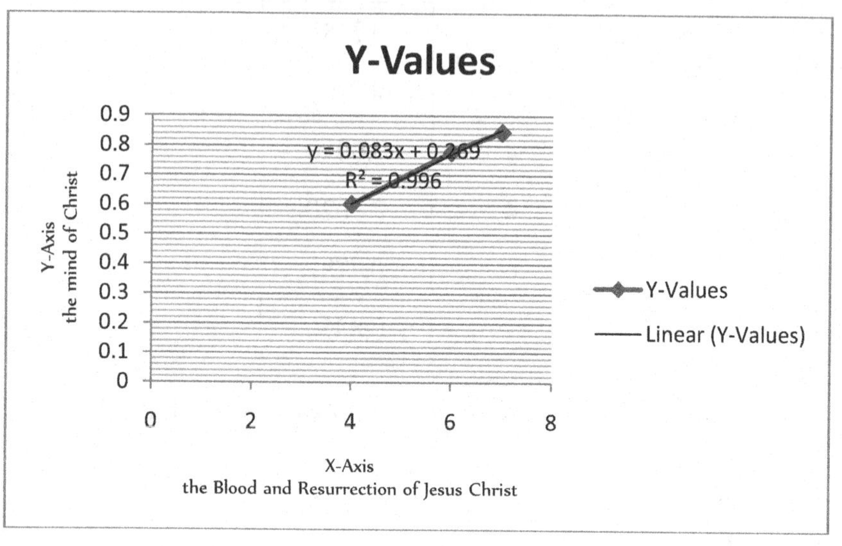

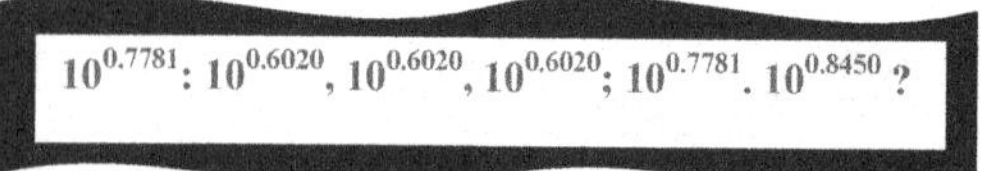

Pilled Poplar, Hazel, and Chestnut bible rods 2

27. Which of you by taking thought can add one 1 x 1; singleness **cubit** 18 inches; 45.72 cm **unto his stature?**

13? Bible Matrices

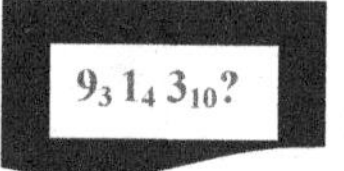

Pilled Poplar, Hazel, and Chestnut bible rods 1

$\text{Log}_{10} 3 = 0.4771$

$\text{Log}_3 9 = y$

$3^y = 9$

$3^y = 3^2$

$y = 2$

$\text{Log}_4 1 = y$

$4^y = 1$

$4^y = 4^0$

$y = 0$

13? Deep calls unto Deep study bible 1

2 0 0.4771? Deep calls unto Deep study bible 2

x-axis	y-axis
13	2.4771

Water Spout *(lightning; combinatorics)* Study bible 1

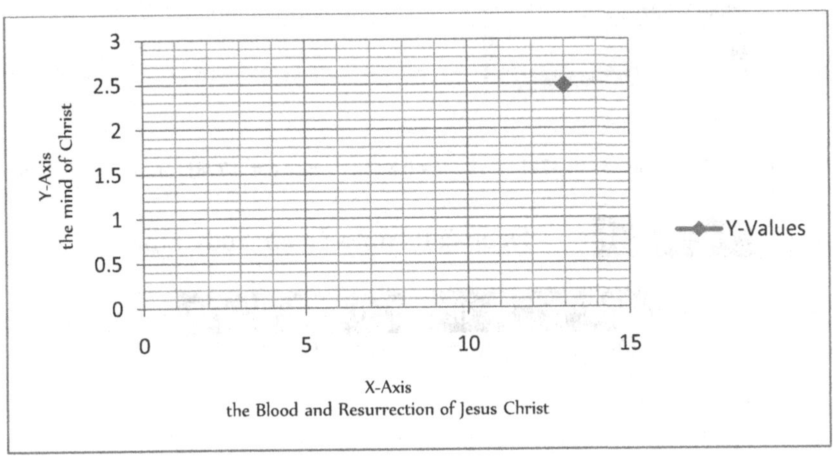

Water Spout *(lightning; combinatorics)* Study bible 2

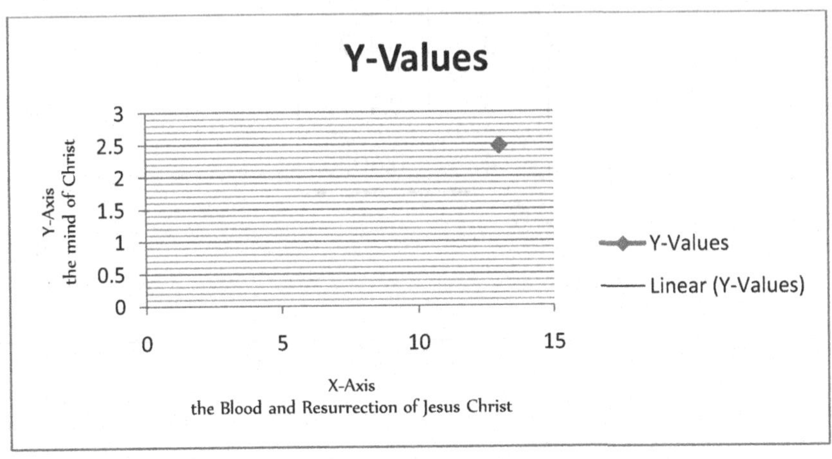

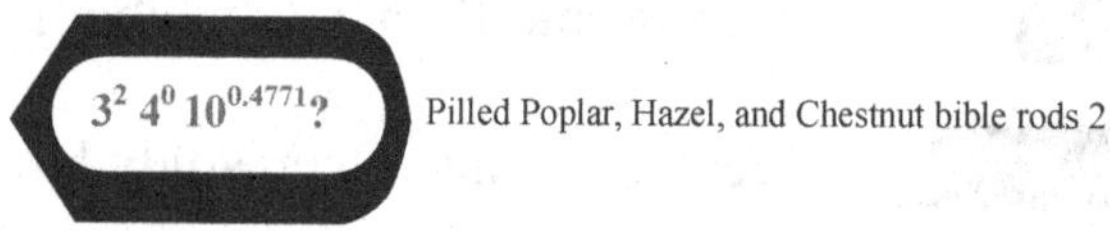

Pilled Poplar, Hazel, and Chestnut bible rods 2

28. And why take ye thought for raiment? Consider the lilies of the field, how they grow; they toil not, neither do they spin:

7? 6, 3; 3, 4: Bible Matrices

Pilled Poplar, Hazel, and Chestnut bible rods 1

$\text{Log}_{10}3 = 0.4771$ $\text{Log}_{10}3 = 0.4771$ $\text{Log}_{10}7 = 0.8450$ $\text{Log}_{10}6 = 0.7781$ $\text{Log}_{10}4 = 0.6020$

7? 6, 3; 3, 4: Deep calls unto Deep study bible 1

0.8450? 0.7781, 0.4771; 0.4771, 0.6020:
Deep calls unto Deep study bible 2

x-axis	y-axis
7	0.8450
6	0.7781
3	0.4771
3	0.4771
4	0.6020

Water Spout *(lightning; combinatorics)* Study bible 1

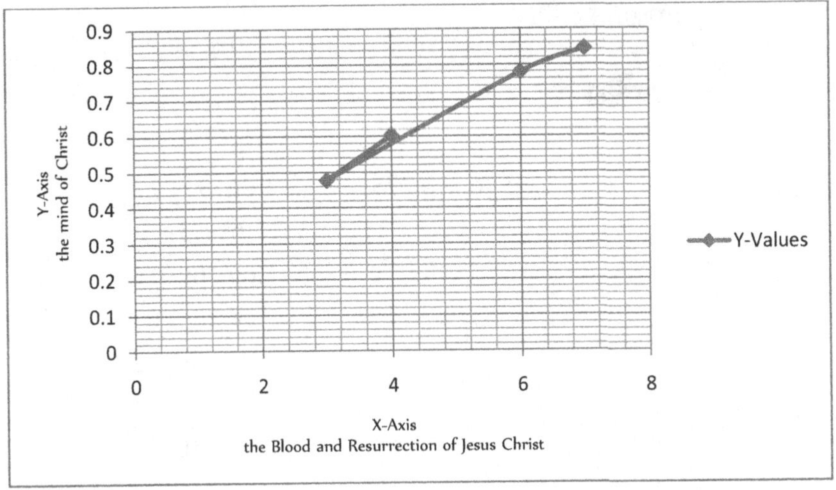

Water Spout *(lightning; combinatorics)*Study bible 2

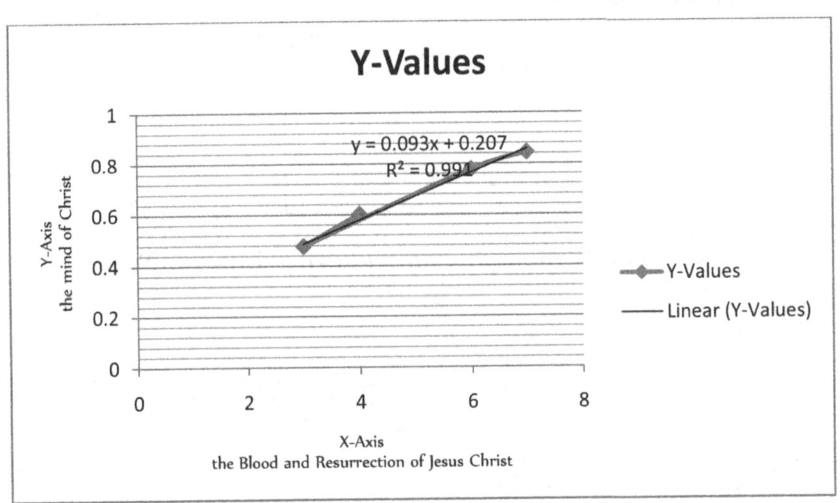

Pilled Poplar, Hazel, and Chestnut bible rods 2

29. And yet I say unto you, That even Solomon peaceable, perfect, peaceful, one who recompenses **in all his glory was not arrayed like one of these.**

6,14. Bible Matrices

Pilled Poplar, Hazel, and Chestnut bible rods 1

$\text{Log}_{10} 11 = 1.0413$ $\text{Log}_{10} 6 = 0.7781$

$$\text{Log}_6 3 = y$$
$$6^y = 3$$
$$\text{Log}_{10} 6y = \log_{10} 3$$
$$y \log_{10} 6 = \log_{10} 3$$
$$y = \log_{10}3/\log_{10}6$$
$$y = 0.4771/ 0.7781$$
$$y = 0.6131$$

6, 14. Deep calls unto Deep study bible 1

0.7781, 0.6131 1.0413 . Deep calls unto Deep study bible 2

x-axis	y-axis
6	0.7781
14	1.6544

Water Spout *(lightning; combinatorics)* Study bible 1

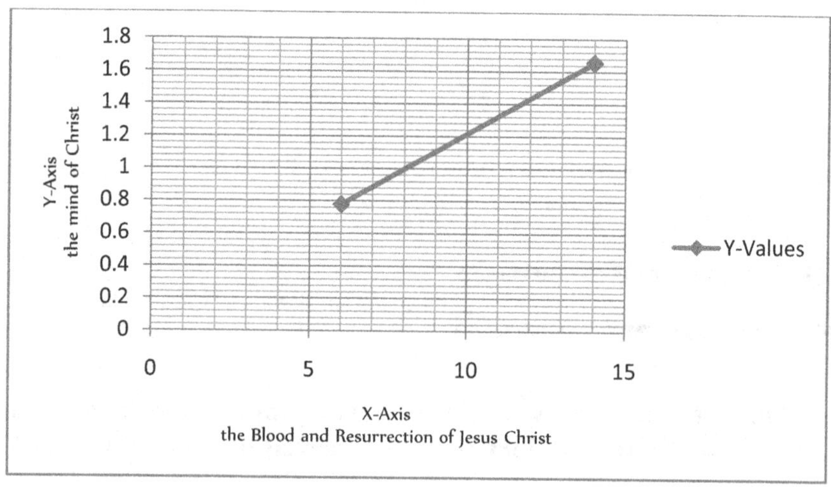

Water Spout *(lightning; combinatorics)* Study bible 2

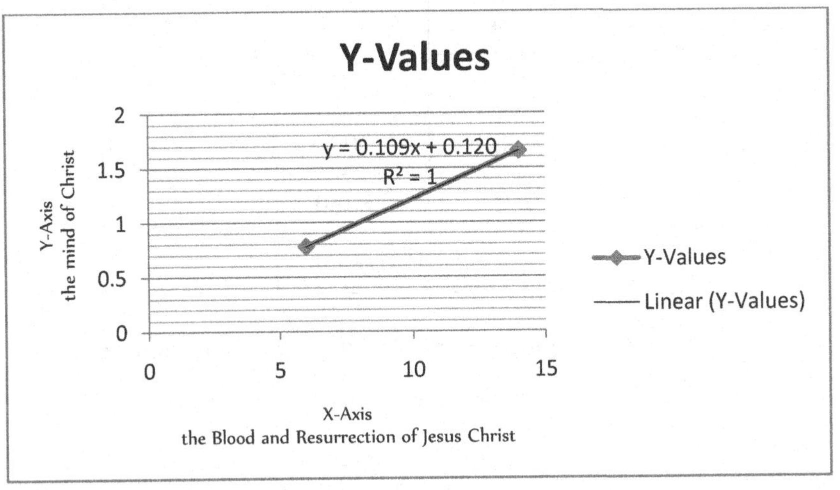

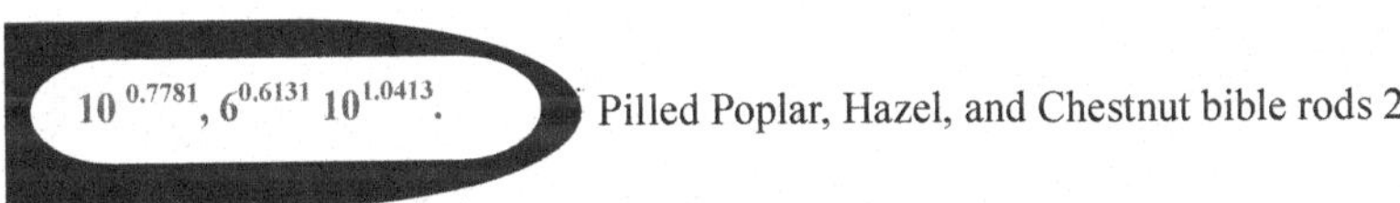

Pilled Poplar, Hazel, and Chestnut bible rods 2

30. Wherefore, if God so clothe the grass of the field, which to day is, and to morrow is cast into the oven, shall he not much more clothe you, O ye of little faith?

1, 9, 4, 8, 7, 5? Bible Matrices

1_{10}, 9_{10}, 4_{10}, 8_{10}, 7_{10}, 5_{10}?

Pilled Poplar, Hazel, and Chestnut bible rods 1

$\text{Log}_{10} 1 = 0$ $\text{Log}_{10} 5 = 0.6989$ $\text{Log}_{10} 7 = 0.8450$ $\text{Log}_{10} 9 = 0.9542$ $\text{Log}_{10} 4 = 0.6020$ $\text{Log}_{10} 8 = 0.9030$

1, 9, 4, 8, 7, 5? Deep calls unto Deep study bible 1

0, 0.9542, 0.6020, 0.9030, 0.8450, 0.6989?

Deep calls unto Deep study bible 2

x-axis	y-axis

1	0
9	0.9542
4	0.6020
8	0.9030
7	0.8450
5	0.6989

Water Spout *(lightning; combinatorics)* Study bible 1

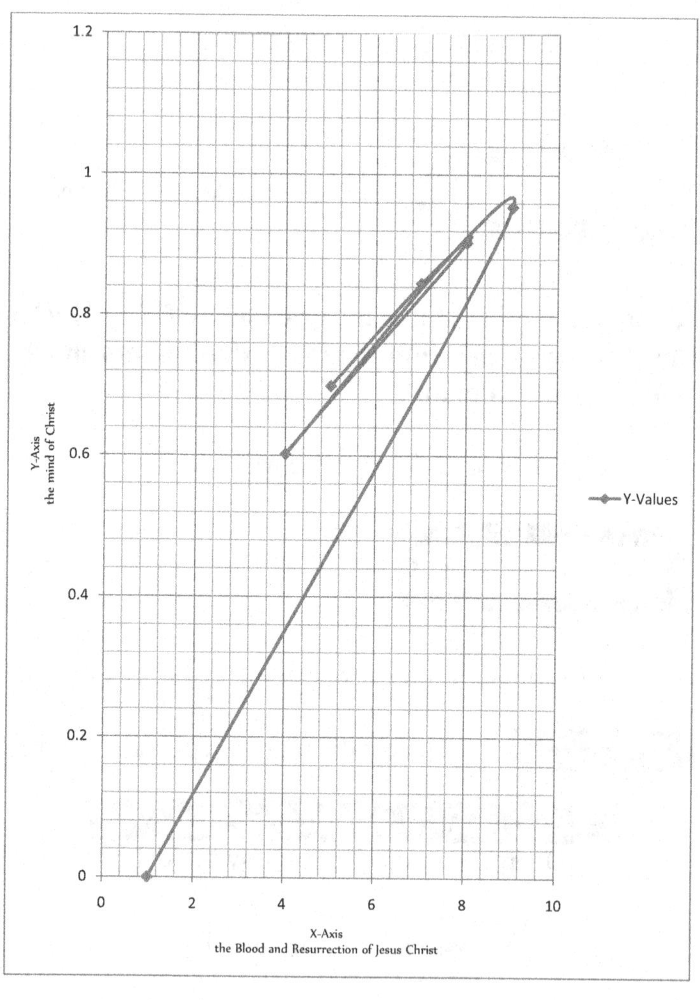

Water Spout *(lightning; combinatorics)* Study bible 2

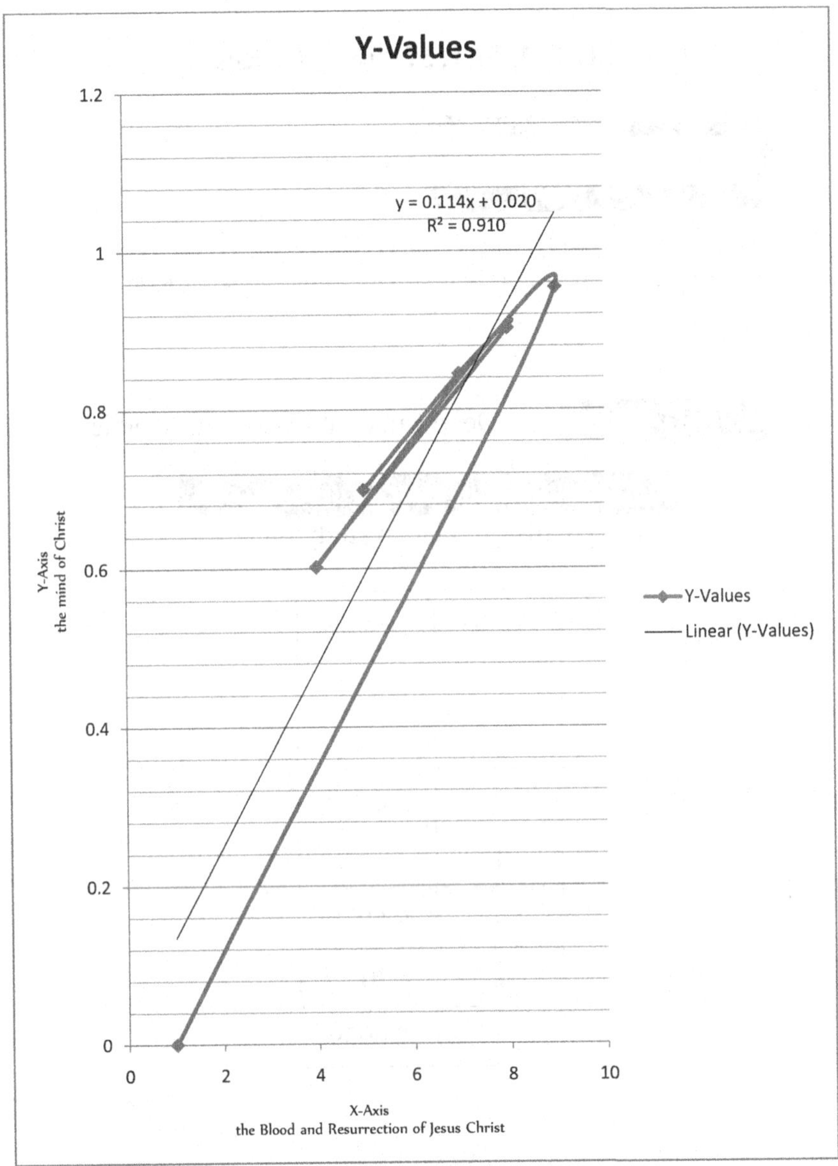

10^{0}, $10^{0.9542}$, $10^{0.6020}$, $10^{0.9030}$, $10^{0.8450}$, $10^{0.6989}$? Pilled Poplar, Hazel, and Chestnut bible rods 2

31. Therefore take no thought, saying, What shall we eat? or, What shall we drink? or, Wherewithal shall we be clothed?

4, 1, 4? 1, 4? 1, 5? Bible Matrices

$4_{10}, 1_{10}, 4_{10}? 1_{10}, 4_{10}? 1_{10}, 5_{10}?$ Pilled Poplar, Hazel, and Chestnut bible rods 1

$\text{Log}_{10} 4 = 0.6020$ $\text{Log}_{10} 1 = 0$ $\text{Log}_{10} 4 = 0.6020$ $\text{Log}_{10} 1 = 0$ $\text{Log}_{10} 4 = 0.6020$ $\text{Log}_{10} 1 = 0$

$\text{Log}_{10} 5 = 0.6989$

4, 1, 4? 1, 4? 1, 5? Deep calls unto Dccp study bible 1

0.6020, 0, 0.6020? 0, 0.6020, 0, 0.6989?
Deep calls unto Deep study bible 2

x-axis	y-axis
4	0.6020
1	0
4	0.6020
1	0
4	0.6020
1	0
5	0.6989

Water Spout *(lightning; combinatorics)* Study bible 1

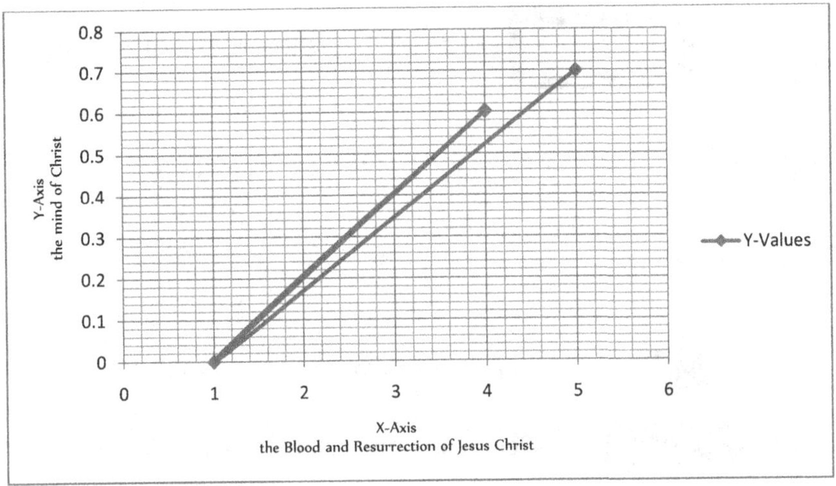

Water Spout *(lightning; combinatorics)* Study bible 2

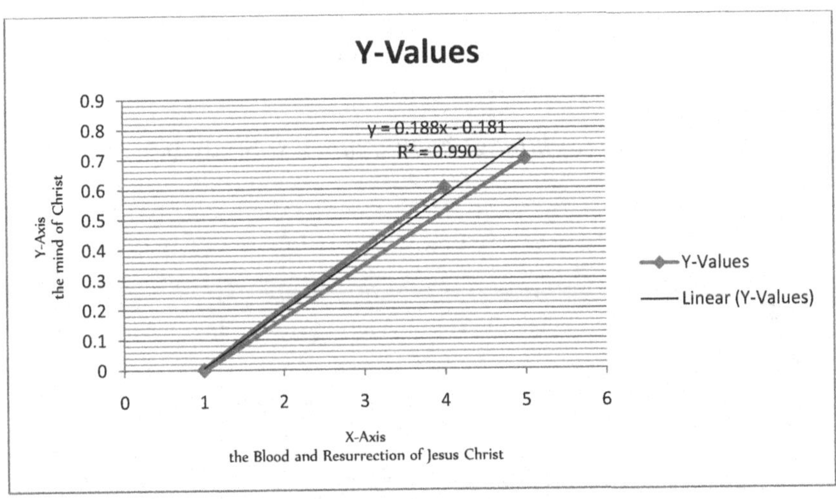

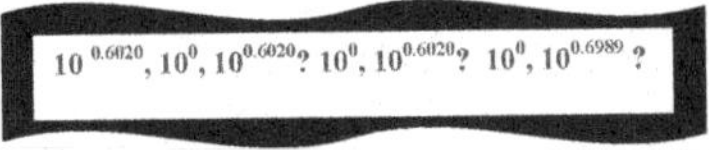

Pilled Poplar, Hazel, and Chestnut bible rods 2

32. For after all these things do the Gentiles non_jews **seek: for your heavenly Father knoweth that ye have need of all these things.**

9: 13. Bible Matrices

$8_2\ 1_{10}: 13_{10}.$ Pilled Poplar, Hazel, and Chestnut bible rods 1

$\text{Log}_{10} 1 = 0$ $\text{Log}_{10} 13 = 1.1139$ $\text{Log}_2 8 = y$

$2^y = 8$

$2^y = 2^3$

$y = 3$

9: 13. Deep calls unto Deep study bible 1

3 0: 1.1139. Deep calls unto Deep study bible 2

x-axis	y-axis
9	3
13	1.1139

Water Spout *(lightning; combinatorics)* Study bible 1

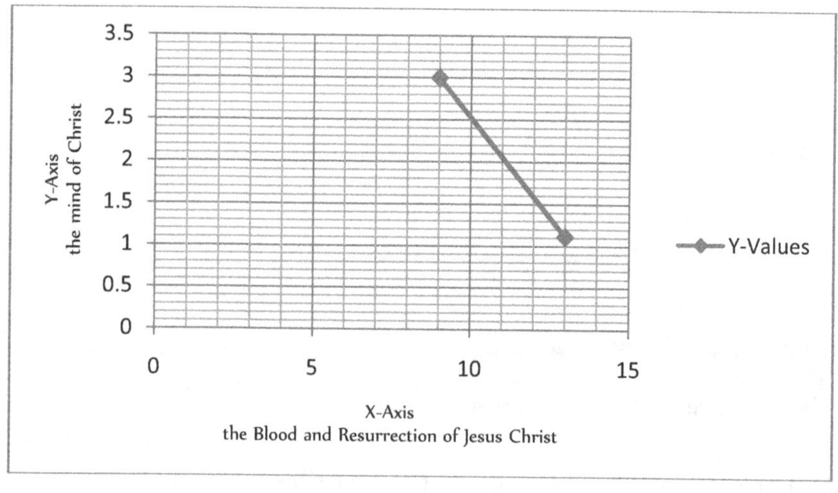

Water Spout *(lightning; combinatorics)* Study bible 2

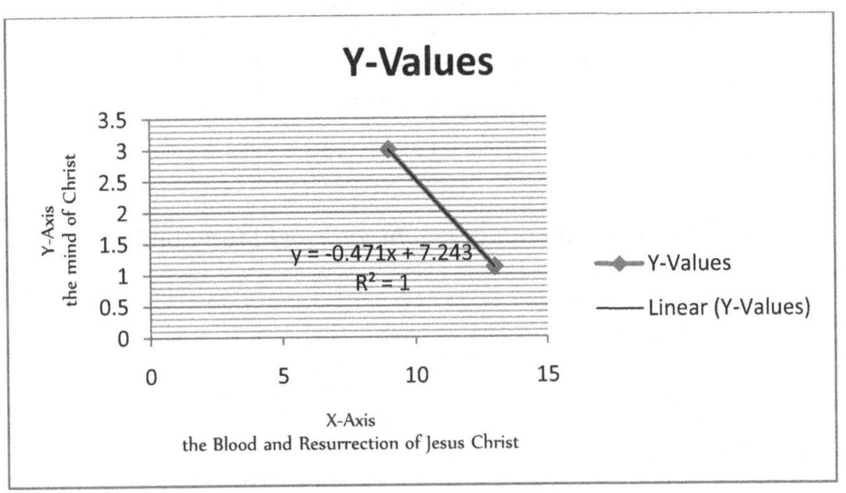

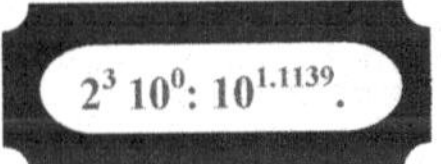

Pilled Poplar, Hazel, and Chestnut bible rods 2

33. But seek ye first $_{1}{}^{x}{}_{1;}$ earliest, initial, original, foremost, opening, primary **the kingdom of God, and his righteousness; and all these things shall be added unto you.**

8, 3; 9. Bible Matrices

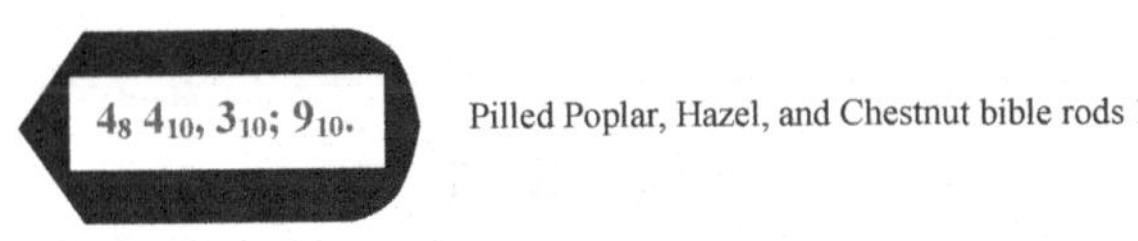

Pilled Poplar, Hazel, and Chestnut bible rods 1

$\text{Log}_8 4 = y$ $\text{Log}_{10} 4 = 0.6020$ $\text{Log}_{10} 3 = 0.4771$ $\text{Log}_{10} 9 = 0.9542$

$8^y = 4$

$2^{3y} = 2^2$

$3y = 2$

$y = 2/3$

8, 3; 9. Deep calls unto Deep study bible 1

0.6667 0.6020, 0.4771; 0.9542.

Deep calls unto Deep study bible 2

x-axis	y-axis
8	1.2687
3	0.4771
9	0.9542

Water Spout *(lightning; combinatorics)* Study bible 1

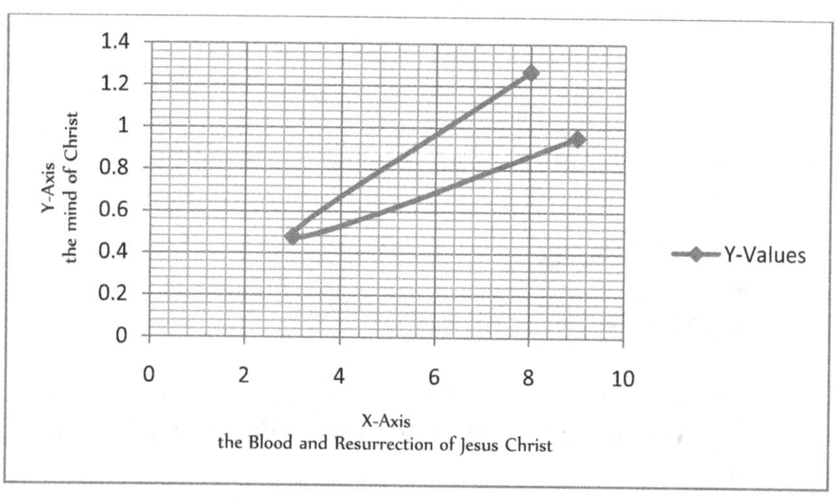

Water Spout *(lightning; combinatorics)* Study bible 2

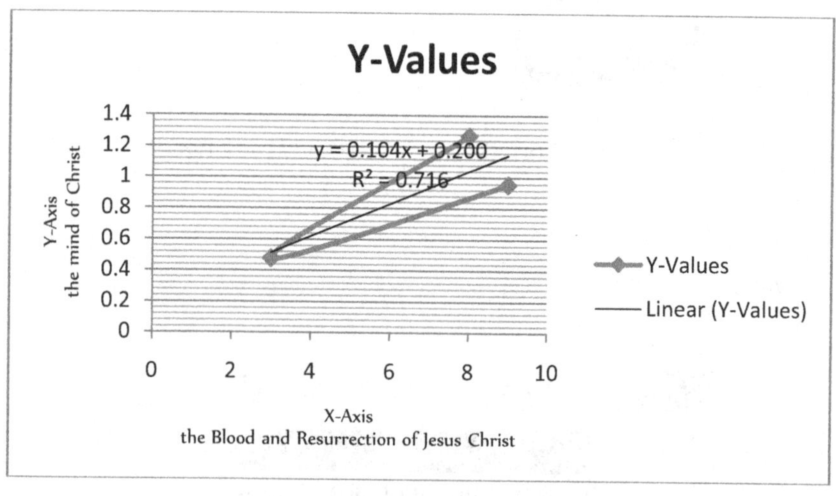

$8^{0.6667}\ 10^{0.6020},\ 10^{0.4771};\ 10^{0.9542}.$

Pilled Poplar, Hazel, and Chestnut bible rods 2

34. Take therefore no thought for the morrow: for the morrow shall take thought for the things of itself. Sufficient unto the day is the evil thereof.

7: 11. 8. Bible Matrices

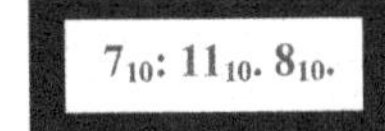
$7_{10}: 11_{10}. 8_{10}.$

Pilled Poplar, Hazel, and Chestnut bible rods 1

$\text{Log}_{10} 7 = 0.8450$ $\text{Log}_{10} 11 = 1.0413$ $\text{Log}_{10} 8 = 0.9030$

7: 11. 8. Deep calls unto Deep study bible 1

0.8450 : 1.0413. 0.9030. Deep calls unto Deep study bible 2

x-axis	y-axis
7	0.8450
11	1.0413
8	0.9030

Water Spout *(lightning; combinatorics)* Study bible 1

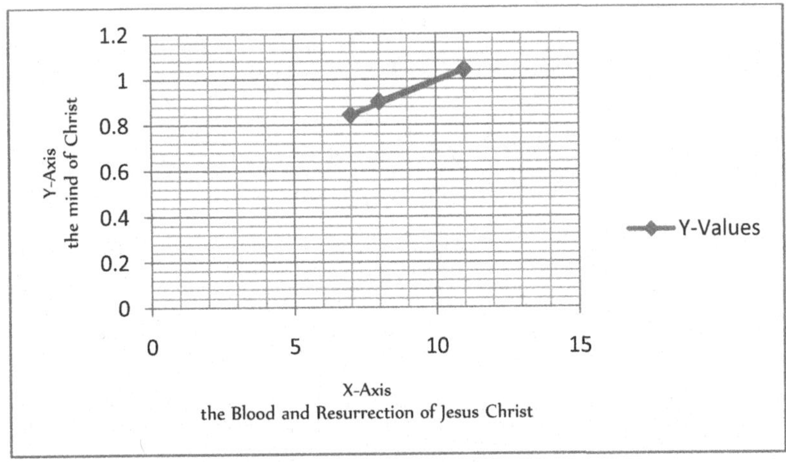

Water Spout *(lightning; combinatorics)* Study bible 2

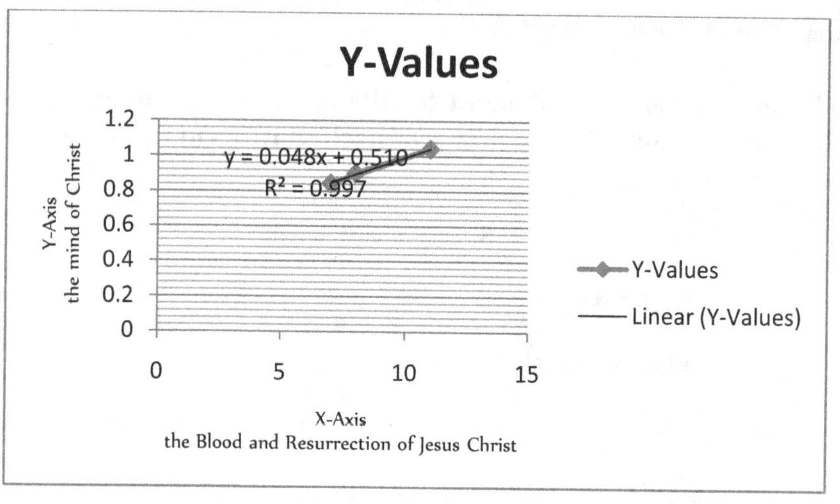

Pilled Poplar, Hazel, and Chestnut bible rods 2

CHAPTER 7

1. Judge not, that ye be not judged.

2, 5. Bible Matrices

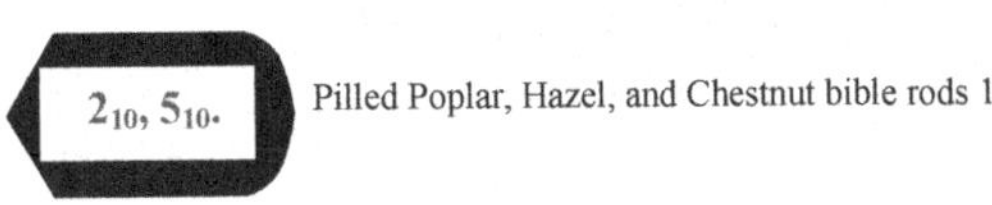

$\text{Log}_{10} 2 = 0.3010$ $\text{Log}_{10} 5 = 0.6989$

2, 5. Deep calls unto Deep study bible 1

0.3010, 0.6989. Deep calls unto Deep study bible 2

x-axis	y-axis
2	0.3010
5	0.6989

Water Spout *(lightning; combinatorics)* Study bible 1

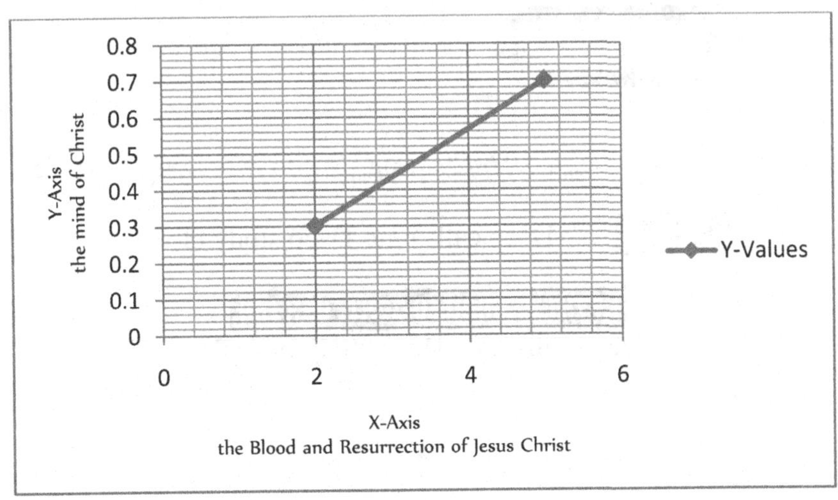

Water Spout *(lightning; combinatorics)* Study bible 2

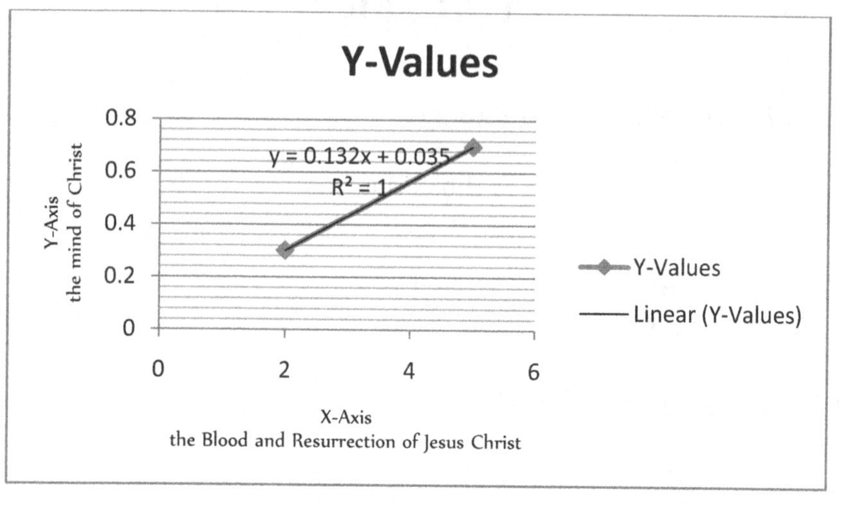

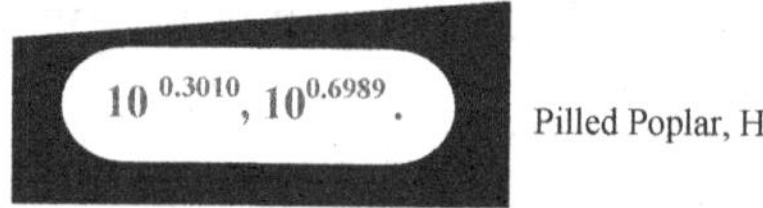

Pilled Poplar, Hazel, and Chestnut bible rods 2

2. For with what judgment ye judge, ye shall be judged: and with what measure ye mete, it shall be measured to you again.

6, 4: 6, 7. Bible Matrices

Pilled Poplar, Hazel, and Chestnut bible rods 1

$\text{Log}_{10} 6 = 0.7781$ $\text{Log}_{10} 4 = 0.6020$ $\text{Log}_{10} 6 = 0.7781$ $\text{Log}_{10} 7 = 0.8450$

6, 4: 6, 7. Deep calls unto Deep study bible 1

0.7781, 0.6020: 0.7781, 0. 8450.
Deep calls unto Deep study bible 2

x-axis	y-axis
6	0.7781
4	0.6020
6	0.7781
7	0.8450

Water Spout *(lightning; combinatorics)* Study bible 1

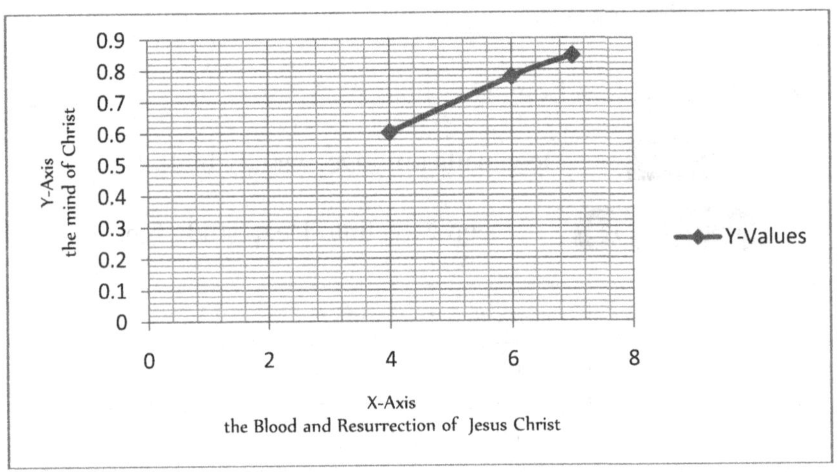

Water Spout *(lightning; combinatorics)* Study bible 2

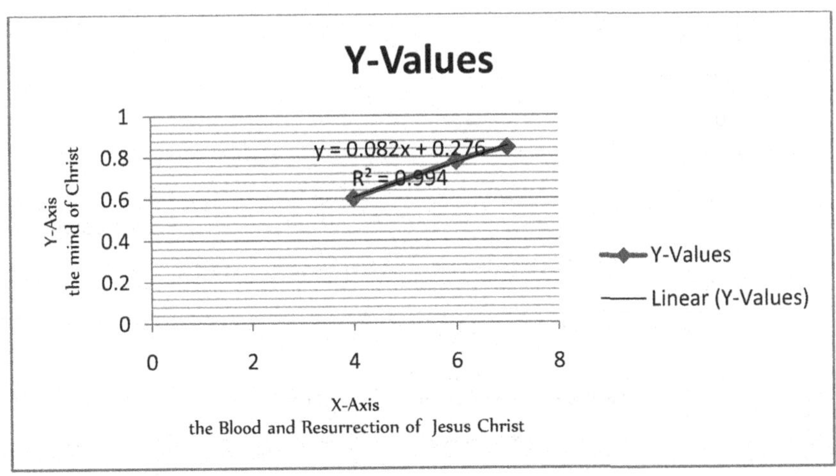

Pilled Poplar, Hazel, and Chestnut bible rods 2

3. And why beholdest thou the mote that is in thy brother's eye, but considerest not the beam that is in thine own eye?

12, 11? Bible Matrices

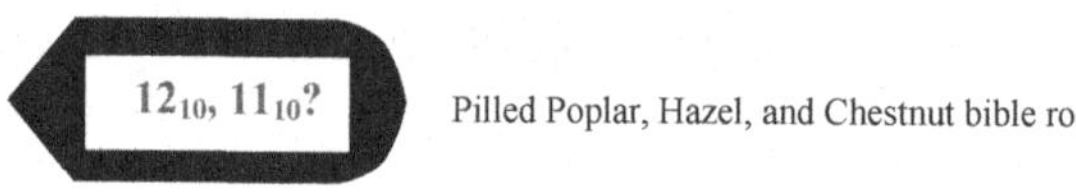

Pilled Poplar, Hazel, and Chestnut bible rods 1

$\text{Log}_{10} 12 = 1.0791$ $\text{Log}_{10} 11 = 1.0413$

12, 11? Deep calls unto Deep study bible 1

1.0791, 1.0413? Deep calls unto Deep study bible 2

x-axis	y-axis
12	1.0791
11	1.0413

Water Spout *(lightning; combinatorics)* Study bible 1

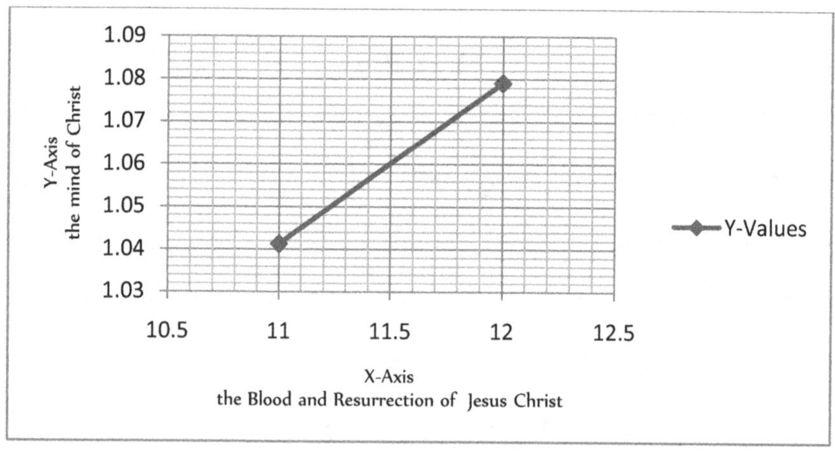

Water Spout *(lightning; combinatorics)* Study bible 2

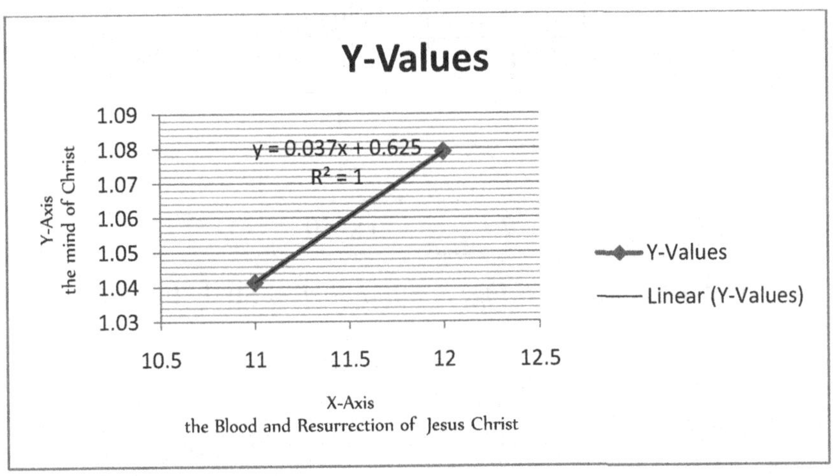

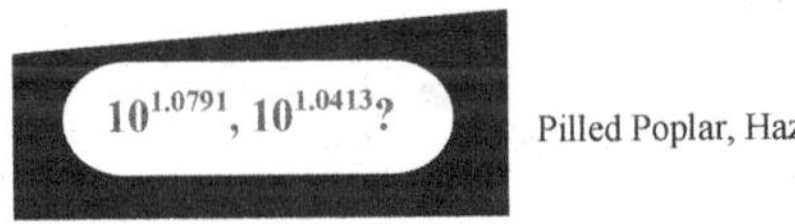

Pilled Poplar, Hazel, and Chestnut bible rods 2

4. Or how wilt thou say to thy brother, Let me pull out the mote out of thine eye; and, behold, a beam is in thine own eye?

8, 10; 1, 1, 7? Bible Matrices

8_{10}, 10_{10}; 1_{10}, 1_{10}, 7_{10}?

Pilled Poplar, Hazel, and Chestnut bible rods 1

$\text{Log}_{10} 8 = 0.9030 \quad \text{Log}_{10} 10 = 1 \quad \text{Log}_{10} 1 = 0 \quad \text{Log}_{10} 1 = 0 \quad \text{Log}_{10} 7 = 0.8450$

8, 10; 1, 1, 7? Deep calls unto Deep study bible 1

0.9030, 1; 0, 0, 0.8450? Deep calls unto Deep study bible 2

x-axis	y-axis
8	0.9030
10	1
1	0
1	0
7	0.8450

Water Spout *(lightning; combinatorics)* Study bible 1

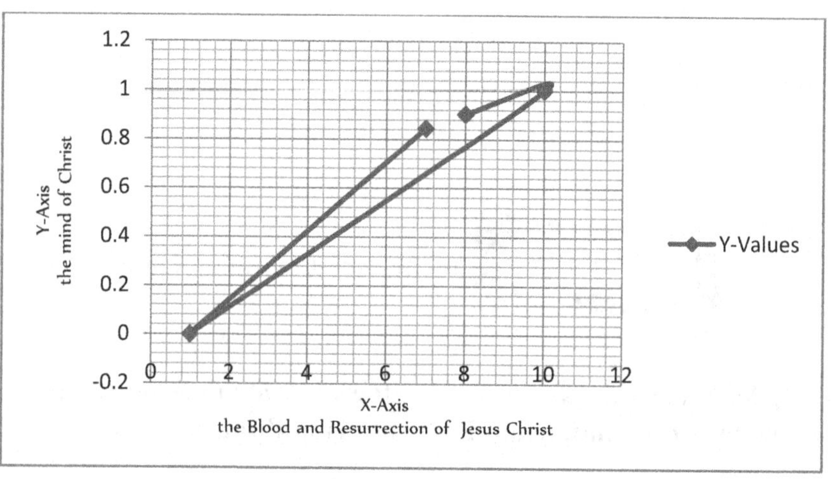

Water Spout *(lightning; combinatorics)* Study bible 2

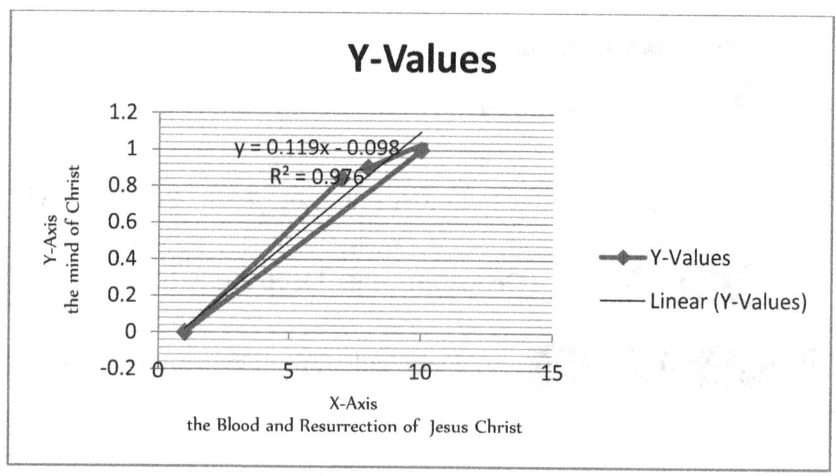

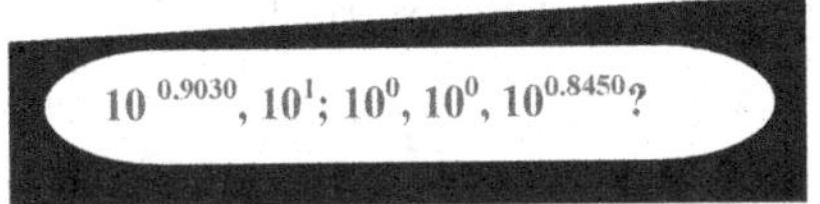

Pilled Poplar, Hazel, and Chestnut bible rods 2

5. Thou hypocrite, first 1 x 1; earliest, initial, original, foremost, opening, primary, former **cast out the beam out of thine own eye; and then shalt thou see clearly to cast out the mote out of thy brother's eye.**

2, 10; 16. Bible Matrices

Pilled Poplar, Hazel, and Chestnut bible rods 1

$\text{Log}_{10} 2 = 0.3010$ $\text{Log}_{10} 9 = 0.9542$ $\text{Log}_{10} 16 = 1.2041$ $\text{Log}_9 1 = y$

$$9^y = 1$$

$$9^y = 9^0$$

$$y = 0$$

2, 10; 16. Deep calls unto Deep study bible 1

0.3010, 0, 0.9542; 1.2041. Deep calls unto Deep study bible 2

x-axis	y-axis
2	0.3010
10	0.9542
16	1.2041

Water Spout *(lightning; combinatorics)* Study bible 1

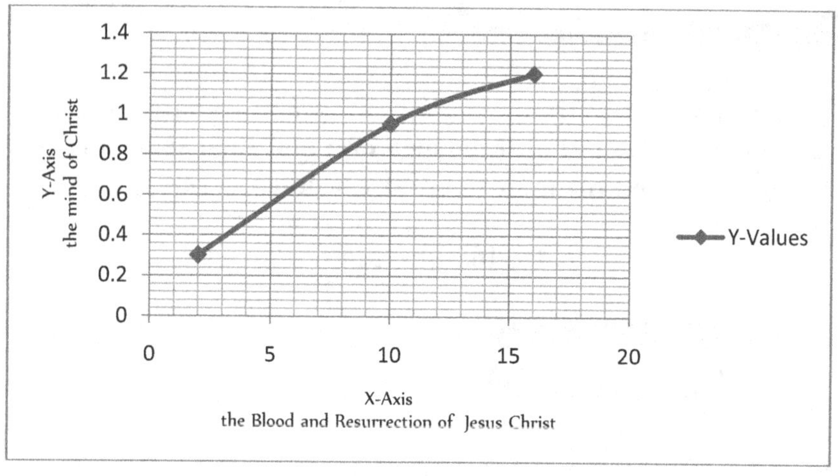

Water Spout *(lightning; combinatorics)* Study bible 2

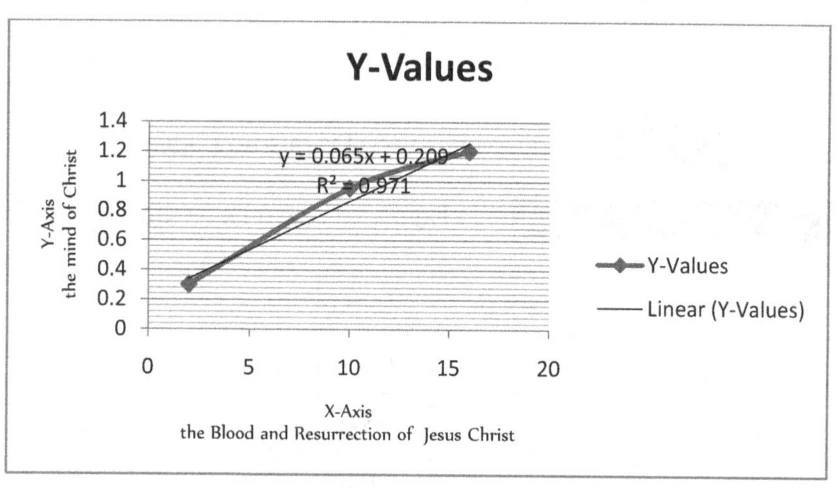

Pilled Poplar, Hazel, and Chestnut bible rods 2

6. Give not that which is holy unto the dogs, neither cast ye your pearls before swine, lest they trample them under their feet, and turn again and rend you.

9, 7, 7, 6. Bible Matrices

$\text{Log}_{10} 9 = 0.9542$ $\text{Log}_{10} 7 = 0.8450$ $\text{Log}_{10} 7 = 0.8450$ $\text{Log}_{10} 6 = 0.7781$

9, 7, 7, 6. Deep calls unto Deep study bible 1

0.9542, 0.8450, 0.8450, 0.7781.
Deep calls unto Deep study bible 2

x-axis	y-axis
9	0.9542
7	0.8450
7	0.8450
6	0.7781

Water Spout *(lightning; combinatorics)* Study bible 1

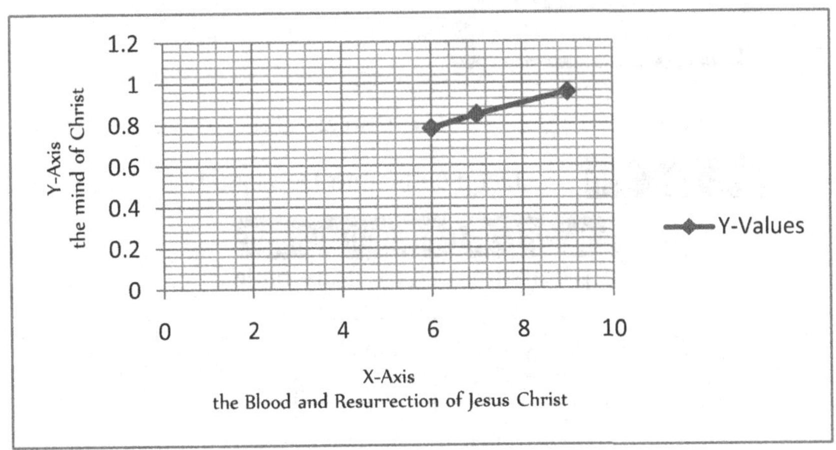

Water Spout *(lightning; combinatorics)* Study bible 2

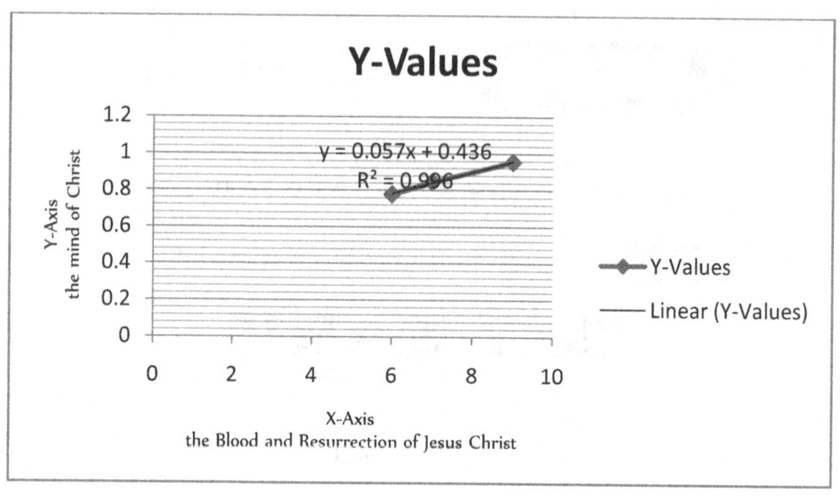

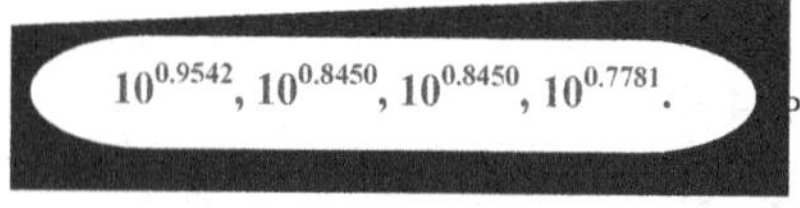

Pilled Poplar, Hazel, and Chestnut bible rods 2

7. Ask, and it shall be given you; seek, and ye shall find; knock, and it shall be opened unto you:

1, 6; 1, 4; 1, 7: Bible Matrices

$1_{10}, 6_{10}; 1_{10}, 4_{10}; 1_{10}, 7_{10}$: Pilled Poplar, Hazel, and Chestnut bible rods 1

$\text{Log}_{10} 1 = 0$ $\text{Log}_{10} 6 = 0.7781$ $\text{Log}_{10} 1 = 0$ $\text{Log}_{10} 4 = 0.6020$ $\text{Log}_{10} 1 = 0$ $\text{Log}_{10} 7 = 0.8450$

1, 6; 1, 4; 1, 7: Deep calls unto Deep study bible 1

0, 0.7781, 0, 0.6020, 0, 0.8450:
Deep calls unto Deep study bible 2

x-axis	y-axis
1	0
6	0.7781
1	0

4	0.6020
1	0
7	0.8450

Water Spout *(lightning; combinatorics)* Study bible 1

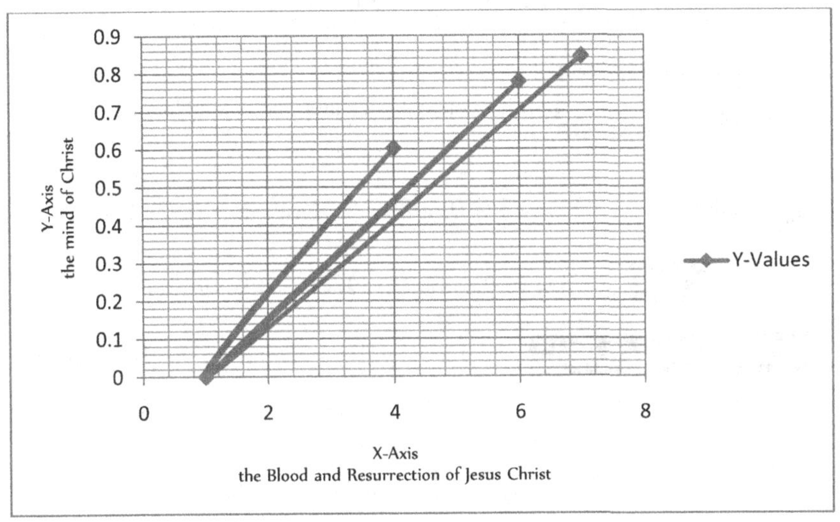

Water Spout *(lightning; combinatorics)* Study bible 2

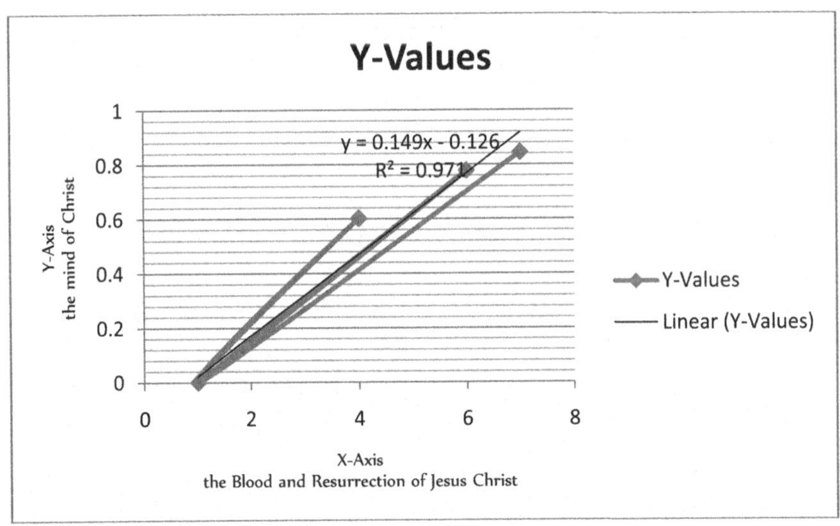

$10^0, 10^{0.7781}; 10^0, 10^{0.6020}; 10^0, 10^{0.8450};$ Pilled Poplar, Hazel, and Chestnut bible rods 2

8. For every one that asketh receiveth; and he that seeketh findeth; and to him that knocketh it shall be opened.

6; 5; 9. Bible Matrices

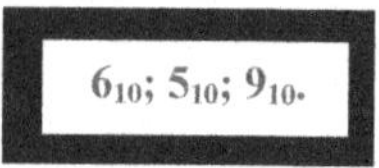

Pilled Poplar, Hazel, and Chestnut bible rods 1

$\text{Log}_{10} 9 = 0.9542$ $\text{Log}_{10} 5 = 0.6989$ $\text{Log}_{10} 6 = 0.7781$

6; 5; 9. Deep calls unto Deep study bible 1

0.7781; 0.6989; 0.9542. Deep calls unto Deep study bible 2

x-axis	y-axis
6	0.7781
5	0.6989
9	0.9542

Water Spout *(lightning; combinatorics)* Study bible 1

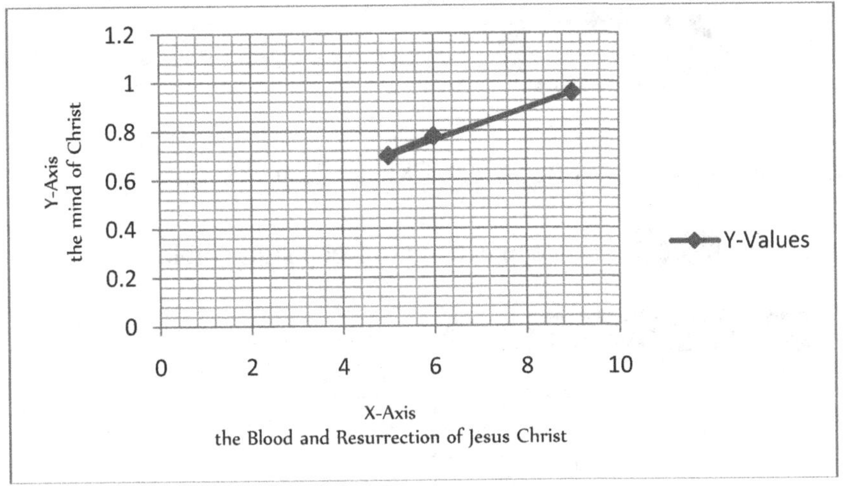

Water Spout *(lightning; combinatorics)* Study bible 2

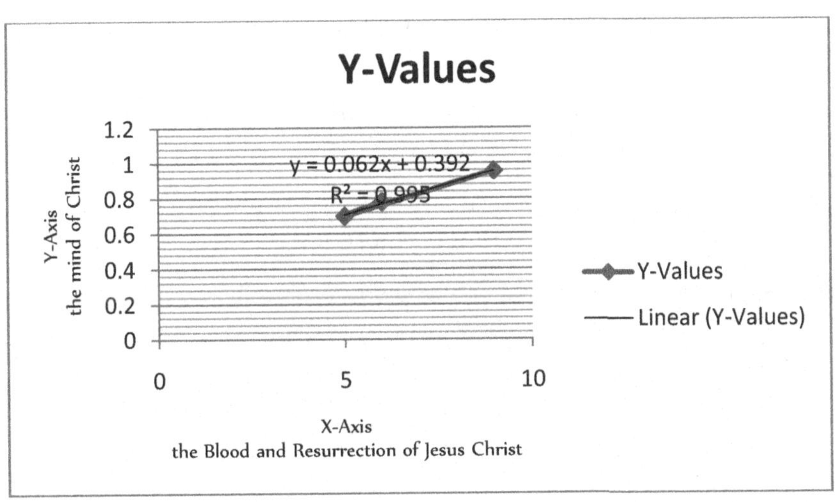

Pilled Poplar, Hazel, and Chestnut bible rods 2

9. Or what man is there of you, whom if his son ask bread, will he give him a stone?

7, 6, 6? Bible Matrices

$Log_{10} 7 = 0.8450$ $Log_{10} 6 = 0.7781$ $Log_{10} 6 = 0.7781$

7, 6, 6? Deep calls unto Deep study bible 1

0.8450, 0.7781, 0.7781? Deep calls unto Deep study bible 2

x-axis	y-axis
7	0.8450
6	0.7781
6	0.7781

Water Spout *(lightning; combinatorics)* Study bible 1

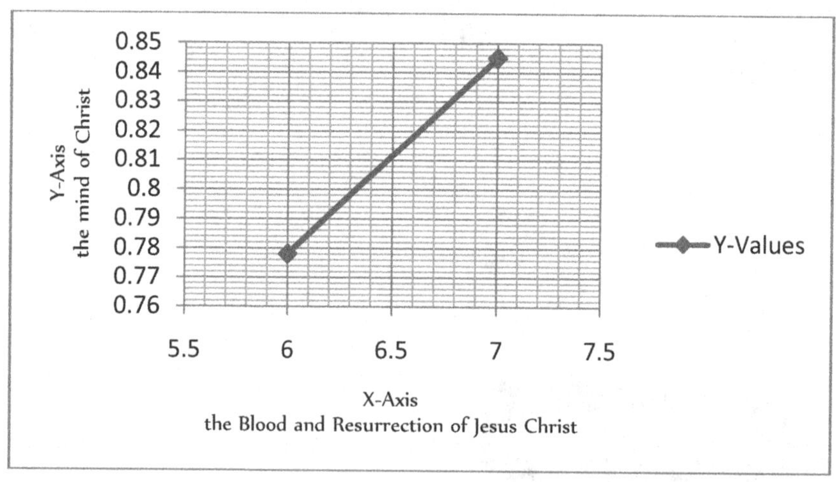

Water Spout *(lightning; combinatorics)* Study bible 2

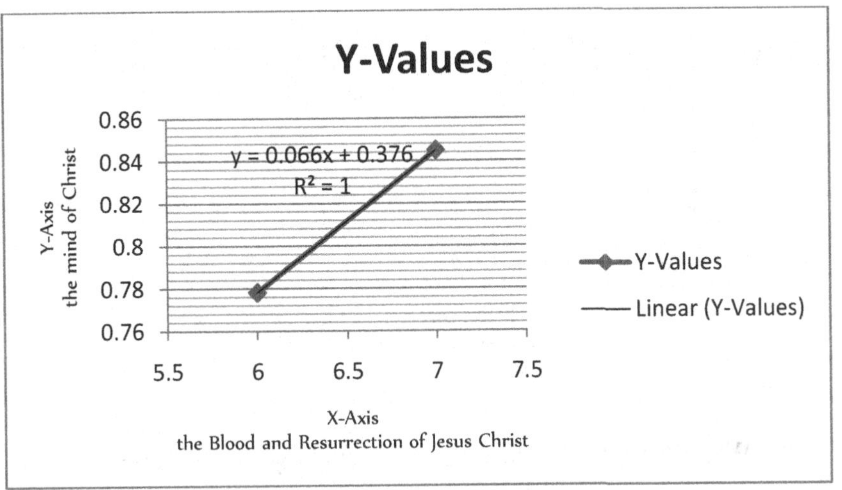

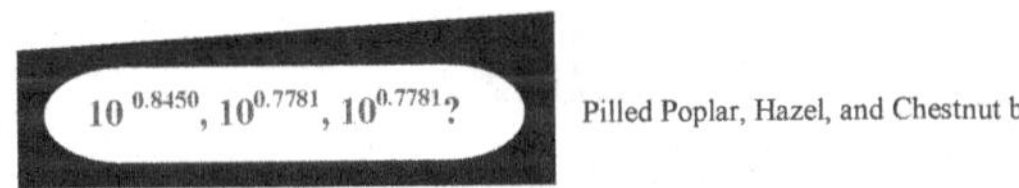

Pilled Poplar, Hazel, and Chestnut bible rods 2

10. Or if he ask a fish, will he give him a serpent?

6, 6? Bible Matrices

Pilled Poplar, Hazel, and Chestnut bible rods 1

$\text{Log}_{10} 6 = 0.7781$ $\text{Log}_{10} 6 = 0.7781$

6, 6? Deep calls unto Deep study bible 1

0.7781, 0.7781? Deep calls unto Deep study bible 2

x-axis	y-axis
6	0.7781
6	0.7781

Water Spout *(lightning; combinatorics)* Study bible 1

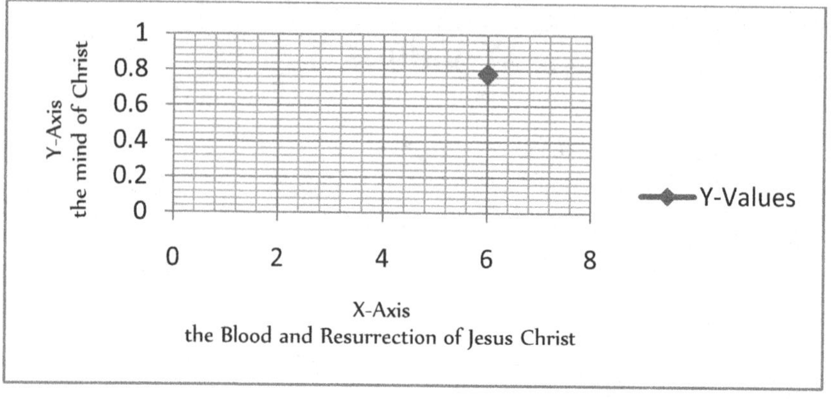

Water Spout *(lightning; combinatorics)* Study bible 2

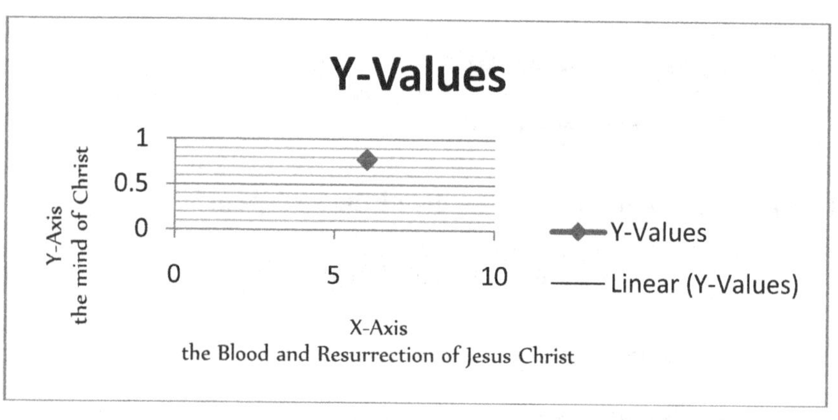

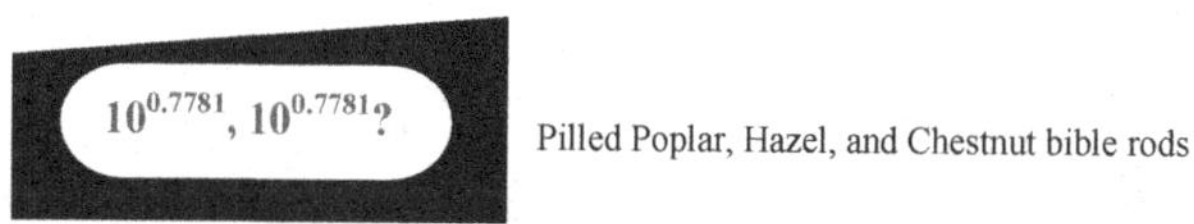

Pilled Poplar, Hazel, and Chestnut bible rods 2

11. If ye then, being evil, know how to give good gifts unto your children, how much more shall your Father which is in heaven give good things to them that ask him?

3, 2, 9, 18? Bible Matrices

3_{10}, 2_{10}, 9_{10}, 18_{10}? Pilled Poplar, Hazel, and Chestnut bible rods 1

$\text{Log}_{10} 3 = 0.4771 \quad \text{Log}_{10} 2 = 0.3010 \quad \log_{10} 9 = 0.9542 \; \log_{10} 18 = 1.2552$

3, 2, 9, 18? Deep calls unto Deep study bible 1

0.4771, 0.3010, 0.9542, 1.2552?

Deep calls unto Deep study bible 2

x-axis	y-axis
3	0.4771
2	0.3010
9	0.9542
18	1.2552

Water Spout *(lightning; combinatorics)* Study bible 1

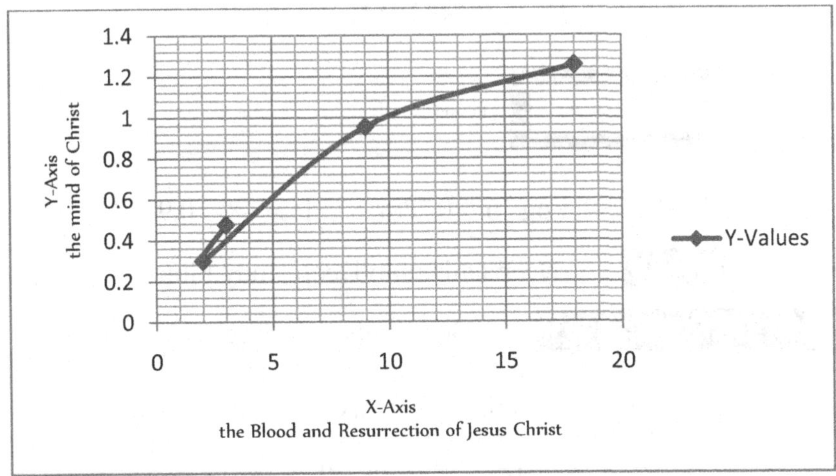

Water Spout *(lightning; combinatorics)* Study bible 2

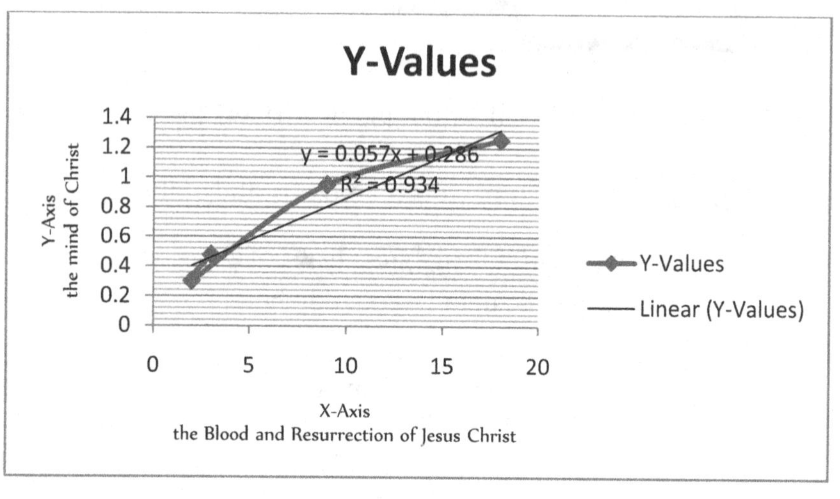

$10^{0.4771}, 10^{0.3010}, 10^{0.9542}, 10^{1.2552}$? Pilled Poplar, Hazel, and Chestnut bible rods 2

12. Therefore all things whatsoever ye would that men should do to you, do ye even so to them: for this is the law and the prophets.

12, 6: 8. Bible Matrices

$12_{10}, 6_{10}: 8_{10}$. Pilled Poplar, Hazel, and Chestnut bible rods 1

$\text{Log}_{10} 12 = 1.0791$ $\text{Log}_{10} 6 = 0.7781$ $\text{Log}_{10} 8 = 0.9030$

12, 6: 8. Deep calls unto Deep study bible 1

1.0791, 0.7781: 0.9030 Deep calls unto Deep study bible 2

x-axis	y-axis
12	1.0791
6	0.7781
8	0.9030

Water Spout *(lightning; combinatorics)* Study bible 1

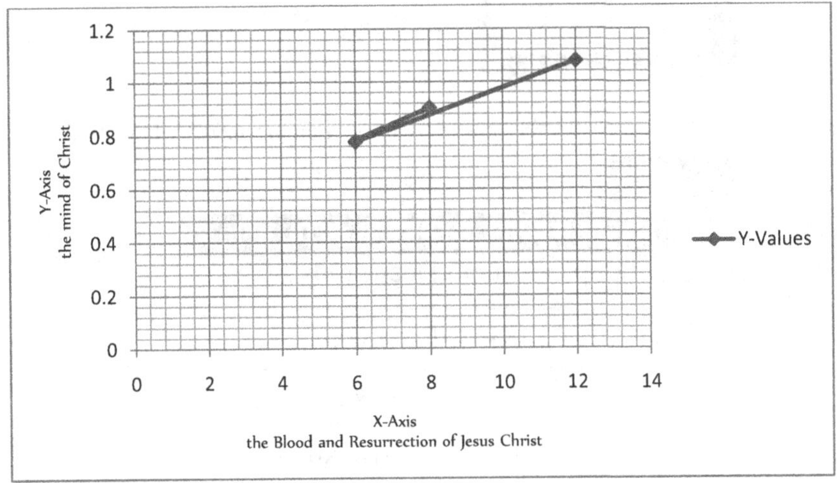

Water Spout *(lightning; combinatorics)* Study bible 2

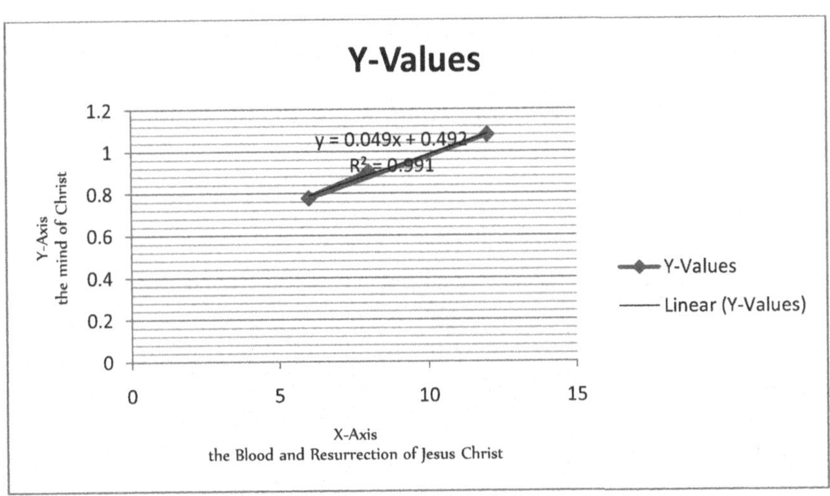

$10^{1.0791}, 10^{0.7781}: 10^{0.9030}$.

Pilled Poplar, Hazel, and Chestnut bible rods 2

13. Enter ye in at the strait gate: for wide is the gate, and broad is the way, that leadeth to destruction, and many there be which go in thereat:

7: 5, 5, 4, 8: Bible Matrices

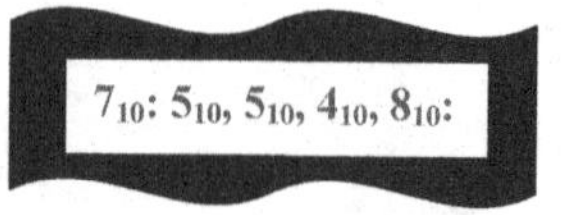

Pilled Poplar, Hazel, and Chestnut bible rods 1

$\text{Log}_{10} 7 = 0.8450$ $\text{Log}_{10} 5 = 0.6989$ $\text{Log}_{10} 5 = 0.6989$ $\text{Log}_{10} 4 = 0.6020$ $\text{Log}_{10} 8 = 0.9030$

7: 5, 5, 4, 8: Deep calls unto Deep study bible 1

0.8450: 0.6989, 0.6989, 0.6020, 0.9030:

Deep calls unto Deep study bible 2

x-axis	y-axis
7	0.8450
5	0.6989
5	0.6989
4	0.6020
8	0.9030

Water Spout *(lightning; combinatorics)* Study bible 1

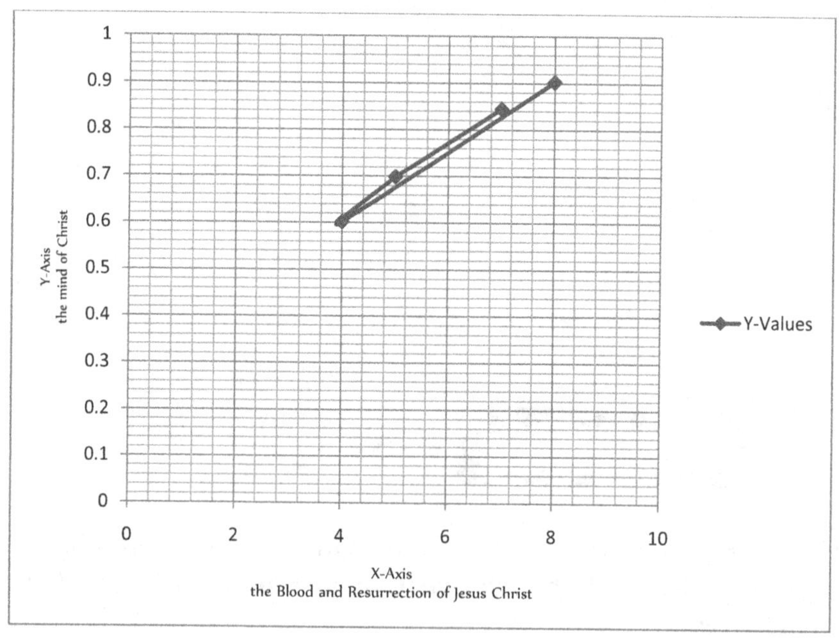

Water Spout *(lightning; combinatorics)* Study bible 2

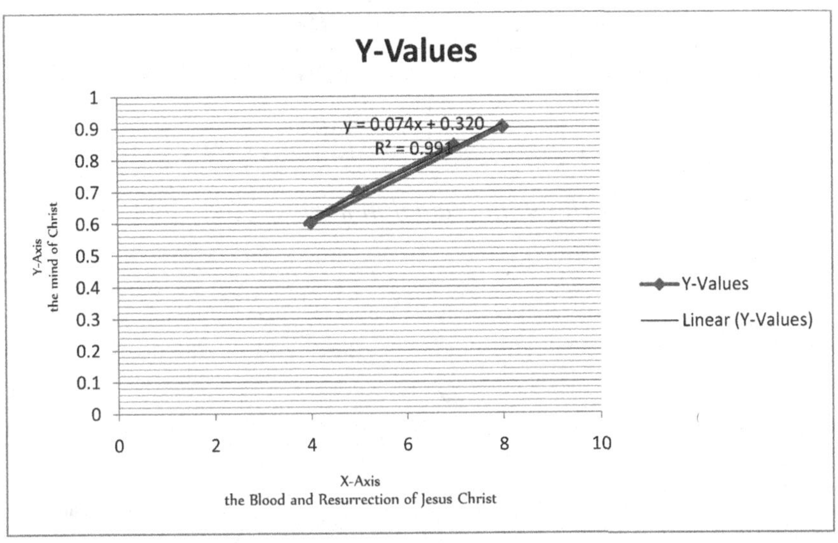

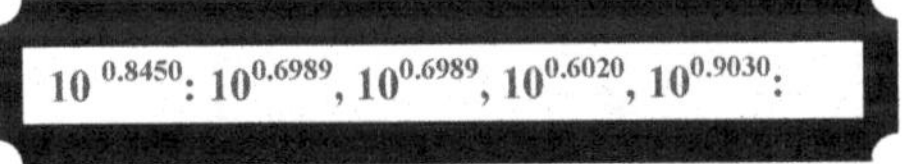

Pilled Poplar, Hazel, and Chestnut bible rods 2

14. Because strait is the gate, and narrow is the way, which leadeth unto life, and few there be that find it.

5, 5, 4, 7. Bible Matrices

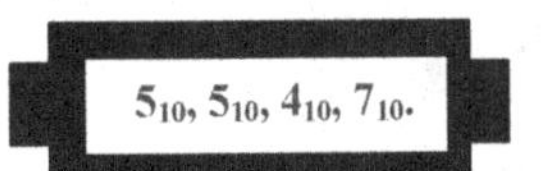

Pilled Poplar, Hazel, and Chestnut bible rods 1

$\text{Log}_{10} 7 = 0.8450$ $\text{Log}_{10} 5 = 0.6989$ $\text{Log}_{10} 5 = 0.6989$ $\text{Log}_{10} 4 = 0.6020$

5, 5, 4, 7. Deep calls unto Deep study bible 1

0.6989, 0.6989, 0.6020, 0.8450.

Deep calls unto Deep study bible 2

x-axis	y-axis

5	0.6989
5	0.6989
4	0.6020
7	0.8450

Water Spout *(lightning; combinatorics)* Study bible 1

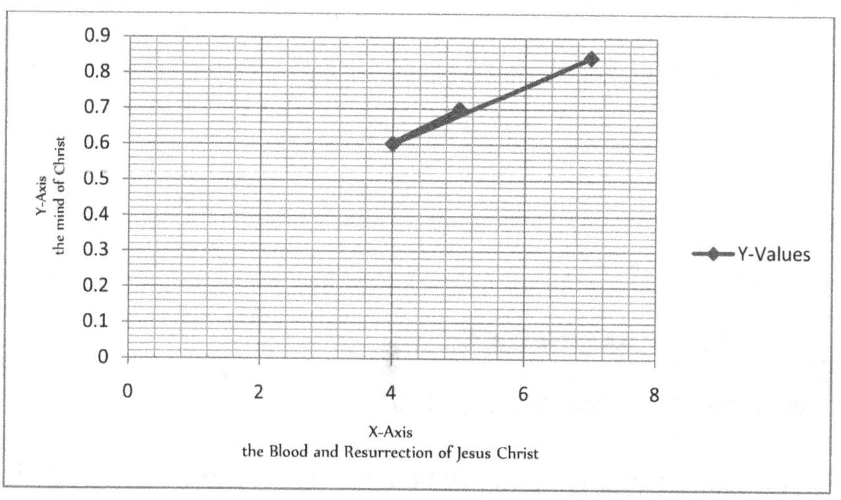

Water Spout *(lightning; combinatorics)* Study bible 2

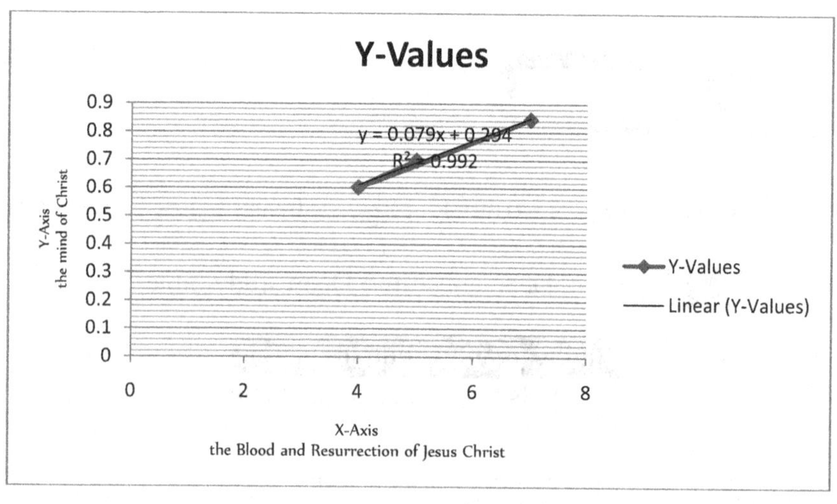

$10^{0.6989}, 10^{0.6989}, 10^{0.6020}, 10^{0.8450}$. Pilled Poplar, Hazel, and Chestnut bible rods 2

15. Beware of false prophets to bubble forth, as from a fountain; utter, **which come to you in sheep's clothing, but inwardly they are ravening wolves.**

4, 7, 6. Bible Matrices

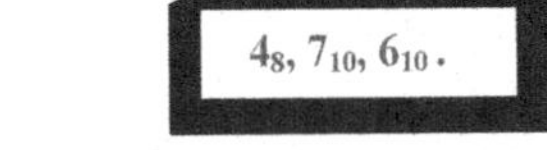
$4_8, 7_{10}, 6_{10}$. Pilled Poplar, Hazel, and Chestnut bible rods 1

$\text{Log}_{10} 7 = 0.8450$ $\text{Log}_{10} 6 = 0.7781$ $\text{Log}_8 4 = y$

$8^y = 4$

$2^{3y} = 2^2$

$3y = 2$

$y = 2/3$

4, 7, 6. Deep calls unto Deep study bible 1

0.6667, 0.8450, 0.7781. Deep calls unto Deep study bible 2

x-axis	y-axis
4	0.6667
7	0.8450
6	0.7781

Water Spout *(lightning; combinatorics)* Study bible 1

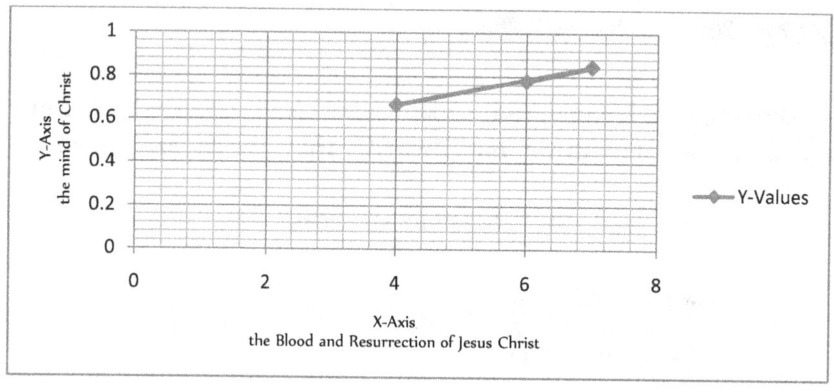

Water Spout *(lightning; combinatorics)* Study bible 2

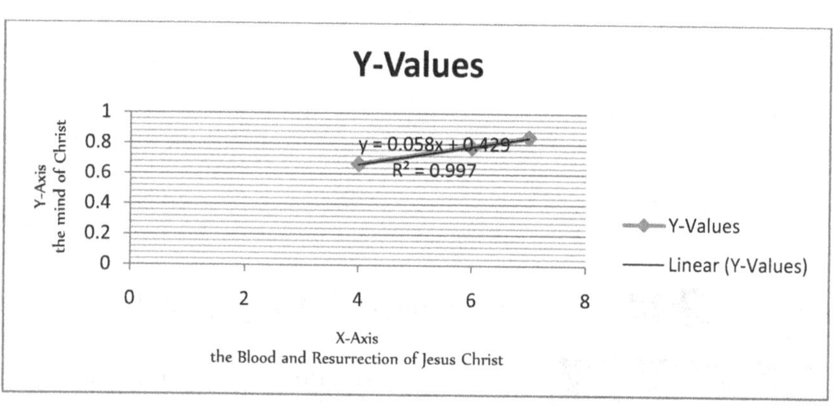

Pilled Poplar, Hazel, and Chestnut bible rods 2

16. Ye shall know them by their fruits. Do men gather grapes of thorns, or figs of thistles?

7. 6, 4? Bible Matrices

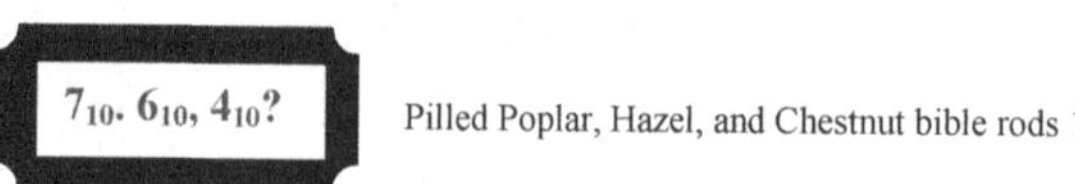

Pilled Poplar, Hazel, and Chestnut bible rods 1

$\text{Log}_{10} 7 = 0.8450$ $\text{Log}_{10} 6 = 0.7781$ $\text{Log}_{10} 4 = 0.6020$

7. 6, 4? Deep calls unto Deep study bible 1

0.8450. 0.7781, 0.6020? Deep calls unto Deep study bible 2

x-axis	y-axis
7	0.8450
6	0.7781
4	0.6020

Water Spout *(lightning; combinatorics)* Study bible 1

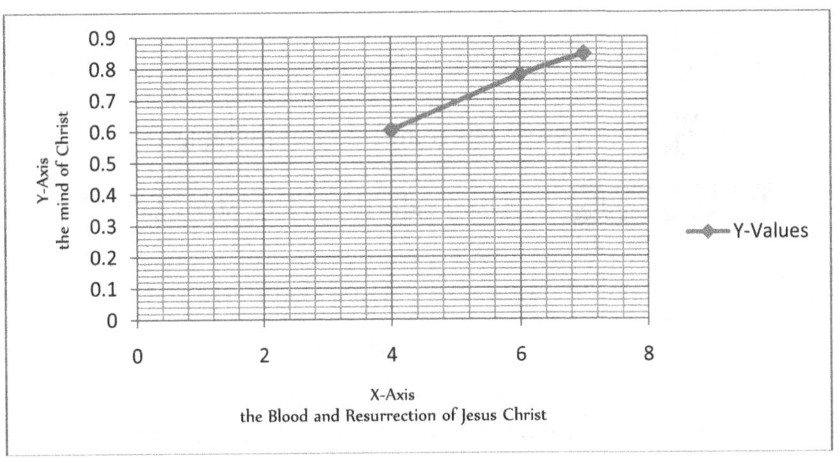

Water Spout *(lightning; combinatorics)* Study bible 2

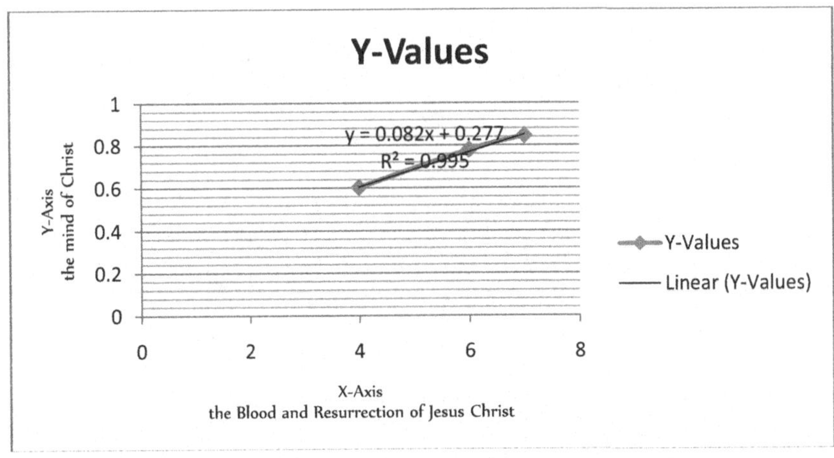

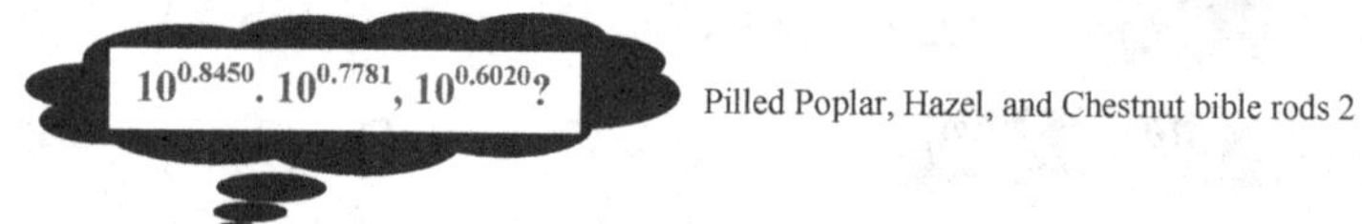

Pilled Poplar, Hazel, and Chestnut bible rods 2

17. Even so every good tree bringeth forth good fruit; but a corrupt tree bringeth forth evil fruit.

9; 8. Bible Matrices

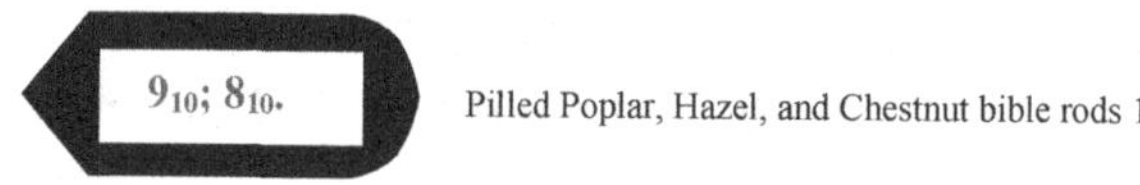

Pilled Poplar, Hazel, and Chestnut bible rods 1

$\text{Log}_{10} 9 = 0.9542$ $\text{Log}_{10} 8 = 0.9030$

9, 8. Deep calls unto Deep study bible 1

0.9542, 0.9030? Deep calls unto Deep study bible 2

x-axis	y-axis
9	0.9542
8	0.9030

Water Spout *(lightning; combinatorics)* Study bible 1

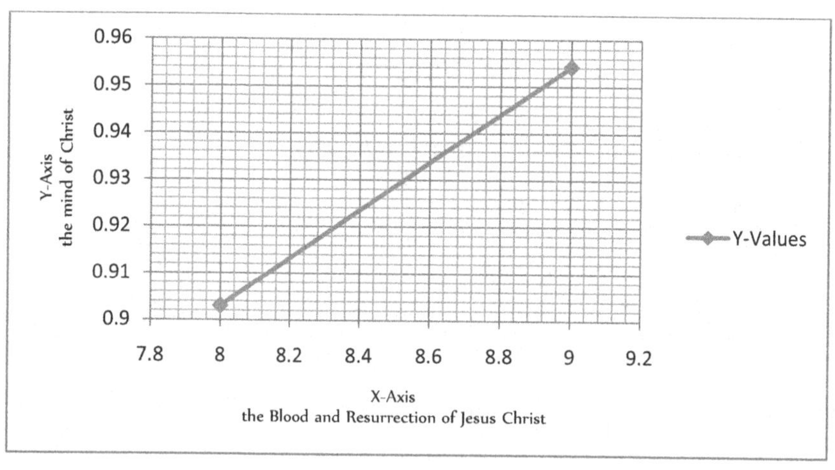

Water Spout *(lightning; combinatorics)* Study bible 2

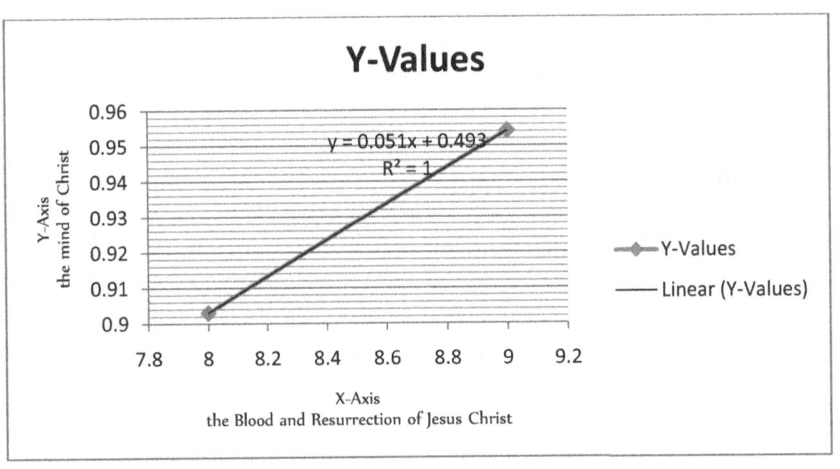

Pilled Poplar, Hazel, and Chestnut bible rods 2

18. A good tree cannot bring forth evil fruit, neither can a corrupt tree bring forth good fruit.

8, 9. Bible Matrices

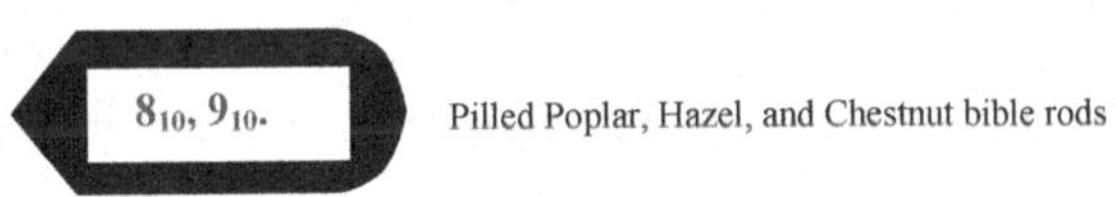

Pilled Poplar, Hazel, and Chestnut bible rods 1

$\text{Log}_{10} 9 = 0.9542$ $\text{Log}_{10} 8 = 0.9030$

8, 9. Deep calls unto Deep study bible 1

0.9030, 0.9542. Deep calls unto Deep study bible 2

x-axis	y-axis
8	0.9030
9	0.9542

Water Spout *(lightning; combinatorics)* Study bible 1

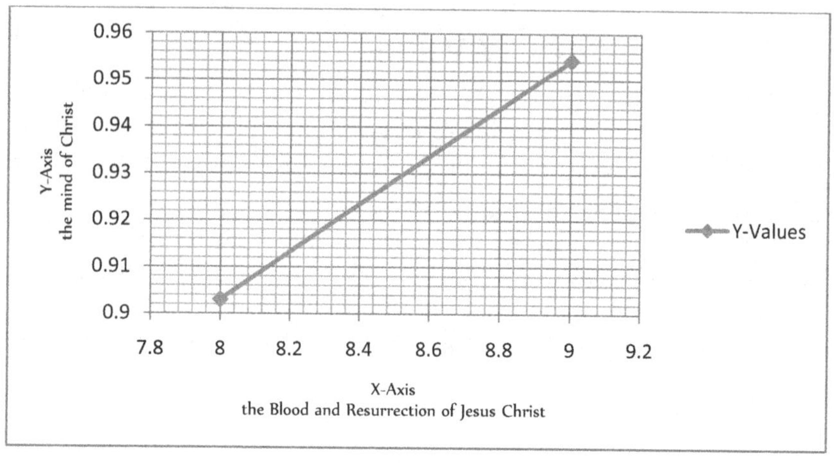

Water Spout *(lightning; combinatorics)* Study bible 2

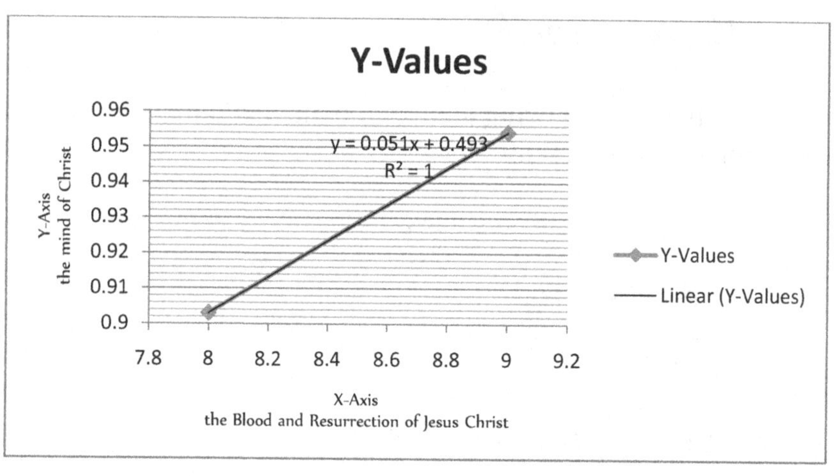

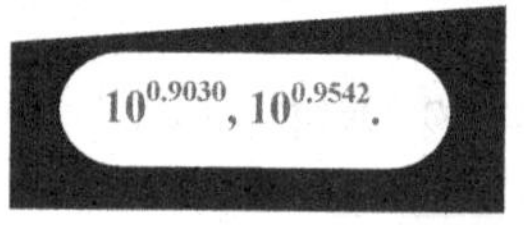

Pilled Poplar, Hazel, and Chestnut bible rods 2

19. Every tree that bringeth not forth good fruit is hewn down, and cast into the fire.

11, 5. Bible Matrices

Pilled Poplar, Hazel, and Chestnut bible rods 1

$\text{Log}_{10} 5 = 0.6989$ $\text{Log}_{10} 11 = 1.0413$

11, 5. Deep calls unto Deep study bible 1

1.0413, 0.6989. Deep calls unto Deep study bible 2

x-axis	y-axis
11	1.0413
5	0.6989

Water Spout *(lightning; combinatorics)* Study bible 1

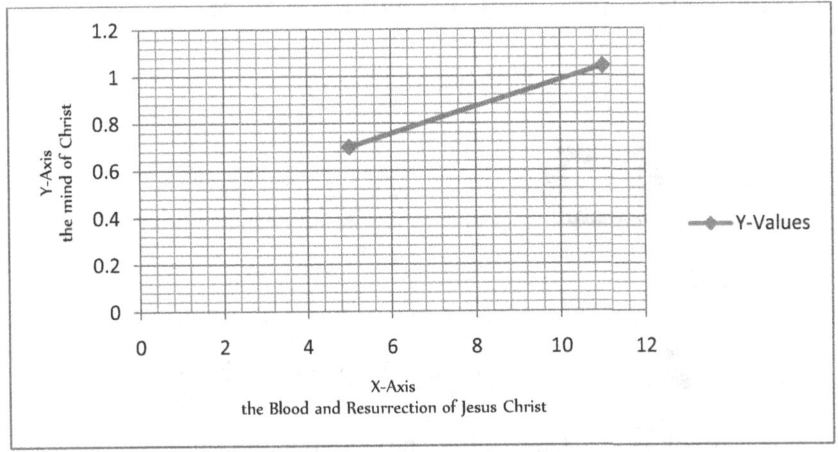

Water Spout *(lightning; combinatorics)* Study bible 2

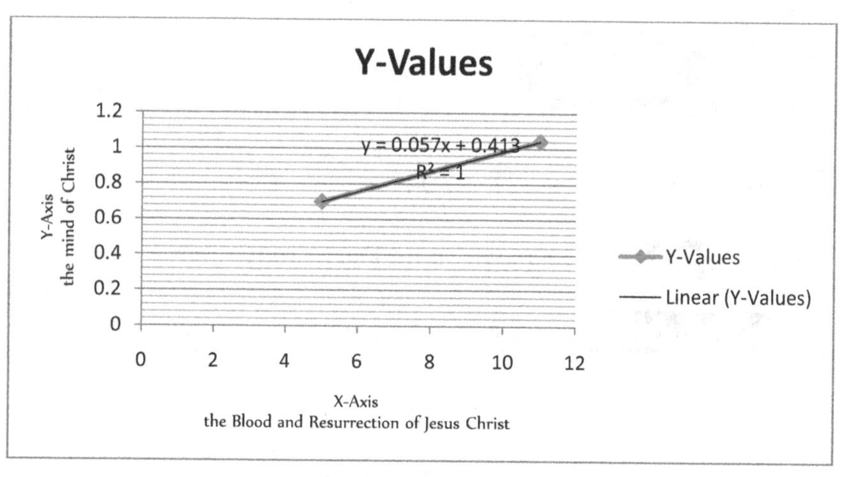

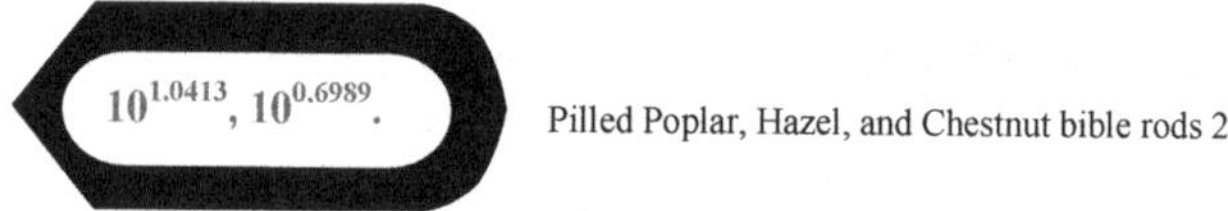

20. Wherefore by their fruits ye shall know them.

8. Bible Matrices

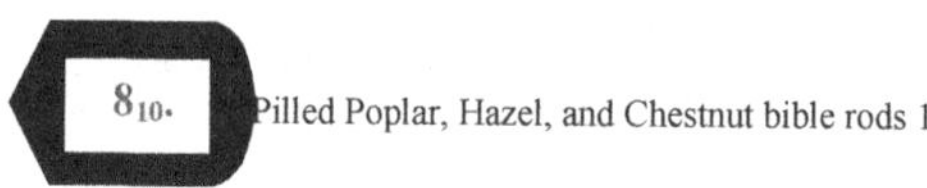

$\text{Log}_{10} 8 = 0.9030$

8. Deep calls unto Deep study bible 1

0.9030. Deep calls unto Deep study bible 2

x-axis	y-axis
8	0.9030

Water Spout *(lightning; combinatorics)* Study bible 1

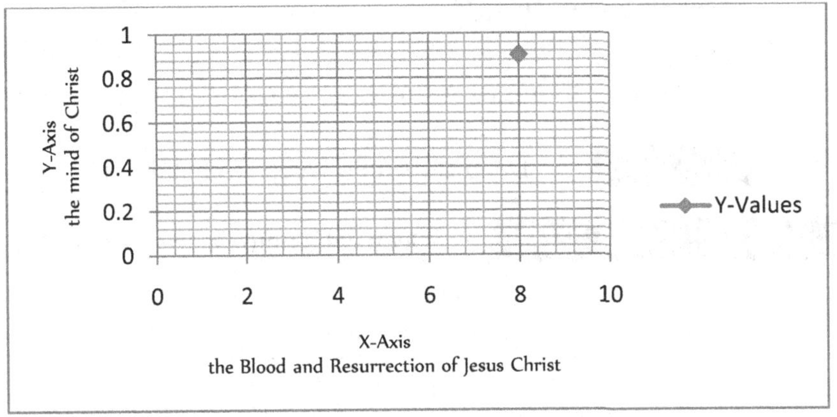

Water Spout *(lightning; combinatorics)* Study bible 2

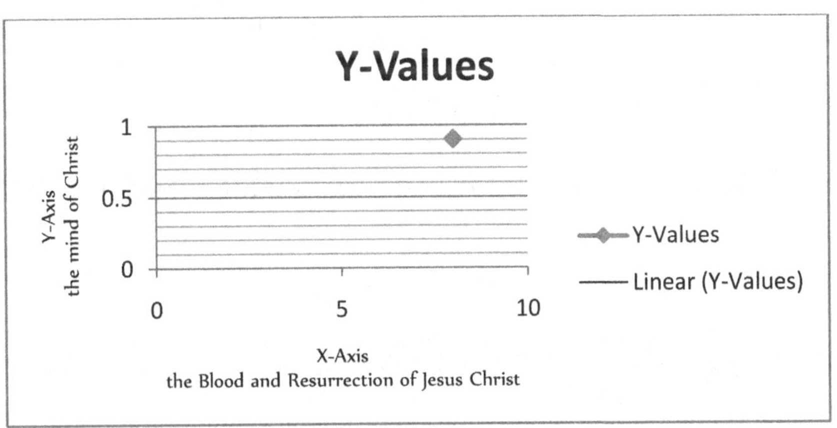

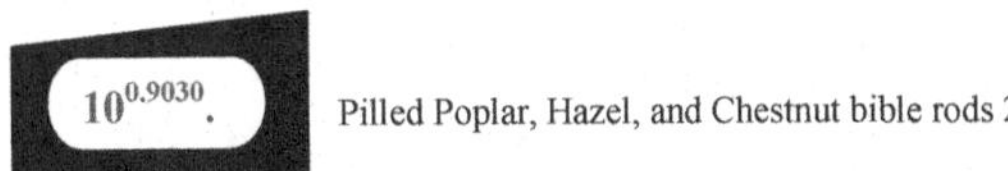

Pilled Poplar, Hazel, and Chestnut bible rods 2

21. Not every one that saith unto me, Lord, Lord, shall enter into the kingdom of heaven; but he that doeth the will of my Father which is in heaven.

7, 1, 1, 7; 13. Bible Matrices

7_{10}, 1_{10}, 1_{10}, 7_{10}; 13_{10}. Pilled Poplar, Hazel, and Chestnut bible rods 1

$\text{Log}_{10} 7 = 0.8450$ $\text{Log}_{10} 1 = 0$ $\text{Log}_{10} 1 = 0$ $\text{Log}_{10} 7 = 0.8450$ $\text{Log}_{10} 13 = 1.1139$

7, 1, 1, 7; 13. Deep calls unto Deep study bible 1

0.8450, 0, 0, 0.8450; 1.1139. Deep calls unto Deep study bible 2

x-axis	y-axis
7	0.8450
1	0
1	0
7	0.8450
13	1.1139

Water Spout *(lightning; combinatorics)* Study bible 1

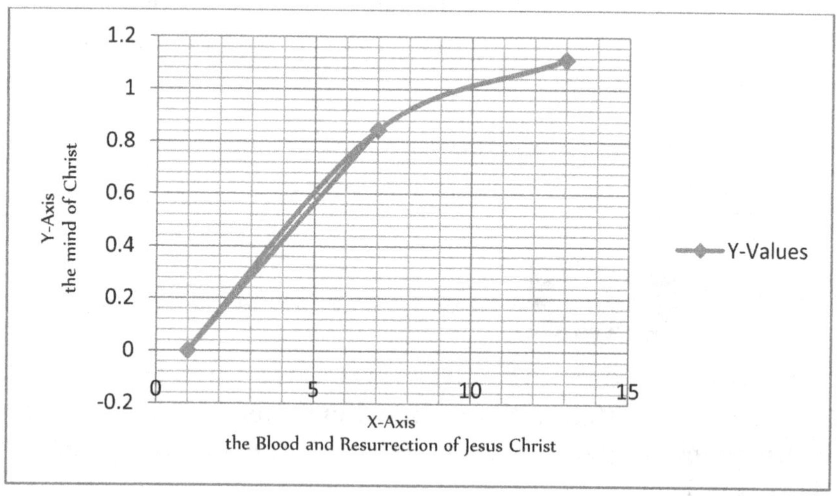

Water Spout *(lightning; combinatorics)* Study bible 2

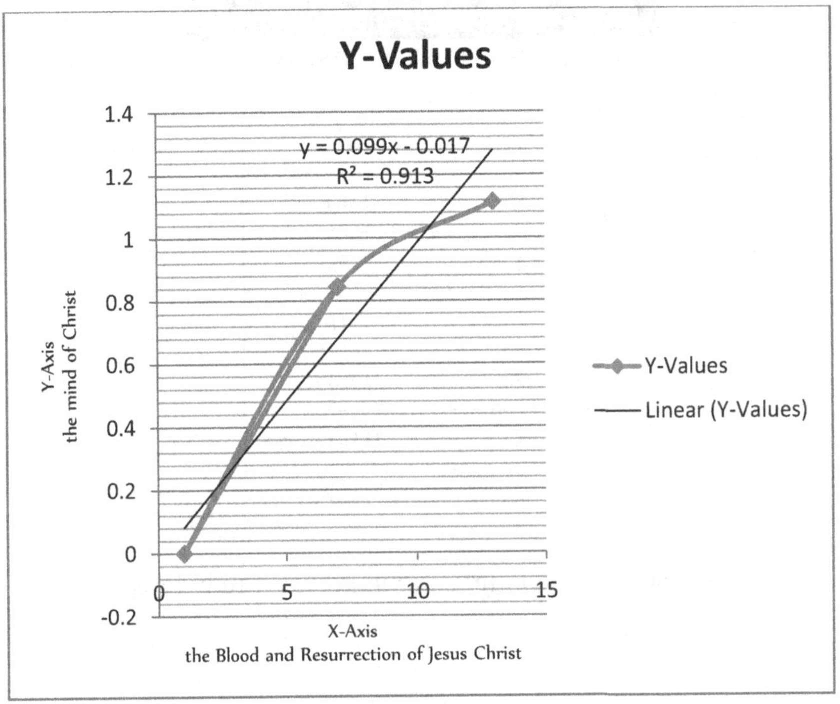

$10^{0.8450}$, 10^{0}, 10^{0}, $10^{0.8450}$; $10^{1.1139}$.

Pilled Poplar, Hazel, and Chestnut bible rods 2

22. Many will say to me in that day, Lord, Lord, have we not prophesied in thy name? and in thy name have cast out devils slanderers, false accusers, the arch-enemy of man's spiritual interest? **and in thy name done many wonderful works?**

8, 1, 1, 7? 8? 8? Bible Matrices

8_{10}, 1_{10}, 1_{10}, 7_{10}? 8_{10}? 8_{10}?

Pilled Poplar, Hazel, and Chestnut bible rods 1

$\text{Log}_{10} 8 = 0.9030$ $\text{Log}_{10} 1 = 0$ $\text{Log}_{10} 1 = 0$ $\text{Log}_{10} 7 = 0.8450$ $\text{Log}_{10} 8 = 0.9030$ $\text{Log}_{10} 8 = 0.9030$

8, 1, 1, 7? 8? 8? Deep calls unto Deep study bible 1

0.9030, 0, 0, 0.8450? 0.9030? 0.9030?
Deep calls unto Deep study bible 2

x-axis	y-axis
8	0.9030
1	0
1	0
7	0.8450
8	0.9030
8	0.9030

Water Spout *(lightning; combinatorics)* Study bible 1

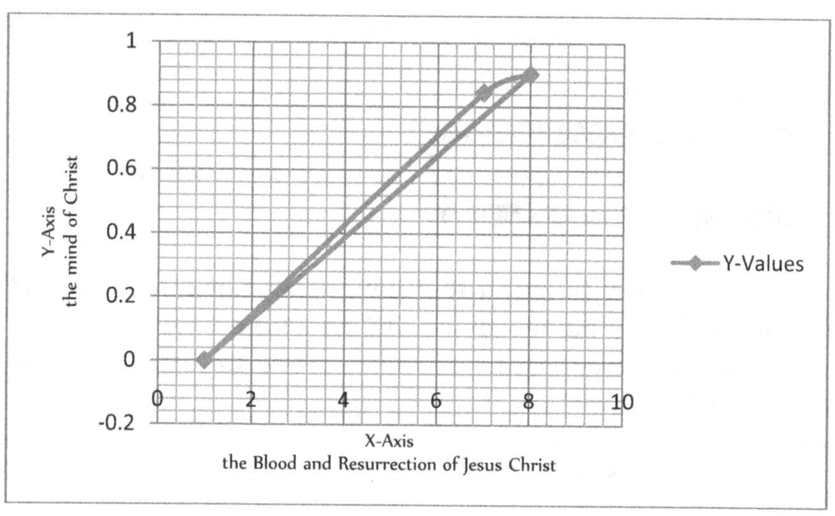

Water Spout *(lightning; combinatorics)* Study bible 2

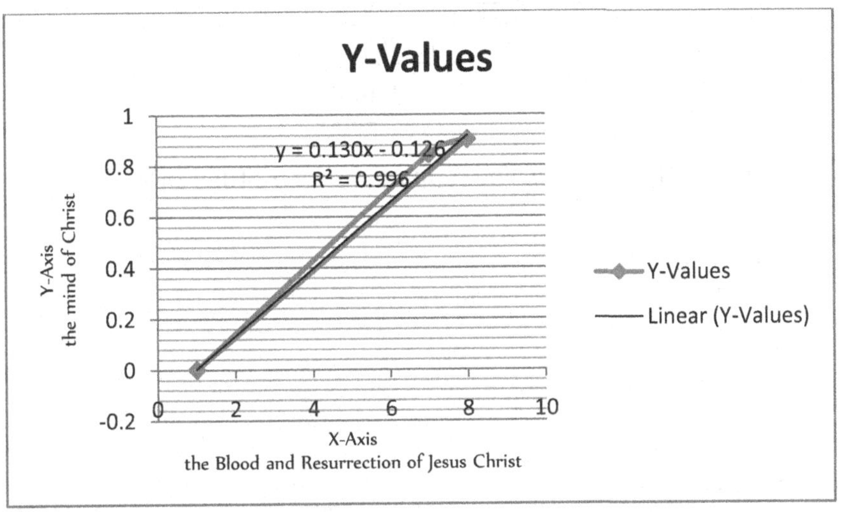

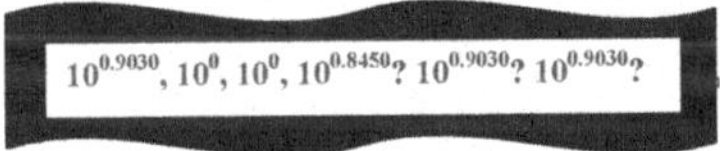

Pilled Poplar, Hazel, and Chestnut bible rods 2

23. And then will I profess unto them, I never knew you: depart from me, ye that work iniquity.

7, 4: 3, 4. Bible Matrices

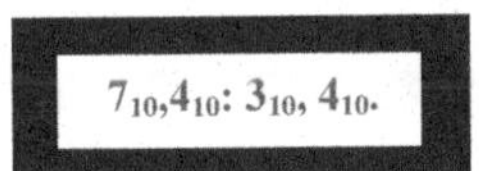

Pilled Poplar, Hazel, and Chestnut bible rods 1

$\text{Log}_{10} 4 = 0.6020$ $\text{Log}_{10} 7 = 0.8450$ $\text{Log}_{10} 3 = 0.4771$ $\text{Log}_{10} 4 = 0.6020$

7, 4: 3, 4. Deep calls unto Deep study bible 1

0.8450, 0.6020: 0.4711, 0.6020.

Deep calls unto Deep study bible 2

x-axis	y-axis
7	0.8450

4	0.6020
3	0.4771
4	0.6020

Water Spout *(lightning; combinatorics)* Study bible 1

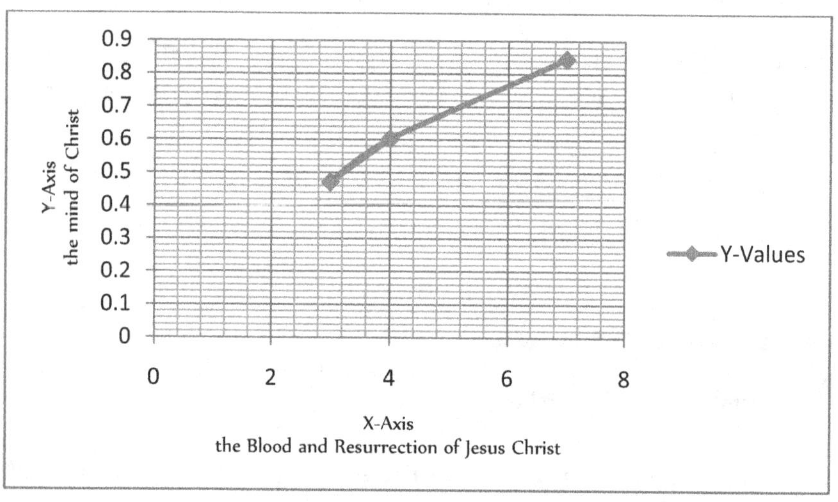

Water Spout *(lightning; combinatorics)* Study bible 2

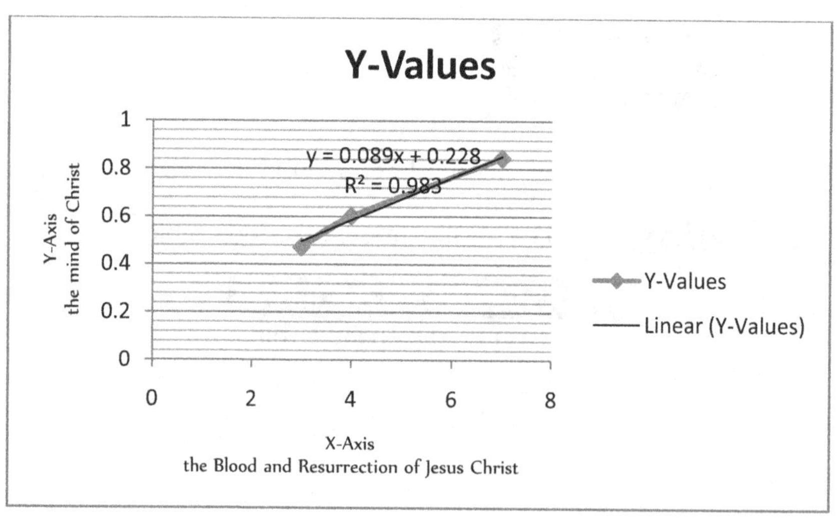

$10^{0.8450}, 10^{0.6020}: 10^{0.4771}, 10^{0.6020}.$

Pilled Poplar, Hazel, and Chestnut bible rods 2

24. Therefore whosoever heareth these sayings of mine, and doeth them, I will liken him unto a wise man, which built his house upon a rock:

7, 3, 8, 7: Bible Matrices

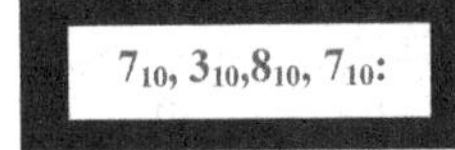

Pilled Poplar, Hazel, and Chestnut bible rods 1

$\text{Log}_{10} 7 = 0.8450$ $\text{Log}_{10} 7 = 0.8450$ $\text{Log}_{10} 3 = 0.4771$ $\text{Log}_{10} 8 = 0.9030$

7, 3, 8, 7: Deep calls unto Deep study bible 1

0.8450, 0.4771, 0.9030, 0.8450: Deep calls unto Deep study bible 2

x-axis	y-axis
7	0.8450
3	0.4771
8	0.9030
7	0.8450

Water Spout *(lightning; combinatorics)* Study bible 1

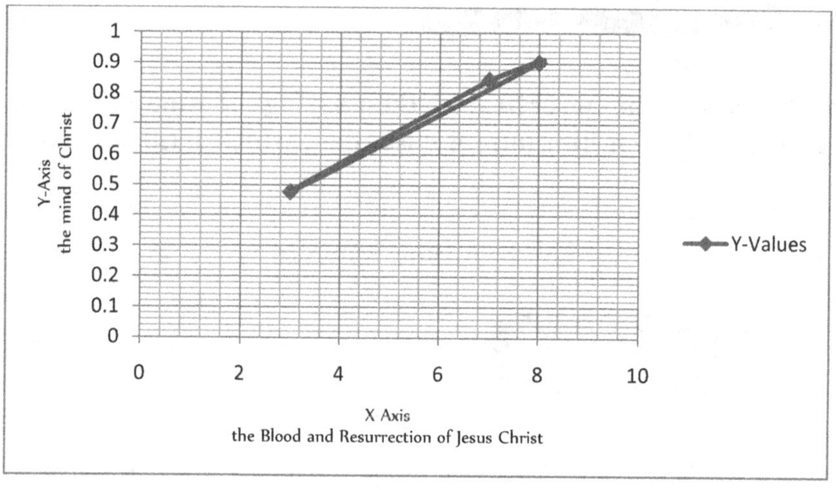

Water Spout *(lightning; combinatorics)* Study bible 2

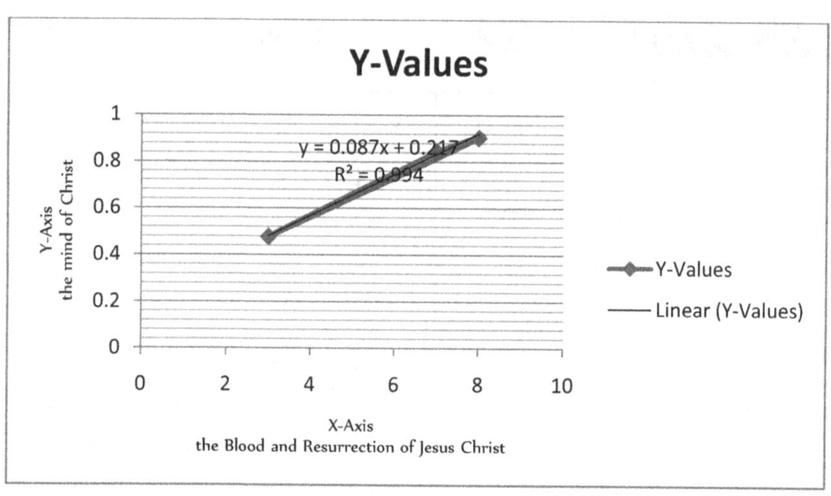

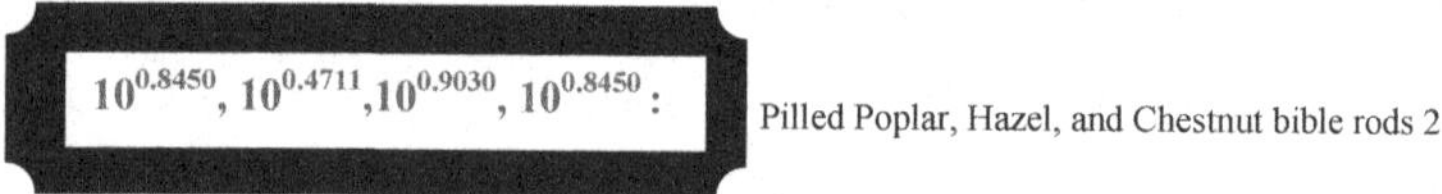
$10^{0.8450}$, $10^{0.4711}$,$10^{0.9030}$, $10^{0.8450}$:

Pilled Poplar, Hazel, and Chestnut bible rods 2

25. And the rain descended, and the floods came, and the winds blew, and beat upon that house; and it fell not: for it was founded upon a rock.

4, 4, 4, 5; 4: 7. Bible Matrices

$4_{10}, 4_{10}, 4_{10}, 5_{10}; 4_{10}: 7_{10}$ Pilled Poplar, Hazel, and Chestnut bible rods 1

$Log_{10}4 = 0.6020$ $Log_{10}4 = 0.6020$ $Log_{10}4 = 0.6020$ $Log_{10}7 = 0.8450$ $Log_{10}5 = 0.6989$ $Log_{10}4 = 0.6020$

4, 4, 4, 5; 4: 7. Deep calls unto Deep study bible 1

0.6020, 0.6020, 0.6020, 0.6989; 0.6020: 0.8450.
Deep calls unto Deep study bible 2

x-axis	y-axis
4	0.6020
4	0.6020
4	0.6020
5	0.6989
4	0.6020
7	0.8450

Water Spout *(lightning; combinatorics)* Study bible 1

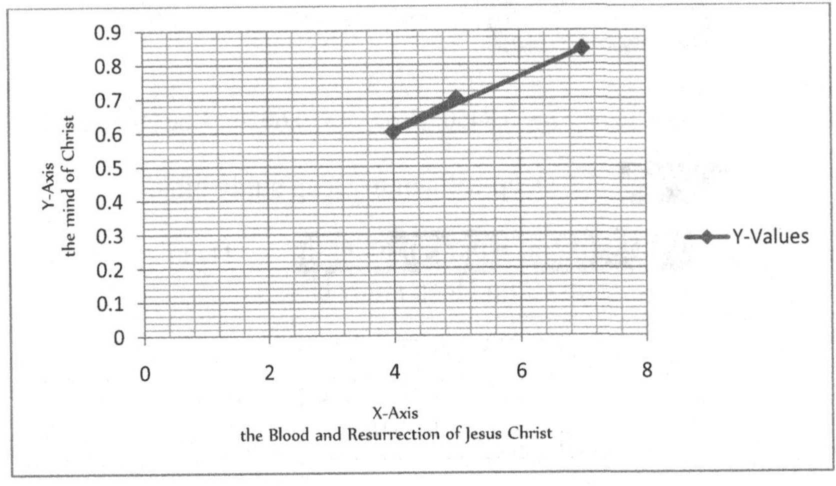

Water Spout *(lightning; combinatorics)* Study bible 2

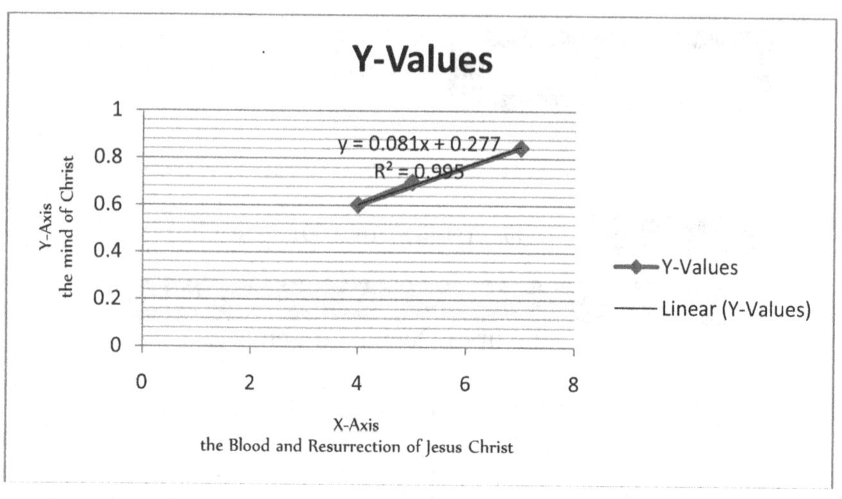

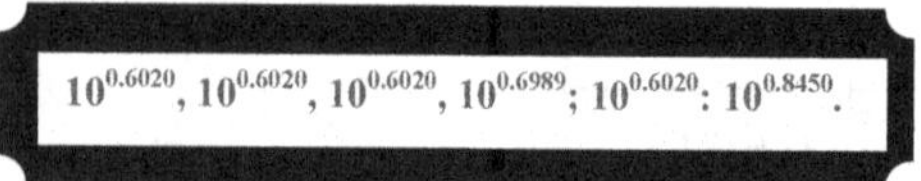
$10^{0.6020}$, $10^{0.6020}$, $10^{0.6020}$, $10^{0.6989}$; $10^{0.6020}$: $10^{0.8450}$.

Pilled Poplar, Hazel, and Chestnut bible rods 2

26. And every one that heareth these sayings of mine, and doeth them not, shall be likened unto a foolish man, which built his house upon the sand:

9, 4, 7, 7: Bible Matrices

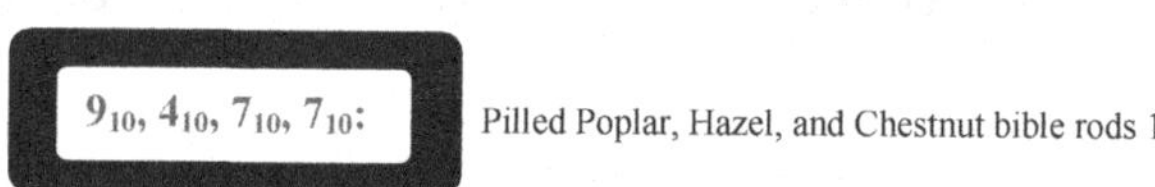
9_{10}, 4_{10}, 7_{10}, 7_{10}:

Pilled Poplar, Hazel, and Chestnut bible rods 1

$\text{Log}_{10} 7 = 0.8450$ $\text{Log}_{10} 7 = 0.8450$ $\text{Log}_{10} 4 = 0.6020$ $\text{Log}_{10} 9 = 0.9542$

9, 4, 7, 7: Deep calls unto Deep study bible 1

0.9542, 0.6020, 0.8450, 0.8450: Deep calls unto Deep study bible 2

x-axis	y-axis
9	0.9542

4	0.6020
7	0.8450
7	0.8450

Water Spout *(lightning; combinatorics)* Study bible 1

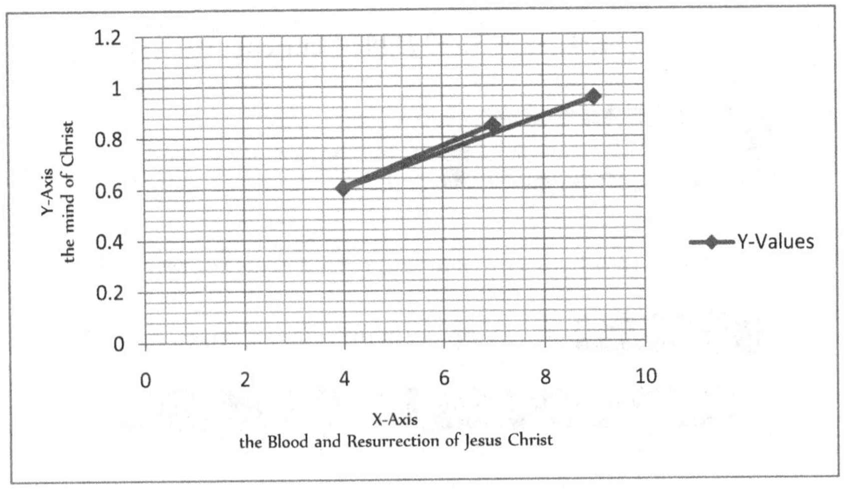

Water Spout *(lightning; combinatorics)* Study bible 2

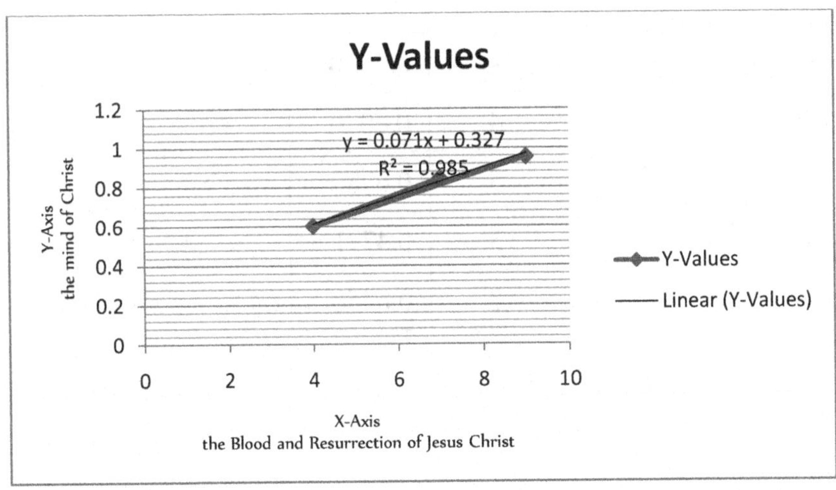

$10^{0.9542}, 10^{0.6020}, 10^{0.8450}, 10^{0.8450}$: Pilled Poplar, Hazel, and Chestnut bible rods 2

27. And the rain descended, and the floods came, and the winds blew, and beat upon that house; and it fell: and great was the fall of it.

4, 4, 4, 5; 3: 7? Bible Matrices

$4_{10}, 4_{10}, 4_{10}, 5_{10}; 3_{10}: 7_{10}$? Pilled Poplar, Hazel, and Chestnut bible rods 1

$\text{Log}_{10} 4 = 0.6020$ $\text{Log}_{10} 4 = 0.6020$ $\text{Log}_{10} 4 = 0.6020$ $\text{Log}_{10} 7 = 0.8450$ $\text{Log}_{10} 5 = 0.6989$ $\text{Log}_{10} 3 = 0.4771$

4, 4, 4, 5; 3 : 7? Deep calls unto Deep study bible 1

0.6020, 0.6020, 0.6020, 0.6989; 0.4771: 0.8450 ?
Deep calls unto Deep study bible 2

x-axis	y-axis
4	0.6020
4	0.6020
4	0.6020
5	0.6989
3	0.4771
7	0.8450

Water Spout *(lightning; combinatorics)* Study bible 1

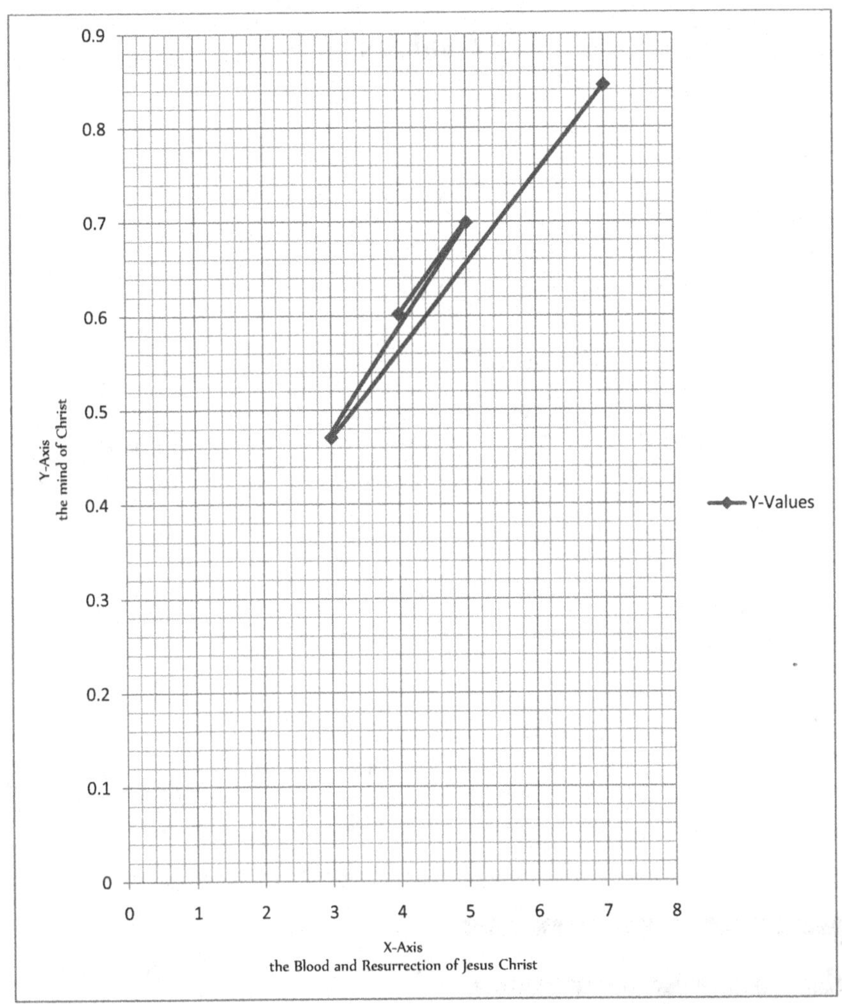

Water Spout *(lightning; combinatorics)* Study bible 2

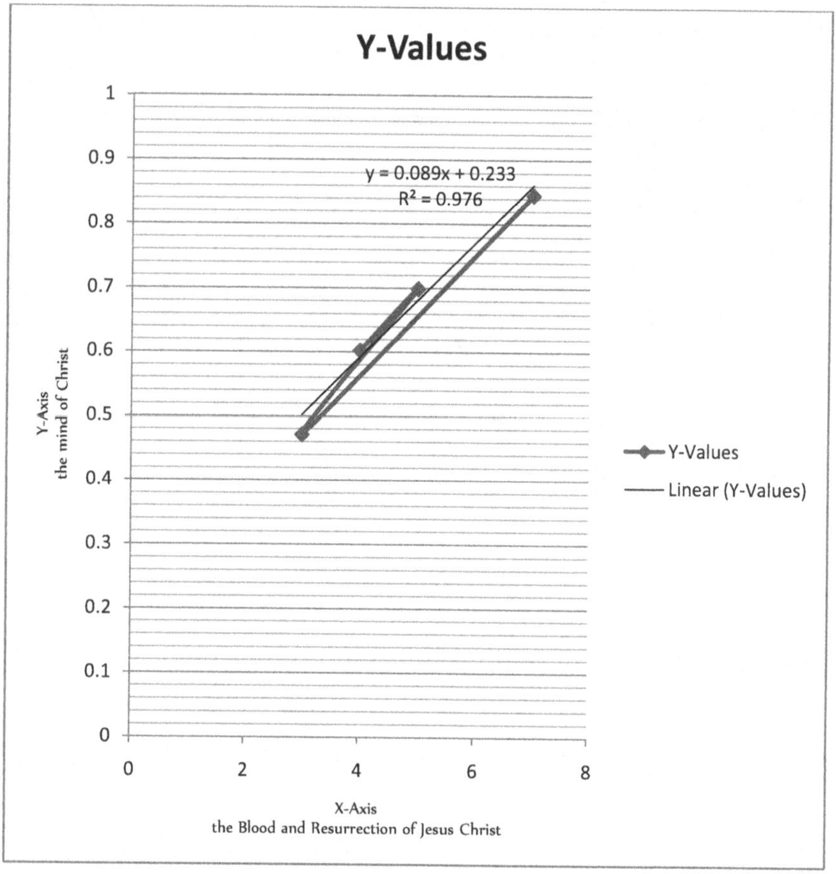

Y-Values

$y = 0.089x + 0.233$
$R^2 = 0.976$

Y-Axis
the mind of Christ

X-Axis
the Blood and Resurrection of Jesus Christ

Y-Values
Linear (Y-Values)

$10^{0.6020}, 10^{0.6020}, 10^{0.6020}, 10^{0.6989}; 10^{0.4771}: 10^{0.8450}$?

Pilled Poplar, Hazel, and Chestnut bible rods 2

28. And it came to pass, when Jesussavior; deliverer **had ended these sayings, the people were astonished at his doctrine:**

5, 6, 7: Bible Matrices

Pilled Poplar, Hazel, and Chestnut bible rods 1

$\text{Log}_2 2 = y$ $\text{Log}_{10} 5 = 0.6989$ $\text{Log}_{10} 4 = 0.6020$ $\text{Log}_{10} 7 = 0.8450$

$2^y = 2^1$

$y = 1$

5, 6, 7: Deep calls unto Deep study bible 1

0.6989, 1 0.6020, 0.8450: Deep calls unto Deep study bible 2

x-axis	y-axis
5	0.6989
6	1.6020
7	0.8450

Water Spout *(lightning; combinatorics)* Study bible 1

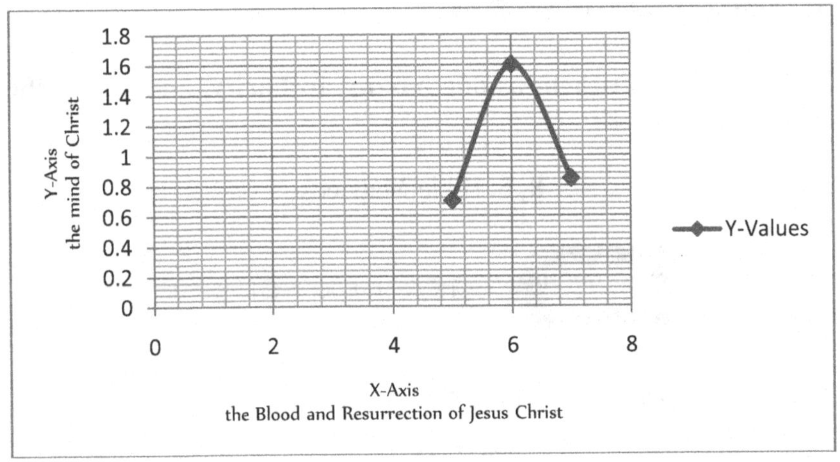

Water Spout *(lightning; combinatorics)* Study bible 2

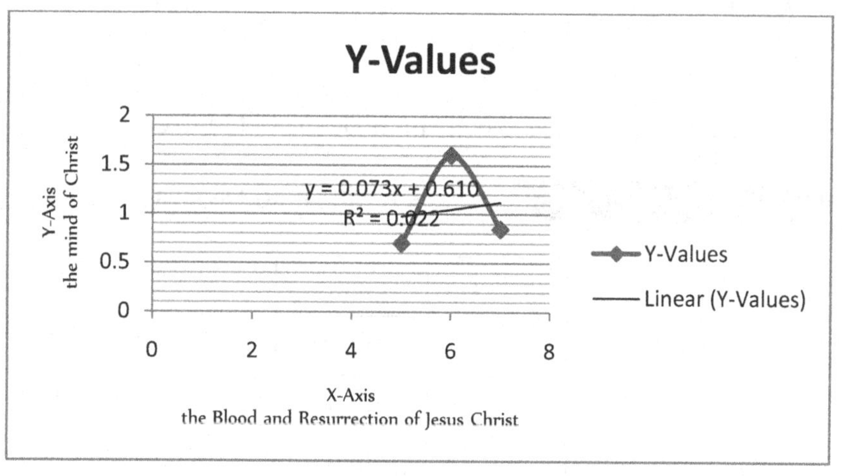

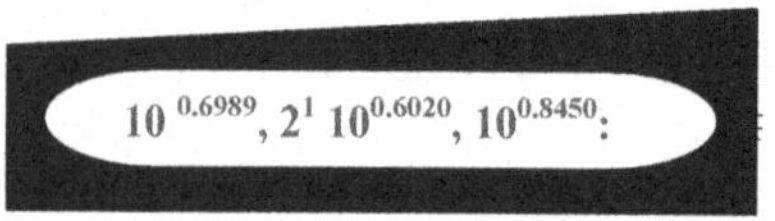

Pilled Poplar, Hazel, and Chestnut bible rods 2

29. For he taught them as one having authority, and not as the scribes lawyers; transcriber.

8, 5. Bible Matrices

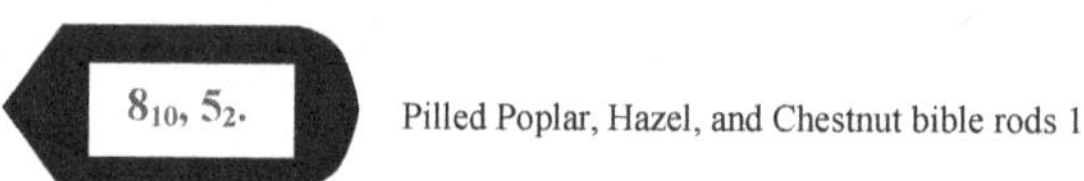

Pilled Poplar, Hazel, and Chestnut bible rods 1

$\text{Log}_{10} 8 = 0.9030$

$$\text{Log}_2 5 = y$$
$$2^y = 5$$
$$y \log_{10} 2 = \log_{10} 5$$
$$y = \log_{10} 5/ \log_{10} 2$$
$$y = 0.6989/ 0.3010$$
$$y = 2.3219$$

8, 5. Deep calls unto Deep study bible 1

0.9030, 2.3219. Deep calls unto Deep study bible 2

x-axis	y-axis
8	0.9030
5	2.3219

Water Spout *(lightning; combinatorics)* Study bible 1

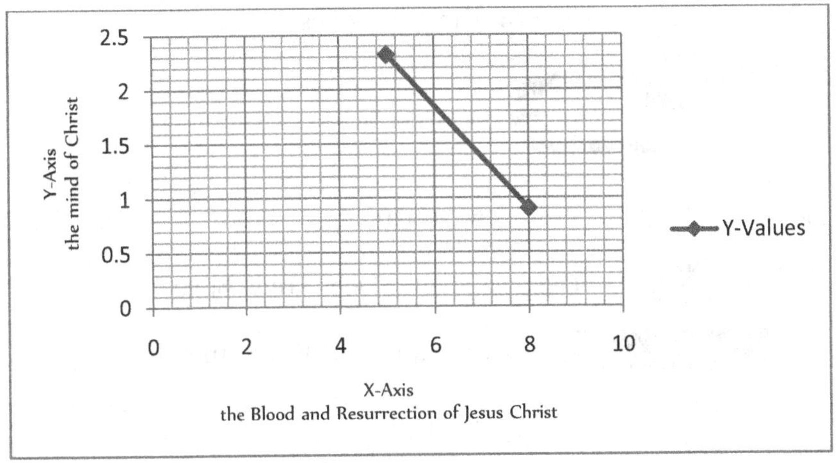

Water Spout *(lightning; combinatorics)* Study bible 2

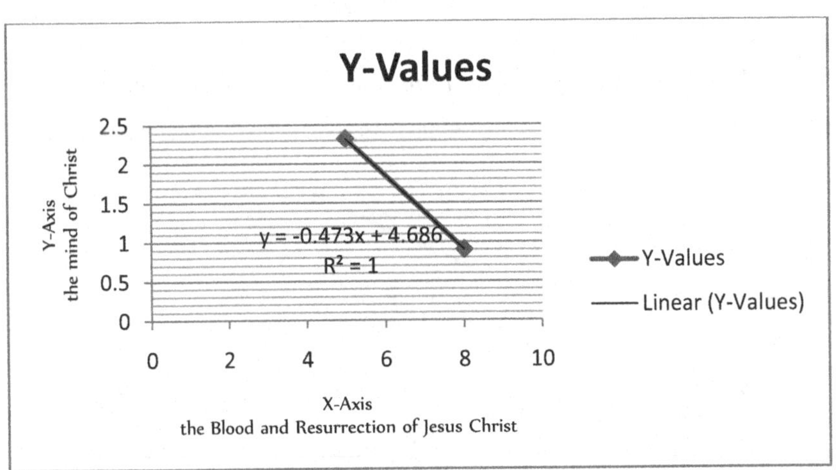

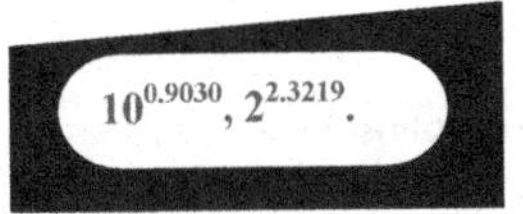

Pilled Poplar, Hazel, and Chestnut bible rods 2

CHAPTER 8

1. When he was come down from the mountain, great multitudes followed him.

8, 4. Bible Matrices

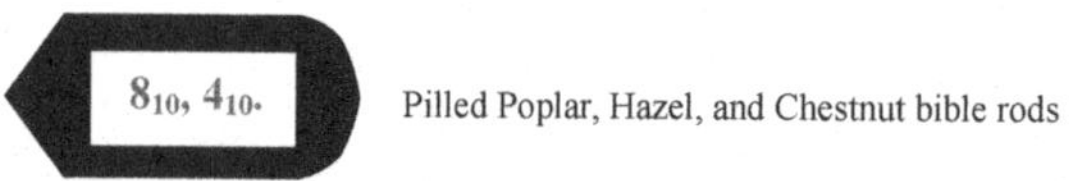

Pilled Poplar, Hazel, and Chestnut bible rods 1

$Log_{10} 8 = 0.9030$ $Log_{10} 4 = 0.6020$

8, 4. Deep calls unto Deep study bible 1

0.9030, 0.6020. Deep calls unto Deep study bible 2

x-axis	y-axis
8	0.9030
4	0.6020

Water Spout *(lightning; combinatorics)* Study bible 1

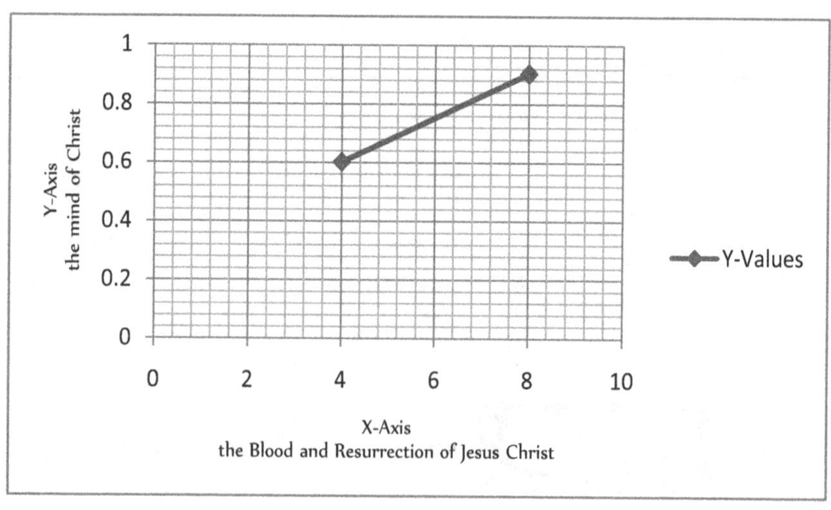

Water Spout *(lightning; combinatorics)* Study bible 2

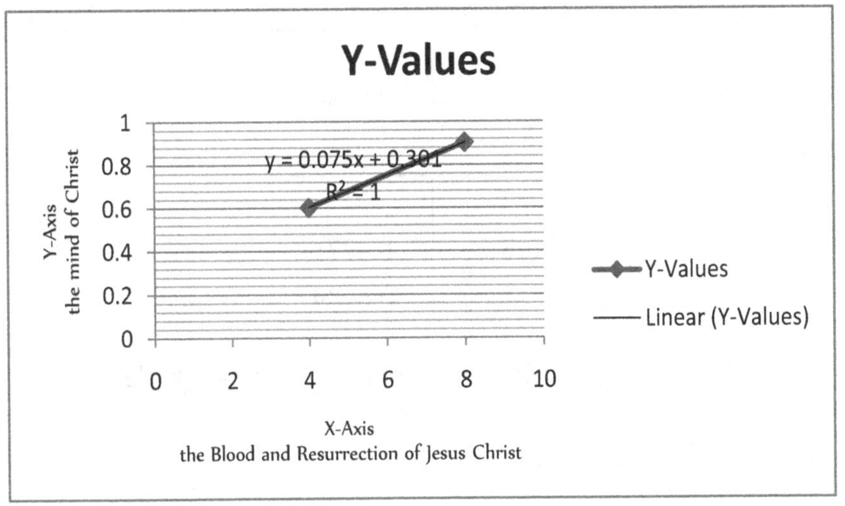

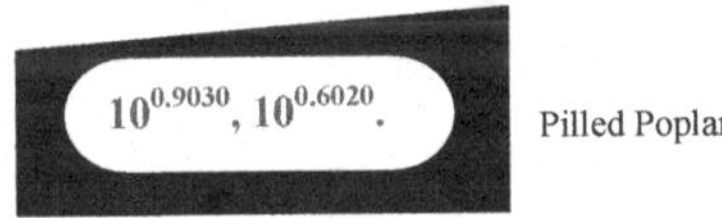

Pilled Poplar, Hazel, and Chestnut bible rods 2

2. And, behold, there came a leper and worshipped him, saying, Lord, if thou wilt, thou canst make me clean.

1, 1, 7, 1, 1, 3, 5. Bible Matrices

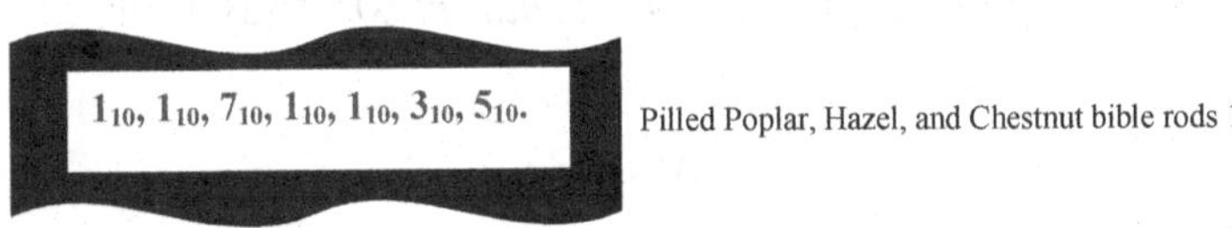

Pilled Poplar, Hazel, and Chestnut bible rods 1

$\text{Log}_{10} 1 = 0$ $\text{Log}_{10} 1 = 0$ $\text{Log}_{10} 7 = 0.8450$ $\text{Log}_{10} 1 = 0$ $\text{Log}_{10} 1 = 0$ $\text{Log}_{10} 5 = 0.6989$ $\text{Log}_{10} 3 = 0.4771$

1, 1, 7, 1, 1, 3, 5. Deep calls unto Deep study bible 1

0, 0, 0.8450, 0, 0, 0.4771, 0.6989.

Deep calls unto Deep study bible 2

x-axis	y-axis
1	0
1	0
7	0.8450
1	0
1	0
3	0.4771
5	0.6989

Water Spout *(lightning; combinatorics)* Study bible 1

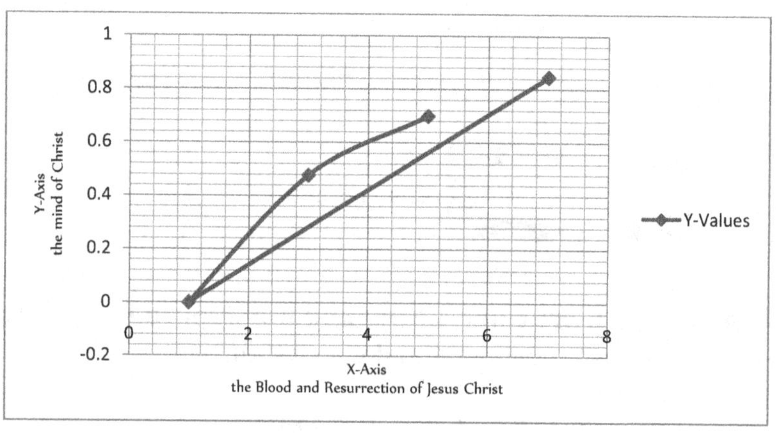

Water Spout *(lightning; combinatorics)* Study bible 2

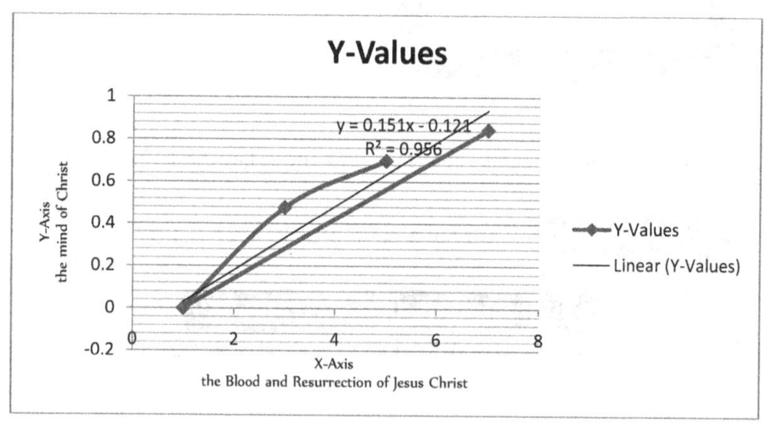

10^{0}, 10^{0}, $10^{0.8450}$, 10^{0}, 10^{0}, $10^{0.4771}$, $10^{0.6989}$. Pilled Poplar, Hazel, and Chestnut bible rods 2

3. And Jesus savior; deliverer **put forth his hand, and touched him, saying, I will; be thou clean. And immediately his leprosy was cleansed.**

6, 3, 1, 2; 3. 6. Bible Matrices

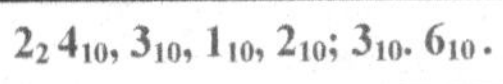

Pilled Poplar, Hazel, and Chestnut bible rods 1

$\text{Log}_2 2 = y$ $\text{Log}_{10} 4 = 0.6020$ $\text{Log}_{10} 3 = 0.4771$ $\text{Log}_{10} 1 = 0$ $\text{Log}_{10} 2 = 0.3010$ $\text{Log}_{10} 6 = 0.7781$ $\text{Log}_{10} 3 = 0.4771$

$2^{y} = 2^{1}$

$y = 1$

6, 3, 1, 2; 3. 6. Deep calls unto Deep study bible 1

1 0.6020, 0.4771, 0, 0.3010; 0.4771. 0.7781.
Deep calls unto Deep study bible 2

x-axis	y-axis
6	1.6020
3	0.4771
1	0
2	0.3010
3	0.4771
6	0.7781

Water Spout *(lightning; combinatorics)* Study bible 1

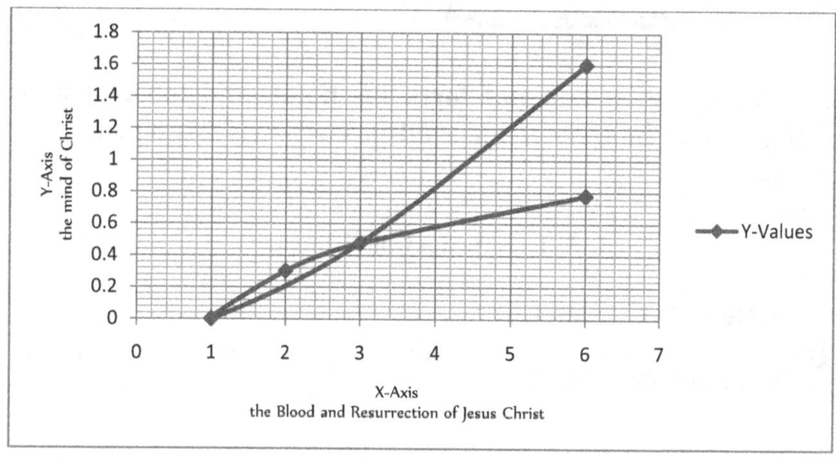

Water Spout *(lightning; combinatorics)* Study bible 2

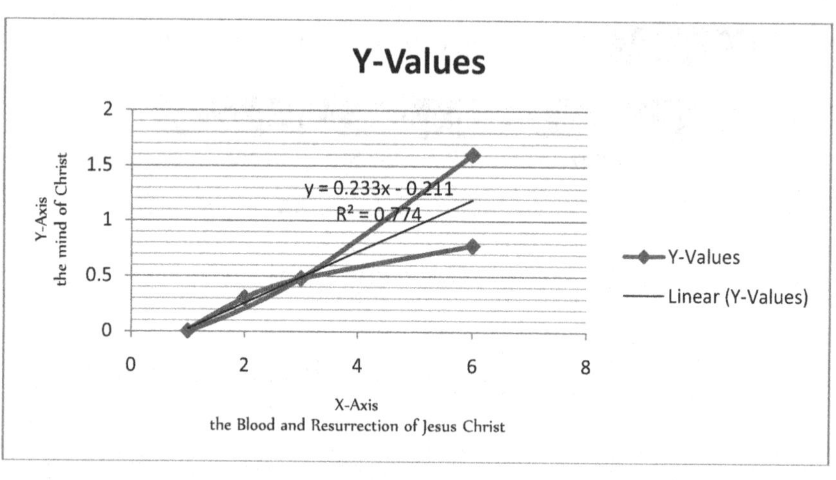

$2^1\ 10^{0.6020}, 10^{0.4771}, 10^0, 10^{0.3010}; 10^{0.4771}. 10^{0.7781}$. Pilled Poplar, Hazel, and Chestnut bible rods 2

4. And Jesussavior; deliverer **saith unto him, See thou tell no man; but go thy way, shew thyself to the priest, and offer the gift that Moses** taken out; drawn forth; drawer out; one born **commanded, for a testimony unto them.**

5, 5; 4, 5, 7, 5. Bible Matrices

$2_2\ 3_{10},\ 5_{10};\ 4_{10},\ 5_{10},\ 6_8\ 1_{10},\ 5_{10}.$ Pilled Poplar, Hazel, and Chestnut bible rods 1

$\text{Log}_2 2 = y$ $\text{Log}_{10} 5 = 0.6989$ $\text{Log}_{10} 3 = 0.4771$ $\text{Log}_{10} 1 = 0$ $\text{Log}_{10} 5 = 0.6989$ $\text{Log}_{10} 5 = 0.6989$ $\text{Log}_{10} 4 = 0.6020$

$2^y = 2^1$

$y = 1$

$\text{Log}_8 6 = y$

$8^y = 6$

$y \log_{10} 8 = \log_{10} 6$

$y = \log_{10} 6 / \log_{10} 8$

$y = 0.7781/0.9030$

$y = 0.8616$

5, 5; 4, 5, 7, 5. Deep calls unto Deep study bible 1

1 0.4771, 0.6989; 0.6020, 0.6989, 0.8616 0, 0.6989.

Deep calls unto Deep study bible 2

x-axis	y-axis
5	1.4771
5	0.6989
4	0.6020
5	0.6989
7	0.8616
5	0.6989

Water Spout *(lightning; combinatorics)* Study bible 1

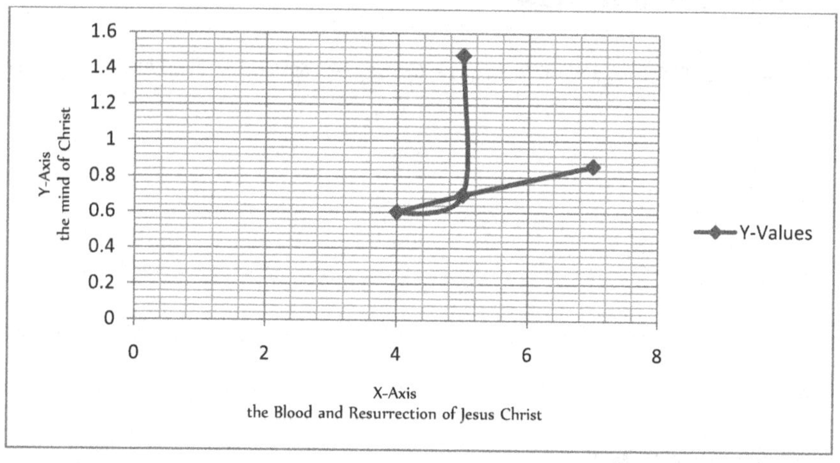

Water Spout *(lightning; combinatorics)* Study bible 2

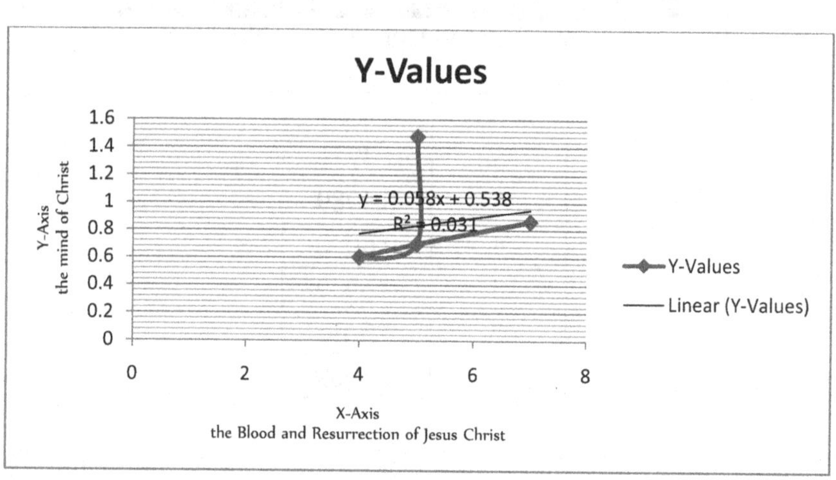

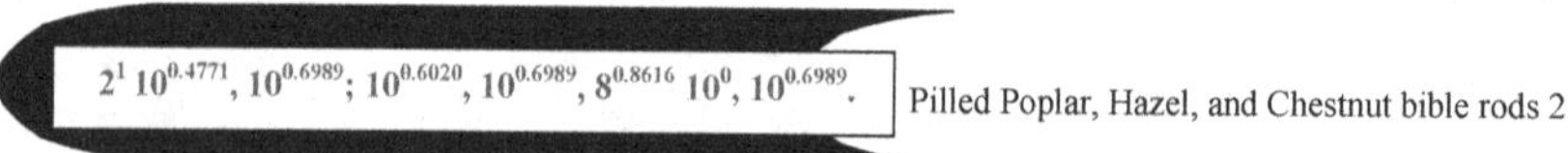
$2^1\ 10^{0.4771},\ 10^{0.6989};\ 10^{0.6020},\ 10^{0.6989},\ 8^{0.8616}\ 10^0,\ 10^{0.6989}.$

Pilled Poplar, Hazel, and Chestnut bible rods 2

5. And when Jesus savior; deliverer**was entered into Capernaum**the field of repentance; city of comfort, **there came unto him a centurion**Commander of a hundred men, **beseeching him,**

7, 6, 2, Bible Matrices

$3_2 4_7, 6_5, 2_{10},$ Pilled Poplar, Hazel, and Chestnut bible rods 1

$\text{Log}_{10} 2 = 0.3010$

$\text{Log}_5 6 = y$
$5^y = 6$
$y \log_{10} 5 = \log_{10} 6$
$y = \log_{10} 6 / \log_{10} 5$
$y = 0.7781/0.6989$
$y = 1.1133$

$\text{Log}_7 4 = y$
$7^y = 4$
$y \log_{10} 7 = \log_{10} 4$
$y = \log_{10} 4 / \log_{10} 7$
$y = 0.6020/0.8450$
$y = 0.7124$

$\text{Log}_2 3 = y$
$2^y = 3$
$y \log_{10} 2 = \log_{10} 3$
$y = \log_{10} 3 / \log_{10} 2$
$y = 0.4771/ 0.3010$
$y = 1.5850$

7, 6, 2, Deep calls unto Deep study bible 1

1.5850 0.7124, 1.1133, 0.3010, Deep calls unto Deep study bible 2

x-axis	y-axis
7	2.2974
6	1.1133
2	0.3010

Water Spout *(lightning; combinatorics)* Study bible 1

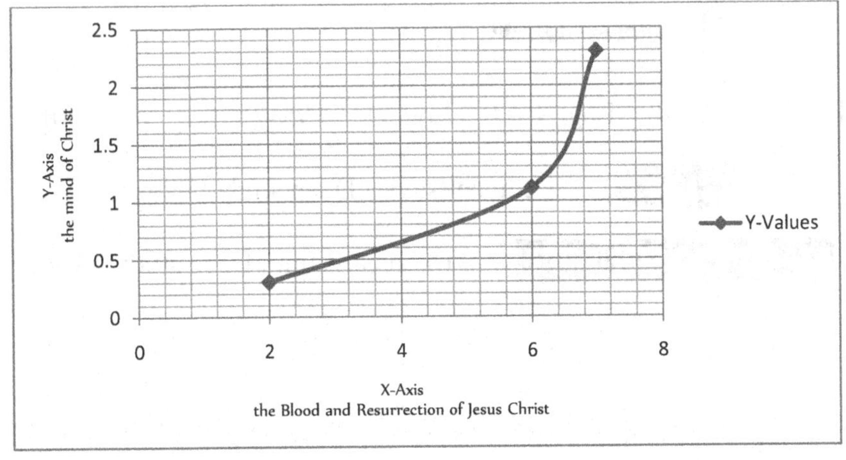

Water Spout *(lightning; combinatorics)* Study bible 2

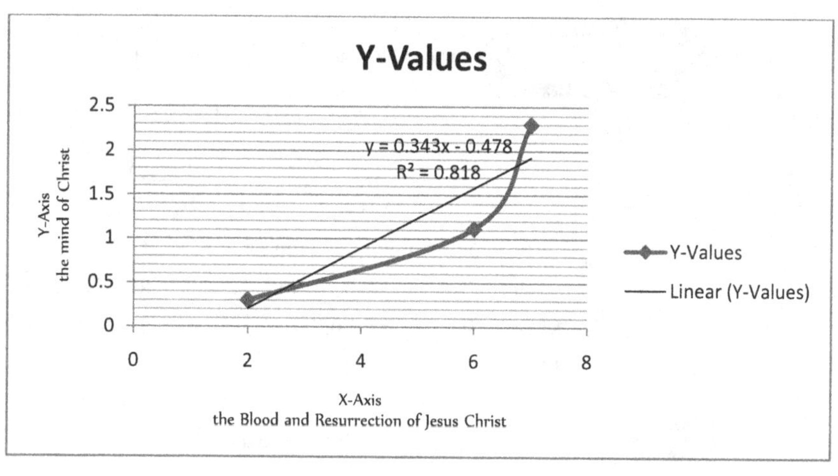

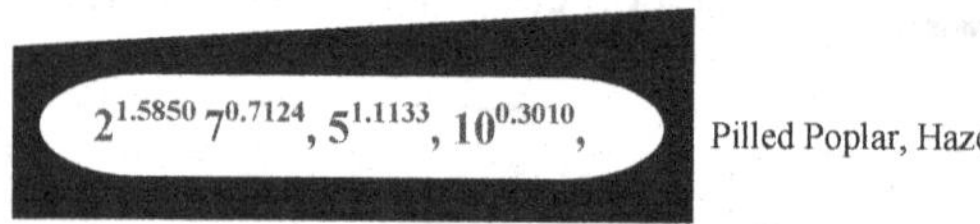

Pilled Poplar, Hazel, and Chestnut bible rods 2

6. And saying, Lord, my servant lieth at home sick of the palsy, grievously tormented.

2, 1, 9, 2. Bible Matrices

Pilled Poplar, Hazel, and Chestnut bible rods 1

$\text{Log}_{10} 2 = 0.3010$ $\text{Log}_{10} 1 = 0$ $\text{Log}_{10} 9 = 0.9542$ $\text{Log}_{10} 2 = 0.3010$

2, 1, 9, 2. Deep calls unto Deep study bible 1

0.3010, 0, 0.9542, 0.3010. Deep calls unto Deep study bible 2

x-axis	y-axis
2	0.3010
1	0
9	0.9542
2	0.3010

Water Spout *(lightning; combinatorics)* Study bible 1

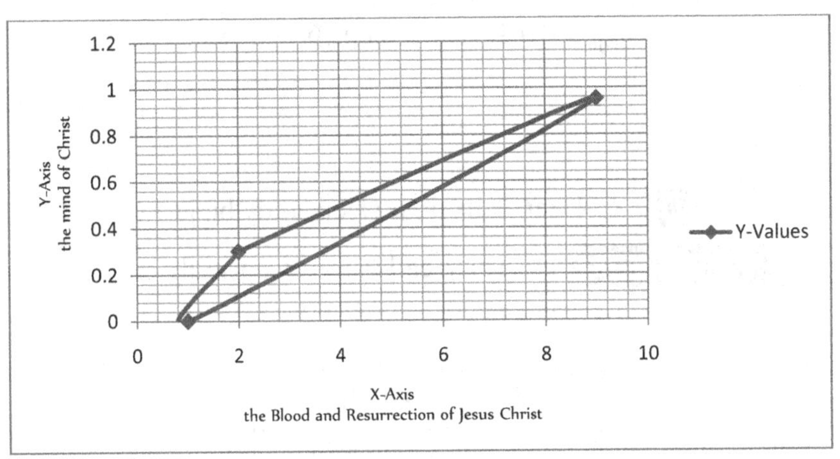

Water Spout *(lightning; combinatorics)* Study bible 2

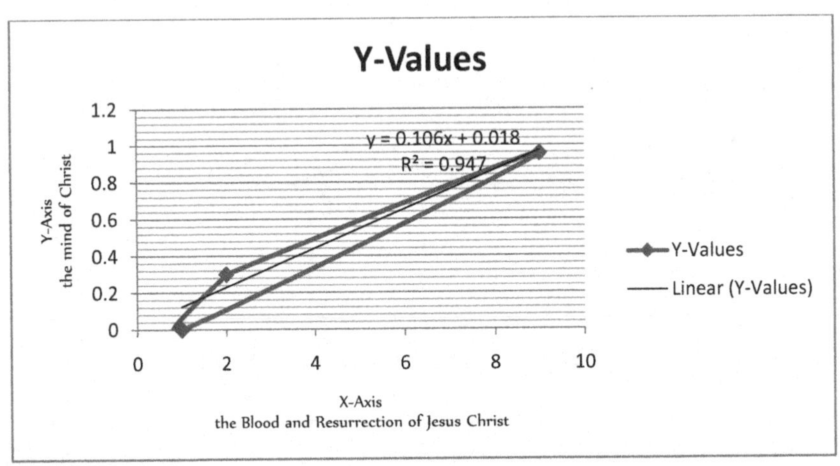

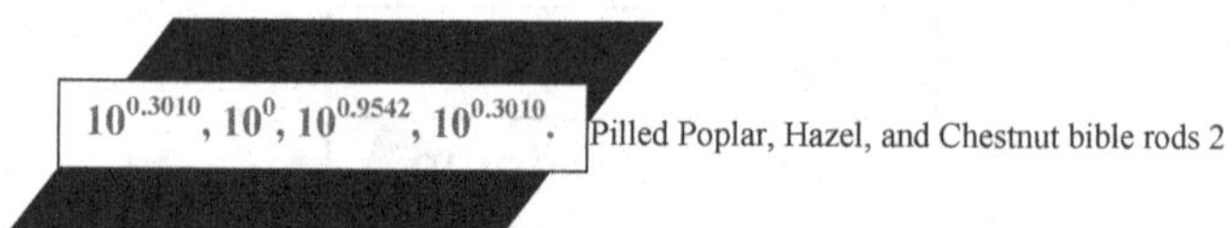

7. And Jesussavior; deliverer **saith unto him, I will come and heal him.**

5, 6. Bible Matrices

$\text{Log}_2 2 = y$ $\quad\text{Log}_{10} 3 = 0.4771$ $\quad\text{Log}_{10} 6 = 0.7781$

$2^y = 2^1$

$y = 1$

5, 6. Deep calls unto Deep study bible 1

1 0.4771, 0.7781. Deep calls unto Deep study bible 2

x-axis	y-axis
5	1.4771
6	0.7781

Water Spout *(lightning; combinatorics)* Study bible 1

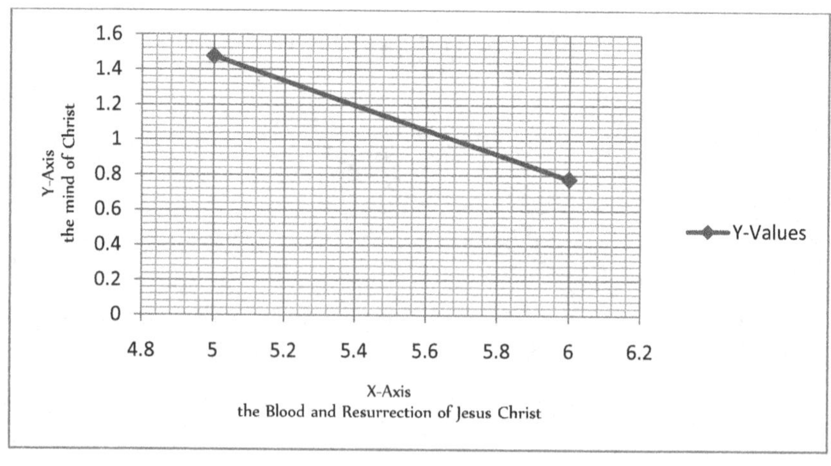

Water Spout *(lightning; combinatorics)* Study bible 2

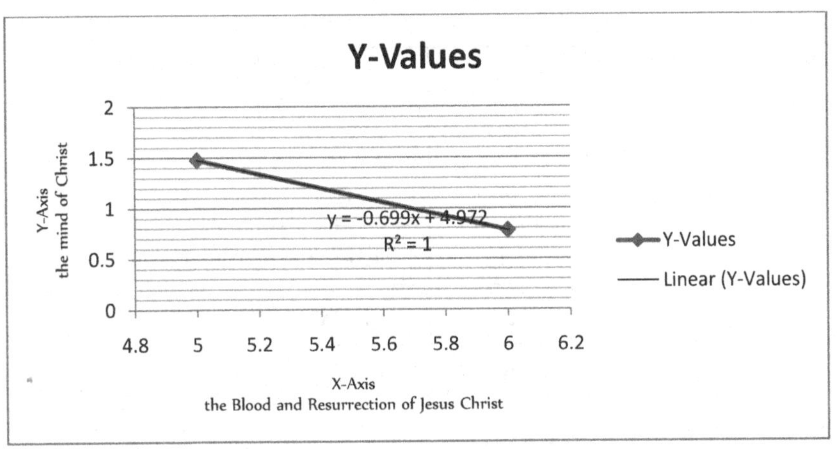

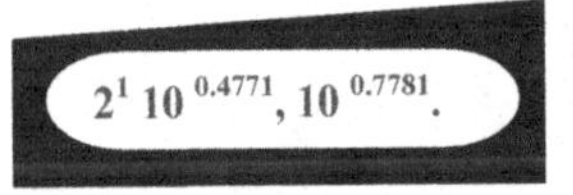

Pilled Poplar, Hazel, and Chestnut bible rods 2

8. The centurion Commander of a hundred men**answered and said, Lord, I am not worthy that thou shouldest come under my roof: but speak the word only, and my servant shall be healed.**

5, 1, 11: 5, 6. Bible Matrices

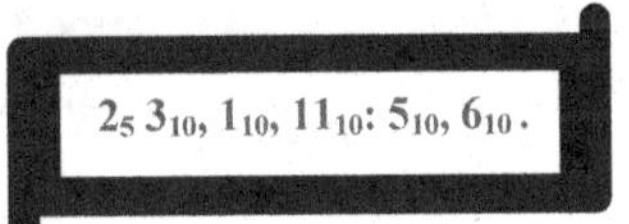

Pilled Poplar, Hazel, and Chestnut bible rods 1

$\text{Log}_{10} 3 = 0.4771$ $\text{Log}_5 2 = y$ $\text{Log}_{10} 1 = 0$ $\text{Log}_{10} 11 = 1.0413$ $\text{Log}_{10} 5 = 0.6989$ $\text{Log}_{10} 6 = 0.7781$

$5^y = 2$

$y \log_{10} 5 = \log_{10} 2$

$y = \log_{10} 2 / \log_{10} 5$

$y = 0.3010 / 0.6989$

$y = 0.4306$

5, 1, 11: 5, 6. Deep calls unto Deep study bible 1

0.4306 0.4771, 0, 1.0413: 0.6989, 0.7781.

Deep calls unto Deep study bible 2

x-axis	y-axis
5	0.9077
1	0
11	1.0413
5	0.6989
6	0.7781

Water Spout *(lightning; combinatorics)* Study bible 1

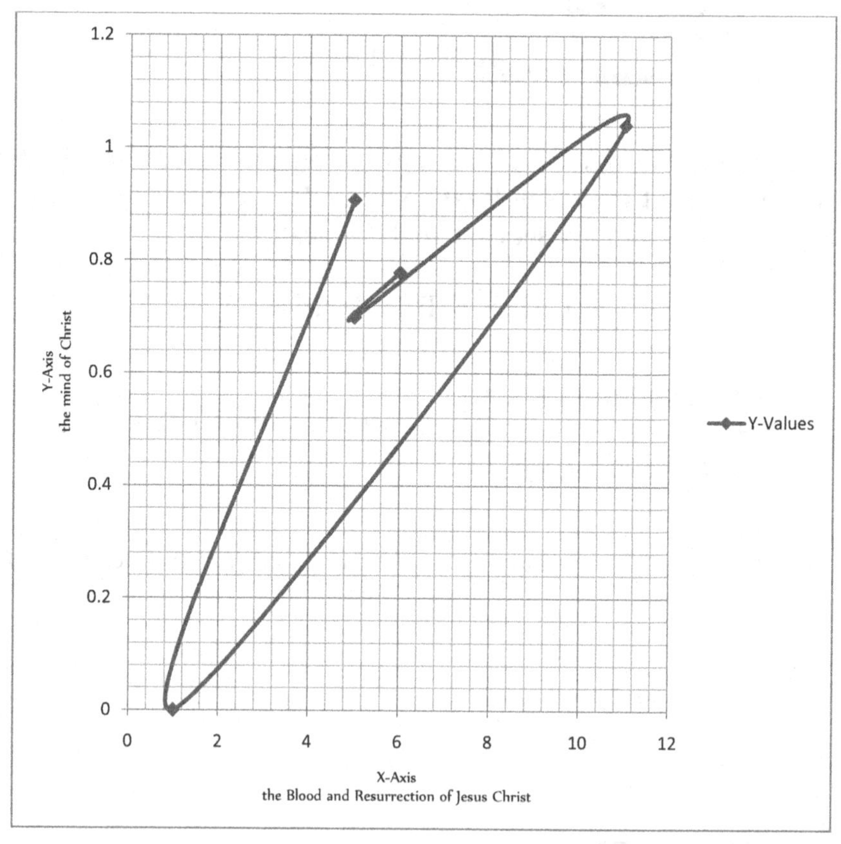

Water Spout *(lightning; combinatorics)* Study bible 2

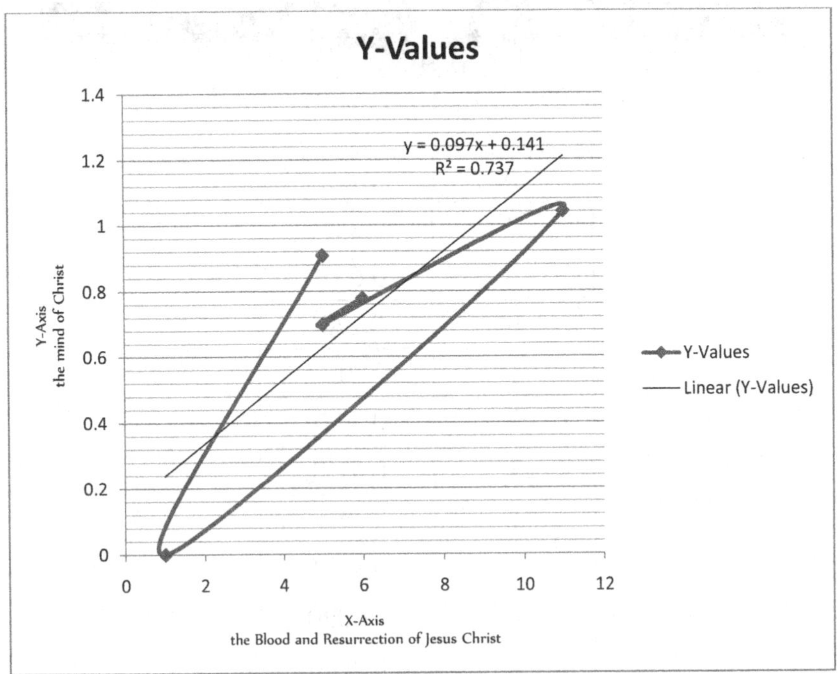

$5^{0.4771}$ $10^{0.4771}$, 10^{0}, $10^{1.0413}$: $10^{0.6989}$, $10^{0.7781}$. Pilled Poplar, Hazel, and Chestnut bible rods 2

9. For I am a man under authority, having soldiers under me: and I say to this man, Go, and he goeth; and to another, Come, and he cometh; and to my servant, Do this, and he doeth it.

7, 4: 6, 1, 3; 3, 1, 3; 4, 2, 4. Bible Matrices

7_{10}, 4_{10}: 6_{10}, 1_{10}, 3_{10}; 3_{10}, 1_{10}, 3_{10}; 4_{10}, 2_{10}, 4_{10}. Pilled Poplar, Hazel, and Chestnut bible rods 1

$\text{Log}_{10} 3 = 0.4771$ $\text{Log}_{10} 2 = 0.3010$ $\text{Log}_{10} 1 = 0$ $\text{Log}_{10} 7 = 0.8450$ $\text{Log}_{10} 4 = 0.6020$ $\text{Log}_{10} 6 = 0.7781$

$\text{Log}_{10} 3 = 0.4771$ $\text{Log}_{10} 3 = 0.4771$ $\text{Log}_{10} 1 = 0$ $\text{Log}_{10} 4 = 0.6020$ $\text{Log}_{10} 4 = 0.6020$

7, 4: 6, 1, 3; 3, 1, 3; 4, 2, 4. Deep calls unto Deep study bible 1

0.8450, 0.6020: 0.7781, 0, 0.4771; 0.4771, 0, 0.4771; 0.6020, 0.3010, 0.6020.

Deep calls unto Deep study bible 2

x-axis	y-axis
7	0.8450
4	0.6020
6	0.7781
1	0
3	0.4771
3	0.4771
1	0
3	0.4771
4	0.6020
2	0.3010
4	0.6020

Water Spout *(lightning; combinatorics)* Study bible 1

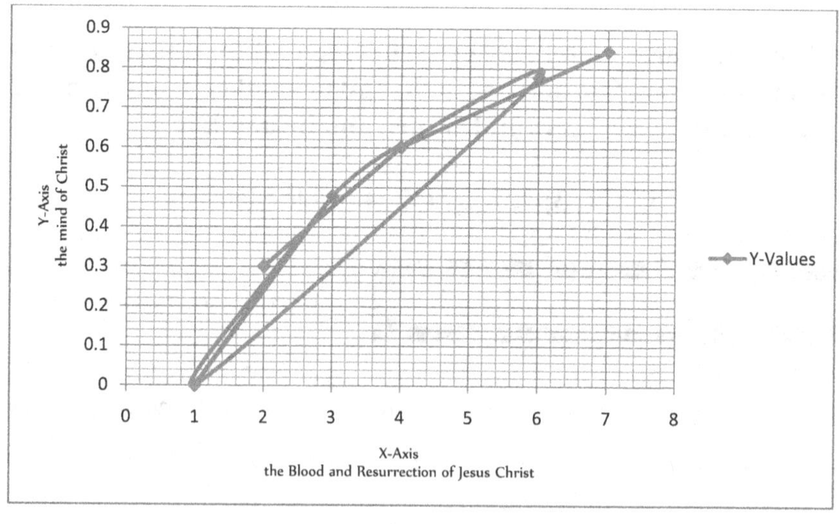

Water Spout *(lightning; combinatorics)* Study bible 2

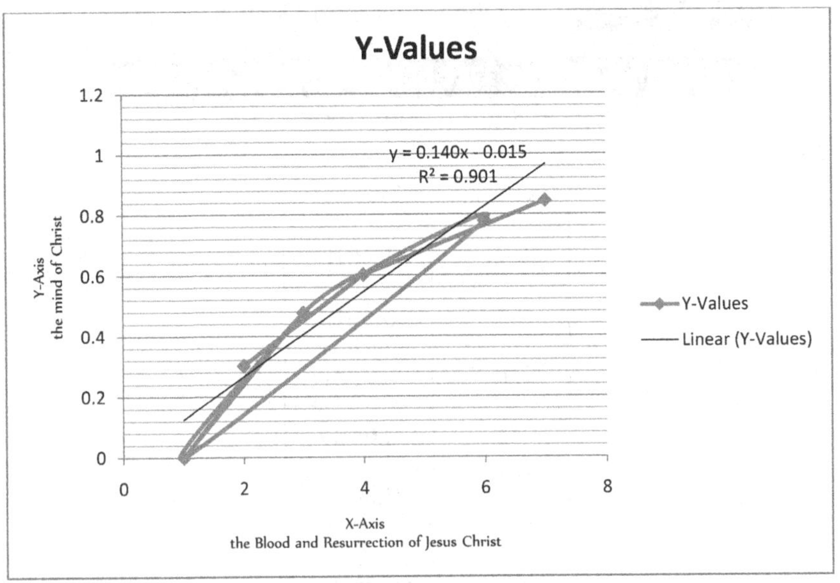

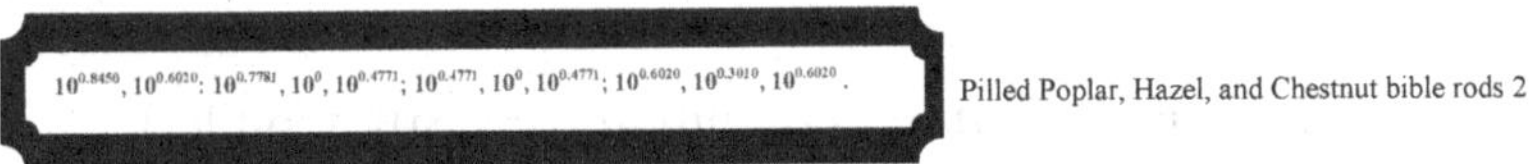

$10^{0.8450}, 10^{0.6020}: 10^{0.7781}, 10^{0}, 10^{0.4771}; 10^{0.4771}, 10^{0}, 10^{0.4771}; 10^{0.6020}, 10^{0.3010}, 10^{0.6020}$.

Pilled Poplar, Hazel, and Chestnut bible rods 2

10. When Jesussavior; deliverer**heard it, he marvelled, and said to them that followed, Verily I say unto you, I have not found so great faith, no, not in Israel** who prevails with God; God strives.

4, 2, 6, 5, 7, 1, 3. Bible Matrices

$2_2\, 2_{10}, 2_{10}, 6_{10}, 5_{10}, 7_{10}, 1_{10}, 3_6$.

Pilled Poplar, Hazel, and Chestnut bible rods 1

$\text{Log}_2 2 = y$ $\quad$ $\text{Log}_6 3 = y$ $\quad$ $\text{Log}_{10} 1 = 0$ $\quad$ $\text{Log}_{10} 2 = 0.3010$ $\quad$ $\text{Log}_{10} 2 = 0.3010$

$2^y = 2^1$ $\quad$ $6^y = 3$

$y = 1$ $\quad$ $y \log_{10} 6 = \log_{10} 3$

$y = \log_{10} 3 / \log_{10} 6$

$y = 0.4771 / 0.7781$

$y = 0.6131$

$\text{Log}_{10} 6 = 0.7781$ $\text{Log}_{10} 5 = 0.6989$ $\text{Log}_{10} 7 = 0.8450$

4, 2, 6, 5, 7, 1, 3. Deep calls unto Deep study bible 1

1 0.3010, 0.3010, 0.7781, 0.6989, 0.8450, 0, 0.6131.
Deep calls unto Deep study bible 2

x-axis	y-axis
4	1.3010
2	0.3010
6	0.7781
5	0.6989
7	0.8450
1	0
3	0.6131

Water Spout *(lightning; combinatorics)* Study bible 1

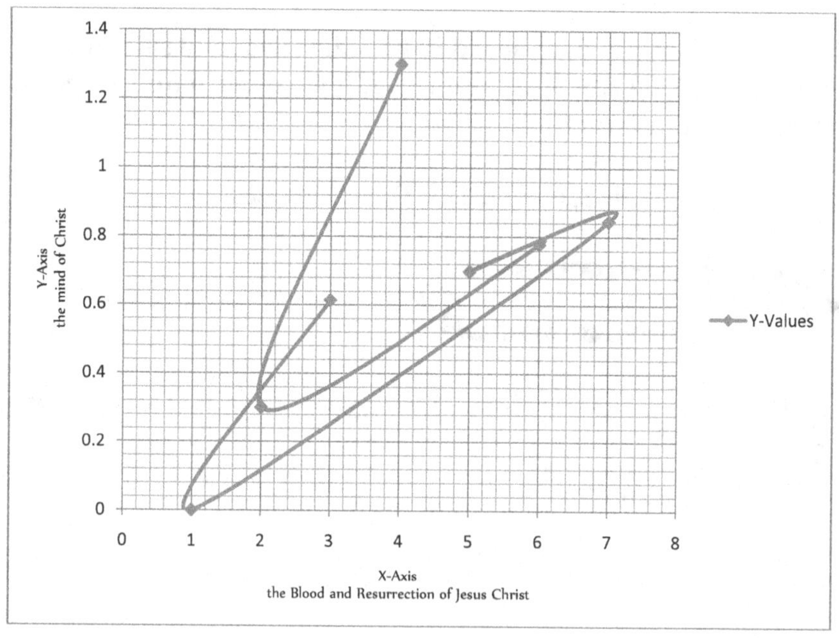

Water Spout *(lightning; combinatorics)* Study bible 2

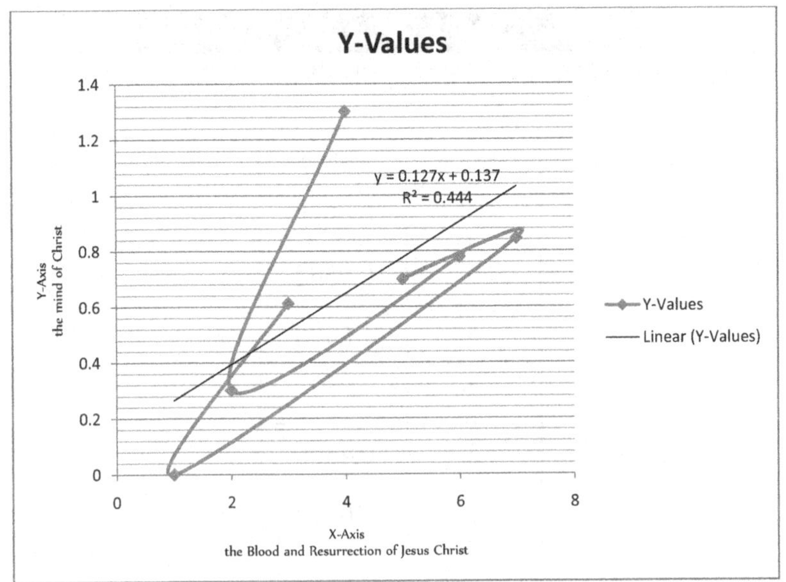

$2^1\ 10^{0.3010}, 10^{0.3010}, 10^{0.7781}, 10^{0.6989}, 10^{0.8450}, 10^0, 6^{0.6131}.$

Pilled Poplar, Hazel, and Chestnut bible rods 2

11. And I say unto you, That many shall come from the east and west, and shall sit down with Abraham father of multitudes, **and Isaac** laughter; sound, **and Jacob**that supplants, undermines; the heel, **in the kingdom of heaven.**

5, 9, 6, 2, 2, 5. Bible Matrices

Pilled Poplar, Hazel, and Chestnut bible rods 1

$\text{Log}_{10} 5 = 0.6989$

$\text{Log}_3 6 = y$

$3^y = 6$

$y \log_{10} 3 = \log_{10} 6$

$y = \log_{10} 6 / \log_{10} 3$

$y = 0.7781/0.4771$

$y = 1.6308\ y = 0.4306$

$\text{Log}_5 2 = y$

$5^y = 2$

$y \log_{10} 5 = \log_{10} 2$

$y = \log_{10} 2 / \log_{10} 5$

$y = 0.3010/0.6989$

$\text{Log}_2 2 = y$

$2^y = 2$

$2^y = 2^1$

$y = 1$

$\text{Log}_{10} 5 = 0.6989$

$\text{Log}_{10} 9 = 0.9542$

5, 9, 6, 2, 2, 5. Deep calls unto Deep study bible 1

0.6989, 0.9542, 1.6308, 1, 0.4306, 0.6989.
Deep calls unto Deep study bible 2

x-axis	y-axis
5	0.6989
9	0.9542
6	1.6308
2	1
2	0.4306
5	0.6989

Water Spout *(lightning; combinatorics)* Study bible 1

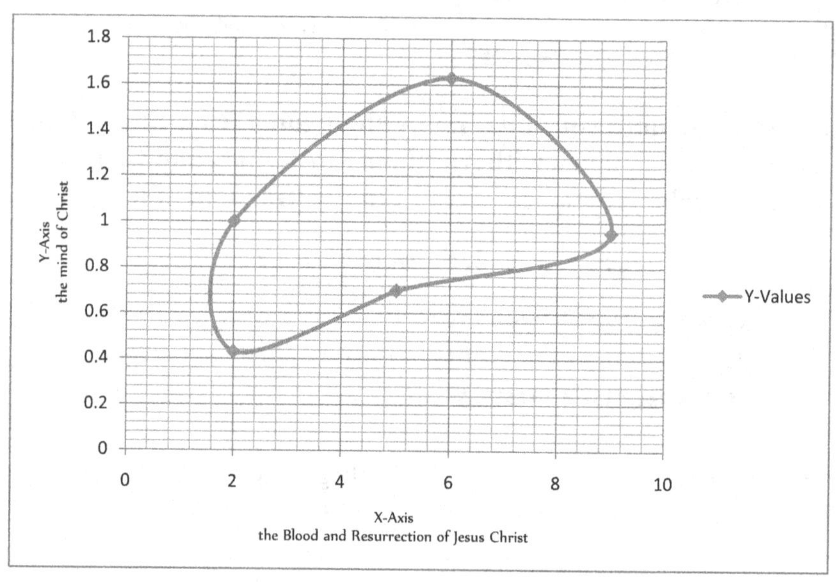

Water Spout *(lightning; combinatorics)* Study bible 2

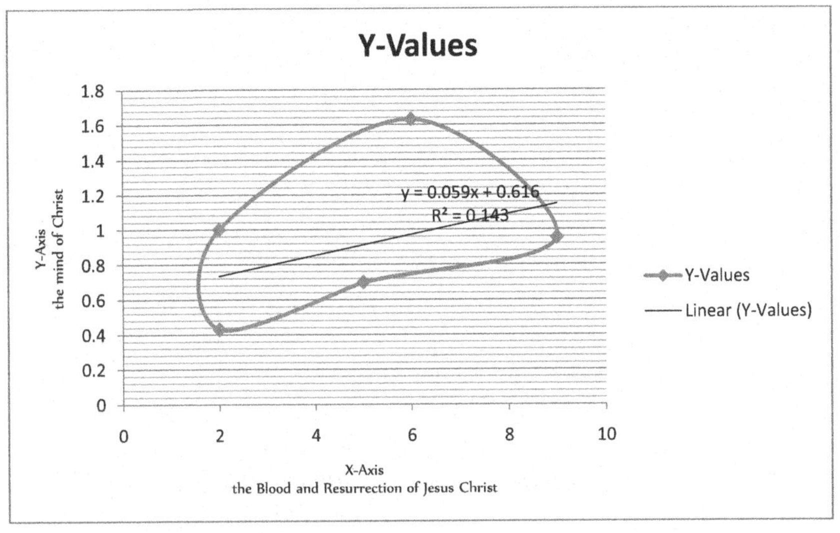

$10^{0.6989}, 10^{0.9542}, 3^{1.6308}, 2^{1}, 5^{0.4306}, 10^{0.6989}.$ Pilled Poplar, Hazel, and Chestnut bible rods 2

12. But the children of the kingdom shall be cast out into outer darkness: there shall be weeping and gnashing of teeth.

13: 8. Bible Matrices

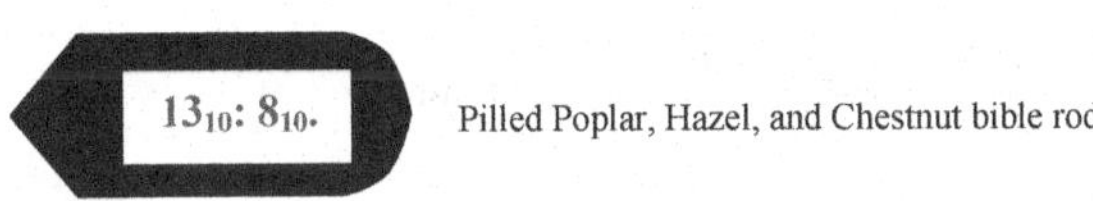

$\text{Log}_{10} 8 = 0.9030$ $\text{Log}_{10} 13 = 1.1139$

13: 8. Deep calls unto Deep study bible 1

1.1139: 0.9030. Deep calls unto Deep study bible 2

x-axis	y-axis
13	1.1139
8	0.9030

Water Spout *(lightning; combinatorics)* Study bible 1

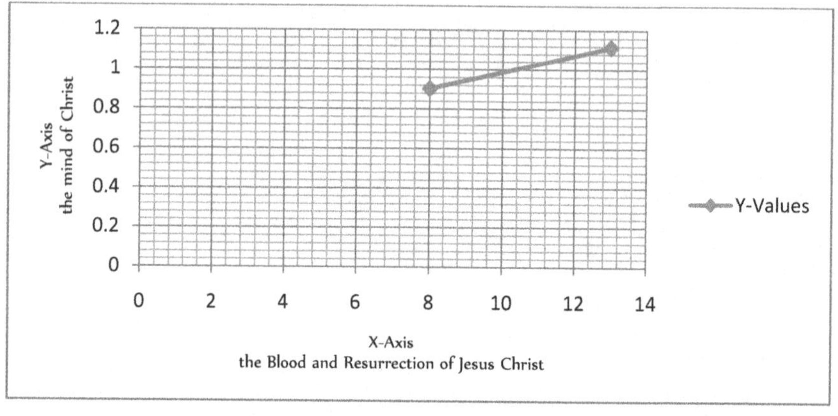

Water Spout *(lightning; combinatorics)* Study bible 2

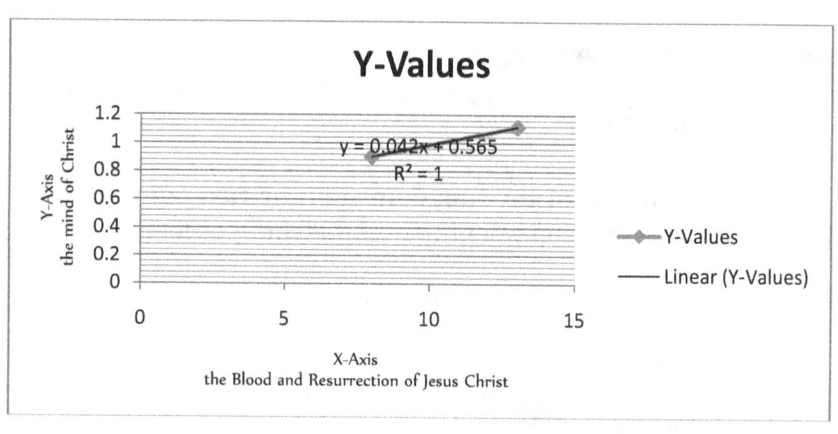

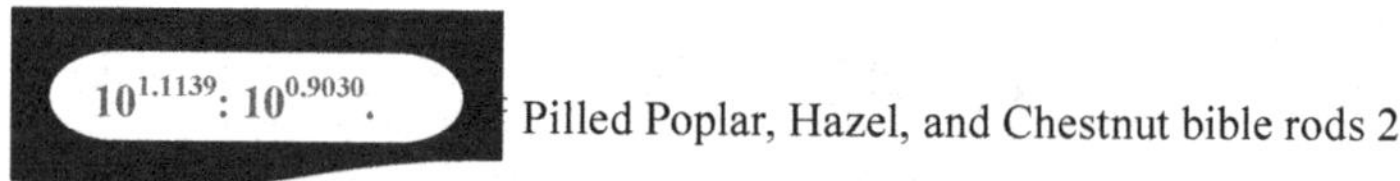

Pilled Poplar, Hazel, and Chestnut bible rods 2

13. And Jesussavior; deliverer **said unto the centurion** Commander of a hundred men, **Go thy way; and as thou hast believed, so be it done unto thee. And his servant was healed in the selfsame hour.**

6, 3; 5, 6. 9. Bible Matrices

$2_2\ 4_5,\ 3_{10};\ 5_{10},\ 6_{10}.\ 9_{10}.$ Pilled Poplar, Hazel, and Chestnut bible rods 1

$\text{Log}_{10} 5 = 0.6989$ $\text{Log}_{10} 3 = 0.4771$

$\text{Log}_5 4 = y$
$5^y = 4$
$y \log_{10} 5 = \log_{10} 4$
$y = \log_{10} 4 / \log_{10} 5$
$y = 0.6020 / 0.6989$
$y = 0.8613$

$\text{Log}_2 2 = y$
$2^y = 2$
$2^y = 2^1$
$y = 1$

$\text{Log}_{10} 6 = 0.7781$ $\text{Log}_{10} 9 = 0.9542$

6, 3; 5, 6. 9. Deep calls unto Deep study bible 1

1 0.8613 . 0.4771; 0.6989, 0.7781. 0.9542.

Deep calls unto Deep study bible 2

x-axis	y-axis
6	1.8613
3	0.4771
5	0.6989
6	0.7781
9	0.9542

Water Spout *(lightning; combinatorics)* Study bible 1

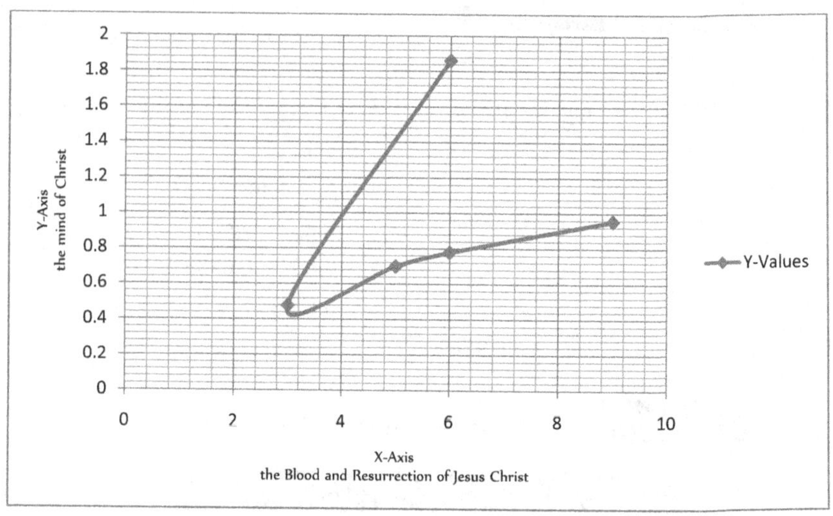

Water Spout *(lightning; combinatorics)* Study bible 2

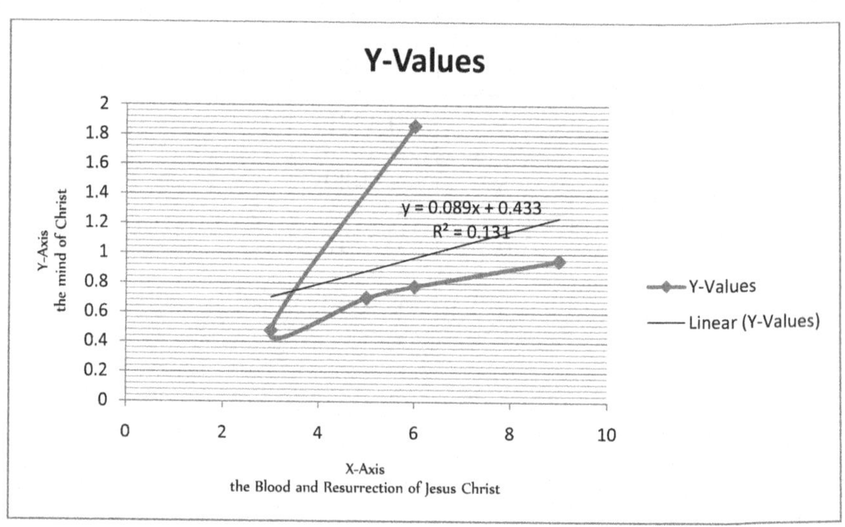

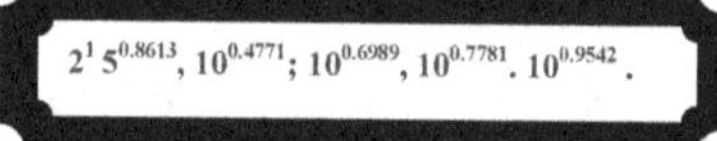

Pilled Poplar, Hazel, and Chestnut bible rods 2

14. And when Jesus savior; deliverer **was come into Peter's** a rock or stone **house, he saw his wife's mother laid, and sick of a fever.**

8, 6, 5. Bible Matrices

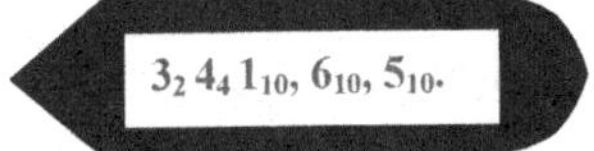

Pilled Poplar, Hazel, and Chestnut bible rods 1

$Log_{10} 1 = 0$ $Log_2 3 = y$ $Log_4 4 = y$ $Log_{10} 6 = 0.7781$ $Log_{10} 5 = 0.6989$

$2^y = 3$ $4^y = 4^1$

$y \log_{10} 2 = \log_{10} 3$ $y = 1$

$y = \log_{10} 3 / \log_{10} 2$

$y = 0.4771/0.0.3010$

$y = 1.5850$

8, 6, 5. Deep calls unto Deep study bible 1

1.5850 1 0, 0.7781, 0.6989. Deep calls unto Deep study bible 2

x-axis	y-axis
8	2.5850
6	0.7781
5	0.6989

Water Spout *(lightning; combinatorics)* Study bible 1

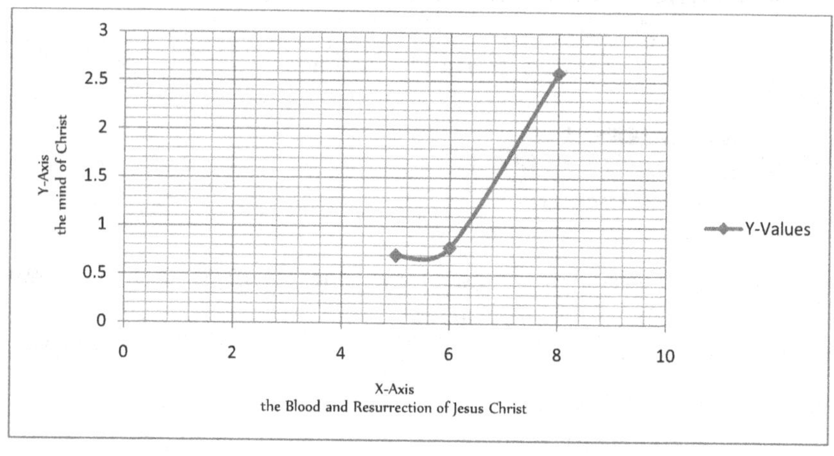

Water Spout *(lightning; combinatorics)* Study bible 2

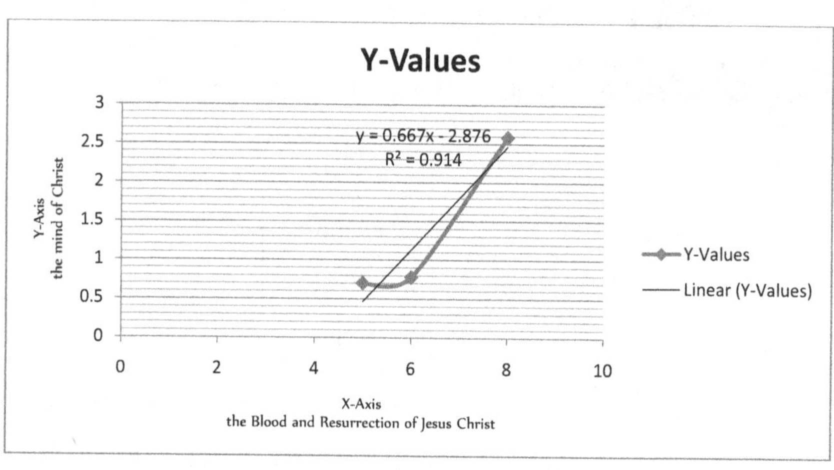

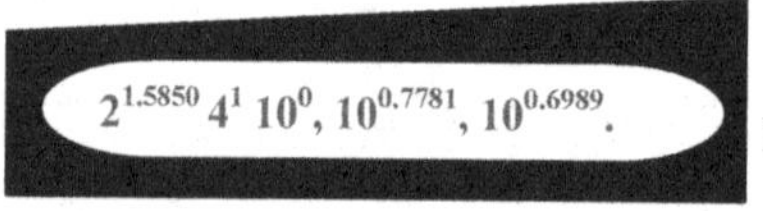

Pilled Poplar, Hazel, and Chestnut bible rods 2

15. And he touched her hand, and the fever left her: and she arose, and ministered unto them.

5, 5: 3, 4. Bible Matrices

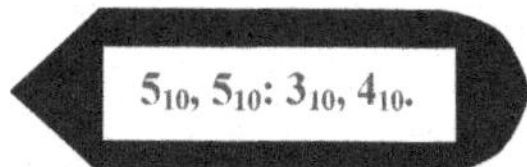

Pilled Poplar, Hazel, and Chestnut bible rods 1

$\text{Log}_{10} 5 = 0.6989$ $\text{Log}_{10} 5 = 0.6989$ $\text{Log}_{10} 3 = 0.4771$ $\text{Log}_{10} 4 = 0.6020$

5, 5: 3, 4. Deep calls unto Deep study bible 1

0.6989, 0.6989: 0.4771, 0.6020. Deep calls unto Deep study bible 2

x-axis	y-axis
5	0.6989
5	0.6989
3	0.4771
4	0.6020

Water Spout *(lightning; combinatorics)* Study bible 1

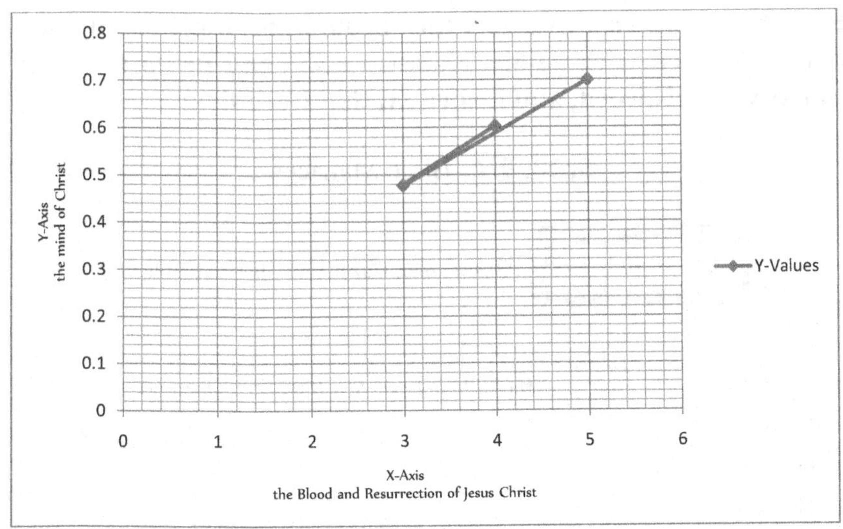

Water Spout *(lightning; combinatorics)* Study bible 2

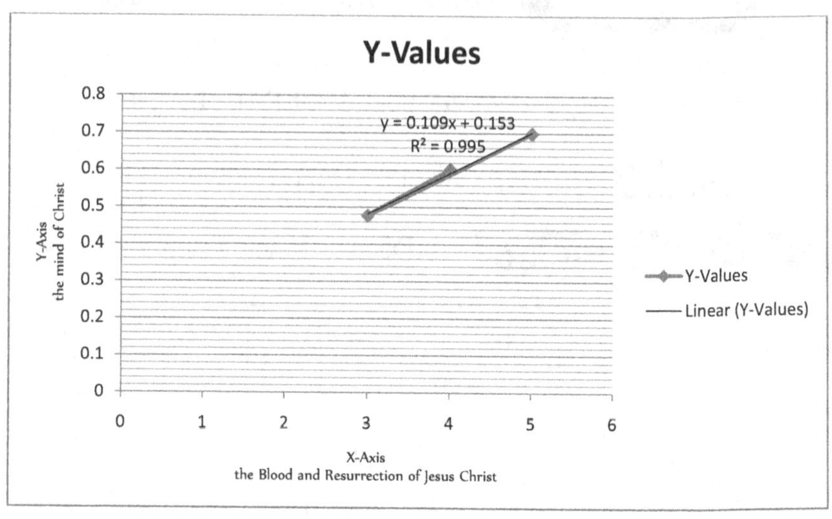

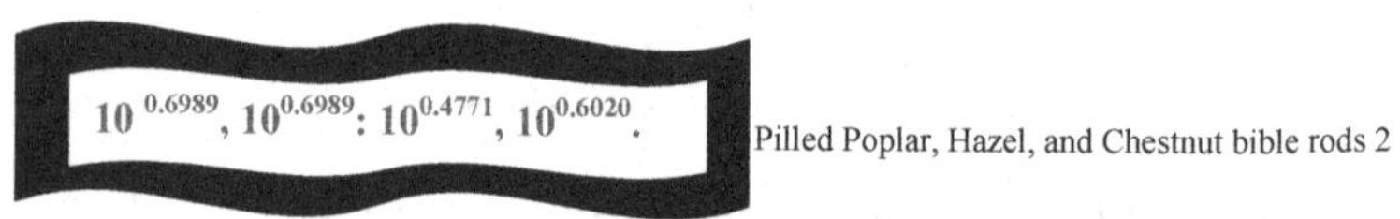

Pilled Poplar, Hazel, and Chestnut bible rods 2

16. When the even was come, they brought unto him many that were possessed with devils slanderers, false accusers: **and he cast out the spirits with his word, and healed all that were sick:**

5, 10: 9, 6: Bible Matrices

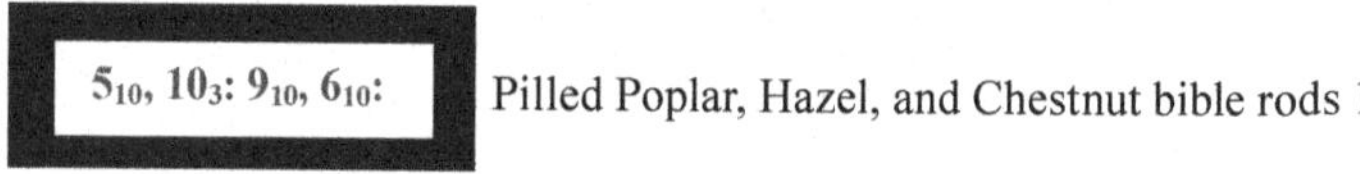

Pilled Poplar, Hazel, and Chestnut bible rods 1

$Log_3 10 = y$ $Log_{10} 5 = 0.6989$ $Log_{10} 9 = 0.9542$ $Log_{10} 6 = 0.7781$

$3^y = 10$

$y \log_{10} 3 = \log_{10} 10$

$y = \log_{10} 10 / \log_{10} 3$

$y = 1 / 0.0.4771$

$y = 2.0959$

5, 10: 9, 6: Deep calls unto Deep study bible 1

0.6989, 2.0959: 0.9542, 0.7781: Deep calls unto Deep study bible 2

x-axis	y-axis
5	0.6989
10	2.0959
9	0.9542
6	0.7781

Water Spout *(lightning; combinatorics)* Study bible 1

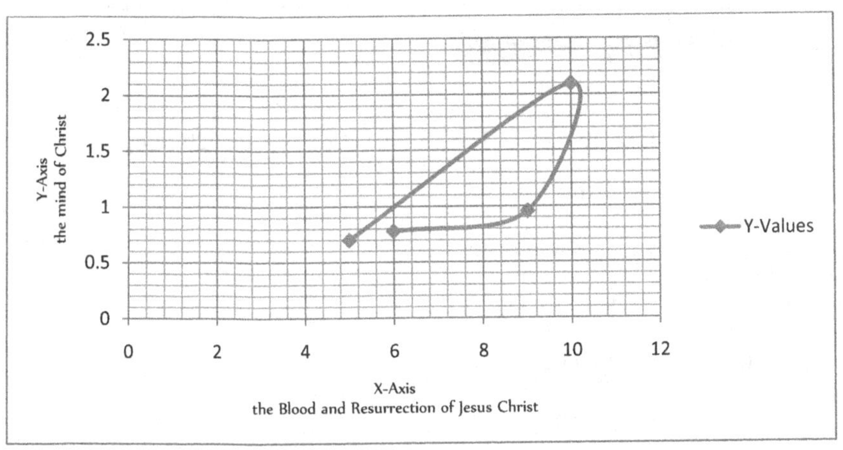

Water Spout *(lightning; combinatorics)* Study bible 2

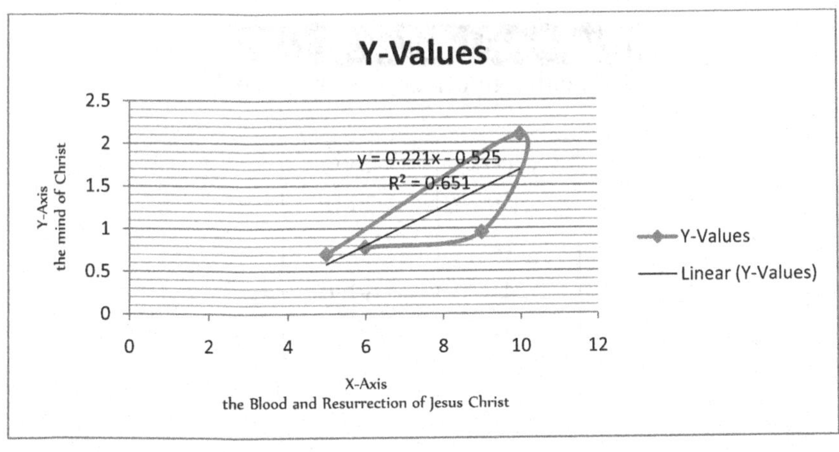

$10^{0.6989}, 3^{2.0959}: 10^{0.9542}, 10^{0.7781}:$

Pilled Poplar, Hazel, and Chestnut bible rods 2

17. That it might be fulfilled which was spoken by Esaias the salvation of the Lord **the prophet** to bubble forth, as from a fountain; utter, **saying, Himself took our infirmities, and bare our sicknesses.**

12, 1, 4, 4. Bible Matrices

$10_5\ 2_8, 1_{10}, 4_{10}, 4_{10}$.

Pilled Poplar, Hazel, and Chestnut bible rods 1

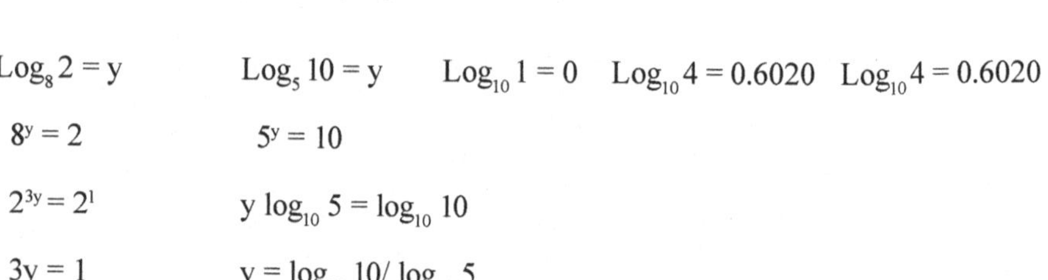

$\text{Log}_8 2 = y$ $\text{Log}_5 10 = y$ $\text{Log}_{10} 1 = 0$ $\text{Log}_{10} 4 = 0.6020$ $\text{Log}_{10} 4 = 0.6020$

$8^y = 2$ $5^y = 10$

$2^{3y} = 2^1$ $y \log_{10} 5 = \log_{10} 10$

$3y = 1$ $y = \log_{10} 10 / \log_{10} 5$

$y = 1/3$ or 0.3333 $y = 1/0.6989$

$y = 1.4308$

12, 1, 4, 4. Deep calls unto Deep study bible 1

1.4308 0.3333, 0, 0.6020, 0.6020 .

Deep calls unto Deep study bible 2

x-axis	y-axis
12	1.7641
1	0
4	0.6020
4	0.6020

Water Spout *(lightning; combinatorics)* Study bible 1

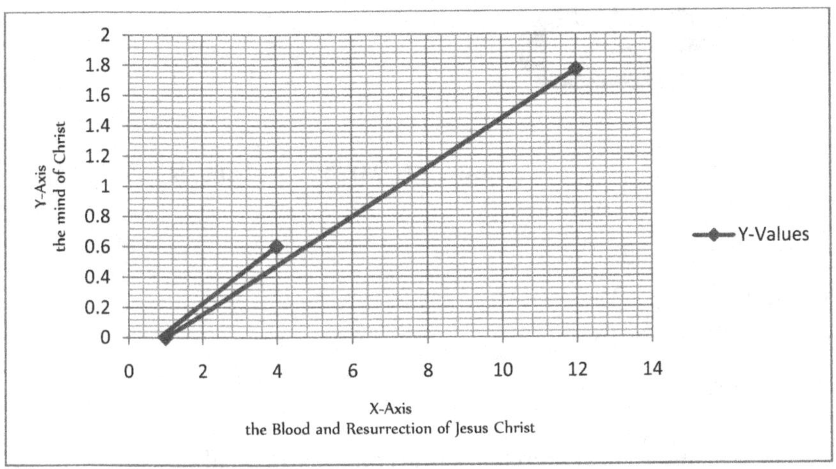

Water Spout *(lightning; combinatorics)* Study bible 2

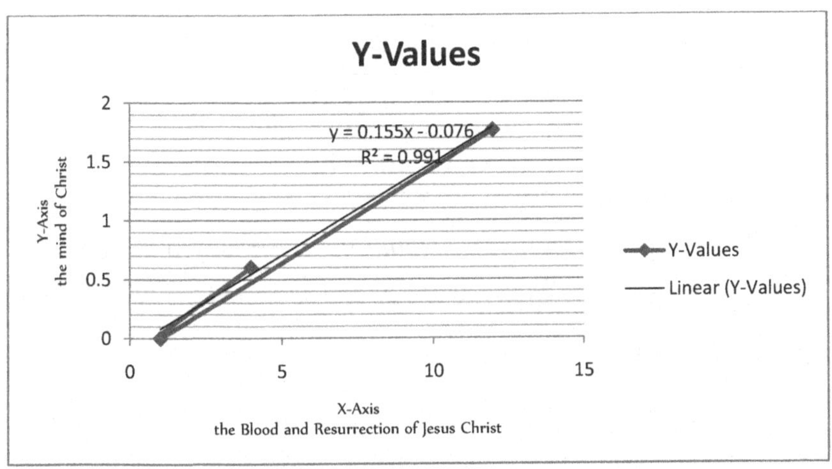

Pilled Poplar, Hazel, and Chestnut bible rods 2

18. Now when Jesus savior; deliverer **saw great multitudes about him, he gave commandment to depart unto the other side.**

8, 9. Bible Matrices

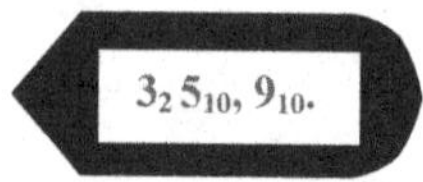

Pilled Poplar, Hazel, and Chestnut bible rods 1

$\text{Log}_2 3 = y$ $\text{Log}_{10} 5 = 0.6989$ $\text{Log}_{10} 9 = 0.9542$

$2^y = 3$

$y \log_{10} 2 = \log_{10} 3$

$y = \log_{10} 3/ \log_{10} 2$

$y = 0.4771/0.0.3010$

$y = 1.5850$

8, 9. Deep calls unto Deep study bible 1

1.5850 0.6989, 0.9542. Deep calls unto Deep study bible 2

x-axis	y-axis
8	2.2839
9	0.9542

Water Spout *(lightning; combinatorics)* Study bible 1

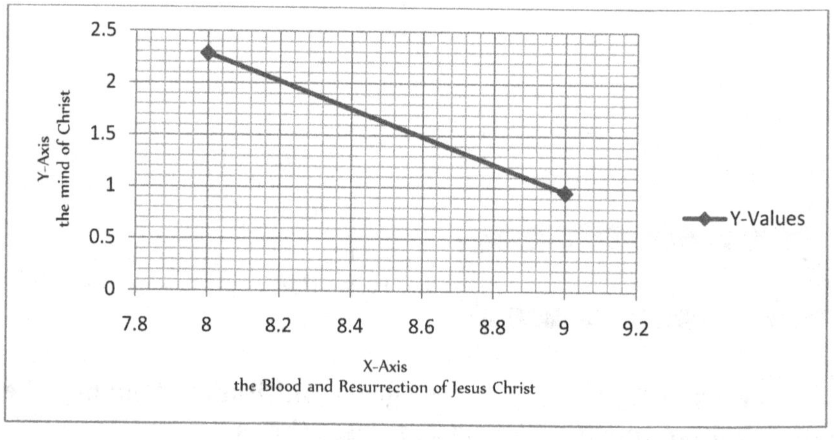

Water Spout *(lightning; combinatorics)* Study bible 2

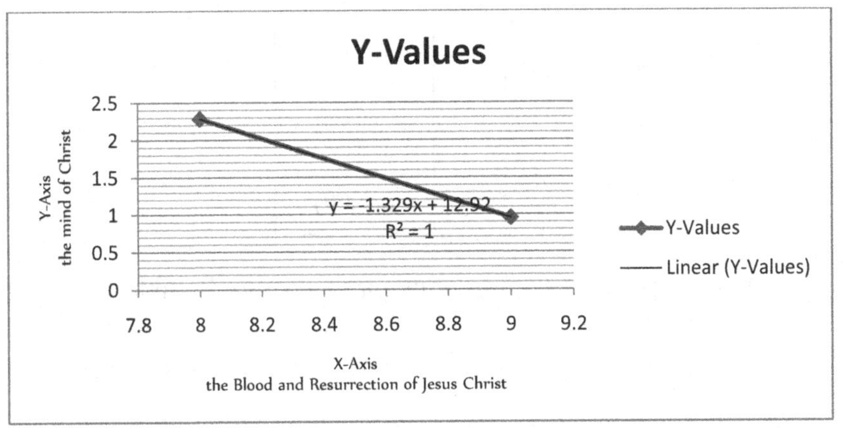

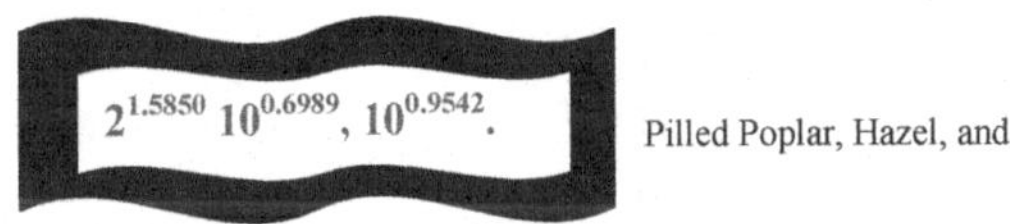

Pilled Poplar, Hazel, and Chestnut bible rods 2

19. And a certain scribe lawyer; transcriber **came, and said unto him, Master, I will follow thee whithersoever thou goest.**

5, 4, 1, 7. Bible Matrices

Pilled Poplar, Hazel, and Chestnut bible rods 1

$\text{Log}_2 4 = y$ $\text{Log}_{10} 4 = 0.6020$ $\text{Log}_{10} 1 = 0$ $\text{Log}_{10} 1 = 0$ $\text{Log}_{10} 7 = 0.8450$

$2^y = 2^2$

$y = 2$

5, 4, 1, 7. Deep calls unto Deep study bible 1

2 0, 0.6020, 0, 0.8450. Deep calls unto Deep study bible 2

x-axis	y-axis
5	2
4	0.6020
1	0
7	0.8450

Water Spout *(lightning; combinatorics)* Study bible 1

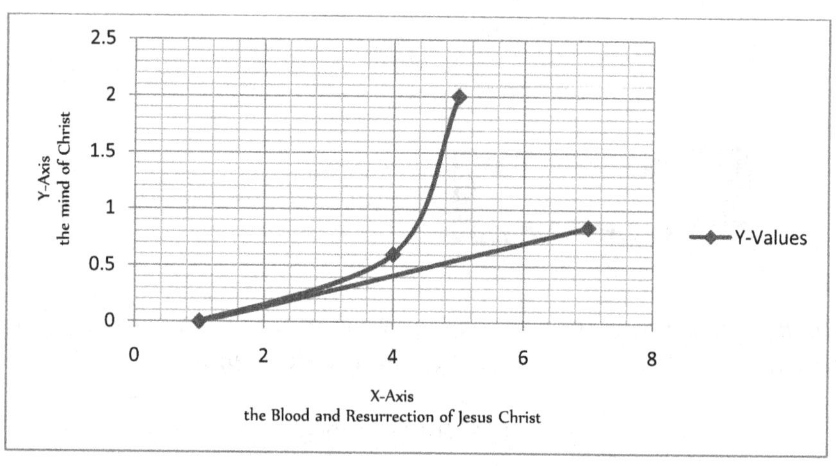

Water Spout *(lightning; combinatorics)* Study bible 2

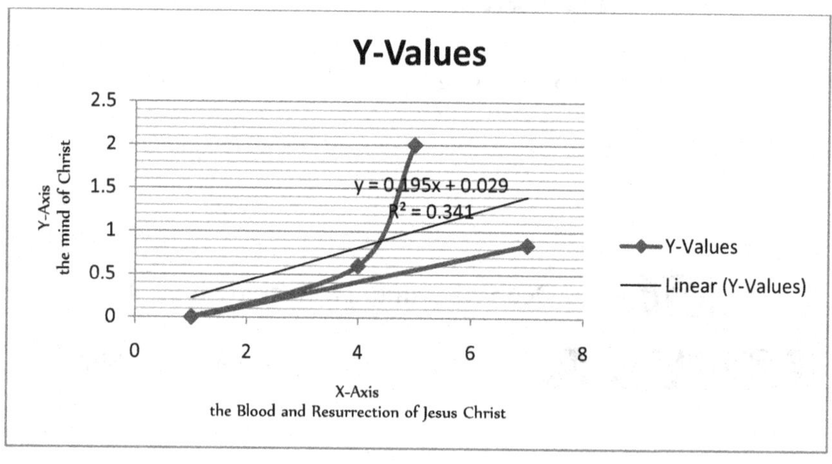

$2^2\ 10^0, 10^{0.6020}, 10^0, 10^{0.8450}.$ Pilled Poplar, Hazel, and Chestnut bible rods 2

20. And Jesussavior; deliverer**saith unto him, The foxes have holes, and the birds of the air have nests; but the Son of man hath not where to lay his head.**

5, 4, 8; 12. Bible Matrices

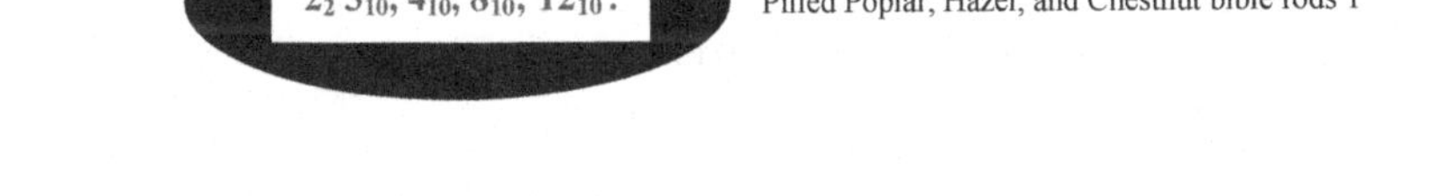

Pilled Poplar, Hazel, and Chestnut bible rods 1

$\text{Log}_2 2 = y$ $\text{Log}_{10} 3 = 0.4771$ $\text{Log}_{10} 4 = 0.6020$ $\text{Log}_{10} 8 = 0.9030$ $\text{Log}_{10} 12 = 1.0791$

$2^y = 2^1$

$y = 1$

5, 4, 8; 12. Deep calls unto Deep study bible 1

1 0.4771, 0.6020, 0.9030; 1.0791.

Deep calls unto Deep study bible 2

x-axis	y-axis
5	1.4771
4	0.6020
8	0.9030
12	1.0791

Water Spout *(lightning; combinatorics)* Study bible 1

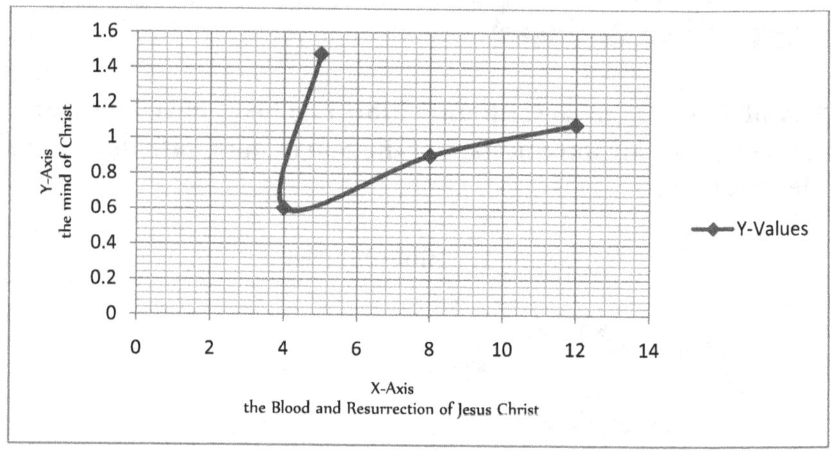

Water Spout *(lightning; combinatorics)* Study bible 2

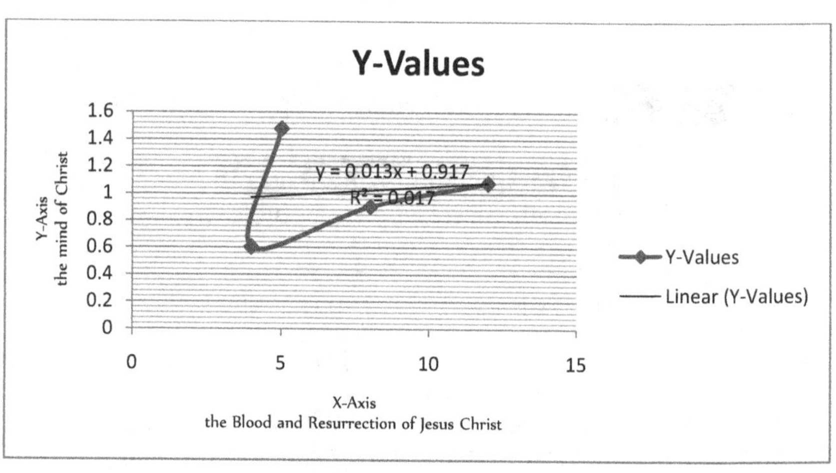

2^{1} $10^{0.4771}$, $10^{0.6020}$, $10^{0.9030}$; $10^{1.0791}$.

Pilled Poplar, Hazel, and Chestnut bible rods 2

21. And another of his disciples said unto him, Lord, suffer me first to go and bury my father.

8, 1, 9. Bible Matrices

$8_{10}, 1_{10}, 9_{10}.$ Pilled Poplar, Hazel, and Chestnut bible rods 1

$\text{Log}_{10} 8 = 0.9030$ $\text{Log}_{10} 9 = 0.9542$ $\text{Log}_{10} 1 = 0$

8, 1, 9. Deep calls unto Deep study bible 1

0.9030, 0, 0.9542. Deep calls unto Deep study bible 2

x-axis	y-axis
8	0.9030
1	0
9	0.9542

Water Spout *(lightning; combinatorics)* Study bible 1

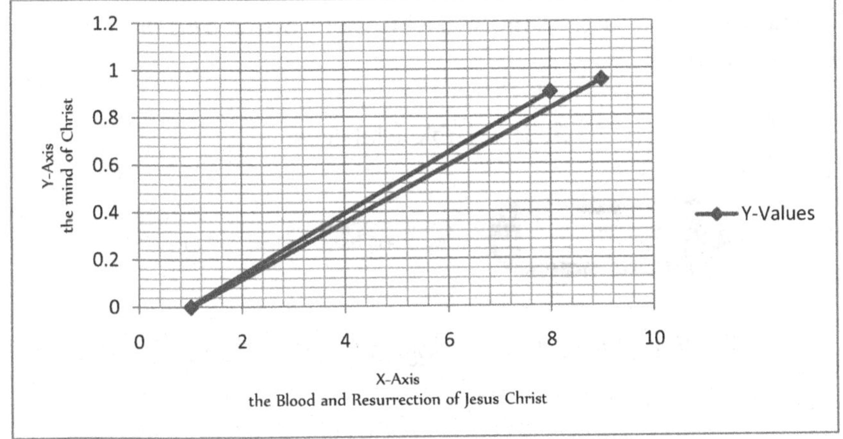

Water Spout *(lightning; combinatorics)* Study bible 2

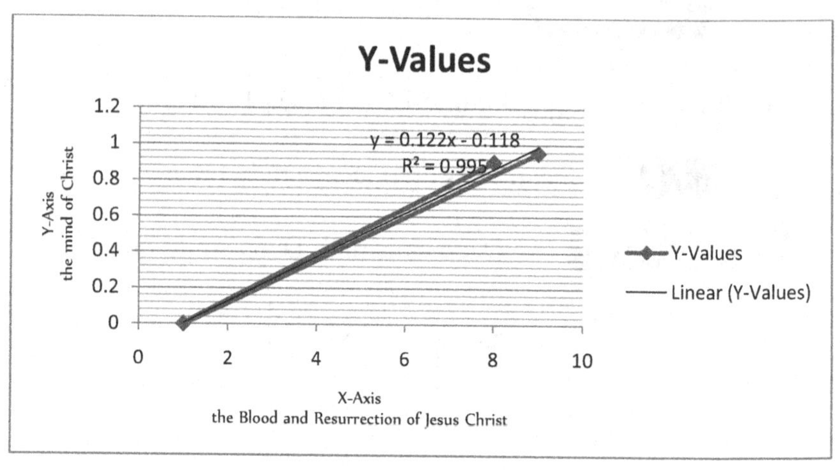

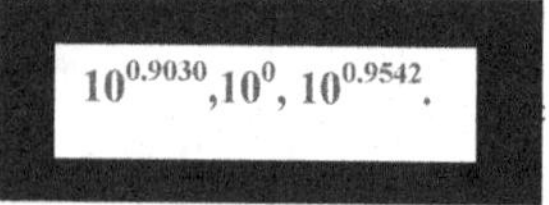

Pilled Poplar, Hazel, and Chestnut bible rods 2

22. But Jesussavior; deliverer**said unto him, Follow me; and let the dead bury their dead.**

5, 2; 7. Bible Matrices

Pilled Poplar, Hazel, and Chestnut bible rods 1

$\text{Log}_2 2 = y$ $\log_{10} 3 = 0.\ 0.4771$ $\log_{10} 2 = 0.3010$ $\log_{10} 7 = 0.8450$

$2^y = 2^1$

$y = 1$

5, 2; 7. Deep calls unto Deep study bible 1

1 0.4771, 0.3010; 0.8450. Deep calls unto Deep study bible 2

x-axis	y-axis
5	1.4771
2	0.3010
7	0.8450

Water Spout *(lightning; combinatorics)* Study bible 1

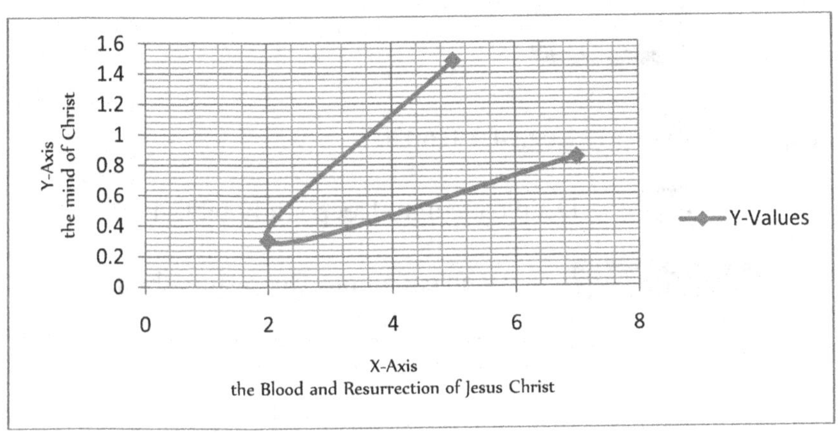

Water Spout *(lightning; combinatorics)* Study bible 2

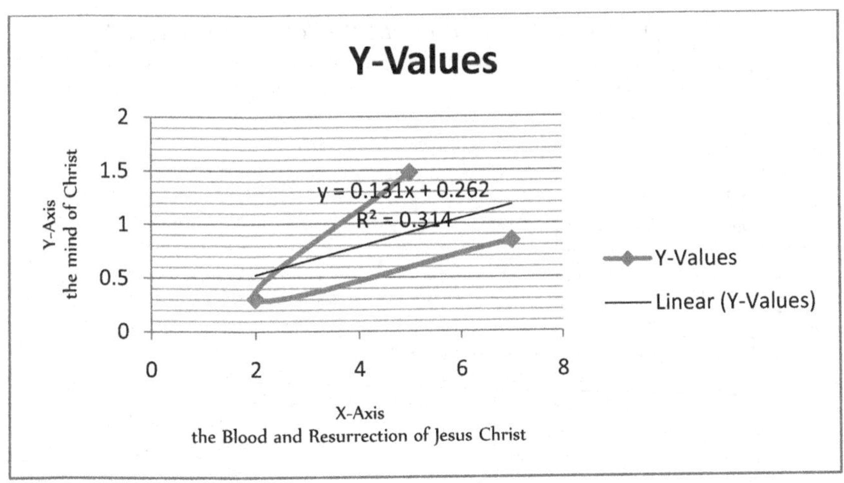

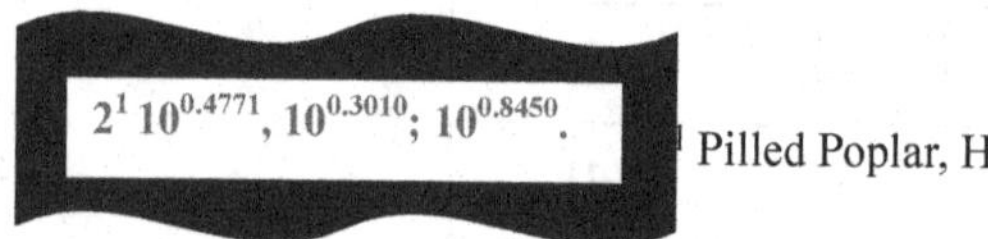

$2^1\ 10^{0.4771},\ 10^{0.3010};\ 10^{0.8450}.$

Pilled Poplar, Hazel, and Chestnut bible rods 2

23. And when he was entered into a ship, his disciples followed him.

8, 4. Bible Matrices

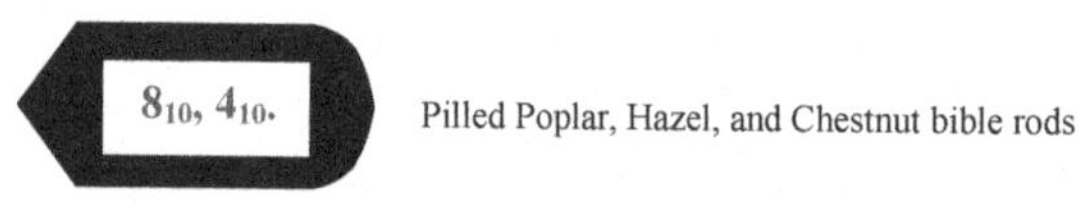

$8_{10},\ 4_{10}.$

Pilled Poplar, Hazel, and Chestnut bible rods 1

$\text{Log}_{10}\ 8 = 0.9030$ $\quad$ $\text{Log}_{10}\ 4 = 0.6020$

8, 4. Deep calls unto Deep study bible 1

0.9030, 0.6020. Deep calls unto Deep study bible 2

x-axis	y-axis
8	0.9030
4	0.6020

Water Spout *(lightning; combinatorics)* Study bible 1

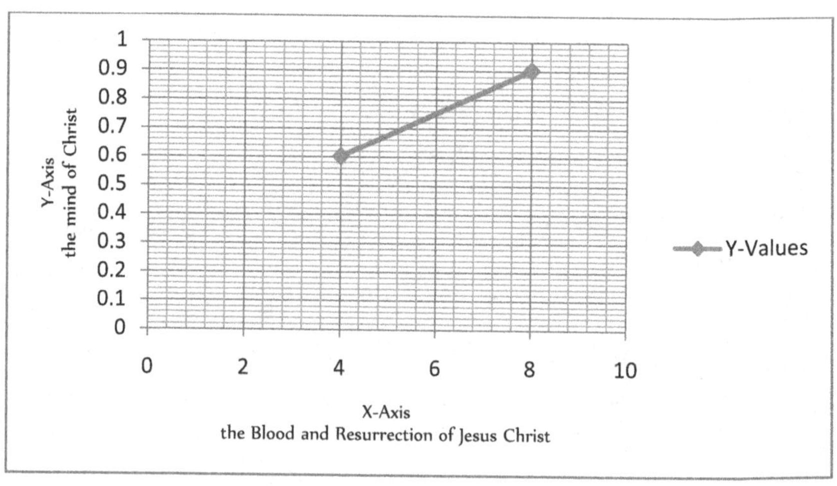

Water Spout *(lightning; combinatorics)* Study bible 2

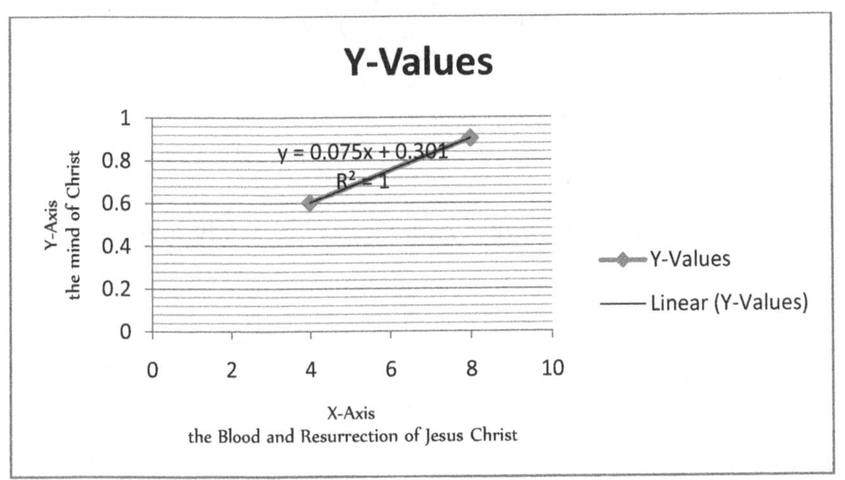

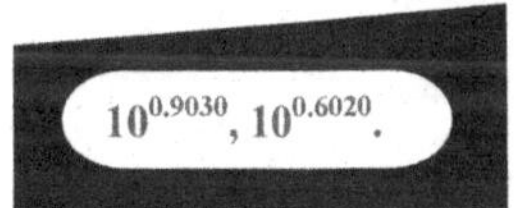

Pilled Poplar, Hazel, and Chestnut bible rods 2

24. And, behold, there arose a great tempest in the sea, insomuch that the ship was covered with the waves: but he was asleep.

1, 1, 8, 9: 4. Bible Matrices

$1_{10}, 1_{10}, 8_{10}, 9_{10}: 4_{10}$.

Pilled Poplar, Hazel, and Chestnut bible rods 1

$\text{Log}_{10} 8 = 0.9030$ $\text{Log}_{10} 1 = 0$ $\text{Log}_{10} 1 = 0$ $\text{Log}_{10} 9 = 0.9542$ $\text{Log}_{10} 4 = 0.6020$

1, 1, 8, 9: 4. Deep calls unto Deep study bible 1

0, 0, 0.9030, 0.9542: 0.6020. Deep calls unto Deep study bible 2

x-axis	y-axis
1	0

1	0
8	0.9030
9	0.9542
4	0.6020

Water Spout *(lightning; combinatorics)* Study bible 1

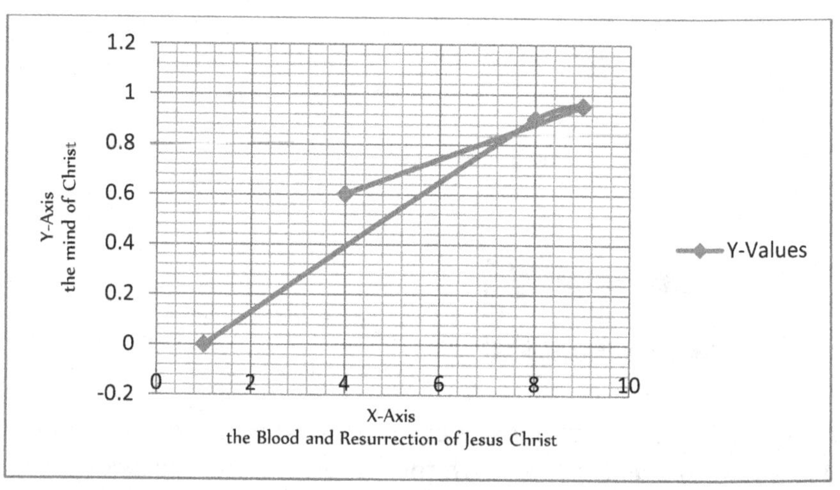

Water Spout *(lightning; combinatorics)* Study bible 2

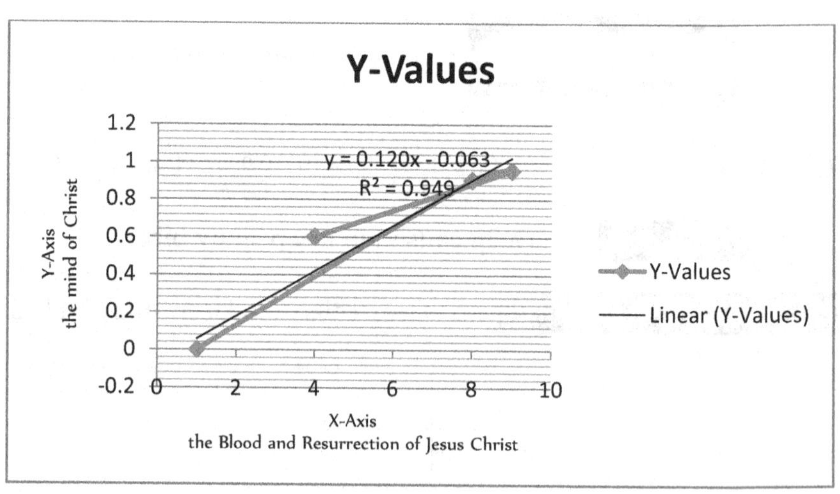

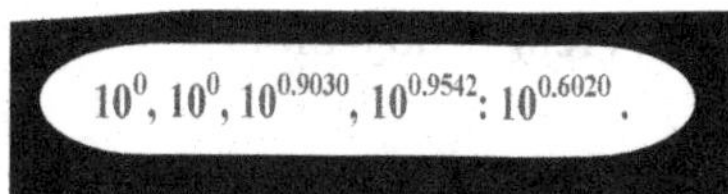

Pilled Poplar, Hazel, and Chestnut bible rods 2

25. And his disciples came to him, and awoke him, saying, Lord, save us: we perish.

6, 3, 1, 1, 2: 2. Bible Matrices

$6_{10}, 3_{10}, 1_{10}, 1_{10}, 2_{10}: 2_{10}.$

Pilled Poplar, Hazel, and Chestnut bible rods 1

$\text{Log}_{10} 1 = 0$ $\text{Log}_{10} 1 = 0$ $\text{Log}_{10} 2 = 0.3010$ $\text{Log}_{10} 2 = 0.3010$ $\text{Log}_{10} 3 = 0.4771$ $\text{Log}_{10} 6 = 0.7781$

6, 3, 1, 1, 2: 2. Deep calls unto Deep study bible 1

0.7781, 0.4771, 0, 0, 0.3010: 0.3010.

Deep calls unto Deep study bible 2

x-axis	y-axis
6	0.7781
3	0.4771
1	0
1	0
2	0.3010
2	0.3010

Water Spout *(lightning; combinatorics)* Study bible 1

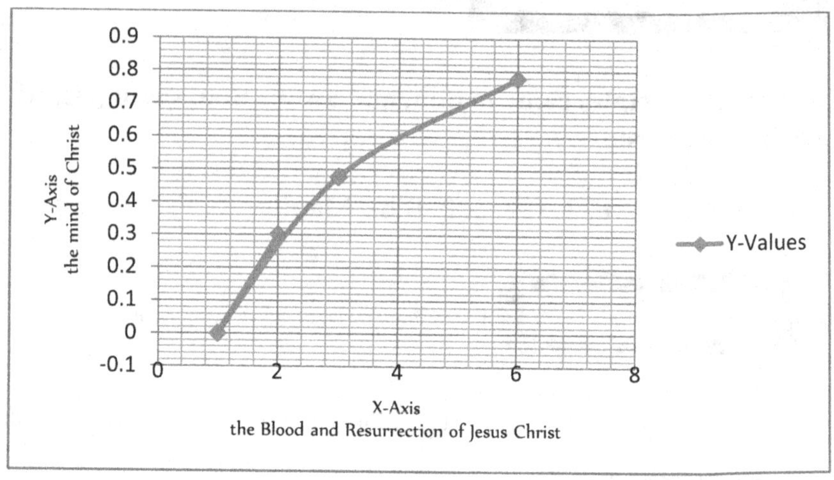

Water Spout *(lightning; combinatorics)* Study bible 2

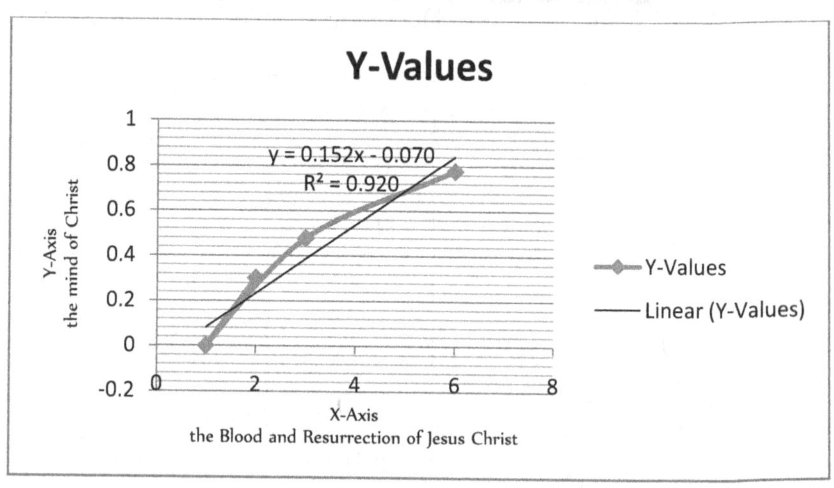

$10^{0.7781}, 10^{0.4771}, 10^{0}, 10^{0}, 10^{0.3010}: 10^{0.3010}$.

Pilled Poplar, Hazel, and Chestnut bible rods 2

26. And he saith unto them, Why are ye fearful, O ye of little faith? Then he arose, and rebuked the winds and the sea; and there was a great calm.

5, 4, 5? 3, 7; 6. Bible Matrices

$5_{10}, 4_{10}, 5_{10}? \ 3_{10}, 7_{10}; 6_{10}.$ Pilled Poplar, Hazel, and Chestnut bible rods 1

$\text{Log}_{10} 5 = 0.6989$ $\text{Log}_{10} 4 = 0.6020$ $\text{Log}_{10} 5 = 0.6989$ $\text{Log}_{10} 3 = 0.4771$ $\text{Log}_{10} 7 = 0.8450$

$\text{Log}_{10} 6 = 0.7781$

5, 4, 5? 3, 7; 6. Deep calls unto Deep study bible 1

0.6989, 0.6020, 0.6989? 0.4771, 0.8450; 0.7781
Deep calls unto Deep study bible 2

x-axis	y-axis
5	0.6989
4	0.6020
5	0.6989
3	0.4771
7	0.8450
6	0.7781

Water Spout *(lightning; combinatorics)* Study bible 1

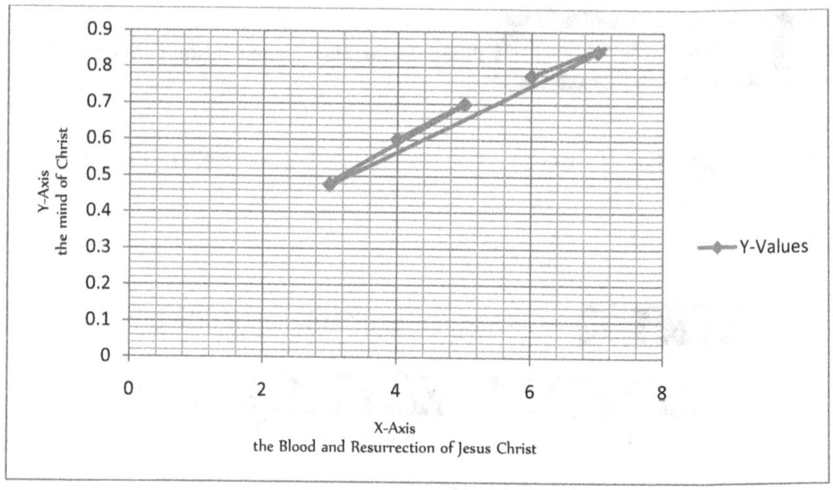

Water Spout *(lightning; combinatorics)* Study bible 2

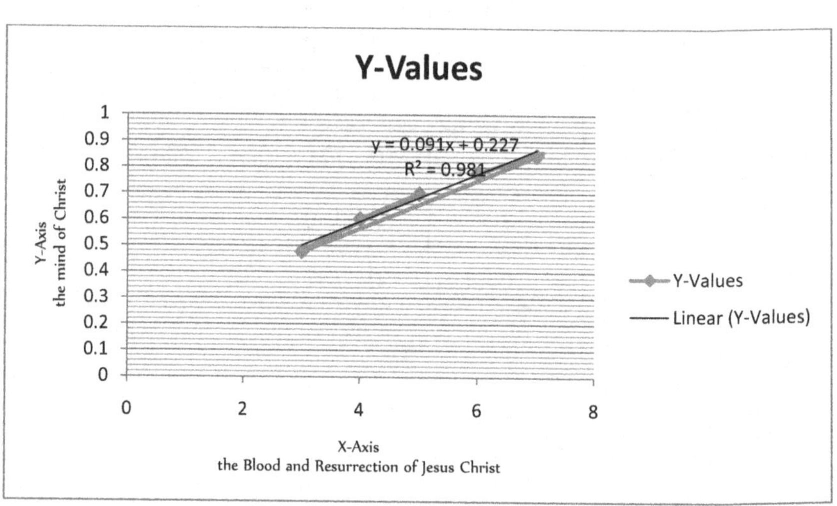

$10^{0.6989}$, $10^{0.6020}$, $10^{0.6989}$? $10^{0.4771}$, $10^{0.8450}$; $10^{0.7781}$. Pilled Poplar, Hazel, and Chestnut bible rods 2

27. But the men marvelled, saying, What manner of man is this, that even the winds and the sea obey him!

4, 1, 6, 9! Bible Matrices

$4_{10}, 1_{10}, 6_{10}, 9_{10}$! Pilled Poplar, Hazel, and Chestnut bible rods 1

$\text{Log}_{10} 4 = 0.6020$ $\text{Log}_{10} 1 = 0$ $\text{Log}_{10} 6 = 0.7781$ $\text{Log}_{10} 9 = 0.9542$

4, 1, 6, 9! Deep calls unto Deep study bible 1

0.6020, 0, 0.7781, 0.9542! Deep calls unto Deep study bible 2

x-axis	y-axis
4	0.6020
1	0
6	0.7781
9	0.9542

Water Spout *(lightning; combinatorics)* Study bible 1

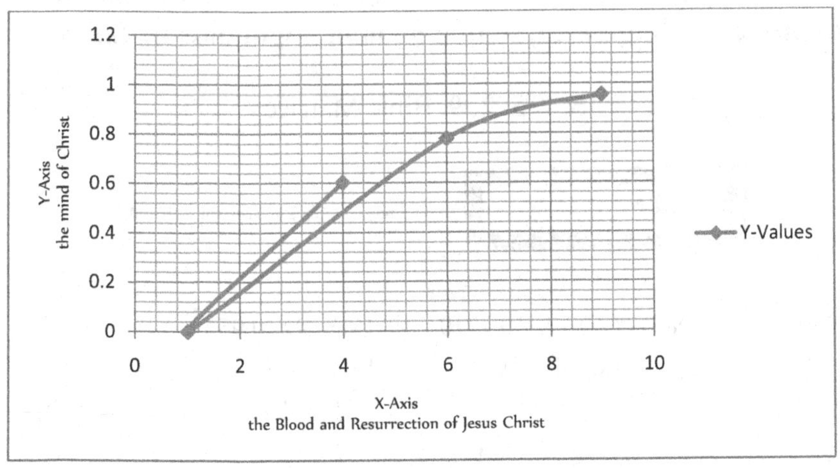

Water Spout *(lightning; combinatorics)* Study bible 2

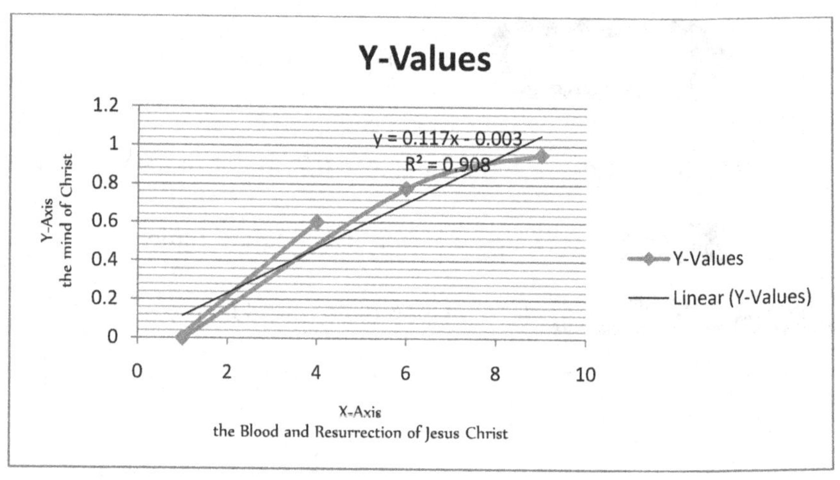

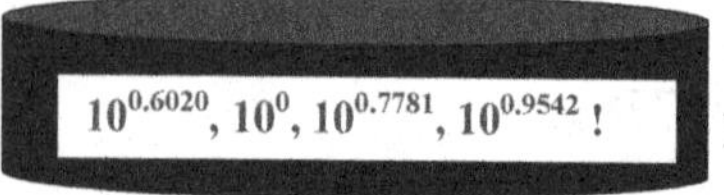

Pilled Poplar, Hazel, and Chestnut bible rods 2

28. And when he was come to the other side into the country of the Gergesenesthose who come from pilgrimage or fight, **there met him two** witness & support; 2 x 1 **possessed with devils** slanderers, false accusers, **coming out of the tombs, exceeding fierce, so that no man might pass by that way.**

15, 7, 5, 2, 9. Bible Matrices

$15_7, 4_4 3_3, 5_{10}, 2_{10}, 9_{10}$.

Pilled Poplar, Hazel, and Chestnut bible rods 1

$\text{Log}_{10} 5 = 0.6989$ $\text{Log}_{10} 2 = 0.3010$ $\text{Log}_{10} 9 = 0.9542$

$\text{Log}_7 15 = y$ $\text{Log}_4 4 = y$ $\text{Log}_3 3 = y$

$7^y = 15$ $4^y = 4$ $3^y = 3^1$

$y \log_{10} 7 = \log_{10} 15$ $2^{2y} = 2^2$ $y = 1$

$y = \log_{10} 15 / \log_{10} 7$ $2y = 2$

$y = 1.1760 / 0.8450$ $y = 1$

$y = 1.3917$

15, 7, 5, 2, 9. Deep calls unto Deep study bible 1

1.3917, 1 1, 0.6989, 0.3010, 0.9542.
Deep calls unto Deep study bible 2

x-axis	y-axis
15	1.3917
7	2
5	0.6989
2	0.3010
9	0.9542

Water Spout *(lightning; combinatorics)* Study bible 1

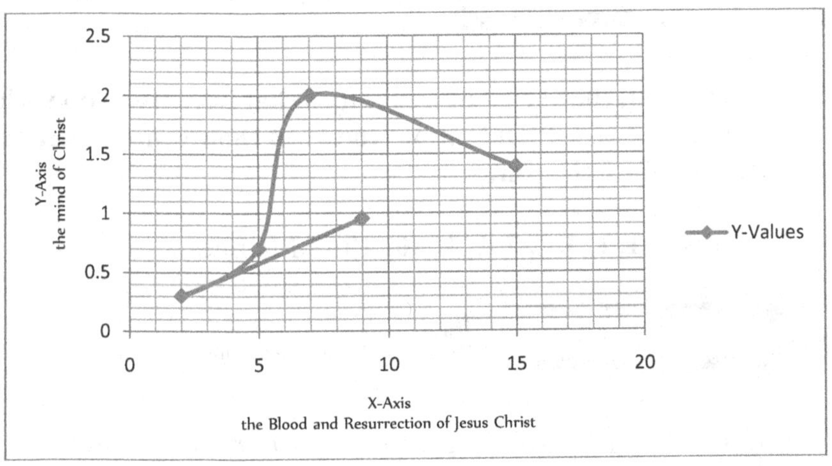

Water Spout *(lightning; combinatorics)* Study bible 2

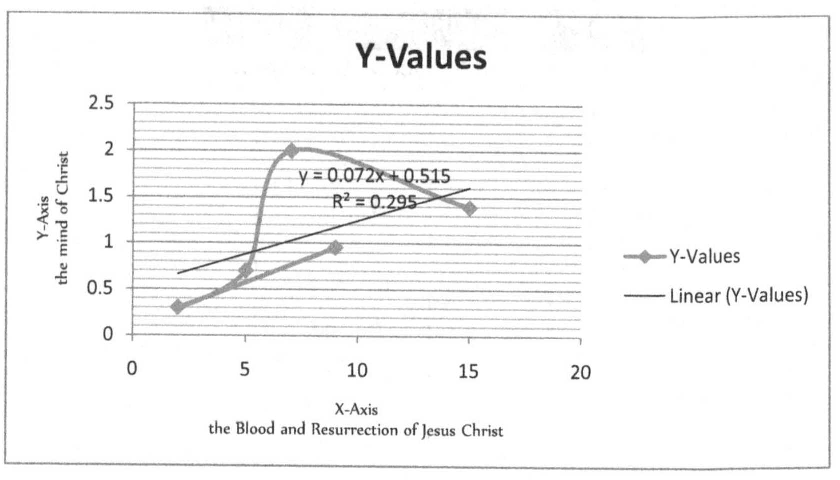

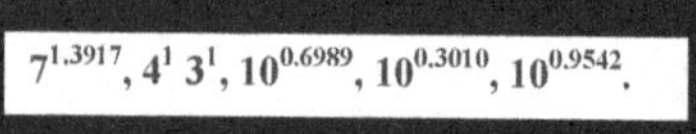

Pilled Poplar, Hazel, and Chestnut bible rods 2

29. And, behold, they cried out, saying, What have we to do with thee, Jesussavior; deliverer, **thou Son of God? art thou come hither to torment us before the time?**

1, 1, 3, 1, 7, 1, 4? 10? Bible Matrices

1_{10}, 1_{10}, 3_{10}, 1_{10}, 7_{10}, 1_2, 4_{10}? 10_{10}?

Pilled Poplar, Hazel, and Chestnut bible rods 1

$\text{Log}_{10} 1 = 0$ $\text{Log}_{10} 1 = 0$ $\text{Log}_{10} 1 = 0$ $\text{Log}_{10} 3 = 0.4771$ $\text{Log}_{10} 7 = 0.8450$

$\text{Log}_{10} 4 = 0.6020$ $\text{Log}_{10} 10 = 1$ $\log_2 1 = y$

$$2^y = 1$$

$$2^y = 2^0$$

$$y = 0$$

1, 1, 3, 1, 7, 1, 4? 10? Deep calls unto Deep study bible 1

0, 0, 0.4771, 0, 0.8450, 0, 0.6020? 1?

Deep calls unto Deep study bible 2

x-axis	y-axis
1	0
1	0
3	0.4771
1	0
7	0.8450
1	0
4	0.6020
10	1

Water Spout *(lightning; combinatorics)* Study bible 1

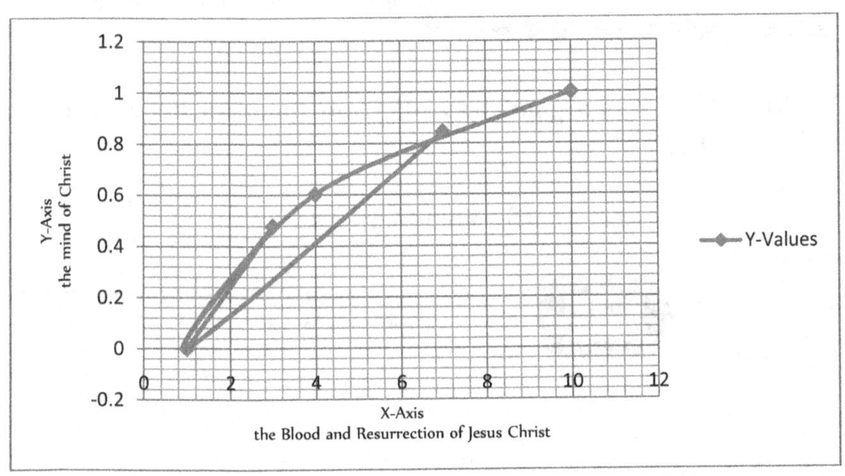

Water Spout *(lightning; combinatorics)* Study bible 2

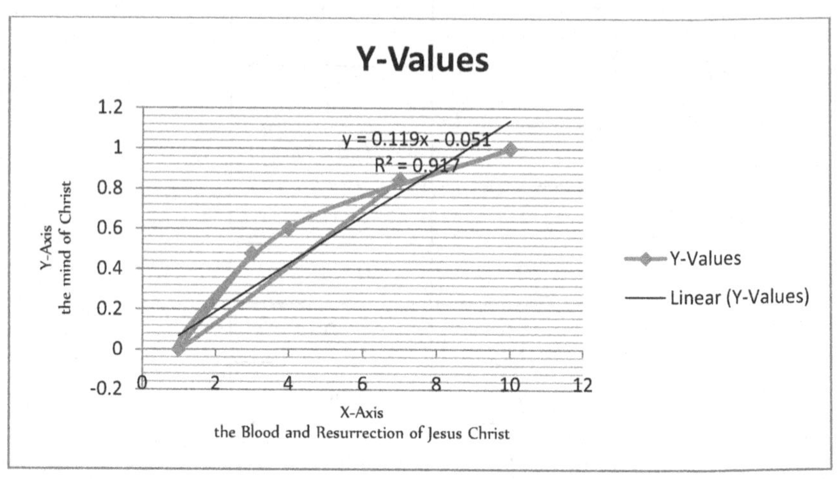

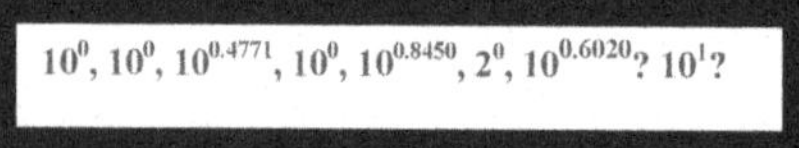

Pilled Poplar, Hazel, and Chestnut bible rods 2

30. And there was a good way off from them an herd of many swine feeding.

15. Bible Matrices

Pilled Poplar, Hazel, and Chestnut bible rods 1

Log_{10} 15 = 1.1760

15. Deep calls unto Deep study bible 1

1.1760 . Deep calls unto Deep study bible 2

x-axis	y-axis
15	1.1760

Water Spout *(lightning; combinatorics)* Study bible 1

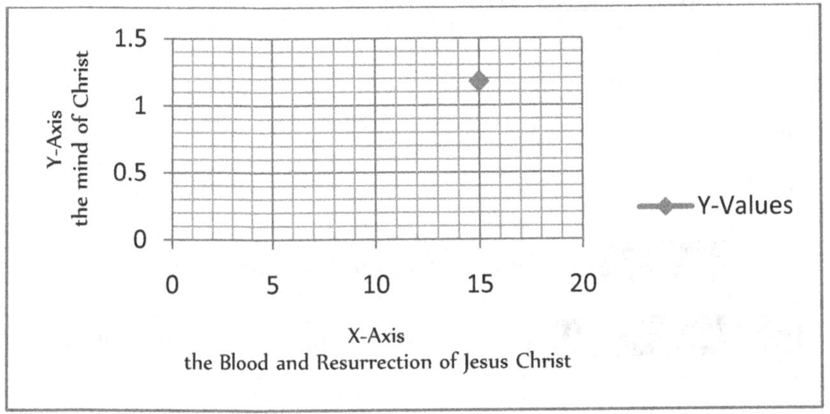

Water Spout *(lightning; combinatorics)* Study bible 2

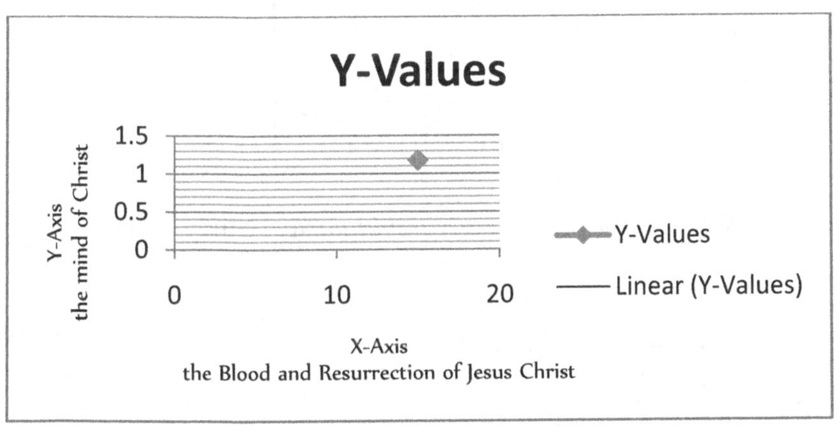

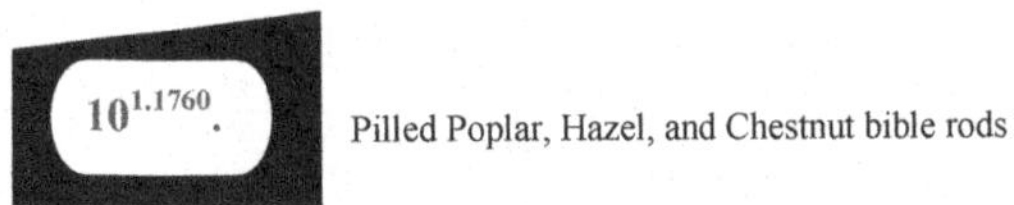

Pilled Poplar, Hazel, and Chestnut bible rods 2

31. So the devils slanderers, false accusers **besought him, saying, If thou cast us out, suffer us to go away into the herd of swine.**

5, 1, 5, 10. Bible Matrices

3_3 2_{10}, 1_{10}, 5_{10}, 10_{10}. Pilled Poplar, Hazel, and Chestnut bible rods 1

$Log_3 3 = y$ $Log_{10} 2 = 0.3010$ $Log_{10} 1 = 0$ $Log_{10} 5 = 0.4771$ $Log_{10} 10 = 1$

$3^y = 3^1$

$y = 1$

5, 1, 5, 10. Deep calls unto Deep study bible 1

1 0.3010, 0, 0.4771, 1. Deep calls unto Deep study bible 2

x-axis	y-axis
5	1.3010
1	0
5	0.4771
10	1

Water Spout *(lightning; combinatorics)* Study bible 1

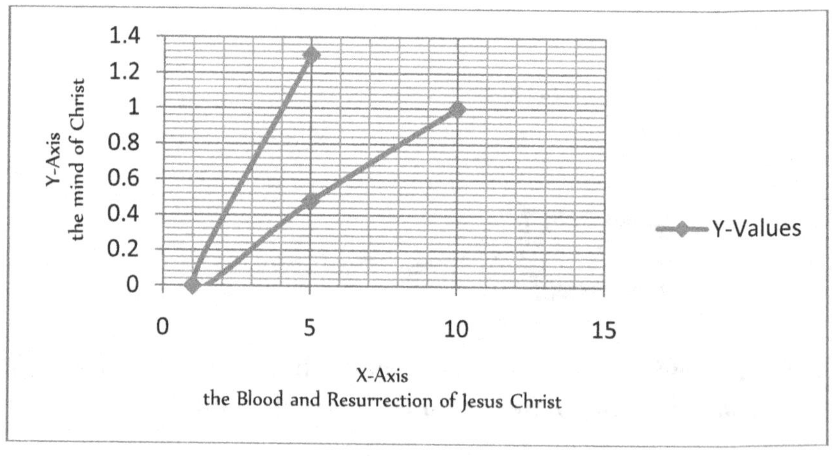

Water Spout *(lightning; combinatorics)* Study bible 2

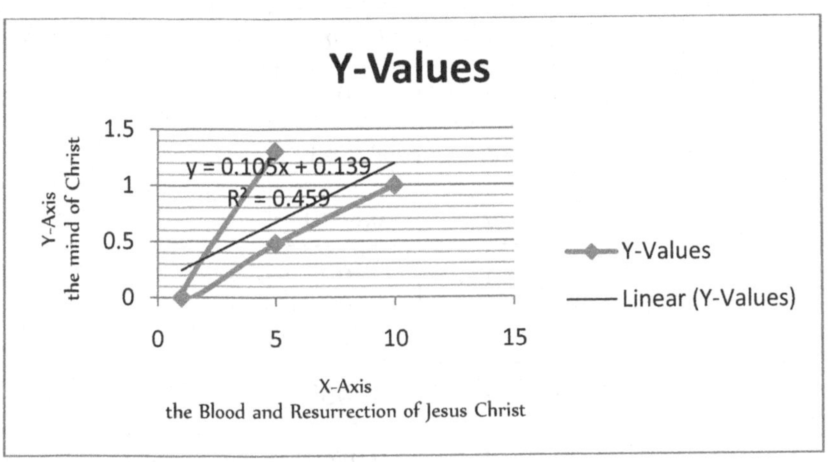

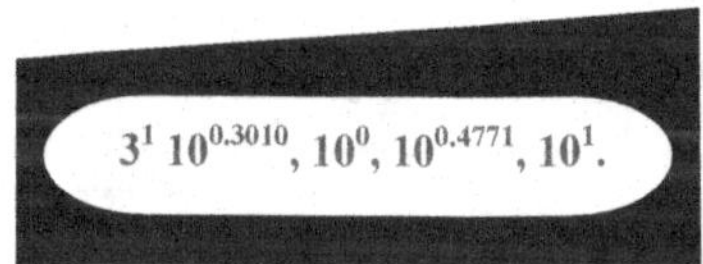

Pilled Poplar, Hazel, and Chestnut bible rods 2

32. And he said unto them, Go. And when they were come out, they went into the herd of swine: and, behold, the whole herd of swine ran violently down a steep place into the sea, and perished in the waters.

5, 1. 6, 7: 1, 1, 14, 5. Bible Matrices

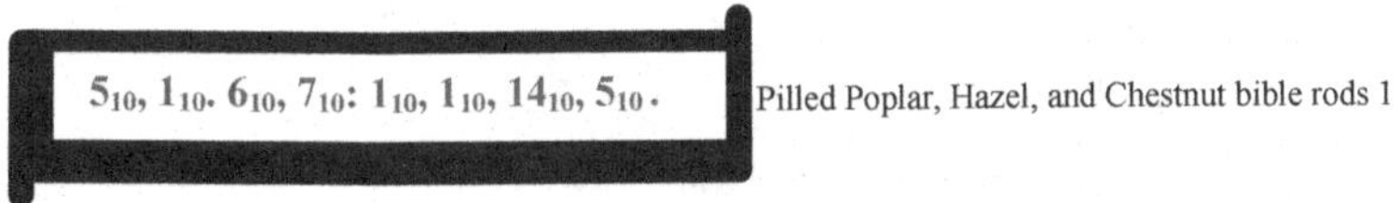

Pilled Poplar, Hazel, and Chestnut bible rods 1

$\text{Log}_{10} 5 = 0.6989$ $\text{Log}_{10} 1 = 0$ $\text{Log}_{10} 6 = 0.7781$ $\text{Log}_{10} 7 = 0.8450$ $\text{Log}_{10} 1 = 0$ $\text{Log}_{10} 1 = 0$

$\text{Log}_{10} 14 = 1.1461$ $\text{Log}_{10} 5 = 0.6989$

5, 1. 6, 7: 1, 1, 14, 5. Deep calls unto Deep study bible 1

0.6989, 0, 0.7781, 0.8450: 0, 0, 1.1461, 0.6989.

Deep calls unto Deep study bible 2

x-axis	y-axis
5	0.6989
1	0
6	0.7781
7	0.8450
1	0
1	0
14	1.1461
5	0.6989

Water Spout *(lightning; combinatorics)* Study bible 1

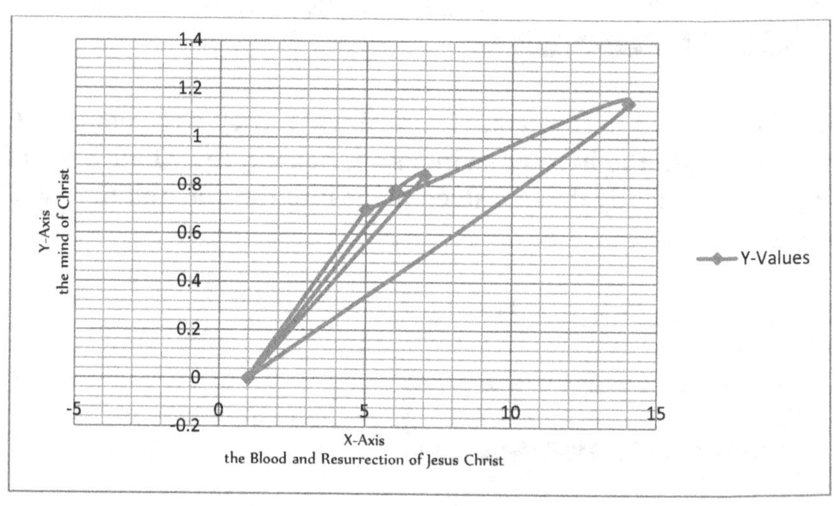

Water Spout *(lightning; combinatorics)* Study bible 2

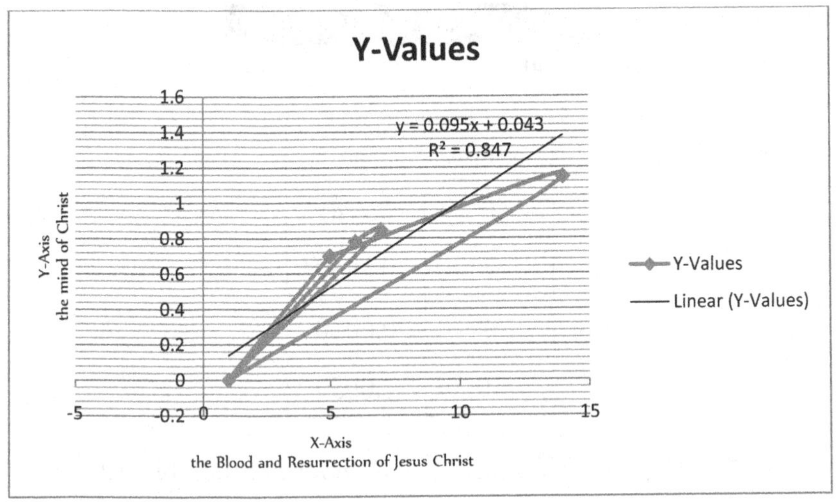

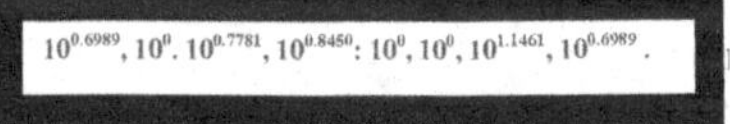

Pilled Poplar, Hazel, and Chestnut bible rods 2

33. And they that kept them fled, and went their ways into the city, and told every thing, and what was befallen to the possessed of the devils slanderers, false accusers.

6, 7, 4, 10. Bible Matrices

Pilled Poplar, Hazel, and Chestnut bible rods 1

$\text{Log}_{10} 6 = 0.7781$ $\text{Log}_{10} 7 = 0.8450$ $\text{Log}_{10} 4 = 0.6020$

$$\text{Log}_3 10 = y$$

$$3^y = 10$$

$$y \log_{10} 3 = \log_{10} 10$$

$$y = \log_{10} 10 / \log_{10} 3$$

$$y = 1 / 0.4771$$

$$y = 2.0959$$

6, 7, 4, 10. Deep calls unto Deep study bible 1

0.7781, 0.8450, 0.6020, 2.0959.
Deep calls unto Deep study bible 2

x-axis	y-axis
6	0.7781
7	0.8450
4	0.6020
10	2.0959

Water Spout *(lightning; combinatorics)* Study bible 1

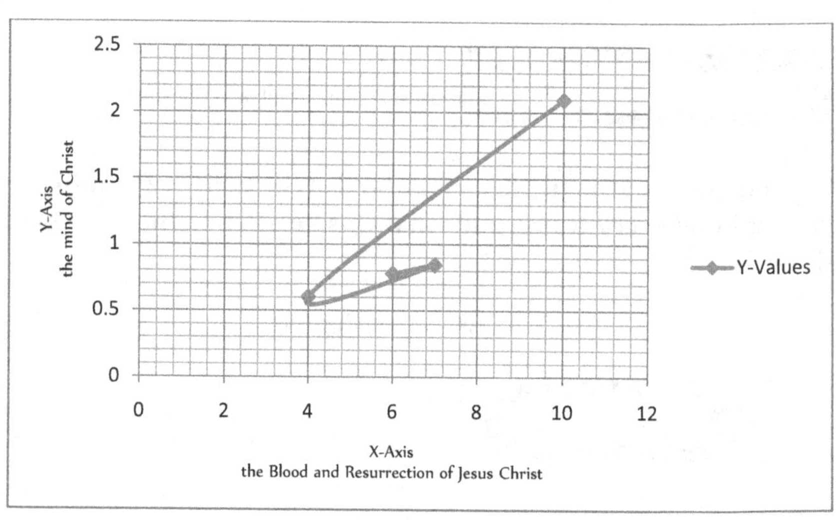

Water Spout *(lightning; combinatorics)* Study bible 2

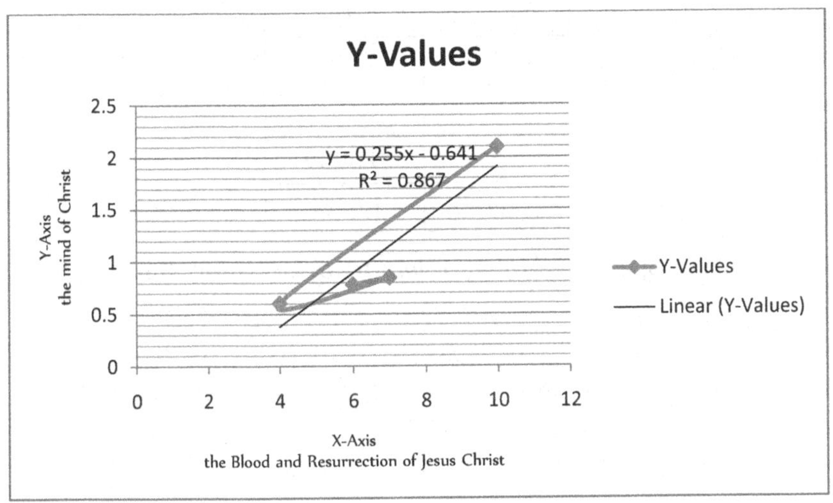

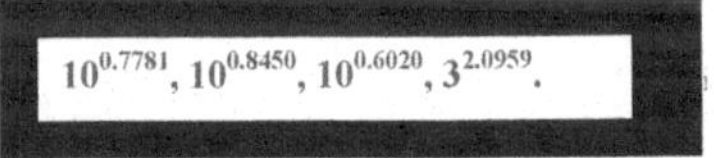
$10^{0.7781}, 10^{0.8450}, 10^{0.6020}, 3^{2.0959}.$

Pilled Poplar, Hazel, and Chestnut bible rods 2

34. And, behold, the whole city came out to meet Jesus savior; deliverer: **and when they saw him, they besought him that he would depart out of their coasts.**

1, 1, 8: 5, 11. Bible Matrices

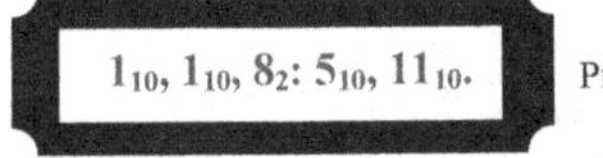
$1_{10}, 1_{10}, 8_2: 5_{10}, 11_{10}.$

Pilled Poplar, Hazel, and Chestnut bible rods 1

$\text{Log}_2 8 = y \quad \text{Log}_{10} 1 = 0 \quad \text{Log}_{10} 1 = 0 \quad \text{Log}_{10} 5 = 0.6989 \quad \text{Log}_{10} 11 = 1.0413$

$2^y = 8$

$2^y = 2^3$

$y = 3$

1, 1, 8: 5, 11. Deep calls unto Deep study bible 1

0, 0, 3: 0.6989, 1.0413. Deep calls unto Deep study bible 2

x-axis	y-axis
1	0
1	0
8	3
5	0.6989
11	1.0413

Water Spout *(lightning; combinatorics)* Study bible 1

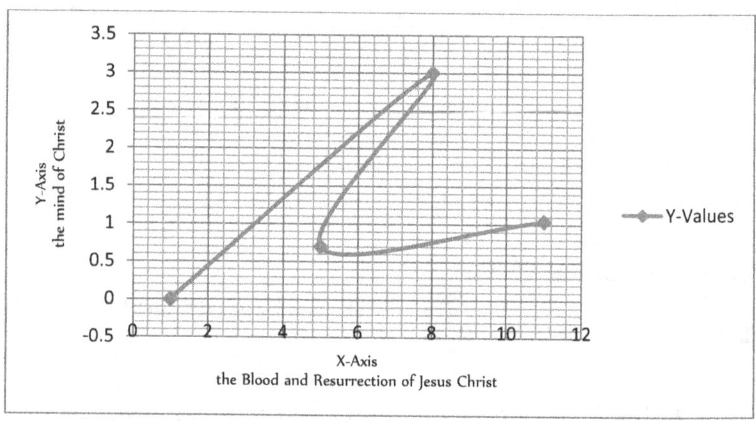

Water Spout *(lightning; combinatorics)* Study bible 2

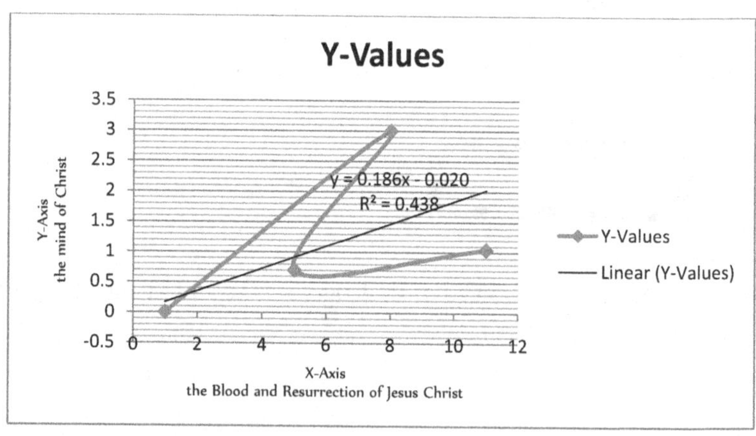

10^0, 10^0, 2^3: $10^{0.6989}$, $10^{1.0413}$.

Pilled Poplar, Hazel, and Chestnut bible rods 2

CHAPTER 9

1. And he entered into a ship, and passed over, and came into his own city.

6, 3, 6. Bible Matrices

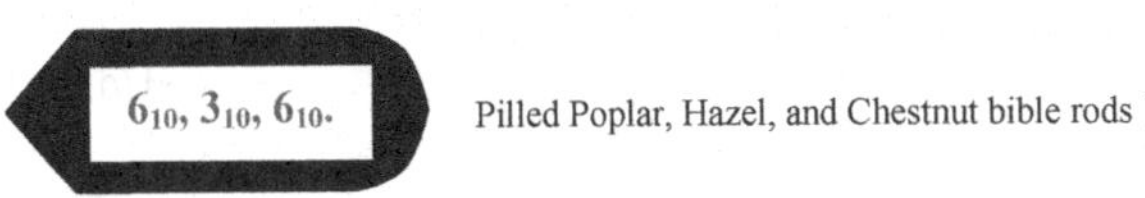

Pilled Poplar, Hazel, and Chestnut bible rods 1

$\text{Log}_{10} 6 = 0.7781$ $\text{Log}_{10} 3 = 0.4771$ $\text{Log}_{10} 6 = 0.7781$

6, 3, 6. Deep calls unto Deep study bible 1

0.7781, 0.4771, 0.7781. Deep calls unto Deep study bible 2

x-axis	y-axis
6	0.7781
3	0.4771
6	0.7781

Water Spout *(lightning; combinatorics)* Study bible 1

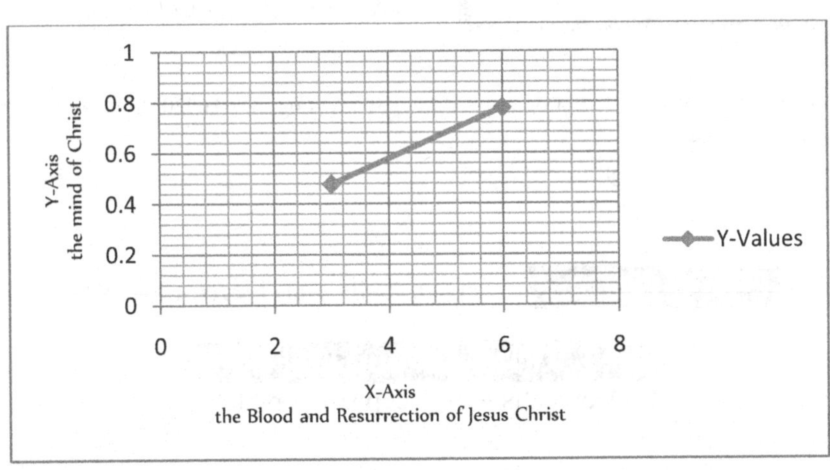

Water Spout *(lightning; combinatorics)* Study bible 2

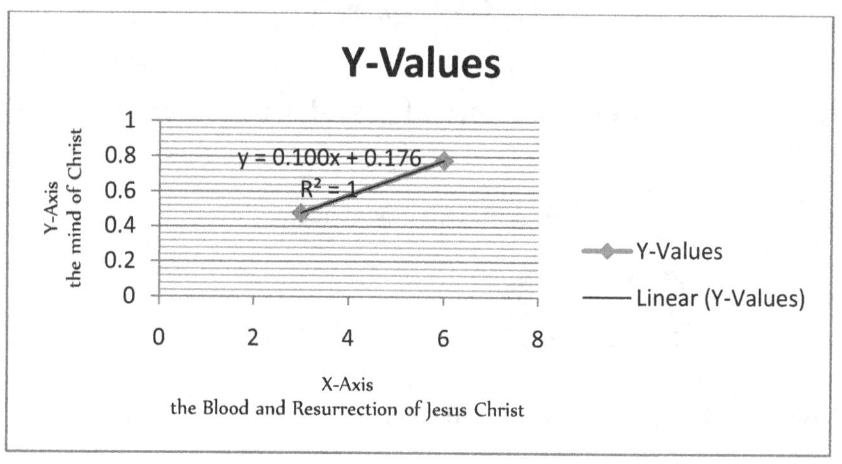

Pilled Poplar, Hazel, and Chestnut bible rods 2

2. And, behold, they brought to him a man sick of the palsy, lying on a bed: and Jesussavior; deliverer**seeing their faith said unto the sick of the palsy; Son, be of good cheer; thy sins be forgiven thee.**

1, 1, 10, 4: 12; 1, 4; 5. Bible Matrices

1_{10}, 1_{10}, 10_{10}, 4_{10}: $2_2 10_{10}$; 1_{10}, 4_{10}; 5_{10}.

Pilled Poplar, Hazel, and Chestnut bible rods 1

$\log_{10} 1 = 0$ $\log_{10} 1 = 0$ $\log_{10} 10 = 1$ $\log_{10} 10 = 1$ $\log_{10} 4 = 0.6020$ $\log_{10} 4 = 0.6020$

$\log_{10} 5 = 0.6989$ $\log_2 2 = y$

$2^y = 2^1$

$y = 1$

1, 1, 10, 4: 12; 1, 4; 5. Deep calls unto Deep study bible 1

0, 0, 1, 0.6020: 1 1; 0, 0.6020; 0.6989.

Deep calls unto Deep study bible 2

x-axis	y-axis
1	0
1	0
10	1
4	0.6020
12	2
1	0
4	0.6020
5	0.6989

Water Spout *(lightning; combinatorics)* Study bible 1

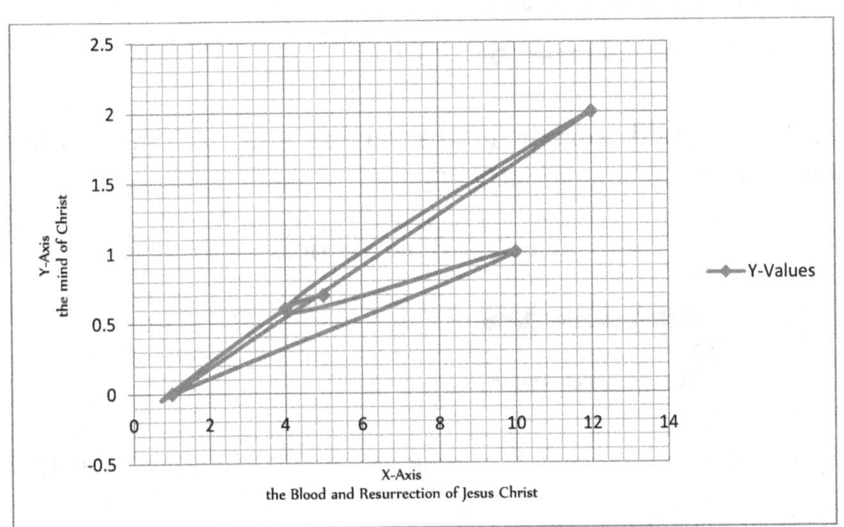

Water Spout *(lightning; combinatorics)* Study bible 2

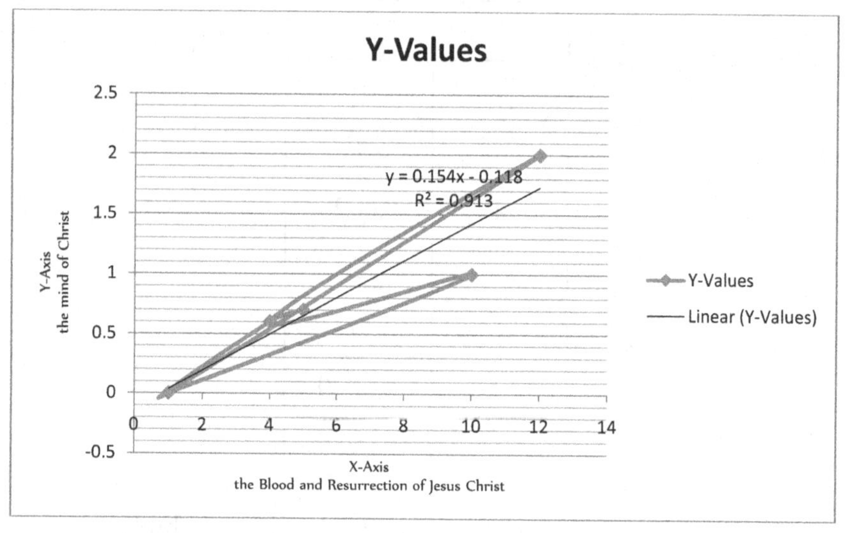

$10^0, 10^0, 10^1, 10^{0.6020}: 2^1\ 10^1; 10^0, 10^{0.6020}; 10^{0.6989}.$ Pilled Poplar, Hazel, and Chestnut bible rods 2

3. And, behold, certain of the scribes lawyers; copiers **said within themselves, This man blasphemeth.**

1, 1, 7, 3. Bible Matrices

$1_{10}, 1_{10}, 4_2\ 3_{10}, 3_{10}.$ Pilled Poplar, Hazel, and Chestnut bible rods 1

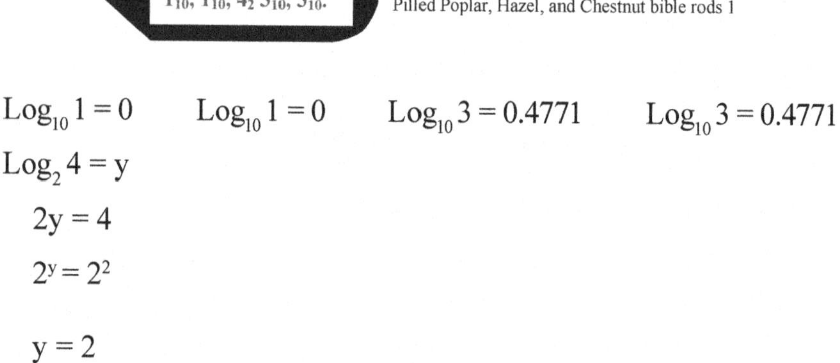

$\text{Log}_{10} 1 = 0$ $\text{Log}_{10} 1 = 0$ $\text{Log}_{10} 3 = 0.4771$ $\text{Log}_{10} 3 = 0.4771$

$\text{Log}_2 4 = y$

$2y = 4$

$2^y = 2^2$

$y = 2$

1, 1, 7, 3. Deep calls unto Deep study bible 1

0, 0, 2 0.4771, 0.4771. Deep calls unto Deep study bible 2

x-axis	y-axis
1	0
1	0
7	2.4771
3	0.4771

Water Spout *(lightning; combinatorics)* Study bible 1

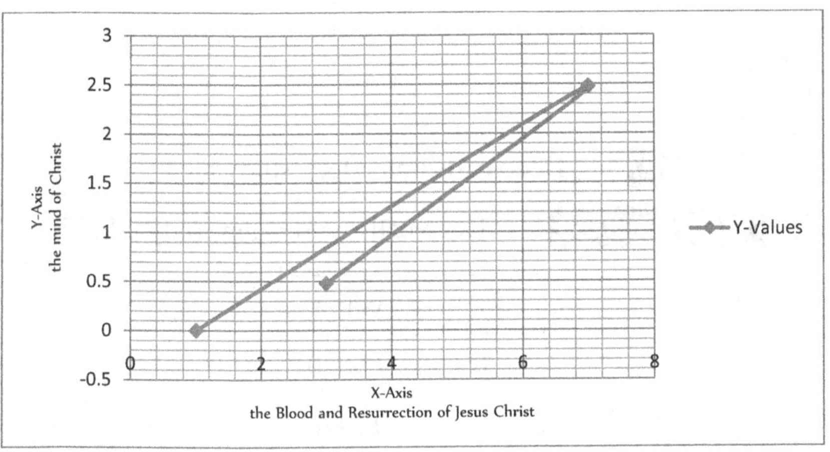

Water Spout *(lightning; combinatorics)* Study bible 2

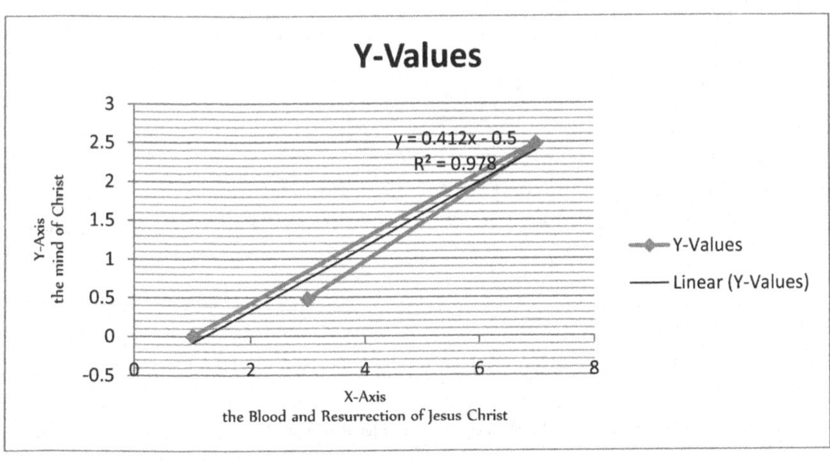

$10^0, 10^0, 2^2\ 10^{0.4771}, 10^{0.4771}.$ Pilled Poplar, Hazel, and Chestnut bible rods 2

4: And Jesussavior; deliverer **knowing their thoughts said, Wherefore think ye evil in your hearts?**

6, 7? Bible Matrices

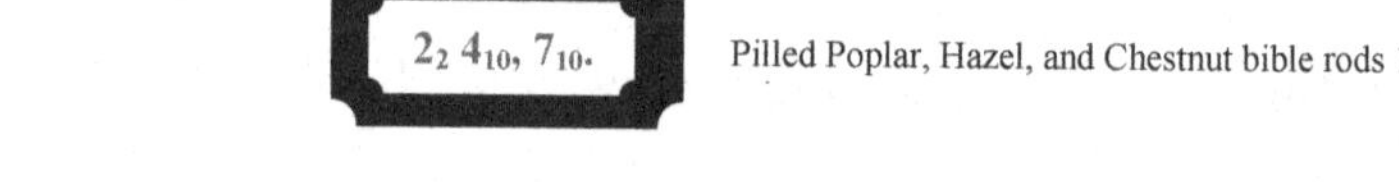

Pilled Poplar, Hazel, and Chestnut bible rods 1

$\text{Log}_2 2 = y$ $\text{Log}_{10} 7 = 0.8450$ $\text{Log}_{10} 4 = 0.6020$

$2^y = 2^1$

$y = 1$

6, 7? Deep calls unto Deep study bible 1

1 0.6020, 0.8450. Deep calls unto Deep study bible 2

x-axis	y-axis
6	1.6020
7	0.8450

Water Spout *(lightning; combinatorics)* Study bible 1

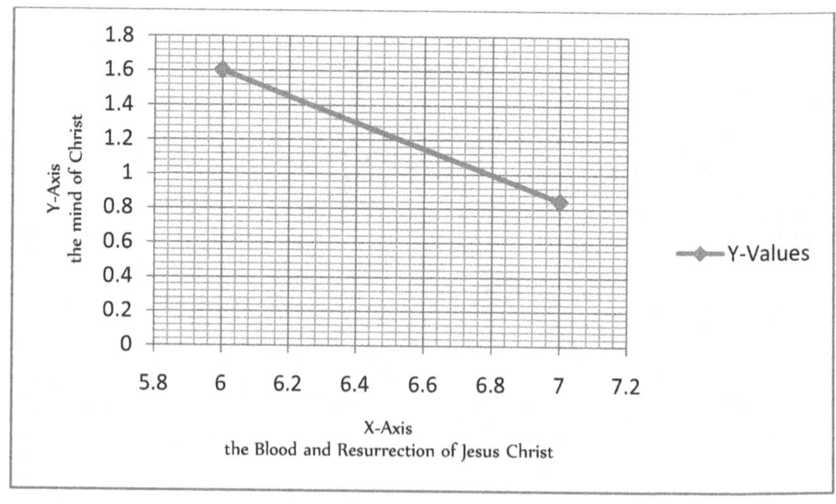

Water Spout *(lightning; combinatorics)* Study bible 2

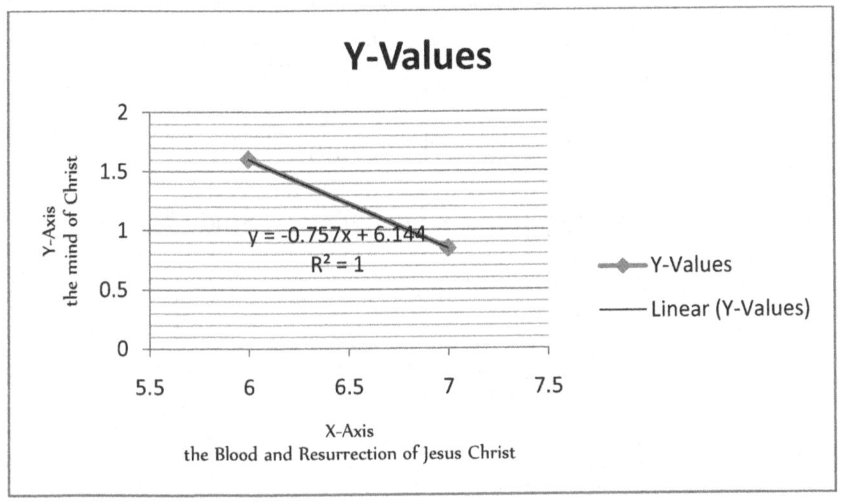

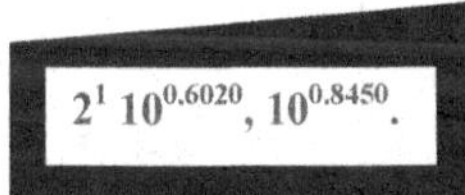

Pilled Poplar, Hazel, and Chestnut bible rods 2

5. For whether is easier, to say, Thy sins be forgiven thee; or to say, Arise, and walk?

4, 2, 5; 3, 1, 2? Bible Matrices

$4_{10}, 2_{10}, 5_{10}; 3_{10}, 1_{10}, 2_{10}?$ Pilled Poplar, Hazel, and Chestnut bible rods 1

$\text{Log}_{10} 1 = 0$ $\text{Log}_{10} 4 = 0.6020$ $\text{Log}_{10} 2 = 0.3010$ $\text{Log}_{10} 5 = 0.6989$ $\text{Log}_{10} 3 = 0.4771$ $\text{Log}_{10} 2 = 0.3010$

4, 2, 5; 3, 1, 2? Deep calls unto Deep study bible 1

0.6020, 0.3010, 0.6989; 0.4771, 0, 0.3010?

Deep calls unto Deep study bible 2

x-axis	y-axis
4	0.6020
2	0.3010

5	0.6989
3	0.4771
1	0
2	0.3010

Water Spout *(lightning; combinatorics)* Study bible 1

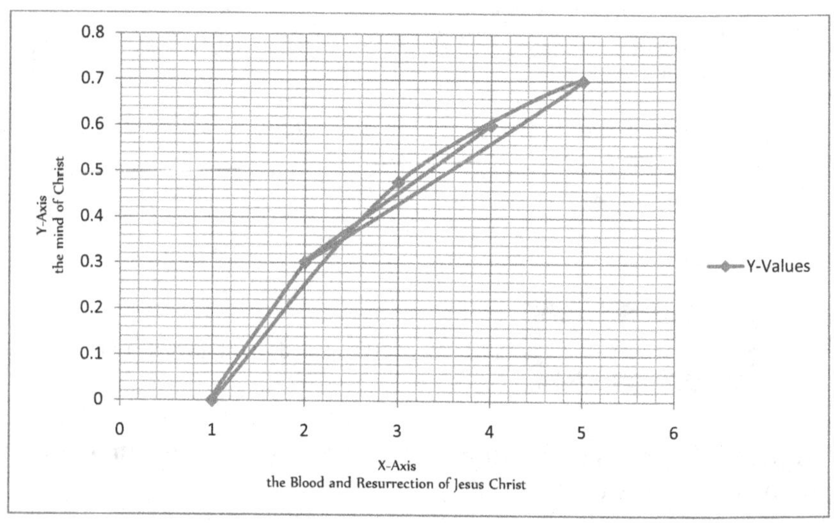

Water Spout *(lightning; combinatorics)* Study bible 2

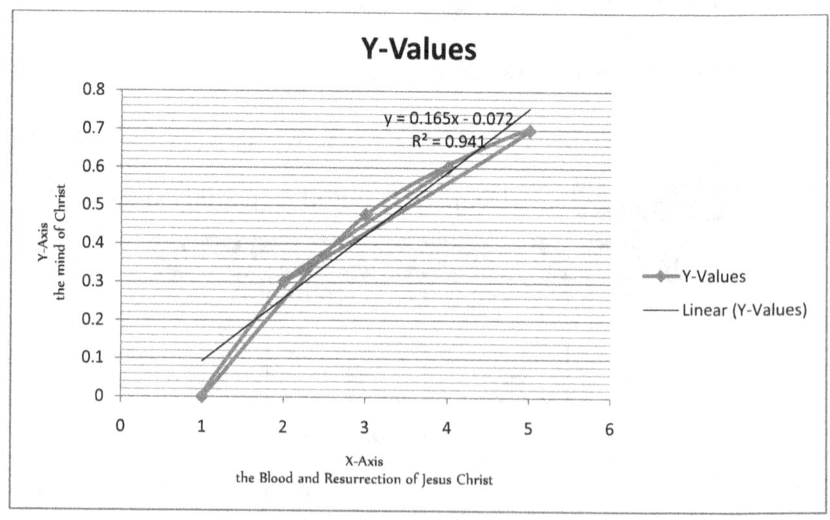

$10^{0.6020}, 10^{0.3010}, 10^{0.6989}; 10^{0.4771}, 10^{0}, 10^{0.3010}$? Pilled Poplar, Hazel, and Chestnut bible rods 2

6. But that ye may know that the Son of man hath power on earth to forgive sins, then saith he to the sick of the palsy, Arise, take up thy bed, and go unto thine house.

17, 9, 1, 4, 5. Bible Matrices

$17_{10}, 9_{10}, 1_{10}, 4_{10}, 5_{10}$. Pilled Poplar, Hazel, and Chestnut bible rods 1

$\mathrm{Log}_{10} 17 = 1.2304$ $\mathrm{Log}_{10} 9 = 0.9542$ $\mathrm{Log}_{10} 4 = 0.6020$ $\mathrm{Log}_{10} 1 = 0$ $\mathrm{Log}_{10} 5 = 0.6989$

17, 9, 1, 4, 5. Deep calls unto Deep study bible 1

1.2304, 0.9542, 0, 0.6020, 0.6989.
Deep calls unto Deep study bible 2

x-axis	y-axis
17	1.2304
9	0.9542
1	0
4	0.6020
5	0.6989

Water Spout *(lightning; combinatorics)* Study bible 1

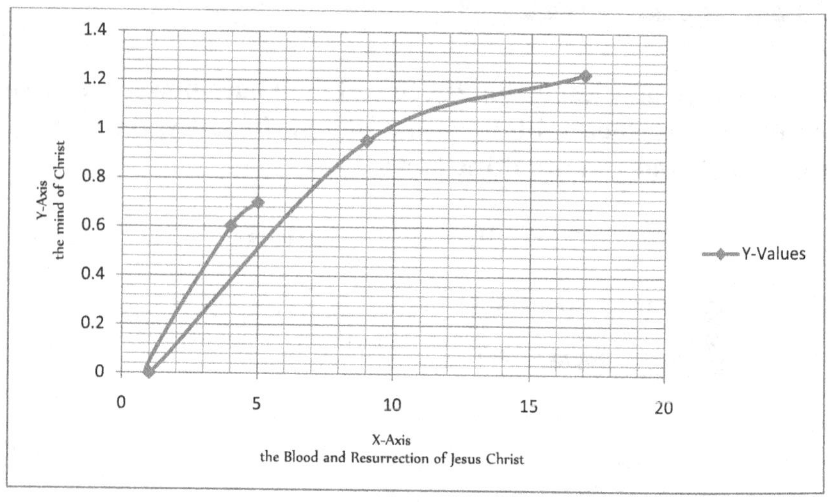

Water Spout *(lightning; combinatorics)* Study bible 2

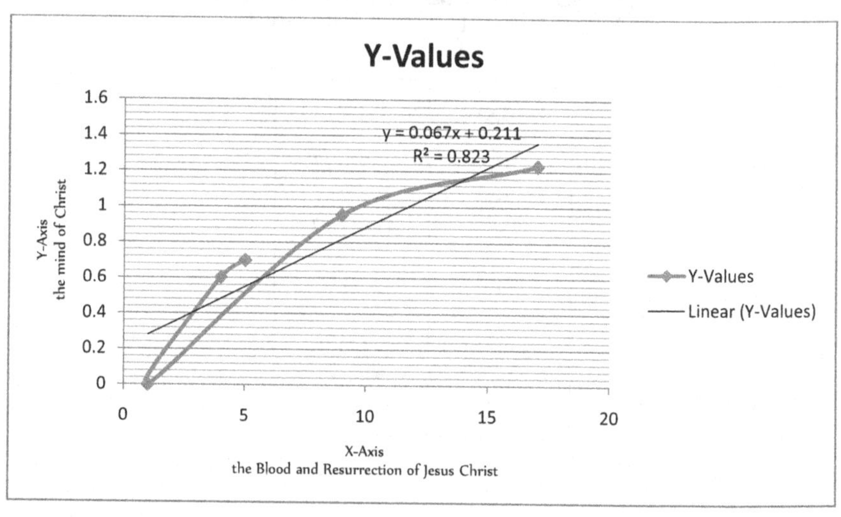

$10^{1.2304}, 10^{0.9542}, 10^{0}, 10^{0.6020}, 10^{0.6989}$. Pilled Poplar, Hazel, and Chestnut bible rods 2

7. And he arose, and departed to his house.

3, 5. Bible Matrices

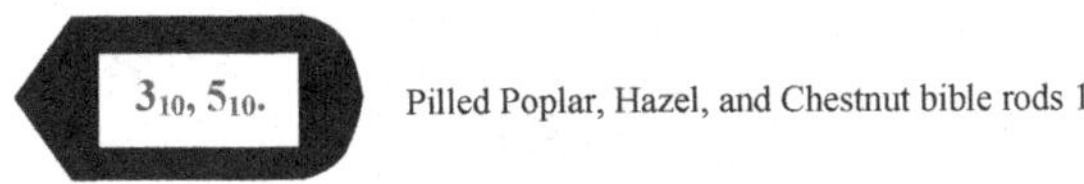

$Log_{10} 3 = 0.4771$ $Log_{10} 5 = 0.6989$

3, 5. Deep calls unto Deep study bible 1

0.4771, 0.6989. Deep calls unto Deep study bible 2

x-axis	y-axis
3	0.4771
5	0.6989

Water Spout *(lightning; combinatorics)* Study bible 1

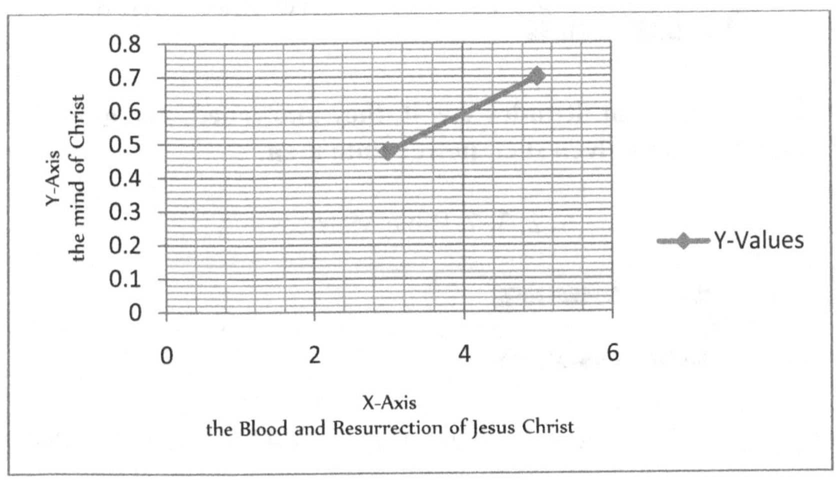

Water Spout *(lightning; combinatorics)* Study bible 2

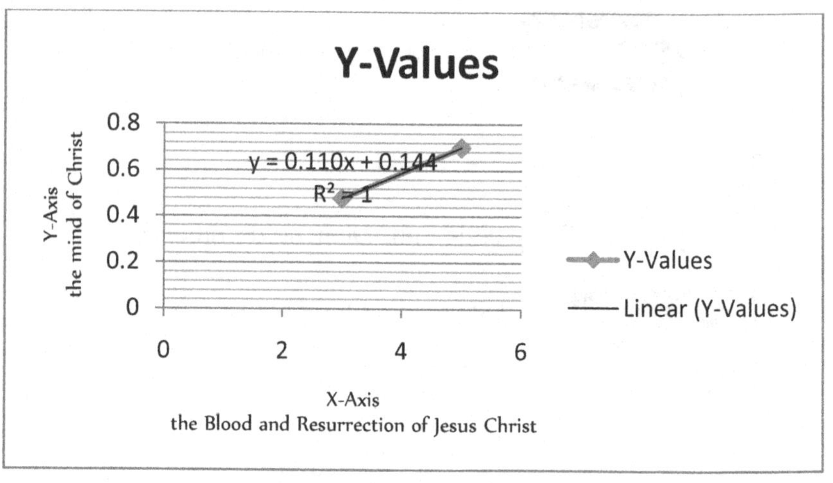

Pilled Poplar, Hazel, and Chestnut bible rods 2

8. But when the multitudes saw it, they marvelled, and glorified God, which had given such power unto men.

6, 2, 3, 7. Bible Matrices

Pilled Poplar, Hazel, and Chestnut bible rods 1

$\text{Log}_{10}6 = 0.7781$ $\text{Log}_{10}2 = 0.3010$ $\text{Log}_{10}3 = 0.4771$ $\text{Log}_{10}7 = 0.8450$

6, 2, 3, 7. Deep calls unto Deep study bible 1

0.7781, 0.3010, 0.4771, 0.8450. Deep calls unto Deep study bible 2

x-axis	y-axis
6	0.7781
2	0.3010
3	0.4771
7	0.8450

Water Spout *(lightning; combinatorics)* Study bible 1

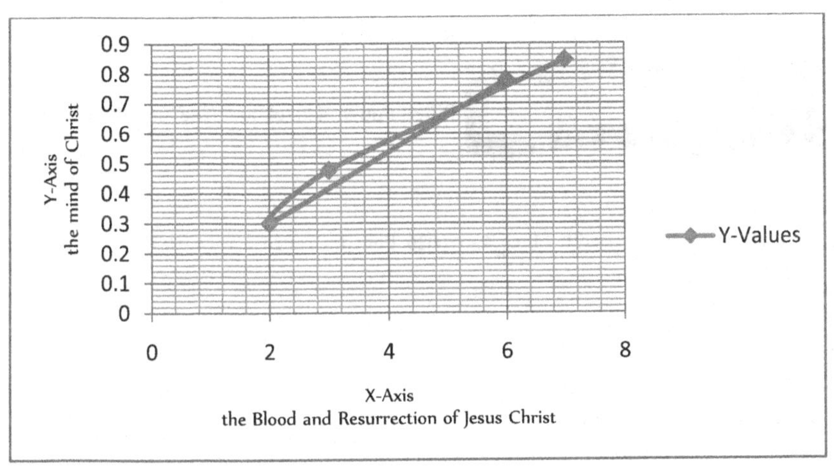

Water Spout *(lightning; combinatorics)* Study bible 2

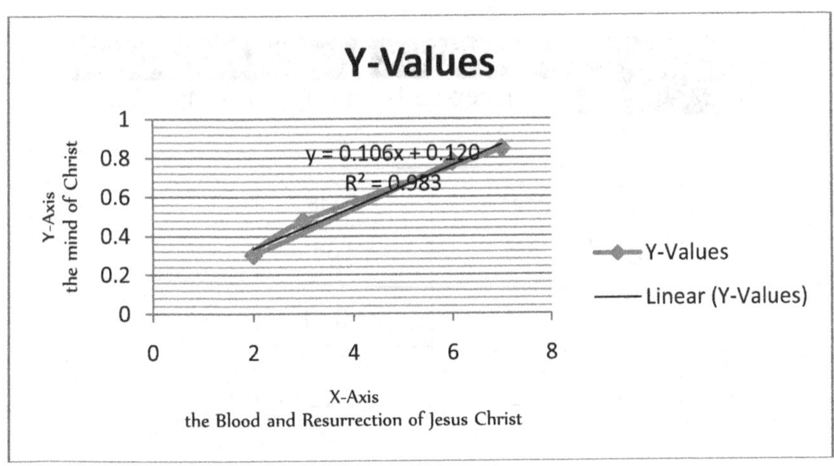

$10^{0.7781}, 10^{0.3010}, 10^{0.4771}, 10^{0.8450}$. Pilled Poplar, Hazel, and Chestnut bible rods 2

9.And as Jesussavior; deliverer**passed forth from thence, he saw a man, named Matthew**given; a reward; gift of God,**sitting at the receipt of custom: and he saith unto him, Follow me. And he arose, and followed him.**

7, 4, 2, 6: 5, 2. 3, 3. Bible Matrices

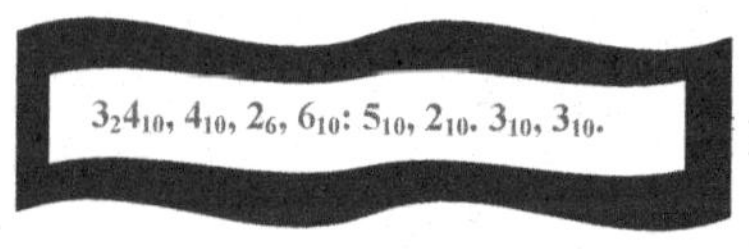

Pilled Poplar, Hazel, and Chestnut bible rods 1

$Log_{10} 3 = 0.4771$ $Log_{10} 3 = 0.4771$ $Log_{10} 4 = 0.6020$ $Log_{10} 4 = 0.6020$ $Log_{10} 6 = 0.7781$ $Log_{10} 5 = 0.6989$

$Log_2 3 = y$ $Log_6 2 = y$

$2^y = 3$ $6^y = 2$

$y \log_{10} 2 = \log_{10} 3$ $y\log_{10} 6 = \log_{10} 2$

$y = \log_{10} 3 / \log_{10} 2$ $y = \log_{10} 2 / \log_{10} 6$

$y = 0.4771 / 0.3010$ $y = 0.3010 / 0.7781$

$y = 1.5850$ $y = 0.3868$

7, 4, 2, 6: 5, 2. 3, 3. Deep calls unto Deep study bible 1

1.5850 0.6020, 0.6020, 0.3868, 0.7781: 0.6989, 0.3010. 0.4771, 0.4771. Deep calls unto Deep study bible 2

x-axis	y-axis
7	2.187
4	0.6020
2	0.3868

6	0.7781
5	0.6989
2	0.3010
3	0.4771
3	0.4771

Water Spout *(lightning; combinatorics)* Study bible 1

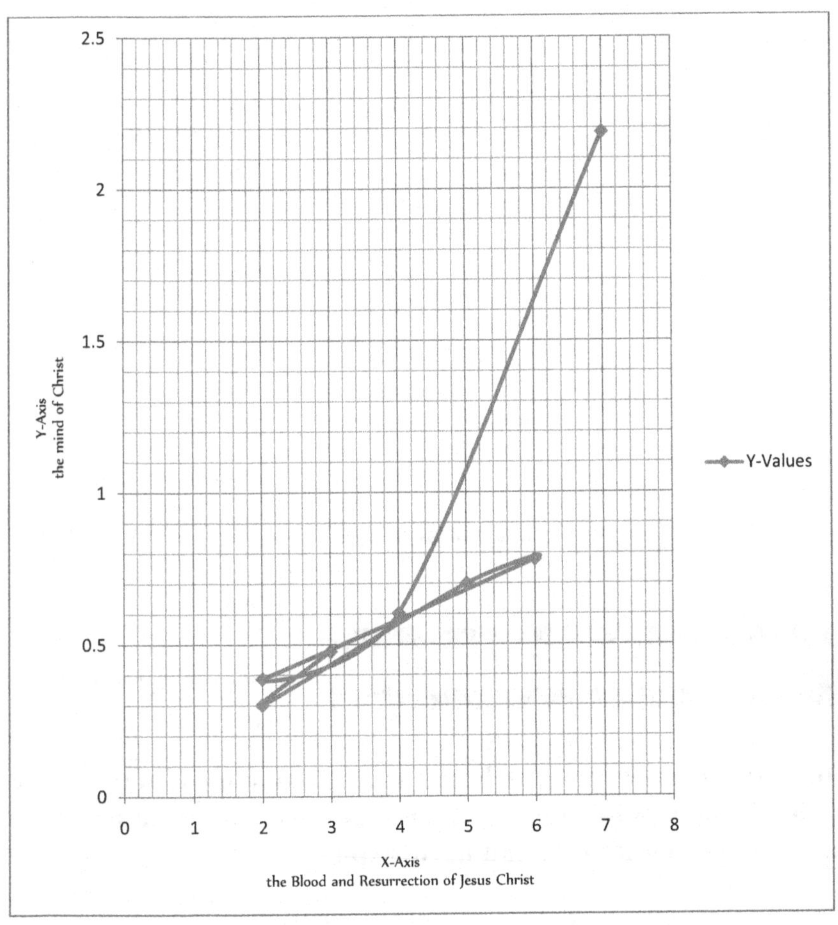

Water Spout *(lightning; combinatorics)* Study bible 2

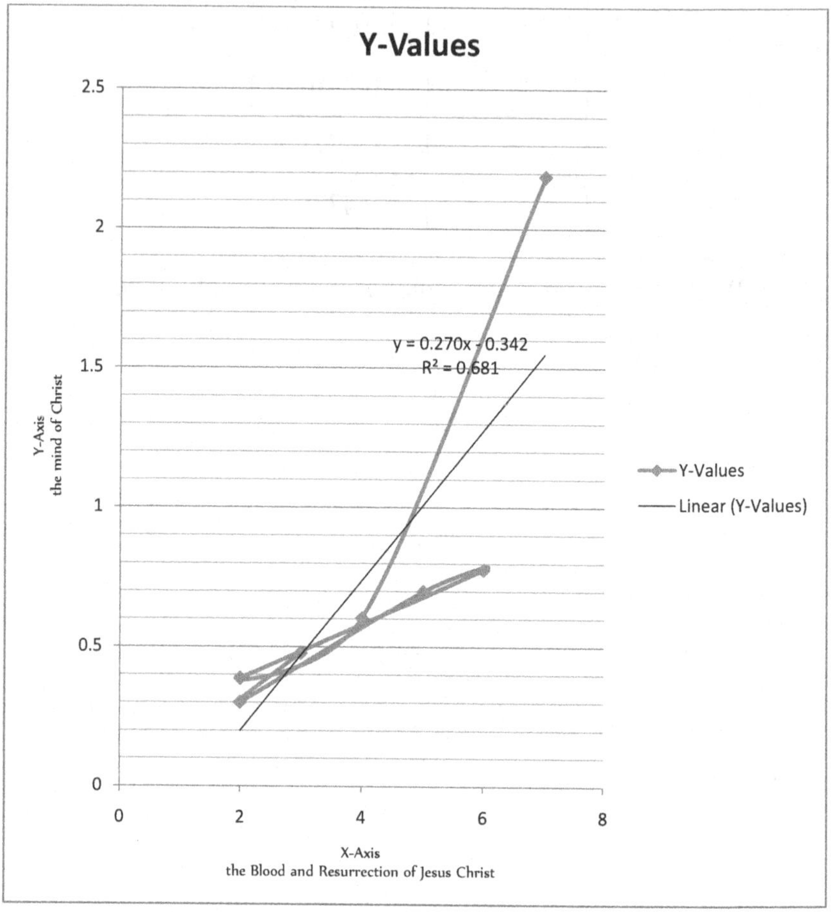

Y-Values

2.5
2
1.5
1
0.5
0

Y-Axis
the mind of Christ

y = 0.270x - 0.342
$R^2 = 0.681$

Y-Values
Linear (Y-Values)

0 2 4 6 8

X-Axis
the Blood and Resurrection of Jesus Christ

$2^{1.5850}\ 10^{0.6020}, 10^{0.6020}, 6^{0.3868}, 10^{0.7781}: 10^{0.6989}, 10^{0.3010}. 10^{0.4771}, 10^{0.4771}.$

Pilled Poplar, Hazel, and Chestnut bible rods 2

10. And it came to pass, as Jesussavior; deliverer**sat at meat in the house, behold, many publicans**one who farmed the taxes; a tax collector **and sinners came and sat down with him and his disciples.**

5, 8, 1, 13. Bible Matrices

$5_{10}, 2_2 6_{10}, 1_{10}, 2_8 11_{10}$. Pilled Poplar, Hazel, and Chestnut bible rods 1

$\text{Log}_{10} 5 = 0.6989$ $\text{Log}_{10} 6 = 0.7781$ $\text{Log}_{10} 1 = 0$ $\text{Log}_{10} 11 = 1.0413$

$\text{Log}_{2} 2 = y$
$2^y = 2$
$2^y = 2^1$
$y = 1$

$\text{Log}_{8} 2 = y$
$8^y = 2$
$y \log_{10} 8 = \log_{10} 2$
$y = \log_{10} 2 / \log_{10} 8$
$y = 0.3010 / 0.9030$
$y = 0.3333$

5, 8, 1, 13. Deep calls unto Deep study bible 1

0.6989, 1 0.7781, 0, 0.3333 1.0413.
Deep calls unto Deep study bible 2

x-axis	y-axis
5	0.6989
8	1.7781
1	0
13	1.3746

Water Spout *(lightning; combinatorics)* Study bible 1

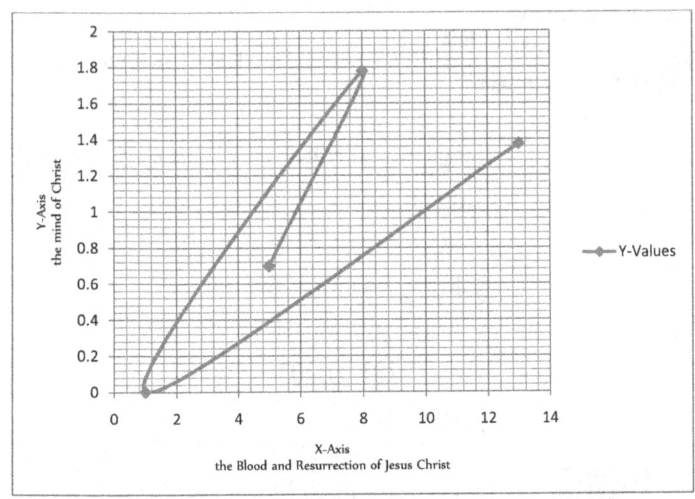

Water Spout *(lightning; combinatorics)* Study bible 2

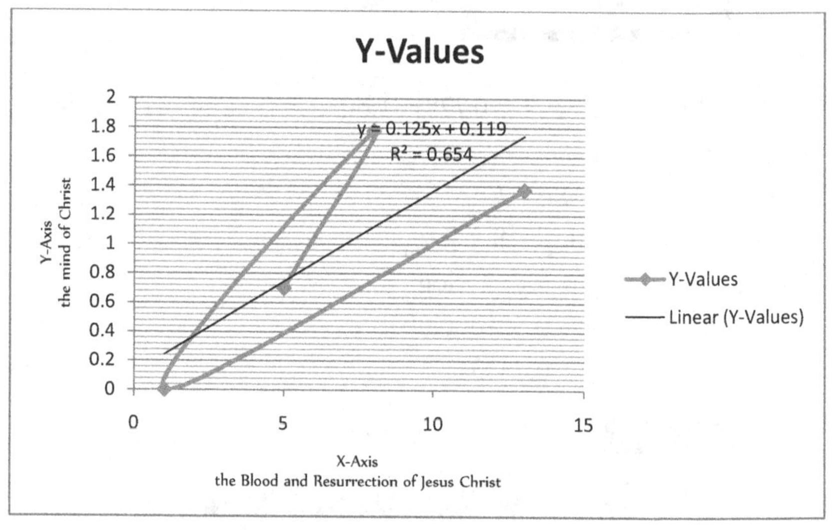

$10^{0.6989}$, 2^1 $10^{0.7781}$, 10^0, $8^{0.3333}$ $10^{1.0413}$. Pilled Poplar, Hazel, and Chestnut bible rods 2

11. And when the Phariseesseparated ones; set apart **saw it, they said unto his disciples, Why eateth your Master with publicans**one who farmed the taxes; a tax collector **and sinners?**

6, 5, 8? Bible Matrices

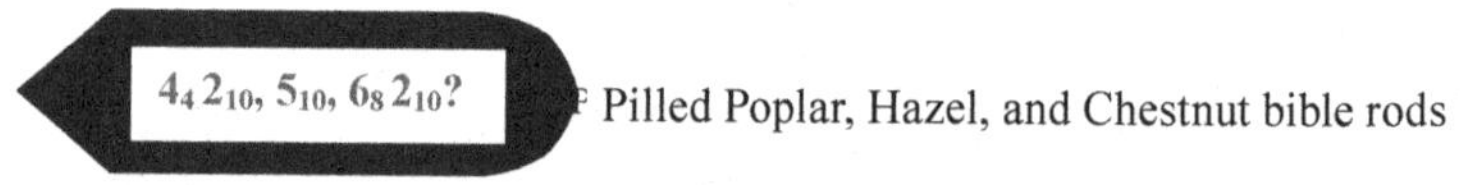

Pilled Poplar, Hazel, and Chestnut bible rods 1

$\text{Log}_{10} 2 = 0.3010$

$\text{Log}_4 4 = y$

$4^y = 4$

$2^{2y} = 2^2$

$y = 1$

$\text{Log}_{10} 5 = 0.6989$

$\text{Log}_8 6 = y$

$8^y = 6$

$y \log_{10} 8 = \log_{10} 6$

$y = \log_{10} 6 / \log_{10} 8$

$y = 0.7781 / 0.9030$

$y = 0.8616$

$\text{Log}_{10} 2 = 0.3010$

6, 5, 8? Deep calls unto Deep study bible 1

1 0.3010, 0.6989, 0.8616 0.3010?

Deep calls unto Deep study bible 2

x-axis	y-axis
6	1.3010
5	0.6989
8	1.1626

Water Spout *(lightning; combinatorics)* Study bible 1

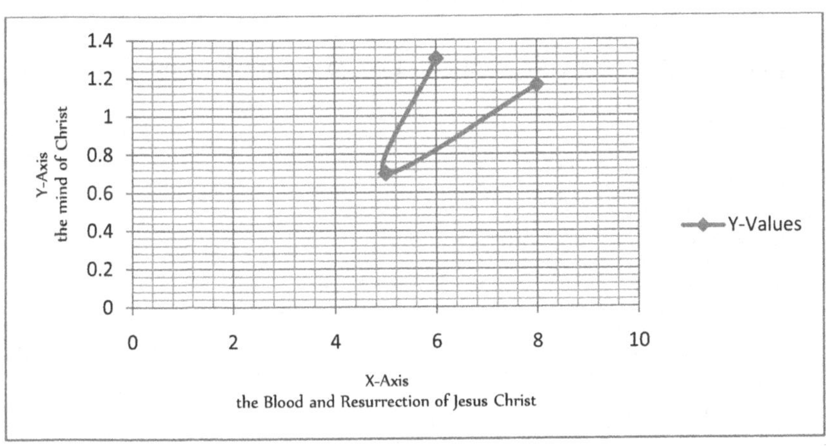

Water Spout *(lightning; combinatorics)* Study bible 2

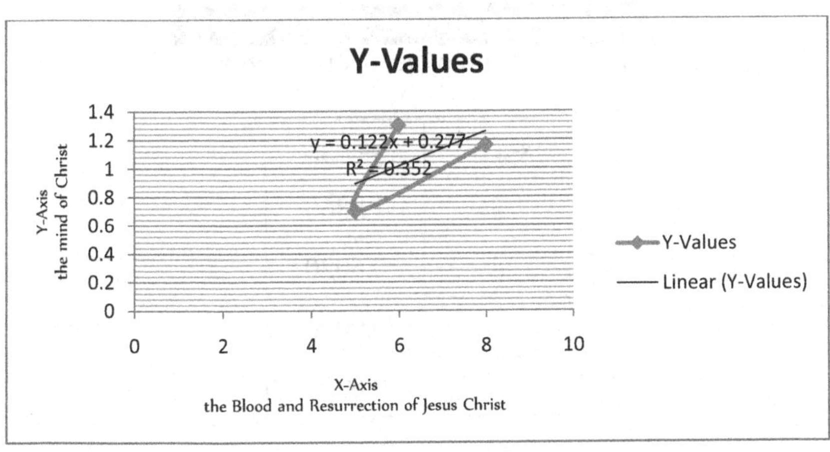

$4^1\ 10^{0.3010}, 10^{0.6989}, 8^{0.8616}\ 10^{0.3010}$? Pilled Poplar, Hazel, and Chestnut bible rods 2

12. But when Jesussavior; deliverer**heard that, he said unto them, They that be whole need not a physician, but they that are sick.**

5, 4, 8, 5. Bible Matrices

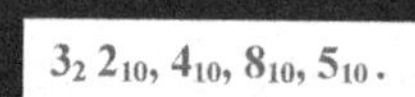

Pilled Poplar, Hazel, and Chestnut bible rods 1

$\text{Log}_{10} 8 = 0.9030$ $\text{Log}_{10} 4 = 0.6020$ $\text{Log}_{10} 5 = 0.6989$ $\text{Log}_{10} 2 = 0.3010$

$\text{Log}_2 3 = y$

$2^y = 3$

$y \log_{10} 2 = \log_{10} 3$

$y = \log_{10} 3 / \log_{10} 2$

$y = 0.4771 / 0.3010$

$y = 1.5850$

5, 4, 8, 5. Deep calls unto Deep study bible 1

1.5850 0.3010, 0.6020, 0.9030, 0.6989.
Deep calls unto Deep study bible 2

x-axis	y-axis
5	1.8860
4	0.6020
8	0.9030
5	0.6989

Water Spout *(lightning; combinatorics)* Study bible 1

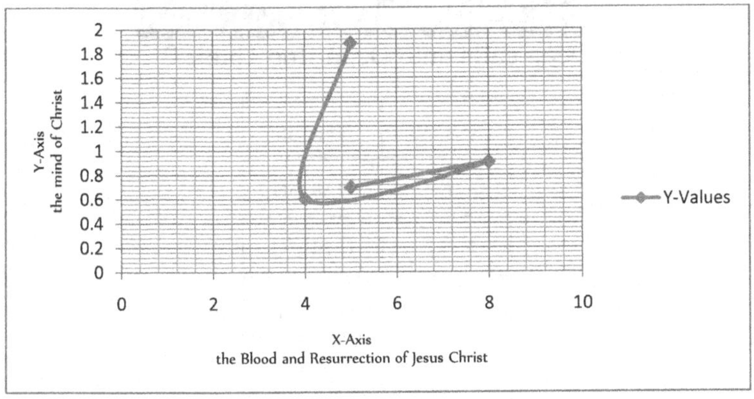

Water Spout *(lightning; combinatorics)* Study bible 2

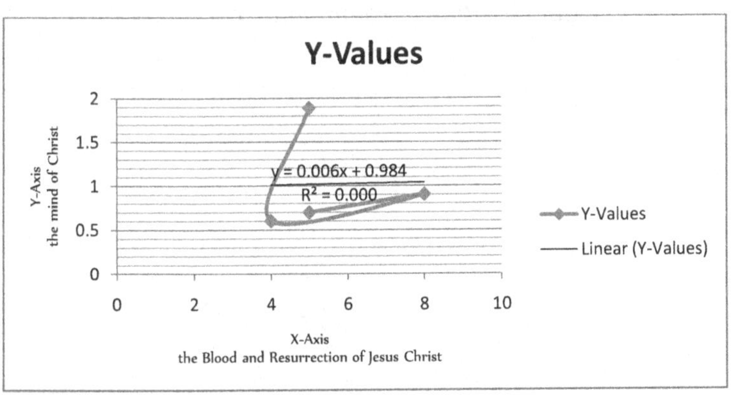

$2^{1.5850}\ 10^{0.3010},\ 10^{0.6020},\ 10^{0.9030},\ 10^{0.6989}$. Pilled Poplar, Hazel, and Chestnut bible rods 2

13. But go ye and learn what that meaneth, I will have mercy, and not sacrifice: for I am not come to call the righteous, but sinners to repentance.

8, 4, 3: 9, 4. Bible Matrices

Pilled Poplar, Hazel, and Chestnut bible rods 1

$\text{Log}_{10} 8 = 0.9030$ $\text{Log}_{10} 4 = 0.6020$ $\text{Log}_{10} 4 = 0.6020$ $\text{Log}_{10} 3 = 0.4771$ $\text{Log}_{10} 9 = 0.9542$

8, 4, 3: 9, 4. Deep calls unto Deep study bible 1

0.9030, 0.6020, 0.4771: 0.9542, 0.6020

Deep calls unto Deep study bible 2

x-axis	y-axis
8	0.9030
4	0.6020
3	0.4771
9	0.9542
4	0.6020

Water Spout *(lightning; combinatorics)* Study bible 1

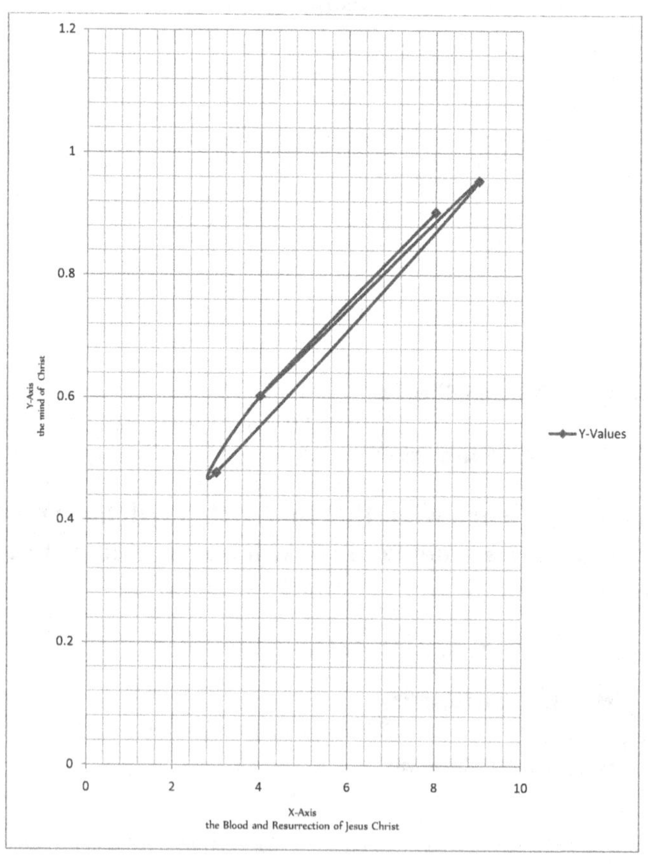

Water Spout *(lightning; combinatorics)* Study bible 2

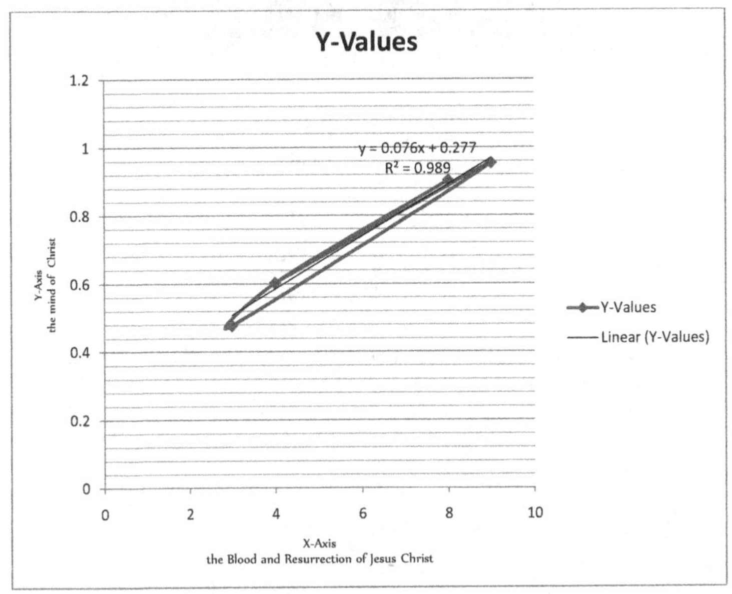

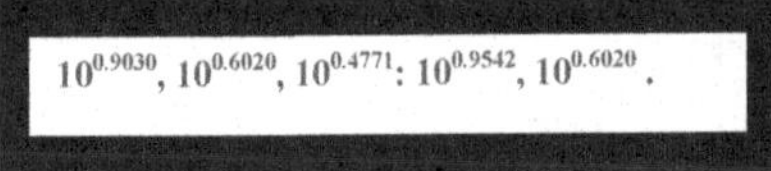
$10^{0.9030}, 10^{0.6020}, 10^{0.4771}: 10^{0.9542}, 10^{0.6020}.$

Pilled Poplar, Hazel, and Chestnut bible rods 2

14. Then came to him the disciples of John the grace or mercy of the Lord, **saying, Why do we and the Pharisees** separated ones; set apart **fast oft, but thy disciples fast not?**

8, 1, 8, 5? Bible Matrices

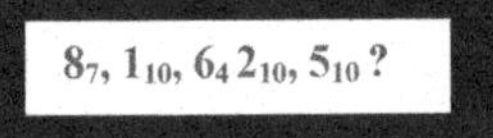
$8_7, 1_{10}, 6_4 2_{10}, 5_{10}$?

Pilled Poplar, Hazel, and Chestnut bible rods 1

$\text{Log}_{10} 1 = 0$ $\qquad$ $\text{Log}_{10} 5 = 0.6989$ $\qquad$ $\text{Log}_{10} 2 = 0.3010$

$\text{Log}_7 8 = y$

$7^y = 8$

$y \log_{10} 7 = \log_{10} 8$

$y = \log_{10} 8 / \log_{10} 7$

$y = 0.9030 / 0.8450$

$y = 1.0686$

$\text{Log}_4 6 = y$

$4^y = 6$

$y \log_{10} 4 = \log_{10} 6$

$y = \log_{10} 6 / \log_{10} 4$

$y = 0.7781 / 0.6020$

$y = 1.2925$

8, 1, 8, 5? Deep calls unto Deep study bible 1

1.0686, 0, 1.2925 0.3010, 0.6989?
Deep calls unto Deep study bible 2

x-axis	y-axis
8	1.0686
1	0
8	1.5935
5	0.6989

Water Spout *(lightning; combinatorics)* Study bible 1

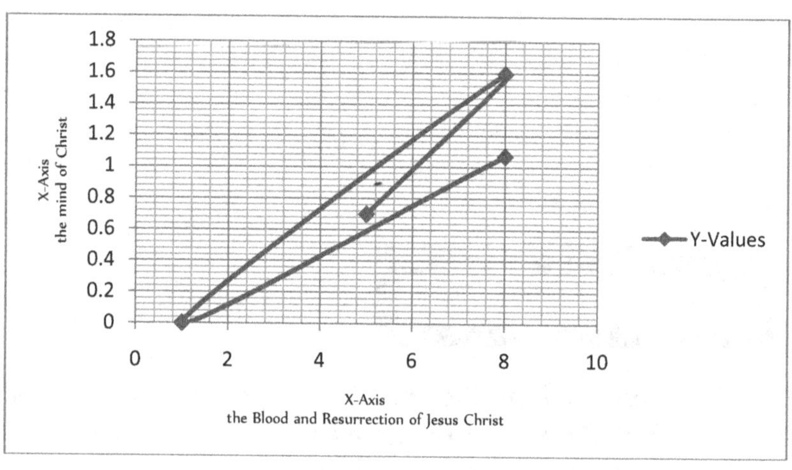

Water Spout *(lightning; combinatorics)* Study bible 2

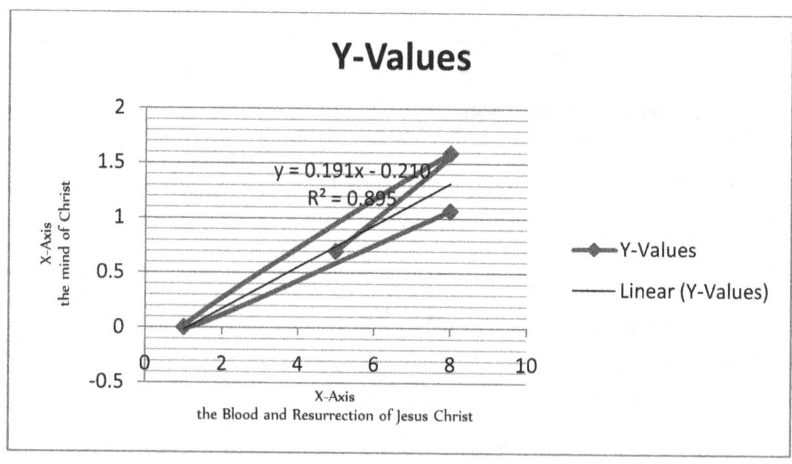

$7^{1.0686}, 10^{0}, 4^{1.2925}$ $10^{0.3010}, 10^{0.6989}$?

Pilled Poplar, Hazel, and Chestnut bible rods 2

15.And Jesussavior; deliverer**said unto them, Can the children of the bridechamber mourn, as long as the bridegroom is with them? but the days will come, when the bridegroom shall be taken from them, and then shall they fast.**

5, 7, 8? 5, 8, 5. Bible Matrices

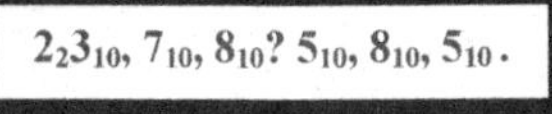

Pilled Poplar, Hazel, and Chestnut bible rods 1

$\text{Log}_{10}5 = 0.6989$ $\text{Log}_{10}8 = 0.9030$ $\text{Log}_{10}5 = 0.6989$ $\text{Log}_{10}8 = 0.9030$ $\text{Log}_{10}7 = 0.8450$ $\text{Log}_{10}3 = 0.4771$

$\text{Log}_2 2 = y$

$2^y = 2^1$

$y = 1$

5, 7, 8? 5, 8, 5. Deep calls unto Deep study bible 1

1 0.4771, 0.8450, 0.9030? 0.6989, 0.9030, 0.6989.

Deep calls unto Deep study bible 2

x-axis	y-axis
5	1.4771
7	0.8450
8	0.9030
5	0.6989
8	0.9030
5	0.6989

Water Spout *(lightning; combinatorics)* Study bible 1

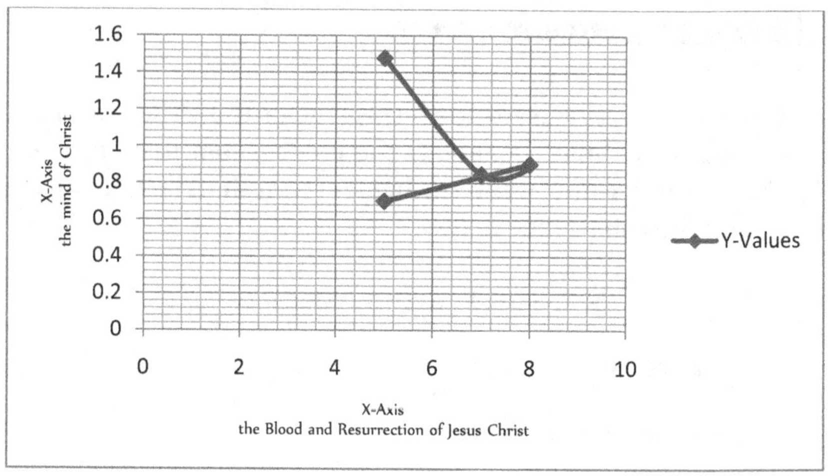

Water Spout *(lightning; combinatorics)* Study bible 2

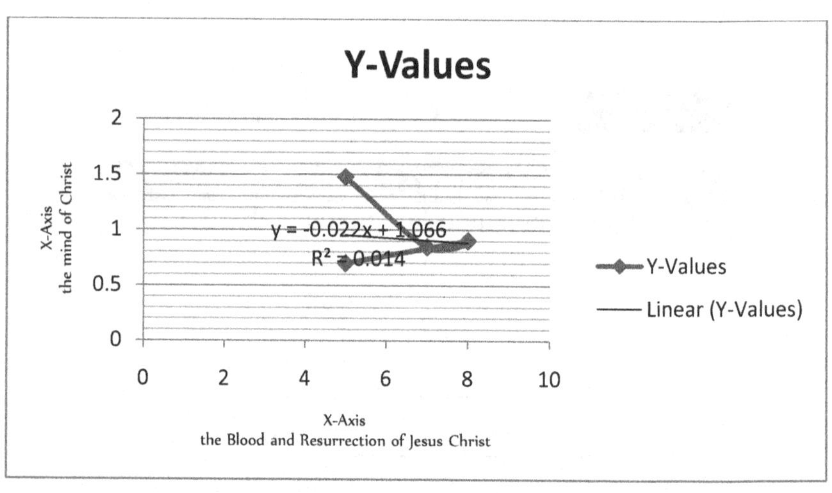

2^1 $10^{0.4771}$, $10^{0.8450}$, $10^{0.9030}$? $10^{0.6989}$, $10^{0.9030}$, $10^{0.6989}$.

Pilled Poplar, Hazel, and Chestnut bible rods 2

16. No man putteth a piece of new cloth unto an old garment, for that which is put in to fill it up taketh from the garment, and the rent is made worse.

12, 14, 6. Bible Matrices

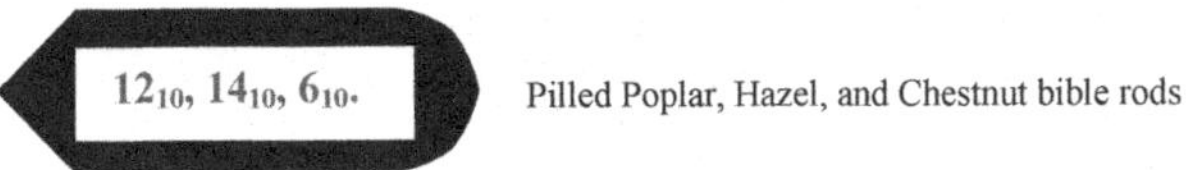

Pilled Poplar, Hazel, and Chestnut bible rods 1

$\text{Log}_{10} 12 = 1.0791$ $\text{Log}_{10} 14 = 1.1461$ $\text{Log}_{10} 6 = 0.7781$

12, 14, 6. Deep calls unto Deep study bible 1

1.0791, 1.1461, 0.7781. Deep calls unto Deep study bible 2

x-axis	y-axis
12	1.0791
14	1.1461
6	0.7781

Water Spout *(lightning; combinatorics)* Study bible 1

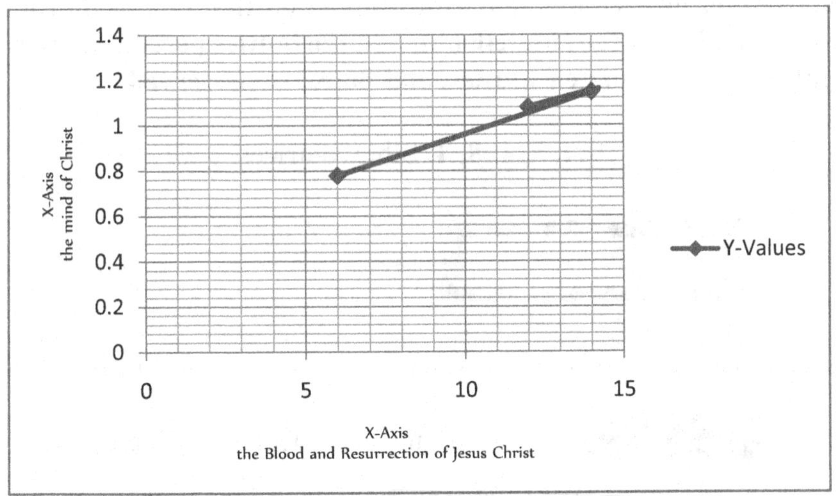

Water Spout *(lightning; combinatorics)* Study bible 2

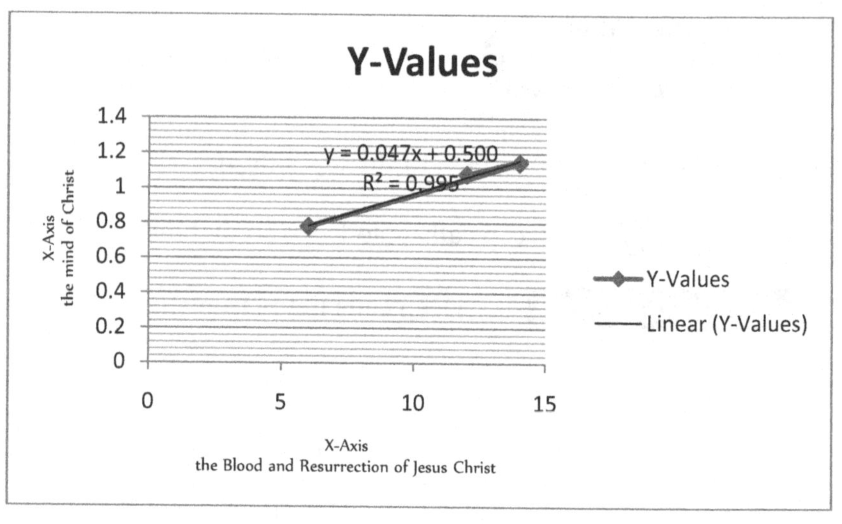

$10^{1.0791}$, $10^{1.1461}$, $10^{0.7781}$. Pilled Poplar, Hazel, and Chestnut bible rods 2

17. Neither do men put new wine into old bottles: else the bottles break, and the wine runneth out, and the bottles perish: but they put new wine into new bottles, and both are preserved.

9:4, 5, 4: 8, 4. Bible Matrices

9_{10}: 4_{10}, 5_{10}, 4_{10}: 8_{10}, 4_{10}. Pilled Poplar, Hazel, and Chestnut bible rods 1

$\text{Log}_{10} 8 = 0.9030$ $\text{Log}_{10} 4 = 0.6020$ $\text{Log}_{10} 4 = 0.6020$ $\text{Log}_{10} 4 = 0.6020$ $\text{Log}_{10} 9 = 0.9542$ $\text{Log}_{10} 5 = 0.6989$

9: 4, 5, 4: 8, 4. Deep calls unto Deep study bible 1

0.9542: 0.6020, 0.6989, 0.6020: 0.9030, 0.6020.
Deep calls unto Deep study bible 2

x-axis	y-axis
9	0.9542
4	0.6020
5	0.6989
4	0.6020
8	0.9030
4	0.6020

Water Spout *(lightning; combinatorics)* Study bible 1

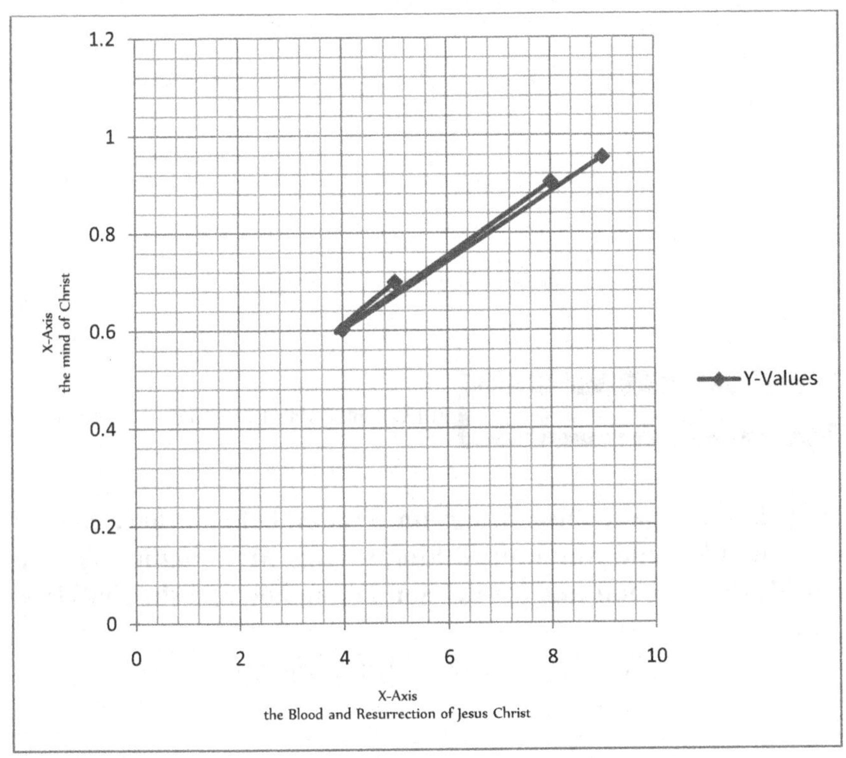

Water Spout *(lightning; combinatorics)* Study bible 2

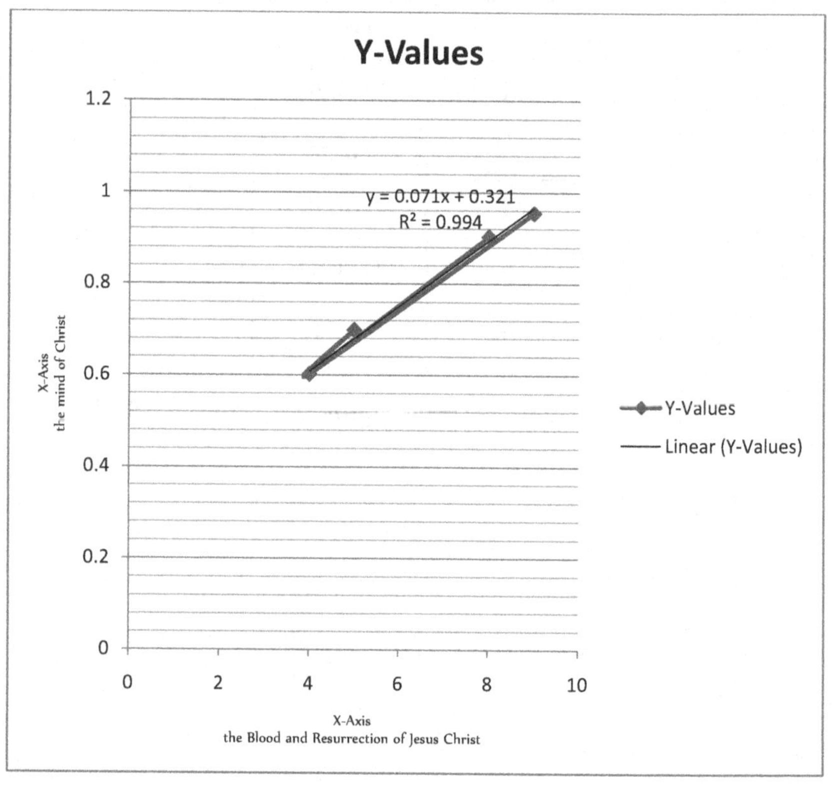

$10^{0.9542}: 10^{0.6020}, 10^{0.6989}, 10^{0.6020}: 10^{0.9030}, 10^{0.6020}.$ Pilled Poplar, Hazel, and Chestnut bible rods 2

18. While he spake these things unto them, behold, there came a certain ruler, and worshipped him, saying, My daughter is even now dead: but come and lay thy hand upon her, and she shall live.

7, 1, 5, 3, 1, 6: 8, 4. Bible Matrices

$7_{10}, 1_{10}, 5_{10}, 3_{10}, 1_{10}, 6_{10}: 8_{10}, 4_{10}.$ Pilled Poplar, Hazel, and Chestnut bible rods 1

$\text{Log}_{10} 1 = 0$ $\text{Log}_{10} 1 = 0$ $\text{Log}_{10} 8 = 0.9030$ $\text{Log}_{10} 4 = 0.6020$ $\text{Log}_{10} 5 = 0.6989$ $\text{Log}_{10} 3 = 0.4771$

$\text{Log}_{10} 6 = 0.7781$ $\text{Log}_{10} 7 = 0.8450$

7, 1, 5, 3, 1, 6: 8, 4. Deep calls unto Deep study bible 1

0.8450, 0, 0.6989, 0.4771, 0, 0.7781: 0.9030, 0.6020.
Deep calls unto Deep study bible 2

x-axis	y-axis
7	0.8450
1	0
5	0.6989
3	0.4771
1	0
6	0.7781
8	0.9030
4	0.6020

Water Spout *(lightning; combinatorics)* Study bible 1

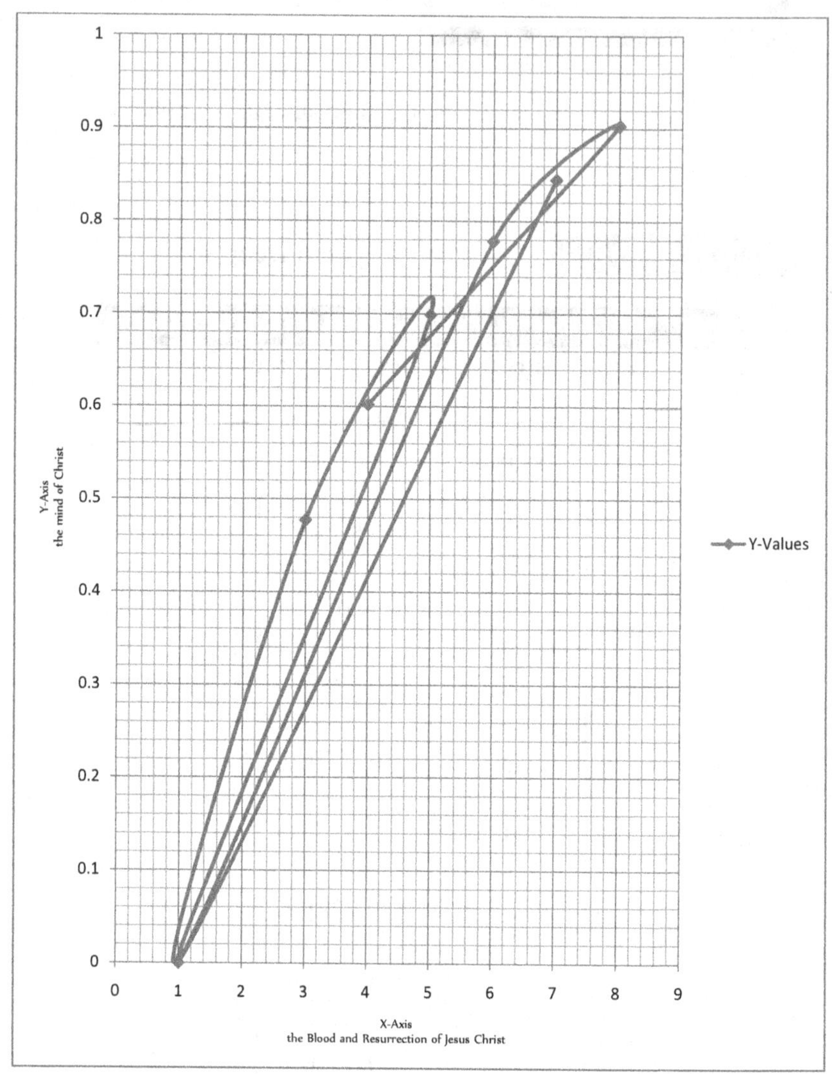

Water Spout *(lightning; combinatorics)* Study bible 2

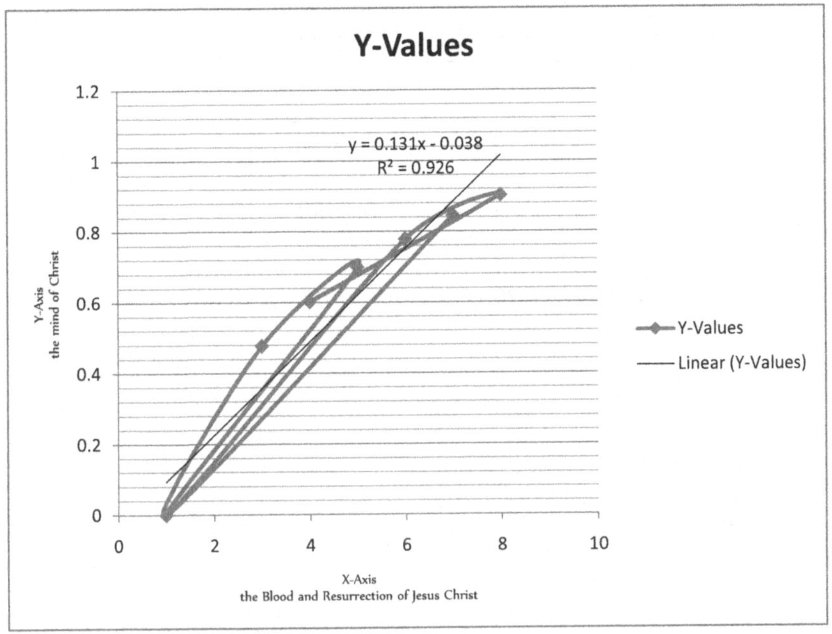

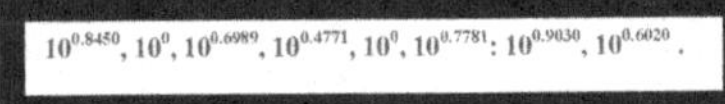
$10^{0.8450}, 10^{0}, 10^{0.6989}, 10^{0.4771}, 10^{0}, 10^{0.7781}: 10^{0.9030}, 10^{0.6020}.$

Pilled Poplar, Hazel, and Chestnut bible rods 2

19.And Jesussavior; deliverer**arose, and followed him, and so did his disciples.**

3, 3, 5. Bible Matrices

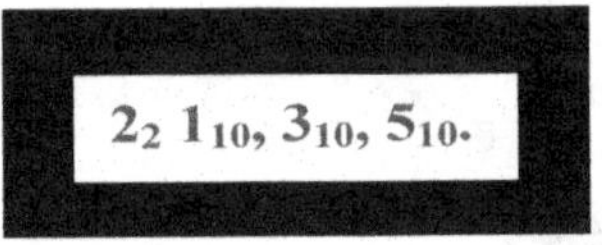
$2_2\ 1_{10}, 3_{10}, 5_{10}.$

Pilled Poplar, Hazel, and Chestnut bible rods 1

$\text{Log}_2 2 = y$ $\text{Log}_{10} 3 = 0.4771$ $\text{Log}_{10} 5 = 0.6989$ $\text{Log}_{10} 1 = 0$

$2^y = 2^1$

$y = 1$

3, 3, 5. Deep calls unto Deep study bible 1

1 0, 0.4771, 0.6989. Deep calls unto Deep study bible 2

x-axis	y-axis
3	1
3	0.4771
5	0.6989

Water Spout *(lightning; combinatorics)* Study bible 1

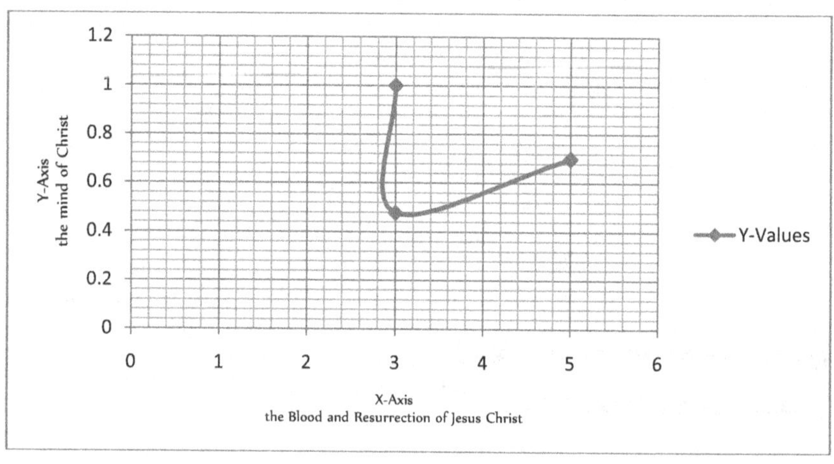

Water Spout *(lightning; combinatorics)* Study bible 2

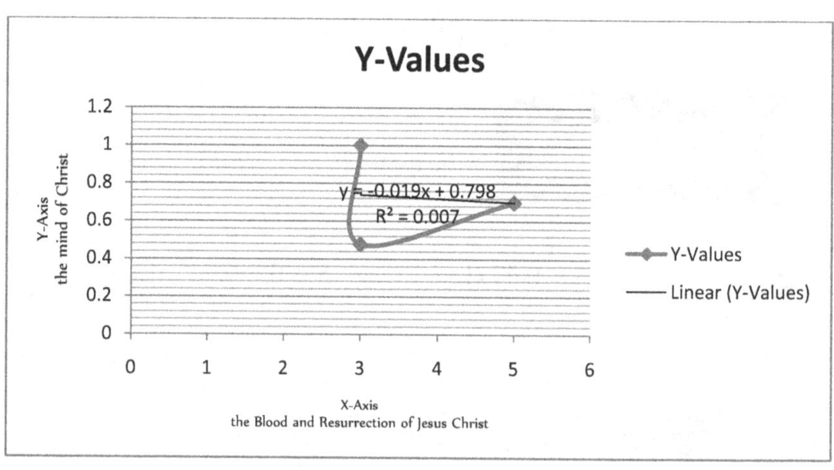

$2^1\ 10^0, 10^{0.4771}, 10^{0.6989}.$ Pilled Poplar, Hazel, and Chestnut bible rods 2

20. And, behold, a woman, which was diseased with an issue of blood twelve dominion or divine government; 2 x 2 x 3 **years, came behind him, and touched the hem of his garment:**

1, 1, 2, 10, 3, 7: Bible Matrices

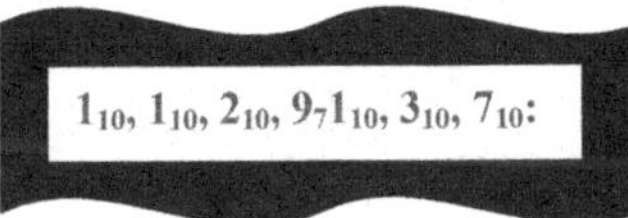

Pilled Poplar, Hazel, and Chestnut bible rods 1

$\text{Log}_{10} 7 = 0.8450 \quad \text{Log}_{10} 3 = 0.4771 \quad \text{Log}_{10} 2 = 0.3010 \quad \text{Log}_{10} 1 = 0 \quad \text{Log}_{10} 1 = 0 \quad \text{Log}_{10} 1 = 0$

$\text{Log}_7 9 = y$

$7^y = 9$

$y \log_{10} 7 = \log_{10} 9$

$y = \log_{10} 9 / \log_{10} 7$

$y = 0.9542 / 0.8450$

$y = 1.1292$

1, 1, 2, 10, 3, 7: Deep calls unto Deep study bible 1

0, 0, 0.3010, 1.1292 0, 0.4771, 0.8450:
Deep calls unto Deep study bible 2

x-axis	y-axis
1	0
1	0
2	0.3010
10	1.1292
3	0.4771
7	0.8450

Water Spout *(lightning; combinatorics)* Study bible 1

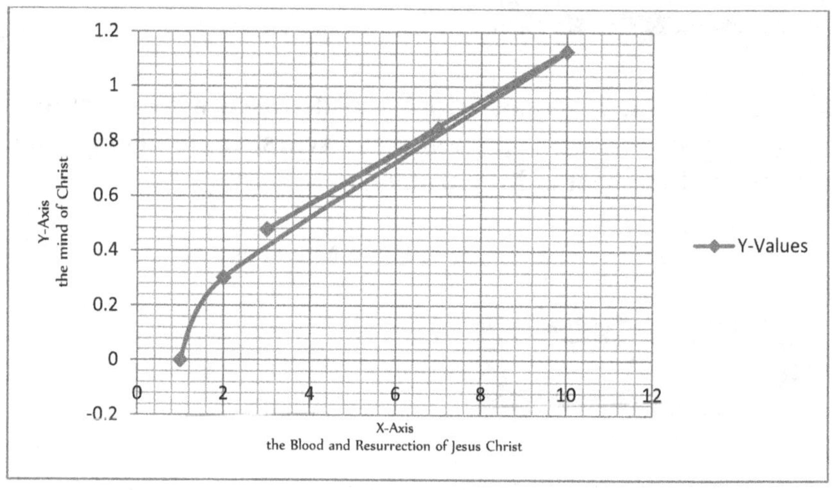

Water Spout *(lightning; combinatorics)* Study bible 2

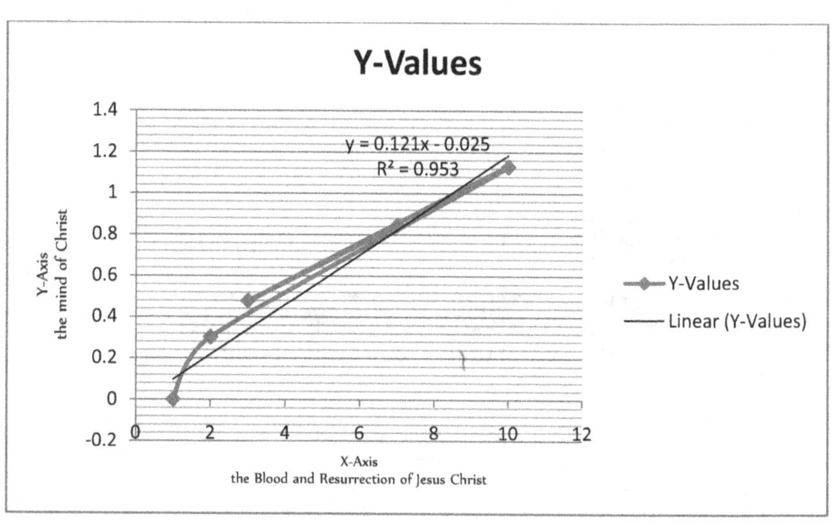

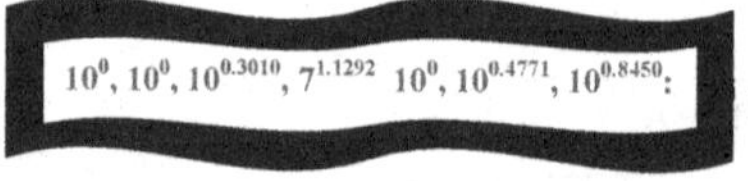

Pilled Poplar, Hazel, and Chestnut bible rods 2

21. For she said within herself, If I may but touch his garment, I shall be whole.

5, 7, 4. Bible Matrices

$\text{Log}_{10} 7 = 0.8450$ $\text{Log}_{10} 4 = 0.6020$ $\text{Log}_{10} 5 = 0.6989$

5, 7, 4. Deep calls unto Deep study bible 1

0.6989, 0.8450, 0.6020. Deep calls unto Deep study bible 2

x-axis	y-axis
5	0.6989
7	0.8450
4	0.6020

Water Spout *(lightning; combinatorics)* Study bible 1

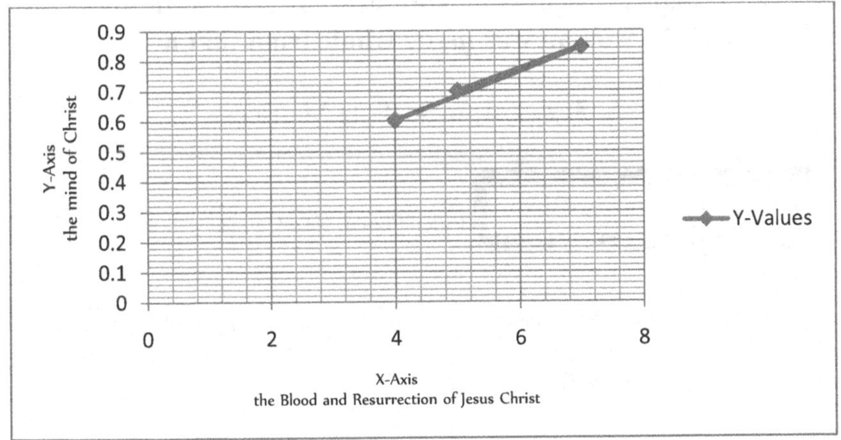

Water Spout *(lightning; combinatorics)* Study bible 2

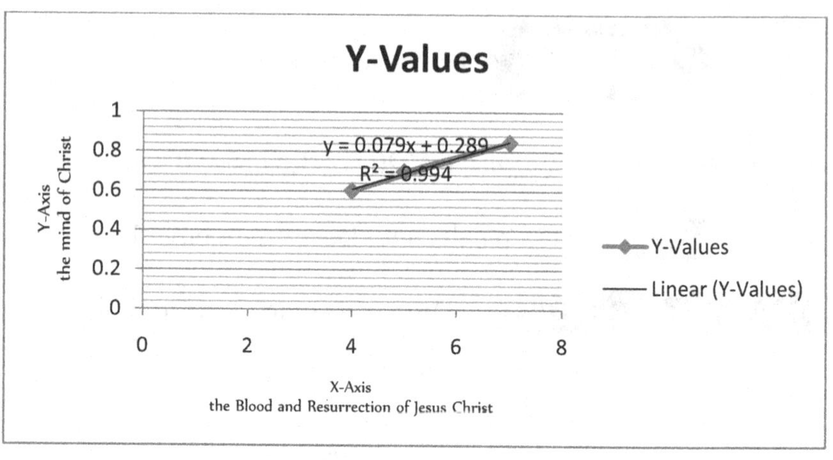

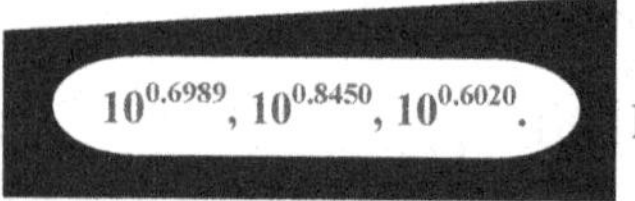

Pilled Poplar, Hazel, and Chestnut bible rods 2

22.But Jesussavior; deliverer**turned him about, and when he saw her, he said, Daughter, be of good comfort; thy faith hath made thee whole. And the woman was made whole from that hour.**

5, 5, 2, 1, 4; 6. 9. Bible Matrices

$2_2 3_{10}$, 5_{10}, 2_{10}, 1_{10}, 4_{10}; 6_{10}. 9_{10}.

Pilled Poplar, Hazel, and Chestnut bible rods 1

$\text{Log}_{10} 9 = 0.9542$ $\text{Log}_{10} 6 = 0.7781$ $\text{Log}_{10} 4 = 0.6020$ $\text{Log}_{10} 1 = 0$ $\text{Log}_{10} 2 = 0.3010$ $\text{Log}_{10} 5 = 0.6989$

$\text{Log}_2 2 = y$ $\text{Log}_{10} 3 = 0.4771$

$2^y = 2^1$

$2 = 1$

5, 5, 2, 1, 4; 6. 9. Deep calls unto Deep study bible 1

1 0.4771, 0.6989, 0.3010, 0, 0.6020; 0.7781. 0.9542.
Deep calls unto Deep study bible 2

x-axis	y-axis
5	1.4771
5	0.6989
2	0.3010
1	0
4	0.6020
6	0.7781
9	0.9542

Water Spout *(lightning; combinatorics)* Study bible 1

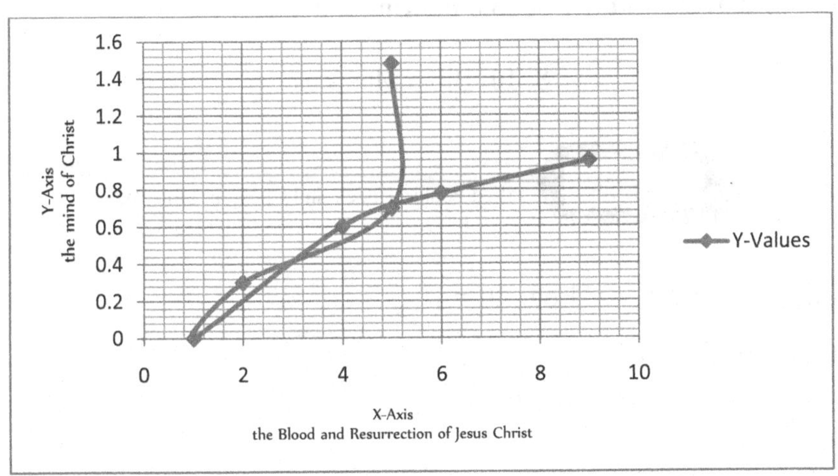

Water Spout *(lightning; combinatorics)* Study bible 2

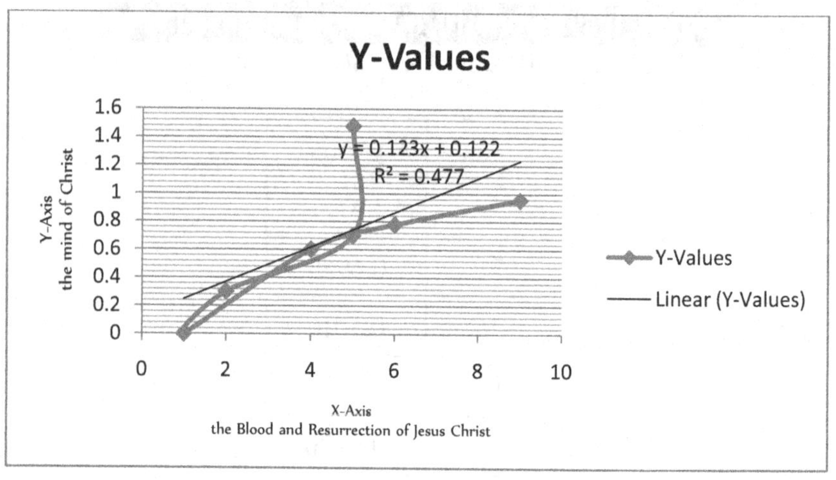

Pilled Poplar, Hazel, and Chestnut bible rods 2

23. And when Jesussavior; deliverer**came into the ruler's house, and saw the minstrels and the people making a noise,**

8, 10, Bible Matrices

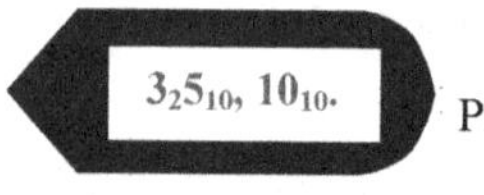

Pilled Poplar, Hazel, and Chestnut bible rods 1

$\text{Log}_{10} 5 = 0.6989$ $\quad$ $\text{Log}_{10} 10 = 1$

$\text{Log}_2 3 = y$

$2^y = 3$

$y \log_{10} 2 = \log_{10} 3$

$y = \log_{10}3 / \log_{10}2$

$y = 0.4771 / 0.3010$

$y = 1.5850$

8, 10, Deep calls unto Deep study bible 1

1.5850 0.6989, 1, Deep calls unto Deep study bible 2

x-axis	y-axis
8	2.2839
10	1

Water Spout *(lightning; combinatorics)* Study bible 1

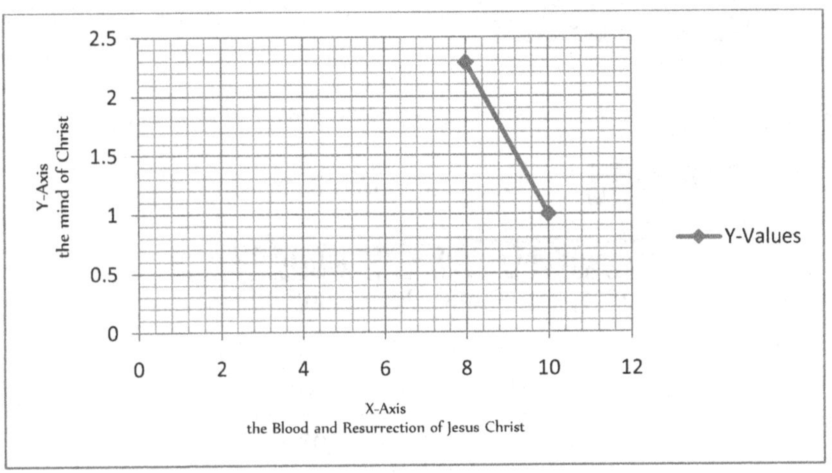

Water Spout *(lightning; combinatorics)* Study bible 2

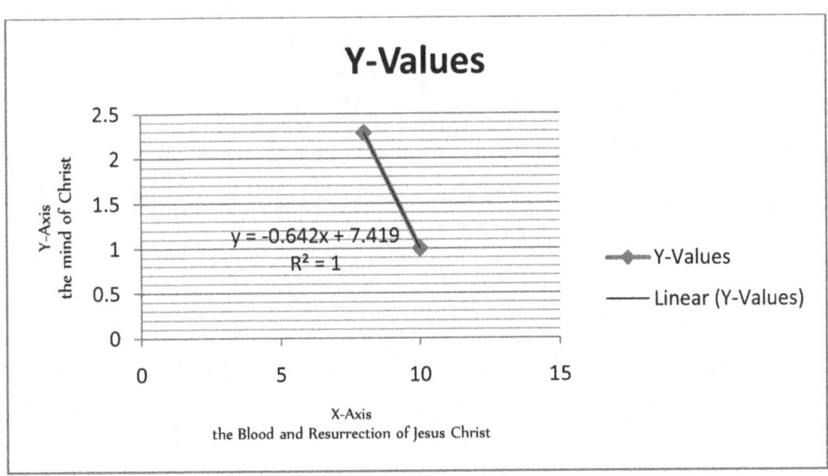

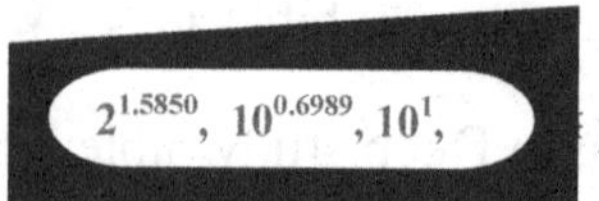

Pilled Poplar, Hazel, and Chestnut bible rods 2

24. He said unto them, Give place: for the maid is not dead, but sleepeth. And they laughed him to scorn.

4, 2: 6, 2. 6. Bible Matrices

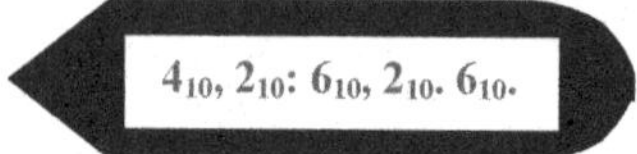

Pilled Poplar, Hazel, and Chestnut bible rods 1

$\text{Log}_{10} 6 = 07781$ $\text{Log}_{10} 4 = 0.6020$ $\text{Log}_{10} 6 = 07781$ $\text{Log}_{10} 2 = 0.3010$ $\text{Log}_{10} 2 = 0.3010$

4, 2: 6, 2. 6. Deep calls unto Deep study bible 1

0.6020, 0.3010: 0.7781, 0.3010. 0.7781.
Deep calls unto Deep study bible 2

x-axis	y-axis
4	0.6020
2	0.3010
6	0.7781
2	0.3010
6	0.7781

Water Spout *(lightning; combinatorics)* Study bible 1

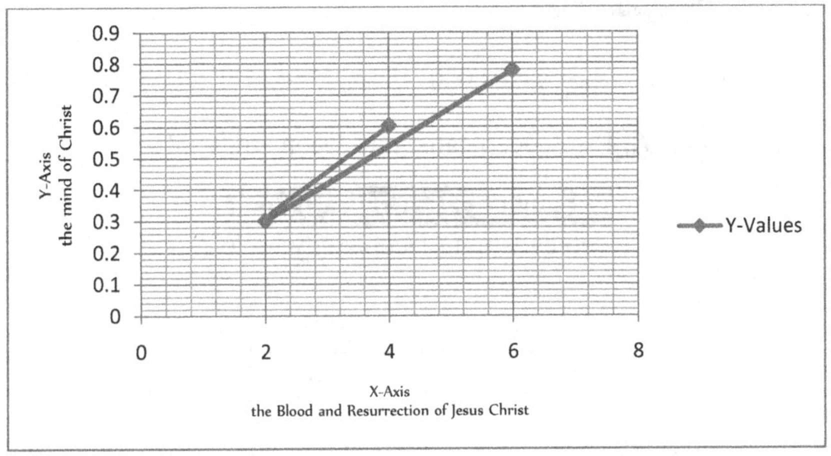

Water Spout *(lightning; combinatorics)* Study bible 2

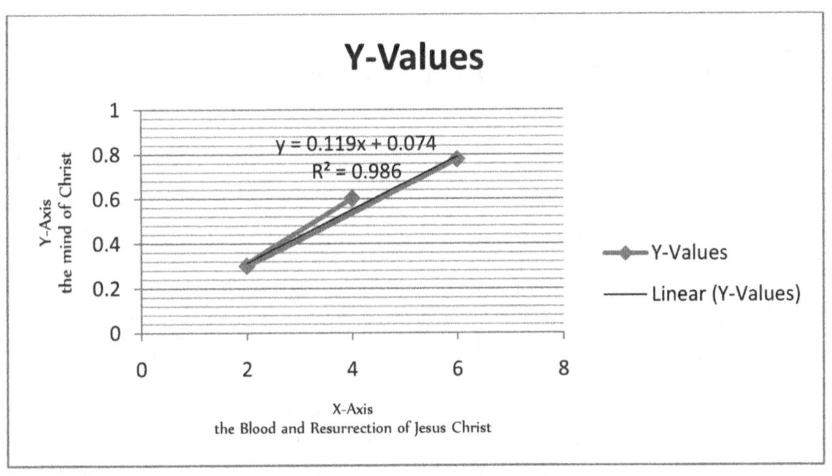

$10^{0.6020}, 10^{0.3010}: 10^{0.7781}, 10^{0.3010}. 10^{0.7781}.$ Pilled Poplar, Hazel, and Chestnut bible rods 2

25. But when the people were put forth, he went in, and took her by the hand, and the maid arose.

7, 3, 6, 4. Bible Matrices

$7_{10}, 3_{10}, 6_{10}, 4_{10}$. Pilled Poplar, Hazel, and Chestnut bible rods 1

$\log_{10} 7 = 0.8450$ $\log_{10} 4 = 0.6020$ $\log_{10} 3 = 0.4771$ $\log_{10} 6 = 0.7781$

7, 3, 6, 4. Deep calls unto Deep study bible 1

0.8450, 0.4771, 0.7781, 0.6020.
Deep calls unto Deep study bible 2

x-axis	y-axis
7	0.8450
3	0.4771
6	0.7781
4	0.6020

Water Spout *(lightning; combinatorics)* Study bible 1

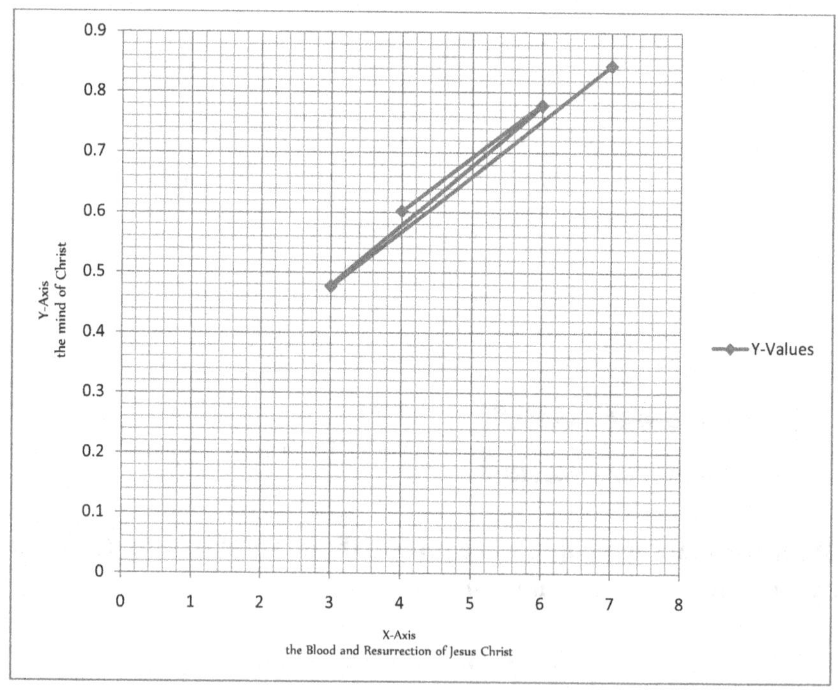

Water Spout *(lightning; combinatorics)* Study bible 2

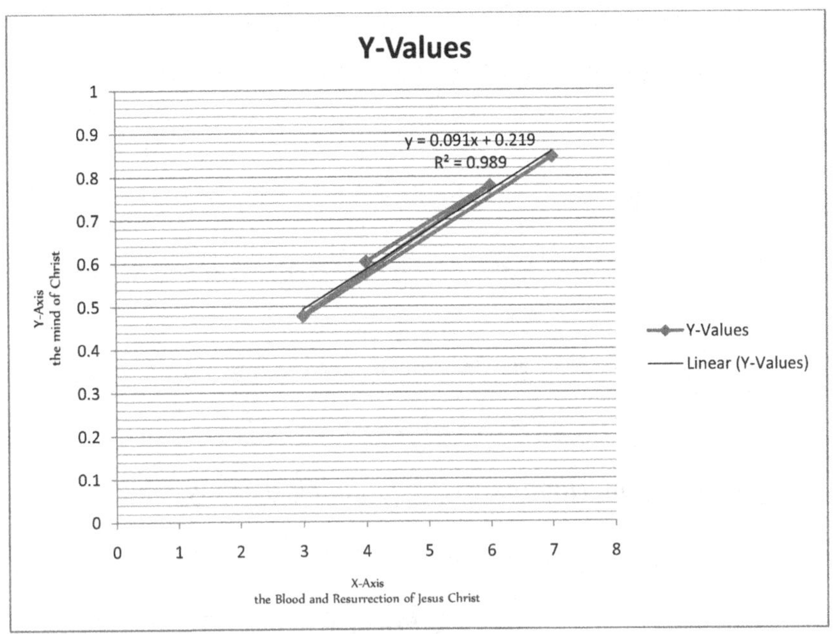

Pilled Poplar, Hazel, and Chestnut bible rods 2

26. And the fame hereof went abroad into all that land.

10. Bible Matrices

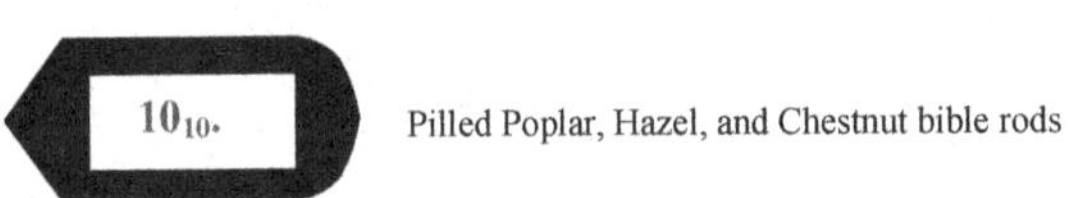

$\text{Log}_{10}\ 10 = 1$

10. Deep calls unto Deep study bible 1

1. Deep calls unto Deep study bible 2

x-axis	y-axis
10	1

Water Spout *(lightning; combinatorics)* Study bible 1

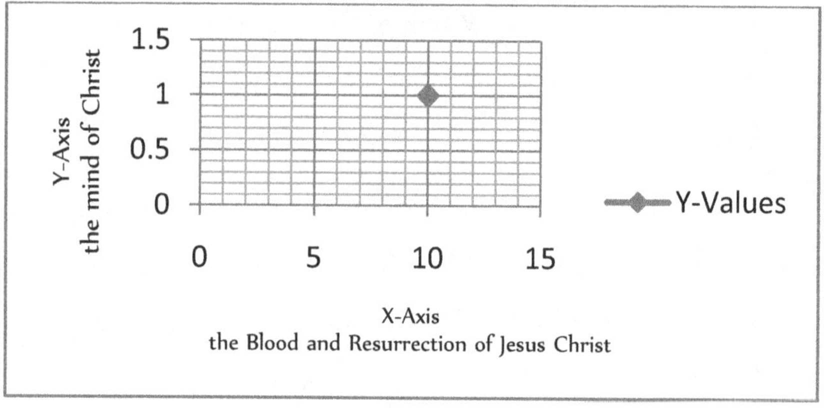

Water Spout *(lightning; combinatorics)* Study bible 2

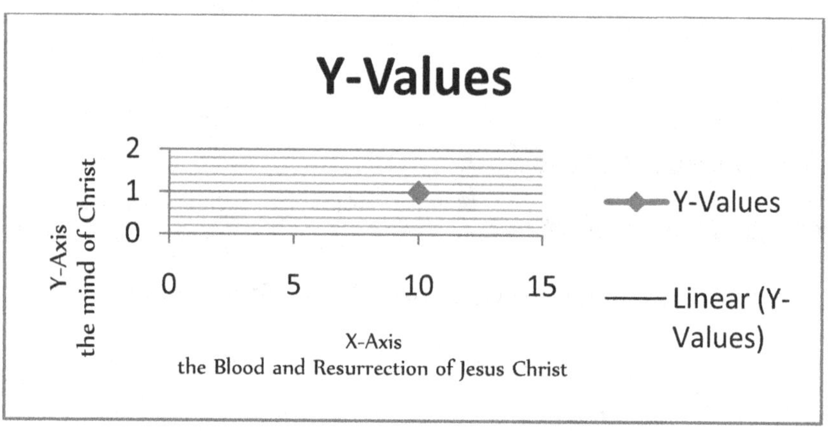

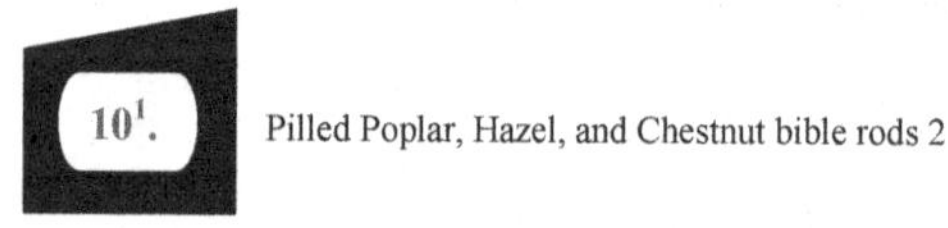

Pilled Poplar, Hazel, and Chestnut bible rods 2

27. And when Jesussavior; deliverer**departed thence, two** witness and support; 2 x 1 **blind men followed him, crying, and saying, Thou Son of David**beloved; dear, **have mercy on us.**

5, 5, 1, 2, 4, 4. Bible Matrices

$3_2\ 2_{10},\ 1_5\ 4_{10},\ 1_{10},\ 2_{10},\ 4_2,\ 4_{10}.$ Pilled Poplar, Hazel, and Chestnut bible rods 1

$Log_{10} 4 = 0.6020$ $Log_{10} 2 = 0.3010$ $Log_{10} 1 = 0$ $Log_{10} 2 = 0.3010$ $Log_{10} 4 = 0.6020$

$Log_2 3 = y$	$log_2 4 = y$	$log_5 1 = y$
$2^y = 3$	$2^y = 4$	$5^y = 1$
$y \log_{10} 2 = \log_{10} 3$	$2^y = 2^2$	$5^y = 5^0$
$y = \log_{10} 3 / \log_{10} 2$	$y = 2$	$y = 0$
$y = 0.4771 / 0.3010$		
$y = 1.5850$		

5, 5, 1, 2, 4, 4. Deep calls unto Deep study bible 1

1.5850 0.3010, 0 0.6020, 0, 0.3010, 2, 0.6020
Deep calls unto Deep study bible 2

x-axis	y-axis
5	1.8860
5	0.6020
1	0
2	0.3010
4	2
4	0.6020

Water Spout *(lightning; combinatorics)* Study bible 1

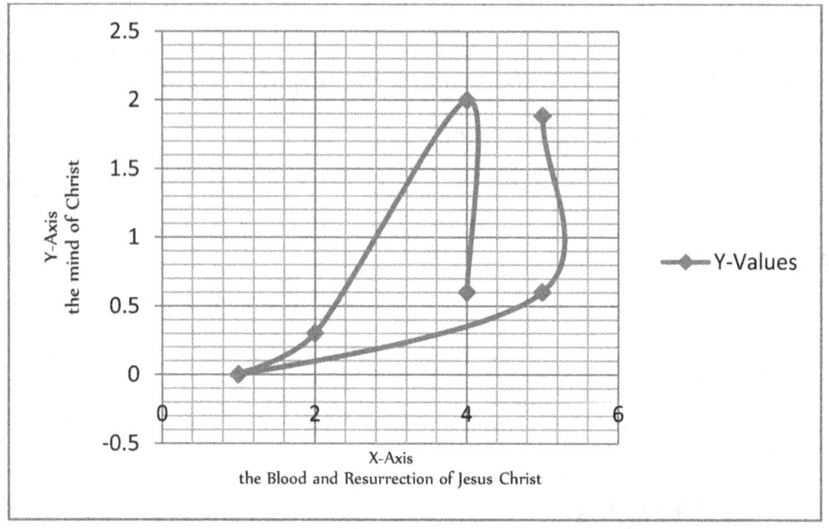

Water Spout *(lightning; combinatorics)* Study bible 2

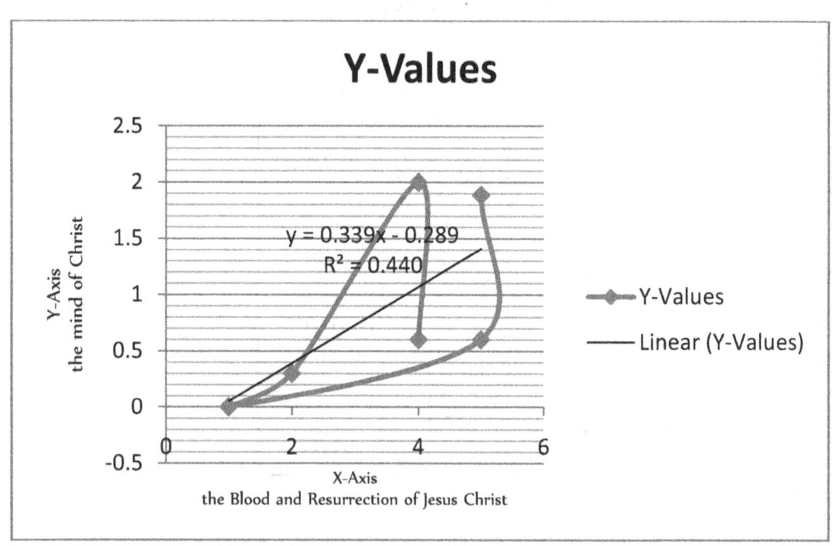

$2^{1.5850}\ 10^{0.3010}, 5^{0}\ 10^{0.6020}, 10^{0}, 10^{0.3010}, 2^{2}, 10^{0.6020}$. Pilled Poplar, Hazel, and Chestnut bible rods 2

28. And when he was come into the house, the blind men came to him: and Jesussavior; deliverer **saith unto them, Believe ye that I am able to do this? They said unto him, Yea, Lord.**

8, 6: 5, 9? 4, 1, 1. Bible Matrices

$8_{10}, 6_{10}: 2_2 3_{10}, 9_{10}? 4_{10}, 1_{10}, 1_{10}.$ Pilled Poplar, Hazel, and Chestnut bible rods 1

$\text{Log}_{10} 8 = 0.9030$ $\text{Log}_{10} 6 = 0.7781$ $\text{Log}_{10} 9 = 0.9542$ $\text{Log}_{10} 1 = 0$ $\text{Log}_{10} 1 = 0$ $\text{Log}_{10} 4 = 0.6020$

$\text{Log}_2 2 = y$ $\text{Log}_{10} 3 = 0.4771$

$2^y = 2^1$

$2 = 1$

8, 6: 5, 9? 4, 1, 1. Deep calls unto Deep study bible 1

0.9030, 0.7781: 1 0.4771, 0.9542? 0.6020, 0, 0.

Deep calls unto Deep study bible 2

x-axis	y-axis
8	0.9030
6	0.7781
5	1.4771
9	0.9542
4	0.6020
1	0
1	0

Water Spout *(lightning; combinatorics)* Study bible 1

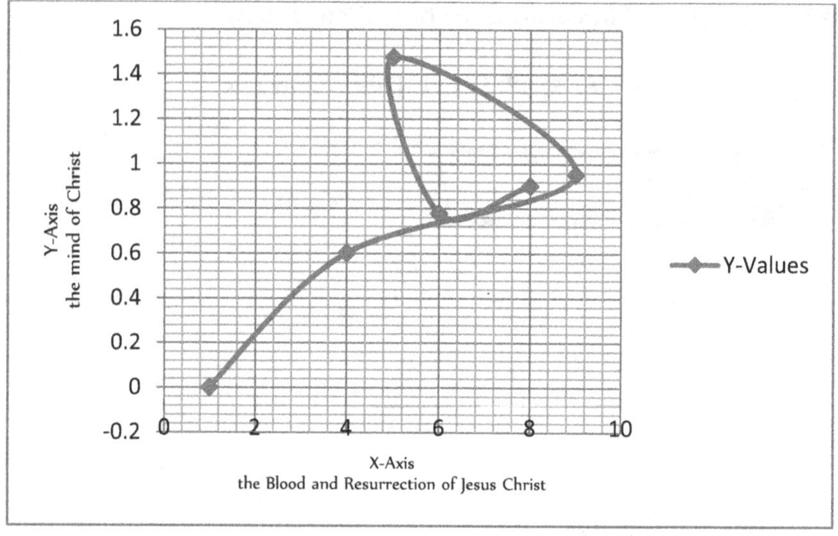

Water Spout *(lightning; combinatorics)* Study bible 2

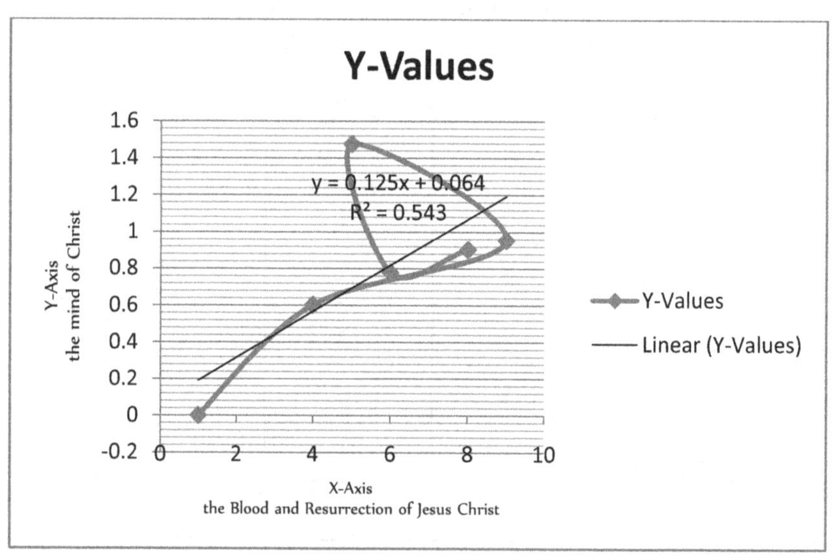

$10^{0.9030}, 10^{0.7781}: 2^{1}\ 10^{0.4771}, 10^{0.9542}?\ 10^{0.6020}, 10^{0}, 10^{0}.$

Pilled Poplar, Hazel, and Chestnut bible rods 2

29. Then touched he their eyes, saying, According to your faith be it unto you.

5, 1, 8. Bible Matrices

$\text{Log}_{10} 8 = 0.9030$ $\text{Log}_{10} 5 = 0.6989$ $\text{Log}_{10} 1 = 0$

5, 1, 8. Deep calls unto Deep study bible 1

0.6989, 0, 0.9030. Deep calls unto Deep study bible 2

x-axis	y-axis
5	0.6989
1	0
8	0.9030

Water Spout *(lightning; combinatorics)* Study bible 1

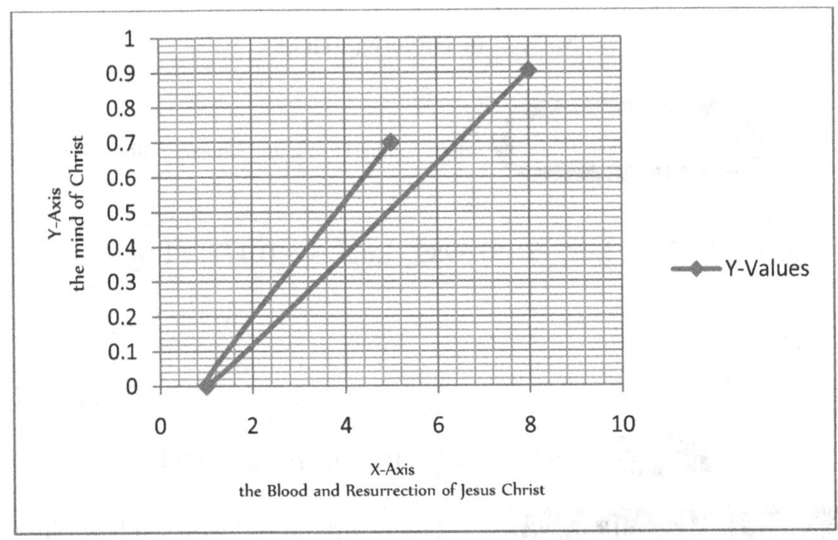

Water Spout *(lightning; combinatorics)* Study bible 2

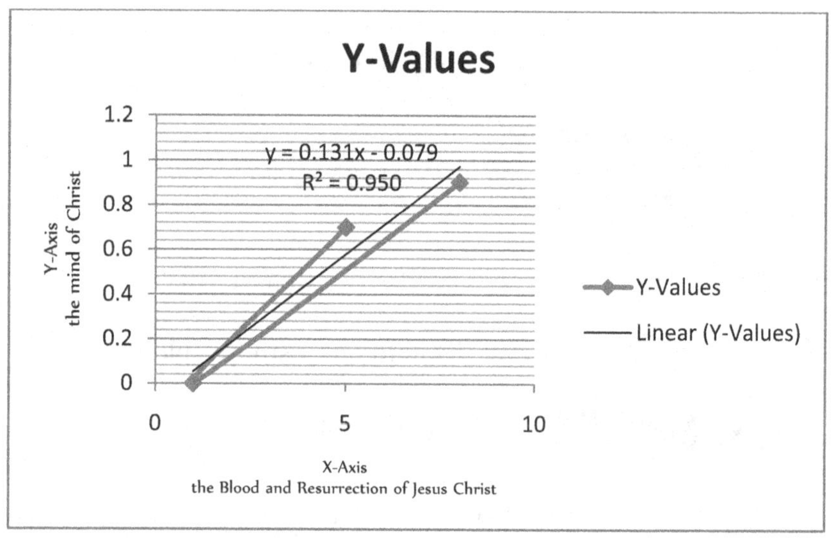

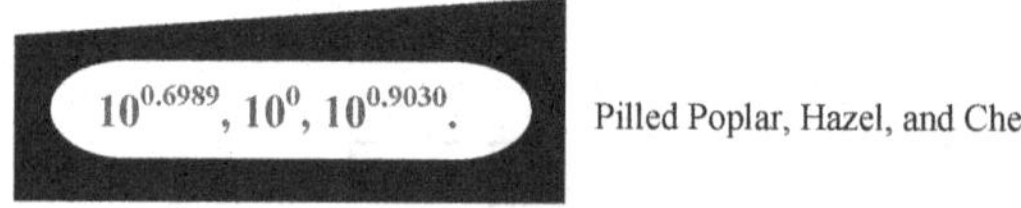

Pilled Poplar, Hazel, and Chestnut bible rods 2

30. And their eyes were opened; and Jesussavior; deliverer **straitly charged them, saying, See that no man know it.**

5; 5, 1, 6. Bible Matrices

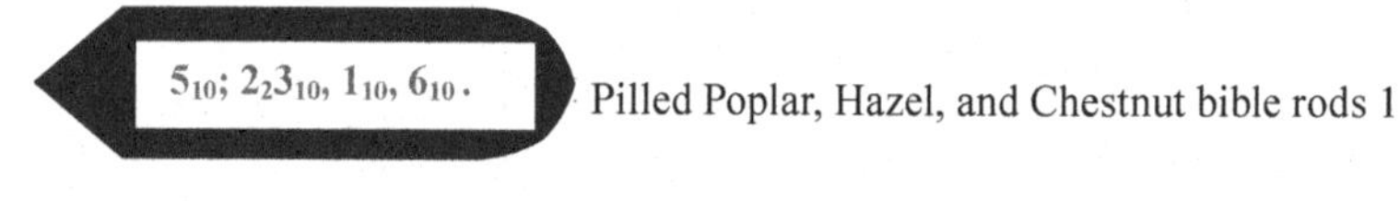

Pilled Poplar, Hazel, and Chestnut bible rods 1

$\text{Log}_{10} 6 = 0.7781$ $\text{Log}_{10} 5 = 0.6989$ $\text{Log}_{10} 3 = 0.4771$ $\text{Log}_{10} 1 = 0$

$\text{Log}_2 2 = y$

$2^y = 2^1$

$y = 1$

5; 5, 1, 6. Deep calls unto Deep study bible 1

0.6989; 1 0.4771, 0, 0.7781. Deep calls unto Deep study bible 2

x-axis	y-axis
5	0.6989
5	1.4771
1	0
6	0.7781

Water Spout *(lightning; combinatorics)* Study bible 1

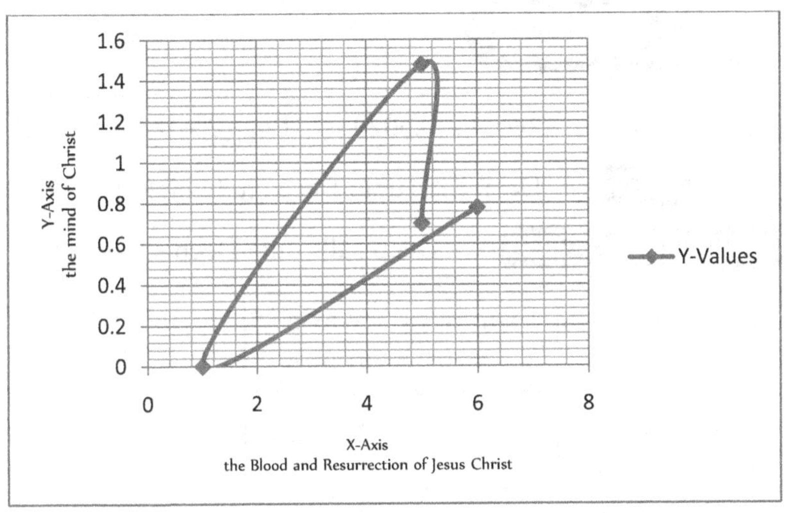

Water Spout *(lightning; combinatorics)* Study bible 2

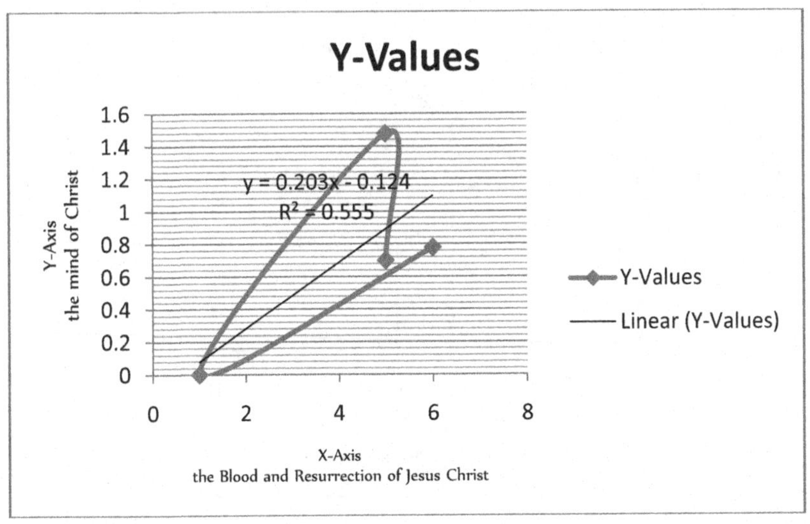

$10^{0.6989}$; 2^1 $10^{0.4771}$, 10^0, $10^{0.7781}$. Pilled Poplar, Hazel, and Chestnut bible rods 2

31. But they, when they were departed, spread abroad his fame in all that country.

2, 4, 8. Bible Matrices

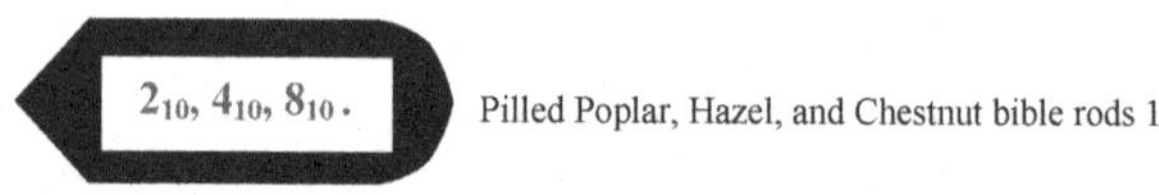

Pilled Poplar, Hazel, and Chestnut bible rods 1

$\text{Log}_{10} 8 = 0.9030$ $\text{Log}_{10} 4 = 0.6020$ $\text{Log}_{10} 2 = 0.3010$

2, 4, 8. Deep calls unto Deep study bible 1

0.3010, 0.6020, 0.9030. Deep calls unto Deep study bible 2

x-axis	y-axis
2	0.3010
4	0.6020
8	0.9030

Water Spout *(lightning; combinatorics)* Study bible 1

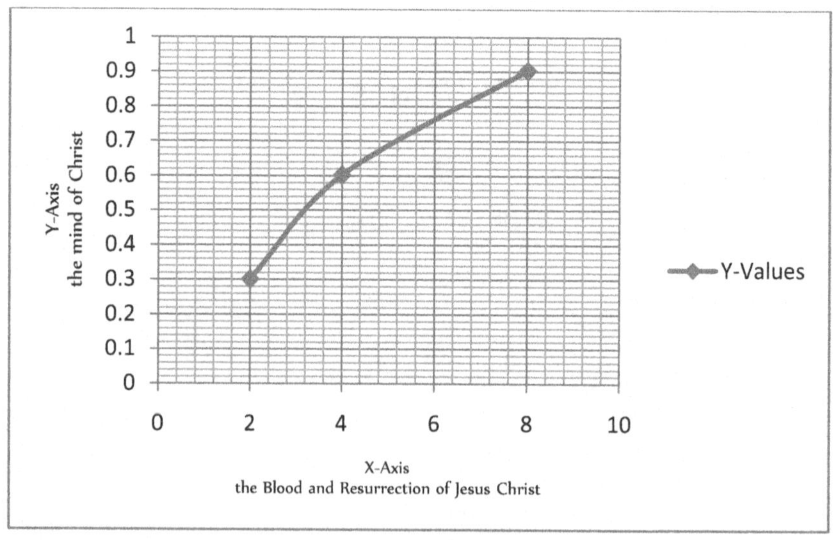

Water Spout *(lightning; combinatorics)* Study bible 2

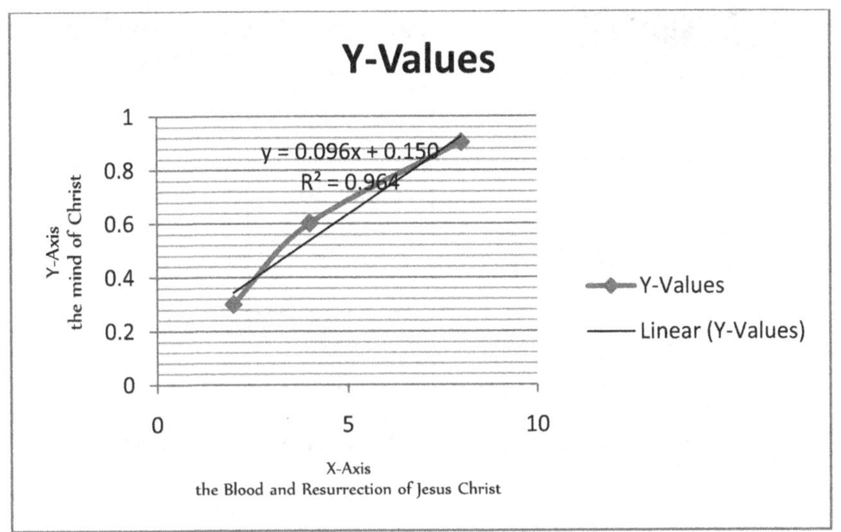

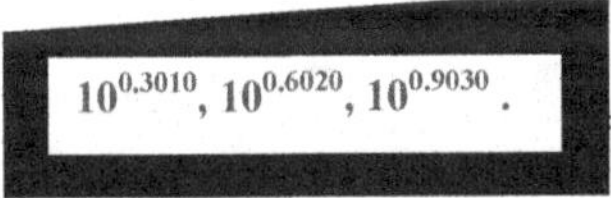

Pilled Poplar, Hazel, and Chestnut bible rods 2

32. As they went out, behold, they brought to him a dumb man possessed with a devil Slanderer; false accuser.

4, 1, 11. Bible Matrices

Pilled Poplar, Hazel, and Chestnut bible rods 1

$\text{Log}_{10} 1 = 0$ $\quad$ $\text{Log}_{10} 4 = 0.6020$

$\text{Log}_3 11 = y$

$3^y = 11$

$y \log_{10} 3 = \log_{10} 11$

$y = \log_{10}11 / \log_{10}3$

$y = 1.0413 / 0.4771$

$y = 2.1825$

4, 1, 11. Deep calls unto Deep study bible 1

0.6020, 0, 2.1825. Deep calls unto Deep study bible 2

x-axis	y-axis
4	0.6020
1	0
11	2.1825

Water Spout *(lightning; combinatorics)* Study bible 1

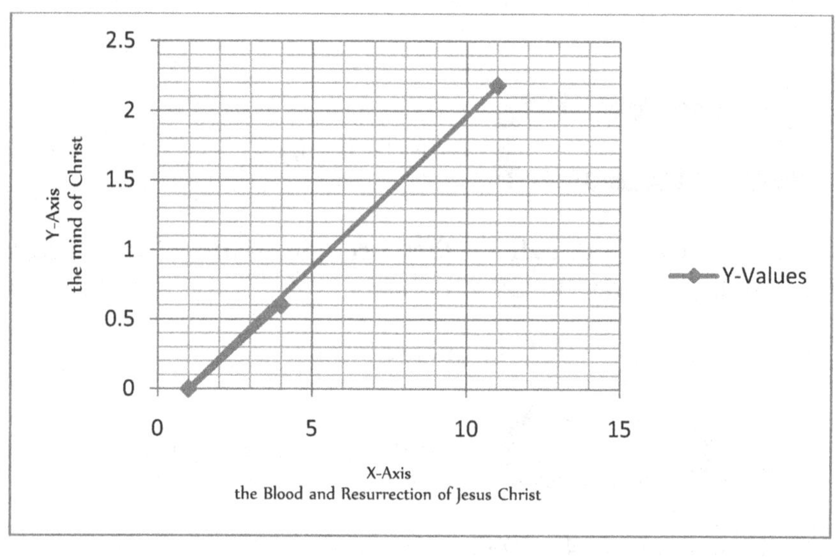

Water Spout *(lightning; combinatorics)* Study bible 2

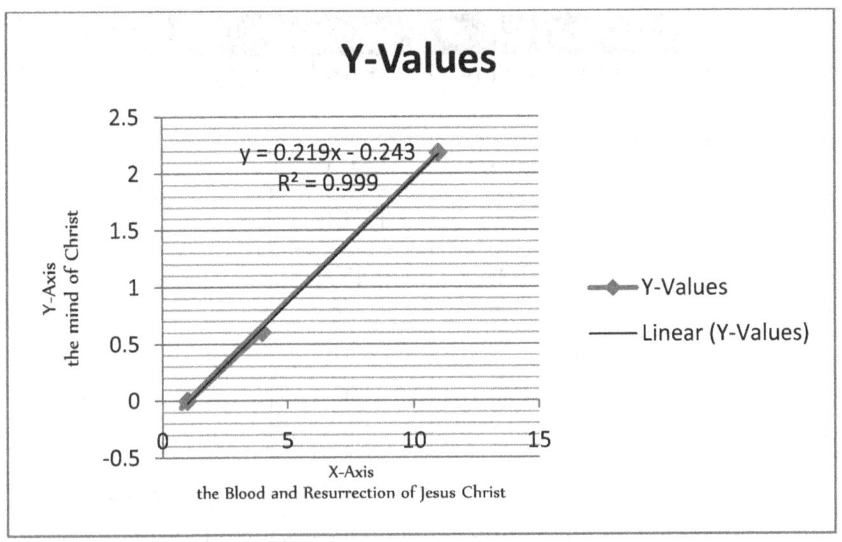

$10^{0.6020}$, 10^{0}, $3^{2.1825}$. Pilled Poplar, Hazel, and Chestnut bible rods 2

33. And when the devil Slanderer; false accuser **was cast out, the dumb spake: and the multitudes marvelled, saying, It was never so seen in Israel** who prevails with God; God strives.

7, 3: 4, 1, 7. Bible Matrices

$4_3\, 3_{10}, 3_{10} : 4_{10}, 1_{10}, 7_6$. Pilled Poplar, Hazel, and Chestnut bible rods 1

$\text{Log}_{10} 3 = 0.4771$ $\quad$ $\text{Log}_{10} 4 = 0.6020$ $\quad$ $\text{Log}_{10} 3 = 0.4771$ $\quad$ $\text{Log}_{10} 1 = 0$

$\text{Log}_6 7 = y$	$\log_3 4 = y$
$6^y = 7$	$3^y = 4$
$y \log_{10} 6 = \log_{10} 7$	$y \log_{10} 3 = \log_{10} 4$
$y = \log_{10} 7 / \log_{10} 6$	$y = \log_{10} 4 / \log_{10} 3$
$y = 0.8450 / 0.7781$	$y = 0.6020 / 0.4771$
$y = 1.0859$	$y = 1.2617$

7, 3: 4, 1, 7. Deep calls unto Deep study bible 1

1.2617 0.4771, 0.4771: 0,6020, 0, 1.0859.
Deep calls unto Deep study bible 2

x-axis	y-axis
7	1.7388
3	0.4771
4	0.6020
1	0
7	1.0859

Water Spout *(lightning; combinatorics)* Study bible 1

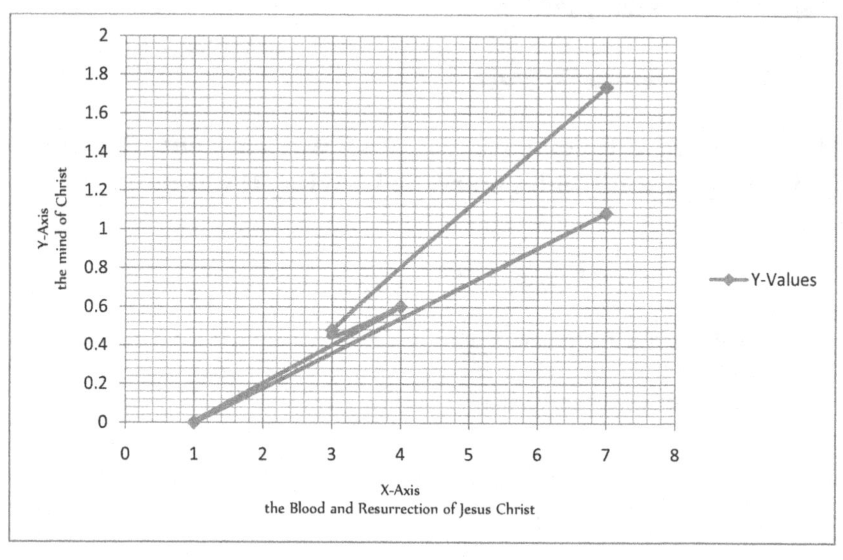

Water Spout *(lightning; combinatorics)* Study bible 2

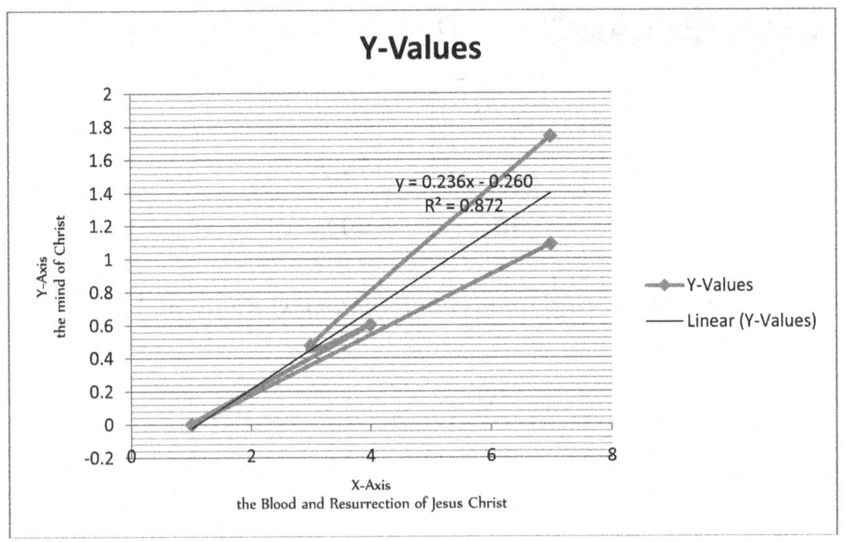

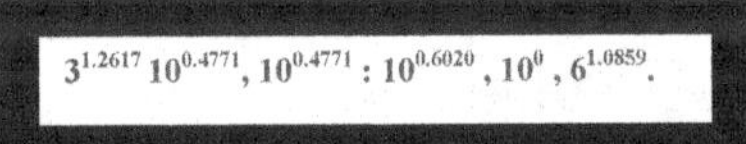

Pilled Poplar, Hazel, and Chestnut bible rods 2

34.But the Pharisees separated ones; set apart **said, He casteth out devils**Slanderers; false accusers**through the prince of the devils**Slanderers; false accusers.

4, 10. Bible Matrices

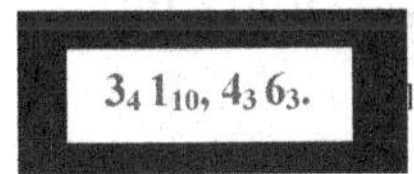

Pilled Poplar, Hazel, and Chestnut bible rods 1

$\text{Log}_{10} 1 = 0$

$\text{Log}_4 3 = y$

$4^y = 3$

$y \log_{10} 4 = \log_{10} 3$

$y = \log_{10} 3/ \log_{10} 4$

$y = 0.4771/ 0.6020$

$y = 0.7925$

$\log_3 4 = y$

$3^y = 4$

$y \log_{10} 3 = \log_{10} 4$

$y = \log_{10} 4/ \log_{10} 3$

$y = 0.6020/ 0.4771$

$y = 1.2617$

$\log_3 6 = y$

$3^y = 6$

$y \log_{10} 3 = \log_{10} 6$

$y = \log_{10} 6/ \log_{10} 3$

$y = 0.7781/ 0.4771$

$y = 1.6308$

4, 10. Deep calls unto Deep study bible 1

0.7925 0, 1.2617 1.6308. Deep calls unto Deep study bible 2

x-axis	y-axis
4	0.7925
10	2.8925

Water Spout *(lightning; combinatorics)* Study bible 1

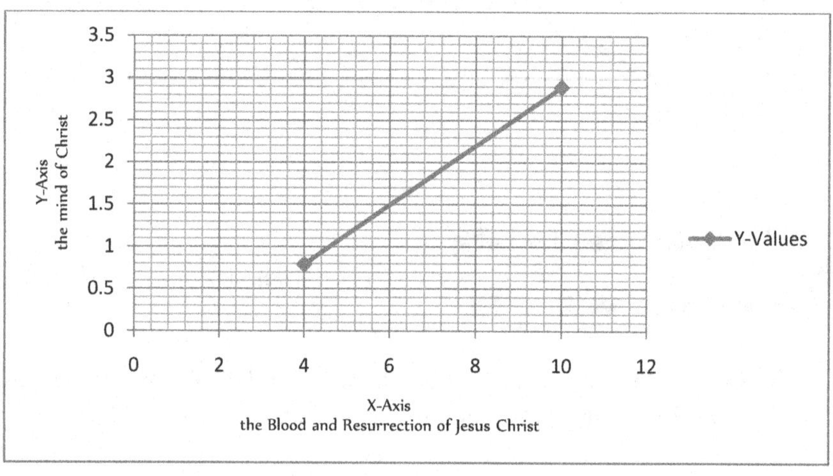

Water Spout *(lightning; combinatorics)* Study bible 2

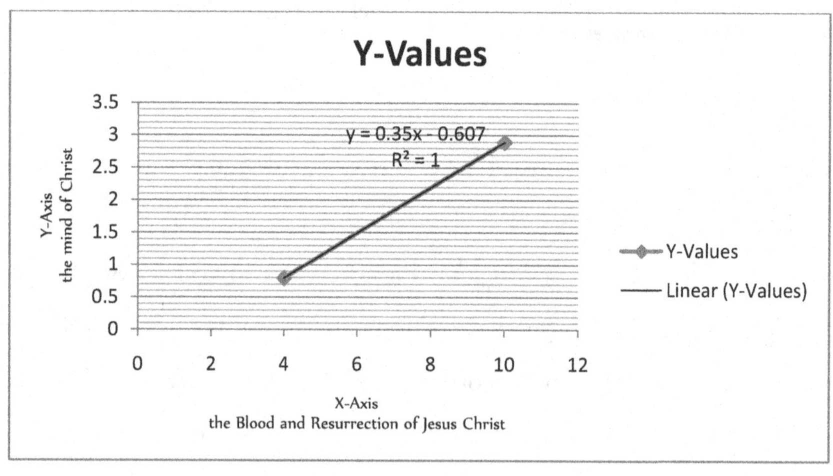

$4^{0.7925}\ 10^{0},\ 3^{1.2617}\ \ 3^{1.6308}.$ Pilled Poplar, Hazel, and Chestnut bible rods 2

35.And Jesussavior; deliverer **went about all the cities and villages, teaching in their synagogues, and preaching the gospel of the kingdom, and healing every sickness and every disease among the people.**

9, 4, 7, 10. Bible Matrices

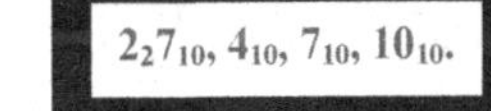

Pilled Poplar, Hazel, and Chestnut bible rods 1

$\text{Log}_{10} 7 = 0.8450 \quad \text{Log}_{10} 4 = 0.6020 \quad \text{Log}_{10} 10 = 1 \quad \text{Log}_{10} 7 = 0.8450$

$\text{Log}_{\,2} 2 = y$

$2^y = 2^1$

$y = 1$

9, 4, 7, 10. Deep calls unto Deep study bible 1

1 0.8450, 0.6020, 0.8450, 1. Deep calls unto Deep study bible 2

x-axis	y-axis
9	1.8450
4	0.6020
7	0.8450
10	1

Water Spout *(lightning; combinatorics)* Study bible 1

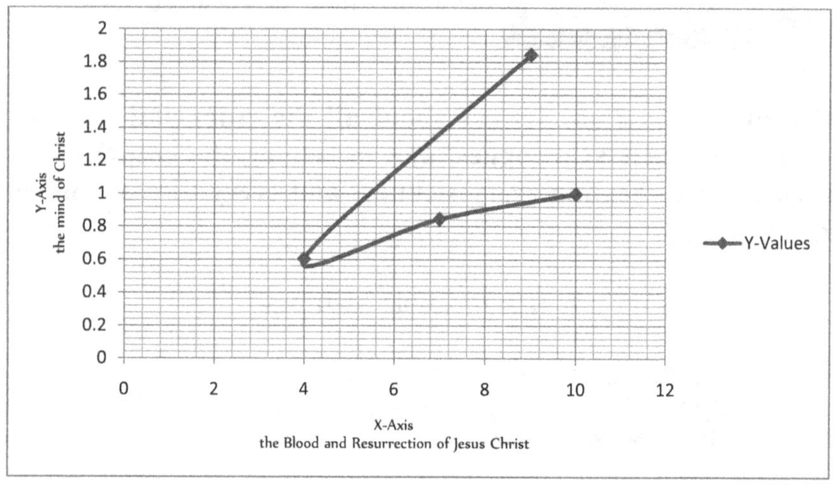

Water Spout *(lightning; combinatorics)* Study bible 2

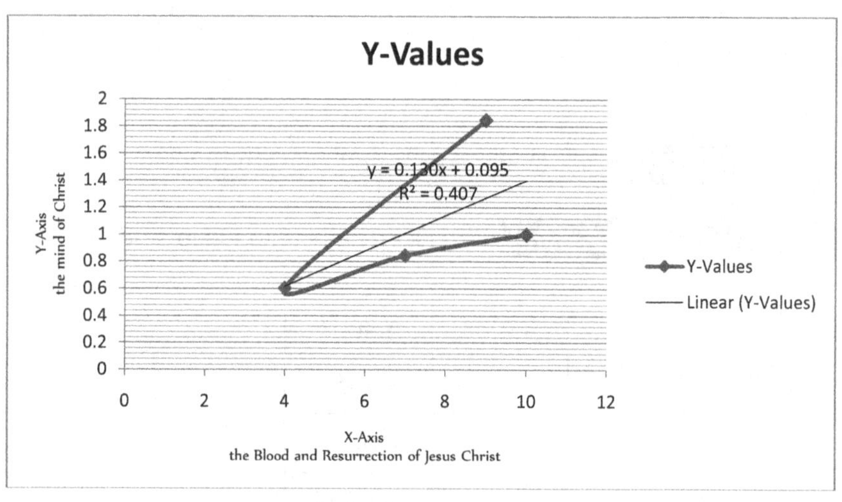

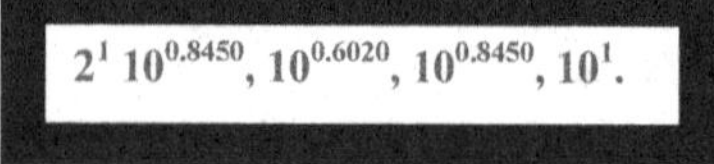
2^1 $10^{0.8450}$, $10^{0.6020}$, $10^{0.8450}$, 10^1.

Pilled Poplar, Hazel, and Chestnut bible rods 2

36. But when he saw the multitudes, he was moved with compassion on them, because they fainted, and were scattered abroad, as sheep having no shepherd.

6, 7, 3, 4, 5. Bible Matrices

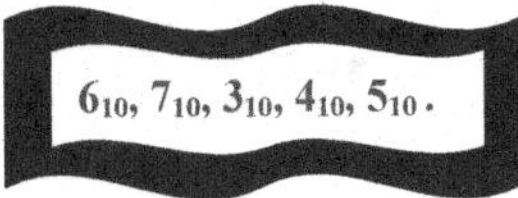

Pilled Poplar, Hazel, and Chestnut bible rods 1

$\text{Log}_{10} 7 = 0.8450$ $\text{Log}_{10} 4 = 0.6020$ $\text{Log}_{10} 3 = 0.4771$ $\text{Log}_{10} 5 = 0.6989$ $\text{Log}_{10} 6 = 0.7781$

6, 7, 3, 4, 5. Deep calls unto Deep study bible 1

0.7781, 0.8450, 0.4771, 0.6020, 0.6989.
Deep calls unto Deep study bible 2

x-axis	y-axis
6	0.7781
7	0.8450
3	0.4771
4	0.6020
5	0.6989

Water Spout *(lightning; combinatorics)* Study bible 1

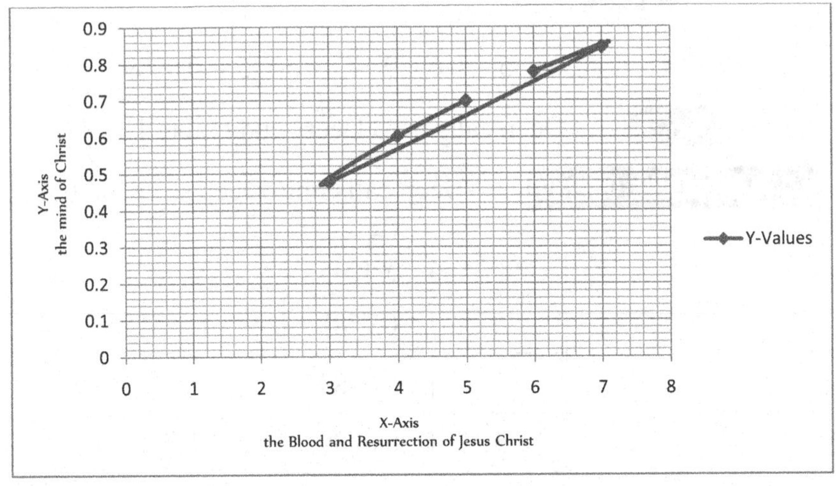

Water Spout *(lightning; combinatorics)* Study bible 2

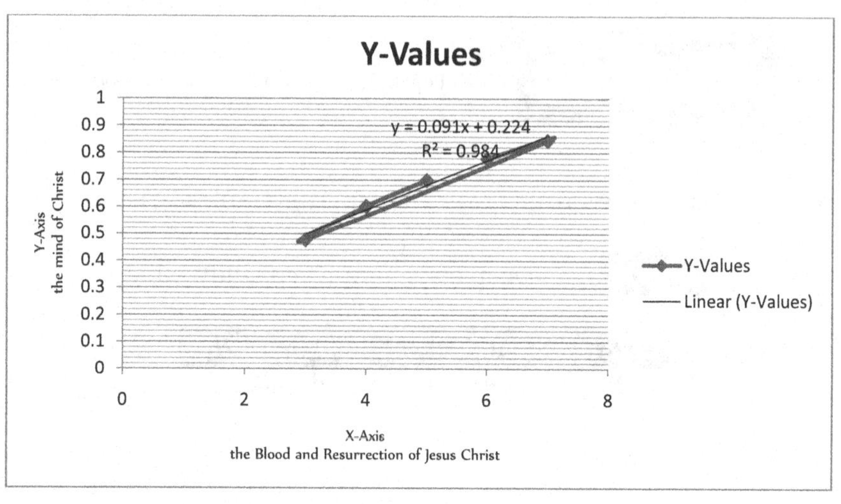

Pilled Poplar, Hazel, and Chestnut bible rods 2

37. Then saith he unto his disciples, The harvest truly is plenteous, but the labourers are few;

6, 5, 5; Bible Matrices

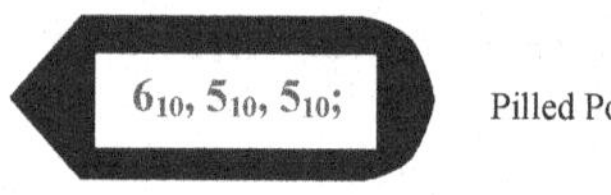

Pilled Poplar, Hazel, and Chestnut bible rods 1

$\text{Log}_{10} 6 = 0.7781$ $\text{Log}_{10} 5 = 0.6989$ $\text{Log}_{10} 5 = 0.6989$

6, 5, 5; Deep calls unto Deep study bible 1

0.7781, 0.6989, 0.6989; Deep calls unto Deep study bible 2

x-axis	y-axis
6	0.7781
5	0.6989
5	0.6989

Water Spout *(lightning; combinatorics)* Study bible 1

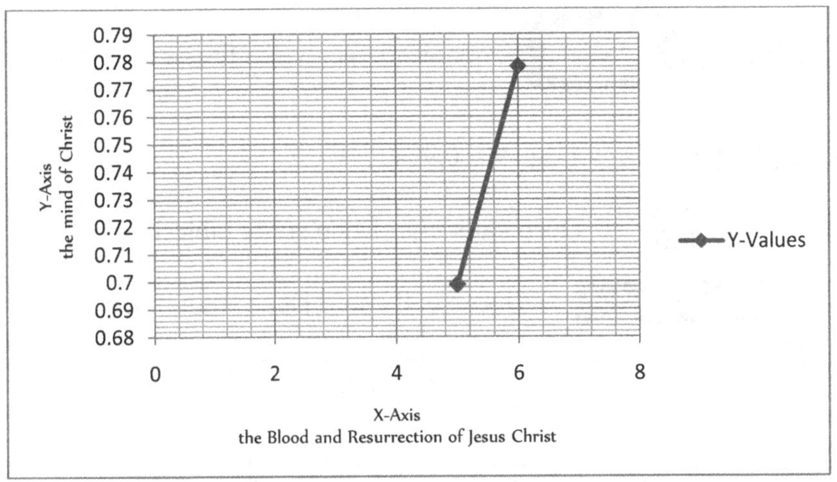

Water Spout *(lightning; combinatorics)* Study bible 2

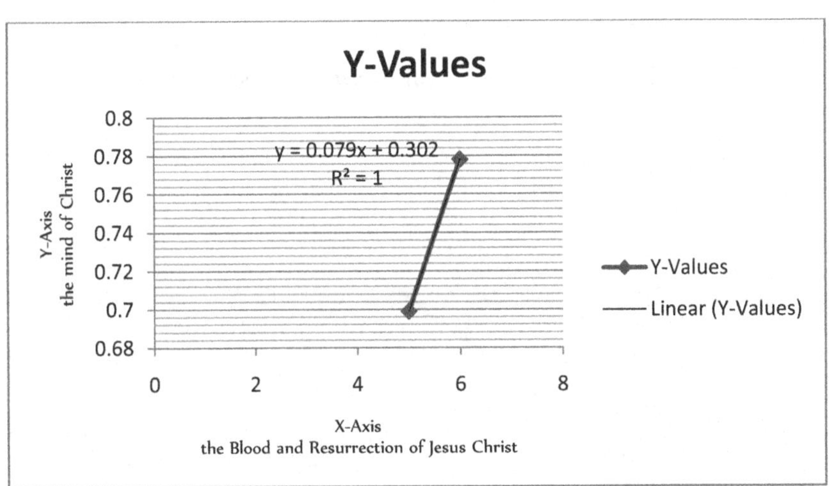

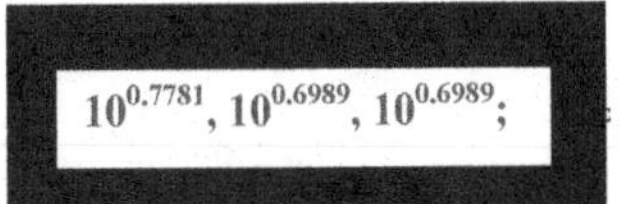
$10^{0.7781}$, $10^{0.6989}$, $10^{0.6989}$;

Pilled Poplar, Hazel, and Chestnut bible rods 2

38. Pray ye therefore the Lord of the harvest, that he will send forth labourers into his harvest.

8, 9. Bible Matrices

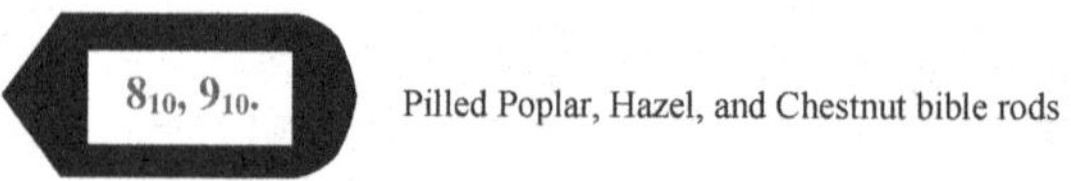

$\text{Log}_{10} 8 = 0.9030$ $\text{Log}_{10} 9 = 0.9542$

8, 9. Deep calls unto Deep study bible 1

0.9030, 0.9542. Deep calls unto Deep study bible 2

x-axis	y-axis
8	0.9030
9	0.9542

Water Spout *(lightning; combinatorics)* Study bible 1

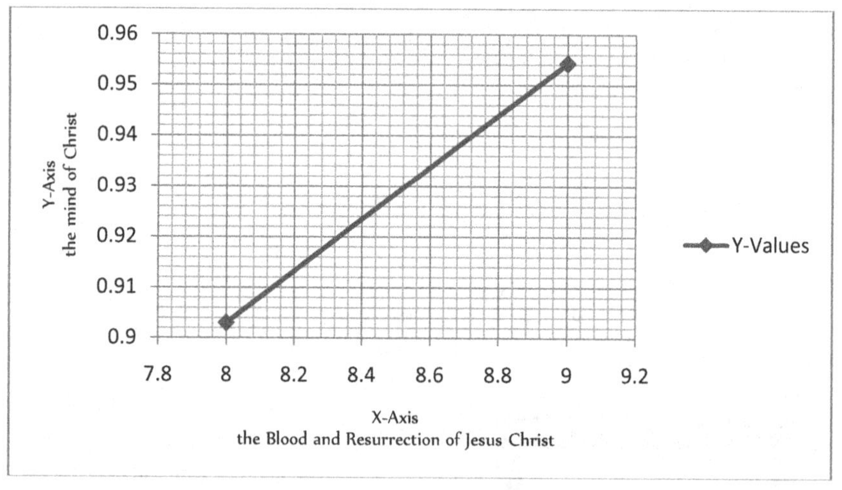

Water Spout *(lightning; combinatorics)* Study bible 2

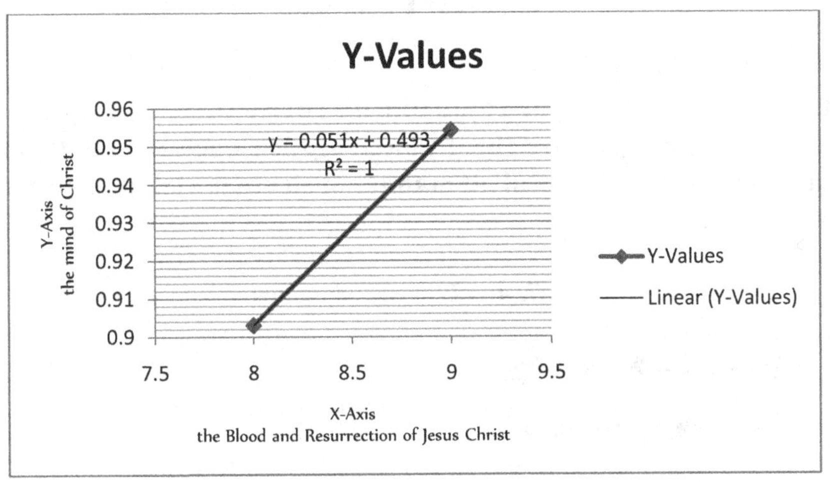

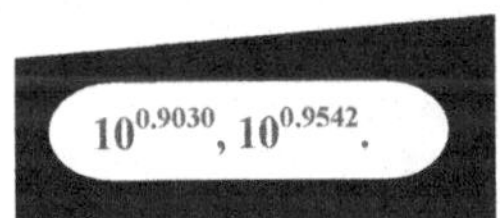

Pilled Poplar, Hazel, and Chestnut bible rods 2

CHAPTER 10

1. And when he had called unto him his twelve dominion or divine government; 2 x 2 x 3 **disciples, he gave them power against unclean spirits, to cast them out, and to heal all manner of sickness and all manner of disease.**

10, 7, 4, 12. Bible Matrices

$9_7\, 1_{10}, 7_{10}, 4_{10}, 12_{10}.$ Pilled Poplar, Hazel, and Chestnut bible rods 1

$\text{Log}_{10} 1 = 0$ $\text{Log}_{10} 7 = 0.8450$ $\text{Log}_{10} 4 = 0.6020$ $\text{Log}_{10} 12 = 1.0791$

$$\text{Log}_7 9 = y$$
$$7^y = 9$$
$$y \log_{10} 7 = \log_{10} 9$$
$$y = \log_{10} 9 / \log_{10} 7$$
$$y = 0.9542 / 0.8450$$
$$y = 1.1292$$

10, 7, 4, 12. Deep calls unto Deep study bible 1

1.1292 0, 0.8450, 0.6020, 1.0791.

Deep calls unto Deep study bible 2

x-axis	y-axis
10	1.1292
7	0.8450
4	0.6020
12	1.0791

Water Spout *(lightning; combinatorics)* Study bible 1

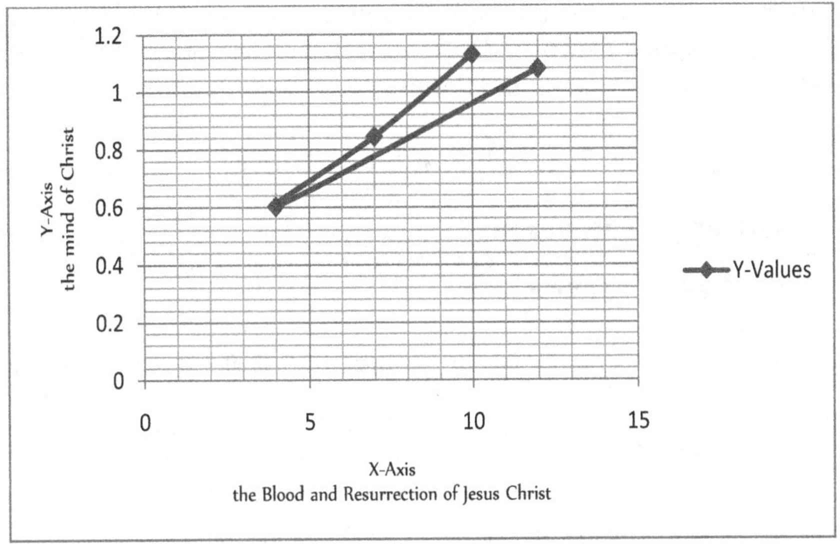

Water Spout *(lightning; combinatorics)* Study bible 2

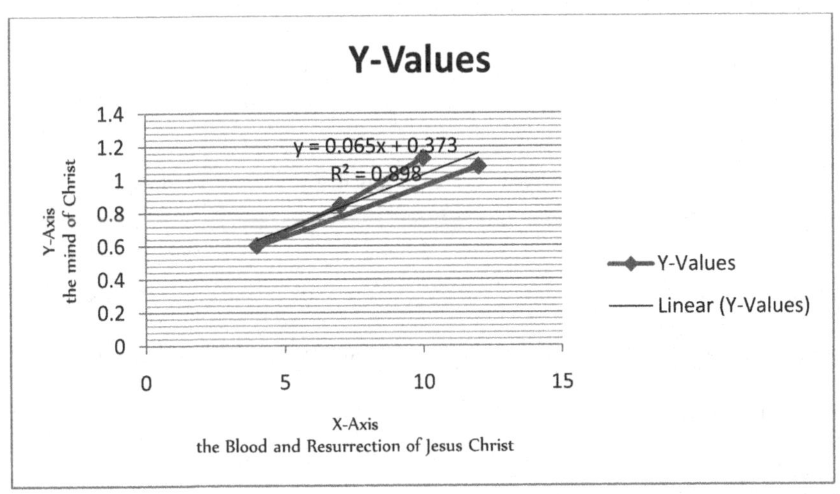

$7^{1.1292}$ 10^{0}, $10^{0.8450}$, $10^{0.6020}$, $10^{1.0791}$. Pilled Poplar, Hazel, and Chestnut bible rods 2

2. Now the names of the twelve dominion or divine government; 2 x 2 x 3 **apostles are these; The first** 1 x 1 ; earliest, initial, original, foremost, opening, primary, former, **Simon**that hears; that obeys, **who is called Peter**a rock or stone, **and Andrew**a strong man; manly; manliness **his brother; James** that supplants, undermines; the heel **the son of Zebedee**abundant; portion;my gift, **and John**the grace or mercy of the Lord**his brother;**

9; 2, 1, 4, 4; 5, 4; Bible Matrices

$6_7\,3_{10}$; 2_9, 1_4, 4_4, $2_5\,2_{10}$; $1_5\,4_{10}$, $2_7\,2_{10}$; Pilled Poplar, Hazel, and Chestnut bible rods 1

$\text{Log}_{10}3 = 0.4771$ $\text{Log}_{10}2 = 0.3010$ $\text{Log}_{10}4 = 0.6020$ $\text{Log}_{10}2 = 0.3010$

$\text{Log}_7 6 = y$ $\log_9 2 = y$ $\log_5 2 = y$

$7^y = 6$ $9^y = 2$ $5^y = 2$

$y \log_{10} 7 = \log_{10} 6$ $y \log_{10} 9 = \log_{10} 2$ $y \log_{10} 5 = \log_{10} 2$

$y = \log_{10} 6 / \log_{10} 7$ $y = \log_{10} 2 / \log_{10} 9$ $y = \log_{10} 2 / \log_{10} 5$

$y = 0.7781 / 0.8450$ $y = 0.3010 / 0.9542$ $y = 0.3010 / 0.6989$

$y = 0.9208$ $y = 0.3154$ $y = 0.4306$

$\text{Log}_7 2 = y$ $\log_4 1 = y$ $\log_4 4 = y$ $\log_5 1 = y$

$7^y = 2$ $4^y = 1$ $4^y = 4$ $5^y = 1$

$y \log_{10} 7 = \log_{10} 2$ $4^y = 4^0$ $2^{2y} = 2^2$ $5^y = 5^0$

$y = \log_{10} 2 / \log_{10} 7$ $y = 0$ $2y = 2$ $y = 0$

$y = 0.3010 / 0.8450$ $y = 1$

$y = 0.3562$

9; 2, 1, 4, 4; 5, 4; Deep calls unto Deep study bible 1

0.9208 0.4771; 0.3154, 0, 1, 0.4306 0.3010; 0 0.6020, 0.3562 0.3010;
Deep calls unto Deep study bible 2

x-axis	y-axis
9	1.3979
2	0.3154
1	0
4	1
4	0.7316
5	0.6020
4	0.6572

Water Spout *(lightning; combinatorics)* Study bible 1

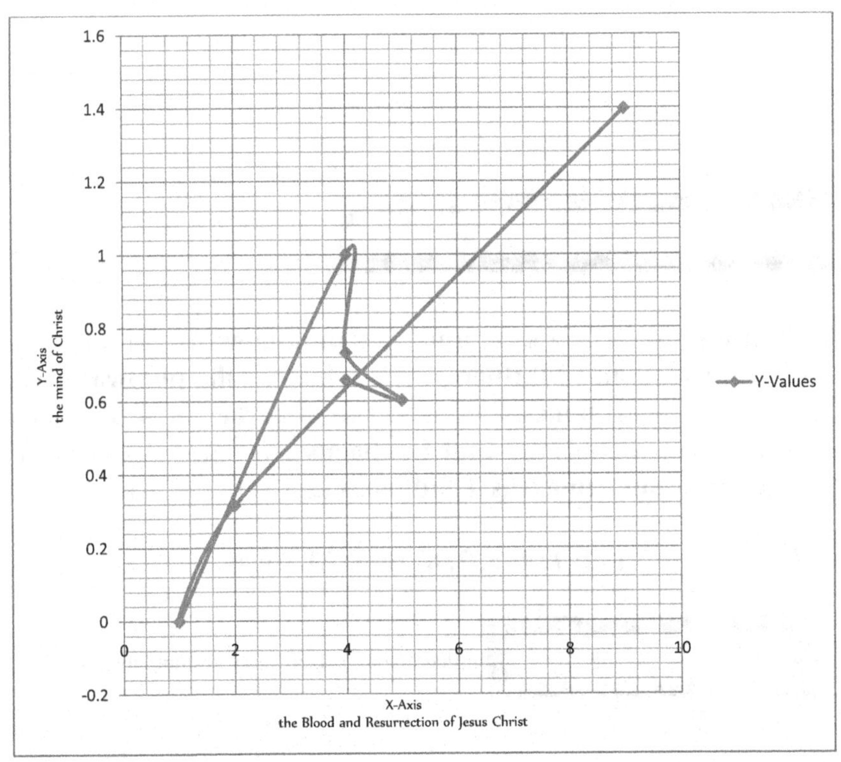

Water Spout *(lightning; combinatorics)* Study bible 2

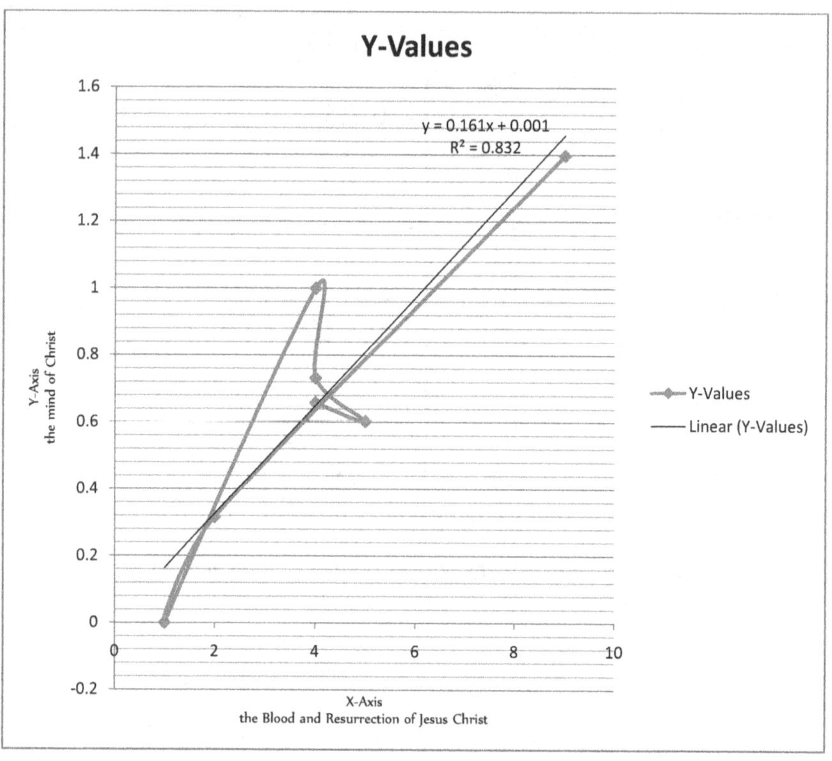

$7^{0.9208}\ 10^{0.4771};\ 9^{0.3154},\ 4^{0},\ 4^{1},\ 5^{0.4306}\ 10^{0.3010};\ 5^{0}\ 10^{0.6020},\ 7^{0.3562}\ 10^{0.3010};$	Pilled Poplar, Hazel, and Chestnut bible rods 2

3. Philipwarlike; a lover of horses, **and Bartholomew**a son that suspends the waters;**Thomas**a twin, **and Matthew**given; a reward; gift of God **the publican**one who farmed the taxes; a tax collector; **James**that supplants, undermines; the heel **the son of Alphaeus** changing; a thousand; learned; chief; leader, **and Lebbaeus** a man of heart; praising; confessing; courageous, **whose surname was Thaddaeus** breast; that praises or confesses;

1, 2; 1, 4; 5, 2, 4; Bible Matrices

$1_{5},\ 2_{6};\ 1_{2},\ 2_{6}\ 2_{8};\ 1_{5}\ 4_{6},\ 2_{7},\ 4_{5};$	Pilled Poplar, Hazel, and Chestnut bible rods 1

$\text{Log}_8 2 = y$	$\log_6 2 = y$	$\log_6 4 = y$
$8^y = 2$	$6^y = 2$	$6^y = 4$
$y \log_{10} 8 = \log_{10} 2$	$y \log_{10} 6 = \log_{10} 2$	$y \log_{10} 6 = \log_{10} 4$
$y = \log_{10} 2 / \log_{10} 8$	$y = \log_{10} 2 / \log_{10} 6$	$y = \log_{10} 4 / \log_{10} 6$
$y = 0.3010 / 0.9030$	$y = 0.3010 / 0.7781$	$y = 0.6020 / 0.7781$
$y = 0.3333$	$y = 0.3868$	$y = 0.7736$

$\text{Log}_7 2 = y$	$\log_5 1 = y$	$\log_2 1 = y$	$\log_5 1 = y$
$7^y = 2$	$5^y = 1$	$2^y = 1$	$5^y = 1$
$y \log_{10} 7 = \log_{10} 2$	$5^y = 5^0$	$2^y = 2^0$	$5^y = 5^0$
$y = \log_{10} 2 / \log_{10} 7$	$y = 0$	$y = 0$	$y = 0$
$y = 0.3010 / 0.8450$			
$y = 0.3562$			

$\text{Log}_5 4 = y$	$\log_6 2 = y$
$5^y = 4$	$6^y = 2$
$y \log_{10} 5 = \log_{10} 4$	$y \log_{10} 6 = \log_{10} 2$
$y = \log_{10} 4 / \log_{10} 5$	$y = \log_{10} 2 / \log_{10} 6$
$y = 0.6020 / 0.6989$	$y = 0.3010 / 0.7781$
$y = 0.8613$	$y = 0.3868$

1, 2; 1, 4; 5, 2, 4; Deep calls unto Deep study bible 1

0, 0.3868; 0, 0.3868 0.3333; 0 0.7736, 0.3562, 0.8613;
Deep calls unto Deep study bible 2

x-axis	y-axis
1	0
2	0.3868
1	0
4	0.7201
5	0.7736
2	0.3562
4	0.8613

Water Spout *(lightning; combinatorics)* Study bible 1

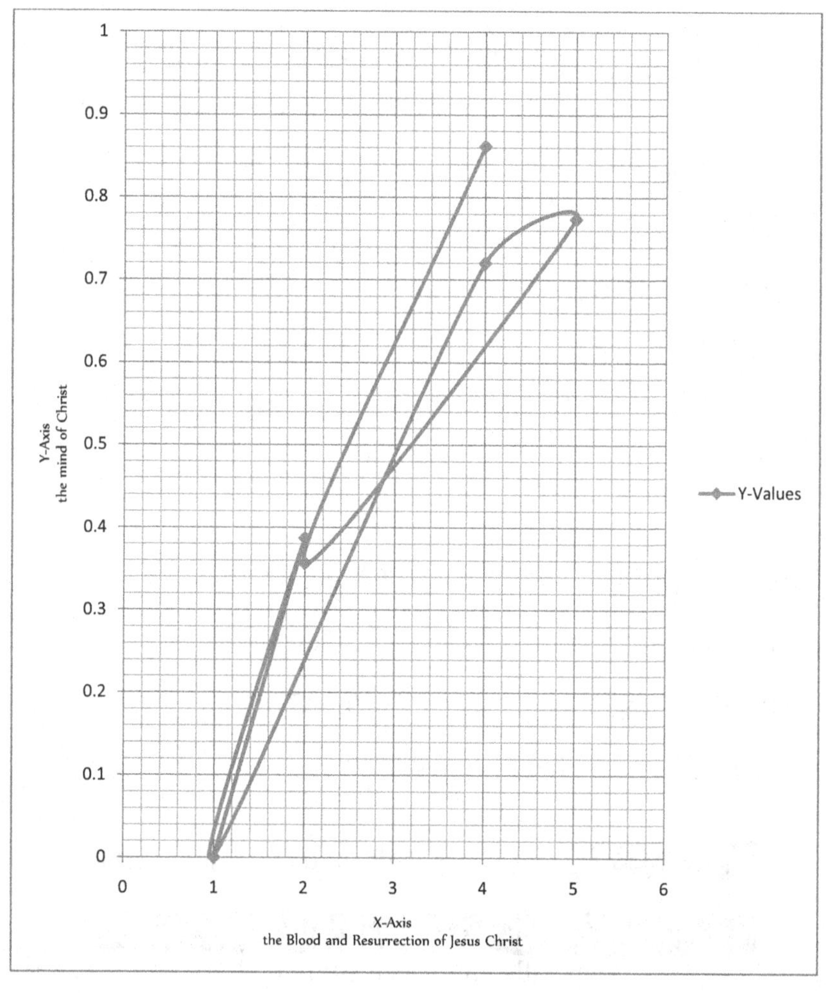

Water Spout *(lightning; combinatorics)* Study bible 2

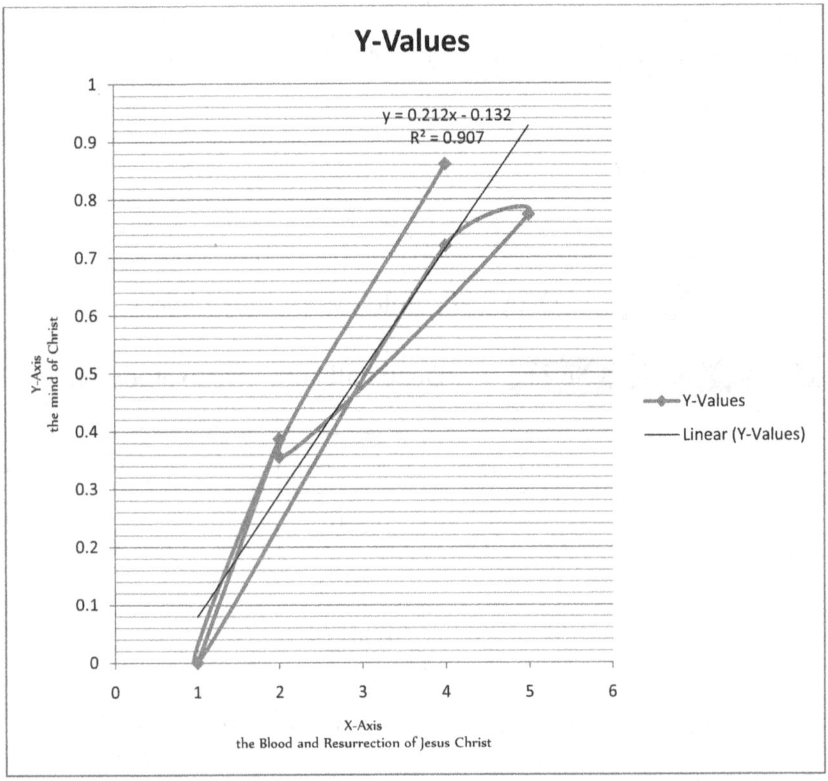

Y-Values

$y = 0.212x - 0.132$
$R^2 = 0.907$

Y-Axis
the mind of Christ

X-Axis
the Blood and Resurrection of Jesus Christ

Y-Values
Linear (Y-Values)

$5^0, 6^{0.3868}; 2^0, 6^{0.3868}\ 8^{0.3333}; 5^0\ 6^{0.7736}, 7^{0.3562}, 5^{0.8613};$ Pilled Poplar, Hazel, and Chestnut bible rods 2

4. Simonthat hears; that obeys **the Canaanite, and Judas Iscariot** a man of murder; a hireling, **who also betrayed him.**

3, 3, 4. Bible Matrices

$\text{Log}_{10} 2 = 0.3010$ $\text{Log}_{10} 4 = 0.6020$

$\log_6 3 = y$

$6^y = 3$

$y \log_{10} 6 = \log_{10} 3$

$y = \log_{10} 3 / \log_{10} 6$

$y = 0.4771 / 0.7781$

$y = 0.6131$

$\log_4 1 = y$

$4^y = 1$

$4^y = 4^0$

$y = 0$

3, 3, 4. Deep calls unto Deep study bible 1

0 0.3010, 0.6131, 0.6020. Deep calls unto Deep study bible 2

x-axis	y-axis
3	0.3010
3	0.6131
4	0.6020

Water Spout *(lightning; combinatorics)* Study bible 1

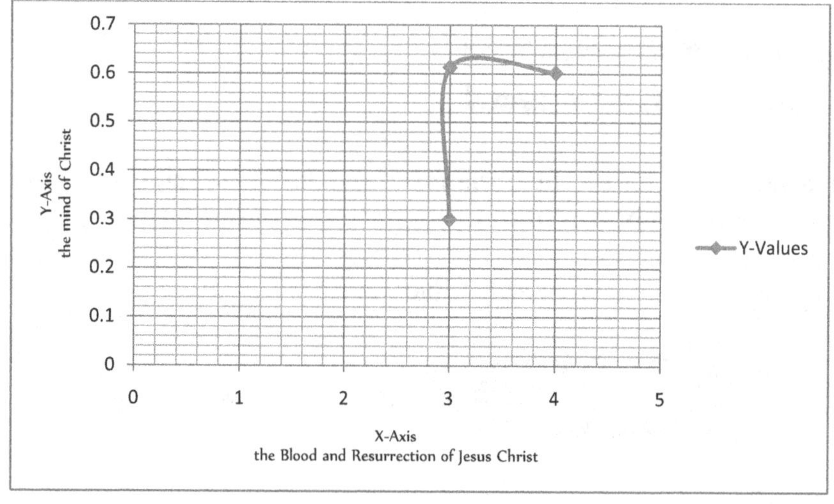

Water Spout *(lightning; combinatorics)* Study bible 2

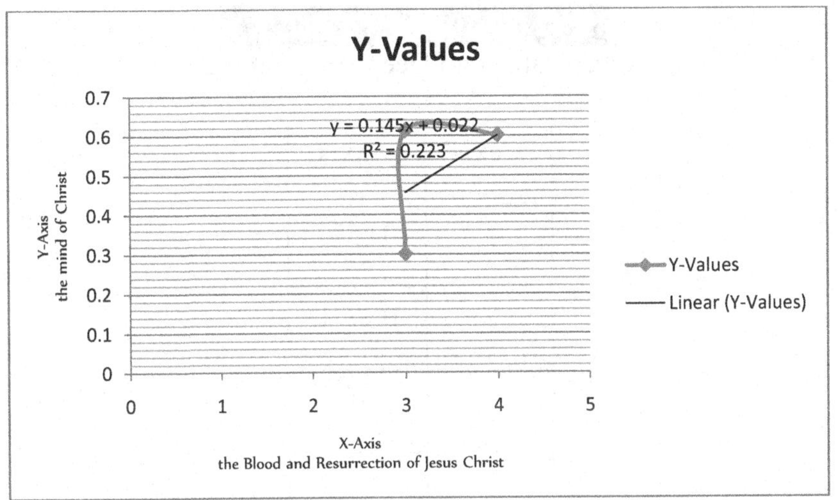

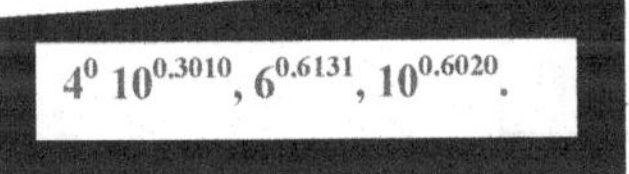
4^0 $10^{0.3010}$, $6^{0.6131}$, $10^{0.6020}$.

Pilled Poplar, Hazel, and Chestnut bible rods 2

5. These twelve dominion or divine government; 2 x 2 x 3 **Jesus**savior; deliverer **sent forth, and commanded them, saying, Go not into the way of the Gentiles** non--jews, **and into any city of the Samaritans enter ye not:**

5, 3, 1, 8, 10: Bible Matrices

$2_7 1_2\ 2_{10}, 3_{10}, 1_{10}, 8_2, 10_{10}$:

Pilled Poplar, Hazel, and Chestnut bible rods 1

$\text{Log}_{10} 10 = 1$ $\text{Log}_{10} 3 = 0.4771$ $\text{Log}_{10} 2 = 0.3010$

$\text{Log}_7 2 = y$ $\log_{10} 1 = y$ $\log_2 1 = y$ $\log_2 8 = y$

$7^y = 2$ $10^y = 1$ $2^y = 1$ $2^y = 8$

$y \log_{10} 7 = \log_{10} 2$ $10^y = 10^0$ $2^y = 2^0$ $2^y = 2^3$

$y = \log_{10} 2 / \log_{10} 7$ $y = 0$ $y = 0$ $y = 3$

$y = 0.3010 / 0.8450$

$y = 0.3562$

5, 3, 1, 8, 10: Deep calls unto Deep study bible 1

0.3562 0 0.3010, 0.4771, 0, 3, 1:
Deep calls unto Deep study bible 2

x-axis	y-axis
5	0.6572
3	0.4771
1	0
8	3
10	1

Water Spout *(lightning; combinatorics)* Study bible 1

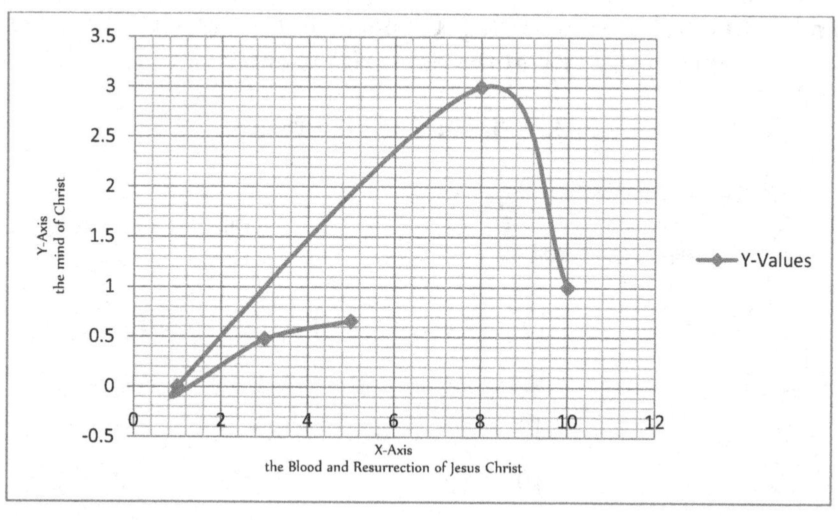

Water Spout *(lightning; combinatorics)* Study bible 2

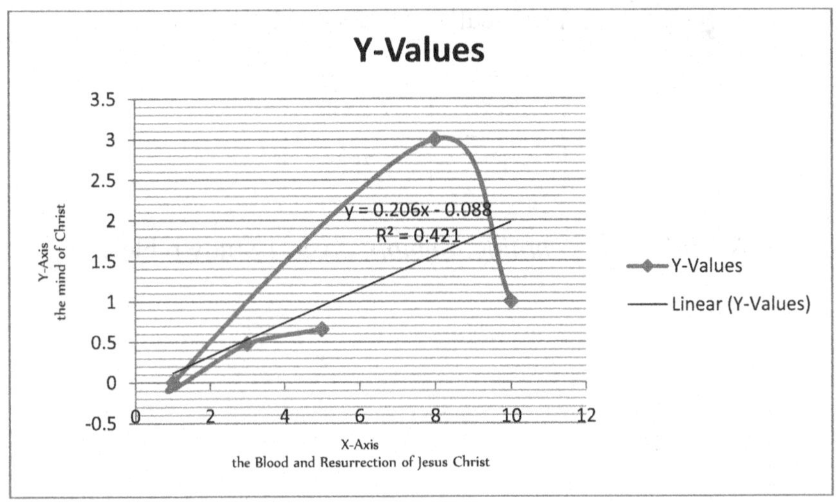

Pilled Poplar, Hazel, and Chestnut bible rods 2

6. But go rather to the lost sheep of the house of Israel who prevails with God; God strives.

12. Bible Matrices

Pilled Poplar, Hazel, and Chestnut bible rods 1

$\text{Log}_6\, 12 = y$

$6^y = 12$

$y \log_{10} 6 = \log_{10} 12$

$y = \log_{10} 12 / \log_{10} 6$

$y = 1.0791 / 0.7781$

$y = 1.3868$

12. Deep calls unto Deep study bible 1

1.3868 Deep calls unto Deep study bible 2

x-axis	y-axis
12	1.3868

Water Spout *(lightning; combinatorics)* Study bible 1

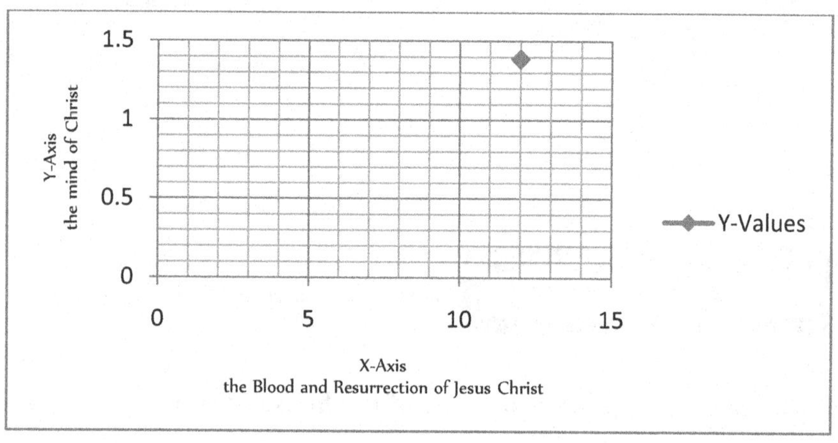

Water Spout *(lightning; combinatorics)* Study bible 2

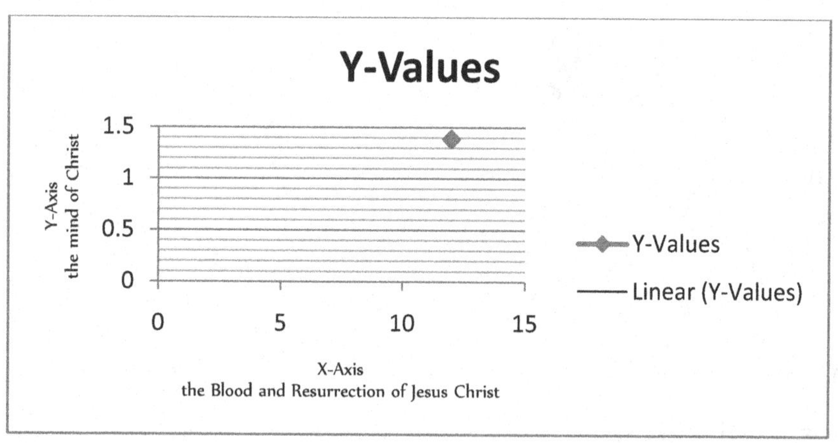

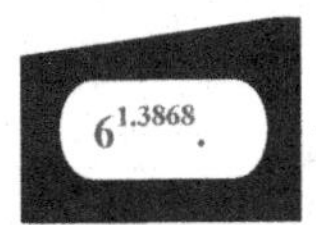

Pilled Poplar, Hazel, and Chestnut bible rods 2

7. And as ye go, preach, saying, The kingdom of heaven is at hand.

4, 1, 1, 7. Bible Matrices

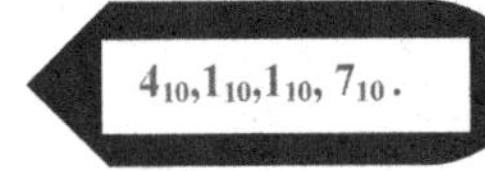

Pilled Poplar, Hazel, and Chestnut bible rods 1

$\text{Log}_{10} 4 = 0.6020$

$\log_{10} 1 = y$

$10^y = 1$

$10^y = 10^0$

$y = 0$

$\text{Log}_{10} 7 = 0.8450$

$\log_{10} 1 = y$

$10^y = 1$

$10^y = 10^0$

$y = 0$

4, 1, 1, 7. Deep calls unto Deep study bible 1

0.6020, 0, 0, 0.8450. Deep calls unto Deep study bible 2

x-axis	y-axis
4	0.6020
1	0
1	0
7	0.8450

Water Spout *(lightning; combinatorics)* Study bible 1

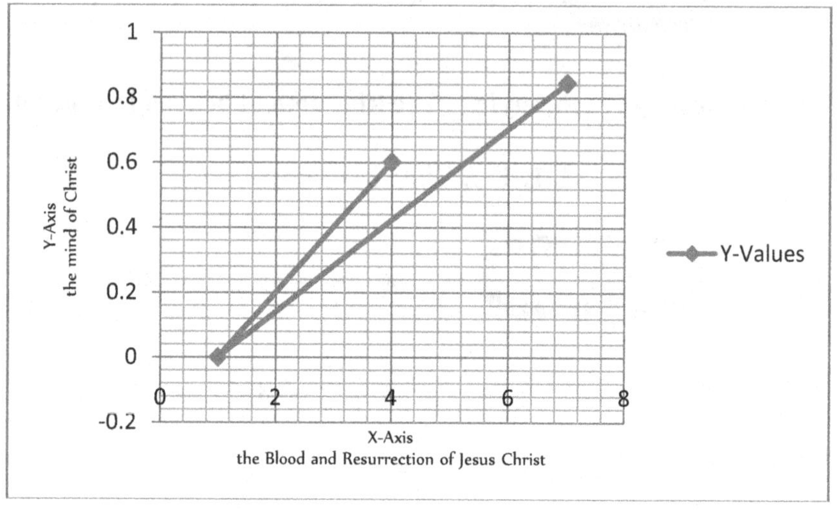

Water Spout *(lightning; combinatorics)* Study bible 2

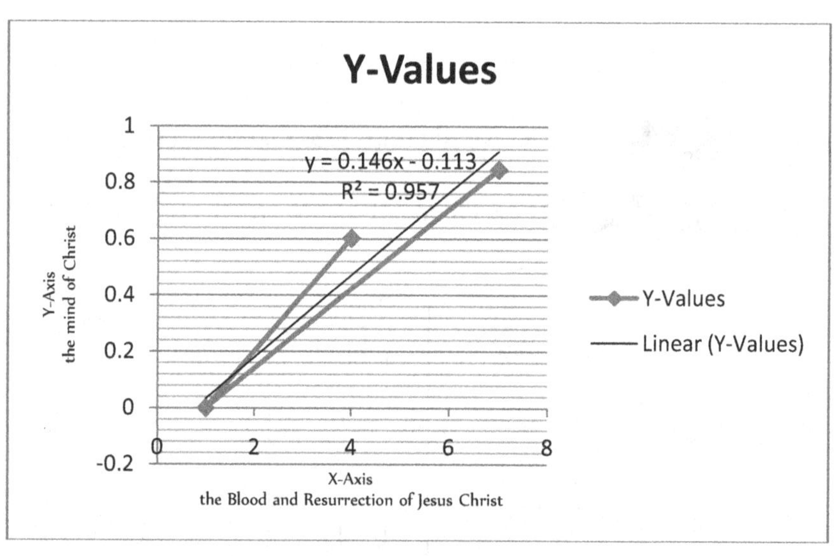

$10^{0.6020}, 10^{0}, 10^{0}, 10^{0.8450}$. Pilled Poplar, Hazel, and Chestnut bible rods 2

8. Heal the sick, cleanse the lepers, raise the dead, cast out devils slanderers; false accusers : **freely ye have received, freely give.**

3, 3, 3, 3: 4, 2. Bible Matrices

$3_{10}, 3_{10}, 3_{10}, 3_{3}: 4_{10}, 2_{10}.$ Pilled Poplar, Hazel, and Chestnut bible rods 1

$\text{Log}_{10} 3 = 0.4771$ $\text{Log}_{10} 4 = 0.6020$ $\text{Log}_{10} 2 = 0.3010$ $\text{Log}_{10} 3 = 0.4771$ $\text{Log}_{10} 3 = 0.4771$

$\log_{3} 3 = y$

$3^{y} = 3$

$3^{y} = 3^{1}$

$y = 1$

3, 3, 3, 3: 4, 2. Deep calls unto Deep study bible 1

0.4771, 0.4771, 0.4771, 1: 0.6020, 0.3010.
Deep calls unto Deep study bible 2

x-axis	y-axis
3	0.4771
3	0.4771
3	0.4771
3	1
4	0.6020
2	0.3010

Water Spout *(lightning; combinatorics)* Study bible 1

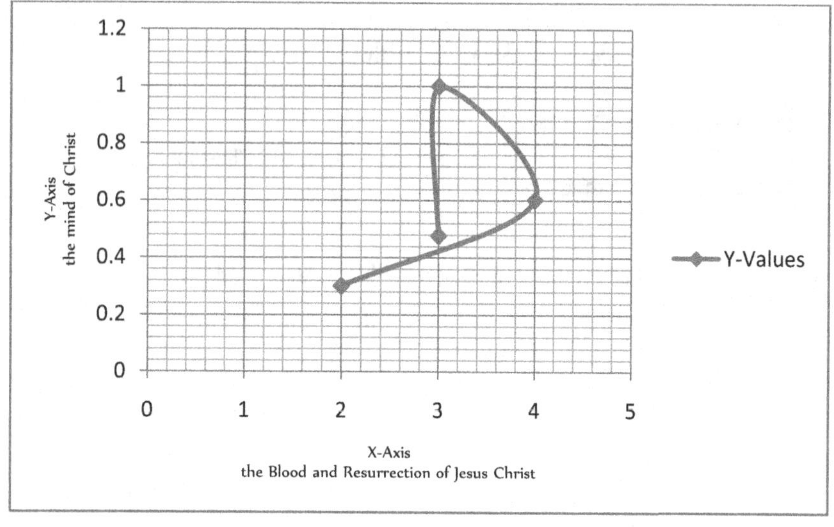

Water Spout *(lightning; combinatorics)* Study bible 2

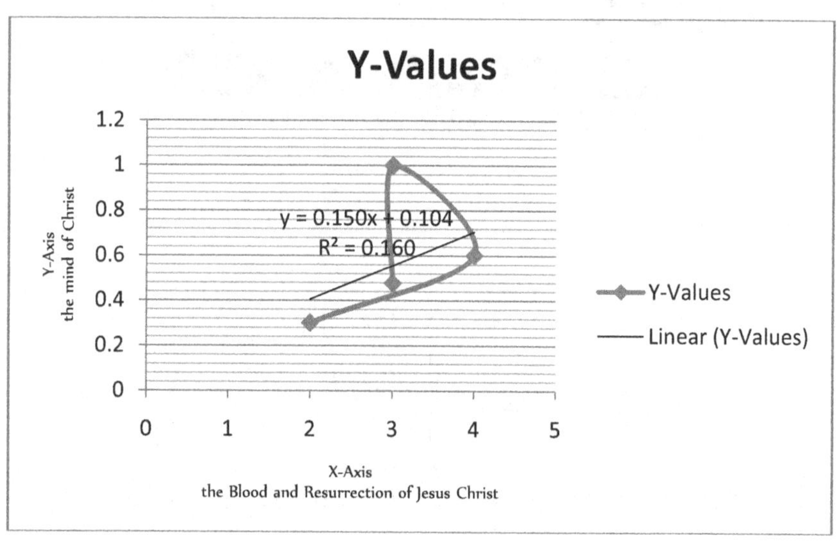

$10^{0.4771}$, $10^{0.4771}$, $10^{0.4771}$, 3^1: $10^{0.6020}$, $10^{0.3010}$.

Pilled Poplar, Hazel, and Chestnut bible rods 2

9. Provide neither gold, nor silver, nor brass in your purses,

3, 2, 5, Bible Matrices

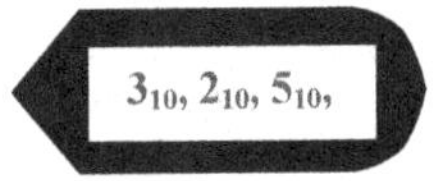

Pilled Poplar, Hazel, and Chestnut bible rods 1

$\text{Log}_{10} 3 = 0.4771$ $\text{Log}_{10} 2 = 0.3010$ $\text{Log}_{10} 5 = 0.6989$

3, 2, 5, Deep calls unto Deep study bible 1

0.4771, 0.3010, 0.6989, Deep calls unto Deep study bible 2

x-axis	y-axis
3	0.4771
2	0.3010
5	0.6989

Water Spout *(lightning; combinatorics)* Study bible 1

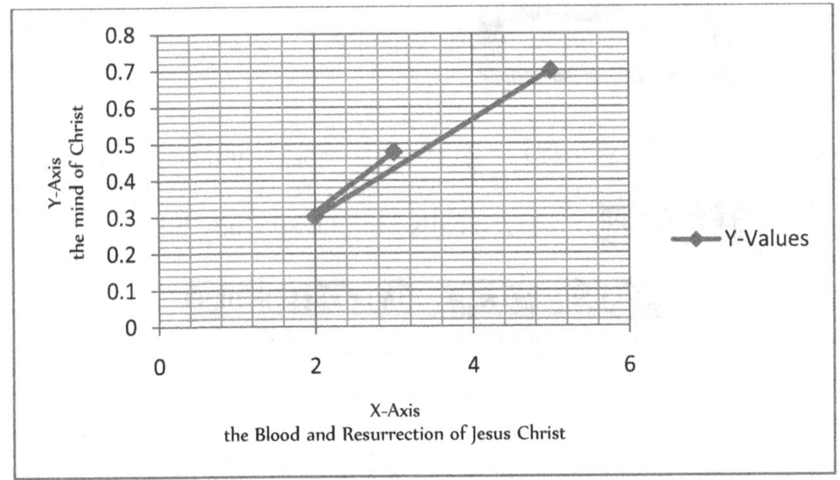

Water Spout *(lightning; combinatorics)* Study bible 2

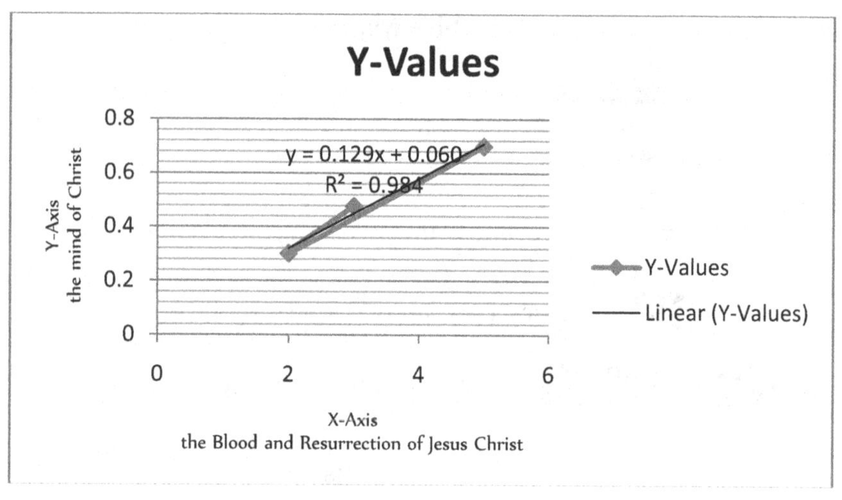

$10^{0.4771}$, $10^{0.3010}$, $10^{0.6989}$, Pilled Poplar, Hazel, and Chestnut bible rods 2

10. Nor scrip for your journey, neither two coats, neither shoes, nor yet staves: for the workman is worthy of his meat.

5, 3, 2, 3: 8. Bible Matrices

5_{10}, 3_{10}, 2_{10}, 3_{10}: 8_{10}. Pilled Poplar, Hazel, and Chestnut bible rods 1

$\text{Log}_{10} 8 = 0.9030$ $\text{Log}_{10} 5 = 0.6989$ $\text{Log}_{10} 3 = 0.4771$ $\text{Log}_{10} 3 = 0.4771$ $\text{Log}_{10} 2 = 0.3010$

5, 3, 2, 3: 8. Deep calls unto Deep study bible 1

0.6989, 0.4771, 0.3010, 0.4771: 0.9030.
Deep calls unto Deep study bible 2

x-axis	y-axis
5	0.6989

3	0.4771
2	0.3010
3	0.4771
8	0.9030

Water Spout *(lightning; combinatorics)* Study bible 1

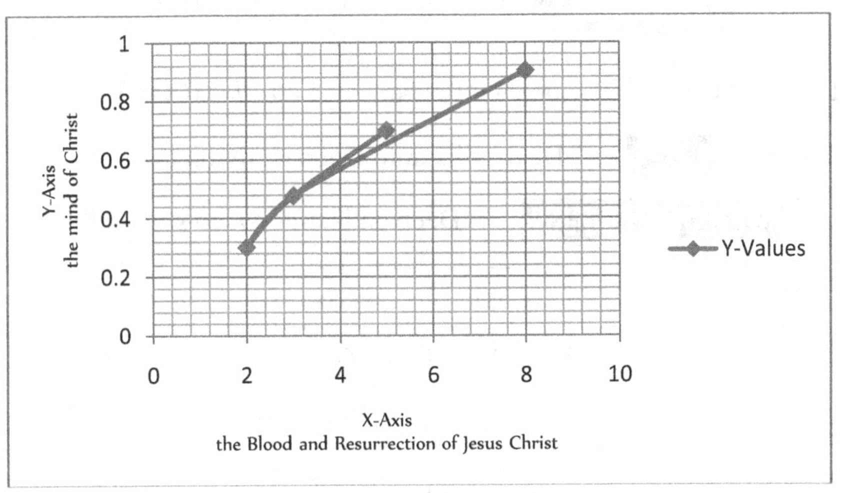

Water Spout *(lightning; combinatorics)* Study bible 2

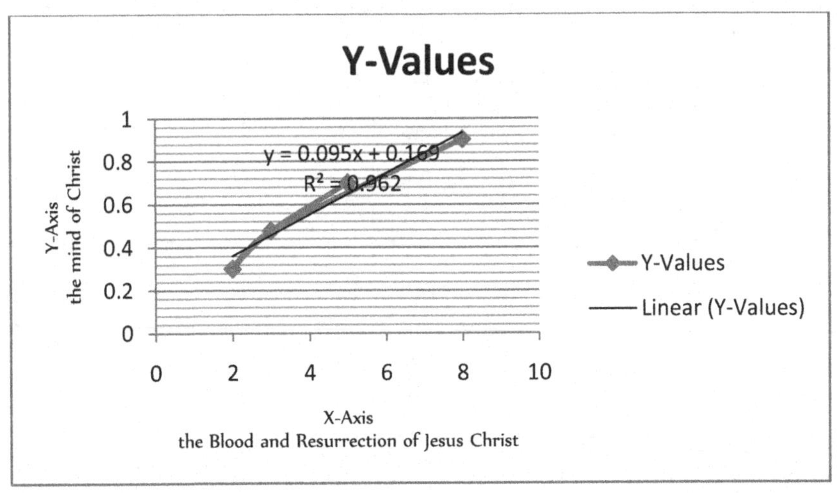

Pilled Poplar, Hazel, and Chestnut bible rods 2

11. And into whatsoever city or town ye shall enter, enquire who in it is worthy; and there abide till ye go thence.

9, 6; 7. Bible Matrices

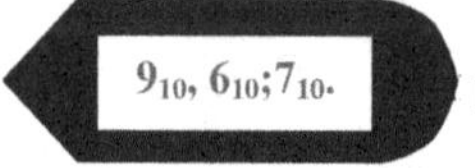

Pilled Poplar, Hazel, and Chestnut bible rods 1

$\text{Log}_{10} 6 = 0.7781$ $\text{Log}_{10} 9 = 0.9542$ $\text{Log}_{10} 7 = 0.8450$

9, 6; 7. Deep calls unto Deep study bible 1

0.9542, 0.7781; 0.8450. Deep calls unto Deep study bible 2

x-axis	y-axis
9	0.9542
6	0.7781
7	0.8450

Water Spout *(lightning; combinatorics)* Study bible 1

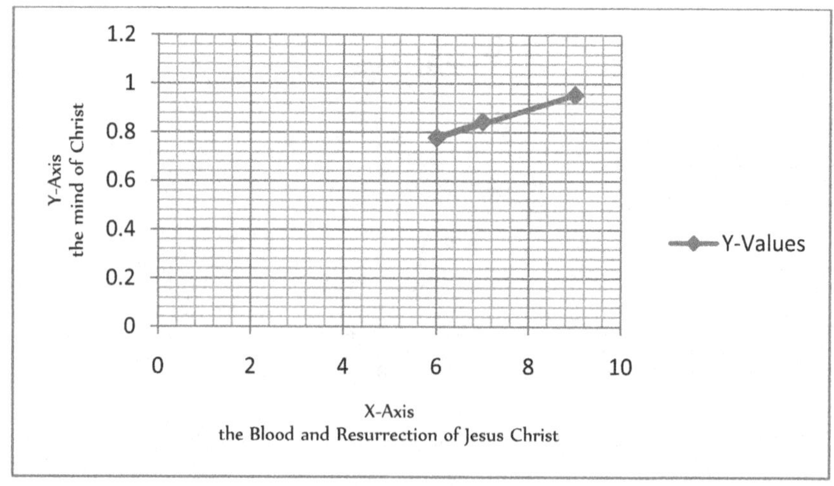

Water Spout *(lightning; combinatorics)* Study bible 2

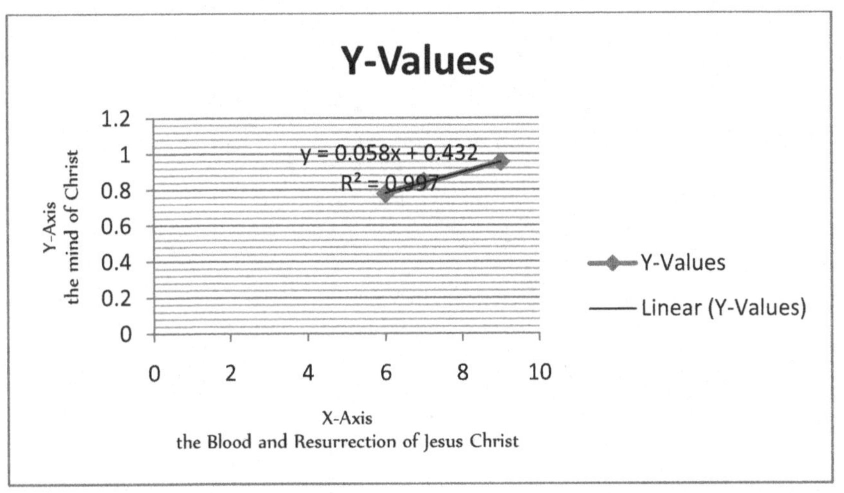

Pilled Poplar, Hazel, and Chestnut bible rods 2

12. And when ye come into an house, salute it.

7, 2. Bible Matrices

$\text{Log}_{10} 7 = 0.8450$ $\text{Log}_{10} 2 = 0.3010$

7, 2. Deep calls unto Deep study bible 1

0.8450, 0.3010. Deep calls unto Deep study bible 2

x-axis	y-axis
7	0.8450
2	0.3010

Water Spout *(lightning; combinatorics)* Study bible 1

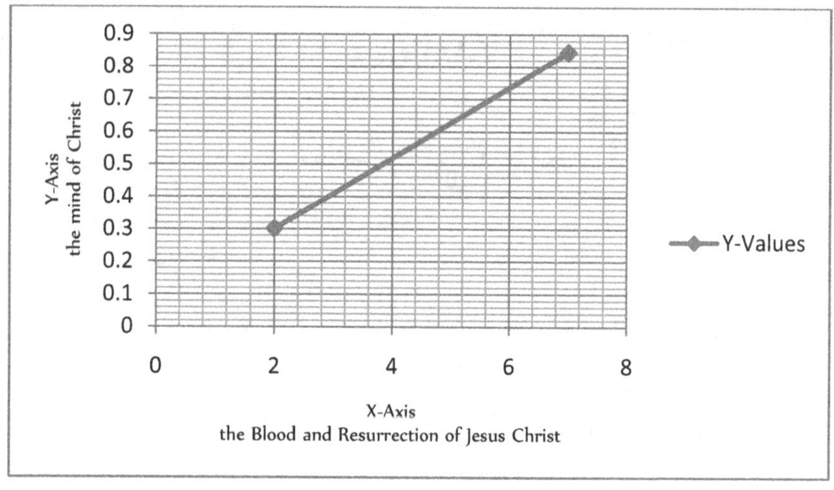

Water Spout *(lightning; combinatorics)* Study bible 2

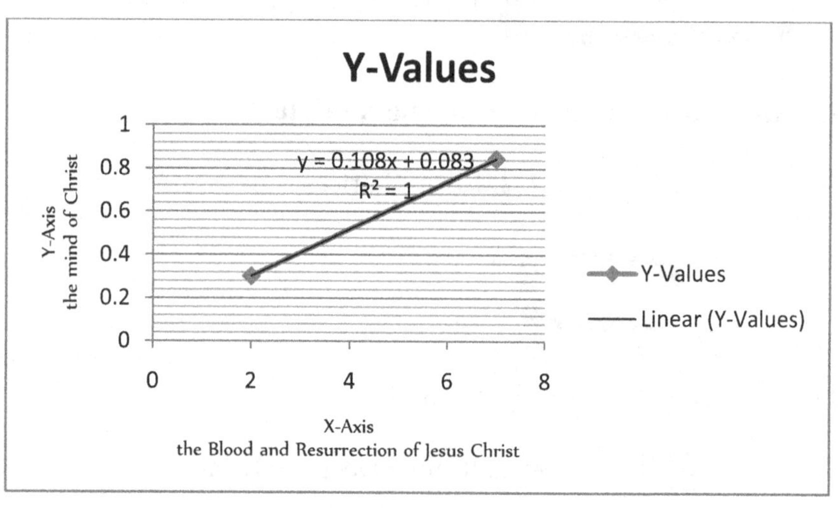

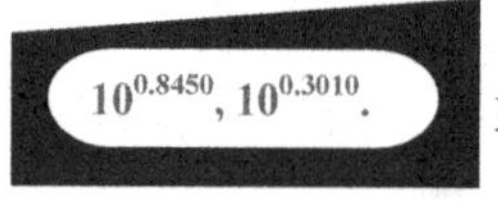

Pilled Poplar, Hazel, and Chestnut bible rods 2

13. And if the house be worthy, let your peace come upon it: but if it be not worthy, let your peace return to you.

6, 6: 6, 6. Bible Matrices

$6_{10}, 6_{10}: 6_{10}, 6_{10}.$ Pilled Poplar, Hazel, and Chestnut bible rods 1

$\text{Log}_{10} 6 = 0.7781 \quad \text{Log}_{10} 6 = 0.7781 \quad \text{Log}_{10} 6 = 0.7781 \quad \text{Log}_{10} 6 = 0.7781$

6, 6: 6, 6. Deep calls unto Deep study bible 1

0.7781, 0.7781: 0.7781, 0.7781.
Deep calls unto Deep study bible 2

x-axis	y-axis
6	0.7781
6	0.7781
6	0.7781
6	0.7781

Water Spout *(lightning; combinatorics)* Study bible 1

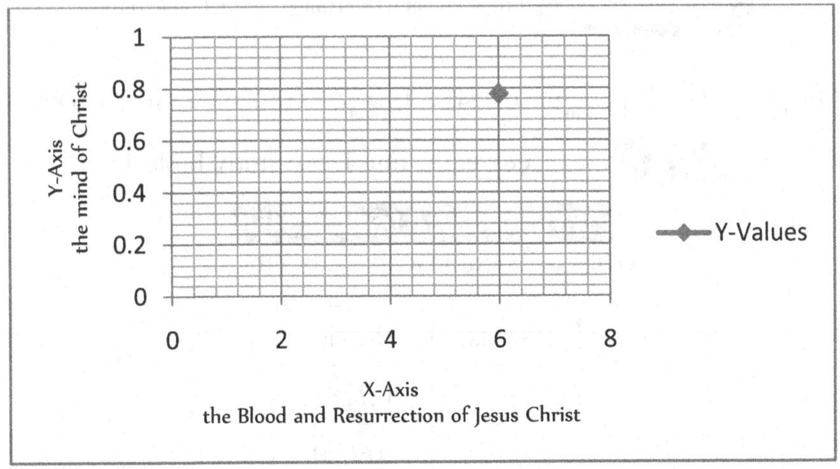

Water Spout *(lightning; combinatorics)* Study bible 2

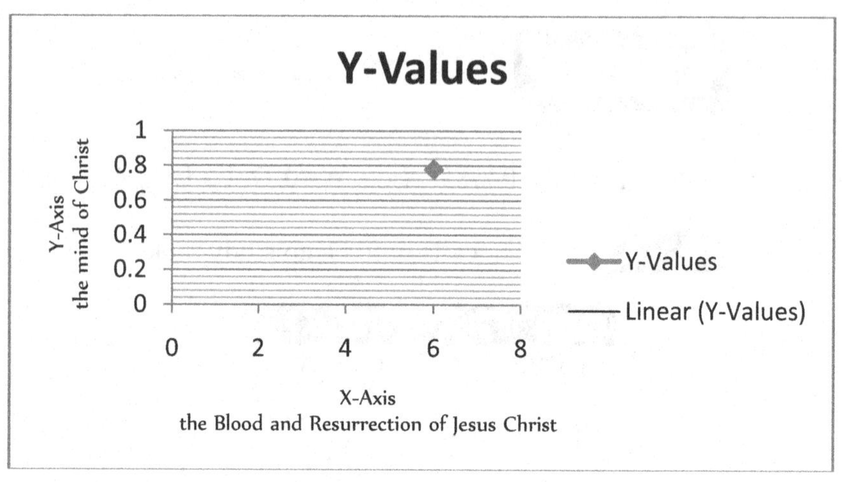

$10^{0.7781}, 10^{0.7781}: 10^{0.7781}, 10^{0.7781}.$

Pilled Poplar, Hazel, and Chestnut bible rods 2

14. And whosoever shall not receive you, nor hear your words, when ye depart out of that house or city, shake off the dust of your feet.

6, 4, 9, 7. Bible Matrices

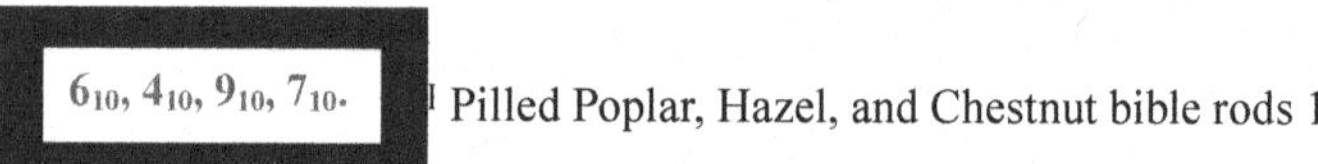
$6_{10}, 4_{10}, 9_{10}, 7_{10}.$

Pilled Poplar, Hazel, and Chestnut bible rods 1

$\text{Log}_{10} 6 = 0.7781 \quad \text{Log}_{10} 9 = 0.9542 \quad \text{Log}_{10} 4 = 0.6020 \quad \text{Log}_{10} 7 = 0.8450$

6, 4, 9, 7. Deep calls unto Deep study bible 1

0.7781, 0.6020, 0.9542, 0.8450.

Deep calls unto Deep study bible 2

x-axis	y-axis
6	0.7781
4	0.6020

9	0.9542
7	0.8450

Water Spout *(lightning; combinatorics)* Study bible 1

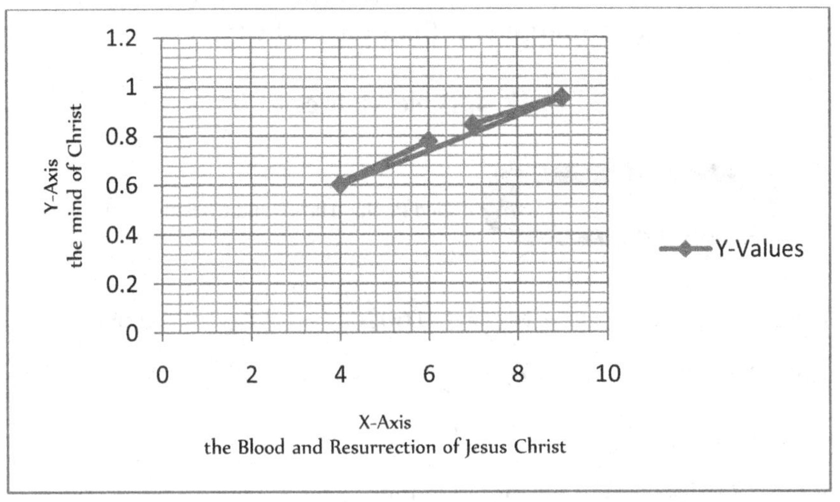

Water Spout *(lightning; combinatorics)* Study bible 2

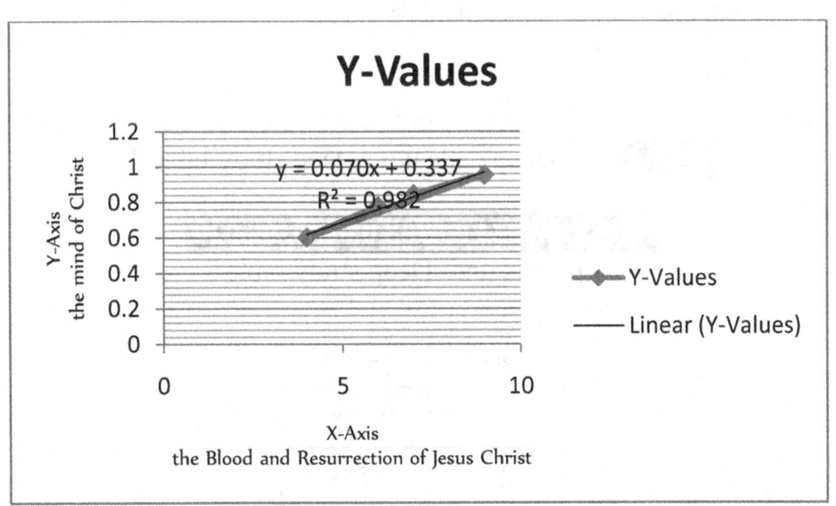

$10^{0.7781}$, $10^{0.6020}$, $10^{0.9542}$, $10^{0.8450}$. Pilled Poplar, Hazel, and Chestnut bible rods 2

15. Verily I say unto you, It shall be more tolerable for the land of Sodomtheir secret; their cement; burning; the walled**and Gomorrha**rebellious people; submersion**in the day of judgment, than for that city.**

5, 17, 4. Bible Matrices

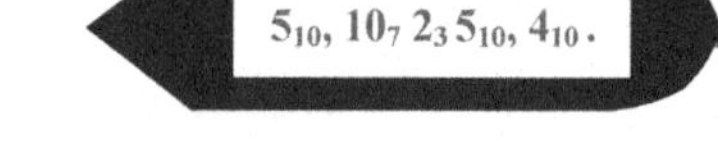

Pilled Poplar, Hazel, and Chestnut bible rods 1

$\text{Log}_{10} 5 = 0.6989$ $\quad$ $\text{Log}_{10} 4 = 0.6020$ $\quad$ $\text{Log}_{10} 5 = 0.6989$

$\text{Log}_{7} 10 = y$ $\quad$ $\log_3 2 = y$

$7^y = 10$ $\quad$ $3^y = 2$

$y \log_{10} 7 = \log_{10} 10$ $\quad$ $y \log_{10} 3 = \log_{10} 2$

$y = \log_{10} 10 / \log_{10} 7$ $\quad$ $y = \log_{10} 2 / \log_{10} 3$

$y = 1 / 0.8450$ $\quad$ $y = 0.3010/ 0.4771$

$y = 1.1834$ $\quad$ $y = 0.6308$

5, 17, 4. Deep calls unto Deep study bible 1

0.6989, 1.1834 0.6308 0.6989, 0.6020.

Deep calls unto Deep study bible 2

x-axis	y-axis
5	0.6989
17	2.5131
4	0.6020

Water Spout *(lightning; combinatorics)* Study bible 1

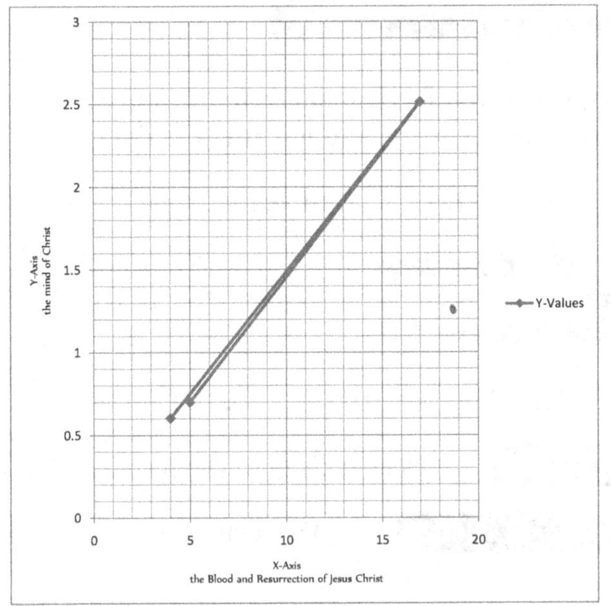

Water Spout *(lightning; combinatorics)* Study bible 2

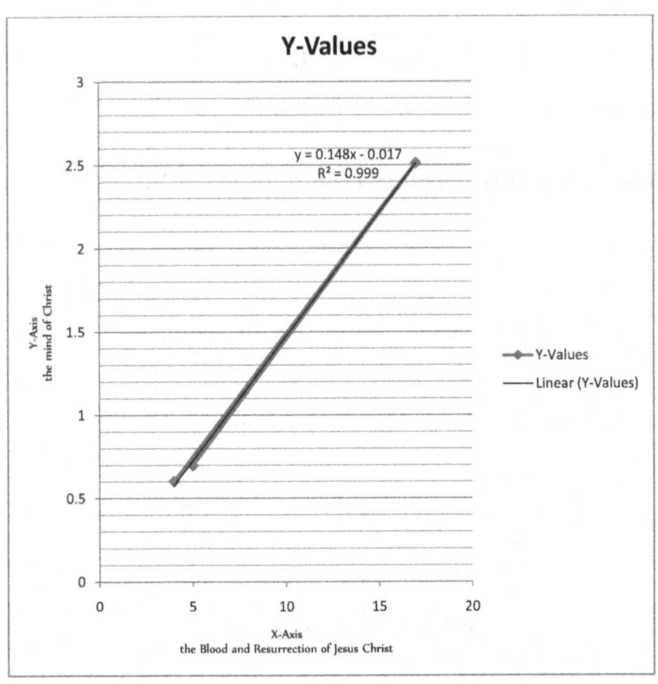

$10^{0.6989}, 7^{1.1834}\ 3^{0.6308}\ 10^{0.6989}, 10^{0.6020}.$

Pilled Poplar, Hazel, and Chestnut bible rods 2

16. Behold, I send you forth as sheep in the midst of wolves: be ye therefore wise as serpents, and harmless as doves.

1, 11: 6, 4. Bible Matrices

$1_{10}, 11_{10}: 6_{10}, 4_{10}.$

Pilled Poplar, Hazel, and Chestnut bible rods 1

$\text{Log}_{10} 6 = 0.7781 \quad \text{Log}_{10} 4 = 0.6020 \quad \text{Log}_{10} 11 = 1.0413 \quad \text{Log}_{10} 1 = 0$

1, 11: 6, 4. Deep calls unto Deep study bible 1

0, 1.0413: 0.7781, 0.6020. Deep calls unto Deep study bible 2

x-axis	y-axis
1	0
11	1.0413
6	0.7781
4	0.6020

Water Spout *(lightning; combinatorics)* Study bible 1

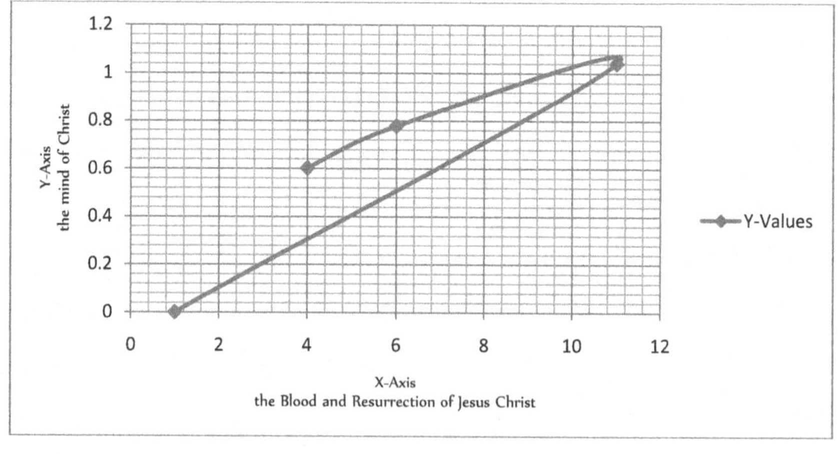

Water Spout *(lightning; combinatorics)* Study bible 2

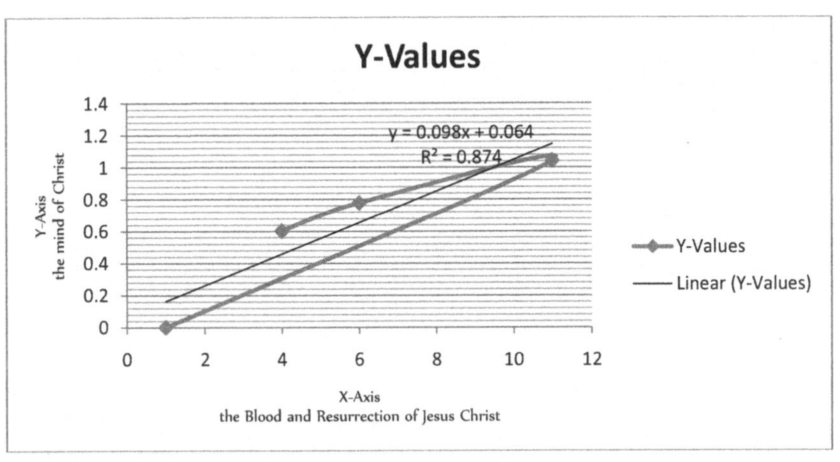

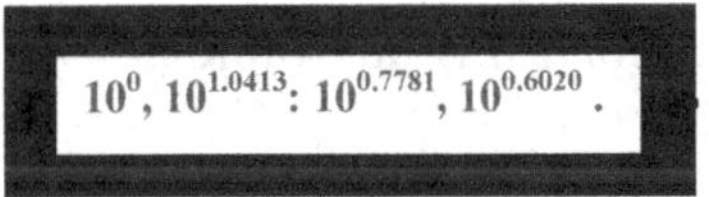

Pilled Poplar, Hazel, and Chestnut bible rods 2

17. But beware of men: for they will deliver you up to the councils, and they will scourge you in their synagogues;

4: 9, 8; Bible Matrices

Pilled Poplar, Hazel, and Chestnut bible rods 1

$\text{Log}_{10} 8 = 0.9030$ $\text{Log}_{10} 9 = 0.9542$ $\text{Log}_{10} 4 = 0.6020$

4: 9, 8; Deep calls unto Deep study bible 1

0.6020: 0.9542, 0.9030; Deep calls unto Deep study bible 2

x-axis	y-axis
4	0.6020
9	0.9542
8	0.9030

Water Spout *(lightning; combinatorics)* Study bible 1

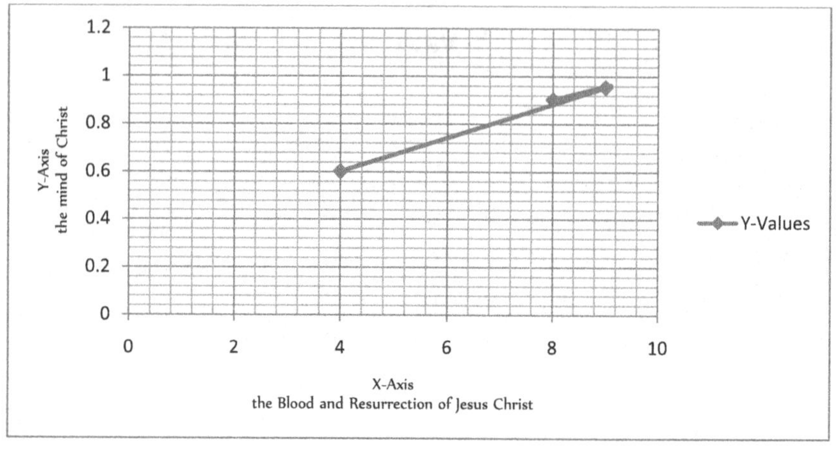

Water Spout *(lightning; combinatorics)* Study bible 2

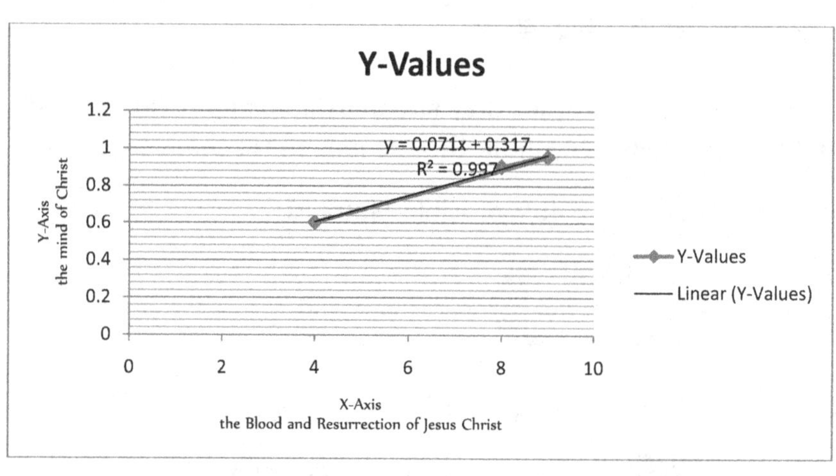

$10^{0.6020}$: $10^{0.9542}$, $10^{0.9030}$; Pilled Poplar, Hazel, and Chestnut bible rods 2

18. And ye shall be brought before governors and kings for my sake, for a testimony against them and the Gentiles non- jews.

12, 8. Bible Matrices

$\text{Log}_2 8 = y \quad \text{Log}_{10} 12 = 1.0791$

$2^y = 8$

$2^y = 2^3$

$y = 3$

12, 8. Deep calls unto Deep study bible 1

1.0791, 3. Deep calls unto Deep study bible 2

x-axis	y-axis
12	1.0791
8	3

Water Spout *(lightning; combinatorics)* Study bible 1

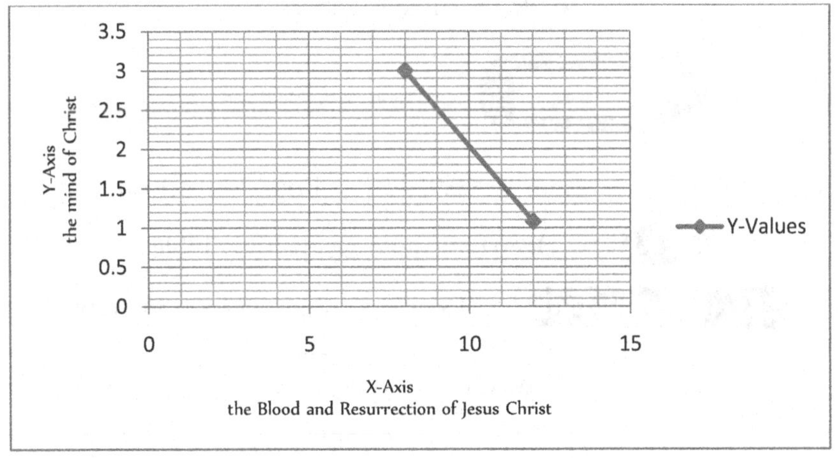

Water Spout *(lightning; combinatorics)* Study bible 2

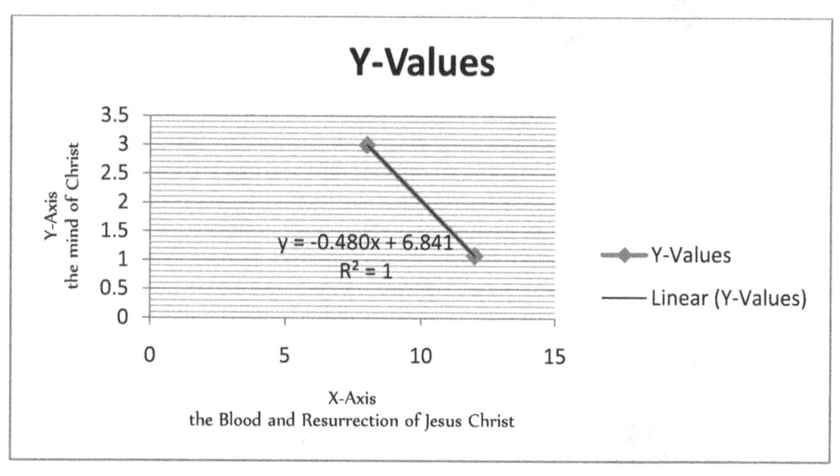

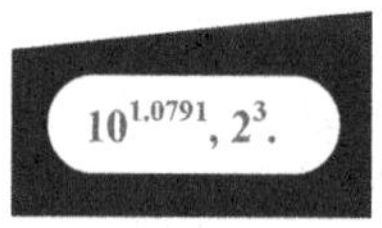

Pilled Poplar, Hazel, and Chestnut bible rods 2

19. But when they deliver you up, take no thought how or what ye shall speak: for it shall be given you in that same hour what ye shall speak.

6, 9: 14. Bible Matrices

$\text{Log}_{10} 6 = 0.7781$ $\text{Log}_{10} 9 = 0.9542$ $\text{Log}_{10} 14 = 1.1461$

6, 9: 14. Deep calls unto Deep study bible 1

0.7781, 0.9542: 1.1461. Deep calls unto Deep study bible 2

x-axis	y-axis
6	0.7781
9	0.9542
14	1.1461

Water Spout *(lightning; combinatorics)* Study bible 1

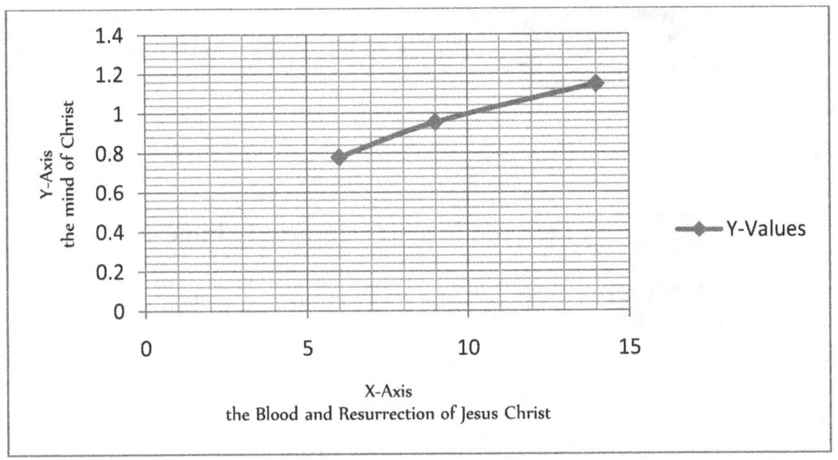

Water Spout *(lightning; combinatorics)* Study bible 2

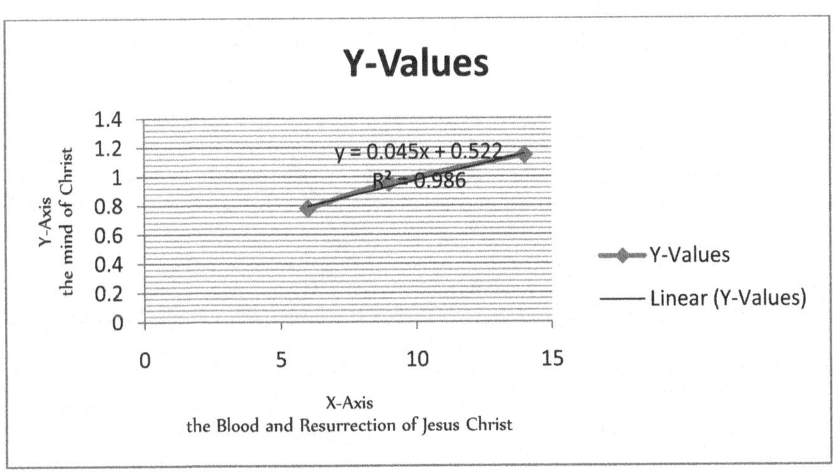

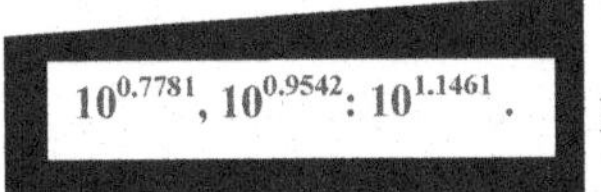

Pilled Poplar, Hazel, and Chestnut bible rods 2

20. For it is not ye that speak, but the Spirit of your Father which speaketh in you.

7, 10. Bible Matrices

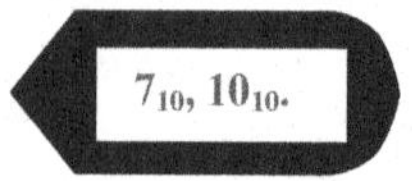

Pilled Poplar, Hazel, and Chestnut bible rods 1

$\text{Log}_{10} 7 = 0.8450$ $\text{Log}_{10} 10 = 1$

7, 10. Deep calls unto Deep study bible 1

0.8450, 1 Deep calls unto Deep study bible 2

x-axis	y-axis
7	0.8450
10	1

Water Spout *(lightning; combinatorics)* Study bible 1

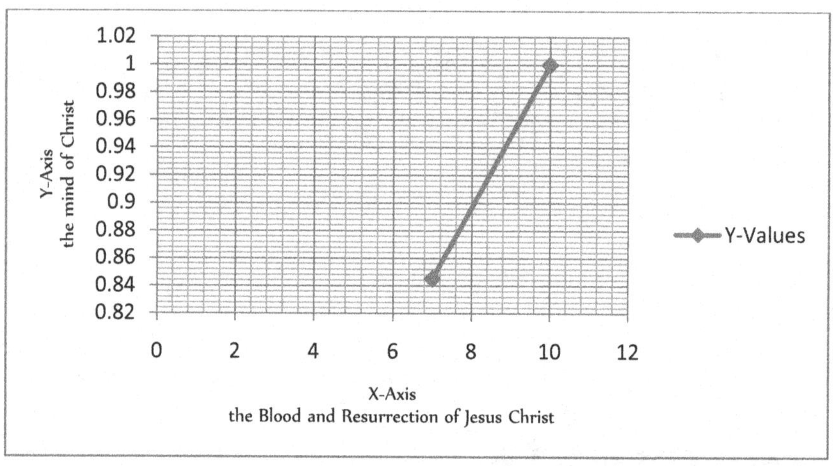

Water Spout *(lightning; combinatorics)* Study bible 2

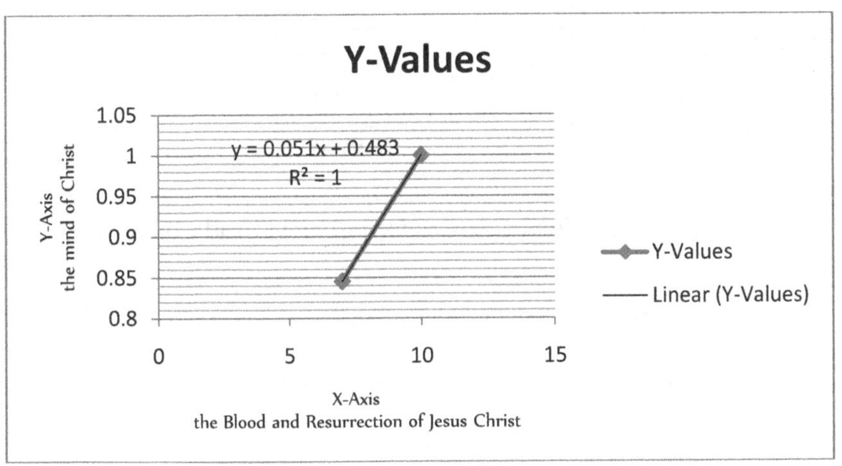

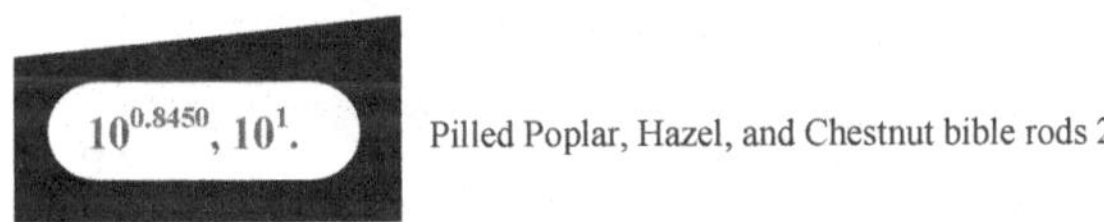

Pilled Poplar, Hazel, and Chestnut bible rods 2

21. And the brother shall deliver up the brother to death, and the father the child: and the children shall rise up against their parents, and cause them to be put to death.

10, 5: 9, 8. Bible Matrices

$10_{10}, 5_{10}: 9_{10}, 8_{10}$. Pilled Poplar, Hazel, and Chestnut bible rods 1

$\text{Log}_{10} 8 = 0.9030$ $\text{Log}_{10} 9 = 0.9542$ $\text{Log}_{10} 5 = 0.6989$ $\text{Log}_{10} 10 = 1$

10, 5: 9, 8. Deep calls unto Deep study bible 1

1, 0.6989: 0.9542, 0.9030. Deep calls unto Deep study bible 2

x-axis	y-axis
10	1
5	0.6989
9	0.9542
8	0.9030

Water Spout *(lightning; combinatorics)* Study bible 1

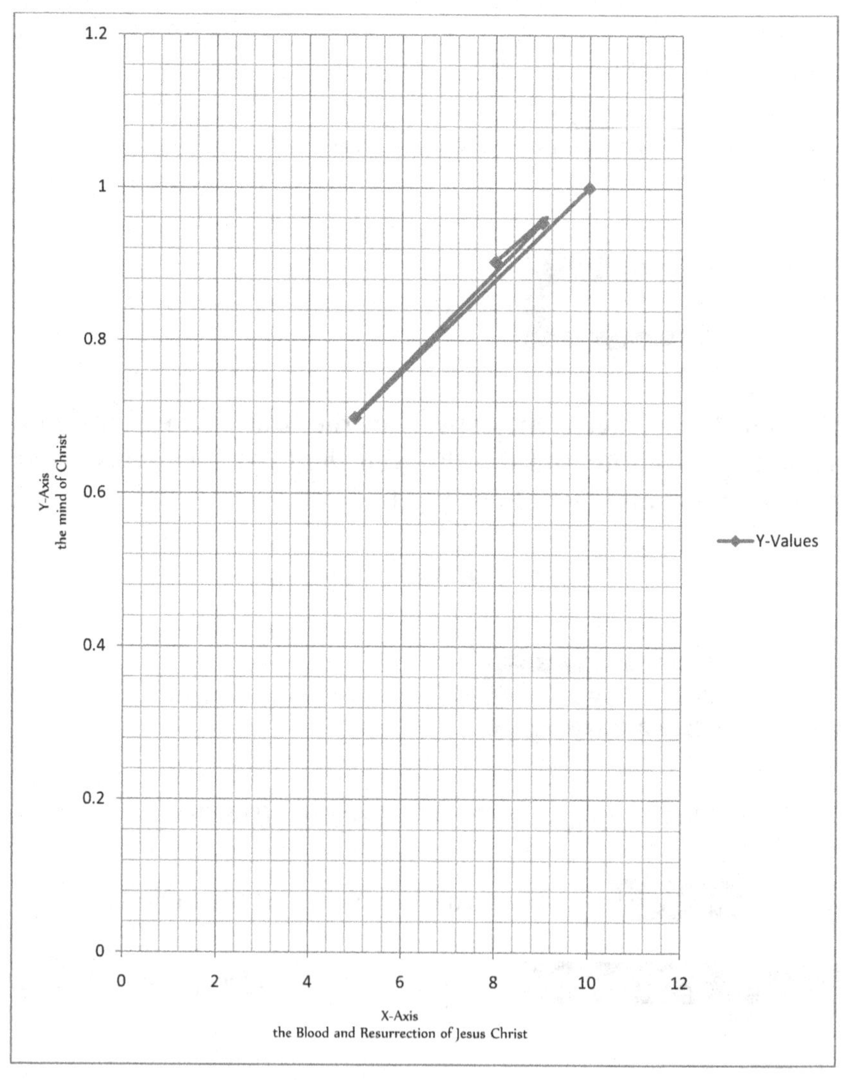

Water Spout *(lightning; combinatorics)* Study bible 2

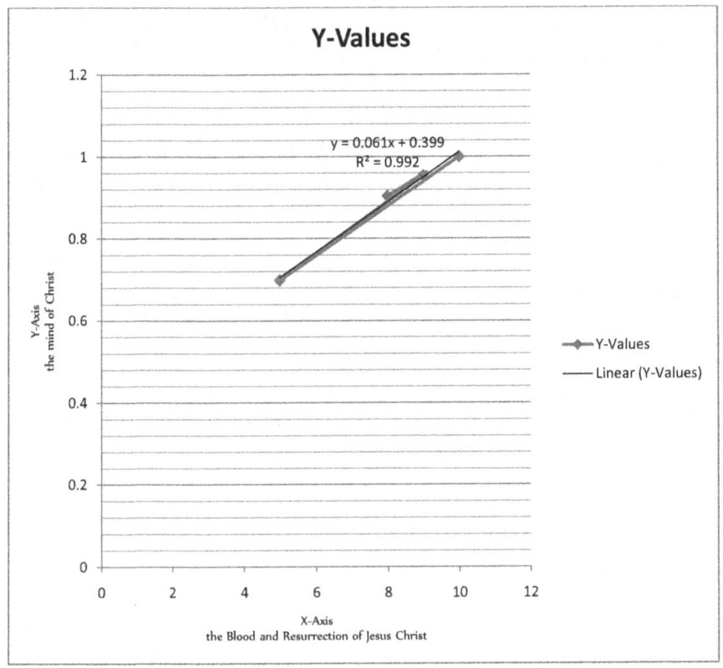

$10^1, 10^{0.6989}: 10^{0.9542}, 10^{0.9030}$.

Pilled Poplar, Hazel, and Chestnut bible rods 2

22. And ye shall be hated of all men for my name's sake: but he that endureth to the end shall be saved.

12: 10. Bible Matrices

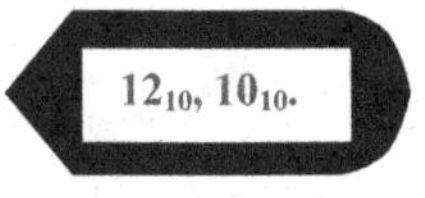
$12_{10}, 10_{10}$.

Pilled Poplar, Hazel, and Chestnut bible rods

$\text{Log}_{10}\ 12 = 1.0791$ $\text{Log}_{10}\ 10 = 1$

12: 10. Deep calls unto Deep study bible 1

1.0791, 1 Deep calls unto Deep study bible 2

x-axis	y-axis
12	1.0791
10	1

Water Spout *(lightning; combinatorics)* Study bible 1

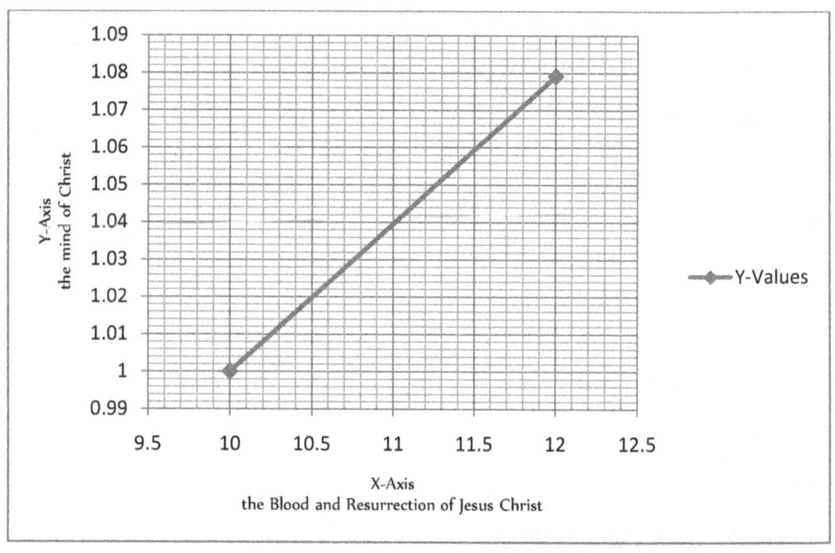

Water Spout *(lightning; combinatorics)* Study bible 2

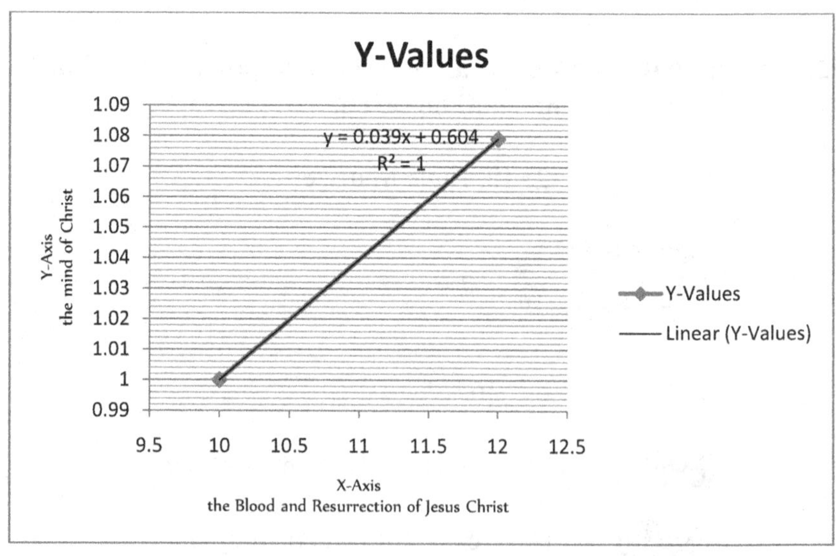

$10^{1.0791}, 10^{1}.$

Pilled Poplar, Hazel, and Chestnut bible rods 2

23. But when they persecute you in this city, flee ye into another: for verily I say unto you, Ye shall not have gone over the cities of Israel who prevails with God; God strives, **till the Son of man be come.**

8, 4: 6, 10, 7. Bible Matrices

$8_{10}, 4_{10}: 6_{10}, 10_{6}, 7_{10}.$ Pilled Poplar, Hazel, and Chestnut bible rods 1

$Log_{10} 8 = 0.9030$ $Log_{10} 4 = 0.6020$ $Log_{10} 6 = 0.7781$ $Log_{10} 7 = 0.8450$

$Log_{6} 10 = y$

$6^{y} = 10$

$y \log_{10} 6 = \log_{10} 10$

$y = \log_{10} 10 / \log_{10} 6$

$y = 1 / 0.7781$

$y = 1.2851$

8, 4: 6, 10, 7. Deep calls unto Deep study bible 1

0.9030, 0.6020: 0.7781, 1.2851, 0.8450.

Deep calls unto Deep study bible 2

x-axis	y-axis
8	0.9030
4	0.6020
6	0.7781
10	1.2851
7	0.8450

Water Spout *(lightning; combinatorics)* Study bible 1

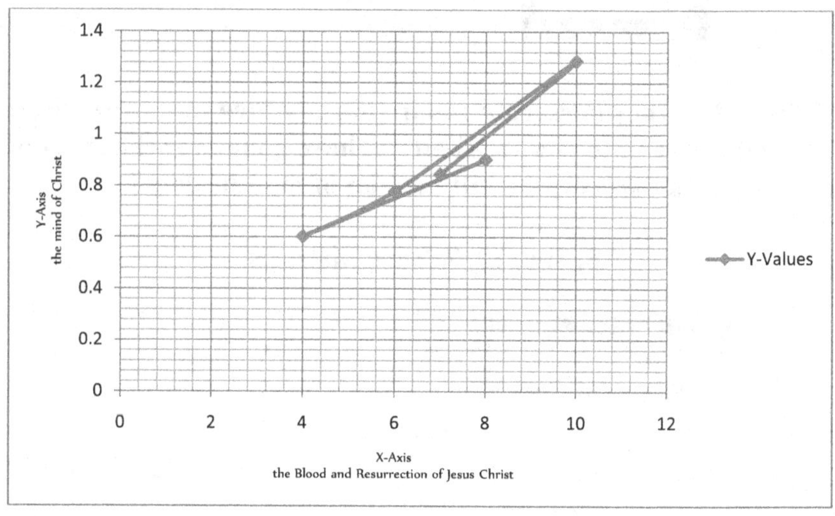

Water Spout *(lightning; combinatorics)* Study bible 2

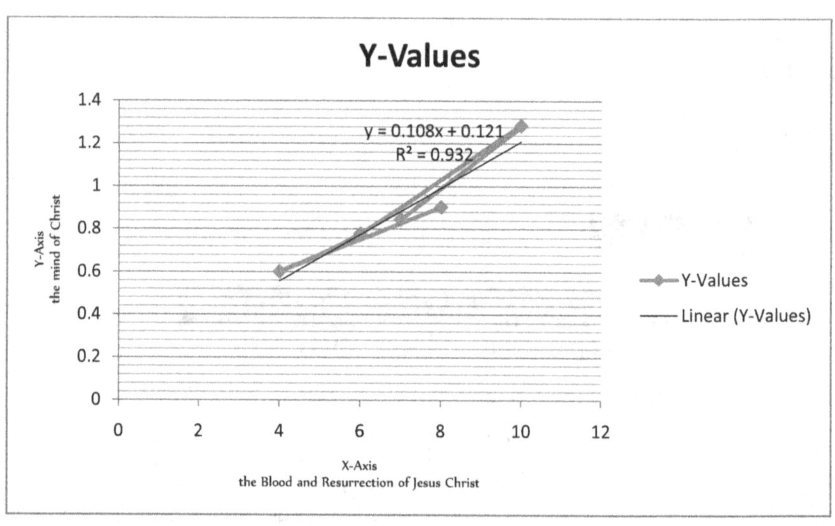

$10^{0.9030}, 10^{0.6020}: 10^{0.7781}, 6^{1.2851}, 10^{0.8450}$. Pilled Poplar, Hazel, and Chestnut bible rods 2

24. The disciple is not above his master, nor the servant above his lord.

7, 6. Bible Matrices

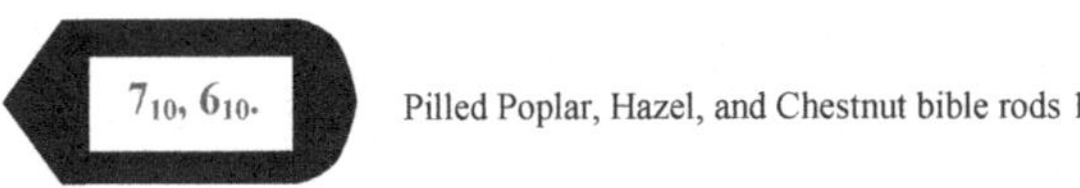

$\text{Log}_{10} 7 = 0.8450$ $\text{Log}_{10} 6 = 0.7781$

7, 6. Deep calls unto Deep study bible 1

0.8450, 0.7781. Deep calls unto Deep study bible 2

x-axis	y-axis
7	0.8450
6	0.7781

Water Spout *(lightning; combinatorics)* Study bible 1

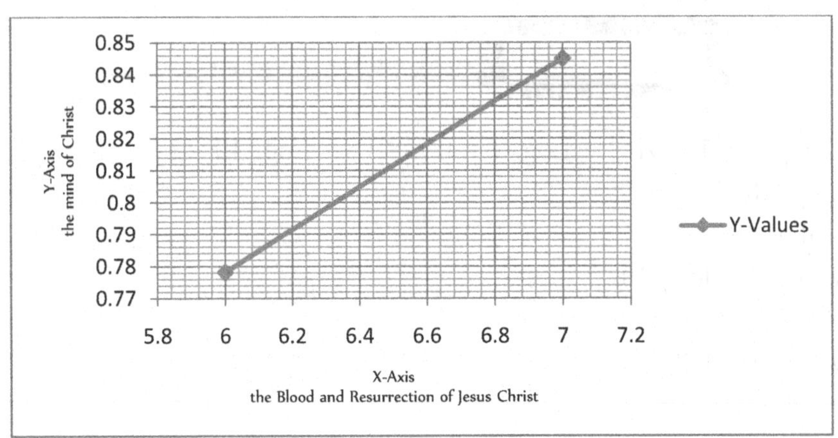

Water Spout *(lightning; combinatorics)* Study bible 2

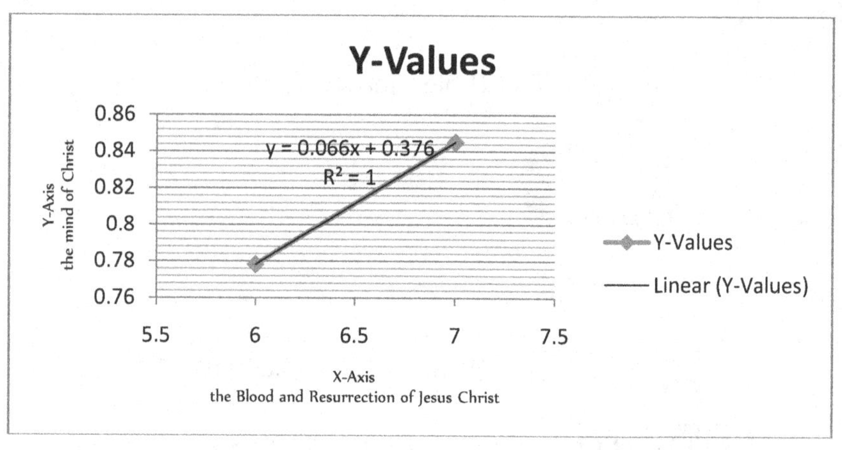

Pilled Poplar, Hazel, and Chestnut bible rods 2

25. It is enough for the disciple that he be as his master, and the servant as his lord. If they have called the master of the house Beelzebubgod of the fly, **how much more shall they call them of his household?**

12, 6.10, 10? Bible Matrices

Pilled Poplar, Hazel, and Chestnut bible rods 1

$\text{Log}_{10}\ 12 = 1.0791$ $\text{Log}_{10}\ 6 = 0.7781$ $\text{Log}_{10}\ 10 = 1$

$\text{Log}_{4}\ 10 = y$

$4^y = 10$

$y \log_{10} 4 = \log_{10} 10$

$y = \log_{10} 10 / \log_{10} 4$

$y = 1 / 0.6020$

$y = 1.6611$

12, 6. 10, 10? Deep calls unto Deep study bible 1

1.0791, 0.7781. 1.6611, 1? Deep calls unto Deep study bible 2

x-axis	y-axis
12	1.0791
6	0.7781
10	1.6611
10	1

Water Spout *(lightning; combinatorics)* Study bible 1

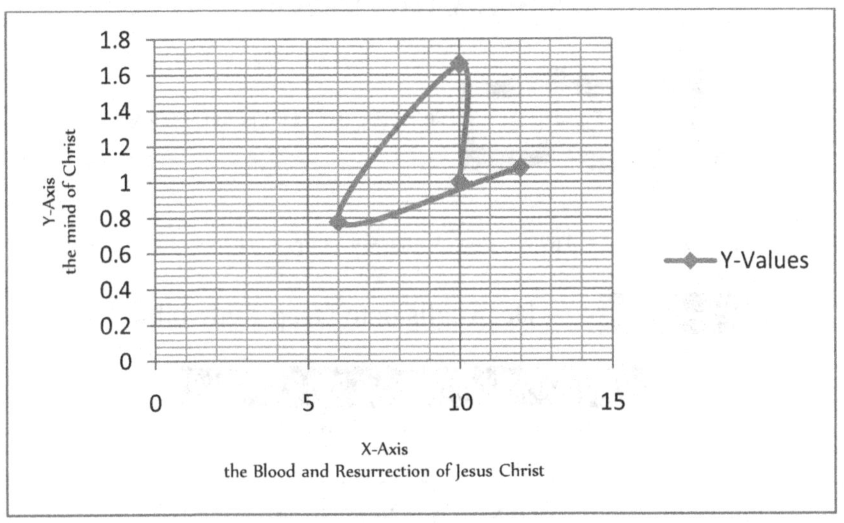

Water Spout *(lightning; combinatorics)* Study bible 2

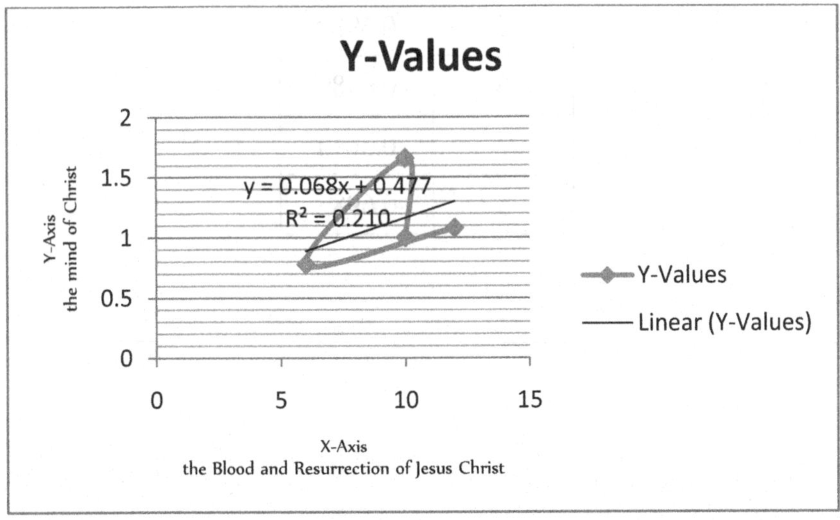

$10^{1.0791}$, $10^{0.7781}$. $4^{1.6611}$, 10^{1}?

Pilled Poplar, Hazel, and Chestnut bible rods 2

26. Fear them not therefore: for there is nothing covered, that shall not be revealed; and hid, that shall not be known.

4: 5, 5; 2, 5. Bible Matrices

Pilled Poplar, Hazel, and Chestnut bible rods 1

$\text{Log}_{10}4 = 0.6020$ $\text{Log}_{10}5 = 0.6989$ $\text{Log}_{10}5 = 0.6989$ $\text{Log}_{10}5 = 0.6989$ $\text{Log}_{10}2 = 0.3010$

4: 5, 5; 2, 5. Deep calls unto Deep study bible 1

0.6020: 0.6989, 0.6989; 0.3010, 0.6989.

Deep calls unto Deep study bible 2

x-axis	y-axis
4	0.6020
5	0.6989
5	0.6989
2	0.3010
5	0.6989

Water Spout *(lightning; combinatorics)* Study bible 1

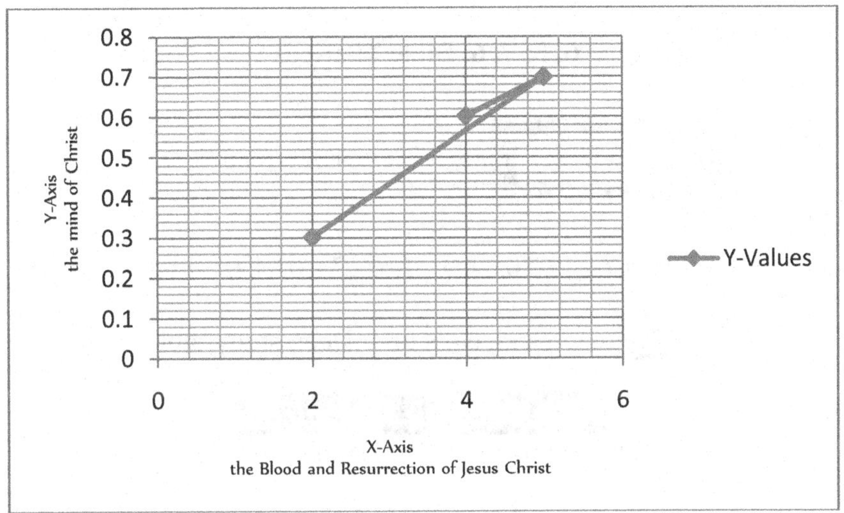

Water Spout *(lightning; combinatorics)* Study bible 2

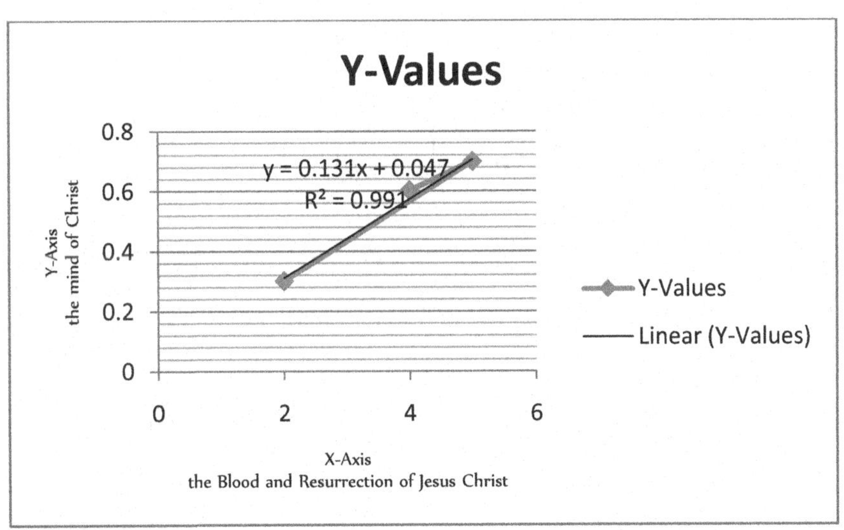

$10^{0.6020}$: $10^{0.6989}$, $10^{0.6989}$; $10^{0.3010}$, $10^{0.6989}$. Pilled Poplar, Hazel, and Chestnut bible rods 2

27. What I tell you in darkness, that speak ye in light: and what ye hear in the ear, that preach ye upon the housetops.

6, 5: 7, 6. Bible Matrices

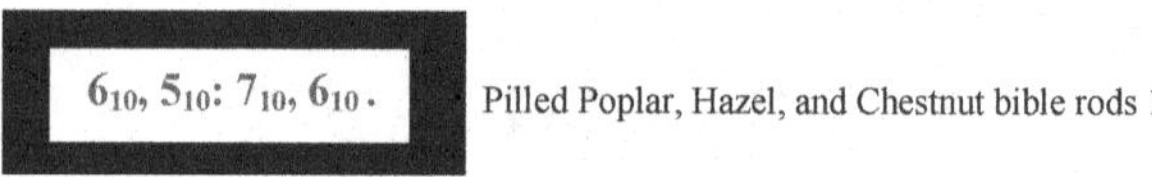
$6_{10}, 5_{10}: 7_{10}, 6_{10}.$ Pilled Poplar, Hazel, and Chestnut bible rods 1

$\text{Log}_{10} 6 = 0.7781$ $\text{Log}_{10} 5 = 0.6989$ $\text{Log}_{10} 7 = 0.8450$ $\text{Log}_{10} 6 = 0.7781$

6, 5: 7, 6. Deep calls unto Deep study bible 1

0.7781, 0.6989: 0.8450, 0.7781.
Deep calls unto Deep study bible 2

x-axis	y-axis
6	0.7781
5	0.6989
7	0.8450
6	0.7781

Water Spout *(lightning; combinatorics)* Study bible 1

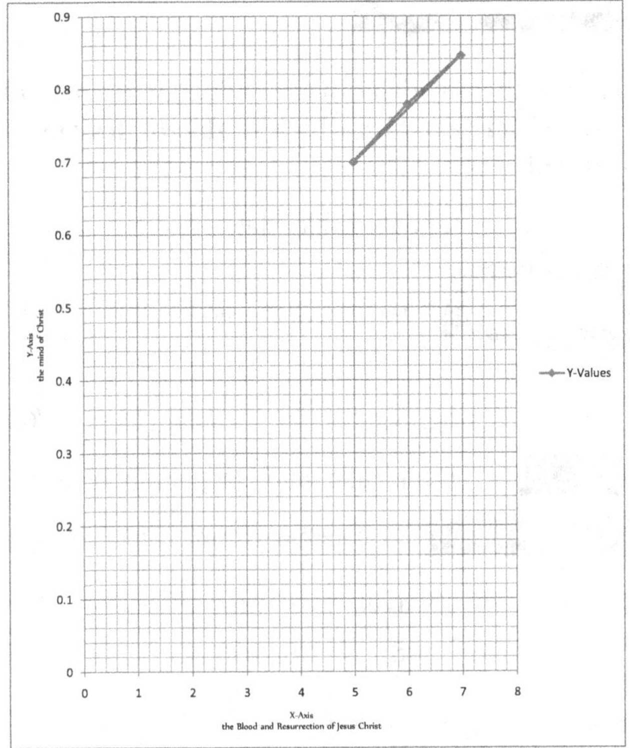

Water Spout *(lightning; combinatorics)* Study bible 2

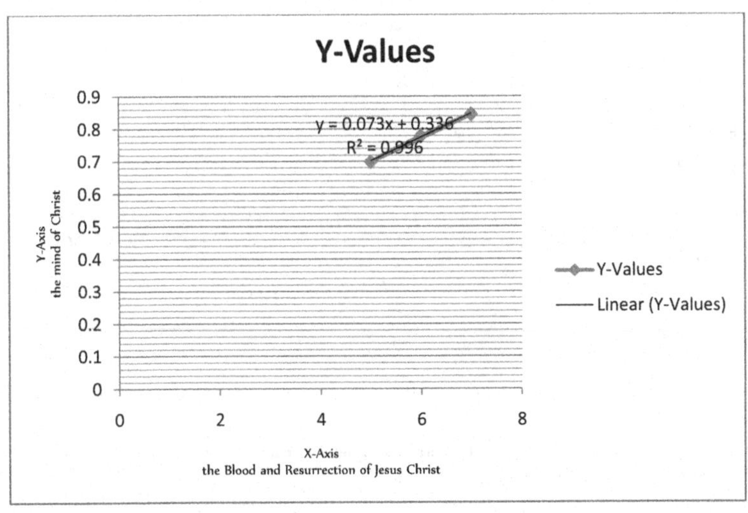

$10^{0.7781}, 10^{0.6989}: 10^{0.8450}, 10^{0.7781}$. Pilled Poplar, Hazel, and Chestnut bible rods 2

28. And fear not them which kill the body, but are not able to kill the soul: but rather fear him which is able to destroy both soul and body in hell.

8, 8: 15. Bible Matrices

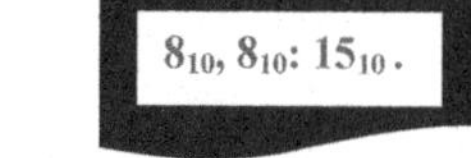
$8_{10}, 8_{10}: 15_{10}$.

Pilled Poplar, Hazel, and Chestnut bible rods 1

$Log_{10} 8 = 0.9030$ $Log_{10} 8 = 0.9030$ $Log_{10} 15 = 1.1760$

8, 8: 15. Deep calls unto Deep study bible 1

0.9030, 0.9030: 1.1760. Deep calls unto Deep study bible 2

x-axis	y-axis
8	0.9030
8	0.9030
15	1.1760

Water Spout *(lightning; combinatorics)* Study bible 1

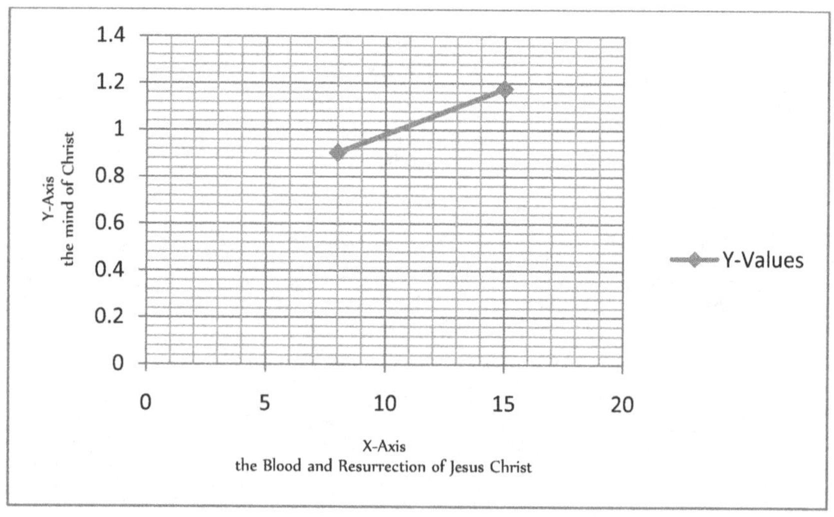

Water Spout *(lightning; combinatorics)* Study bible 2

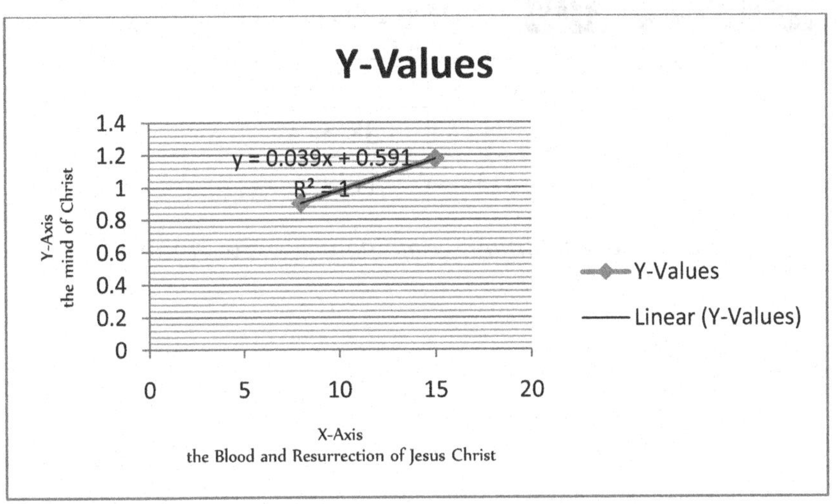

Pilled Poplar, Hazel, and Chestnut bible rods 2

29. Are not two witness and support; 2 x 1 **sparrows sold for a farthing? and one of them shall not fall on the ground without your Father.**

8? 13. Bible Matrices

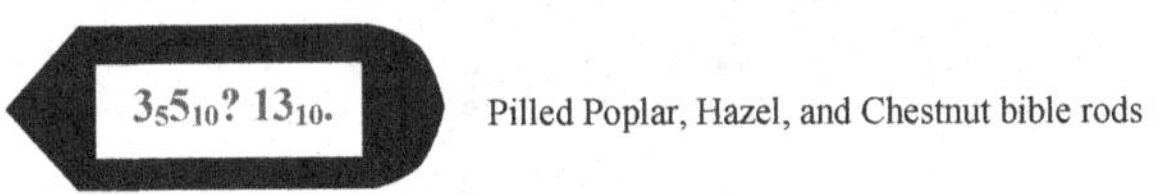

$\text{Log}_{10} 5 = 0.6989$ $\text{Log}_{10} 13 = 1.1139$

$\text{Log}_5 3 = y$

$5^y = 3$

$y \log_{10} 5 = \log_{10} 3$

$y = \log_{10} 3 / \log_{10} 5$

$y = 0.4771 / 0.6989$

$y = 0.6826$

8? 13. Deep calls unto Deep study bible 1

0.6826 0.6989? 1.1139. Deep calls unto Deep study bible 2

x-axis	y-axis
8	1.3815
13	1.1139

Water Spout *(lightning; combinatorics)* Study bible 1

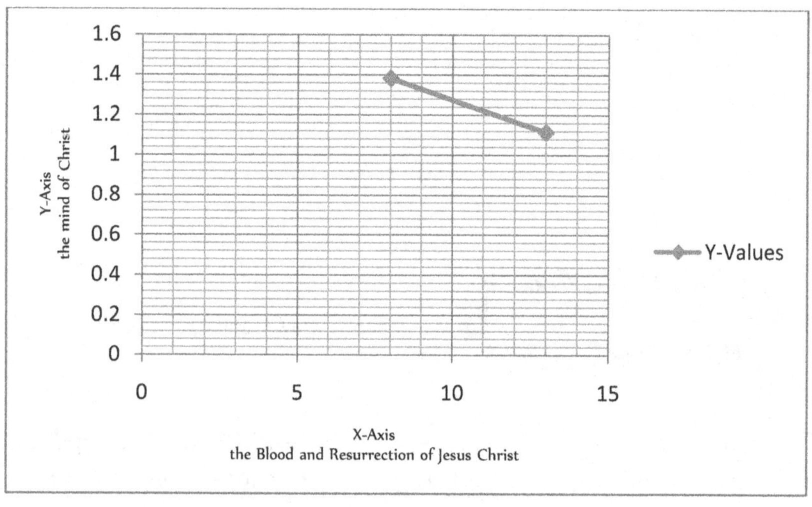

Water Spout *(lightning; combinatorics)* Study bible 2

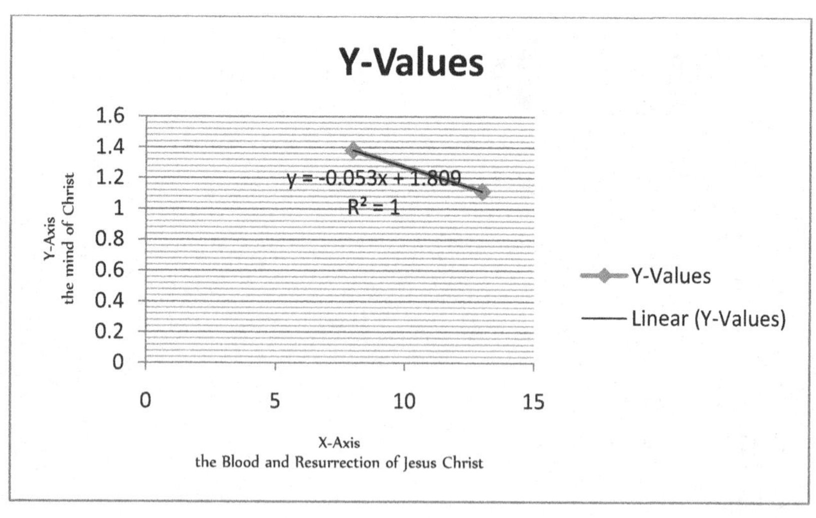

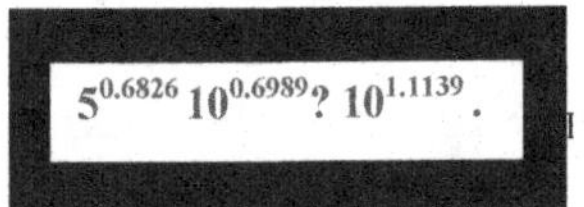

Pilled Poplar, Hazel, and Chestnut bible rods 2

30. But the very hairs of your head are all numbered.

10. Bible Matrices

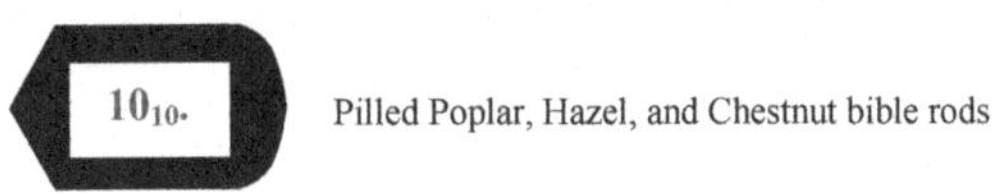

$\text{Log}_{10} 10 = 1$

10. Deep calls unto Deep study bible 1

1. Deep calls unto Deep study bible 2

x-axis	y-axis
10	1

Water Spout *(lightning; combinatorics)* Study bible 1

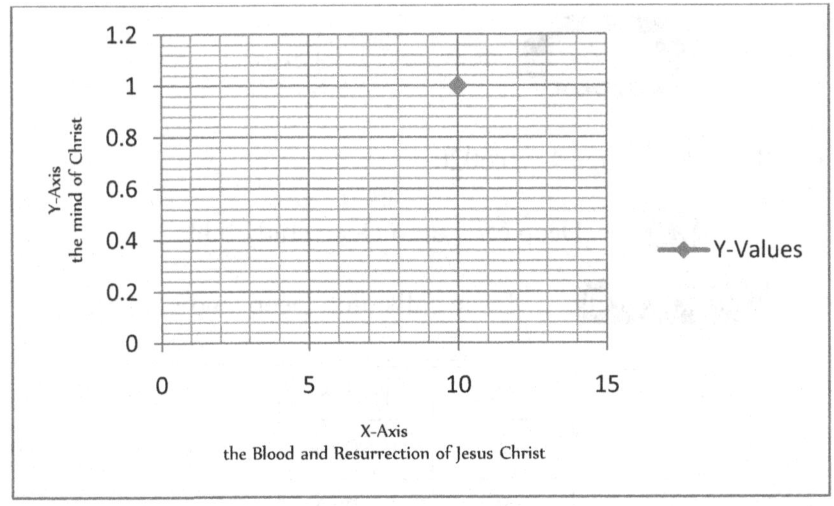

Water Spout *(lightning; combinatorics)* Study bible 2

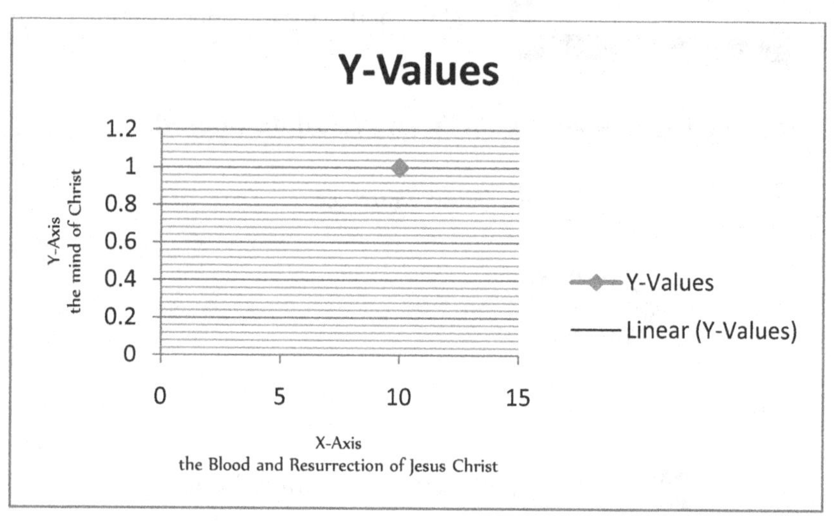

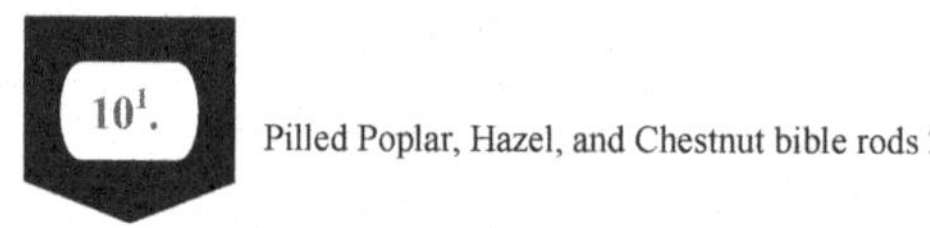

Pilled Poplar, Hazel, and Chestnut bible rods 2

31. Fear ye not therefore, ye are of more value than many sparrows.

4, 8. Bible Matrices

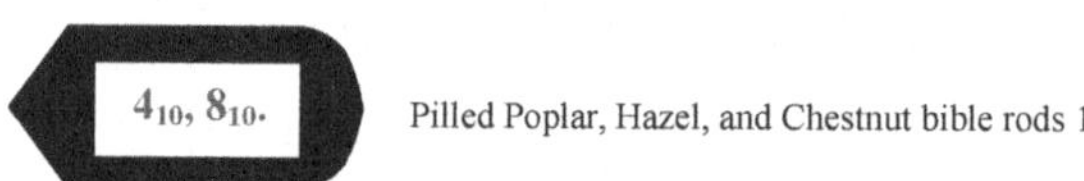

Pilled Poplar, Hazel, and Chestnut bible rods 1

$\text{Log}_{10} 8 = 0.9030$ $\text{Log}_{10} 4 = 0.6020$

4, 8. Deep calls unto Deep study bible 1

0.6020, 0.9030. Deep calls unto Deep study bible 2

x-axis	y-axis
4	0.6020
8	0.9030

Water Spout *(lightning; combinatorics)* Study bible 1

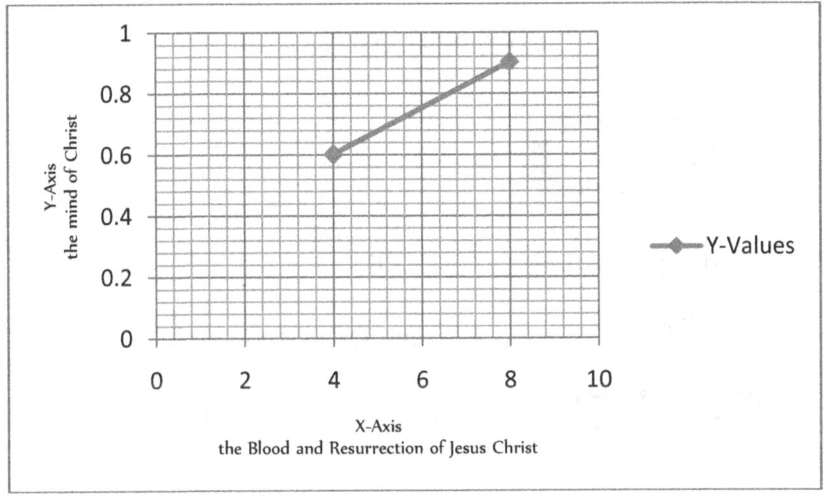

Water Spout *(lightning; combinatorics)* Study bible 2

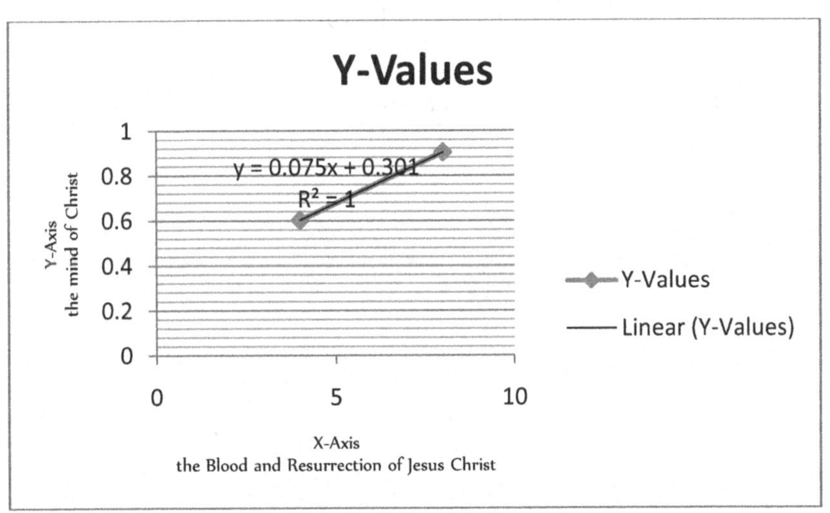

$10^{0.6020}$, $10^{0.9030}$.	Pilled Poplar, Hazel, and Chestnut bible rods 2

32. Whosoever therefore shall confess me before men, him will I confess also before my Father which is in heaven.

7, 12. Bible Matrices

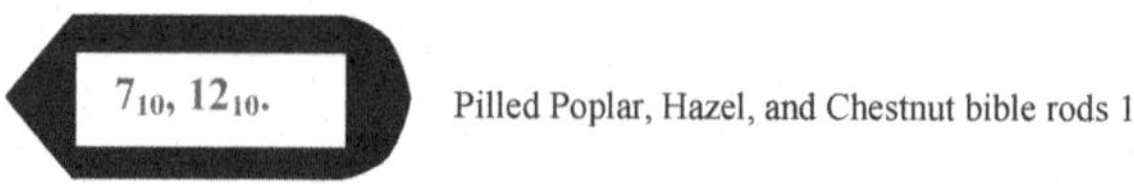

$\text{Log}_{10} 7 = 0.8450$ $\text{Log}_{10} 12 = 1.0791$

7, 12. Deep calls unto Deep study bible 1

0.8450, 1.0791 Deep calls unto Deep study bible 2

x-axis	y-axis
7	0.8450
12	1.0791

Water Spout *(lightning; combinatorics)* Study bible 1

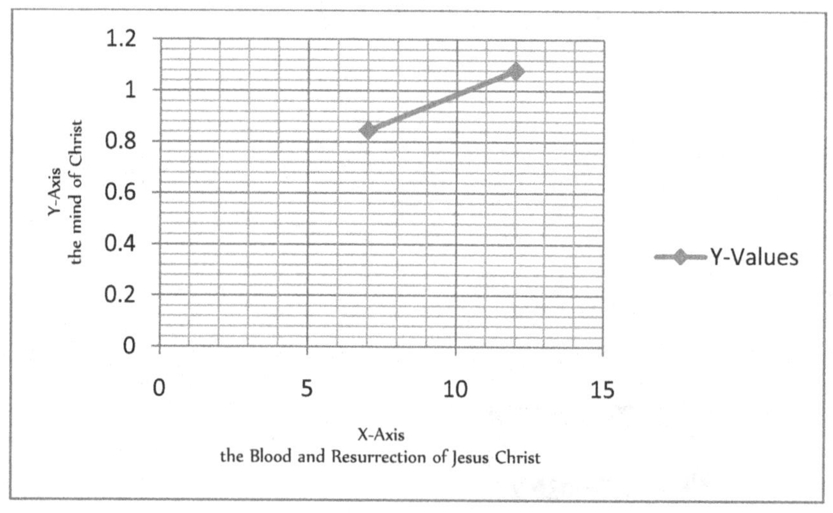

Water Spout *(lightning; combinatorics)* Study bible 2

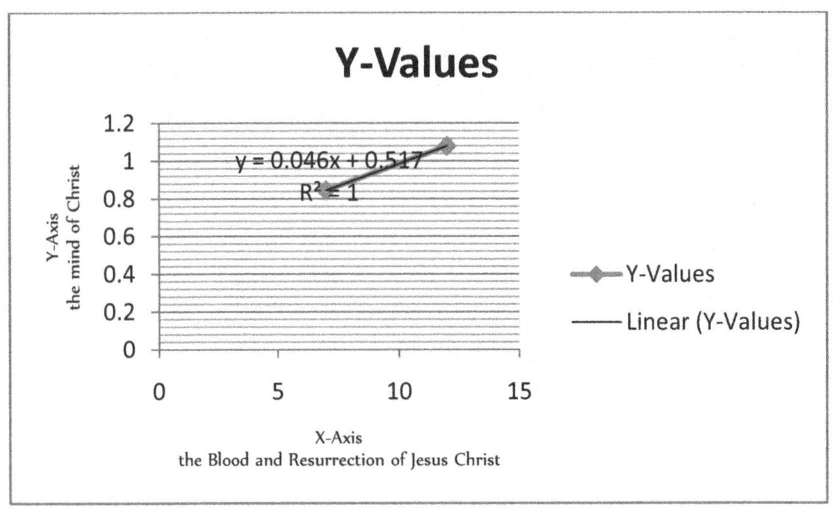

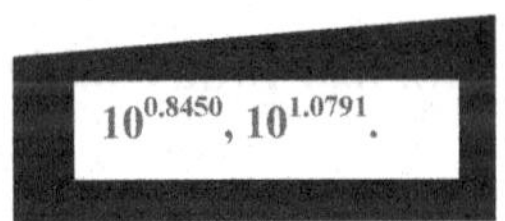

Pilled Poplar, Hazel, and Chestnut bible rods 2

33. But whosoever shall deny me before men, him will I also deny before my Father which is in heaven.

7, 12. Bible Matrices

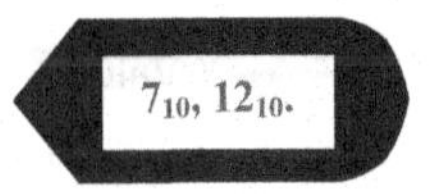

Pilled Poplar, Hazel, and Chestnut bible rods 1

$\text{Log}_{10} 7 = 0.8450$ $\text{Log}_{10} 12 = 1.0791$

7, 12. Deep calls unto Deep study bible 1

0.8450, 1.0791 Deep calls unto Deep study bible 2

x-axis	y-axis
7	0.8450
12	1.0791

Water Spout *(lightning; combinatorics)* Study bible 1

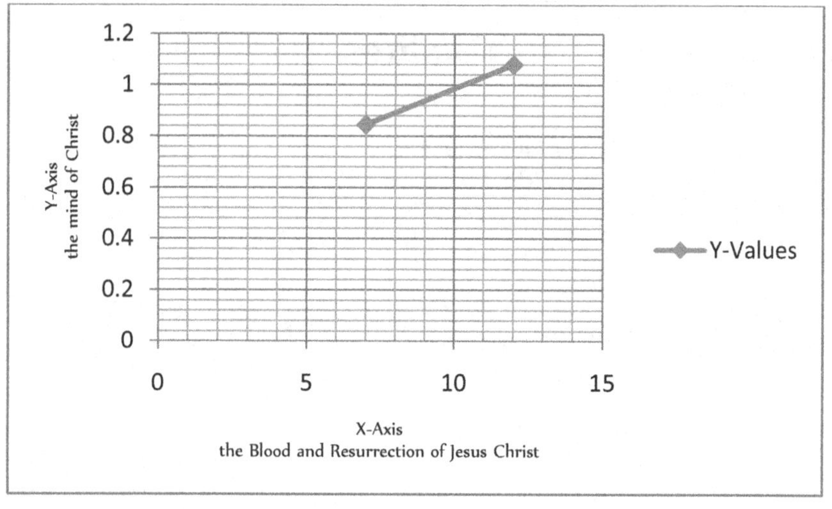

Water Spout *(lightning; combinatorics)* Study bible 2

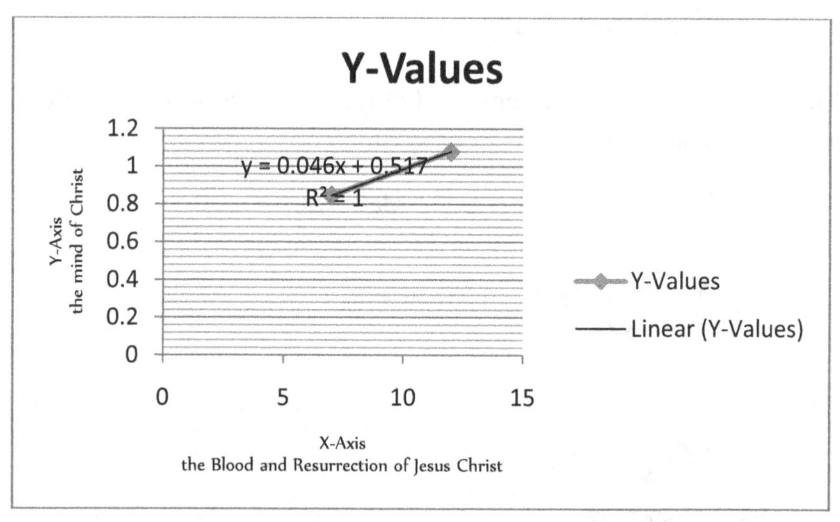

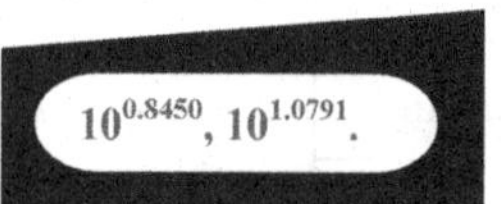

Pilled Poplar, Hazel, and Chestnut bible rods 2

34. Think not that I am come to send peace on earth: I came not to send peace, but a sword.

11: 6, 3. Bible Matrices

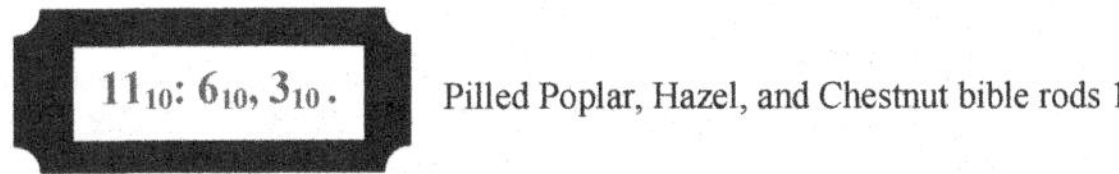

Pilled Poplar, Hazel, and Chestnut bible rods 1

$Log_{10} 11 = 1.0413$ $Log_{10} 6 = 0.7781$ $Log_{10} 3 = 0.4771$

11: 6, 3. Deep calls unto Deep study bible 1

1.0413: 0.7781, 0.4771. Deep calls unto Deep study bible 2

x-axis	y-axis
11	1.0413
6	0.7781
3	0.4771

Water Spout *(lightning; combinatorics)* Study bible 1

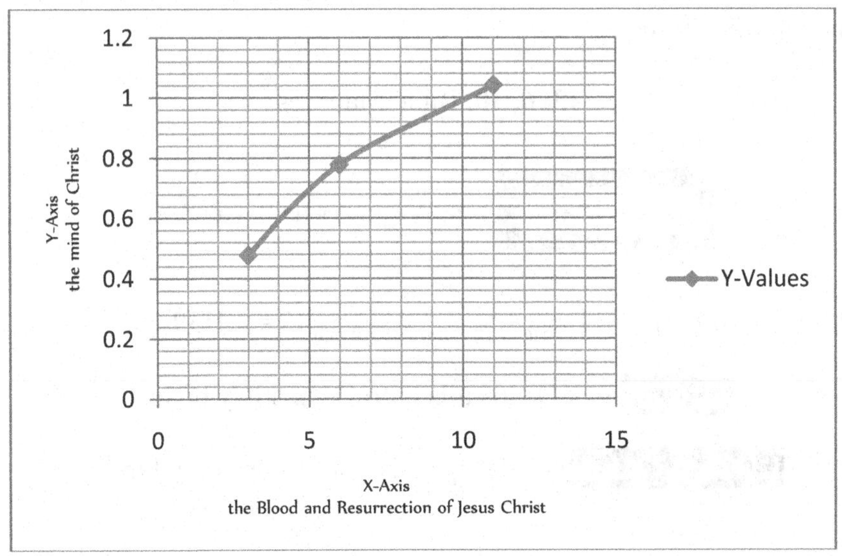

Water Spout *(lightning; combinatorics)* Study bible 2

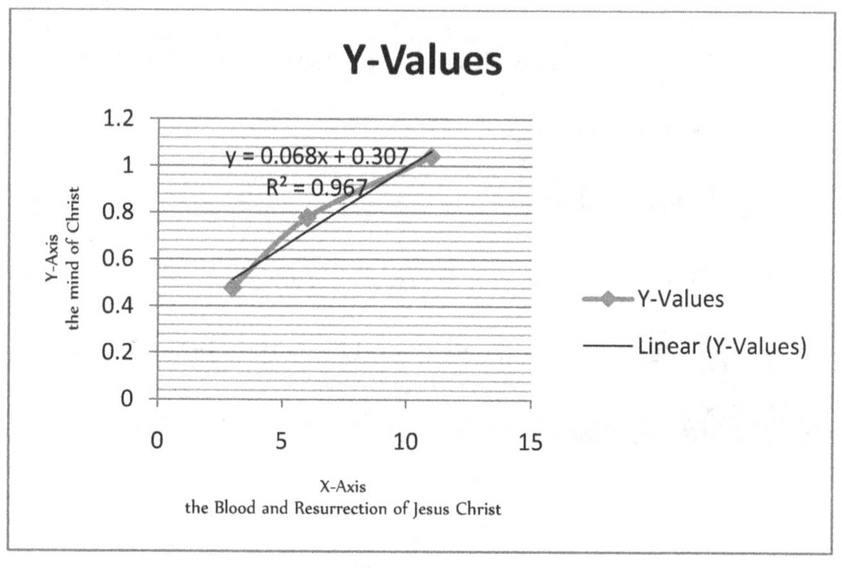

Pilled Poplar, Hazel, and Chestnut bible rods 2

35. For I am come to set a man at variance against his father, and the daughter against her mother, and the daughter in law against her mother in law.

13, 6, 10. Bible Matrices

Pilled Poplar, Hazel, and Chestnut bible rods 1

$\text{Log}_{10} 6 = 0.7781$ $\text{Log}_{10} 10 = 1$ $\text{Log}_{10} 13 = 1.1139$

13, 6, 10. Deep calls unto Deep study bible 1

1.1139, 0.7781, 1. Deep calls unto Deep study bible 2

x-axis	y-axis
13	1.1139
6	0.7781
10	1

Water Spout *(lightning; combinatorics)* Study bible 1

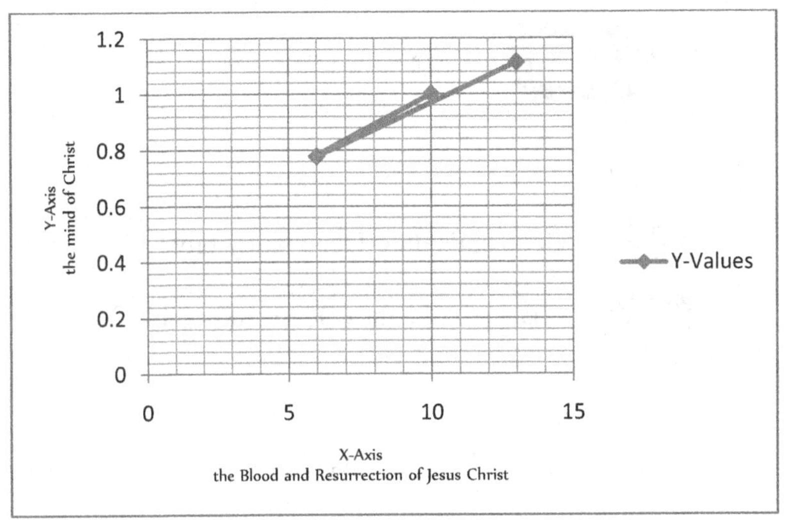

Water Spout *(lightning; combinatorics)* Study bible 2

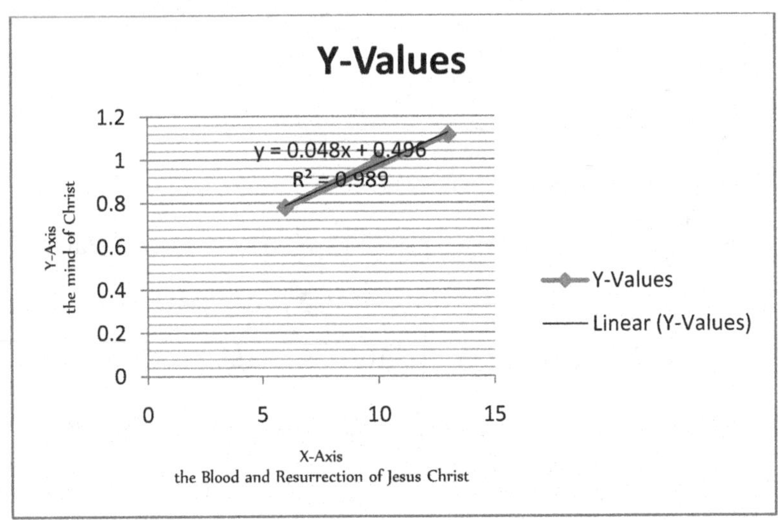

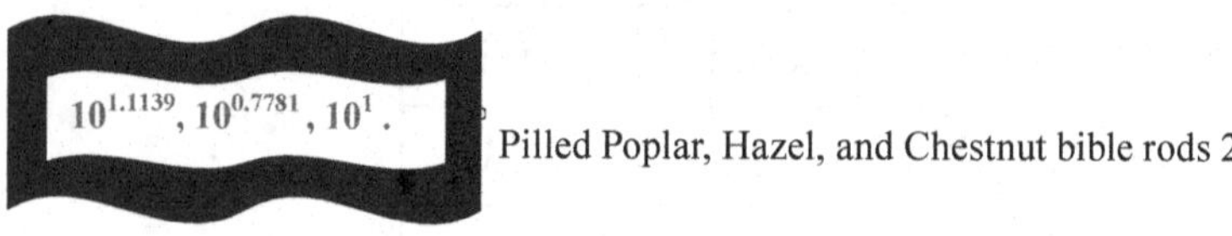

36. And a man's foes shall be they of his own household.

11. Bible Matrices

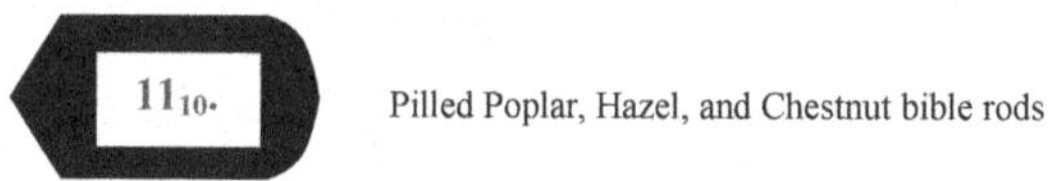

$\text{Log}_{10} 11 = 1.0413$

11. Deep calls unto Deep study bible 1

1.0413. Deep calls unto Deep study bible 2

x-axis	y-axis
11	1.0413

Water Spout *(lightning; combinatorics)* Study bible 1

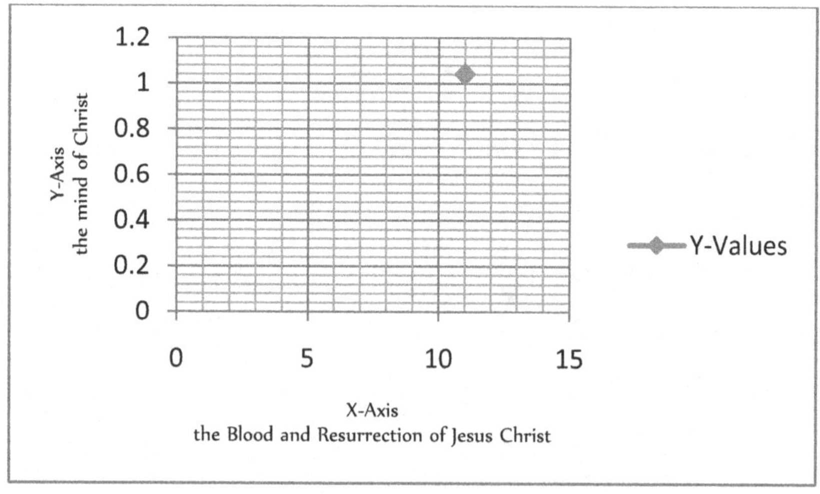

Water Spout *(lightning; combinatorics)* Study bible 2

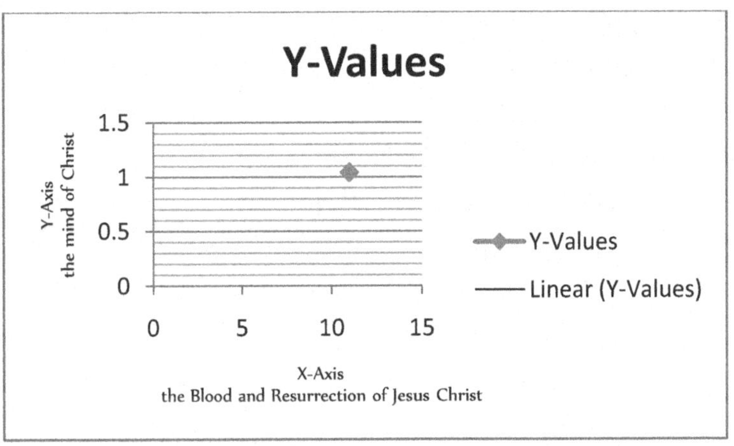

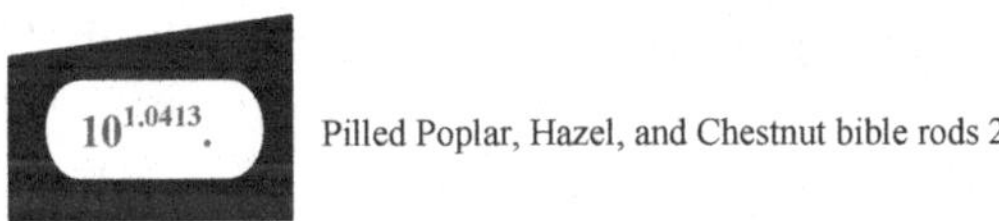

Pilled Poplar, Hazel, and Chestnut bible rods 2

37. He that loveth father or mother more than me is not worthy of me: and he that loveth son or daughter more than me is not worthy of me.

14: 15. Bible Matrices

14_{10}, 15_{10}.

Pilled Poplar, Hazel, and Chestnut bible rods 1

$\text{Log}_{10}\ 14 = 1.1461$ $\text{Log}_{10}\ 15 = 1.1760$

14, 15. Deep calls unto Deep study bible 1

1.1461, 1.1760. Deep calls unto Deep study bible 2

x-axis	y-axis
14	1.1461
15	1.1760

Water Spout *(lightning; combinatorics)* Study bible 1

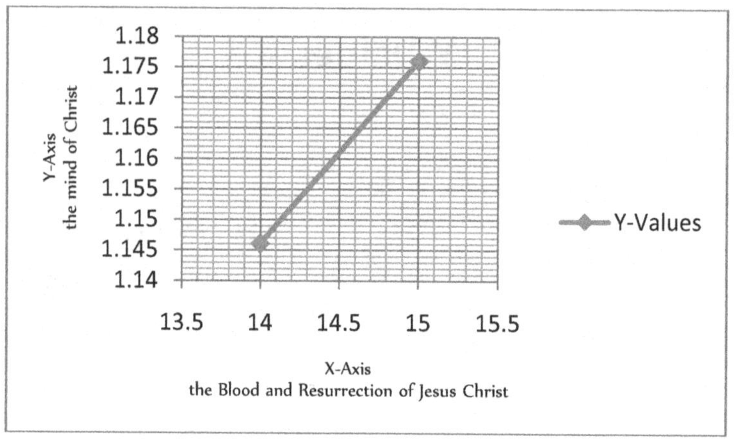

Water Spout *(lightning; combinatorics)* Study bible 2

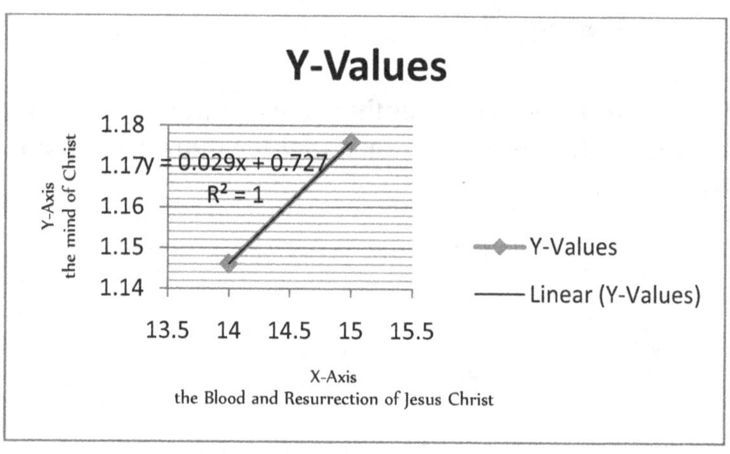

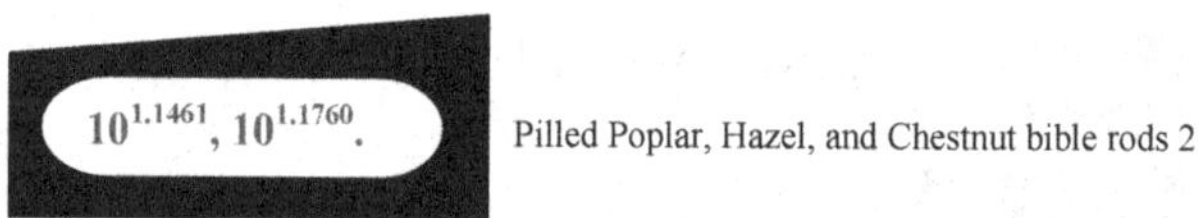

Pilled Poplar, Hazel, and Chestnut bible rods 2

38. And he that taketh not his cross, and followeth after me, is not worthy of me.

7, 4, 5. Bible Matrices

$\text{Log}_{10} 7 = 0.8450$ $\text{Log}_{10} 4 = 0.6020$ $\text{Log}_{10} 5 = 0.6989$

7, 4, 5. Deep calls unto Deep study bible 1

0.8450, 0.6020, 0.6989. Deep calls unto Deep study bible 2

x-axis	y-axis
7	0.8450
4	0.6020
5	0.6989

Water Spout *(lightning; combinatorics)* Study bible 1

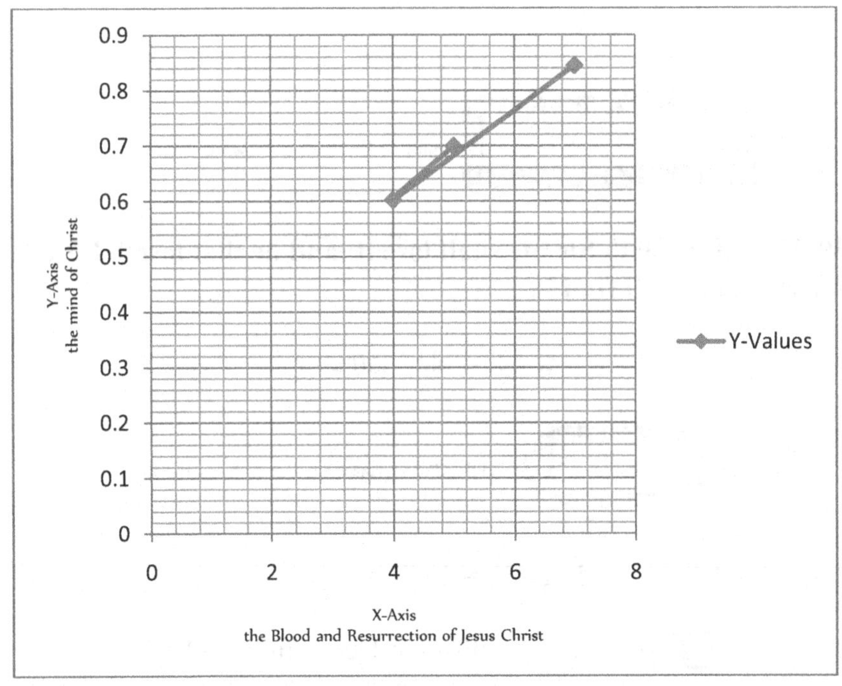

Water Spout *(lightning; combinatorics)* Study bible 2

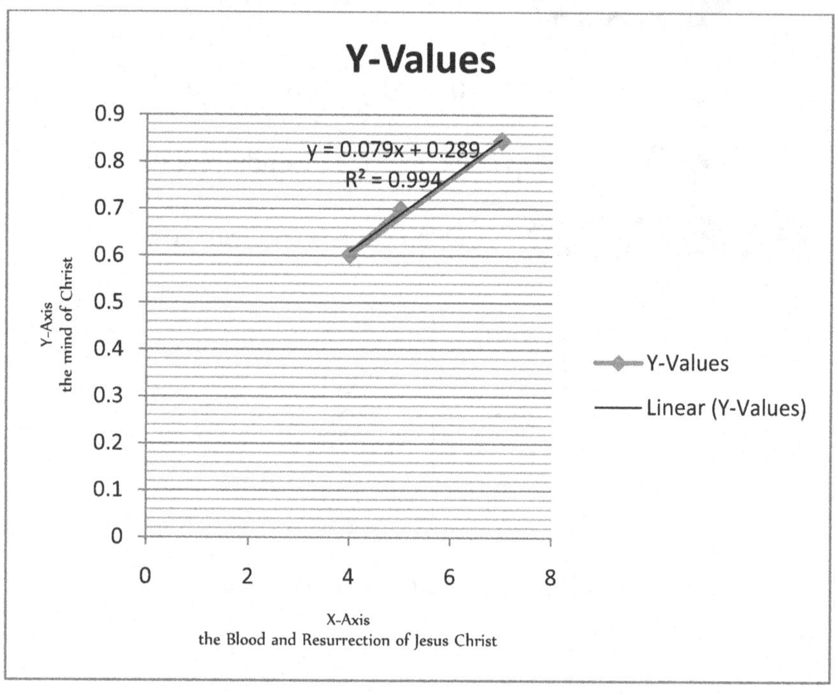

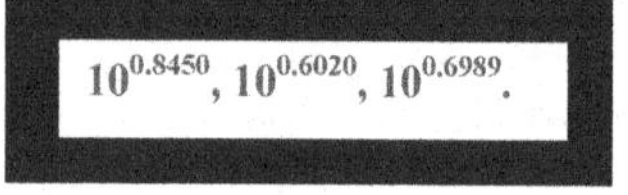

Pilled Poplar, Hazel, and Chestnut bible rods 2

39. He that findeth his life shall lose it: and he that loseth his life for my sake shall find it.

8: 12. Bible Matrices

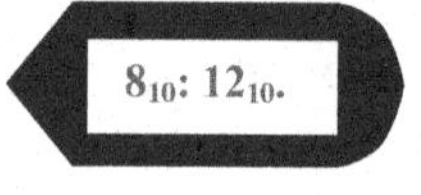

Pilled Poplar, Hazel, and Chestnut bible rods 1

$\text{Log}_{10} 8 = 0.9030$ $\quad$ $\text{Log}_{10} 12 = 1.0791$

8: 12. Deep calls unto Deep study bible 1

0.9030, 1.0791. Deep calls unto Deep study bible 2

x-axis	y-axis
8	0.9030
12	1.0791

Water Spout *(lightning; combinatorics)* Study bible 1

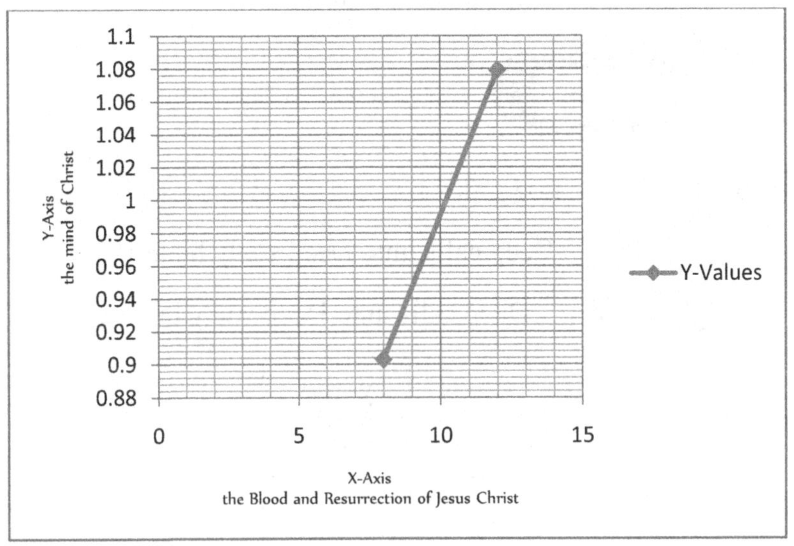

Water Spout *(lightning; combinatorics)* Study bible 2

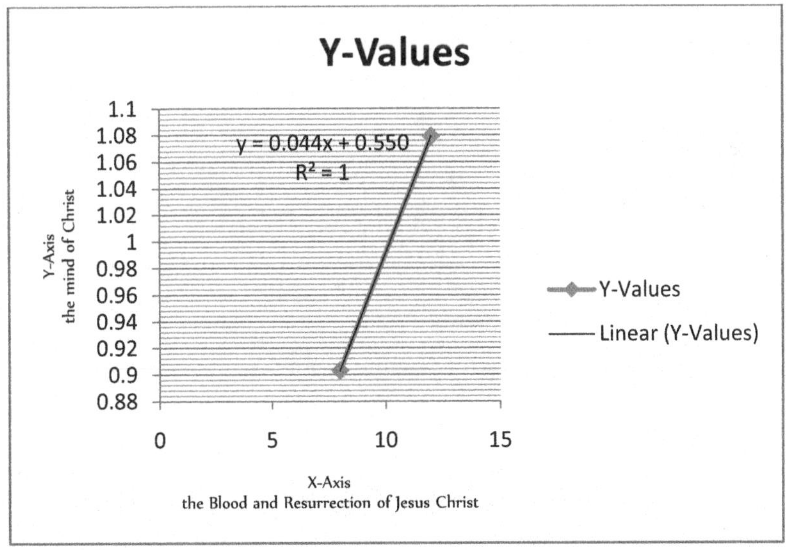

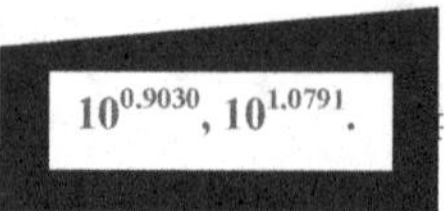

Pilled Poplar, Hazel, and Chestnut bible rods 2

40. He that receiveth you receiveth me, and he that receiveth me receiveth him that sent me.

6, 10. Bible Matrices

$\text{Log}_{10} 6 = 0.7781$ $\text{Log}_{10} 10 = 1$

6, 10. Deep calls unto Deep study bible 1

0.7781, 1. Deep calls unto Deep study bible 2

x-axis	y-axis
6	0.7781
10	1

Water Spout *(lightning; combinatorics)* Study bible 1

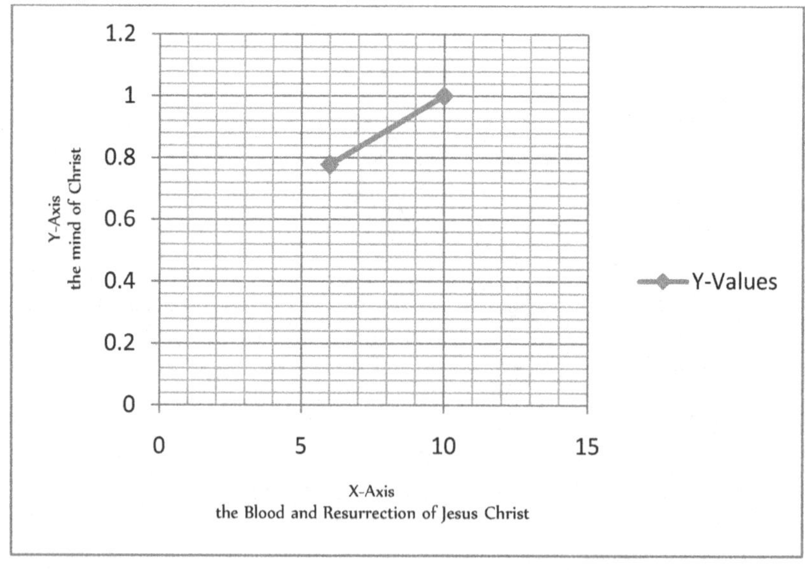

Water Spout *(lightning; combinatorics)* Study bible 2

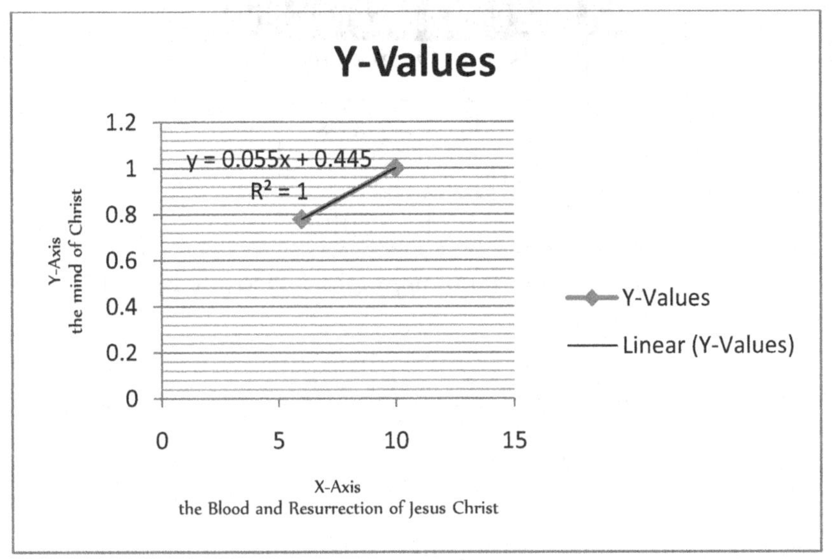

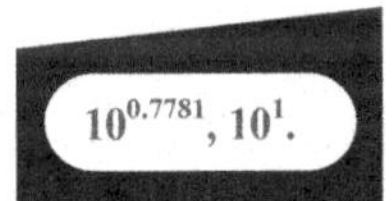

Pilled Poplar, Hazel, and Chestnut bible rods 2

41. He that receiveth a prophet to bubble forth, as from a fountain; utter **in the name of a prophet** to bubble forth, as from a fountain; utter **shall receive a prophet's** to bubble forth, as from a fountain; utter **reward; and he that receiveth a righteous man in the name of a righteous man shall receive a righteous man's reward.**

16; 20. Bible Matrices

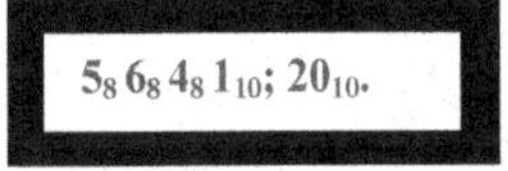

Pilled Poplar, Hazel, and Chestnut bible rods 1

$\text{Log}_{10} 20 = 1.3010$

$\text{Log } 1_{10} = 0$

$\text{Log}_8 5 = y$
$8^y = 5$
$y \log_{10} 8 = \log_{10} 5$
$y = \log_{10} 5 / \log_{10} 8$
$y = 0.6989 / 0.9030$
$y = 0.7739$

$\text{Log}_8 6 = y$
$8^y = 6$
$y \log_{10} 8 = \log_{10} 6$
$y = \log_{10} 6 / \log_{10} 8$
$y = 0.7781 / 0.9030$
$y = 0.8616$

$\text{Log}_8 4 = y$
$8^y = 4$
$y \log_{10} 8 = \log_{10} 4$
$y = \log_{10} 4 / \log_{10} 8$
$y = 0.6020 / 0.9030$
$y = 0.6666$

16; 20. Deep calls unto Deep study bible 1

0.7739 0.8616 0.6666 0; 1.3010.
Deep calls unto Deep study bible 2

x-axis	y-axis
16	2.3021
20	1.3010

Water Spout *(lightning; combinatorics)* Study bible 1

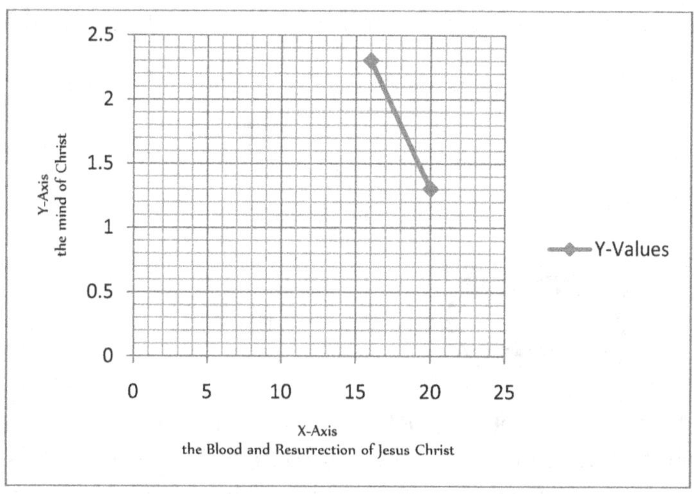

Water Spout *(lightning; combinatorics)* Study bible 2

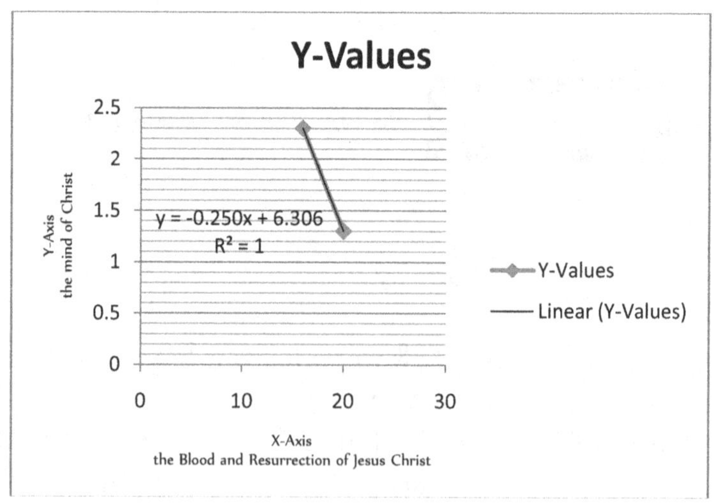

$8^{0.7739}\ 8^{0.8616}\ 8^{0.6666}\ 10^{0};\ 10^{1.3010}.$ Pilled Poplar, Hazel, and Chestnut bible rods 2

42. And whosoever shall give to drink unto one of these little ones a cup of cold water only in the name of a disciple, verily I say unto you, he shall in no wise lose his reward.

24, 5, 8. Bible Matrices

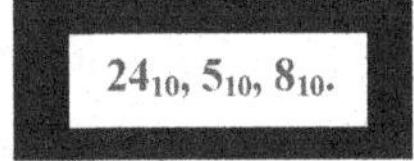
$24_{10}, 5_{10}, 8_{10}.$

Pilled Poplar, Hazel, and Chestnut bible rods 1

$Log_{10} 8 = 0.9030$ $Log_{10} 5 = 0.6989$ $Log_{10} 24 = 1.3802$

24, 5, 8. Deep calls unto Deep study bible 1

1.3802, 0.6989, 0.9030. Deep calls unto Deep study bible 2

x-axis	y-axis
24	1.3802
5	0.6989
8	0.9030

Water Spout *(lightning; combinatorics)* Study bible 1

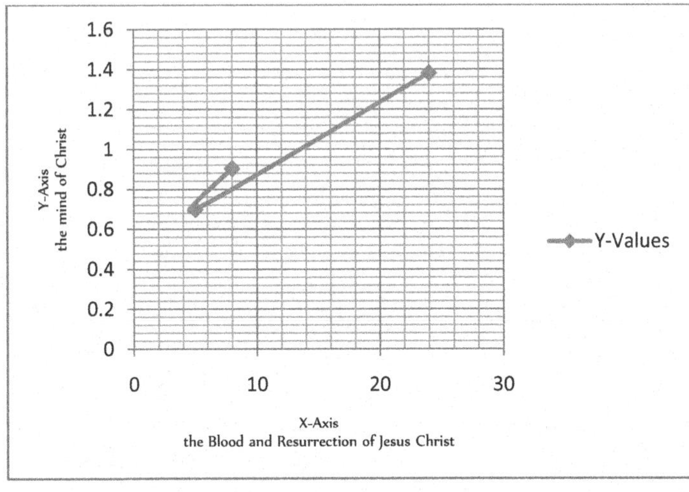

Water Spout *(lightning; combinatorics)* Study bible 2

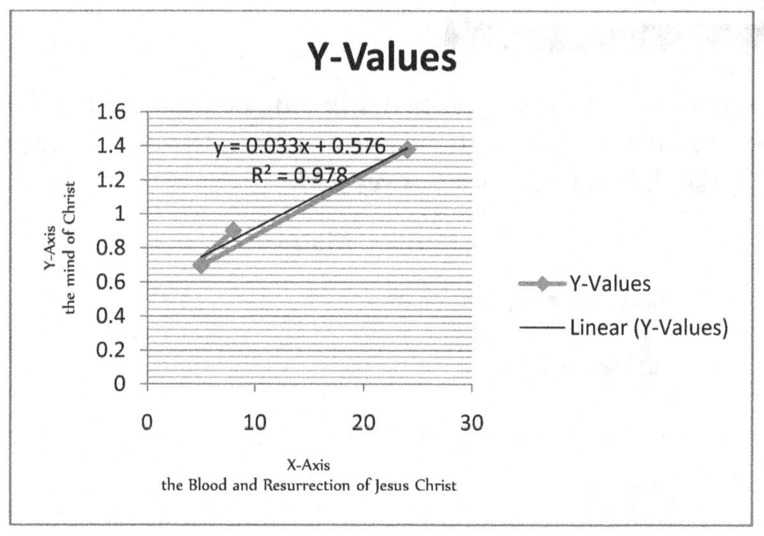

$10^{1.3802}$, $10^{0.6989}$, $10^{0.9030}$.	Pilled Poplar, Hazel, and Chestnut bible rods 2

CHAPTER 11

1. And it came to pass, when Jesussavior; deliverer **had made an end of commanding his twelve** dominion or divine government; 2 x 2 x 3 **disciples, he departed thence to teach and to preach in their cities.**

5, 11, 11. Bible Matrices

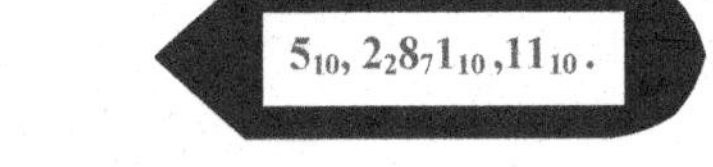

Pilled Poplar, Hazel, and Chestnut bible rods 1

$\text{Log}_{10} 5 = 0.6989$ $\text{Log}_{10} 1 = 0$ $\text{Log}_{10} 11 = 1.0413$

$\text{Log}_7 8 = y$

$7^y = 8$

$y \log_{10} 7 = \log_{10} 8$

$y = \log_{10} 8 / \log_{10} 7$

$y = 0.9030 / 0.8450$

$y = 1.0686$

$\text{Log}_2 2 = y$

$2^y = 2^1$

$y = 1$

5, 11, 11. Deep calls unto Deep study bible 1

0.6989, 1 1.0686 0, 1.0413. Deep calls unto Deep study bible 2

x-axis	y-axis
5	0.6989
11	2.0686
11	1.0413

Water Spout *(lightning; combinatorics)* Study bible 1

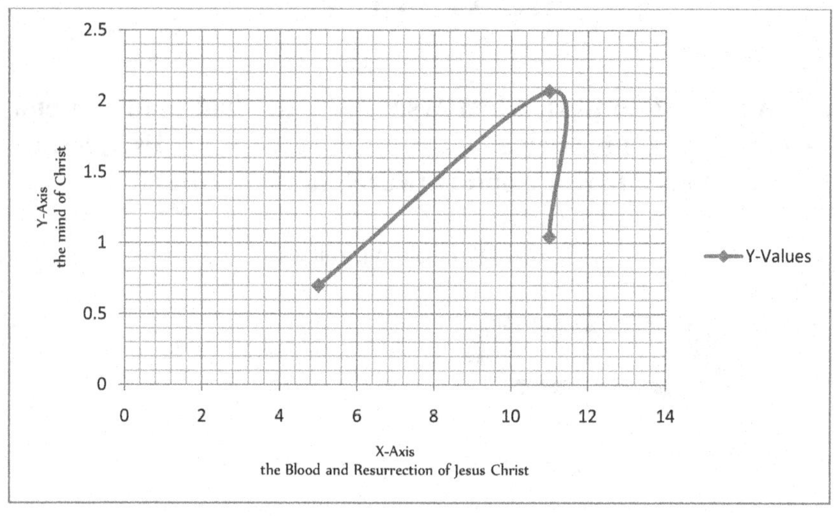

Water Spout *(lightning; combinatorics)* Study bible 2

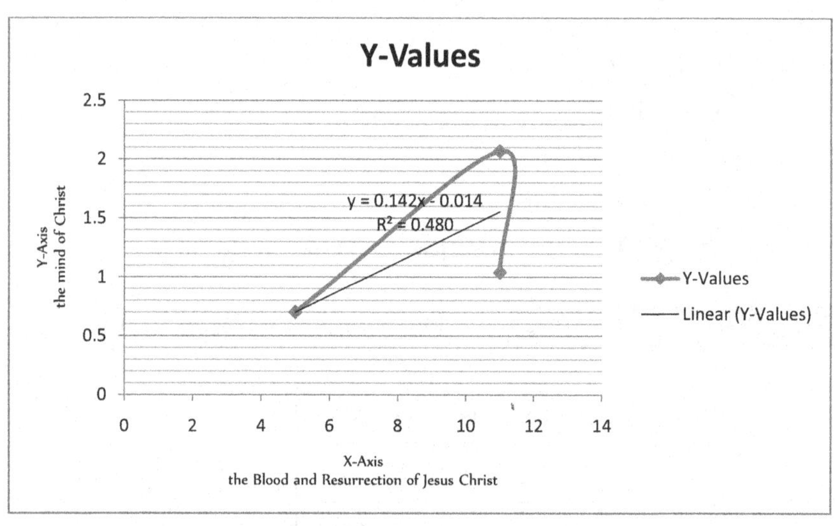

$10^{0.6989}, 2^{1}\ 7^{1.0686}\ 10^{0}, 10^{1.0413}.$

Pilled Poplar, Hazel, and Chestnut bible rods 2

2. Now when John the grace or mercy of the Lord **had heard in the prison the works of Christ**anointed; smear, **he sent two** witness and support; 2 x 1 **of his disciples,**

12, 6, Bible Matrices

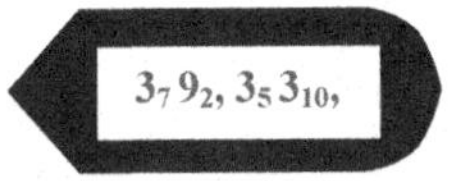

Pilled Poplar, Hazel, and Chestnut bible rods 1

$\text{Log}_{10} 3 = 0.4771$

$\text{Log}_7 3 = y$	$\text{Log}_2 9 = y$	$\text{Log}_5 3 = y$
$7^y = 3$	$2^y = 9$	$5^y = 3$
$y \log_{10} 7 = \log_{10} 3$	$y \log_{10} 2 = \log_{10} 9$	$y \log_{10} 5 = \log_{10} 3$
$y = \log_{10} 3 / \log_{10} 7$	$y = \log_{10} 9 / \log_{10} 2$	$y = \log_{10} 3 / \log_{10} 5$
$y = 0.4771 / 0.8450$	$y = 0.9542 / 0.3010$	$y = 0.4771/0.6989$
$y = 0.5646$	$y = 3.1700$	$y = 0.6826$

12, 6, Deep calls unto Deep study bible 1

0.5646 3.1700, 0.6826 0.4771, Deep calls unto Deep study bible 2

x-axis	y-axis
12	3.7346
6	1.1597

Water Spout *(lightning; combinatorics)* Study bible 1

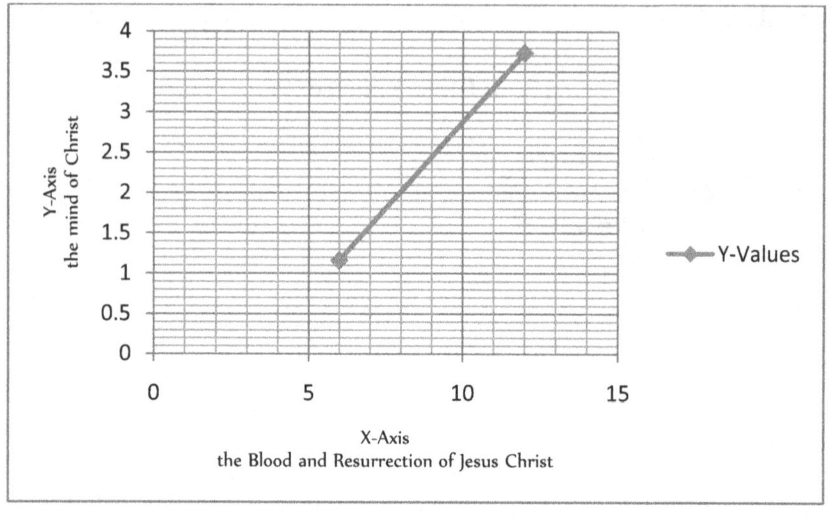

Water Spout *(lightning; combinatorics)* Study bible 2

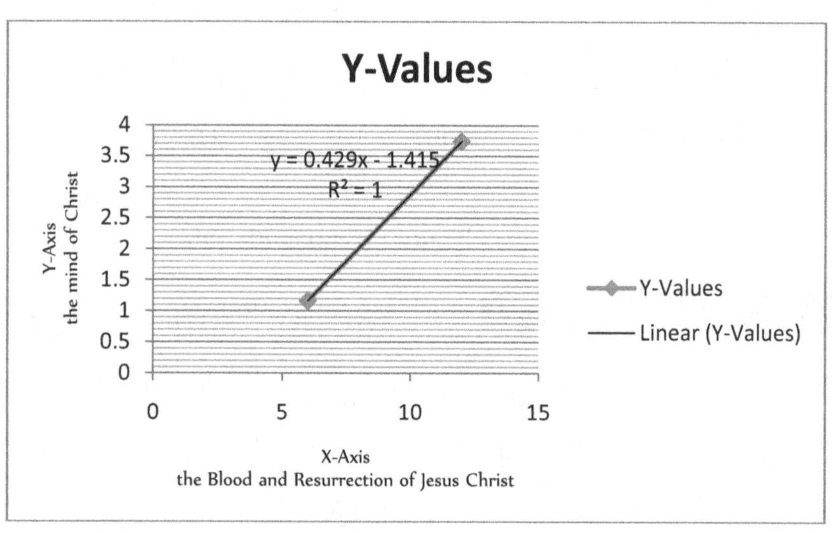

$7^{0.5646}$ $2^{3.1700}$, $5^{0.6826}$ $10^{0.4771}$,

Pilled Poplar, Hazel, and Chestnut bible rods 2

3. And said unto him, Art thou he that should come, or do we look for another?

4, 6, 6? Bible Matrices

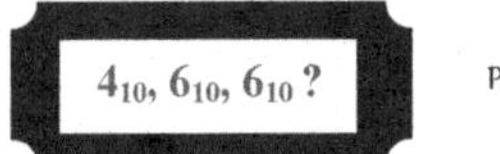

Pilled Poplar, Hazel, and Chestnut bible rods 1

$\text{Log}_{10} 6 = 0.7781$ $\text{Log}_{10} 4 = 0.6020$ $\text{Log}_{10} 6 = 0.7781$

4, 6, 6? Deep calls unto Deep study bible 1

0.6020, 0.7781, 0.7781? Deep calls unto Deep study bible 2

x-axis	y-axis
4	0.6020
6	0.7781
6	0.7781

Water Spout *(lightning; combinatorics)* Study bible 1

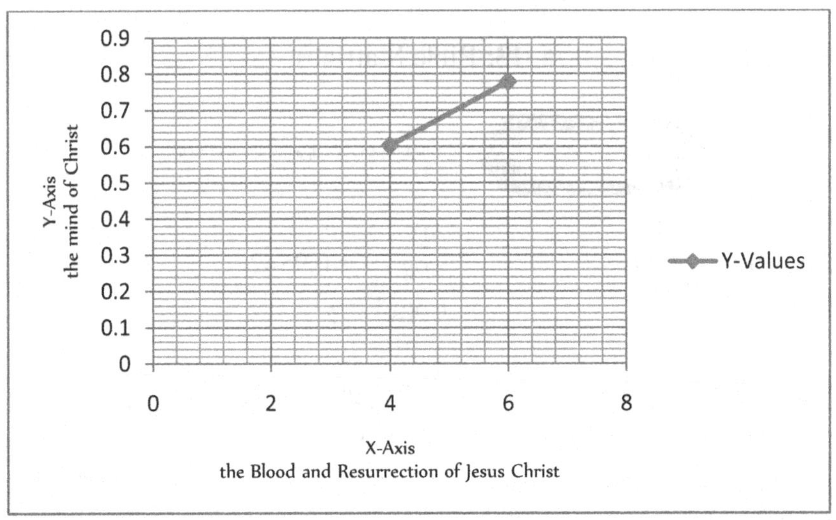

Water Spout *(lightning; combinatorics)* Study bible 2

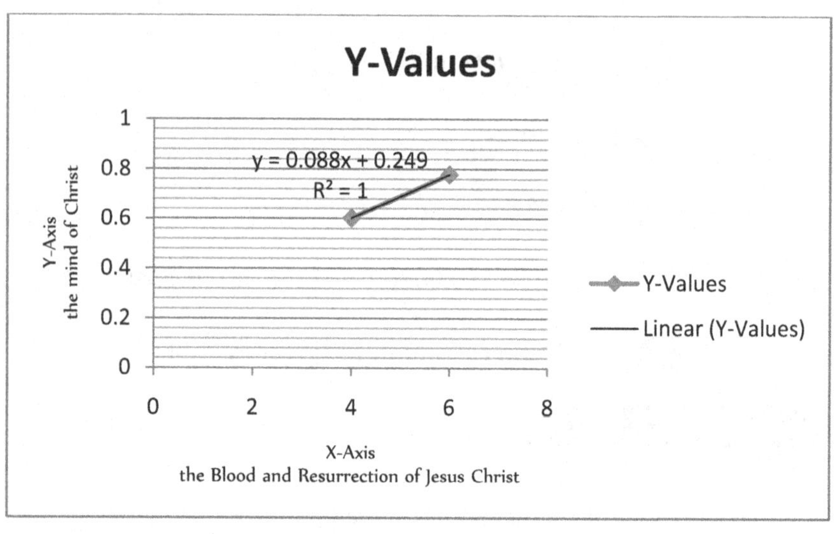

4. Jesussavior; deliverer**answered and said unto them, Go and shew John**the grace or mercy of the Lord**again those things which ye do hear and see:**

6, 13: Bible Matrices

$1_2 5_{10}, 4_7 9_{10}$:

Pilled Poplar, Hazel, and Chestnut bible rods 1

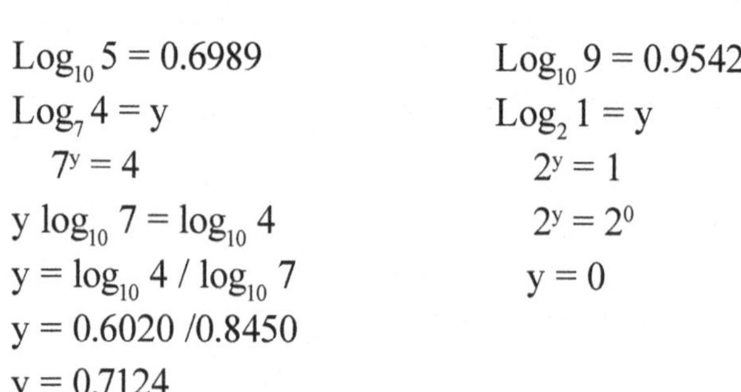

$\text{Log}_{10} 5 = 0.6989$

$\text{Log}_7 4 = y$

$7^y = 4$

$y \log_{10} 7 = \log_{10} 4$

$y = \log_{10} 4 / \log_{10} 7$

$y = 0.6020 / 0.8450$

$y = 0.7124$

$\text{Log}_{10} 9 = 0.9542$

$\text{Log}_2 1 = y$

$2^y = 1$

$2^y = 2^0$

$y = 0$

6, 13: Deep calls unto Deep study bible 1

0 0.6989, 0.7124 0.9542: Deep calls unto Deep study bible 2

x-axis	y-axis
6	0.6989
13	1.6666

Water Spout *(lightning; combinatorics)* Study bible 1

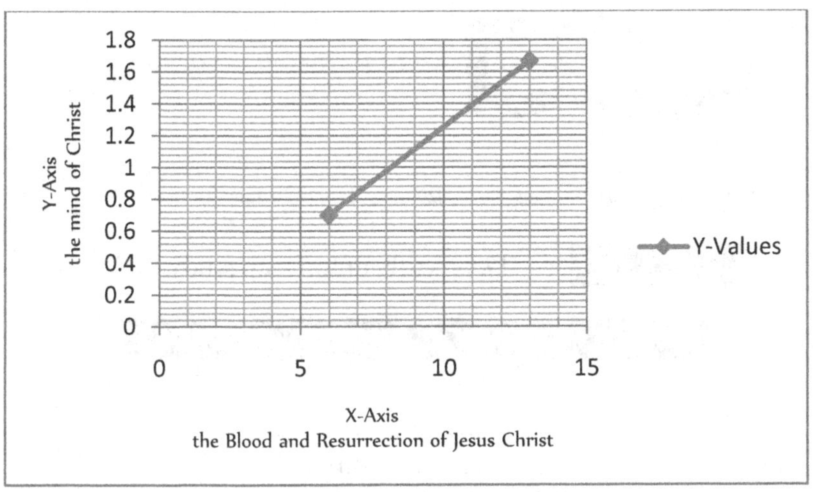

Water Spout *(lightning; combinatorics)* Study bible 2

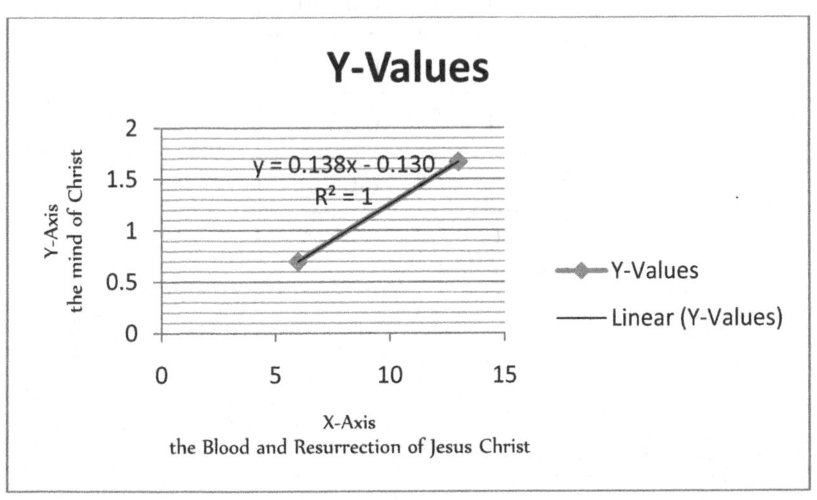

$2^{0}\ 10^{0.6989},\ 7^{0.7124}\ 10^{0.9542}$:

Pilled Poplar, Hazel, and Chestnut bible rods 2

5. The blind receive their sight, and the lame walk, the lepers are cleansed, and the deaf hear, the dead are raised up, and the poor have the gospel preached to them.

5, 4, 4, 4, 5, 9. Bible Matrices

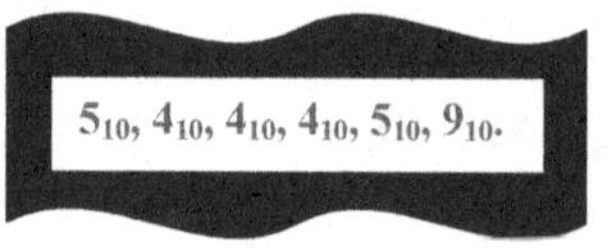

Pilled Poplar, Hazel, and Chestnut bible rods 1

$\text{Log}_{10}5 = 0.6989$ $\text{Log}_{10}5 = 0.6989$ $\text{Log}_{10}4 = 0.6020$ $\text{Log}_{10}4 = 0.6020$ $\text{Log}_{10}4 = 0.6020$ $\text{Log}_{10}9 = 0.9542$

5, 4, 4, 4, 5, 9. Deep calls unto Deep study bible 1

0.6989, 0.6020, 0.6020, 0.6020, 0.6989, 0.9542.

Deep calls unto Deep study bible 2

x-axis	y-axis
5	0.6989
4	0.6020
4	0.6020
4	0.6020
5	0.6989
9	0.9542

Water Spout *(lightning; combinatorics)* Study bible 1

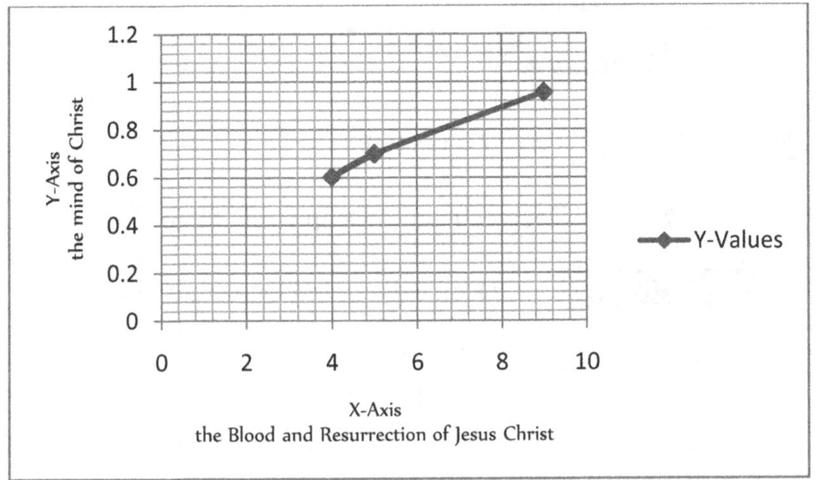

Water Spout *(lightning; combinatorics)* Study bible 2

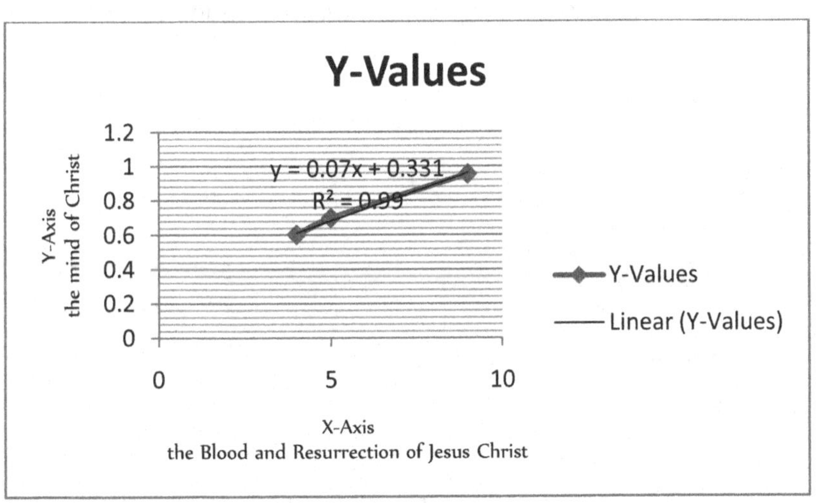

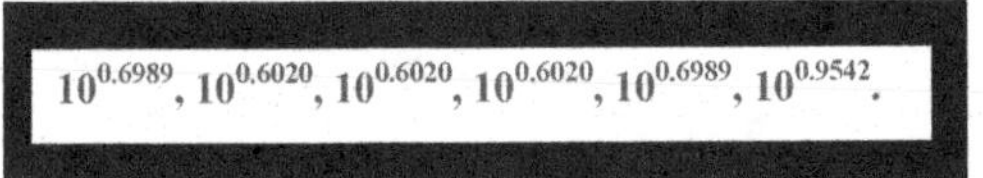

$10^{0.6989}$, $10^{0.6020}$, $10^{0.6020}$, $10^{0.6020}$, $10^{0.6989}$, $10^{0.9542}$.

Pilled Poplar, Hazel, and Chestnut bible rods 2

6. And blessed is he, whosoever shall not be offended in me.

4, 7. Bible Matrices

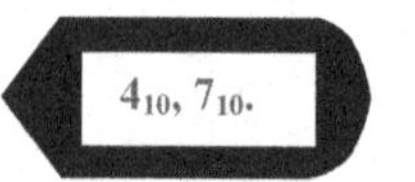

Pilled Poplar, Hazel, and Chestnut bible rods 1

$\text{Log}_{10} 4 = 0.6020$ $\text{Log}_{10} 7 = 0.8450$

4, 7. Deep calls unto Deep study bible 1

0.6020, 0.8450. Deep calls unto Deep study bible 2

x-axis	y-axis
4	0.6020
7	0.8450

Water Spout *(lightning; combinatorics)* Study bible 1

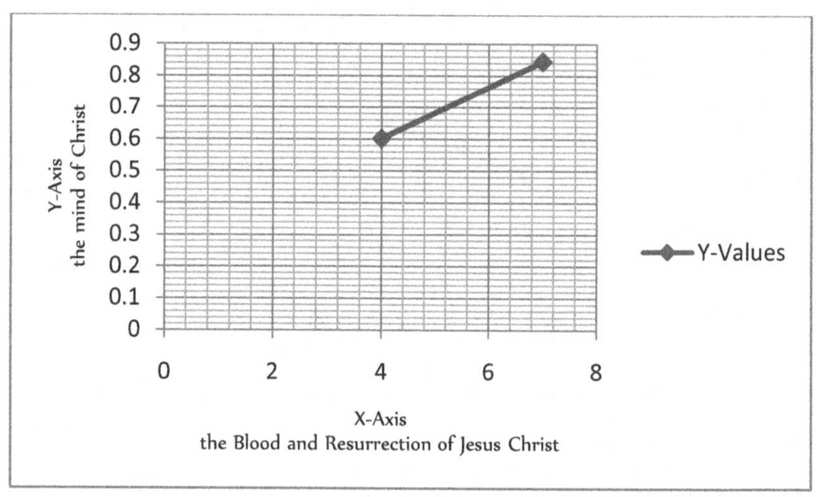

Water Spout *(lightning; combinatorics)* Study bible 2

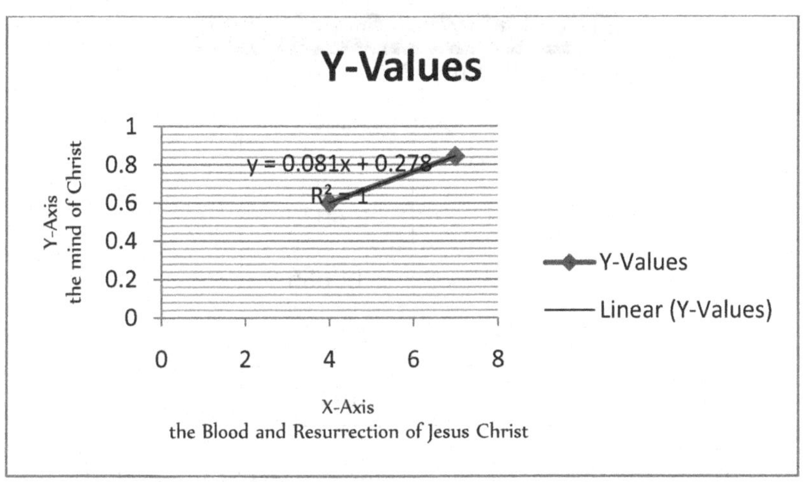

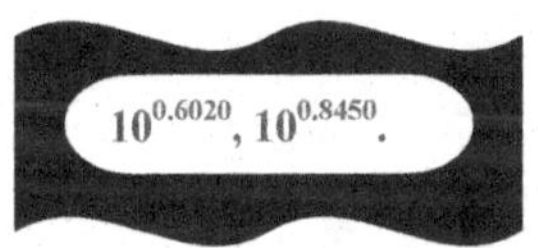

Pilled Poplar, Hazel, and Chestnut bible rods 2

7. And as they departed, Jesussavior; deliverer**began to say unto the multitudes concerning John**the grace or mercy of the Lord, **What went ye out into the wilderness to see? A reed shaken with the wind?**

4, 9, 9? 6? Bible Matrices

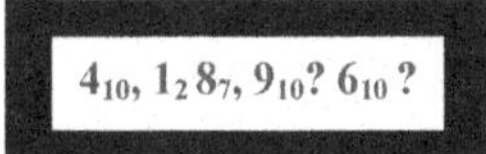

Pilled Poplar, Hazel, and Chestnut bible rods 1

$\text{Log}_{10} 6 = 0.7781$ $\text{Log}_{10} 4 = 0.6020$ $\text{Log}_{10} 9 = 0.9542$

$\text{Log}_7 8 = y$

$7^y = 8$

$y \log_{10} 7 = \log_{10} 8$

$y = \log_{10} 8 / \log_{10} 7$

$y = 0.9030 / 0.8450$

$y = 1.0686$

$\text{Log}_2 1 = y$

$2^y = 1$

$2^y = 2^0$

$y = 0$

4, 9, 9? 6? Deep calls unto Deep study bible 1

0.6020, 0 1.0686, 0.9542? 0.7781?
Deep calls unto Deep study bible 2

x-axis	y-axis
4	0.6020
9	1.0686
9	0.9542
6	0.7781

Water Spout *(lightning; combinatorics)* Study bible 1

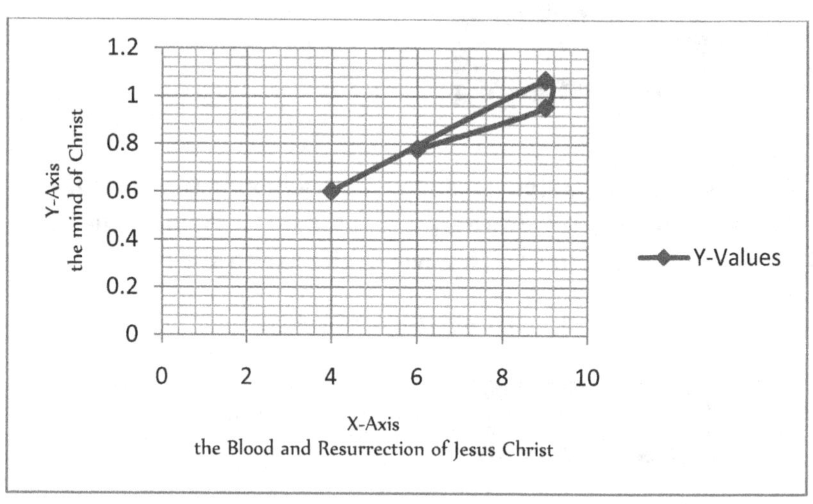

Water Spout *(lightning; combinatorics)* Study bible 2

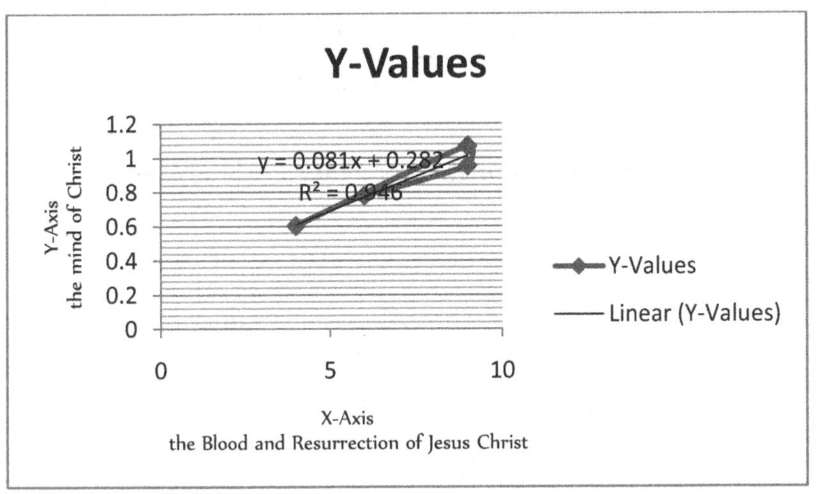

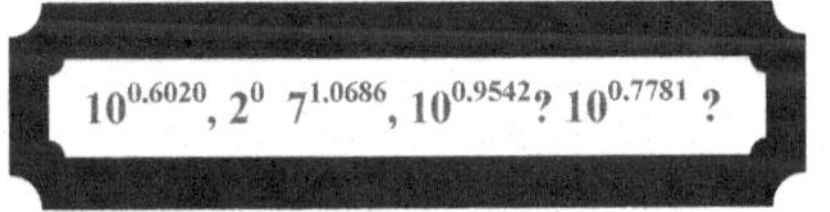

Pilled Poplar, Hazel, and Chestnut bible rods 2

8. But what went ye out for to see? A man clothed in soft raiment? behold, they that wear soft clothing are in kings' houses.

8? 6? 1, 9. Bible Matrices

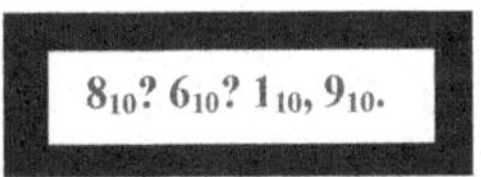

Pilled Poplar, Hazel, and Chestnut bible rods 1

$\text{Log}_{10} 6 = 0.7781$ $\text{Log}_{10} 1 = 0$ $\text{Log}_{10} 8 = 0.9030$ $\text{Log}_{10} 9 = 0.9542$

8? 6? 1, 9. Deep calls unto Deep study bible 1

0.9030? 0.7781? 0, 0.9542. Deep calls unto Deep study bible 2

x-axis	y-axis
8	0.9030

6	0.7781
1	0
9	0.9542

Water Spout *(lightning; combinatorics)* Study bible 1

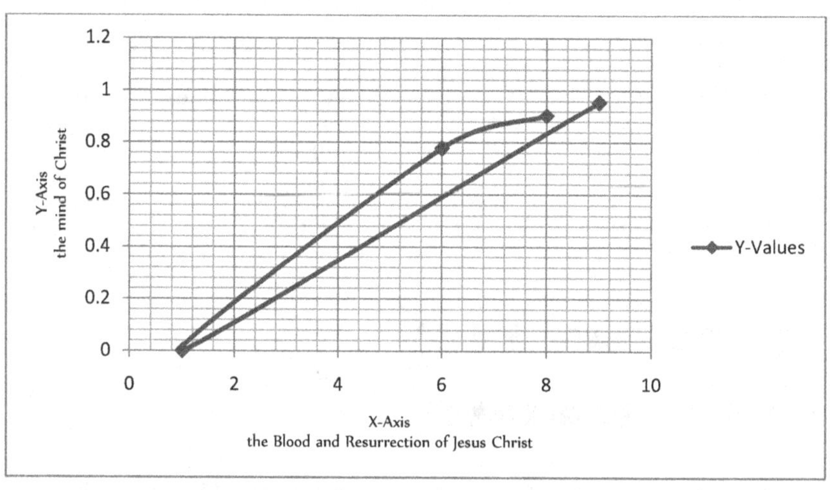

Water Spout *(lightning; combinatorics)* Study bible 2

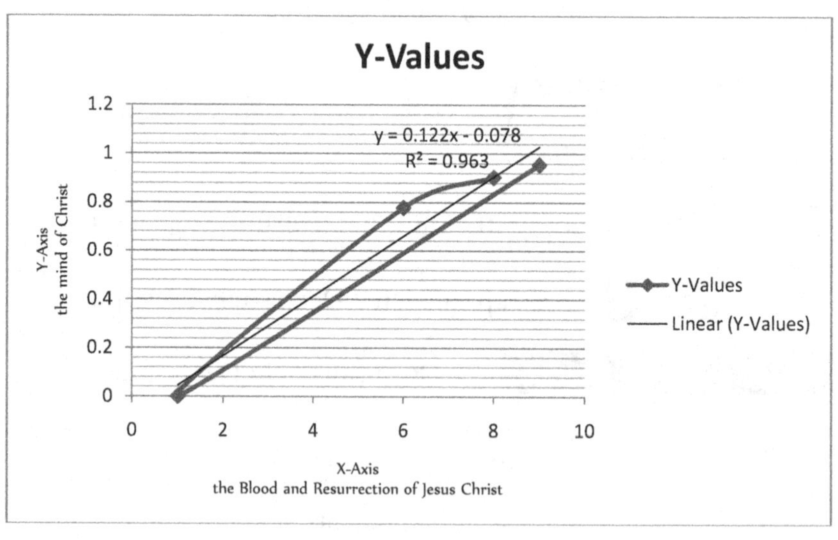

$10^{0.9030}$? $10^{0.7781}$? 10^{0}, $10^{0.9542}$.

Pilled Poplar, Hazel, and Chestnut bible rods 2

9. But what went ye out for to see? A prophet to bubble forth, as from a fountain; utter? **yea, I say unto you, and more than a prophet** to bubble forth, as from a fountain; utter.

8? 2? 1, 4, 5. Bible Matrices

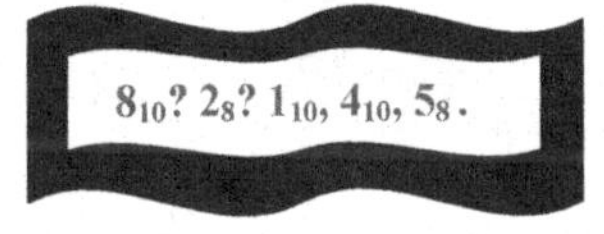

Pilled Poplar, Hazel, and Chestnut bible rods 1

$Log_{10} 4 = 0.6020$
$Log_8 2 = y$
$8^y = 2$
$y \log_{10} 8 = \log_{10} 2$
$y = \log_{10} 2 / \log_{10} 8$
$y = 0.3010 / 0.9030$
$y = 0.3333$

$Log_{10} 1 = 0$
$Log_8 5 = y$
$8^y = 5$
$y \log_{10} 8 = \log_{10} 5$
$y = \log_{10} 5 / \log_{10} 8$
$y = 0.6989 / 0.9030$
$y = 0.7739$

$Log_{10} 8 = 0.9030$

8? 2? 1, 4, 5. Deep calls unto Deep study bible 1

0.9030? 0.3333? 0, 0.6020, 0.7739.

Deep calls unto Deep study bible 2

x-axis	y-axis
8	0.9030
2	0.3333
1	0
4	0.6020
5	0.7739

Water Spout *(lightning; combinatorics)* Study bible 1

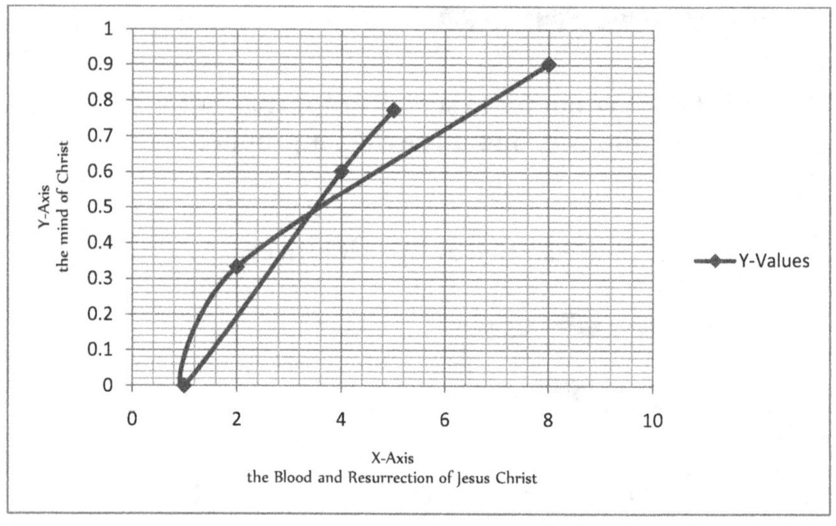

Water Spout *(lightning; combinatorics)* Study bible 2

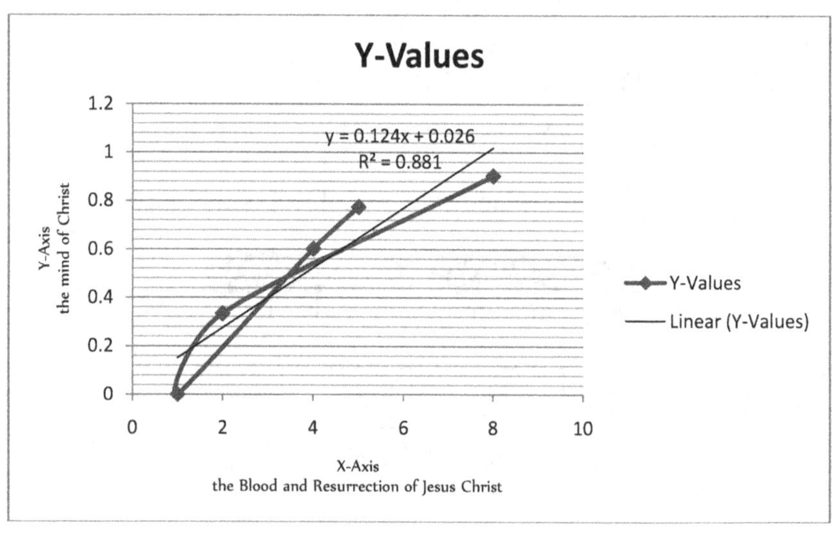

$10^{0.9030}$? $8^{0.3333}$? 10^{0}, $10^{0.6020}$, $8^{0.7739}$.

Pilled Poplar, Hazel, and Chestnut bible rods 2

10. For this is he, of whom it is written, Behold, I send my messenger before thy face, which shall prepare thy way before thee.

4, 5, 1, 7, 7. Bible Matrices

$4_{10}, 5_{10}, 1_{10}, 7_{10}, 7_{10}$.

Pilled Poplar, Hazel, and Chestnut bible rods 1

$\text{Log}_{10} 4 = 0.6020$ $\text{Log}_{10} 5 = 0.6989$ $\text{Log}_{10} 1 = 0$ $\text{Log}_{10} 7 = 0.8450$ $\text{Log}_{10} 7 = 0.8450$

4, 5, 1, 7, 7. Deep calls unto Deep study bible 1

0.6020, 0.6989, 0, 0.8450, 0.8450.
Deep calls unto Deep study bible 2

x-axis	y-axis
4	0.6020
5	0.6989
1	0
7	0.8450
7	0.8450

Water Spout *(lightning; combinatorics)* Study bible 1

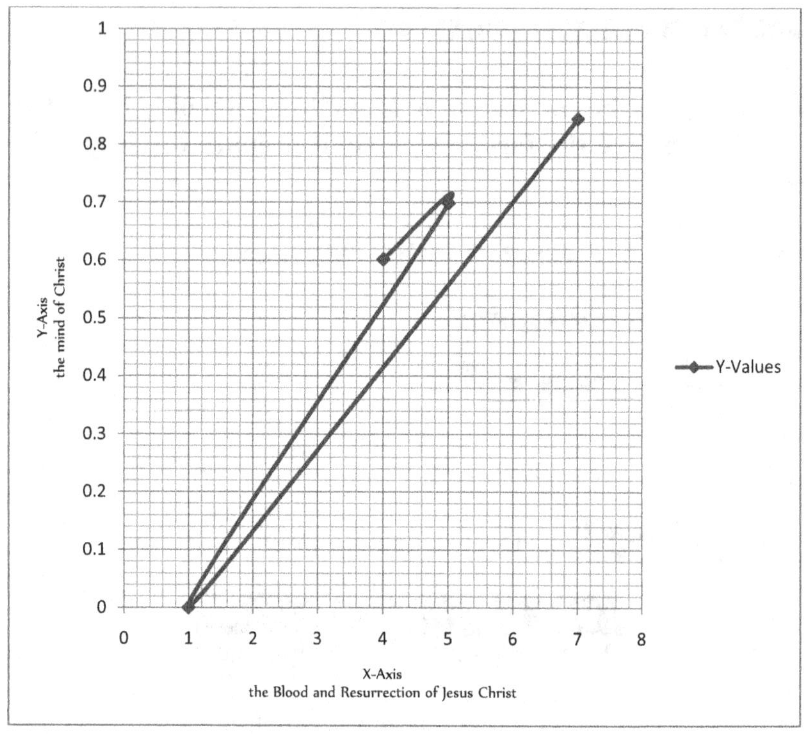

Water Spout *(lightning; combinatorics)* Study bible 2

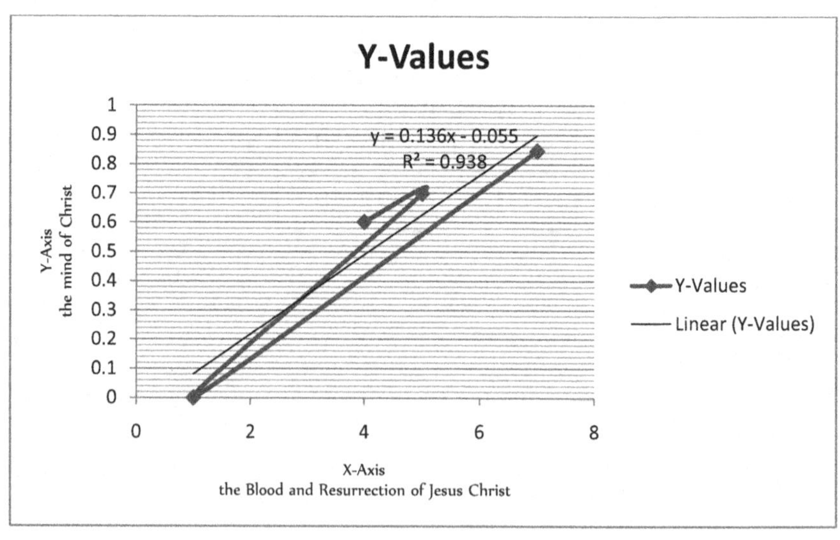

$10^{0.6020}, 10^{0.6989}, 10^{0}, 10^{0.8450}, 10^{0.8450}$.

Pilled Poplar, Hazel, and Chestnut bible rods 2

11. Verily I say unto you, Among them that are born of women there hath not risen a greater than Johnthe grace or mercy of the Lord **the Baptist: notwithstanding he that is least in the kingdom of heaven is greater than he.**

5, 17: 14. Bible Matrices

$5_{10}, 15_{7}\, 2_{10}: 14_{10}$.

Pilled Poplar, Hazel, and Chestnut bible rods 1

$\text{Log}_{10} 5 = 0.6989$ $\text{Log}_{10} 2 = 0.3010$ $\text{Log}_{10} 14 = 1.1461$

$\text{Log}_{7} 15 = y$

$7^{y} = 15$

$y \log_{10} 7 = \log_{10} 15$

$y = \log_{10} 15 / \log_{10} 7$

$y = 1.1760 / 0.8450$

$y = 1.3917$

5, 17: 14. Deep calls unto Deep study bible 1

0.6989, 1.3917 0.3010: 1.1461.

Deep calls unto Deep study bible 2

x-axis	y-axis
5	0.6989
17	1.6927
14	1.1461

Water Spout *(lightning; combinatorics)* Study bible 1

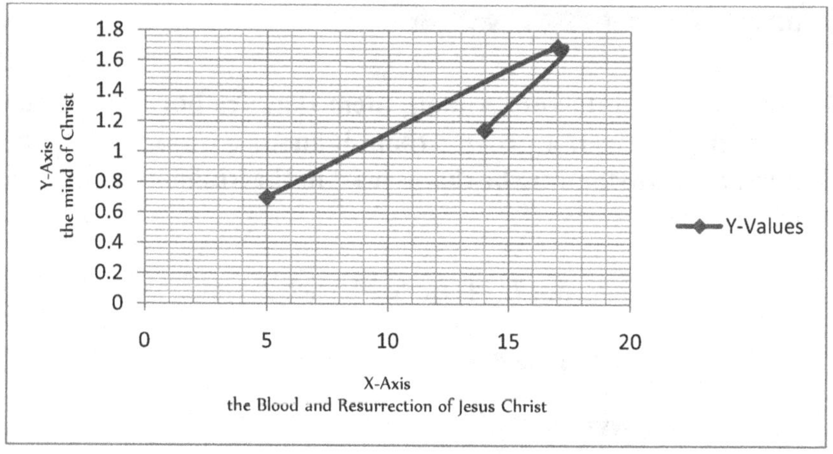

Water Spout *(lightning; combinatorics)* Study bible 2

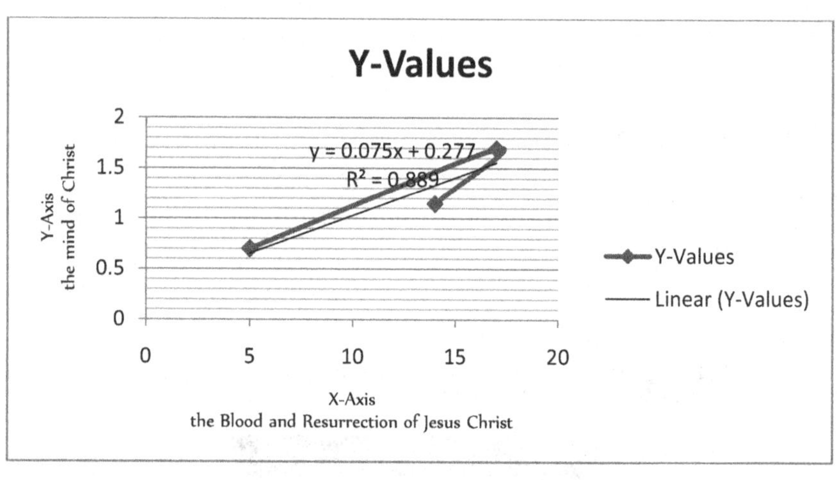

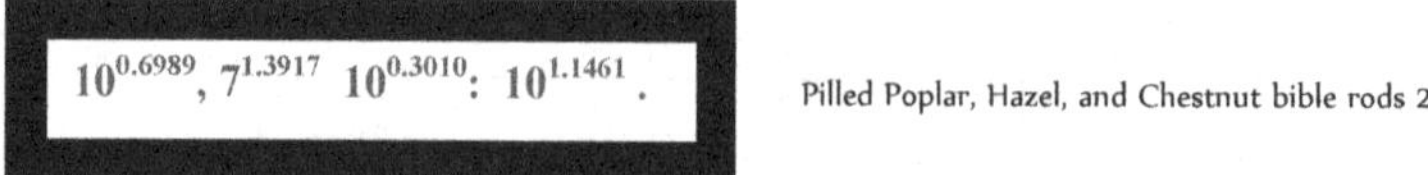

Pilled Poplar, Hazel, and Chestnut bible rods 2

12. And from the days of John the grace or mercy of the Lord **the Baptist until now the kingdom of heaven suffereth violence, and the violent take it by force.**

16, 7. Bible Matrices

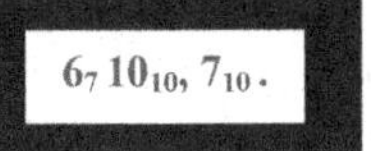

Pilled Poplar, Hazel, and Chestnut bible rods 1

$\text{Log}_{10} 7 = 0.8450$ $\text{Log}_{10} 10 = 1$

$\text{Log}_7 6 = y$

$7^y = 6$

$y \log_{10} 7 = \log_{10} 6$

$y = \log_{10} 6 / \log_{10} 7$

$y = 0.7781 / 0.8450$

$y = 0.9208$

16, 7. Deep calls unto Deep study bible 1

0.9208 1, 0.8450. Deep calls unto Deep study bible 2

x-axis	y-axis
16	1.9208
7	0.8450

Water Spout *(lightning; combinatorics)* Study bible 1

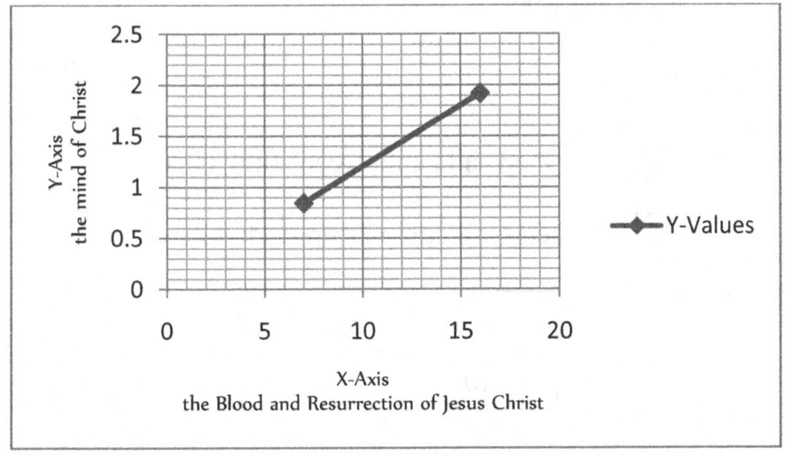

Water Spout *(lightning; combinatorics)* Study bible 2

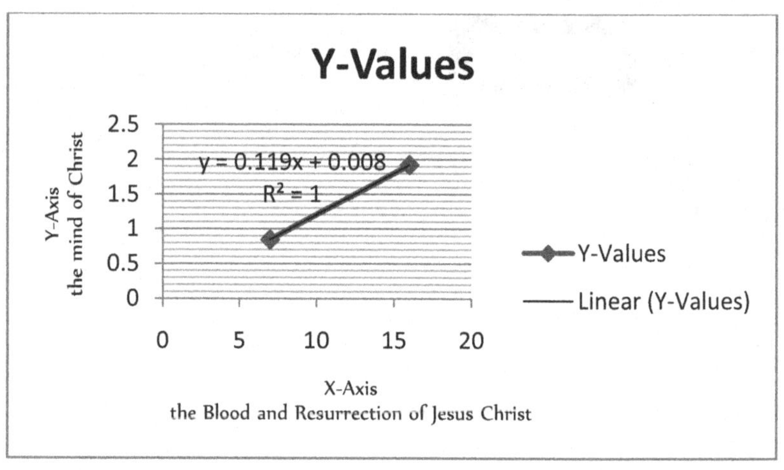

Pilled Poplar, Hazel, and Chestnut bible rods 2

13. For all the prophets and the law prophesied until Johnthe grace or mercy of the Lord.

10. Bible Matrices

Pilled Poplar, Hazel, and Chestnut bible rods 1

$\text{Log}_{10} 10 = 1$

10. Deep calls unto Deep study bible 1

1. Deep calls unto Deep study bible 2

x-axis	y-axis
10	1

Water Spout *(lightning; combinatorics)* Study bible 1

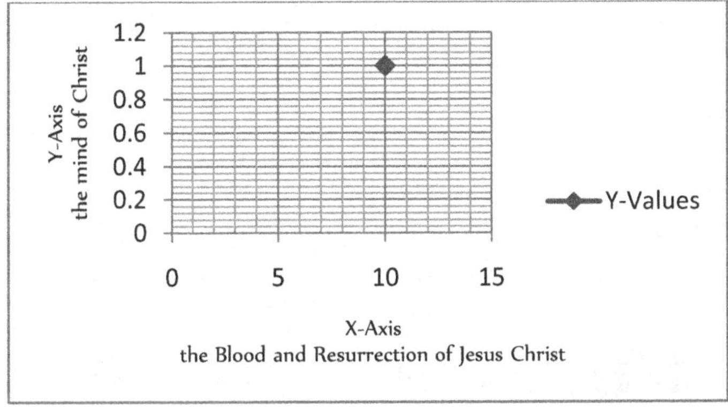

Water Spout *(lightning; combinatorics)* Study bible 2

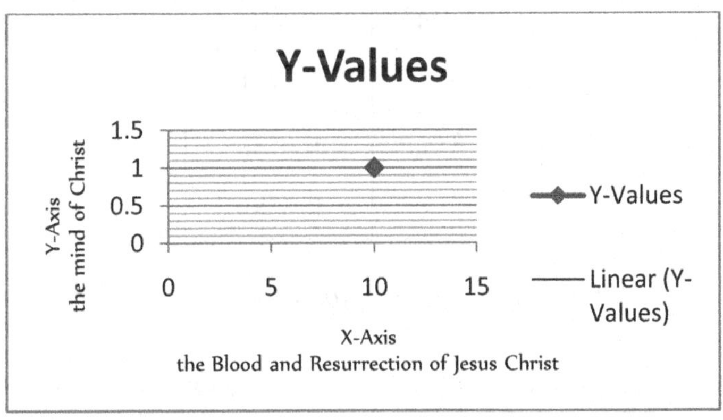

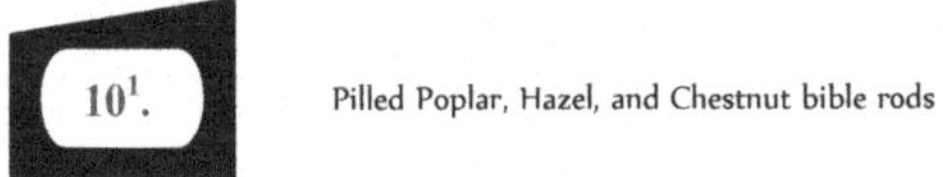

Pilled Poplar, Hazel, and Chestnut bible rods 2

14. And if ye will receive it, this is Elias God the Lord, the strong Lord, **which was for to come.**

6, 3, 5. Bible Matrices

Pilled Poplar, Hazel, and Chestnut bible rods 1

$\mathrm{Log}_{10} 6 = 0.7781$ $\mathrm{Log}_{10} 5 = 0.6989$

$\mathrm{Log}_{6} 3 = y$

$6^{y} = 3$

$y \log_{10} 6 = \log_{10} 3$

$y = \log_{10} 3 / \log_{10} 6$

$y = 0.4771 / 0.7781$

$y = 0.6131$

6, 3, 5. Deep calls unto Deep study bible 1

0.7781, 0.6131, 0.6989. Deep calls unto Deep study bible 2

x-axis	y-axis
6	0.7781
3	0.6131
5	0.6989

Water Spout *(lightning; combinatorics)* Study bible 1

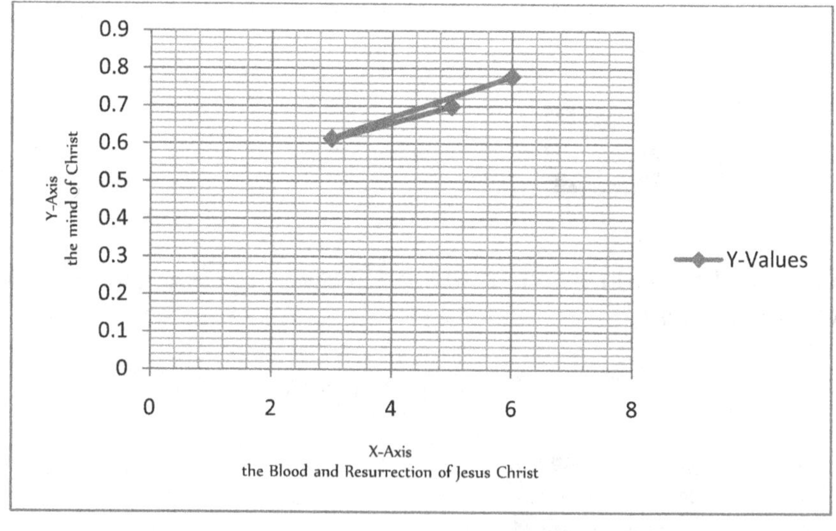

Water Spout *(lightning; combinatorics)* Study bible 2

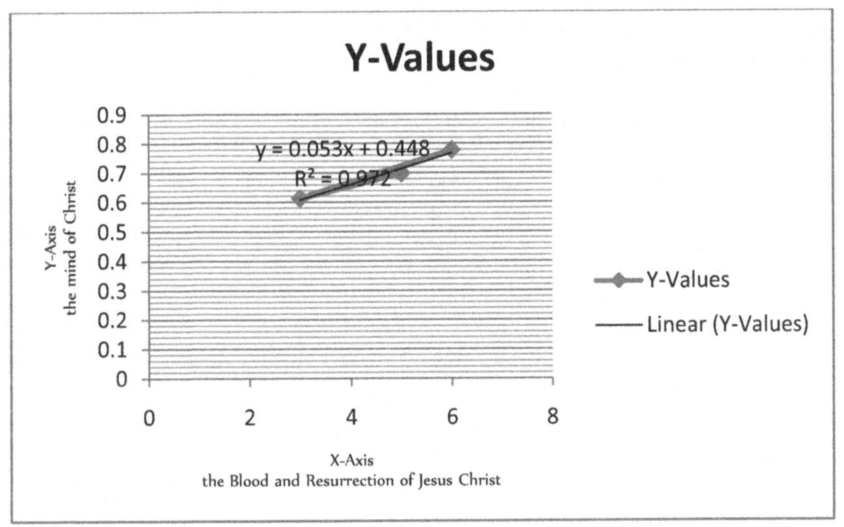

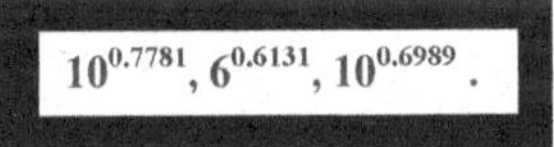

Pilled Poplar, Hazel, and Chestnut bible rods 2

15. He that hath ears to hear, let him hear.

6, 3. Bible Matrices

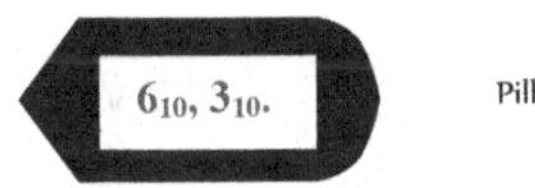

Pilled Poplar, Hazel, and Chestnut bible rods 1

$\text{Log}_{10} 6 = 0.7781$ $\text{Log}_{10} 3 = 0.4771$

6, 3. Deep calls unto Deep study bible 1

0.7781, 0.4771. Deep calls unto Deep study bible 2

x-axis	y-axis
6	0.7781
3	0.4771

Water Spout *(lightning; combinatorics)* Study bible 1

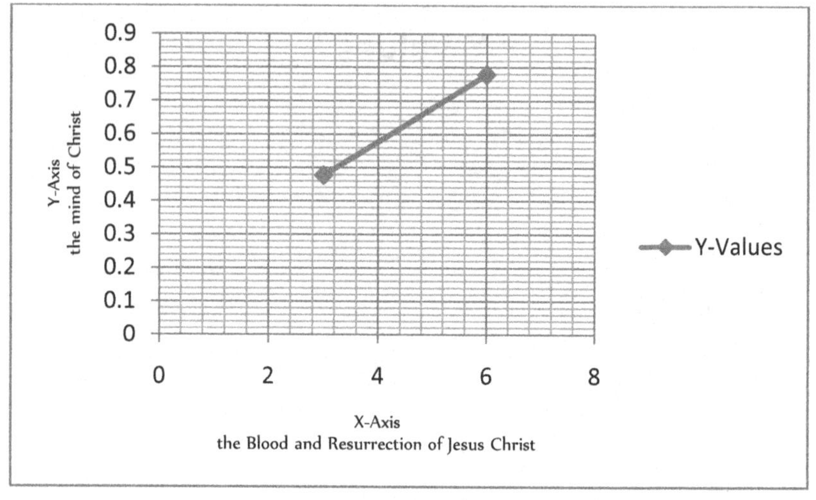

Water Spout *(lightning; combinatorics)* Study bible 2

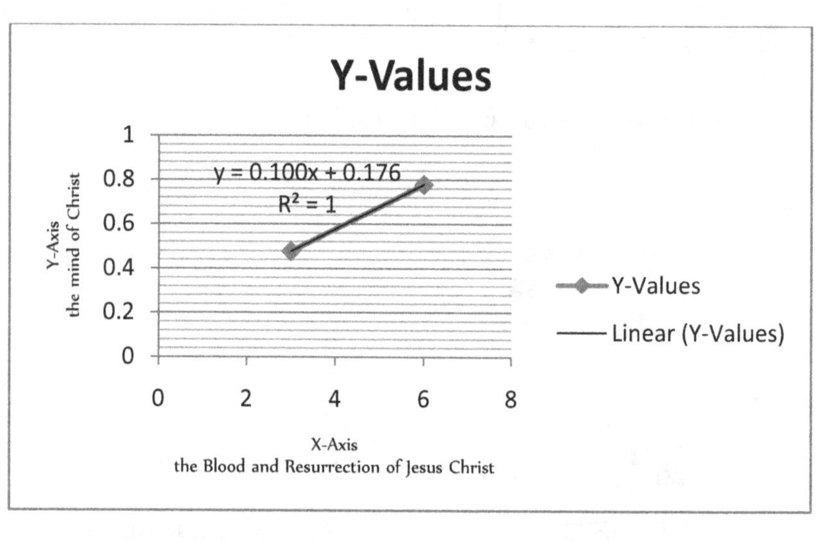

Pilled Poplar, Hazel, and Chestnut bible rods 2

16. But whereunto shall I liken this generation? It is like unto children sitting in the markets, and calling unto their fellows,

7? 9, 5, Bible Matrices

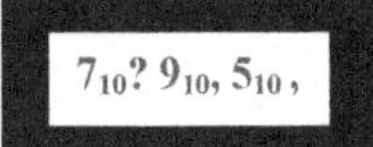

Pilled Poplar, Hazel, and Chestnut bible rods 1

$Log_{10} 5 = 0.6989$ $Log_{10} 7 = 0.8450$ $Log_{10} 9 = 0.9542$

7? 9, 5, Deep calls unto Deep study bible 1

0.8450? 0.9542, 0.6989, Deep calls unto Deep study bible 2

x-axis	y-axis
7	0.8450
9	0.9542
5	0.6989

Water Spout *(lightning; combinatorics)* Study bible 1

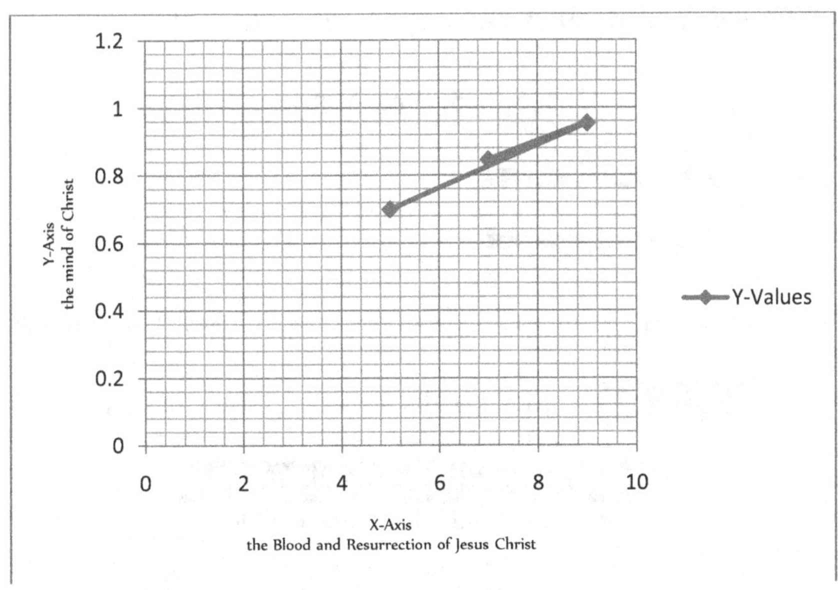

Water Spout *(lightning; combinatorics)* Study bible 2

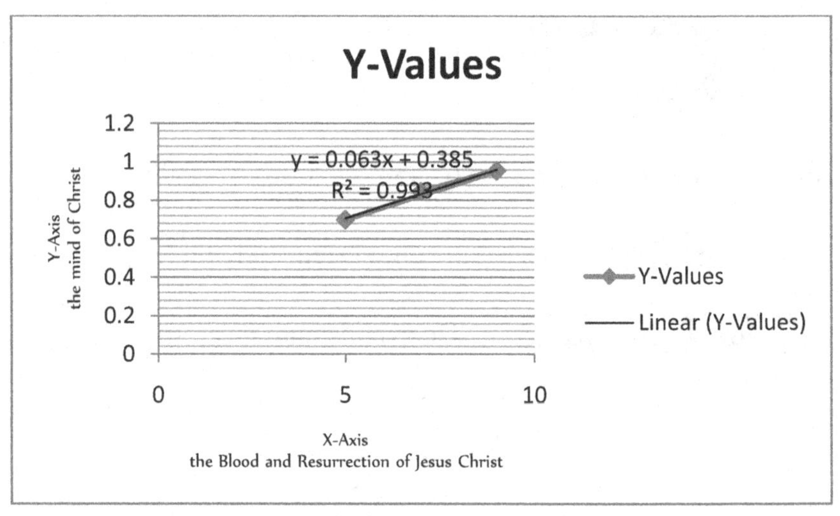

$10^{0.8450}$? $10^{0.9542}$, $10^{0.6989}$,

Pilled Poplar, Hazel, and Chestnut bible rods 2

17. And saying, We have piped unto you, and ye have not danced; we have mourned unto you, and ye have not lamented.

2, 5, 5; 5, 5. Bible Matrices

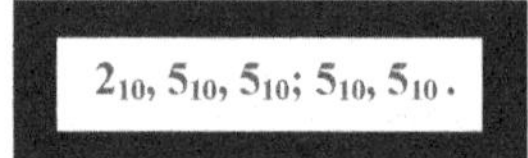
2_{10}, 5_{10}, 5_{10}; 5_{10}, 5_{10} .

Pilled Poplar, Hazel, and Chestnut bible rods 1

$\mathrm{Log}_{10} 2 = 0.3010$ $\mathrm{Log}_{10} 5 = 0.6989$ $\mathrm{Log}_{10} 5 = 0.6989$ $\mathrm{Log}_{10} 5 = 0.6989$ $\mathrm{Log}_{10} 5 = 0.6989$

2, 5, 5; 5, 5. Deep calls unto Deep study bible 1

0.3010, 0.6989, 0.6989; 0.6989, 0.6989.
Deep calls unto Deep study bible 2

x-axis	y-axis
2	0.3010
5	0.6989
5	0.6989
5	0.6989
5	0.6989

Water Spout *(lightning; combinatorics)* Study bible 1

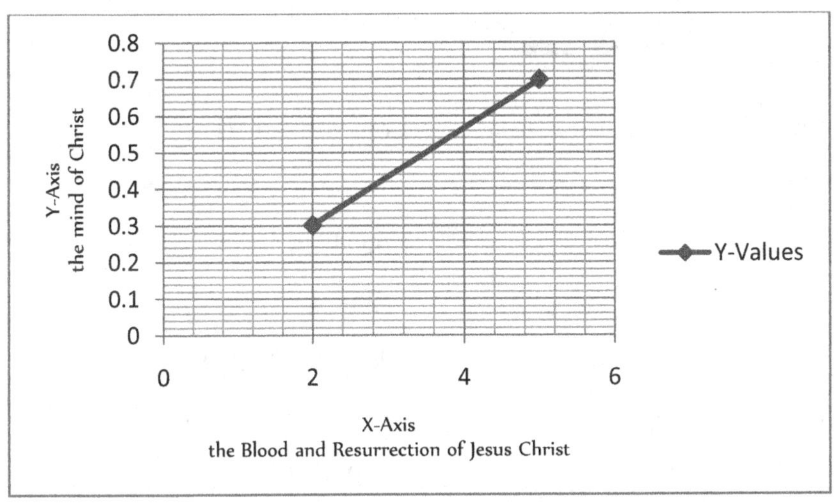

Water Spout *(lightning; combinatorics)* Study bible 2

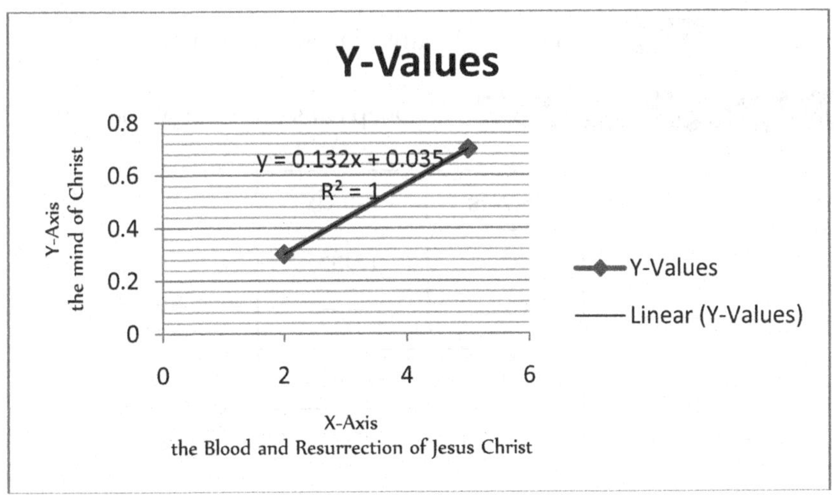

$10^{0.3010}, 10^{0.6989}, 10^{0.6989}; 10^{0.6989}, 10^{0.6989}$. Pilled Poplar, Hazel, and Chestnut bible rods 2

18. For Johnthe grace or mercy of the Lord**came neither eating nor drinking, and they say, He hath a devil** slanderer, false accuser.

7, 3, 4. Bible Matrices

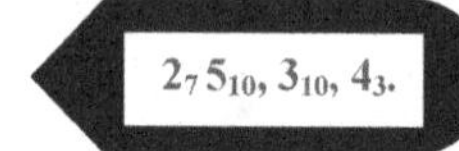

Pilled Poplar, Hazel, and Chestnut bible rods 1

$\mathrm{Log}_{10} 5 = 0.6989$

$\mathrm{Log}_{10} 3 = 0.4771$

$\mathrm{Log}_7 2 = y$

$7^y = 2$

$y \log_{10} 7 = \log_{10} 2$

$y = \log_{10} 2 / \log_{10} 7$

$y = 0.3010 / 0.8450$

$y = 0.3562$

$\mathrm{Log}_3 4 = y$

$3^y = 4$

$y \log_{10} 3 = \log_{10} 4$

$y = \log_{10} 4 / \log_{10} 3$

$y = 0.6020 / 0.4771$

$y = 1.2617$

7, 3, 4. Deep calls unto Deep study bible 1

0.3562 0.6989, 0.4771, 1.2617. Deep calls unto Deep study bible 2

x-axis	y-axis
7	1.0551
3	0.4771
4	1.2617

Water Spout *(lightning; combinatorics)* Study bible 1

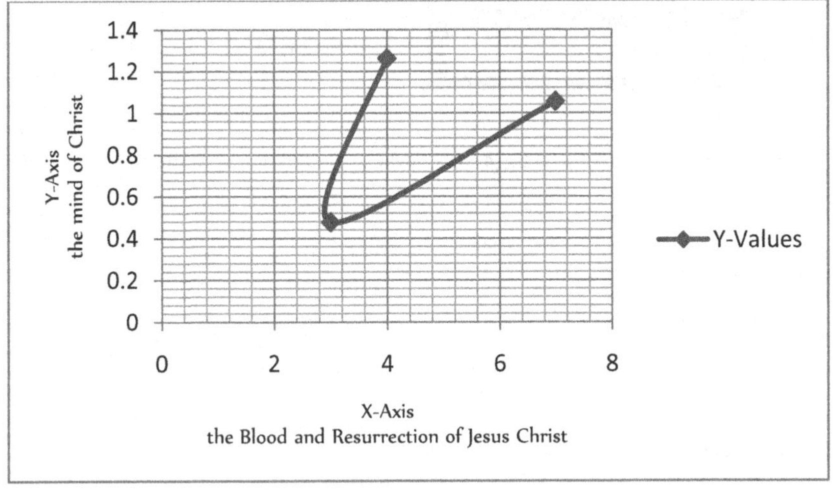

Water Spout *(lightning; combinatorics)* Study bible 2

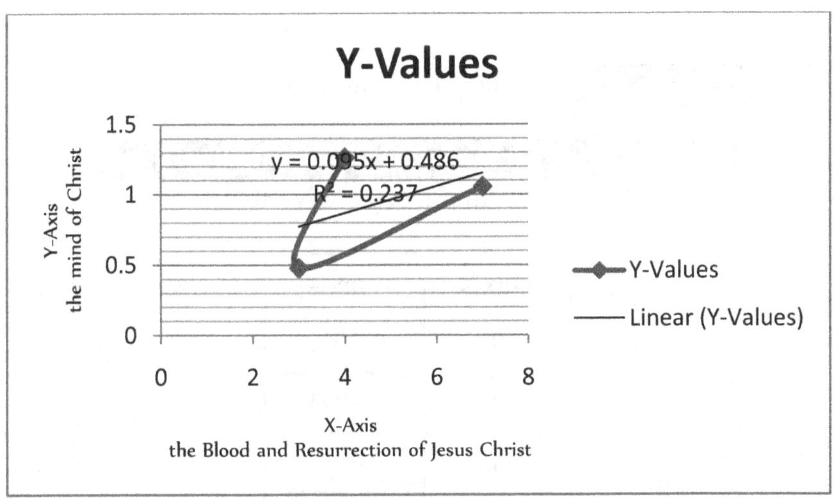

$7^{0.3562}$ $10^{0.6989}$, $10^{0.4771}$, $3^{1.2617}$.

Pilled Poplar, Hazel, and Chestnut bible rods 2

19. The Son of man came eating and drinking, and they say, Behold a man gluttonous, and a winebibber, a friend of publicansone who farmed the taxes; a tax collector **and sinners. But wisdom is justified of her children.**

8, 3, 4, 3, 6. 7. Bible Matrices

$8_{10}, 3_{10}, 4_{10}, 3_{10}, 4_8 2_{10}. 7_{10}.$

Pilled Poplar, Hazel, and Chestnut bible rods 1

$\text{Log}_{10} 8 = 0.9030$ $\text{Log}_{10} 3 = 0.4771$ $\text{Log}_{10} 4 = 0.6020$ $\text{Log}_{10} 3 = 0.4771$ $\text{Log}_{10} 2 = 0.3010$ $\text{Log}_{10} 7 = 0.8450$

$\text{Log}_8 4 = y$

$8^y = 4$

$y \log_{10} 8 = \log_{10} 4$

$y = \log_{10} 4 / \log_{10} 8$

$y = 0.6020 / 0.9030$

$y = 0.6666$

8, 3, 4, 3, 6. 7. Deep calls unto Deep study bible 1

0.9030, 0.4771, 0.6020, 0.4771, 0.6666 0.3010. 0.8450.
Deep calls unto Deep study bible 2

x-axis	y-axis
8	0.9030
3	0.4771
4	0.6020
3	0.4771
6	0.9676
7	0.8450

Water Spout *(lightning; combinatorics)* Study bible 1

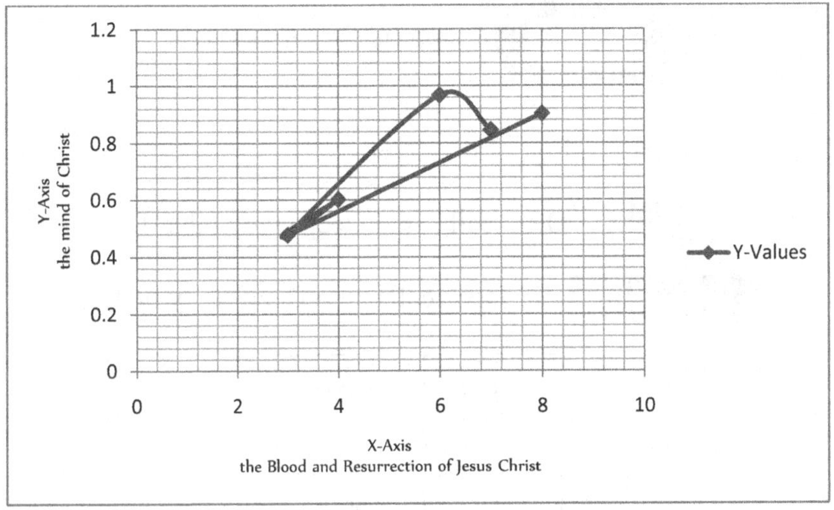

Water Spout *(lightning; combinatorics)* Study bible 2

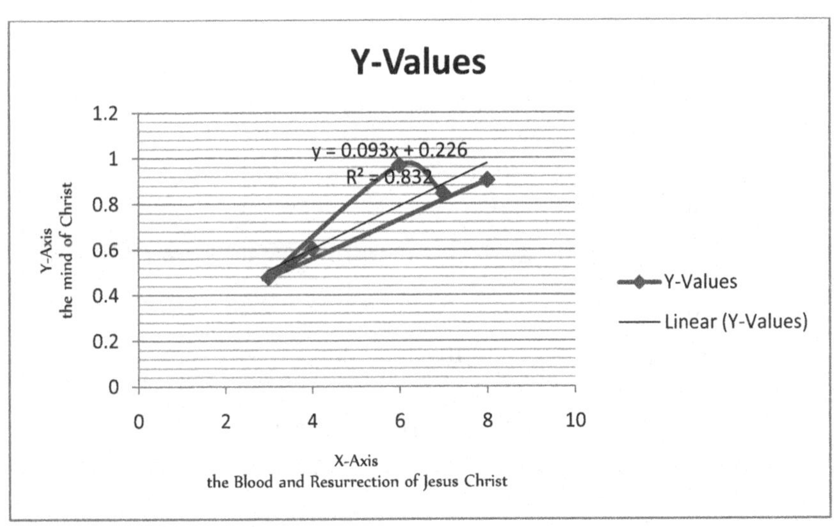

$10^{0.9030}, 10^{0.4771}, 10^{0.6020}, 10^{0.4771}, 8^{0.6666}\ 10^{0.3010}. 10^{0.8450}$.	Pilled Poplar, Hazel, and Chestnut bible rods 2

20. Then began he to upbraid the cities wherein most of his mighty works were done, because they repented not:

15, 4: Bible Matrices

$Log_{10} 4 = 0.6020$ $Log_{10} 15 = 1.1760$

15, 4: Deep calls unto Deep study bible 1

1.1760, 0.6020: Deep calls unto Deep study bible 2

x-axis	y-axis
15	1.1760
4	0.6020

Water Spout *(lightning; combinatorics)* Study bible 1

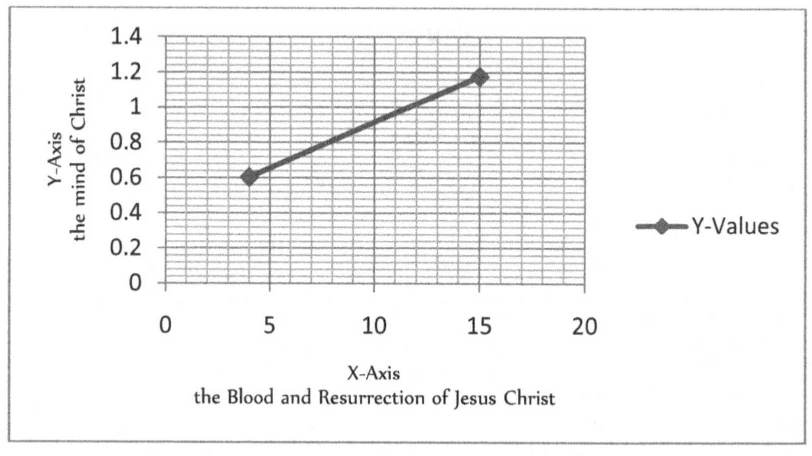

Water Spout *(lightning; combinatorics)* Study bible 2

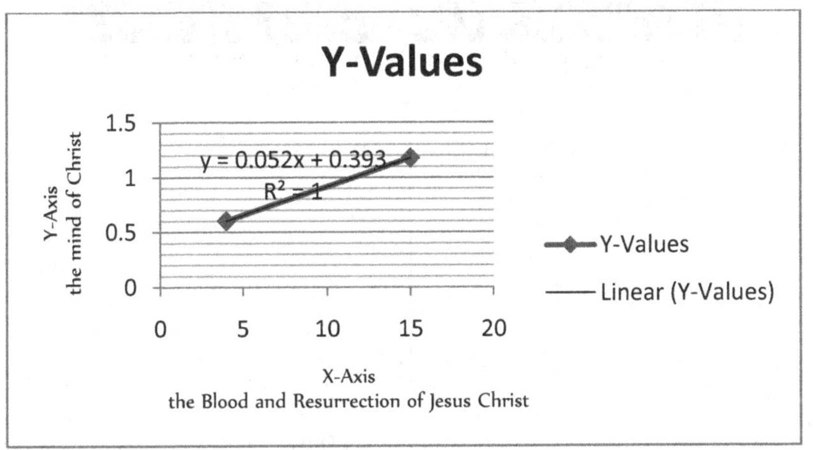

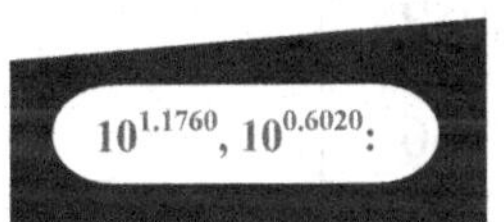

Pilled Poplar, Hazel, and Chestnut bible rods 2

21. Woe unto thee, Chorazinthe secret; here is a mystery!**woe unto thee, Bethsaida**house of fruits; house of fish! **for if the mighty works, which were done in you, had been done in Tyre**strength; rock; sharp**and Sidon**hunting; fishing; venison, **they would have repented long ago in sackcloth and ashes.**

3, 1! 3, 1! 5, 5, 7, 10. Bible Matrices

3_{10}, 1_6! 3_{10}, 1_6! 5_{10}, 5_{10}, $5_3 2_3$, 10_{10}.

Pilled Poplar, Hazel, and Chestnut bible rods 1

$\text{Log}_{10} 3 = 0.4771$ $\text{Log}_{10} 1 = 0$ $\text{Log}_{10} 3 = 0.4771$ $\text{Log}_{10} 1 = 0$ $\text{Log}_{10} 5 = 0.6989$ $\text{Log}_{10} 5 = 0.6989$ $\log_{10} 10 = 1$

$\text{Log}_3 5 = y$

$3^y = 5$

$y \log_{10} 3 = \log_{10} 5$

$y = \log_{10} 5 / \log_{10} 3$

$y = 0.6989 / 0.4771$

$y = 1.4648$

$\text{Log}_3 2 = y$

$3^y = 2$

$y \log_{10} 3 = \log_{10} 2$

$y = \log_{10} 2 / \log_{10} 3$

$y = 0.3010 / 0.4771$

$y = 0.6308$

$\text{Log}_6 1 = y$

$6y = 60$

$y = 0$

$\text{Log}_6 1 = y$

$6y = 60$

$y = 0$

3, 1! 3, 1! 5, 5, 7, 10. Deep calls unto Deep study bible 1

0.4771, 0! 0.4771, 0! 0.6989, 0.6989, 1.4648 0.6308, 1.
Deep calls unto Deep study bible 2

x-axis	y-axis
3	0.4771
1	0
3	0.4771
1	0
5	0.6989
5	0.6989
7	2.0956
10	1

Water Spout *(lightning; combinatorics)* Study bible 1

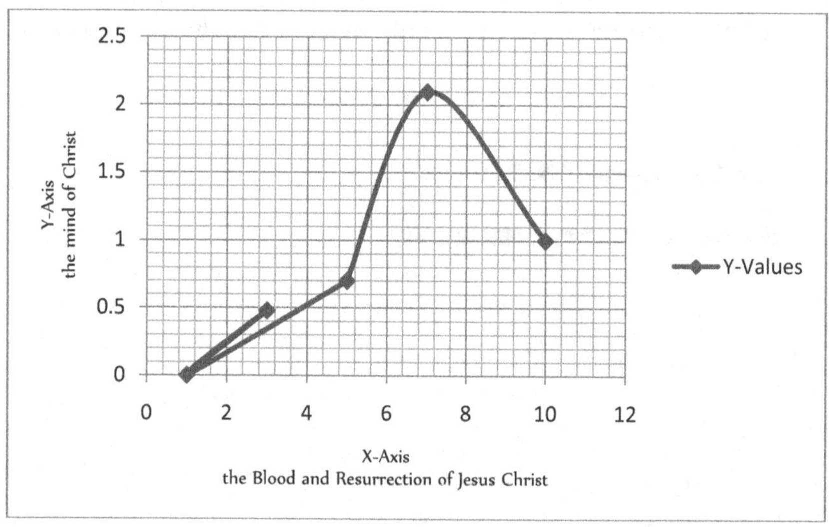

Water Spout *(lightning; combinatorics)* Study bible 2

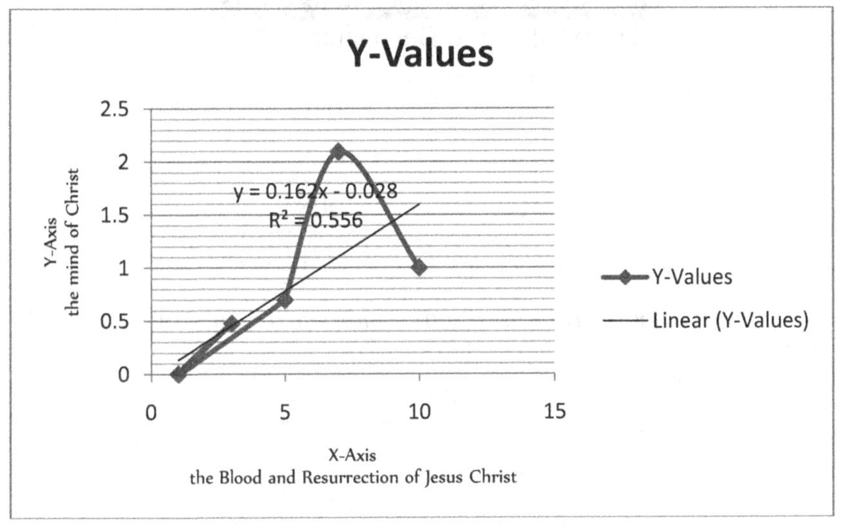

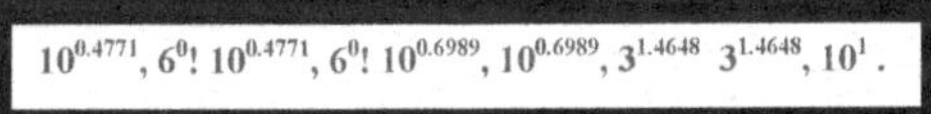

Pilled Poplar, Hazel, and Chestnut bible rods 2

22. But I say unto you, It shall be more tolerable for Tyrestrength; rock;
sharp**and Sidon**hunting; fishing; venison**at the day of judgment, than for you.**

5, 14, 3. Bible Matrices

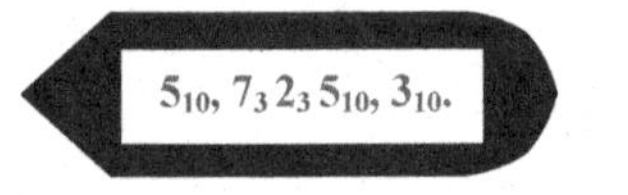

Pilled Poplar, Hazel, and Chestnut bible rods 1

$\text{Log}_{10} 5 = 0.6989$

$\text{Log}_{3} 7 = y$

$3^{y} = 7$

$y \log_{10} 3 = \log_{10} 7$

$y = \log_{10} 7 / \log_{10} 3$

$y = 0.8450 / 0.4771$

$y = 1.7711$

$\text{Log}_{10} 3 = 0.4771$

$\text{Log}_{3} 2 = y$

$3^{y} = 2$

$y \log_{10} 3 = \log_{10} 2$

$y = \log_{10} 2 / \log_{10} 3$

$y = 0.3010 / 0.4771$

$y = 0.6308$

$\text{Log}_{10} 5 = 0.6989$

5, 14, 3. Deep calls unto Deep study bible 1

0.6989, 1.7711 0.6308 0.6989, 0.4771.

Deep calls unto Deep study bible 2

x-axis	y-axis
5	0.6989
14	3.1008
3	0.4771

Water Spout *(lightning; combinatorics)* Study bible 1

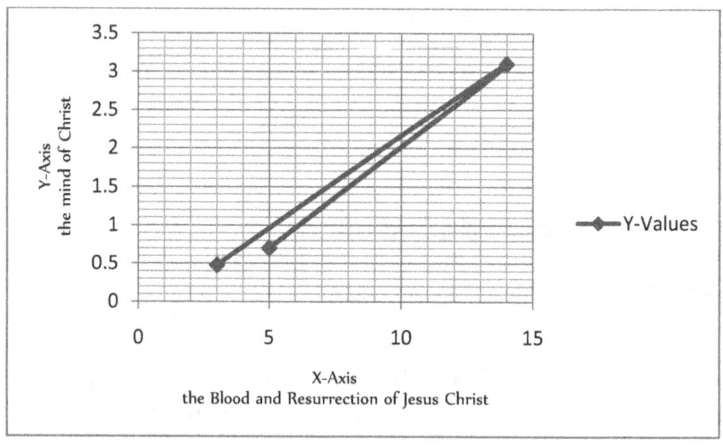

Water Spout *(lightning; combinatorics)* Study bible 2

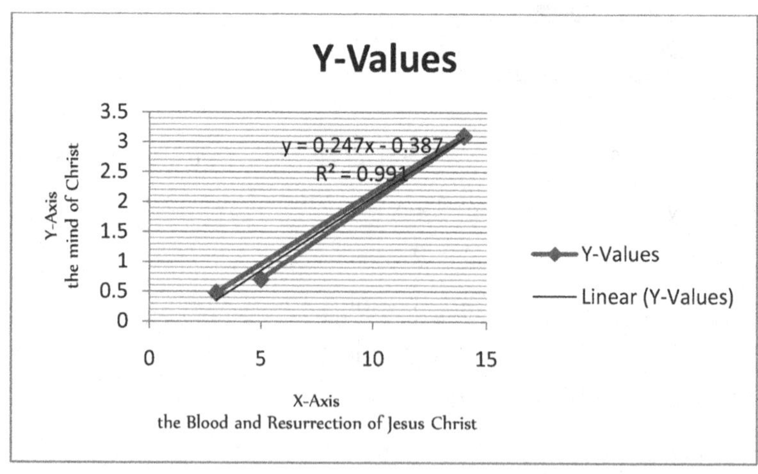

$10^{0.6989}, 3^{1.7711}\ 3^{0.6308}\ 10^{0.6989}, 10^{0.4771}.$

Pilled Poplar, Hazel, and Chestnut bible rods 2

23. And thou, Capernaum the field of repentance; city of comfort, **which art exalted unto heaven, shalt be brought down to hell: for if the mighty works, which have been done in thee, had been done in Sodom** their secret; their cement; burning; the walled, **it would have remained until this day.**

2, 1, 5, 6: 5, 6, 5, 7. Bible Matrices

$2_{10}, 1_7, 5_{10}, 6_{10}: 5_{10}, 6_{10}, 5_7, 7_{10}.$

Pilled Poplar, Hazel, and Chestnut bible rods 1

$\text{Log}_{10}6 = 0.7781$ $\text{Log}_{10}2 = 0.3010$ $\text{Log}_{10}6 = 0.7781$ $\text{Log}_{10}5 = 0.6989$ $\text{Log}_{10}5 = 0.6989$ $\text{Log}_{10}7 = 0.8450$

$\text{Log}_7 5 = y$

$7^y = 5$

$y \log_{10} 7 = \log_{10} 5$

$y = \log_{10} 5 / \log_{10} 7$

$y = 0.6989 / 0.8450$

$y = 0.8271$

$\text{Log}_7 1 = y$

$7^y = 1$

$7^y = 7^0$

$y = 0$

2, 1, 5, 6: 5, 6, 5, 7. Deep calls unto Deep study bible 1

0.3010, 0, 0.6989, 0.7781: 0.6989, 0.7781, 0.8271, 0.8450.

Deep calls unto Deep study bible 2

x-axis	y-axis
2	0.3010
1	0
5	0.6989
6	0.7781
5	0.6989
6	0.7781
5	0.8271
7	0.8450

Water Spout *(lightning; combinatorics)* Study bible 1

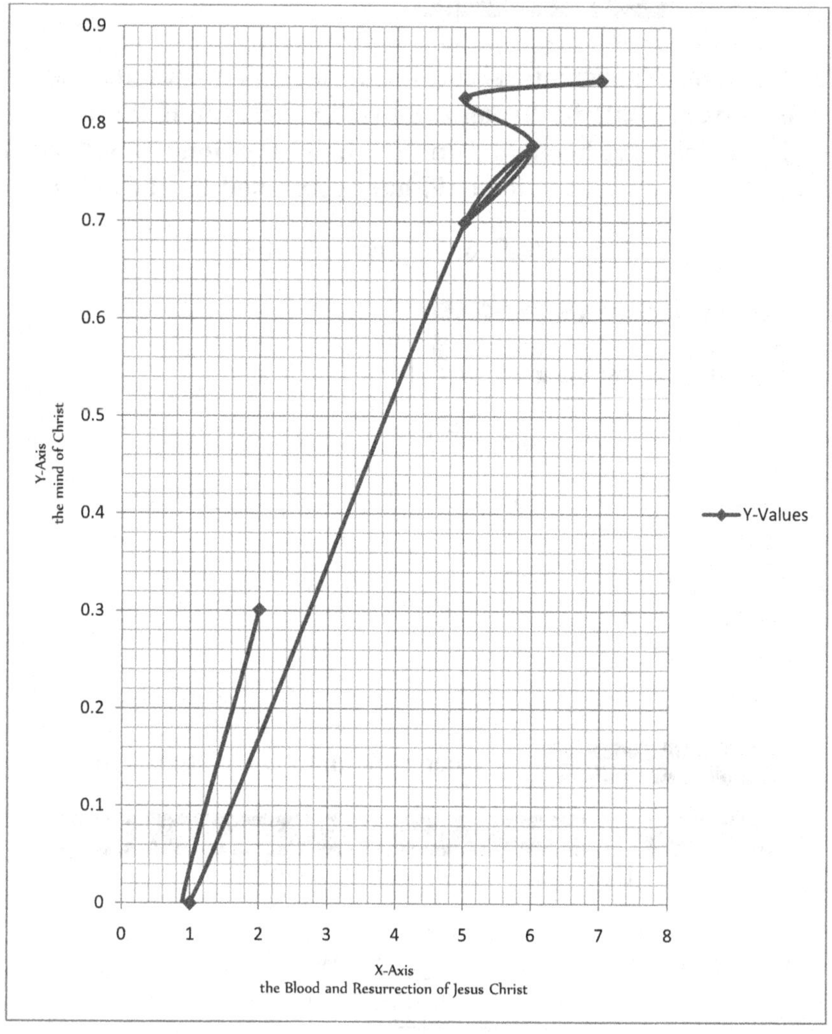

Water Spout *(lightning; combinatorics)* Study bible 2

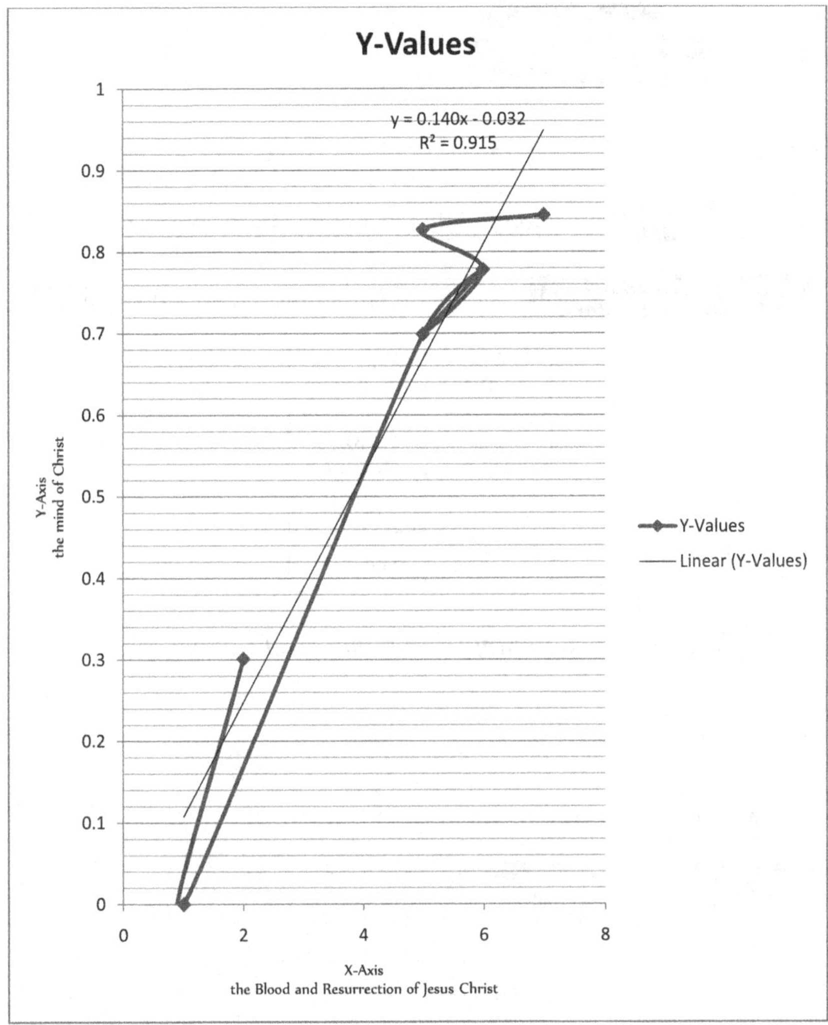

$10^{0.3010}, 7^{0}, 10^{0.6989}, 10^{0.7781} : 10^{0.6989}, 10^{0.7781}, 7^{0.8271}, 10^{0.8450}.$

Pilled Poplar, Hazel, and Chestnut bible rods 2

24. But I say unto you, That it shall be more tolerable for the land of Sodomtheir secret; their cement; burning; the walled**in the day of judgment, than for thee.**

5, 16, 3. Bible Matrices

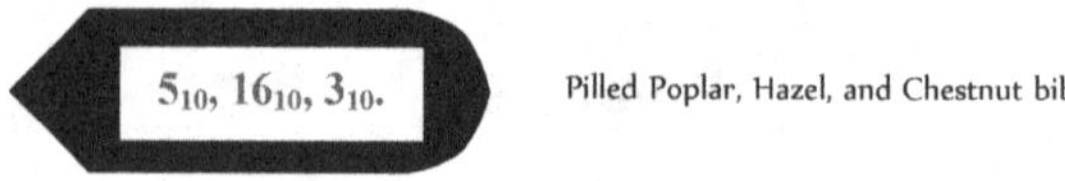

Pilled Poplar, Hazel, and Chestnut bible rods 1

$\text{Log}_{10} 5 = 0.6989$ $\text{Log}_{10} 3 = 0.4771$ $\text{Log}_{10} 16 = 1.2041$

5, 16, 3. Deep calls unto Deep study bible 1

0.6989, 1.2041, 0.4771. Deep calls unto Deep study bible 2

x-axis	y-axis
5	0.6989
16	1.2041
3	0.4771

Water Spout *(lightning; combinatorics)* Study bible 1

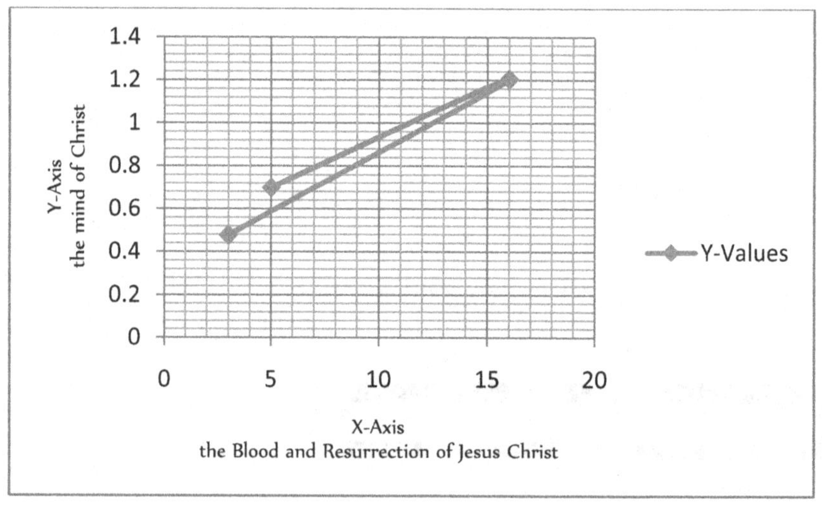

Water Spout *(lightning; combinatorics)* Study bible 2

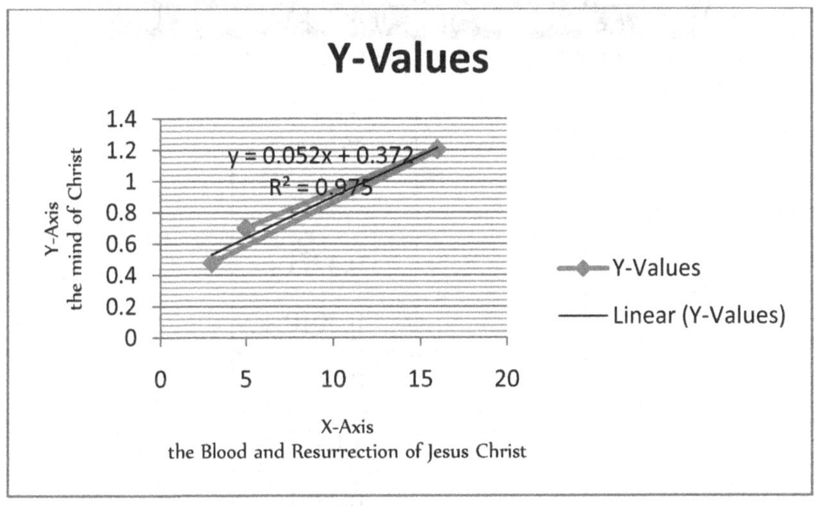

$10^{0.6989}$, $10^{1.2041}$, $10^{0.4771}$.

Pilled Poplar, Hazel, and Chestnut bible rods 2

25. At that time Jesussavior; deliverer **answered and said, I thank thee, O Father, Lord of heaven and earth, because thou hast hid these things from the wise and prudent, and hast revealed them unto babes.**

7, 3, 2, 5, 11, 6. Bible Matrices

$4_2\ 3_{10}$, 3_{10}, 2_{10}, 5_{10}, 11_{10}, 6_{10}.

Pilled Poplar, Hazel, and Chestnut bible rods 1

$\text{Log}_{10}6 = 0.7781$ $\text{Log}_{10}5 = 0.6989$ $\text{Log}_{10}3 = 0.4771$ $\text{Log}_{10}3 = 0.4771$ $\text{Log}_{10}2 = 0.3010$ $\text{Log}_{10}11 = 1.0413$

$\text{Log}_2 4 = y$

$2^y = 4$

$2^y = 2^2$

$y = 2$

7, 3, 2, 5, 11, 6. Deep calls unto Deep study bible 1

2 0.4771, 0.4771, 0.3010, 0.6989, 1.0413, 0.7781.
Deep calls unto Deep study bible 2

x-axis	y-axis
7	2.4771
3	0.4771
2	0.3010
5	0.6989
11	1.0413
6	0.7781

Water Spout *(lightning; combinatorics)* Study bible 1

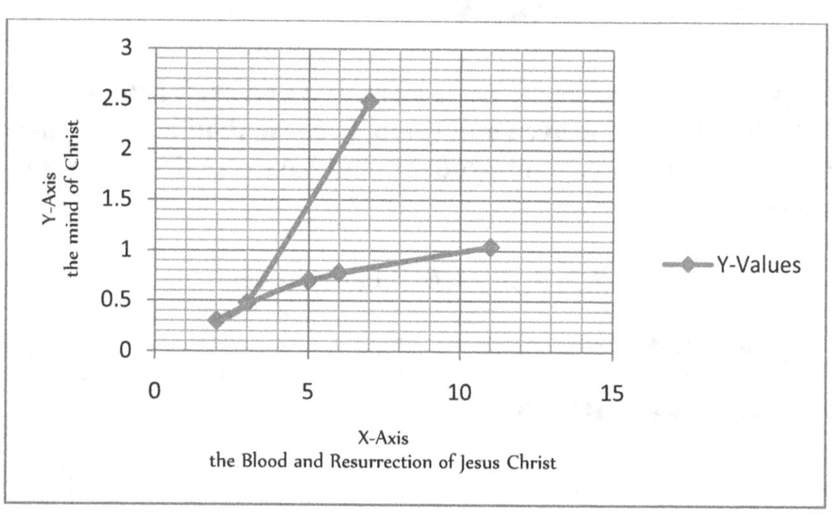

Water Spout *(lightning; combinatorics)* Study bible 2

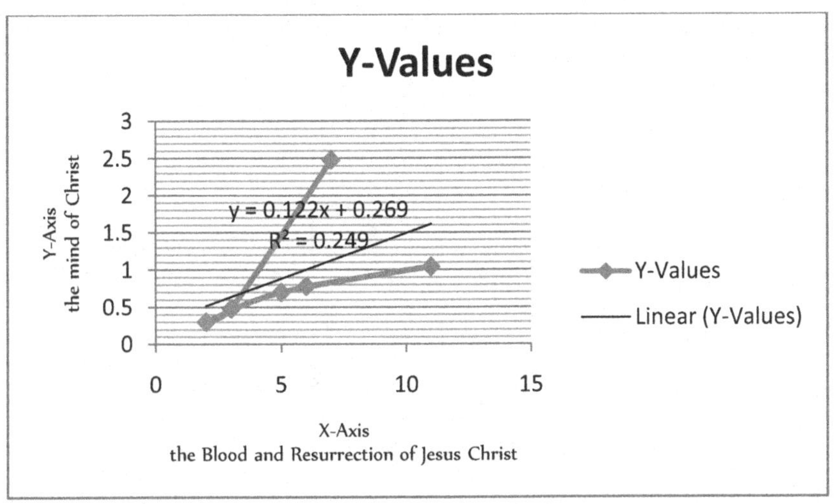

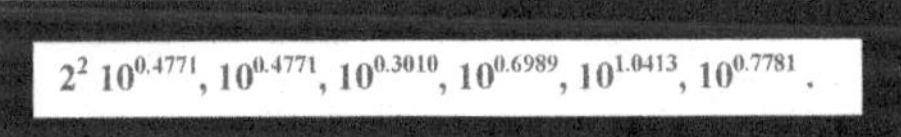

Pilled Poplar, Hazel, and Chestnut bible rods 2

26. Even so, Father: for so it seemed good in thy sight.

2, 1: 8. Bible Matrices

Pilled Poplar, Hazel, and Chestnut bible rods 1

$\text{Log}_{10} 2 = 0.3010$ $\text{Log}_{10} 1 = 0$ $\text{Log}_{10} 8 = 0.9030$

2, 1: 8. Deep calls unto Deep study bible 1

0.3010, 0: 0.9030. Deep calls unto Deep study bible 2

x-axis	y-axis
2	0.3010
1	0
8	0.9030

Water Spout *(lightning; combinatorics)* Study bible 1

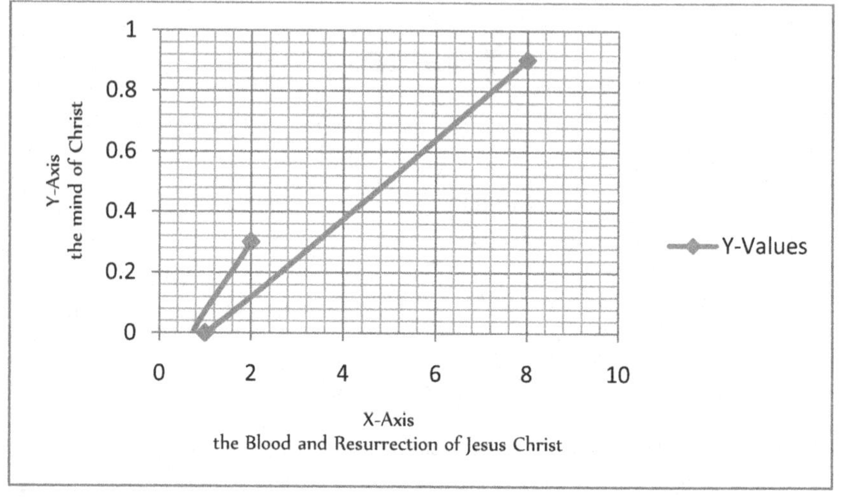

Water Spout *(lightning; combinatorics)* Study bible 2

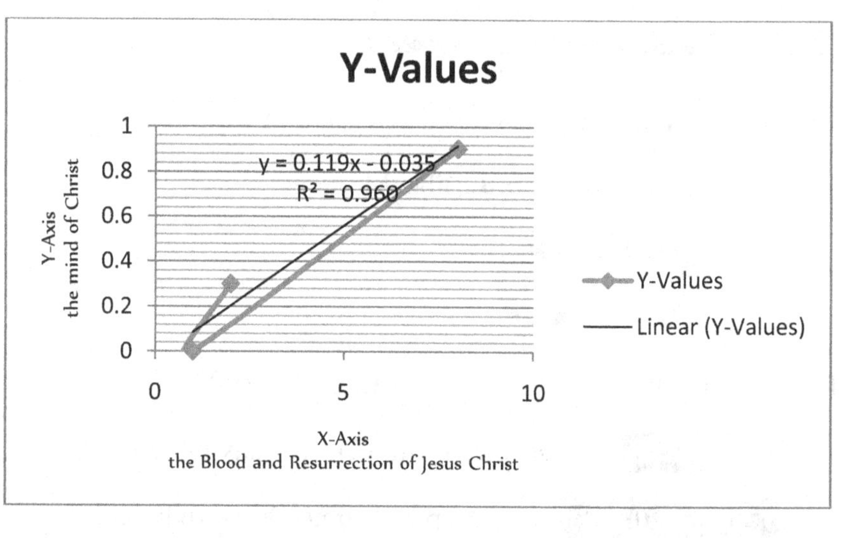

$10^{0.3010}, 10^{0}: 10^{0.9030}$.

Pilled Poplar, Hazel, and Chestnut bible rods 2

27. All things are delivered unto me of my Father: and no man knoweth the Son, but the Father; neither knoweth any man the Father, save the Son, and he to whomsoever the Son will reveal him.

9: 6, 3; 6, 3, 9. Bible Matrices

$9_{10}: 6_{10}, 3_{10}; 6_{10}, 3_{10}, 9_{10}$. Pilled Poplar, Hazel, and Chestnut bible rods 1

$Log_{10}6 = 0.7781$ $Log_{10}3 = 0.4771$ $Log_{10}3 = 0.4771$ $Log_{10}9 = 0.9542$ $Log_{10}6 = 0.7781$ $Log_{10}9 = 0.9542$

9: 6, 3; 6, 3, 9. Deep calls unto Deep study bible 1

0. 9542: 0.7781, 0.4771; 0.7781, 0.4771, 0.9542.
Deep calls unto Deep study bible 2

x-axis	y-axis
9	0.9542
6	0.7781
3	0.4771
6	0.7781
3	0.4771
9	0.9542

Water Spout *(lightning; combinatorics)* Study bible 1

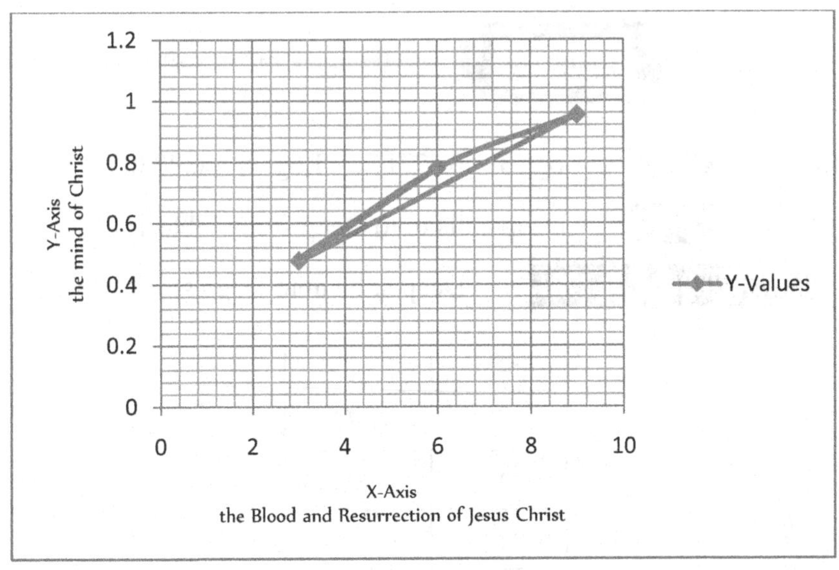

Water Spout *(lightning; combinatorics)* Study bible 2

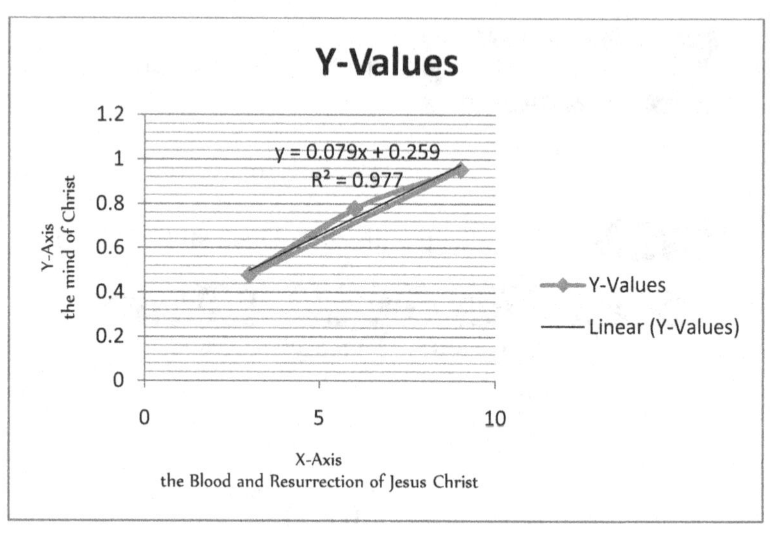

Pilled Poplar, Hazel, and Chestnut bible rods 2

28. Come unto me, all ye that labour and are heavy laden, and I will give you rest.

3, 8, 6. Bible Matrices

Pilled Poplar, Hazel, and Chestnut bible rods 1

$\text{Log}_{10} 6 = 0.7781$ $\text{Log}_{10} 3 = 0.4771$ $\text{Log}_{10} 8 = 0.9030$

3, 8, 6. Deep calls unto Deep study bible 1

0.4771, 0.9030, 0.7781. Deep calls unto Deep study bible 2

x-axis	y-axis
3	0.4771
8	0.9030
6	0.7781

Water Spout *(lightning; combinatorics)* Study bible 1

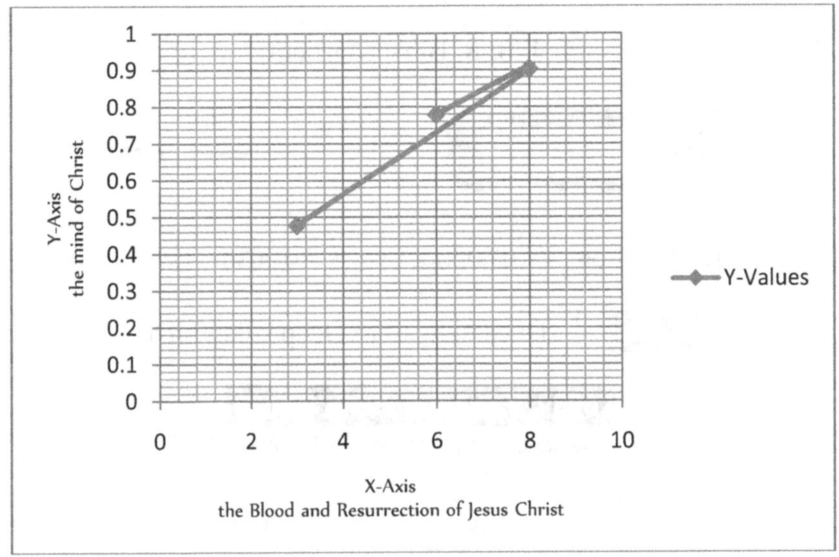

Water Spout *(lightning; combinatorics)* Study bible 2

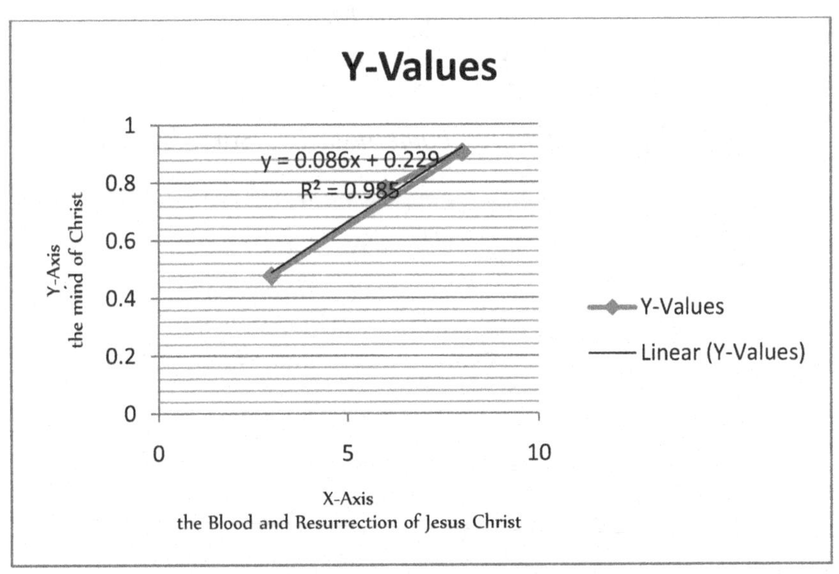

$10^{0.4771}$, $10^{0.9030}$, $10^{0.7781}$.

Pilled Poplar, Hazel, and Chestnut bible rods 2

29. Take my yoke upon you, and learn of me; for I am meek and lowly in heart: and ye shall find rest unto your souls.

5, 4; 8: 8. Bible Matrices

Pilled Poplar, Hazel, and Chestnut bible rods 1

$Log_{10}5 = 0.6989$ $Log_{10}4 = 0.6020$ $Log_{10}8 = 0.9030$ $Log_{10}8 = 0.9030$

5, 4; 8: 8. Deep calls unto Deep study bible 1

0.6989, 0.6020; 0.9030: 0.9030.
Deep calls unto Deep study bible 2

x-axis	y-axis
5	0.6989
.4	0.6020
8	0.9030
8	0.9030

Water Spout *(lightning; combinatorics)* Study bible 1

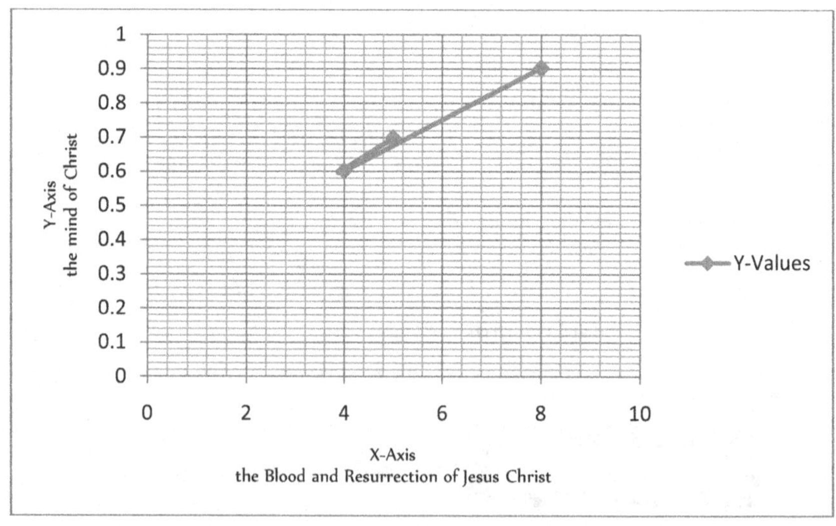

Water Spout *(lightning; combinatorics)* Study bible 2

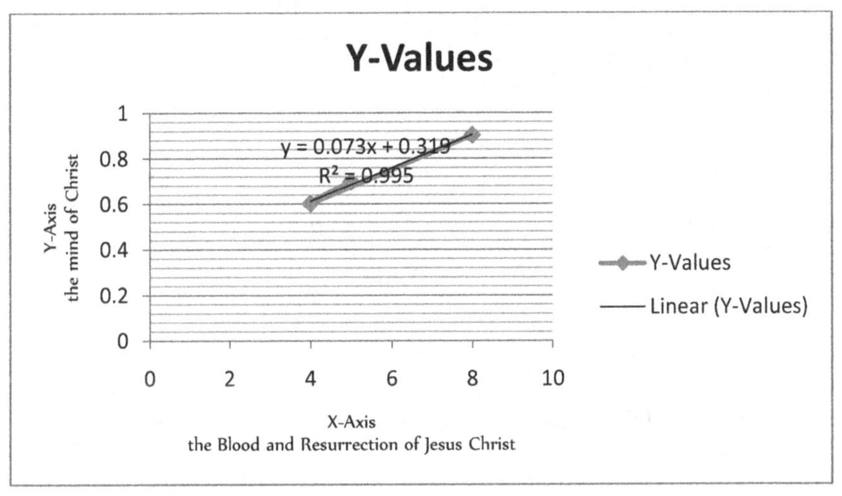

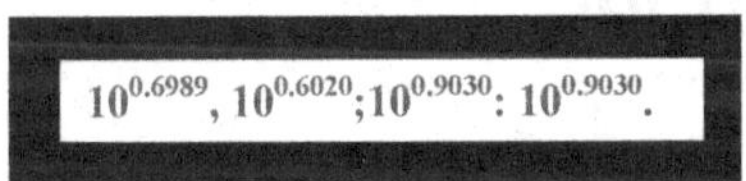

Pilled Poplar, Hazel, and Chestnut bible rods 2

30. For my yoke is easy, and my burden is light.

5, 5. Bible Matrices

Pilled Poplar, Hazel, and Chestnut bible rods 1

$\text{Log}_{10} 5 = 0.6989$ $\text{Log}_{10} 5 = 0.6989$

5, 5. Deep calls unto Deep study bible 1

0.6989, 0.6989. Deep calls unto Deep study bible 2

x-axis	y-axis
5	0.6989
5	0.6989

Water Spout *(lightning; combinatorics)* Study bible 1

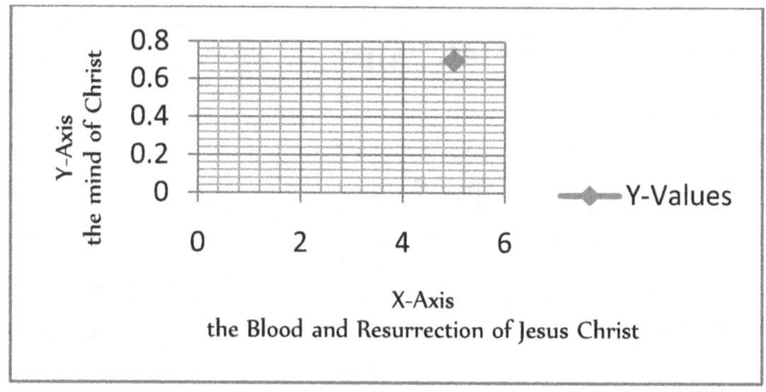

Water Spout *(lightning; combinatorics)* Study bible 2

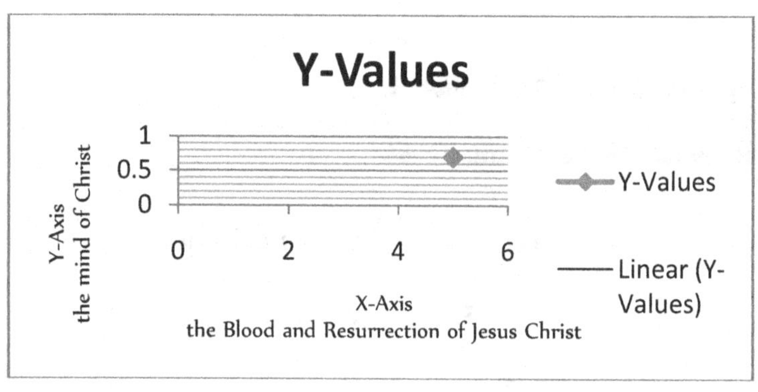

CHAPTER 12

1. At that time Jesussavior; deliverer **went on the Sabbath** jewish day of worship & rest **day through the corn; and his disciples were an hungred, and began to pluck the ears of corn, and to eat.**

12, 6, 8, 3. Bible Matrices

$4_2\, 4_6\, 4_{10},\, 6_{10},\, 8_{10},\, 3_{10}.$

Pilled Poplar, Hazel, and Chestnut bible rods 1

$\text{Log}_{10} 6 = 0.7781 \quad \text{Log}_{10} 3 = 0.4771 \quad \text{Log}_{10} 4 = 0.6020 \quad \text{Log}_{10} 8 = 0.9030$

$$\text{Log}_6 4 = y$$
$$6^y = 4$$
$$y \log_{10} 6 = \log_{10} 4$$
$$y = \log_{10} 4 / \log_{10} 6$$
$$y = 0.6020 / 0.7781$$
$$y = 0.7736$$

$$\text{Log}_2 4 = y$$
$$2^y = 4$$
$$2^y = 2^2$$
$$y = 2$$

12, 6, 8, 3. Deep calls unto Deep study bible 1

2 0.7736 0.6020, 0.7781, 0.9030, 0.4771

Deep calls unto Deep study bible 2

x-axis	y-axis
12	3.3756
6	0.7781
8	0.9030
3	0.4771

Water Spout *(lightning; combinatorics)* Study bible 1

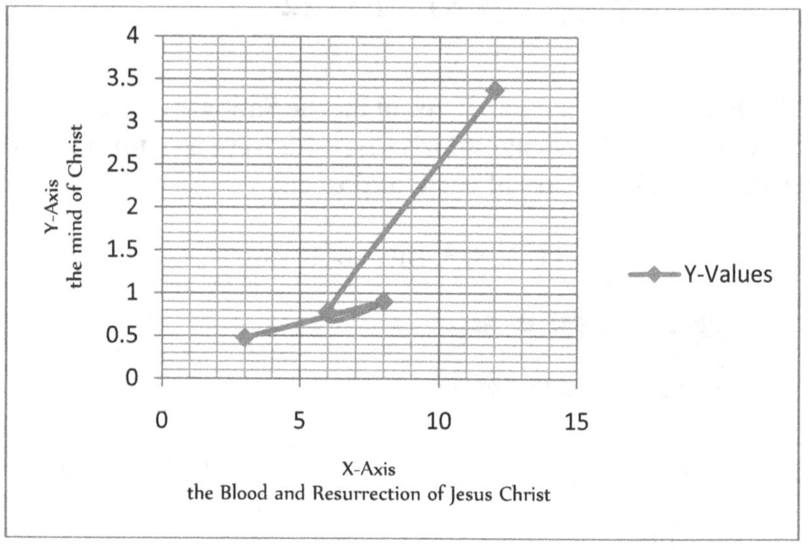

Water Spout *(lightning; combinatorics)* Study bible 2

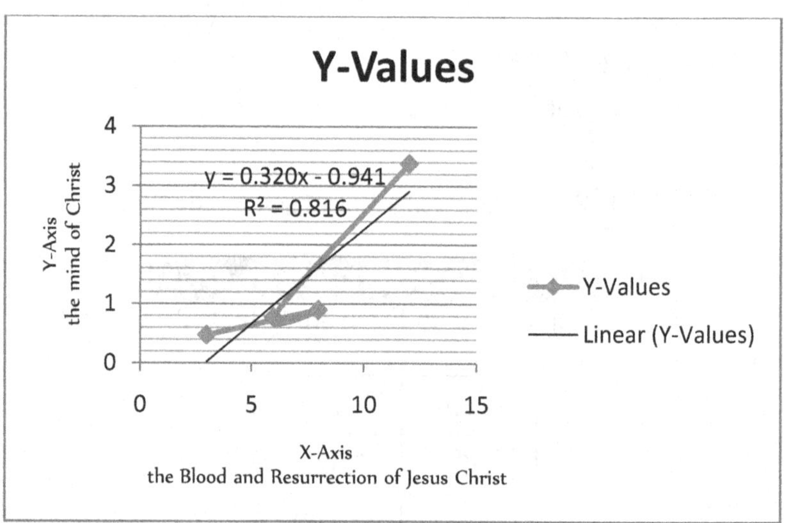

2^2 $6^{0.7736}$ $10^{0.6020}$, $10^{0.7781}$, $10^{0.9030}$, $10^{0.4771}$.

Pilled Poplar, Hazel, and Chestnut bible rods 2

2. But when the Phariseesset apart; separatists**saw it, they said unto him, Behold, thy disciples do that which is not lawful to do upon the Sabbath** jewish day of worship & rest **day.**

6, 4, 1, 14. Bible Matrices

$4_3\, 2_{10},\, 4_{10},\, 1_{10},\, 13_6\, 1_{10}.$

Pilled Poplar, Hazel, and Chestnut bible rods 1

$\log_{10} 2 = 0.3010$ $\log_{10} 4 = 0.6020$ $\log_{10} 1 = 0$ $\log_{10} 1 = 0$

$$\log_6 13 = y$$
$$6^y = 13$$
$$y \log_{10} 6 = \log_{10} 13$$
$$y = \log_{10} 13 / \log_{10} 6$$
$$y = 1.1139 / 0.7781$$
$$y = 1.4315$$

$$\log_3 4 = y$$
$$3^y = 4$$
$$y \log_{10} 3 = \log_{10} 4$$
$$y = \log_{10} 4 / \log_{10} 3$$
$$y = 0.6020 / 0.4771$$
$$y = 1.2617$$

6, 4, 1, 14. Deep calls unto Deep study bible 1

1.2617 0.3010, 0.6020, 0, 1.4315 0.

Deep calls unto Deep study bible 2

x-axis	y-axis
6	1.5627
4	0.6020
1	0
14	1.4315

Water Spout *(lightning; combinatorics)* Study bible 1

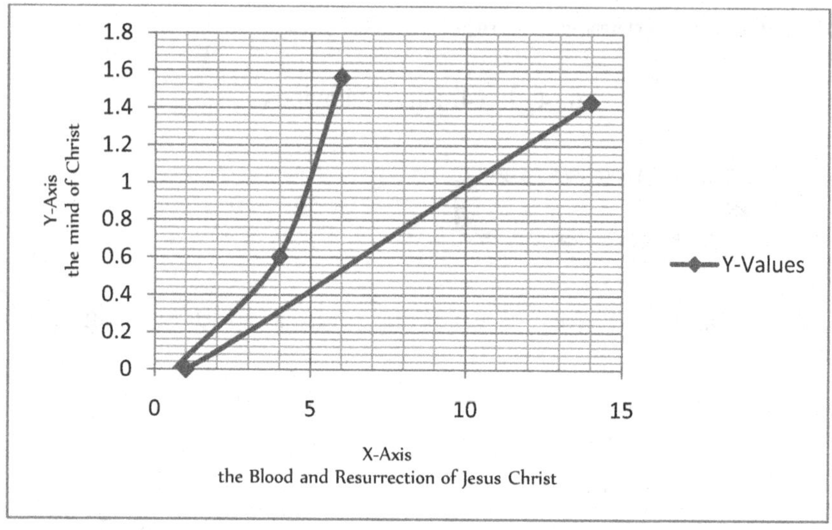

Water Spout *(lightning; combinatorics)* Study bible 2

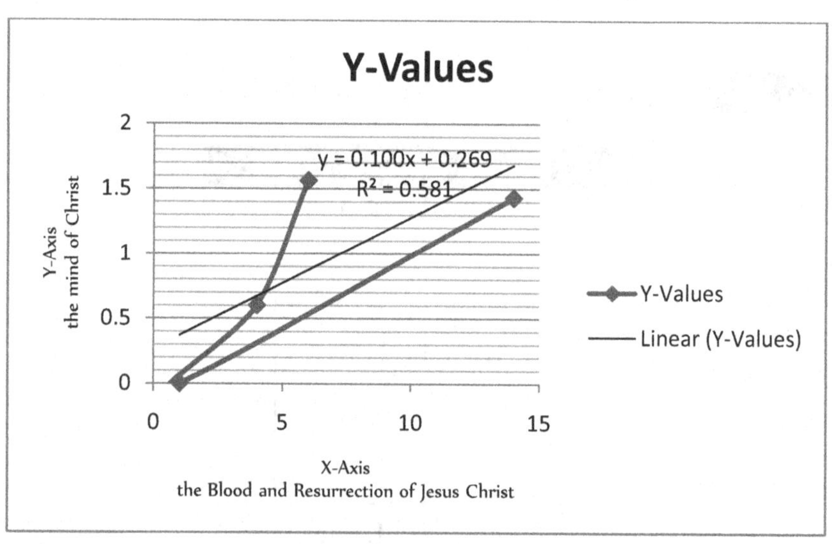

$3^{1.2617}\ 10^{0.3010}, 10^{0.6020}, 10^{0}, 6^{1.4315}\ 10^{0}$.

Pilled Poplar, Hazel, and Chestnut bible rods 2

3. But he said unto them, Have ye not read what Davidbeloved;dear **did, when he was an hungred, and they that were with him;**

5, 7, 5, 6; Bible Matrices

$5_{10}, 6_{2}1_{10}, 5_{10}, 6_{10}$;

Pilled Poplar, Hazel, and Chestnut bible rods 1

$\text{Log}_{10} 5 = 0.6989$ $\text{Log}_{10} 6 = 0.7781$ $\text{Log}_{10} 5 = 0.6989$ $\text{Log}_{10} 1 = 0$

$\text{Log}_{2} 6 = y$

$2^{y} = 6$

$y \log_{10} 2 = \log_{10} 6$

$y = \log_{10} 6 / \log_{10} 2$

$y = 0.7781 / 0.3010$

$y = 2.5850$

5, 7, 5, 6; Deep calls unto Deep study bible 1

0.6989, 2.5850 0, 0.6989, 0.7781;

Deep calls unto Deep study bible 2

x-axis	y-axis
5	0.6989
7	2.5850
5	0.6989
6	0.7781

Water Spout *(lightning; combinatorics)* Study bible 1

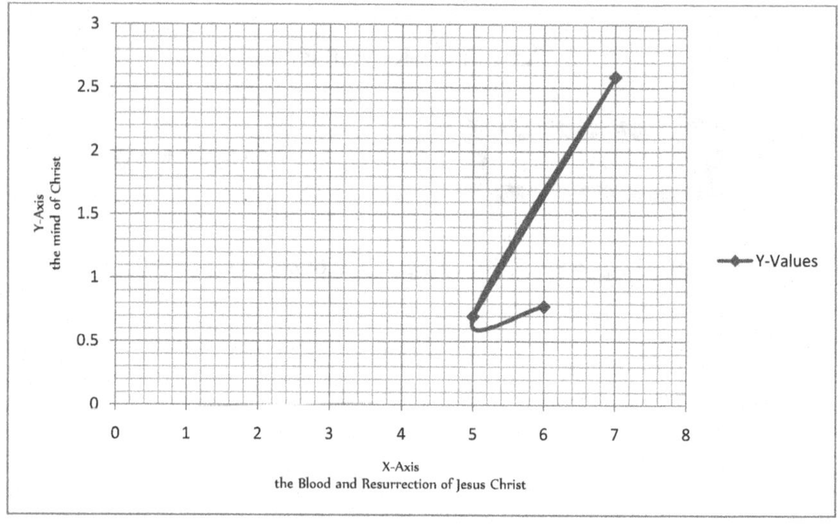

Water Spout *(lightning; combinatorics)* Study bible 2

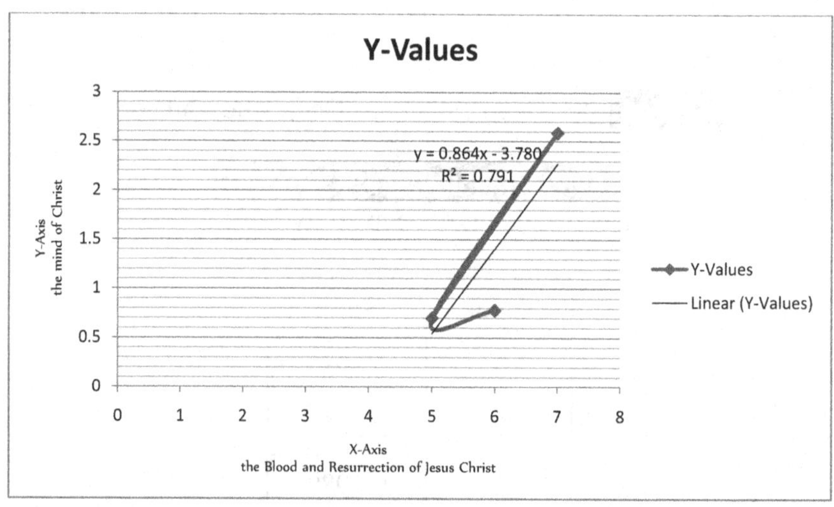

$10^{0.6989}$, $2^{2.5850}$ 10^{0}, $10^{0.6989}$, $10^{0.7781}$;

Pilled Poplar, Hazel, and Chestnut bible rods 2

4. How he entered into the house of God, and did eat the shewbread, which was not lawful for him to eat, neither for them which were with him, but only for the priests?

8, 5, 8, 7, 5? Bible Matrices

$8_{10}, 5_{10}, 8_{10}, 7_{10}, 5_{10}$?

Pilled Poplar, Hazel, and Chestnut bible rods 1

$Log_{10} 5 = 0.6989$ $Log_{10} 5 = 0.6989$ $Log_{10} 8 = 0.9030$ $Log_{10} 8 = 0.9030$ $Log_{10} 7 = 0.8450$

8, 5, 8, 7, 5? Deep calls unto Deep study bible 1

0.9030, 0.6989, 0.9030, 0.8450, 0.6989?
Deep calls unto Deep study bible 2

x-axis	y-axis
8	0.9030
5	0.6989
8	0.9030
7	0.8450
5	0.6989

Water Spout *(lightning; combinatorics)* Study bible 1

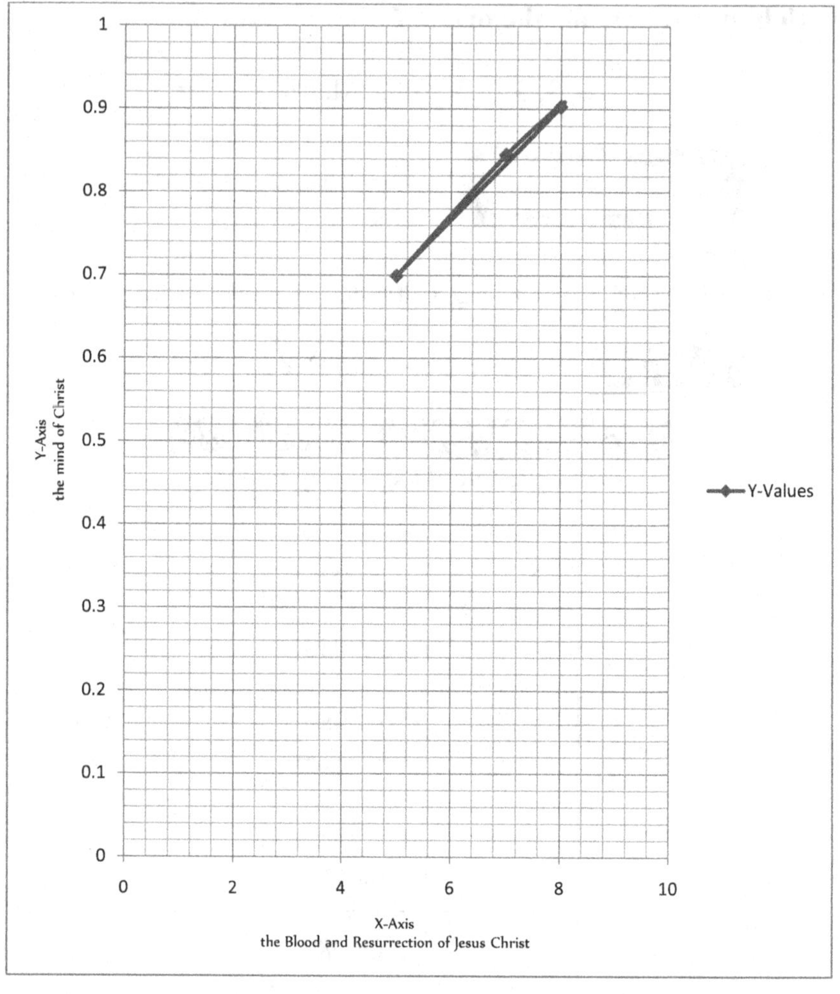

Water Spout *(lightning; combinatorics)* Study bible 2

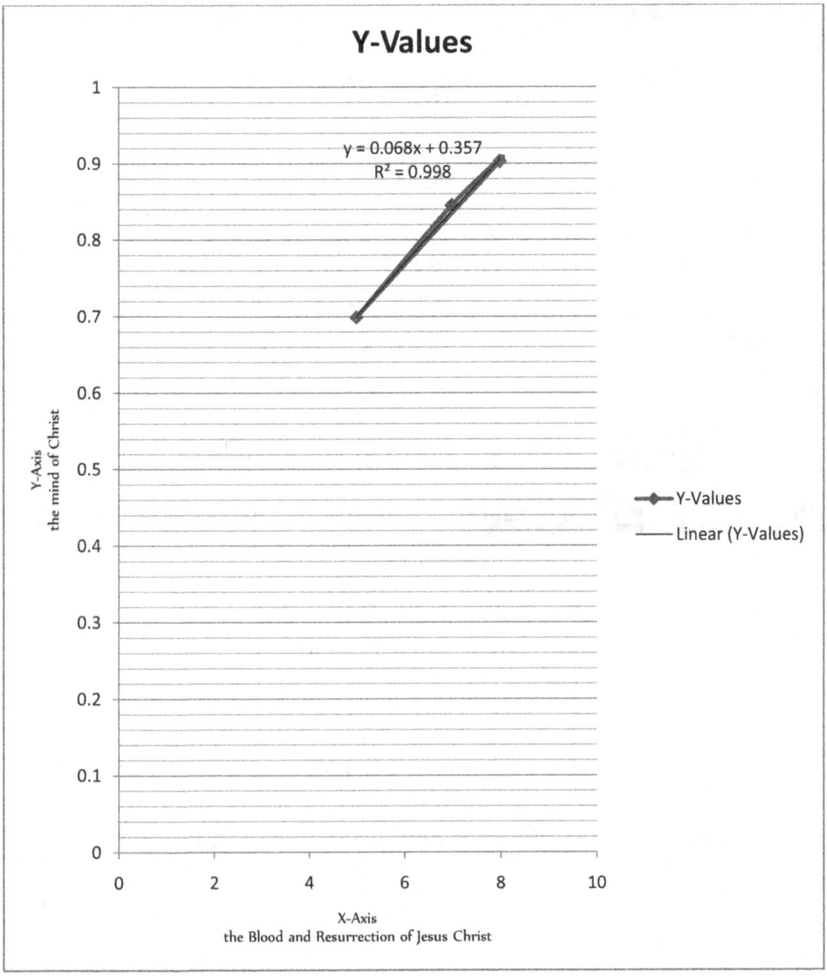
Y-Values
y = 0.068x + 0.357
R² = 0.998
1
0.9
0.8
0.7
0.6
0.5
0.4
0.3
0.2
0.1
0
0
2
4
6
8
10
Y-Axis
the mind of Christ
X-Axis
the Blood and Resurrection of Jesus Christ
Y-Values
Linear (Y-Values)

$10^{0.9030}$, $10^{0.6989}$, $10^{0.9030}$, $10^{0.8450}$, $10^{0.6989}$?

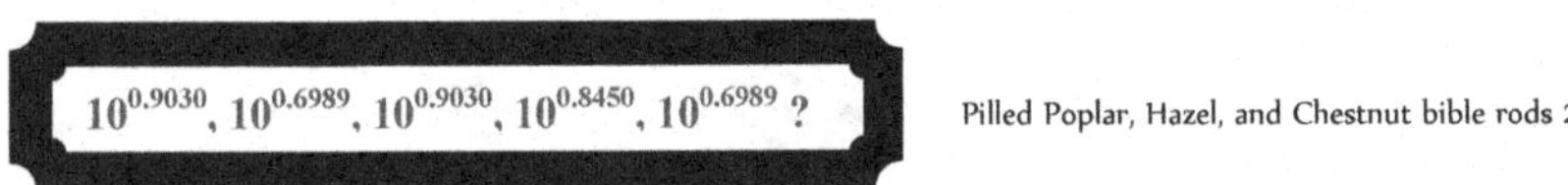

Pilled Poplar, Hazel, and Chestnut bible rods 2

5. Or have ye not read in the law, how that on the Sabbath jewish day of worship & rest **days the priests in the temple profane the Sabbath** jewish day of worship & rest, **and are blameless?**

8, 14, 3? Bible Matrices

$8_{10}, 5_6 9_6, 3_{10}$? Pilled Poplar, Hazel, and Chestnut bible rods 1

$\text{Log}_{10} 8 = 0.9030$ $\text{Log}_{10} 3 = 0.4771$

$\text{Log}_6 5 = y$

$6^y = 5$

$y \log_{10} 6 = \log_{10} 5$

$y = \log_{10} 5 / \log_{10} 6$

$y = 0.6989 / 0.7781$

$y = 0.8982$

$\text{Log}_6 9 = y$

$6^y = 9$

$y \log_{10} 6 = \log_{10} 9$

$y = \log_{10} 9 / \log_{10} 6$

$y = 0.9542 / 0.7781$

$y = 1.2263$

8, 14, 3? Deep calls unto Deep study bible 1

0.9030, 0.8982 1.2263, 0.4771 ? Deep calls unto Deep study bible 2

x-axis	y-axis
8	0.9030
14	2.1245
3	0.4771

Water Spout *(lightning; combinatorics)* Study bible 1

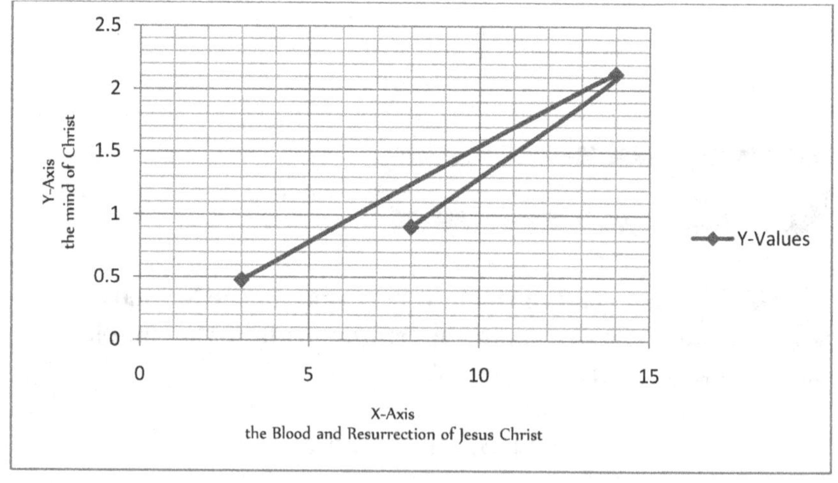

Water Spout *(lightning; combinatorics)* Study bible 2

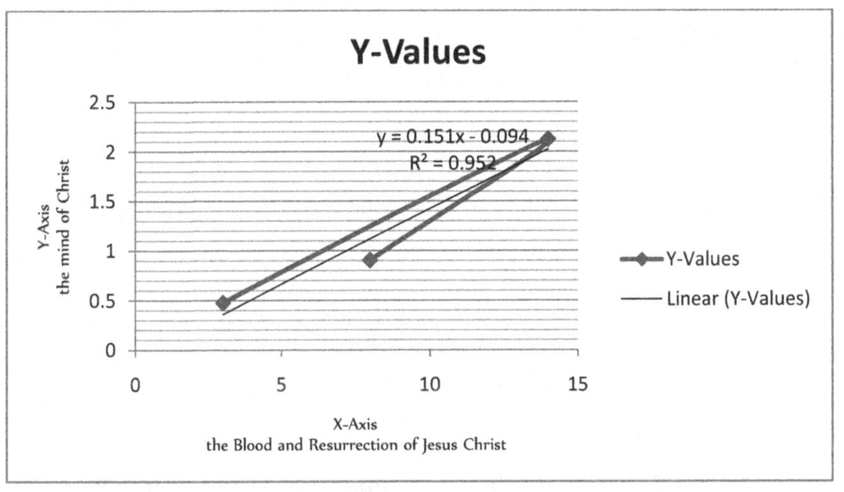

Pilled Poplar, Hazel, and Chestnut bible rods 2

6. But I say unto you, That in this place is one greater than the temple.

5, 10. Bible Matrices

Pilled Poplar, Hazel, and Chestnut bible rods 1

$\text{Log}_{10} 5 = 0.6989$ $\text{Log}_{10} 10 = 1$

5, 10. Deep calls unto Deep study bible 1

0.6989, 1. Deep calls unto Deep study bible 2

x-axis	y-axis
5	0.6989
10	1

Water Spout *(lightning; combinatorics)* Study bible 1

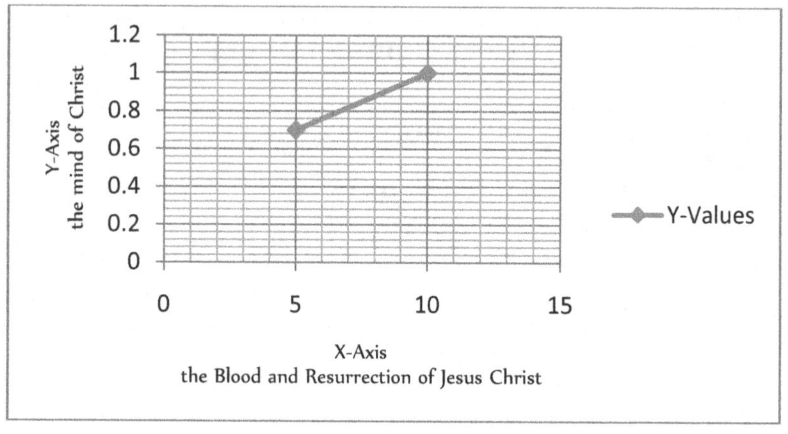

Water Spout *(lightning; combinatorics)* Study bible 2

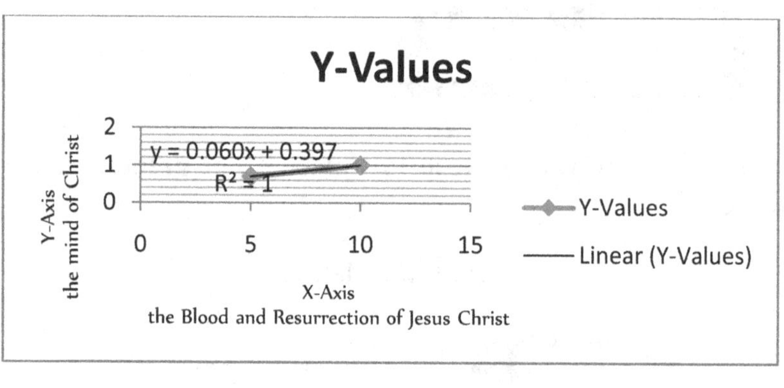

Pilled Poplar, Hazel, and Chestnut bible rods 2

7. But if ye had known what this meaneth, I will have mercy, and not sacrifice, ye would not have condemned the guiltless.

8, 4, 3, 7. Bible Matrices

Pilled Poplar, Hazel, and Chestnut bible rods 1

$Log_{10} 8 = 0.9030$ $Log_{10} 4 = 0.6020$ $Log_{10} 3 = 0.4771$ $Log_{10} 7 = 0.8450$

8, 4, 3, 7. Deep calls unto Deep study bible 1

0.9030, 0.6020, 0.4771, 0.8450.
Deep calls unto Deep study bible 2

x-axis	y-axis
8	0.9030
4	0.6020
3	0.4771
7	0.8450

Water Spout *(lightning; combinatorics)* Study bible 1

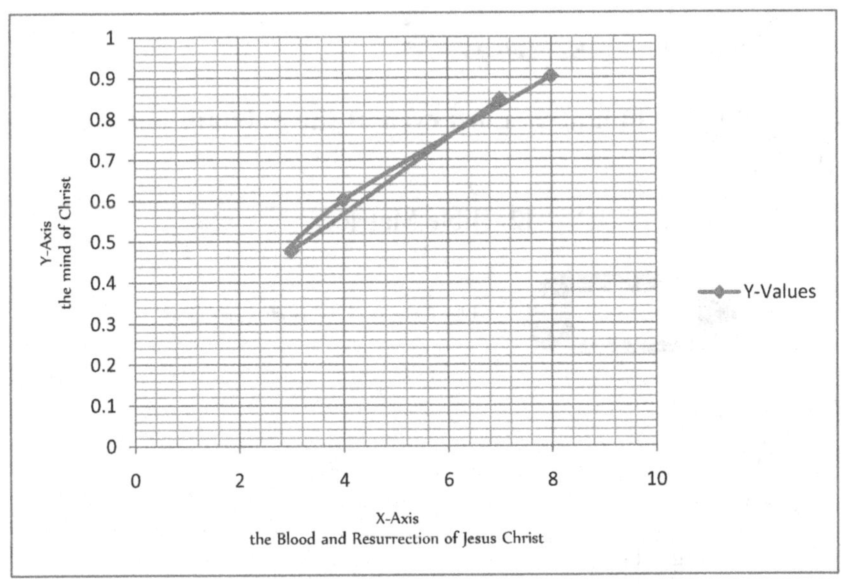

Water Spout *(lightning; combinatorics)* Study bible 2

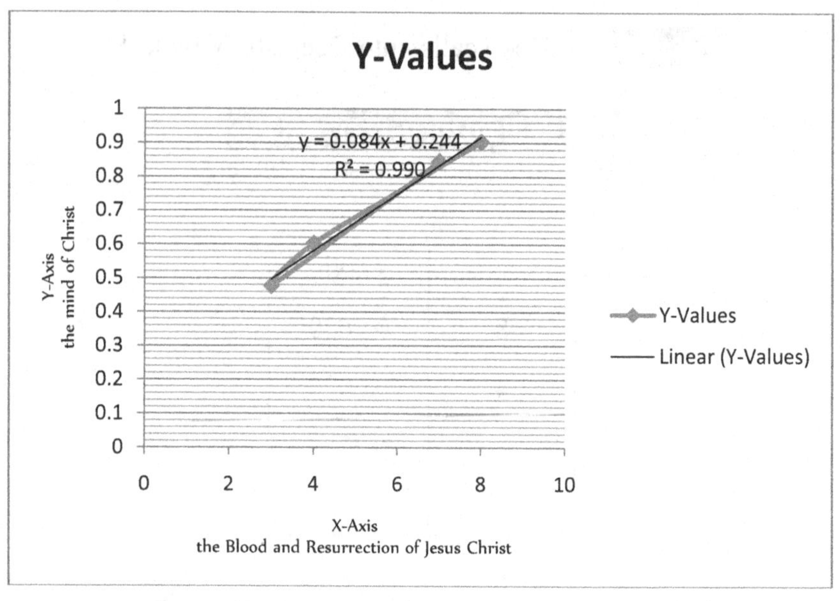

Pilled Poplar, Hazel, and Chestnut bible rods 2

8. For the Son of man is Lord even of the Sabbath jewish day of worship & rest **day.**

12. Bible Matrices

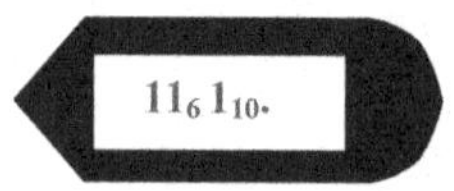

Pilled Poplar, Hazel, and Chestnut bible rods 1

$\text{Log}_{10} 1 = 0$

$\text{Log}_6 11 = y$

$6^y = 11$

$y \log_{10} 6 = \log_{10} 11$

$y = \log_{10} 11 / \log_{10} 6$

$y = 1.0413 / 0.7781$

$y = 1.3382$

12. Deep calls unto Deep study bible 1

1.3382 0. Deep calls unto Deep study bible 2

x-axis	y-axis
12	1.3382

Water Spout *(lightning; combinatorics)* Study bible 1

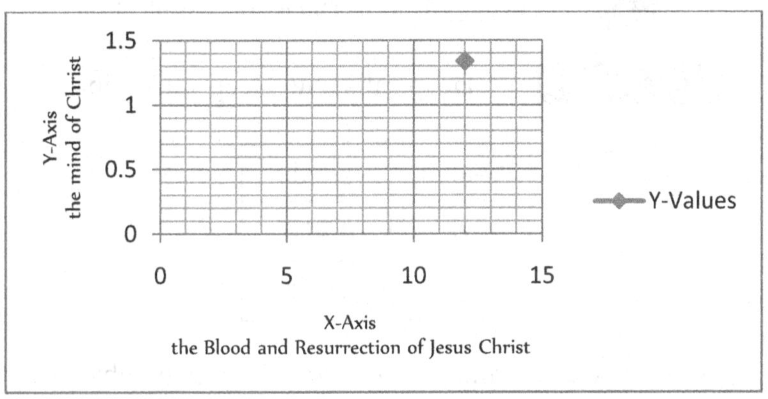

Water Spout *(lightning; combinatorics)* Study bible 2

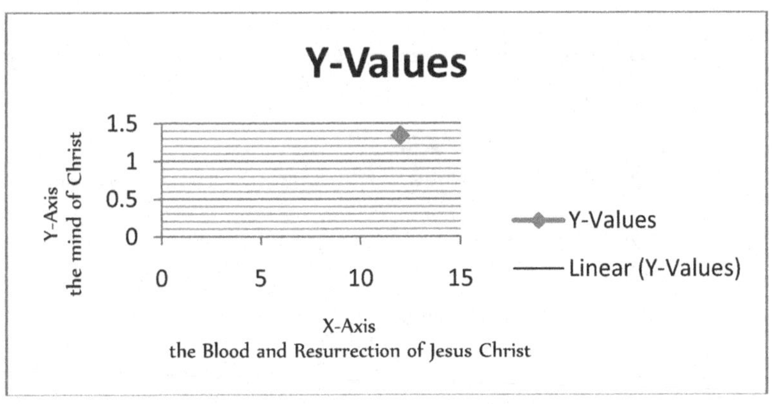

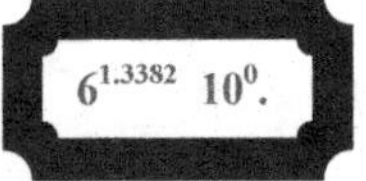

Pilled Poplar, Hazel, and Chestnut bible rods 2

9. And when he was departed thence, he went into their synagogue:

6, 5: Bible Matrices

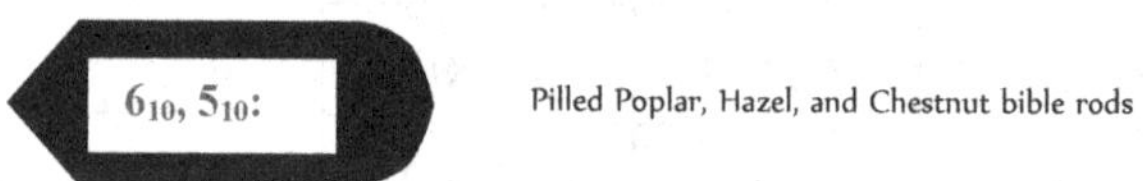

$\text{Log}_{10} 5 = 0.6989$ $\text{Log}_{10} 6 = 0.7781$

6, 5: Deep calls unto Deep study bible 1

0.7781, 0.6989: Deep calls unto Deep study bible 2

x-axis	y-axis
6	0.7781
5	0.6989

Water Spout *(lightning; combinatorics)* Study bible 1

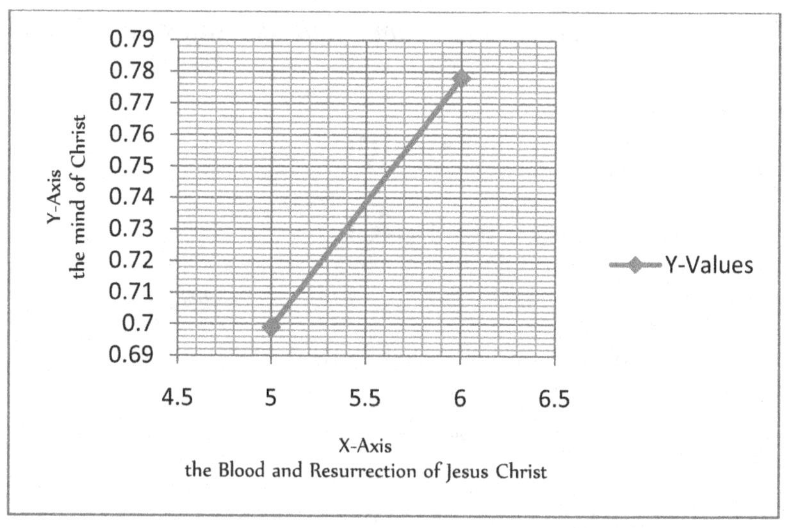

Water Spout *(lightning; combinatorics)* Study bible 2

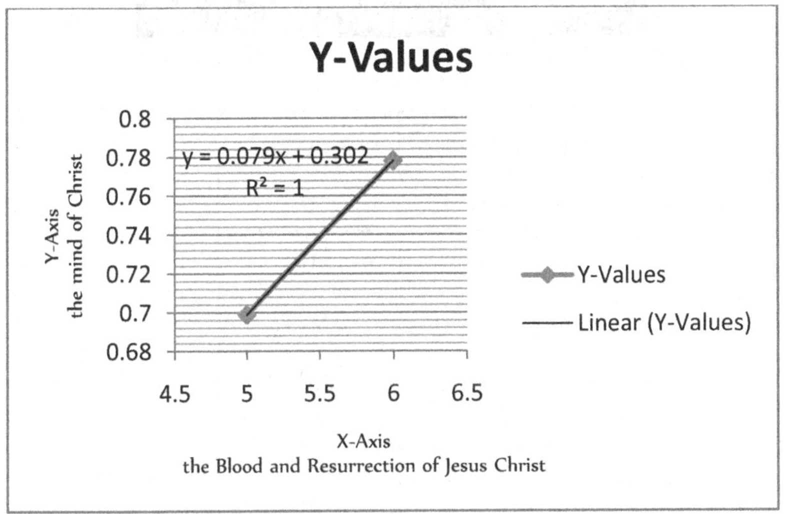

$10^{0.7781}$, $10^{0.6989}$:

Pilled Poplar, Hazel, and Chestnut bible rods 2

10. And, behold, there was a man which had his hand withered. And they asked him, saying, Is it lawful to heal on the Sabbath jewish day of worship & rest **days? that they might accuse him.**

1, 1, 9. 4, 1, 9? 5. Bible Matrices

1_{10}, 1_{10}, 9_{10}. 4_{10}, 1_{10}, $8_6 1_{10}$? 5_{10}.

Pilled Poplar, Hazel, and Chestnut bible rods 1

$\text{Log}_{10} 5 = 0.6989$ $\text{Log}_{10} 4 = 0.6020$ $\text{Log}_{10} 9 = 0.9542$ $\text{Log}_{10} 1 = 0$ $\text{Log}_{10} 1 = 0$ $\text{Log}_{10} 1 = 0$ $\text{Log}_{10} 1 = 0$

$\text{Log}_6 8 = y$

$6^y = 8$

$y \log_{10} 6 = \log_{10} 8$

$y = \log_{10} 8 / \log_{10} 6$

$y = 0.9030 / 0.7781$

$y = 1.1605$

1, 1, 9. 4, 1, 9? 5. Deep calls unto Deep study bible 1

0, 0, 0.9542. 0.6020, 0, 1.1605 0? 0.6989.
Deep calls unto Deep study bible 2

x-axis	y-axis
1	0
1	0
9	0.9542
4	0.6020
1	0
9	1.1605
5	0.6989

Water Spout *(lightning; combinatorics)* Study bible 1

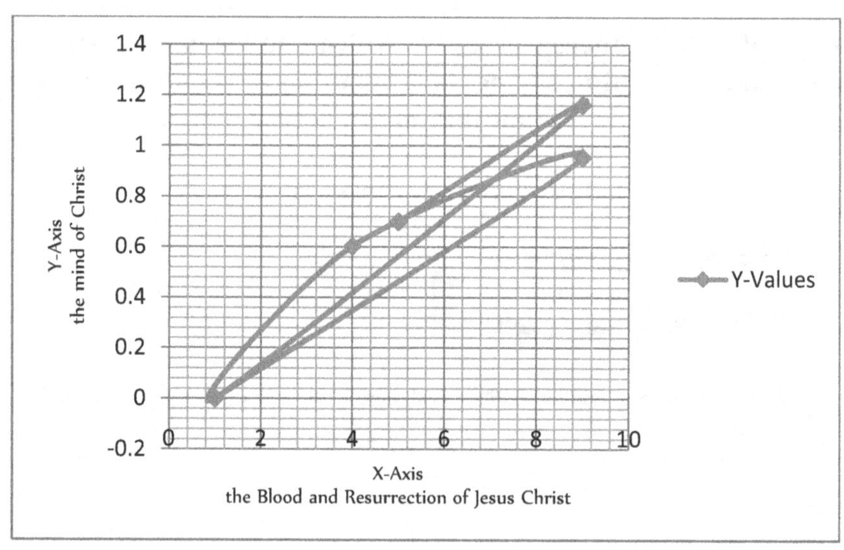

Water Spout *(lightning; combinatorics)* Study bible 2

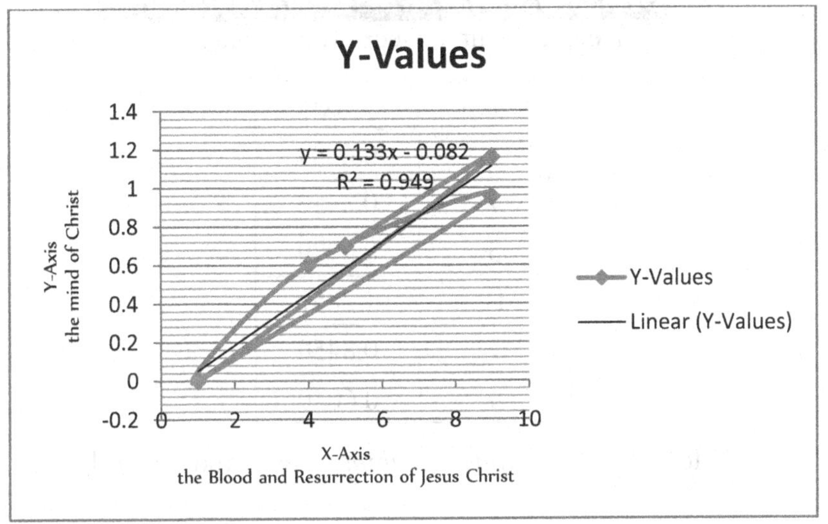

$10^{0}, 10^{0}, 10^{0.9542}. 10^{0.6020}, 10^{0}, 6^{1.1605}$ 10^{0}? $10^{0.6989}$.

Pilled Poplar, Hazel, and Chestnut bible rods 2

11. And he said unto them, What man shall there be among you, that shall have one sheep, and if it fall into a pit on the Sabbath jewish day of worship & rest **day, will he not lay hold on it, and lift it out?**

5, 7, 5, 11, 7, 4? Bible Matrices

$5_{10}, 7_{10}, 5_{10}, 10_{6}\, 1_{10}, 7_{10}, 4_{10}$?

Pilled Poplar, Hazel, and Chestnut bible rods 1

$\text{Log}_{10} 5 = 0.6989$ $\text{Log}_{10} 5 = 0.6989$ $\text{Log}_{10} 7 = 0.8450$ $\text{Log}_{10} 7 = 0.8450$ $\text{Log}_{10} 4 = 0.6020$ $\text{Log}_{10} 1 = 0$

$\text{Log}_{6} 10 = y$

$6^{y} = 10$

$y \log_{10} 6 = \log_{10} 10$

$y = \log_{10} 10 / \log_{10} 6$

$y = 1 / 0.7781$

$y = 1.2851$

5, 7, 5, 11, 7, 4? Deep calls unto Deep study bible 1

0.6989, 0.8450, 0.6989, 1.2851 0, 0.8450, 0.6020?
Deep calls unto Deep study bible 2

x-axis	y-axis
5	0.6989
7	0.8450
5	0.6989
11	1.2851
7	0.8450
4	0.6020

Water Spout *(lightning; combinatorics)* Study bible 1

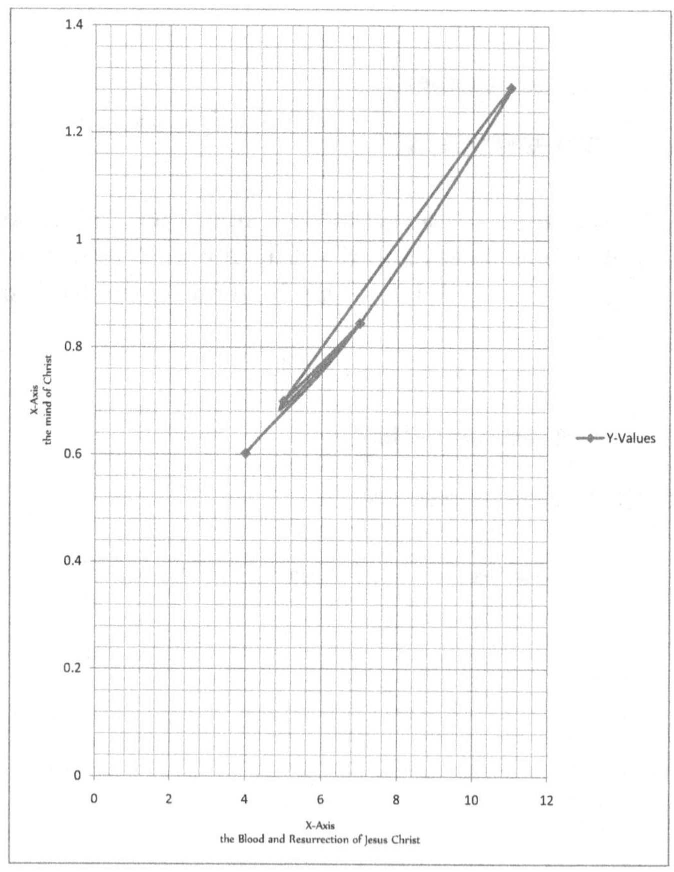

Water Spout *(lightning; combinatorics)* Study bible 2

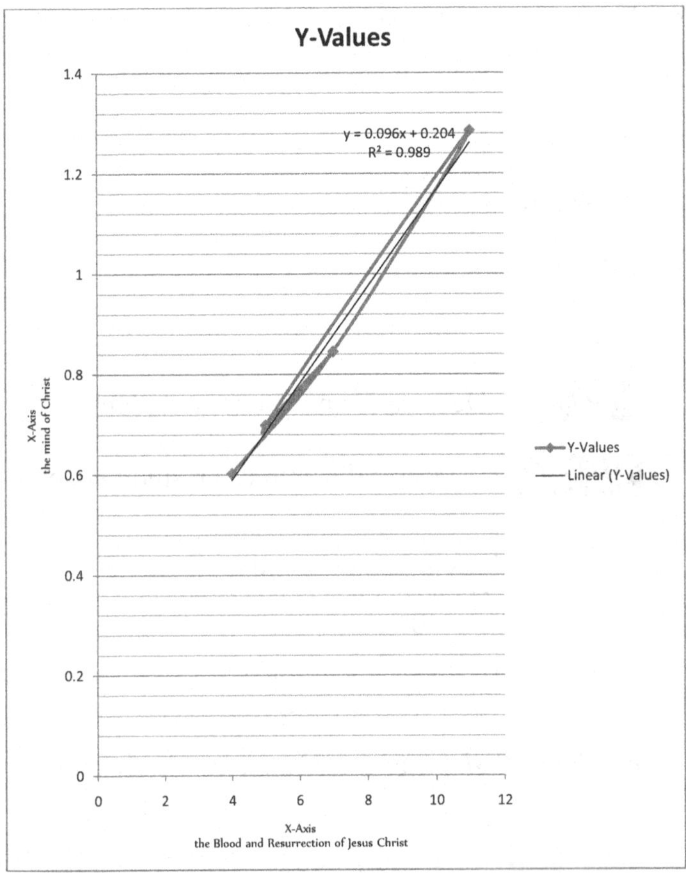

$10^{0.6989}$, $10^{0.8450}$, $10^{0.6989}$, $6^{1.2851}$ 10^{0}, $10^{0.8450}$, $10^{0.6020}$?

Pilled Poplar, Hazel, and Chestnut bible rods 2

12. How much then is a man better than a sheep? Wherefore it is lawful to do well on the Sabbath jewish day of worship & rest **days.**

10? 11. Bible Matrices

Pilled Poplar, Hazel, and Chestnut bible rods 1

$Log_{10} 10 = 1$ $Log_{10} 1 = 0$

$Log_6 10 = y$

$6^y = 10$

$y \log_{10} 6 = \log_{10} 10$

$y = \log_{10} 10 / \log_{10} 6$

$y = 1 / 0.7781$

$y = 1.2851$

10? 11. Deep calls unto Deep study bible 1

1? 1.2851 0. Deep calls unto Deep study bible 2

x-axis	y-axis
10	1
11	1.2851

Water Spout *(lightning; combinatorics)* Study bible 1

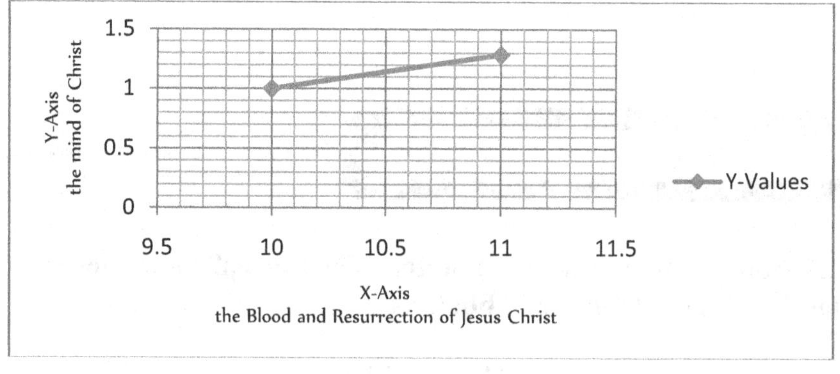

Water Spout *(lightning; combinatorics)* Study bible 2

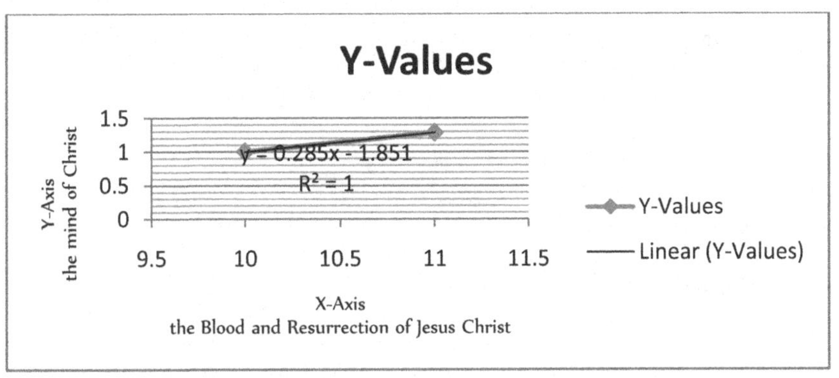

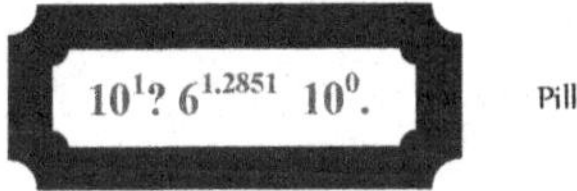

Pilled Poplar, Hazel, and Chestnut bible rods 2

13. Then saith he to the man, Stretch forth thine hand. And he stretched it forth; and it was restored whole, like as the other.

6, 4. 5; 5, 4. Bible Matrices

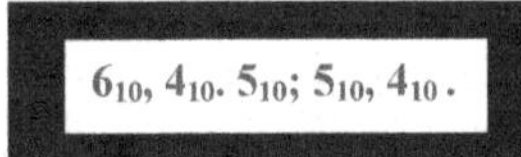

Pilled Poplar, Hazel, and Chestnut bible rods 1

$Log_{10}5 = 0.6989$ $Log_{10}6 = 0.7781$ $Log_{10}5 = 0.6989$ $Log_{10}4 = 0.6020$ $Log_{10}4 = 0.6020$

6, 4. 5; 5, 4. Deep calls unto Deep study bible 1

0.7781, 0.6020. 0.6989; 0.6989, 0.6020.
Deep calls unto Deep study bible 2

x-axis	y-axis
6	0.7781
4	0.6020
5	0.6989
5	0.6989
4	0.6020

Water Spout *(lightning; combinatorics)* Study bible 1

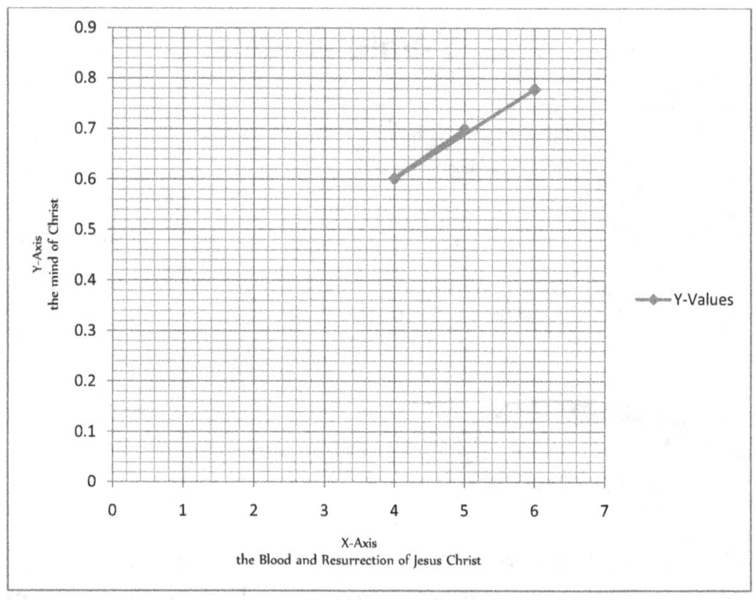

Water Spout *(lightning; combinatorics)* Study bible 2

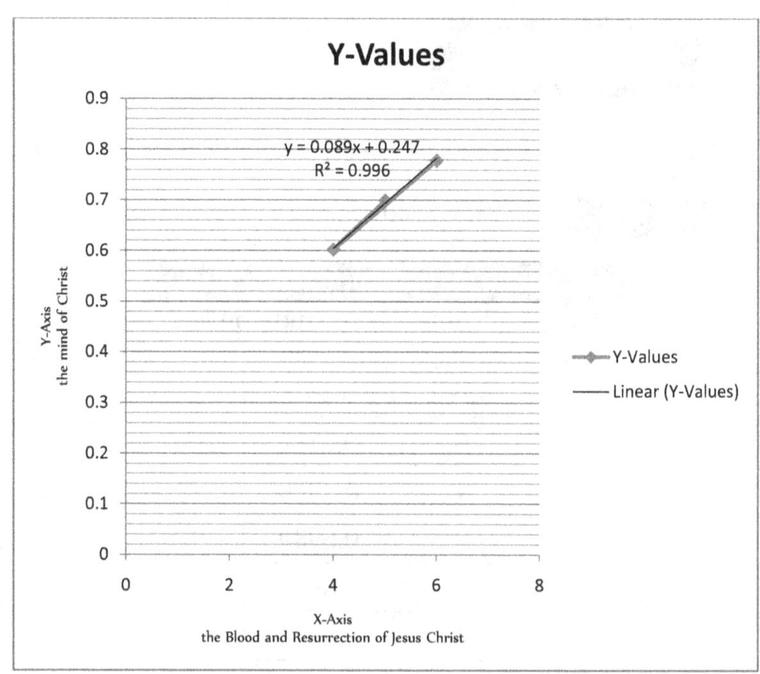

$10^{0.7781}$, $10^{0.6020}$. $10^{0.6989}$; $10^{0.6989}$, $10^{0.6020}$.

Pilled Poplar, Hazel, and Chestnut bible rods 2

14. Then the Phariseesset apart; separatists **went out, and held a council against him, how they might destroy him.**

5, 6, 5. Bible Matrices

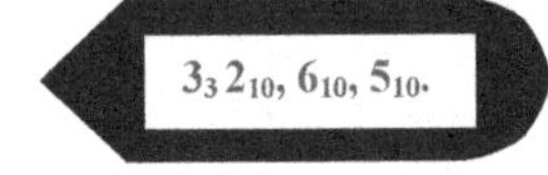

Pilled Poplar, Hazel, and Chestnut bible rods 1

$\text{Log}_{10} 5 = 0.6989$ $\text{Log}_{10} 6 = 0.7781$ $\text{Log}_{10} 2 = 0.3010$

$\text{Log}_3 3 = y$

$3^y = 3^1$

$y = 1$

5, 6, 5. Deep calls unto Deep study bible 1

1 0.3010, 0.7781, 0.6989. Deep calls unto Deep study bible 2

x-axis	y-axis
5	1.3010
6	0.7781
5	0.6989

Water Spout *(lightning; combinatorics)* Study bible 1

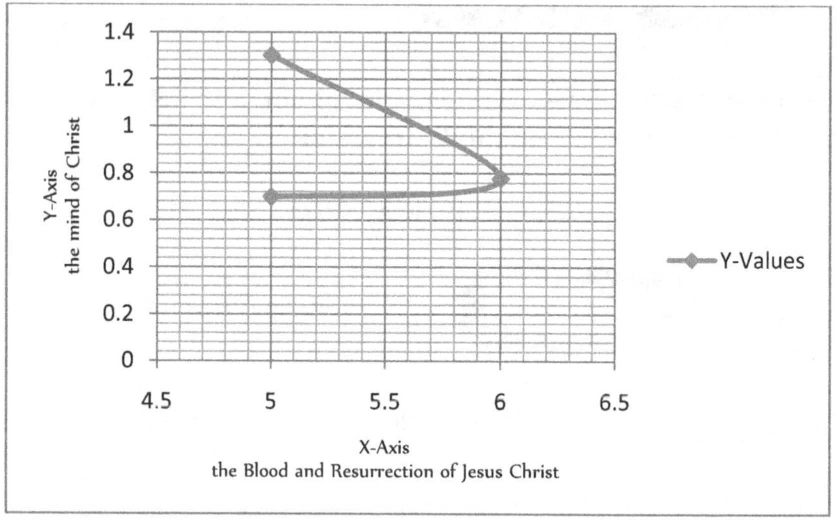

Water Spout *(lightning; combinatorics)* Study bible 2

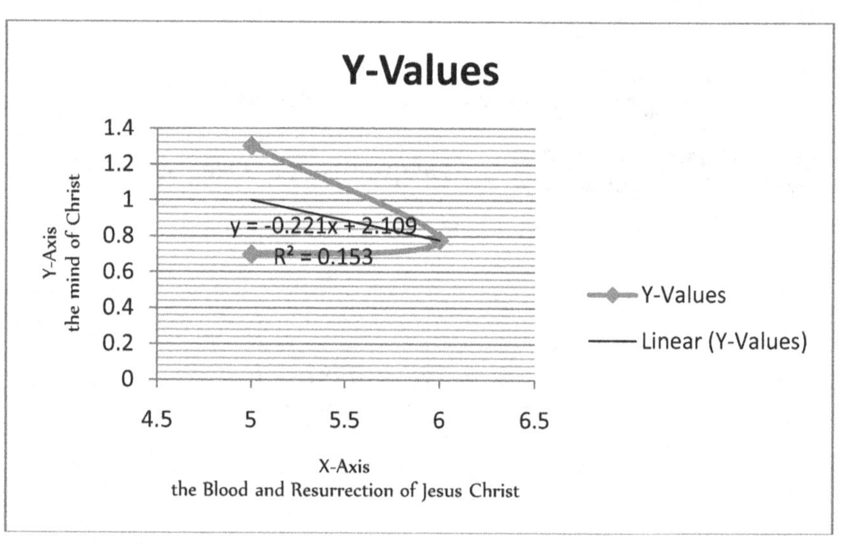

Pilled Poplar, Hazel, and Chestnut bible rods 2

15. But when Jesussavior; deliverer **knew it, he withdrew himself from thence: and great multitudes followed him, and he healed them all;**

5, 5:5, 5; Bible Matrices

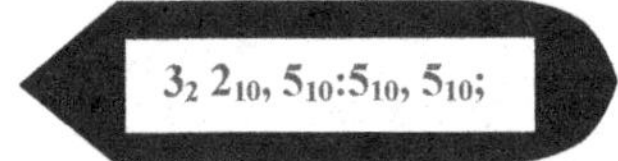

Pilled Poplar, Hazel, and Chestnut bible rods 1

$\text{Log}_{10} 5 = 0.6989$ $\text{Log}_{10} 5 = 0.6989$ $\text{Log}_{10} 5 = 0.6989$ $\text{Log}_{10} 2 = 0.3010$

$\text{Log}_2 3 = y$

$2^y = 3$

$y \log_{10} 2 = \log_{10} 3$

$y = \log_{10} 3 / \log_{10} 2$

$y = 0.4771 / 0.3010$

$y = 1.5850$

5, 5: 5, 5; Deep calls unto Deep study bible 1

1.5850 0.3010, 0.6989: 0.6989, 0.6989;
Deep calls unto Deep study bible 2

x-axis	y-axis
5	1.8860
5	0.6989
5	0.6989
5	0.6989

Water Spout *(lightning; combinatorics)* Study bible 1

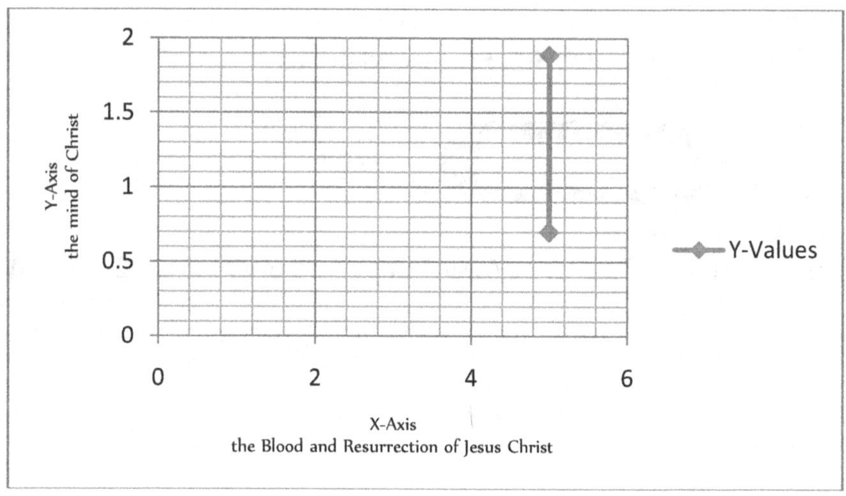

Water Spout *(lightning; combinatorics)* Study bible 2

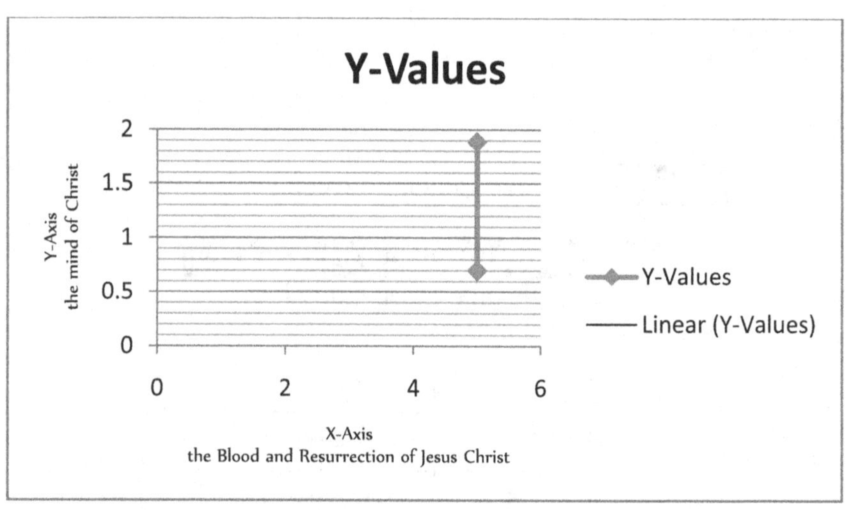

$2^{1.5850}$ $10^{0.3010}$, $10^{0.6989}$:$10^{0.6989}$, $10^{0.6989}$;

Pilled Poplar, Hazel, and Chestnut bible rods 2

16. And charged them that they should not make him known:

10: Bible Matrices

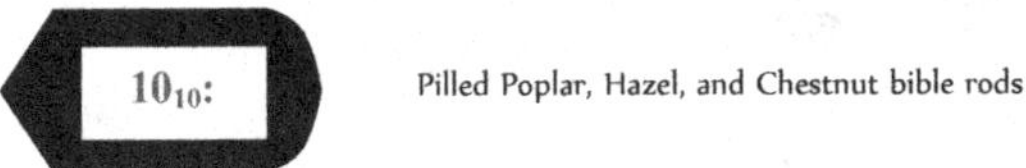

$\text{Log}_{10} 10 = 1$

10: Deep calls unto Deep study bible 1

1: Deep calls unto Deep study bible 2

x-axis	y-axis
10	1

Water Spout *(lightning; combinatorics)* Study bible 1

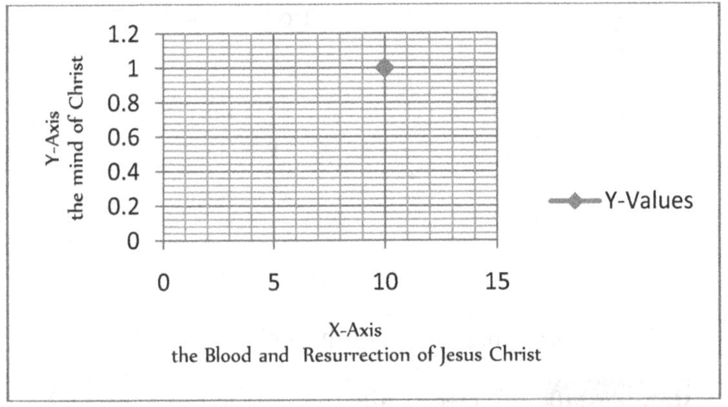

Water Spout *(lightning; combinatorics)* Study bible 2

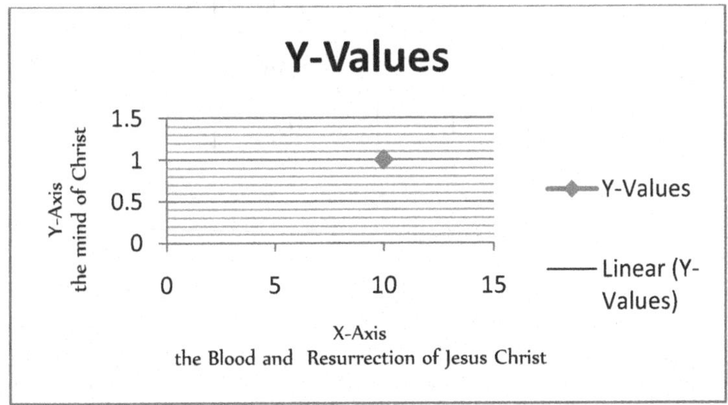

Pilled Poplar, Hazel, and Chestnut bible rods 2

17. That it might be fulfilled which was spoken by Esaiasthe salvation of the Lord**the prophet** to bubble forth, as from a fountain; utter, **saying,**

12, 1, Bible Matrices

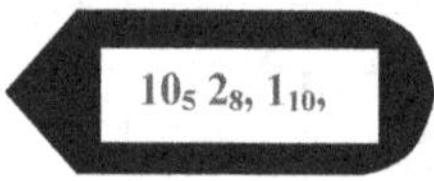

Pilled Poplar, Hazel, and Chestnut bible rods 1

$\text{Log}_{10} 1 = 0$

$$\text{Log}_5 10 = y$$
$$5^y = 10$$
$$y \log_{10} 5 = \log_{10} 10$$
$$y = \log_{10} 10 / \log_{10} 5$$
$$y = 1 / 0.6989$$
$$y = 1.4308$$

$$\text{Log}_2 8 = y$$
$$2^y = 8$$
$$2^y = 2^3$$
$$y = 3$$

12, 1, Deep calls unto Deep study bible 1

1.4308 3, 0, Deep calls unto Deep study bible 2

x-axis	y-axis
12	4.4308
1	0

Water Spout *(lightning; combinatorics)* Study bible 1

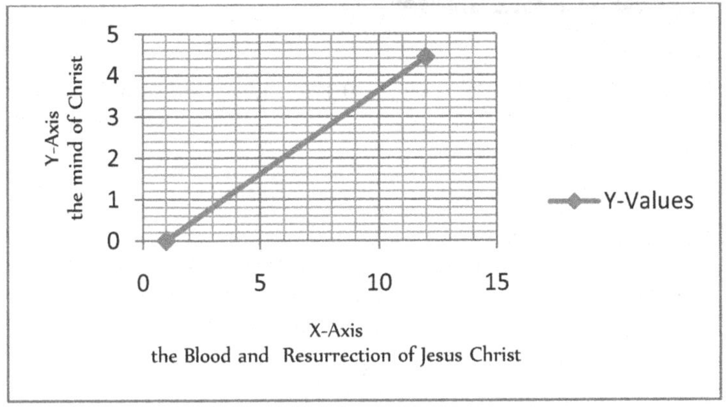

Water Spout *(lightning; combinatorics)* Study bible 2

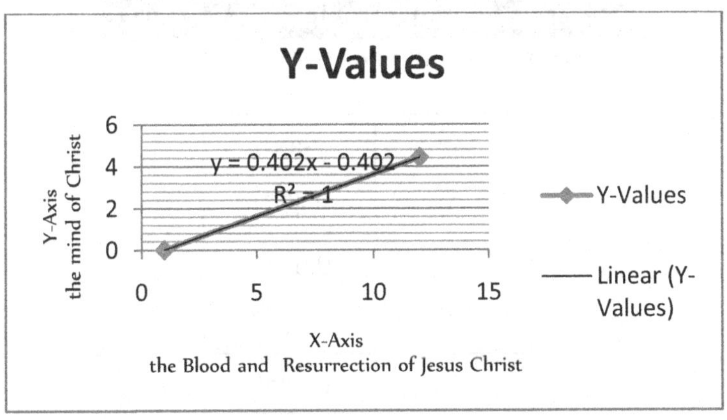

Pilled Poplar, Hazel, and Chestnut bible rods 2

18. Behold my servant, whom I have chosen; my beloved, in whom my soul is well pleased: I will put my spirit upon him, and he shall shew judgment to the Gentiles non-jews.

3, 4; 2, 7: 7, 8. Bible Matrices

$3_{10}, 4_{10}; 2_{10}, 7_{10}: 7_{10}, 8_{2}.$ Pilled Poplar, Hazel, and Chestnut bible rods 1

$\text{Log}_{10}3 = 0.4771$ $\text{Log}_{10}4 = 0.6020$ $\text{Log}_{10}2 = 0.3010$ $\text{Log}_{10}7 = 0.8450$ $\text{Log}_{10}7 = 0.8450$

$\text{Log}_2 8 = y$

$2^y = 8$

$2^y = 2^3$

$y = 3$

3, 4; 2, 7: 7, 8. Deep calls unto Deep study bible 1

0.4771, 0.6020; 0.3010, 0.8450: 0.8450, 3.
Deep calls unto Deep study bible 2

x-axis	y-axis
3	0.4771
4	0.6020
2	0.3010
7	0.8450
7	0.8450
8	3

Water Spout *(lightning; combinatorics)* Study bible 1

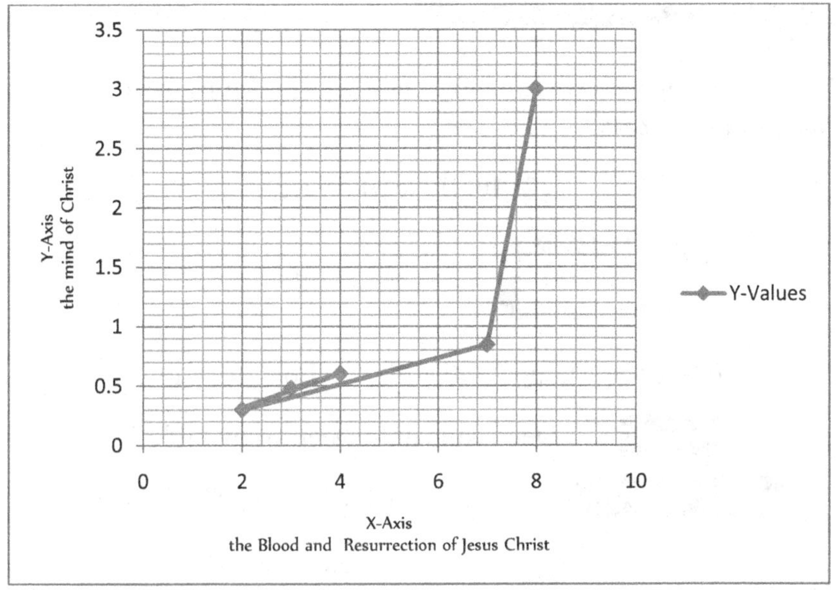

Water Spout *(lightning; combinatorics)* Study bible 2

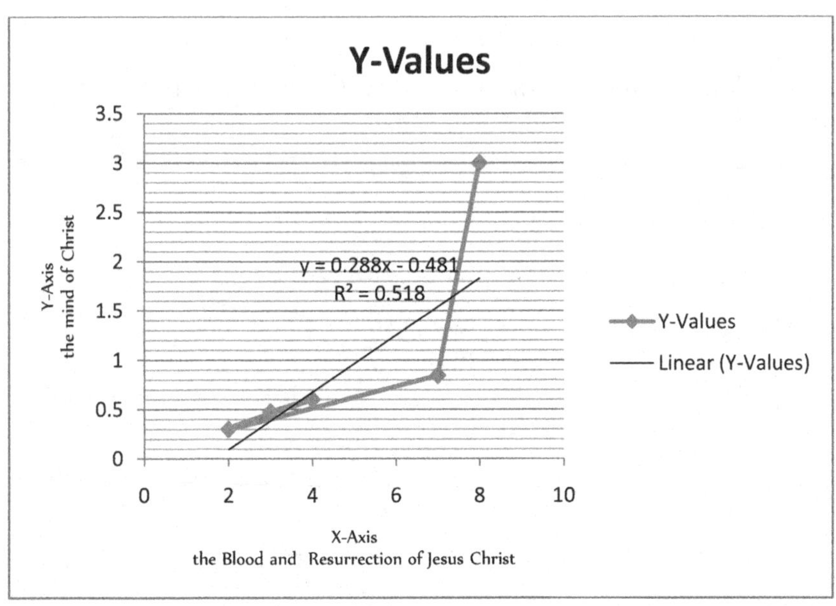

$10^{0.4771}, 10^{0.6020}; 10^{0.3010}, 10^{0.8450}: 10^{0.8450}, 2^3.$

Pilled Poplar, Hazel, and Chestnut bible rods 2

19. He shall not strive, nor cry; neither shall any man hear his voice in the streets.

4, 2; 10. Bible Matrices

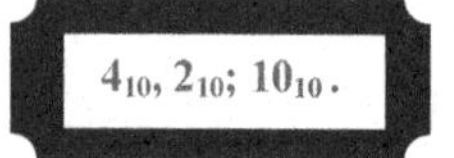

Pilled Poplar, Hazel, and Chestnut bible rods 1

$\text{Log}_{10} 4 = 0.6020$ $\text{Log}_{10} 2 = 0.3010$ $\text{Log}_{10} 10 = 1$

4, 2; 10. Deep calls unto Deep study bible 1

0.6020, 0.3010; 1. Deep calls unto Deep study bible 2

x-axis	y-axis
4	0.6020
2	0.3010
10	1

Water Spout *(lightning; combinatorics)* Study bible 1

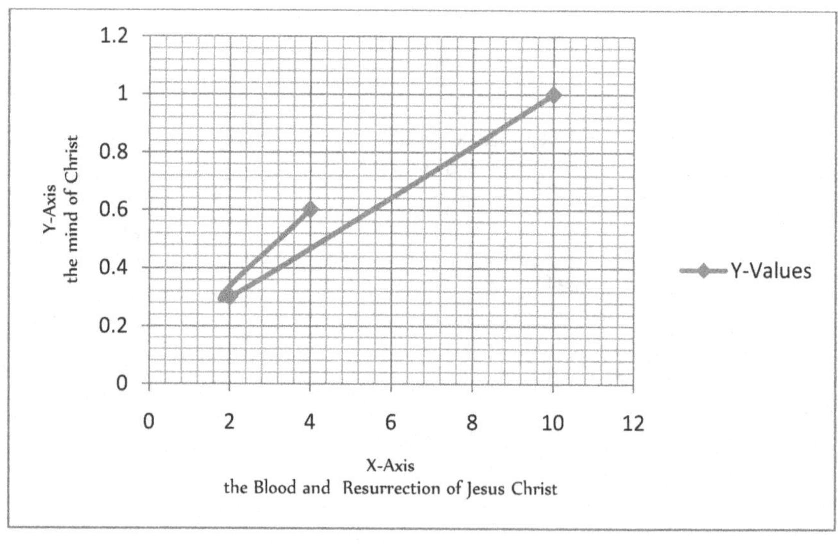

Water Spout *(lightning; combinatorics)* Study bible 2

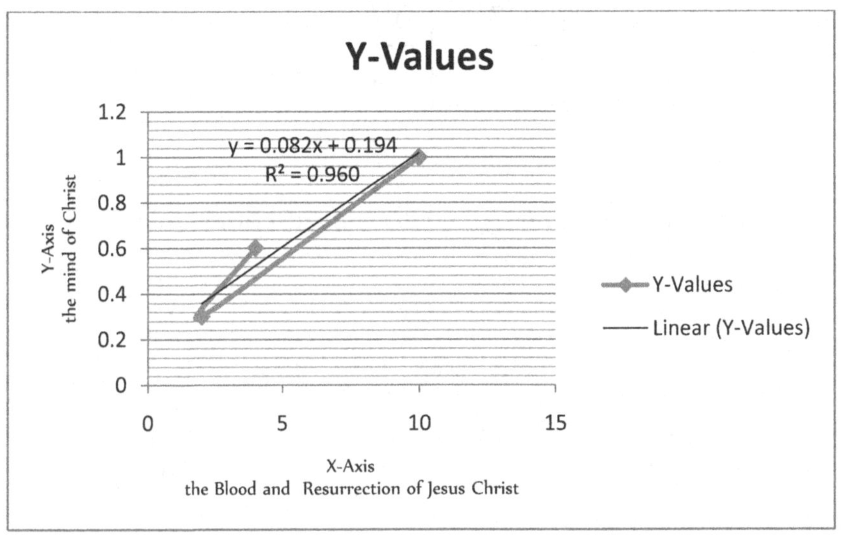

Pilled Poplar, Hazel, and Chestnut bible rods 2

20. A bruised reed shall he not break, and smoking flax shall he not quench, till he send forth judgment unto victory.

7, 7, 7. Bible Matrices

Pilled Poplar, Hazel, and Chestnut bible rods 1

$\text{Log}_{10} 7 = 0.8450$ $\text{Log}_{10} 7 = 0.8450$ $\text{Log}_{10} 7 = 0.8450$

7, 7, 7. Deep calls unto Deep study bible 1

0.8450, 0.8450, 0.8450. Deep calls unto Deep study bible 2

x-axis	y-axis
7	0.8450
7	0.8450
7	0.8450

Water Spout *(lightning; combinatorics)* Study bible 1

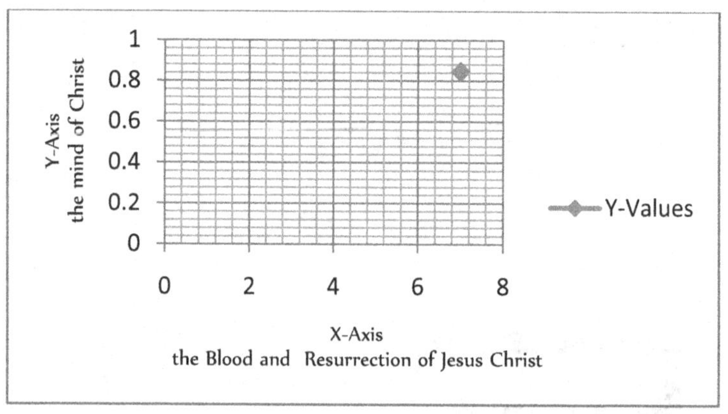

Water Spout *(lightning; combinatorics)* Study bible 2

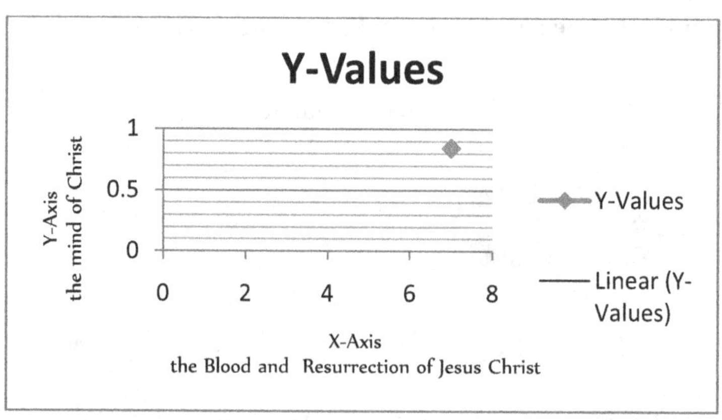

$10^{0.8450}$, $10^{0.8450}$, $10^{0.8450}$.

Pilled Poplar, Hazel, and Chestnut bible rods 2

21. And in his name shall the Gentiles non-jews **trust.**

8. Bible Matrices

$\text{Log}_{10} 1 = 0$

$\text{Log}_2 7 = y$

$2^y = 7$

$y \log_{10} 2 = \log_{10} 7$

$y = \log_{10} 7 / \log_{10} 2$

$y = 0.8450 / 0.3010$

$y = 2.8073$

8. Deep calls unto Deep study bible 1

2.8073 0. Deep calls unto Deep study bible 2

x-axis	y-axis
8	2.8073

Water Spout *(lightning; combinatorics)* Study bible 1

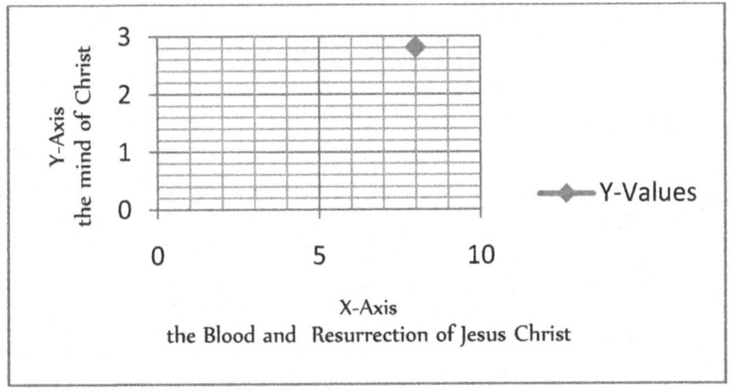

Water Spout *(lightning; combinatorics)* Study bible 2

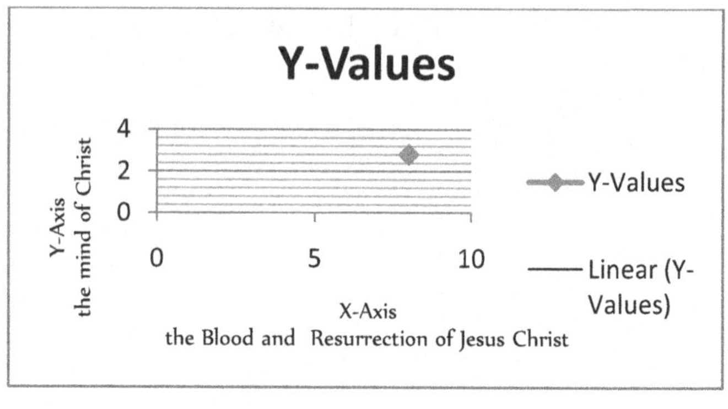

$2^{2.8073}$ 10^{0}. Pilled Poplar, Hazel, and Chestnut bible rods 2

22. Then was brought unto him one possessed with a devil slanderer, false accuser, **blind, and dumb: and he healed him, insomuch that the blind and dumb both spake and saw.**

10, 1, 2: 4, 10. Bible Matrices

10_3, 1_{10}, 2_{10}: 4_{10}, 10_{10}. Pilled Poplar, Hazel, and Chestnut bible rods 1

$\text{Log}_{10} 1 = 0$ $\text{Log}_{10} 4 = 0.6020$ $\text{Log}_{10} 2 = 0.3010$ $\text{Log}_{10} 10 = 1$

$\text{Log}_3 10 = y$

$3^y = 10$

$y \log_{10} 3 = \log_{10} 10$

$y = \log_{10} 10 / \log_{10} 3$

$y = 1 / 0.4771$

$y = 2.0959$

10, 1, 2: 4, 10. Deep calls unto Deep study bible 1

2.0959, 0, 0.3010: 0.6020, 1. Deep calls unto Deep study bible 2

x-axis	y-axis
10	2.0959
1	0
2	0.3010
4	0.6020
10	1

Water Spout *(lightning; combinatorics)* Study bible 1

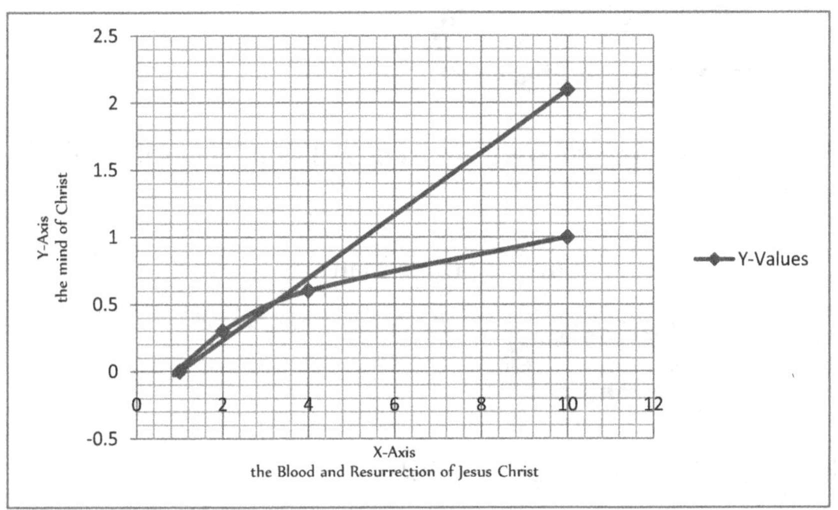

Water Spout *(lightning; combinatorics)* Study bible 2

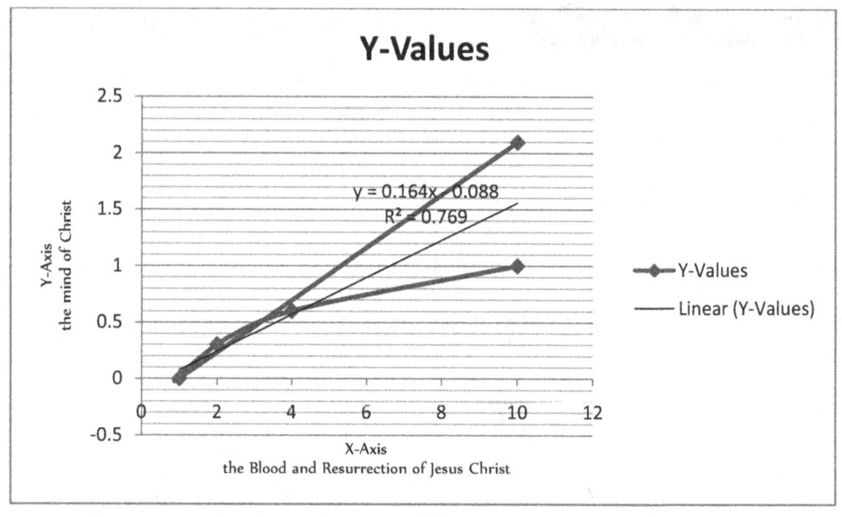

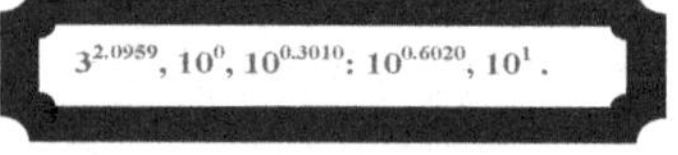

Pilled Poplar, Hazel, and Chestnut bible rods 2

23. And all the people were amazed, and said, Is not this the son of Davidbeloved;dear?

6, 2, 7? Bible Matrices

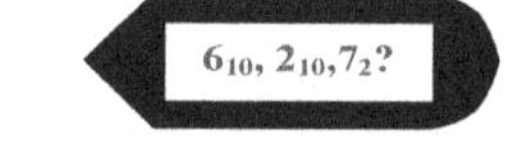

Pilled Poplar, Hazel, and Chestnut bible rods 1

$\text{Log}_{10} 6 = 0.7781$ $\text{Log}_{10} 2 = 0.3010$

$\text{Log}_2 7 = y$

$2^y = 7$

$y \log_{10} 2 = \log_{10} 7$

$y = \log_{10} 7 / \log_{10} 2$

$y = 0.8450 / 0.3010$

$y = 2.8073$

6, 2, 7? Deep calls unto Deep study bible 1

0.7781, 0.3010, 2.8073? Deep calls unto Deep study bible 2

x-axis	y-axis
6	0.7781
2	0.3010
7	2.8073

Water Spout *(lightning; combinatorics)* Study bible 1

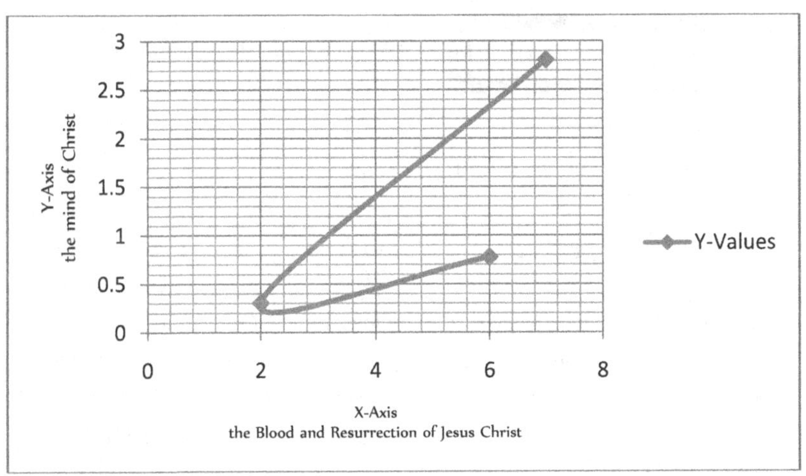

Water Spout *(lightning; combinatorics)* Study bible 2

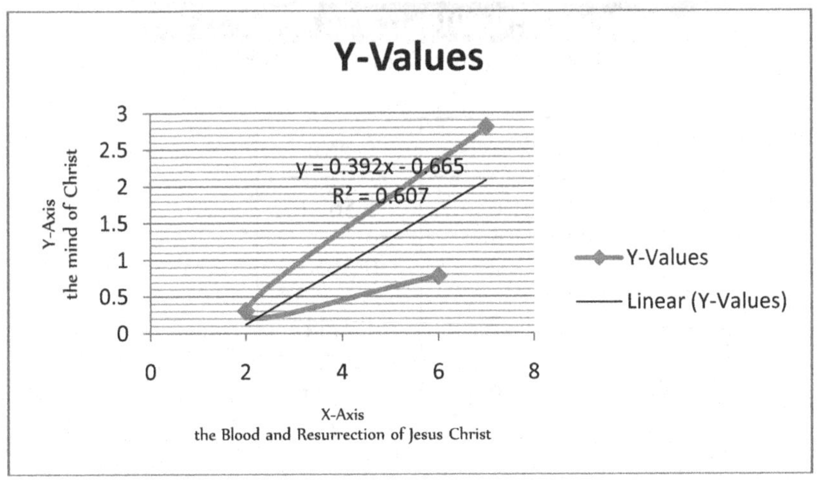

$10^{0.7781}$, $10^{0.3010}$, $2^{2.8073}$?

Pilled Poplar, Hazel, and Chestnut bible rods 2

24. But when the Phariseesset apart; separatists**heard it, they said, This fellow doth not cast out devils** slanderers, false accusers, **but by Beelzebub**god of the fly **the prince of the devils**slanderers; accusers.

6, 2, 7, 8. Bible Matrices

4_3 2_{10}, 2_{10},7_3, 3_4 5_2.

Pilled Poplar, Hazel, and Chestnut bible rods I

$Log_{10} 2 = 0.3010$ $Log_{10} 2 = 0.3010$

$Log_3 4 = y$	$Log_3 7 = y$	$Log_4 3 = y$	$Log_2 5 = y$
$3^y = 4$	$3^y = 7$	$4^y = 3$	$2^y = 5$
$y \log_{10} 3 = \log_{10} 4$	$y \log_{10} 3 = \log_{10} 7$	$y \log_{10} 4 = \log_{10} 3$	$y \log_{10} 2 = \log_{10} 5$
$y = \log_{10} 4 / \log_{10} 3$	$y = \log_{10} 7 / \log_{10} 3$	$y = \log_{10} 3 / \log_{10} 4$	$y = \log_{10} 5 / \log_{10} 2$
$y = 0.6020 / 0.4771$	$y = 0.8450 / 0.4771$	$y = 0.4771 / 0.6020$	$y = 0.6989 / 0.3010$
$y = 1.2617$	$y = 1.7711$	$y = 0.7925$	$y = 2.3219$

6, 2, 7, 8. Deep calls unto Deep study bible 1

1.2617 0.3010, 0.3010, 1.7711, 0.7925 2.3219.

Deep calls unto Deep study bible 2

x-axis	y-axis
6	1.5627
2	0.3010
7	1.7711
8	3.1144

Water Spout *(lightning; combinatorics)* Study bible 1

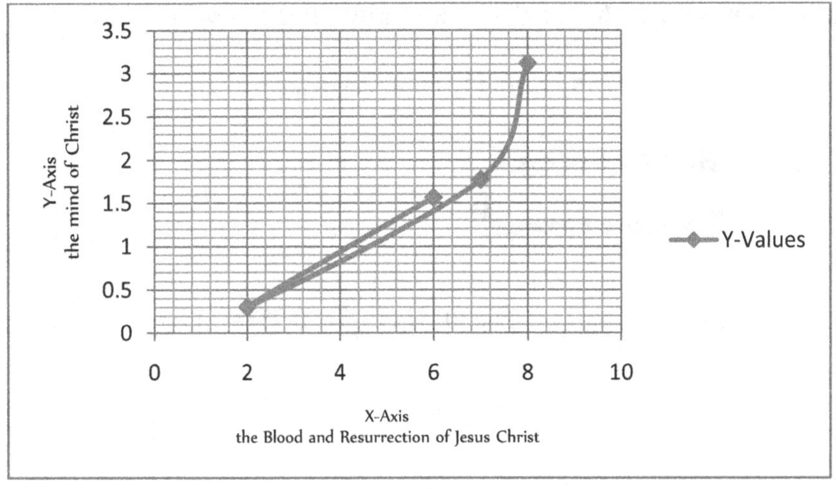

Water Spout *(lightning; combinatorics)* Study bible 2

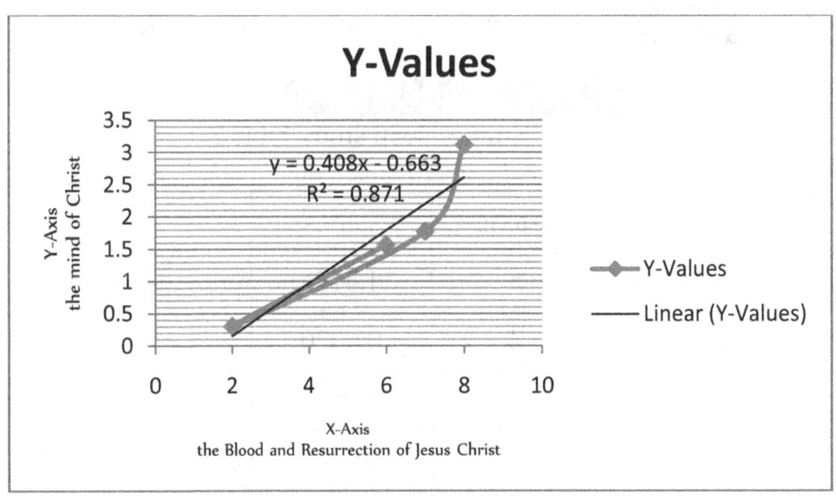

$3^{1.2617}$ $10^{0.3010}$, $10^{0.3010}$, $3^{1.7711}$, $4^{0.7925}$ $2^{2.3219}$.

Pilled Poplar, Hazel, and Chestnut bible rods 2

25. And Jesussavior; deliverer**knew their thoughts, and said unto them, Every kingdom divided against itself is brought to desolation; and every city or house divided against itself shall not stand:**

5, 4, 9; 11: Bible Matrices

$2_2\, 3_{10}, 4_{10}, 9_{10}; 11_{10}$: Pilled Poplar, Hazel, and Chestnut bible rods 1

$Log_{10} 3 = 0.4771$ $Log_{10} 4 = 0.6020$ $Log_{10} 9 = 0.9542$ $Log_{10} 11 = 1.0413$

$Log_2 2 = y$

$2^y = 2^1$

$y = 1$

5, 4, 9; 11: Deep calls unto Deep study bible 1

1 0.4771, 0.6020, 0.9542; 1.0413:
Deep calls unto Deep study bible 2

x-axis	y-axis
5	1.4771
4	0.6020
9	0.9542
11	1.0413

Water Spout *(lightning; combinatorics)* Study bible 1

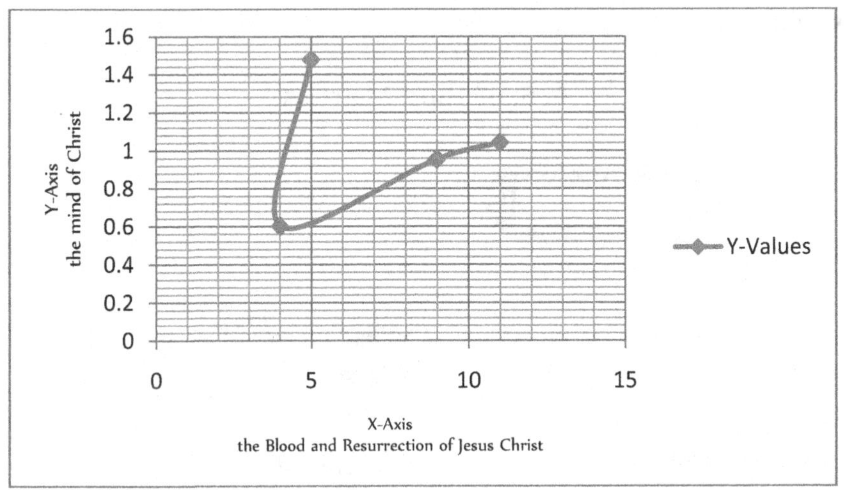

Water Spout *(lightning; combinatorics)* Study bible 2

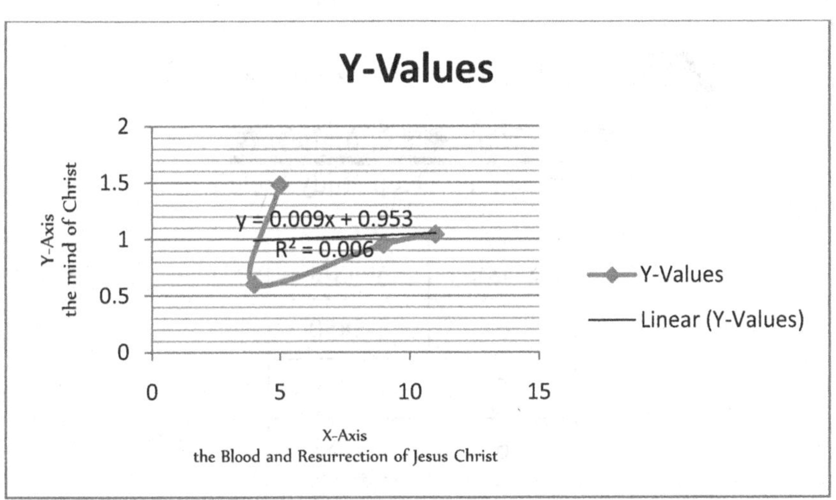

2^1 $10^{0.4771}$, $10^{0.6020}$, $10^{0.9542}$; $10^{1.0413}$:

Pilled Poplar, Hazel, and Chestnut bible rods 2

26. And if Satancontrary; adversary; enemy; accuser**cast out Satan** contrary; adversary; enemy; accuser, **he is divided against himself; how shall then his kingdom stand?**

6, 5; 6? Bible Matrices

$3_4\,3_4, 5_{10}; 6_{10}?$

Pilled Poplar, Hazel, and Chestnut bible rods 1

$\text{Log}_{10} 5 = 0.6989$	$\text{Log}_{10} 6 = 0.7781$
$\text{Log}_4 3 = y$	$\text{Log}_4 3 = y$
$4^y = 3$	$4^y = 3$
$y \log_{10} 4 = \log_{10} 3$	$y \log_{10} 4 = \log_{10} 3$
$y = \log_{10} 3 / \log_{10} 4$	$y = \log_{10} 3 / \log_{10} 4$
$y = 0.4771 / 0.6020$	$y = 0.4771 / 0.6020$
$y = 0.7925$	$y = 0.7925$

6, 5; 6? Deep calls unto Deep study bible 1

0.7925 0.7925, 0.6989; 0.7781?
Deep calls unto Deep study bible 2

x-axis	y-axis
6	1.5850
5	0.6989
6	0.7781

Water Spout *(lightning; combinatorics)* Study bible 1

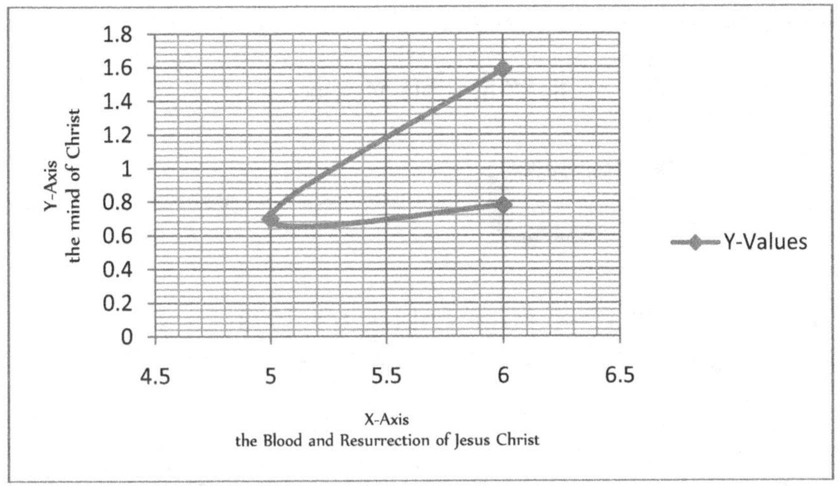

Water Spout *(lightning; combinatorics)* Study bible 2

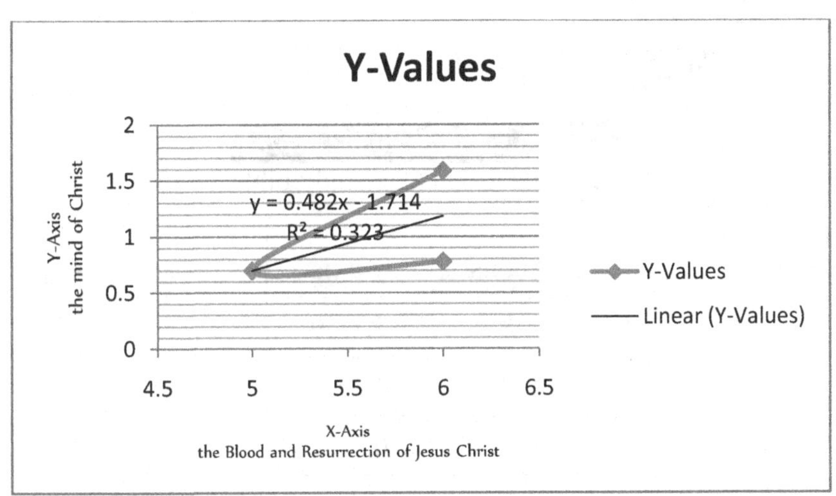

$4^{0.7925}$ $4^{0.7925}$, $10^{0.6989}$; $10^{0.7781}$?

Pilled Poplar, Hazel, and Chestnut bible rods 2

27. And if I by Beelzebubgod of the fly **cast out devils** slanderers; accusers, **by whom do your children cast them out? therefore they shall be your judges.**

8, 8? 6. Bible Matrices

$5_4\, 3_2,\, 8_{10}?\, 6_{10}.$

Pilled Poplar, Hazel, and Chestnut bible rods 1

$\text{Log}_{10} 8 = 0.\ 9030$
$\text{Log}_4 5 = y$
$4^y = 5$
$y \log_{10} 4 = \log_{10} 5$
$y = \log_{10} 5 / \log_{10} 4$
$y = 0.6989 / 0.6020$
$y = 1.1609$

$\text{Log}_{10} 6 = 0.7781$
$\text{Log}_2 3 = y$
$2^y = 3$
$y \log_{10} 2 = \log_{10} 3$
$y = \log_{10} 3 / \log_{10} 2$
$y = 0.4771 / 0.3010$
$y = 1.5850$

8, 8? 6. Deep calls unto Deep study bible 1

1.1609 1.5850, 0.9030? 0.7781.
Deep calls unto Deep study bible 2

x-axis	y-axis
8	2.7459
8	0.9030
6	0.7781

Water Spout *(lightning; combinatorics)* Study bible 1

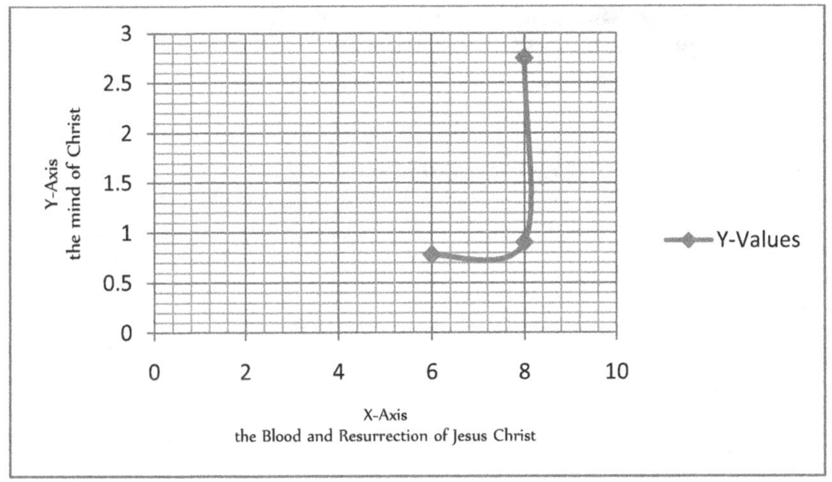

Water Spout *(lightning; combinatorics)* Study bible 2

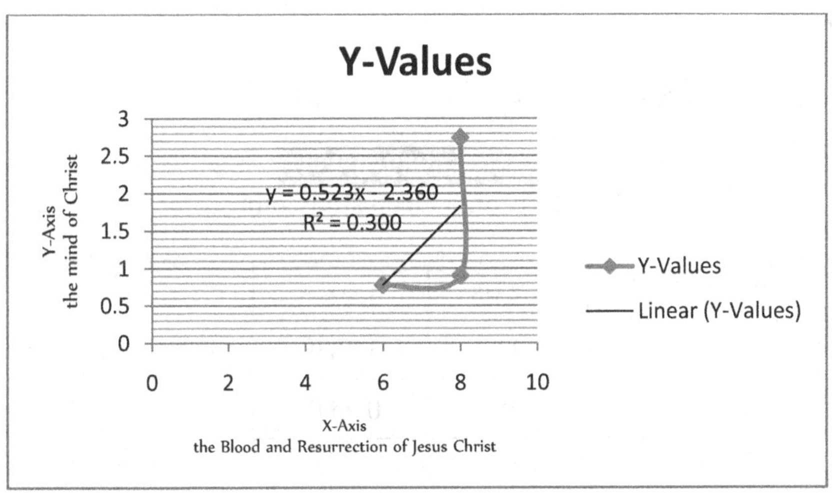

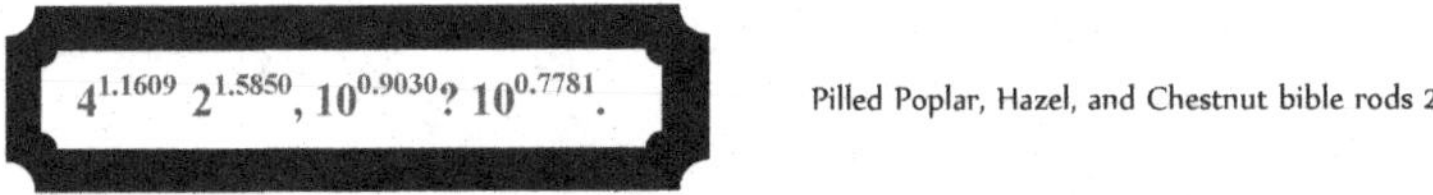
$4^{1.1609}$ $2^{1.5850}$, $10^{0.9030}$? $10^{0.7781}$.

Pilled Poplar, Hazel, and Chestnut bible rods 2

28. But if I cast out devils slanderers; accusers **by the Spirit of God, then the kingdom of God is come unto you.**

11, 9. Bible Matrices

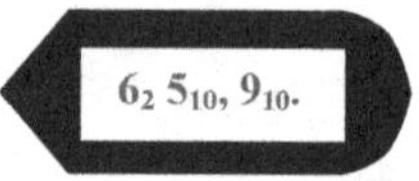

Pilled Poplar, Hazel, and Chestnut bible rods 1

$Log_{10} 5 = 0.6989$ $Log_{10} 9 = 0.9542$

$Log_2 6 = y$

$2^y = 6$

$y \log_{10} 2 = \log_{10} 6$

$y = \log_{10} 6 / \log_{10} 2$

$y = 0.7781 / 0.3010$

$y = 2.5850$

11, 9. Deep calls unto Deep study bible 1

2.5850 0.6989, 0.9542.

Deep calls unto Deep study bible 2

x-axis	y-axis
11	3.2839
9	0.9542

Water Spout *(lightning; combinatorics)* Study bible 1

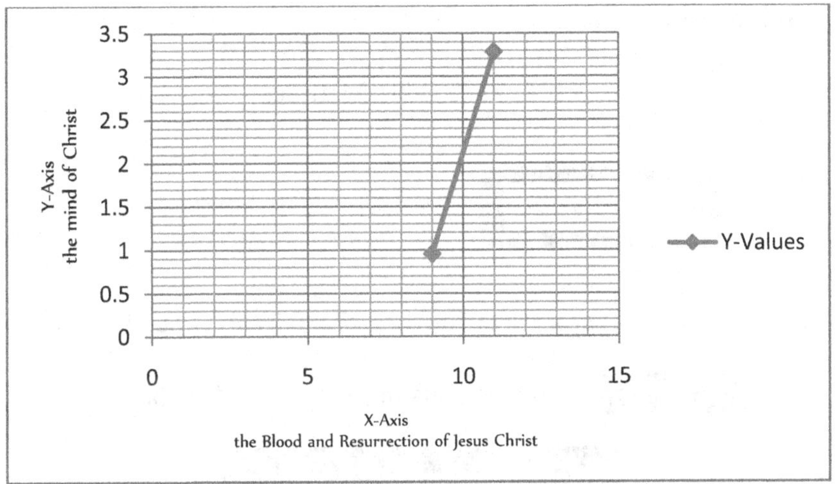

Water Spout *(lightning; combinatorics)* Study bible 2

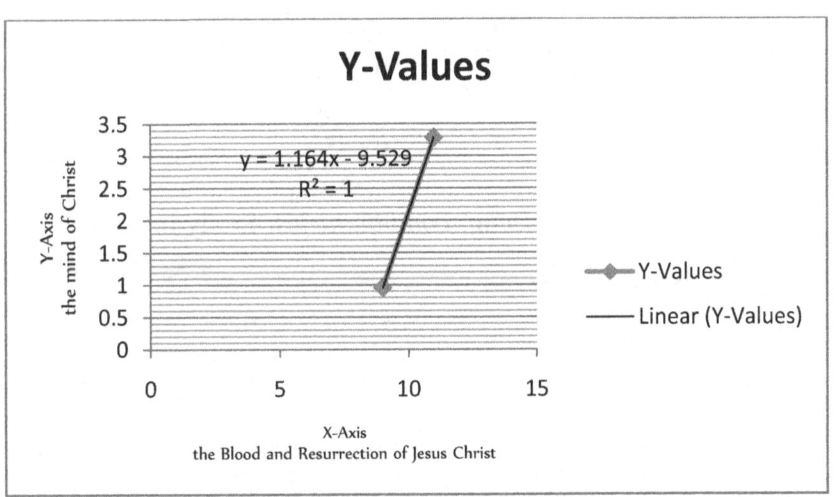

$2^{2.5850}$ $10^{0.6989}$, $10^{0.9542}$.

Pilled Poplar, Hazel, and Chestnut bible rods 2

29. Or else how can one enter into a strong man's house, and spoil his goods, except he first bind the strong man? and then he will spoil his house.

11, 4, 7? 7. Bible Matrices

$\text{Log}_{10} 7 = 0.8450$ $\text{Log}_{10} 4 = 0.6020$ $\text{Log}_{10} 7 = 0.8450$ $\text{Log}_{10} 11 = 1.0413$

11, 4, 7? 7. Deep calls unto Deep study bible 1

1.0413, 0.6020, 0.8450? 0.8450.
Deep calls unto Deep study bible 2

x-axis	y-axis
11	1.0413
4	0.6020
7	0.8450
7	0.8450

Water Spout *(lightning; combinatorics)* Study bible 1

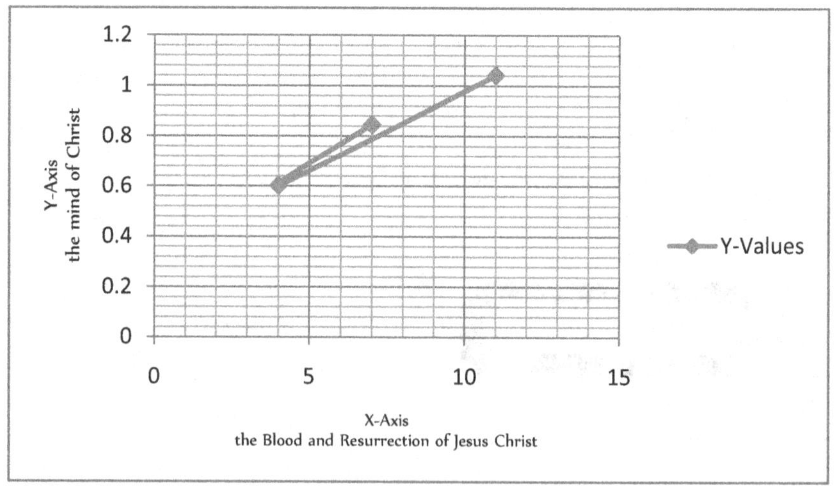

Water Spout *(lightning; combinatorics)* Study bible 2

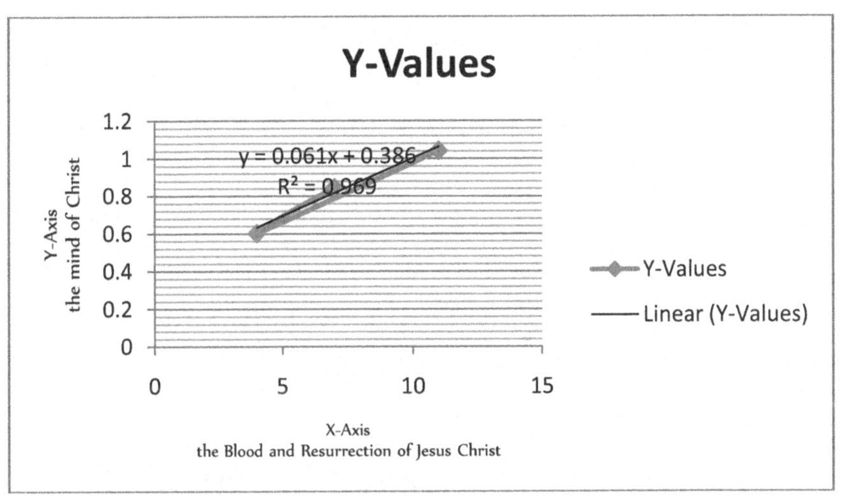

Pilled Poplar, Hazel, and Chestnut bible rods 2

30. He that is not with me is against me; and he that gathereth not with me scattereth abroad.

9; 9. Bible Matrices

Pilled Poplar, Hazel, and Chestnut bible rods 1

$\text{Log}_{10} 9 = 0.9542$ $\text{Log}_{10} 9 = 0.9542$

9; 9. Deep calls unto Deep study bible 1

0.9542; 0.9542. Deep calls unto Deep study bible 2

x-axis	y-axis
9	0.9542
9	0.9542

Water Spout *(lightning; combinatorics)* Study bible 1

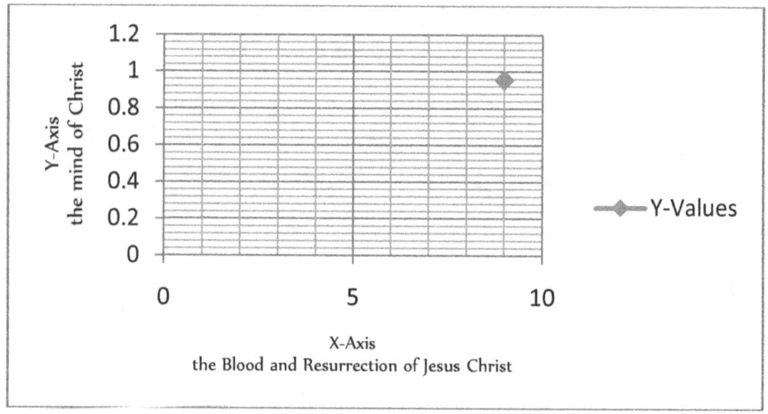

Water Spout *(lightning; combinatorics)* Study bible 2

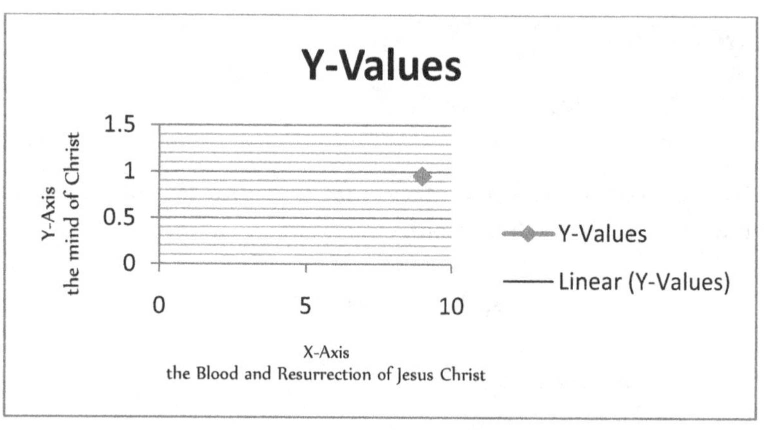

$10^{0.9542}$, $10^{0.9542}$.

Pilled Poplar, Hazel, and Chestnut bible rods 2

31. Wherefore I say unto you, All manner of sin and blasphemy shall be forgiven unto men: but the blasphemy against the Holy Ghost shall not be forgiven unto men.

5, 11: 13. Bible Matrices

$5_{10}, 11_{10}: 13_{10}$.

Pilled Poplar, Hazel, and Chestnut bible rods 1

$\text{Log}_{10} 5 = 0.6989$ $\text{Log}_{10} 11 = 1.0413$ $\text{Log}_{10} 13 = 1.1139$

5, 11: 13. Deep calls unto Deep study bible 1

0.6989, 1.0413: 1.1139. Deep calls unto Deep study bible 2

x-axis	y-axis
5	0.6989
11	1.0413
13	1.1139

Water Spout *(lightning; combinatorics)* Study bible 1

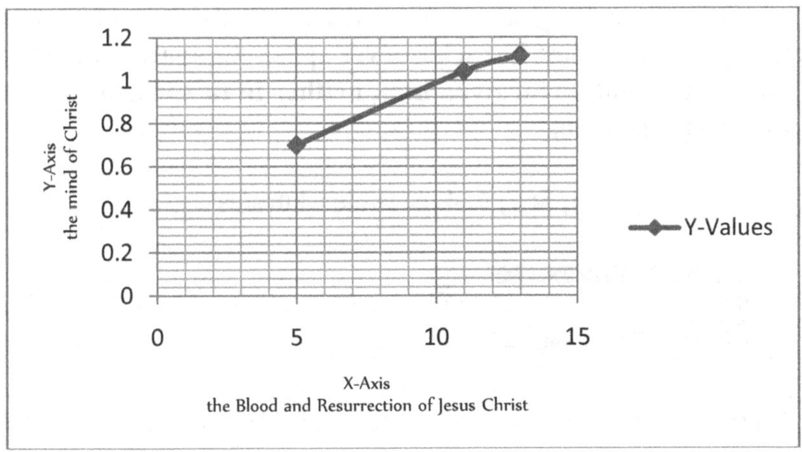

Water Spout *(lightning; combinatorics)* Study bible 2

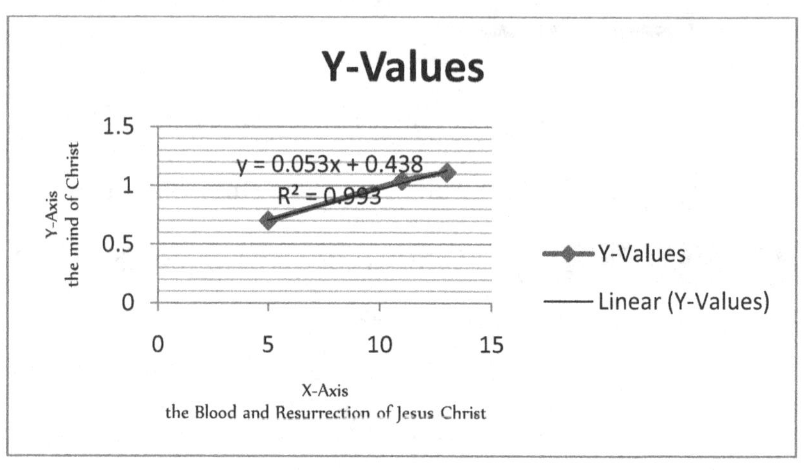

$10^{0.6989}$, $10^{1.0413}$: $10^{1.1139}$.

Pilled Poplar, Hazel, and Chestnut bible rods 2

32. And whosoever speaketh a word against the Son of man, it shall be forgiven him: but whosoever speaketh against the Holy Ghost, it shall not be forgiven him, neither in this world, neither in the world to come.

10, 5: 7, 6, 4, 6. Bible Matrices

10_{10}, 5_{10}: 7_{10}, 6_{10}, 4_{10}, 6_{10}.

Pilled Poplar, Hazel, and Chestnut bible rods 1

$\text{Log}_{10} 5 = 0.6989$ $\text{Log}_{10} 6 = 0.7781$ $\text{Log}_{10} 6 = 0.7781$ $\text{Log}_{10} 4 = 0.6020$ $\text{Log}_{10} 10 = 1$ $\text{Log}_{10} 7 = 0.8450$

10, 5: 7, 6, 4, 6. Deep calls unto Deep study bible 1

1, 0.6989: 0.8450, 0.7781, 0.6020, 0.7781.
Deep calls unto Deep study bible 2

x-axis	y-axis
10	1
5	0.6989
7	0.8450
6	0.7781
4	0.6020
6	0.7781

Water Spout *(lightning; combinatorics)* Study bible 1

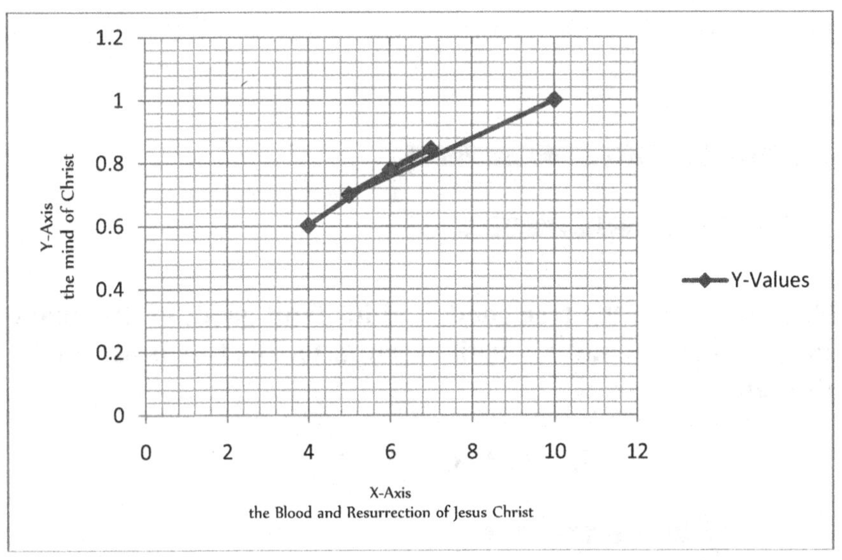

Water Spout *(lightning; combinatorics)* Study bible 2

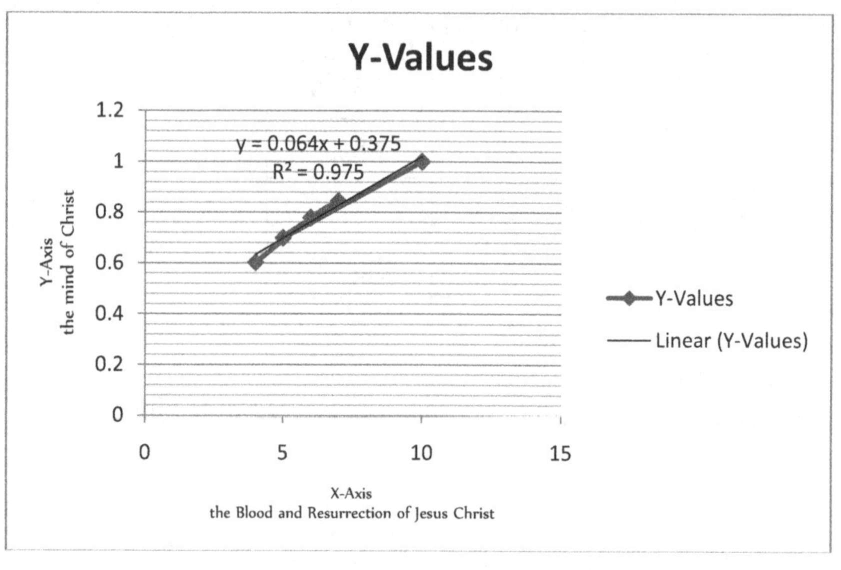

$10^{1}, 10^{0.6989}: 10^{0.8450}, 10^{0.7781}, 10^{0.6020}, 10^{0.7781}$.

Pilled Poplar, Hazel, and Chestnut bible rods 2

33. Either make the tree good, and his fruit good; or else make the tree corrupt, and his fruit corrupt: for the tree is known by his fruit.

5, 4; 6, 4: 8. Bible Matrices

$5_{10}, 4_{10}; 6_{10}, 4_{10}: 8_{10}$.

Pilled Poplar, Hazel, and Chestnut bible rods 1

$Log_{10} 5 = 0.6989$ $Log_{10} 4 = 0.6020$ $Log_{10} 6 = 0.7781$ $Log_{10} 4 = 0.6020$ $Log_{10} 8 = 0.9030$

5, 4; 6, 4: 8. Deep calls unto Deep study bible 1

0.6989, 0.6020; 0.7781, 0.6020: 0.9030.
Deep calls unto Deep study bible 2

x-axis	y-axis
5	0.6989
4	0.6020
6	0.7781
4	0.6020
8	0.9030

Water Spout *(lightning; combinatorics)* Study bible 1

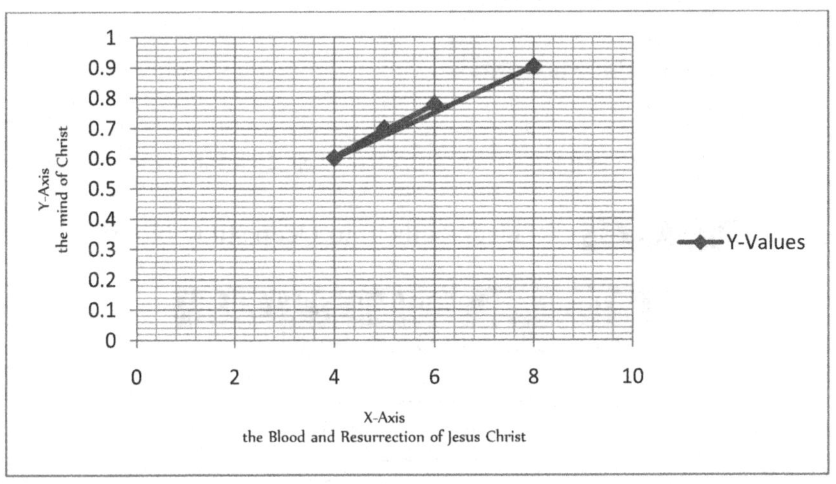

Water Spout *(lightning; combinatorics)* Study bible 2

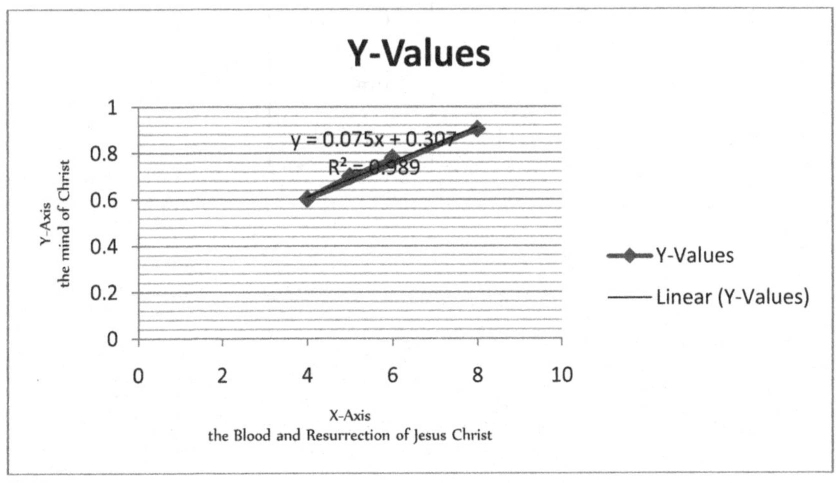

$10^{0.6989}$, $10^{0.6020}$; $10^{0.7781}$, $10^{0.6020}$: $10^{0.9030}$.

Pilled Poplar, Hazel, and Chestnut bible rods 2

34. O generation of vipers, how can ye, being evil, speak good things? for out of the abundance of the heart the mouth speaketh.

4, 3, 2, 3? 11. Bible Matrices

4_{10}, 3_{10}, 2_{10}, 3_{10}? 11_{10}.

Pilled Poplar, Hazel, and Chestnut bible rods 1

$\text{Log}_{10} 4 = 0.6020$ $\text{Log}_{10} 3 = 0.4771$ $\text{Log}_{10} 3 = 0.4771$ $\text{Log}_{10} 2 = 0.3010$ $\text{Log}_{10} 11 = 1.0413$

4, 3, 2, 3? 11. Deep calls unto Deep study bible 1

0.6020, 0.4771, 0.3010, 0.4771? 1.0413.

Deep calls unto Deep study bible 2

x-axis	y-axis
4	0.6020
3	0.4771
2	0.3010
3	0.4771
11	1.0413

Water Spout *(lightning; combinatorics)* Study bible 1

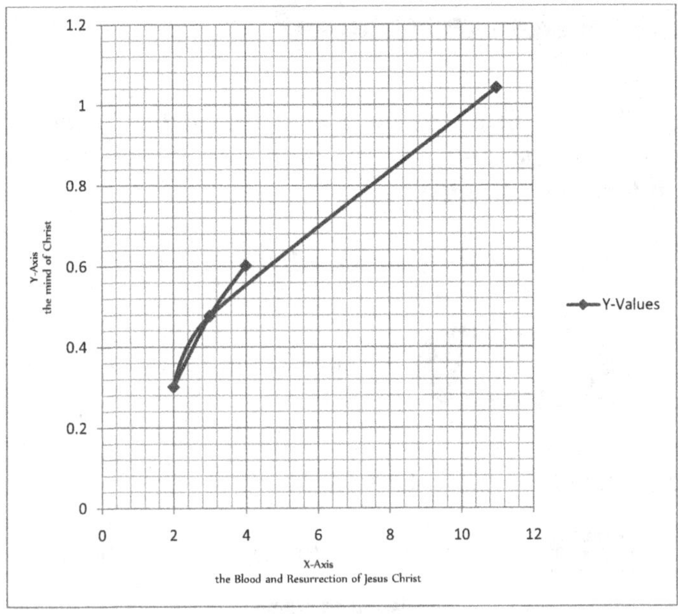

Water Spout *(lightning; combinatorics)* Study bible 2

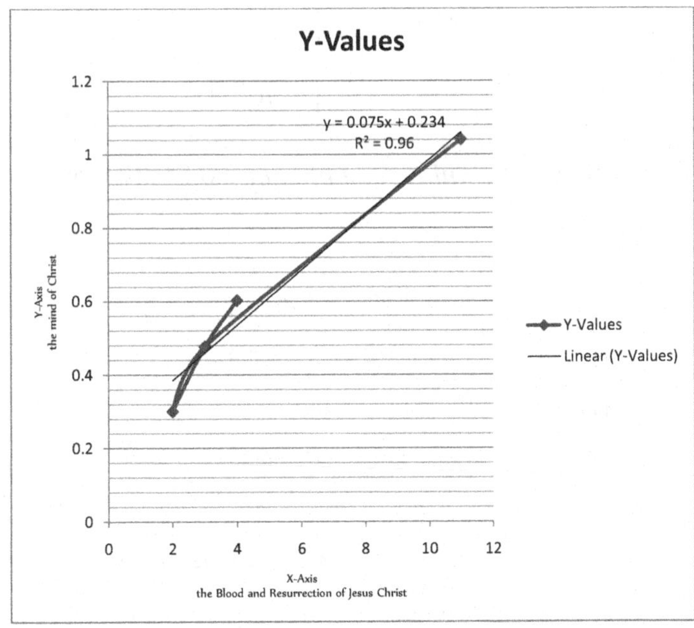

$10^{0.6020}$, $10^{0.4771}$, $10^{0.3010}$, $10^{0.4771}$? $10^{1.0413}$.

Pilled Poplar, Hazel, and Chestnut bible rods 2

35. A good man out of the good treasure of the heart bringeth forth good things: and an evil man out of the evil treasure bringeth forth evil things.

15: 13. Bible Matrices

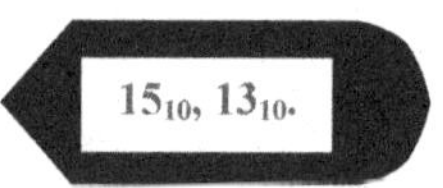

Pilled Poplar, Hazel, and Chestnut bible rods 1

$\text{Log}_{10}\ 15 = 1.1760$ $\text{Log}_{10}\ 13 = 1.1139$

15, 13. Deep calls unto Deep study bible 1

1.1760, 1.1139.
Deep calls unto Deep study bible 2

x-axis	y-axis
15	1.1760
13	1.1139

Water Spout *(lightning; combinatorics)* Study bible 1

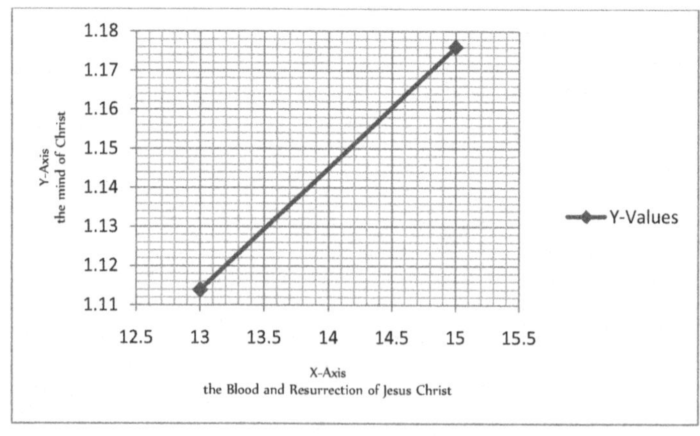

Water Spout *(lightning; combinatorics)* Study bible 2

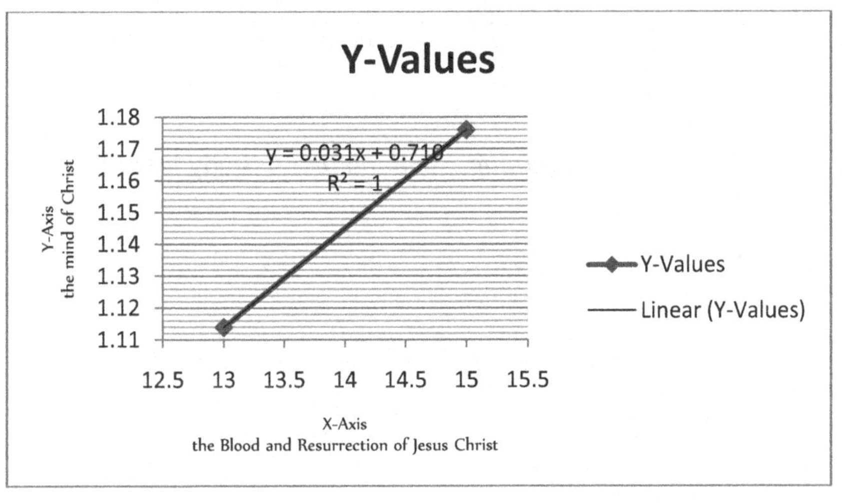

$10^{1.1760}, 10^{1.1139}$. Pilled Poplar, Hazel, and Chestnut bible rods 2

36. But I say unto you, That every idle word that men shall speak, they shall give account thereof in the day of judgment.

5, 8, 10. Bible Matrices

$\log_{10} 5 = 0.6989$ $\log_{10} 8 = 0.9030$ $\log_{10} 10 = 1$

5, 8, 10. Deep calls unto Deep study bible 1

0.6989, 0.9030, 1 Deep calls unto Deep study bible 2

x-axis	y-axis
5	0.6989
8	0.9030
10	1

Water Spout *(lightning; combinatorics)* Study bible 1

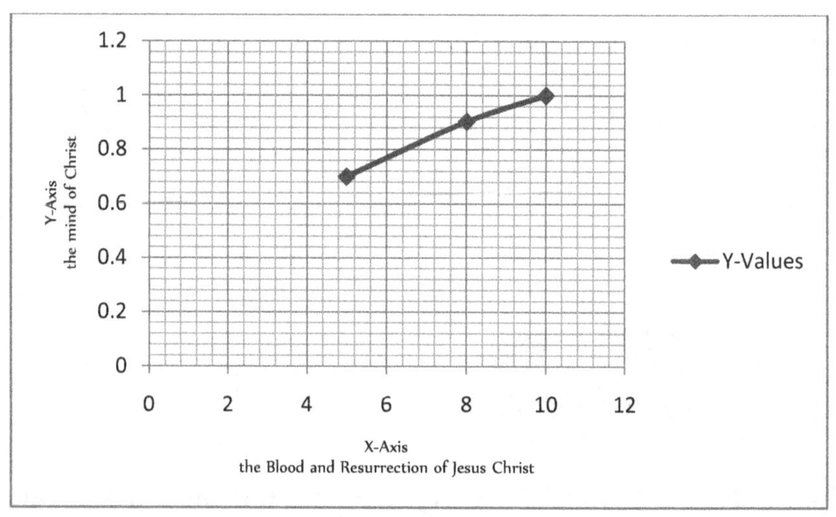

Water Spout *(lightning; combinatorics)* Study bible 2

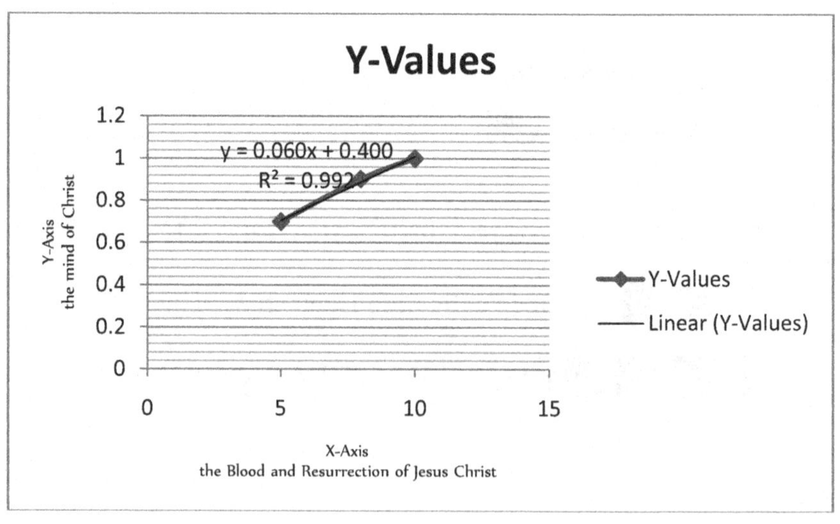

37. For by thy words thou shalt be justified, and by thy words thou shalt be condemned.

8, 8. Bible Matrices

$\text{Log}_{10} 8 = 0.9030$ $\text{Log}_{10} 8 = 0.9030$

8, 8. Deep calls unto Deep study bible 1

0.9030, 0.9030. Deep calls unto Deep study bible 2

x-axis	y-axis
8	0.9030
8	0.9030

Water Spout *(lightning; combinatorics)* Study bible 1

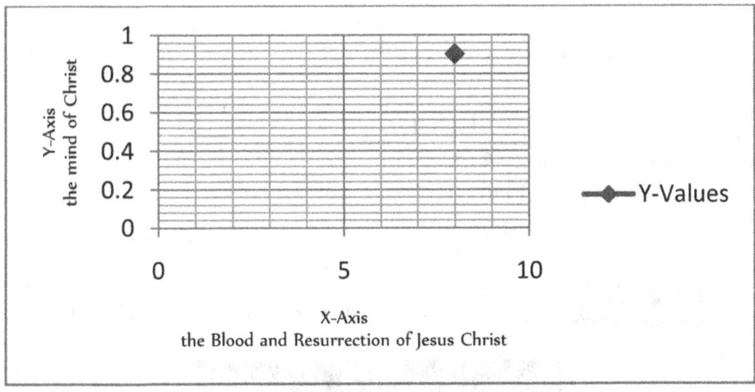

Water Spout *(lightning; combinatorics)* Study bible 2

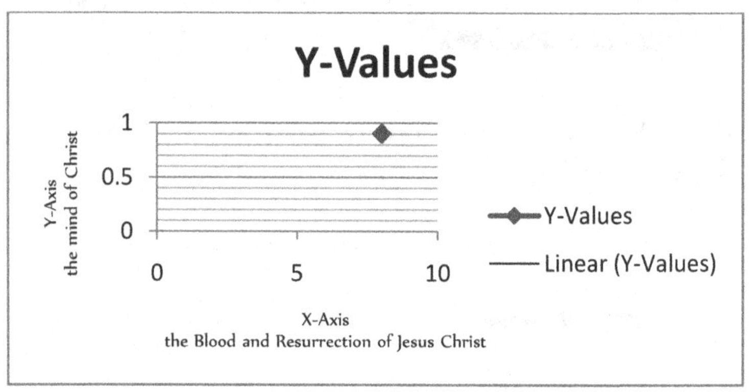

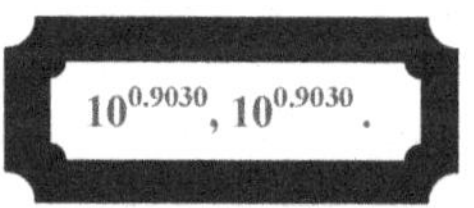

Pilled Poplar, Hazel, and Chestnut bible rods 2

38. Then certain of the scribes lawyers; copyist; transcribers **and of the Pharisees**set apart; separatists**answered, saying, Master, we would see a sign from thee.**

10, 1, 1, 7. Bible Matrices

Pilled Poplar, Hazel, and Chestnut bible rods 1

$\text{Log}_{10} 7 = 0.8450$	$\text{Log}_{10} 1 = 0$	$\text{Log}_{10} 1 = 0$	$\text{Log}_{10} 1 = 0$
$\text{Log}_3 5 = y$	$\text{Log}_3 4 = y$		
$3^y = 5$	$3^y = 4$		
$y \log_{10} 3 = \log_{10} 5$	$y \log_{10} 3 = \log_{10} 4$		
$y = \log_{10} 5 / \log_{10} 3$	$y = \log_{10} 4 / \log_{10} 3$		
$y = 0.6989 / 0.4771$	$y = 0.6020 / 0.4771$		
$y = 1.4648$	$y = 1.2617$		

10, 1, 1, 7. Deep calls unto Deep study bible 1

1.4648 1.2617 0, 0, 0, 0.8450.

Deep calls unto Deep study bible 2

x-axis	y-axis
10	2.7265
1	0
1	0
7	0.8450

Water Spout *(lightning; combinatorics)* Study bible 1

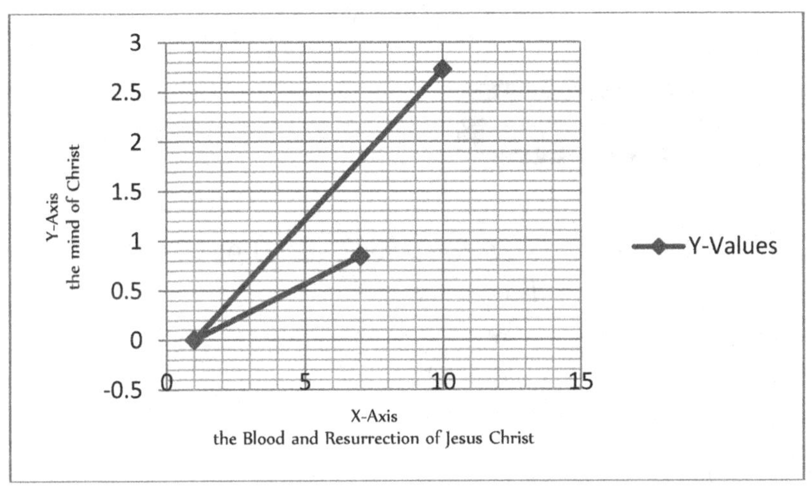

Water Spout *(lightning; combinatorics)* Study bible 2

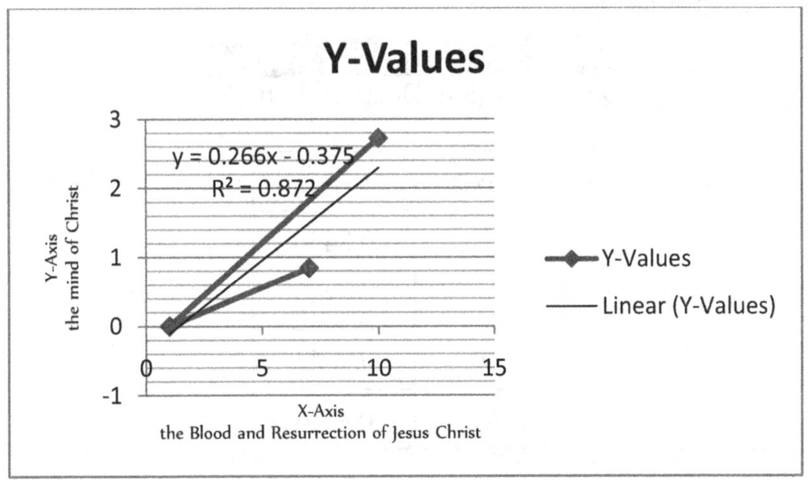

$3^{1.4648}\ 3^{1.2617}\ 10^{0}, 10^{0}, 10^{0}, 10^{0.8450}$.

Pilled Poplar, Hazel, and Chestnut bible rods 2

39. But he answered and said unto them, An evil and adulterous generation seeketh after a sign; and there shall no sign be given to it, but the sign of the prophet to bubble forth, as from a fountain; utter **Jonas** a dove; he that oppresses; destroyer:

7, 9; 9, 7: Bible Matrices

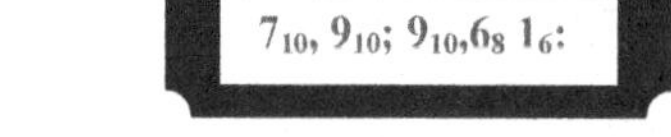

Pilled Poplar, Hazel, and Chestnut bible rods 1

$\text{Log}_{10} 7 = 0.8450$

$\text{Log}_{8} 6 = y$

$8^{y} = 6$

$y \log_{10} 8 = \log_{10} 6$

$y = \log_{10} 6 / \log_{10} 8$

$y = 0.7781 / 0.9030$

$y = 0.8616$

$\text{Log}_{10} 9 = 0.9542$

$\text{Log}_{6} 1 = y$

$6^{y} = 1$

$6^{y} = 6^{0}$

$y = 0$

$\text{Log}_{10} 9 = 0.9542$

7, 9; 9, 7: Deep calls unto Deep study bible 1

0.8450, 0.9542; 0.9542, 0.8616 0:
Deep calls unto Deep study bible 2

x-axis	y-axis
7	0.8450
9	0.9542
9	0.9542
7	0.8616

Water Spout *(lightning; combinatorics)* Study bible 1

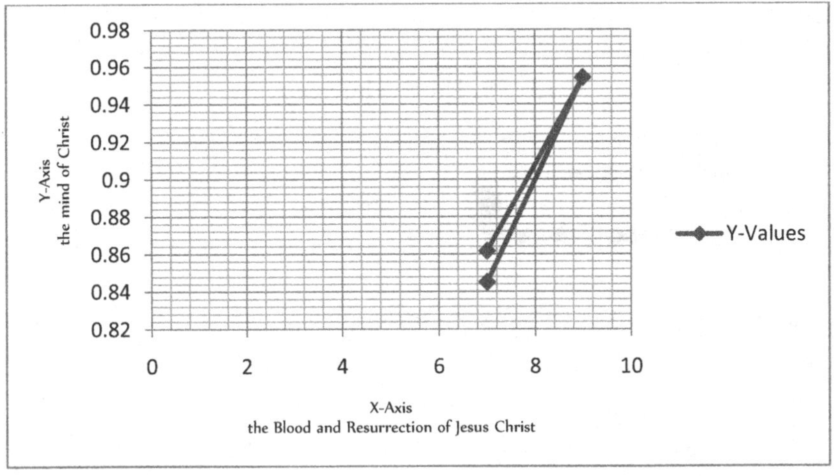

Water Spout *(lightning; combinatorics)* Study bible 2

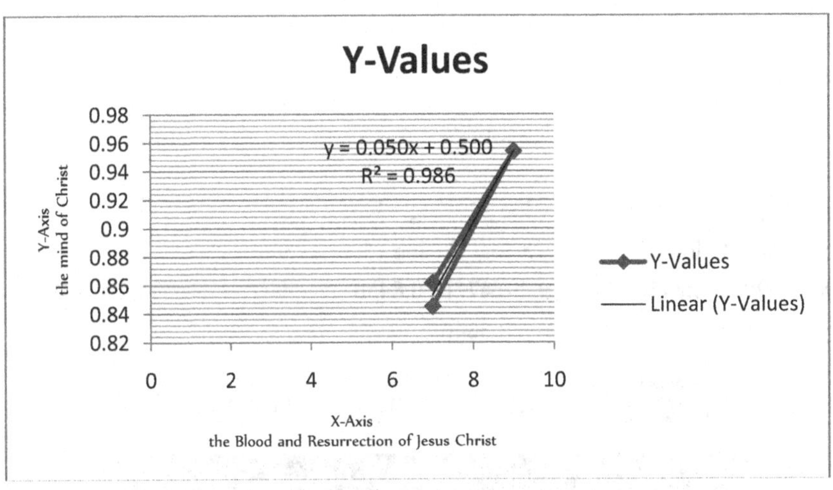

Pilled Poplar, Hazel, and Chestnut bible rods 2

40. For as Jonasa dove; he that oppresses; destroyer**was three** completion or perfection, and unity; 3 x 1 **days and three** completion or perfection, and unity; 3 x 1 **nights in the**

whale's belly; so shall the Son of man be three completion or perfection, and unity; 3 x 1 **days and three** completion or perfection, and unity; 3 x 1 **nights in the heart of the earth.**

13; 18. Bible Matrices

$3_6 2_7 3_7 5_{10}, 8_7 3_7 7_{10}.$

Pilled Poplar, Hazel, and Chestnut bible rods 1

$\text{Log}_{10} 7 = 0.8450$

$\text{Log}_6 3 = y$

$6^y = 3$

$y \log_{10} 6 = \log_{10} 3$

$y = \log_{10} 3 / \log_{10} 6$

$y = 0.4771 / 0.7781$

$y = 0.6131$

$\text{Log}_{10} 5 = 0.6989$

$\text{Log}_7 2 = y$

$7^y = 2$

$y \log_{10} 7 = \log_{10} 2$

$y = \log_{10} 2 / \log_{10} 7$

$y = 0.3010 / 0.8450$

$y = 0.3562$

$\text{Log}_7 3 = y$

$7^y = 3$

$y \log_{10} 7 = \log_{10} 3$

$y = \log_{10} 3 / \log_{10} 7$

$y = 0.4771 / 0.8450$

$y = 0.5646$

$\text{Log}_7 8 = y$

$7^y = 8$

$y \log_{10} 7 = \log_{10} 8$

$y = \log_{10} 8 / \log_{10} 7$

$y = 0.9030 / 0.8450$

$y = 1.0686$

$\text{Log}_7 3 = y$

$7^y = 3$

$y \log_{10} 7 = \log_{10} 3$

$y = \log_{10} 3 / \log_{10} 7$

$y = 0.4771 / 0.8450$

$y = 0.5646$

13, 18. Deep calls unto Deep study bible 1

0.6131 0.3562 0.5646 0.6989, 1.0686 0.5646 0.8450.

Deep calls unto Deep study bible 2

x-axis	y-axis
13	2.2328
18	2.4782

Water Spout *(lightning; combinatorics)* Study bible 1

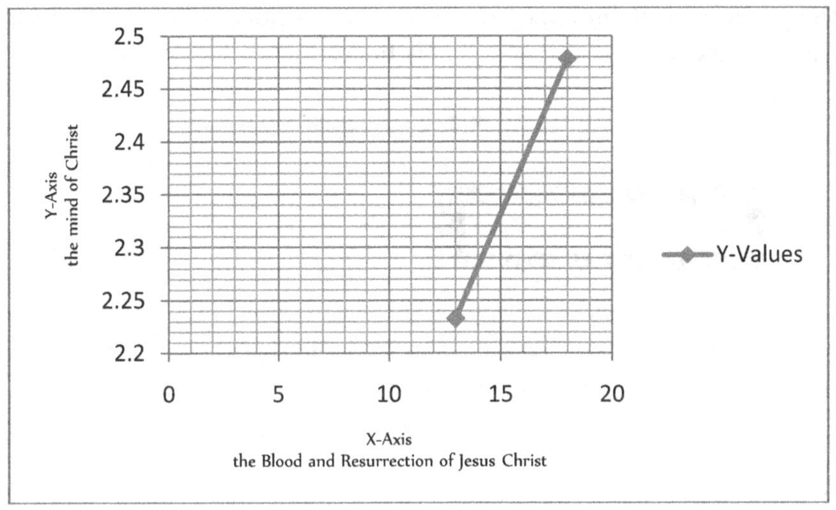

Water Spout *(lightning; combinatorics)* Study bible 2

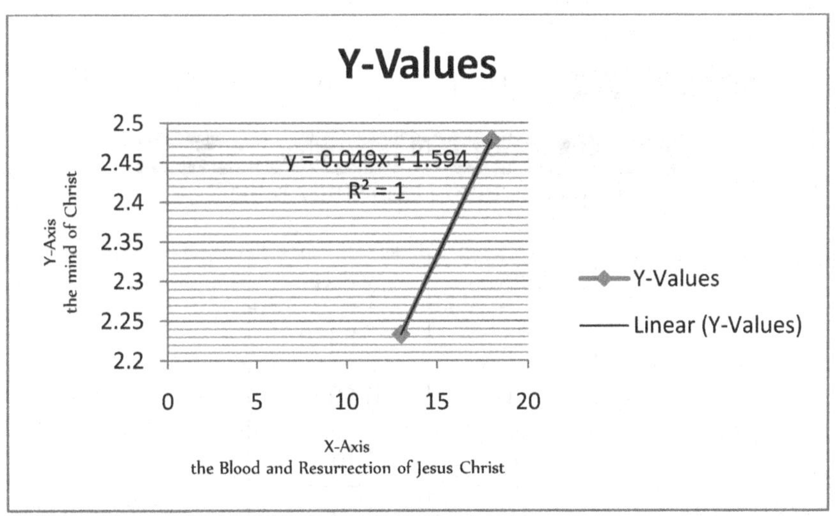

$6^{0.6131}\ 7^{0.3562}\ 7^{0.5646}\ 10^{0.6989},\ 7^{1.0686}\ 7^{0.5646}\ 10^{0.8450}$.

Pilled Poplar, Hazel, and Chestnut bible rods 2

41. The men of Ninevehhandsome; agreeable**shall rise in judgment with this generation, and shall condemn it: because they repented at the preaching of Jonas**a dove; he that oppresses; destroyer;**and, behold, a greater than Jonas**a dove; he that oppresses; destroyer **is here.**

11, 4: 8;1, 1, 6. Bible Matrices

$4_2 7_{10}, 4_{10}: 8_6; 1_{10}, 1_{10}, 4_6 2_{10}$.

Pilled Poplar, Hazel, and Chestnut bible rods 1

$Log_{10} 7 = 0.8450$	$Log_{10} 4 = 0.6020$	$Log_{10} 2 = 0.3010$	$Log_{10} 1 = 0$	$Log_{10} 1 = 0$
$Log_6 8 = y$	$Log_6 4 = y$	$Log_2 4 = y$		
$6^y = 8$	$6^y = 4$	$2^y = 4$		
$y \log_{10} 6 = \log_{10} 8$	$y \log_{10} 6 = \log_{10} 4$	$2^y = 2^2$		
$y = \log_{10} 8 / \log_{10} 6$	$y = \log_{10} 4 / \log_{10} 6$	$y = 2$		
$y = 0.9030 / 0.7781$	$y = 0.6020 / 0.7781$			
$y = 1.1605$	$y = 0.7736$			

11, 4: 8; 1, 1, 6. Deep calls unto Deep study bible 1

2 0.8450, 0.6020: 1.1605; 0, 0, 0.7736 0.3010.

Deep calls unto Deep study bible 2

x-axis	y-axis
11	2.8450
4	0.6020
8	1.1605
1	0
1	0
6	1.0746

Water Spout *(lightning; combinatorics)* Study bible 1

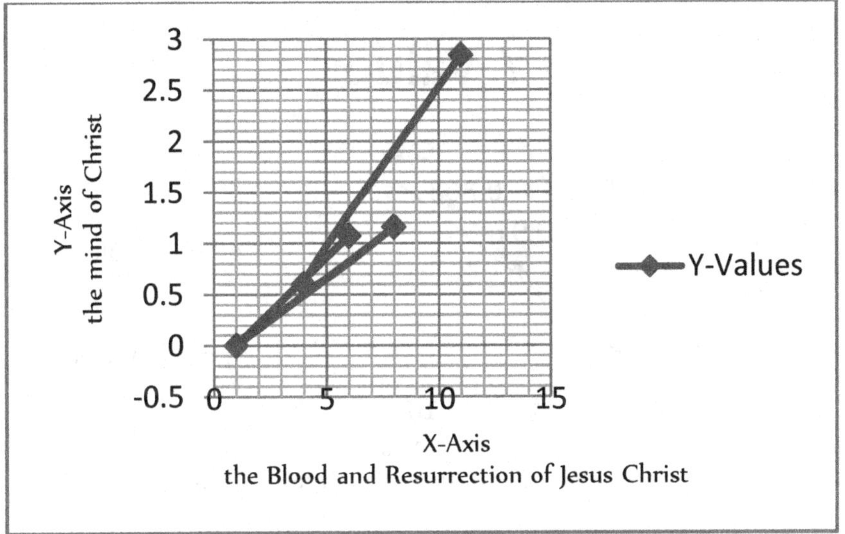

Water Spout *(lightning; combinatorics)* Study bible 2

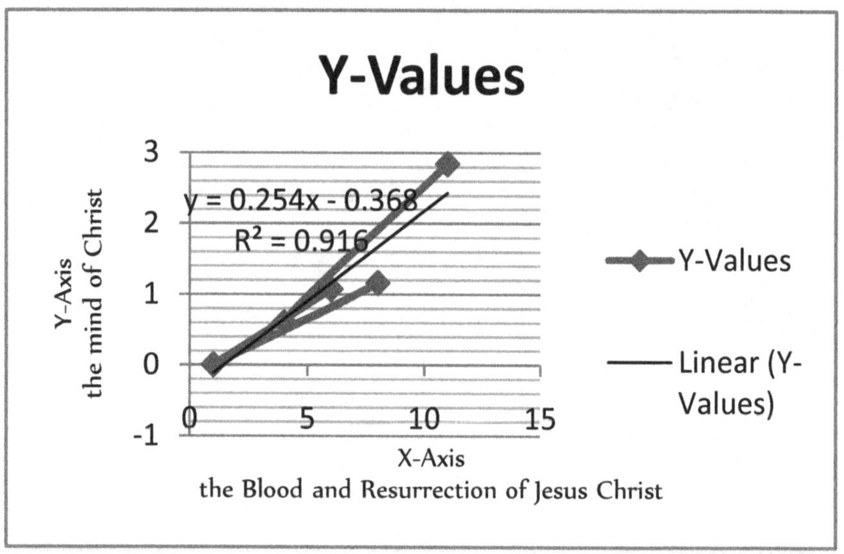

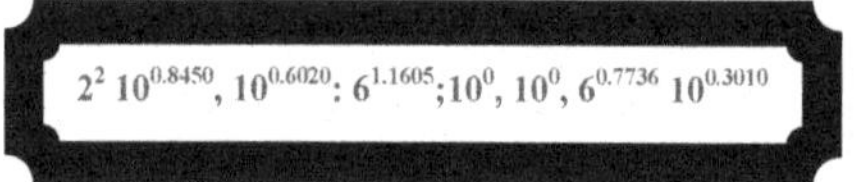
2^2 $10^{0.8450}$, $10^{0.6020}$: $6^{1.1605}$;10^0, 10^0, $6^{0.7736}$ $10^{0.3010}$

Pilled Poplar, Hazel, and Chestnut bible rods 2

42. The queen of the south shall rise up in the judgment with this generation, and shall condemn it: for she came from the uttermost parts of the earth to hear the wisdom of Solomonpeaceable; peaceful; perfect; one who recompenses; **and, behold, a greater than Solomon**peaceable; peaceful; perfect; one who recompenses **is here.**

14, 4: 16; 1, 1, 6. Bible Matrices

14_{10}, 4_{10}: 16_{10}; 1_{10}, 1_{10}, 4_6 2_{10}.

Pilled Poplar, Hazel, and Chestnut bible rods 1

$Log_{10} 14 = 1.1461$ $Log_{10} 4 = 0.6020$ $Log_{10} 16 = 1.2041$ $Log_{10} 1 = 0$ $Log_{10} 1 = 0$ $Log_{10} 2 = 0.3010$

$Log_6 4 = y$

$6^y = 4$

$y \log_{10} 6 = \log_{10} 4$

$y = \log_{10} 4 / \log_{10} 6$

$y = 0.6020 / 0.7781$

$y = 0.7736$

14, 4: 16; 1, 1, 6. Deep calls unto Deep study bible 1

1.1461, 0.6020: 1.1041; 0, 0, 0.7736 0.3010.
Deep calls unto Deep study bible 2

x-axis	y-axis
14	1.1461
4	0.6020
16	1.1041
1	0
1	0
6.	1.0746

Water Spout *(lightning; combinatorics)* Study bible 1

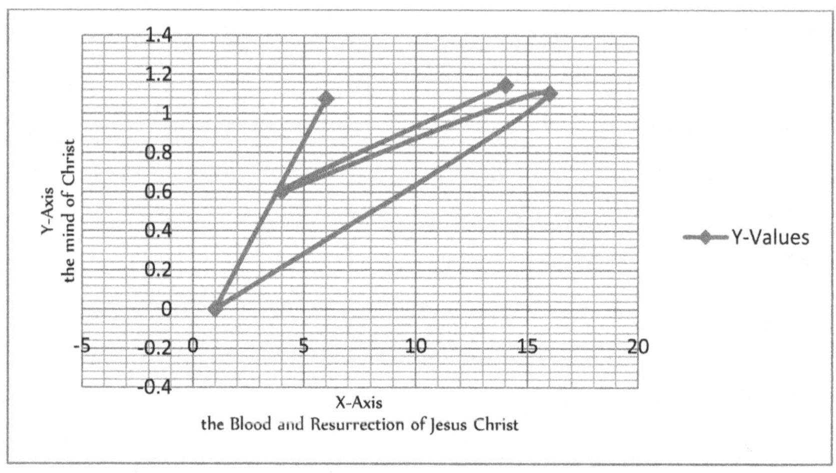

Water Spout *(lightning; combinatorics)* Study bible 2

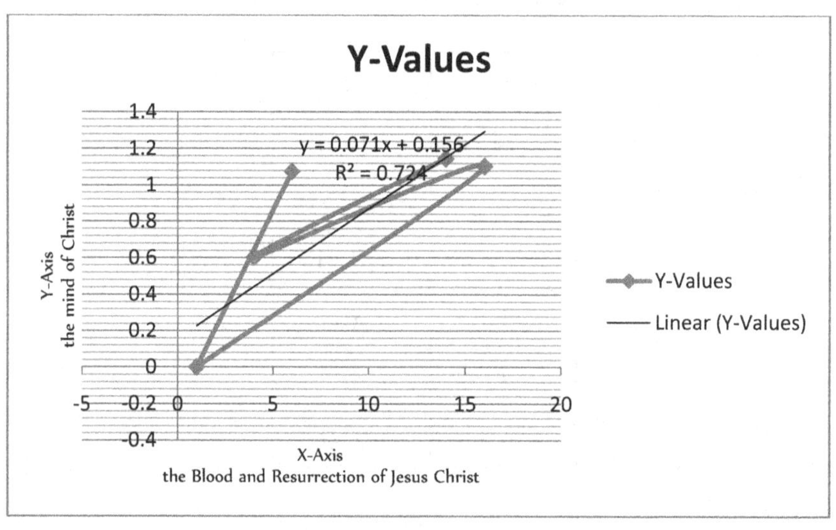

$10^{1.1461}, 10^{0.6020}: 10^{1.1041}; 10^{0}, 10^{0}, 6^{0.7736}\ 10^{0.3010}.$

Pilled Poplar, Hazel, and Chestnut bible rods 2

43. When the unclean spirit is gone out of a man, he walketh through dry places, seeking rest, and findeth none.

10, 5, 2, 3. Bible Matrices

$10_{10}, 5_{10}, 2_{10}, 3_{10}.$

Pilled Poplar, Hazel, and Chestnut bible rods 1

$\text{Log}_{10} 10 = 1 \quad \text{Log}_{10} 5 = 0.6989. \quad \text{Log}_{10} 2 = 0.3010 \quad \text{Log}_{10} 3 = 0.4771$

10, 5, 2, 3. Deep calls unto Deep study bible 1

1, 0.6989, 0.3010, 0.4771.
Deep calls unto Deep study bible 2

x-axis	y-axis
10	1
5	0.6989
2	0.3010
3	0.4771

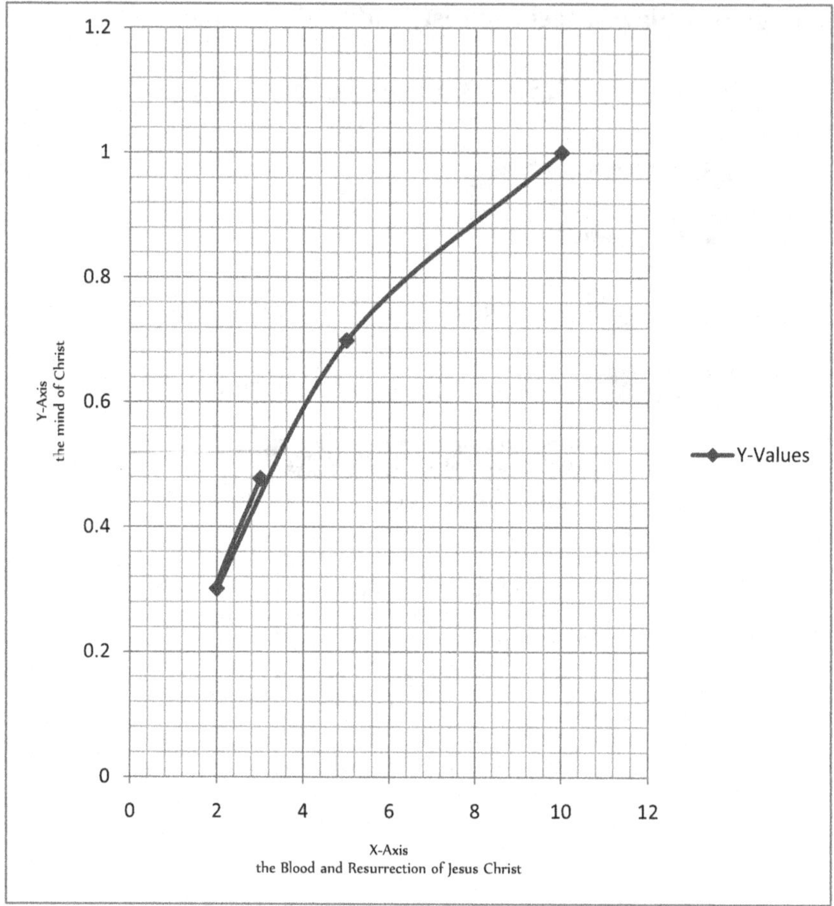
Water Spout (lightning; combinatorics) Study bible 1
1.2
1
0.8
0.6
0.4
0.2
0
0
2
4
6
8
10
12
Y-Axis
the mind of Christ
X-Axis
the Blood and Resurrection of Jesus Christ
Y-Values

Water Spout *(lightning; combinatorics)* Study bible 2

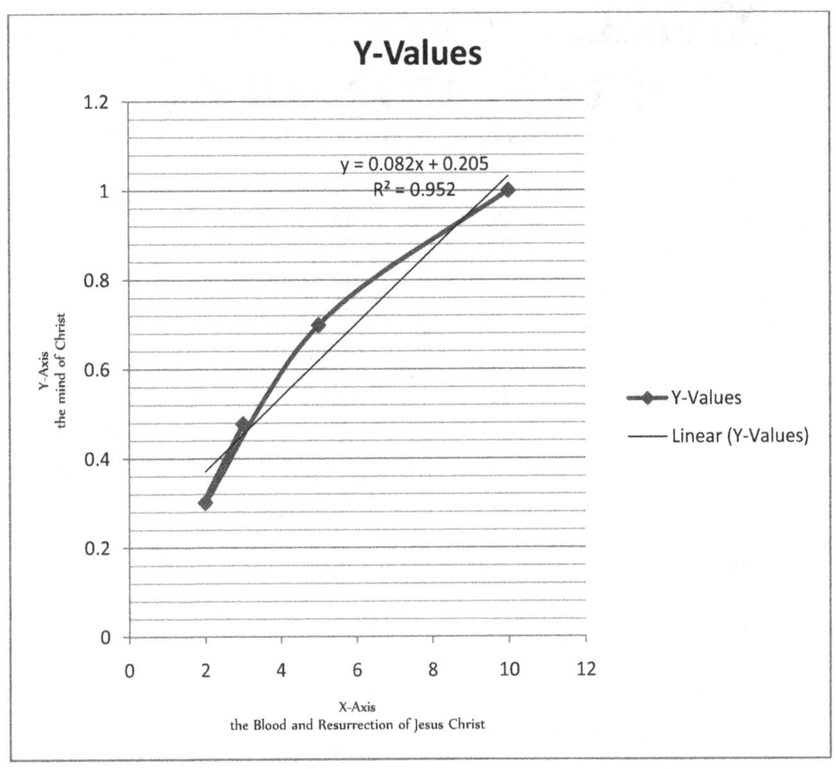

$10^{1}, 10^{0.6989}, 10^{0.3010}, 10^{0.4771}$.

Pilled Poplar, Hazel, and Chestnut bible rods 2

44. Then he saith, I will return into my house from whence I came out; and when he is come, he findeth it empty, swept, and garnished.

3, 11; 5, 4, 1, 2. Bible Matrices

$3_{10}, 11_{10}; 5_{10}, 4_{10}, 1_{10}, 2_{10}$.

Pilled Poplar, Hazel, and Chestnut bible rods 1

$\text{Log}_{10} 5 = 0.6989$ $\text{Log}_{10} 4 = 0.6020$ $\text{Log}_{10} 3 = 0.4771$ $\text{Log}_{10} 2 = 0.3010$ $\text{Log}_{10} 1 = 0$ $\text{Log}_{10} 11 = 1.0413$

3, 11; 5, 4, 1, 2. Deep calls unto Deep study bible 1

0.4771, 1.0413; 0.6989, 0.6020, 0, 0.3010
Deep calls unto Deep study bible 2

x-axis	y-axis
3	0.4771
11	1.0413
5	0.6989
4	0.6020
1	0
2	0.3010

Water Spout *(lightning; combinatorics)* Study bible 1

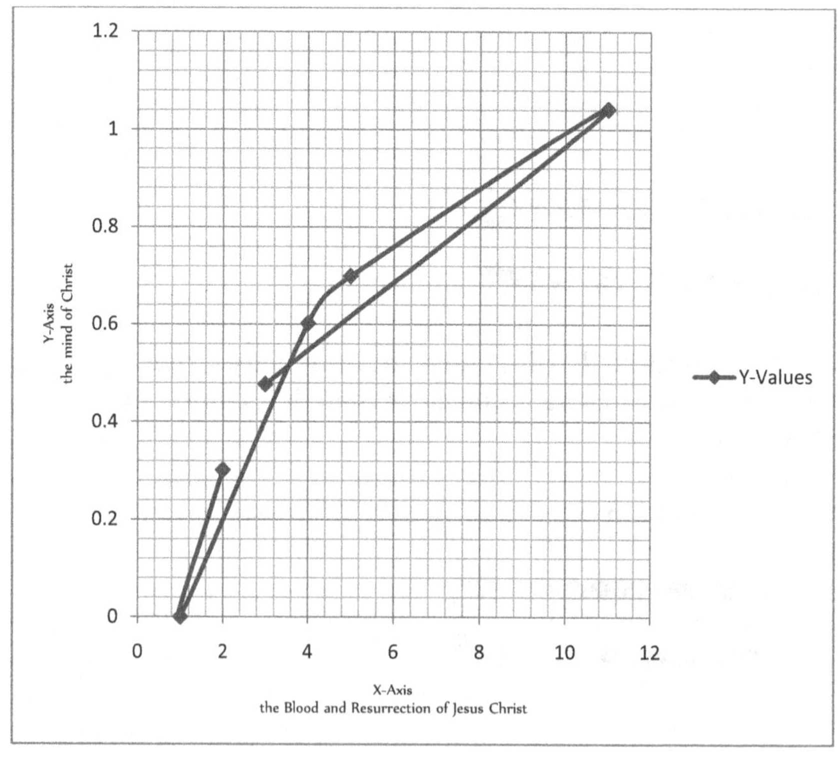

Water Spout *(lightning; combinatorics)* Study bible 2

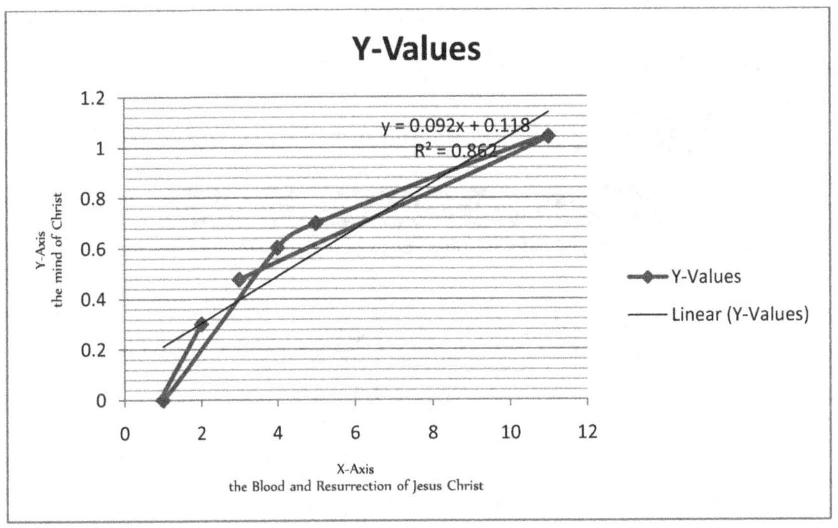

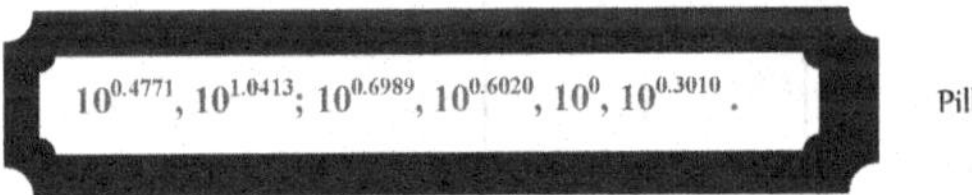

Pilled Poplar, Hazel, and Chestnut bible rods 2

45. Then goeth he, and taketh with himself seven divine perfection or completeness; 7 x 1 **other spirits more wicked than himself, and they enter in and dwell there: and the last state of that man is worse than the first. Even so shall it be also unto this wicked generation.**

3, 11, 7:12.10. Bible Matrices

3_{10},5_6 6_{10},7_{10}:12_{10}.10_{10} .

Pilled Poplar, Hazel, and Chestnut bible rods 1

$\text{Log}_{10} 3 = 0.4771$ $\text{Log}_{10} 6 = 0.7781$ $\text{Log}_{10} 7 = 0.8450$ $\text{Log}_{10} 12 = 1.0791$ $\text{Log}_{10} 10 = 1$

$\text{Log}_6 5 = y$

$6^y = 5$

$y \log_{10} 6 = \log_{10} 5$

$y = \log_{10} 5 / \log_{10} 6$

$y = 0.6989 / 0.7781$

$y = 0.8982$

3, 11, 7: 12. 10. Deep calls unto Deep study bible 1

0.4771, 0.8982 0.7781, 0.8450: 1.0791. 1.
Deep calls unto Deep study bible 2

x-axis	y-axis
3	0.4771
11	1.6763
7	0.8450
12	1.0791
10	1

Water Spout *(lightning; combinatorics)* Study bible 1

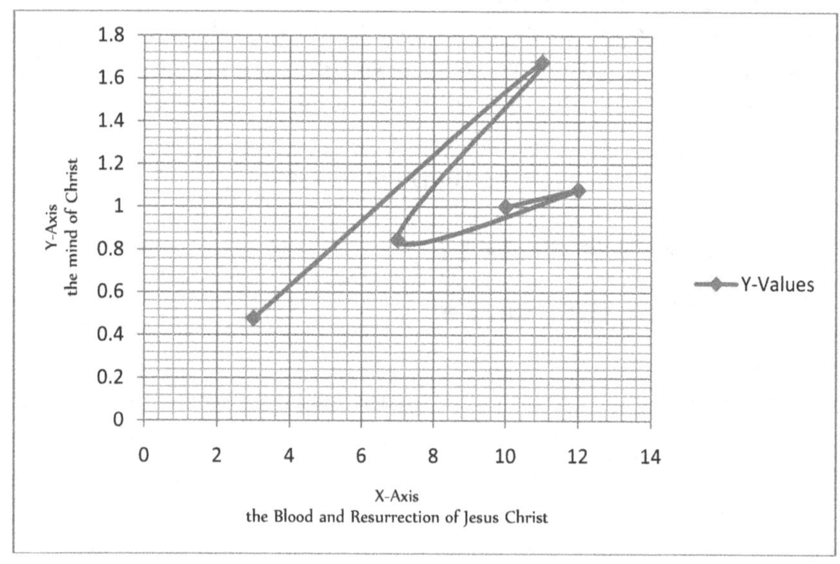

Water Spout *(lightning; combinatorics)* Study bible 2

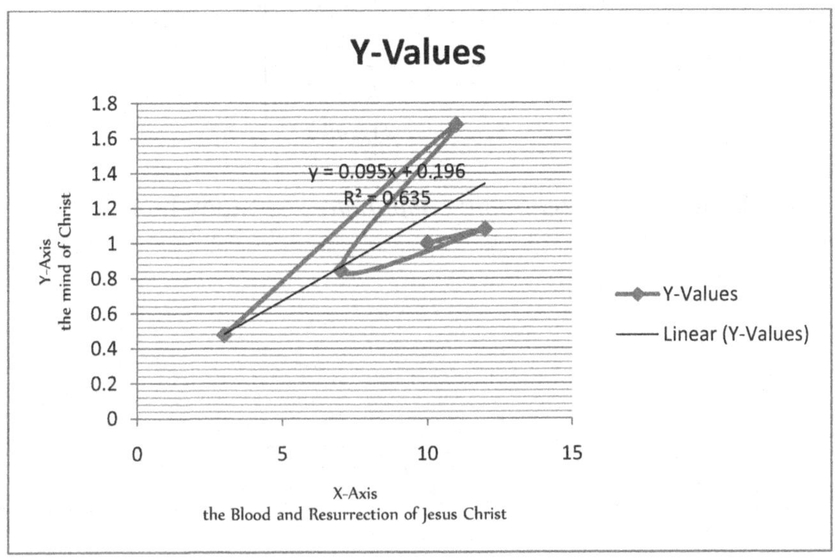

$10^{0.4771}, 6^{0.8982}$ $10^{0.7781}, 10^{0.8450}$: $10^{1.0791}$. 10^{1} .

Pilled Poplar, Hazel, and Chestnut bible rods 2

46. While he yet talked to the people, behold, his mother and his brethren stood without, desiring to speak with him.

7, 1, 7, 5. Bible Matrices

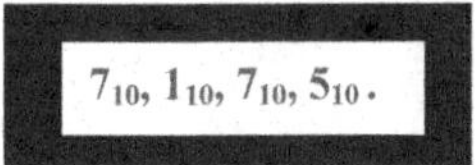
$7_{10}, 1_{10}, 7_{10}, 5_{10}$.

Pilled Poplar, Hazel, and Chestnut bible rods 1

$\text{Log}_{10} 5 = 0.6989$ $\text{Log}_{10} 7 = 0.8450$ $\text{Log}_{10} 7 = 0.8450$ $\text{Log}_{10} 1 = 0$

7, 1, 7, 5. Deep calls unto Deep study bible 1

0.8450, 0, 0.8450, 0.6989.

Deep calls unto Deep study bible 2

x-axis	y-axis
7	0.8450
1	0
7	0.8450
5	0.6989

Water Spout *(lightning; combinatorics)* Study bible 1

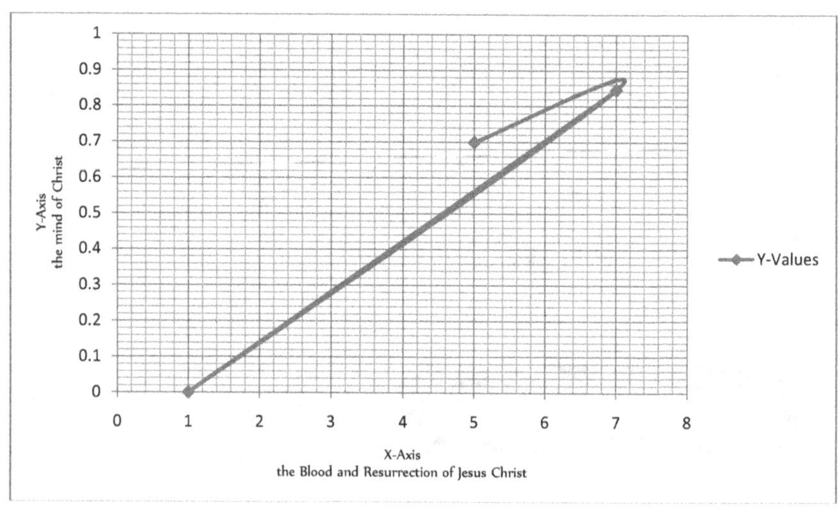

Water Spout *(lightning; combinatorics)* Study bible 2

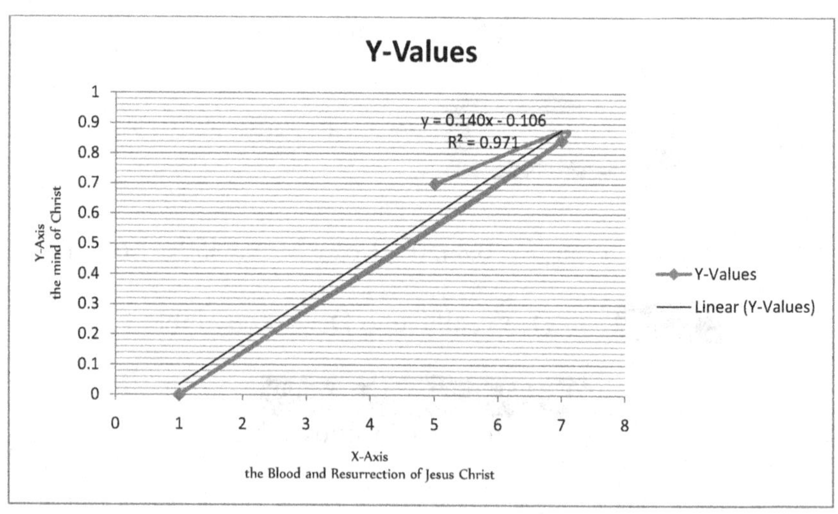

$10^{0.8450}, 10^{0}, 10^{0.8450}, 10^{0.6989}.$

Pilled Poplar, Hazel, and Chestnut bible rods 2

47. Then one said unto him, Behold, thy mother and thy brethren stand without, desiring to speak with thee.

5, 1, 7, 5. Bible Matrices

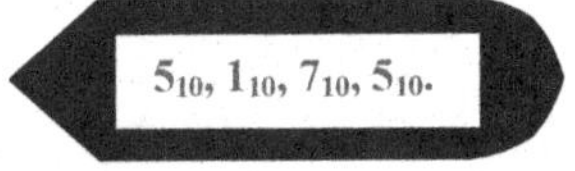

Pilled Poplar, Hazel, and Chestnut bible rods 1

$\text{Log}_{10} 5 = 0.6989$ $\text{Log}_{10} 5 = 0.6989$ $\text{Log}_{10} 7 = 0.8450$ $\text{Log}_{10} 1 = 0$

5, 1, 7, 5. Deep calls unto Deep study bible 1

0.6989, 0, 0.8450, 0.6989.

Deep calls unto Deep study bible 2

x-axis	y-axis
5	0.6989
1	0
7	0.8450
5	0.6989

Water Spout *(lightning; combinatorics)* Study bible 1

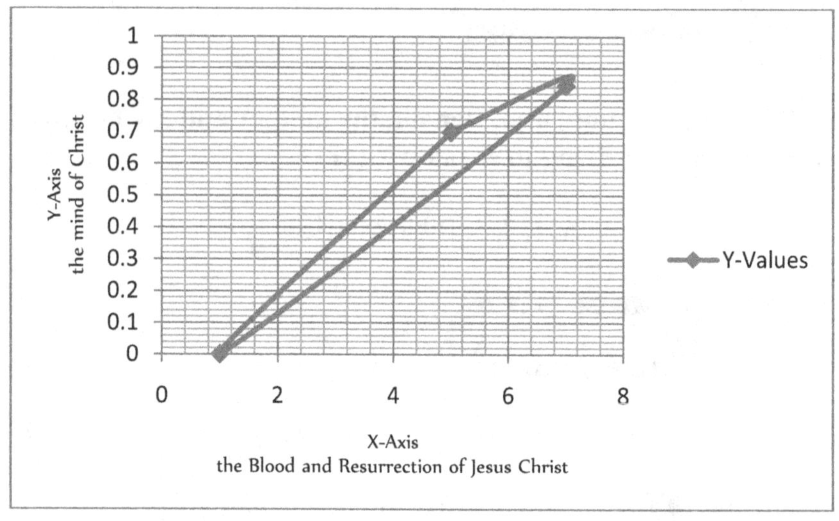

Water Spout *(lightning; combinatorics)* Study bible 2

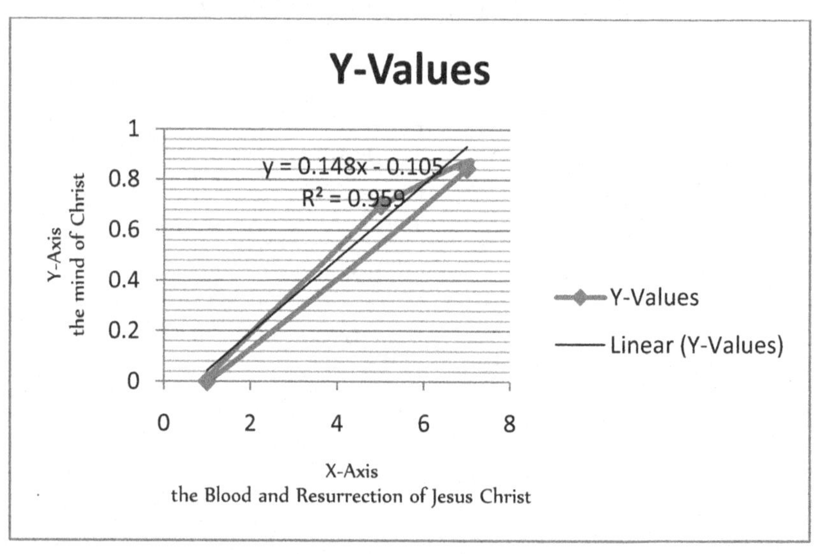

$10^{0.6989}, 10^{0}, 10^{0.8450}, 10^{0.6989}$.

Pilled Poplar, Hazel, and Chestnut bible rods 2

48. But he answered and said unto him that told him, Who is my mother? and who are my brethren?

10, 4? 5? Bible Matrices

$\text{Log}_{10} 5 = 0.6989$ $\text{Log}_{10} 4 = 0.6020$ $\text{Log}_{10} 10 = 1$

10, 4? 5? Deep calls unto Deep study bible 1

1, 0.6020? 0.6989? Deep calls unto Deep study bible 2

x-axis	y-axis
10	1
4	0.6020
5	0.6989

Water Spout *(lightning; combinatorics)* Study bible 1

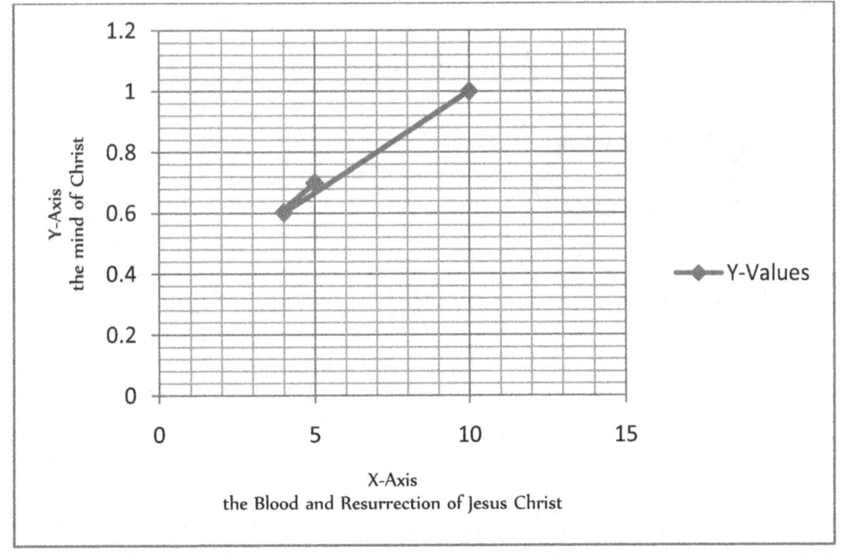

Water Spout *(lightning; combinatorics)* Study bible 2

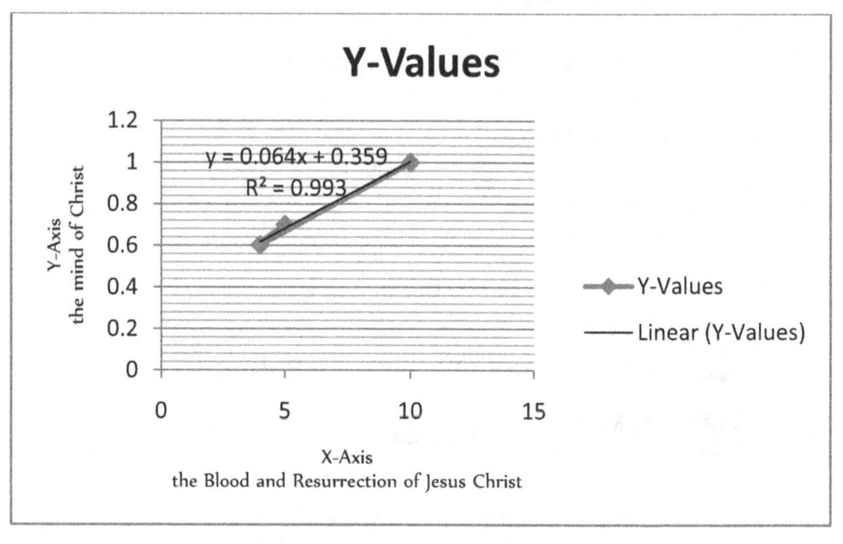

49. And he stretched forth his hand toward his disciples, and said, Behold my mother and my brethren!

9, 2, 6! Bible Matrices

$\text{Log}_{10} 9 = 0.9542$ $\text{Log}_{10} 2 = 0.3010$ $\text{Log}_{10} 6 = 0.7781$

9, 2, 6! Deep calls unto Deep study bible 1

0.9542, 0.3010, 0.7781!
Deep calls unto Deep study bible 2

x-axis	y-axis
9	0.9542
2	0.3010
6	0.7781

Water Spout *(lightning; combinatorics)* Study bible 1

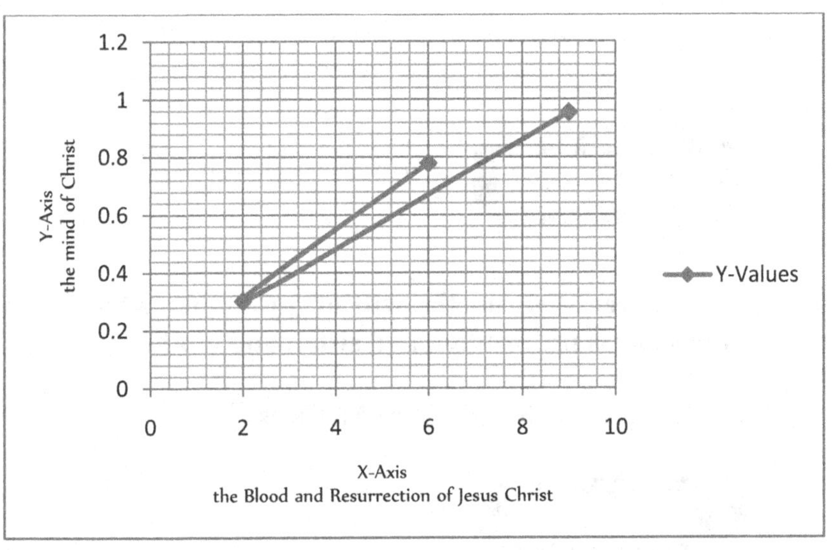

Water Spout *(lightning; combinatorics)* Study bible 2

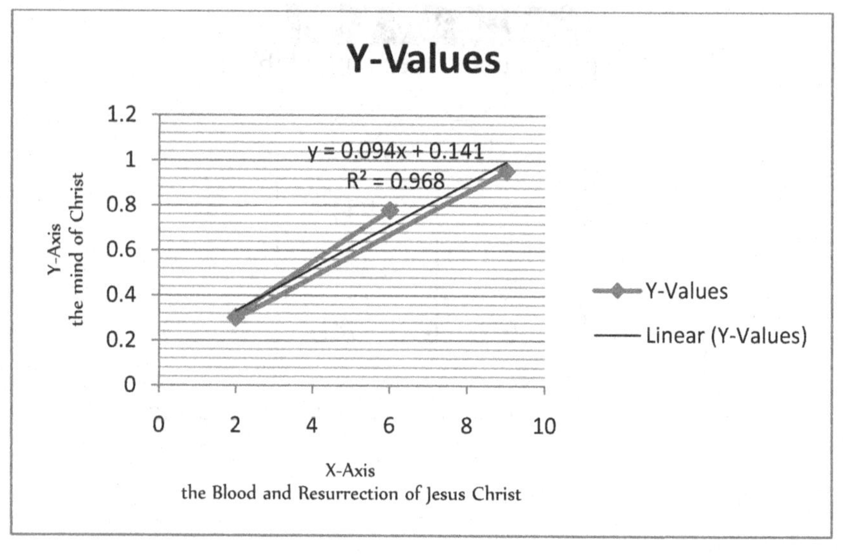

Pilled Poplar, Hazel, and Chestnut bible rods 2

50. For whosoever shall do the will of my Father which is in heaven, the same is my brother, and sister, and mother.

13, 5, 2, 2. Bible Matrices

Pilled Poplar, Hazel, and Chestnut bible rods 1

$\text{Log}_{10}\,13 = 1.1139$ $\text{Log}_{10}\,5 = 0.6989$ $\text{Log}_{10}\,2 = 0.3010$ $\text{Log}_{10}\,2 = 0.3010$

13, 5, 2, 2. Deep calls unto Deep study bible 1

1.1139, 0.6989, 0.3010, 0.3010.
Deep calls unto Deep study bible 2

x-axis	y-axis
13	1.1139
5	0.6989
2	0.3010
2	0.3010

Water Spout *(lightning; combinatorics)* Study bible 1

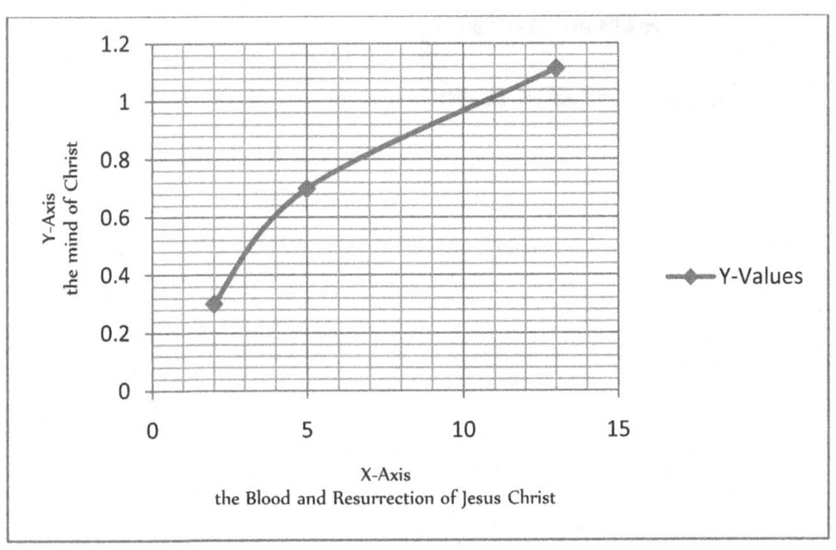

Water Spout *(lightning; combinatorics)* Study bible 2

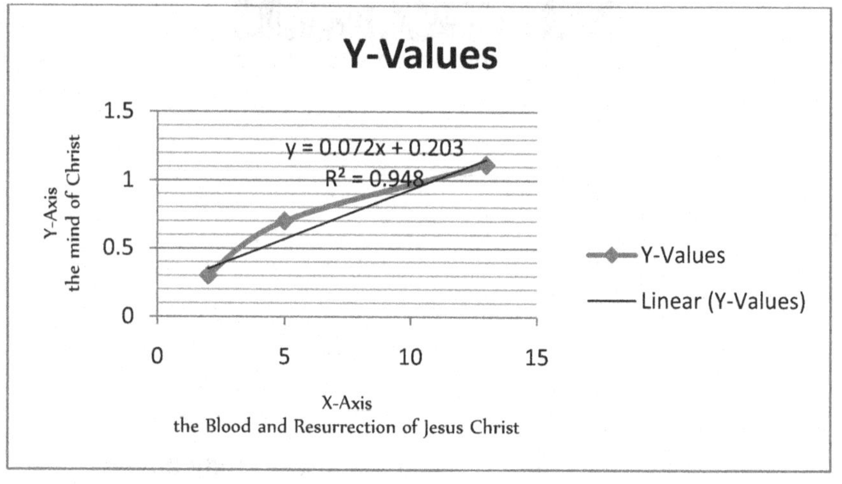

$10^{1.1139}$, $10^{0.6989}$, $10^{0.3010}$, $10^{0.3010}$.

Pilled Poplar, Hazel, and Chestnut bible rods 2

CHAPTER 13

1. The same day went Jesussavior; deliverer**out of the house, and sat by the sea side.**

9, 6. Bible Matrices

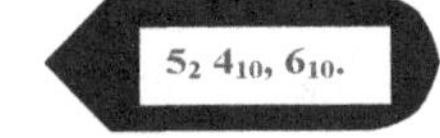

Pilled Poplar, Hazel, and Chestnut bible rods 1

$\text{Log}_{10} 4 = 0.6020$ $\text{Log}_{10} 6 = 0.7781$

$\text{Log}_2 5 = y$

$2^y = 5$

$y \log_{10} 2 = \log_{10} 5$

$y = \log_{10} 5 / \log_{10} 2$

$y = 0.6989 / 0.3010$

$y = 2.3219$

9, 6. Deep calls unto Deep study bible 1

2.3219 0.6020, 0.7781. Deep calls unto Deep study bible 2

x-axis	y-axis
9	2.9239
6	0.7781

Water Spout *(lightning; combinatorics)* Study bible 1

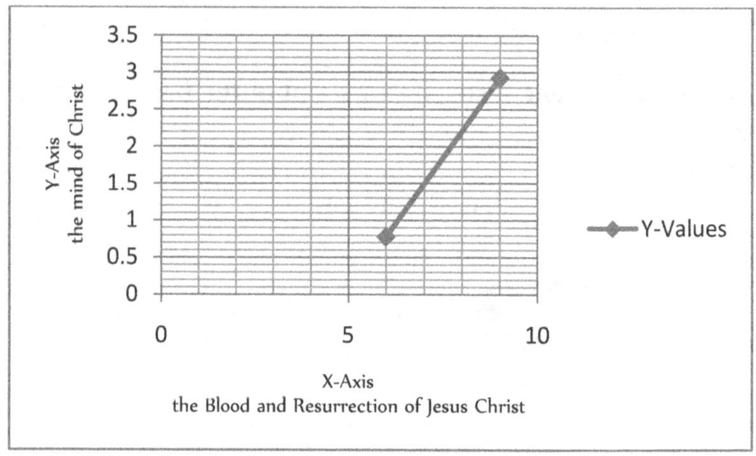

Water Spout *(lightning; combinatorics)* Study bible 2

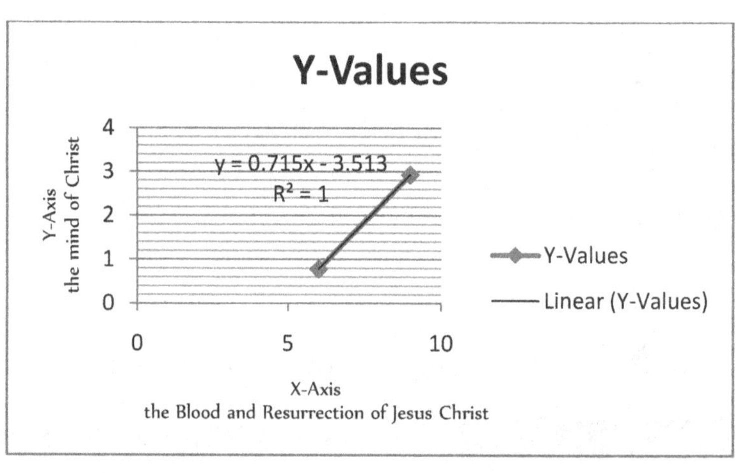

$2^{2.3219}$ $10^{0.6020}$, $10^{0.7781}$.

Pilled Poplar, Hazel, and Chestnut bible rods 2

2. And great multitudes were gathered together unto him, so that he went into a ship, and sat; and the whole multitude stood on the shore.

8, 7, 2; 8. Bible Matrices

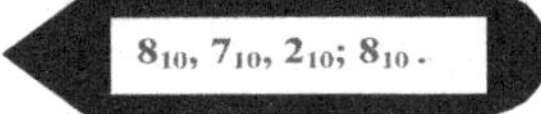

Pilled Poplar, Hazel, and Chestnut bible rods 1

$Log_{10} 7 = 0.8450$ $Log_{10} 8 = 0.9030$ $Log_{10} 2 = 0.3010$ $Log_{10} 8 = 0.9030$

8, 7, 2; 8. Deep calls unto Deep study bible 1

0.9030, 0.8450, 0.3010; 0.9030.
Deep calls unto Deep study bible 2

x-axis	y-axis
8	0.9030
7	0.8450
2	0.3010
8	0.9030

Water Spout *(lightning; combinatorics)* Study bible 1

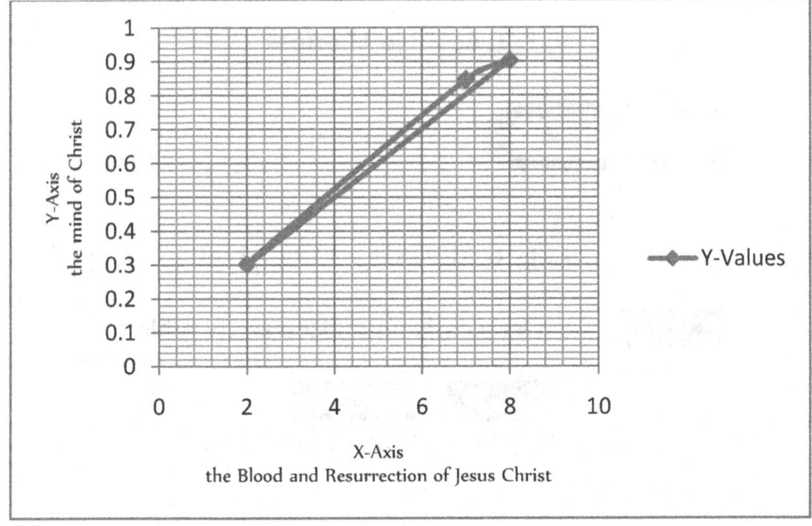

Water Spout *(lightning; combinatorics)* Study bible 2

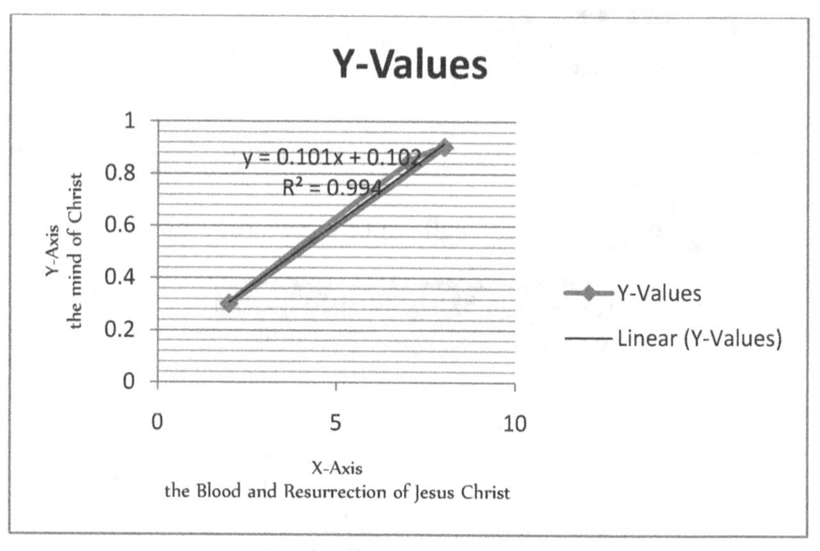

3. And he spake many things unto them in parables, saying, Behold, a sower went forth to sow;

9, 1, 1, 6; Bible Matrices

$\text{Log}_{10} 9 = 0.9542.$ $\text{Log}_{10} 6 = 0.7781$ $\text{Log}_{10} 1 = 0$ $\text{Log}_{10} 1 = 0$

9, 1, 1, 6; Deep calls unto Deep study bible 1

0.9542, 0, 0, 0.7781;
Deep calls unto Deep study bible 2

x-axis	y-axis
9	0.9542
1	0
1	0
6	0.7781

Water Spout *(lightning; combinatorics)* Study bible 1

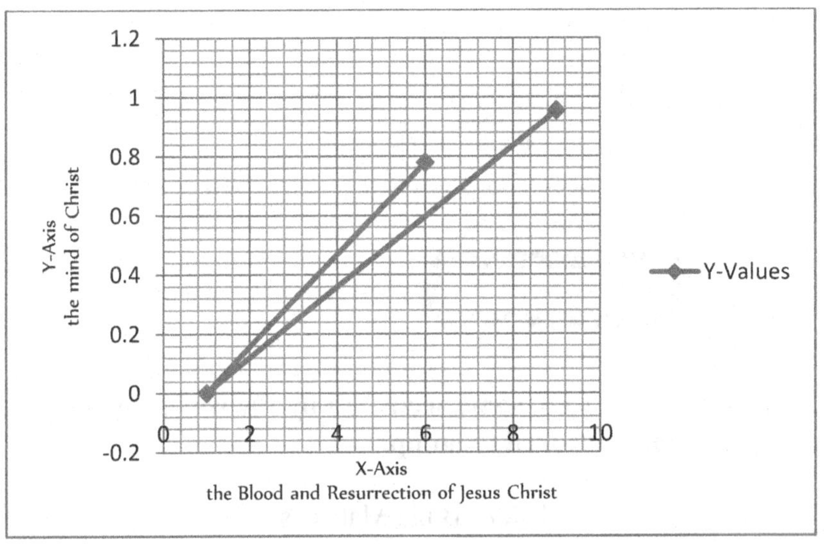

Water Spout *(lightning; combinatorics)* Study bible 2

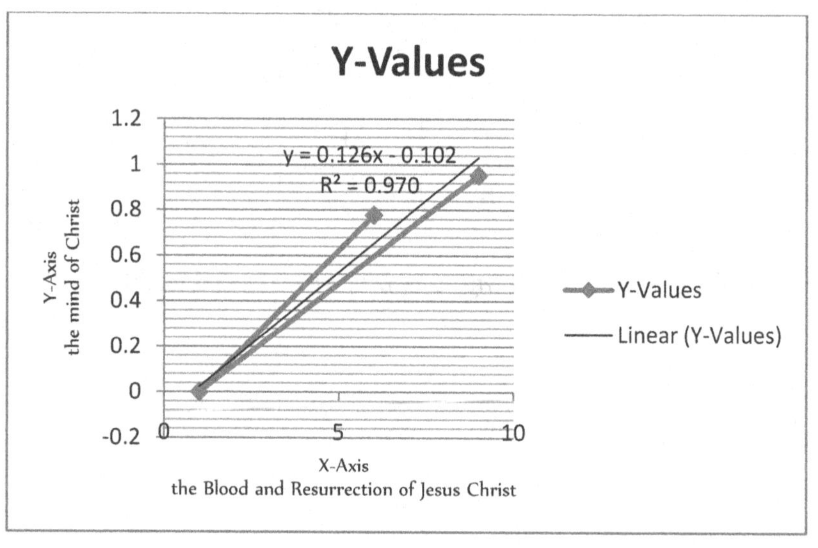

4. And when he sowed, some seeds fell by the way side, and the fowls came and devoured them up:

4, 7, 8: Bible Matrices

$\text{Log}_{10} 4 = 0.6020$ $\text{Log}_{10} 7 = 0.8450$ $\text{Log}_{10} 8 = 0.9030$

4, 7, 8: Deep calls unto Deep study bible 1

0.6020, 0.8450, 0.9030:
Deep calls unto Deep study bible 2

x-axis	y-axis
4	0.6020
7	0.8450
8	0.9030

Water Spout *(lightning; combinatorics)* Study bible 1

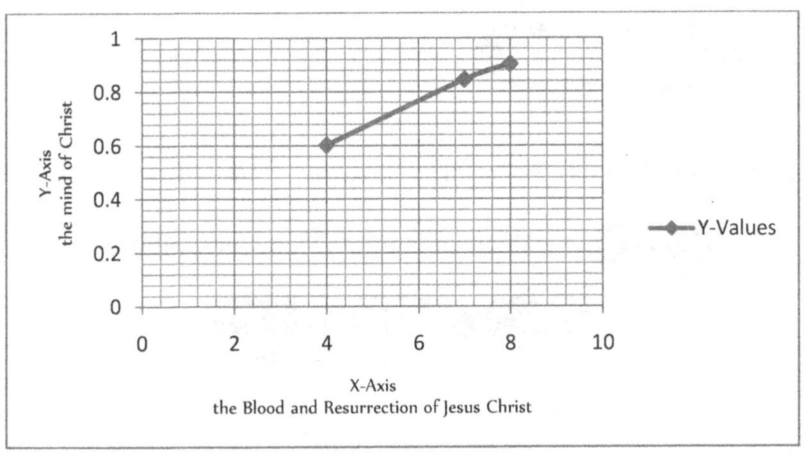

Water Spout *(lightning; combinatorics)* Study bible 2

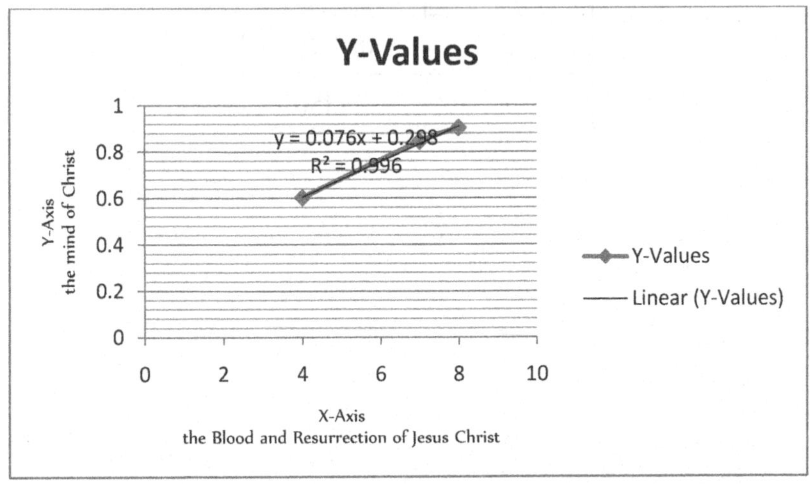

$10^{0.6020}$, $10^{0.8450}$, $10^{0.9030}$:

Pilled Poplar, Hazel, and Chestnut bible rods 2

5. Some fell upon stony places, where they had not much earth: and forthwith they sprung up, because they had no deepness of earth:

5, 6: 5, 7: Bible Matrices

Pilled Poplar, Hazel, and Chestnut bible rods 1

$\log_{10} 5 = 0.6989$ $\log_{10} 5 = 0.6989$ $\log_{10} 6 = 0.7781$ $\log_{10} 7 = 0.8450$

5, 6: 5, 7: Deep calls unto Deep study bible 1

0.6989, 0.7781: 0.6989, 0.8450:
Deep calls unto Deep study bible 2

x-axis	y-axis
5	0.6989
6	0.7781
5	0.6989
7	0.8450

Water Spout *(lightning; combinatorics)* Study bible 1

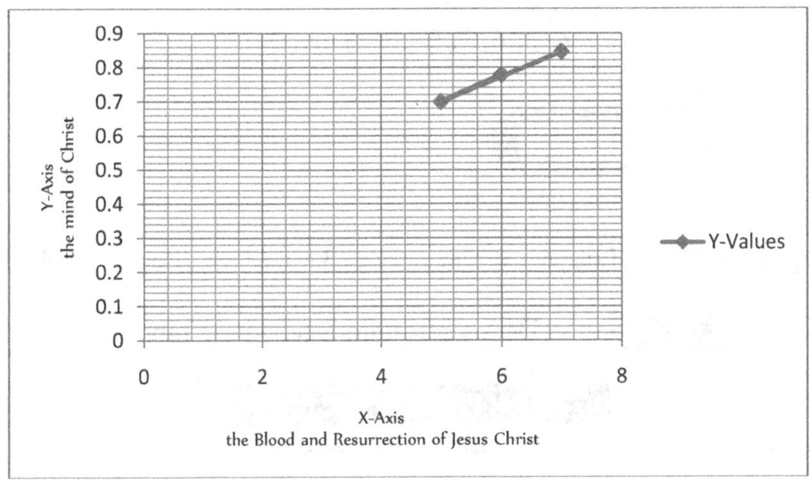

Water Spout *(lightning; combinatorics)* Study bible 2

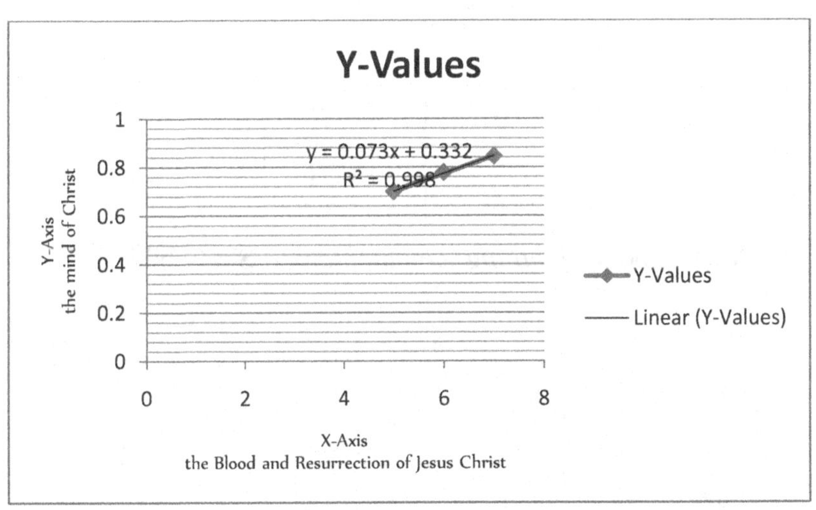

$10^{0.6989}$, $10^{0.7781}$: $10^{0.6989}$, $10^{0.8450}$:

Pilled Poplar, Hazel, and Chestnut bible rods 2

6. And when the sun was up, they were scorched; and because they had no root, they withered away.

6, 3; 6, 3. Bible Matrices

$\text{Log}_{10} 6 = 0.7781$ $\text{Log}_{10} 6 = 0.7781$ $\text{Log}_{10} 3 = 0.4771$ $\text{Log}_{10} 3 = 0.4771$

6, 3; 6, 3. Deep calls unto Deep study bible 1

0.7781, 0.4771; 0.7781, 0.4771.

Deep calls unto Deep study bible 2

x-axis	y-axis
6	0.7781
3	0.4771
6	0.7781
3	0.4771

Water Spout *(lightning; combinatorics)* Study bible 1

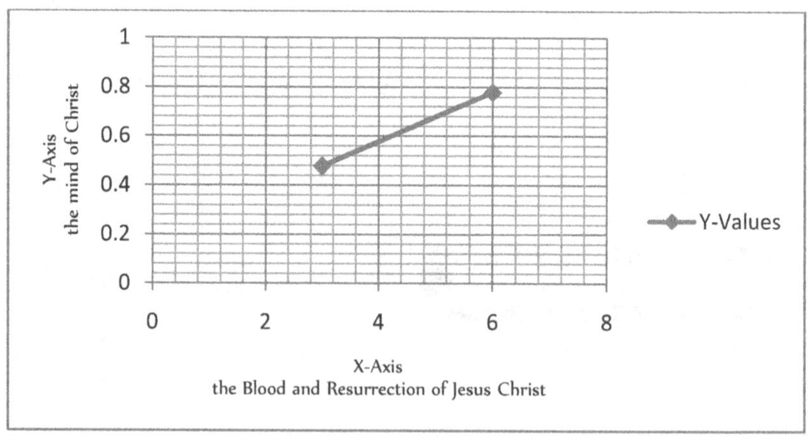

Water Spout *(lightning; combinatorics)* Study bible 2

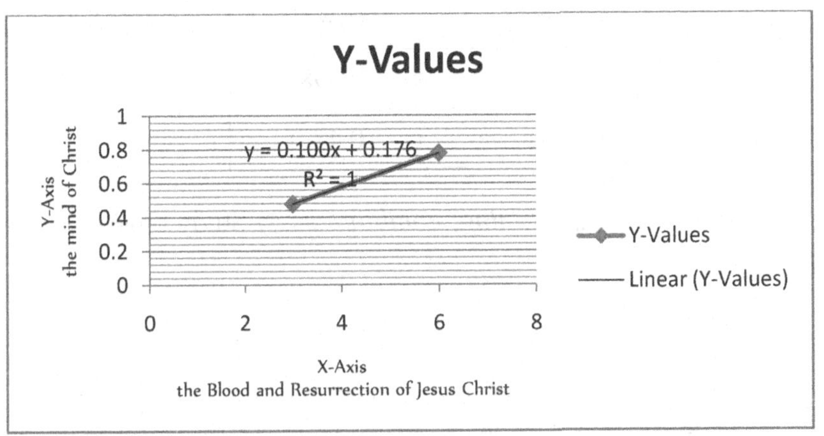

7. And some fell among thorns; and the thorns sprung up, and choked them:

5; 5, 3: Bible Matrices

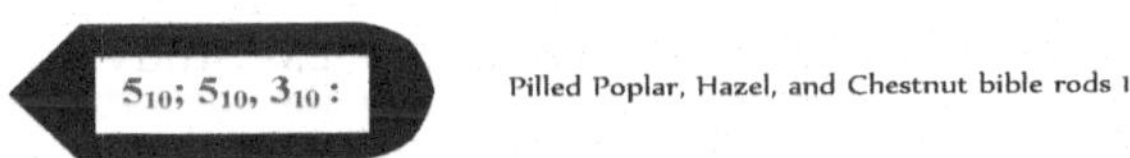

$\text{Log}_{10} 5 = 0.6989$ $\text{Log}_{10} 5 = 0.6989$ $\text{Log}_{10} 3 = 0.4771$

5; 5, 3: Deep calls unto Deep study bible 1

0.6989; 0.6989, 0.4771:
Deep calls unto Deep study bible 2

x-axis	y-axis
5	0.6989
5	0.6989
3	0.4771

Water Spout *(lightning; combinatorics)* Study bible 1

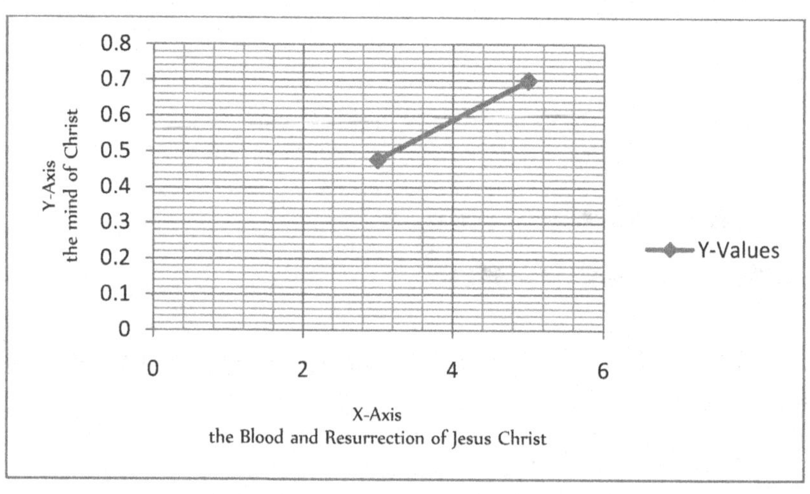

Water Spout *(lightning; combinatorics)* Study bible 2

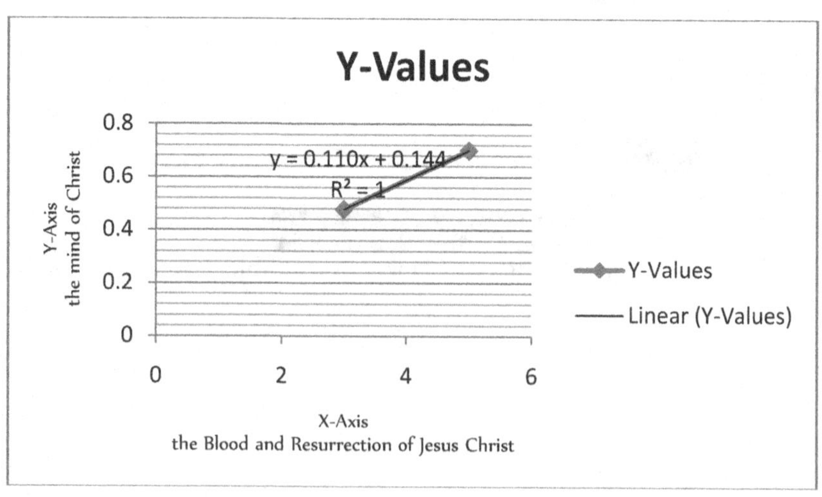

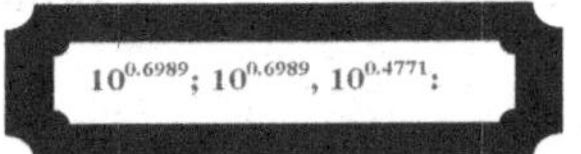

Pilled Poplar, Hazel, and Chestnut bible rods 2

8. But other fell into good ground, and brought forth fruit, some an hundred 2 x 2 x 5 x 5 fold, some sixty 2 x 2 x 3 x 5 fold, some thirty 2 x 3 x 5 fold.

6, 4, 4, 3, 3. Bible Matrices

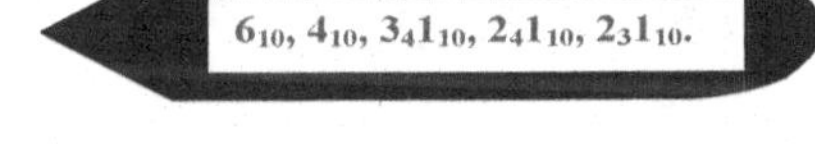

Pilled Poplar, Hazel, and Chestnut bible rods 1

$Log_{10} 6 = 0.7781$ $Log_{10} 4 = 0.6020$ $Log_{10} 1 = 0$ $Log_{10} 1 = 0$ $Log_{10} 1 = 0$

$Log_4 3 = y$ $Log_3 2 = y$ $Log_4 2 = y$

$4^y = 3$ $3^y = 2$ $4^y = 2$

$y \log_{10} 4 = \log_{10} 3$ $y \log_{10} 3 = \log_{10} 2$ $2^{2y} = 2^1$

$y = \log_{10} 3 / \log_{10} 4$ $y = \log_{10} 2 / \log_{10} 3$ $2y = 1$

$y = 0.4771 / 0.6020$ $y = 0.3010 / 0.4771$ $y = ½$ or 0.5

$y = 0.7925$ $y = 0.6308$

6, 4, 4, 3, 3. Deep calls unto Deep study bible 1

0.7781, 0.6020, 0.7925 0, 0.5 0, 0.6308 0.

Deep calls unto Deep study bible 2

x-axis	y-axis
6	0.7781
4	0.6020
4	0.7925
3	0.5
3	0.6308

Water Spout *(lightning; combinatorics)* Study bible 1

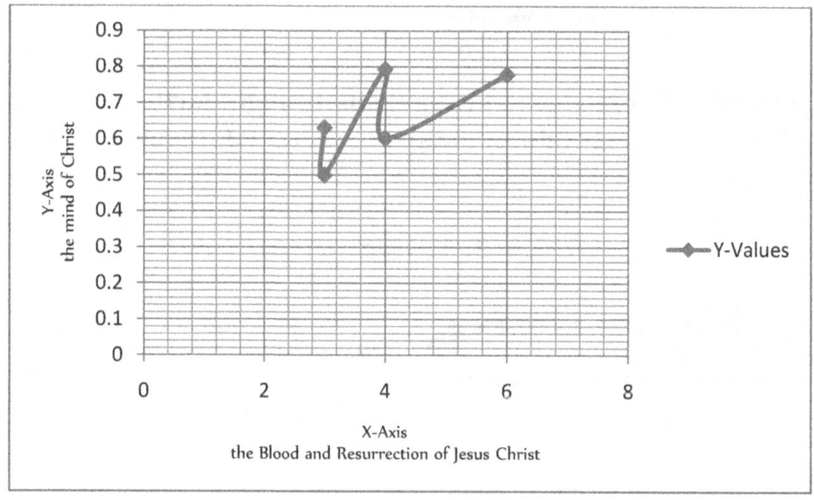

Water Spout *(lightning; combinatorics)* Study bible 2

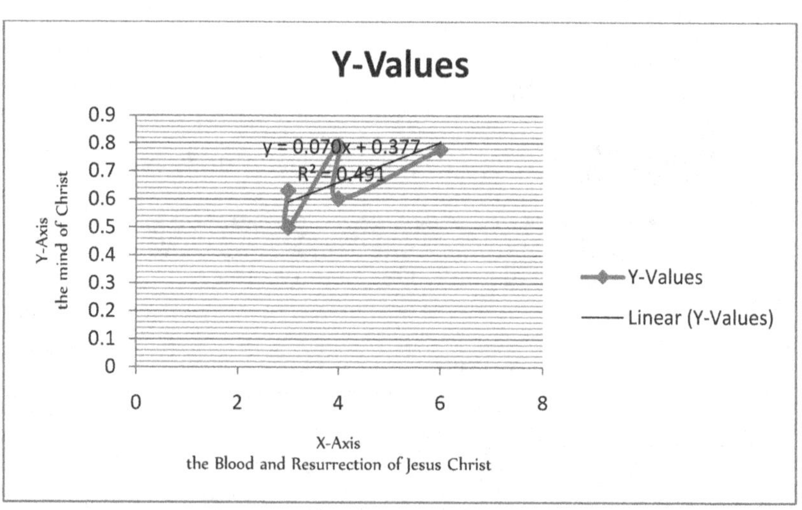

$10^{0.7781}, 10^{0.6020}, 4^{0.7925}\ 10^{0}, 4^{0.5}\ 10^{0}, 3^{0.6308}10^{0}.$

Pilled Poplar, Hazel, and Chestnut bible rods 2

9. Who hath ears to hear, let him hear.

5, 3. Bible Matrices

$5_{10}, 3_{10}.$ Pilled Poplar, Hazel, and Chestnut bible rods 1

$\text{Log}_{10} 5 = 0.6989$ $\text{Log}_{10} 3 = 0.4771$

5, 3. Deep calls unto Deep study bible 1

0.6989, 0.4771. Deep calls unto Deep study bible 2

x-axis	y-axis
5	0.6989
3	0.4771

Water Spout *(lightning; combinatorics)* Study bible 1

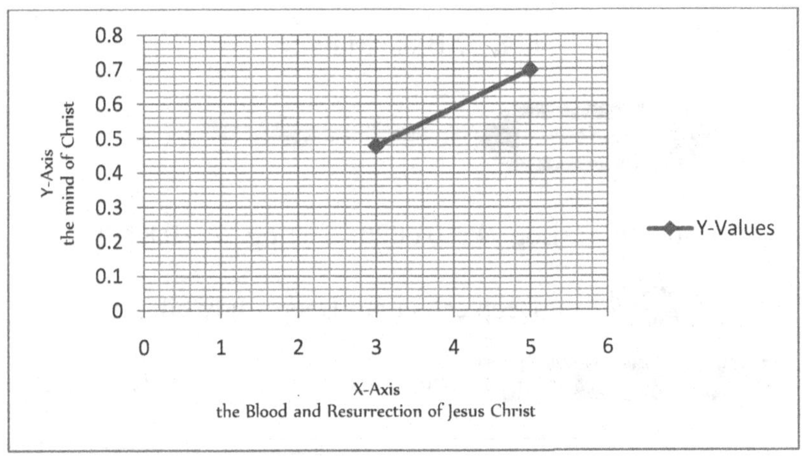

Water Spout *(lightning; combinatorics)* Study bible 2

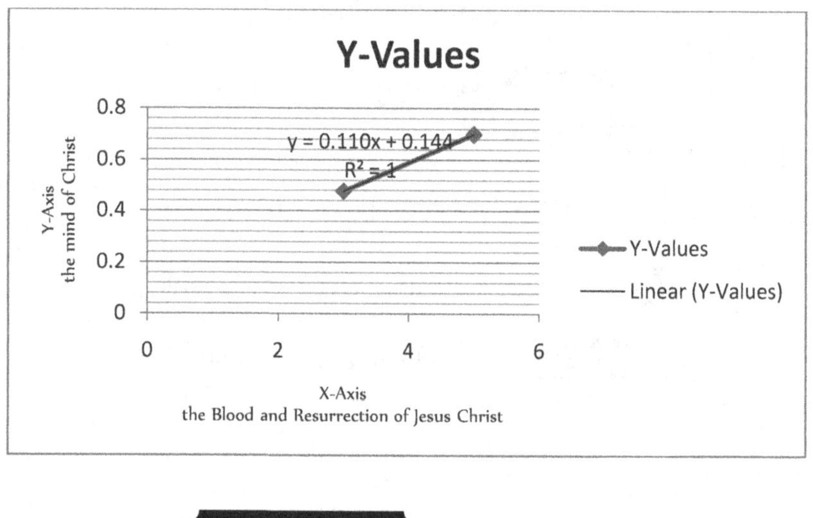

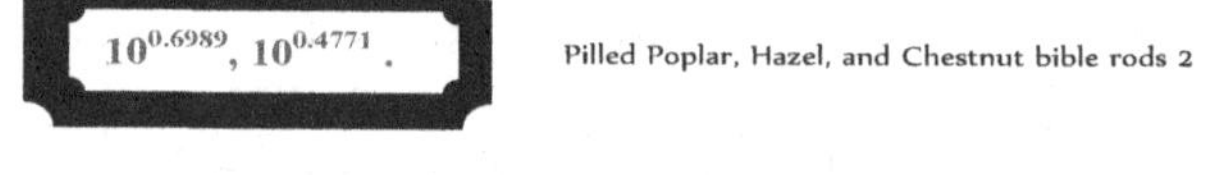

10. And the disciples came, and said unto him, Why speakest thou unto them in parables?

4, 4, 7? Bible Matrices

$\text{Log}_{10} 4 = 0.6020$ $\text{Log}_{10} 4 = 0.6020$ $\text{Log}_{10} 7 = 0.8450$

4, 4, 7? Deep calls unto Deep study bible 1

0.6020, 0.6020, 0.8450? Deep calls unto Deep study bible 2

x-axis	y-axis
4	0.6020
4	0.6020
7	0.8450

Water Spout *(lightning; combinatorics)* Study bible 1

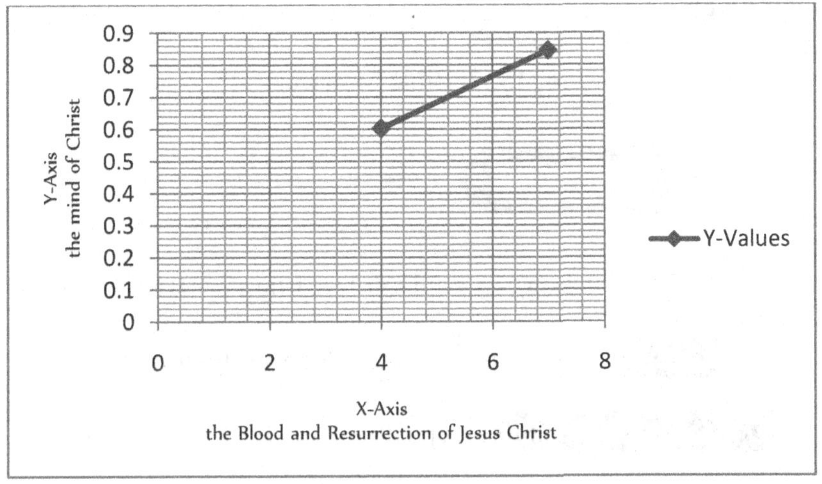

Water Spout *(lightning; combinatorics)* Study bible 2

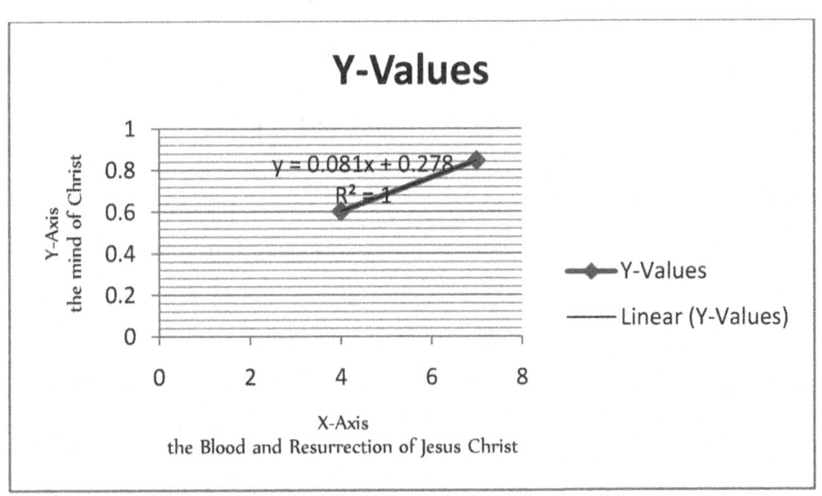

$10^{0.6020}$, $10^{0.6020}$, $10^{0.8450}$?

Pilled Poplar, Hazel, and Chestnut bible rods 2

11. He answered and said unto them, Because it is given unto you to know the mysteries of the kingdom of heaven, but to them it is not given.

6, 15, 7. Bible Matrices

$Log_{10} 6 = 0.7781$ $Log_{10} 15 = 1.1760$ $Log_{10} 7 = 0.8450$

6, 15, 7. Deep calls unto Deep study bible 1

0.7781, 1.1760, 0.8450. Deep calls unto Deep study bible 2

x-axis	y-axis
6	0.7781
15	1.1760
7	0.8450

Water Spout *(lightning; combinatorics)* Study bible 1

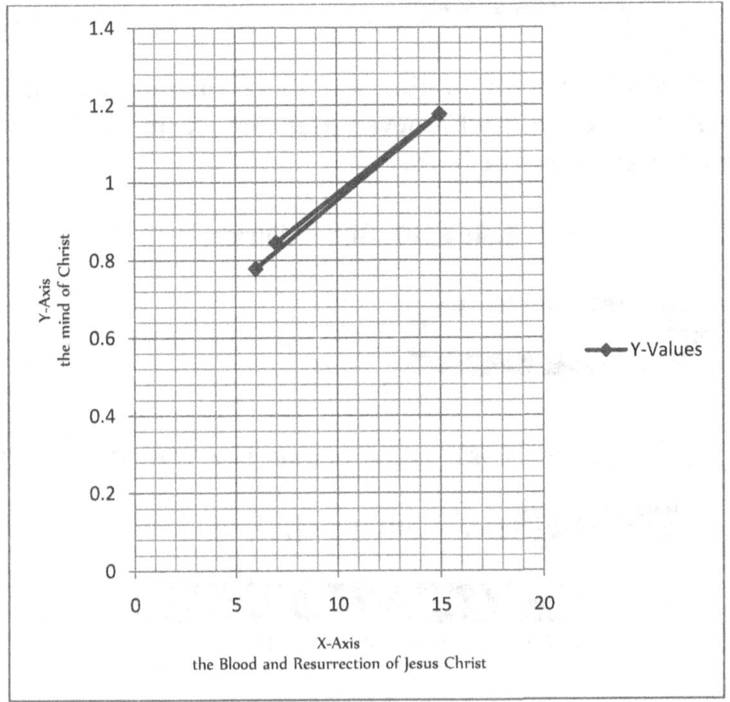

Water Spout *(lightning; combinatorics)* Study bible 2

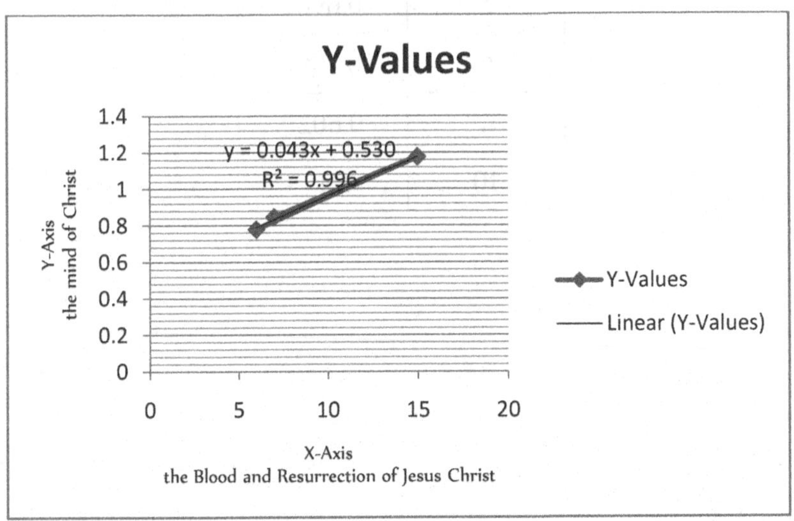

$10^{0.7781}, 10^{1.1760}, 10^{0.8450}.$

Pilled Poplar, Hazel, and Chestnut bible rods 2

12. For whosoever hath, to him shall be given, and he shall have more abundance: but whosoever hath not, from him shall be taken away even that he hath.

3, 5, 6: 4, 10. Bible Matrices

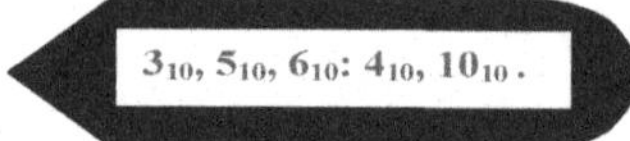

Pilled Poplar, Hazel, and Chestnut bible rods 1

$\text{Log}_{10}3 = 0.4771$ $\text{Log}_{10}5 = 0.6989$ $\text{Log}_{10}6 = 0.7781$ $\text{Log}_{10}4 = 0.6020$ $\text{Log}_{10}10 = 1$

3, 5, 6: 4, 10. Deep calls unto Deep study bible 1

0.4771, 0.6989, 0.7781: 0.6020, 1.
Deep calls unto Deep study bible 2

x-axis	y-axis
3	0.4771
5	0.6989
6	0.7781
4	0.6020
10	1

Water Spout *(lightning; combinatorics)* Study bible 1

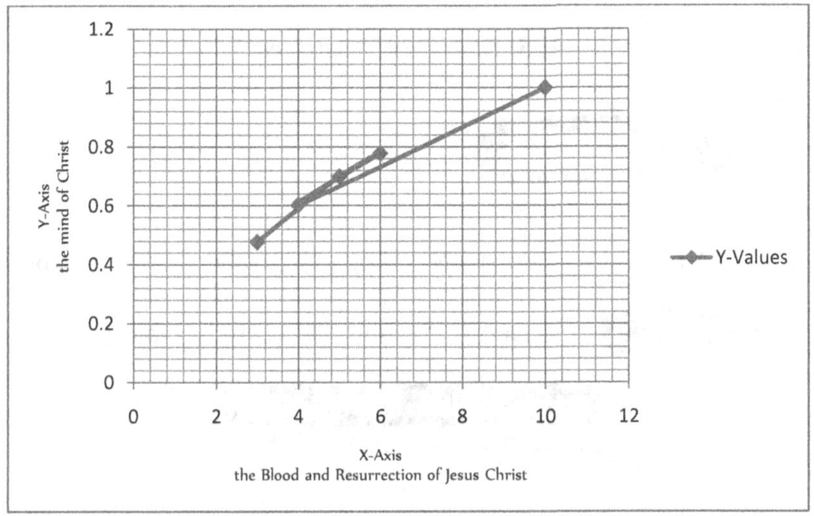

Water Spout *(lightning; combinatorics)* Study bible 2

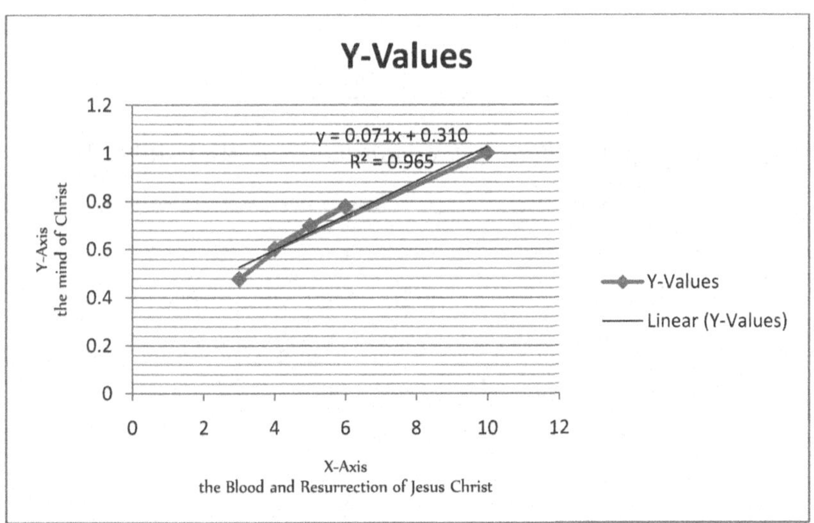

$10^{0.4771}$, $10^{0.6989}$, $10^{0.7781}$; $10^{0.6020}$, 10^{1}.

Pilled Poplar, Hazel, and Chestnut bible rods 2

13. Therefore speak I to them in parables: because they seeing see not; and hearing they hear not, neither do they understand.

7: 5; 5, 4. Bible Matrices

$\text{Log}_{10} 7 = 0.8450$ $\text{Log}_{10} 5 = 0.6989$ $\text{Log}_{10} 5 = 0.6989$ $\text{Log}_{10} 4 = 0.6020$

7: 5; 5, 4. Deep calls unto Deep study bible 1

0.8450: 0.6989; 0.6989, 0.6020.
Deep calls unto Deep study bible 2

x-axis	y-axis
7	0.8450
5	0.6989
5	0.6989
4	0.6020

Water Spout *(lightning; combinatorics)* Study bible 1

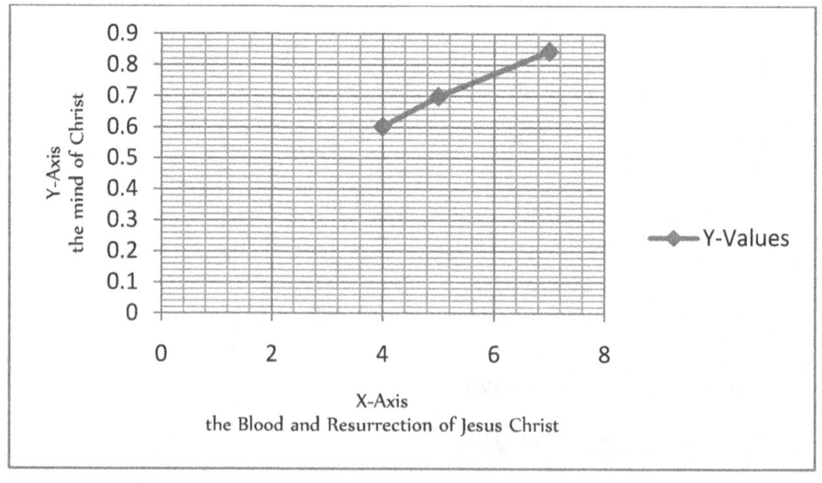

Water Spout *(lightning; combinatorics)* Study bible 2

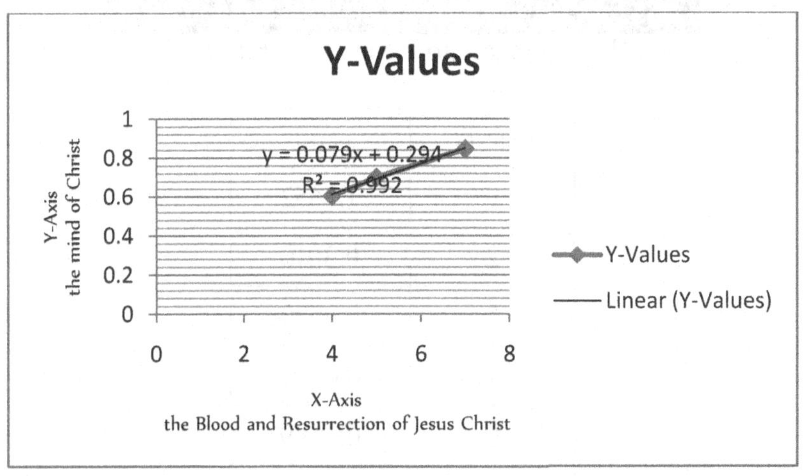

Pilled Poplar, Hazel, and Chestnut bible rods 2

14. And in them is fulfilled the prophecy of Esaiasthe salvation of the Lord, **which saith, By hearing ye shall hear, and shall not understand; and seeing ye shall see, and shall not perceive:**

9, 2, 5, 4; 5, 4: Bible Matrices

Pilled Poplar, Hazel, and Chestnut bible rods 1

$\mathrm{Log}_{10} 4 = 0.6020$ $\mathrm{Log}_{10} 5 = 0.6989$ $\mathrm{Log}_{10} 2 = 0.3010$ $\mathrm{Log}_{10} 5 = 0.6989$ $\mathrm{Log}_{10} 4 = 0.6020$

$\mathrm{Log}_5 9 = y$

$5^y = 9$

$y \log_{10} 5 = \log_{10} 9$

$y = \log_{10} 9 / \log_{10} 5$

$y = 0.9542 / 0.6989$

$y = 1.3652$

9, 2, 5, 4; 5, 4: Deep calls unto Deep study bible 1

1.3652, 0.3010, 0.6989, 0.6020; 0.6989, 0.6020: Deep calls unto Deep study bible 2

x-axis	y-axis
9	1.3652
2	0.3010
5	0.6989
4	0.6020
5	0.6989
4	0.6020

Water Spout *(lightning; combinatorics)* Study bible 1

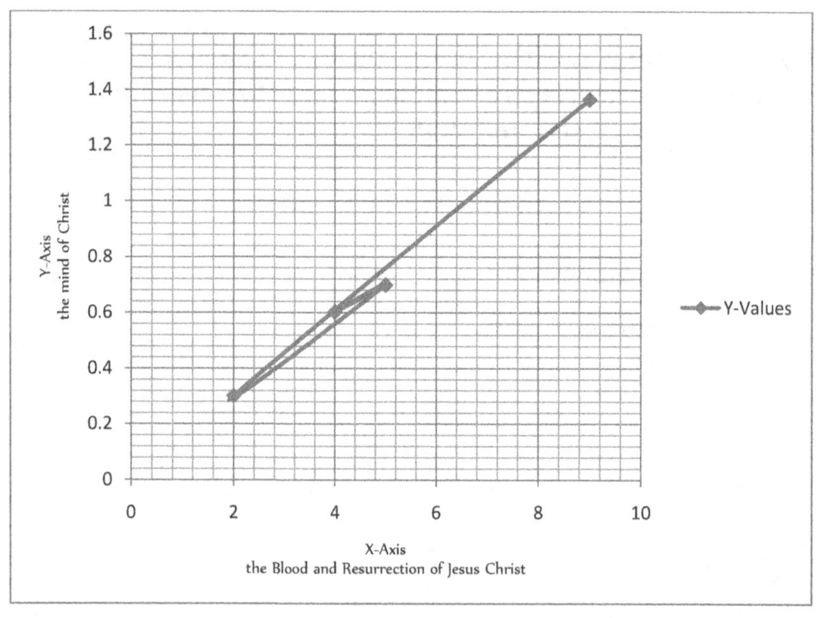

Water Spout *(lightning; combinatorics)* Study bible 2

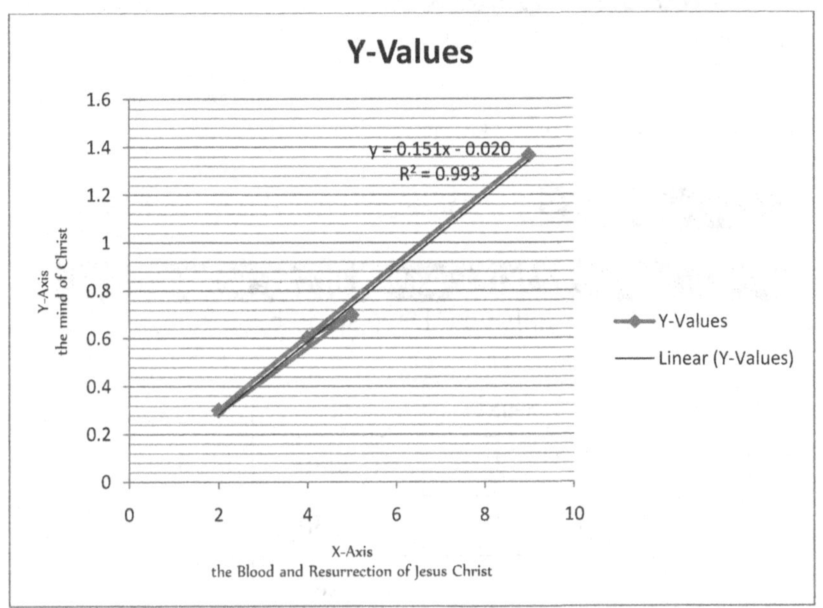

$5^{1.3652}$, $10^{0.3010}$, $10^{0.6989}$, $10^{0.6020}$; $10^{0.6989}$, $10^{0.6020}$:

Pilled Poplar, Hazel, and Chestnut bible rods 2

15. For this people's heart is waxed gross, and their ears are dull of hearing, and their eyes they have closed; lest at any time they should see with their eyes, and hear with their ears, and should understand with their heart, and should be converted, and I should heal them.

7, 7, 6; 10, 5, 6, 4, 5. Bible Matrices

7_{10}, 7_{10}, 6_{10}; 10_{10}, 5_{10}, 6_{10}, 4_{10}, 5_{10}. Pilled Poplar, Hazel, and Chestnut bible rods 1

$Log_{10} 7 = 0.8450$ $Log_{10} 7 = 0.8450$ $Log_{10} 5 = 0.6989$ $Log_{10} 5 = 0.6989$ $Log_{10} 6 = 0.7781$
$Log_{10} 6 = 0.7781$ $Log_{10} 4 = 0.6020$ $Log_{10} 10 = 1$

7, 7, 6; 10, 5, 6, 4, 5. Deep calls unto Deep study bible 1

0.8450, 0.8450, 0.7781; 1, 0.6989, 0.7781, 0.6020, 0.6989.
Deep calls unto Deep study bible 2

x-axis	y-axis
7	0.8450
7	0.8450
6	0.7781
10	1
5	0.6989
6	0.7781
4	0.6020
5	0.6989

Water Spout *(lightning; combinatorics)* Study bible 1

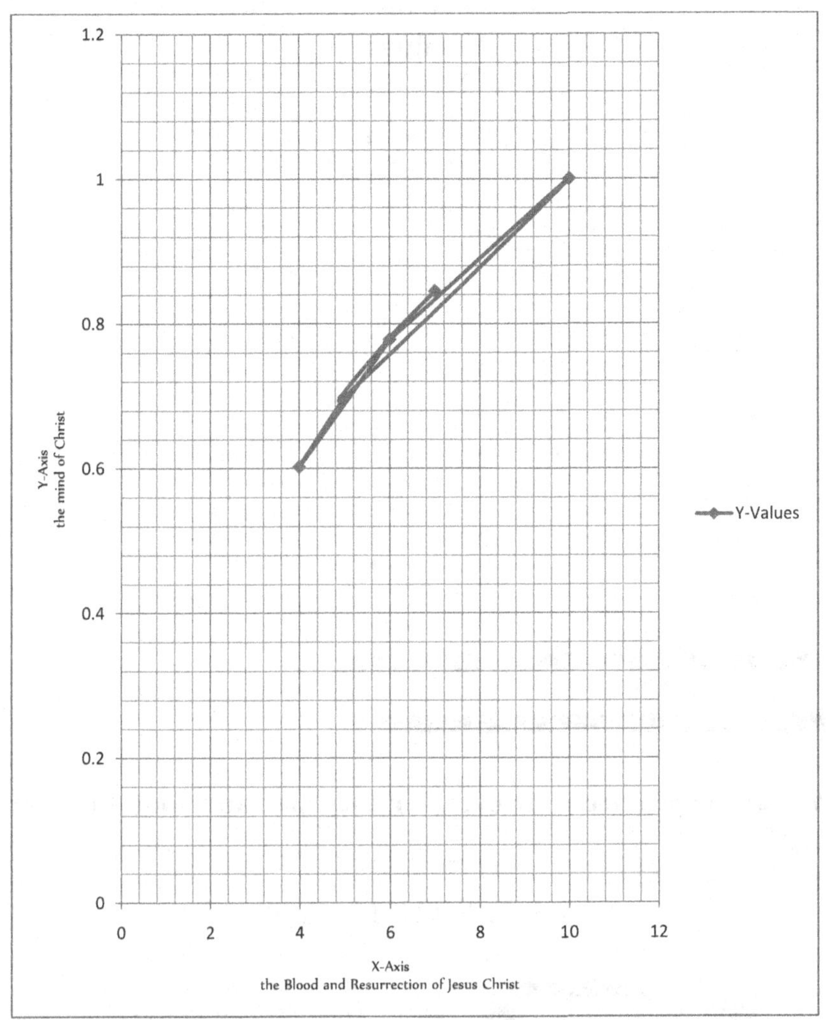

Water Spout *(lightning; combinatorics)* Study bible 2

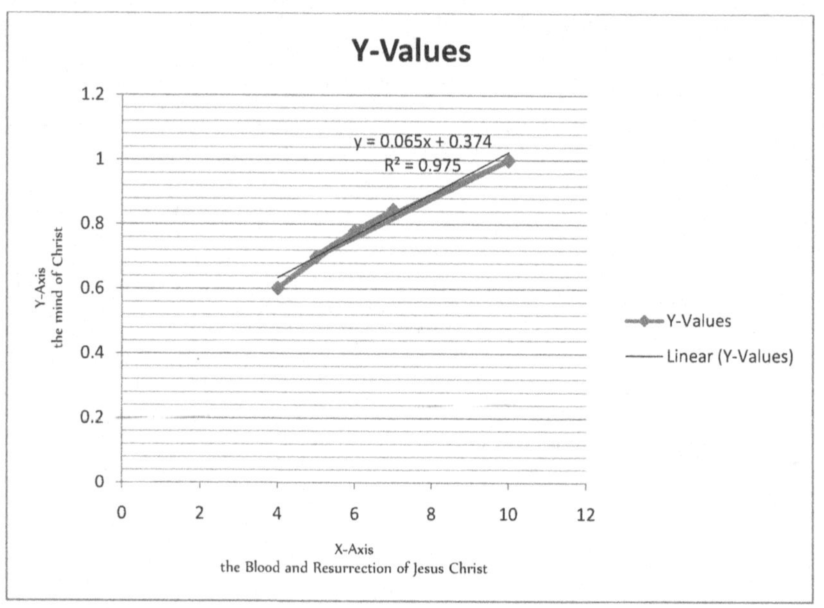

$10^{0.8450}, 10^{0.8450}, 10^{0.7781}; 10^{1}, 10^{0.6989}, 10^{0.7781}, 10^{0.6020}, 10^{0.6989}$.

Pilled Poplar, Hazel, and Chestnut bible rods 2

16. But blessed are your eyes, for they see: and your ears, for they hear.

5, 3: 3, 3. Bible Matrices

$5_{10}, 3_{10}: 3_{10}, 3_{10}$.

Pilled Poplar, Hazel, and Chestnut bible rods 1

$\text{Log}_{10} 5 = 0.6989 \quad \text{Log}_{10} 3 = 0.4771 \quad \text{Log}_{10} 3 = 0.4771 \quad \text{Log}_{10} 3 = 0.4771$

5, 3: 3, 3. Deep calls unto Deep study bible 1

0.6989, 0.4771: 0.4771, 0.4771.
Deep calls unto Deep study bible 2

x-axis	y-axis
5	0.6989
3	0.4771
3	0.4771
3	0.4771

Water Spout *(lightning; combinatorics)* Study bible 1

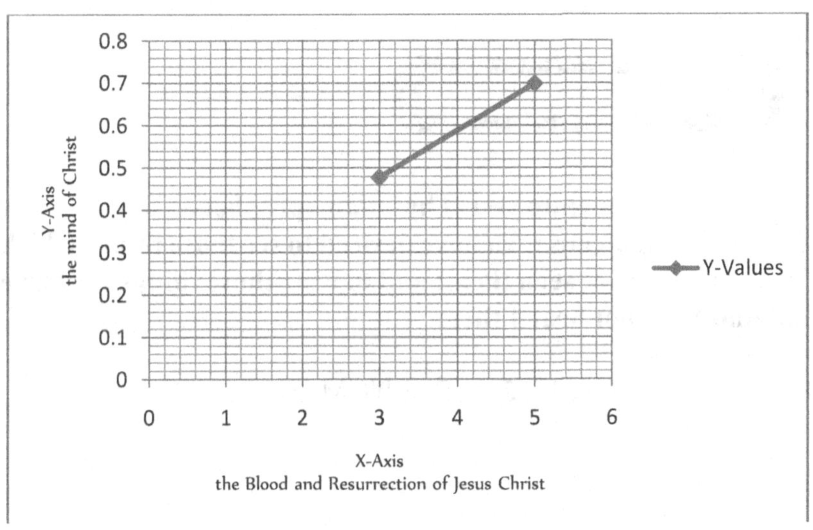

Water Spout *(lightning; combinatorics)* Study bible 2

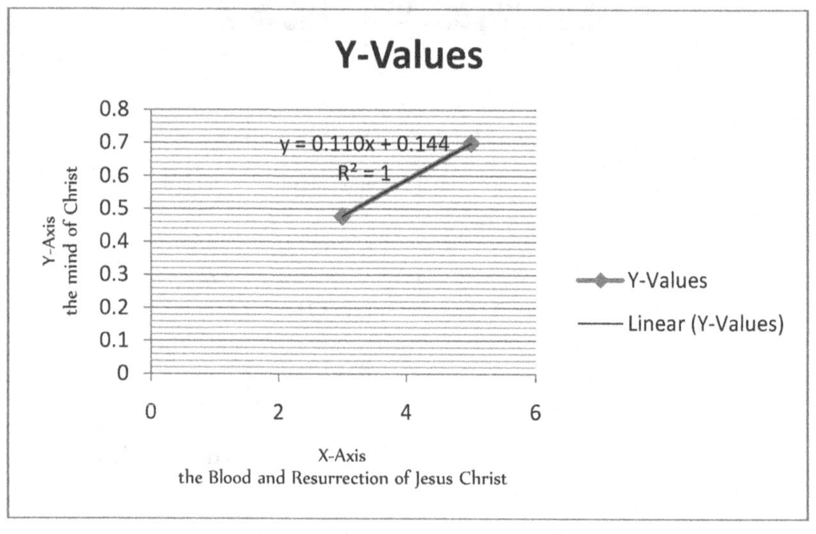

Pilled Poplar, Hazel, and Chestnut bible rods 2

17. For verily I say unto you, That many prophets to bubble forth, as from a fountain; utter **and righteous men have desired to see those things which ye see, and have not seen them; and to hear those things which ye hear, and have not heard them.**

6, 15, 5; 8, 5. Bible Matrices

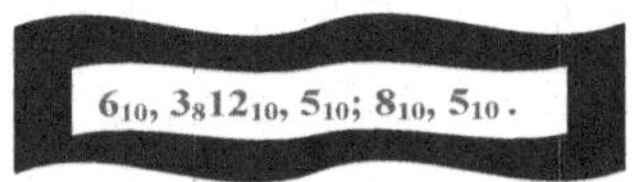

Pilled Poplar, Hazel, and Chestnut bible rods 1

$\text{Log}_{10} 5 = 0.6989$ $\text{Log}_{10} 5 = 0.6989$ $\text{Log}_{10} 8 = 0.9030$ $\text{Log}_{10} 6 = 0.7781$ $\text{Log}_{10} 12 = 1.0791$

$\text{Log}_8 3 = y$

$8^y = 3$

$y \log_{10} 8 = \log_{10} 3$

$y = \log_{10} 3 / \log_{10} 8$

$y = 0.4771 / 0.9030$

$y = 0.5283$

6, 15, 5; 8, 5. Deep calls unto Deep study bible 1

0.7781, 0.5283 1.0791, 0.6989; 0.9030, 0.6989.

Deep calls unto Deep study bible 2

x-axis	y-axis
6	0.7781
15	1.6074
5	0.6989
8	0.9030
5	0.6989

Water Spout *(lightning; combinatorics)* Study bible 1

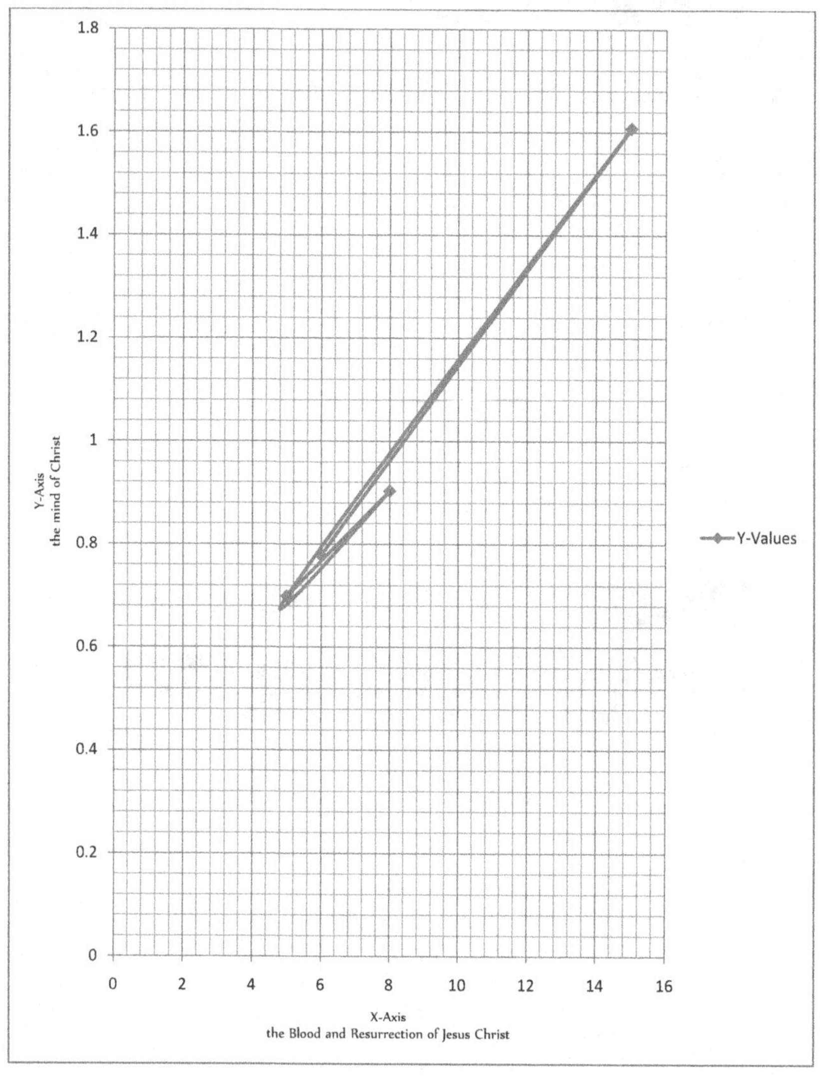

Water Spout *(lightning; combinatorics)* Study bible 2

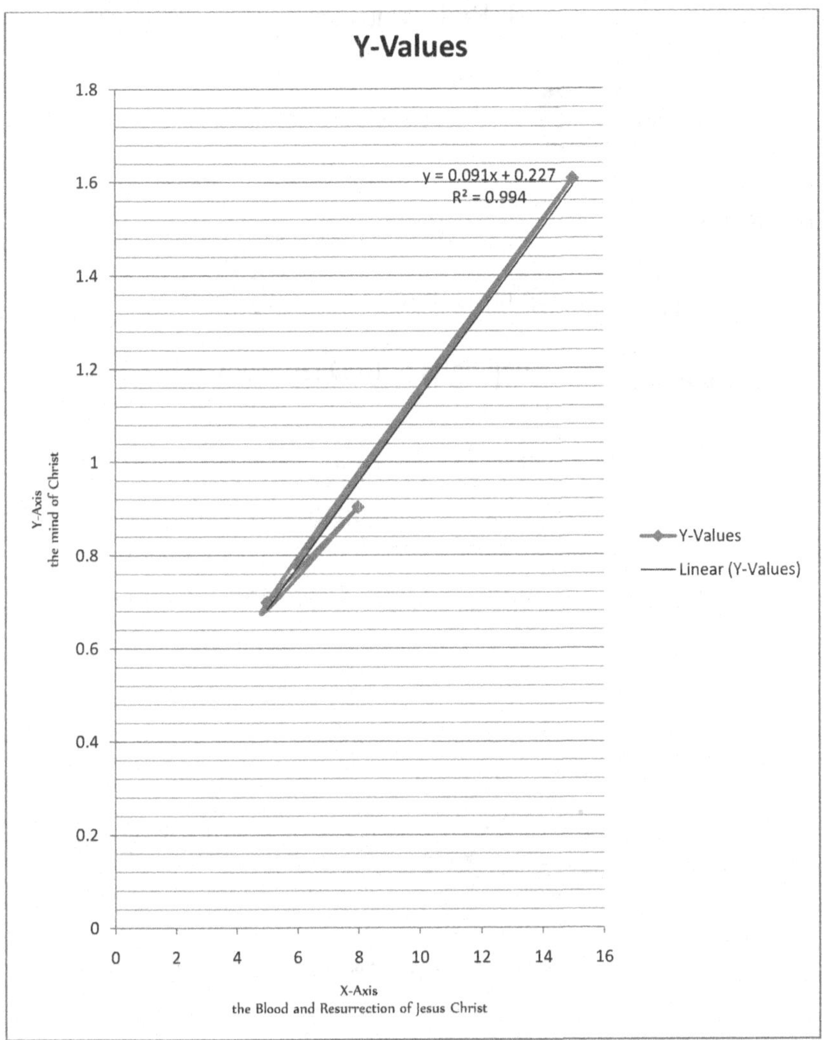

$10^{0.7781}$, $8^{0.5283}$ $10^{1.0791}$, $10^{0.6989}$; $10^{0.9030}$, $10^{0.6989}$.

Pilled Poplar, Hazel, and Chestnut bible rods 2

18. Hear ye therefore the parable of the sower.

8. Bible Matrices

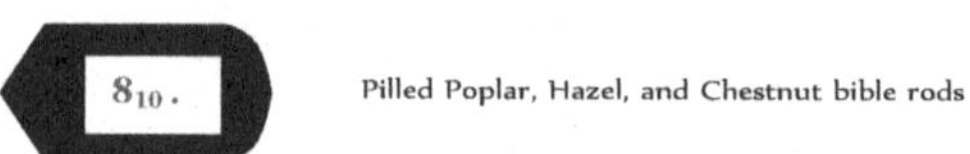

$\text{Log}_{10} 8 = 0.9030$

8. Deep calls unto Deep study bible 1

0.9030. Deep calls unto Deep study bible 2

x-axis	y-axis
8	0.9030

Water Spout *(lightning; combinatorics)* Study bible 1

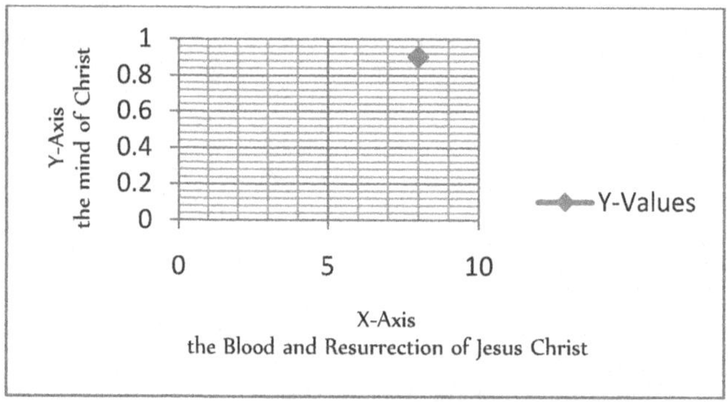

Water Spout *(lightning; combinatorics)* Study bible 2

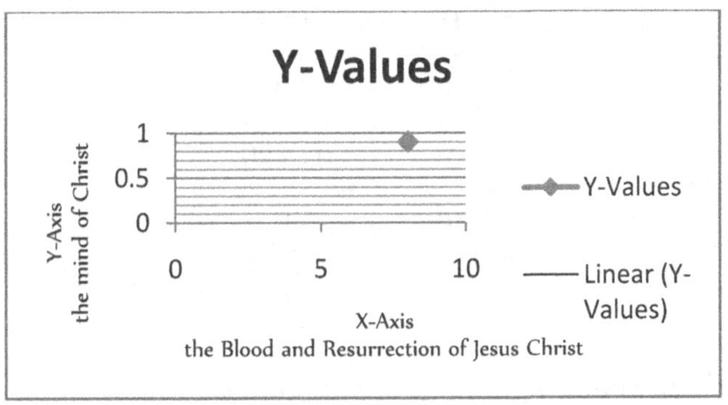

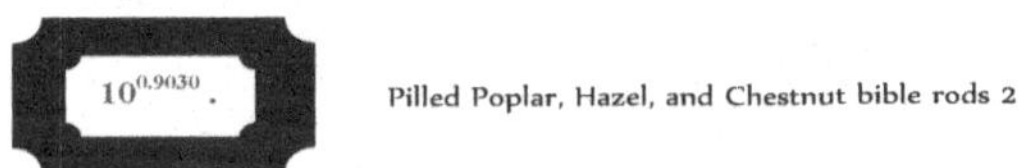

Pilled Poplar, Hazel, and Chestnut bible rods 2

19. When any one heareth the word of the kingdom, and understandeth it not, then cometh the wicked one, and catcheth away that which was sown in his heart. This is he which received seed by the way side.

9, 4, 5, 10. 10. Bible Matrices

Pilled Poplar, Hazel, and Chestnut bible rods 1

$\text{Log}_{10} 9 = 0.9542$ $\text{Log}_{10} 5 = 0.6989$ $\text{Log}_{10} 4 = 0.6020$ $\text{Log}_{10} 10 = 1$ $\text{Log}_{10} 10 = 1$

9, 4, 5, 10. 10. Deep calls unto Deep study bible 1

0.9542, 0.6020, 0.6989, 1. 1. Deep calls unto Deep study bible 2

x-axis	y-axis
9	0.9542
4	0.6020
5	0.6989
10	1
10	1

Water Spout *(lightning; combinatorics)* Study bible 1

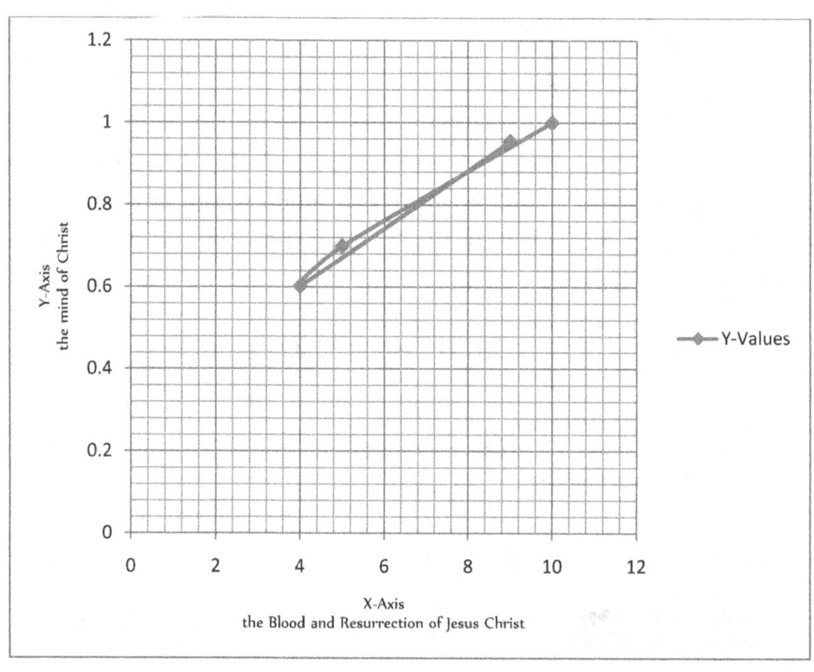

Water Spout *(lightning; combinatorics)* Study bible 2

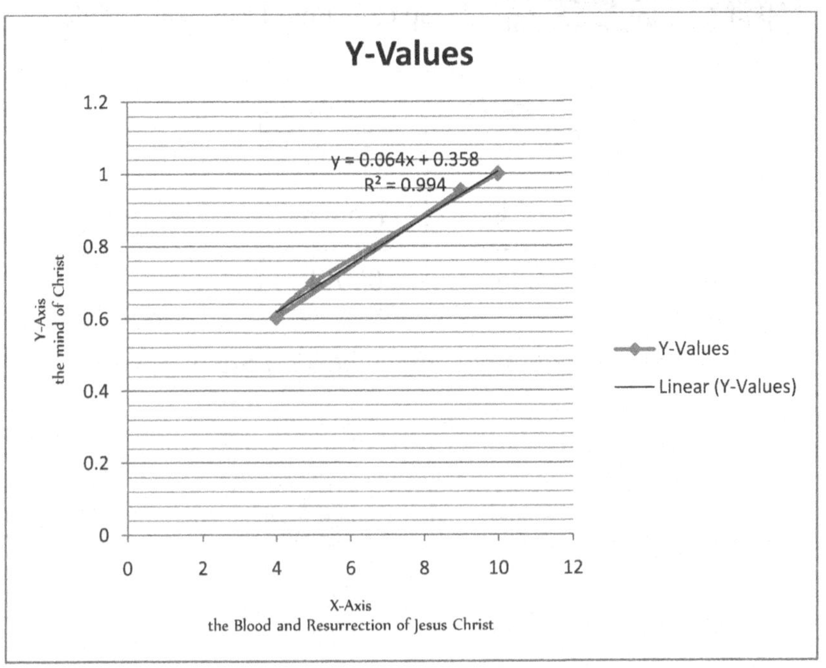

Pilled Poplar, Hazel, and Chestnut bible rods 2

20. But he that received the seed into stony places, the same is he that heareth the word, and anon with joy receiveth it;

9, 8, 6; Bible Matrices

Pilled Poplar, Hazel, and Chestnut bible rods 1

$\text{Log}_{10} 9 = 0.9542$ $\text{Log}_{10} 8 = 0.9030$ $\text{Log}_{10} 6 = 0.7781$

9, 8, 6; Deep calls unto Deep study bible 1

0.9542, 0.9030, 0.7781; Deep calls unto Deep study bible 2

x-axis	y-axis
9	0.9542
8	0.9030
6	0.7781

Water Spout *(lightning; combinatorics)* Study bible 1

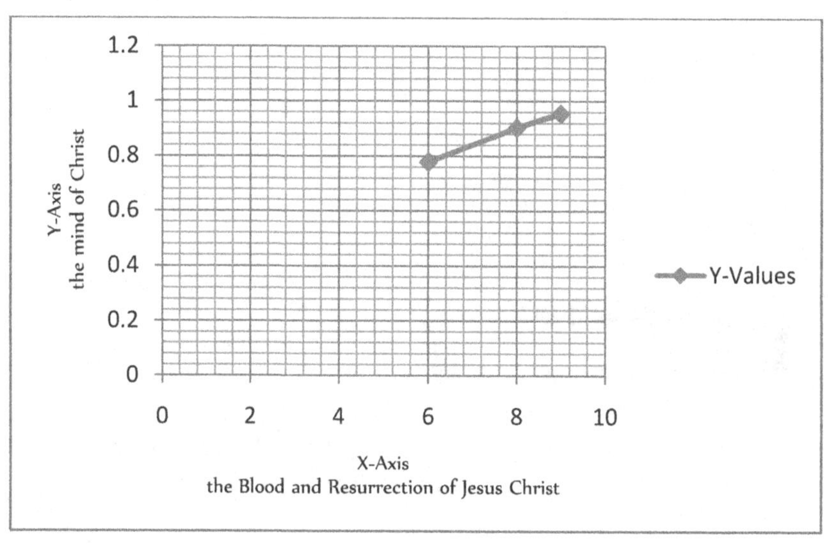

Water Spout *(lightning; combinatorics)* Study bible 2

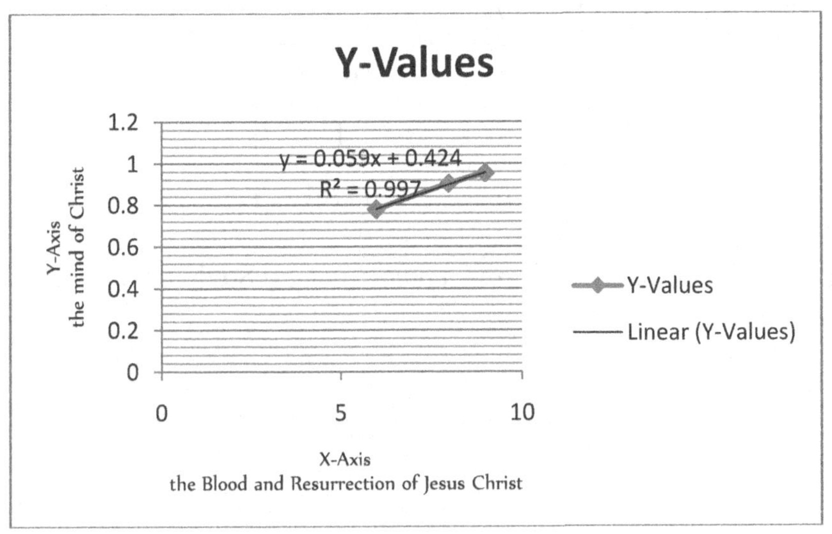

21. Yet hath he not root in himself, but dureth for a while: for when tribulation or persecution ariseth because of the word, by and by he is offended.

7, 5: 10, 6. Bible Matrices

$\log_{10} 10 = 1$ $\log_{10} 5 = 0.6989$ $\log_{10} 6 = 0.7781$ $\log_{10} 7 = 0.8450$

7, 5: 10, 6. Deep calls unto Deep study bible 1

0.8450, 0.6989: 1, 0.7781.
Deep calls unto Deep study bible 2

x-axis	y-axis
7	0.8450
5	0.6989
10	1
6	0.7781

Water Spout *(lightning; combinatorics)* Study bible 1

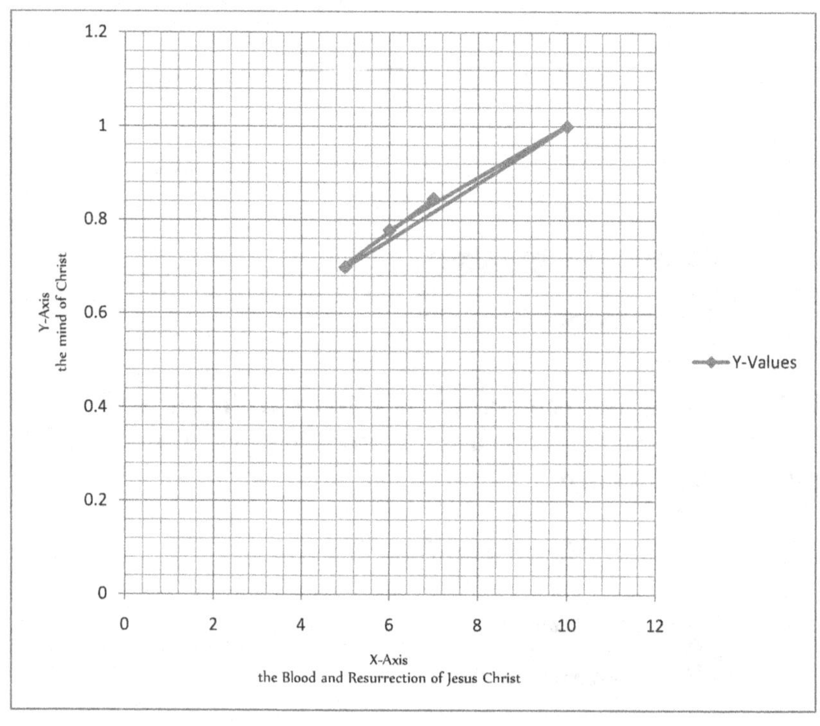

Water Spout *(lightning; combinatorics)* Study bible 2

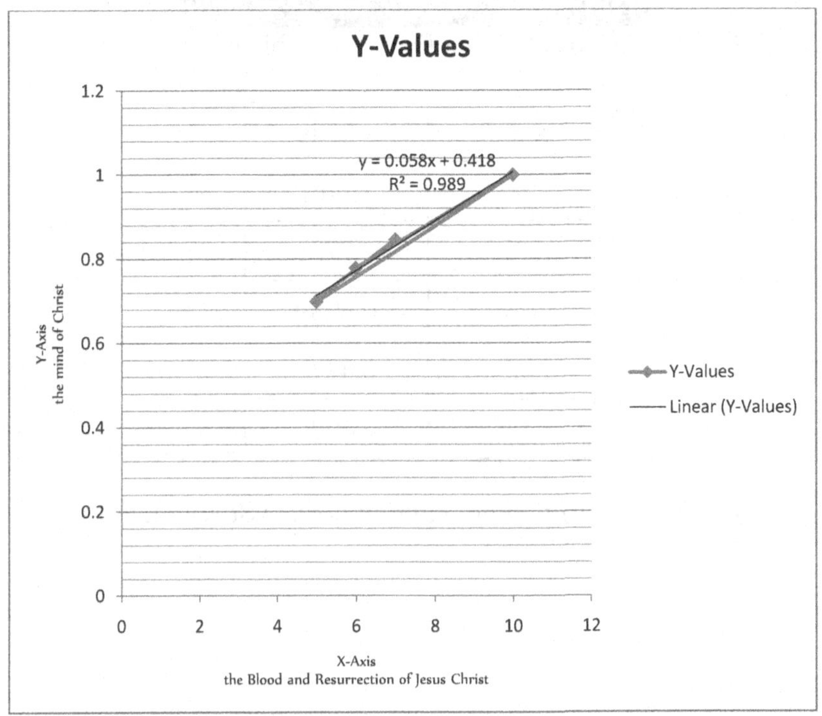

$10^{0.8450}$, $10^{0.6989}$: 10^{1}, $10^{0.7781}$.

Pilled Poplar, Hazel, and Chestnut bible rods 2

22. He also that received seed among the thorns is he that heareth the word; and the care of this world, and the deceitfulness of riches, choke the word, and he becometh unfruitful.

14; 6, 5, 3, 4. Bible Matrices

14_{10}; 6_{10}, 5_{10}, 3_{10}, 4_{10}.

Pilled Poplar, Hazel, and Chestnut bible rods 1

$Log_{10} 14 = 1.1461$ $Log_{10} 5 = 0.6989$ $Log_{10} 3 = 0.4771$ $Log_{10} 4 = 0.6020$ $Log_{10} 6 = 0.7781$

14; 6, 5, 3, 4. Deep calls unto Deep study bible 1

1.1461; 0.7781, 0.6989, 0.4771, 0.6020.
Deep calls unto Deep study bible 2

x-axis	y-axis
14	1.1461
6	0.7781
5	0.6989
3	0.4771
4	0.6020

Water Spout *(lightning; combinatorics)* Study bible 1

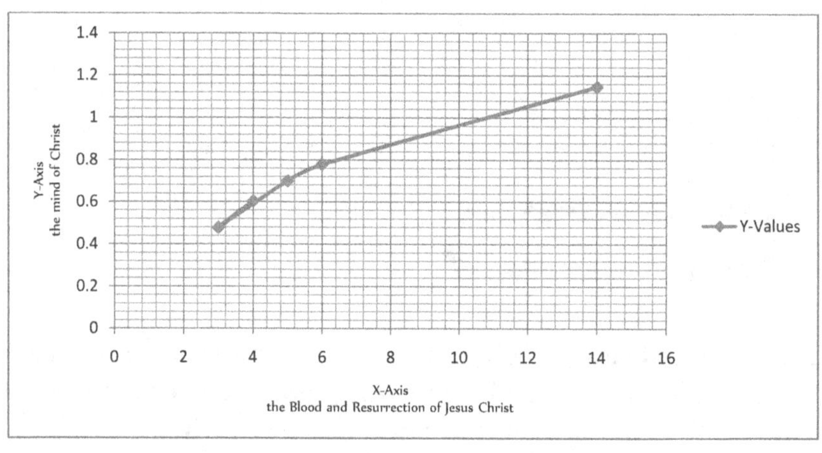

Water Spout *(lightning; combinatorics)* Study bible 2

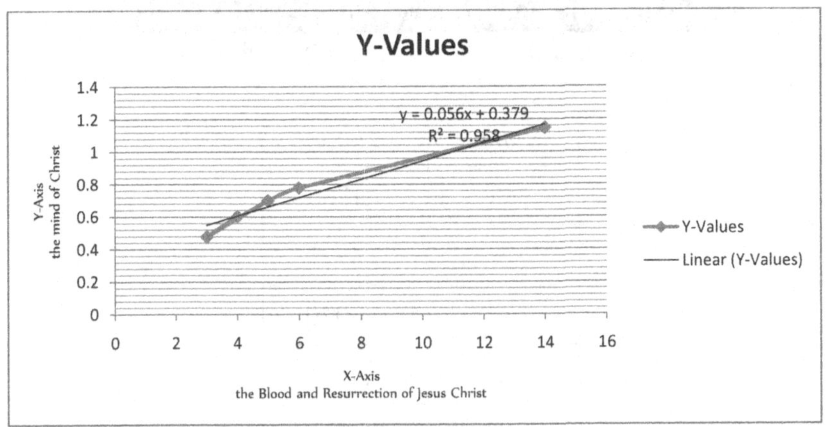

$10^{1.1461}$; $10^{0.7781}$, $10^{0.6989}$, $10^{0.4771}$, $10^{0.6020}$.

Pilled Poplar, Hazel, and Chestnut bible rods 2

23. But he that received seed into the good ground is he that heareth the word, and understandeth it; which also beareth fruit, and bringeth forth, some an hundred 2 x 2 x 5 x 5 **fold, some sixty** 2 x 2 x 3 x 5, **some thirty** 2 x 3 x 5.

15, 3; 4, 3, 4, 2, 2. Bible Matrices

15_{10}, 3_{10}; 4_{10}, 3_{10}, $3_4 1_{10}$, 2_4, 2_3 .

Pilled Poplar, Hazel, and Chestnut bible rods 1

$\text{Log}_{10} 15 = 1.1760$	$\text{Log}_{10} 3 = 0.4771$	$\text{Log}_{10} 4 = 0.6020$	$\text{Log}_{10} 3 = 0.4771$	$\text{Log}_{10} 1 = 0$
$\text{Log}_4 3 = y$	$\text{Log}_3 2 = y$	$\text{Log}_4 2 = y$		
$4^y = 3$ $3^y = 2$	$4^y = 2$			
$y \log_{10} 4 = \log_{10} 3$	$y \log_{10} 3 = \log_{10} 2$	$2^{2y} = 2^1$		
$y = \log_{10} 3 / \log_{10} 4$	$y = \log_{10} 2 / \log_{10} 3$	$2y = 1$		
$y = 0.4771 / 0.6020$	$y = 0.3010 / 0.4771$	$y = ½$ or 0.5		
$y = 0.7925$	$y = 0.6308$			

15, 3; 4, 3, 4, 2, 2. Deep calls unto Deep study bible 1

1.1760, 0.4771; 0.6020, 0.4771, 0.7925 0, 0.5, 0.6308.
Deep calls unto Deep study bible 2

x-axis	y-axis
15	1.1760
3	0.4771
4	0.6020
3	0.4771
4	0.7925
2	0.5
2	0.6308

Water Spout *(lightning; combinatorics)* Study bible 1

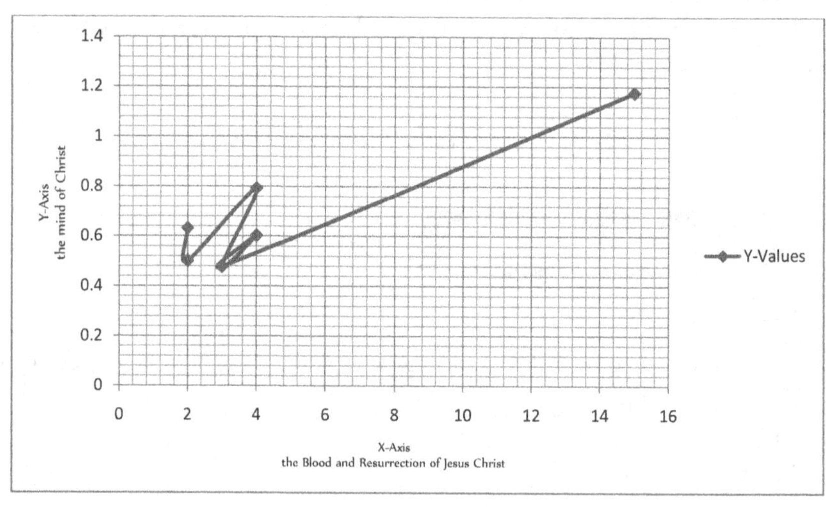

Water Spout *(lightning; combinatorics)* Study bible 2

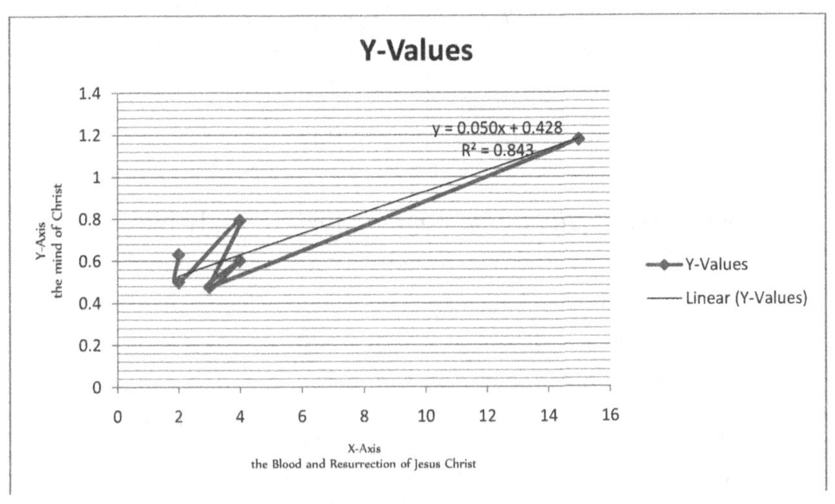

$10^{1.1760}$, $10^{0.4771}$; $10^{0.6020}$, $10^{0.4771}$, $4^{0.7925}$ 10^{0}, $4^{0.5}$, $3^{0.6308}$.

Pilled Poplar, Hazel, and Chestnut bible rods 2

24. Another parable put he forth unto them, saying, The kingdom of heaven is likened unto a man which sowed good seed in his field:

7, 1, 16: Bible Matrices

Pilled Poplar, Hazel, and Chestnut bible rods 1

$\text{Log}_{10} 7 = 0.8450$ $\text{Log}_{10} 1 = 0$ $\text{Log}_{10} 16 = 1.2041$

7, 1, 16: Deep calls unto Deep study bible 1

0.8450, 0, 1.2041: Deep calls unto Deep study bible 2

x-axis	y-axis
7	0.8450
1	0
16	1.2041

Water Spout *(lightning; combinatorics)* Study bible 1

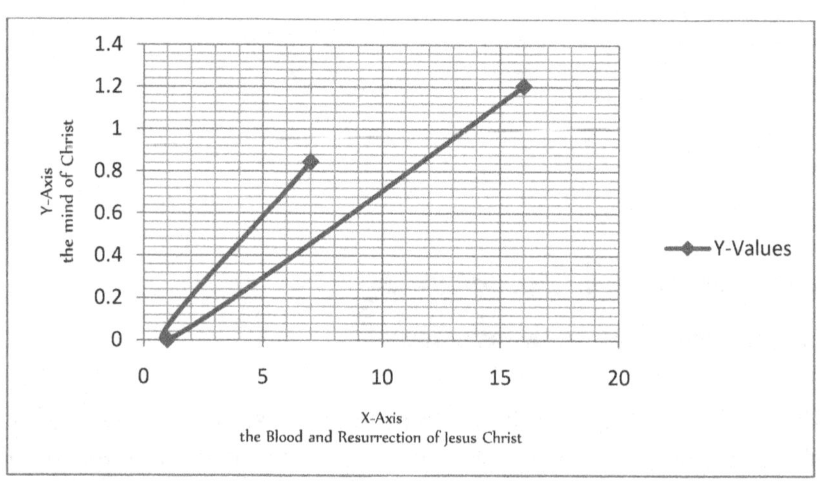

Water Spout *(lightning; combinatorics)* Study bible 2

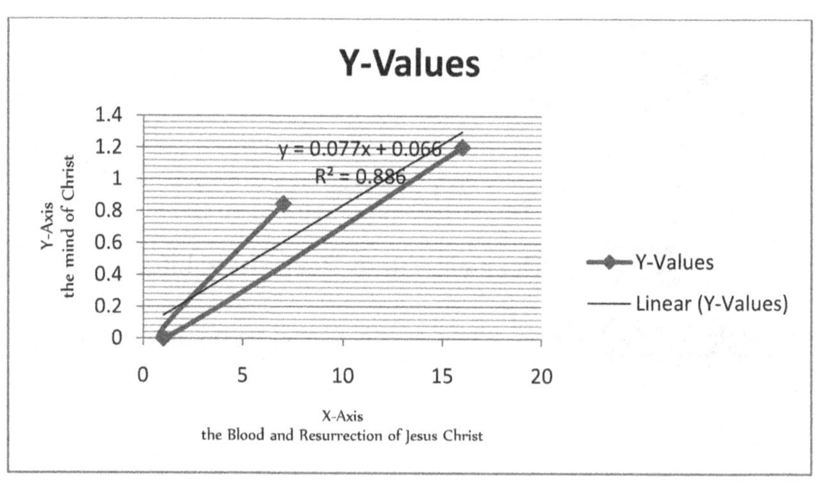

$10^{0.8450}$, 10^{0}, $10^{1.2041}$:

Pilled Poplar, Hazel, and Chestnut bible rods 2

25. But while men slept, his enemy came and sowed tares among the wheat, and went his way.

4, 9, 4. Bible Matrices

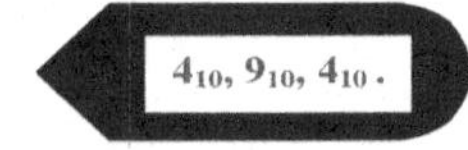

Pilled Poplar, Hazel, and Chestnut bible rods 1

$\log_{10} 9 = 0.9542$ $\log_{10} 4 = 0.6020$ $\log_{10} 4 = 0.6020$

4, 9, 4. Deep calls unto Deep study bible 1

0.6020, 0.9542, 0.6020. Deep calls unto Deep study bible 2

x-axis	y-axis
4	0.6020
9	0.9542
4	0.6020

Water Spout *(lightning; combinatorics)* Study bible 1

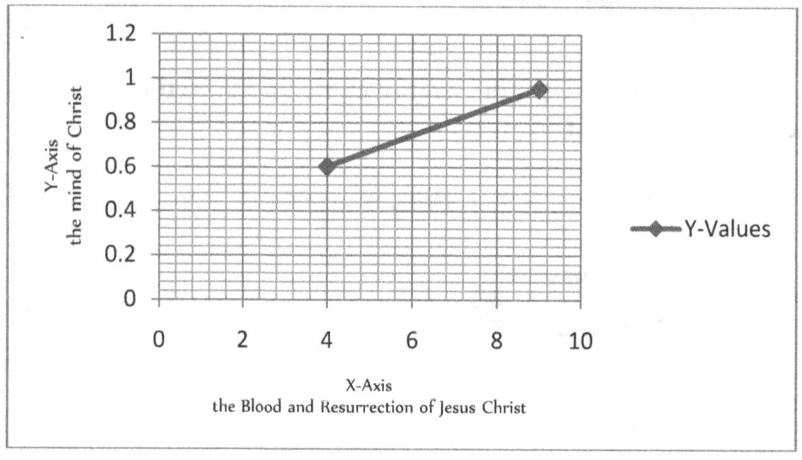

Water Spout *(lightning; combinatorics)* Study bible 2

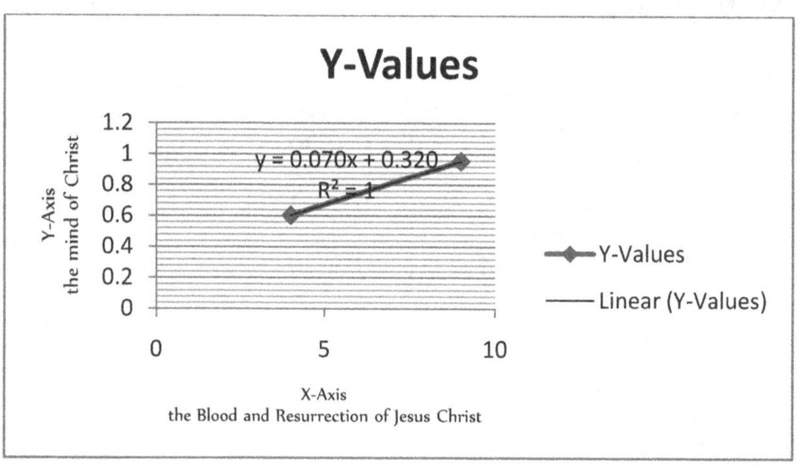

$10^{0.6020}, 10^{0.9542}, 10^{0.6020}$.

Pilled Poplar, Hazel, and Chestnut bible rods 2

26. But when the blade was sprung up, and brought forth fruit, then appeared the tares also.

7, 4, 5. Bible Matrices

$\text{Log}_{10} 7 = 0.8450$ $\text{Log}_{10} 5 = 0.6989$ $\text{Log}_{10} 4 = 0.6020$

7, 4, 5. Deep calls unto Deep study bible 1

0.8450, 0.6020, 0.6989. Deep calls unto Deep study bible 2

x-axis	y-axis
7	0.8450
4	0.6020
5	0.6989

Water Spout *(lightning; combinatorics)* Study bible 1

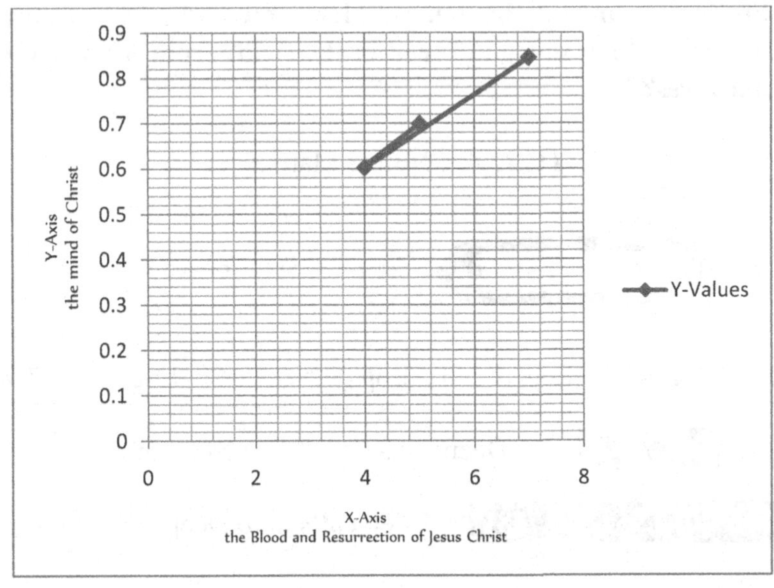

Water Spout *(lightning; combinatorics)* Study bible 2

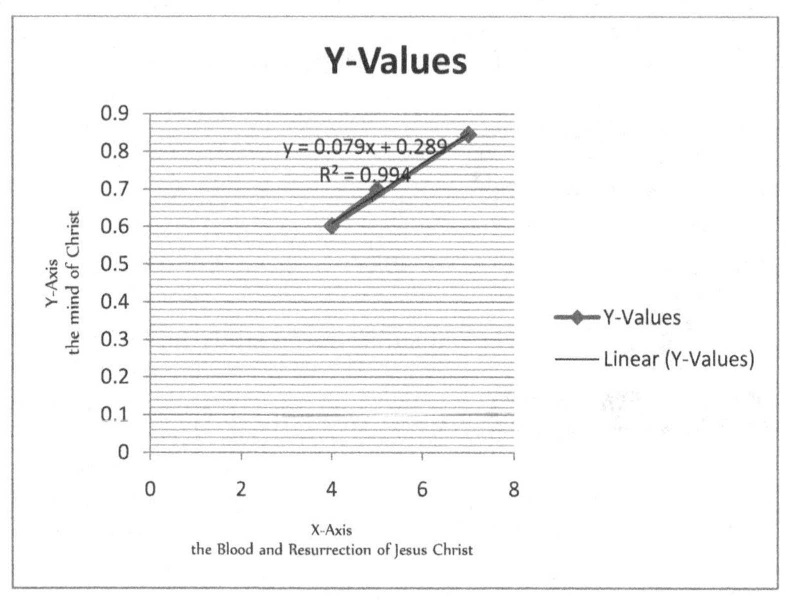

27. So the servants of the householder came and said unto him, Sir, didst not thou sow good seed in thy field? from whence then hath it tares?

11, 1, 9? 6? Bible Matrices

$\text{Log}_{10}\,11 = 1.0413$ $\text{Log}_{10}\,1 = 0$ $\text{Log}_{10}\,9 = 0.9542$ $\text{Log}_{10}\,6 = 0.7781$

11, 1, 9? 6? Deep calls unto Deep study bible 1

1.0413, 0, 0.9542? 0.7781? Deep calls unto Deep study bible 2

x-axis	y-axis
11	1.0413
1	0
9	0.9542
6	0.7781

Water Spout *(lightning; combinatorics)* Study bible 1

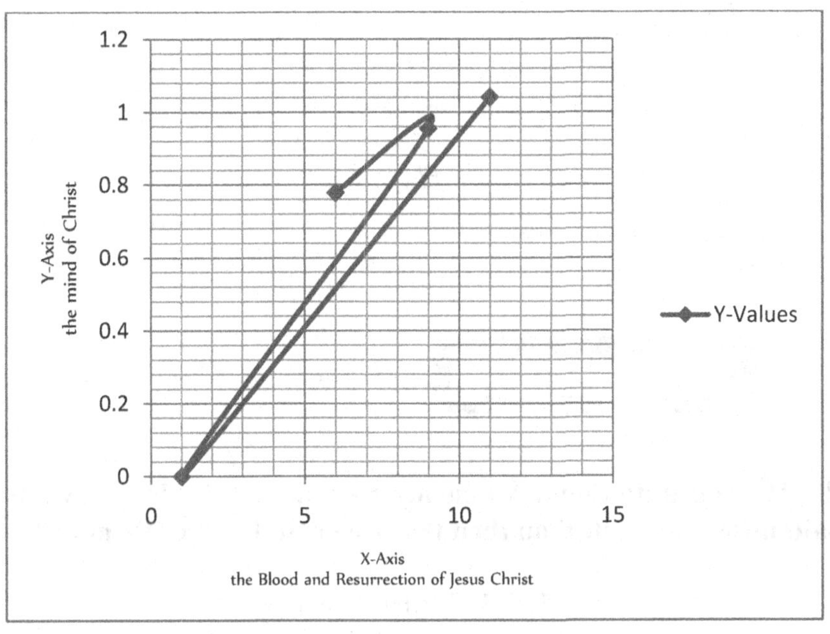

Water Spout *(lightning; combinatorics)* Study bible 2

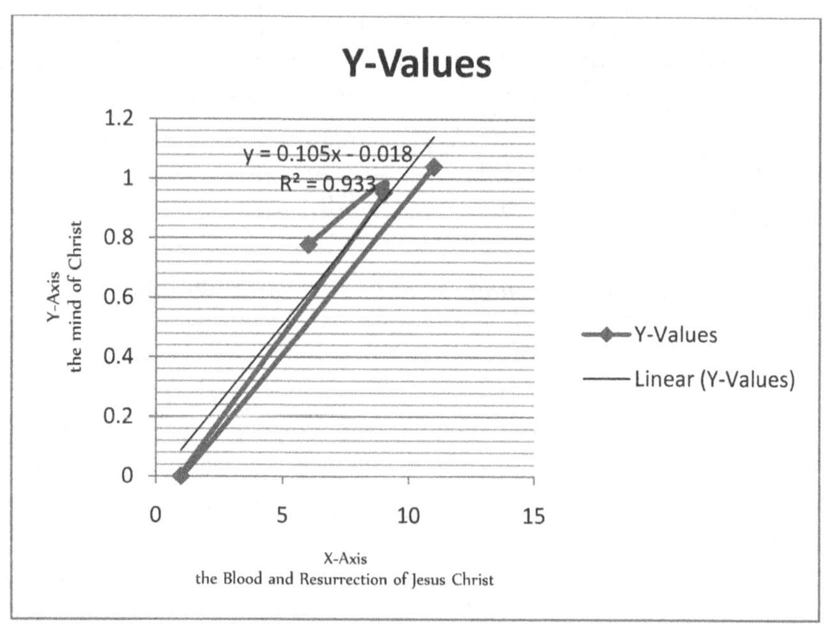

28. He said unto them, An enemy hath done this. The servants said unto him, Wilt thou then that we go and gather them up?

4, 5. 5, 10? Bible Matrices

$\text{Log}_{10} 10 = 1$ $\text{Log}_{10} 5 = 0.6989$ $\text{Log}_{10} 5 = 0.6989$ $\text{Log}_{10} 4 = 0.6020$

4, 5. 5, 10? Deep calls unto Deep study bible 1

0.6020, 0.6989. 0.6989, 1? Deep calls unto Deep study bible 2

x-axis	y-axis
4	0.6020
5	0.6989
5	0.6989
10	1

Water Spout *(lightning; combinatorics)* Study bible 1

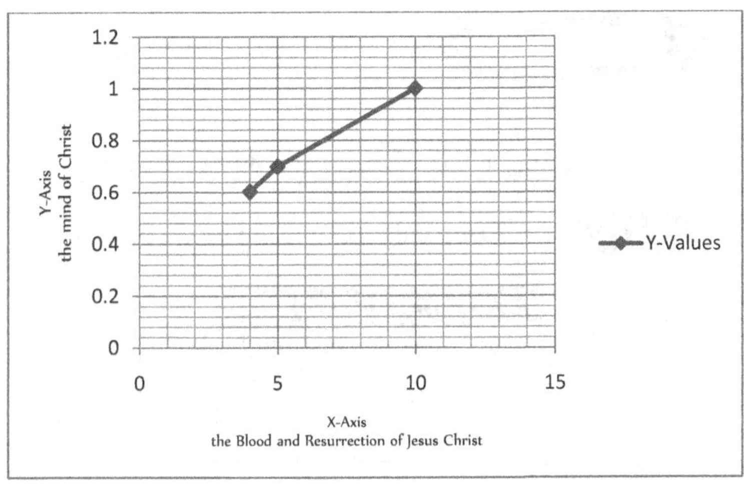

Water Spout *(lightning; combinatorics)* Study bible 2

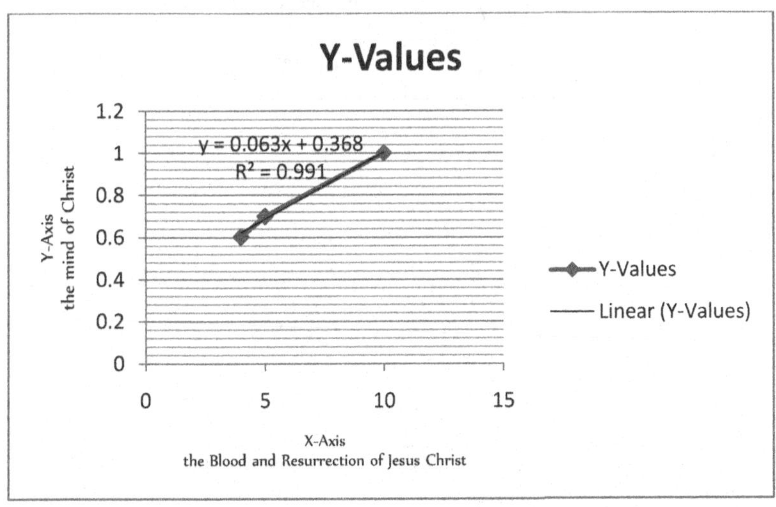

$10^{0.6020}, 10^{0.6989}. 10^{0.6989}, 10^{1}$?

Pilled Poplar, Hazel, and Chestnut bible rods 2

29. But he said, Nay; lest while ye gather up the tares, ye root up also the wheat with them.

3, 1; 7, 8. Bible Matrices

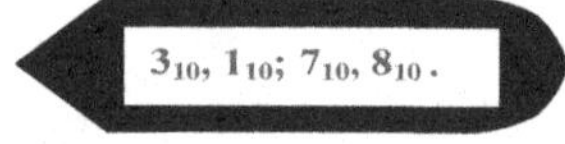

Pilled Poplar, Hazel, and Chestnut bible rods 1

$Log_{10} 3 = 0.4771$ $Log_{10} 1 = 0$ $Log_{10} 7 = 0.8450$ $Log_{10} 8 = 0.9030$

3, 1; 7, 8. Deep calls unto Deep study bible 1

0.4771, 0; 0.8450, 0.9030.

Deep calls unto Deep study bible 2

x-axis	y-axis
3	0.4771
1	0
7	0.8450
8	0.9030

Water Spout *(lightning; combinatorics)* Study bible 1

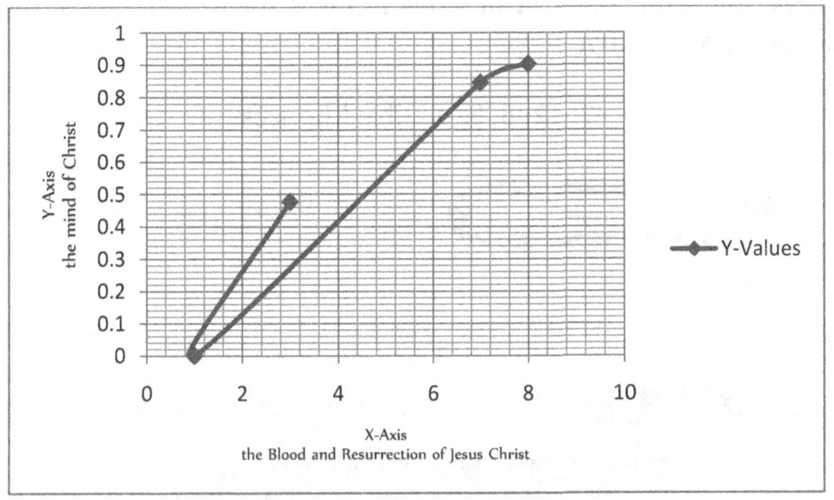

Water Spout *(lightning; combinatorics)* Study bible 2

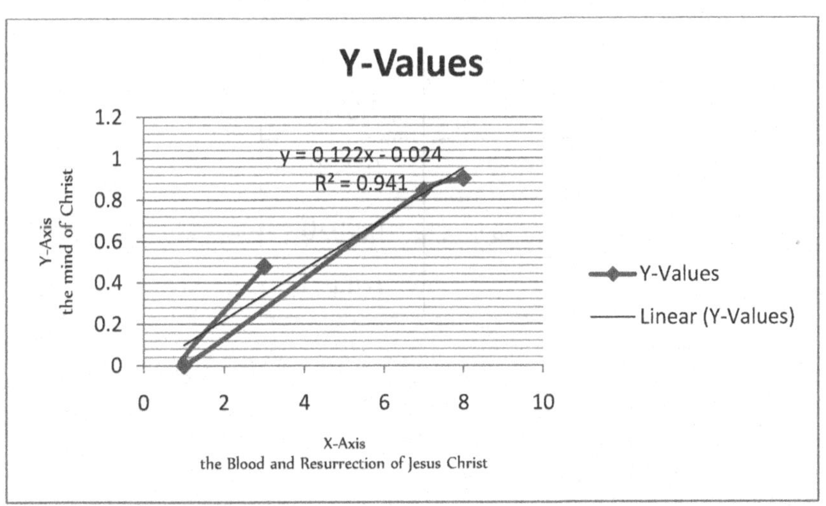

$10^{0.4771}$, 10^{0}; $10^{0.8450}$, $10^{0.9030}$.

Pilled Poplar, Hazel, and Chestnut bible rods 2

30. Let both grow together until the harvest: and in the time of harvest I will say to the reapers, Gather ye together first the tares, and bind them in bundles to burn them: but gather the wheat into my barn.

7: 12, 6, 8: 7. Bible Matrices

7_{10}: 12_{10}, 6_{10}, 8_{10}: 7_{10}.

Pilled Poplar, Hazel, and Chestnut bible rods 1

$\text{Log}_{10} 12 = 1.0791$ $\text{Log}_{10} 7 = 0.8450$ $\text{Log}_{10} 7 = 0.8450$ $\text{Log}_{10} 6 = 0.7781$ $\text{Log}_{10} 8 = 0.9030$

7: 12, 6, 8: 7. Deep calls unto Deep study bible 1

0.8450: 1.0791, 0.7781, 0.9030: 0.8450.
Deep calls unto Deep study bible 2

x-axis	y-axis
7	0.8450
12	1.0791
6	0.7781
8	0.9030
7	0.8450

Water Spout *(lightning; combinatorics)* Study bible 1

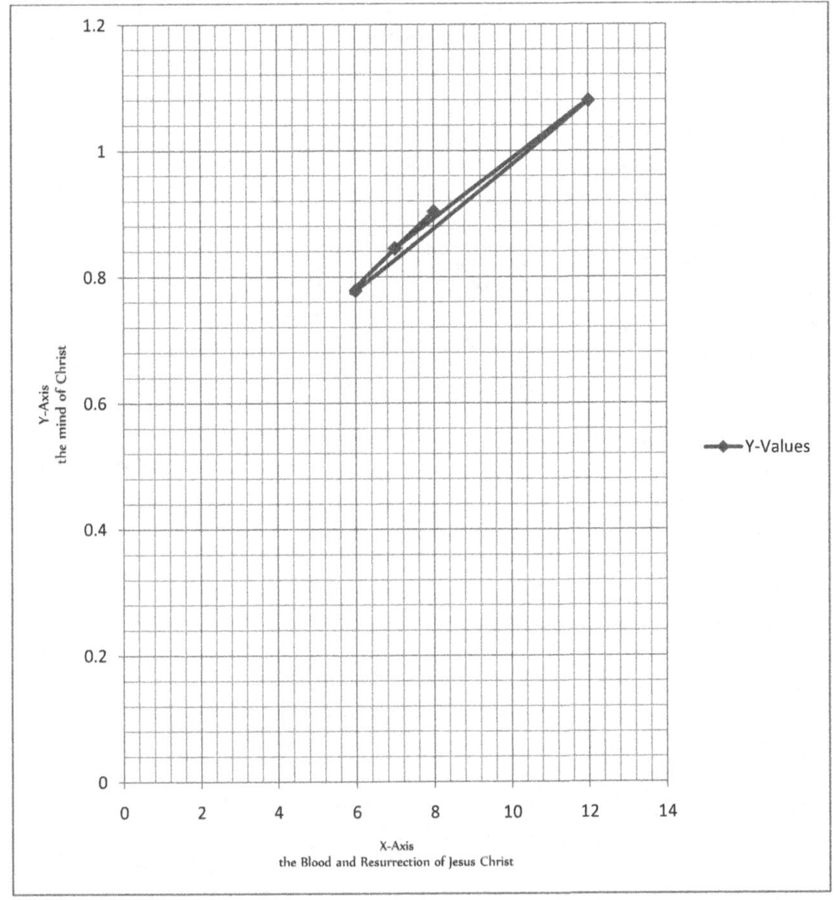

Water Spout *(lightning; combinatorics)* Study bible 2

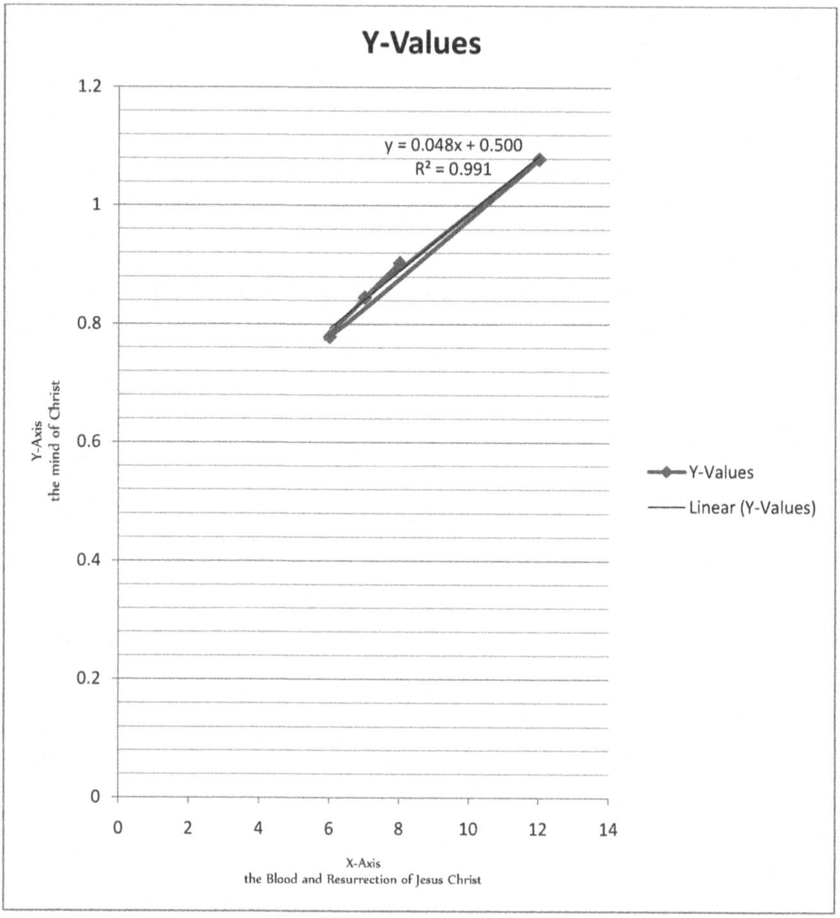
Y-Values
1.2
1
0.8
0.6
0.4
0.2
0
0
2
4
6
8
10
12
14
y = 0.048x + 0.500
R² = 0.991
Y-Axis
the mind of Christ
X-Axis
the Blood and Resurrection of Jesus Christ
Y-Values
Linear (Y-Values)

$10^{0.8450}$: $10^{1.0791}$, $10^{0.7781}$, $10^{0.9030}$: $10^{0.8450}$.

Pilled Poplar, Hazel, and Chestnut bible rods 2

31. Another parable put he forth unto them, saying, The kingdom of heaven is like to a grain of mustard seed, which a man took, and sowed in his field:

7, 1, 12, 4, 5: Bible Matrices

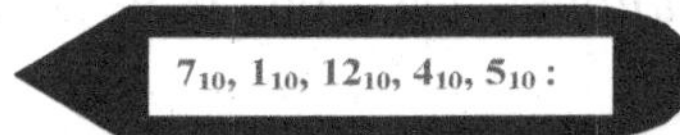

Pilled Poplar, Hazel, and Chestnut bible rods 1

$\text{Log}_{10} 7 = 0.8450 \quad \text{Log}_{10} 5 = 0.6989 \quad \text{Log}_{10} 1 = 0 \quad \text{Log}_{10} 4 = 0.6020 \quad \text{Log}_{10} 12 = 1.0791$

7, 1, 12, 4, 5: Deep calls unto Deep study bible 1

0.8450, 0, 1.0791, 0.6020, 0.6989:
Deep calls unto Deep study bible 2

x-axis	y-axis
7	0.8450
1	0
12	1.0791
4	0.6020
5	0.6989

Water Spout *(lightning; combinatorics)* Study bible 1

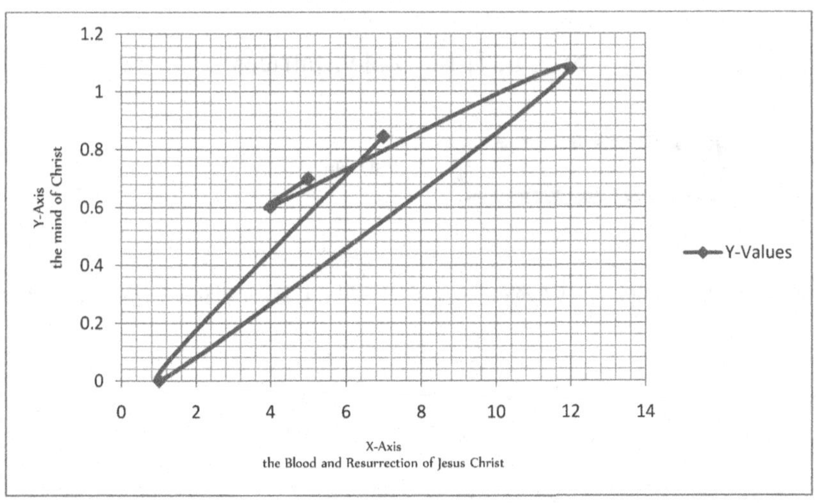

Water Spout *(lightning; combinatorics)* Study bible 2

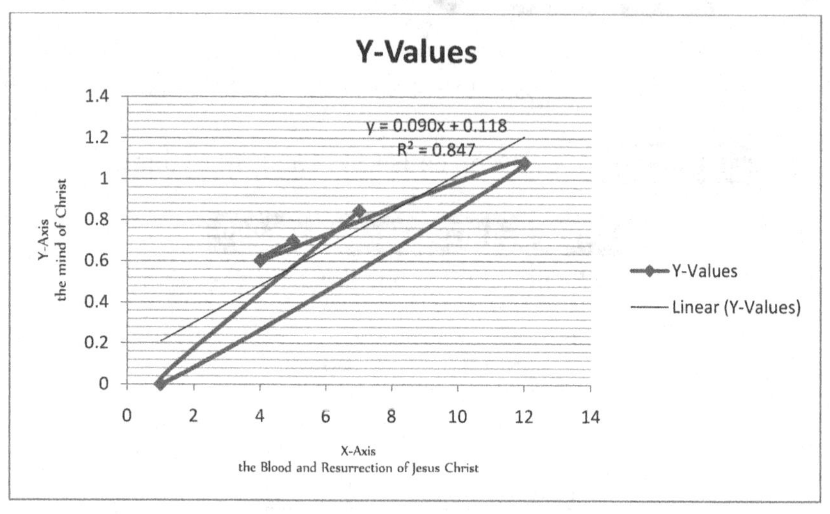

$10^{0.8450}, 10^{0}, 10^{1.0791}, 10^{0.6020}, 10^{0.6989}$: Pilled Poplar, Hazel, and Chestnut bible rods 2

32. Which indeed is the least of all seeds: but when it is grown, it is the greatest among herbs, and becometh a tree, so that the birds of the air come and lodge in the branches thereof.

8: 5, 6, 4, 14. Bible Matrices

$8_{10}: 5_{10}, 6_{10}, 4_{10}, 14_{10}.$ Pilled Poplar, Hazel, and Chestnut bible rods 1

$\text{Log}_{10} 14 = 1.1461$ $\text{Log}_{10} 5 = 0.6989$ $\text{Log}_{10} 6 = 0.7781$ $\text{Log}_{10} 4 = 0.6020$ $\text{Log}_{10} 8 = 0.9030$

8: 5, 6, 4, 14. Deep calls unto Deep study bible 1

0.9030: 0.6989, 0.7781, 0.6020, 1.1461.
Deep calls unto Deep study bible 2

x-axis	y-axis
8	0.9030
5	0.6989
6	0.7781
4	0.6020
14	1.1461

Water Spout *(lightning; combinatorics)* Study bible 1

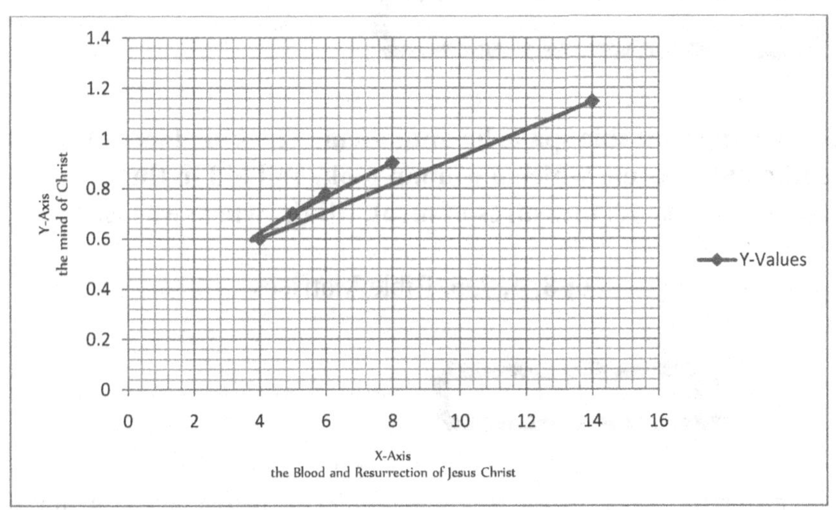

Water Spout *(lightning; combinatorics)* Study bible 2

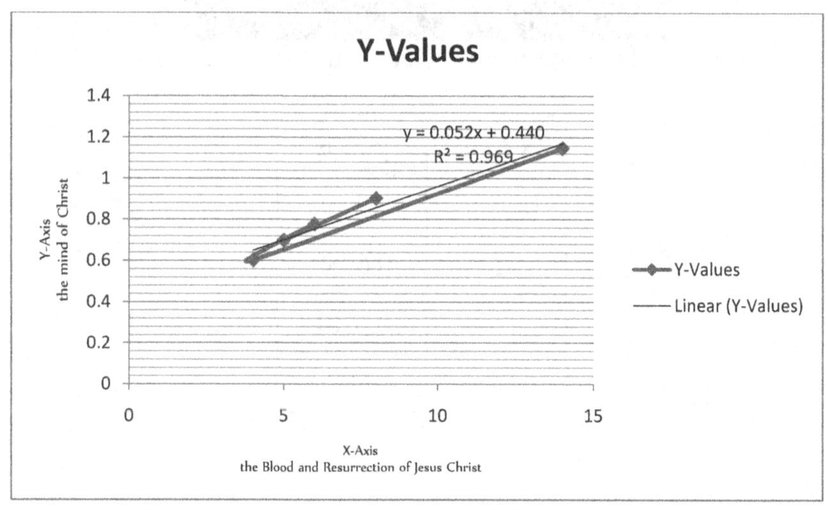

$10^{0.9030}$: $10^{0.6989}$, $10^{0.7781}$, $10^{0.6020}$, $10^{1.1461}$.

Pilled Poplar, Hazel, and Chestnut bible rods 2

33. Another parable spake he unto them; The kingdom of heaven is like unto leaven, which a woman took, and hid in three **completion or perfection, and unity; 3 x 1** **measures of meal, till the whole was leavened.**

6; 8, 4, 7, 5. Bible Matrices

6_{10}; 8_{10}, 4_{10}, 4_7 3_{10}, 5_{10}.

Pilled Poplar, Hazel, and Chestnut bible rods 1

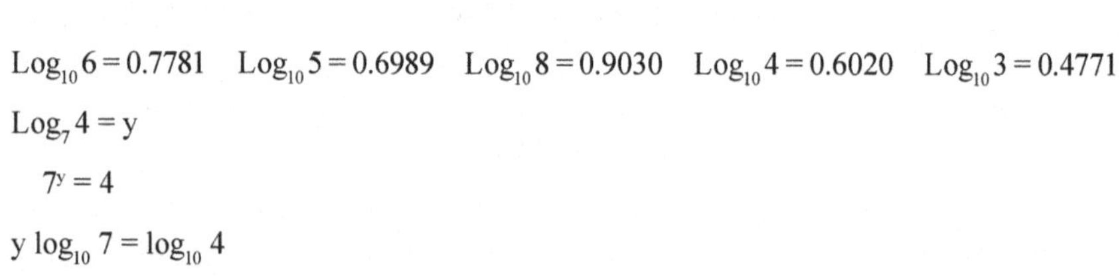
$\mathrm{Log}_{10}6 = 0.7781$ $\mathrm{Log}_{10}5 = 0.6989$ $\mathrm{Log}_{10}8 = 0.9030$ $\mathrm{Log}_{10}4 = 0.6020$ $\mathrm{Log}_{10}3 = 0.4771$

$\mathrm{Log}_7 4 = y$

$7^y = 4$

$y \log_{10} 7 = \log_{10} 4$

$y = \log_{10} 4 / \log_{10} 7$

$y = 0.6020 / 0.8450$

$y = 0.7124$

6; 8, 4, 7, 5. Deep calls unto Deep study bible 1

0.7781; 0.9030, 0.6020, 0.7124 0.4771, 0.6989.
Deep calls unto Deep study bible 2

x-axis	y-axis
6	0.7781
8	0.9030
4	0.6020
7	1.1895
5	0.6989

Water Spout *(lightning; combinatorics)* Study bible 1

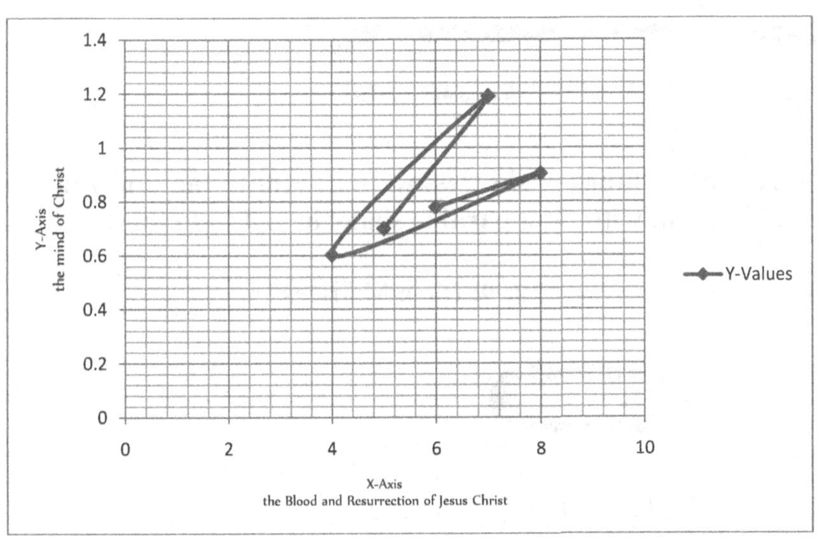

Water Spout *(lightning; combinatorics)* Study bible 2

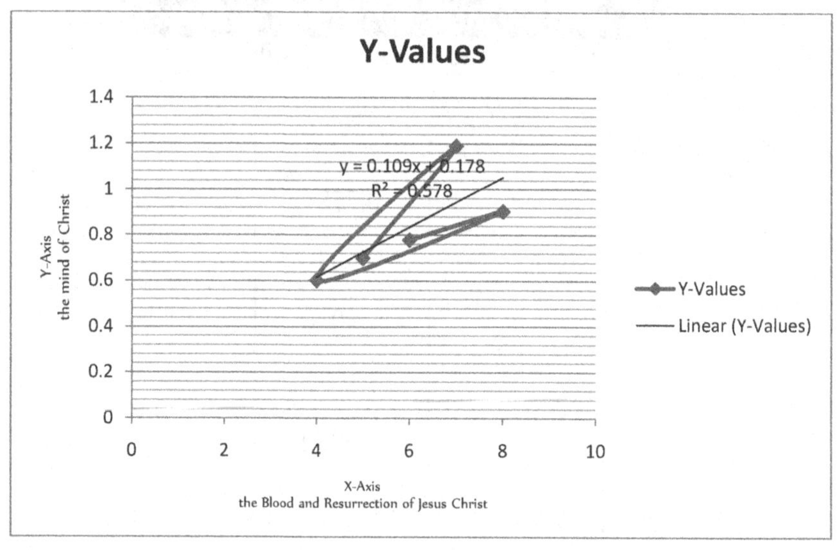

Pilled Poplar, Hazel, and Chestnut bible rods 2

34. All these things spake Jesussavior; deliverer**unto the multitude in parables; and without a parable spake he not unto them:**

10; 9: Bible Matrices

5_2 5_{10}; 9_{10} :

Pilled Poplar, Hazel, and Chestnut bible rods 1

$\mathrm{Log}_{10} 9 = 0.9542$ $\mathrm{Log}_{10} 5 = 0.6989$

$\mathrm{Log}_2 5 = y$

$2^y = 5$

$y \log_{10} 2 = \log_{10} 5$

$y = \log_{10} 5 / \log_{10} 2$

$y = 0.6989 / 0.3010$

$y = 2.3219$

10; 9: Deep calls unto Deep study bible 1

2.3219 0.6989; 0.9542: Deep calls unto Deep study bible 2

x-axis	y-axis
10	3.0208
9	0.9542

Water Spout *(lightning; combinatorics)* Study bible 1

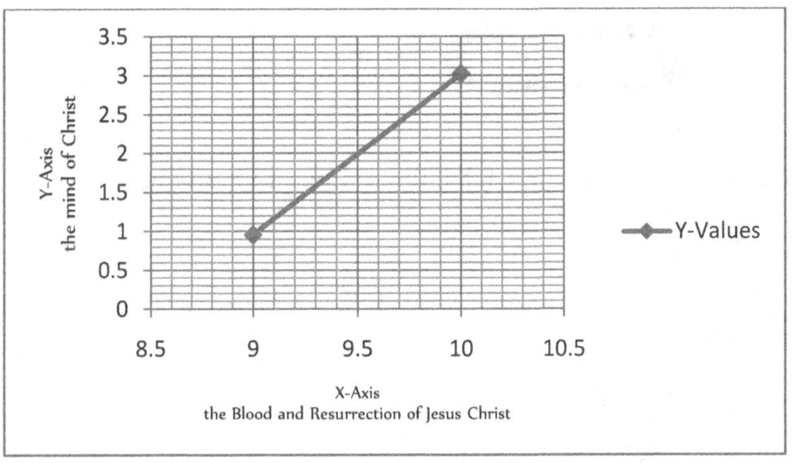

Water Spout *(lightning; combinatorics)* Study bible 2

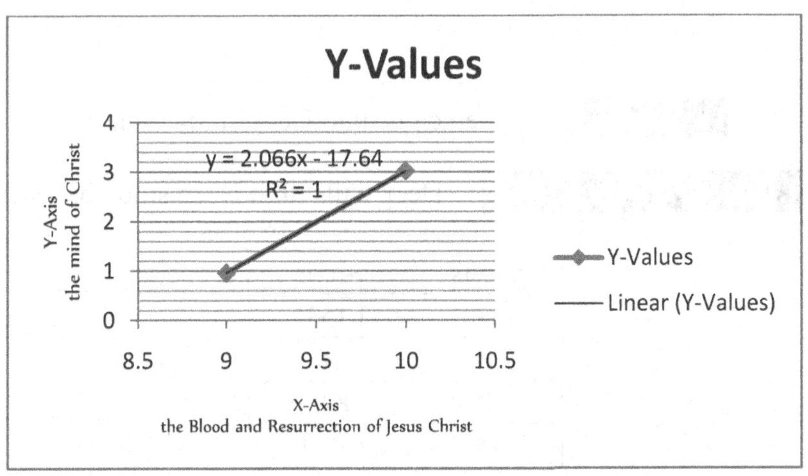

$2^{2.3219}$ $10^{0.6989}$; $10^{0.9542}$: Pilled Poplar, Hazel, and Chestnut bible rods 2

35. That it might be fulfilled which was spoken by the prophet to bubble forth, as from a fountain; utter, **saying, I will open my mouth in parables; I will utter things which have been kept secret from the foundation of the world.**

11, 1, 7; 15. Bible Matrices

11_8, 1_{10}, 7_{10}; 15_{10}. Pilled Poplar, Hazel, and Chestnut bible rods 1

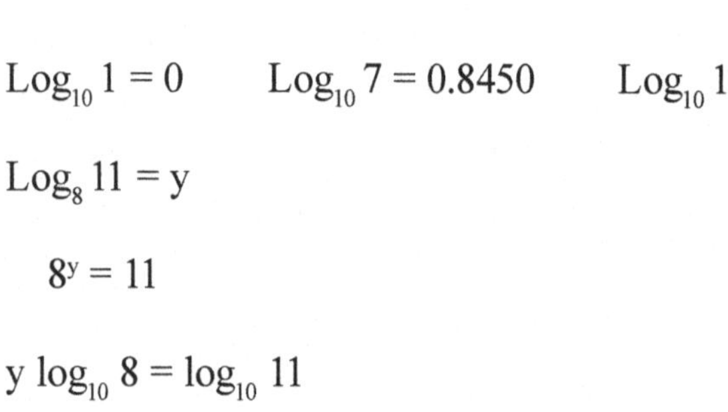

$\text{Log}_{10}\, 1 = 0 \qquad \text{Log}_{10}\, 7 = 0.8450 \qquad \text{Log}_{10}\, 15 = 1.1760$

$\text{Log}_8\, 11 = y$

$8^y = 11$

$y \log_{10} 8 = \log_{10} 11$

$y = \log_{10} 11 / \log_{10} 8$

$y = 1.0413 / 0.9030$

$y = 1.1531$

11, 1, 7; 15. Deep calls unto Deep study bible 1

1.1531, 0, 0.8450; 1.1760. Deep calls unto Deep study bible 2

x-axis	y-axis
11	1.1531
1	0
7	0.8450
15	1.1760

Water Spout *(lightning; combinatorics)* Study bible 1

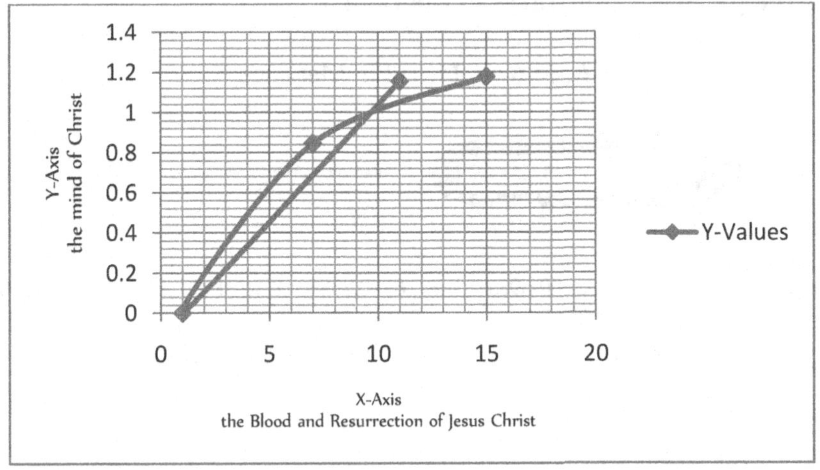

Water Spout *(lightning; combinatorics)* Study bible 2

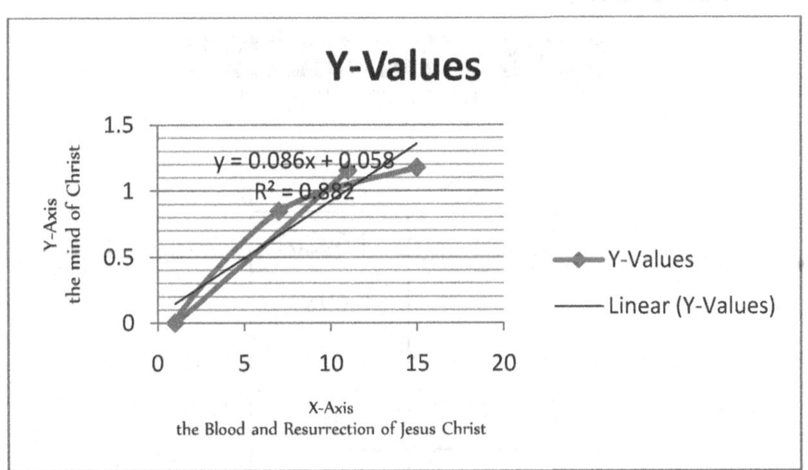

$8^{1.1531}, 10^{0}, 10^{0.8450}; 10^{1.1760}$.

Pilled Poplar, Hazel, and Chestnut bible rods 2

36. Then Jesussavior; deliverer **sent the multitude away, and went into the house: and his disciples came unto him, saying, Declare unto us the parable of the tares of the field.**

6, 5: 6, 1, 11. Bible Matrices

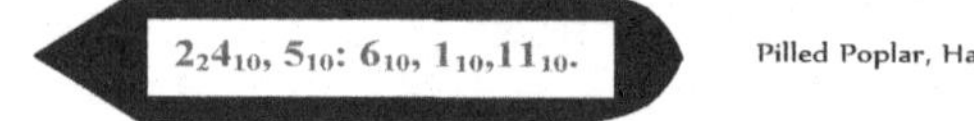

Pilled Poplar, Hazel, and Chestnut bible rods 1

$\text{Log}_{10} 11 = 1.0413$ $\text{Log}_{10} 5 = 0.6989$ $\text{Log}_{10} 6 = 0.7781$ $\text{Log}_{10} 1 = 0$ $\text{Log}_{10} 4 = 0.6020$

$\text{Log}_2 2 = y$

$2^y = 2^1$

$y = 1$

6, 5: 6, 1, 11. Deep calls unto Deep study bible 1

1 0.6020, 0.6989: 0.7781, 0, 1.0413.

Deep calls unto Deep study bible 2

x-axis	y-axis
6	1.6020
5	0.6989
6	0.7781
1	0
11	1.0413

Water Spout *(lightning; combinatorics)* Study bible 1

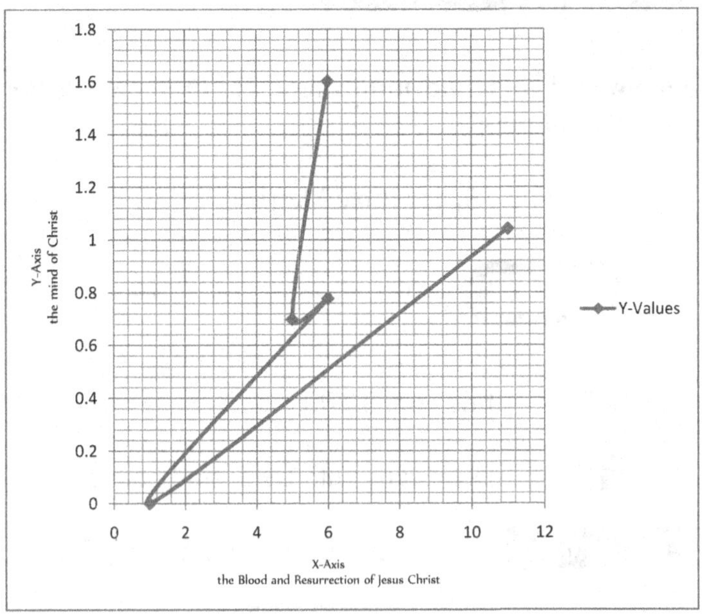

Water Spout *(lightning; combinatorics)* Study bible 2

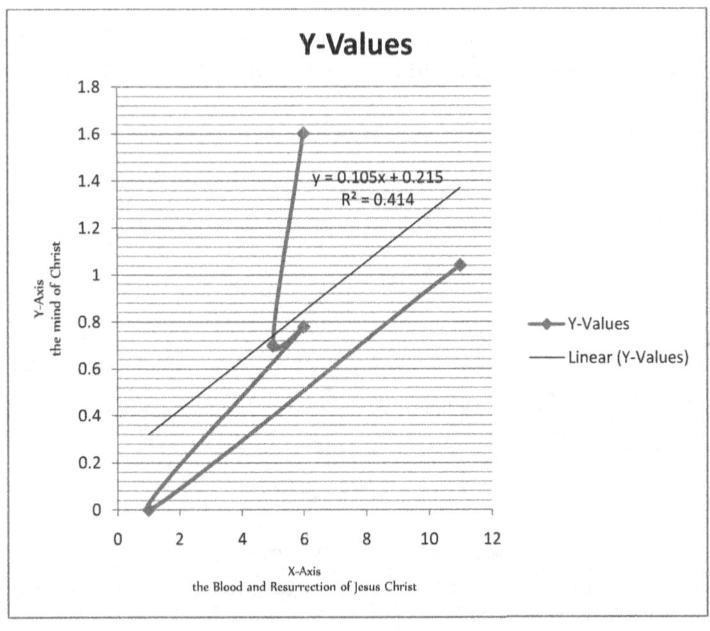

$2^1\ 10^{0.6020}, 10^{0.6989}: 10^{0.7781}, 10^0, 10^{1.0413}.$ Pilled Poplar, Hazel, and Chestnut bible rods 2

37. He answered and said unto them, He that soweth the good seed is the Son of man;

6, 11; Bible Matrices

Pilled Poplar, Hazel, and Chestnut bible rods 1

$Log_{10}\ 11 = 1.0413$ $Log_{10}\ 6 = 0.7781$

6, 11; Deep calls unto Deep study bible 1

0.7781, 1.0413; Deep calls unto Deep study bible 2

x-axis	y-axis
6	0.7781
11	1.0413

Water Spout *(lightning; combinatorics)* Study bible 1

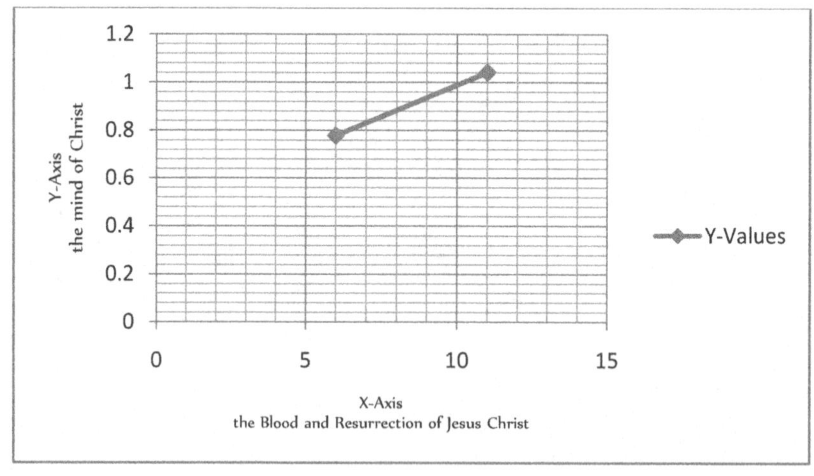

Water Spout *(lightning; combinatorics)* Study bible 2

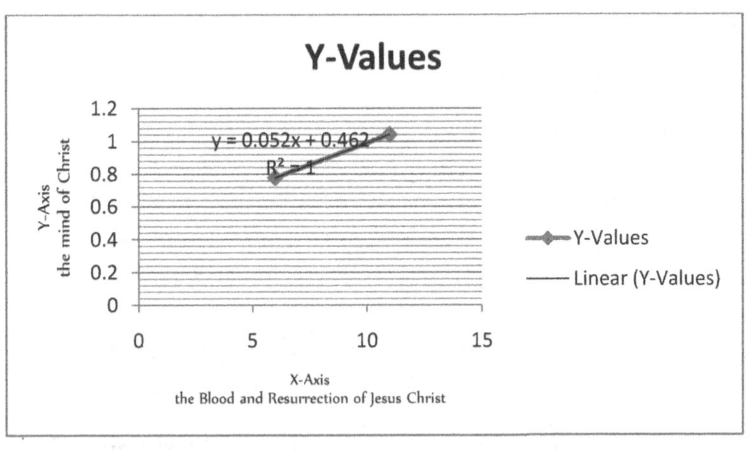

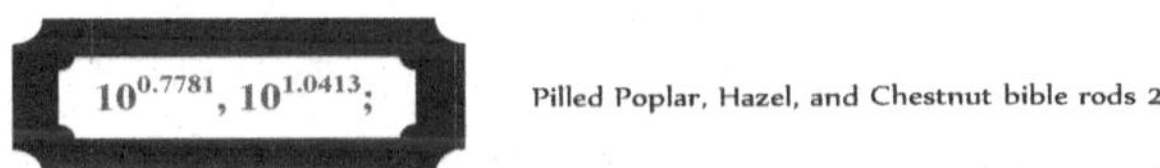

38. The field is the world; the good seed are the children of the kingdom; but the tares are the children of the wicked one;

5; 9; 10; Bible Matrices

5_{10}; 9_{10}; 10_{10} ;

Pilled Poplar, Hazel, and Chestnut bible rods 1

$\text{Log}_{10} 10 = 1$ $\text{Log}_{10} 5 = 0.6989$ $\text{Log}_{10} 9 = 0.9542$

5; 9; 10; Deep calls unto Deep study bible 1

0.6989; 0.9542; 1; Deep calls unto Deep study bible 2

x-axis	y-axis
5	0.6989
9	0.9542
10	1

Water Spout *(lightning; combinatorics)* Study bible 1

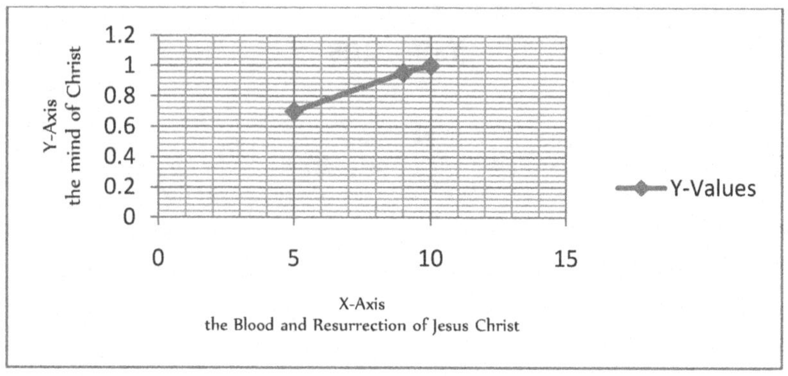

Water Spout *(lightning; combinatorics)* Study bible 2

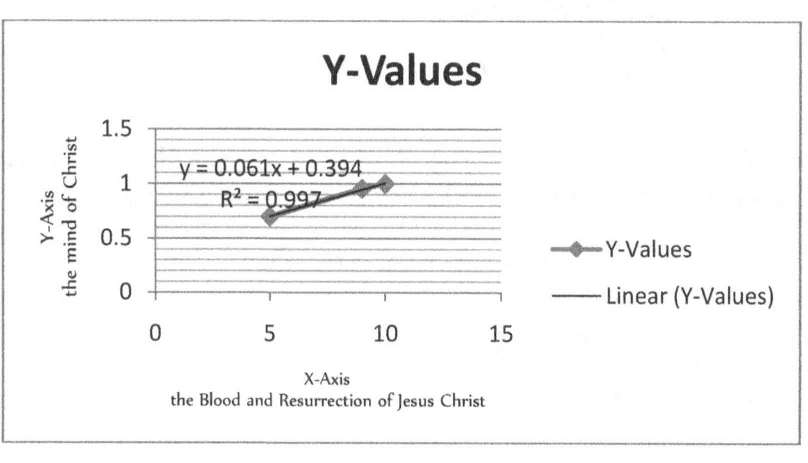

Pilled Poplar, Hazel, and Chestnut bible rods 2

39. The enemy that sowed them is the devil slanderer; false accuser; **the harvest is the end of the world; and the reapers are the angels.**

8; 8; 6. Bible Matrices

8_3; 8_{10}; 6_{10}. Pilled Poplar, Hazel, and Chestnut bible rods 1

$\text{Log}_{10} 8 = 0.9030$ $\text{Log}_{10} 6 = 0.7781$

$\text{Log}_3 8 = y$

$3^y = 8$

$y \log_{10} 3 = \log_{10} 8$

$y = \log_{10} 8 / \log_{10} 3$

$y = 0.9030 / 0.4771$

$y = 1.8926$

8; 8; 6. Deep calls unto Deep study bible 1

1.8926; 0.9030; 0.7781. Deep calls unto Deep study bible 2

x-axis	y-axis
8	1.8926
8	0.9030
6	0.7781

Water Spout *(lightning; combinatorics)* Study bible 1

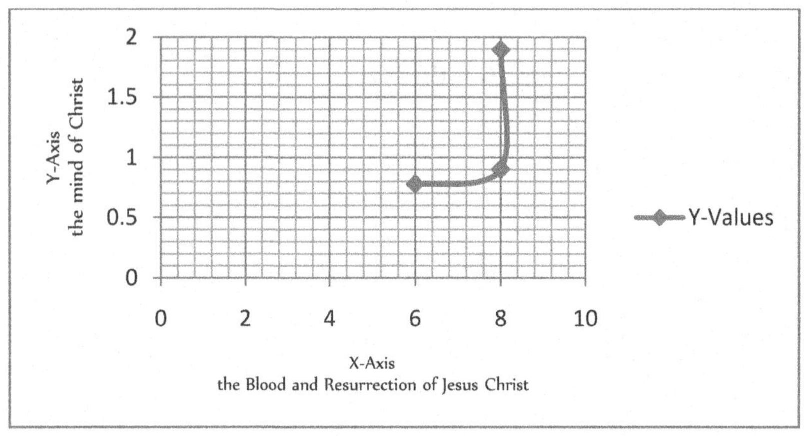

Water Spout *(lightning; combinatorics)* Study bible 2

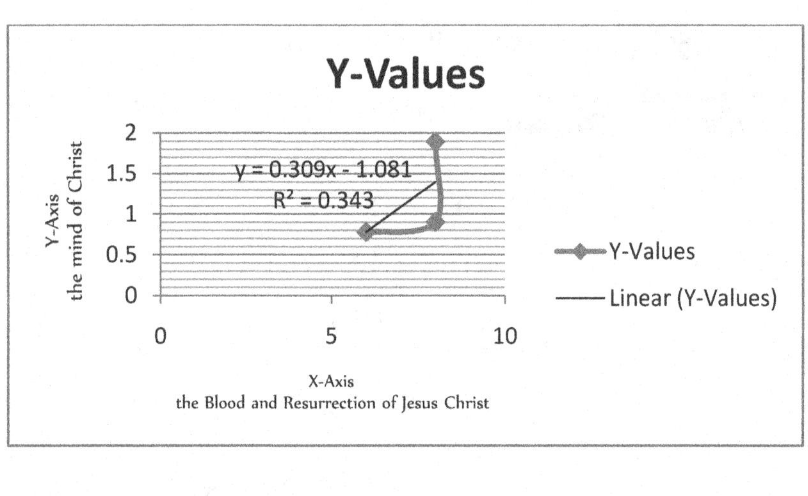

40. As therefore the tares are gathered and burned in the fire; so shall it be in the end of this world.

11; 10. Bible Matrices

Pilled Poplar, Hazel, and Chestnut bible rods 1

$\text{Log}_{10}\,11 = 1.0413$ $\text{Log}_{10}\,10 = 1$

11; 10. Deep calls unto Deep study bible 1

1.0413; 1. Deep calls unto Deep study bible 2

x-axis	y-axis
11	1.0413
10	1

Water Spout *(lightning; combinatorics)* Study bible 1

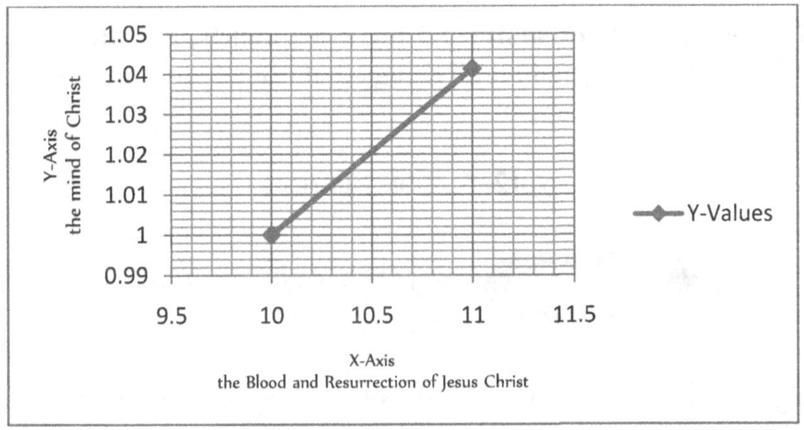

Water Spout *(lightning; combinatorics)* Study bible 2

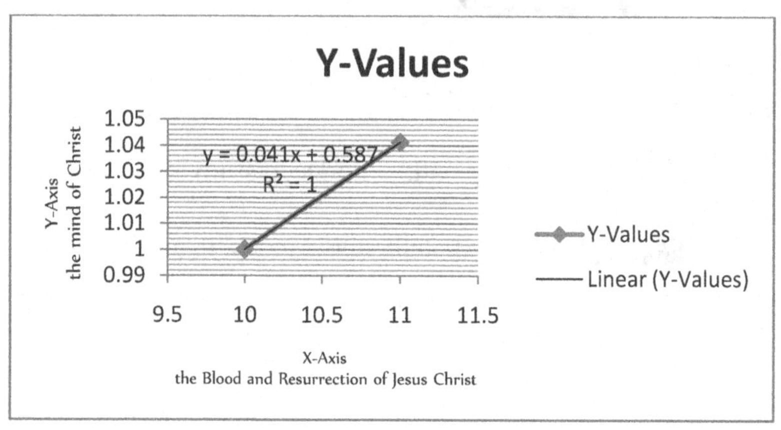

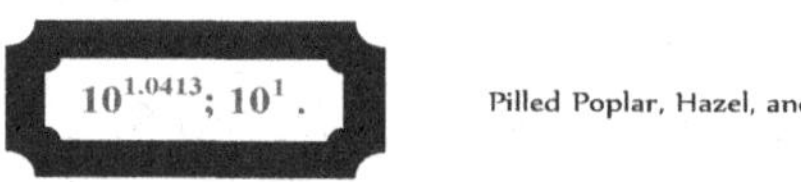

41. The Son of man shall send forth his angels, and they shall gather out of his kingdom all things that offend, and them which do iniquity;

9, 12, 5; Bible Matrices

$\text{Log}_{10} 9 = 0.9542$ $\text{Log}_{10} 5 = 0.6989$ $\text{Log}_{10} 12 = 1.0791$

9, 12, 5; Deep calls unto Deep study bible 1

0.9542, 1.0791, 0.6989; Deep calls unto Deep study bible 2

x-axis	y-axis
9	0.9542
12	1.0791
5	0.6989

Water Spout *(lightning; combinatorics)* Study bible 1

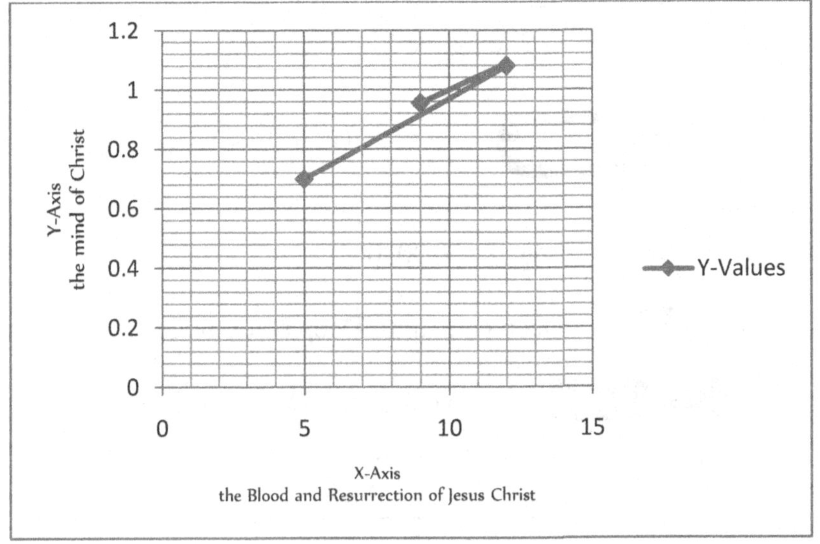

Water Spout *(lightning; combinatorics)* Study bible 2

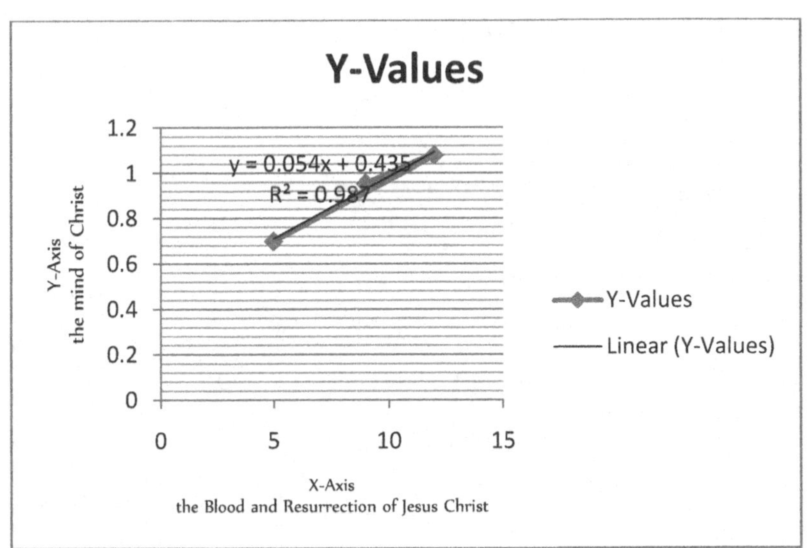

$10^{0.9542}$, $10^{1.0791}$, $10^{0.6989}$;

Pilled Poplar, Hazel, and Chestnut bible rods 2

42. And shall cast them into a furnace of fire: there shall be wailing and gnashing of teeth.

9: 8. Bible Matrices

$\text{Log}_{10} 9 = 0.9542$ $\text{Log}_{10} 8 = 0.9030$

9: 8. Deep calls unto Deep study bible 1

0.9542: 0.9030. Deep calls unto Deep study bible 2

x-axis	y-axis
9	0.9542
8	0.9030

Water Spout *(lightning; combinatorics)* Study bible 1

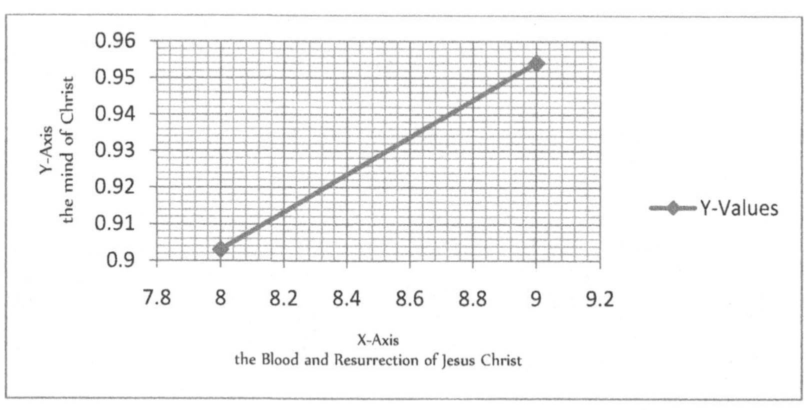

Water Spout *(lightning; combinatorics)* Study bible 2

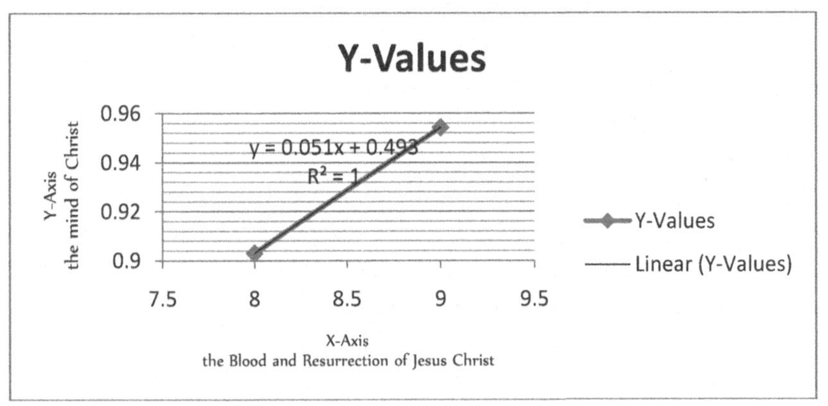

Pilled Poplar, Hazel, and Chestnut bible rods 2

43. Then shall the righteous shine forth as the sun in the kingdom of their Father. Who hath ears to hear, let him hear.

15, 5, 3. Bible Matrices

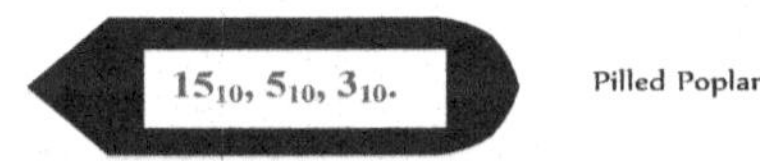

Pilled Poplar, Hazel, and Chestnut bible rods 1

$\text{Log}_{10}\,15 = 1.1760$ $\text{Log}_{10}\,5 = 0.6989$ $\text{Log}_{10}\,3 = 0.4771$

15, 5, 3. Deep calls unto Deep study bible 1

1.1760, 0.6989, 0.4771. Deep calls unto Deep study bible 2

x-axis	y-axis
15	1.1760
5	0.6989
3	0.4771

Water Spout *(lightning; combinatorics)* Study bible 1

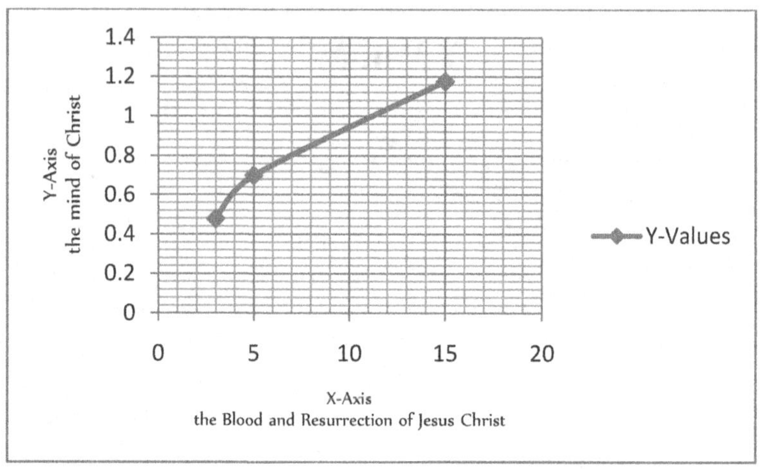

Water Spout *(lightning; combinatorics)* Study bible 2

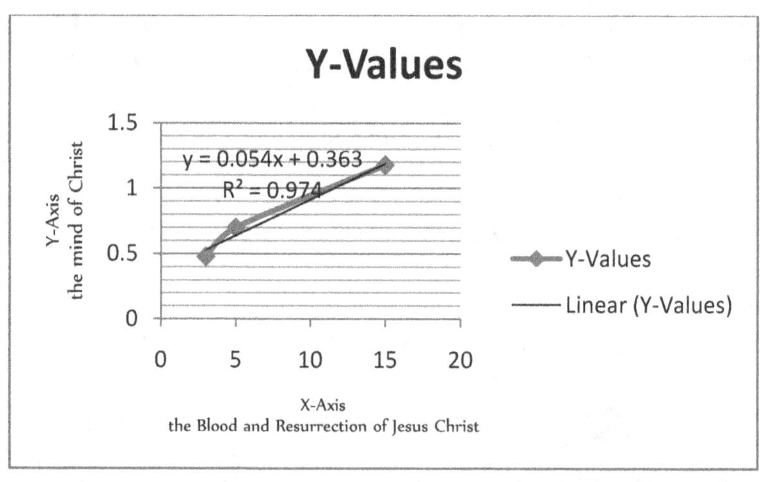

Pilled Poplar, Hazel, and Chestnut bible rods 2

44. Again, the kingdom of heaven is like unto treasure hid in a field; the which when a man hath found, he hideth, and for joy thereof goeth and selleth all that he hath, and buyeth that field.

1, 12; 7, 2, 11, 4. Bible Matrices

$1_{10}, 12_{10}; 7_{10}, 2_{10}, 11_{10}, 4_{10}.$

Pilled Poplar, Hazel, and Chestnut bible rods 1

$\text{Log}_{10} 1 = 0$ $\text{Log}_{10} 11 = 1.0413$ $\text{Log}_{10} 12 = 1.0791$ $\text{Log}_{10} 7 = 0.8450$ $\text{Log}_{10} 2 = 0.3010$ $\text{Log}_{10} 4 = 0.6020$

1, 12; 7, 2, 11, 4. Deep calls unto Deep study bible 1

0, 1.0791; 0.8450, 0.3010, 1.0413, 0.6020.

Deep calls unto Deep study bible 2

x-axis	y-axis
1	0
12	1.0791
7	0.8450
2	0.3010
11	1.0413
4	0.6020

Water Spout *(lightning; combinatorics)* Study bible 1

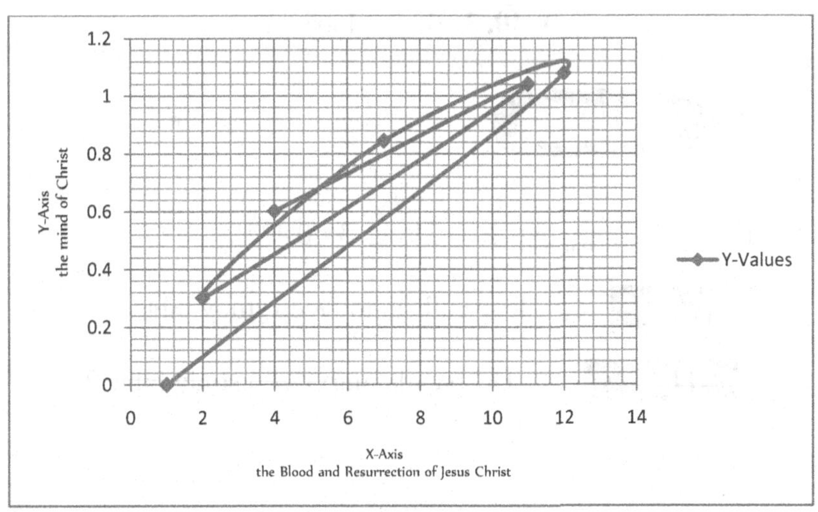

Water Spout *(lightning; combinatorics)* Study bible 2

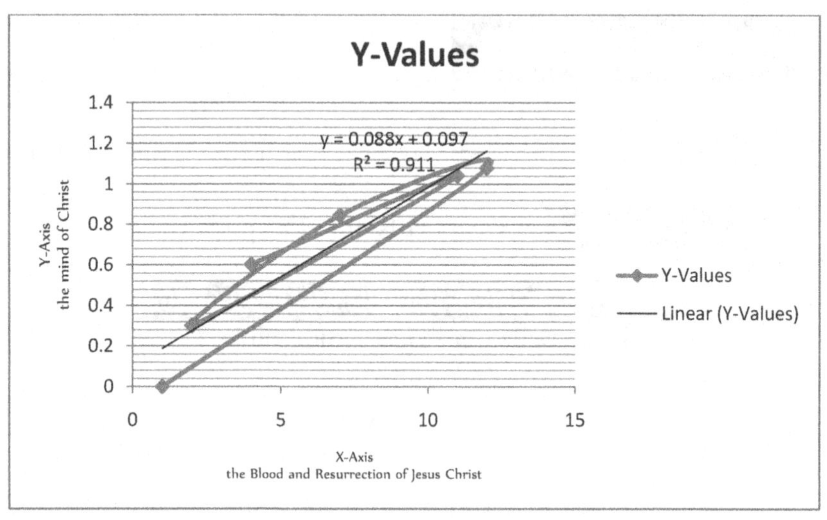

Pilled Poplar, Hazel, and Chestnut bible rods 2

45. Again, the kingdom of heaven is like unto a merchant man, seeking goodly pearls:

1, 10, 3: Bible Matrices

$\text{Log}_{10} 1 = 0$ $\text{Log}_{10} 10 = 1$ $\text{Log}_{10} 3 = 0.4771$

1, 10, 3: Deep calls unto Deep study bible 1

0, 1, 0.4771: Deep calls unto Deep study bible 2

x-axis	y-axis
1	0
10	1
3	0.4771

Water Spout *(lightning; combinatorics)* Study bible 1

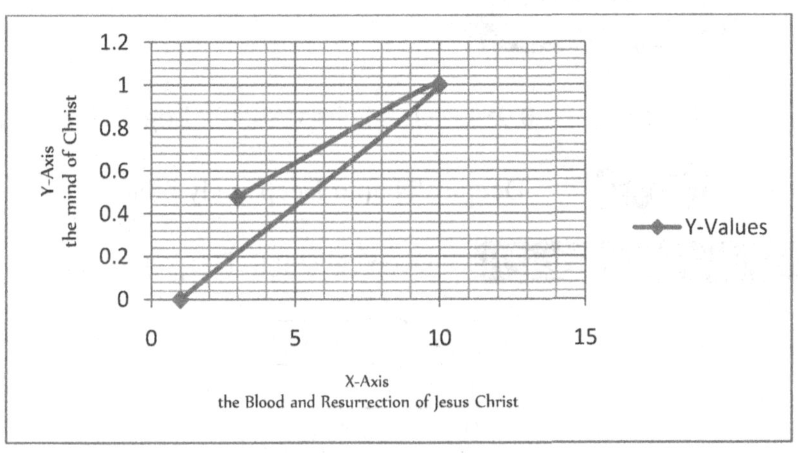

Water Spout *(lightning; combinatorics)* Study bible 2

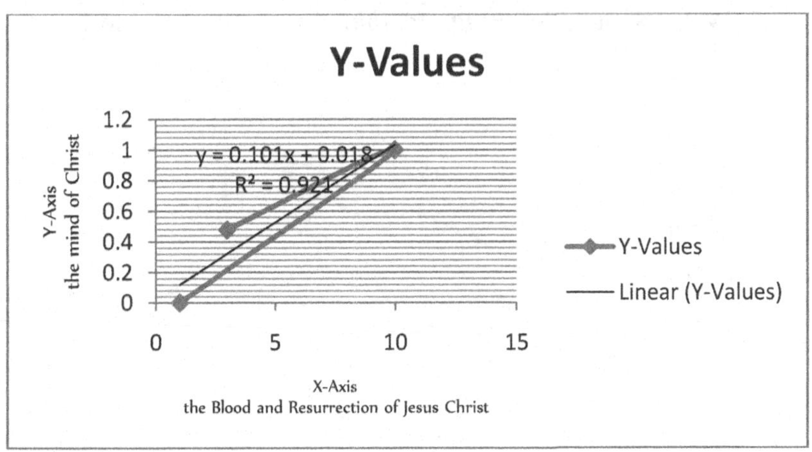

$10^0, 10^1, 10^{0.4771}$: Pilled Poplar, Hazel, and Chestnut bible rods 2

46. Who, when he had found one pearl of great price, went and sold all that he had, and bought it.

1, 9, 7, 3. Bible Matrices

$\mathrm{Log}_{10} 1 = 0$ $\mathrm{Log}_{10} 9 = 0.9542$ $\mathrm{Log}_{10} 7 = 0.8450$ $\mathrm{Log}_{10} 3 = 0.4771$

1, 9, 7, 3. Deep calls unto Deep study bible 1

0, 0.9542, 0.8450, 0.4771. Deep calls unto Deep study bible 2

x-axis	y-axis
1	0
9	0.9542
7	0.8450
3	0.4771

Water Spout *(lightning; combinatorics)* Study bible 1

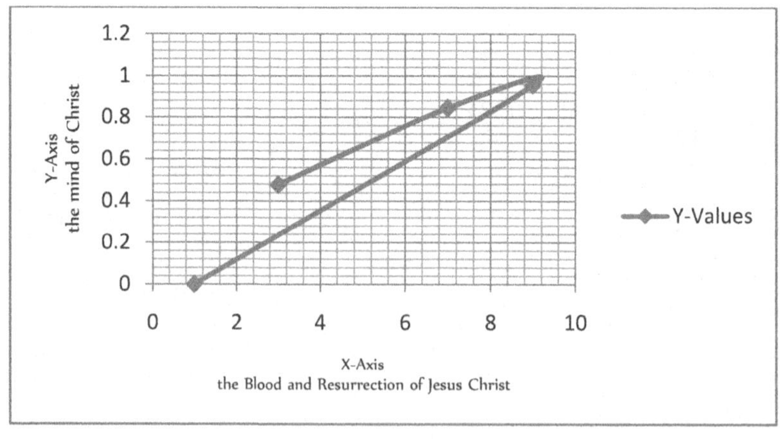

Water Spout *(lightning; combinatorics)* Study bible 2

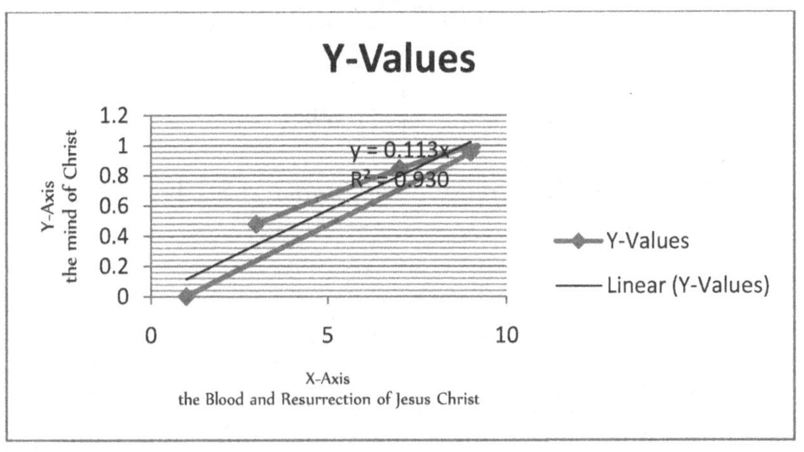

10^{0}, $10^{0.9542}$, $10^{0.8450}$, $10^{0.4771}$.

Pilled Poplar, Hazel, and Chestnut bible rods 2

47. Again, the kingdom of heaven is like unto a net, that was cast into the sea, and gathered of every kind:

1, 9, 6, 5: Bible Matrices

Pilled Poplar, Hazel, and Chestnut bible rods 1

$\text{Log}_{10} 1 = 0$ $\text{Log}_{10} 5 = 0.6989$ $\text{Log}_{10} 9 = 0.9542$ $\text{Log}_{10} 6 = 0.7781$

1, 9, 6, 5: Deep calls unto Deep study bible 1

0, 0.9542, 0.7781, 0.6989:

Deep calls unto Deep study bible 2

x-axis	y-axis
1	0
9	0.9542
6	0.7781
5	0.6989

Water Spout *(lightning; combinatorics)* Study bible 1

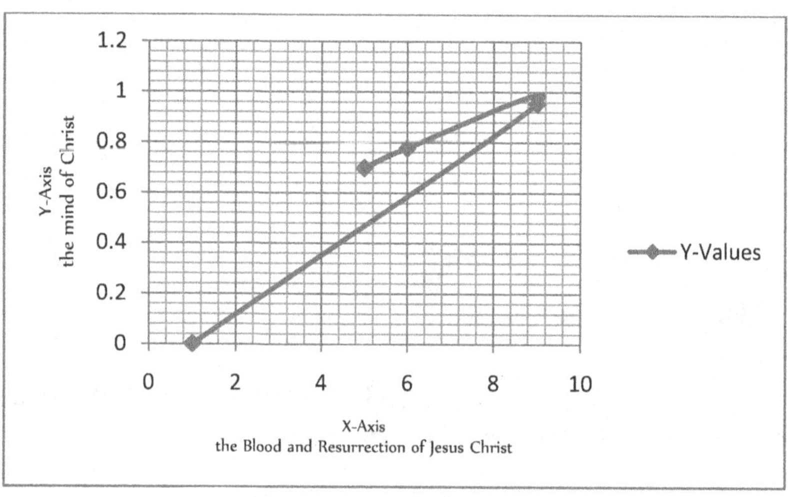

Water Spout *(lightning; combinatorics)* Study bible 2

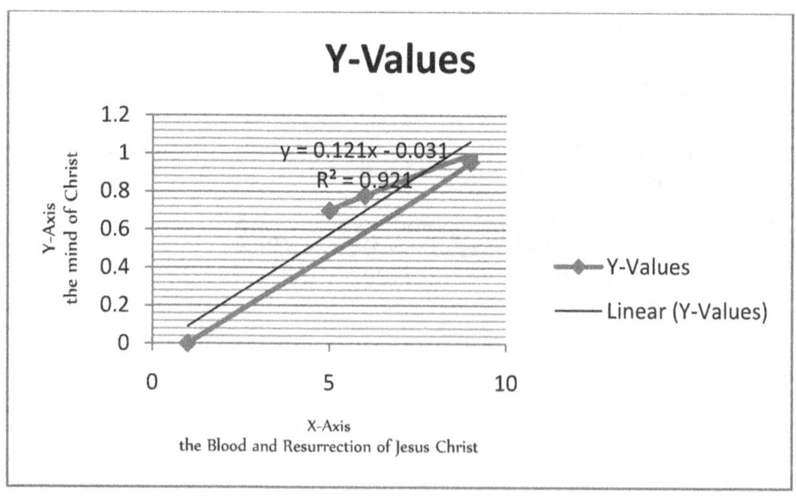

$10^{0}, 10^{0.9542}, 10^{0.7781}, 10^{0.6989}$:

Pilled Poplar, Hazel, and Chestnut bible rods 2

48. Which, when it was full, they drew to shore, and sat down, and gathered the good into vessels, but cast the bad away.

1, 4, 4, 3, 6, 5. Bible Matrices

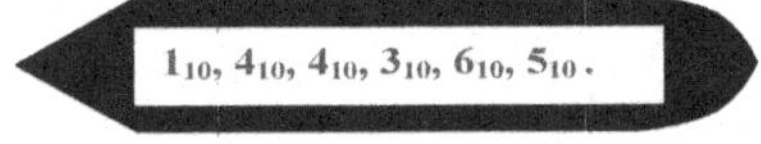

Pilled Poplar, Hazel, and Chestnut bible rods 1

$\text{Log}_{10} 1 = 0$ $\text{Log}_{10} 5 = 0.6989$ $\text{Log}_{10} 4 = 0.6020$ $\text{Log}_{10} 4 = 0.6020$ $\text{Log}_{10} 6 = 0.7781$ $\text{Log}_{10} 3 = 0.4771$

1, 4, 4, 3, 6, 5. Deep calls unto Deep study bible 1

0, 0.6020, 0.6020, 0.4771, 0.7781, 0.6989.

Deep calls unto Deep study bible 2

x-axis	y-axis
1	0
4	0.6020
4	0.6020
3	0.4771
6	0.7781
5	0.6989

Water Spout *(lightning; combinatorics)* Study bible 1

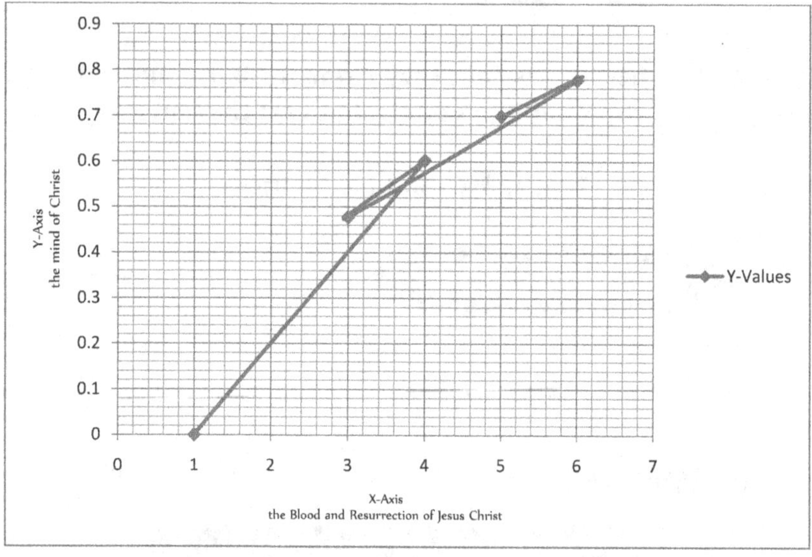

Water Spout (lightning; combinatorics) Study bible 2

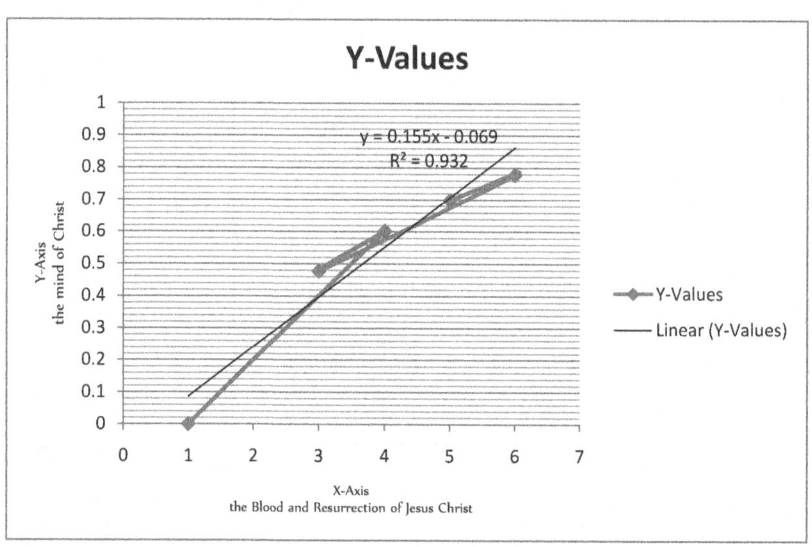

10^0, $10^{0.6020}$, $10^{0.6020}$, $10^{0.4771}$, $10^{0.7781}$, $10^{0.6989}$.

Pilled Poplar, Hazel, and Chestnut bible rods 2

49. So shall it be at the end of the world: the angels shall come forth, and sever the wicked from among the just,

10: 5, 8, Bible Matrices

$\text{Log}_{10} 10 = 1$ $\text{Log}_{10} 5 = 0.6989$ $\text{Log}_{10} 8 = 0.9030$

10: 5, 8, Deep calls unto Deep study bible 1

1, 0.6989, 0.9030, Deep calls unto Deep study bible 2

x-axis	y-axis
10	1
5	0.6989
8	0.9030

Water Spout *(lightning; combinatorics)* Study bible 1

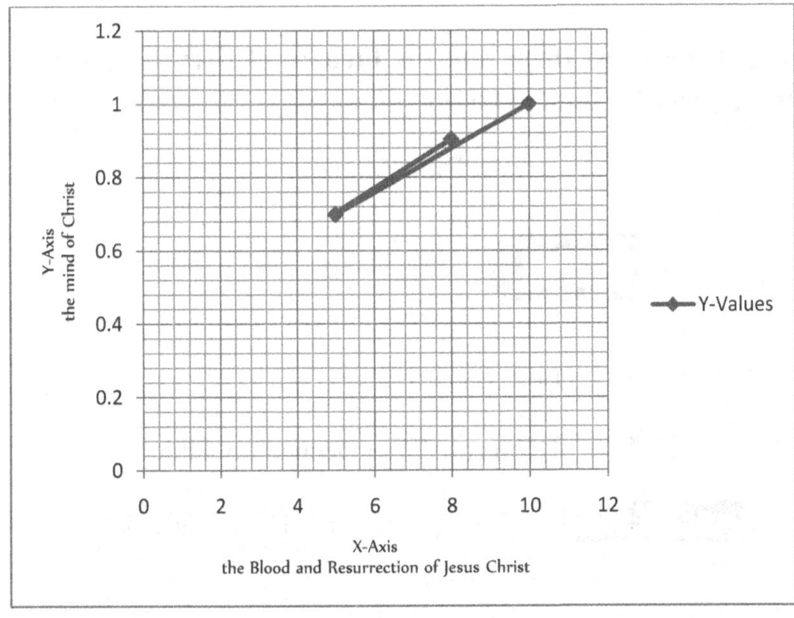

Water Spout *(lightning; combinatorics)* Study bible 2

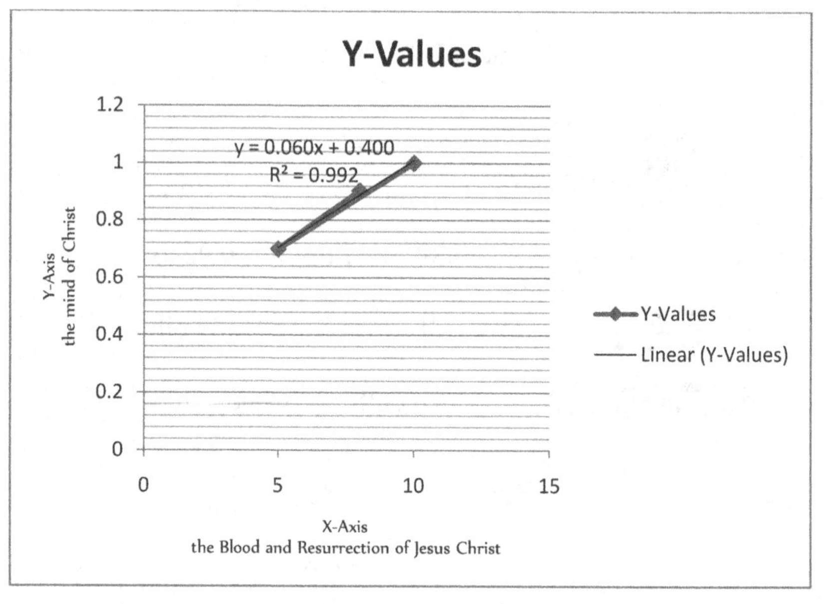

$10^1: 10^{0.6989}, 10^{0.9030},$

Pilled Poplar, Hazel, and Chestnut bible rods 2

50. And shall cast them into the furnace of fire: there shall be wailing and gnashing of teeth.

9: 8. Bible Matrices

$\text{Log}_{10} 9 = 0.9542$ $\text{Log}_{10} 8 = 0.9030$

9: 8. Deep calls unto Deep study bible 1

0.9542: 0.9030. Deep calls unto Deep study bible 2

x-axis	y-axis
9	0.9542
8	0.9030

Water Spout *(lightning; combinatorics)* Study bible 1

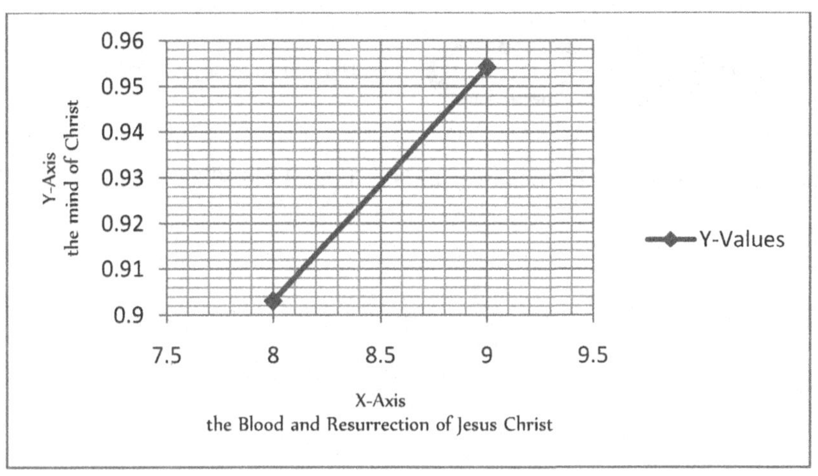

Water Spout *(lightning; combinatorics)* Study bible 2

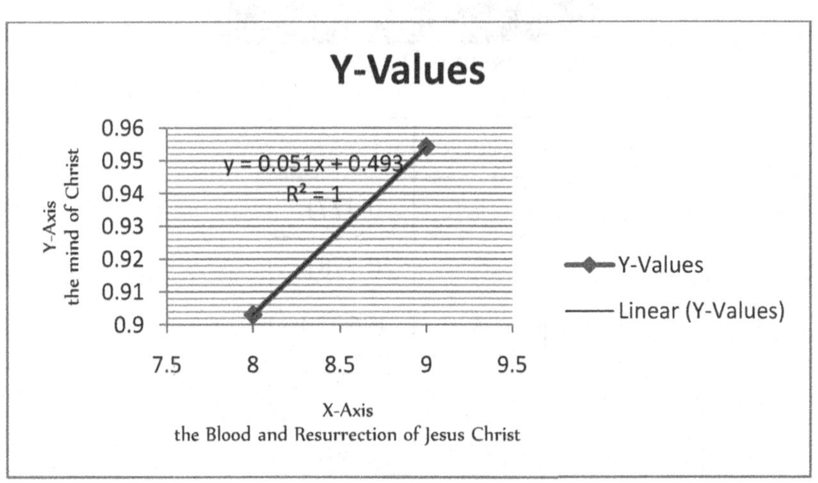

Pilled Poplar, Hazel, and Chestnut bible rods 2

51. Jesussavior; deliverer**saith unto them, Have ye understood all these things? They say unto him, Yea, Lord.**

4, 6? 4, 1, 1. Bible Matrices

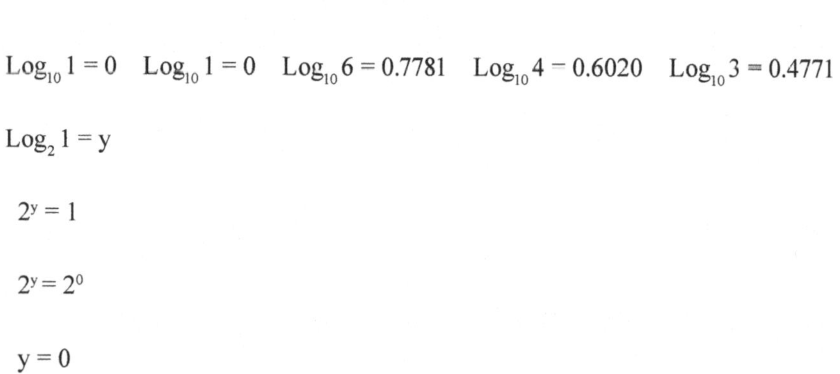

Pilled Poplar, Hazel, and Chestnut bible rods 1

$\text{Log}_{10} 1 = 0$ $\text{Log}_{10} 1 = 0$ $\text{Log}_{10} 6 = 0.7781$ $\text{Log}_{10} 4 = 0.6020$ $\text{Log}_{10} 3 = 0.4771$

$\text{Log}_2 1 = y$

$2^y = 1$

$2^y = 2^0$

$y = 0$

4, 6? 4, 1, 1. Deep calls unto Deep study bible 1

0, 0.4771, 0.7781? 0.6020, 0, 0.
Deep calls unto Deep study bible 2

x-axis	y-axis
4	0.4771
6	0.7781
4	0.6020
1	0
1	0

Water Spout *(lightning; combinatorics)* Study bible 1

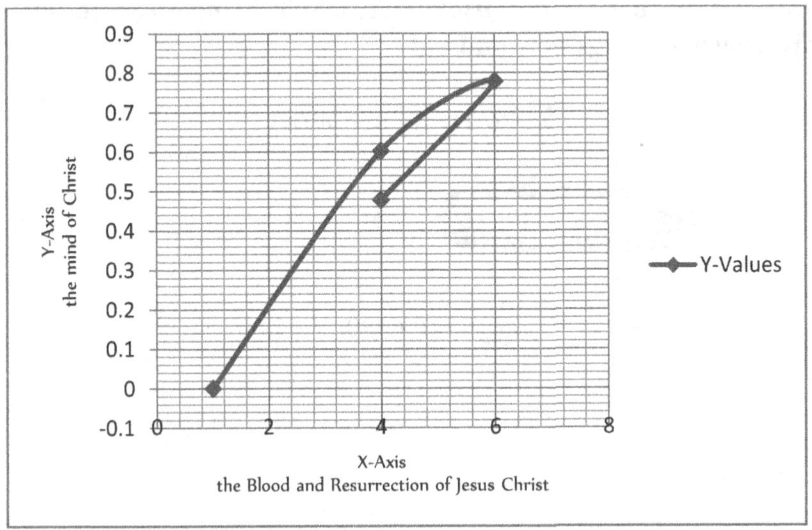

Water Spout *(lightning; combinatorics)* Study bible 2

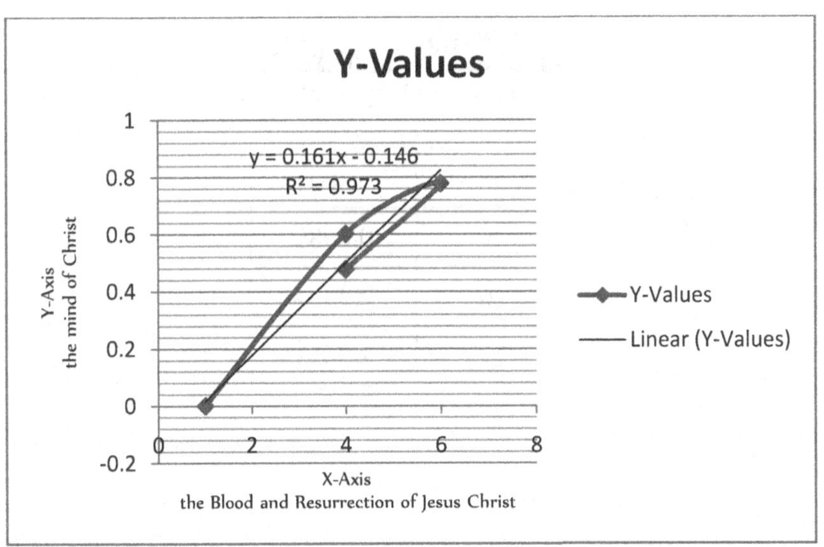

$2^0\ 10^{0.4771},\ 10^{0.7781}?\ 10^{0.6020},\ 10^0,\ 10^0.$

Pilled Poplar, Hazel, and Chestnut bible rods 2

52. Then said he unto them, Therefore every scribe lawyer; copyist; transcriber **which is instructed unto the kingdom of heaven is like unto a man that is an householder, which bringeth forth out of his treasure things new and old.**

5, 20, 11. Bible Matrices

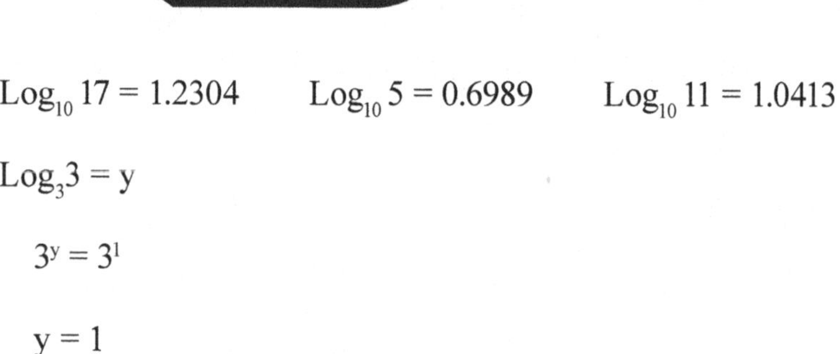

Pilled Poplar, Hazel, and Chestnut bible rods 1

$\text{Log}_{10} 17 = 1.2304$ $\text{Log}_{10} 5 = 0.6989$ $\text{Log}_{10} 11 = 1.0413$

$\text{Log}_3 3 = y$

$3^y = 3^1$

$y = 1$

5, 20, 11. Deep calls unto Deep study bible 1

0.6989, 1 1.2304, 1.0413.

Deep calls unto Deep study bible 2

x-axis	y-axis
5	0.6989
20	2.2304
11	1.0413

Water Spout *(lightning; combinatorics)* Study bible 1

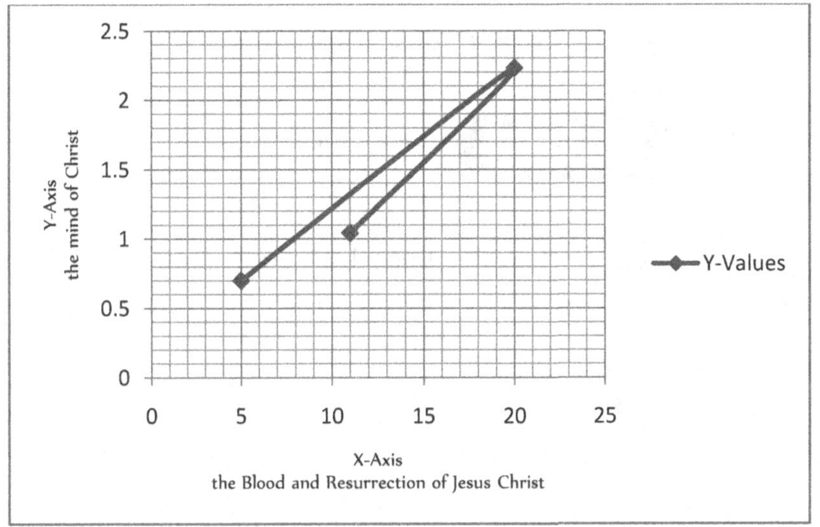

Water Spout *(lightning; combinatorics)* Study bible 2

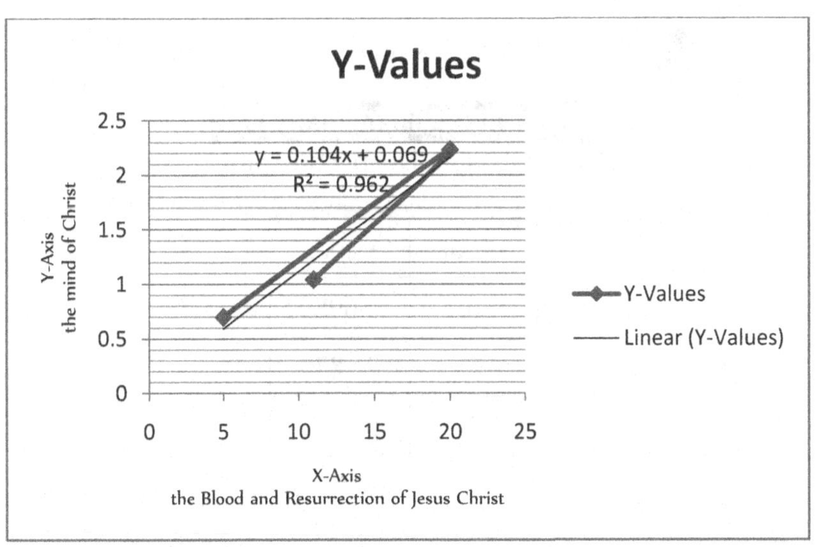

$10^{0.6989}, 3^1\ 10^{1.2304}, 10^{1.0413}$.

Pilled Poplar, Hazel, and Chestnut bible rods 2

53. And it came to pass, that when Jesussavior; deliverer**had finished these parables, he departed thence.**

5, 7, 3. Bible Matrices

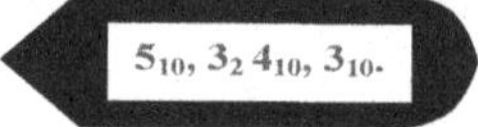

Pilled Poplar, Hazel, and Chestnut bible rods 1

$\text{Log}_2 3 = y$ $\text{Log}_{10} 5 = 0.6989$ $\text{Log}_{10} 4 = 0.6020$ $\text{Log}_{10} 3 = 0.4771$

$2^y = 3$

$y \log_{10} 2 = \log_{10} 3$

$y = \log_{10} 3 / \log_{10} 2$

$y = 0.4771 / 0.3010$

$y = 1.5850$

5, 7, 3. Deep calls unto Deep study bible 1

0.6989, 1.5850 0.6020, 0.4771.

Deep calls unto Deep study bible 2

x-axis	y-axis
5	0.6989
7	2.1870
3	0.4771

Water Spout *(lightning; combinatorics)* Study bible 1

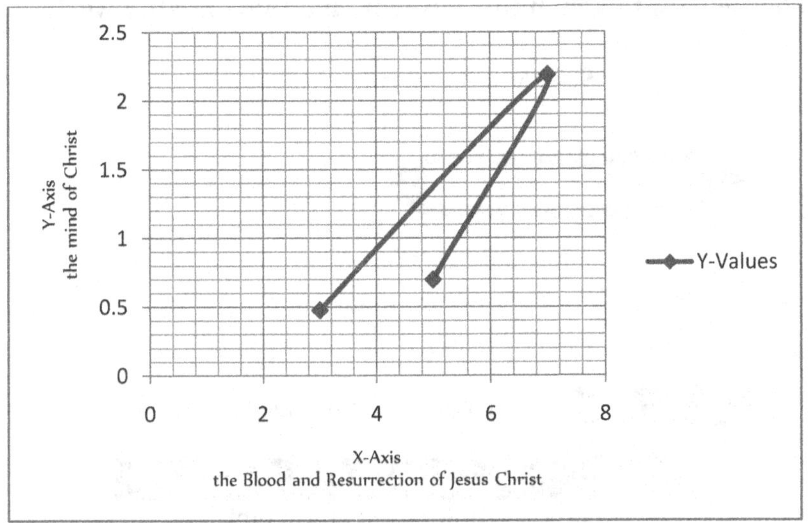

Water Spout *(lightning; combinatorics)* Study bible 2

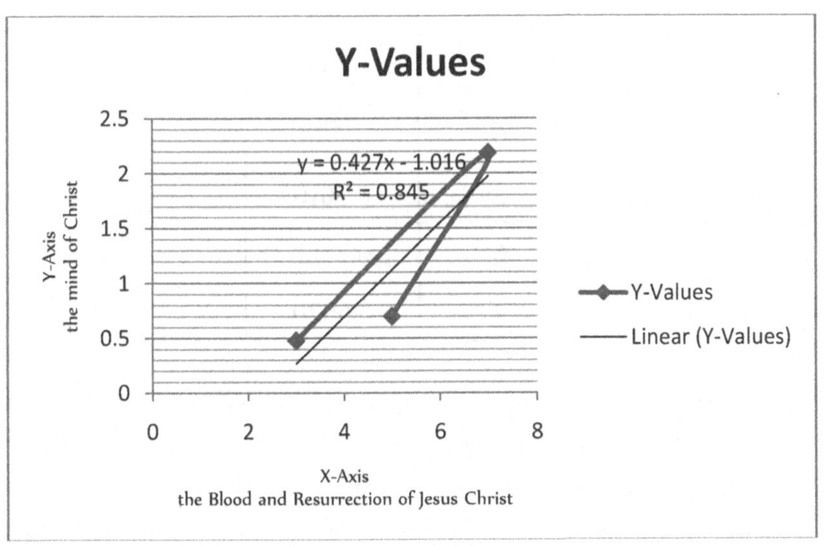

$10^{0.6989}$, $2^{1.5850}$ $10^{0.6020}$, $10^{0.4771}$.

Pilled Poplar, Hazel, and Chestnut bible rods 2

54. And when he was come into his own country, he taught them in their synagogue, in somuch that they were astonished, and said, Whence hath this man this wisdom, and these mighty works?

9, 6, 6, 2, 6, 4? Bible Matrices

Pilled Poplar, Hazel, and Chestnut bible rods 1

$\text{Log}_{10} 9 = 0.9542$ $\text{Log}_{10} 6 = 0.7781$ $\text{Log}_{10} 6 = 0.7781$ $\text{Log}_{10} 6 = 0.7781$

$\text{Log}_{10} 2 = 0.3010$ $\text{Log}_{10} 4 = 0.6020$

9, 6, 6, 2, 6, 4? Deep calls unto Deep study bible 1

0.9542, 0.7781, 0.7781, 0.3010, 0.7781, 0.6020?
Deep calls unto Deep study bible 2

x-axis	y-axis
9	0.9542
6	0.7781
6	0.7781
2	0.3010
6	0.7781
4	0.6020

Water Spout *(lightning; combinatorics)* Study bible 1

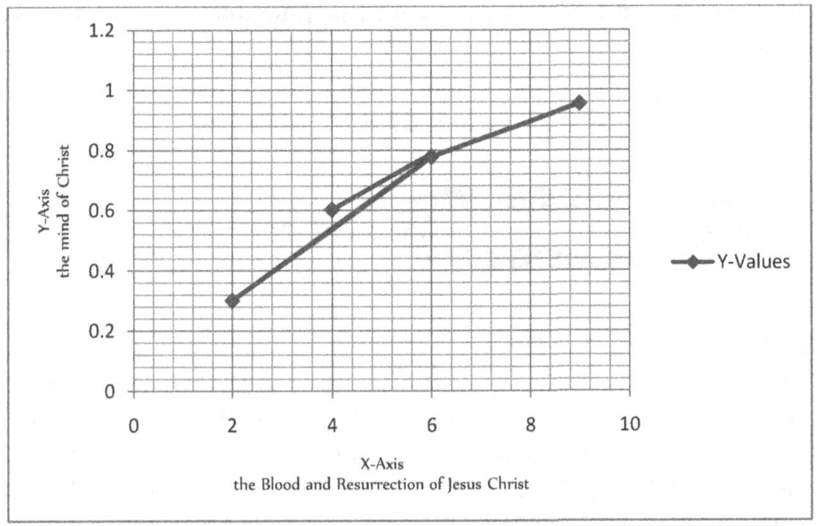

Water Spout *(lightning; combinatorics)* Study bible 2

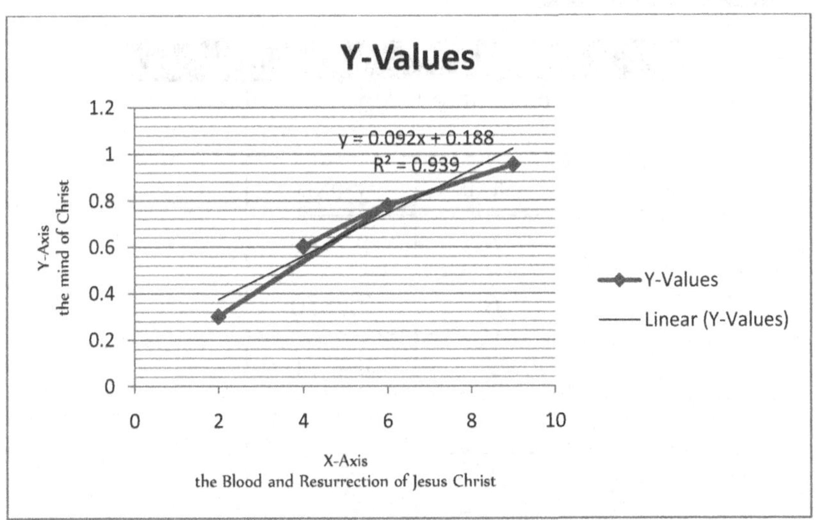

$10^{0.9542}$, $10^{0.7781}$, $10^{0.7781}$, $10^{0.3010}$, $10^{0.7781}$, $10^{0.6020}$?

Pilled Poplar, Hazel, and Chestnut bible rods 2

55. Is not this the carpenter's son? is not his mother called Mary a tear? and his brethren, James that supplants, undermines; the heel, and Joses exalted; raised; who pardons, and Simon that hears; that obeys, and Judas the praise of the Lord; confession?

6? 6? 3, 1, 2, 2, 2? Bible Matrices

6_{10}? 6_2? 3_{10}, 1_5, 2_4, 2_4, 2_6?

Pilled Poplar, Hazel, and Chestnut bible rods 1

$\log_{10} 6 = 0.7781$	$\log_{10} 3 = 0.4771$			
$\log_2 6 = y$	$\log_6 2 = y$	$\log_4 2 = y$	$\log_4 2 = y$	$\log_5 1 = y$
$2^y = 6$	$6^y = 2$	$4^y = 2$	$4^y = 2$	$5^y = 1$
$y \log_{10} 2 = \log_{10} 6$	$y \log_{10} 6 = \log_{10} 2$	$y \log_{10} 4 = \log_{10} 2$	$y \log_{10} 4 = \log_{10} 2$	$5^y = 5^0$
$y = \log_{10} 6 / \log_{10} 2$	$y = \log_{10} 2 / \log_{10} 6$	$y = \log_{10} 2 / \log_{10} 4$	$y = \log_{10} 2 / \log_{10}$	$4 y = 0$
$y = 0.7781 / 0.3010$	$y = 0.3010 / 0.7781$	$y = 0.3010 / 0.6020$	$y = 0.3010 / 0.6020$	
$y = 2.5850$	$y = 0.3868$	$y = 0.5$	$y = 0.5$	

6? 6? 3, 1, 2, 2, 2? Deep calls unto Deep study bible 1

0.7781? 2.5850? 0.4771, 0, 0.5, 0.5, 0.3868?

Deep calls unto Deep study bible 2

x-axis	y-axis
6	0.7781
6	2.5850
3	0.4771
1	0
2	0.5
2	0.5
2	0.3868

Water Spout *(lightning; combinatorics)* Study bible 1

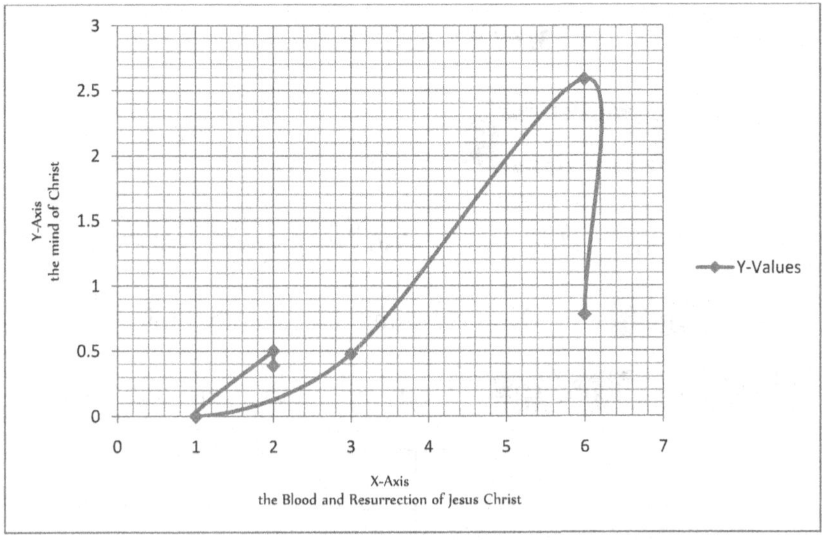

Water Spout *(lightning; combinatorics)* Study bible 2

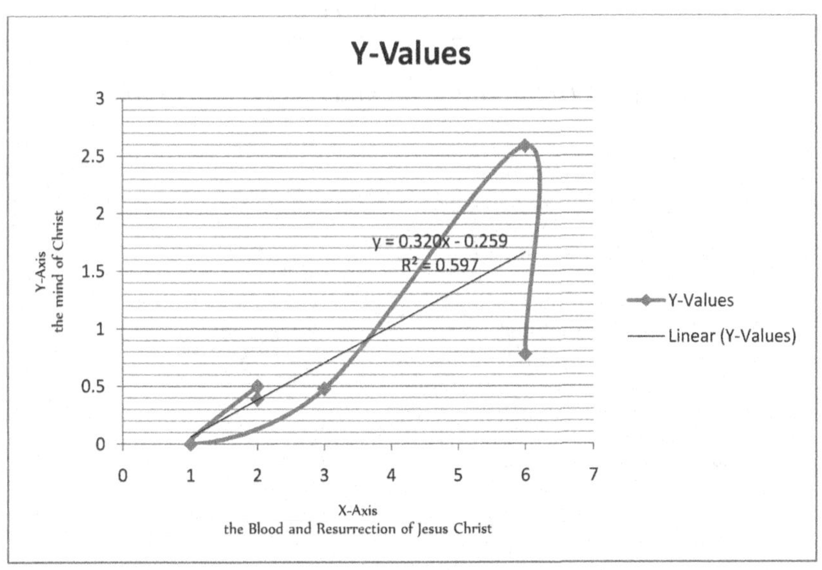

$10^{0.7781}$? $2^{2.5859}$? $10^{0.4771}$, 5^{0}, $4^{0.5}$, $4^{0.5}$, $6^{0.3868}$?

Pilled Poplar, Hazel, and Chestnut bible rods 2

56. And his sisters, are they not all with us? Whence then hath this man all these things?

3, 6? 8? Bible Matrices

$Log_{10} 6 = 0.7781$ $Log_{10} 8 = 0.9030$ $Log_{10} 3 = 0.4771$

3, 6? 8? Deep calls unto Deep study bible 1

0.4771, 0.7781? 0.9030? Deep calls unto Deep study bible 2

x-axis	y-axis
3	0.4771
6	0.7781
8	0.9030

Water Spout *(lightning; combinatorics)* Study bible 1

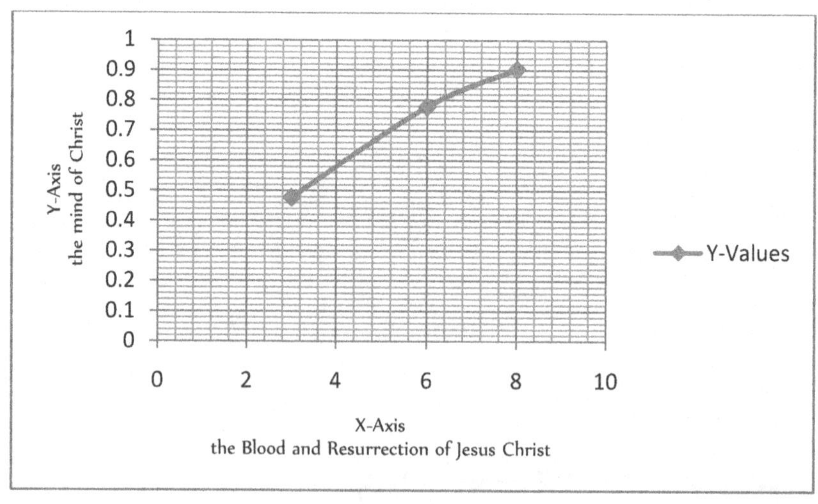

Water Spout *(lightning; combinatorics)* Study bible 2

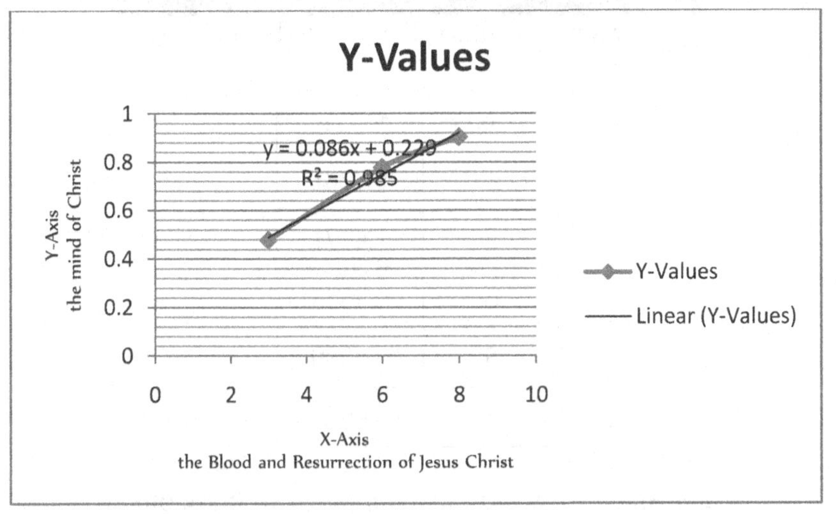

$10^{0.4771}$, $10^{0.7781}$? $10^{0.9030}$?

Pilled Poplar, Hazel, and Chestnut bible rods 2

57. And they were offended in him. But Jesussavior; deliverer**said unto them, A prophet** to bubble forth, as from a fountain; utter **is not without honour, save in his own country, and in his own house.**

6, 5, 6, 5, 5. Bible Matrices

Pilled Poplar, Hazel, and Chestnut bible rods 1

$\text{Log}_{10} 5 = 0.6989$ $\text{Log}_{10} 5 = 0.6989$ $\text{Log}_{10} 6 = 0.7781$ $\text{Log}_{10} 3 = 0.4771$ $\text{Log}_{10} 4 = 0.6020$

$\text{Log}_2 2 = y$

$2^y = 2$

$2^y = 2^1$

$y = 1$

$\text{Log}_8 2 = y$

$8^y = 2$

$2^{3y} = 2^1$

$3y = 1$

$y = 1/3$

6, 5, 6, 5, 5. Deep calls unto Deep study bible 1

0.7781, 1 0.4771, 0.3333 0.6020, 0.6989, 0.6989.
Deep calls unto Deep study bible 2

x-axis	y-axis
6	0.7781
5	1.4771
6	0.9353
5	0.6989
5	0.6989

Water Spout *(lightning; combinatorics)* Study bible 1

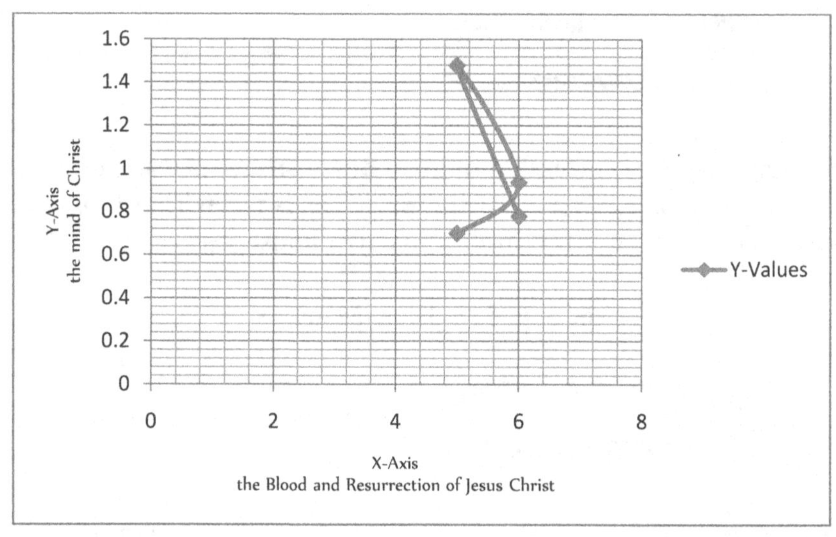

Water Spout *(lightning; combinatorics)* Study bible 2

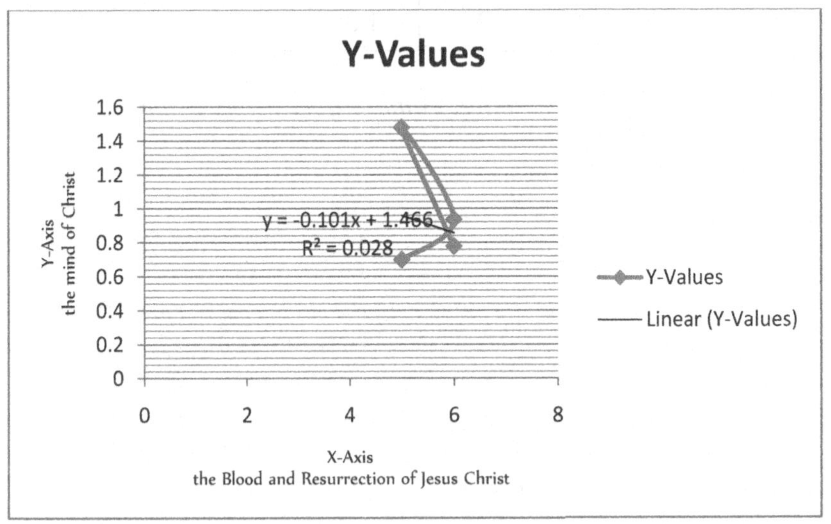

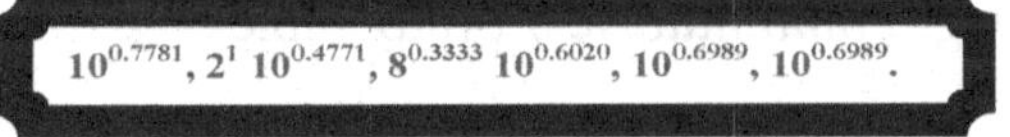

Pilled Poplar, Hazel, and Chestnut bible rods 2

58. And he did not many mighty works there because of their unbelief.

12. Bible Matrices

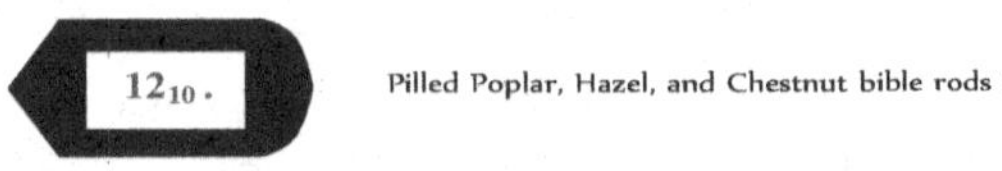

Pilled Poplar, Hazel, and Chestnut bible rods 1

$\text{Log}_{10}\ 12 = 1.0791$

12. Deep calls unto Deep study bible 1

1.0791. Deep calls unto Deep study bible 2

x-axis	y-axis
12	1.0791

Water Spout *(lightning; combinatorics)* Study bible 1

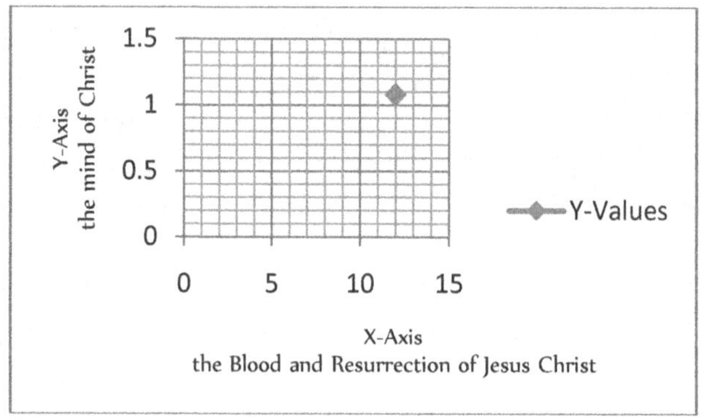

Water Spout *(lightning; combinatorics)* Study bible 2

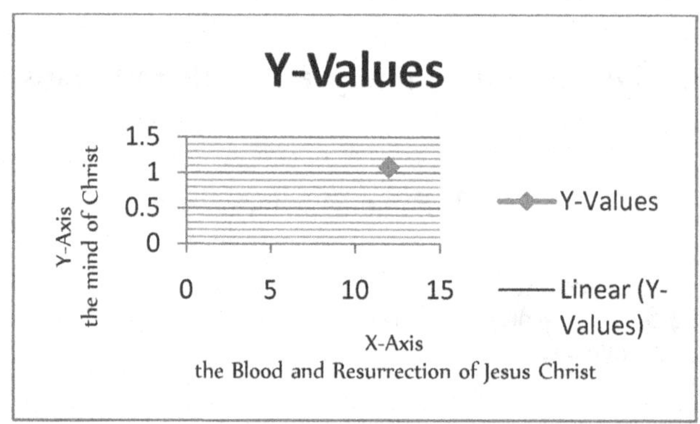

Pilled Poplar, Hazel, and Chestnut bible rods 2

CHAPTER 14

1. At that time Herod **son of a hero** **the tetrarch** **the ruler over the fourth part of a province** **heard of the fame of Jesus** **savior; deliverer**,

12, Bible Matrices

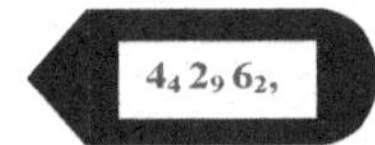

Pilled Poplar, Hazel, and Chestnut bible rods 1

$\text{Log}_2 6 = y$

$2^y = 6$

$y \log_{10} 2 = \log_{10} 6$

$y = \log_{10} 6 / \log_{10} 2$

$y = 0.7781 / 0.3010$

$y = 2.5850$

$\text{Log}_9 2 = y$

$9^y = 2$

$y \log_{10} 9 = \log_{10} 2$

$y = \log_{10} 2 / \log_{10} 9$

$y = 0.3010 / 0.9542$

$y = 0.3154$

$\text{Log}_4 4 = y$

$4^y = 4$

$2^{2y} = 2^2$

$2y = 2$

$y = 1$

12, Deep calls unto Deep study bible 1

1 0.3154 2.5850, Deep calls unto Deep study bible 2

x-axis	y-axis
12	3.9004

Water Spout *(lightning; combinatorics)* Study bible 1

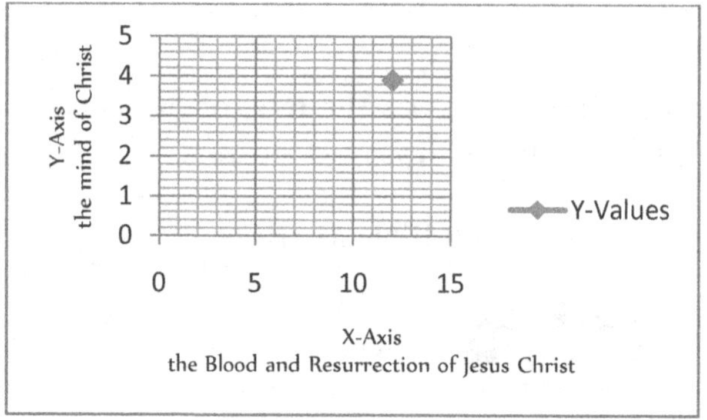

Water Spout *(lightning; combinatorics)* Study bible 2

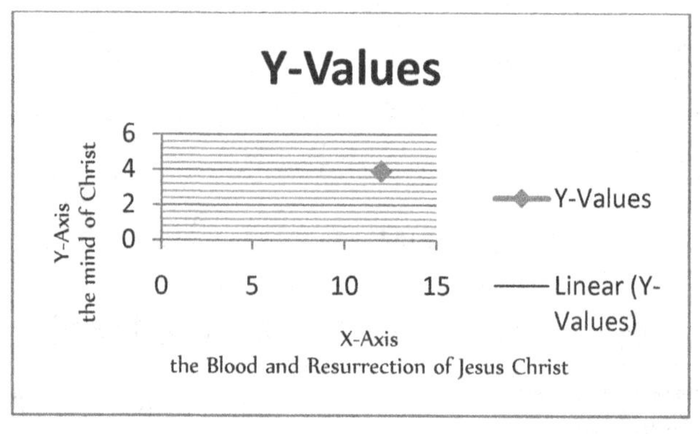

2. And said unto his servants, This is John

2. And said unto his servants, This is John the grace or mercy of the Lord **the Baptist; he is risen from the dead; and therefore mighty works do shew forth themselves in him.**

5, 5; 6;10. Bible Matrices

5_{10}, 3_7 2_{10}; 6_{10}; 10_{10}.

Pilled Poplar, Hazel, and Chestnut bible rods 1

$\text{Log}_{10} 6 = 0.7781$ $\text{Log}_{10} 5 = 0.6989$ $\text{Log}_{10} 10 = 1$ $\text{Log}_{10} 2 = 0.3010$

$\text{Log}_7 3 = y$

$7^y = 3$

$y \log_{10} 7 = \log_{10} 3$

$y = \log_{10} 3 / \log_{10} 7$

$y = 0.4771 / 0.8450$

$y = 0.5646$

5, 5; 6; 10. Deep calls unto Deep study bible 1

0.6989, 0.5646 0.3010; 0.7781; 1.

Deep calls unto Deep study bible 2

x-axis	y-axis
5	0.6989
5	0.8656
6	0.7781
10	1

Water Spout *(lightning; combinatorics)* Study bible 1

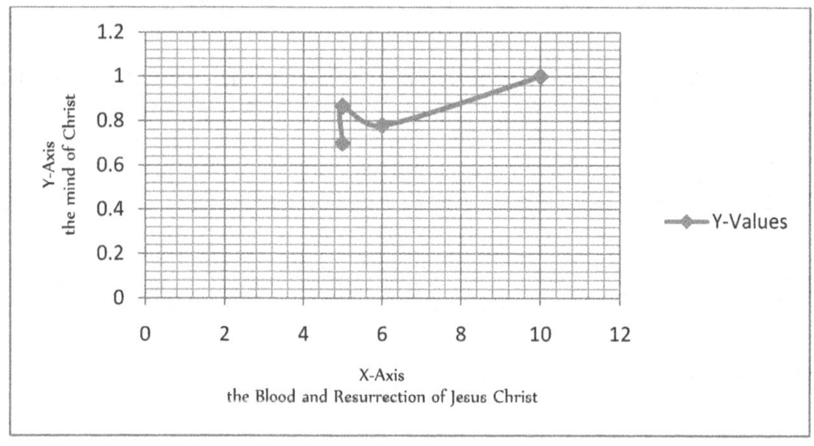

Water Spout *(lightning; combinatorics)* Study bible 2

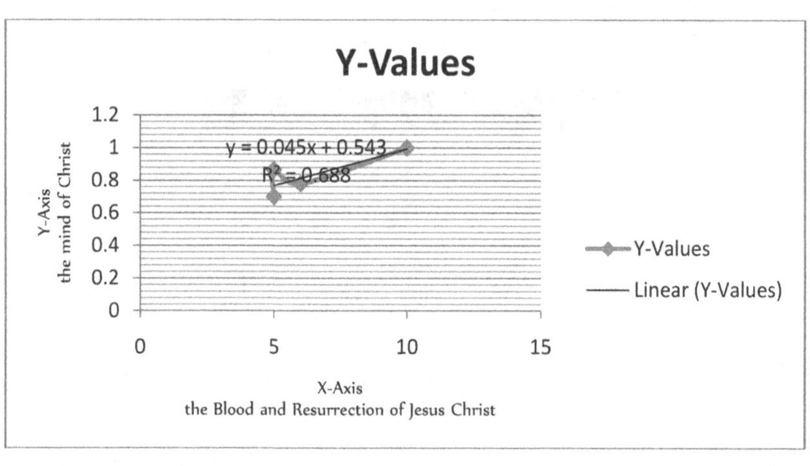

Pilled Poplar, Hazel, and Chestnut bible rods 2

3. For Herodson of a hero **had laid hold on John**the grace or mercy of the Lord, **and bound him, and put him in prison for Herodias' sake, his brother Philip's**warlike; a lover of horses**wife.**

7, 3, 8, 4. Bible Matrices

$2_4\ 5_7,\ 3_{10},\ 8_{10},\ 3_5 1_{10}.$

Pilled Poplar, Hazel, and Chestnut bible rods 1

$\mathrm{Log}_{10} 3 = 0.4771$

$\mathrm{Log}_7 5 = y$

$7^y = 5$

$y \log_{10} 7 = \log_{10} 5$

$y = \log_{10} 5 / \log_{10} 7$

$y = 0.6989 / 0.8450$

$y = 0.8271$

$\mathrm{Log}_{10} 8 = 0.9030$

$\mathrm{Log}_5 3 = y$

$5^y = 3$

$y \log_{10} 5 = \log_{10} 3$

$y = \log_{10} 3 / \log_{10} 5$

$y = 0.4771 / 0.6989$

$y = 0.6826$

$\mathrm{Log}_{10} 1 = 0$

$\mathrm{Log}_4 2 = y$

$4^y = 2$

$2^{2y} = 2^1$

$2y = 1$

$y = ½$ or 0.5

7, 3, 8, 4. Deep calls unto Deep study bible 1

0.5 0.8271, 0.4771, 0.9030, 0.6826 0.

Deep calls unto Deep study bible 2

x-axis	y-axis
7	1.3271
3	0.4771
8	0.9030
4	0.6826

Water Spout *(lightning; combinatorics)* Study bible 1

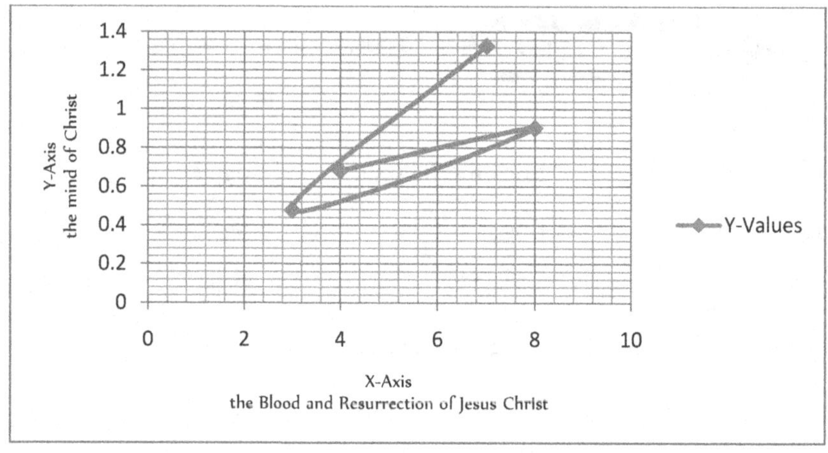

Water Spout *(lightning; combinatorics)* Study bible 2

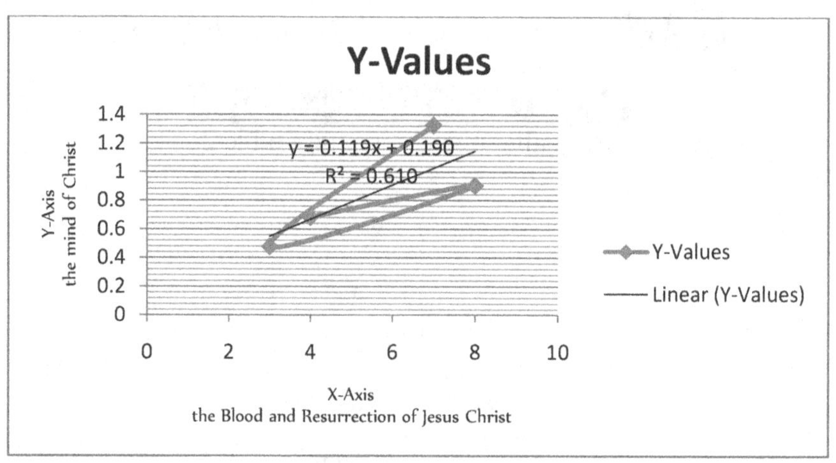

$4^{0.5}\ 7^{0.8271},\ 10^{0.4771},\ 10^{0.9030},\ 5^{0.6826}\ 10^{0}$.

Pilled Poplar, Hazel, and Chestnut bible rods 2

4. For John the grace or mercy of the Lord **said unto him, It is not lawful for thee to have her.**

5, 9. Bible Matrices

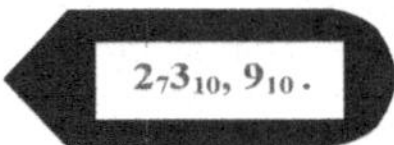

Pilled Poplar, Hazel, and Chestnut bible rods 1

$\log_{10} 9 = 0.9542$ $\log_{10} 3 = 0.4771$

$\log_7 2 = y$

$7^y = 2$

$y \log_{10} 7 = \log_{10} 2$

$y = \log_{10} 2 / \log_{10} 7$

$y = 0.3010 / 0.8450$

$y = 0.3562$

5, 9. Deep calls unto Deep study bible 1

0.3562 0.4771, 0.9542. Deep calls unto Deep study bible 2

x-axis	y-axis
5	0.8333
9	0.9542

Water Spout *(lightning; combinatorics)* Study bible 1

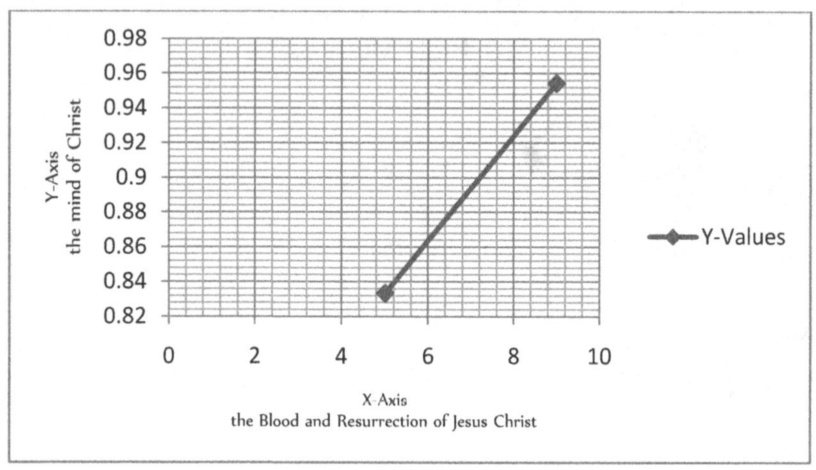

Water Spout *(lightning; combinatorics)* Study bible 2

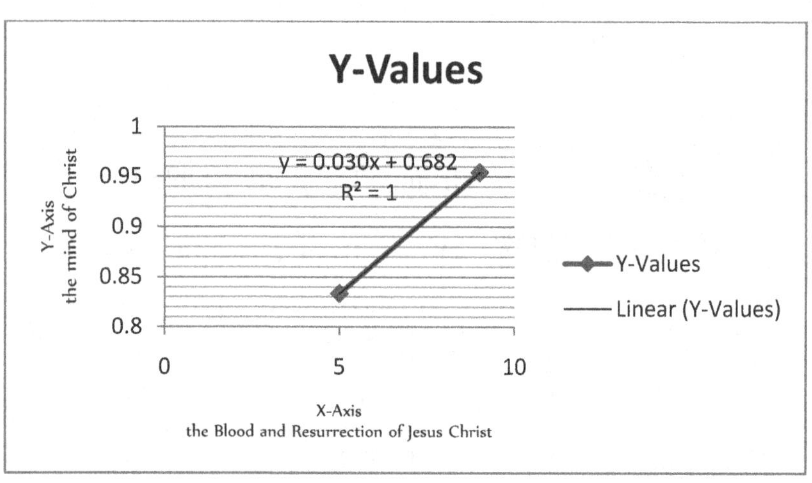

$7^{0.3562}$ $10^{0.4771}$, $10^{0.9542}$. Pilled Poplar, Hazel, and Chestnut bible rods 2

5. And when he would have put him to death, he feared the multitude, because they counted him as a prophet to bubble forth, as from a fountain; utter.

9, 4, 7. Bible Matrices

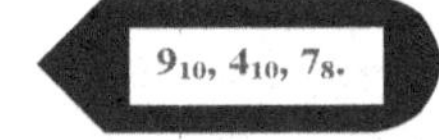

Pilled Poplar, Hazel, and Chestnut bible rods 1

$\text{Log}_{10} 9 = 0.9542$ $\text{Log}_{10} 4 = 0.6020$

$\text{Log}_{8} 7 = y$

$8^{y} = 7$

$y \log_{10} 8 = \log_{10} 7$

$y = \log_{10} 7 / \log_{10} 8$

$y = 0.8450 / 0.9030$

$y = 0.9357$

9, 4, 7. Deep calls unto Deep study bible 1

0.9542, 0.6020, 0.9357. Deep calls unto Deep study bible 2

x-axis	y-axis
9	0.9542
4	0.6020
7	0.9357

Water Spout *(lightning; combinatorics)* Study bible 1

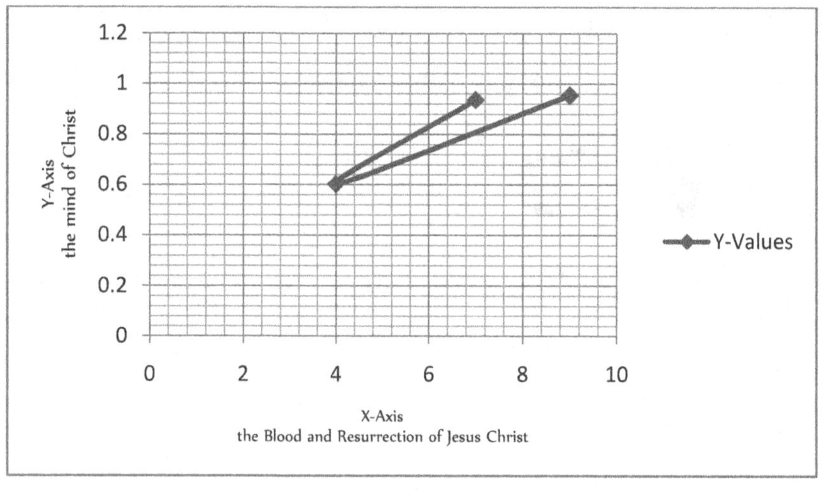

Water Spout *(lightning; combinatorics)* Study bible 2

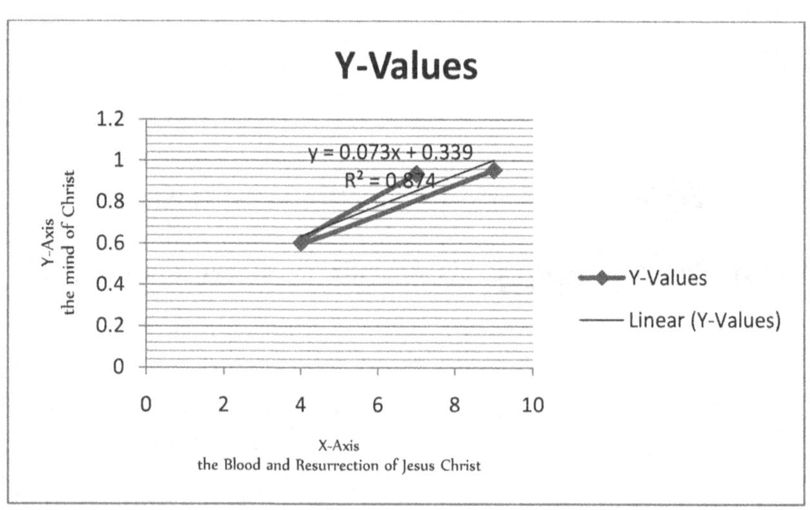

$10^{0.9542}$, $10^{0.6020}$, $8^{0.9357}$. Pilled Poplar, Hazel, and Chestnut bible rods 2

6. But when Herod'sson of a hero **birthday was kept, the daughter of Herodias danced before them, and pleased Herod**son of a hero.

6, 7, 3. Bible Matrices

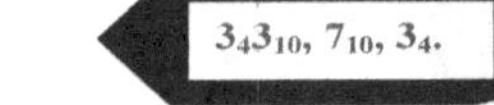

Pilled Poplar, Hazel, and Chestnut bible rods 1

$\text{Log}_{10} 3 = 0.4771$

$\text{Log}_4 3 = y$

$4^y = 3$

$y \log_{10} 4 = \log_{10} 3$

$y = \log_{10} 3 / \log_{10} 4$

$y = 0.4771 / 0.6020$

$y = 0.7925$

$\text{Log}_{10} 7 = 0.8450$

$\text{Log}_4 3 = y$

$4^y = 3$

$y \log_{10} 4 = \log_{10} 3$

$y = \log_{10} 3 / \log_{10} 4$

$y = 0.4771 / 0.6020$

$y = 0.7925$

6, 7, 3. Deep calls unto Deep study bible 1

0.7925 0.4771, 0.8450, 0.7925.
Deep calls unto Deep study bible 2

x-axis	y-axis
6	1.2696
7	0.8450
3	0.7925

Water Spout *(lightning; combinatorics)* Study bible 1

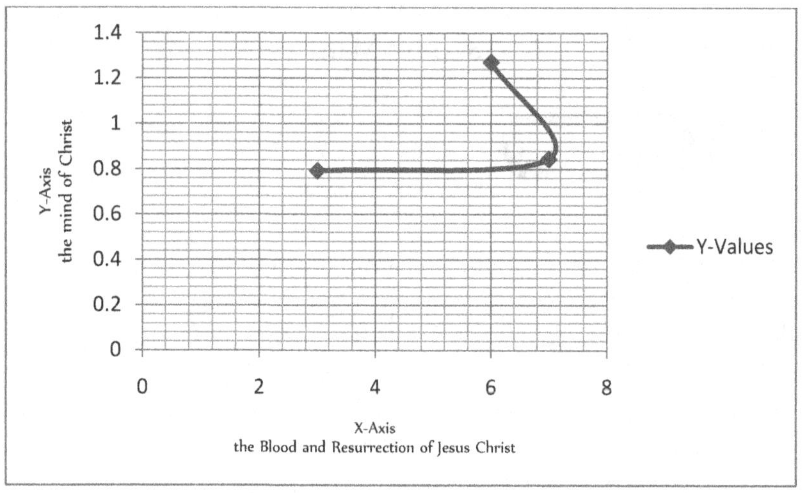

Water Spout *(lightning; combinatorics)* Study bible 2

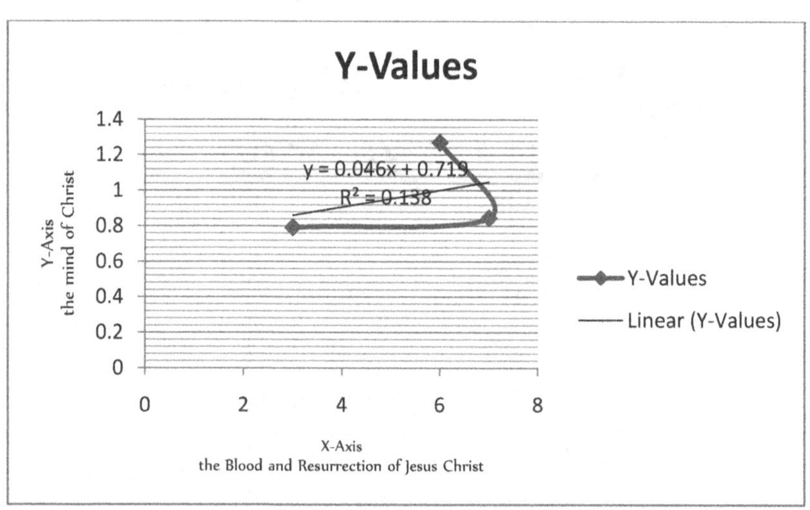

$4^{0.7925}$ $10^{0.4771}$, $10^{0.8450}$, $4^{0.7925}$.

Pilled Poplar, Hazel, and Chestnut bible rods 2

7. Whereupon he promised with an oath to give her whatsoever she would ask.

13. Bible Matrices

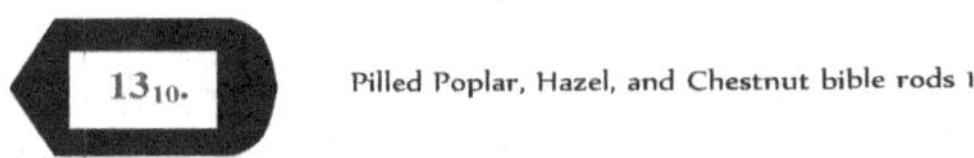

$\text{Log}_{10} 13 = 1.1139$

13. Deep calls unto Deep study bible 1

1.1139. Deep calls unto Deep study bible 2

x-axis	y-axis
13	1.1139

Water Spout *(lightning; combinatorics)* Study bible 1

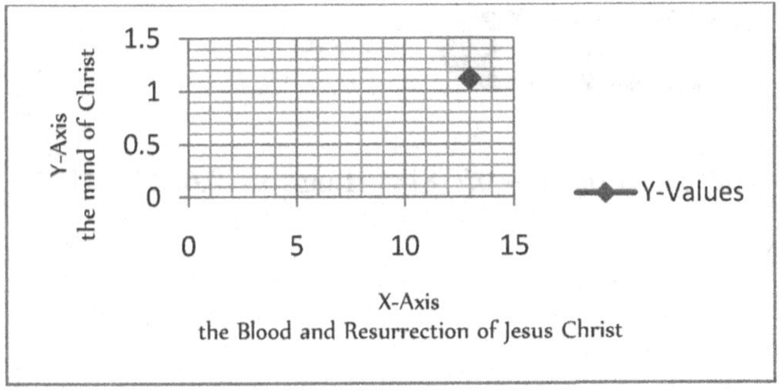

Water Spout *(lightning; combinatorics)* Study bible 2

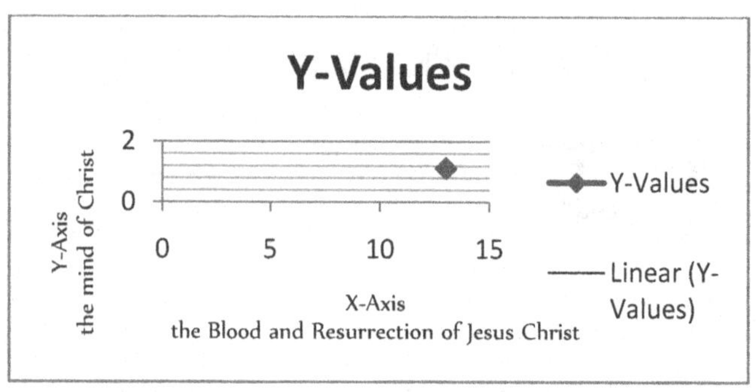

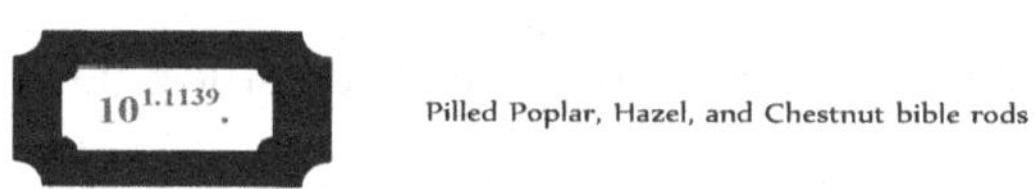

8. And she, being before instructed of her mother, said, Give me here John Baptist'sforerunner of our Lord**head in a charger.**

2, 6, 1, 9. Bible Matrices

$\text{Log}_{10} 2 = 0.3010$ $\text{Log}_{10} 6 = 0.7781$ $\text{Log}_{10} 4 = 0.6020$ $\text{Log}_{10} 1 = 0$

$\text{Log}_4 5 = y$

$4^y = 5$

$y \log_{10} 4 = \log_{10} 5$

$y = \log_{10} 5 / \log_{10} 4$

$y = 0.6989 / 0.6020$

$y = 1.1609$

2, 6, 1, 9. Deep calls unto Deep study bible 1

0.3010, 0.7781, 0, 1.1609 0.6020.

Deep calls unto Deep study bible 2

x-axis	y-axis
2	0.3010
6	0.7781
1	0
9	1.7629

Water Spout *(lightning; combinatorics)* Study bible 1

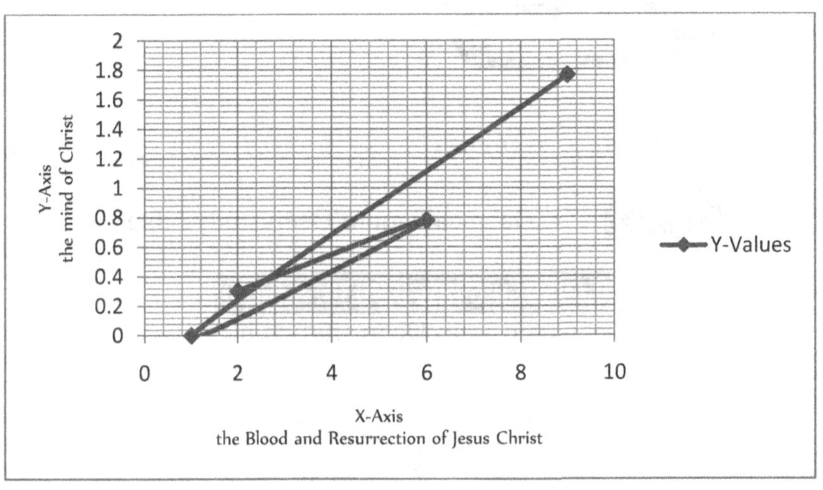

Water Spout *(lightning; combinatorics)* Study bible 2

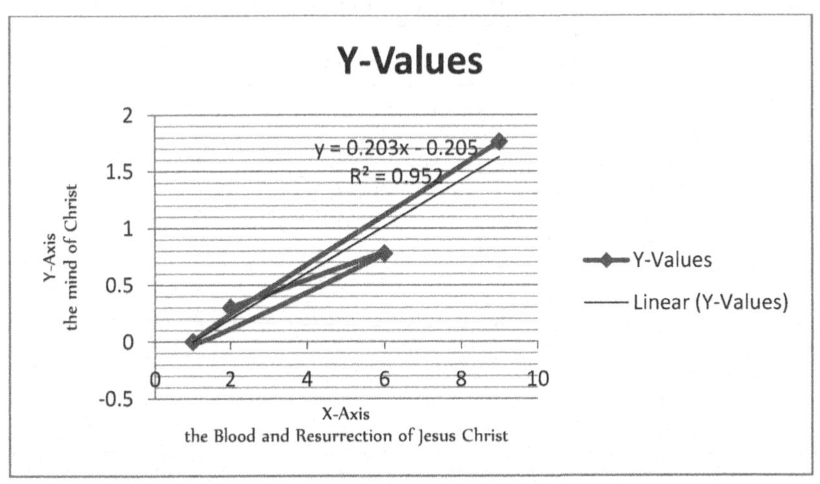

$10^{0.3010}$, $10^{0.7781}$, 10^{0}, $4^{1.1609}$ $10^{0.6020}$.

Pilled Poplar, Hazel, and Chestnut bible rods 2

9. And the king was sorry: nevertheless for the oath's sake, and them which sat with him at meat, he commanded it to be given her.

5: 5, 8, 7. Bible Matrices

Pilled Poplar, Hazel, and Chestnut bible rods 1

$\text{Log}_{10} 8 = 0.9030$ $\text{Log}_{10} 5 = 0.6989$ $\text{Log}_{10} 5 = 0.6989$ $\text{Log}_{10} 7 = 0.8450$

5: 5, 8, 7. Deep calls unto Deep study bible 1

0.6989: 0.6989, 0.9030, 0.8450.

Deep calls unto Deep study bible 2

x-axis	y-axis
5	0.6989
5	0.6989
8	0.9030
7	0.8450

Water Spout *(lightning; combinatorics)* Study bible 1

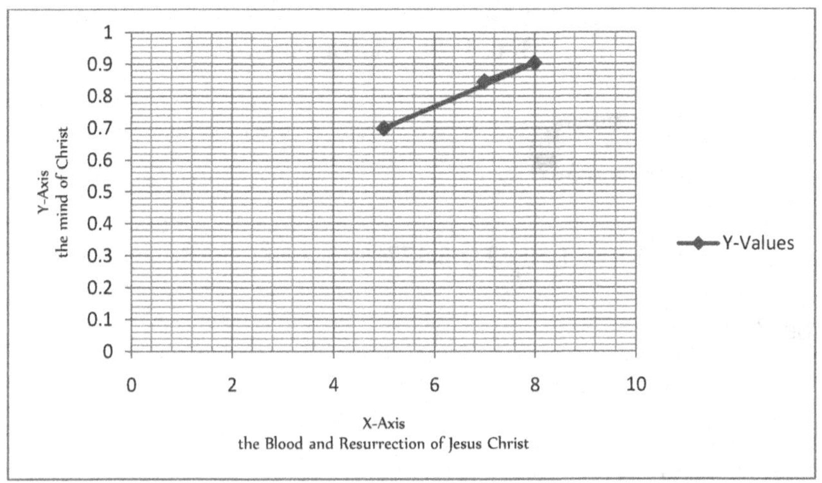

Water Spout *(lightning; combinatorics)* Study bible 2

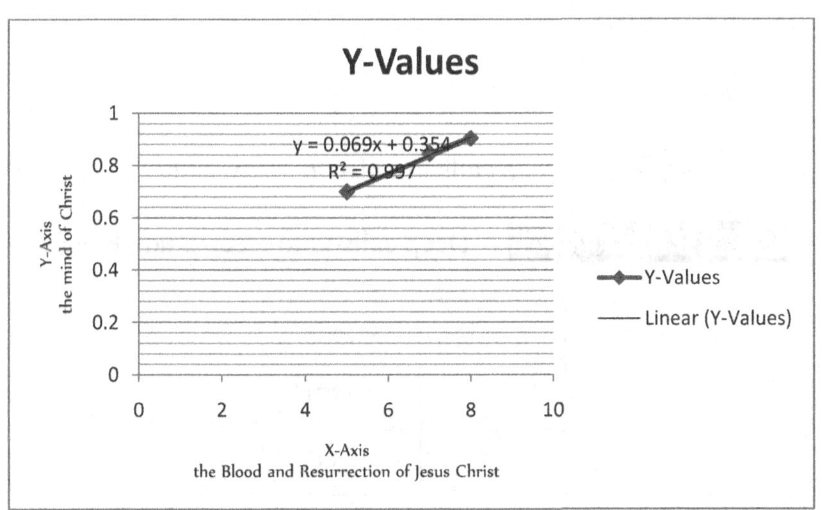

$10^{0.6989}$: $10^{0.6989}$, $10^{0.9030}$, $10^{0.8450}$.

Pilled Poplar, Hazel, and Chestnut bible rods 2

10. And he sent, and beheaded Johnthe grace or mercy of the Lord **in the prison.**

3, 6. Bible Matrices

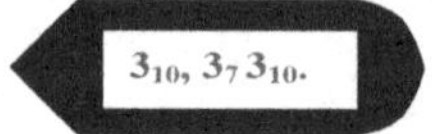

Pilled Poplar, Hazel, and Chestnut bible rods 1

$\text{Log}_{10} 3 = 0.4771$ $\text{Log}_{10} 3 = 0.4771$

$\text{Log}_7 3 = y$

$7^y = 3$

$y \log_{10} 7 = \log_{10} 3$

$y = \log_{10} 3 / \log_{10} 7$

$y = 0.3010 / 0.8450$

$y = 0.3562$

3, 6. Deep calls unto Deep study bible 1

0.4771, 0.3562 0.4771. Deep calls unto Deep study bible 2

x-axis	y-axis
3	0.4771
6	0.8333

Water Spout *(lightning; combinatorics)* Study bible 1

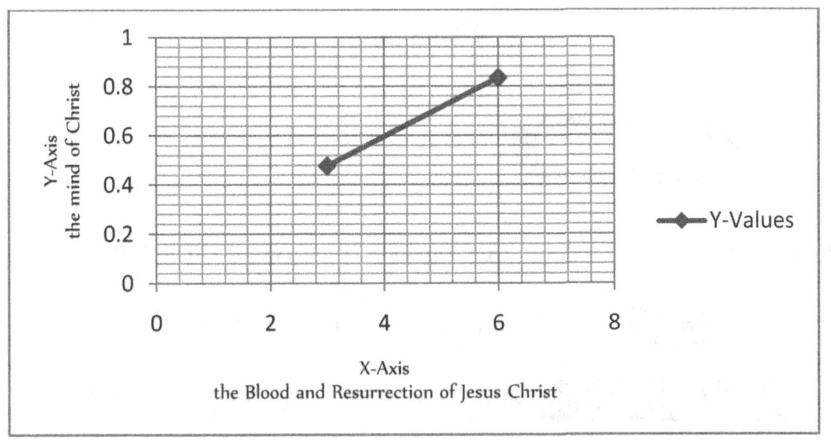

Water Spout *(lightning; combinatorics)* Study bible 2

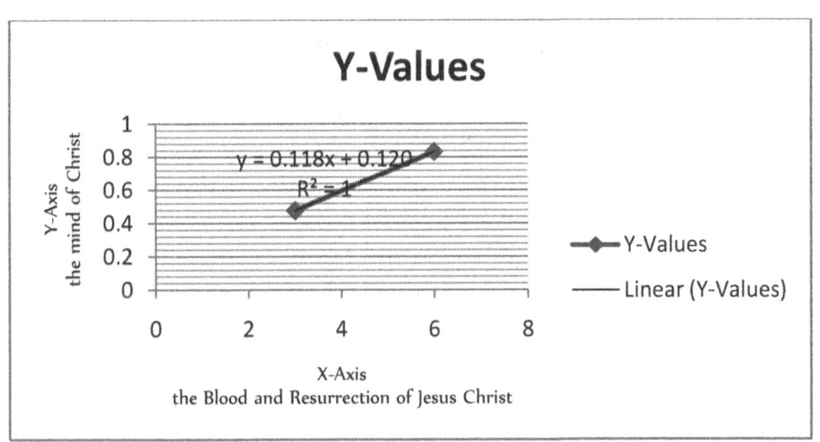

$10^{0.4771}$, $7^{0.3562}$ $10^{0.4771}$. Pilled Poplar, Hazel, and Chestnut bible rods 2

11. And his head was brought in a charger, and given to the damsel: and she brought it to her mother.

8, 5: 7. Bible Matrices

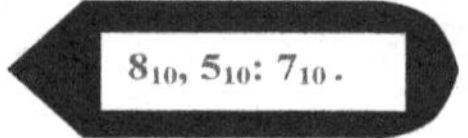

Pilled Poplar, Hazel, and Chestnut bible rods 1

$\text{Log}_{10} 8 = 0.9030$ $\text{Log}_{10} 5 = 0.6989$ $\text{Log}_{10} 7 = 0.8450$

8, 5: 7. Deep calls unto Deep study bible 1

0.9030, 0.6989: 0.8450. Deep calls unto Deep study bible 2

x-axis	y-axis
8	0.9030
5	0.6989
7	0.8450

Water Spout *(lightning; combinatorics)* Study bible 1

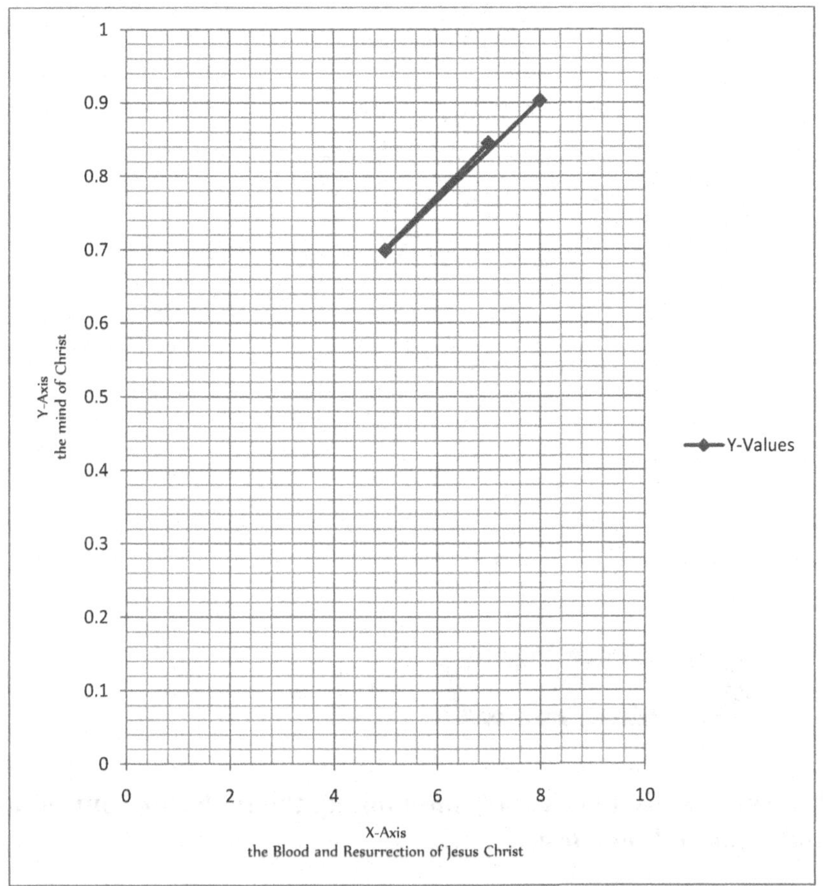

Water Spout *(lightning; combinatorics)* Study bible 2

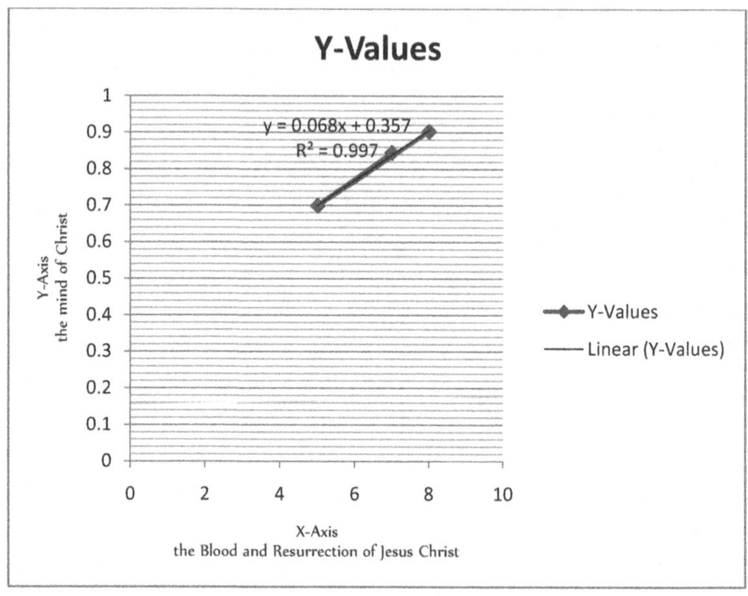

Pilled Poplar, Hazel, and Chestnut bible rods 2

12. And his disciples came, and took up the body, and buried it, and went and told Jesussavior; deliverer.

4, 5, 3, 5. Bible Matrices

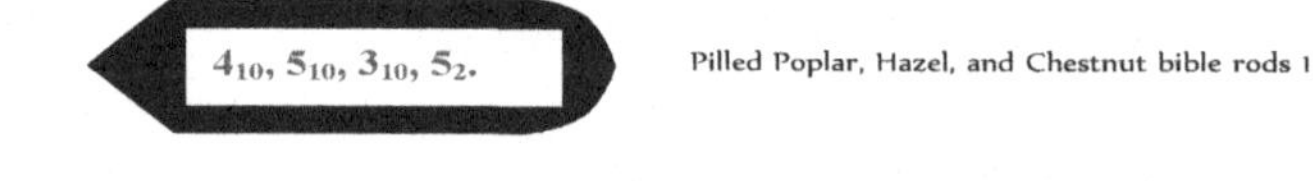

Pilled Poplar, Hazel, and Chestnut bible rods 1

$\text{Log}_{10} 4 = 0.6020$ $\text{Log}_{10} 5 = 0.6989$ $\text{Log}_{10} 3 = 0.4771$

$\text{Log}_2 5 = y$

$2^y = 5$

$y \log_{10} 2 = \log_{10} 5$

$y = \log_{10} 5 / \log_{10} 2$

$y = 0.6989 / 0.3010$

$y = 2.3219$

4, 5, 3, 5. Deep calls unto Deep study bible 1

0.6020, 0.6989, 0.4771, 2.3219.
Deep calls unto Deep study bible 2

x-axis	y-axis
4	0.6020
5	0.6989
3	0.4771
5	2.3219

Water Spout *(lightning; combinatorics)* Study bible 1

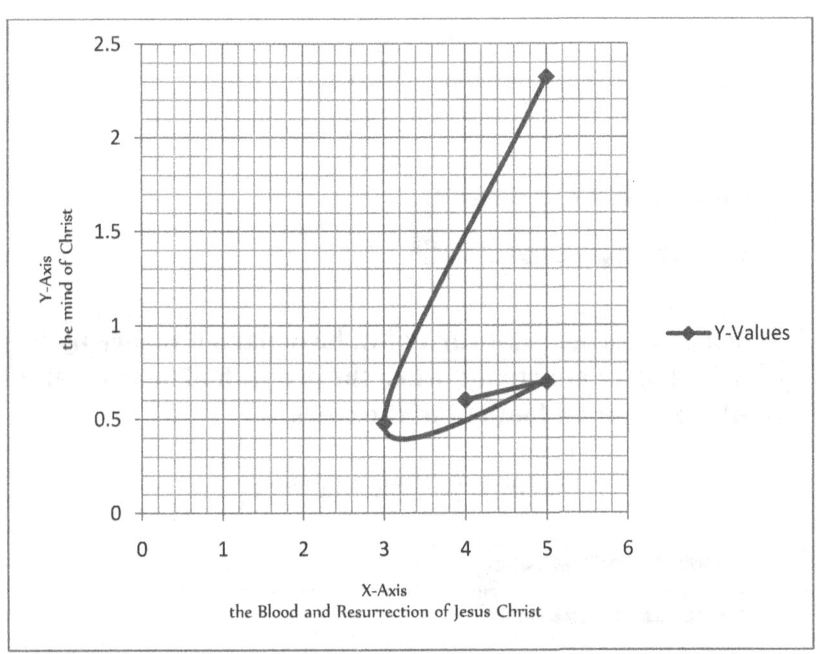

Water Spout *(lightning; combinatorics)* Study bible 2

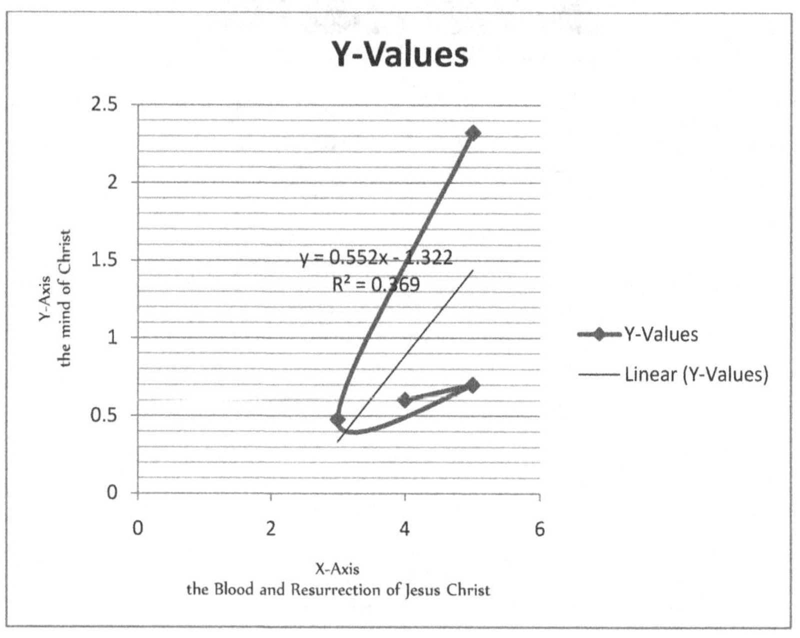

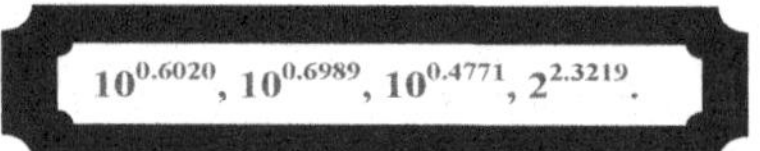

Pilled Poplar, Hazel, and Chestnut bible rods 2

13. When Jesussavior; deliverer**heard of it, he departed thence by ship into a desert place apart: and when the people had heard thereof, they followed him on foot out of the cities.**

5, 10: 7, 9. Bible Matrices

$2_2\ 3_{10},\ 10_{10}: 7_{10},\ 9_{10}.$

Pilled Poplar, Hazel, and Chestnut bible rods 1

$\text{Log}_{10} 9 = 0.9542$ $\text{Log}_{10} 3 = 0.4771$ $\text{Log}_{10} 10 = 1$ $\text{Log}_{10} 7 = 0.8450$

$\text{Log}_2 2 = y$

$2^y = 2$

$2^y = 2^1$

$y = 1$

5, 10: 7, 9. Deep calls unto Deep study bible 1

1 0.4771, 1: 0.8450, 0.9542.
Deep calls unto Deep study bible 2

x-axis	y-axis
5	1.4771
10	1
7	0.8450
9	0.9542

Water Spout *(lightning; combinatorics)* Study bible 1

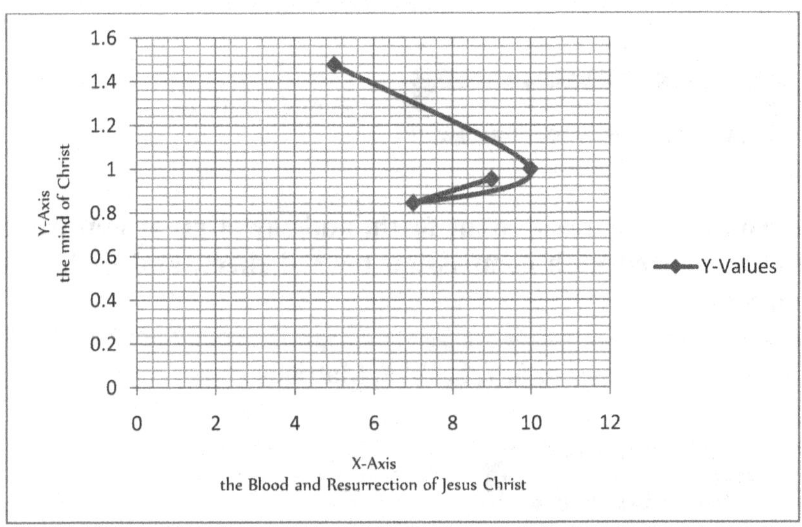

Water Spout *(lightning; combinatorics)* Study bible 2

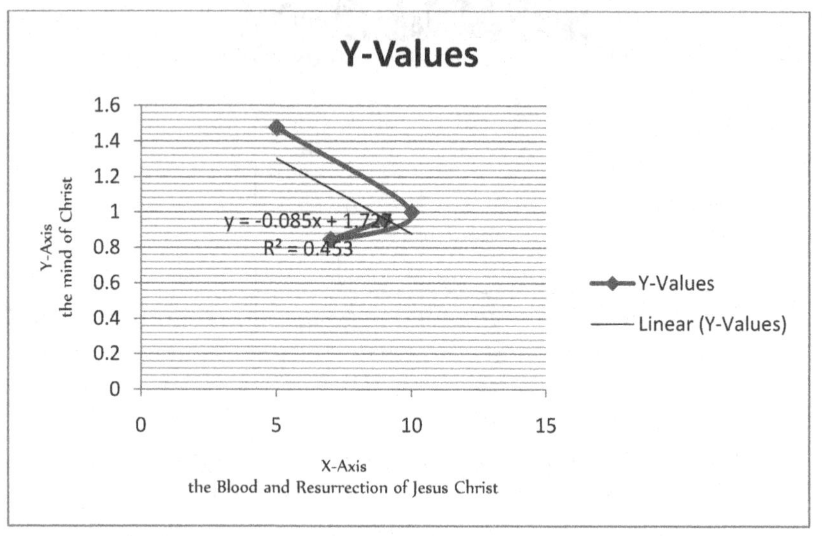

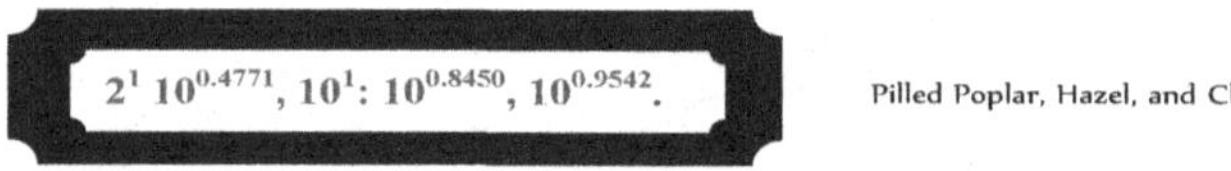

Pilled Poplar, Hazel, and Chestnut bible rods 2

14. And Jesussavior; delivererwent forth, and saw a great multitude, and was moved with compassion toward them, and he healed their sick.

4, 5, 7, 5. Bible Matrices

$2_2 2_{10}, 5_{10}, 7_{10}, 5_{10}.$

Pilled Poplar, Hazel, and Chestnut bible rods 1

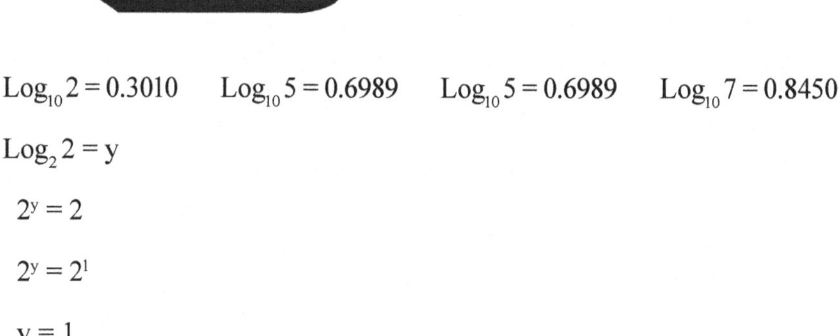

$\text{Log}_{10} 2 = 0.3010 \quad \text{Log}_{10} 5 = 0.6989 \quad \text{Log}_{10} 5 = 0.6989 \quad \text{Log}_{10} 7 = 0.8450$

$\text{Log}_2 2 = y$

$2^y = 2$

$2^y = 2^1$

$y = 1$

4, 5, 7, 5. Deep calls unto Deep study bible 1

1 0.3010, 0.6989, 0.8450, 0.6989.
Deep calls unto Deep study bible 2

x-axis	y-axis
4	1.3010
5	0.6989
7	0.8450
5	0.6989

Water Spout *(lightning; combinatorics)* Study bible 1

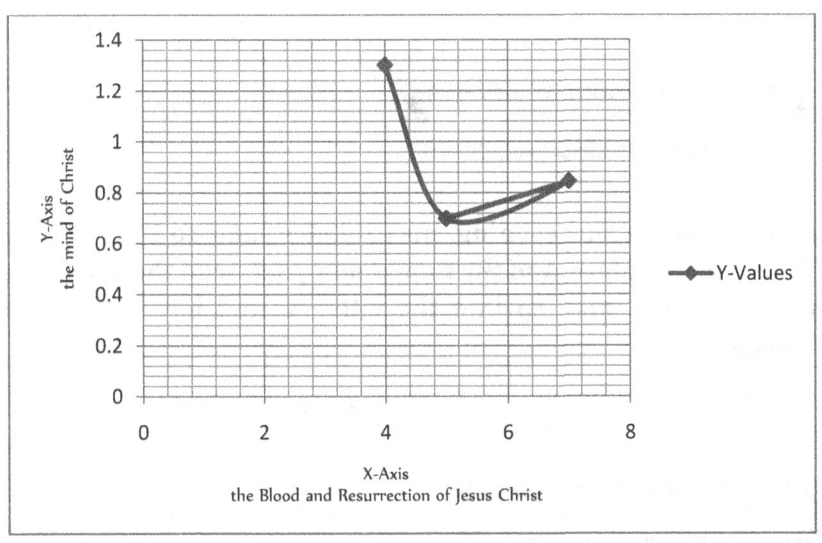

Water Spout *(lightning; combinatorics)* Study bible 2

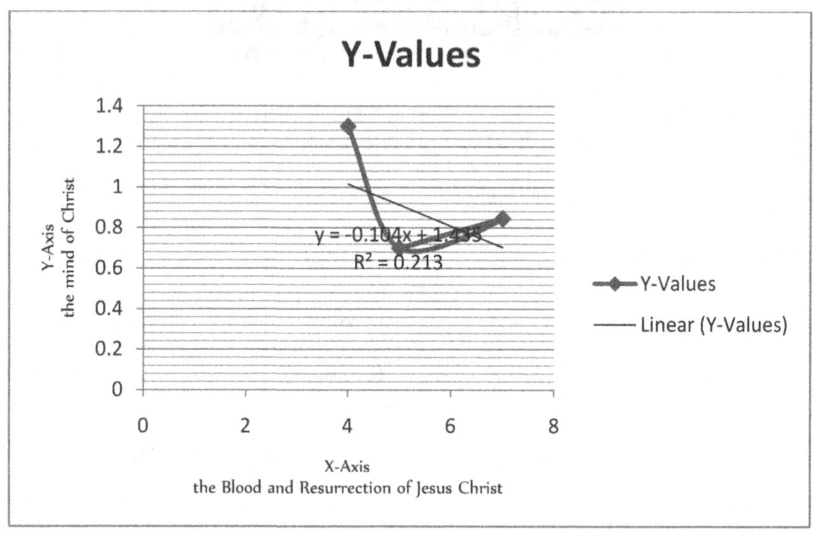

2^1 $10^{0.3010}$, $10^{0.6989}$, $10^{0.8450}$, $10^{0.6989}$.

Pilled Poplar, Hazel, and Chestnut bible rods 2

15. And when it was evening, his disciples came to him, saying, This is a desert place, and the time is now past; send the multitude away, that they may go into the villages, and buy themselves victuals.

5, 5, 1, 5, 6; 4, 7, 4. Bible Matrices

5_{10}, 5_{10}, 1_{10}, 5_{10}, 6_{10}; 4_{10}, 7_{10}, 4_{10} .

Pilled Poplar, Hazel, and Chestnut bible rods 1

$Log_{10} 4 = 0.6020$ $Log_{10} 5 = 0.6989$ $Log_{10} 4 = 0.6020$ $Log_{10} 5 = 0.6989$

$Log_{10} 5 = 0.6989$ $Log_{10} 6 = 0.7781$ $Log_{10} 7 = 0.8450$ $Log_{10} 1 = 0$

5, 5, 1, 5, 6; 4, 7, 4. Deep calls unto Deep study bible 1

0.6989, 0.6989, 0, 0.6989, 0.7781; 0.6020, 0.8450, 0.6020.
Deep calls unto Deep study bible 2

x-axis	y-axis
5	0.6989
5	0.6989
1	0
5	0.6989
6	0.7781
4	0.6020
7	0.8450
4	0.6020

Water Spout (lightning; combinatorics) Study bible 1

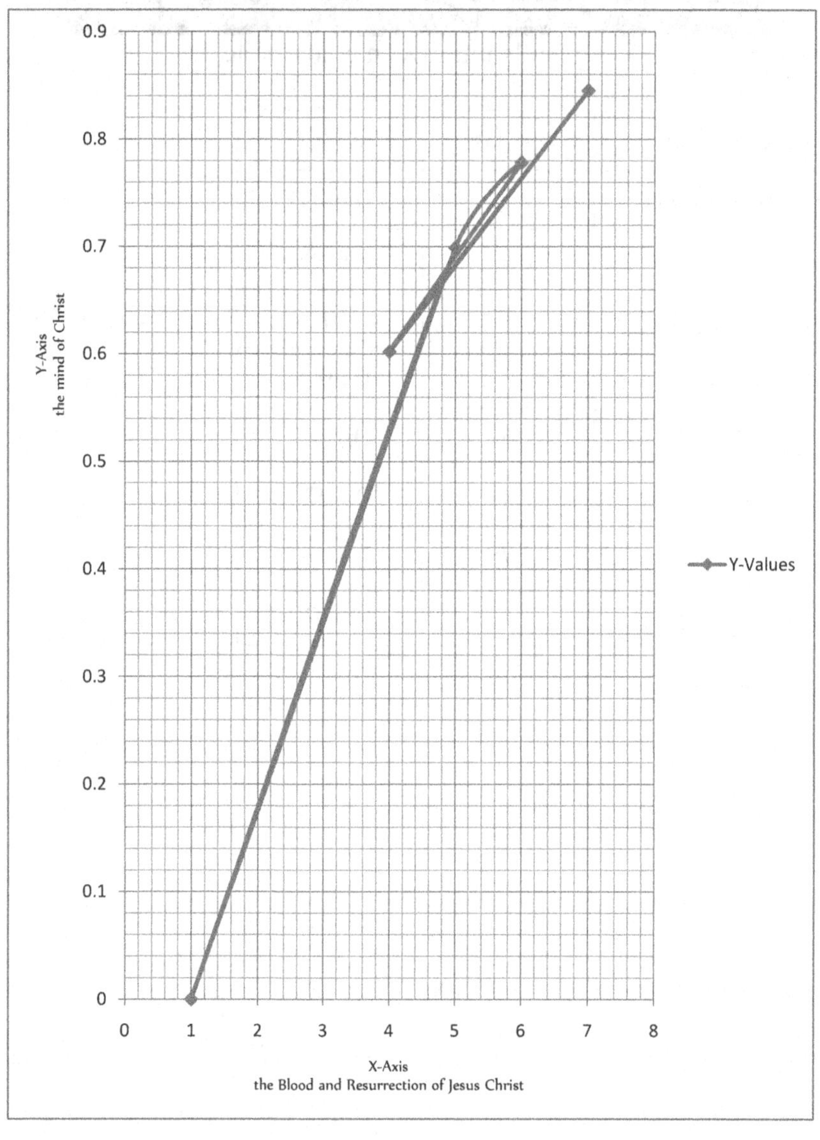

Water Spout *(lightning; combinatorics)* Study bible 2

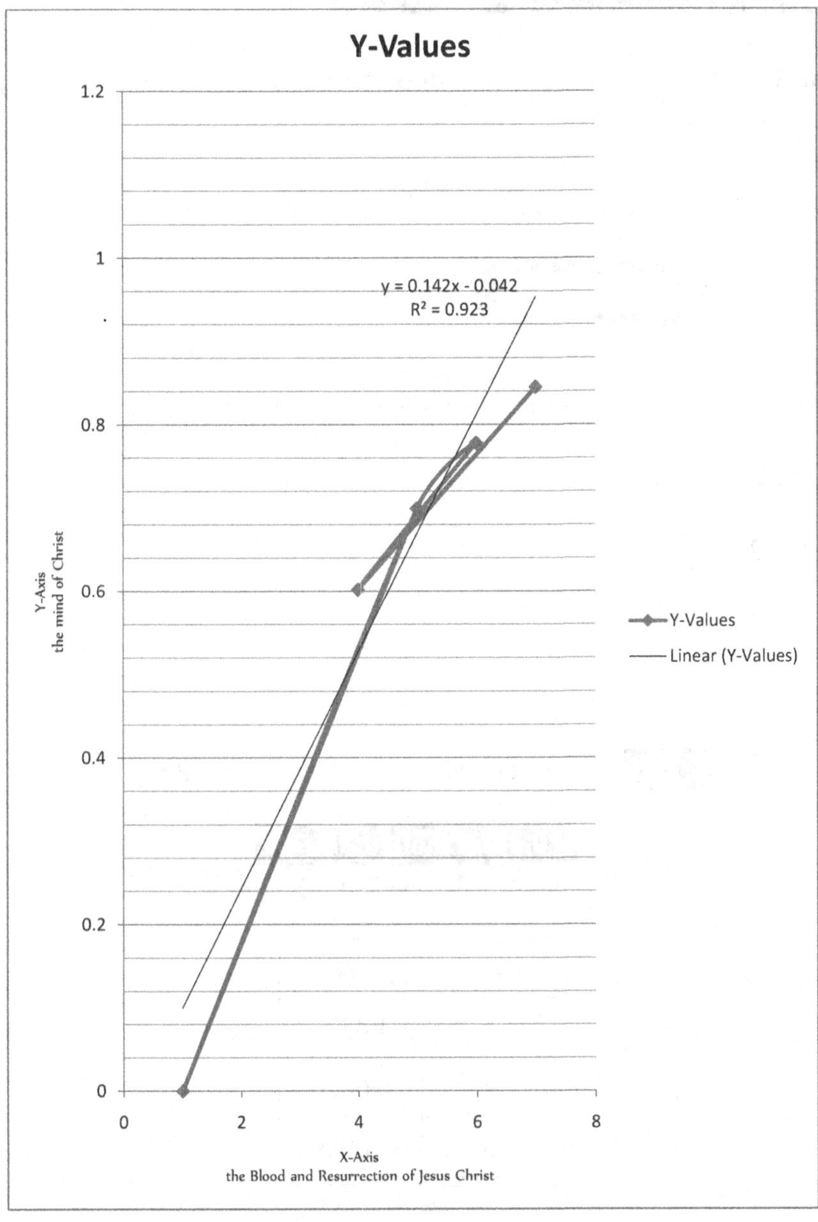

$10^{0.6989}, 10^{0.6989}, 10^{0}, 10^{0.6989}, 10^{0.7781}; 10^{0.6020}, 10^{0.8450}, 10^{0.6020}$.

Pilled Poplar, Hazel, and Chestnut bible rods 2

16. But Jesussavior; deliverer**said unto them, They need not depart; give ye them to eat.**

5, 4; 5. Bible Matrices

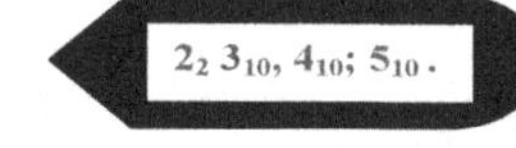

Pilled Poplar, Hazel, and Chestnut bible rods 1

$\text{Log}_{10} 4 = 0.6020$ $\text{Log}_{10} 5 = 0.6989$ $\text{Log}_{10} 3 = 0.4771$

$\text{Log}_2 2 = y$

$2^y = 2$

$2^y = 2^1$

$y = 1$

5, 4; 5. Deep calls unto Deep study bible 1

1, 0.4771, 0.6020; 0.6989.
Deep calls unto Deep study bible 2

x-axis	y-axis
5	1.4771
4	0.6020
5	0.6989

Water Spout *(lightning; combinatorics)* Study bible 1

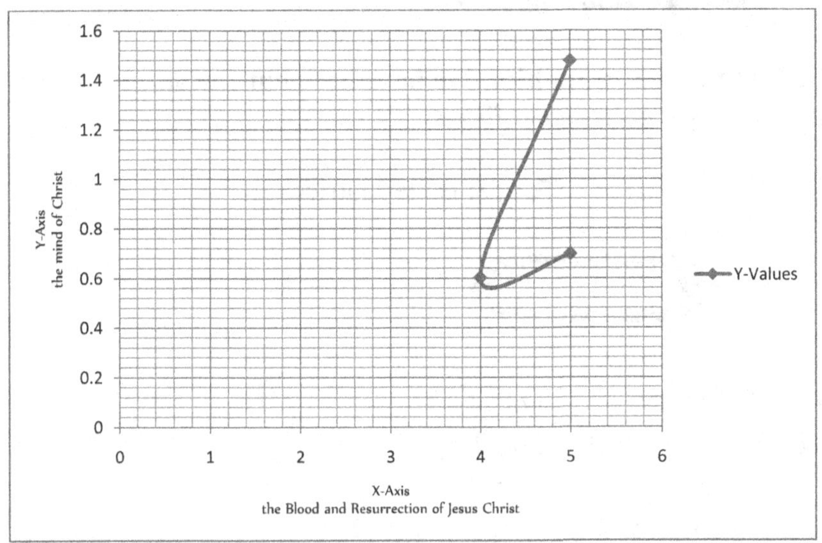

Water Spout *(lightning; combinatorics)* Study bible 2

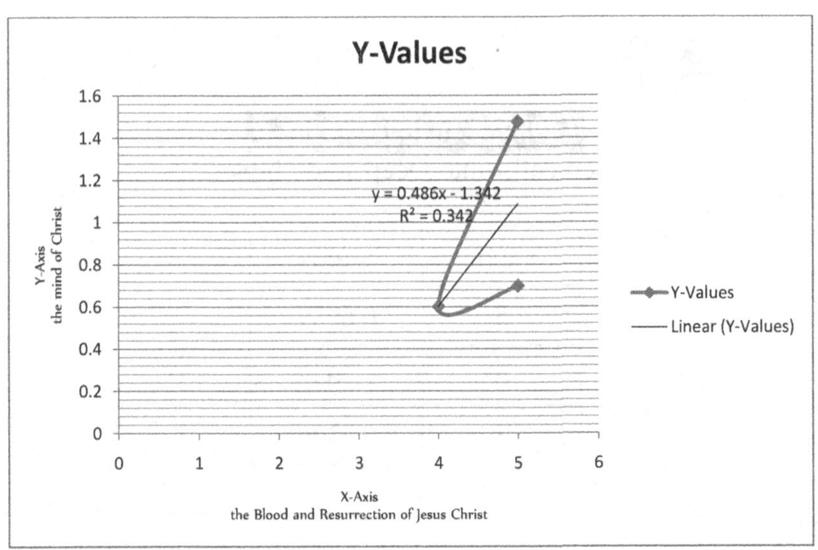

$2^1 \, 10^{0.4771}, 10^{0.6020}; 10^{0.6989}$.

Pilled Poplar, Hazel, and Chestnut bible rods 2

17. And they say unto him, We have here but five grace; 5 x 1 **loaves, and two** witness and support; 2 x 1 **fishes.**

5, 6, 3. Bible Matrices

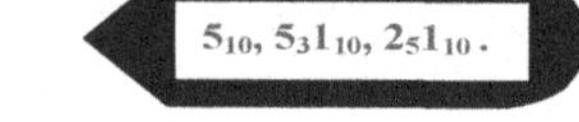

Pilled Poplar, Hazel, and Chestnut bible rods 1

$Log_{10} 5 = 0.6989$
$Log_3 5 = y$
$3^y = 5$
$y \log_{10} 3 = \log_{10} 5$
$y = \log_{10} 5 / \log_{10} 3$
$y = 0.6989 / 0.4771$
$y = 1.4648$

$Log_{10} 1 = 0$
$Log_5 2 = y$
$5^y = 2$
$y \log_{10} 5 = \log_{10} 2$
$y = \log_{10} 2 / \log_{10} 5$
$y = 0.3010 / 0.6989$
$y = 0.4306$

$Log_{10} 1 = 0$

5, 6, 3. Deep calls unto Deep study bible 1

0.6989, 1.4648 0, 0.4306 0.

Deep calls unto Deep study bible 2

x-axis	y-axis
5	0.6989
6	1.4648
3	0.4306

Water Spout *(lightning; combinatorics)* Study bible 1

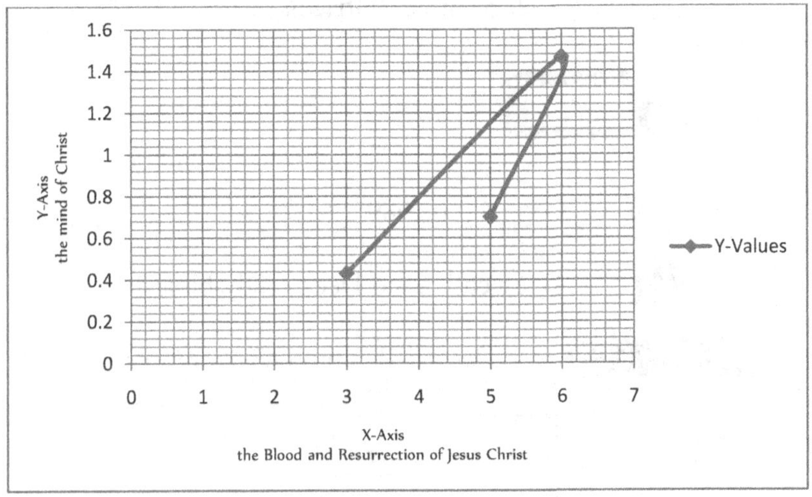

Water Spout *(lightning; combinatorics)* Study bible 2

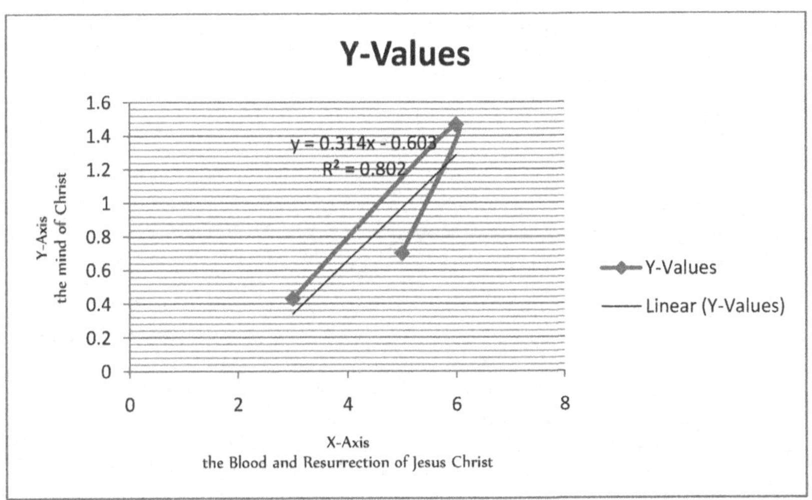

$10^{0.6989}$, $3^{1.4648}$ 10^{0}, $5^{0.4306}$ 10^{0}.

Pilled Poplar, Hazel, and Chestnut bible rods 2

18. He said, Bring them hither to me.

2, 5. Bible Matrices

$\text{Log}_{10} 2 = 0.3010$ $\text{Log}_{10} 5 = 0.6989$

2, 5. Deep calls unto Deep study bible 1

0.3010, 0.6989. Deep calls unto Deep study bible 2

x-axis	y-axis
2	0.3010
5	0.6989

Water Spout *(lightning; combinatorics)* Study bible 1

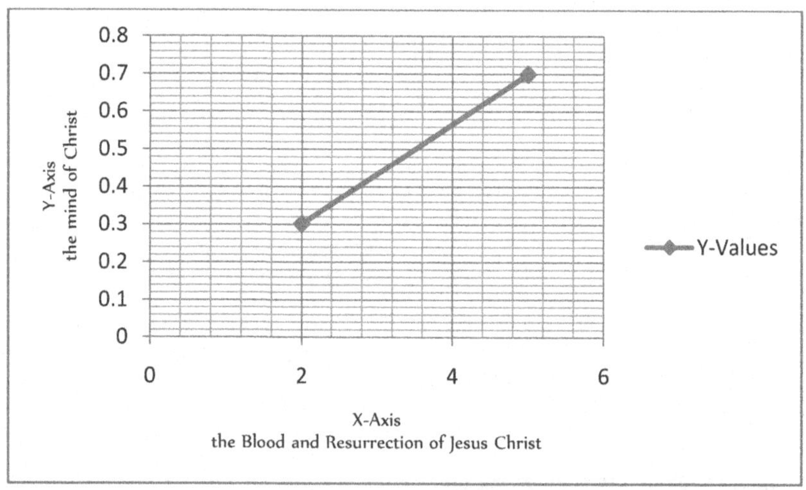

Water Spout *(lightning; combinatorics)* Study bible 2

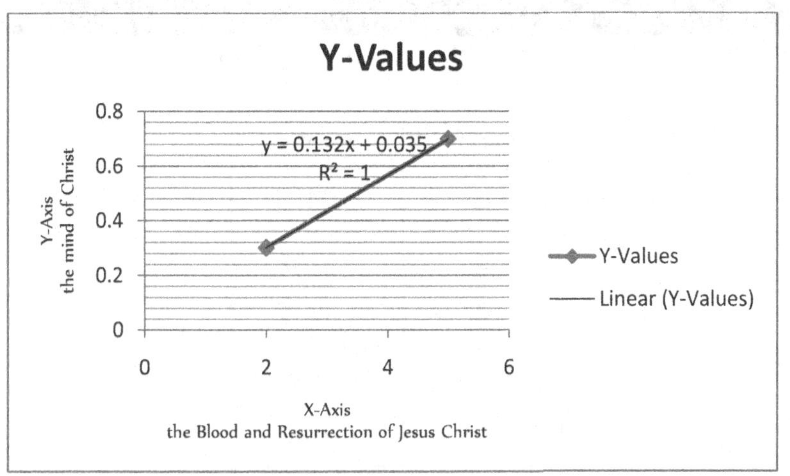

$10^{0.3010}, 10^{0.6989}$.

Pilled Poplar, Hazel, and Chestnut bible rods 2

19. And he commanded the multitude to sit down on the grass, and took the five grace; 5 x 1 **loaves, and the two** witness and support; 2 x 1 **fishes, and looking up to heaven, he blessed, and brake, and gave the loaves to his disciples, and the disciples to the multitude.**

11, 5, 4, 5, 2, 2, 7, 6. Bible Matrices

$11_{10}, 4_3 1_{10}, 3_5 1_{10}, 5_{10}, 2_{10}, 2_{10}, 7_{10}, 6_{10}$.

Pilled Poplar, Hazel, and Chestnut bible rods 1

$Log_{10} 5 = 0.6989$	$Log_{10} 2 = 0.3010$	$Log_{10} 2 = 0.3010$	$Log_{10} 7 = 0.8450$
$Log_{10} 6 = 0.7781$	$Log_{10} 11 = 1.0413$	$Log_{10} 1 = 0$	$Log_{10} 1 = 0$
$Log_3 5 = y$	$Log_3 4 = y$		
$3^y = 5$	$3^y = 4$		
$y \log_{10} 3 = \log_{10} 5$	$y \log_{10} 3 = \log_{10} 4$		
$y = \log_{10} 5 / \log_{10} 3$	$y = \log_{10} 4 / \log_{10} 3$		
$y = 0.6989 / 0.4771$	$y = 0.6020 / 0.4771$		
$y = 1.4648$	$y = 1.2617$		

11, 5, 4, 5, 2, 2, 7, 6. Deep calls unto Deep study bible 1

1.0413, 1.2617 0, 1.4648 0, 0.6989, 0.3010, 0.3010, 0.8450, 0.7781.
Deep calls unto Deep study bible 2

x-axis	y-axis
11	1.0413
5	1.2617
4	1.4648
5	0.6989
2	0.3010
2	0.3010
7	0.8450
6	0.7781

Water Spout *(lightning; combinatorics)* Study bible 1

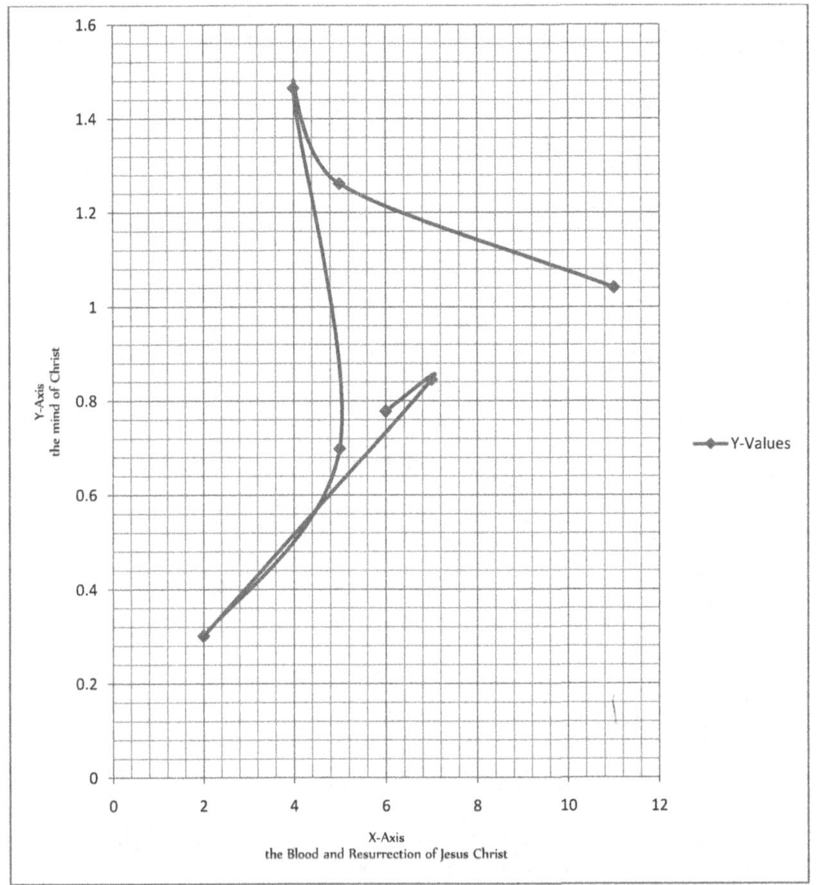

Water Spout *(lightning; combinatorics)* Study bible 2

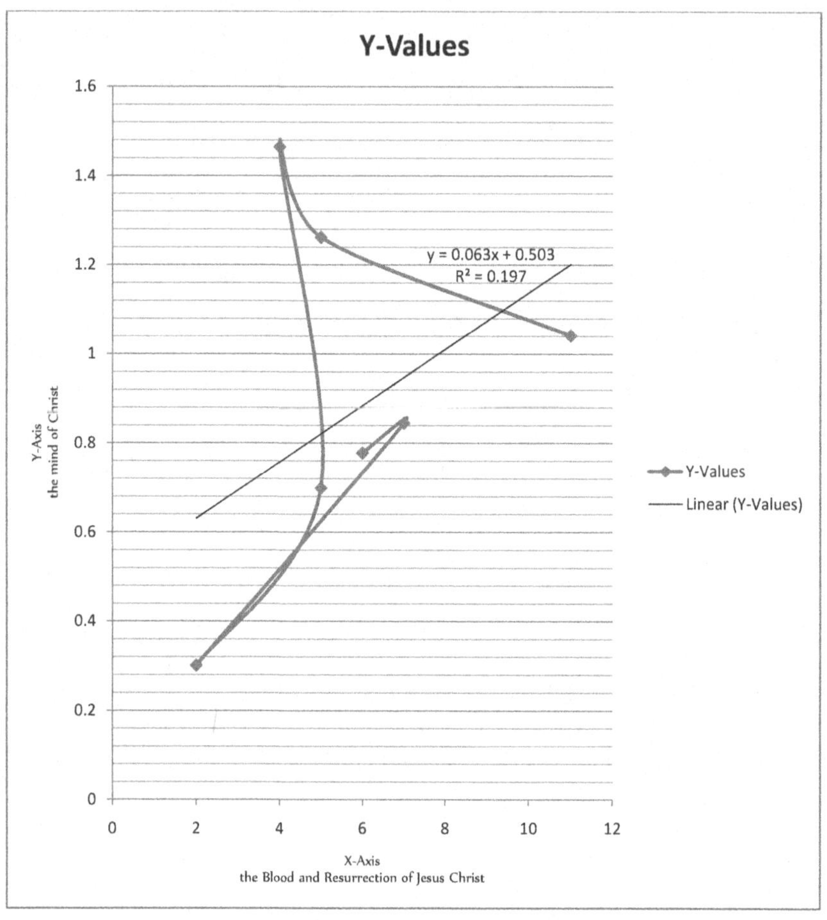

$10^{1.0413}$, $3^{1.2617}$ 10^{0}, $5^{1.4648}$ 10^{0} . $10^{0.6989}$, $10^{0.3010}$, $10^{0.3010}$,$10^{0.8450}$, $10^{0.7781}$.

Pilled Poplar, Hazel, and Chestnut bible rods 2

20. And they did all eat, and were filled: and they took up of the fragments that remained twelve **dominion or divine government; 2 x 2 x 3** **baskets full.**

5, 3: 12. Bible Matrices

$5_{10}, 3_{10}: 10_7 2_{10}.$

Pilled Poplar, Hazel, and Chestnut bible rods 1

$Log_{10} 3 = 0.4771$ $Log_{10} 5 = 0.6989$ $Log_{10} 2 = 0.3010$

$$Log_7 10 = y$$

$$7^y = 10$$

$$y \log_{10} 7 = \log_{10} 10$$

$$y = \log_{10} 10 / \log_{10} 7$$

$$y = 1/0.8450$$

$$y = 1.1834$$

5, 3: 12. Deep calls unto Deep study bible 1

0.6989, 4771: 1.1834 0.3010.

Deep calls unto Deep study bible 2

x-axis	y-axis
5	0.6989
3	0.4771
12	1.4844

Water Spout *(lightning; combinatorics)* Study bible 1

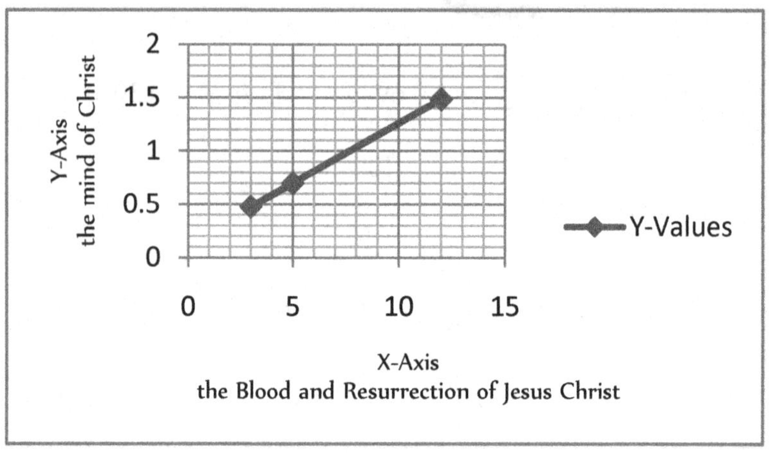

Water Spout *(lightning; combinatorics)* Study bible 2

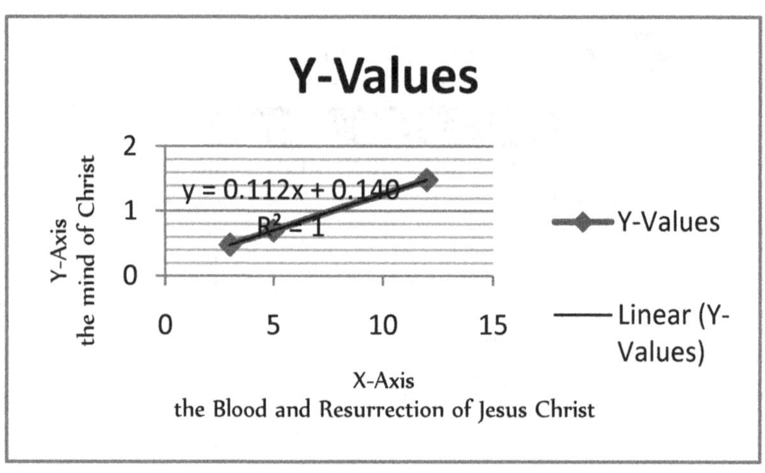

Pilled Poplar, Hazel, and Chestnut bible rods 2

21. And they that had eaten were about five thousand 2 x 2 x 2 x 5 x 5 x 5 x 5 **men, beside women and children.**

10, 4. Bible Matrices

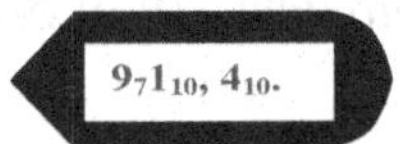

Pilled Poplar, Hazel, and Chestnut bible rods 1

$\text{Log}_{10} 4 = 0.6020$ $\text{Log}_{10} 1 = 0$

$\text{Log}_7 9 = y$

$7^y = 9$

$y \log_{10} 7 = \log_{10} 9$

$y = \log_{10} 9 / \log_{10} 7$

$y = 0.9542 / 0.8450$

$y = 1.1292$

10, 4. Deep calls unto Deep study bible 1

1.1292 0, 0.6020. Deep calls unto Deep study bible 2

x-axis	y-axis
10	1.1292
4	0.6020

Water Spout *(lightning; combinatorics)* Study bible 1

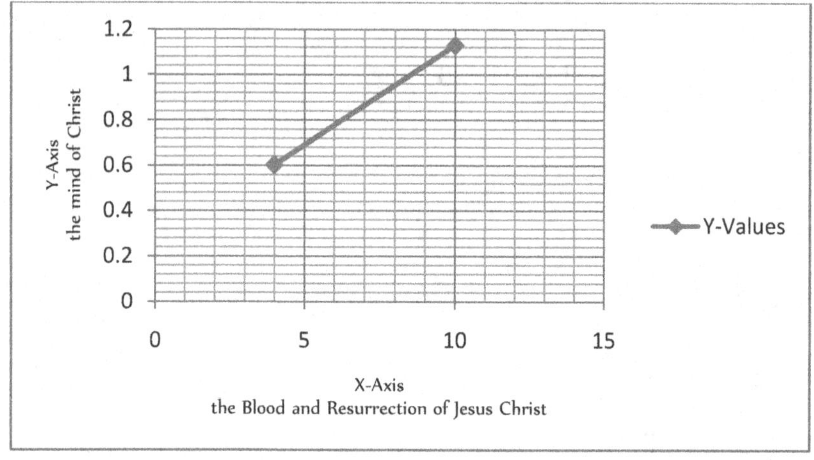

Water Spout *(lightning; combinatorics)* Study bible 2

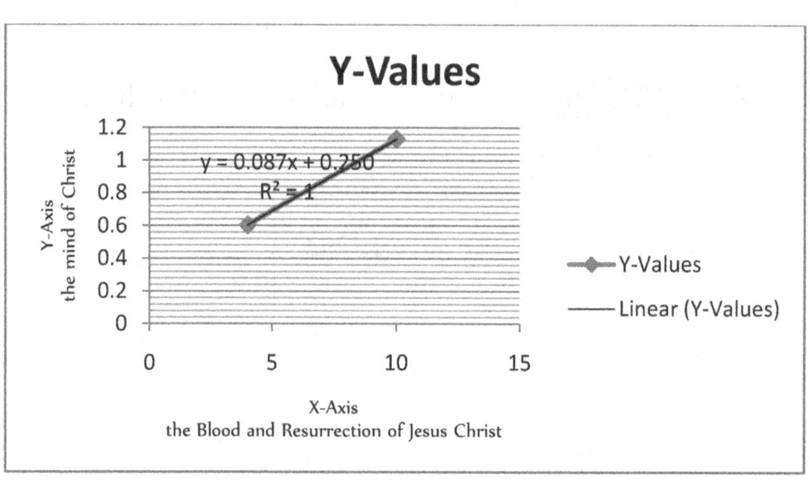

$7^{1.1292}$ 10^{0}, $10^{0.6020}$.

Pilled Poplar, Hazel, and Chestnut bible rods 2

22. And straightway Jesussavior; deliverer**constrained his disciples to get into a ship, and to go before him unto the other side, while he sent the multitudes away.**

11, 9, 6. Bible Matrices

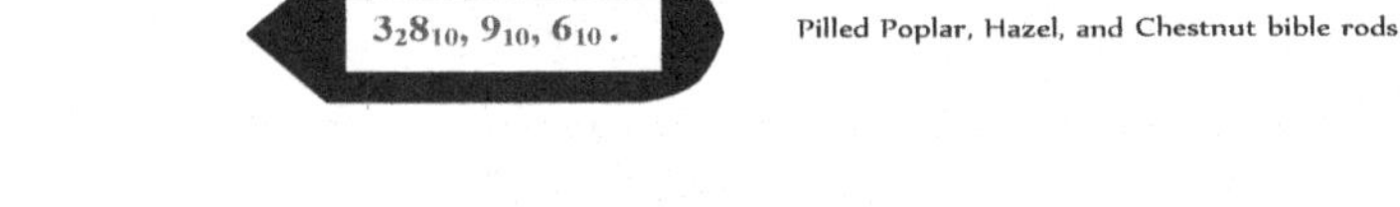

$\log_{10} 9 = 0.9542$ $\log_{10} 6 = 0.7781$ $\log_{10} 8 = 0.9030$

$\log_2 3 = y$

$2^y = 3$

$y \log_{10} 2 = \log_{10} 3$

$y = \log_{10} 3 / \log_{10} 2$

$y = 0.4771 / 0.3010$

$y = 1.5850$

11, 9, 6. Deep calls unto Deep study bible 1

1.5850 0.9030, 0.9542, 0.7781.
Deep calls unto Deep study bible 2

x-axis	y-axis
11	2.4880
9	0.9542
6	0.7781

Water Spout *(lightning; combinatorics)* Study bible 1

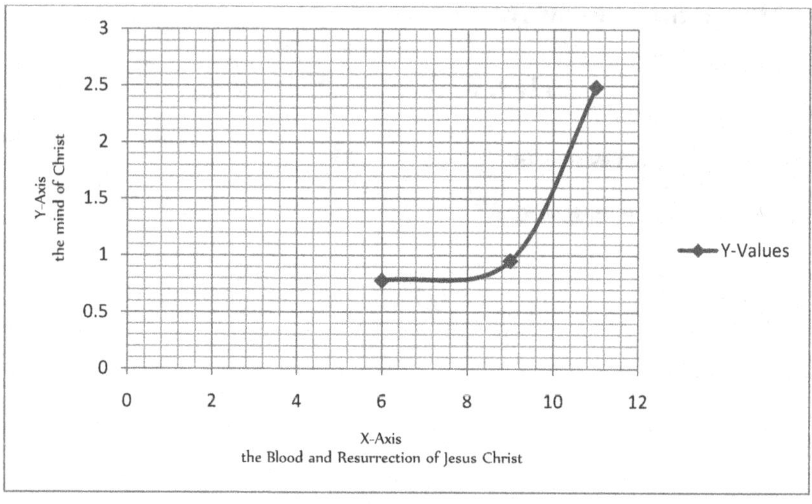

Water Spout *(lightning; combinatorics)* Study bible 2

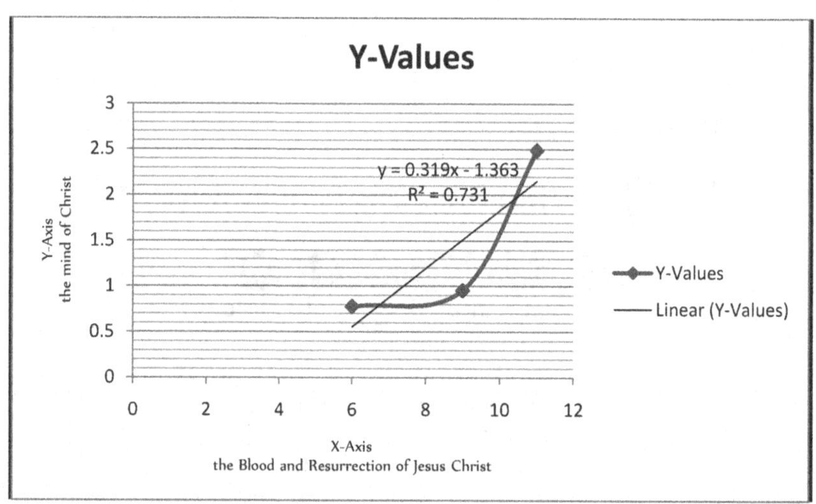

$2^{1.5850}$ $10^{0.9030}$, $10^{0.9542}$, $10^{0.7781}$.

Pilled Poplar, Hazel, and Chestnut bible rods 2

23. And when he had sent the multitudes away, he went up into a mountain apart to pray: and when the evening was come, he was there alone.

8, 9: 6, 4. Bible Matrices

$8_{10}, 9_{10}: 6_{10}, 4_{10}.$

Pilled Poplar, Hazel, and Chestnut bible rods 1

$\text{Log}_{10} 9 = 0.9542$ $\text{Log}_{10} 8 = 0.9030$ $\text{Log}_{10} 6 = 0.7781$ $\text{Log}_{10} 4 = 0.6020$

8, 9: 6, 4. Deep calls unto Deep study bible 1

0.9030, 0.9542: 0.7781, 0.6020.
Deep calls unto Deep study bible 2

x-axis	y-axis
8	0.9030
9	0.9542
6	0.7781
4	0.6020

Water Spout *(lightning; combinatorics)* Study bible 1

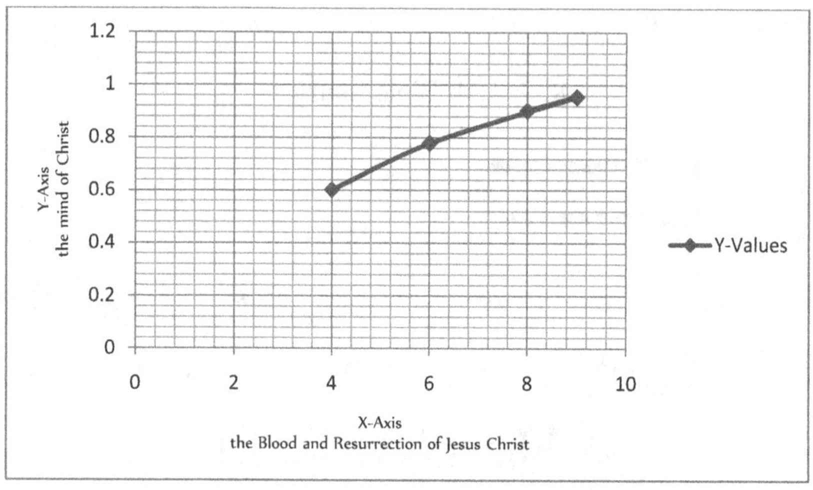

Water Spout *(lightning; combinatorics)* Study bible 2

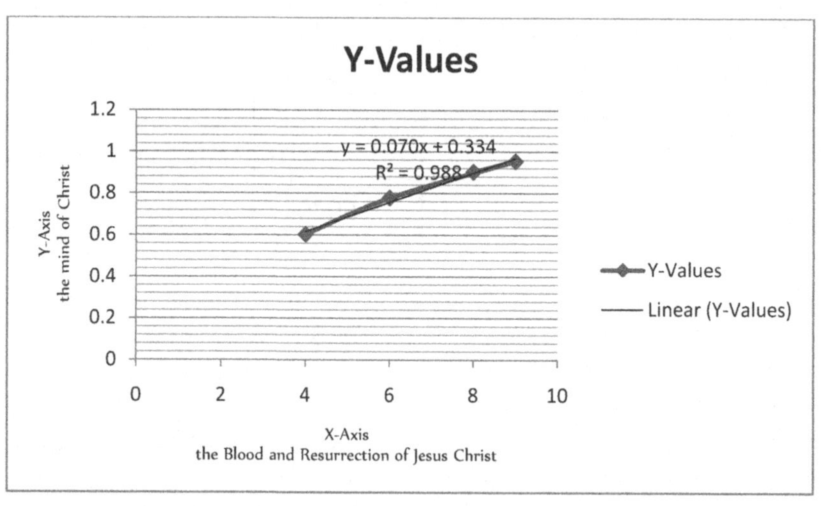

$10^{0.9030}$, $10^{0.9542}$: $10^{0.7781}$, $10^{0.6020}$.

Pilled Poplar, Hazel, and Chestnut bible rods 2

24. But the ship was now in the midst of the sea, tossed with waves: for the wind was contrary.

11, 3: 5. Bible Matrices

$Log_{10} 11 = 1.0413$ $Log_{10} 5 = 0.6989$ $Log_{10} 3 = 0.4771$

11, 3: 5. Deep calls unto Deep study bible 1

1.0413, 0.4771: 0.6989.
Deep calls unto Deep study bible 2

x-axis	y-axis
11	1.0413
3	0.4771
5	0.6989

Water Spout *(lightning; combinatorics)* Study bible 1

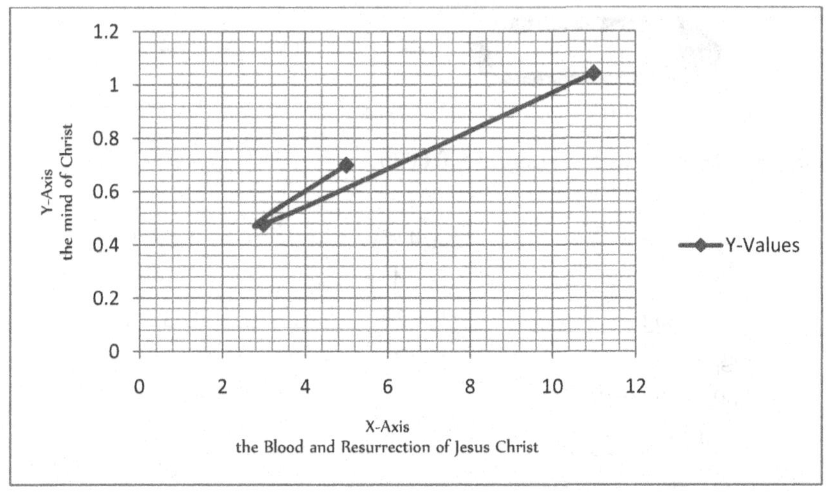

Water Spout *(lightning; combinatorics)* Study bible 2

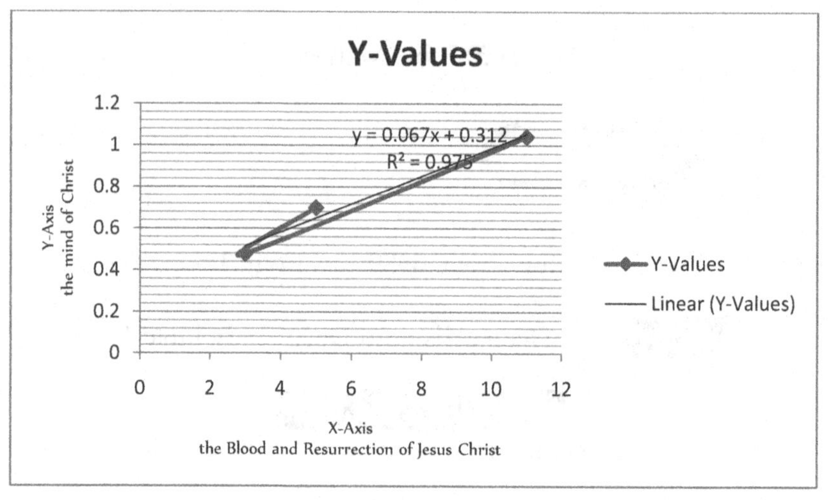

Pilled Poplar, Hazel, and Chestnut bible rods 2

25. And in the fourth balance or earth ; 2 x 2 **watch** 3am to 6am **of the night Jesus** savior; deliverer **went unto them, walking on the sea.**

12, 4. Bible Matrices

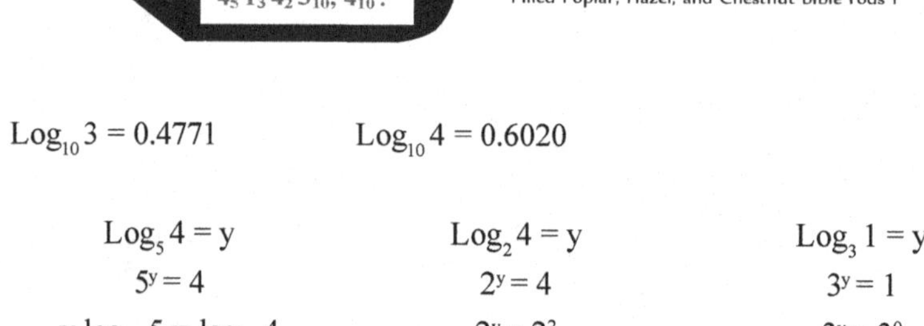

Pilled Poplar, Hazel, and Chestnut bible rods 1

$\text{Log}_{10} 3 = 0.4771$ $\text{Log}_{10} 4 = 0.6020$

$\text{Log}_5 4 = y$

$5^y = 4$

$y \log_{10} 5 = \log_{10} 4$

$y = \log_{10} 4 / \log_{10} 5$

$y = 0.6020 / 0.6989$

$y = 0.8613$

$\text{Log}_2 4 = y$

$2^y = 4$

$2^y = 2^2$

$y = 2$

$\text{Log}_3 1 = y$

$3^y = 1$

$3^y = 3^0$

$y = 0$

12, 4. Deep calls unto Deep study bible 1

0.8613 0 2 0.4771, 0.6020.

Deep calls unto Deep study bible 2

x-axis	y-axis
12	3.3384
4	0.6020

Water Spout *(lightning; combinatorics)* Study bible 1

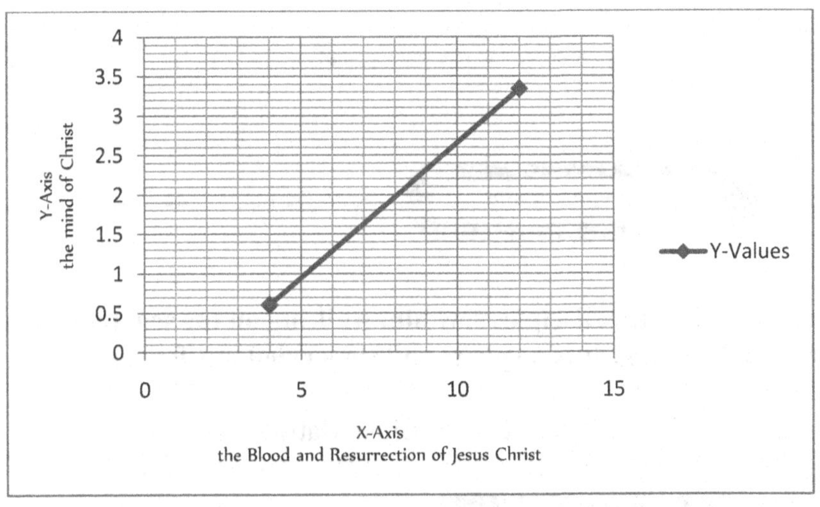

Water Spout *(lightning; combinatorics)* Study bible 2

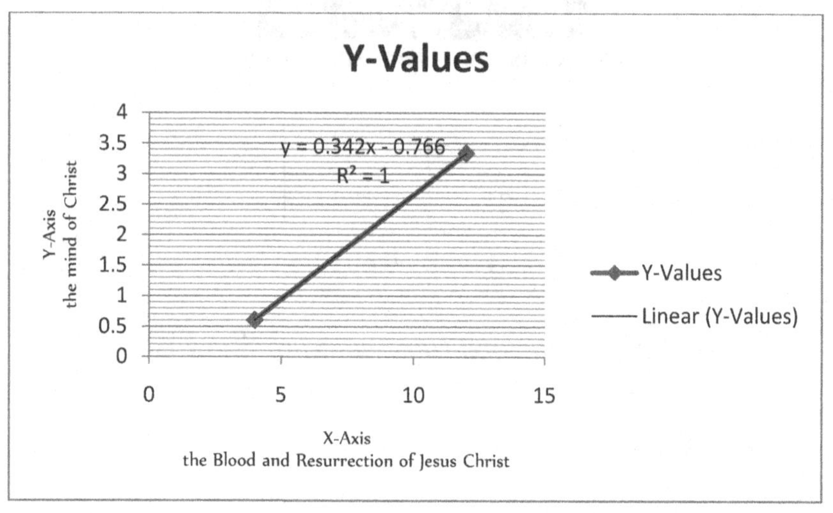

Pilled Poplar, Hazel, and Chestnut bible rods 2

26. And when the disciples saw him walking on the sea, they were troubled, saying, It is a spirit; and they cried out for fear.

10, 3, 1, 4; 6. Bible Matrices

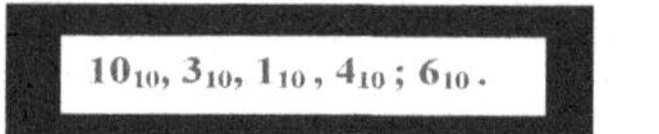

Pilled Poplar, Hazel, and Chestnut bible rods 1

$\text{Log}_{10} 10 = 1$ $\text{Log}_{10} 3 = 0.4771$ $\text{Log}_{10} 4 = 0.6020$ $\text{Log}_{10} 6 = 0.7781$ $\text{Log}_{10} 1 = 0$

10, 3, 1, 4; 6. Deep calls unto Deep study bible 1

1, 0.4771, 0, 0.6020; 0.7781.
Deep calls unto Deep study bible 2

x-axis	y-axis
10	1
3	0.4771
1	0
4	0.6020
6	0.7781

Water Spout *(lightning; combinatorics)* Study bible 1

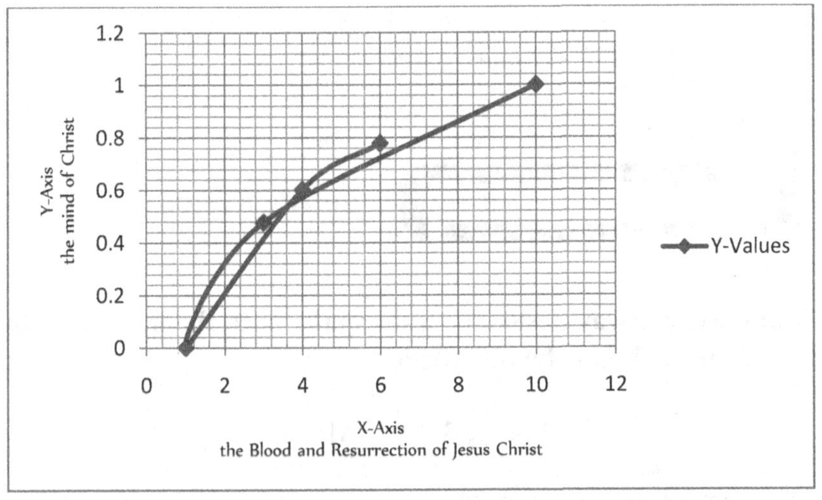

Water Spout *(lightning; combinatorics)* Study bible 2

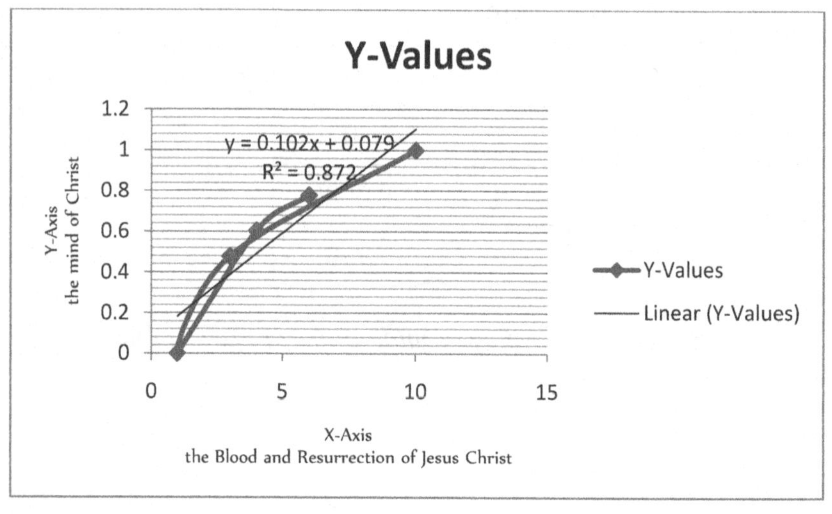

27. But straightway Jesussavior; deliverer**spake unto them, saying, Be of good cheer; it is I; be not afraid.**

6, 1, 4; 3; 3. Bible Matrices

$3_2\, 3_{10}$, 1_{10}, 4_{10}; 3_{10}; 3_{10}.

Pilled Poplar, Hazel, and Chestnut bible rods 1

$\text{Log}_{10} 3 = 0.4771$ $\text{Log}_{10} 3 = 0.4771$ $\text{Log}_{10} 3 = 0.4771$ $\text{Log}_{10} 4 = 0.6020$ $\text{Log}_{10} 1 = 0$

$\text{Log}_2 3 = y$

$2^y = 3$

$y \log_{10} 2 = \log_{10} 3$

$y = \log_{10} 3 / \log_{10} 2$

$y = 0.4771 / 0.3010$

$y = 1.5850$

6, 1, 4; 3; 3. Deep calls unto Deep study bible 1

1.5850 0.4771, 0, 0.6020; 0.4771; 0.4771.
Deep calls unto Deep study bible 2

x-axis	y-axis
6	2.0621
1	0
4	0.6020
3	0.4771
3	0.4771

Water Spout *(lightning; combinatorics)* Study bible 1

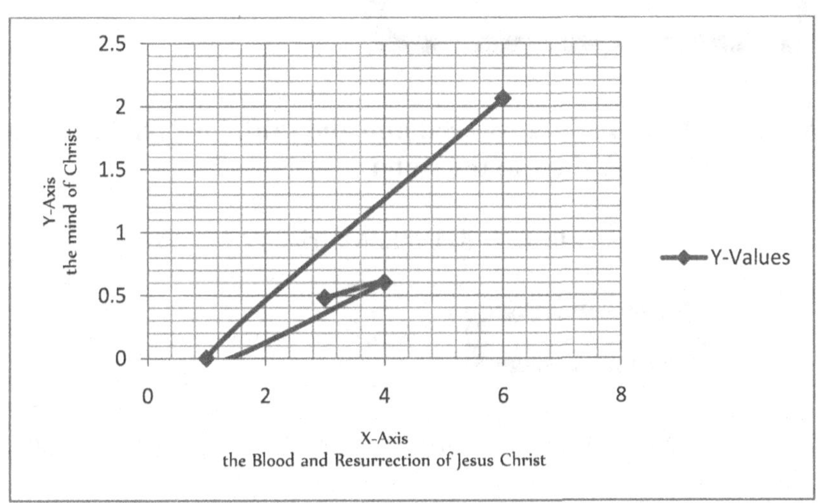

Water Spout *(lightning; combinatorics)* Study bible 2

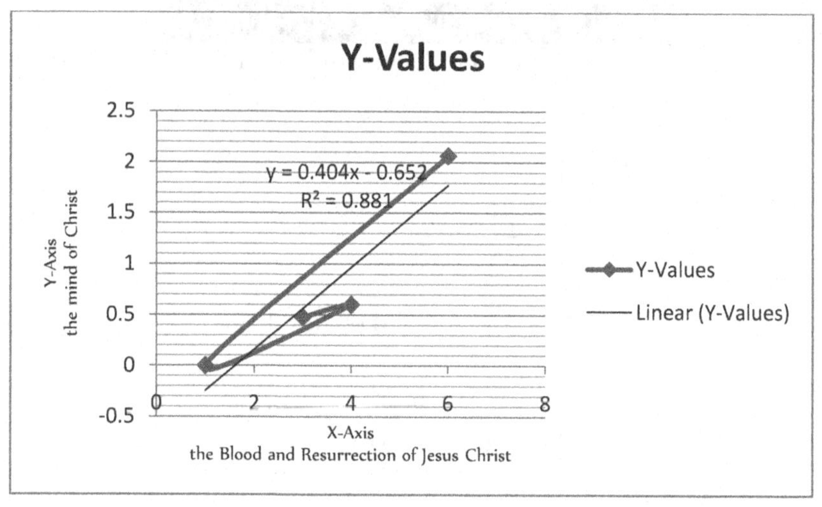

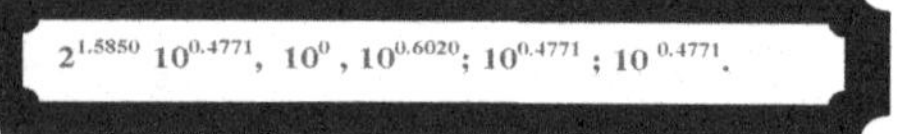
$2^{1.5850}\ 10^{0.4771},\ 10^{0},\ 10^{0.6020};\ 10^{0.4771};\ 10^{0.4771}.$

Pilled Poplar, Hazel, and Chestnut bible rods 2

28. And Petera rock or stone**answered him and said, Lord, if it be thou, bid me come unto thee on the water.**

6, 1, 4, 8. Bible Matrices

$2_4\ 4_{10},\ 1_{10},\ 4_{10},\ 8_{10}.$

Pilled Poplar, Hazel, and Chestnut bible rods 1

$\text{Log}_{10} 4 = 0.6020$ $\text{Log}_{10} 8 = 0.9030$ $\text{Log}_{10} 1 = 0$ $\text{Log}_{10} 4 = 0.6020$

$\text{Log}_4 2 = y$

$4^y = 2$

$2^{2y} = 2^1$

$2y = 1$

$y = ½ \text{ or } 0.5$

6, 1, 4, 8. Deep calls unto Deep study bible 1

0.5 0.6020, 0, 0.6020, 0.9030.
Deep calls unto Deep study bible 2

x-axis	y-axis
6	1.1020
1	0
4	0.6020
8	0.9030

Water Spout *(lightning; combinatorics)* Study bible 1

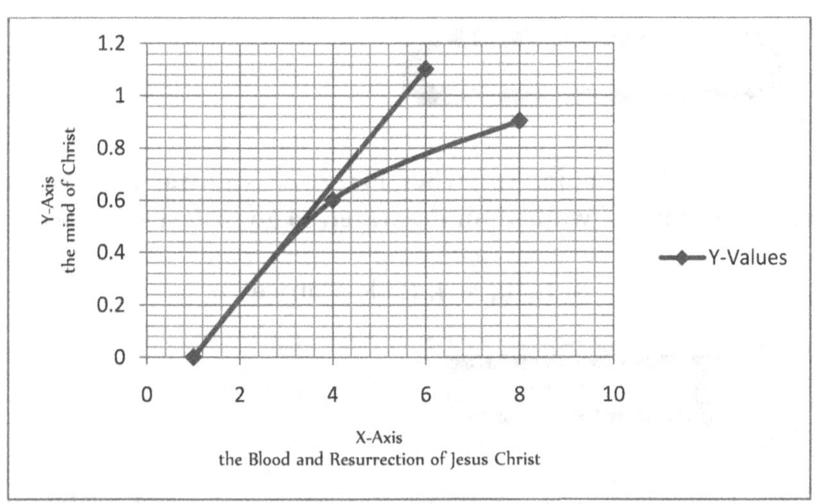

Water Spout *(lightning; combinatorics)* Study bible 2

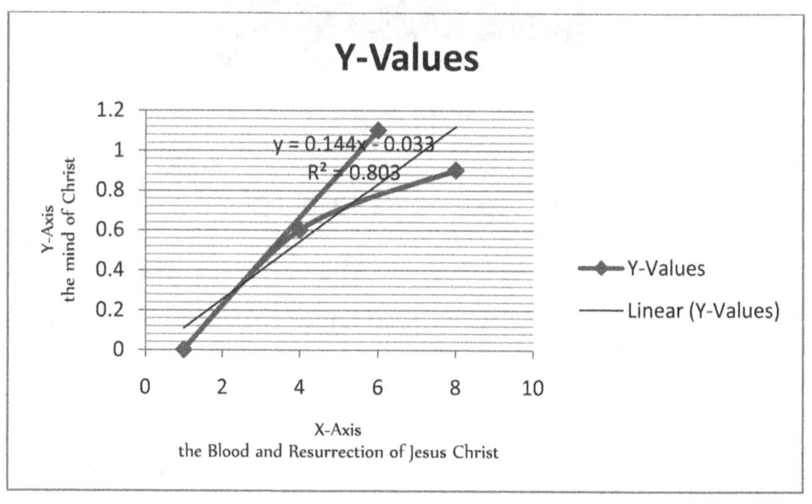

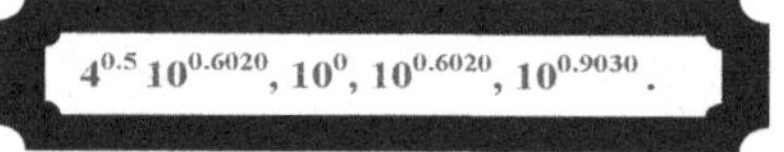
$4^{0.5}$ $10^{0.6020}$, 10^{0}, $10^{0.6020}$, $10^{0.9030}$.

Pilled Poplar, Hazel, and Chestnut bible rods 2

29. And he said, Come. And when Peter a rock or stone**was come down out of the ship, he walked on the water, to go to Jesus**savior; deliverer.

3, 1. 10, 5, 4. Bible Matrices

3_{10}, 1_{10}. $3_4 7_{10}$, 5_{10}, 4_2.

Pilled Poplar, Hazel, and Chestnut bible rods 1

$Log_{10} 3 = 0.4771$ $Log_{10} 5 = 0.6989$ $Log_{10} 1 = 0$ $Log_{10} 7 = 0.8450$

$Log_4 3 = y$

$4^y = 3$

$y \log_{10} 4 = \log_{10}$

$y = \log_{10} 3 / \log_{10}$

$y = 0.4771 / 0.6020$

$y = 0.7925$

$Log_2 4 = y$

$2^y = 4$

$3\ 2^y = 2^2$

$4\ y = 2$

3, 1. 10, 5, 4. Deep calls unto Deep study bible 1

0.4771, 0, 0.7925 0.8450, 0.6989, 2.
Deep calls unto Deep study bible 2

x-axis	y-axis
3	0.4771
1	0
10	1.6375
5	0.6989
4	2

Water Spout *(lightning; combinatorics)* Study bible 1

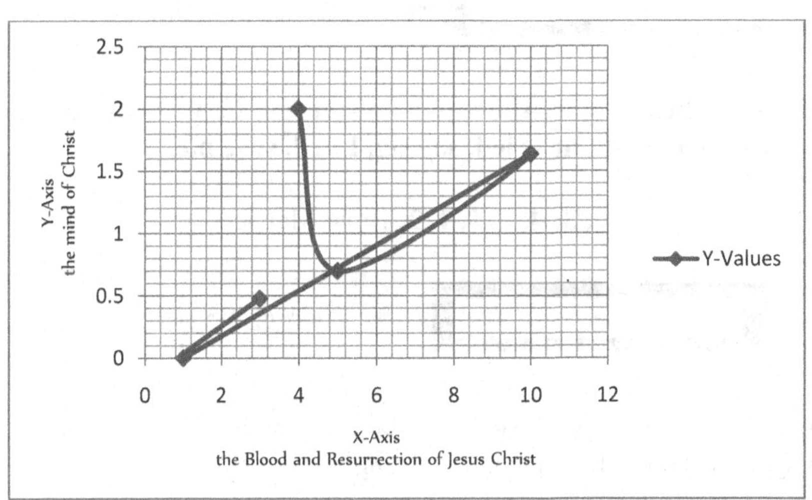

Water Spout *(lightning; combinatorics)* Study bible 2

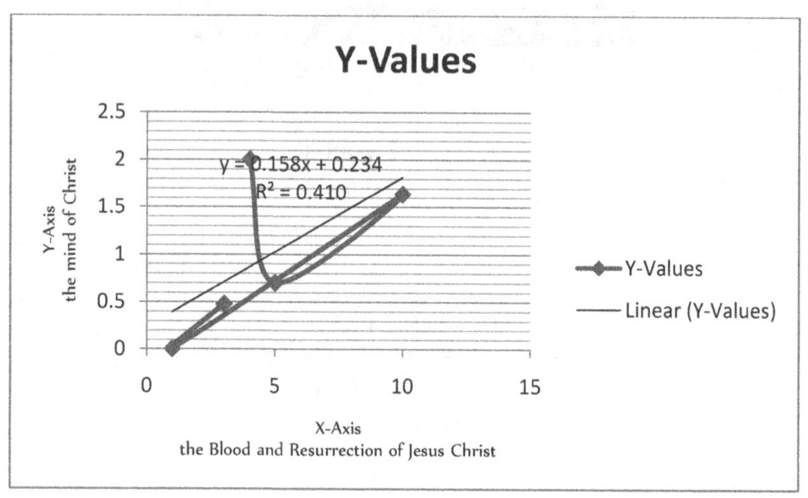

$10^{0.4771}$, 10^{0}. $4^{0.7925}$ $10^{0.8450}$, $10^{0.6989}$, 2^{2}. Pilled Poplar, Hazel, and Chestnut bible rods 2

30. But when he saw the wind boisterous, he was afraid; and beginning to sink, he cried, saying, Lord, save me.

7, 3; 4, 2, 1, 1, 2. Bible Matrices

7_{10}, 3_{10}; 4_{10}, 2_{10}, 1_{10}, 1_{10}, 2_{10}. Pilled Poplar, Hazel, and Chestnut bible rods 1

$Log_{10} 7 = 0.8450$ $Log_{10} 3 = 0.4771$ $Log_{10} 4 = 0.6020$ $Log_{10} 2 = 0.3010$
$Log_{10} 2 = 0.3010$ $Log_{10} 1 = 0$ $Log_{10} 1 = 0$

7, 3; 4, 2, 1, 1, 2. Deep calls unto Deep study bible 1

0.8450, 0.4771; 0.6020, 0.3010, 0, 0, 0.3010.
Deep calls unto Deep study bible 2

x-axis	y-axis
7	0.8450
3	0.4771
4	0.6020
2	0.3010
1	0
1	0
2	0.3010

Water Spout *(lightning; combinatorics)* Study bible 1

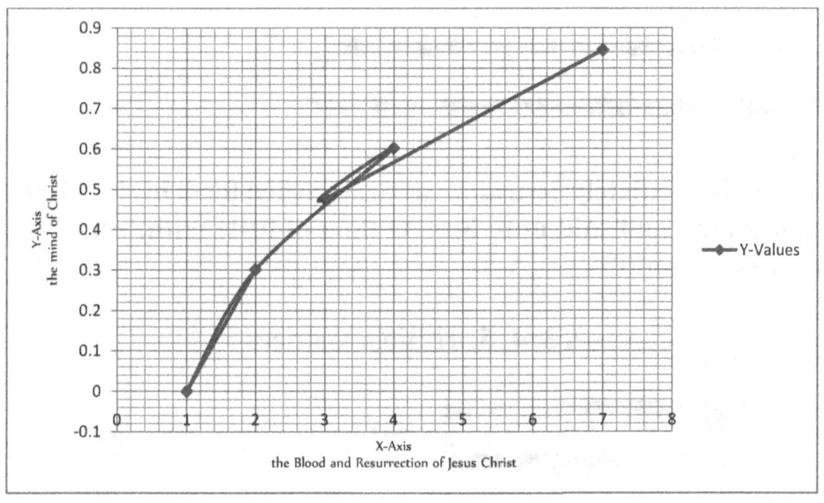

Water Spout *(lightning; combinatorics)* Study bible 2

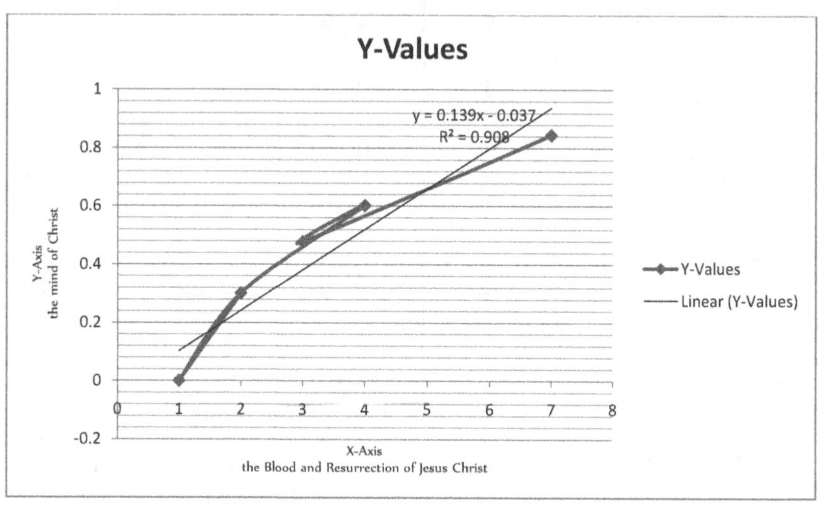

$10^{0.8450}$, $10^{0.4771}$; $10^{0.6020}$, $10^{0.3010}$, 10^{0}, 10^{0}, $10^{0.3010}$.

Pilled Poplar, Hazel, and Chestnut bible rods 2

31. And immediately Jesussavior; deliverer **stretched forth his hand, and caught him, and said unto him, O thou of little faith, wherefore didst thou doubt?**

7, 3, 4, 5, 4? Bible Matrices

$3_2\ 4_{10}$, 3_{10}, 4_{10}, 5_{10}, 4_{10} ?

Pilled Poplar, Hazel, and Chestnut bible rods 1

$\text{Log}_{10} 3 = 0.4771$ $\text{Log}_{10} 5 = 0.6989$ $\text{Log}_{10} 4 = 0.6020$ $\text{Log}_{10} 4 = 0.6020$ $\text{Log}_{10} 4 = 0.6020$

$\text{Log}_2 3 = y$

$2^y = 3$

$y \log_{10} 2 = \log_{10} 3$

$y = \log_{10} 3 / \log_{10} 2$

$y = 0.4771 / 0.3010$

$y = 1.5850$

7, 3, 4, 5, 4? Deep calls unto Deep study bible 1

1.5850 0.6020, 0.4771, 0.6020, 0.6989, 0.6020?
Deep calls unto Deep study bible 2

x-axis	y-axis
7	2.1870
3	0.4771
4	0.6020
5	0.6989
4	0.6020

Water Spout *(lightning; combinatorics)* Study bible 1

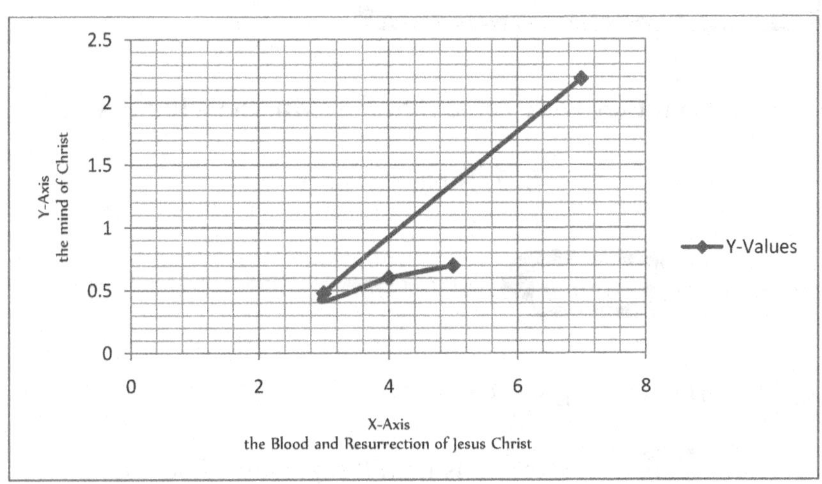

Water Spout *(lightning; combinatorics)* Study bible 2

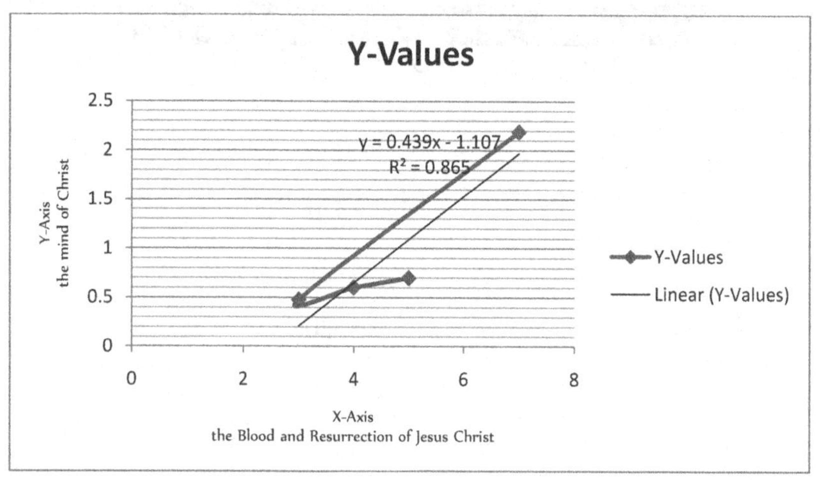

Pilled Poplar, Hazel, and Chestnut bible rods 2

32. And when they were come into the ship, the wind ceased.

8, 3. Bible Matrices

$\text{Log}_{10} 8 = 0.9030$ $\text{Log}_{10} 3 = 0.4771$

8, 3. Deep calls unto Deep study bible 1

0.9030, 0.4771. Deep calls unto Deep study bible 2

x-axis	y-axis
8	0.9030
3	0.4771

Water Spout *(lightning; combinatorics)* Study bible 1

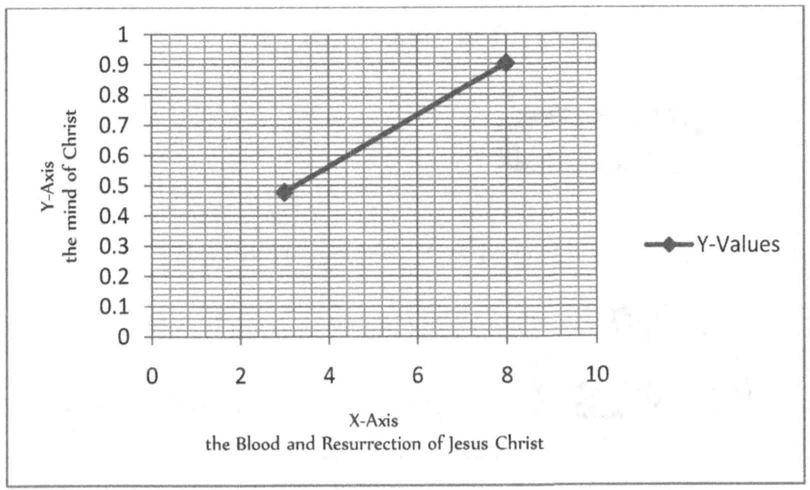

Water Spout *(lightning; combinatorics)* Study bible 2

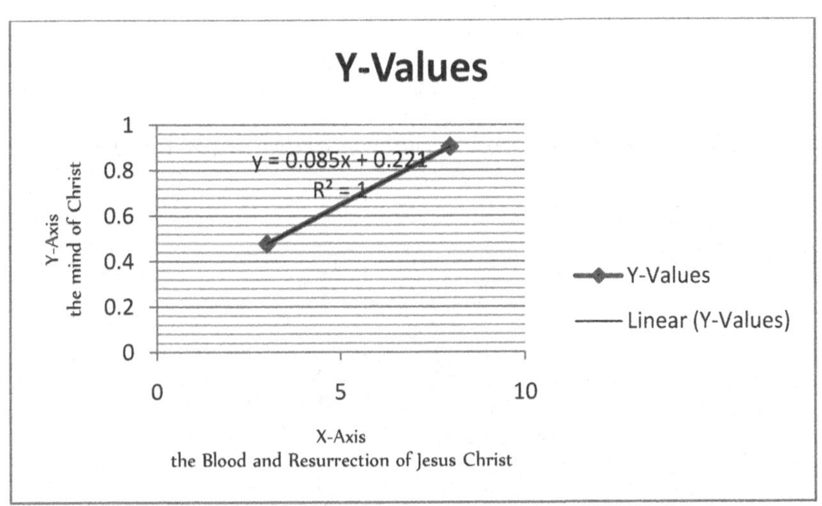

$10^{0.9030}$, $10^{0.4771}$.

Pilled Poplar, Hazel, and Chestnut bible rods 2

33. Then they that were in the ship came and worshipped him, saying, Of a truth thou art the Son of God.

11, 1, 9. Bible Matrices

$\log_{10} 9 = 0.9542$ $\log_{10} 1 = 0$ $\log_{10} 11 = 1.0413$

11, 1, 9. Deep calls unto Deep study bible 1

1.0413, 0, 0.9542. Deep calls unto Deep study bible 2

x-axis	y-axis
11	1.0413
1	0
9	0.9542

Water Spout *(lightning; combinatorics)* Study bible 1

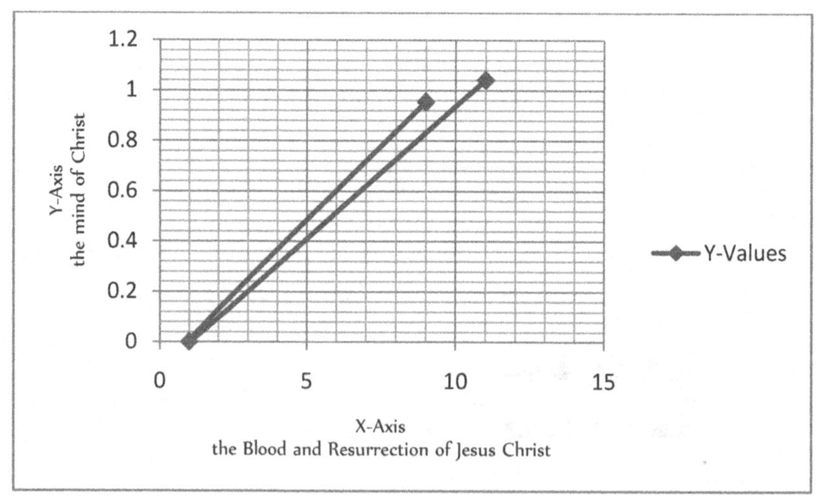

Water Spout *(lightning; combinatorics)* Study bible 2

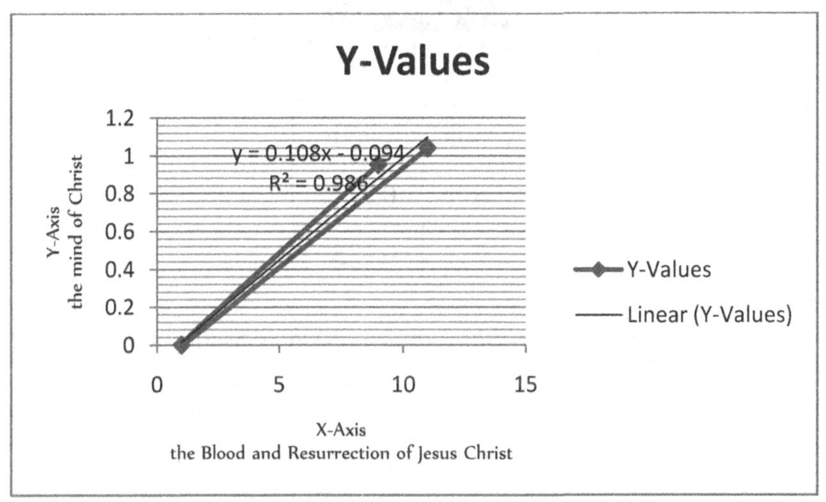

Pilled Poplar, Hazel, and Chestnut bible rods 2

34. And when they were gone over, they came into the land of Gennesaretgarden of the prince; a garden of riches.

6, 7. Bible Matrices

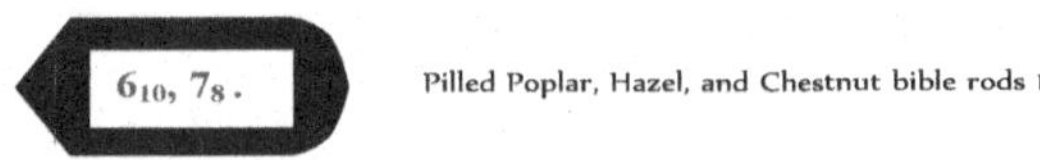

Pilled Poplar, Hazel, and Chestnut bible rods 1

$\text{Log}_{10} 6 = 0.7781$

$\text{Log}_{8} 7 = y$

$8^{y} = 7$

$y \log_{10} 8 = \log_{10} 7$

$y = \log_{10} 7 / \log_{10} 8$

$y = 0.8450 / 0.9030$

$y = 0.9357$

6, 7. Deep calls unto Deep study bible 1

0.7781, 0.9357.
Deep calls unto Deep study bible 2

x-axis	y-axis
6	0.7781
7	0.9357

Water Spout *(lightning; combinatorics)* Study bible 1

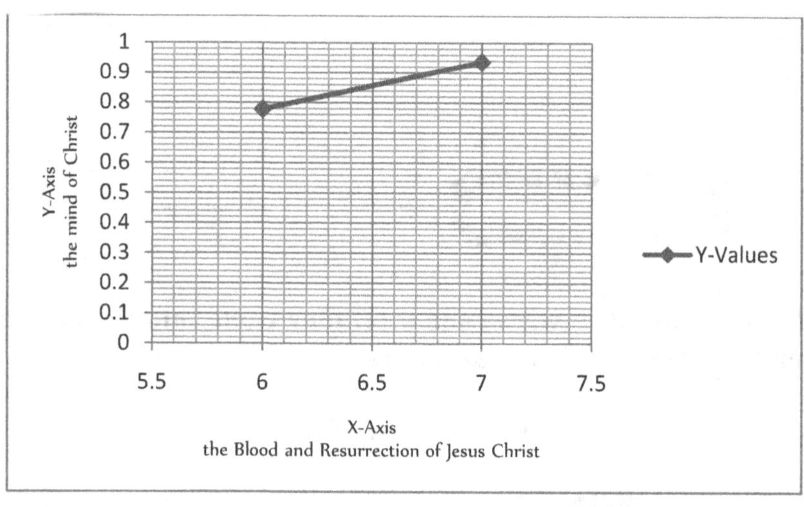

Water Spout *(lightning; combinatorics)* Study bible 2

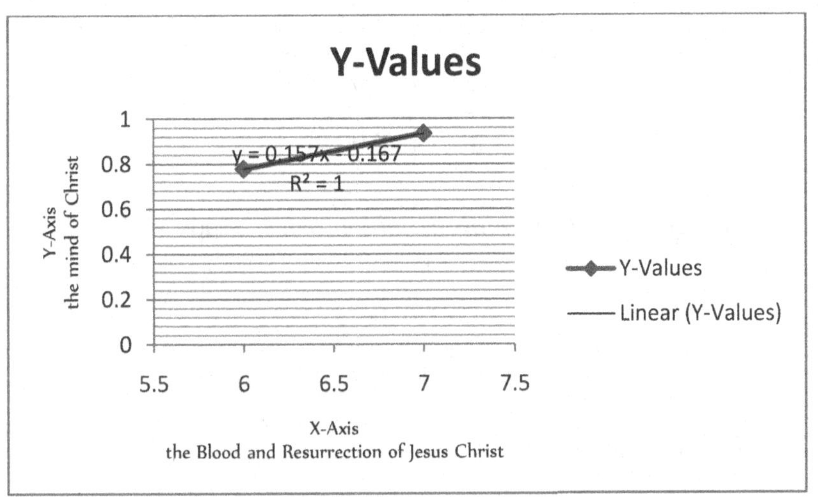

35. And when the men of that place had knowledge of him, they sent out into all that country round about, and brought unto him all that were diseased;

11, 9, 8; Bible Matrices

$\text{Log}_{10} 9 = 0.9542$ $\text{Log}_{10} 8 = 0.9030$ $\text{Log}_{10} 11 = 1.0413$

11, 9, 8; Deep calls unto Deep study bible 1

1.0413, 0.9542, 0.9030; Deep calls unto Deep study bible 2

x-axis	y-axis
11	1.0413
9	0.9542
8	0.9030

Water Spout *(lightning; combinatorics)* Study bible 1

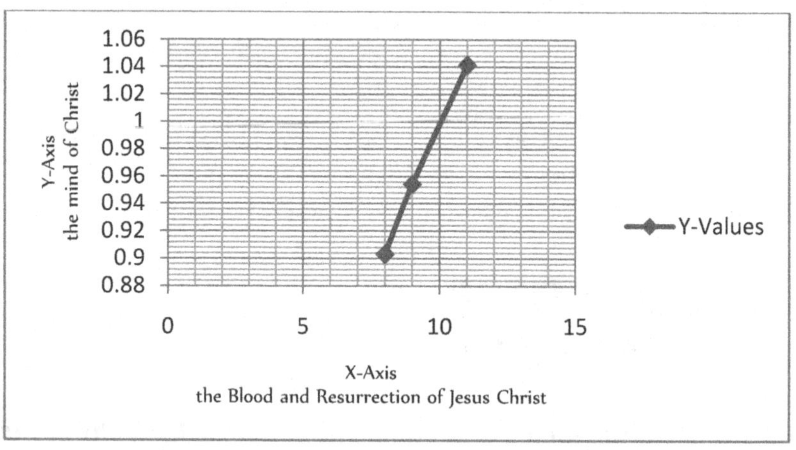

Water Spout *(lightning; combinatorics)* Study bible 2

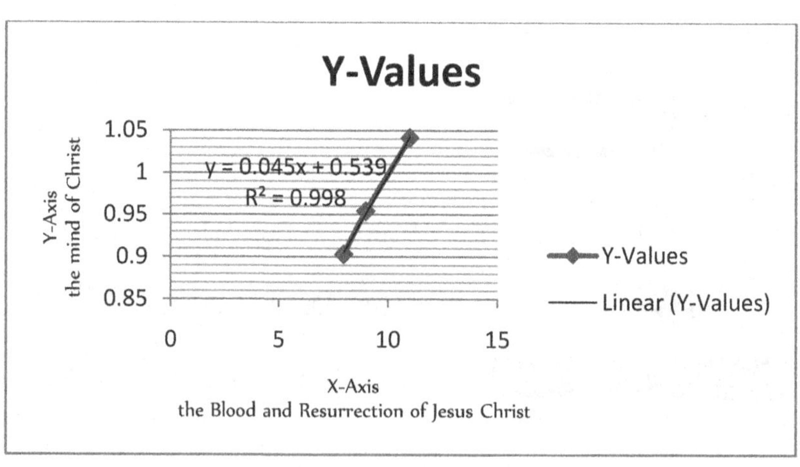

$10^{1.0413}$, $10^{0.9542}$, $10^{0.9030}$;

Pilled Poplar, Hazel, and Chestnut bible rods 2

36. And besought him that they might only touch the hem of his garment: and as many as touched were made perfectly whole.

13: 9. Bible Matrices

Pilled Poplar, Hazel, and Chestnut bible rods 1

$\text{Log}_{10} 9 = 0.9542$ $\text{Log}_{10} 13 = 1.1139$

13: 9. Deep calls unto Deep study bible 1

1.1139: 0.9542. Deep calls unto Deep study bible 2

x-axis	y-axis
13	1.1139
9	0.9542

Water Spout *(lightning; combinatorics)* Study bible 1

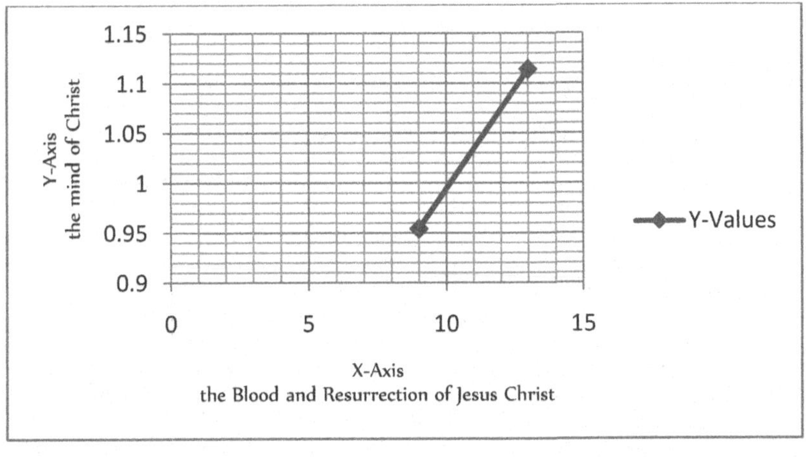

Water Spout *(lightning; combinatorics)* Study bible 2

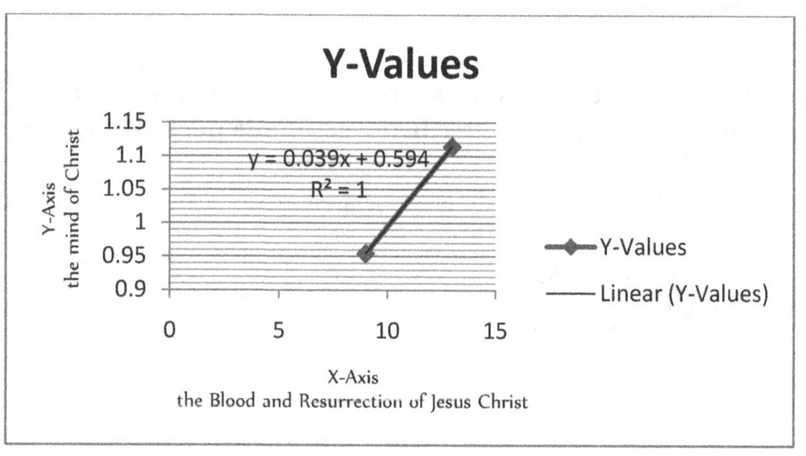

$10^{1.1139}$: $10^{0.9542}$.

Pilled Poplar, Hazel, and Chestnut bible rods 2

CHAPTER 15

1. Then came to Jesussavior; deliverer **scribes** lawyers **and Pharisees**set apart; separatists, **which were of Jerusalem** habitation of peace;vision of peace;possession of peace, **saying,**

7, 4, 1, Bible Matrices

$4_2\ 1_1\ 2_3,\ 4_9,\ 1_{10},$

Pilled Poplar, Hazel, and Chestnut bible rods 1

$\mathrm{Log}_{10} 1 = 0$

$\mathrm{Log}_3 2 = y$

$3^y = 2$

$y \log_{10} 3 = \log_{10} 2$

$y = \log_{10} 2 / \log_{10} 3$

$y = 0.3010 / 0.4771$

$y = 0.6308$

$\mathrm{Log}_9 4 = y$

$9^y = 4$

$y \log_{10} 9 = \log_{10} 4$

$y = \log_{10} 4 / \log_{10} 9$

$y = 0.6020 / 0.9542$

$y = 0.6308$

$\mathrm{Log}_1 1 = y$

$1^y = 1$

$1^y = 1^1$

$y = 1\ y = 2$

$\mathrm{Log}_2 4 = y$

$2^y = 4$

$2^y = 2^2$

7, 4, 1, Deep calls unto Deep study bible 1

2 1 0.6308, 0.6308, 0,

Deep calls unto Deep study bible 2

x-axis	y-axis
7	3.6308
4	0.6308
1	0

Water Spout *(lightning; combinatorics)* Study bible 1

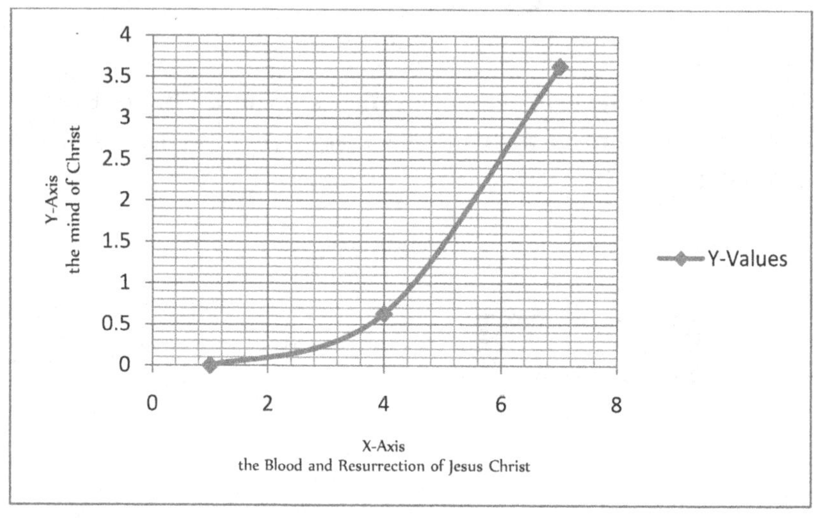

Water Spout *(lightning; combinatorics)* Study bible 2

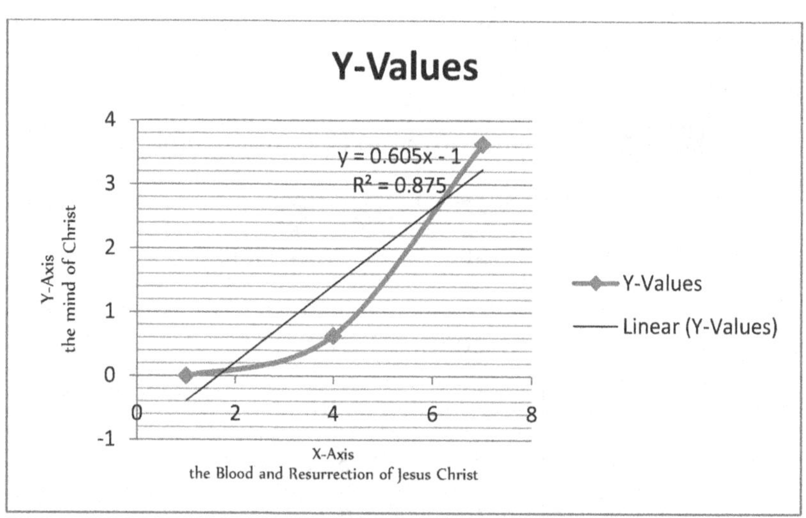

$2^2\ 1^1\ 3^{0.6308},\ 9^{0.6308},\ 10^0,$

Pilled Poplar, Hazel, and Chestnut bible rods 2

2. Why do thy disciples transgress the tradition of the elders? for they wash not their hands when they eat bread.

10? 10. Bible Matrices

$\text{Log}_{10} 10 = 1$ $\text{Log}_{10} 10 = 1$

10? 10. Deep calls unto Deep study bible 1

1? 1. Deep calls unto Deep study bible 2

x-axis	y-axis
10	1
10	1

Water Spout *(lightning; combinatorics)* Study bible 1

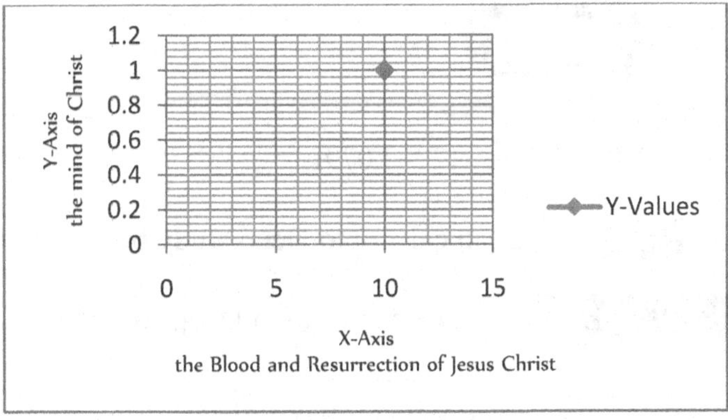

Water Spout *(lightning; combinatorics)* Study bible 2

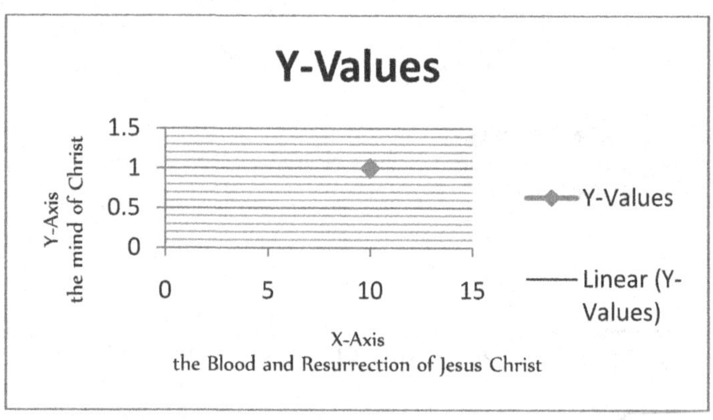

Pilled Poplar, Hazel, and Chestnut bible rods 2

3. But he answered and said unto them, Why do ye also transgress the commandment of God by your tradition?

7, 12? Bible Matrices

$\text{Log}_{10} 7 = 0.8450$ $\text{Log}_{10} 12 = 1.0791$

7, 12? Deep calls unto Deep study bible 1

0.8450, 1.0791? Deep calls unto Deep study bible 2

x-axis	y-axis
7	0.8450
12	1.0791

Water Spout *(lightning; combinatorics)* Study bible 1

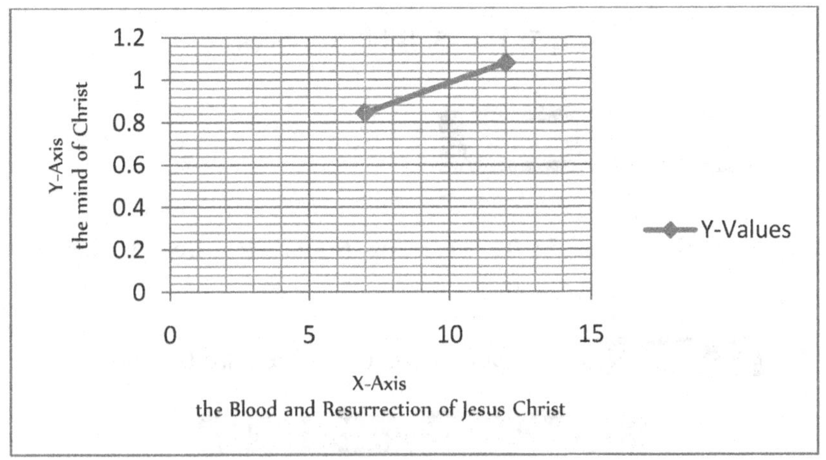

Water Spout *(lightning; combinatorics)* Study bible 2

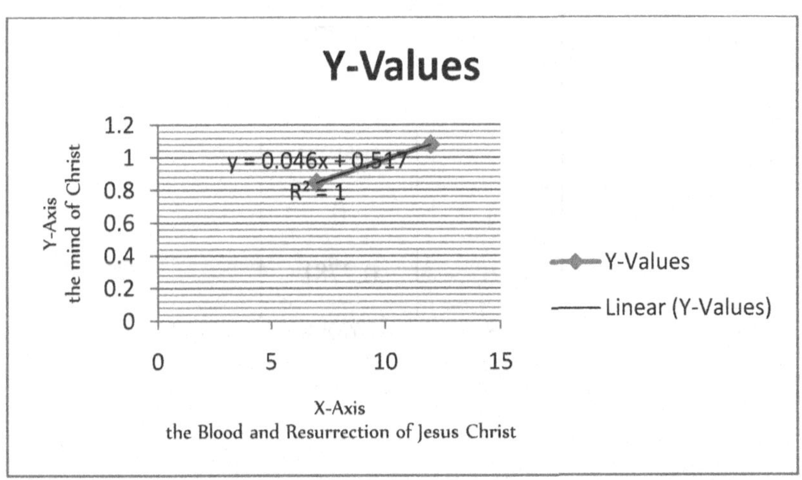

$10^{0.8450}$, $10^{1.0791}$?

Pilled Poplar, Hazel, and Chestnut bible rods 2

4. For God commanded, saying, Honour thy father and mother: and, He that curseth father or mother, let him die the death.

3, 1, 5: 1, 6, 5. Bible Matrices

$3_{10}, 1_{10}, 5_{10} : 1_{10}, 6_{10}, 5_{10}$.

Pilled Poplar, Hazel, and Chestnut bible rods 1

$Log_{10} 3 = 0.4771$ $Log_{10} 5 = 0.6989$ $Log_{10} 6 = 0.7781$ $Log_{10} 5 = 0.6989$
$Log_{10} 1 = 0$ $Log_{10} 1 = 0$

3, 1, 5: 1, 6, 5. Deep calls unto Deep study bible 1

0.4771, 0, 0.6989: 0, 0.7781, 0.6989.
Deep calls unto Deep study bible 2

x-axis	y-axis
3	0.4771
1	0
5	0.6989
1	0
6	0.7781
5	0.6989

Water Spout *(lightning; combinatorics)* Study bible 1

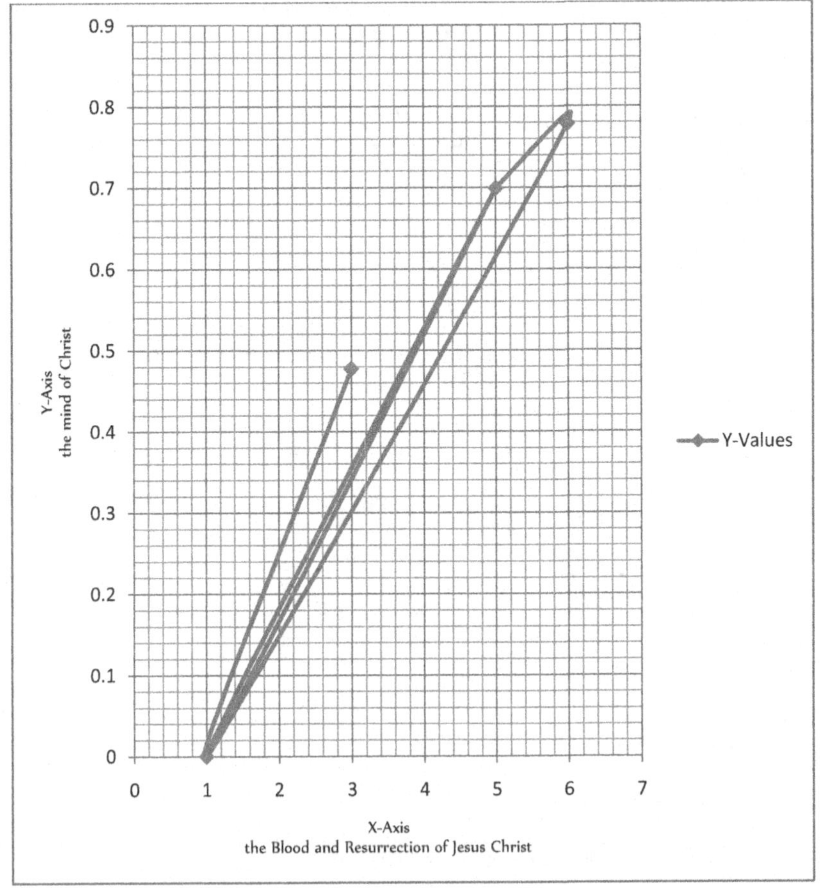

Water Spout *(lightning; combinatorics)* Study bible 2

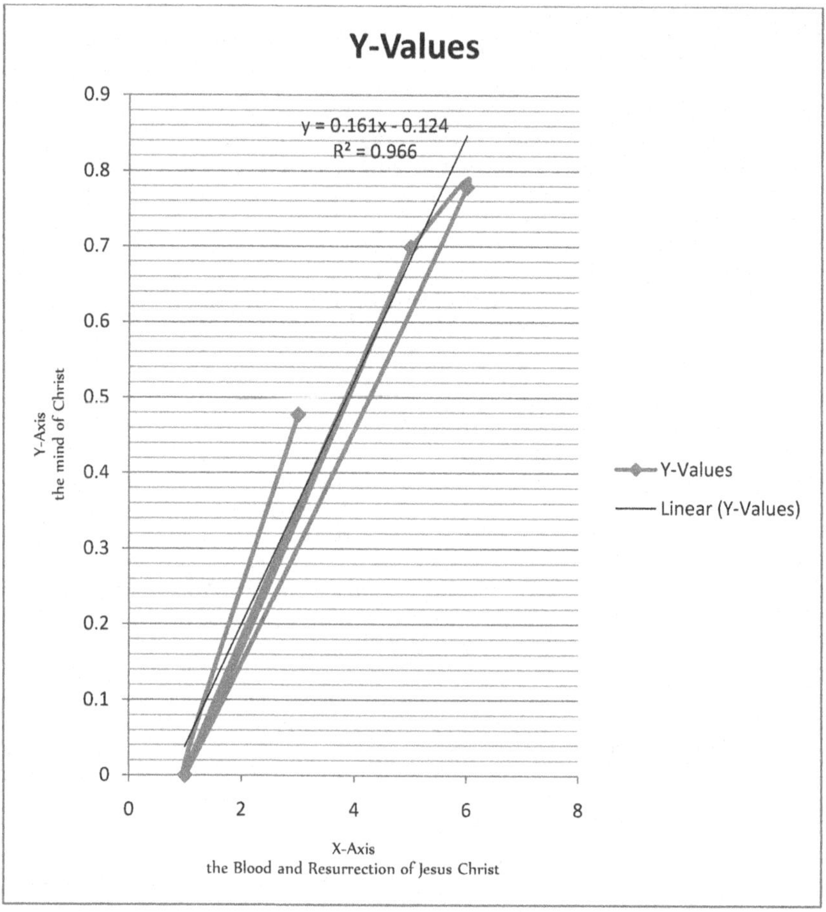
Y-Values
y = 0.161x - 0.124
R² = 0.966
0.9
0.8
0.7
0.6
0.5
0.4
0.3
0.2
0.1
0
0
2
4
6
8
Y-Axis
the mind of Christ
X-Axis
the Blood and Resurrection of Jesus Christ
Y-Values
Linear (Y-Values)

$10^{0.4771}$, 10^{0}, $10^{0.6989}$: 10^{0}, $10^{0.7781}$, $10^{0.6989}$.

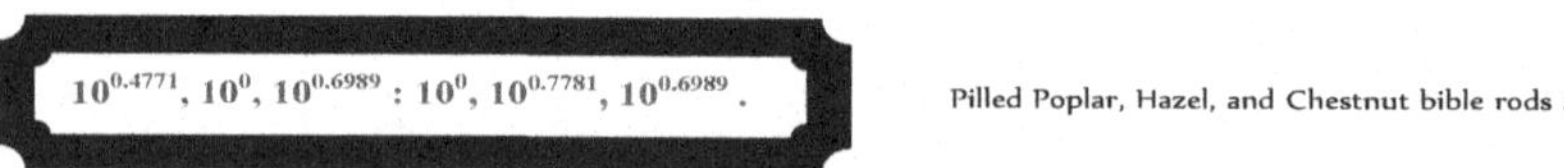

Pilled Poplar, Hazel, and Chestnut bible rods 2

5. But ye say, Whosoever shall say to his father or his mother, It is a gift, by whatsoever thou mightest be profited by me;

3, 9, 4, 8; Bible Matrices

$3_{10}, 9_{10}, 4_{10}, 8_{10}$; Pilled Poplar, Hazel, and Chestnut bible rods 1

$\text{Log}_{10} 9 = 0.9542$ $\text{Log}_{10} 3 = 0.4771$ $\text{Log}_{10} 4 = 0.6020$ $\text{Log}_{10} 8 = 0.9030$

3, 9, 4, 8; Deep calls unto Deep study bible 1

0.4771, 0.9542, 0.6020, 0.9030;
Deep calls unto Deep study bible 2

x-axis	y-axis
3	0.4771
9	0.9542
4	0.6020
8	0.9030

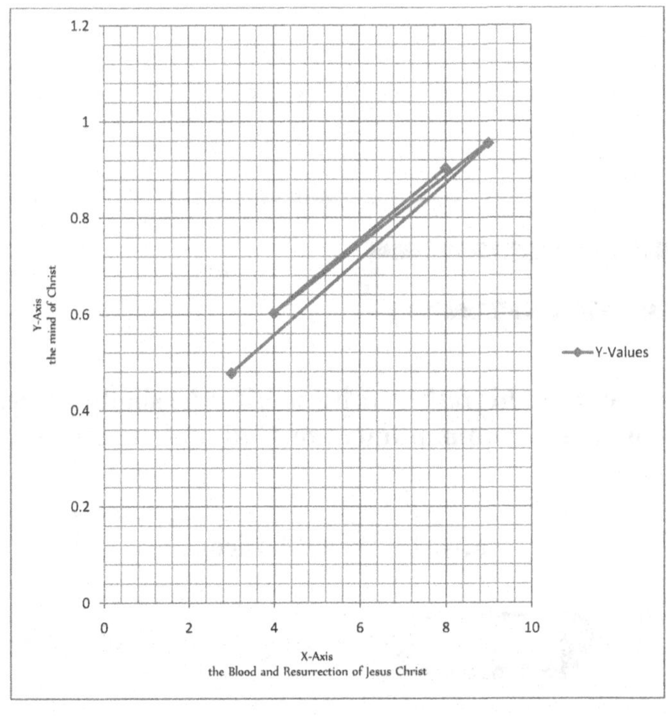

Water Spout *(lightning; combinatorics)* Study bible 2

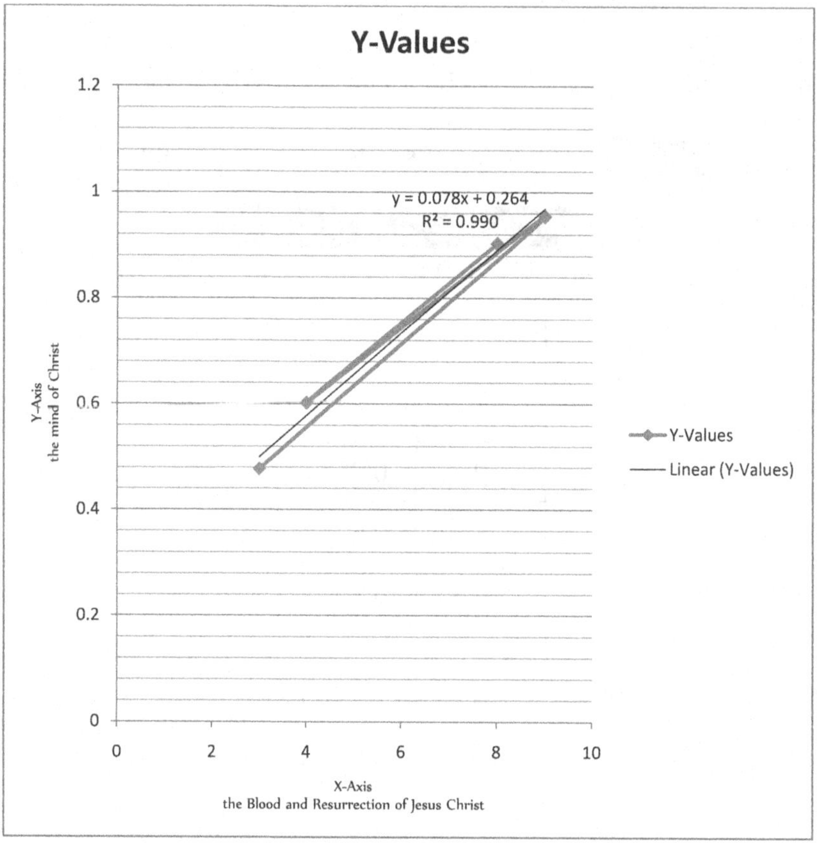
Y-Values
1.2
1
0.8
0.6
0.4
0.2
0
y = 0.078x + 0.264
R² = 0.990
Y-Axis
the mind of Christ
Y-Values
Linear (Y-Values)
0
2
4
6
8
10
X-Axis
the Blood and Resurrection of Jesus Christ

$10^{0.4771}$, $10^{0.9542}$, $10^{0.6020}$, $10^{0.9030}$;

Pilled Poplar, Hazel, and Chestnut bible rods 2

6. And honour not his father or his mother, he shall be free. Thus have ye made the commandment of God of none effect by your tradition.

8, 4. 14. Bible Matrices

8_{10}, 4_{10}. 14_{10}.

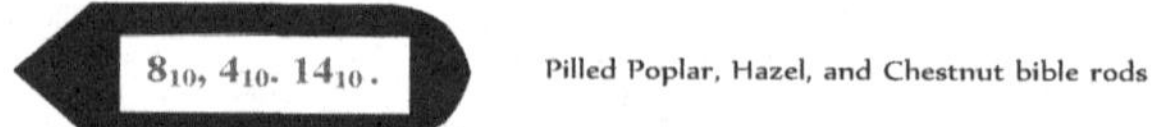

Pilled Poplar, Hazel, and Chestnut bible rods 1

$\text{Log}_{10} 8 = 0.9030$ $\text{Log}_{10} 4 = 0.6020$ $\text{Log}_{10} 14 = 1.1461$

8, 4, 14. Deep calls unto Deep study bible 1

0.9030, 0.6020, 1.1461.
Deep calls unto Deep study bible 2

x-axis	y-axis
8	0.9030
4	0.6020
14	1.1461

Water Spout *(lightning; combinatorics)* Study bible 1

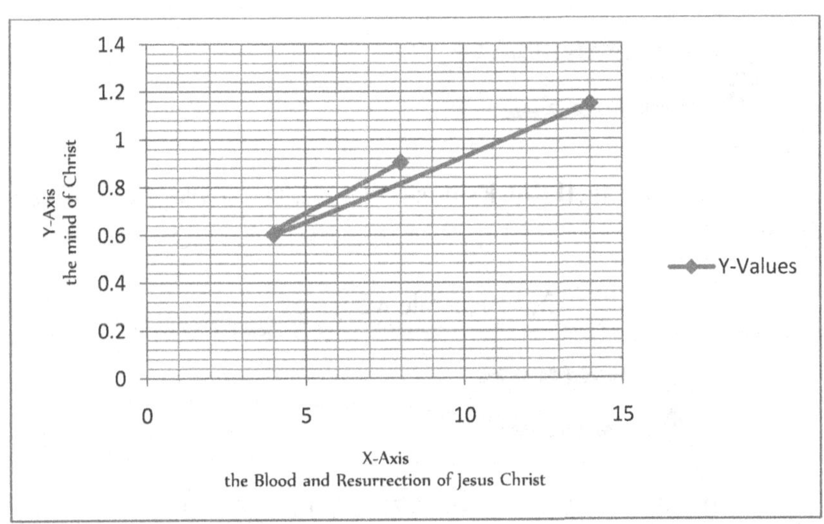

Water Spout *(lightning; combinatorics)* Study bible 2

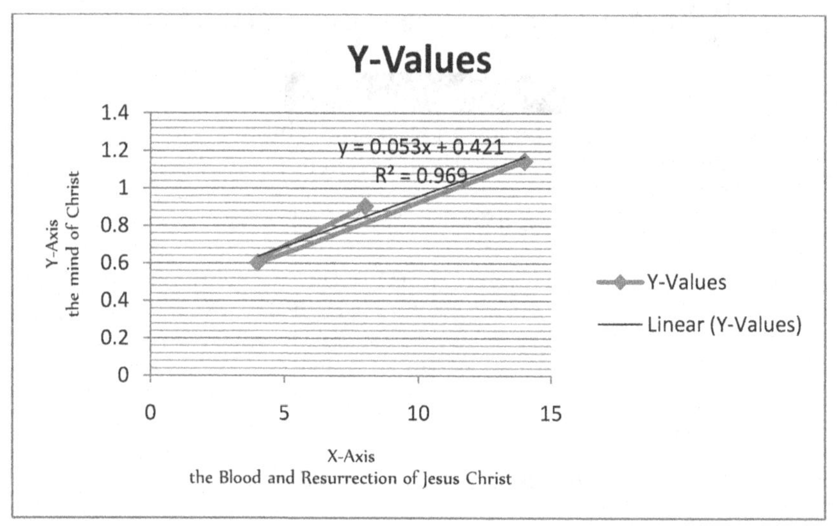

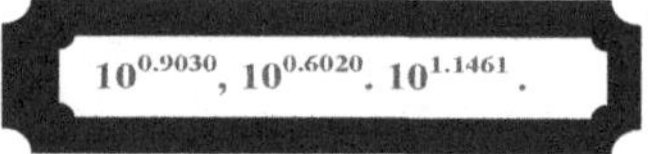

Pilled Poplar, Hazel, and Chestnut bible rods 2

7. Ye hypocrites, well did Esaiasthe salvation of the Lord **prophesy of you, saying,**

2, 6, 1, Bible Matrices

Pilled Poplar, Hazel, and Chestnut bible rods 1

$\text{Log}_{10} 2 = 0.3010$ $\text{Log}_{10} 3 = 0.4771$ $\text{Log}_{10} 1 = 0$

$\text{Log}_5 3 = y$

$5^y = 3$

$y \log_{10} 5 = \log_{10} 3$

$y = \log_{10} 3 / \log_{10} 5$

$y = 0.4771 / 0.6989$

$y = 0.6826$

2, 6, 1, Deep calls unto Deep study bible 1

0.3010, 0.6826 0.4771, 0,
Deep calls unto Deep study bible 2

x-axis	y-axis
2	0.3010
6	1.1597
1	0

Water Spout *(lightning; combinatorics)* Study bible 1

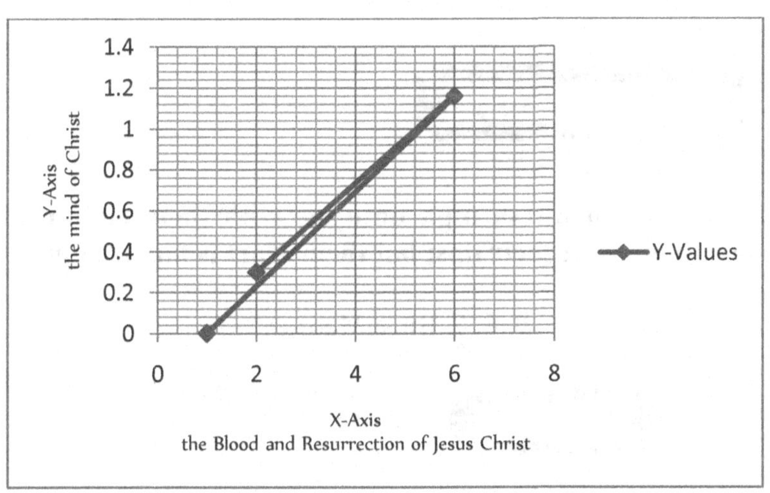

Water Spout *(lightning; combinatorics)* Study bible 2

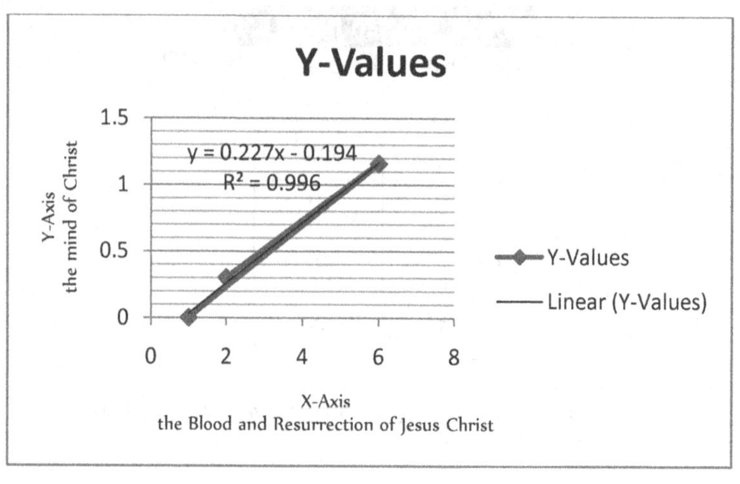

$10^{0.3010}$, $5^{1.4648}$ $10^{0.4771}$, 10^{0},

Pilled Poplar, Hazel, and Chestnut bible rods 2

8. This people draweth nigh unto me with their mouth, and honoureth me with their lips; but their heart is far from me.

9, 6; 7. Bible Matrices

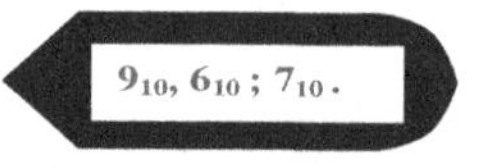

Pilled Poplar, Hazel, and Chestnut bible rods 1

$\text{Log}_{10}\,9 = 0.9542$ $\text{Log}_{10}\,6 = 0.7781$ $\text{Log}_{10}\,7 = 0.8450$

9, 6; 7. Deep calls unto Deep study bible 1

0.9542, 0.7781; 0.8450. Deep calls unto Deep study bible 2

x-axis	y-axis
9	0.9542
6	0.7781
7	0.8450

Water Spout *(lightning; combinatorics)* Study bible 1

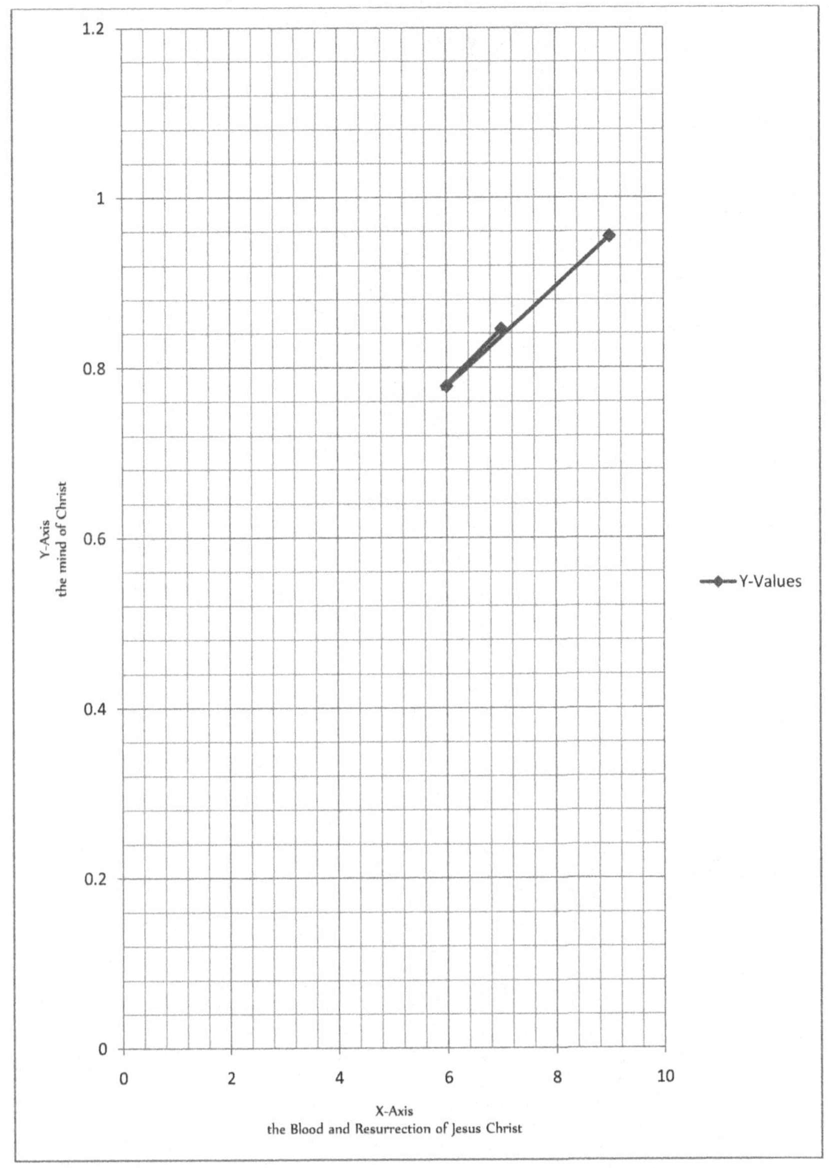

Water Spout *(lightning; combinatorics)* Study bible 2

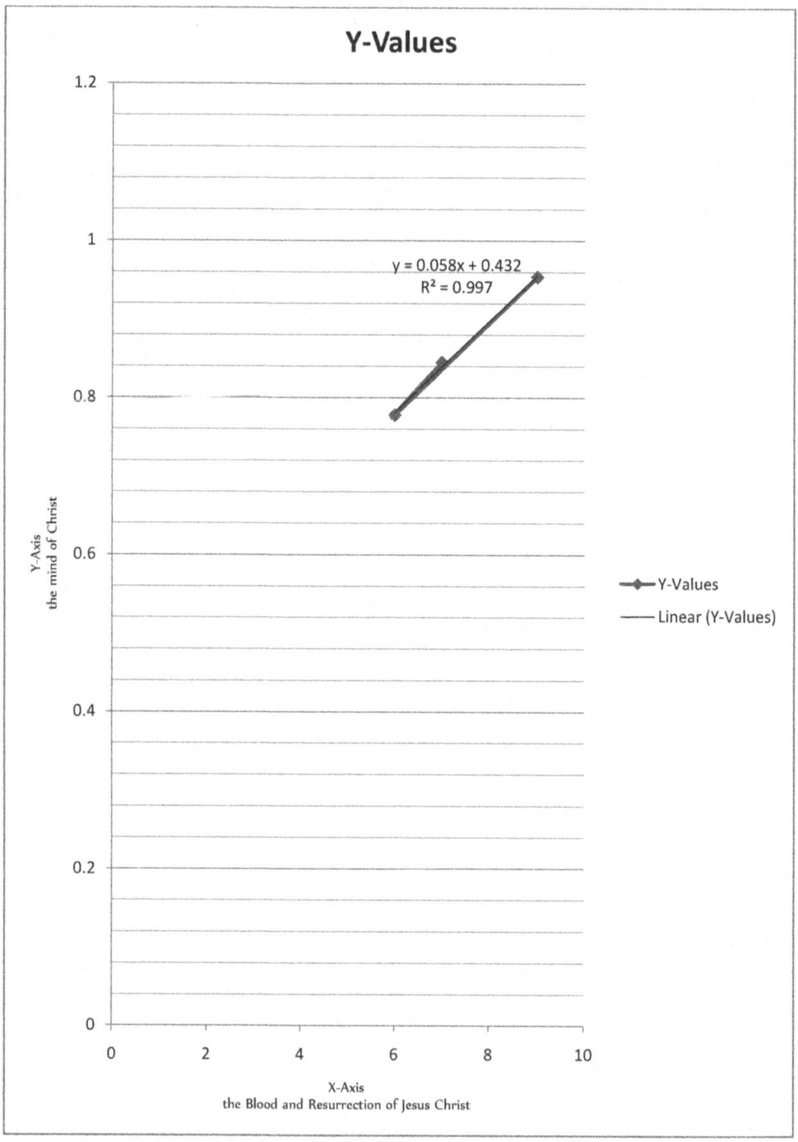

$10^{0.9542}$, $10^{0.7781}$; $10^{0.8450}$.

Pilled Poplar, Hazel, and Chestnut bible rods 2

9. But in vain they do worship me, teaching for doctrines the commandments of men.

7, 7. Bible Matrices

$\text{Log}_{10} 7 = 0.8450$ $\text{Log}_{10} 7 = 0.8450$

7, 7. Deep calls unto Deep study bible 1

0.8450, 0.8450. Deep calls unto Deep study bible 2

x-axis	y-axis
7	0.8450
7	0.8450

Water Spout *(lightning; combinatorics)* Study bible 1

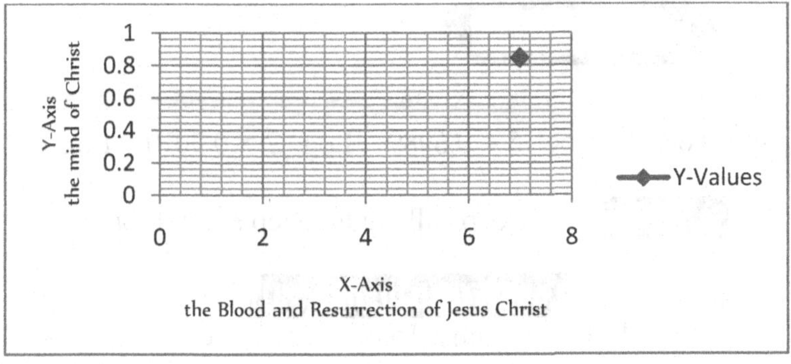

Water Spout *(lightning; combinatorics)* Study bible 2

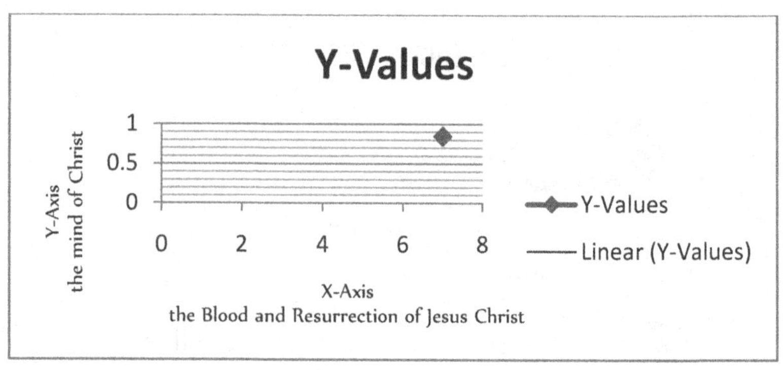

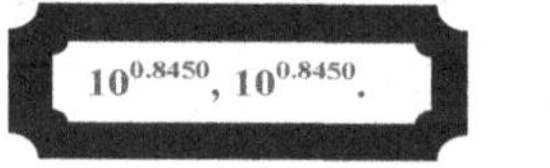

Pilled Poplar, Hazel, and Chestnut bible rods 2

10. And he called the multitude, and said unto them, Hear, and understand:

5, 4, 1, 2: Bible Matrices

$\text{Log}_{10} 4 = 0.6020$ $\text{Log}_{10} 5 = 0.6989$ $\text{Log}_{10} 2 = 0.3010$ $\text{Log}_{10} 1 = 0$

5, 4, 1, 2: Deep calls unto Deep study bible 1

0.6989, 0.6020, 0, 0.3010:
Deep calls unto Deep study bible 2

x-axis	y-axis
5	0.6989
4	0.6020
1	0
2	0.3010

Water Spout *(lightning; combinatorics)* Study bible 1

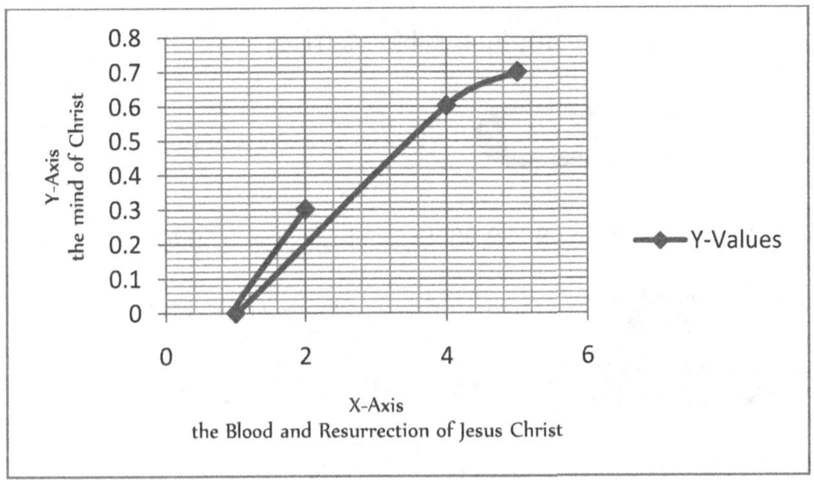

Water Spout *(lightning; combinatorics)* Study bible 2

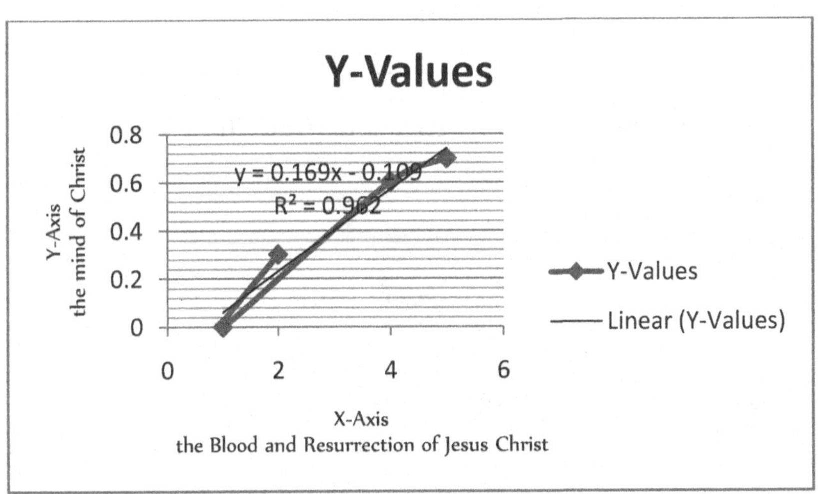

$10^{0.6989}$, $10^{0.6020}$, 10^{0}, $10^{0.3010}$: Pilled Poplar, Hazel, and Chestnut bible rods 2

11. Not that which goeth into the mouth defileth a man; but that which cometh out of the mouth, this defileth a man.

10; 8, 4. Bible Matrices

$\text{Log}_{10} 10 = 1$ $\text{Log}_{10} 8 = 0.9030$ $\text{Log}_{10} 4 = 0.6020$

10; 8, 4. Deep calls unto Deep study bible 1

1; 0.9030, 0.6020. Deep calls unto Deep study bible 2

x-axis	y-axis
10	1
8	0.9030
4	0.6020

Water Spout *(lightning; combinatorics)* Study bible 1

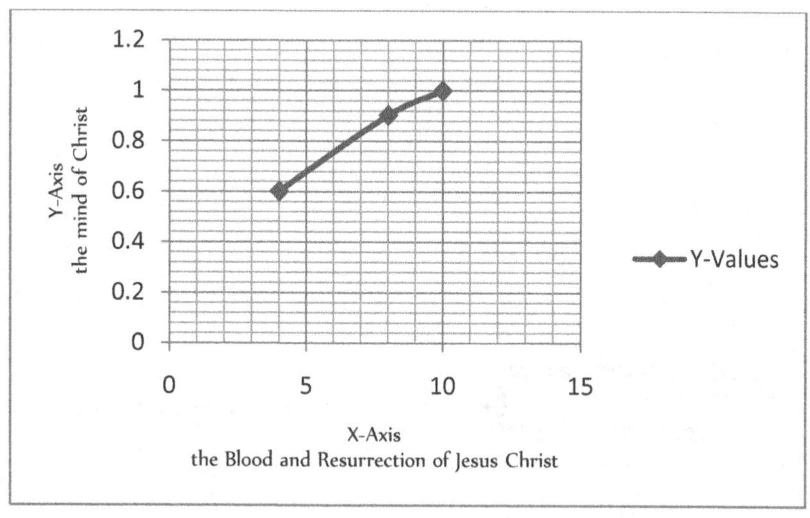

Water Spout *(lightning; combinatorics)* Study bible 2

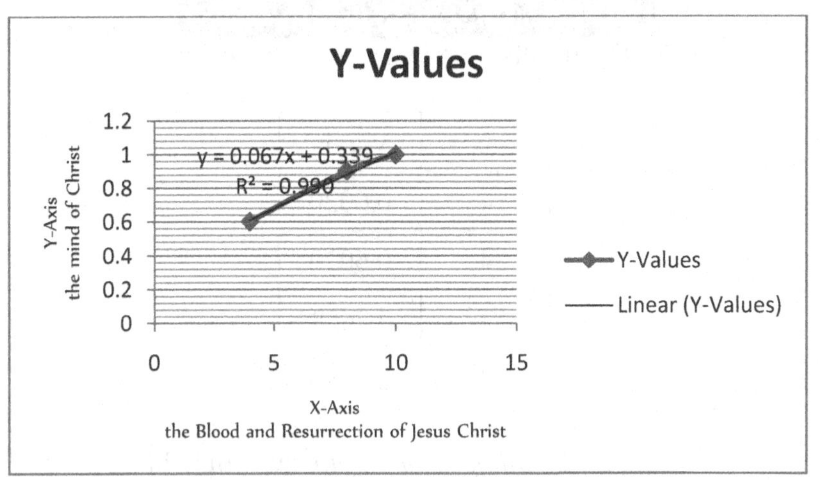

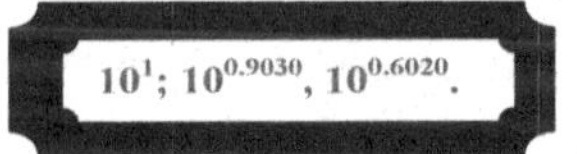

10^1; $10^{0.9030}$, $10^{0.6020}$.

Pilled Poplar, Hazel, and Chestnut bible rods 2

12. Then came his disciples, and said unto him, Knowest thou that the Phariseesset apart; separatists **were offended, after they heard this saying?**

4, 4, 7, 5? Bible Matrices

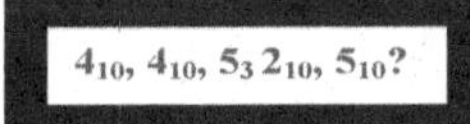

4_{10}, 4_{10}, $5_3\,2_{10}$, 5_{10}?

Pilled Poplar, Hazel, and Chestnut bible rods 1

$\text{Log}_{10} 4 = 0.6020$ $\text{Log}_{10} 5 = 0.6989$ $\text{Log}_{10} 4 = 0.6020$ $\text{Log}_{10} 2 = 0.3010$

$\text{Log}_3 5 = y$

$3^y = 5$

$y \log_{10} 3 = \log_{10} 5$

$y = \log_{10} 5 / \log_{10} 3$

$y = 0.6989 / 0.4771$

$y = 1.4648$

4, 4, 7, 5? Deep calls unto Deep study bible 1

0.6020, 0.6020, 1.4648 0.3010, 0.6989?
Deep calls unto Deep study bible 2

x-axis	y-axis
4	0.6020
4	0.6020
7	1.7658
5	0.6989

Water Spout *(lightning; combinatorics)* Study bible 1

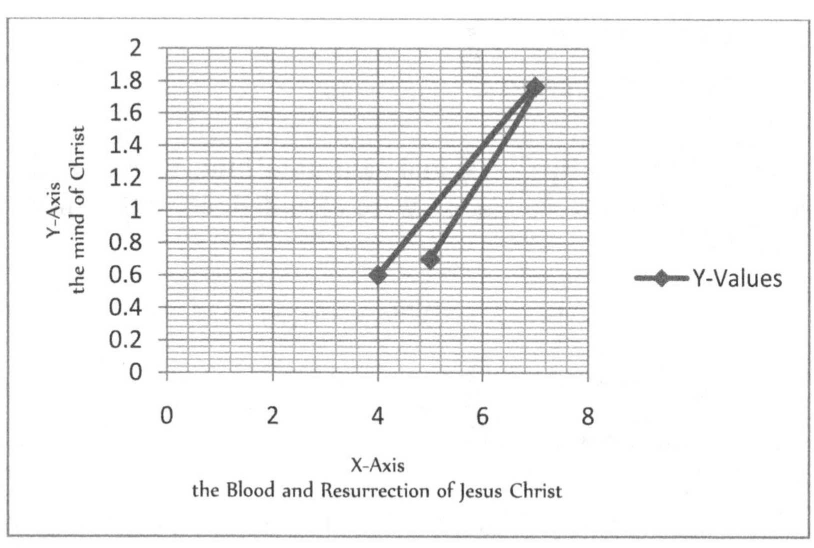

Water Spout *(lightning; combinatorics)* Study bible 2

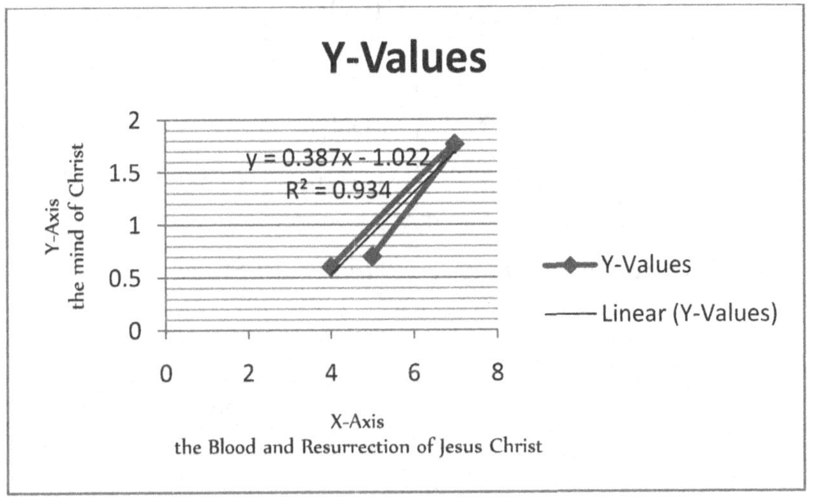

Pilled Poplar, Hazel, and Chestnut bible rods 2

13. But he answered and said, Every plant, which my heavenly Father hath not planted, shall be rooted up.

5, 2, 7, 4. Bible Matrices

Pilled Poplar, Hazel, and Chestnut bible rods 1

$\text{Log}_{10} 7 = 0.8450$ $\text{Log}_{10} 5 = 0.6989$ $\text{Log}_{10} 2 = 0.3010$ $\text{Log}_{10} 4 = 0.6020$

5, 2, 7, 4. Deep calls unto Deep study bible 1

0.6989, 0.3010, 0.8450, 0.6020.
Deep calls unto Deep study bible 2

x-axis	y-axis
5	0.6989
2	0.3010
7	0.8450
4	0.6020

Water Spout *(lightning; combinatorics)* Study bible 1

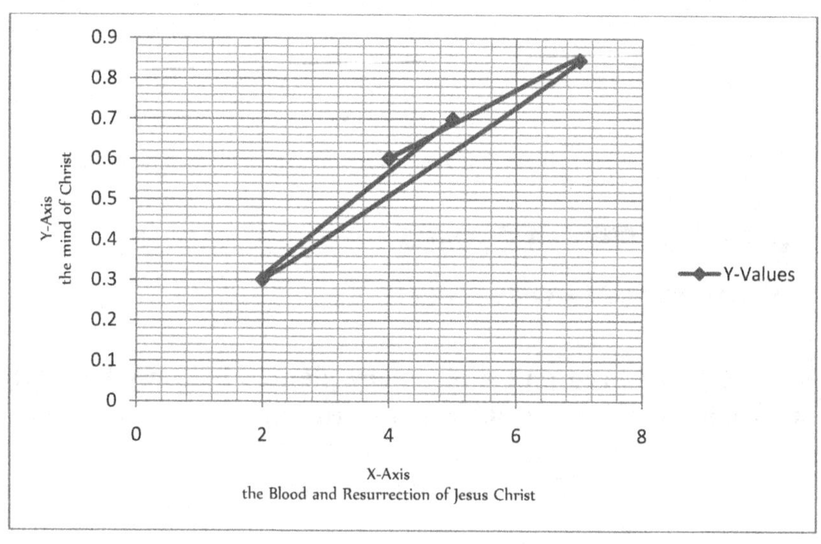

Water Spout *(lightning; combinatorics)* Study bible 2

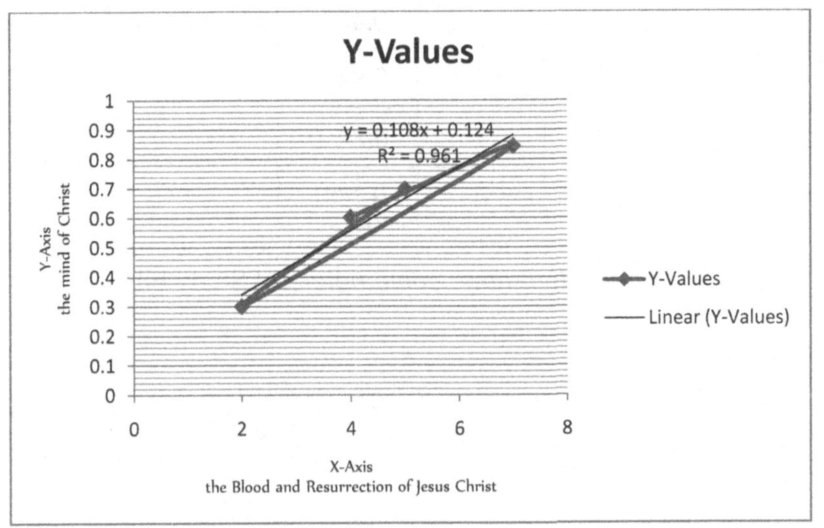

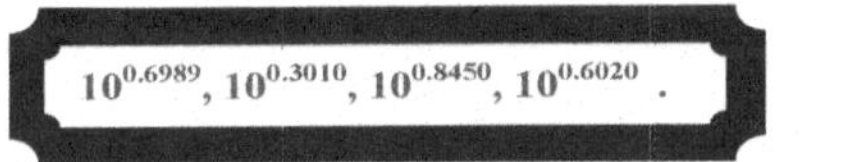

Pilled Poplar, Hazel, and Chestnut bible rods 2

14. Let them alone: they be blind leaders of the blind. And if the blind lead the blind, both shall fall into the ditch.

3: 7. 7, 6. Bible Matrices

Pilled Poplar, Hazel, and Chestnut bible rods 1

$\text{Log}_{10} 7 = 0.8450$ $\text{Log}_{10} 6 = 0.7781$ $\text{Log}_{10} 7 = 0.8450$ $\text{Log}_{10} 3 = 0.4771$

3: 7. 7, 6. Deep calls unto Deep study bible 1

0.4771: 0.8450. 0.8450, 0.7781.

Deep calls unto Deep study bible 2

x-axis	y-axis
3	0.4771
7	0.8450
7	0.8450
6	0.7781

Water Spout *(lightning; combinatorics)* Study bible 1

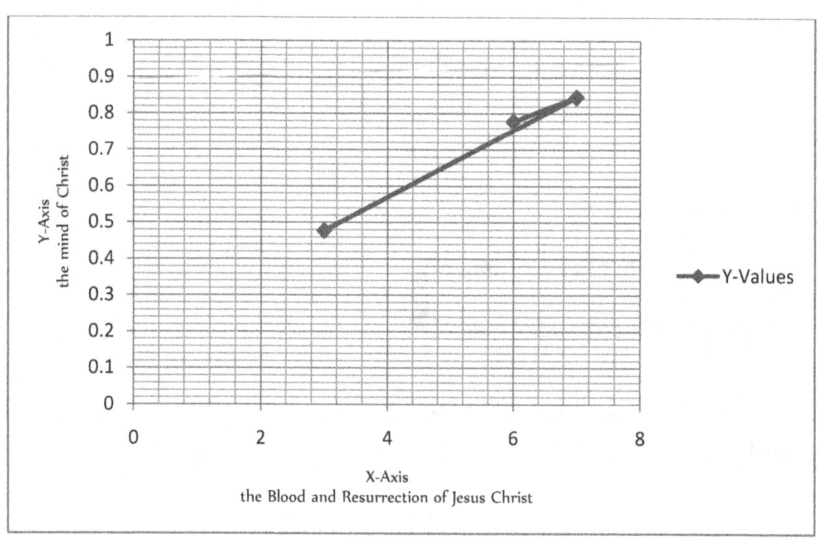

Water Spout *(lightning; combinatorics)* Study bible 2

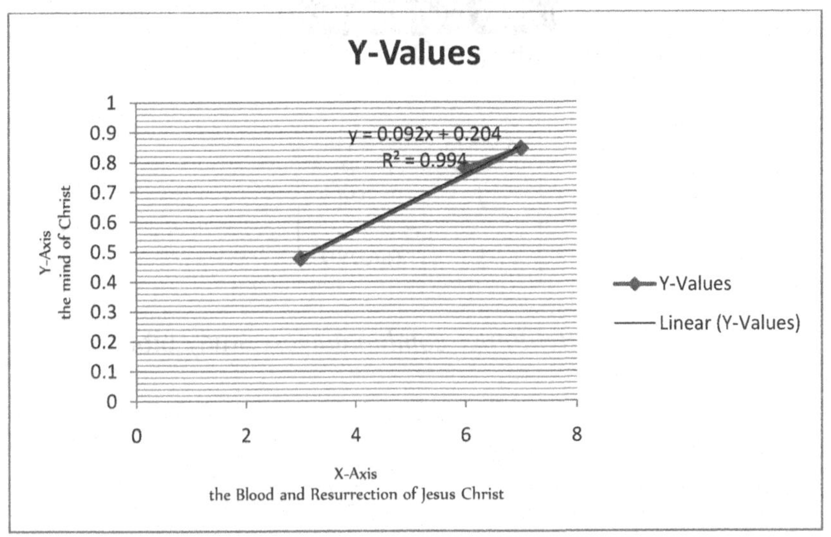

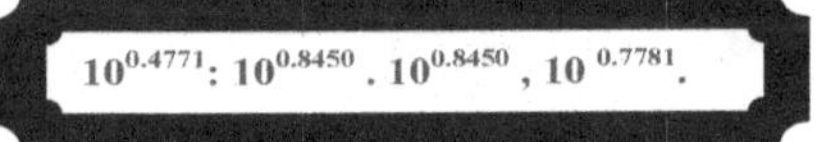

Pilled Poplar, Hazel, and Chestnut bible rods 2

15. Then answered Petera rock or stone **and said unto him, Declare unto us this parable.**

7, 5. Bible Matrices

Pilled Poplar, Hazel, and Chestnut bible rods 1

$\text{Log}_{10} 4 = 0.6020$ $\text{Log}_{10} 5 = 0.6989$

$\text{Log}_4 3 = y$

$4^y = 3$

$y \log_{10} 4 = \log_{10} 3$

$y = \log_{10} 3 / \log_{10} 4$

$y = 0.4771 / 0.6020$

$y = 0.7925$

7, 5. Deep calls unto Deep study bible 1

0.7925 0.6020, 0.6989.

Deep calls unto Deep study bible 2

x-axis	y-axis
7	1.3945
5	0.6989

Water Spout *(lightning; combinatorics)* Study bible 1

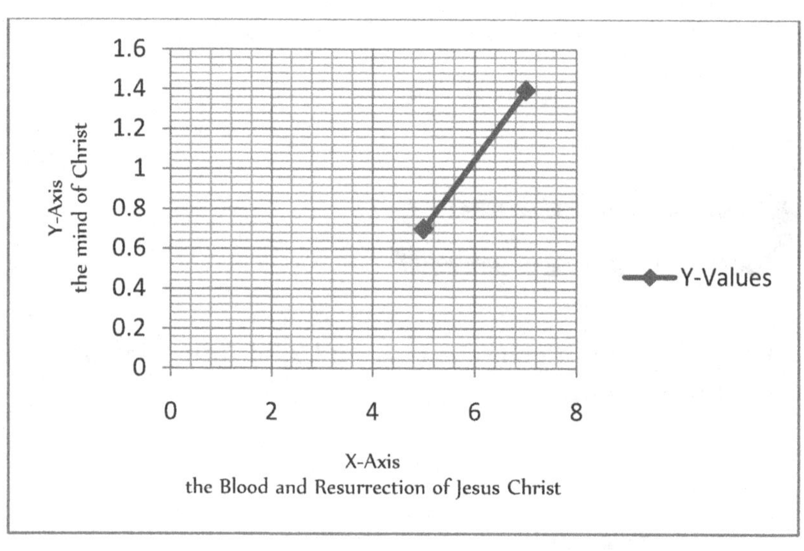

Water Spout *(lightning; combinatorics)* Study bible 2

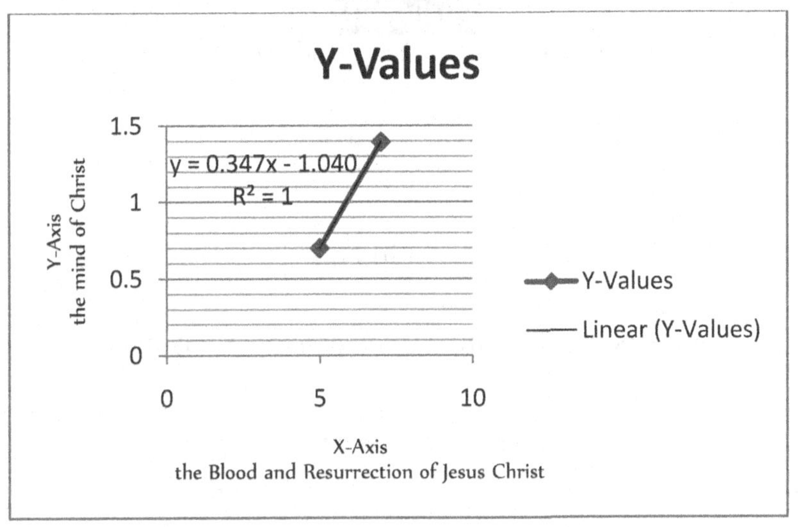

16. And Jesus savior; deliverer **said, Are ye also yet without understanding?**

3, 6? Bible Matrices

$\text{Log}_{10} 1 = 0$ $\text{Log}_{10} 6 = 0.7781$

$\text{Log}_2 2 = y$

$2^y = 2$

$2^y = 2^1$

$y = 1$

3, 6? Deep calls unto Deep study bible 1

1 0, 0.7781?

Deep calls unto Deep study bible 2

x-axis	y-axis
3	1
6	0.7781

Water Spout *(lightning; combinatorics)* Study bible 1

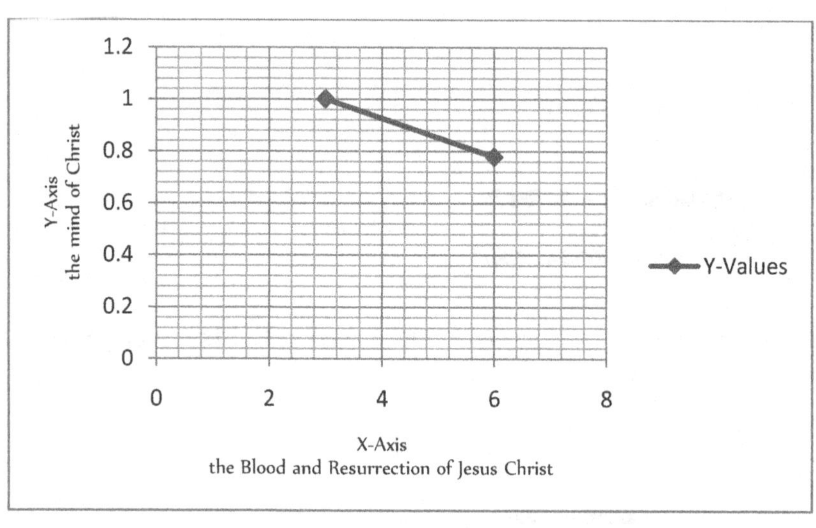

Water Spout *(lightning; combinatorics)* Study bible 2

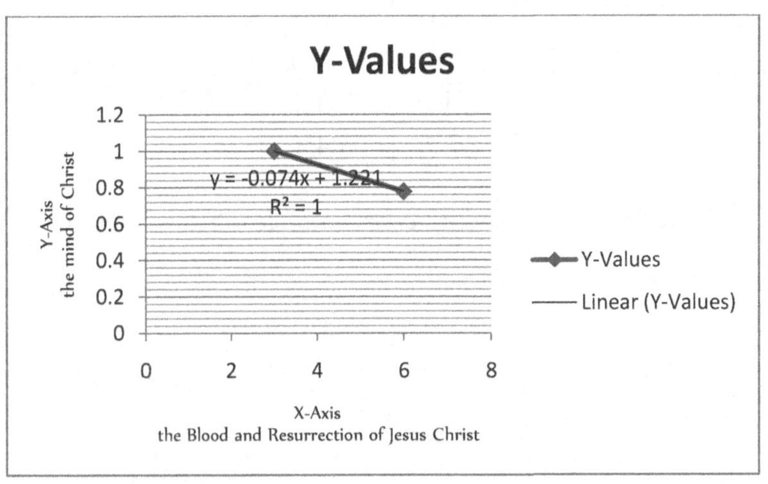

17. Do not ye yet understand, that whatsoever entereth in at the mouth goeth into the belly, and is cast out into the draught?

5, 11, 7? Bible Matrices

$\text{Log}_{10}\ 11 = 1.0413$ $\text{Log}_{10}\ 5 = 0.6989$ $\text{Log}_{10}\ 7 = 0.8450$

5, 11, 7? Deep calls unto Deep study bible 1

0.6989, 1.0413, 0.8450?

Deep calls unto Deep study bible 2

x-axis	y-axis
5	0.6989
11	1.0413
7	0.8450

Water Spout *(lightning; combinatorics)* Study bible 1

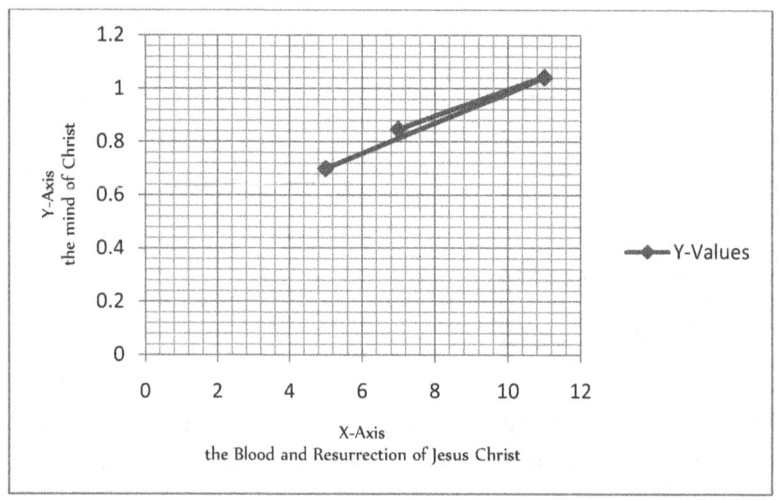

Water Spout *(lightning; combinatorics)* Study bible 2

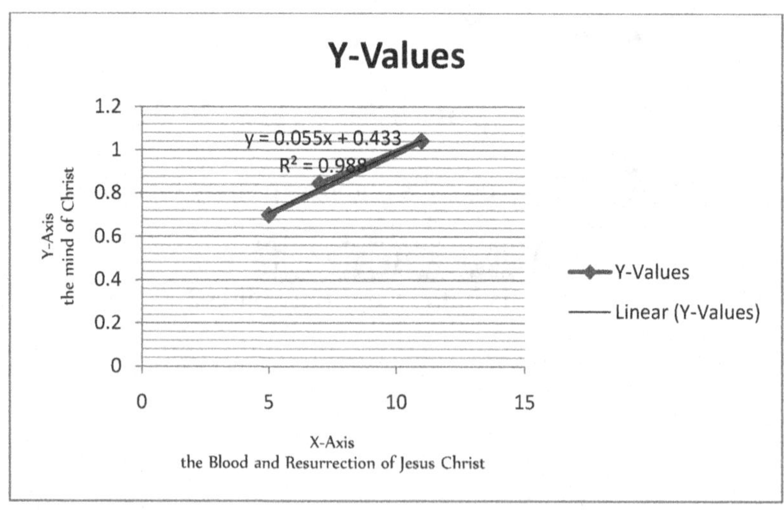

$10^{0.6989}$, $10^{1.0413}$, $10^{0.8450}$?

Pilled Poplar, Hazel, and Chestnut bible rods 2

18. But those things which proceed out of the mouth come forth from the heart; and they defile the man.

14; 5. Bible Matrices

$Log_{10} 14 = 1.1461$ $Log_{10} 5 = 0.6989$

14; 5. Deep calls unto Deep study bible 1

1.1461; 0.6989. Deep calls unto Deep study bible 2

x-axis	y-axis
14	1.1461
5	0.6989

Water Spout *(lightning; combinatorics)* Study bible 1

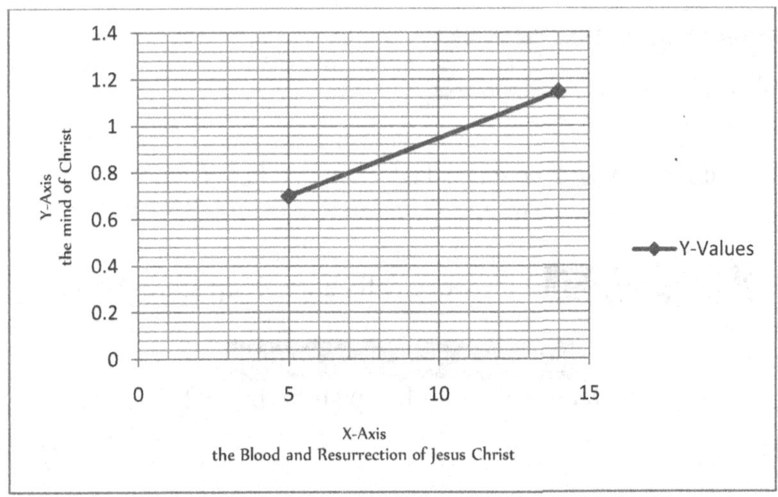

Water Spout *(lightning; combinatorics)* Study bible 2

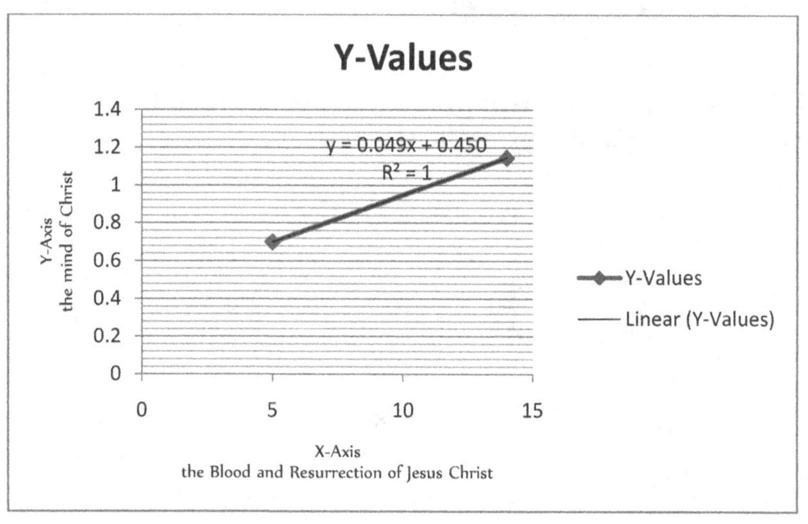

$10^{1.1461}, 10^{0.6989}$. Pilled Poplar, Hazel, and Chestnut bible rods 2

19. For out of the heart proceed evil thoughts, murders, adulteries, fornications, thefts, false witness, blasphemies:

8, 1, 1, 1, 1, 2, 1: Bible Matrices

$8_{10}, 1_{10}, 1_{10}, 1_{10}, 1_{10}, 2_{10}, 1_{10}$: Pilled Poplar, Hazel, and Chestnut bible rods 1

$\text{Log}_{10} 8 = 0.9030$ $\text{Log}_{10} 2 = 0.3010$ $\text{Log}_{10} 1 = 0$ $\text{Log}_{10} 1 = 0$ $\text{Log}_{10} 1 = 0$
$\text{Log}_{10} 1 = 0$ $\text{Log}_{10} 1 = 0$

8, 1, 1, 1, 1, 2, 1: Deep calls unto Deep study bible 1

0.9030, 0, 0, 0, 0, 0.3010, 0:
Deep calls unto Deep study bible 2

x-axis	y-axis
8	0.9030
1	0
1	0
1	0
1	0
2	0.3010
1	0

Water Spout *(lightning; combinatorics)* Study bible 1

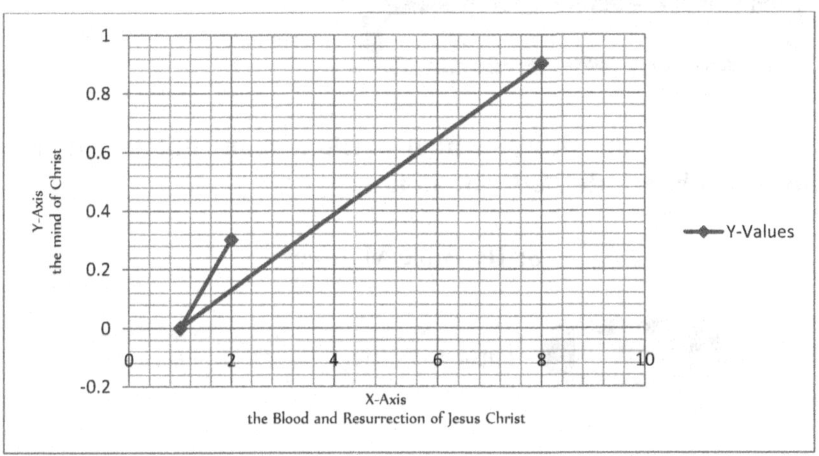

Water Spout *(lightning; combinatorics)* Study bible 2

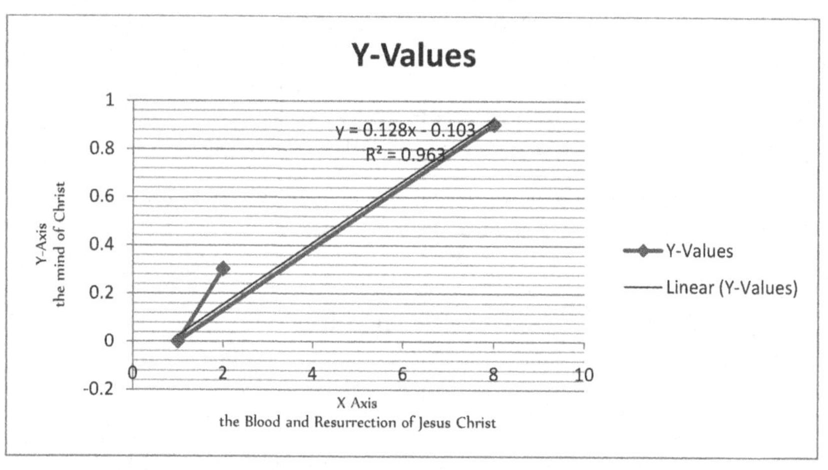

$10^{0.9030}, 10^0, 10^0, 10^0, 10^0, 10^{0.3010}, 10^0$: Pilled Poplar, Hazel, and Chestnut bible rods 2

20. These are the things which defile a man: but to eat with unwashen hands defileth not a man.

8: 10. Bible Matrices

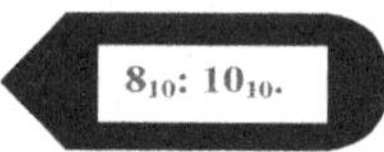

Pilled Poplar, Hazel, and Chestnut bible rods 1

$\text{Log}_{10} 8 = 0.9030$ $\text{Log}_{10} 10 = 1$

8: 10. Deep calls unto Deep study bible 1

0.9030: 1. Deep calls unto Deep study bible 2

x-axis	y-axis
8	0.9030
10	1

Water Spout *(lightning; combinatorics)* Study bible 1

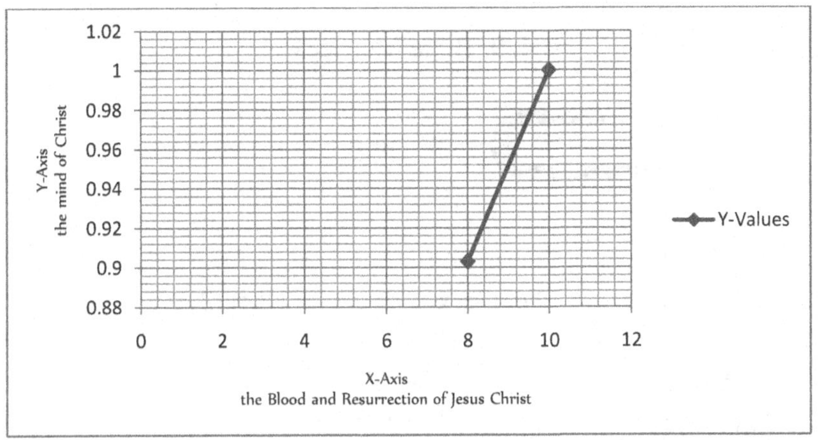

Water Spout *(lightning; combinatorics)* Study bible 2

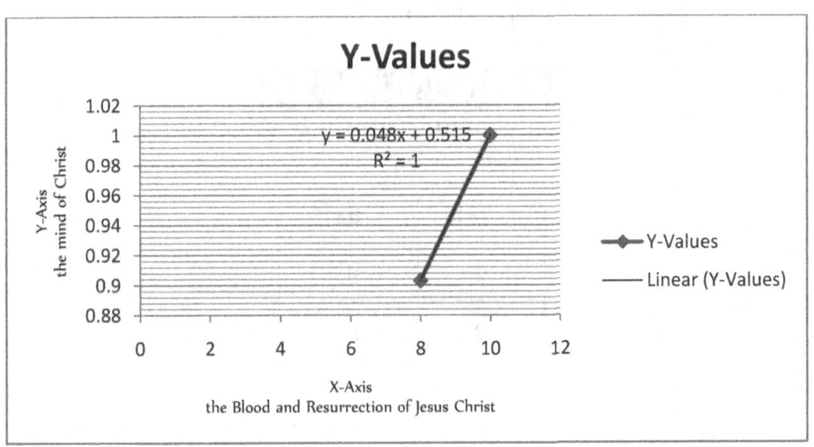

$10^{0.9030}$: 10^{1}.

Pilled Poplar, Hazel, and Chestnut bible rods 2

21. Then Jesussavior; deliverer**went thence, and departed into the coasts of Tyre**strength; rock; sharp**and Sidon**hunting; fishing; venison.

4, 9. Bible Matrices

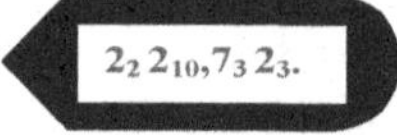

Pilled Poplar, Hazel, and Chestnut bible rods 1

$\text{Log}_{10} 2 = 0.3010$

$\text{Log}_3 2 = y$	$\text{Log}_3 7 = y$	$\text{Log}_2 2 = y$
$3^y = 2$	$3^y = 7$	$2^y = 2$
$y \log_{10} 3 = \log_{10} 2$	$y \log_{10} 3 = \log_{10} 7$	$2^y = 2^1$
$y = \log_{10} 2 / \log_{10} 3$	$y = \log_{10} 7 / \log_{10} 3$	$y = 1$
$y = 0.3010 / 0.4771$	$y = 0.8450 / 0.4771$	
$y = 0.6308$	$y = 1.7711$	

4, 9. Deep calls unto Deep study bible 1

1 0.3010, 1.7711 0.6308.

Deep calls unto Deep study bible 2

x-axis	y-axis
4	1.3010
9	2.4019

Water Spout *(lightning; combinatorics)* Study bible 1

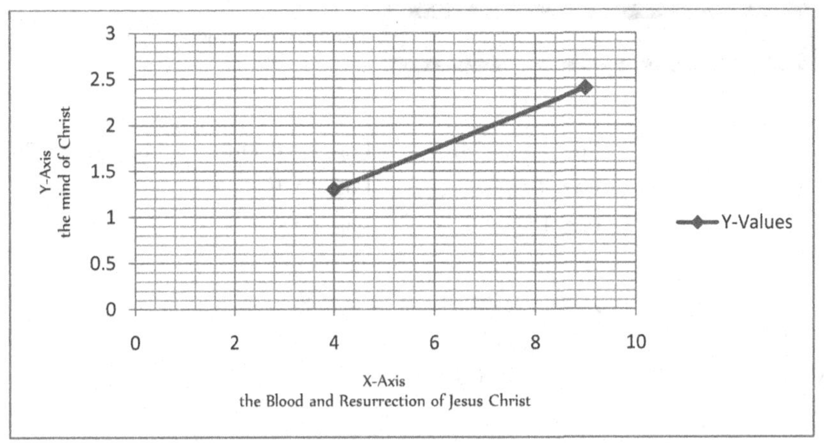

Water Spout *(lightning; combinatorics)* Study bible 2

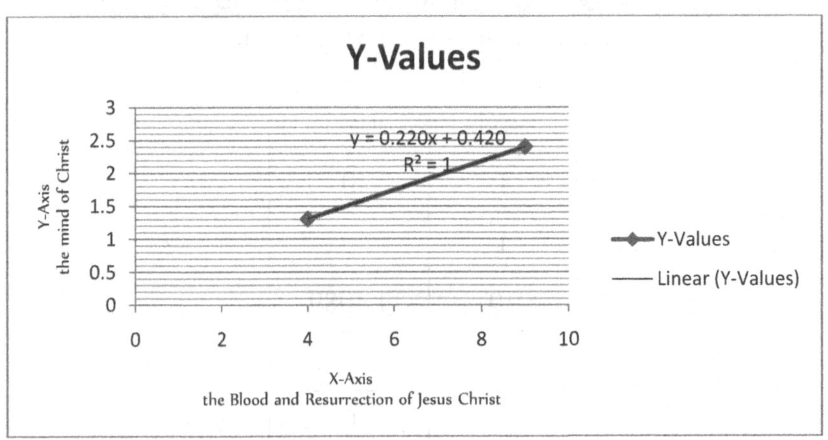

Pilled Poplar, Hazel, and Chestnut bible rods 2

22. And, behold, a woman of Canaanmerchant; trader; or that humbles and subdues; low; flatland **came out of the same coasts, and cried unto him, saying, Have mercy on me, O Lord, thou Son of David**beloved; dear; **my daughter is grievously vexed with a devil** slanderer, false accuser.

1, 1, 10, 4, 1, 4, 2, 4; 8. Bible Matrices

$1_{10}, 1_{10}, 4_{9}\, 6_{10}, 4_{10}, 1_{10}, 4_{10}, 2_{10}, 4_{2}; 8_{3}$.

Pilled Poplar, Hazel, and Chestnut bible rods 1

$Log_{10} 4 = 0.6020$
$Log_{10} 1 = 0$
$Log_3 8 = y$
$3^y = 8$
$y \log_{10} 3 = \log_{10} 8$
$y = \log_{10} 8 / \log_{10} 3$
$y = 0.9030 / 0.4771$
$y = 1.8926$ $y = 0.6308$

$Log_{10} 6 = 0.7781$
$Log_{10} 1 = 0$
$Log_9 4 = y$
$9^y = 4$
$y \log_{10} 9 = \log_{10} 4$
$y = \log_{10} 4 / \log_{10} 9$
$y = 0.6020 / 0.9542$

$Log_{10} 2 = 0.3010$
$Log_{10} 1 = 0$
$Log_2 4 = y$
$2^y = 4$
$2^y = 2^2$
$y = 2$

$Log_{10} 4 = 0.6020$

1, 1, 10, 4, 1, 4, 2, 4; 8. Deep calls unto Deep study bible 1

0, 0, 0.6308 0.7781, 0.6020, 0, 0.6020, 0.3010, 2; 1.8926.
Deep calls unto Deep study bible 2

x-axis	y-axis
1	0
1	0
10	1.4089
4	0.6020
1	0
4	0.6020
2	0.3010
4	2
8	1.8926

Water Spout *(lightning; combinatorics)* Study bible 1

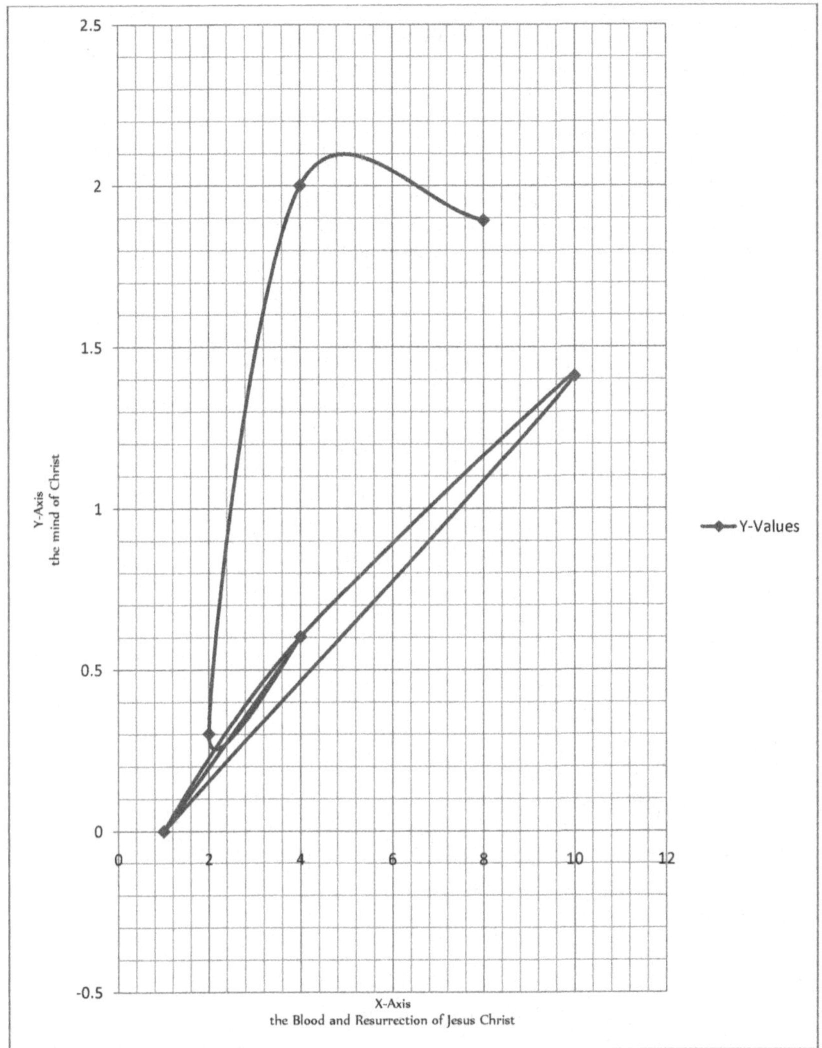

Water Spout *(lightning; combinatorics)* Study bible 2

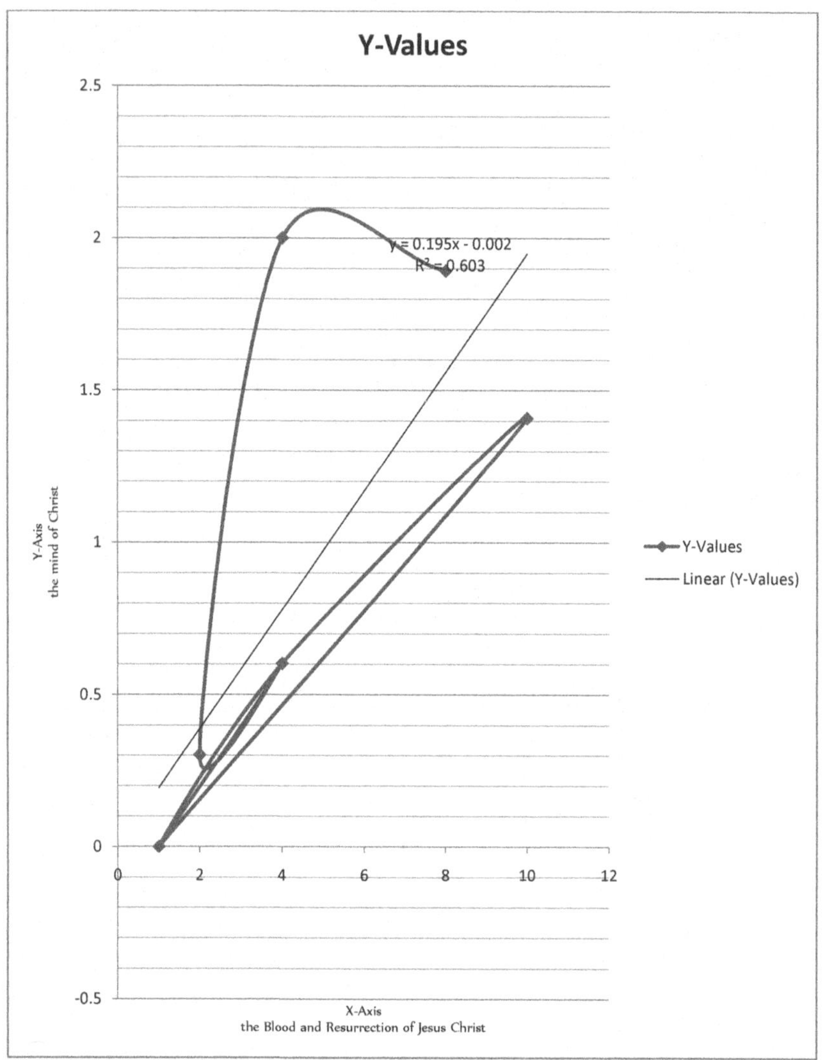

$10^0, 10^0, 9^{0.6308}$ $10^{0.7781}, 10^{0.6020}, 10^0, 10^{0.6020}, 10^{0.3010}, 2^2; 3^{1.8926}$.

Pilled Poplar, Hazel, and Chestnut bible rods 2

23. But he answered her not a word. And his disciples came and besought him, saying, Send her away; for she crieth after us.

7. 7, 1, 3; 5. Bible Matrices

Pilled Poplar, Hazel, and Chestnut bible rods 1

$\text{Log}_{10} 7 = 0.8450$ $\text{Log}_{10} 5 = 0.6989$ $\text{Log}_{10} 7 = 0.8450$ $\text{Log}_{10} 3 = 0.4771$ $\text{Log}_{10} 1 = 0$

7. 7, 1, 3; 5. Deep calls unto Deep study bible 1

0.8450. 0.8450, 0, 0.4771; 0.6989.
Deep calls unto Deep study bible 2

x-axis	y-axis
7	0.8450
7	0.8450
1	0
3	0.4771
5	0.6989

Water Spout *(lightning; combinatorics)* Study bible 1

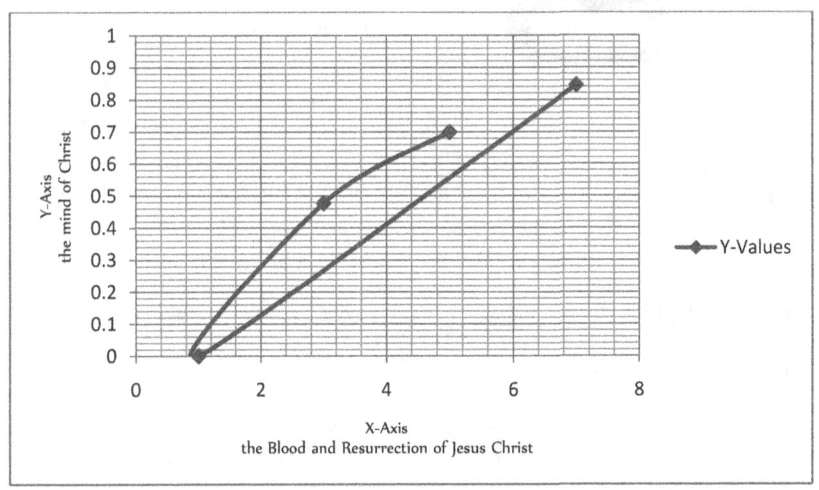

Water Spout *(lightning; combinatorics)* Study bible 2

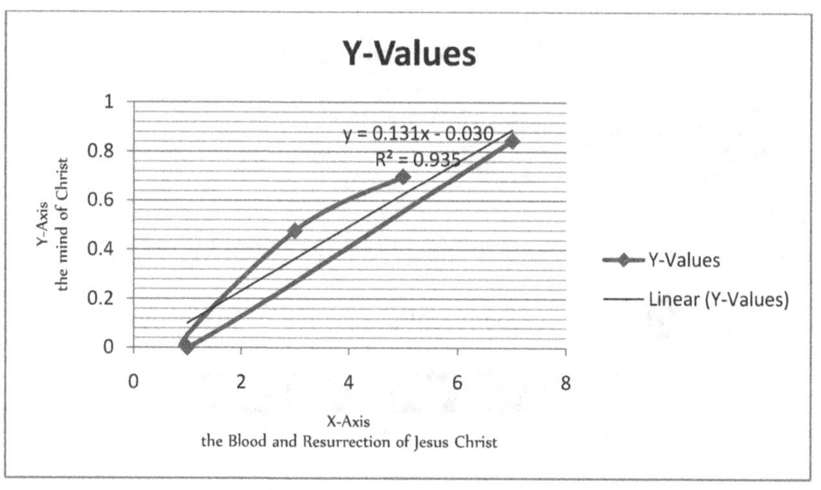

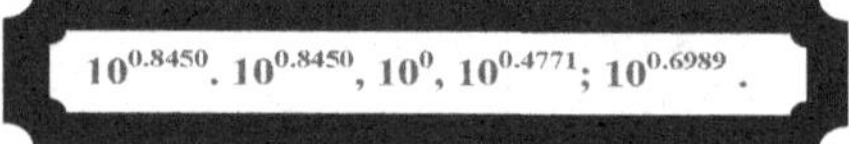

Pilled Poplar, Hazel, and Chestnut bible rods 2

24. But he answered and said, I am not sent but unto the lost sheep of the house of Israel **who prevails with God; God strives**.

5, 14. Bible Matrices

Pilled Poplar, Hazel, and Chestnut bible rods 1

$\text{Log}_{10} 5 = 0.6989$

$\text{Log}_{6} 14 = y$

$6^{y} = 14$

$y \log_{10} 6 = \log_{10} 14$

$y = \log_{10} 14 / \log_{10} 6$

$y = 1.1461 / 0.7781$

$y = 1.4729$

5, 14. Deep calls unto Deep study bible 1

0.6989, 1.4729. Deep calls unto Deep study bible 2

x-axis	y-axis
5	0.6989
14	1.4729

Water Spout *(lightning; combinatorics)* Study bible 1

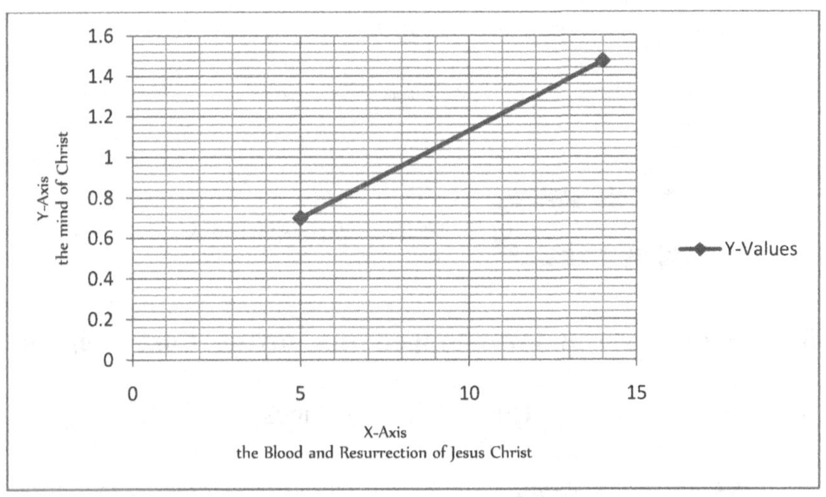

Water Spout *(lightning; combinatorics)* Study bible 2

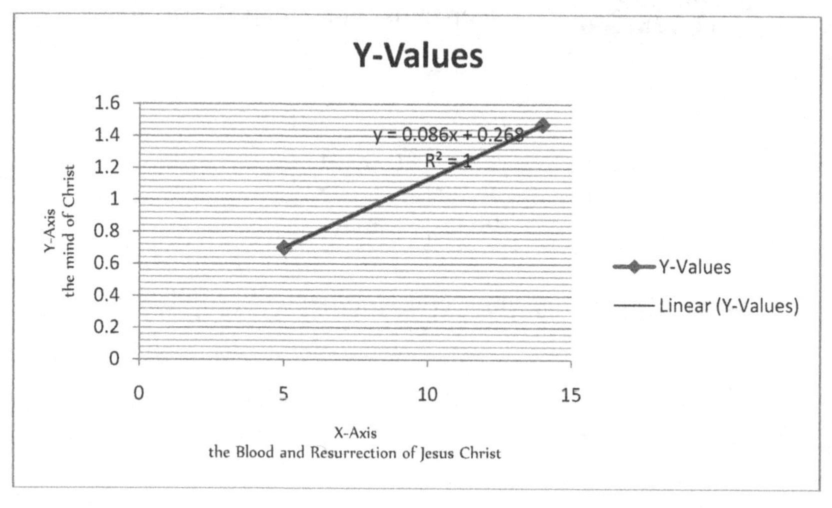

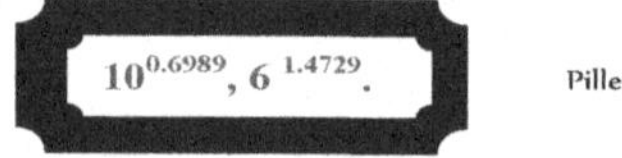

Pilled Poplar, Hazel, and Chestnut bible rods 2

25. Then came she and worshipped him, saying, Lord, help me.

6, 1, 1, 2. Bible Matrices

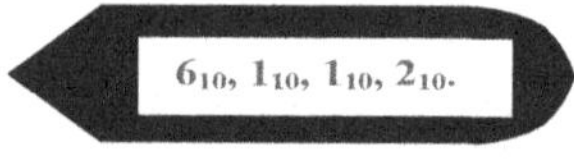

Pilled Poplar, Hazel, and Chestnut bible rods 1

$\text{Log}_{10} 6 = 0.7781$ $\text{Log}_{10} 2 = 0.3010$ $\text{Log}_{10} 1 = 0$ $\text{Log}_{10} 1 = 0$

6, 1, 1, 2. Deep calls unto Deep study bible 1

0.7781, 0, 0, 0.3010.

Deep calls unto Deep study bible 2

x-axis	y-axis
6	0.7781
1	0
1	0
2	0.3010

Water Spout *(lightning; combinatorics)* Study bible 1

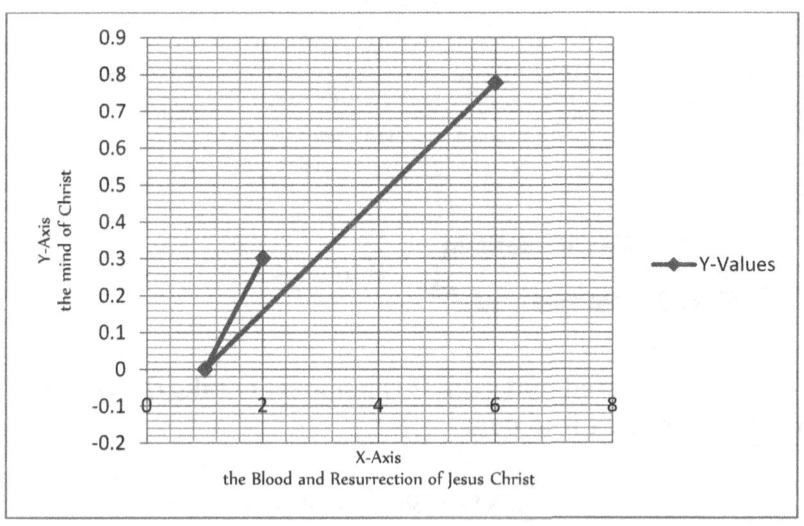

Water Spout *(lightning; combinatorics)* Study bible 2

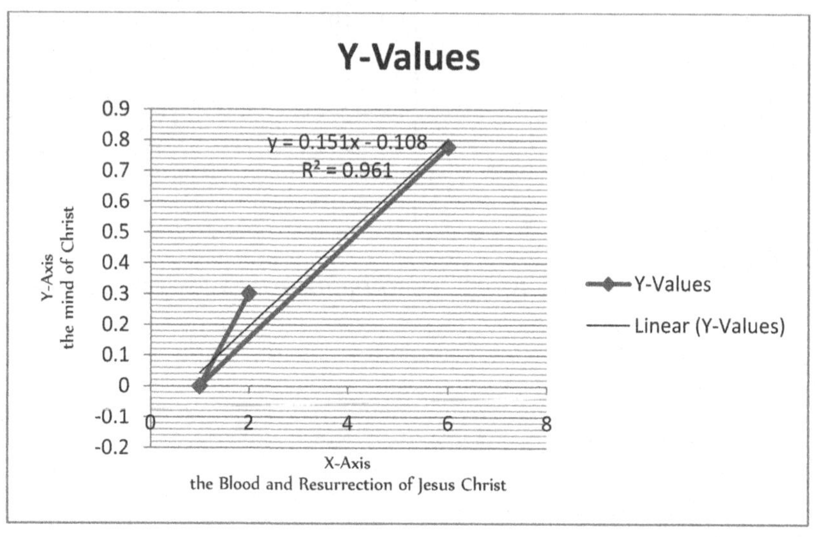

26. But he answered and said, It is not meet to take the children's bread, and to cast it to dogs.

5, 9, 6. Bible Matrices

$\text{Log}_{10} 5 = 0.6989$ $\text{Log}_{10} 9 = 0.9542$ $\text{Log}_{10} 6 = 0.7781$

5, 9, 6. Deep calls unto Deep study bible 1

0.6989, 0.9542, 0.7781.
Deep calls unto Deep study bible 2

x-axis	y-axis
5	0.6989
9	0.9542
6	0.7781

Water Spout *(lightning; combinatorics)* Study bible 1

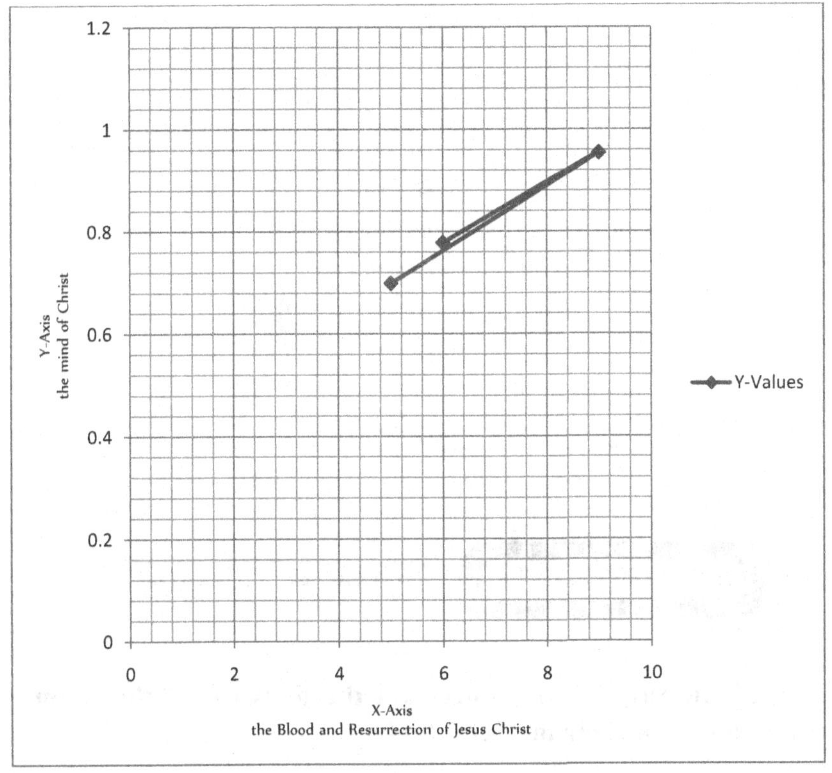

Water Spout *(lightning; combinatorics)* Study bible 2

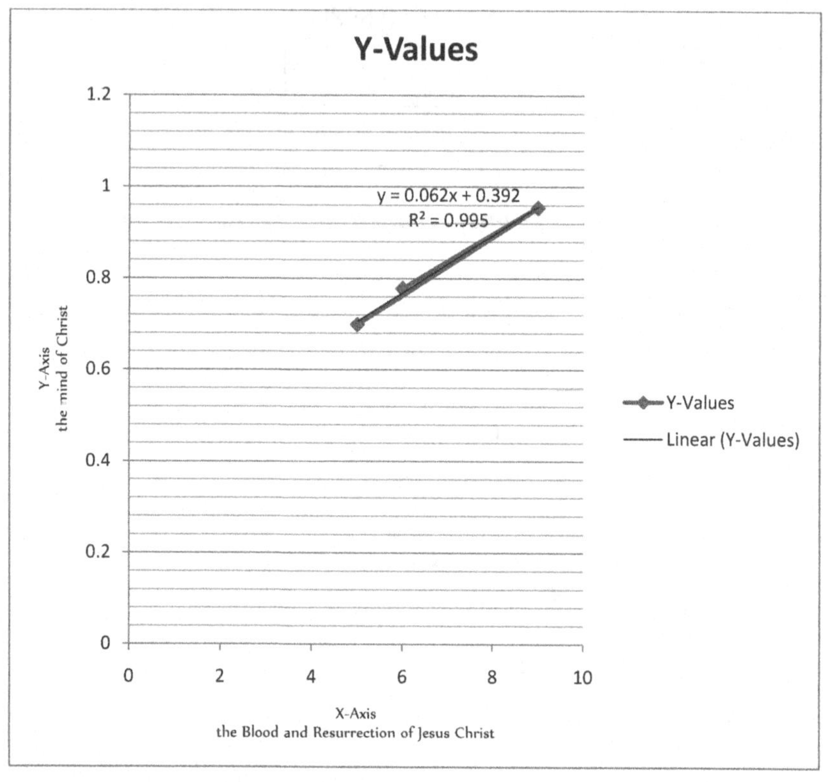

$10^{0.6989}$, $10^{0.9542}$, $10^{0.7781}$.

Pilled Poplar, Hazel, and Chestnut bible rods 2

27. And she said, Truth, Lord: yet the dogs eat of the crumbs which fall from their masters' table.

3, 1, 1: 13. Bible Matrices

3_{10}, 1_{10}, 1_{10}: 13_{10}.

Pilled Poplar, Hazel, and Chestnut bible rods 1

$\text{Log}_{10} 3 = 0.4771$ $\text{Log}_{10} 1 = 0$ $\text{Log}_{10} 13 = 1.1139$ $\text{Log}_{10} 1 = 0$

3, 1, 1: 13. Deep calls unto Deep study bible 1

0.4771, 0, 0: 1.1139.

Deep calls unto Deep study bible 2

x-axis	y-axis
3	0.4771
1	0
1	0
13	1.1139

Water Spout *(lightning; combinatorics)* Study bible 1

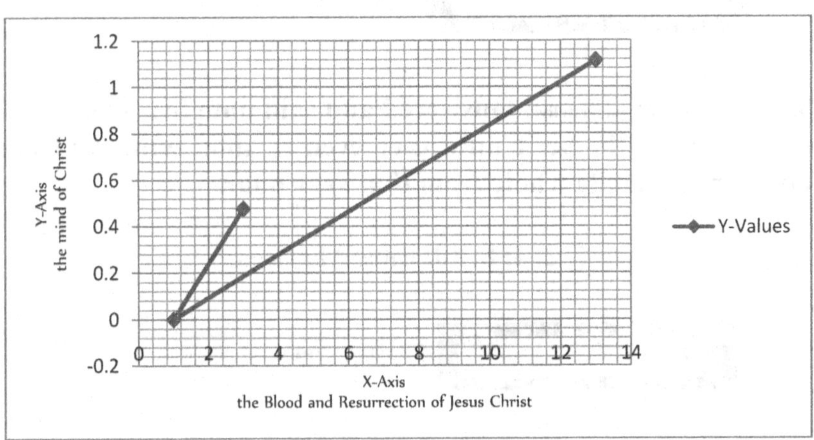

Water Spout *(lightning; combinatorics)* Study bible 2

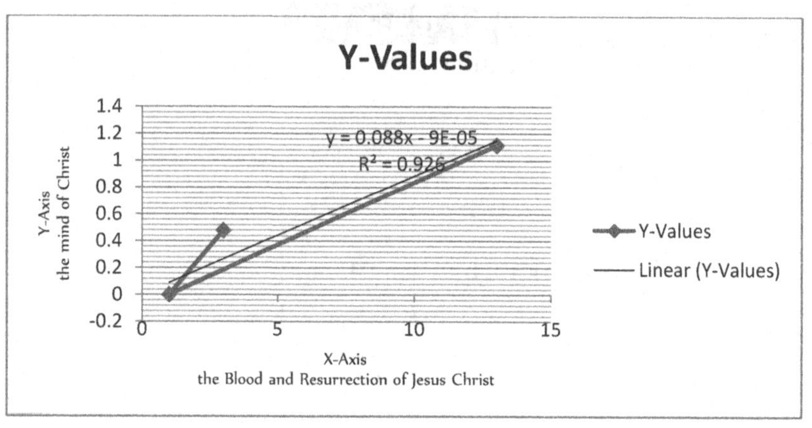

Pilled Poplar, Hazel, and Chestnut bible rods 2

28. Then Jesussavior; deliverer**answered and said unto her, O woman, great is thy faith: be it unto thee even as thou wilt. And her daughter was made whole from that very hour.**

7, 2, 4: 8. 10. Bible Matrices

$2_2\ 5_{10}$, 2_{10}, 4_{10}: 8_{10}. 10_{10} .

Pilled Poplar, Hazel, and Chestnut bible rods 1

$\text{Log}_{10} 10 = 1$ $\text{Log}_{10} 2 = 0.3010$ $\text{Log}_{10} 4 = 0.6020$ $\text{Log}_{10} 8 = 0.9030$ $\text{Log}_{10} 5 = 0.6989$

$\text{Log}_2 2 = y$

$2y = 2$

$2^y = 2^1$

$y = 1$

7, 2, 4: 8. 10. Deep calls unto Deep study bible 1

1 0.6989, 0.3010, 0.6020: 0.9030. 1.
Deep calls unto Deep study bible 2

x-axis	y-axis
7	1.6989
2	0.3010
4	0.6020
8	0.9030
10	1

Water Spout *(lightning; combinatorics)* Study bible 1

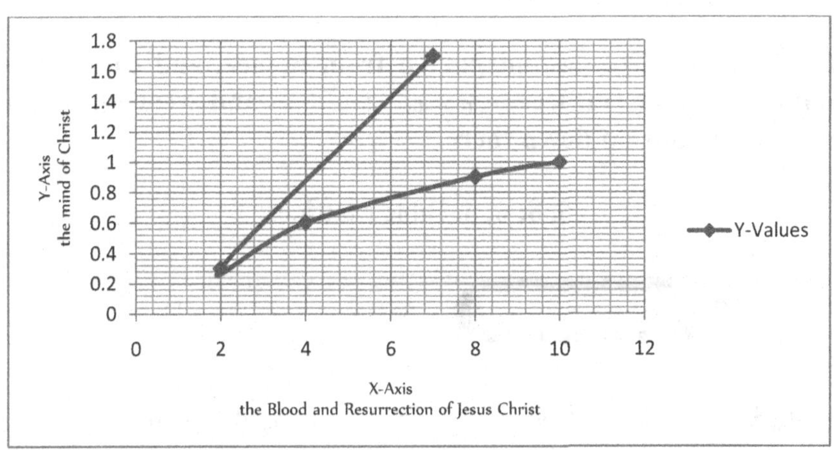

Water Spout *(lightning; combinatorics)* Study bible 2

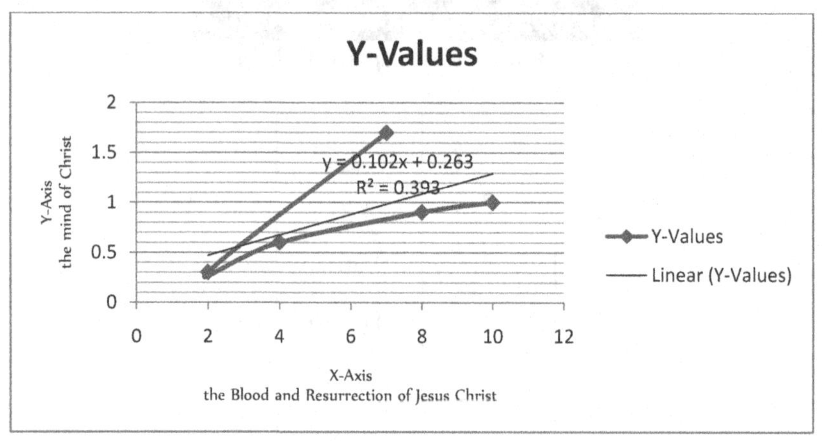

$2^1\ 10^{0.6989},\ 10^{0.3010},\ 10^{0.6020}:\ 10^{0.9030}.\ 10^1.$

Pilled Poplar, Hazel, and Chestnut bible rods 2

29. And Jesussavior; deliverer**departed from thence, and came nigh unto the sea of Galilee**wheel; revolution; circle; circuit; **and went up into a mountain, and sat down there.**

5, 8; 6, 4. Bible Matrices

$2_2 3_{10},\ 8_4;\ 6_{10},\ 4_{10}.$

Pilled Poplar, Hazel, and Chestnut bible rods 1

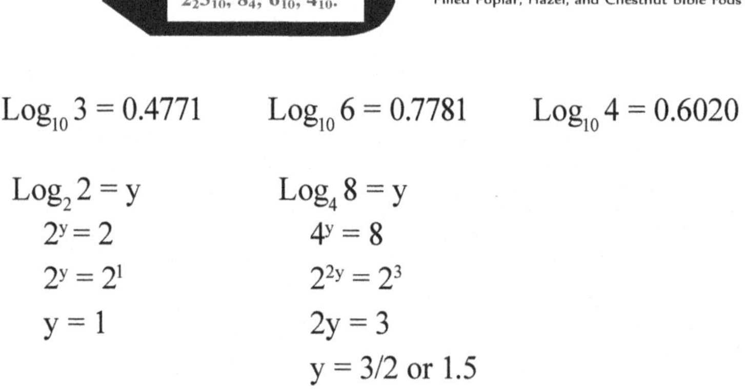

$\text{Log}_{10} 3 = 0.4771$ $\text{Log}_{10} 6 = 0.7781$ $\text{Log}_{10} 4 = 0.6020$

$\text{Log}_2 2 = y$

$2^y = 2$

$2^y = 2^1$

$y = 1$

$\text{Log}_4 8 = y$

$4^y = 8$

$2^{2y} = 2^3$

$2y = 3$

$y = 3/2 \text{ or } 1.5$

5, 8; 6, 4. Deep calls unto Deep study bible 1

1 0.4771, 1.5; 0.7781, 0.6020.
Deep calls unto Deep study bible 2

x-axis	y-axis
5	1.4771
8	1.5
6	0.7781
4	0.6020

Water Spout *(lightning; combinatorics)* Study bible 1

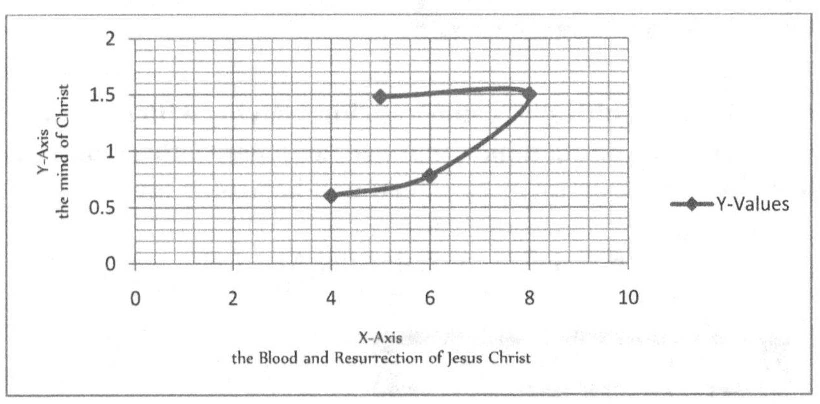

Water Spout *(lightning; combinatorics)* Study bible 2

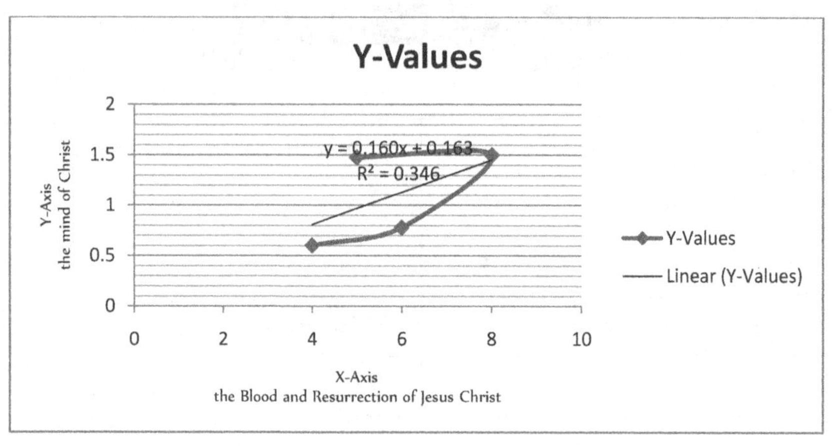

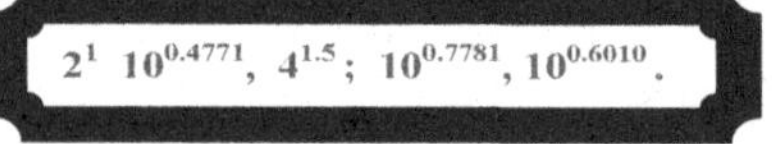

Pilled Poplar, Hazel, and Chestnut bible rods 2

30. And great multitudes came unto him, having with them those that were lame, blind, dumb, maimed, and many others, and cast them down at Jesus'savior; deliverer **feet; and he healed them:**

6, 7, 1, 1, 1, 3, 7; 4: Bible Matrices

6_{10}, 7_{10}, 1_{10}, 1_{10}, 1_{10}, 3_{10}, $6_2 1_{10}$; 4_{10}:

Pilled Poplar, Hazel, and Chestnut bible rods 1

$\text{Log}_{10} 6 = 0.7781$ $\quad$ $\text{Log}_{10} 7 = 0.8450$ $\quad$ $\text{Log}_{10} 3 = 0.4771$ $\quad$ $\text{Log}_{10} 4 = 0.6020$

$\text{Log}_{10} 1 = 0$ $\quad$ $\text{Log}_{10} 1 = 0$

$\text{Log}_{10} 1 = 0$ $\quad$ $\text{Log}_{10} 1 = 0$

$\text{Log}_2 6 = y$

$2^y = 6$

$y \log_{10} 2 = \log_{10} 6$

$y = \log_{10} 6 / \log_{10} 2$

$y = 0.7781 / 0.3010$

$y = 2.5850$

6, 7, 1, 1, 1, 3, 7; 4: Deep calls unto Deep study bible 1

0.7781, 0.8450, 0, 0, 0, 0.4771, 2.5850 0; 0.6020:
Deep calls unto Deep study bible 2

x-axis	y-axis
6	0.7781
7	0.8450
1	0
1	0
1	0
3	0.4771
7	2.5850
4	0.6020

Water Spout *(lightning; combinatorics)* Study bible 1

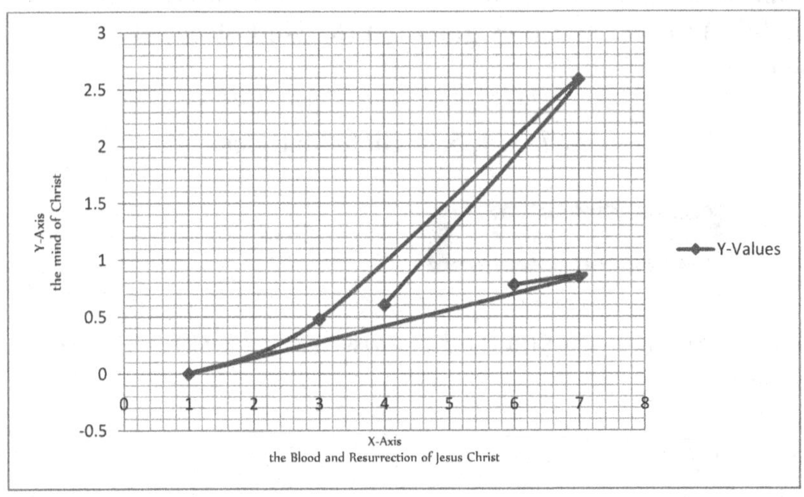

Water Spout *(lightning; combinatorics)* Study bible 2

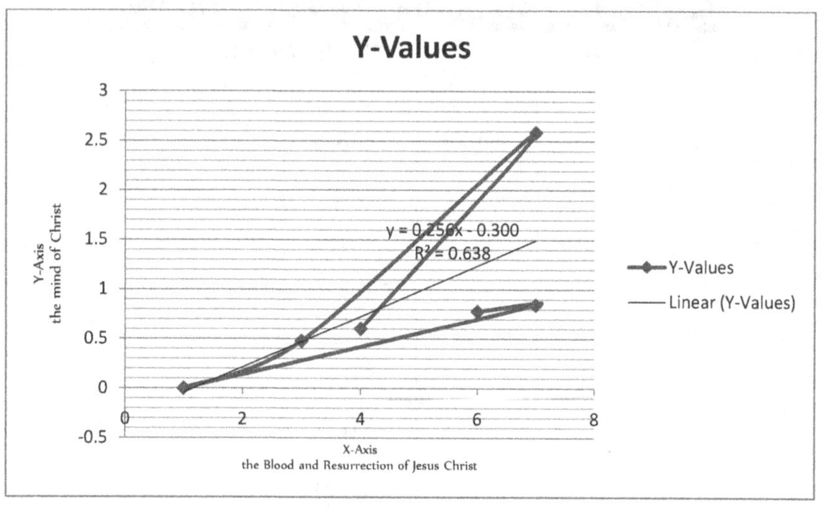

$10^{0.7781}$, $10^{0.8450}$, 10^{0}, 10^{0}, 10^{0}, $10^{0.4771}$, $2^{2.5850}$ 10^{0}; $10^{0.6020}$:

Pilled Poplar, Hazel, and Chestnut bible rods 2

31. Insomuch that the multitude wondered, when they saw the dumb to speak, the maimed to be whole, the lame to walk, and the blind to see: and they glorified the God of Israel **who prevails with God; God strives.**

5, 7, 5, 4, 5: 7. Bible Matrices

5_{10}, 7_{10}, 5_{10}, 4_{10}, 5_{10} : 7_6.

Pilled Poplar, Hazel, and Chestnut bible rods 1

$\text{Log}_{10} 5 = 0.6989$ $\text{Log}_{10} 7 = 0.8450$ $\text{Log}_{10} 5 = 0.6989$ $\text{Log}_{10} 5 = 0.6989$ $\text{Log}_{10} 4 = 0.6020$

$\text{Log}_6 7 = y$

$6^y = 7$

$y \log_{10} 6 = \log_{10} 7$

$y = \log_{10} 7 / \log_{10} 6$

$y = 0.8450 / 0.6020$

$y = 1.4036$

5, 7, 5, 4, 5: 7. Deep calls unto Deep study bible 1

0.6989, 0.8450, 0.6989, 0.6020, 0.6989: 1.4036.
Deep calls unto Deep study bible 2

x-axis	y-axis
5	0.6989
7	0.8450
5	0.6989
4	0.6020
5	0.6989
7	1.4036

Water Spout *(lightning; combinatorics)* Study bible 1

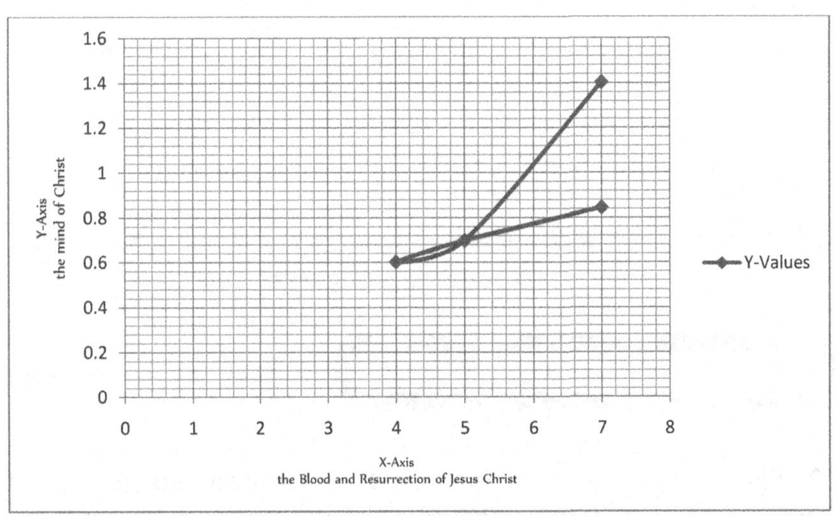

Water Spout *(lightning; combinatorics)* Study bible 2

x-axis	y-axis
3	0.4771
9	0.9542
4	0.6020
8	0.9030

Water Spout *(lightning; combinatorics)* Study bible 1

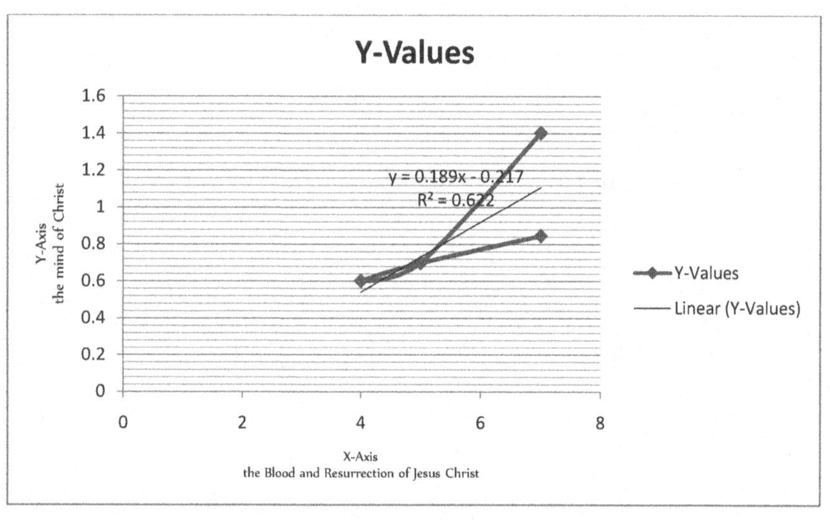

$10^{0.6989}$, $10^{0.8450}$, $10^{0.6989}$, $10^{0.6020}$, $10^{0.6989}$: $6^{1.4036}$. Pilled Poplar, Hazel, and Chestnut bible rods 2

32. Then Jesussavior; deliverer **called his disciples unto him, and said, I have compassion on the multitude, because they continue with me now three** completion or perfection, and unity; 3 x 1 **days, and have nothing to eat: and I will not send them away fasting, lest they faint in the way.**

7, 2, 6, 8, 5: 8, 6. Bible Matrices

$2_2\, 5_{10}, 2_{10}, 6_{10}, 8_{10}, 5_{10}: 7_7\, 1_{10}, 6_{10}.$

Pilled Poplar, Hazel, and Chestnut bible rods 1

$\log_{10} 6 = 0.7781$ $\log_{10} 5 = 0.6989$ $\log_{10} 2 = 0.3010$ $\log_{10} 5 = 0.6989$

$\log_{10} 6 = 0.7781$ $\log_{10} 8 = 0.9030$ $\log_{10} 1 = 0$

$\log_2 2 = y$

$2^y = 2$

$2^y = 2^1$

$y = 1$

$\log_7 7 = y$

$7^y = 7$

$7^y = 7^1$

$y = 1$

7, 2, 6, 8, 5: 8, 6. Deep calls unto Deep study bible 1

1 0.6989, 0.3010, 0.7781, 0.9030, 0.6989: 1 0, 0.7781.

Deep calls unto Deep study bible 2

x-axis	y-axis
7	1.6989
2	0.3010
6	0.7781
8	0.9030
5	0.6989
8	1
6	0.7781

Water Spout *(lightning; combinatorics)* Study bible 1

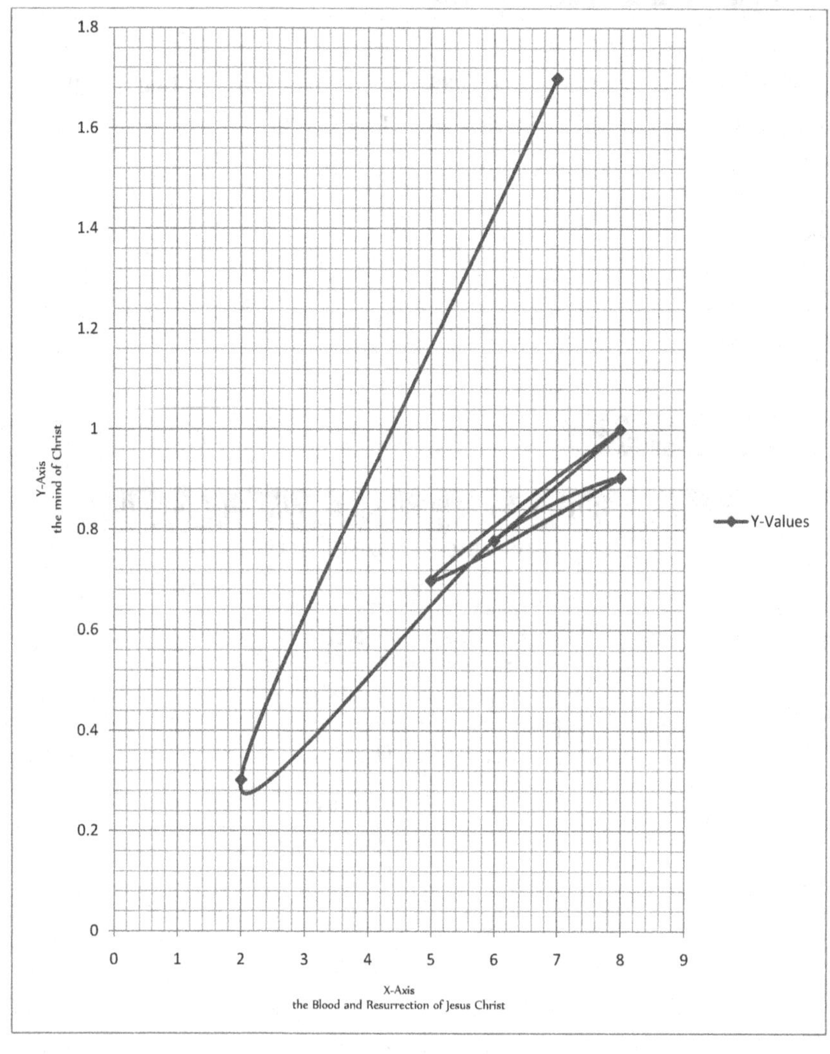

Water Spout *(lightning; combinatorics)* Study bible 2

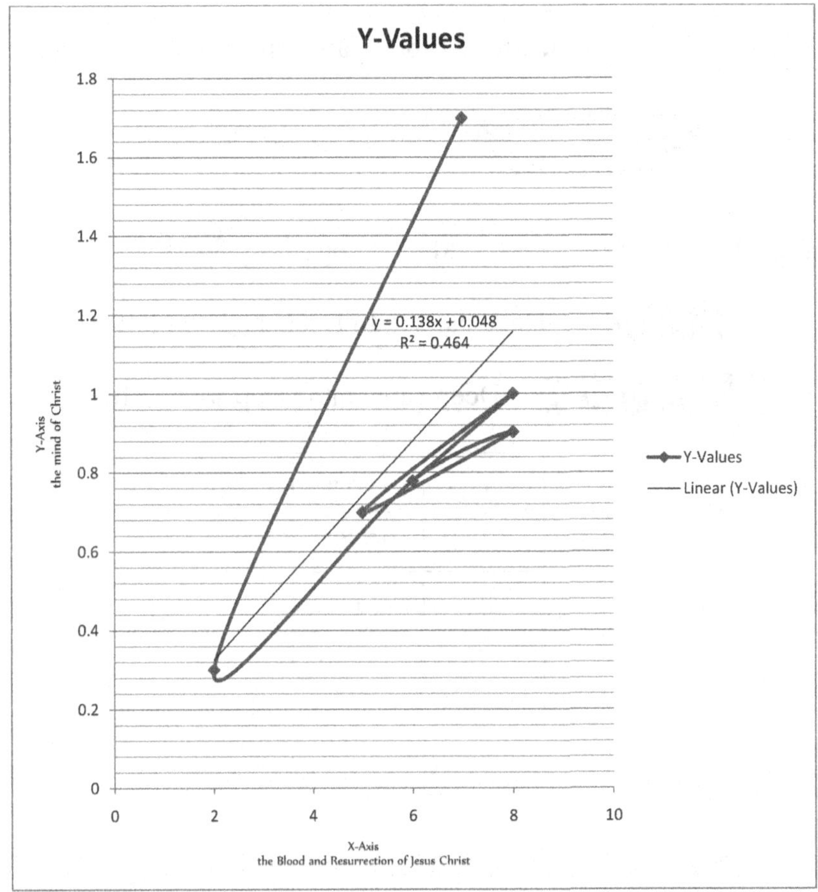

2^1 $10^{0.6989}$, $10^{0.3010}$, $10^{0.7781}$, $10^{0.9030}$, $10^{0.6989}$: 7^1 10^0, $10^{0.7781}$.

Pilled Poplar, Hazel, and Chestnut bible rods 2

33. And his disciples say unto him, Whence should we have so much bread in the wilderness, as to fill so great a multitude?

6, 10, 7? Bible Matrices

$\text{Log}_{10} 10 = 1$ $\text{Log}_{10} 6 = 0.7781$ $\text{Log}_{10} 7 = 0.8450$

6, 10, 7? Deep calls unto Deep study bible 1

0.7781, 1, 0.8450? Deep calls unto Deep study bible 2

x-axis	y-axis
6	0.7781
10	1
7	0.8450

Water Spout *(lightning; combinatorics)* Study bible 1

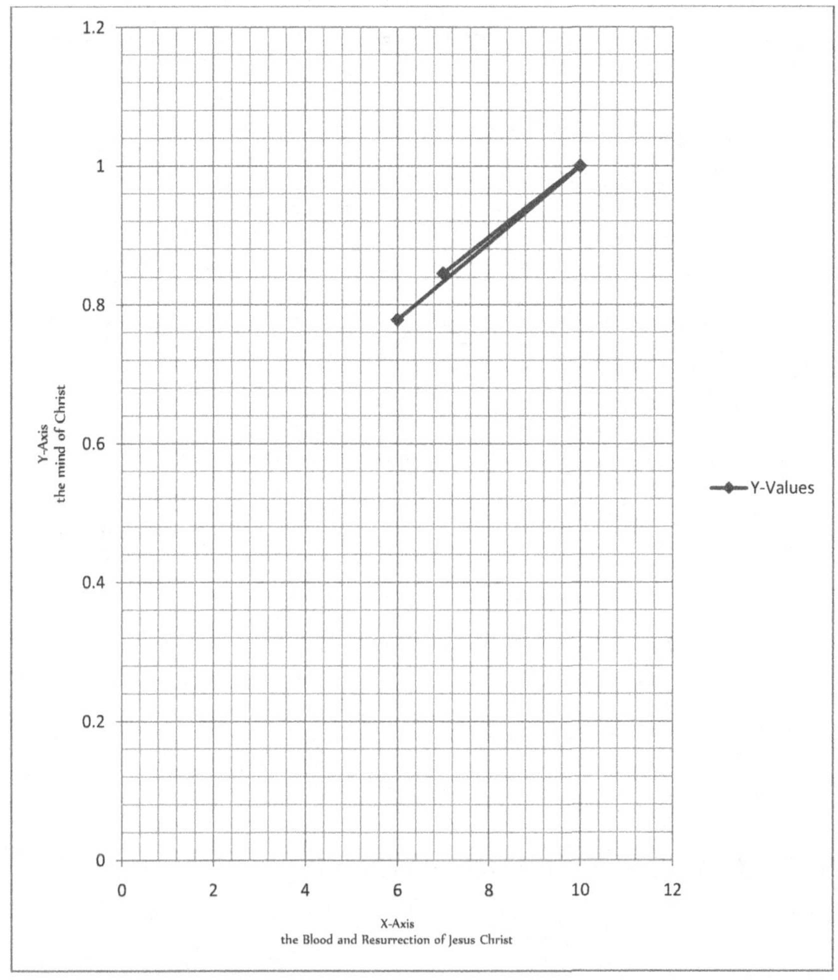

Water Spout *(lightning; combinatorics)* Study bible 2

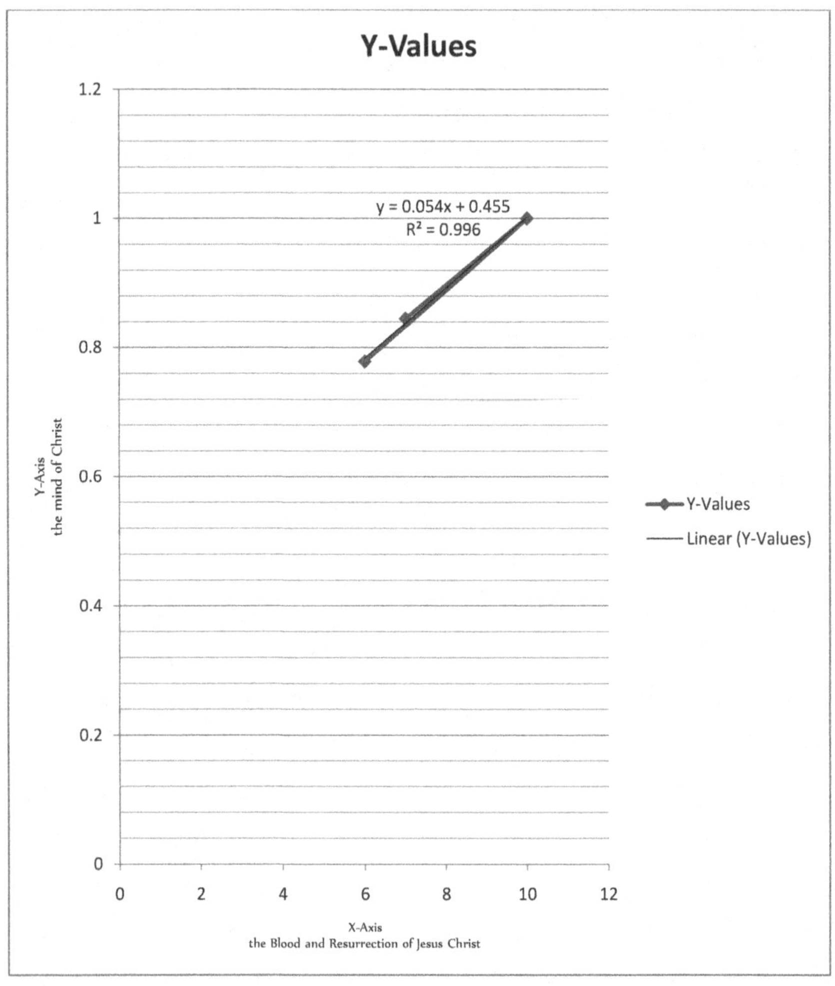

$10^{0.7781}$, 10^{1}, $10^{0.8450}$?

Pilled Poplar, Hazel, and Chestnut bible rods 2

34. And Jesussavior; deliverer**saith unto them, How many loaves have ye? And they said, Seven** divine perfection or completeness; 7 x 1, **and a few little fishes.**

5, 5? 3, 1, 5. Bible Matrices

$2_2\ 3_{10},\ 5_{10}?\ 3_{10},\ 1_6,\ 5_{10}.$ Pilled Poplar, Hazel, and Chestnut bible rods 1

$\text{Log}_{10} 3 = 0.4771$ $\text{Log}_{10} 5 = 0.6989$ $\text{Log}_{10} 3 = 0.4771$ $\text{Log}_{10} 5 = 0.6989$

$$\text{Log}_2 2 = y \qquad 2^y = 2 \qquad 2^y = 2^1 \qquad y = 1$$

$$\text{Log}_6 1 = y \qquad 6^y = 1 \qquad 6^y = 6^0 \qquad y = 0$$

5, 5? 3, 1, 5. Deep calls unto Deep study bible 1

1 0.4771, 0.6989? 0.4771, 0, 0.6989.
Deep calls unto Deep study bible 2

x-axis	y-axis
5	1.4771
5	0.6989
3	0.4771
1	0
5	0.6989

Water Spout *(lightning; combinatorics)* Study bible 1

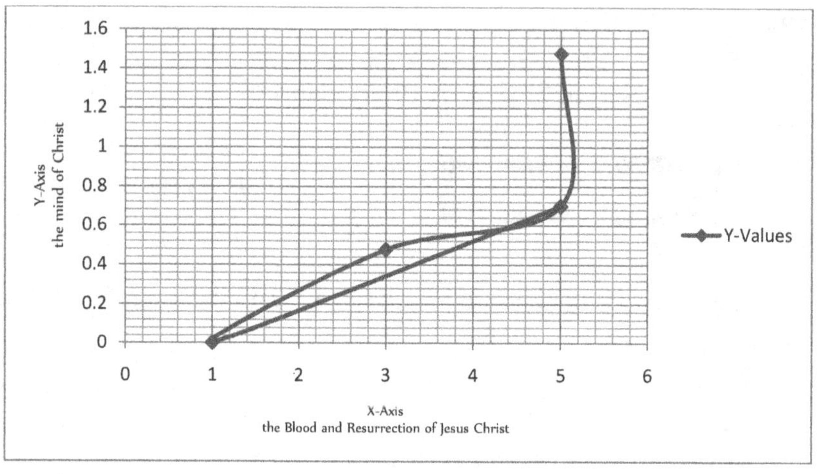

Water Spout *(lightning; combinatorics)* Study bible 2

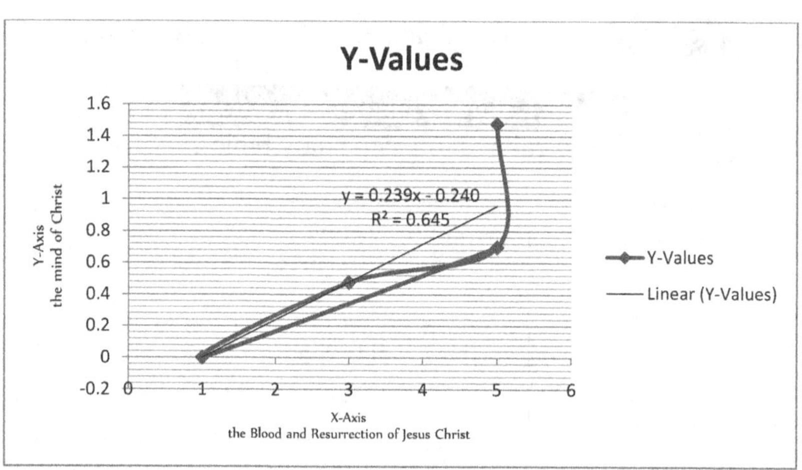

2^1 $10^{0.4771}$, $10^{0.6989}$? $10^{0.4771}$, 6^0, $10^{0.6989}$.

Pilled Poplar, Hazel, and Chestnut bible rods 2

35. And he commanded the multitude to sit down on the ground.

11. Bible Matrices

$\text{Log}_{10}\ 11 = 1.0413$

11. Deep calls unto Deep study bible 1

1.0413. Deep calls unto Deep study bible 2

x-axis	y-axis
11	1.0413

Water Spout *(lightning; combinatorics)* Study bible 1

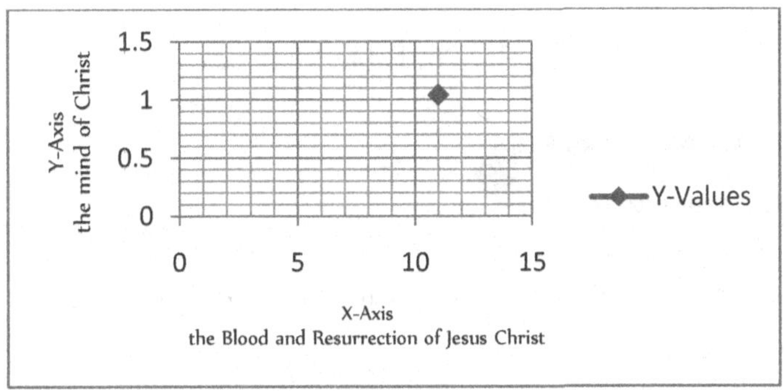

Water Spout *(lightning; combinatorics)* Study bible 2

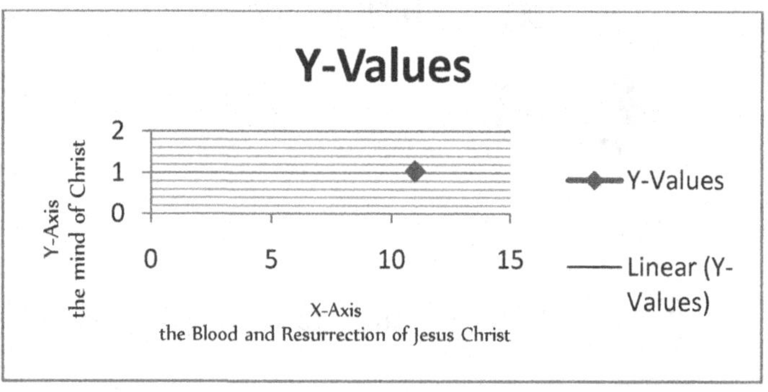

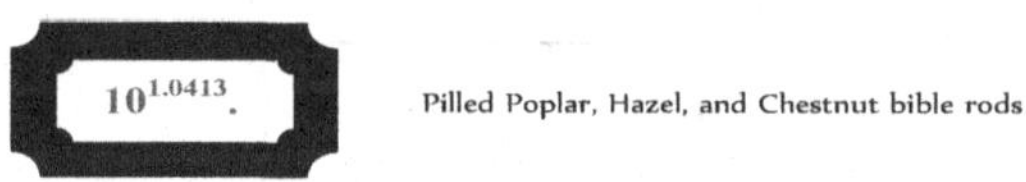

Pilled Poplar, Hazel, and Chestnut bible rods 2

36. And he took the seven divine perfection or completeness; 7 x 1 **loaves and the fishes, and gave thanks, and brake them, and gave to his disciples, and the disciples to the multitude.**

9, 3, 3, 5, 6. Bible Matrices

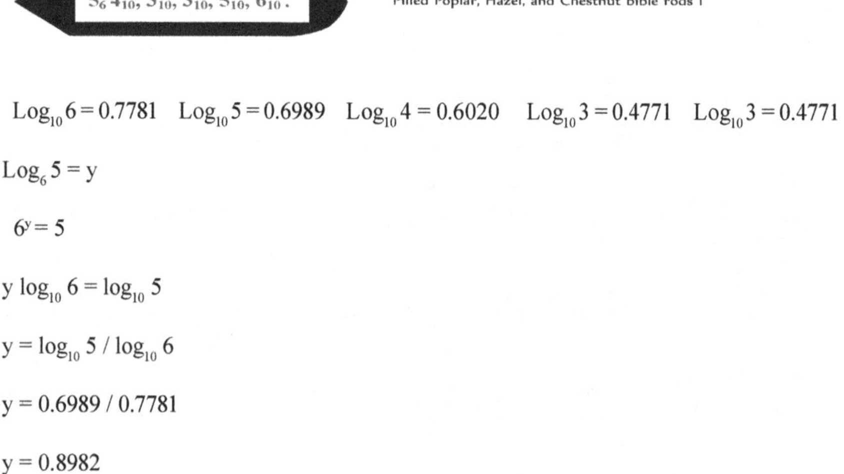

Pilled Poplar, Hazel, and Chestnut bible rods 1

$\mathrm{Log}_{10} 6 = 0.7781$ $\mathrm{Log}_{10} 5 = 0.6989$ $\mathrm{Log}_{10} 4 = 0.6020$ $\mathrm{Log}_{10} 3 = 0.4771$ $\mathrm{Log}_{10} 3 = 0.4771$

$\mathrm{Log}_6 5 = y$

$6^y = 5$

$y \log_{10} 6 = \log_{10} 5$

$y = \log_{10} 5 / \log_{10} 6$

$y = 0.6989 / 0.7781$

$y = 0.8982$

9, 3, 3, 5, 6. Deep calls unto Deep study bible 1

0.8982 0.6020, 0.4771, 0.4771, 0.6989, 0.7781.
Deep calls unto Deep study bible 2

x-axis	y-axis
9	1.5002
3	0.4771
3	0.4771
5	0.6989
6	0.7781

Water Spout *(lightning; combinatorics)* Study bible 1

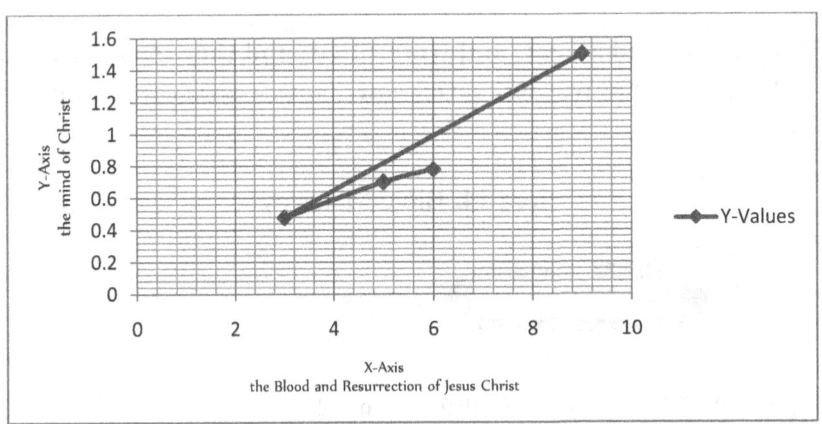

Water Spout *(lightning; combinatorics)* Study bible 2

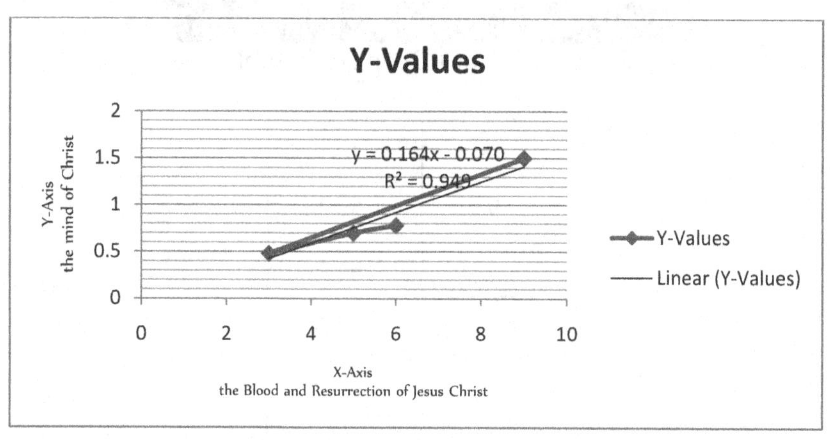

Pilled Poplar, Hazel, and Chestnut bible rods 2

37. And they did all eat, and were filled: and they took up of the broken meat that was left seven divine perfection or completeness; 7 x 1 **baskets full.**

5, 3: 14. Bible Matrices

5_{10}, 3_{10}: 12_6 2_{10} .

Pilled Poplar, Hazel, and Chestnut bible rods 1

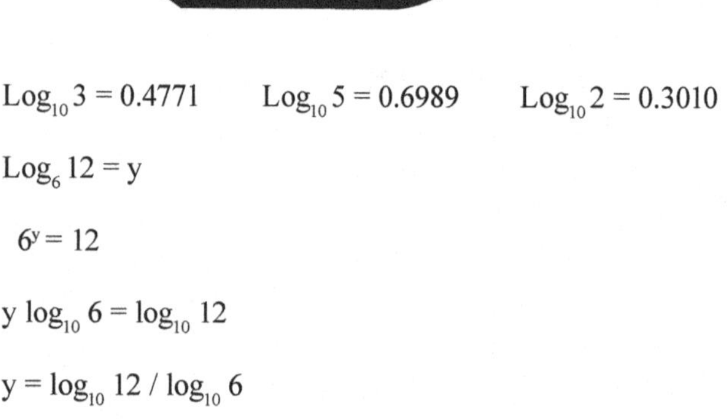

$\text{Log}_{10} 3 = 0.4771$ $\text{Log}_{10} 5 = 0.6989$ $\text{Log}_{10} 2 = 0.3010$

$\text{Log}_6 12 = y$

$6^y = 12$

$y \log_{10} 6 = \log_{10} 12$

$y = \log_{10} 12 / \log_{10} 6$

$y = 1.0791 / 0.7781$

$y = 1.3868$

5, 3: 14. Deep calls unto Deep study bible 1

0.6989, 0.4771: 1.3868 0.3010.
Deep calls unto Deep study bible 2

x-axis	y-axis
5	0.6989
3	0.4771
14	1.6878

Water Spout *(lightning; combinatorics)* Study bible 1

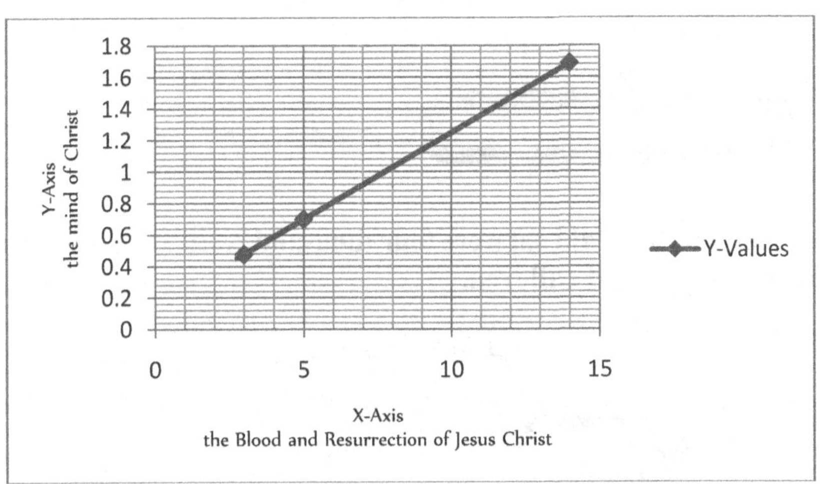

Water Spout *(lightning; combinatorics)* Study bible 2

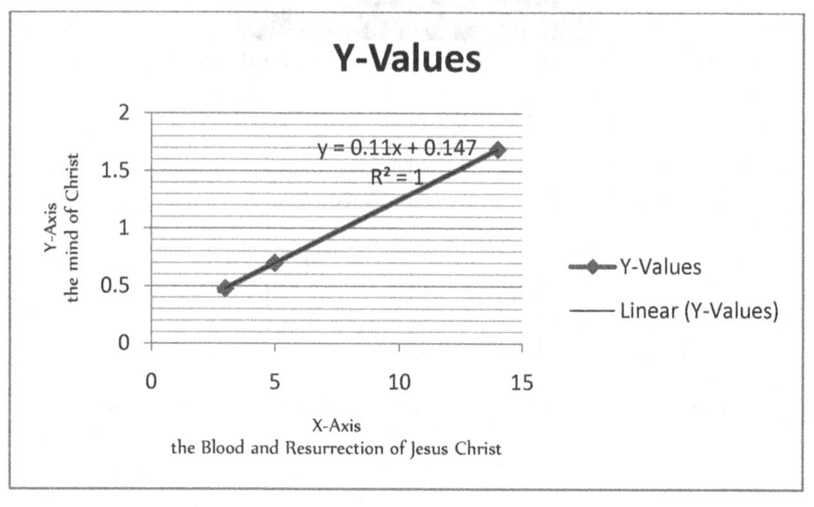

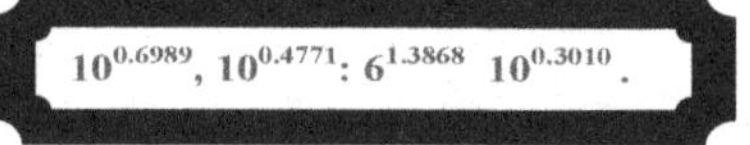

Pilled Poplar, Hazel, and Chestnut bible rods 2

38. And they that did eat were four thousand 2 x 2 x 2 x 2 x 2 x 5 x 5 x 5 **men, beside women and children.**

9, 4. Bible Matrices

Pilled Poplar, Hazel, and Chestnut bible rods 1

$\text{Log}_{10} 1 = 0$ $\text{Log}_{10} 4 = 0.6020$

$\text{Log}_8 8 = y$

$8^y = 8$

$8^y = 8^1$

$y = 1$

9, 4. Deep calls unto Deep study bible 1

1 0, 0.6020. Deep calls unto Deep study bible 2

x-axis	y-axis
9	1
4	0.6020

Water Spout *(lightning; combinatorics)* Study bible 1

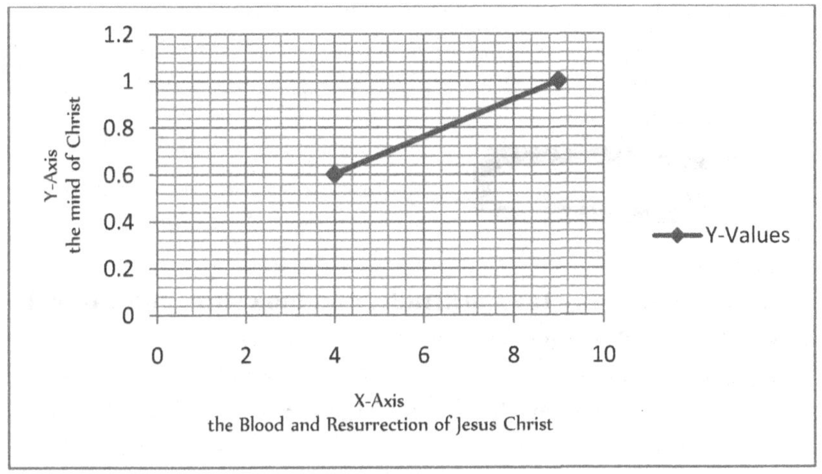

Water Spout *(lightning; combinatorics)* Study bible 2

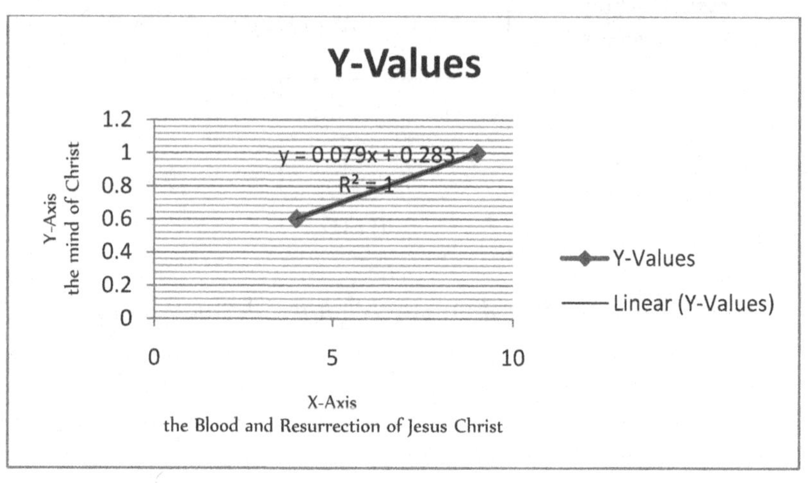

39. And he sent away the multitude, and took ship, and came into the coasts of Magdala tower; greatness.

6, 3, 7. Bible Matrices

$\text{Log}_{10} 6 = 0.7781$ $\text{Log}_{10} 3 = 0.4771$

$\text{Log}_2 7 = y$

$2^y = 7$

$y \log_{10} 2 = \log_{10} 7$

$y = \log_{10} 7 / \log_{10} 2$

$y = 0.8450 / 0.3010$

$y = 2.8073$

6, 3, 7. Deep calls unto Deep study bible 1

0.7781, 0.4771, 2.8073.
Deep calls unto Deep study bible 2

x-axis	y-axis
6	0.7781
3	0.4771
7	2.8073

Water Spout *(lightning; combinatorics)* Study bible 1

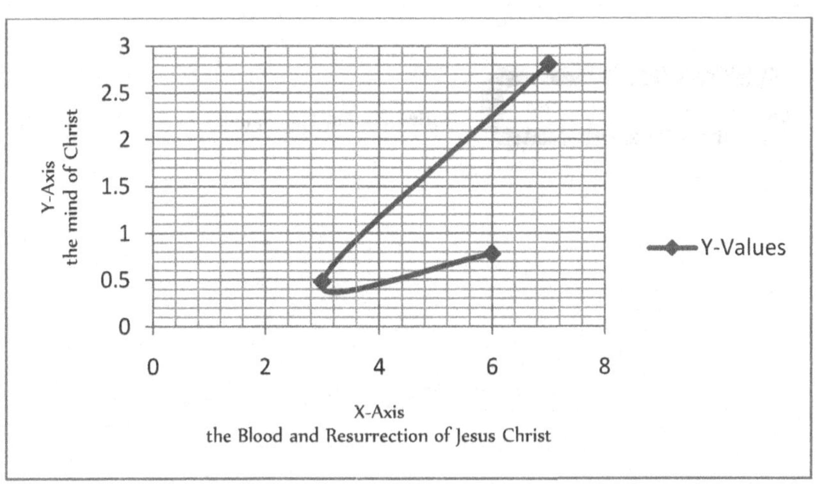

Water Spout *(lightning; combinatorics)* Study bible 2

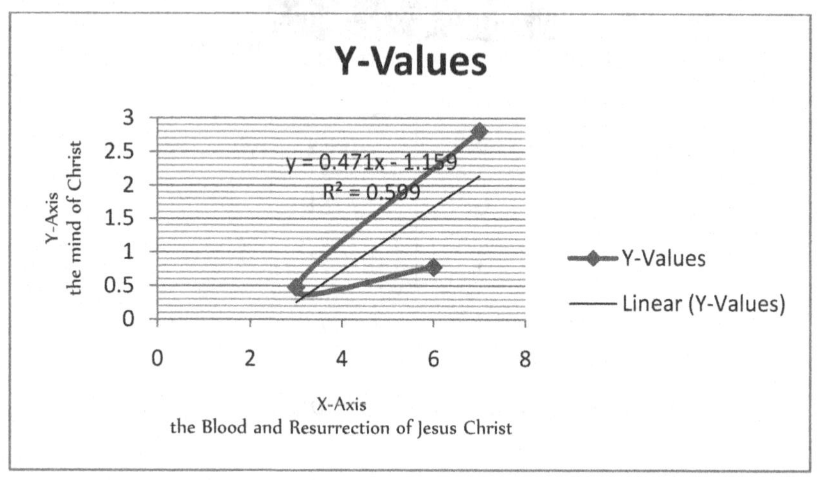

$10^{0.7781}$, $10^{0.4771}$, $2^{2.8073}$.

Pilled Poplar, Hazel, and Chestnut bible rods 2

CHAPTER 16

1. The Pharisees set apart; separatists **also with the Sadducees**followers of Zadok**came, and tempting desired him that he would shew them a sign from heaven.**

7, 13. Bible Matrices

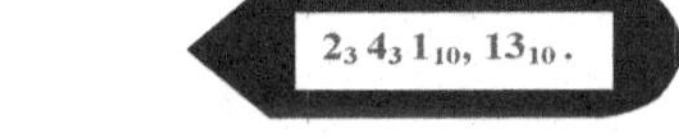

Pilled Poplar, Hazel, and Chestnut bible rods 1

$\text{Log}_{10} 13 = 1.1139$
$\text{Log}_3 2 = y$
$3^y = 2$
$y \log_{10} 3 = \log_{10} 2$
$y = \log_{10} 2 / \log_{10} 3$
$y = 0.3010 / 0.4771$
$y = 0.6308$

$\text{Log}_{10} 1 = 0$
$\text{Log}_3 4 = y$
$3^y = 4$
$y \log_{10} 3 = \log_{10} 4$
$y = \log_{10} 4 / \log_{10} 3$
$y = 0.6020 / 0.4771$
$y = 1.2617$

7, 13. Deep calls unto Deep study bible 1

0.6308 1.2617 0, 1.1139.

Deep calls unto Deep study bible 2

x-axis	y-axis
7	1.8925
13	1.1139

Water Spout *(lightning;combinatorics)* Study bible 1

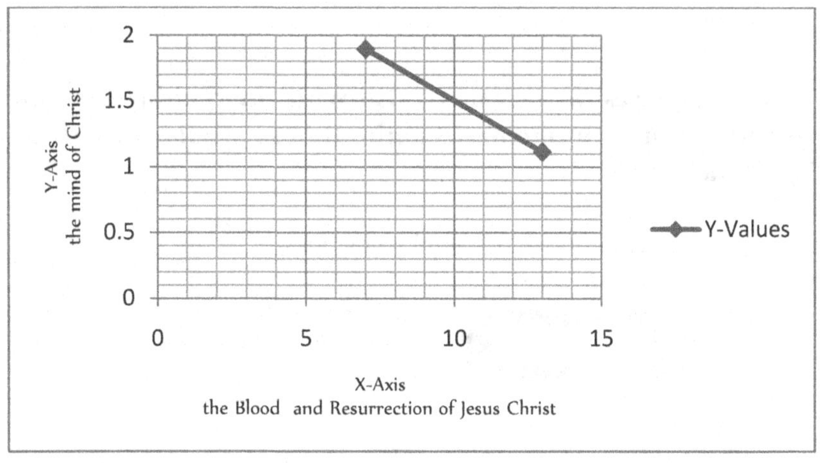

Water Spout *(lightning;combinatorics)* Study bible 2

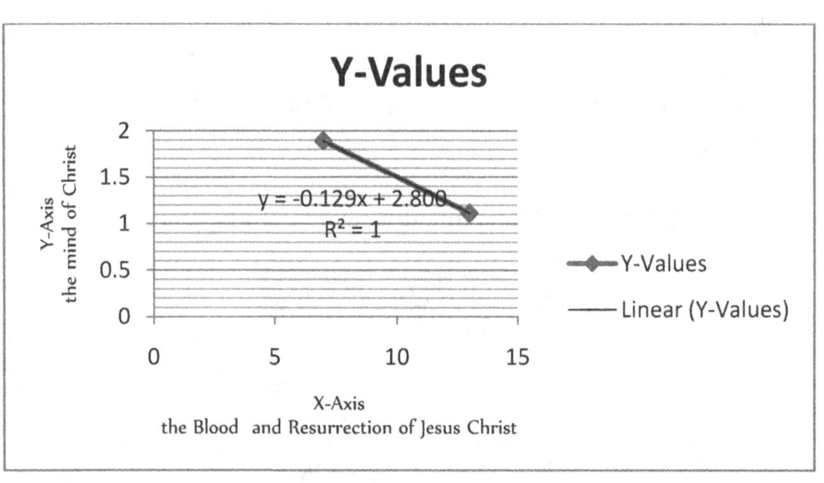

$3^{0.6308}$ $3^{1.2617}$ 10^{0}, $10^{1.1139}$.

Pilled Poplar, Hazel, and Chestnut bible rods 2

2. He answered and said unto them, When it is evening, ye say, It will be fair weather: for the sky is red.

6, 4, 2, 5: 5. Bible Matrices

$6_{10}, 4_{10}, 2_{10}, 5_{10}: 5_{10}$. Pilled Poplar, Hazel, and Chestnut bible rods 1

$\text{Log}_{10} 5 = 0.6989$ $\text{Log}_{10} 4 = 0.6020$ $\text{Log}_{10} 5 = 0.6989$ $\text{Log}_{10} 6 = 0.7781$ $\text{Log}_{10} 2 = 0.3010$

6, 4, 2, 5: 5. Deep calls unto Deep study bible 1

0.7781, 0.6020, 0.3010, 0.6989: 0.6989.
Deep calls unto Deep study bible 2

x-axis	y-axis
6	0.7781
4	0.6020
2	0.3010
5	0.6989
5	0.6989

Water Spout *(lightning;combinatorics)* Study bible 1

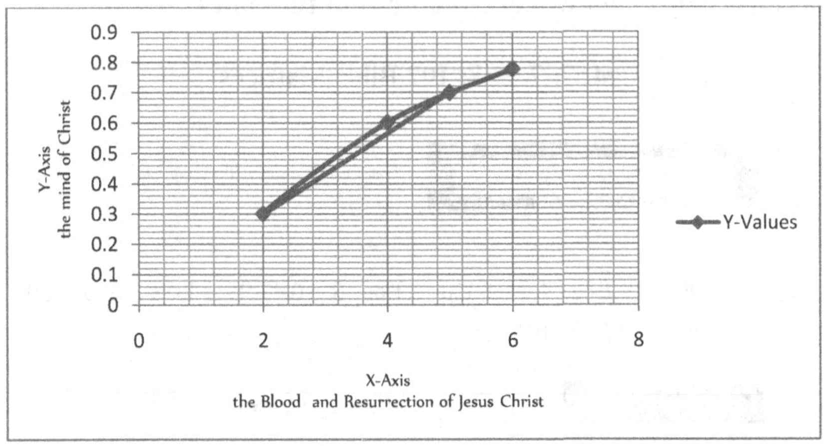

Water Spout *(lightning;combinatorics)* Study bible 2

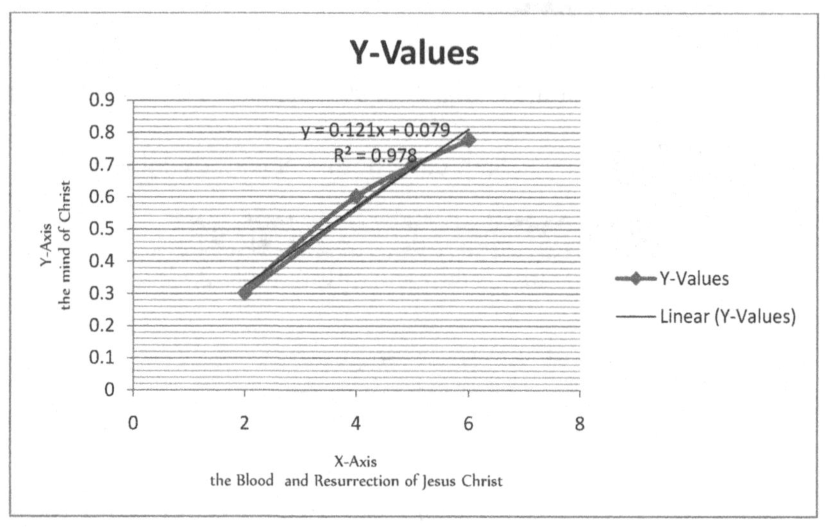

$10^{0.7781}$, $10^{0.6020}$, $10^{0.3010}$, $10^{0.6989}$: $10^{0.6989}$. Pilled Poplar, Hazel, and Chestnut bible rods 2

3. And in the morning, It will be foul weather to day: for the sky is red and lowring. O ye hypocrites, ye can discern the face of the sky; but can ye not discern the signs of the times?

4, 7: 7. 3, 8; 10? Bible Matrices

4_{10}, 7_{10}: 7_{10} . 3_{10}, 8_{10}; 10_{10} ? Pilled Poplar, Hazel, and Chestnut bible rods 1

$\text{Log}_{10} 8 = 0.9030$ $\text{Log}_{10} 4 = 0.6020$ $\text{Log}_{10} 3 = 0.4771$ $\text{Log}_{10} 7 = 0.8450$
$\text{Log}_{10} 7 = 0.8450$ $\text{Log}_{10} 10 = 1$

4, 7: 7. 3, 8; 10? Deep calls unto Deep study bible 1

0.6020, 0.8450: 0.8450. 0.4771, 0.9030; 1?
Deep calls unto Deep study bible 2

x-axis	y-axis
4	0.6020
7	0.8450
7	0.8450
3	0.4771
8	0.9030
10	1

Water Spout *(lightning;combinatorics)* Study bible 1

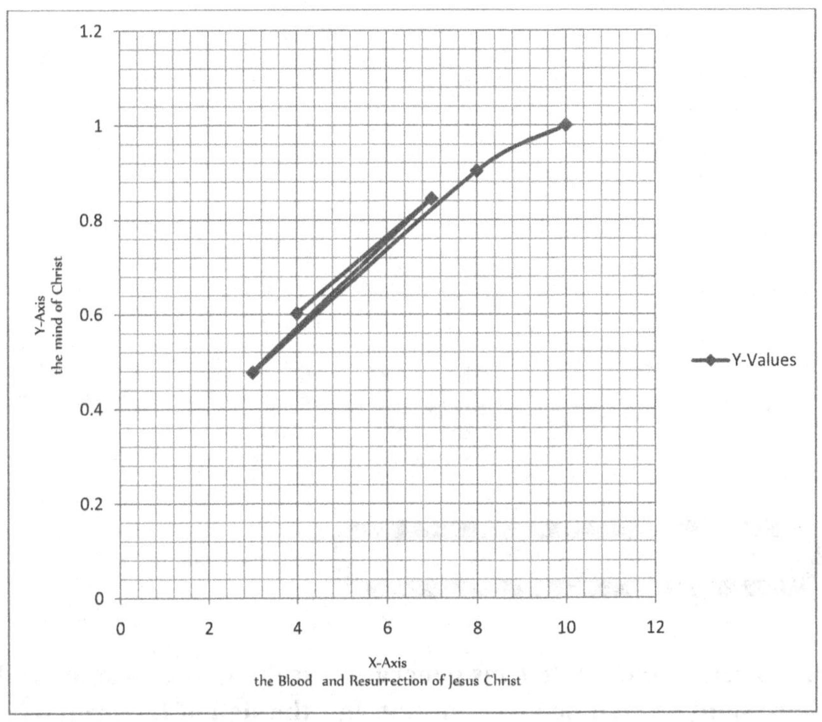

Water Spout *(lightning;combinatorics)* Study bible 2

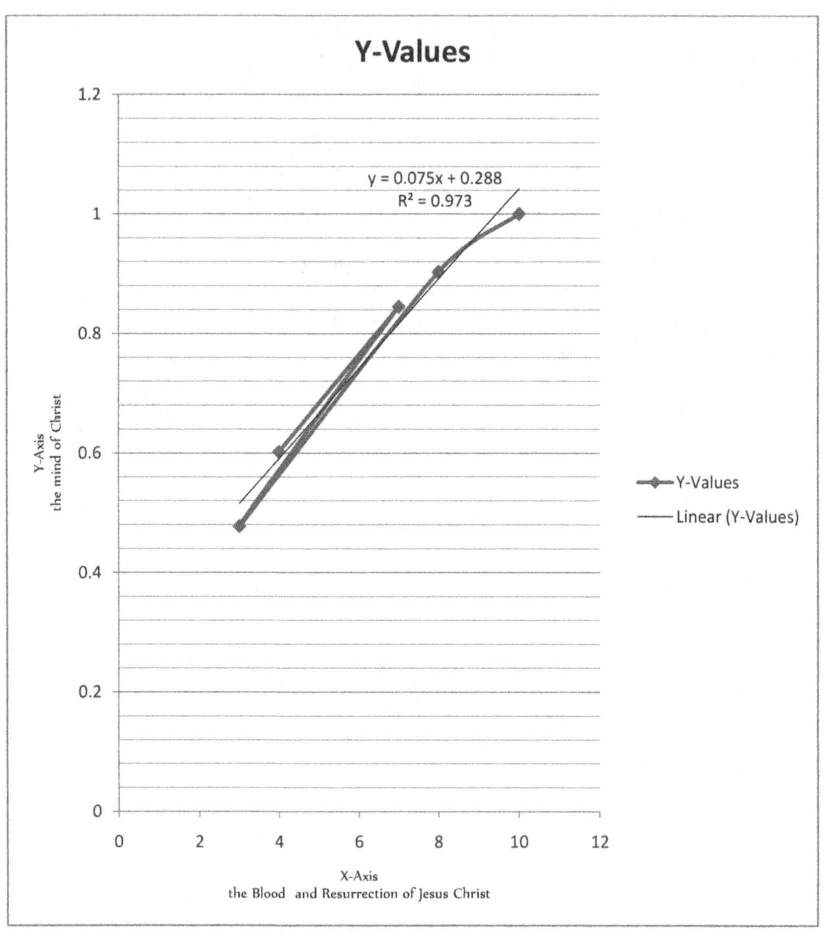

$10^{0.6020}$, $10^{0.8450}$: $10^{0.8450}$. $10^{0.4771}$, $10^{0.9030}$; 10^{1} ?

Pilled Poplar, Hazel, and Chestnut bible rods 2

4. A wicked and adulterous generation seeketh after a sign; and there shall no sign be given unto it, but the sign of the prophet to bubble forth, as from a fountain; utter **Jonas**a dove; he that oppresses; destroyer. **And he left them, and departed.**

9; 9, 7. 4, 2. Bible Matrices

$9_{10}; 9_{10}, 6_8 1_6. 4_{10}, 2_{10}.$ Pilled Poplar, Hazel, and Chestnut bible rods 1

$Log_{10} 9 = 0.9542$ $Log_{10} 9 = 0.9542$ $Log_{10} 4 = 0.6020$ $Log_{10} 2 = 0.3010$

$Log_8 6 = y$

$8^y = 6$

$y \log_{10} 8 = \log_{10}$

$y = \log_{10} 6 / \log_{10} 8$

$y = 0.7781 / 0.9030$

$y = 0.8616$

$Log_6 1 = y$

$6^y = 1$

$6\ 6^y = 6^0$

$y = 0$

9; 9, 7. 4, 2. Deep calls unto Deep study bible 1

0.9542; 0.9542, 0.8616 0, 0.4771, 0.3010.
Deep calls unto Deep study bible 2

x-axis	y-axis
9	0.9542
9	0.9542
7	0.8616
4	0.4771
2	0.3010

Water Spout *(lightning;combinatorics)* Study bible 1

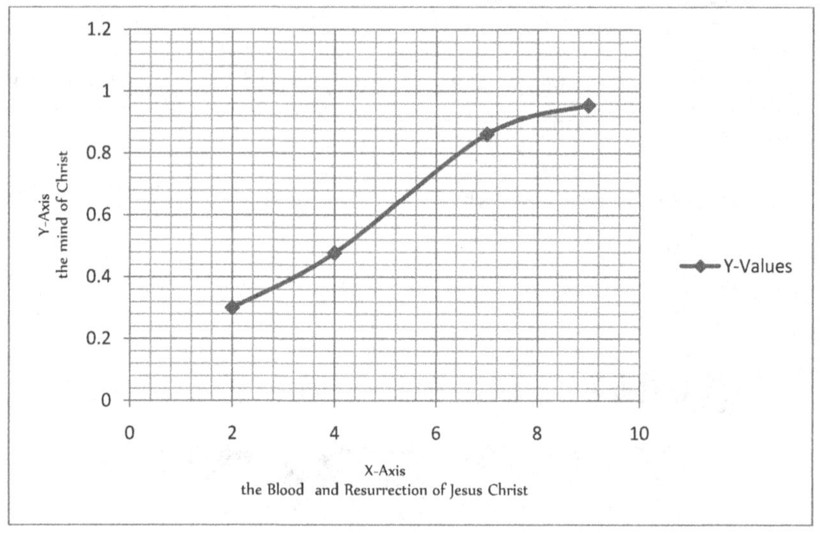

Water Spout *(lightning;combinatorics)* Study bible 2

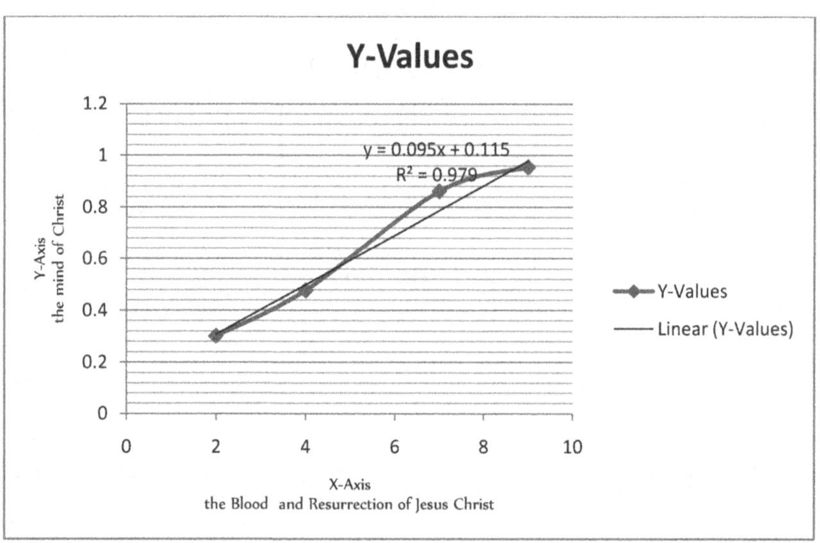

$10^{0.9542}$; $10^{0.9542}$, $8^{0.8616}$ 6^{0}. $10^{0.4771}$, $10^{0.3010}$.

Pilled Poplar, Hazel, and Chestnut bible rods 2

5. And when his disciples were come to the other side, they had forgotten to take bread.

10, 6. Bible Matrices

$\text{Log}_{10} 10 = 1$ $\text{Log}_{10} 6 = 0.7781$

10, 6. Deep calls unto Deep study bible 1

1, 0.7781. Deep calls unto Deep study bible 2

x-axis	y-axis
10	1
6	0.7781

Water Spout *(lightning;combinatorics)* Study bible 1

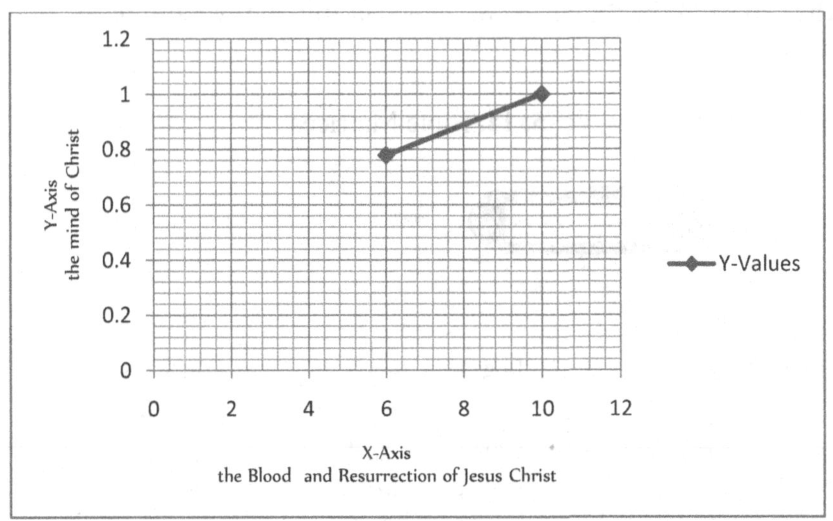

Water Spout *(lightning;combinatorics)* Study bible 2

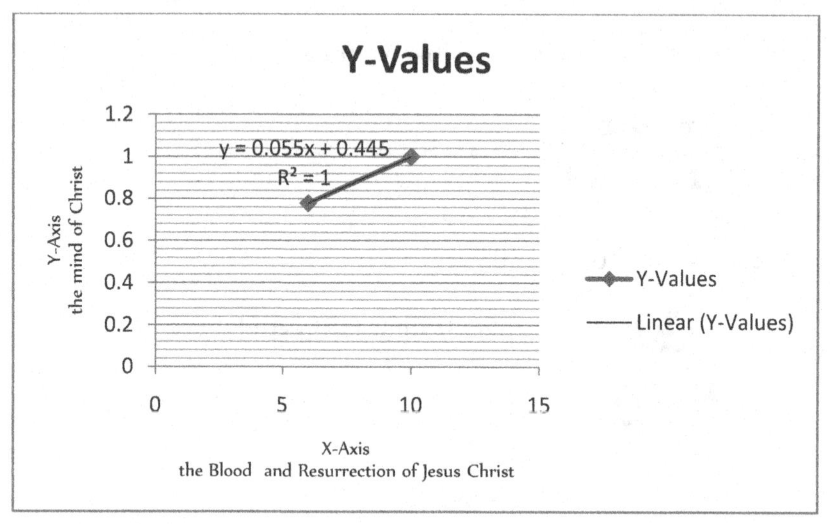

Pilled Poplar, Hazel, and Chestnut bible rods 2

6. Then Jesus **savior; deliverer** **said unto them, Take heed and beware of the leaven of the Pharisees** **set apart; separatists** **and of the Sadducees** **followers of Zadok.**

5, 14. Bible Matrices

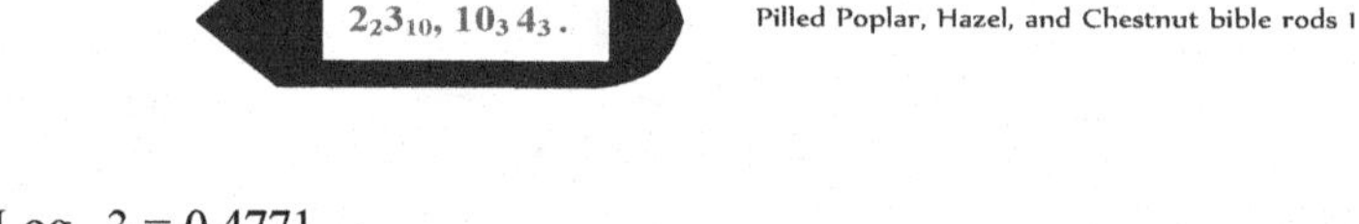

$\text{Log}_{10} 3 = 0.4771$

$\text{Log}_3 10 = y$

$3^y = 10$

$y \log_{10} 3 = \log_{10} 10$

$y = \log_{10} 10 / \log_{10} 3$

$y = 1 / 0.4771$

$y = 2.0959$

$\text{Log}_3 4 = y$

$3^y = 4$

$y \log_{10} 3 = \log_{10} 4$

$y = \log_{10} 4 / \log_{10} 3$

$y = 0.6020 / 0.4771$

$y = 1.2617$

$\text{Log}_2 2 = y$

$2^y = 2$

$2^y = 2^1$

$y = 1$

5, 14. Deep calls unto Deep study bible 1

1 0.4771, 2.0959 1.2617.

Deep calls unto Deep study bible 2

x-axis	y-axis
5	1.4771
14	3.3576

Water Spout *(lightning;combinatorics)* Study bible 1

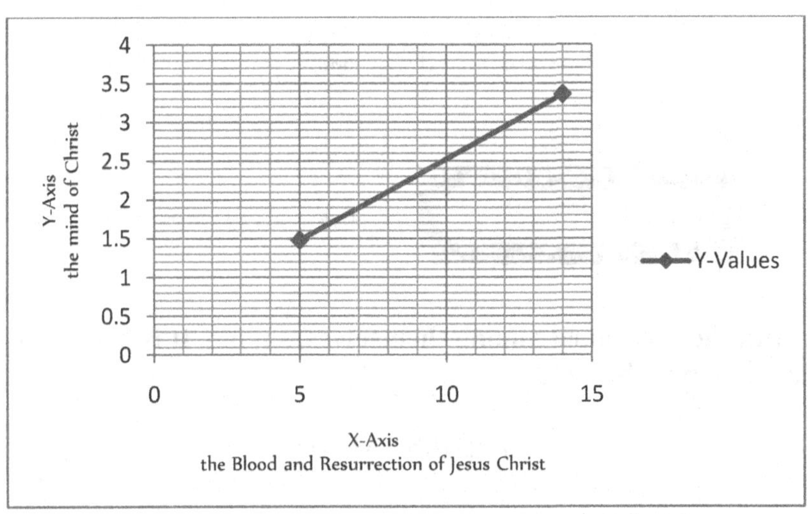

Water Spout *(lightning;combinatorics)* Study bible 2

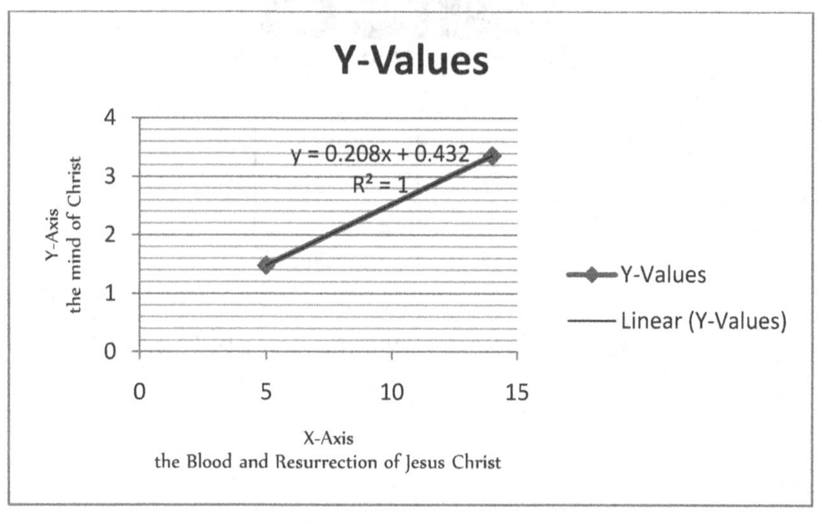

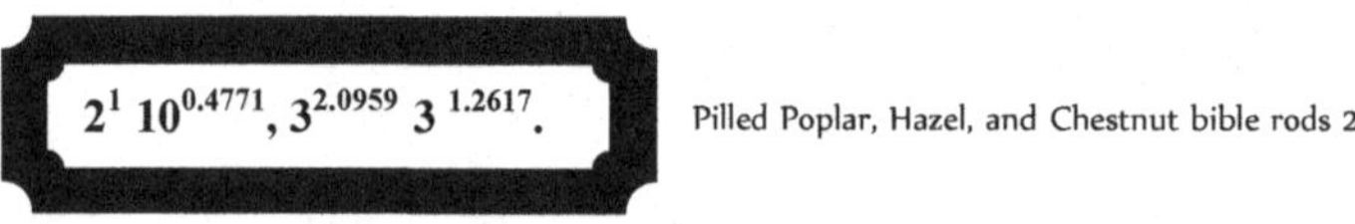

Pilled Poplar, Hazel, and Chestnut bible rods 2

7. And they reasoned among themselves, saying, It is because we have taken no bread.

5, 1, 8. Bible Matrices

Pilled Poplar, Hazel, and Chestnut bible rods 1

$\text{Log}_{10} 8 = 0.9030$ $\text{Log}_{10} 5 = 0.6989$ $\text{Log}_{10} 1 = 0$

5, 1, 8. Deep calls unto Deep study bible 1

0.6989, 0, 0.9030. Deep calls unto Deep study bible 2

x-axis	y-axis
5	0.6989
1	0
8	0.9030

Water Spout *(lightning;combinatorics)* Study bible 1

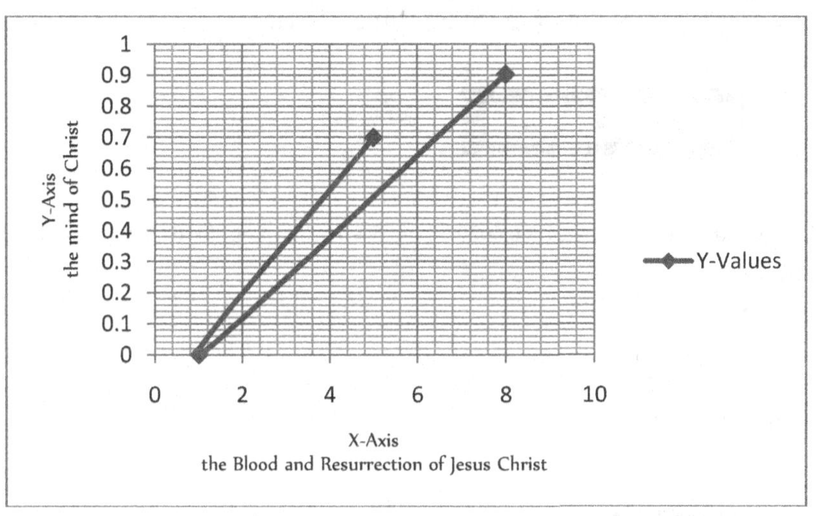

Water Spout *(lightning;combinatorics)* Study bible 2

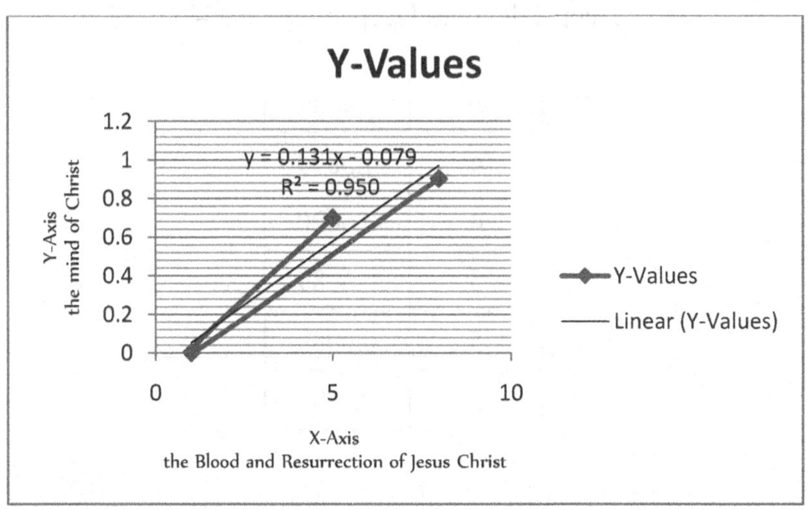

$10^{0.6989}, 10^{0}, 10^{0.9030}$.

Pilled Poplar, Hazel, and Chestnut bible rods 2

8. Which when Jesus savior; deliverer perceived, he said unto them, O ye of little faith, why reason ye among yourselves, because ye have brought no bread?

4, 4, 5, 5, 6? Bible Matrices

$3_2 1_{10}, 4_{10}, 5_{10}, 5_{10}, 6_{10}$?

Pilled Poplar, Hazel, and Chestnut bible rods 1

$\text{Log}_{10} 6 = 0.7781$ $\text{Log}_{10} 4 = 0.6020$ $\text{Log}_{10} 5 = 0.6989$ $\text{Log}_{10} 5 = 0.6989$ $\text{Log}_{10} 1 = 0$

$\text{Log}_2 3 = y$

$2^y = 3$

$y \log_{10} 2 = \log_{10} 3$

$y = \log_{10} 3 / \log_{10} 2$

$y = 0.4771 / 0.3010$

$y = 1.5850$

4, 4, 5, 5, 6? Deep calls unto Deep study bible 1

1.5850 0, 0.6020, 0.6989, 0.6989, 0.7781?

Deep calls unto Deep study bible 2

x-axis	y-axis
4	1.5850
4	0.6020
5	0.6989
5	0.6989
6	0.7781

Water Spout *(lightning;combinatorics)* Study bible 1

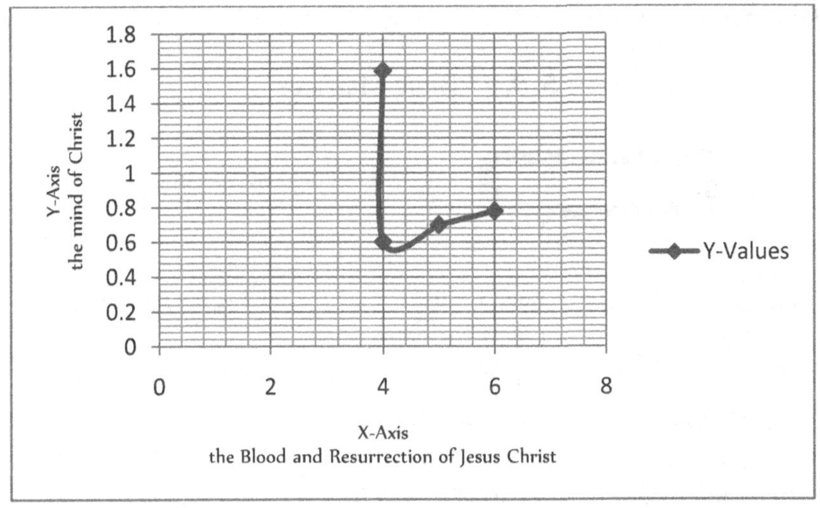

Water Spout *(lightning;combinatorics)* Study bible 2

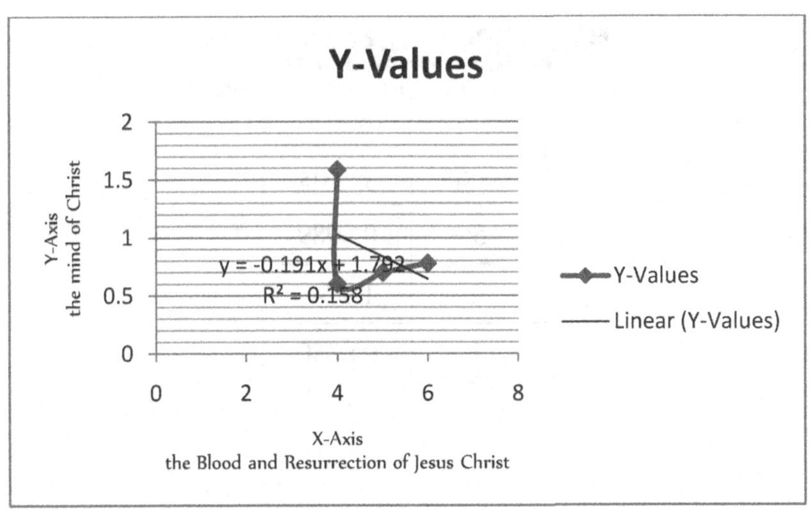

$2^{1.5850}$ 10^{0}, $10^{0.6020}$, $10^{0.6989}$, $10^{0.6989}$, $10^{0.7781}$?

Pilled Poplar, Hazel, and Chestnut bible rods 2

9. Do ye not yet understand, neither remember the five grace; 5 x 1 **loaves of the five** 2 x 2 x 2 x 5 x 5 x 5 x 5 **thousand, and how many baskets ye took up?**

5, 9, 7? Bible Matrices

5_{10}, 4_3 4_7 1_{10}, 7_{10} ?

Pilled Poplar, Hazel, and Chestnut bible rods 1

$\text{Log}_{10} 5 = 0.6989$
$\text{Log}_7 4 = y$
$7^y = 4$
$y \log_{10} 7 = \log_{10} 4$
$y = \log_{10} 4 / \log_{10} 7$
$y = 0.6020 / 0.8450$
$y = 0.7124$

$\text{Log}_{10} 1 = 0$
$\text{Log}_3 4 = y$
$3^y = 4$
$y \log_{10} 3 = \log_{10} 4$
$y = \log_{10} 4 / \log_{10} 3$
$y = 0.6020 / 0.4771$
$y = 1.2617$

$\text{Log}_{10} 7 = 0.8450$

5, 9, 7? Deep calls unto Deep study bible 1

0.6989, 1.2617 0.7124 0, 0.8450?
Deep calls unto Deep study bible 2

x-axis	y-axis
5	0.6989
9	1.9741
7	0.8450

Water Spout *(lightning;combinatorics)* Study bible 1

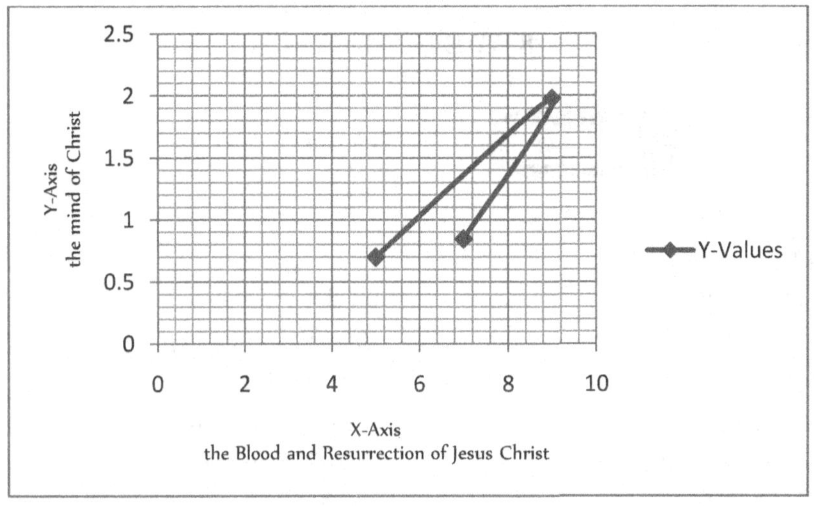

Water Spout *(lightning;combinatorics)* Study bible 2

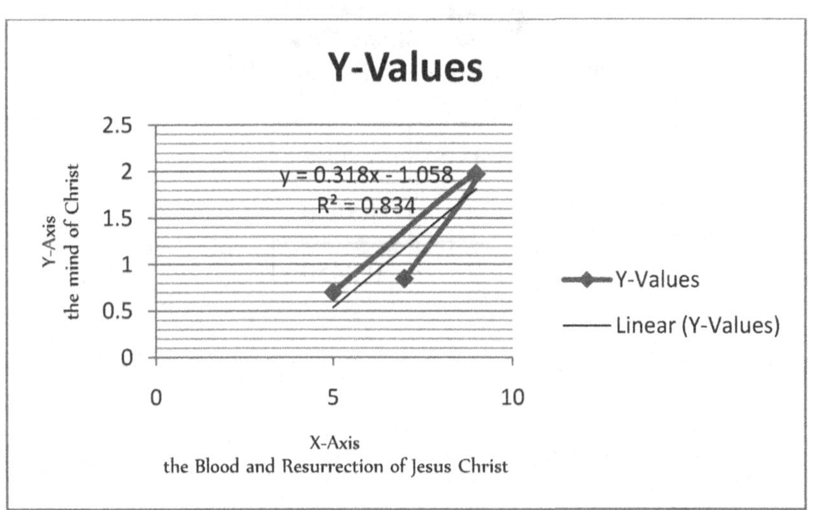

$10^{0.6989}$, $3^{1.2617}$ $7^{0.7124}$ 10^{0}, $10^{0.8450}$?

Pilled Poplar, Hazel, and Chestnut bible rods 2

10. Neither the seven divine perfection or completeness; 7 x 1 **loaves of the four thousand** 2 x 2 x 2 x 2 x 2 x 5 x 5 x 5, **and how many baskets ye took up?**

8, 7? Bible Matrices

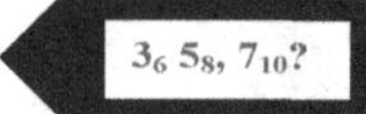

Pilled Poplar, Hazel, and Chestnut bible rods 1

$\log_{10} 7 = 0.8450$

$\log_8 5 = y$	$\log_6 3 = y$
$8^y = 5$	$6^y = 3$
$y \log_{10} 8 = \log_{10} 5$	$y \log_{10} 6 = \log_{10} 3$
$y = \log_{10} 5 / \log_{10} 8$	$y = \log_{10} 3 / \log_{10} 6$
$y = 0.6989 / 0.9030$	$y = 0.4771 / 0.7781$
$y = 0.7739$	$y = 0.6131$

8, 7? Deep calls unto Deep study bible 1

0.6131 0.7739, 0.8450

Deep calls unto Deep study bible 2

x-axis	y-axis
8	1.3870
7	0.8450

Water Spout *(lightning;combinatorics)* Study bible 1

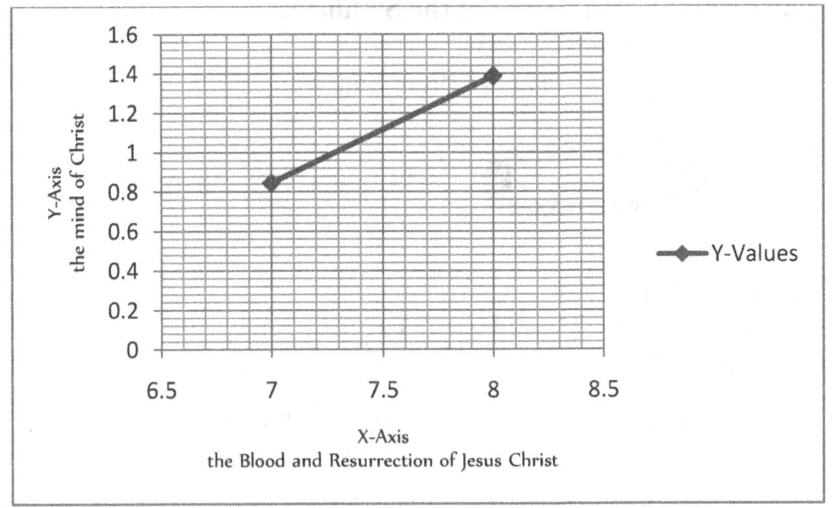

Water Spout *(lightning;combinatorics)* Study bible 2

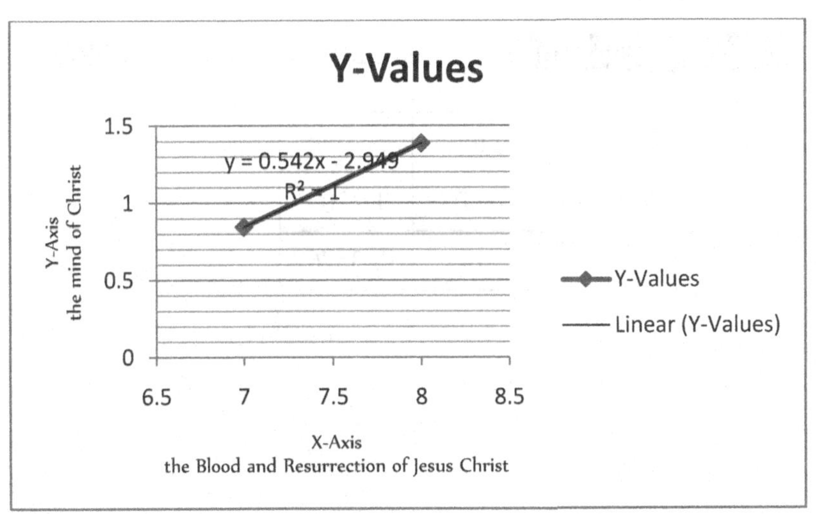

$6^{0.6131}$ $8^{0.7739}$, $10^{0.8450}$?

Pilled Poplar, Hazel, and Chestnut bible rods 2

11. How is it that ye do not understand that I spake it not to you concerning bread, that ye should beware of the leaven of the Phariseesset apart; separatists**and of the Sadducees**followers of Zadok?

17, 14? Bible Matrices

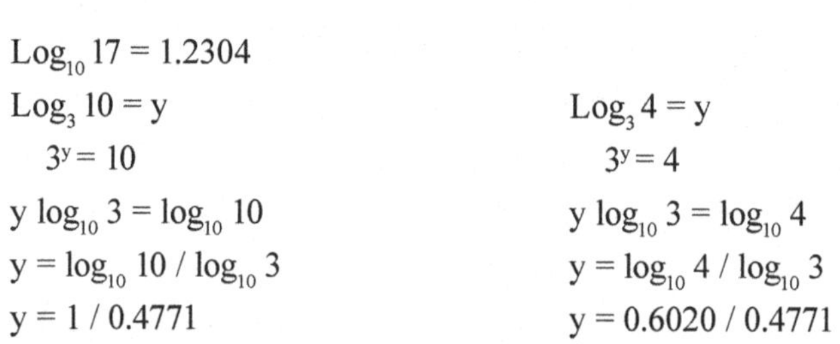

$\text{Log}_{10} 17 = 1.2304$

$\text{Log}_3 10 = y$

$3^y = 10$

$y \log_{10} 3 = \log_{10} 10$

$y = \log_{10} 10 / \log_{10} 3$

$y = 1 / 0.4771$

$y = 2.0959$

$\text{Log}_3 4 = y$

$3^y = 4$

$y \log_{10} 3 = \log_{10} 4$

$y = \log_{10} 4 / \log_{10} 3$

$y = 0.6020 / 0.4771$

$y = 1.2617$

17, 14? Deep calls unto Deep study bible 1

1.2304, 2.0959 1.2617? Deep calls unto Deep study bible 2

x-axis	y-axis
17	1.2304
14	3.3576

Water Spout *(lightning;combinatorics)* Study bible 1

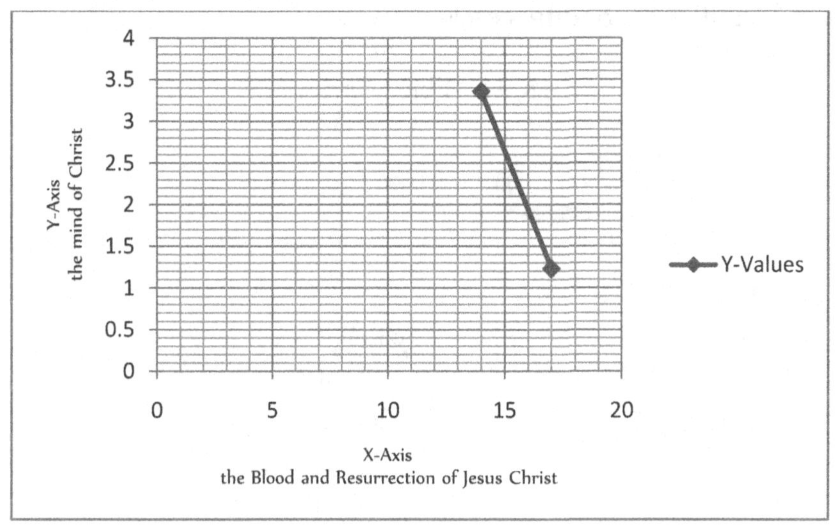

Water Spout *(lightning;combinatorics)* Study bible 2

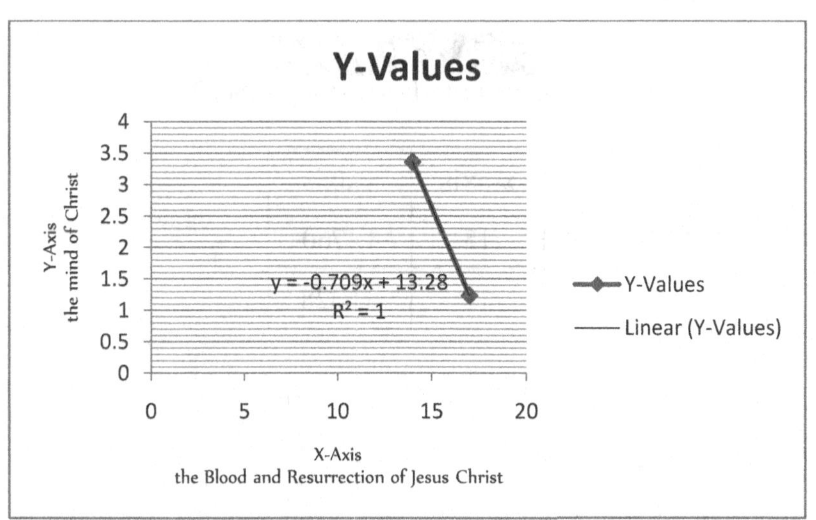

$10^{1.2304}$, $3^{2.0959}$ $3^{1.2617}$?

Pilled Poplar, Hazel, and Chestnut bible rods 2

12. Then understood they how that he bade them not beware of the leaven of bread, but of the doctrine of the Phariseesset apart; separatists**and of the Sadducees**followers of Zadok.

15, 11. Bible Matrices

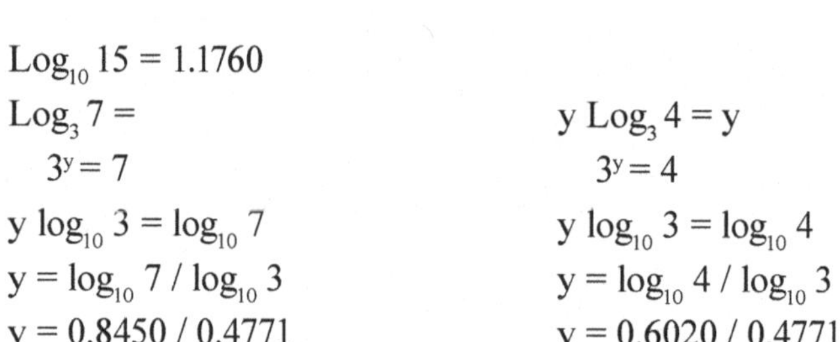

$\text{Log}_{10}\, 15 = 1.1760$

$\text{Log}_3\, 7 =$

$3^y = 7$

$y \log_{10} 3 = \log_{10} 7$

$y = \log_{10} 7 / \log_{10} 3$

$y = 0.8450 / 0.4771$

$y = 1.7711$

$y\ \text{Log}_3\, 4 = y$

$3^y = 4$

$y \log_{10} 3 = \log_{10} 4$

$y = \log_{10} 4 / \log_{10} 3$

$y = 0.6020 / 0.4771$

$y = 1.2617$

15, 11. Deep calls unto Deep study bible 1

1.1760, 1.7711 1.2617.

Deep calls unto Deep study bible 2

x-axis	y-axis
15	1.1760
11	3.0328

Water Spout *(lightning;combinatorics)* Study bible 1

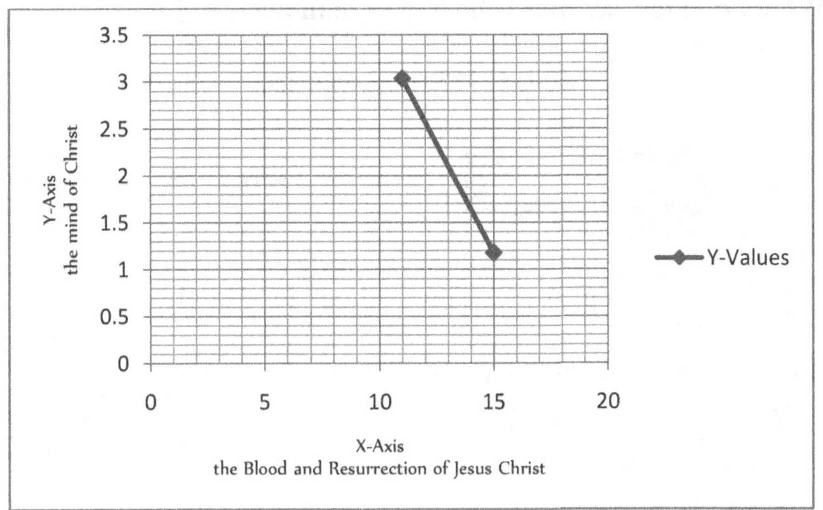

Water Spout *(lightning;combinatorics)* Study bible 2

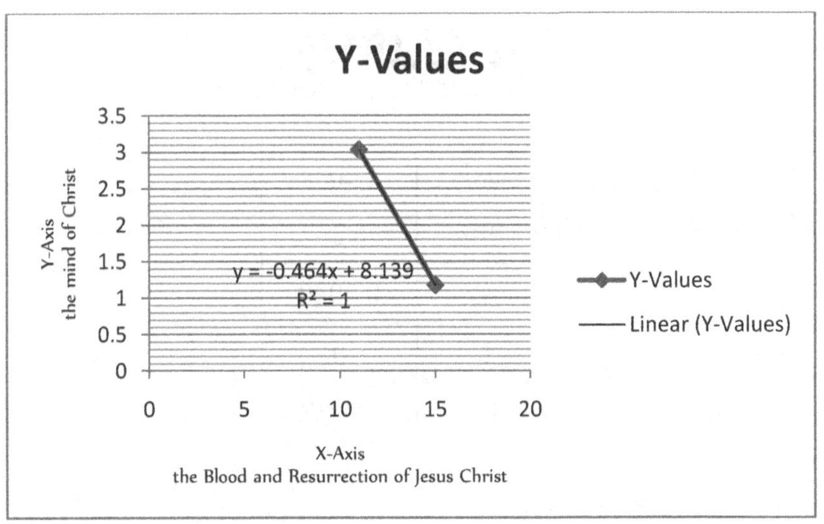

$10^{1.1760}$, $3^{1.7711}$ $3^{1.2617}$.

Pilled Poplar, Hazel, and Chestnut bible rods 2

13. When Jesussavior; deliverer **came into the coasts of Caesarea Philippi**the fountain; warlike; a lover of horses**, he asked his disciples, saying, Whom do men say that I the Son of man am?**

9, 4, 1, 11? Bible Matrices

$2_2 7_7, 4_{10}, 1_{10}, 11_{10}?$

Pilled Poplar, Hazel, and Chestnut bible rods 1

$\text{Log}_{10} 1 = 0$ $\text{Log}_{10} 4 = 0.6020$ $\text{Log}_{10} 11 = 1.0413$

$\text{Log}_2 2 = y$
$2^y = 2$
$2^y = 2^1$
$y = 1$

$\text{Log}_7 7 = y$
$7^y = 7$
$7^y = 7^1$
$y = 1$

9, 4, 1, 11? Deep calls unto Deep study bible 1

1 1, 0.6020, 0, 1.0413?
Deep calls unto Deep study bible 2

x-axis	y-axis
9	2
4	0.6020
1	0
11	1.0413

Water Spout *(lightning;combinatorics)* Study bible 1

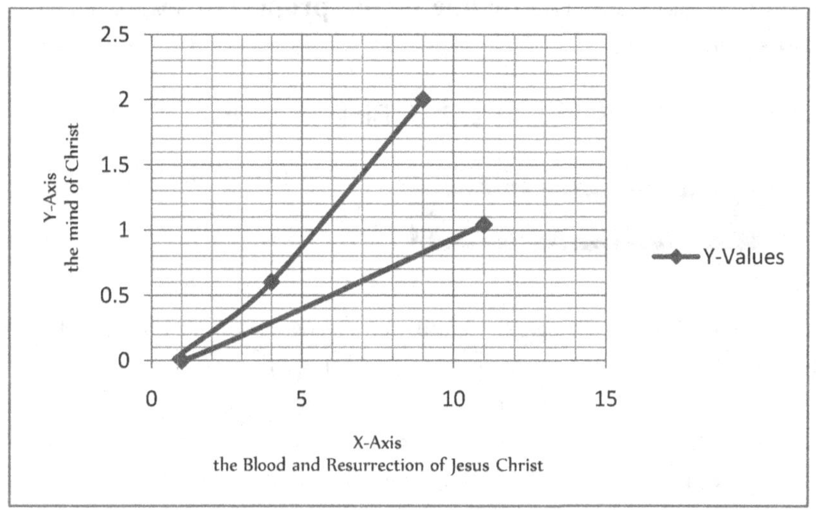

Water Spout *(lightning;combinatorics)* Study bible 2

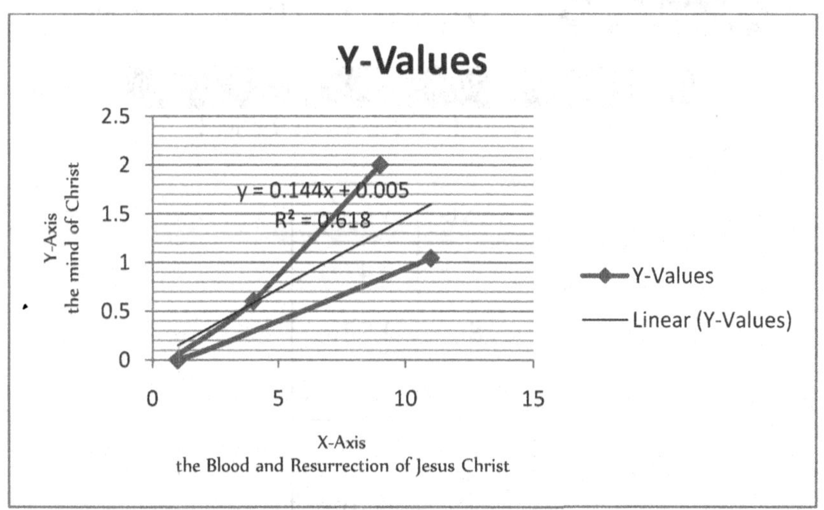

2^1 7^1, $10^{0.6020}$, 10^0, $10^{1.0413}$?

Pilled Poplar, Hazel, and Chestnut bible rods 2

14. And they said, Some say that thou art Johnthe grace or mercy of the Lord**the Baptist: some, Elias**God the Lord; whose God is Jehovah**; and others, Jeremias**exaltation of the Lord, **or one of the prophets** to bubble forth, as from a fountain; utter.

3, 8: 1, 1; 2, 1, 5. Bible Matrices

$3_{10}, 6_7\, 2_{10}: 1_{10}, 1_7; 2_{10}, 1_4, 5_8.$ Pilled Poplar, Hazel, and Chestnut bible rods 1

$\text{Log}_{10} 3 = 0.4771$
$\text{Log}_8 5 = y$
$8^y = 5$
$y \log_{10} 8 = \log_{10} 5$
$y = \log_{10} 5 / \log_{10} 8$
$y = 0.6989 / 0.9030$
$y = 0.7739$

$\text{Log}_{10} 2 = 0.3010$
$\text{Log}_7 6 = y$
$7^y = 6$
$y \log_{10} 7 = \log_{10} 6$
$y = \log_{10} 6 / \log_{10} 7$
$y = 0.7781 / 0.8450$
$y = 0.9208$

$\text{Log}_{10} 1 = 0$
$\text{Log}_4 1 = y$
$4^y = 1$
$4^y = 4^0$
$y = 0$

$\text{Log}_{10} 2 = 0.3010$

3, 8: 1, 1; 2, 1, 5. Deep calls unto Deep study bible 1

0.4771, 0.9208 0.3010: 0, 0; 0.3010, 0, 0.7739.
Deep calls unto Deep study bible 2

x-axis	y-axis
3	0.4771
8	1.2218
1	0
1	0
2	0.3010
1	0
5	0.7739

Water Spout *(lightning;combinatorics)* Study bible 1

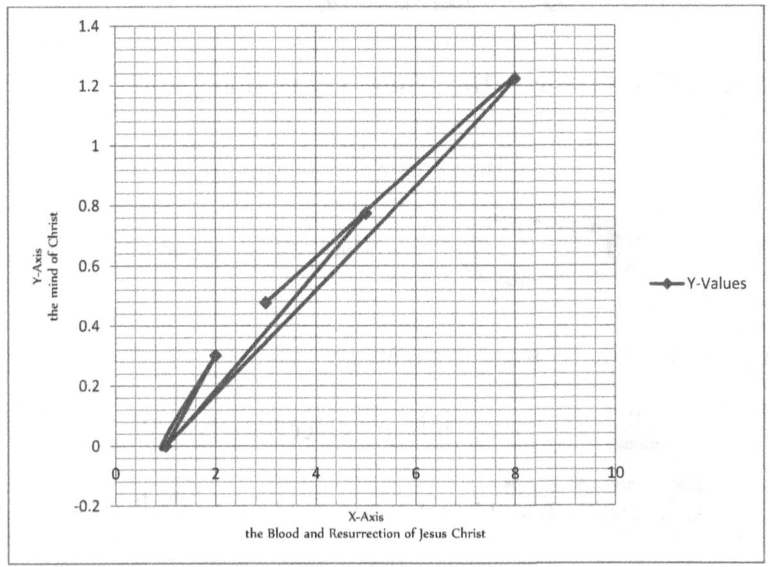

Water Spout *(lightning;combinatorics)* Study bible 2

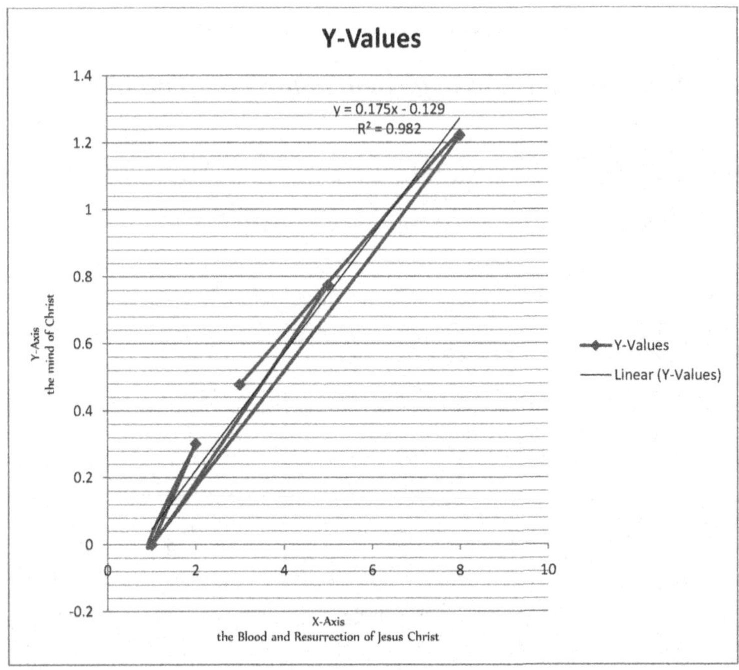

$10^{0.4771}, 7^{0.9208}\ 10^{0.3010}: 10^{0}, 7^{0}; 10^{0.3010}, 4^{0}, 8^{0.7739}.$

Pilled Poplar, Hazel, and Chestnut bible rods 2

15. He saith unto them, But whom say ye that I am?

4, 7? Bible Matrices

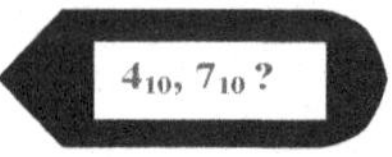

Pilled Poplar, Hazel, and Chestnut bible rods 1

$\text{Log}_{10} 7 = 0.8450 \qquad \text{Log}_{10} 4 = 0.6020$

4, 7? Deep calls unto Deep study bible 1

0.6020, 0.8450? Deep calls unto Deep study bible 2

x-axis	y-axis
4	0.6020
7	0.8450

Water Spout *(lightning;combinatorics)* Study bible 1

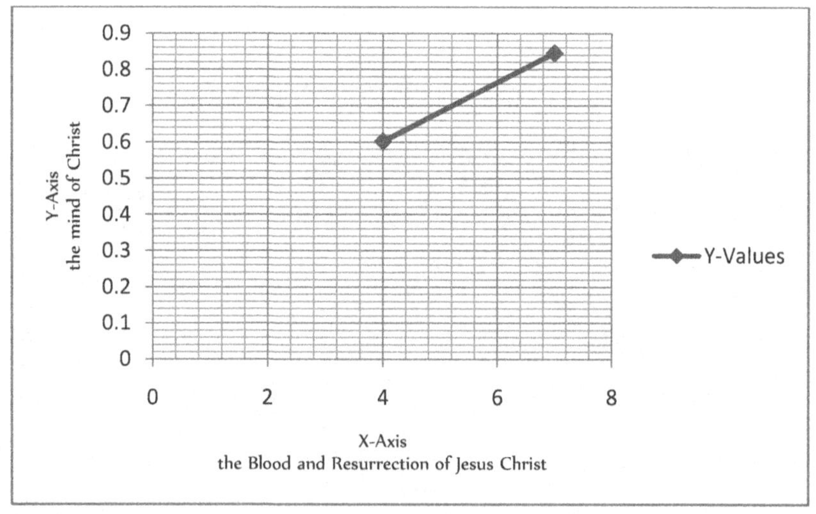

Water Spout *(lightning;combinatorics)* Study bible 2

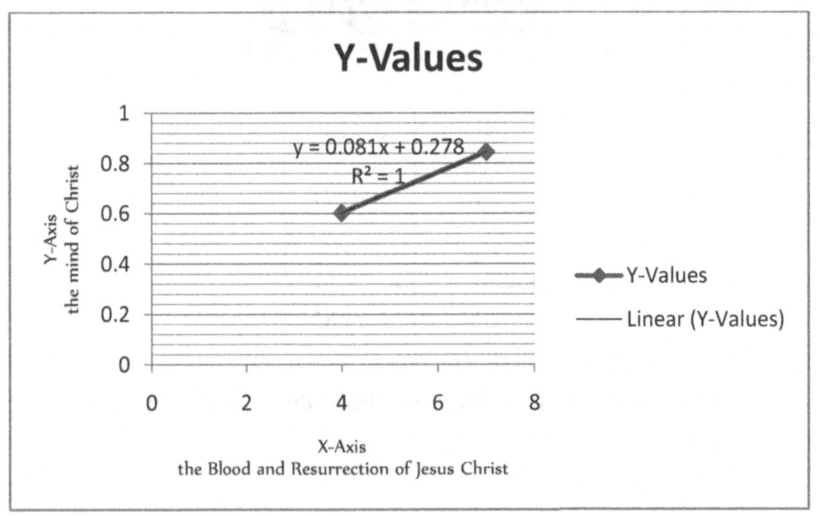

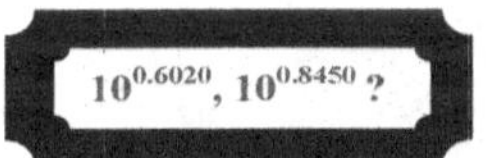

Pilled Poplar, Hazel, and Chestnut bible rods 2

16. And Simonthat hears; that obeys **Peter**a rock or stone **answered and said, Thou art the Christ**anointed; smear, **the Son of the living God.**

6, 4, 6. Bible Matrices

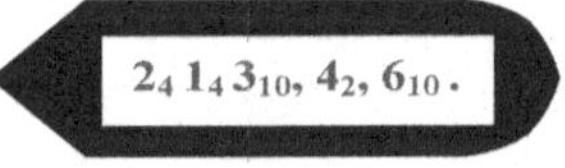

Pilled Poplar, Hazel, and Chestnut bible rods 1

$\text{Log}_{10} 3 = 0.4771$	$\text{Log}_{10} 6 = 0.7781$	
$\text{Log}_4 2 = y$	$\text{Log}_4 1 = y$	$\text{Log}_2 4 = y$
$4^y = 2$	$4^y = 1$	$2^y = 4$
$2^{2y} = 2^1$	$4^y = 4^0$	$2^y = 2^2$
$2y = 1$	$y = 0$	$y = 2$
$y = ½$		

6, 4, 6. Deep calls unto Deep study bible 1

0. 5 0 0.4771, 2, 0.7781.

Deep calls unto Deep study bible 2

x-axis	y-axis
6	0.9771
4	2
6	0.7781

Water Spout *(lightning;combinatorics)* Study bible 1

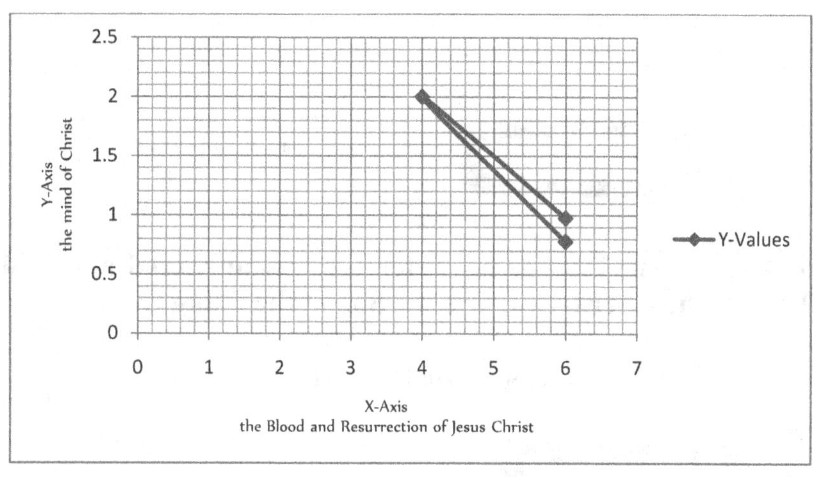

Water Spout *(lightning;combinatorics)* Study bible 2

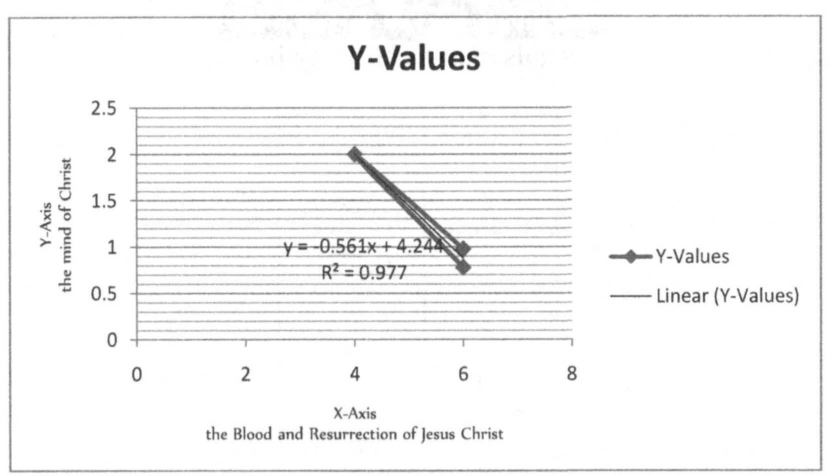

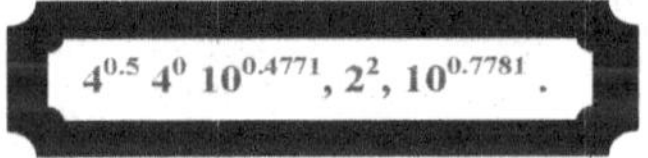

Pilled Poplar, Hazel, and Chestnut bible rods 2

17. And Jesus **savior; deliverer** **answered and said unto him, Blessed art thou, Simon** **that hears; that obeys** **Bar-jona** **son of a Jona; of a dove** **: for flesh and blood hath not revealed it unto thee, but my Father which is in heaven.**

7, 3, 2: 10, 7. Bible Matrices

$2_2 5_{10}$, 3_{10}, $1_4 1_7$: 10_{10}, 7_{10} .

Pilled Poplar, Hazel, and Chestnut bible rods 1

$\text{Log}_{10} 5 = 0.6989$	$\text{Log}_{10} 7 = 0.8450$	$\text{Log}_{10} 10 = 1$	$\text{Log}_{10} 3 = 0.4771$
$\text{Log}_2 2 = y$	$\text{Log}_4 1 = y$	$\text{Log}_7 1 = y$	
$2^y = 2$	$4^y = 1$	$7^y = 1$	
$2^y = 2^1$	$4^y = 4^0$	$7^y = 7^0$	
$y = 1$	$y = 0$	$y = 0$	

7, 3, 2: 10, 7. Deep calls unto Deep study bible 1

1 0.6989, 0.4771, 0 0: 1, 0.8450.
Deep calls unto Deep study bible 2

x-axis	y-axis
7	1.6989
3	0.4771
2	0
10	1
7	0.8450

Water Spout *(lightning;combinatorics)* Study bible 1

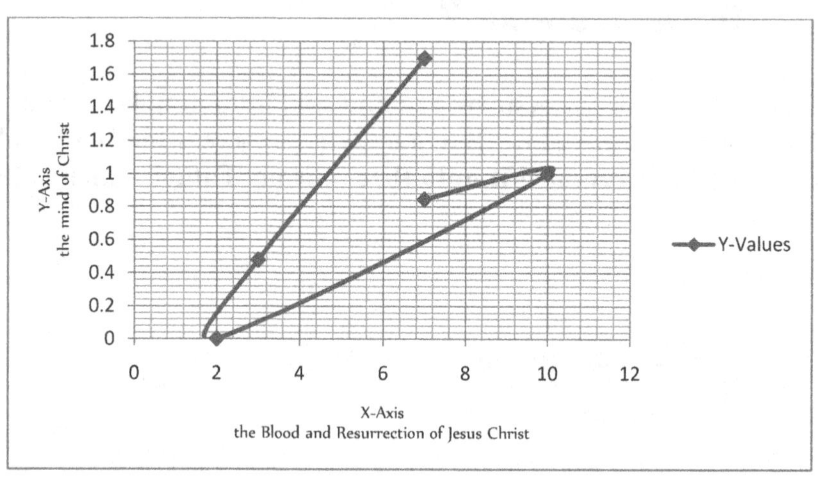

Water Spout *(lightning;combinatorics)* Study bible 2

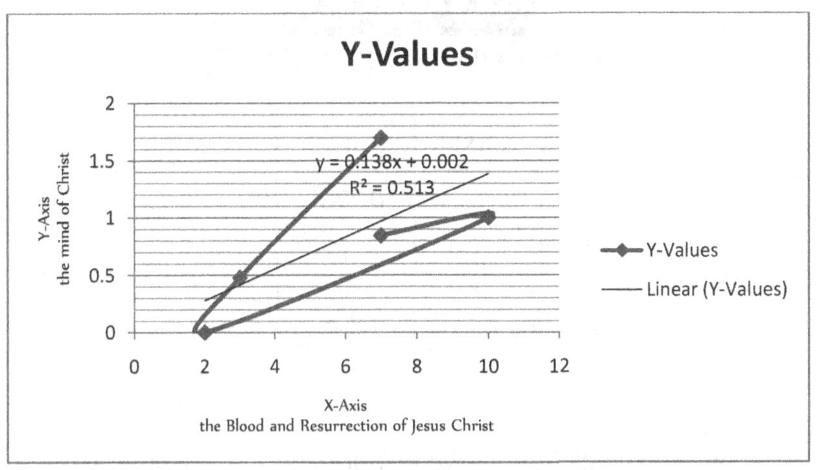

$2^1\ 10^{0.6989},\ 10^{0.4771},\ 4^0\ 7^0:\ 10^1,\ 10^{0.8450}$.

Pilled Poplar, Hazel, and Chestnut bible rods 2

18. And I say also unto thee, That thou art Petera rock or stone**, and upon this rock I will build my church; and the gates of hell shall not prevail against it.**

6, 4, 9; 10. Bible Matrices

$6_{10},\ 4_4,\ 9_{10};\ 10_{10}$.

Pilled Poplar, Hazel, and Chestnut bible rods 1

$\text{Log}_{10} 6 = 0.7781$ $\text{Log}_{10} 9 = 0.9542$ $\text{Log}_{10} 10 = 1$

$\text{Log}_4 4 = y$

$4^y = 4$

$4^y = 4^1$

$y = 1$

6, 4, 9; 10. Deep calls unto Deep study bible 1

0.7781, 1, 0.9542; 1.
Deep calls unto Deep study bible 2

x-axis	y-axis
6	0.7781
4	1
9	0.9542
10	1

Water Spout *(lightning;combinatorics)* Study bible 1

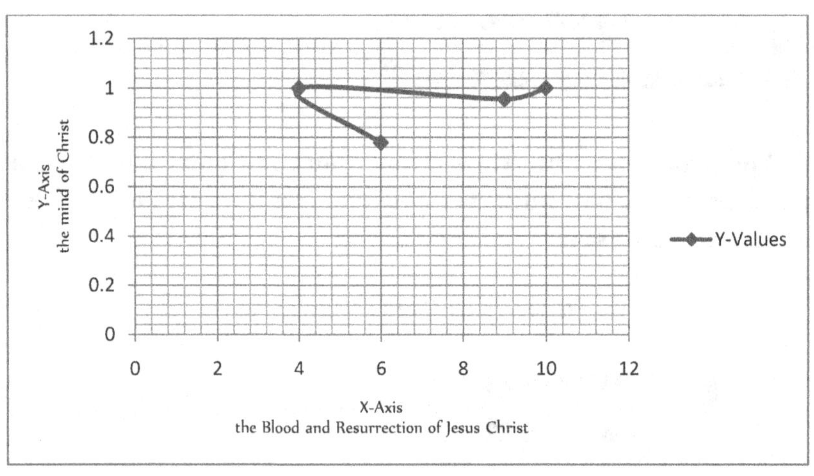

Water Spout *(lightning;combinatorics)* Study bible 2

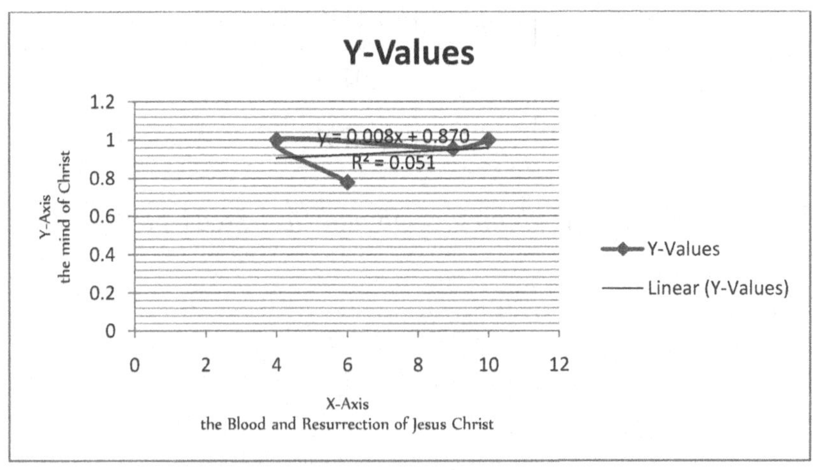

$10^{0.7781}$, 4^1, $10^{0.9542}$; 10^1 .

Pilled Poplar, Hazel, and Chestnut bible rods 2

19. And I will give unto thee the keys of the kingdom of heaven: and whatsoever thou shalt bind on earth shall be bound in heaven: and whatsoever thou shalt loose on earth shall be loosed in heaven.

13: 12: 12. Bible Matrices

$\text{Log}_{10}\ 13 = 1.1139$ $\text{Log}_{10}\ 12 = 1.0791$ $\text{Log}_{10}\ 12 = 1.0791$

13: 12: 12. Deep calls unto Deep study bible 1

1.1139: 1.0791: 1.0791.

Deep calls unto Deep study bible 2

x-axis	y-axis
13	1.1139
12	1.0791
12	1.0791

Water Spout *(lightning;combinatorics)* Study bible 1

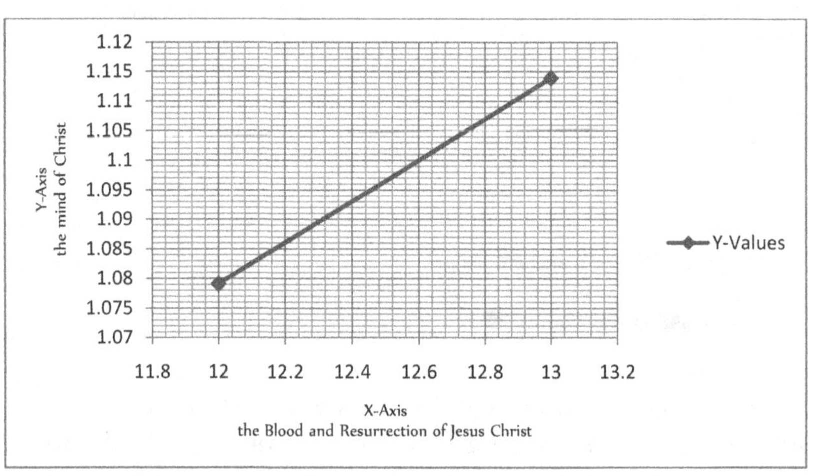

Water Spout *(lightning;combinatorics)* Study bible 2

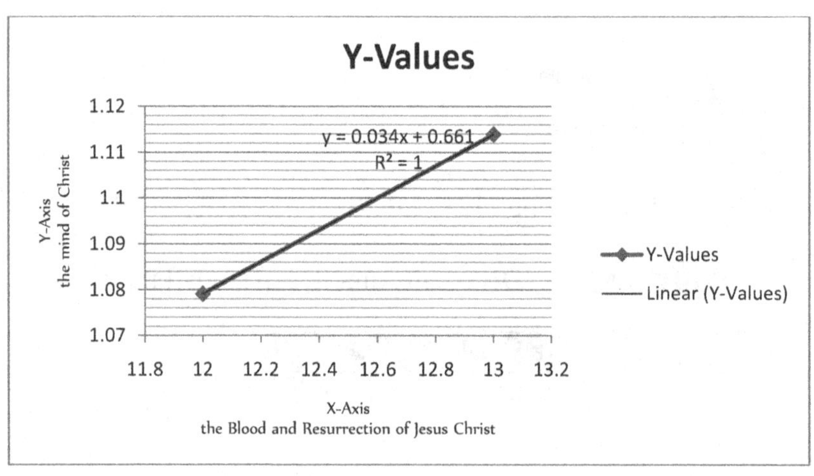

Pilled Poplar, Hazel, and Chestnut bible rods 2

20. Then charged he his disciples that they should tell no man that he was Jesussavior; deliverer**the Christ**anointed; smear.

17. Bible Matrices

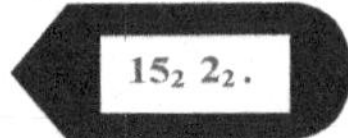

Pilled Poplar, Hazel, and Chestnut bible rods 1

$\text{Log}_2\, 15 = y$

$2^y = 15$

$y \log_{10} 2 = \log_{10} 15$

$y = \log_{10} 15 / \log_{10}$

$y = 1.1760 / 0.3010$

$y = 3.9069$

$\text{Log}_2\, 2 = y$

$2^y = 2$

$2^y = 2^1$

$2\, y = 1$

17. Deep calls unto Deep study bible 1

3.9069 1.

Deep calls unto Deep study bible 2

x-axis	y-axis
17	4.9069

Water Spout *(lightning;combinatorics)* Study bible 1

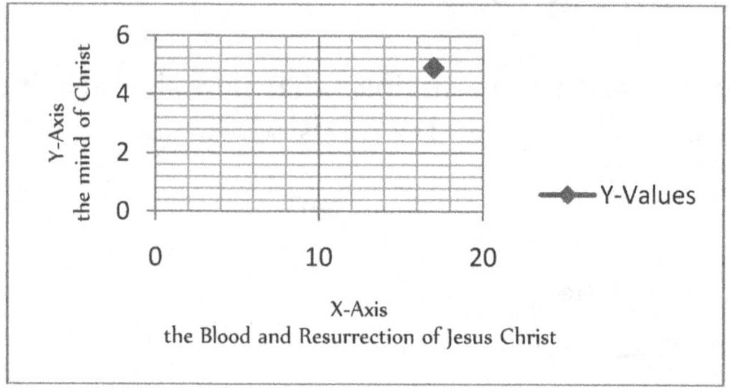

Water Spout *(lightning;combinatorics)* Study bible 2

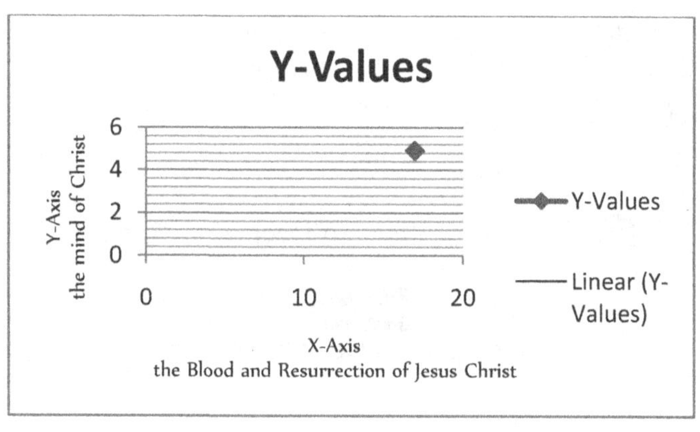

21. From that time forth began Jesussavior; deliverer **to shew unto his disciples, how that he must go unto Jerusalem** habitation of peace; vision of peace;possession of peace, **and suffer many things of the elders and chief priests and scribes**lawyers; transcriber, copyist, **and be killed, and be raised again the third** completion or perfection, and unity; 3 x 1 **day.**

11, 7, 12, 3, 7. Bible Matrices

$6_2\,5_{10},\ 7_9,\ 12_3,\ 3_{10},\ 6_7\,1_{10}.$ Pilled Poplar, Hazel, and Chestnut bible rods 1

$\text{Log}_{10}\,5 = 0.6989$

$\text{Log}_3\,12 = y$

$3^y = 12$

$y \log_{10} 3 = \log_{10} 12$

$y = \log_{10} 12 / \log_{10} 3$

$y = 1.0791 / 0.4771$

$y = 2.2617$ $y = 0.9208$

$\text{Log}_{10}\,3 = 0.4771$

$\text{Log}_7\,6 = y$

$7^y = 6$

$y \log_{10} 7 = \log_{10} 6$

$y = \log_{10} 6 / \log_{10} 7$

$y = 0.7781 / 0.8450$

$\text{Log}_{10}\,1 = 0$

$\text{Log}_9\,7 = y$

$9^y = 7$

$y \log_{10} 9 = \log_{10} 7$

$y = \log_{10} 7 / \log_{10} 9$

$y = 0.8450 / 0.9542$

$y = 0.8855$

$\text{Log}_2\,6 = y$

$2^y = 6$

$y \log_{10} 2 = \log_{10} 6$

$y = \log_{10} 6 / \log_{10} 2$

$y = 0.7781 / 0.3010$

$y = 2.5850$

11, 7, 12, 3, 7. Deep calls unto Deep study bible 1

2.5850 0.6989, 0.8855, 2.2617, 0.4771, 0.9208 0.

Deep calls unto Deep study bible 2

x-axis	y-axis
11	3.2839
7	0.8855
12	2.2617
3	0.4771
7	0.9208

Water Spout *(lightning;combinatorics)* Study bible 1

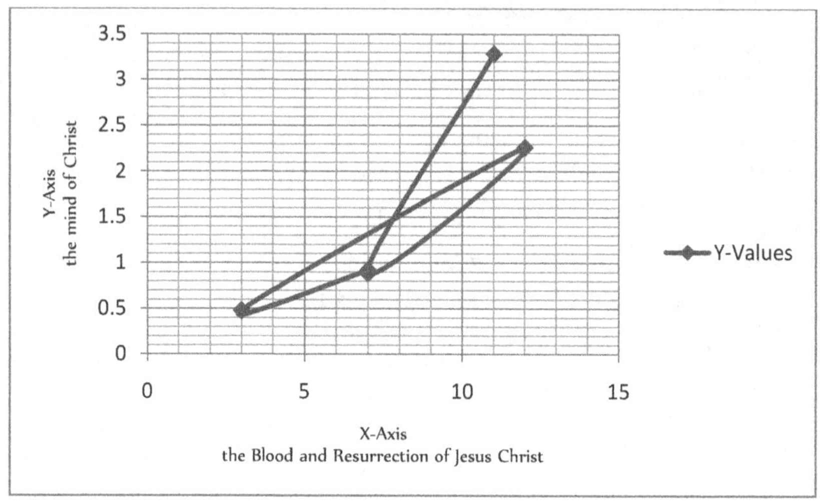

Water Spout *(lightning;combinatorics)* Study bible 2

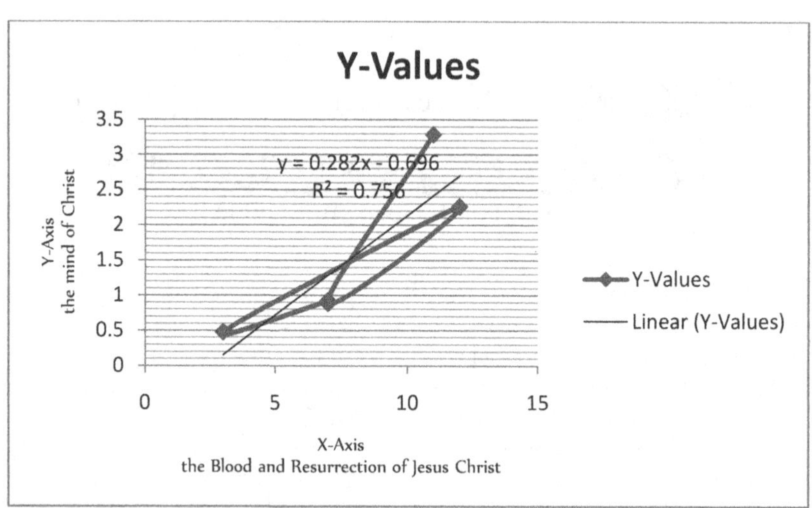

$2^{2.5850}\ 10^{0.6989},\ 9^{0.8855},\ 3^{2.2617},\ 10^{0.4771},\ 7^{0.9208}\ 10^{0}$.

Pilled Poplar, Hazel, and Chestnut bible rods 2

22. Then Petera rock or stone**took him, and began to rebuke him, saying, Be it far from thee, Lord: this shall not be unto thee.**

4, 5, 1, 5, 1: 6. Bible Matrices

$2_4\ 2_{10}, 5_{10}, 1_{10}, 5_{10}, 1_{10}: 6_{10}.$

Pilled Poplar, Hazel, and Chestnut bible rods 1

$\text{Log}_{10} 2 = 0.3010$ $\text{Log}_{10} 5 = 0.6989$ $\text{Log}_{10} 1 = 0$ $\text{Log}_{10} 5 = 0.6989$ $\text{Log}_{10} 1 = 0$ $\text{Log}_{10} 6 = 0.7781$

$\text{Log}_4 2 = y$

$4^y = 2$

$2^{2y} = 2^1$

$2y = 1$

$y = ½$ or 0.5

4, 5, 1, 5, 1: 6. Deep calls unto Deep study bible 1

0.5 0.3010, 0.6989, 0, 0.6989, 0: 0.7781.

Deep calls unto Deep study bible 2

x-axis	y-axis
4	0.8010
5	0.6989
1	0
5	0.6989
1	0
6	0.7781

Water Spout *(lightning;combinatorics)* Study bible 1

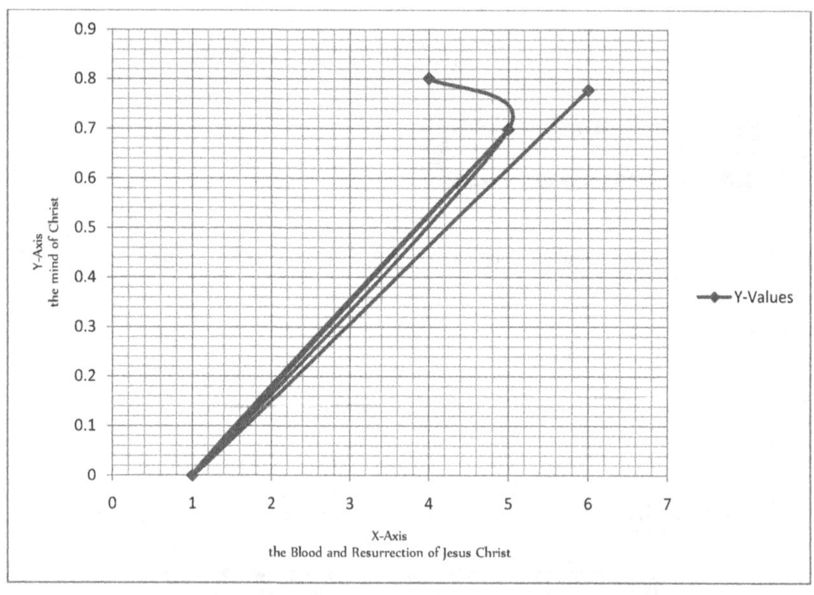

Water Spout *(lightning;combinatorics)* Study bible 2

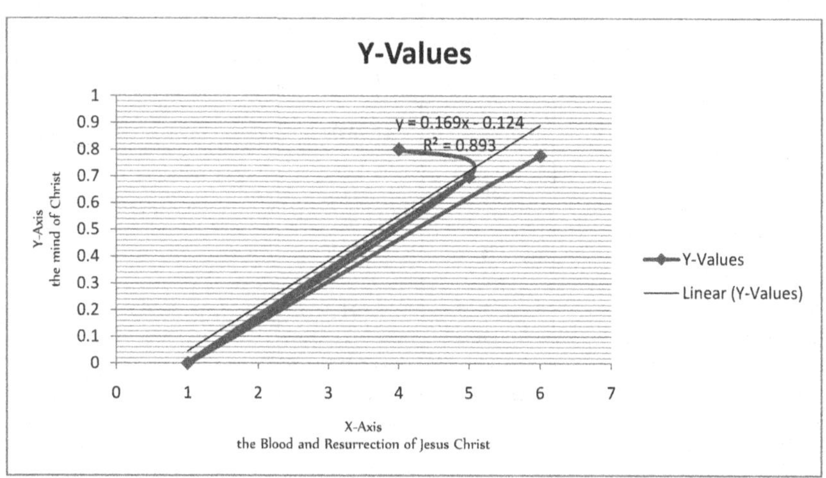

$4^{0.5}$ $10^{0.3010}$, $10^{0.6989}$, 10^{0}, $10^{0.6989}$, 10^{0} : $10^{0.7781}$.

Pilled Poplar, Hazel, and Chestnut bible rods 2

23. But he turned, and said unto Peter a rock or stone, **Get thee behind me, Satan** contrary; adversary; enemy; accuser: **thou art an offence unto me: for thou savourest not the things that be of God, but those that be of men.**

3, 4, 4, 1: 6: 10, 6. Bible Matrices

$3_{10}, 4_4, 4_{10}, 1_4: 6_{10}: 10_{10}, 6_{10}.$ Pilled Poplar, Hazel, and Chestnut bible rods 1

$\log_{10} 3 = 0.4771$ $\log_{10} 4 = 0.6020$ $\log_{10} 4 = 0.6020$ $\log_{10} 10 = 1$ $\log_{10} 6 = 0.7781$ $\log_{10} 6 = 0.7781$

$\log_4 4 = y$ | $\log_4 1 = y$
$4^y = 4$ | $4^y = 1$
$2^{2y} = 2^2$ | $4^y = 4^0$
$2y = 2$ | $y = 0$
$y = 1$

3, 4, 4, 1: 6: 10, 6. Deep calls unto Deep study bible 1

0.4771, 1, 0.6020, 0: 0.7781: 1, 0.7781.
Deep calls unto Deep study bible 2

x-axis	y-axis
3	0.4771
4	1
4	0.6020
1	0
6	0.7781
10	1
6	0.7781

Water Spout *(lightning;combinatorics)* Study bible 1

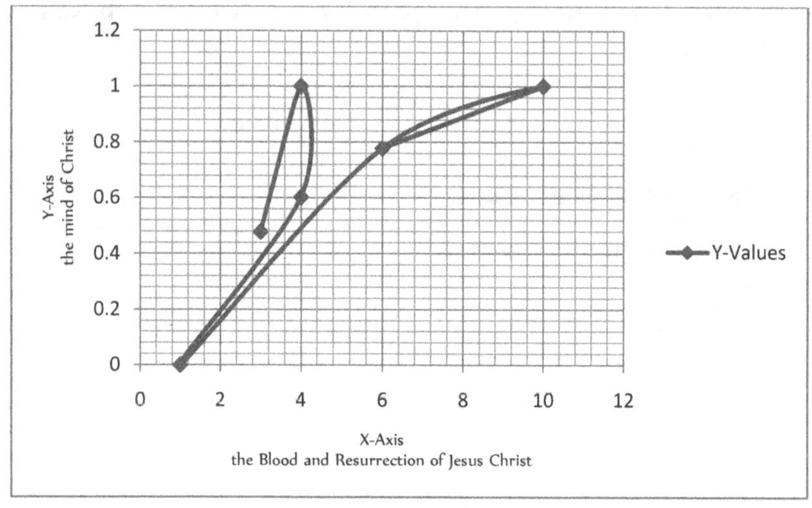

Water Spout *(lightning;combinatorics)* Study bible 2

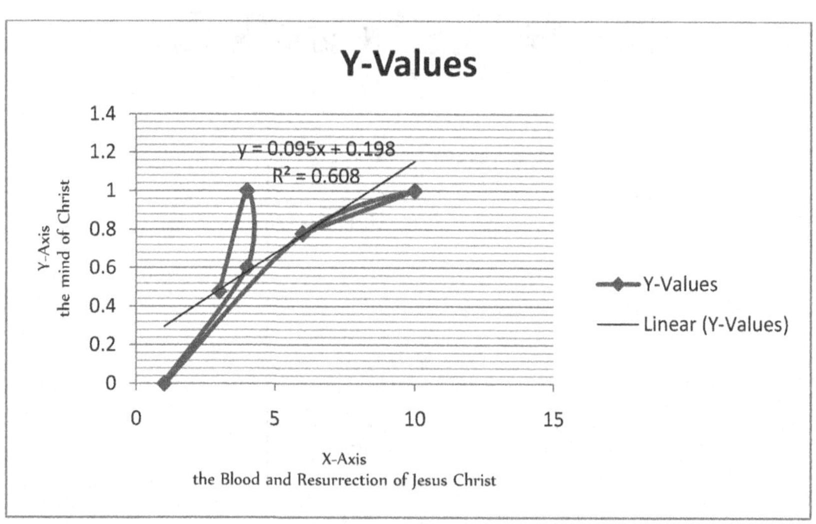

$10^{0.4771}$, 4^1, $10^{0.6020}$, 4^0: $10^{0.7781}$: 10^1, $10^{0.7781}$.

Pilled Poplar, Hazel, and Chestnut bible rods 2

24. Then said Jesus savior; deliverer **unto his disciples, If any man will come after me, let him deny himself, and take up his cross, and follow me.**

6, 7, 4, 5, 3. Bible Matrices

$3_2\ 3_{10},\ 7_{10},\ 4_{10},\ 5_{10},\ 3_{10}.$

Pilled Poplar, Hazel, and Chestnut bible rods 1

$\text{Log}_{10} 3 = 0.4771$ $\text{Log}_{10} 4 = 0.6020$ $\text{Log}_{10} 7 = 0.8450$ $\text{Log}_{10} 3 = 0.4771$ $\text{Log}_{10} 5 = 0.6989$

$\text{Log}_2 3 = y$

$2^y = 3$

$y \log_{10} 2 = \log_{10} 3$

$y = \log_{10} 3 / \log_{10} 2$

$y = 0.4771 / 0.3010$

$y = 1.5850$

6, 7, 4, 5, 3. Deep calls unto Deep study bible 1

1.5850 0.4771, 0.8450, 0.6020, 0.6989, 0.4771.

Deep calls unto Deep study bible 2

x-axis	y-axis
6	2.0621
7	0.8450
4	0.6020
5	0.6989
3	0.4771

Water Spout *(lightning;combinatorics)* Study bible 1

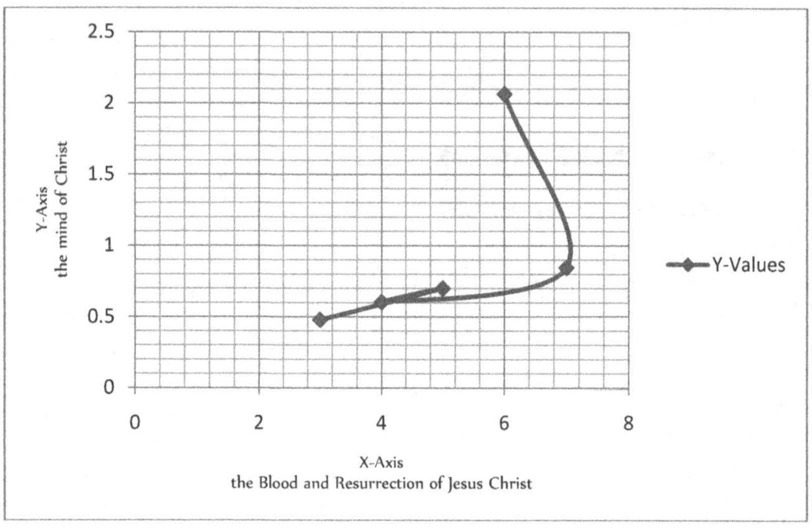

Water Spout *(lightning;combinatorics)* Study bible 2

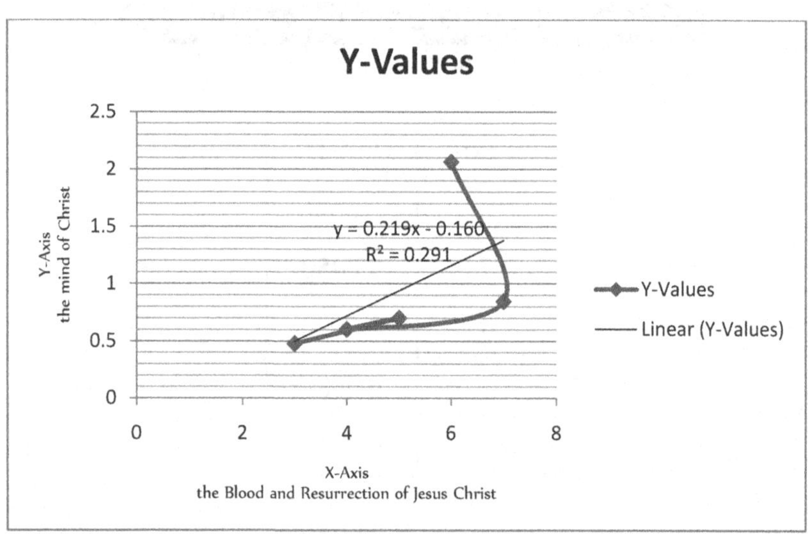

$2^{1.5850}$ $10^{0.4771}$, $10^{0.8450}$, $10^{0.6020}$, $10^{0.6989}$, $10^{0.4771}$.

Pilled Poplar, Hazel, and Chestnut bible rods 2

25. For whosoever will save his life shall lose it: and whosoever will lose his life for my sake shall find it.

9: 12. Bible Matrices

$\text{Log}_{10} 9 = 0.9542$ $\text{Log}_{10} 12 = 1.0791$

9: 12. Deep calls unto Deep study bible 1

0.9542: 1.0791. Deep calls unto Deep study bible 2

x-axis	y-axis
9	0.9542
12	1.0791

Water Spout *(lightning;combinatorics)* Study bible 1

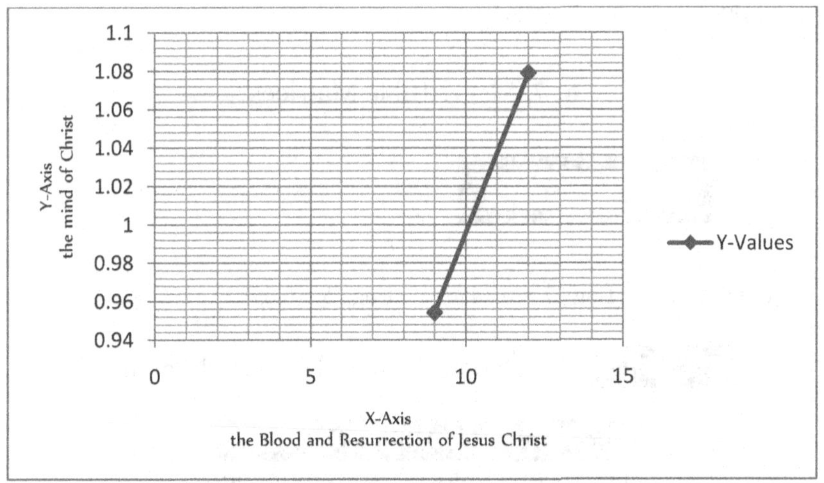

Water Spout *(lightning;combinatorics)* Study bible 2

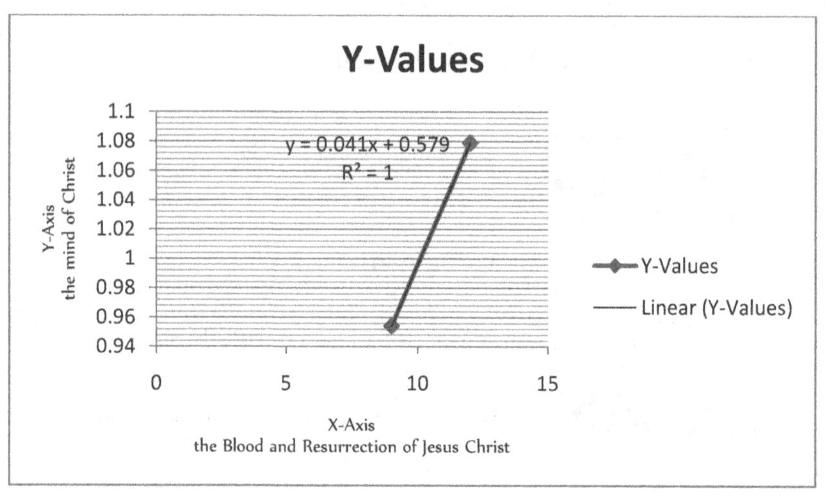

26. For what is a man profited, if he shall gain the whole world, and lose his own soul? or what shall a man give in exchange for his soul?

6, 7, 5? 11? Bible Matrices

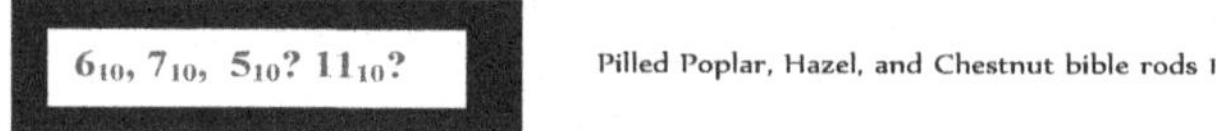

$\text{Log}_{10} 6 = 0.7781$ $\text{Log}_{10} 7 = 0.8450$ $\text{Log}_{10} 5 = 0.6989$ $\text{Log}_{10} 11 = 1.0413$

6, 7, 5? 11? Deep calls unto Deep study bible 1

0.7781, 0.8450, 0.6989? 1.0413?
Deep calls unto Deep study bible 2

x-axis	y-axis
6	0.7781
7	0.8450
5	0.6989
11	1.0413

Water Spout *(lightning;combinatorics)* Study bible 1

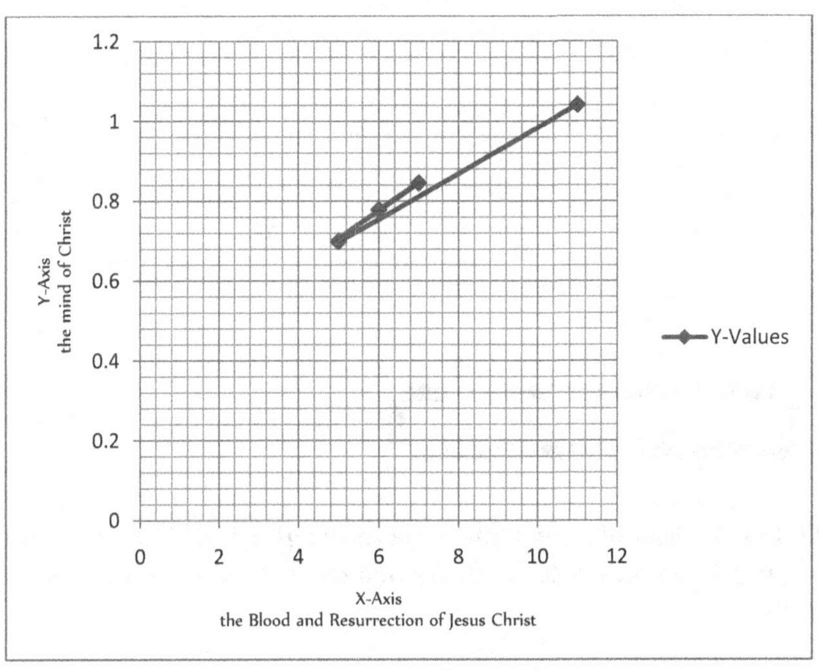

Water Spout *(lightning;combinatorics)* Study bible 2

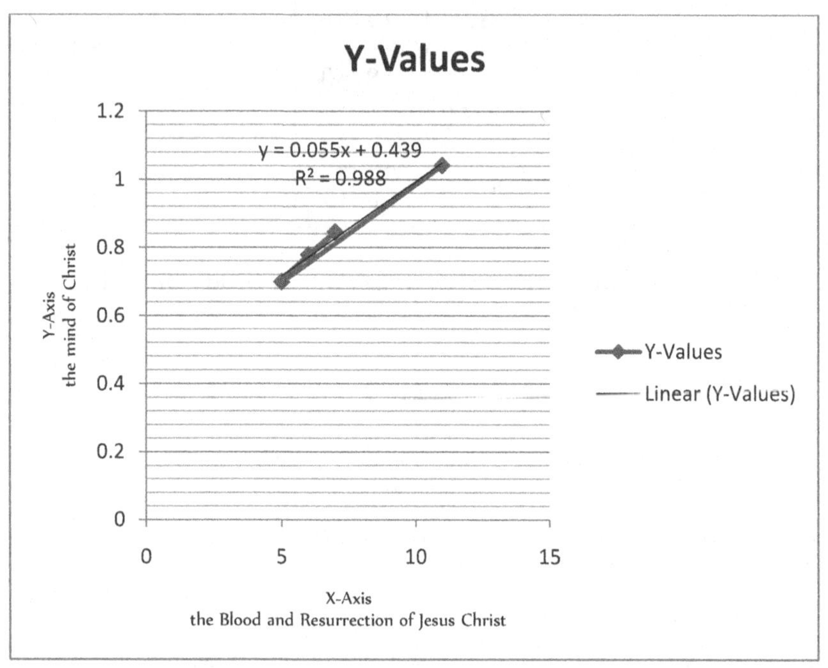

$10^{0.7781}$, $10^{0.8450}$, $10^{0.6989}$? $10^{1.0413}$?

Pilled Poplar, Hazel, and Chestnut bible rods 2

27. For the Son of man shall come in the glory of his Father with his angels; and then he shall reward every man according to his works.

16; 11. Bible Matrices

Pilled Poplar, Hazel, and Chestnut bible rods 1

$\text{Log}_{10}\ 16 = 1.2041$ $\text{Log}_{10}\ 11 = 1.0413$

16; 11. Deep calls unto Deep study bible 1

1.2041; 1.0413. Deep calls unto Deep study bible 2

x-axis	y-axis
16	1.2041
11	1.0413

Water Spout *(lightning;combinatorics)* Study bible 1

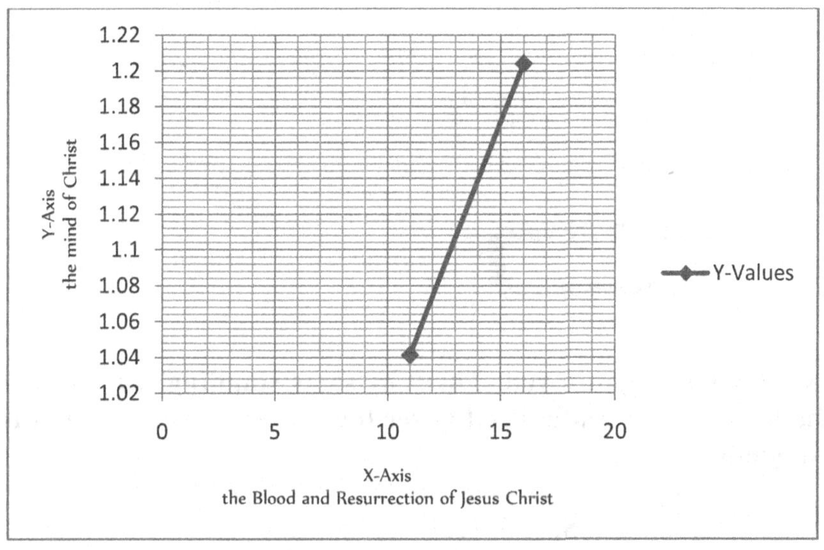

Water Spout *(lightning;combinatorics)* Study bible 2

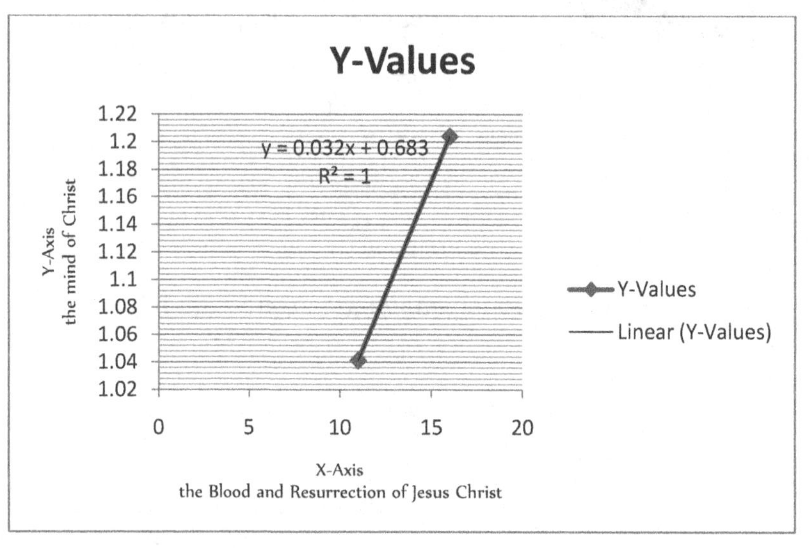

$10^{1.2041}$; $10^{1.0413}$. Pilled Poplar, Hazel, and Chestnut bible rods 2

28. Verily I say unto you, There be some standing here, which shall not taste of death, till they see the Son of man coming in his kingdom.

5, 5, 6, 11. Bible Matrices

$Log_{10} 5 = 0.6989$ $Log_{10} 6 = 0.7781$ $Log_{10} 5 = 0.6989$ $Log_{10} 11 = 1.0413$

5, 5, 6, 11. Deep calls unto Deep study bible 1

0.6989, 0.6989, 0.7781, 1.0413.
Deep calls unto Deep study bible 2

x-axis	y-axis
5	0.6989
5	0.6989
6	0.7781
11	1.0413

Water Spout *(lightning;combinatorics)* Study bible 1

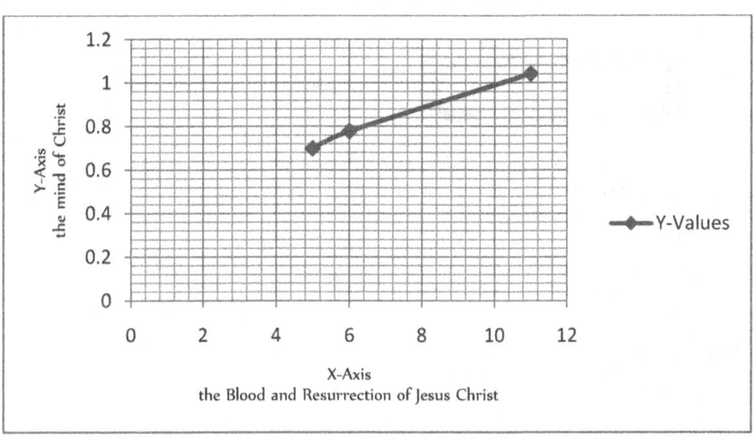

Water Spout *(lightning;combinatorics)* Study bible 2

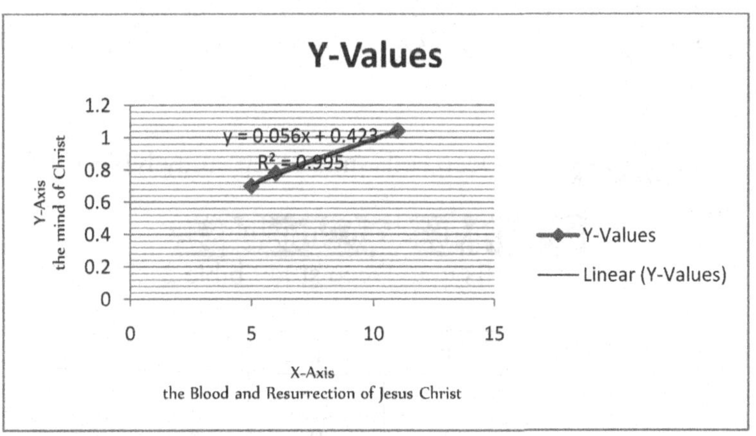

$10^{0.6989}$, $10^{0.6989}$, $10^{0.7781}$, $10^{1.0413}$.

Pilled Poplar, Hazel, and Chestnut bible rods 2

CHAPTER 17

1. And after six man; 2 x 3 **days Jesus** savior; deliverer **taketh Peter** a rock or stone, **James**that supplants, undermines; the heel, **and John**the grace or mercy of the Lord **his brother, and bringeth them up into an high mountain apart,**

7, 1, 4, 9, Bible Matrices

$3_3 2_2 2_4, 1_5, 2_7 2_{10}, 9_{10},$

Pilled Poplar, Hazel, and Chestnut bible rods 1

$Log_{10} 2 = 0.3010$
$Log_7 2 = y$
$7^y = 2$
$y \log_{10} 7 = \log_{10} 2$
$y = \log_{10} 2 / \log_{10} 7$
$y = 0.3010 / 0.8450$
$y = 0.3562$

$Log_{10} 9 = 0.9542$
$Log_4 2 = y$
$4^y = 2$
$2^{2y} = 2^1$
$2y = 1$
$y = ½ \text{ or } 0.5$

$Log_3 3 = y$
$3^y = 3$
$3^y = 3^1 \; 2^y = 2^1$
$y = 1$

$Log_2 2 = y$
$2^y = 2$
$5^y = 5^0$
$y = 1$

$Log_5 1 = y$
$5^y = 1$
$y = 0$

7, 1, 4, 9, Deep calls unto Deep study bible 1

1 1 0.5, 0, 0.3562 0.3010, 0.9542,
Deep calls unto Deep study bible 2

x-axis	y-axis
7	2.5
1	0
4	0.6572
9	0.9542

Water Spout *(lightning;combinatorics)* Study bible 1

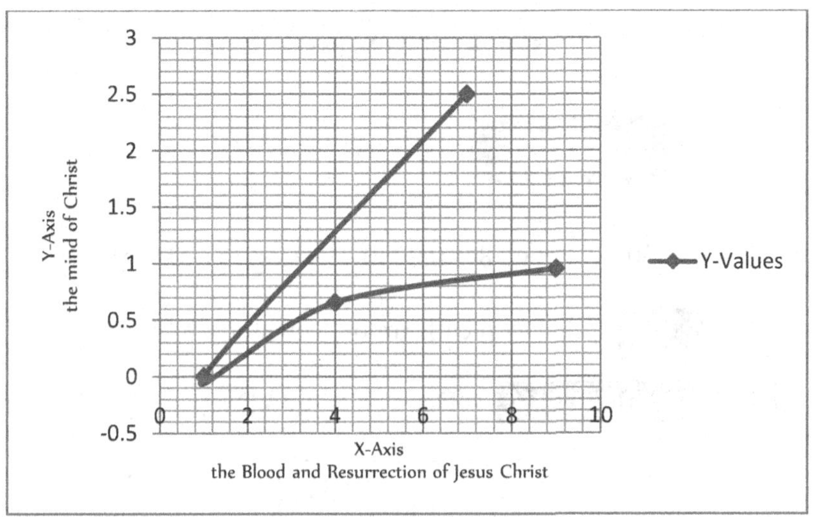

Water Spout *(lightning;combinatorics)* Study bible 2

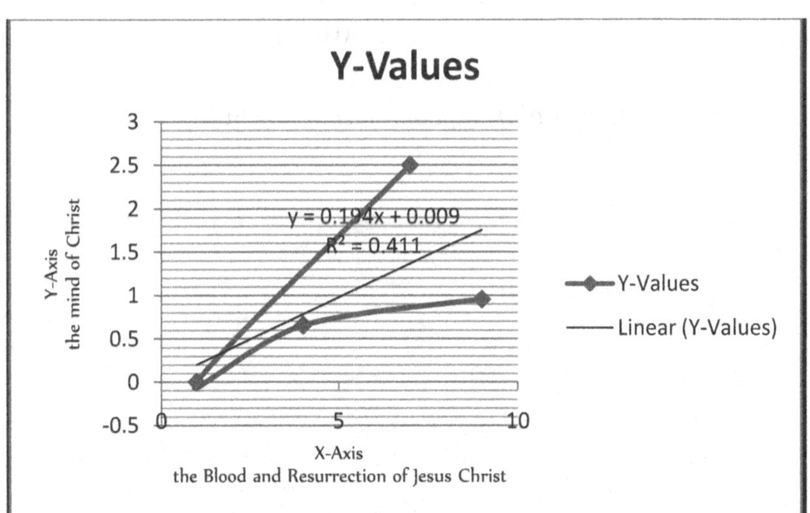

$3^1\ 2^1\ 4^{0.5},\ 5^0,\ 7^{0.3562}\ 10^{0.3010},\ 10^{0.9542},$

Pilled Poplar, Hazel, and Chestnut bible rods 2

2. And was transfigured before them: and his face did shine as the sun, and his raiment was white as the light.

5: 8, 8. Bible Matrices

$\text{Log}_{10} 8 = 0.9030$ $\text{Log}_{10} 8 = 0.9030$ $\text{Log}_{10} 5 = 0.6989$

5: 8, 8. Deep calls unto Deep study bible 1

0.6989: 0.9030, 0.9030. Deep calls unto Deep study bible 2

x-axis	y-axis
5	0.6989
8	0.9030
8	0.9030

Water Spout *(lightning;combinatorics)* Study bible 1

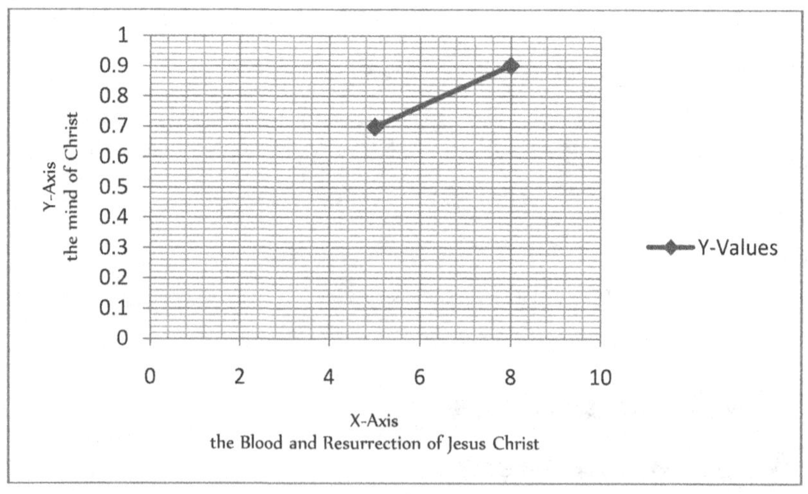

Water Spout *(lightning;combinatorics)* Study bible 2

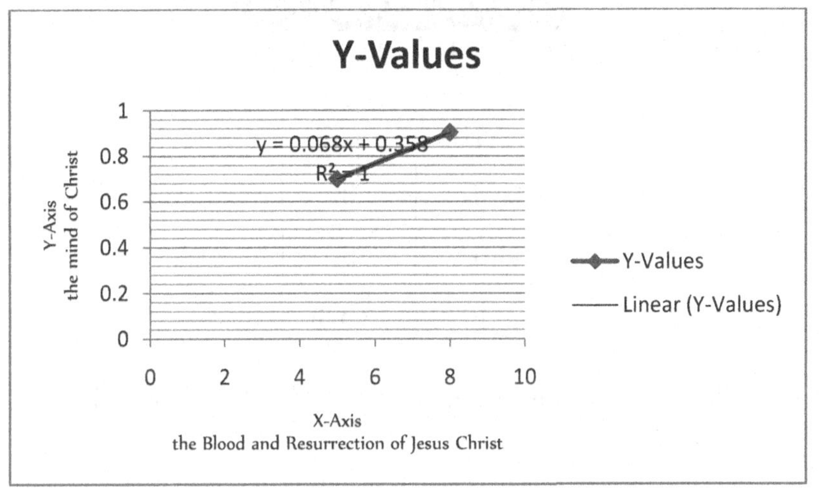

Pilled Poplar, Hazel, and Chestnut bible rods 2

3. And, behold, there appeared unto them Mosestaken out; drawn forth; drawer out; one born **and Elias**God the Lord; the strong Lord **talking with him.**

1, 1, 10. Bible Matrices

Pilled Poplar, Hazel, and Chestnut bible rods 1

$\text{Log}_{10} 1 = 0$
$\text{Log}_8 5 = y$
$8^y = 5$
$y \log_{10} 8 = \log_{10} 5$
$y = \log_{10} 5 / \log_{10} 8$
$y = 0.6989 / 0.9030$
$y = 0.7739$

$\text{Log}_{10} 1 = 0$
$\text{Log}_6 2 = y$
$6^y = 2$
$y \log_{10} 6 = \log_{10} 2$
$y = \log_{10} 2 / \log_{10} 6$
$y = 0.3010 / 0.7781$
$y = 0.3868$

$\text{Log}_{10} 3 = 0.4771$

1, 1, 10. Deep calls unto Deep study bible 1

0, 0, 0.7739 0.3868 0.4771.
Deep calls unto Deep study bible 2

x-axis	y-axis
1	0
1	0
10	1.6378

Water Spout *(lightning;combinatorics)* Study bible 1

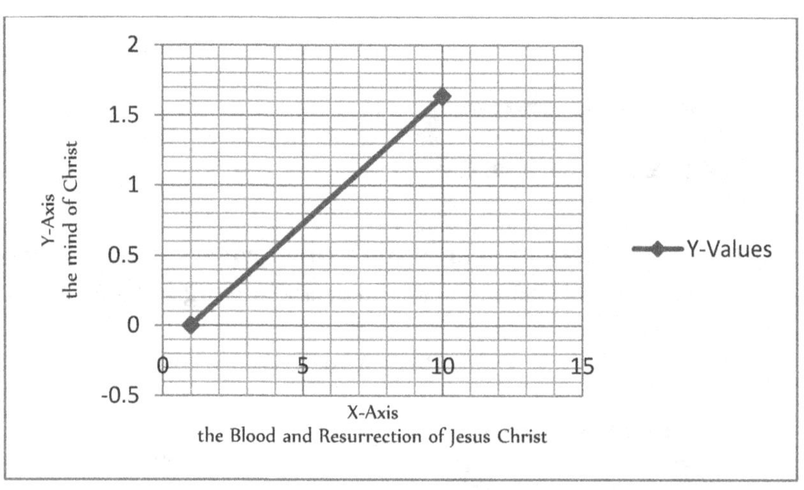

Water Spout *(lightning;combinatorics)* Study bible 2

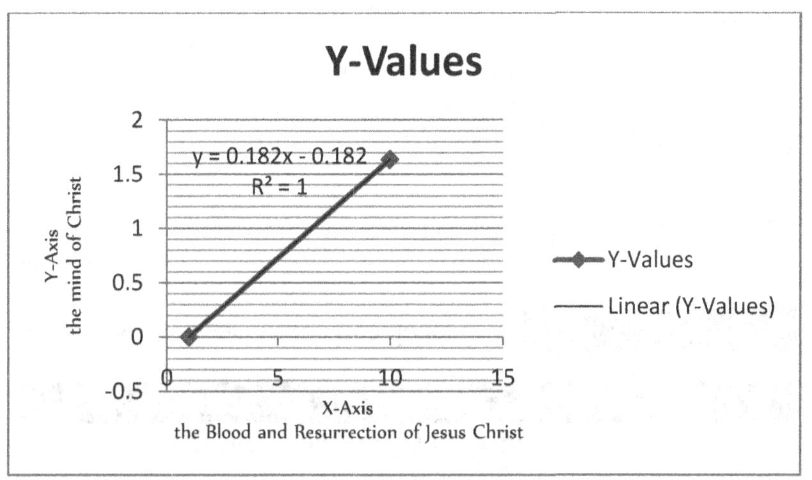

10^{0}, 10^{0}, $8^{0.7739}$ $6^{0.3868}$ $10^{0.4771}$.

Pilled Poplar, Hazel, and Chestnut bible rods 2

4. Then answered Petera rock or stone **, and said unto Jesus**savior; deliverer**, Lord, it is good for us to be here: if thou wilt, let us make here three** completion or perfection, and unity; 3 x 1 **tabernacles; one for thee, and one for Moses** taken out; drawn forth; drawer out; one born**, and one for Elias**God the Lord; the strong Lord.

3, 4, 1, 8: 3, 6; 3, 4, 4. Bible Matrices

3_4, 4_2, 1_{10}, 8_{10}: 3_{10}, 5_7 1_{10} ; 3_{10}, 4_8, 4_6.

Pilled Poplar, Hazel, and Chestnut bible rods 1

$\text{Log}_{10} 8 = 0.9030$ $\text{Log}_{10} 3 = 0.4771$ $\text{Log}_{10} 3 = 0.4771$ $\text{Log}_{10} 1 = 0$ $\text{Log}_{10} 1 = 0$

$\text{Log}_7 5 = y$
$7^y = 5$
$y \log_{10} 7 = \log_{10} 5$
$y = \log_{10} 5 / \log_{10} 7$

$\text{Log}_6 4 = y$
$6^y = 4$
$y \log_{10} 6 = \log_{10} 4$
$y = \log_{10} 4 / \log_{10} 6$

$y = 0.6989 / 0.8450$ $y = 0.6020 / 0.7781$

$y = 0.8271$ $y = 0.7736$

$\text{Log}_4 3 = y$ $\text{Log}_8 4 = y$ $\text{Log}_2 4 = y$

$4^y = 3$ $8^y = 4$ $2^y = 4$

$y \log_{10} 4 = \log_{10} 3$ $2^{3y} = 2^2$ $2^y = 2^2$

$y = \log_{10} 3 / \log_{10} 4$ $3y = 2$ $y = 2$

$y = 0.4771 / 0.6020$ $y = 2/3$

$y = 0.7925$ $y = 0.6666$

3, 4, 1, 8, 3, 6; 3, 4, 4. Deep calls unto Deep study bible 1

0.7925, 2, 0, 0.9030: 0.4771, 0.8271 0; 0.4771, 0.6666, 0.7736.
Deep calls unto Deep study bible 2

x-axis	y-axis
3	0.7925
4	2
1	0
8	0.9030
3	0.4771
6	0.8271
3	0.4771
4	0.6666
4	0.7736

Water Spout *(lightning;combinatorics)* Study bible 1

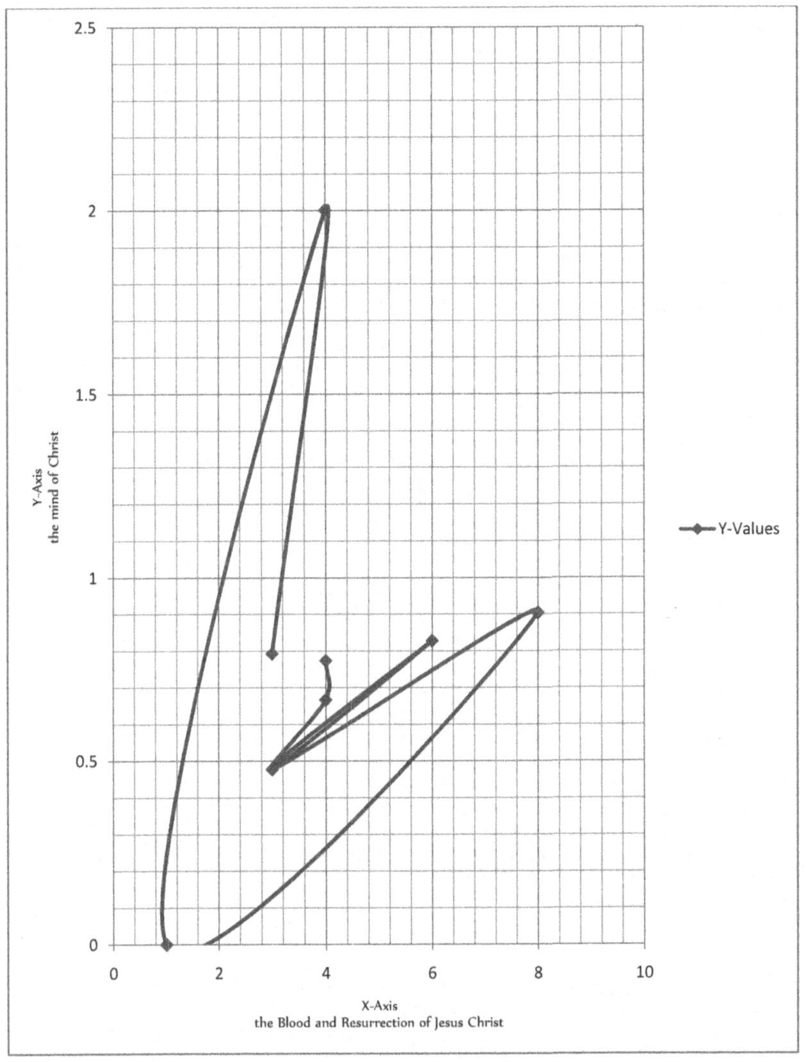

Water Spout *(lightning;combinatorics)* Study bible 2

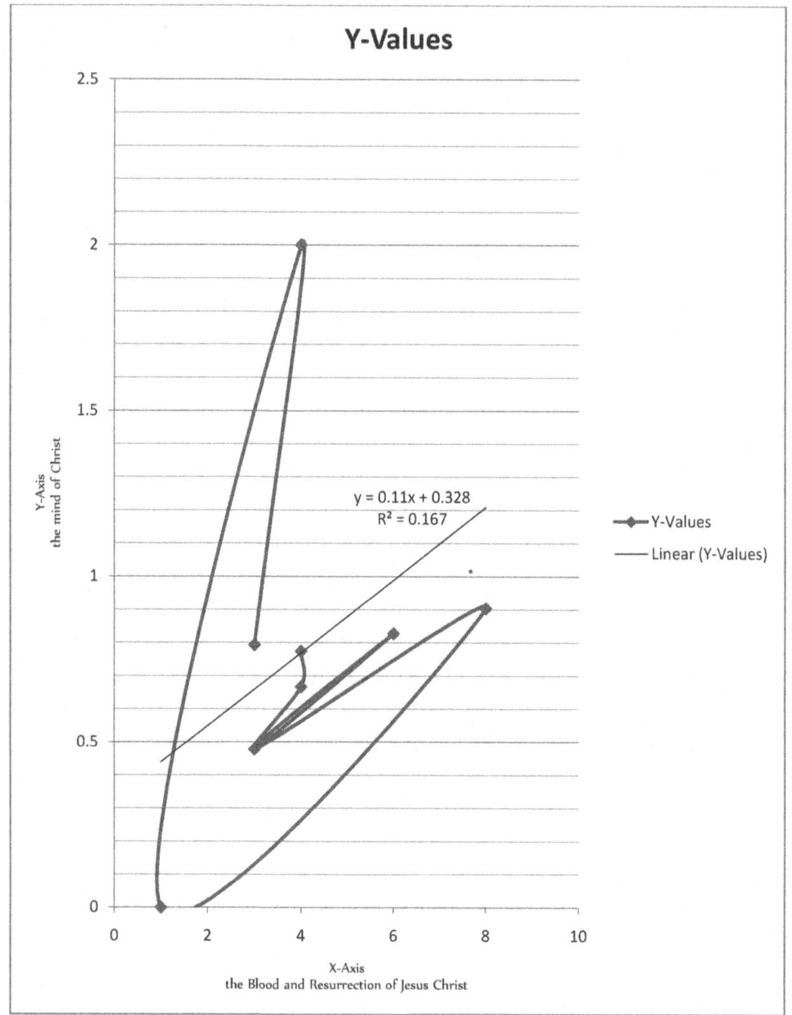

$4^{0.7925}, 2^{2}, 10^{0}, 10^{0.9030}: 10^{0.4771}, 7^{0.8271}\ 10^{0}\ ; 10^{0.4771}, 8^{0.6666}, 6^{0.7736}.$

Pilled Poplar, Hazel, and Chestnut bible rods 2

5. While he yet spake, behold, a bright cloud overshadowed them: and behold a voice out of the cloud, which said, This is my beloved Son, in whom I am well pleased; hear ye him.

4, 1, 5: 8, 2, 5, 6; 3. Bible Matrices

$4_{10}, 1_{10}, 5_{10}: 8_{10}, 2_{10}, 5_{10}, 6_{10}; 3_{10}$.

Pilled Poplar, Hazel, and Chestnut bible rods 1

$\text{Log}_{10} 8 = 0.9030$ $\text{Log}_{10} 4 = 0.6020$ $\text{Log}_{10} 5 = 0.6989$ $\text{Log}_{10} 5 = 0.6989$

$\text{Log}_{10} 1 = 0$ $\text{Log}_{10} 2 = 0.2010$ $\text{Log}_{10} 6 = 0.7781$ $\text{Log}_{10} 3 = 0.4771$

4, 1, 5: 8, 2, 5, 6; 3. Deep calls unto Deep study bible 1

0.6020, 0, 0.6989: 0.9030, 0.3010, 0.6989, 0.7781; 0.4771.
Deep calls unto Deep study bible 2

x-axis	y-axis
4	0.6020
1	0
5	0.6989
8	0.9030
2	0.3010
5	0.6989
6	0.7781
3	0.4771

Water Spout *(lightning;combinatorics)* Study bible 1

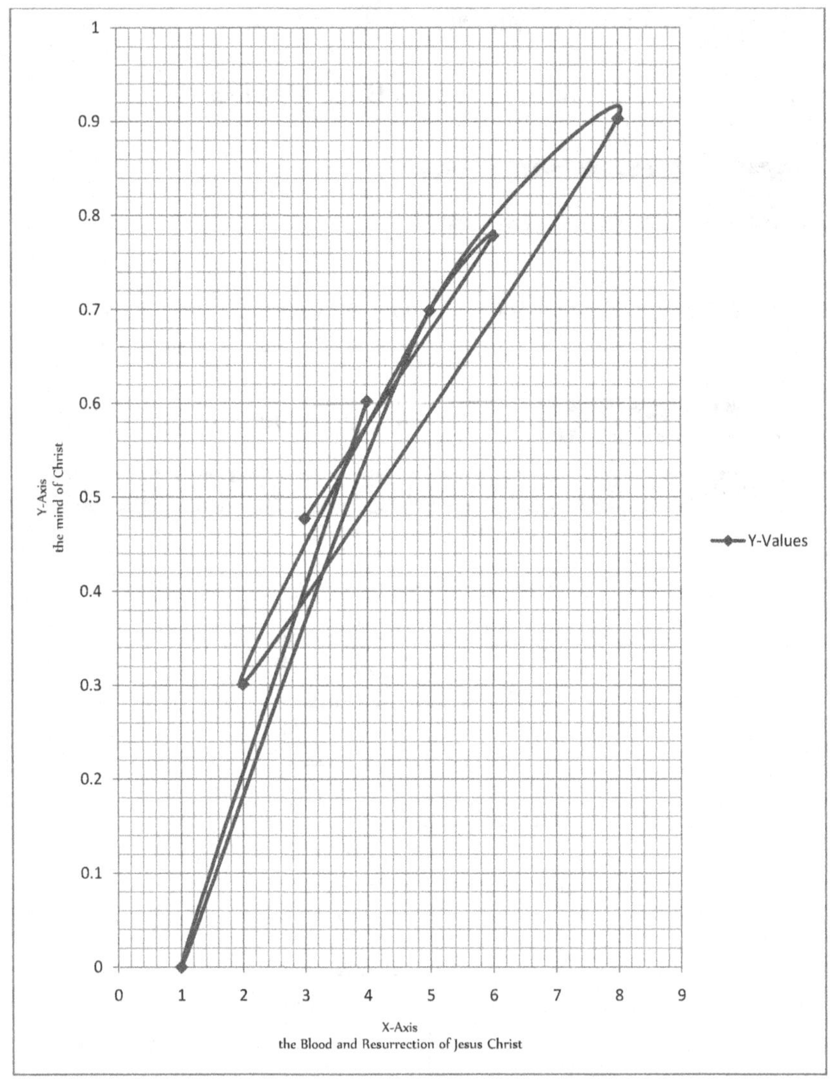

Water Spout *(lightning;combinatorics)* Study bible 2

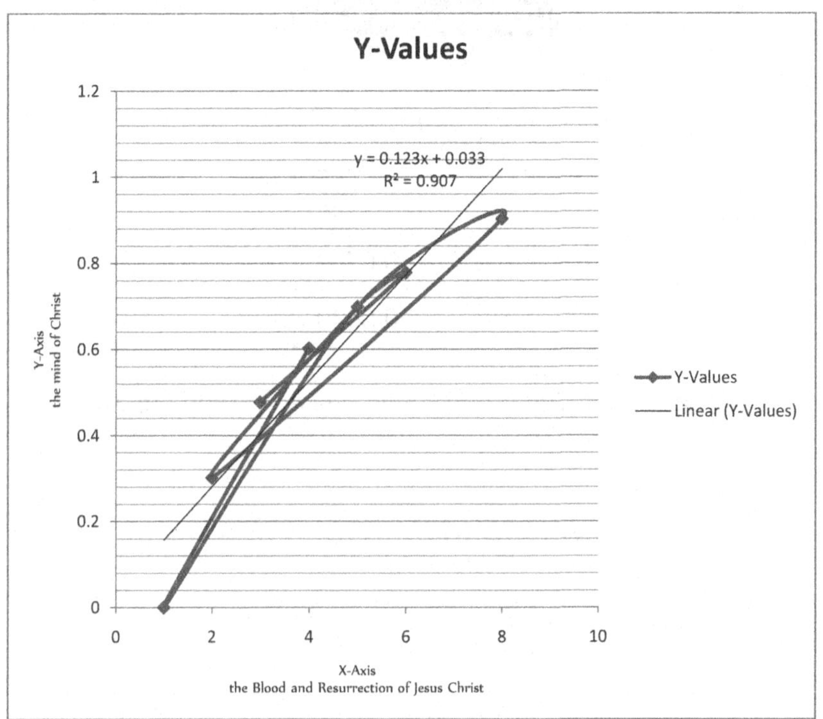

$10^{0.6020}, 10^{0}, 10^{0.6989}: 10^{0.9030}, 10^{0.3010}, 10^{0.6989}, 10^{0.7781}; 10^{0.4771}$.

Pilled Poplar, Hazel, and Chestnut bible rods 2

6. And when the disciples heard it, they fell on their face, and were sore afraid.

6, 5, 4. Bible Matrices

$6_{10}, 5_{10}, 4_{10}$.

Pilled Poplar, Hazel, and Chestnut bible rods 1

$\text{Log}_{10} 6 = 0.7781$ $\text{Log}_{10} 4 = 0.6020$ $\text{Log}_{10} 5 = 0.6989$

6, 5, 4. Deep calls unto Deep study bible 1

0.7781, 0.6989, 0.6020.
Deep calls unto Deep study bible 2

x-axis	y-axis
6	0.7781
5	0.6989
4	0.6020

Water Spout *(lightning;combinatorics)* Study bible 1

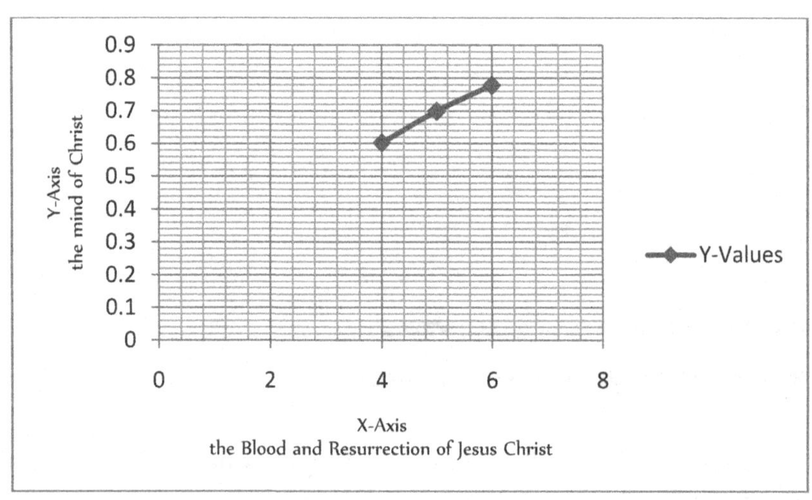

Water Spout *(lightning;combinatorics)* Study bible 2

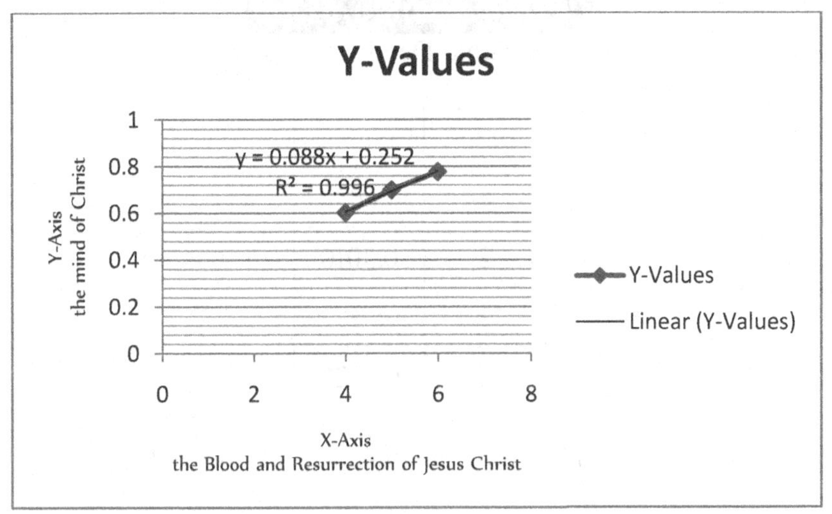

$10^{0.7781}, 10^{0.6989}, 10^{0.6020}$.

Pilled Poplar, Hazel, and Chestnut bible rods 2

7. And Jesussavior; deliverer **came and touched them, and said, Arise, and be not afraid.**

6, 2, 1, 4. Bible Matrices

$2_2\ 4_{10}, 2_{10}, 1_{10}, 4_{10}$.

Pilled Poplar, Hazel, and Chestnut bible rods 1

$\text{Log}_{10} 2 = 0.3010$ $\text{Log}_{10} 4 = 0.6020$ $\text{Log}_{10} 4 = 0.6020$ $\text{Log}_{10} 1 = 0$

$\text{Log}_2 2 = y$

$2^y = 2$

$2^y = 2^1$

$y = 1$

6, 2, 1, 4. Deep calls unto Deep study bible 1

1 0.6020, 0.3010, 0, 0.6020.
Deep calls unto Deep study bible 2

x-axis	y-axis
6	1.6020
2	0.3010
1	0
4	0.6020

Water Spout *(lightning;combinatorics)* Study bible 1

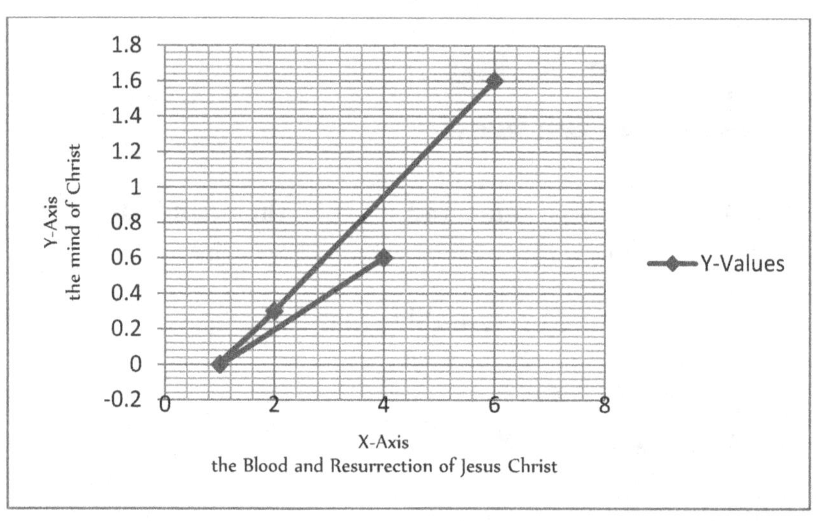

Water Spout *(lightning;combinatorics)* Study bible 2

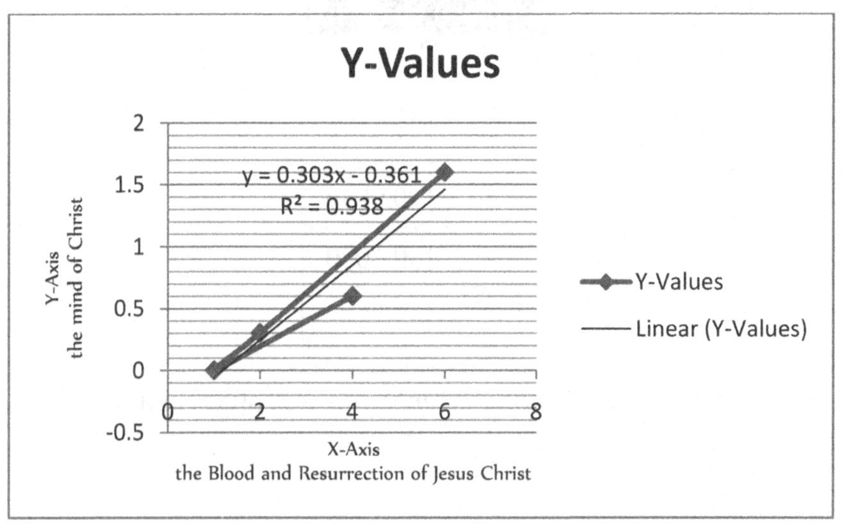

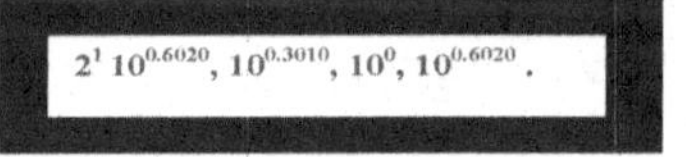
2^1 $10^{0.6020}$, $10^{0.3010}$, 10^{0}, $10^{0.6020}$.

Pilled Poplar, Hazel, and Chestnut bible rods 2

8. And when they had lifted up their eyes, they saw no man, save Jesussavior; deliverer**only.**

8, 4, 3. Bible Matrices

8_{10}, 4_{10}, 2_2 1_{10}.

Pilled Poplar, Hazel, and Chestnut bible rods 1

$\text{Log}_{10} 8 = 0.9030$ $\text{Log}_{10} 4 = 0.6020$ $\text{Log}_{10} 1 = 0$

$\text{Log}_2 2 = y$

$2^y = 2$

$2^y = 2^1$

$y = 1$

8, 4, 3. Deep calls unto Deep study bible 1

0.9030, 0.6020, 1 0.

Deep calls unto Deep study bible 2

x-axis	y-axis
8	0.9030
4	0.6020
3	1

Water Spout *(lightning;combinatorics)* Study bible 1

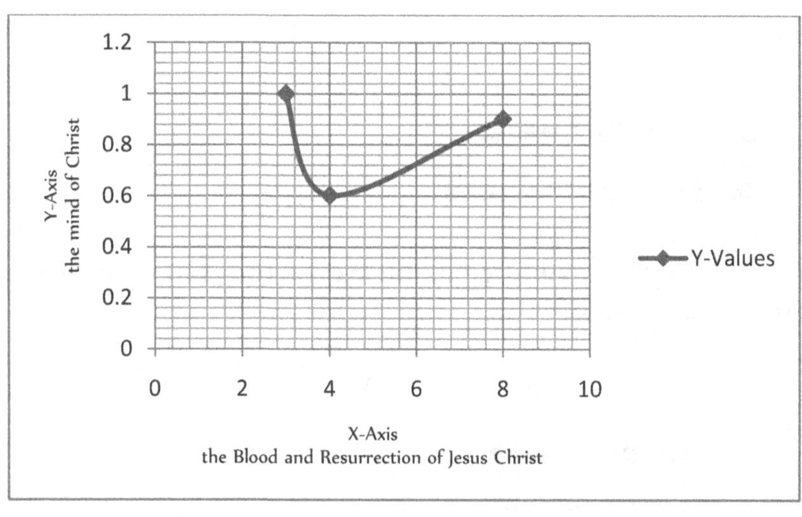

Water Spout *(lightning;combinatorics)* Study bible 2

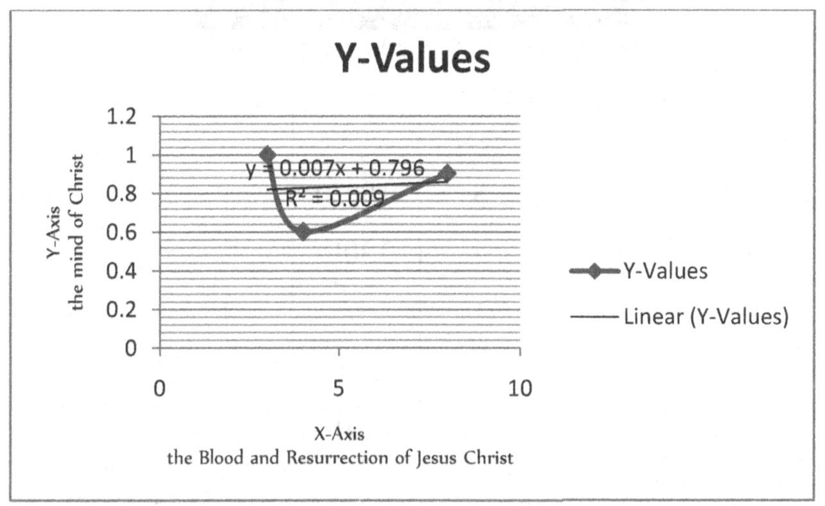

$10^{0.9030}$, $10^{0.6020}$, 2^1 10^0.

Pilled Poplar, Hazel, and Chestnut bible rods 2

9. And as they came down from the mountain, Jesussavior; deliverer**charged them, saying, Tell the vision to no man, until the Son of man be risen again from the dead.**

8, 3, 1, 6, 11. Bible Matrices

8_{10}, 1_2 2_{10}, 1_{10}, 6_{10}, 11_{10}.

Pilled Poplar, Hazel, and Chestnut bible rods 1

$\text{Log}_{10} 8 = 0.9030$ $\text{Log}_{10} 6 = 0.7781$ $\text{Log}_{10} 2 = 0.3010$ $\text{Log}_{10} 11 = 1.0413$ $\text{Log}_{10} 1 = 0$

$\text{Log}_2 1 = y$

$2^y = 1$

$2^y = 2^0$

$y = 0$

8, 3, 1, 6, 11. Deep calls unto Deep study bible 1

0. 9030, 0 0.3010, 0, 0.7781, 1.0413.
Deep calls unto Deep study bible 2

x-axis	y-axis
8	0.9030
3	0.3010
1	0
6	0.7781
11	1.0413

Water Spout *(lightning;combinatorics)* Study bible 1

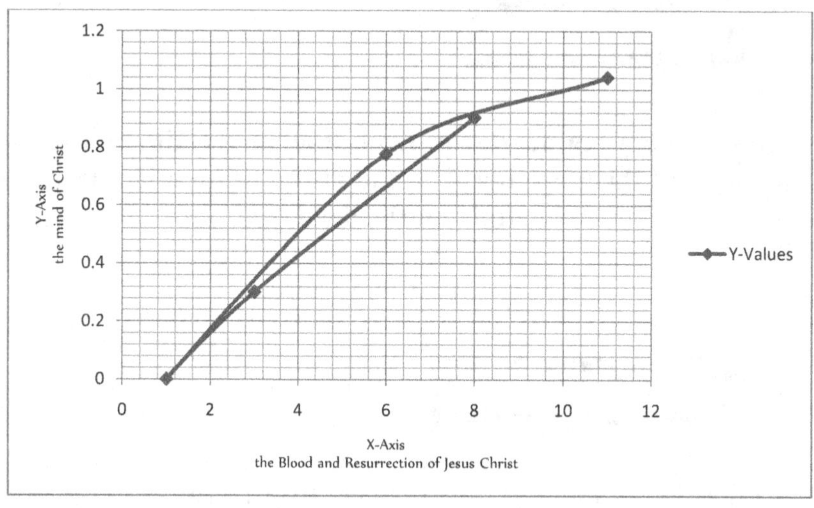

Water Spout *(lightning;combinatorics)* Study bible 2

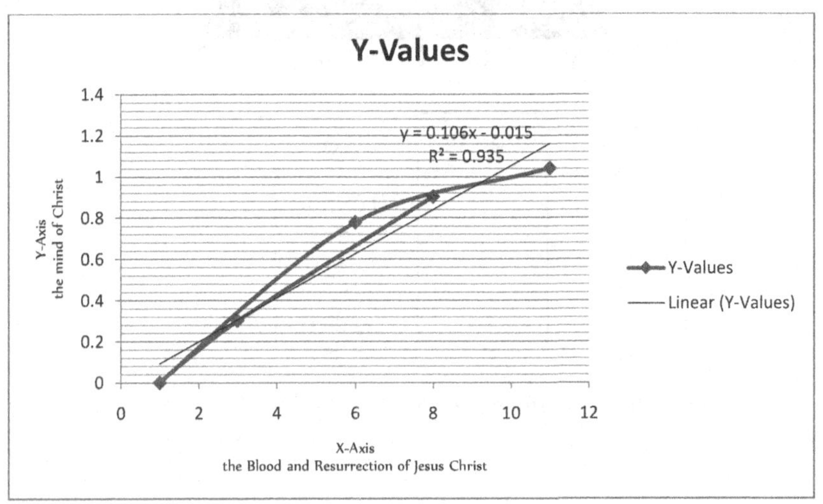

$10^{0.9030}, 2^{0}\ 10^{0.3010}, 10^{0}, 10^{0.7781},\ 10^{1.0413}$. Pilled Poplar, Hazel, and Chestnut bible rods 2

10. And his disciples asked him, saying, Why then say the scribes **lawyers;copyists; transcribers** **that Elias** **God the Lord; whose God is Jehovah** **must first come?**

5, 1, 10? Bible Matrices

$5_{10}, 1_{10}, 5_{3}\ 2_{7}3_{10}$? Pilled Poplar, Hazel, and Chestnut bible rods 1

$Log_{10} 5 = 0.6989$

$Log_{3} 5 = y$

$3^{y} = 5$

$y \log_{10} 3 = \log_{10} 5$

$y = \log_{10} 5 / \log_{10} 3$

$y = 0.6989 / 0.4771$

$y = 1.4648$

$Log_{10} 3 = 0.4771$

$Log_{7} 2 = y$

$7^{y} = 2$

$y \log_{10} 7 = \log_{10} 2$

$y = \log_{10} 2 / \log_{10} 7$

$y = 0.3010 / 0.8450$

$y = 0.3562$

$Log_{10} 1 = 0$

5, 1, 10? Deep calls unto Deep study bible 1

0.6989, 0, 1.4648 0.3562 0.4771?
Deep calls unto Deep study bible 2

x-axis	y-axis
5	0.6989
1	0
10	2.2981

Water Spout *(lightning;combinatorics)* Study bible 1

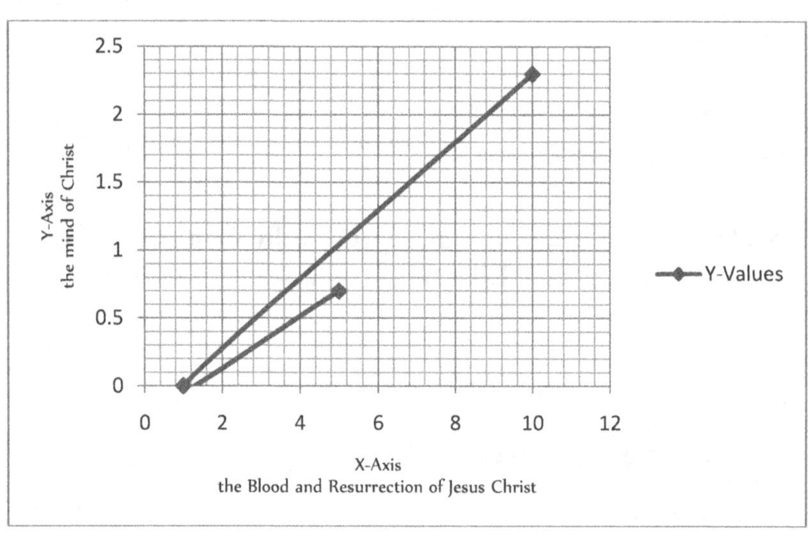

Water Spout *(lightning;combinatorics)* Study bible 2

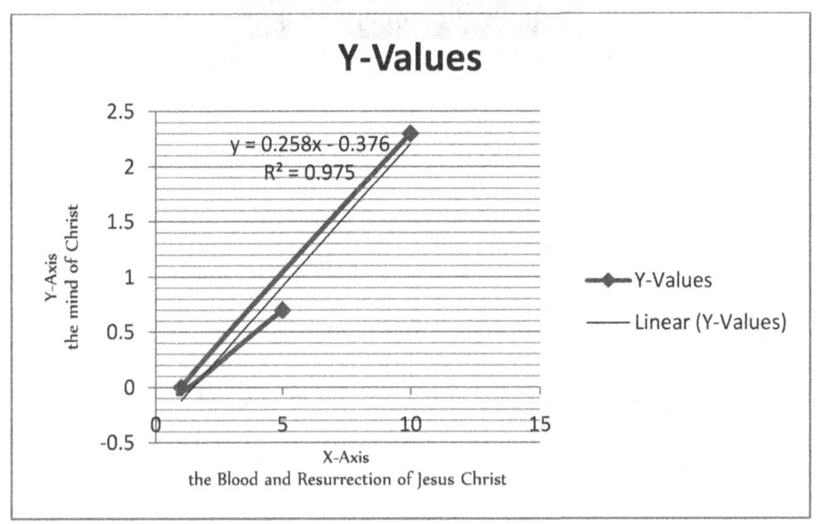

$10^{0.6989}$, 10^{0}, $3^{1.4648}$ $7^{0.3562}$ $10^{0.4771}$?

Pilled Poplar, Hazel, and Chestnut bible rods 2

11. And Jesussavior;deliverer **answered and said unto them, Elias**God the Lord; the strong Lord **truly shall first come, and restore all things.**

7, 5, 4. Bible Matrices

$2_2\, 5_{10}$, $1_6 4_{10}$, 4_{10} .

Pilled Poplar, Hazel, and Chestnut bible rods 1

$\log_{10} 4 = 0.6020$ $\log_{10} 5 = 0.6989$ $\log_{10} 4 = 0.6020$

$\log_6 1 = y$

$6^y = 1$

$6^y = 6^0$

$y = 0$

$\log_2 2 = y$

$2^y = 2$

$2^y = 2^1$

$y = 1$

7, 5, 4. Deep calls unto Deep study bible 1

1 0.6989, 0 0.6020, 0.6020.

Deep calls unto Deep study bible 2

x-axis	y-axis
7	1.6989
5	0.6020
4	0.6020

Water Spout *(lightning;combinatorics)* Study bible 1

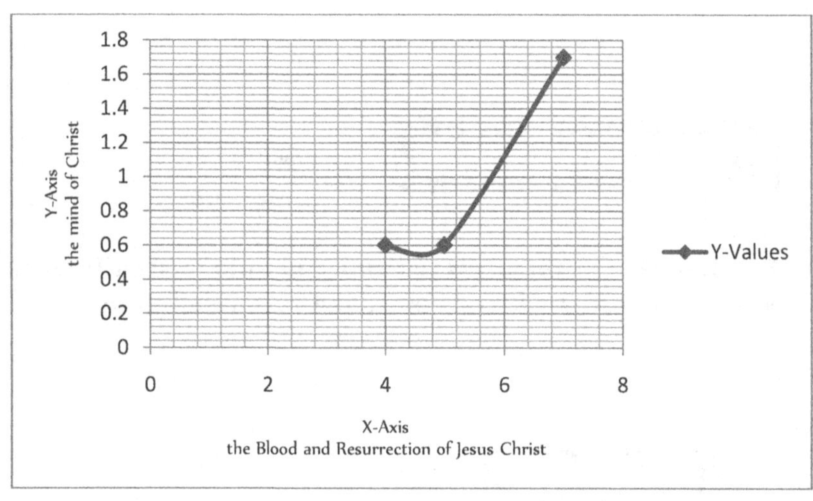

Water Spout *(lightning;combinatorics)* Study bible 2

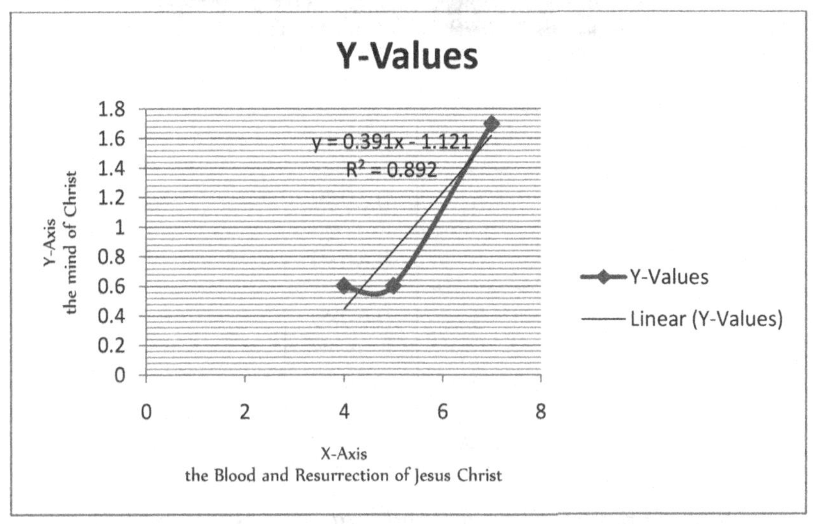

$2^1\ 10^{0.6989}, 6^0\ 10^{0.6020}, 10^{0.6020}$.

Pilled Poplar, Hazel, and Chestnut bible rods 2

12. But I say unto you, That Elias God the Lord; the strong Lord **is come already, and they knew him not, but have done unto him whatsoever they listed. Likewise shall also the Son of man suffer of them.**

5, 5, 5, 8. 10. Bible Matrices

$5_{10}, 2_6\, 3_{10}, 5_{10}, 8_{10}. 10_{10}$.

Pilled Poplar, Hazel, and Chestnut bible rods 1

$\mathrm{Log}_{10} 8 = 0.9030$ $\mathrm{Log}_{10} 5 = 0.6989$ $\mathrm{Log}_{10} 5 = 0.6989$ $\mathrm{Log}_{10} 3 = 0.4771$ $\mathrm{Log}_{10} 10 = 1$

$\mathrm{Log}_6 2 = y$

$6^y = 2$

$y \log_{10} 6 = \log_{10} 2$

$y = \log_{10} 2 / \log_{10} 6$

$y = 0.3010 / 0.7781$

$y = 0.3868$

5, 5, 5, 8. 10. Deep calls unto Deep study bible 1

0.6989, 0.3868 0.4771, 0.6989, 0.9030. 1.
Deep calls unto Deep study bible 2

x-axis	y-axis
5	0.6989
5	0.8639
5	0.6989
8	0.9030
10	1

Water Spout *(lightning;combinatorics)* Study bible 1

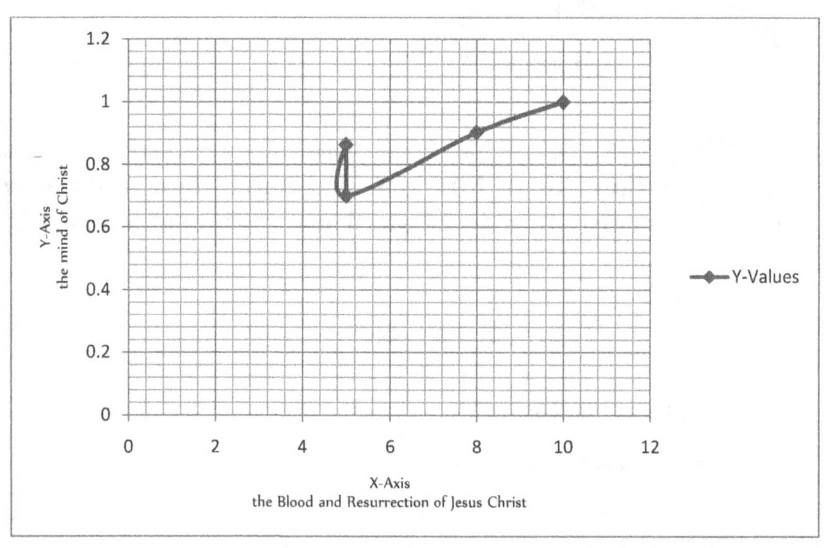

Water Spout *(lightning;combinatorics)* Study bible 2

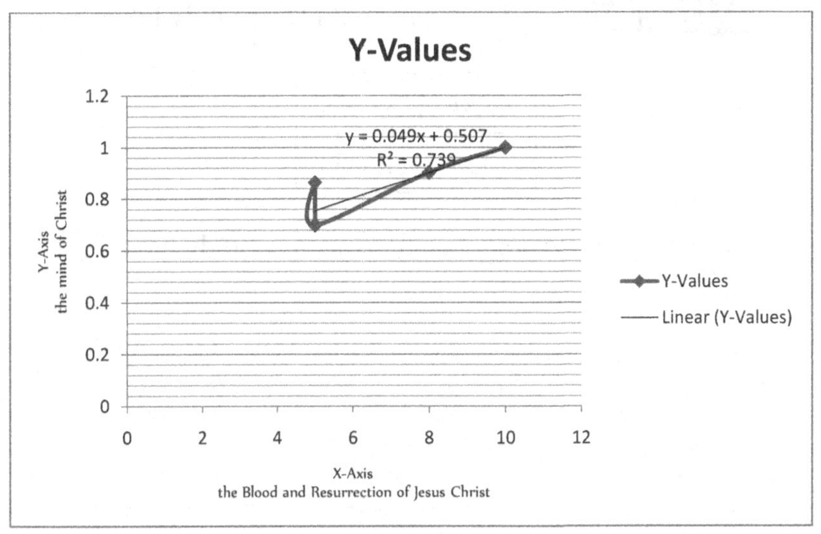

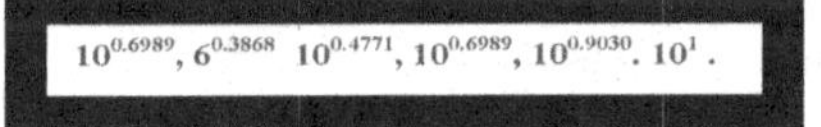

Pilled Poplar, Hazel, and Chestnut bible rods 2

13. Then the disciples understood that he spake unto them of John the grace or mercy of the Lord the Baptist.

13. Bible Matrices

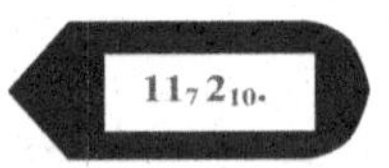

Pilled Poplar, Hazel, and Chestnut bible rods 1

$\text{Log}_{10} 2 = 0.3010$

$\text{Log}_7 11 = y$

$7^y = 11$

$y \log_{10} 7 = \log_{10} 11$

$y = \log_{10} 11 / \log_{10} 7$

$y = 1.0413 / 0.8450$

$y = 1.2323$

13. Deep calls unto Deep study bible 1

1.2323 0.3010 Deep calls unto Deep study bible 2

x-axis	y-axis
13	1.5333

Water Spout *(lightning;combinatorics)* Study bible 1

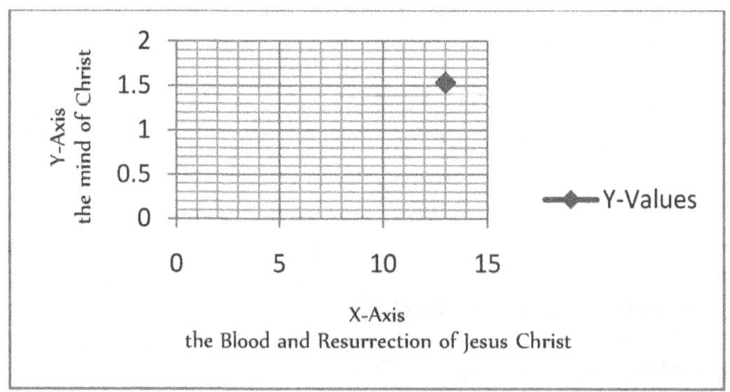

Water Spout *(lightning;combinatorics)* Study bible 2

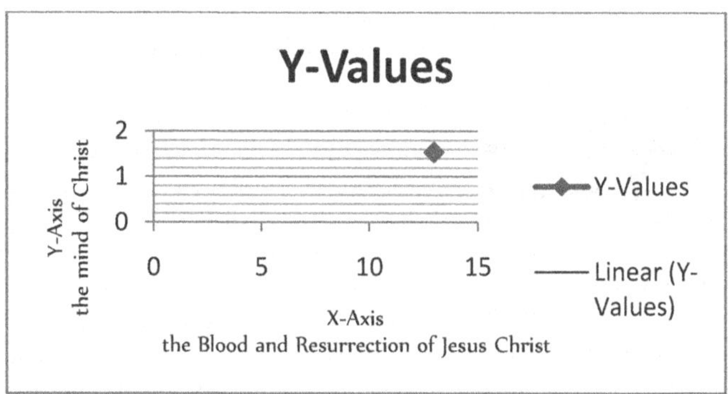

$7^{1.2323}$ $10^{0.3010}$. Pilled Poplar, Hazel, and Chestnut bible rods 2

14. And when they were come to the multitude, there came to him a certain man, kneeling down to him, and saying,

8, 7, 4, 2, Bible Matrices

$8_{10}, 7_{10}, 4_{10}, 2_{10},$ Pilled Poplar, Hazel, and Chestnut bible rods 1

$\text{Log}_{10} 8 = 0.9030$ $\text{Log}_{10} 4 = 0.6020$ $\text{Log}_{10} 7 = 0.8450$ $\text{Log}_{10} 2 = 0.3010$

8, 7, 4, 2, Deep calls unto Deep study bible 1

0.9030, 0.8450, 0.6020, 0.3010,
Deep calls unto Deep study bible 2

x-axis	y-axis
8	0.9030
7	0.8450
4	0.6020
2	0.3010

Water Spout *(lightning;combinatorics)* Study bible 1

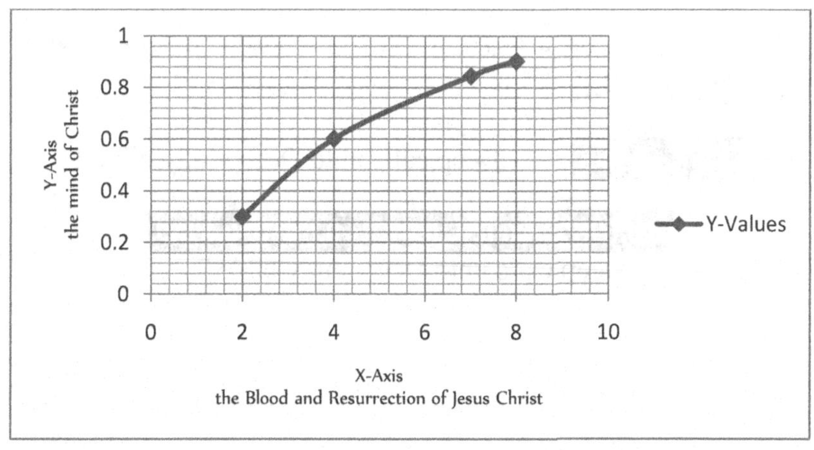

Water Spout *(lightning;combinatorics)* Study bible 2

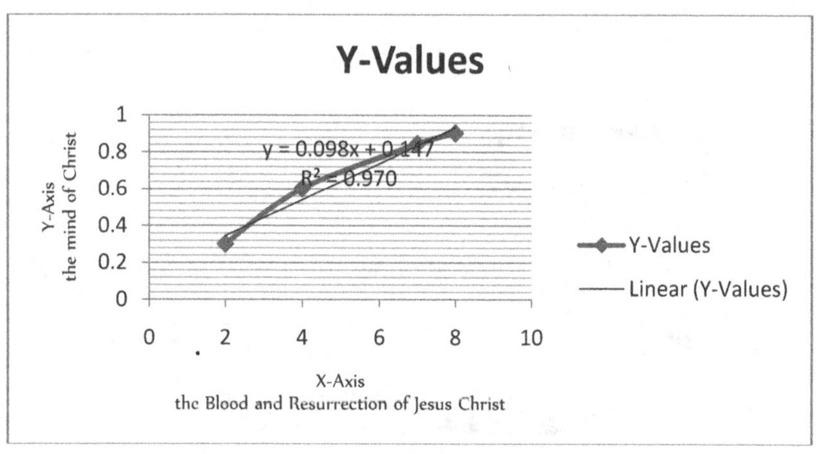

$10^{0.9030}$, $10^{0.8450}$, $10^{0.6020}$, $10^{0.3010}$, Pilled Poplar, Hazel, and Chestnut bible rods 2

15. Lord, have mercy on my son: for he is lunatick, and sore vexed: for ofttimes he falleth into the fire, and oft into the water.

1, 5: 4, 3: 7, 5. Bible Matrices

1_{10}, 5_{10}: 4_{10}, 3_{10}: 7_{10}, 5_{10}. Pilled Poplar, Hazel, and Chestnut bible rods 1

$\mathrm{Log}_{10} 7 = 0.8450$ $\mathrm{Log}_{10} 4 = 0.6020$ $\mathrm{Log}_{10} 5 = 0.6989$ $\mathrm{Log}_{10} 5 = 0.6989$
$\mathrm{Log}_{10} 3 = 0.4771$ $\mathrm{Log}_{10} 1 = 0$

1, 5: 4, 3: 7, 5. Deep calls unto Deep study bible 1

0, 0.6989: 0.6020, 0.4771: 0.8450, 0.6989.
Deep calls unto Deep study bible 2

x-axis	y-axis
1	0
5	0.6989
4	0.6020
3	0.4771
7	0.8450
5	0.6989

Water Spout *(lightning;combinatorics)* Study bible 1

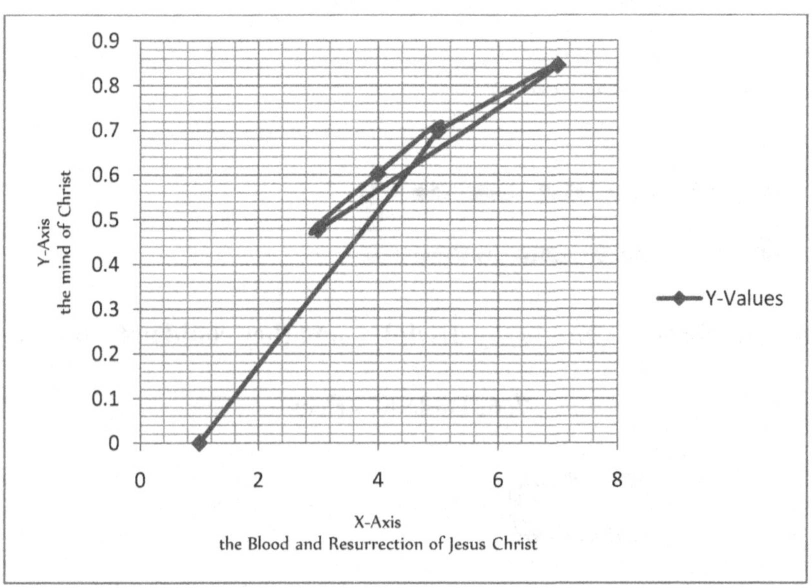

Water Spout *(lightning;combinatorics)* Study bible 2

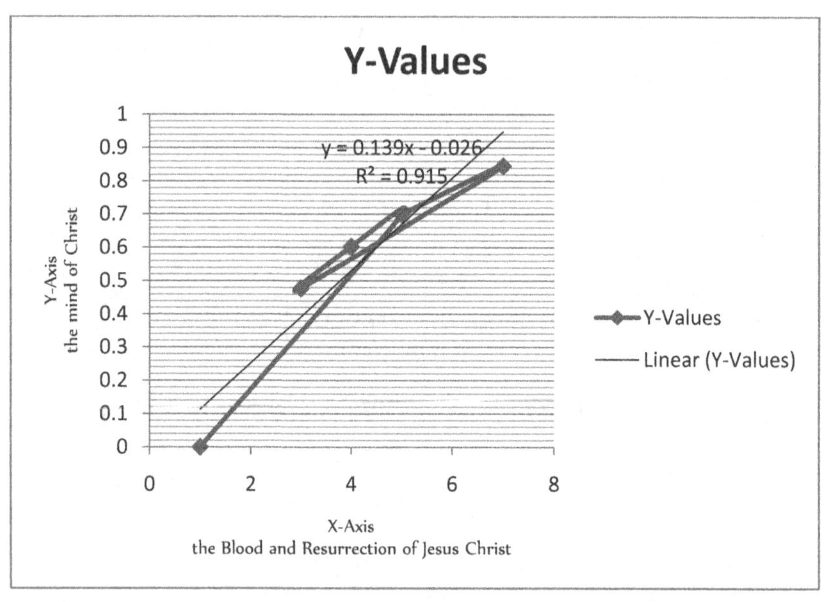

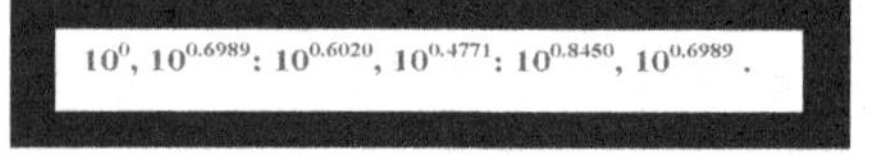

Pilled Poplar, Hazel, and Chestnut bible rods 2

16. And I brought him to thy disciples, and they could not cure him.

7, 6. Bible Matrices

Pilled Poplar, Hazel, and Chestnut bible rods 1

$\text{Log}_{10} 7 = 0.8450$ $\text{Log}_{10} 6 = 0.7781$

7, 6. Deep calls unto Deep study bible 1

0.8450, 0.7781. Deep calls unto Deep study bible 2

x-axis	y-axis
7	0.8450
6	0.7781

Water Spout *(lightning;combinatorics)* Study bible 1

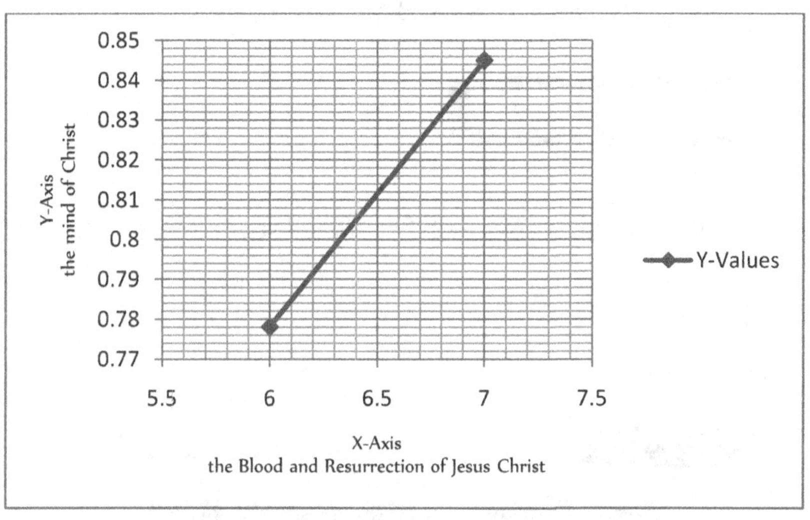

Water Spout *(lightning;combinatorics)* Study bible 2

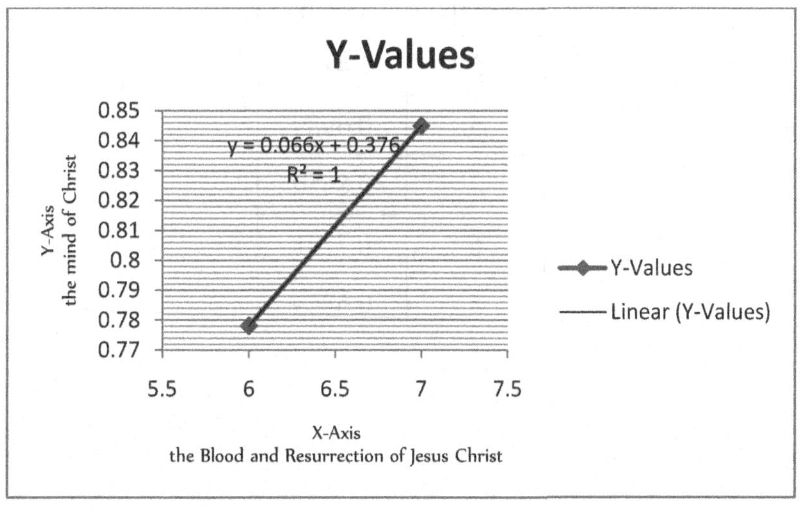

$10^{0.8450}$, $10^{0.7781}$.

Pilled Poplar, Hazel, and Chestnut bible rods 2

17. Then Jesussavior; deliverer**answered and said, O faithless and perverse generation, how long shall I be with you? how long shall I suffer you? bring him hither to me.**

5, 5, 7? 6? 5. Bible Matrices

$2_2 3_{10}$, 5_{10}, 7_{10}? 6_{10}? 5_{10}.

Pilled Poplar, Hazel, and Chestnut bible rods 1

$\text{Log}_{10} 7 = 0.8450$ $\text{Log}_{10} 5 = 0.6989$ $\text{Log}_{10} 5 = 0.6989$ $\text{Log}_{10} 3 = 0.4771$ $\text{Log}_{10} 6 = 0.7781$

$\text{Log}_2 2 = y$

$2^y = 2$

$2^y = 2^1$

$y = 1$

5, 5, 7? 6? 5. Deep calls unto Deep study bible 1

1 0.4771, 0.6989, 0.8450? 0.7781? 0.6989.

Deep calls unto Deep study bible 2

x-axis	y-axis
5	1.4771
5	0.6989
7	0.8450
6	0.7781
5	0.6989

Water Spout *(lightning;combinatorics)* Study bible 1

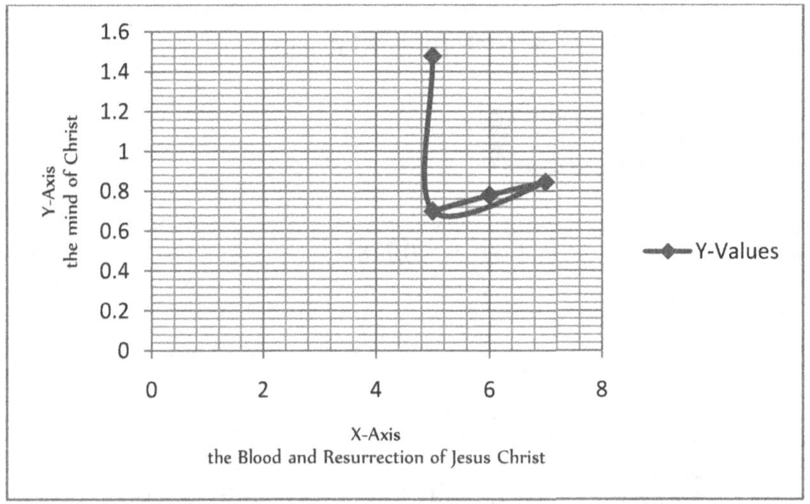

Water Spout *(lightning;combinatorics)* Study bible 2

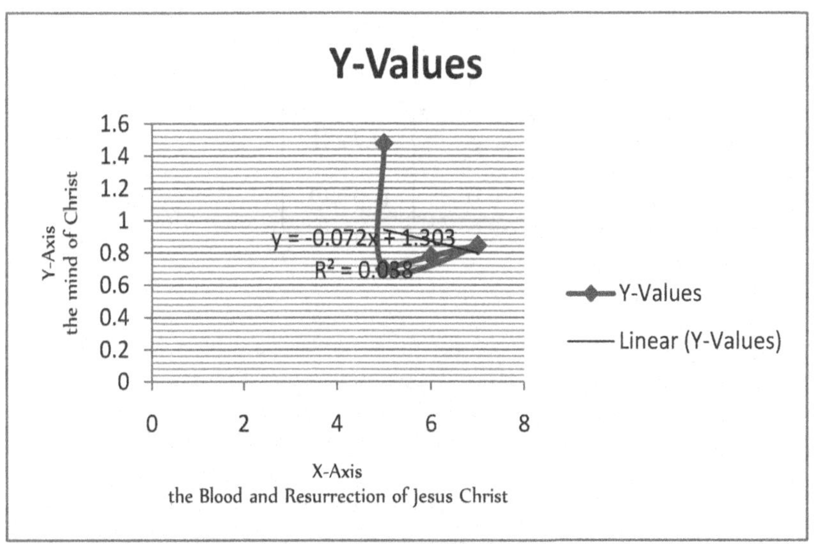

2^1 $10^{0.4771}$, $10^{0.6989}$, $10^{0.8450}$? $10^{0.7781}$? $10^{0.6989}$.

Pilled Poplar, Hazel, and Chestnut bible rods 2

18. And Jesussavior; deliverer**rebuked the devil** slanderer; false accuser; **and he departed out of him: and the child was cured from that very hour.**

5; 6: 9. Bible Matrices

$2_2 3_3$; 6_{10}: 9_{10}.

Pilled Poplar, Hazel, and Chestnut bible rods 1

$\text{Log}_{10} 9 = 0.9542$

$\text{Log}_2 2 = y$

$2^y = 2$

$2^y = 2^1$

$y = 1$

$\text{Log}_{10} 6 = 0.7781$

$\text{Log}_3 3 = y$

$3^y = 3$

$3^y = 3^1$

$y = 1$

5; 6: 9. Deep calls unto Deep study bible 1

1 1; 0.7781: 0.9542. Deep calls unto Deep study bible 2

x-axis	y-axis
5	2
6	0.7781
9	0.9542

Water Spout *(lightning;combinatorics)* Study bible 1

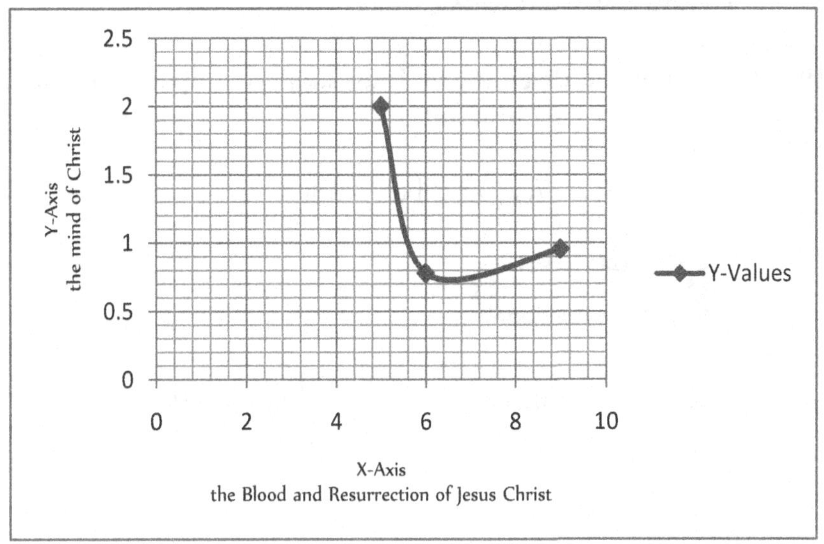

Water Spout *(lightning;combinatorics)* Study bible 2

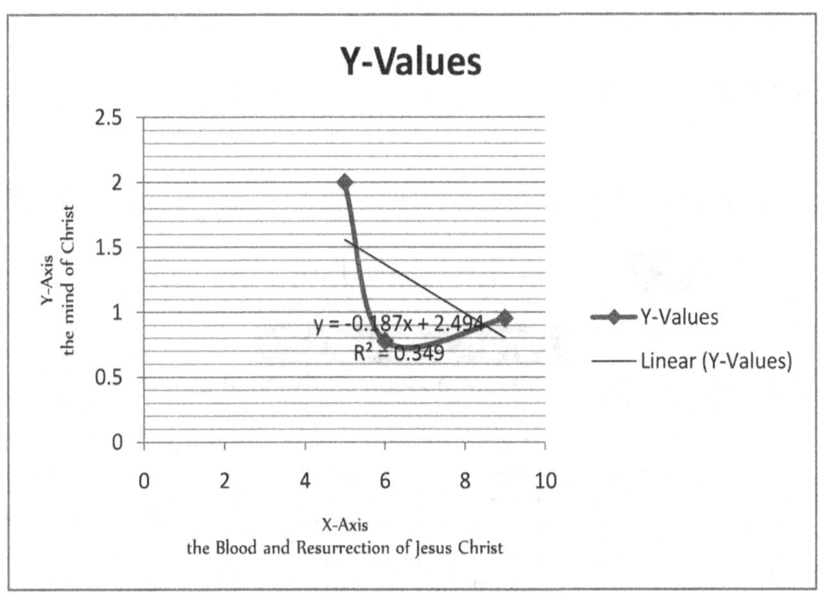

$2^1\ 3^1;\ 10^{0.7781}:\ 10^{0.9542}$.

Pilled Poplar, Hazel, and Chestnut bible rods 2

19. Then came the disciples to Jesussavior; deliverer **apart, and said, Why could not we cast him out?**

7, 2, 7? Bible Matrices

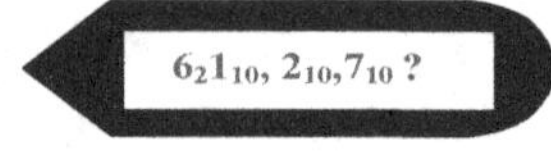

Pilled Poplar, Hazel, and Chestnut bible rods 1

$\text{Log}_{10} 2 = 0.3010$ $\text{Log}_{10} 7 = 0.8450$ $\text{Log}_{10} 1 = 0$

$\text{Log}_2 6 = y$

$2^y = 6$

$y \log_{10} 2 = \log_{10} 6$

$y = \log_{10} 6 / \log_{10} 2$

$y = 0.7781 / 0.3010$

$y = 2.5850$

7, 2, 7? Deep calls unto Deep study bible 1

2.5850 0, 0.3010, 0.8450.

Deep calls unto Deep study bible 2

x-axis	y-axis
7	2.5850
2	0.3010
7	0.8450

Water Spout *(lightning;combinatorics)* Study bible 1

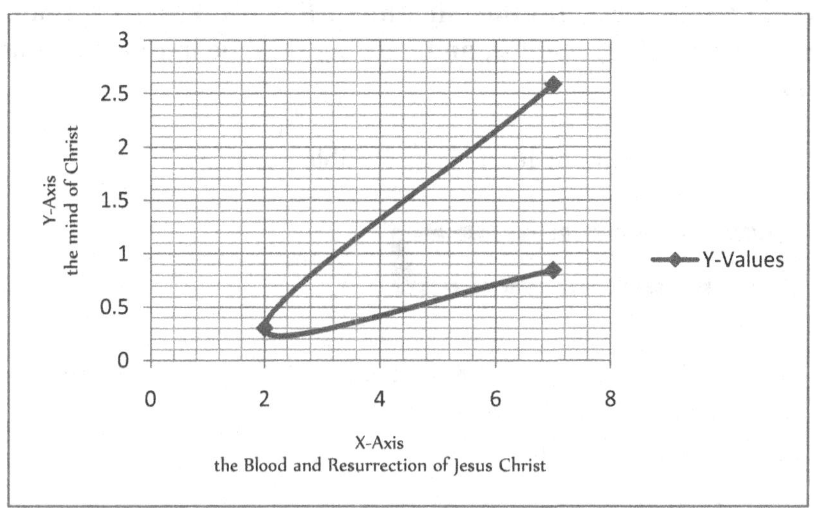

Water Spout *(lightning;combinatorics)* Study bible 2

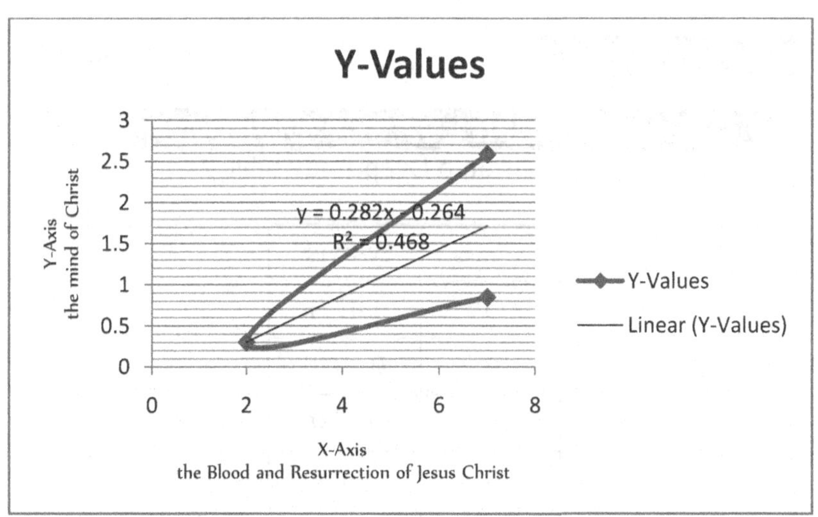

$2^{2.5850}\ 10^{0}, 10^{0.3010}, 10^{0.8450}$?

Pilled Poplar, Hazel, and Chestnut bible rods 2

20. And Jesus savior; deliverer**said unto them, Because of your unbelief: for verily I say unto you, If ye have faith as a grain of mustard seed, ye shall say unto this mountain, Remove hence to yonder place; and it shall remove; and nothing shall be impossible unto you.**

5, 4: 6, 10, 6, 5; 4; 7. Bible Matrices

$2_2\, 3_{10}, 4_{10}: 6_{10}, 10_{10}, 6_{10}, 5_{10}; 4_{10}; 7_{10}.$

Pilled Poplar, Hazel, and Chestnut bible rods 1

$\text{Log}_{10} 6 = 0.7781$ $\text{Log}_{10} 6 = 0.7781$ $\text{Log}_{10} 4 = 0.6020$ $\text{Log}_{10} 5 = 0.6989$

$\text{Log}_{10} 7 = 0.8450$ $\text{Log}_{10} 3 = 0.4771$

$\text{Log}_{10} 4 = 0.6020$ $\text{Log}_{10} 10 = 1$

$\text{Log}_2 2 = y$

$2^y = 2$

$2^y = 2^1$

$y = 1$

5, 4: 6, 10, 6, 5; 4; 7. Deep calls unto Deep study bible 1

1 0.4771, 0.6020: 0.7781, 1, 0.7781, 0.6989; 0.6020; 0.8450.

Deep calls unto Deep study bible 2

x-axis	y-axis
5	1.4771
4	0.6020
6	0.7781
10	1
6	0.7781
5	0.6989
4	0.6020
7	0.8450

Water Spout *(lightning;combinatorics)* Study bible 1

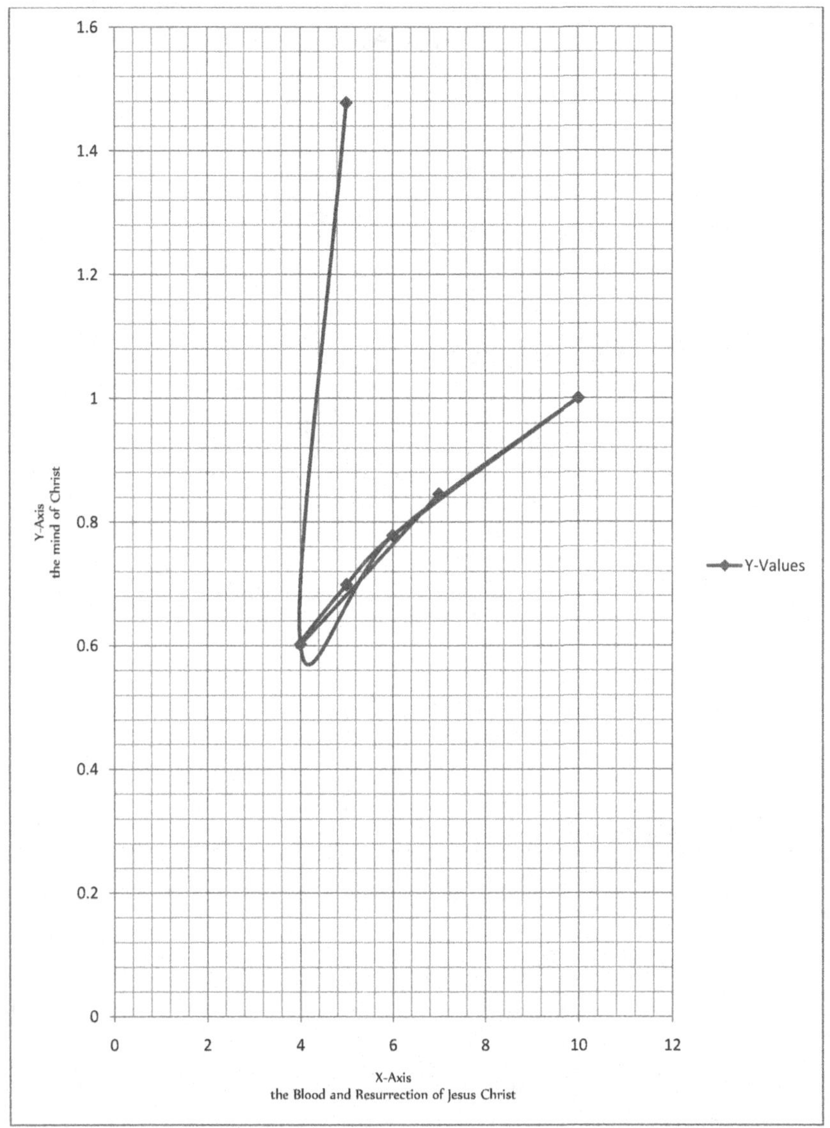

Water Spout *(lightning;combinatorics)* Study bible 2

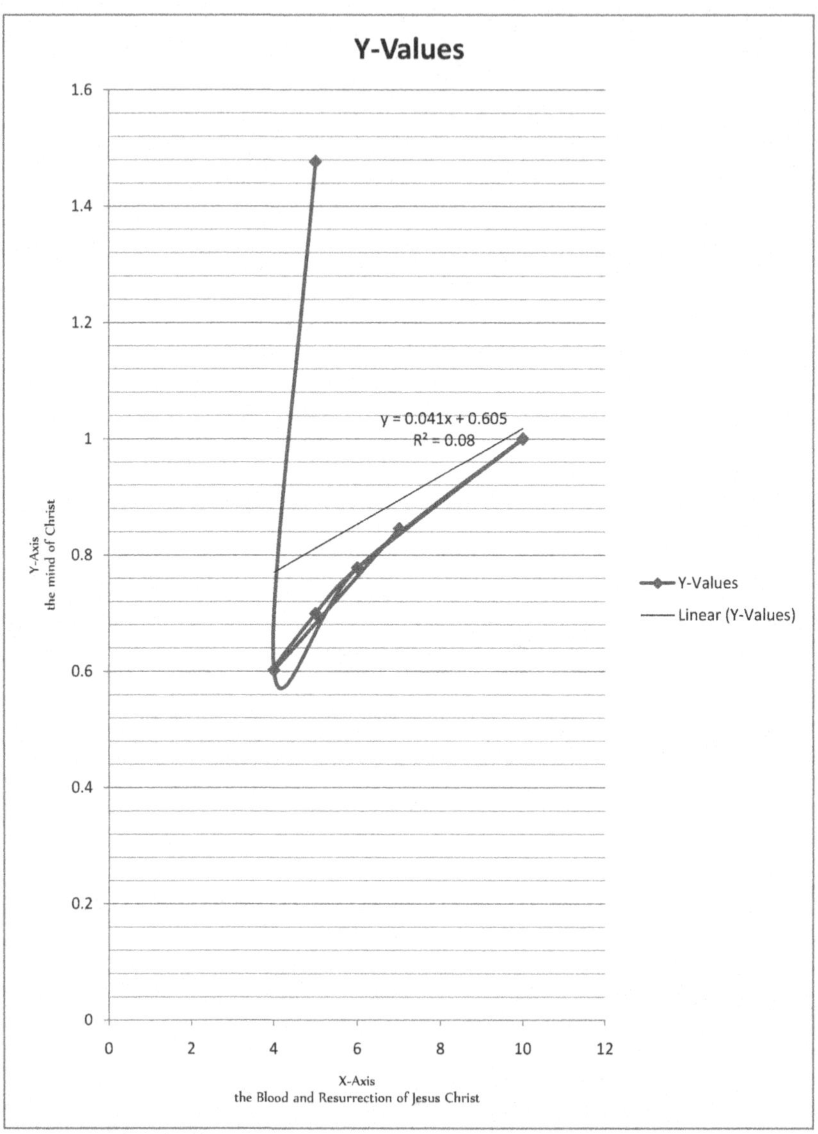

$2^1\ 10^{0.4771}, 10^{0.6020}: 10^{0.7781}, 10^1, 10^{0.7781}, 10^{0.6989}; 10^{0.6020}; 10^{0.8450}.$ Pilled Poplar, Hazel, and Chestnut bible rods 2

21. Howbeit this kind goeth not out but by prayer and fasting.

11. Bible Matrices

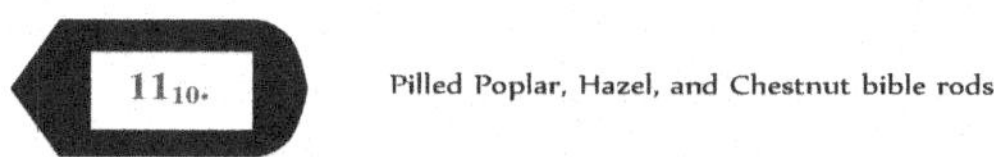

$\text{Log}_{10} 11 = 1.0413$

11. Deep calls unto Deep study bible 1

1.0413. Deep calls unto Deep study bible 2

x-axis	y-axis
11	1.0413

Water Spout *(lightning;combinatorics)* Study bible 1

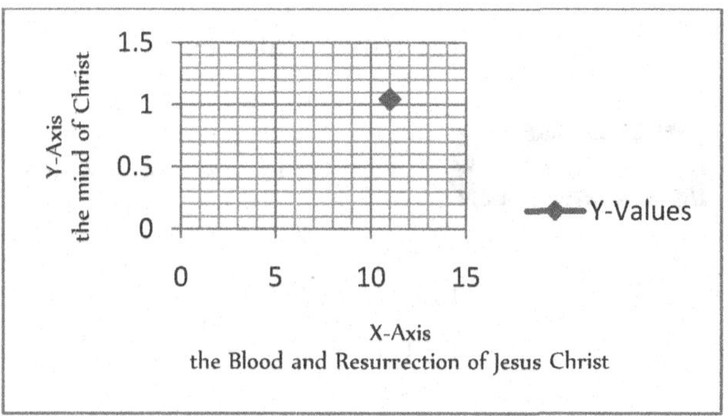

Water Spout *(lightning;combinatorics)* Study bible 2

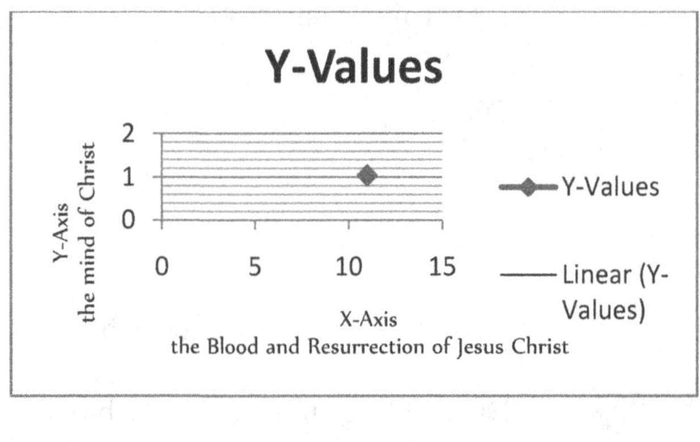

$10^{1.0413}$.

Pilled Poplar, Hazel, and Chestnut bible rods 2

22. And while they abode in Galileewheel; circle; revolution; circuit**, Jesus** savior; deliverer **said unto them, The Son of man shall be betrayed into the hands of men:**

6, 4, 12: Bible Matrices

$6_4, 1_2\, 3_{10}, 12_{10}$:

Pilled Poplar, Hazel, and Chestnut bible rods 1

$Log_{10} 4 = 0.6020$

$Log_4 6 = y$

$4^y = 6$

$y \log_{10} 4 = \log_{10} 6$

$y = \log_{10} 6 / \log_{10}$

$y = 0.7781 / 0.6020$

$y = 1.2925$

$Log_{10} 3 = 0.4771$

$Log_2 1 = y$

$2^y = 1$

$2^y = 2^0$

$4\,y = 0$

6, 4, 12: Deep calls unto Deep study bible 1

1.2925, 0 0.4771, 1.0791:

Deep calls unto Deep study bible 2

x-axis	y-axis
6	1.2925
4	0.4771
12	1.0791

Water Spout *(lightning;combinatorics)* Study bible 1

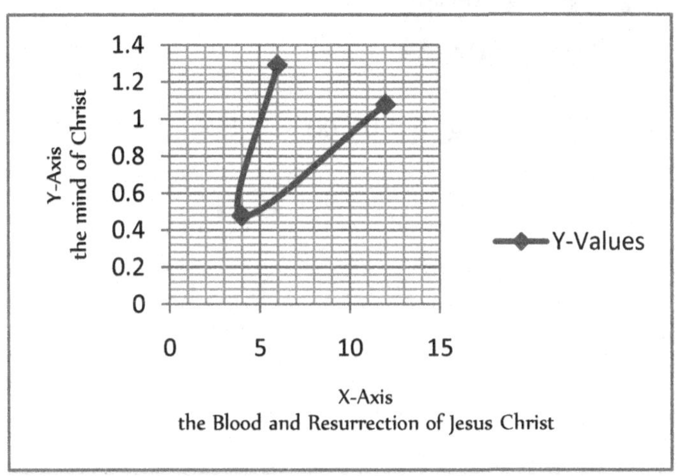

Water Spout *(lightning;combinatorics)* Study bible 2

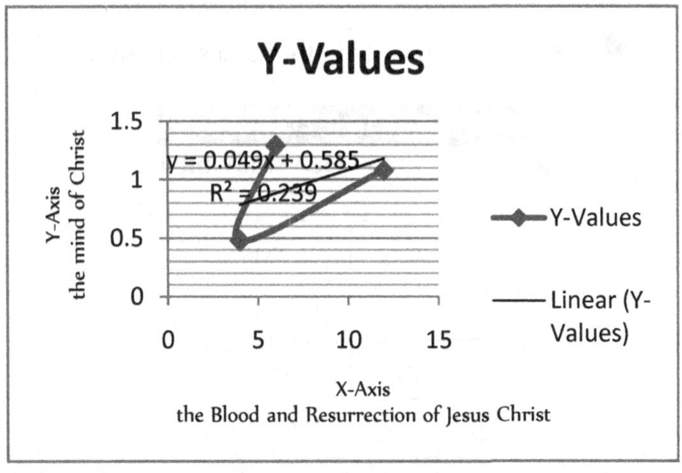

$4^{1.2925}, 2^{0}\ 10^{0.4771}, 10^{1.0791}$:

Pilled Poplar, Hazel, and Chestnut bible rods 2

23. And they shall kill him, and the third **completion or perfection, and unity; 3 x 1** **day he shall be raised again. And they were exceeding sorry.**

5, 9. 5. Bible Matrices

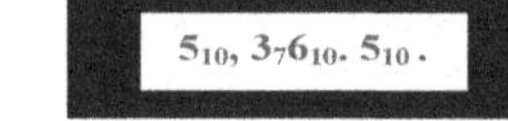

Pilled Poplar, Hazel, and Chestnut bible rods 1

$\text{Log}_{10} 5 = 0.6989$ $\text{Log}_{10} 6 = 0.7781$ $\text{Log}_{10} 5 = 0.6989$

$\text{Log}_{7} 3 = y$

$7^{y} = 3$

$y \log_{10} 7 = \log_{10} 3$

$y = \log_{10} 3 / \log_{10} 7$

$y = 0.4771 / 0.8450$

$y = 0.5646$

5, 9. 5. Deep calls unto Deep study bible 1

0.6989, 0.5646 0.7781. 0.6989.

Deep calls unto Deep study bible 2

x-axis	y-axis
5	0.6989
9	1.3427
5	0.6989

Water Spout *(lightning;combinatorics)* Study bible 1

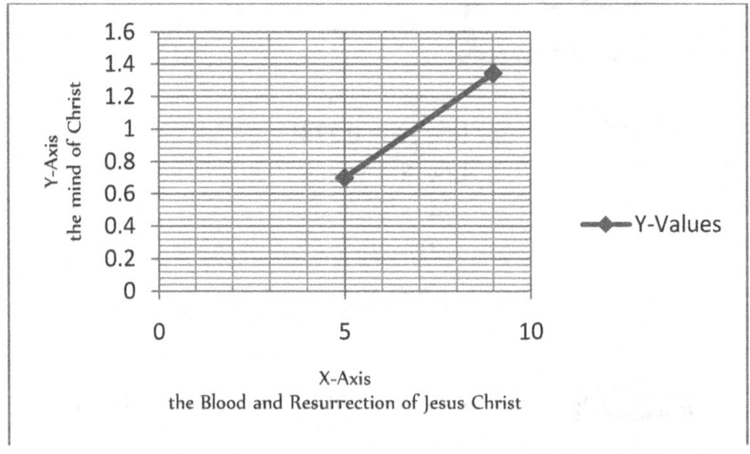

Water Spout *(lightning;combinatorics)* Study bible 2

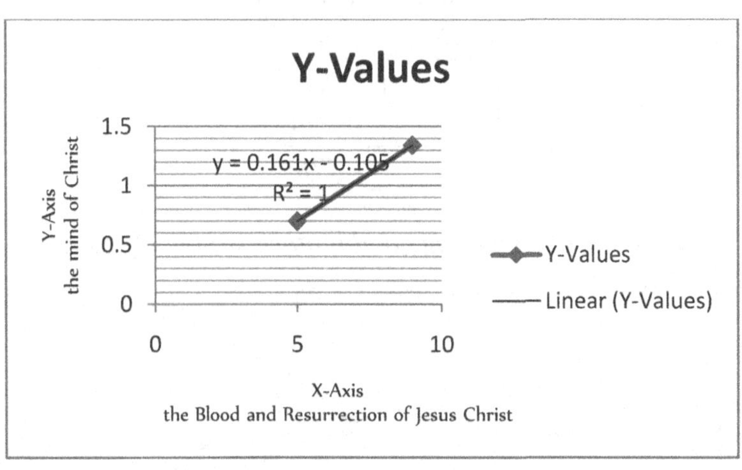

$10^{0.6989}$, $7^{0.5646}$ $10^{0.7781}$. $10^{0.6989}$.

Pilled Poplar, Hazel, and Chestnut bible rods 2

24. And when they were come to Capernaumthe field of repentance; city of comfort, **they that received tribute money came to Peter**a rock or stone, **and said, Doth not your master pay tribute?**

7, 8, 2, 6? Bible Matrices

$7_7, 8_4, 2_{10}, 6_{10}$? Pilled Poplar, Hazel, and Chestnut bible rods 1

$\text{Log}_{10} 2 = 0.3010$

$\text{Log}_7 7 = y$

$7^y = 7$

$7^y = 7^1$

$y = 1$

$y = 3/2$ or 1.5

$\text{Log}_{10} 6 = 0.7781$

$\text{Log}_4 8 = y$

$4^y = 8$

$2^{2y} = 2^3$

$2y = 3$

7, 8, 2, 6? Deep calls unto Deep study bible 1

1, 1.5, 0.3010, 0.7781? Deep calls unto Deep study bible 2

x-axis	y-axis
7	1
8	1.5
2	0.3010
6	0.7781

Water Spout *(lightning;combinatorics)* Study bible 1

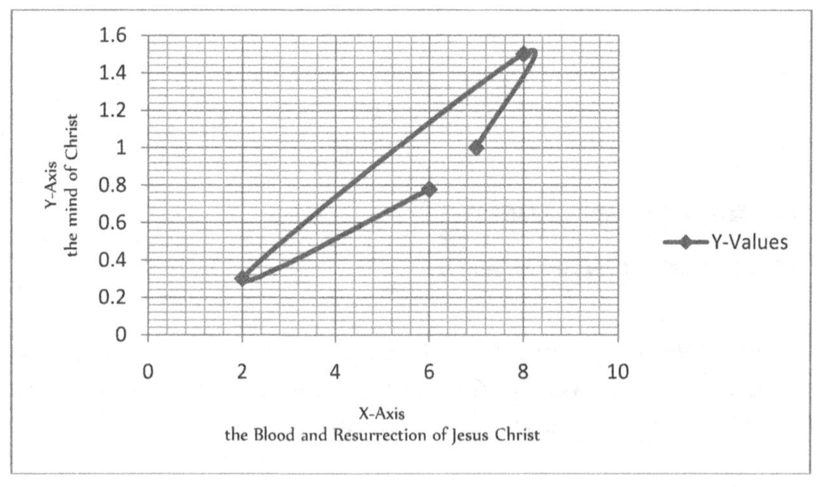

Water Spout *(lightning;combinatorics)* Study bible 2

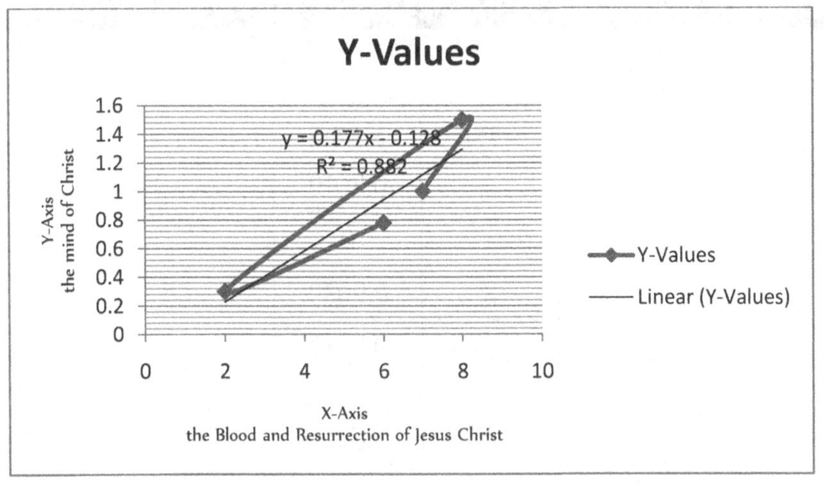

$7^1, 4^{1.5}, 10^{0.3010}, 10^{0.7781}$?

Pilled Poplar, Hazel, and Chestnut bible rods 2

25. He saith, Yes. And when he was come into the house, Jesussavior; deliverer **prevented him, saying, What thinkest thou, Simon**that hears; that obeys, **of whom do the kings of the earth take custom or tribute? of their own children, or of strangers?**

2, 1. 8, 3, 1, 3, 1? 12? 4, 3? Bible Matrices

$2_{10}, 1_{10}. 8_{10}, 1_2\, 2_{10}, 1_{10}, 3_{10}, 1_4? \; 12_{10}? \; 4_{10}, 3_{10}?$

Pilled Poplar, Hazel, and Chestnut bible rods 1

$\text{Log}_{10} 8 = 0.9030$	$\text{Log}_{10} 4 = 0.6020$	$\text{Log}_{10} 2 = 0.3010$	$\text{Log}_{10} 2 = 0.3010$
$\text{Log}_{10} 3 = 0.4771$	$\text{Log}_{10} 3 = 0.4771$		
$\text{Log}_{10} 12 = 1.0791$	$\text{Log}_{10} 1 = 0$	$\text{Log}_{10} 1 = 0$	
$\text{Log}_2 1 = y$	$\text{Log}_4 1 = y$		
$2^y = 1$	$4^y = 1$		
$2^y = 2^0$	$4^y = 4^0$		
$y = 0$	$y = 0$		

2, 1. 8, 3, 1, 3, 1? 12? 4, 3? Deep calls unto Deep study bible 1

0.3010, 0. 0.9030, 0 0.3010, 0, 0.4771, 0? 1.0791? 0.6020, 0.4771?
Deep calls unto Deep study bible 2

x-axis	y-axis
2	0.3010
1	0
8	0.9030
3	0.3010
1	0
3	0.4771
1	0
12	1.0791
4	0.6020
3	0.4771

Water Spout *(lightning;combinatorics)* Study bible 1

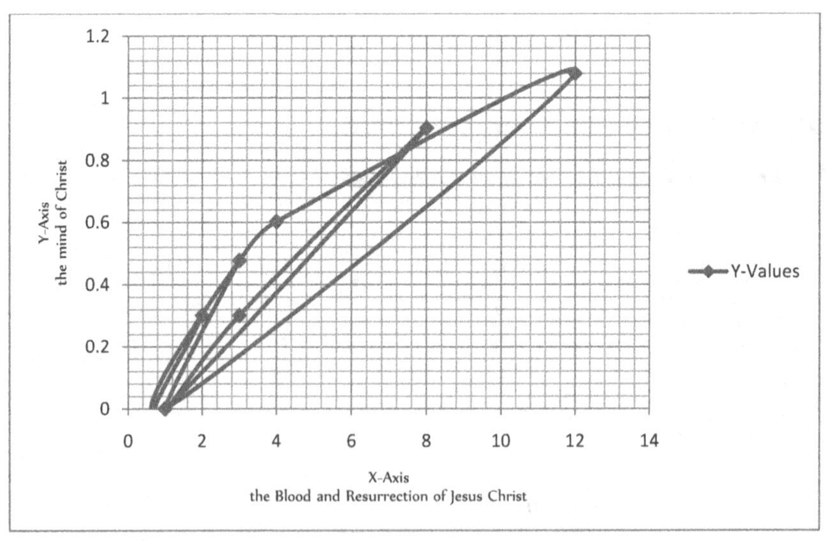

Water Spout *(lightning;combinatorics)* Study bible 2

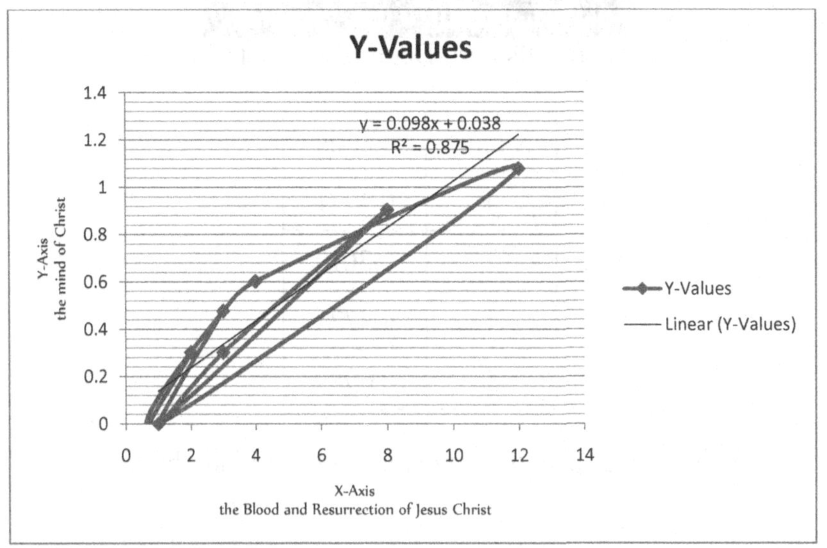

$10^{0.3010}, 10^{0}. 10^{0.9030}, 2^{0}$ $10^{0.3010}, 10^{0}, 10^{0.4771}, 4^{0}? 10^{1.0791}? 10^{0.6020}, 10^{0.4771}?$

Pilled Poplar, Hazel, and Chestnut bible rods 2

26. Peter a rock or stone **saith unto him, Of strangers. Jesus** savior; deliverer **saith unto him, Then are the children free.**

4, 2. 4, 5. Bible Matrices

$1_4 3_{10}, 2_{10}. 1_2 3_{10}, 5_{10}.$

Pilled Poplar, Hazel, and Chestnut bible rods 1

$\text{Log}_{10} 5 = 0.6989$ $\text{Log}_{10} 3 = 0.4771$ $\text{Log}_{10} 3 = 0.4771$ $\text{Log}_{10} 2 = 0.3010$

$\text{Log}_2 1 = y$

$2^y = 1$

$2^y = 2^0$

$y = 0$

$\text{Log}_4 1 = y$

$4^y = 1$

$4^y = 4^0$

$y = 0$

4, 2. 4, 5. Deep calls unto Deep study bible 1

0 0.4771, 0.3010. 0 0.4771, 0.6989.
Deep calls unto Deep study bible 2

x-axis	y-axis
4	0.4771
2	0.3010
4	0.4771
5	0.6989

Water Spout *(lightning;combinatorics)* Study bible 1

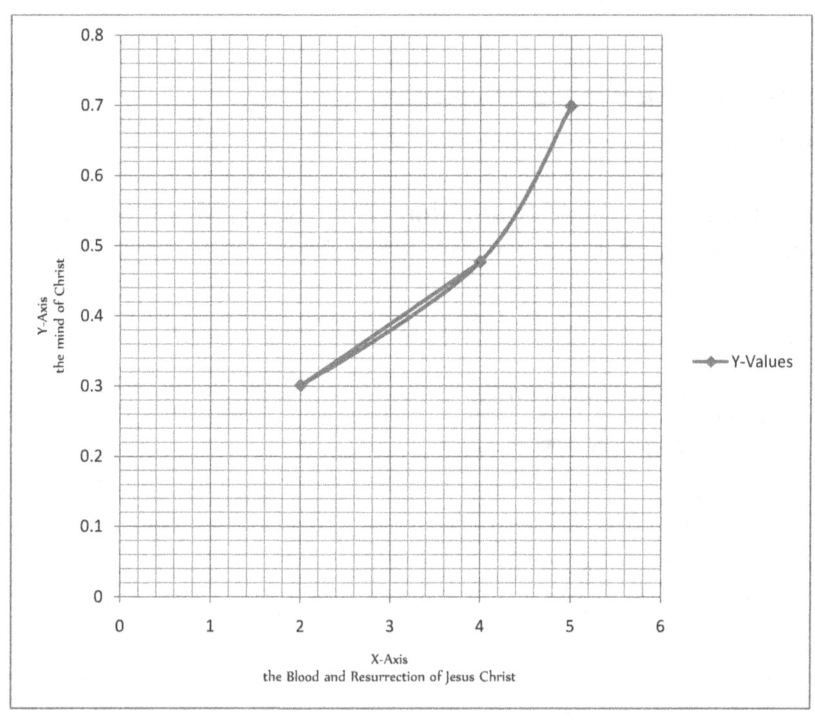

Water Spout *(lightning;combinatorics)* Study bible 2

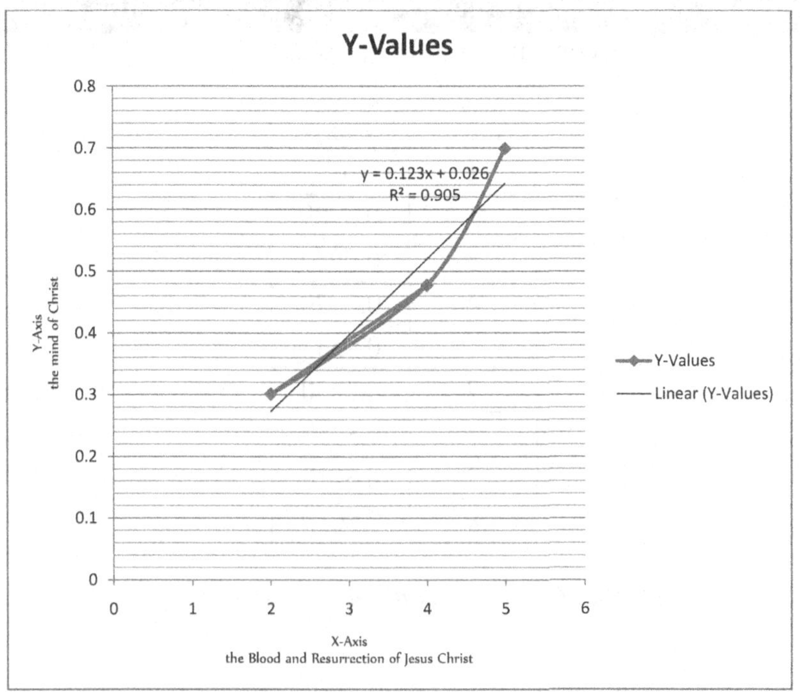

4^0 $10^{0.4771}$, $10^{0.3010}$. 2^0 $10^{0.4771}$, $10^{0.6989}$.

Pilled Poplar, Hazel, and Chestnut bible rods 2

27. Notwithstanding, lest we should offend them, go thou to the sea, and cast an hook, and take up the fish that first cometh up; and when thou hast opened his mouth, thou shalt find a piece of money: that take, and give unto them for me and thee.

1, 5, 5, 4, 9; 7, 7: 2, 8. Bible Matrices

1_{10}, 5_{10}, 5_{10}, 4_{10}, 9_{10}; 7_{10}, 7_{10}: 2_{10}, 8_{10}.

Pilled Poplar, Hazel, and Chestnut bible rods 1

$\text{Log}_{10} 8 = 0.9030$ $\text{Log}_{10} 4 = 0.6020$ $\text{Log}_{10} 5 = 0.6989$ $\text{Log}_{10} 5 = 0.6989$

$\text{Log}_{10} 7 = 0.8450$ $\text{Log}_{10} 7 = 0.8450$

$\text{Log}_{10} 9 = 0.9542$ $\text{Log}_{10} 2 = 0.3010$ $\text{Log}_{10} 1 = 0$

1, 5, 5, 4, 9; 7, 7: 2, 8. Deep calls unto Deep study bible 1

0, 0.6989, 0.6989, 0.6020, 0.9542; 0.8450, 0.8450: 0.3010, 0.9030.
Deep calls unto Deep study bible 2

x-axis	y-axis
1	0
5	0.6989
5	0.6989
4	0.6020
9	0.9542
7	0.8450
7	0.8450
2	0.3010
8	0.9030

Water Spout *(lightning;combinatorics)* Study bible 1

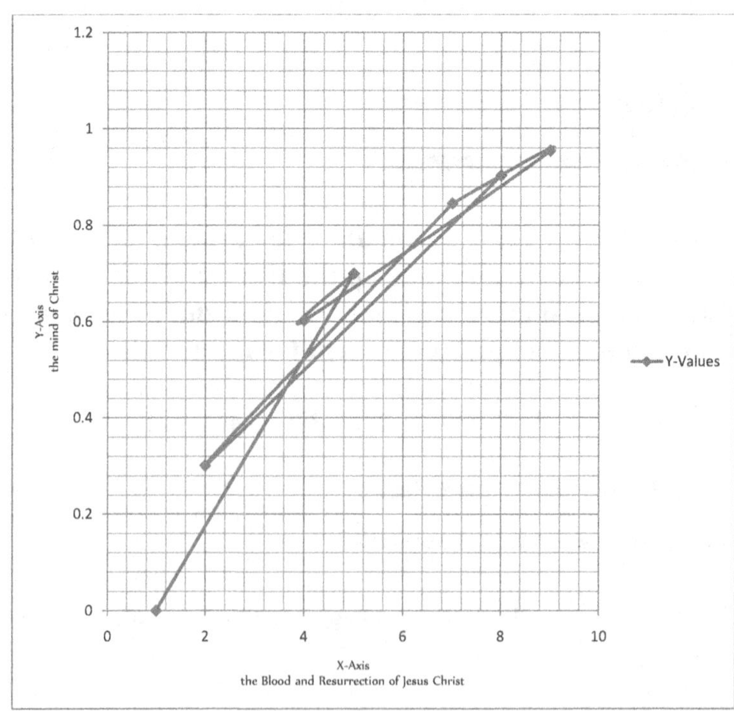

Water Spout *(lightning;combinatorics)* Study bible 2

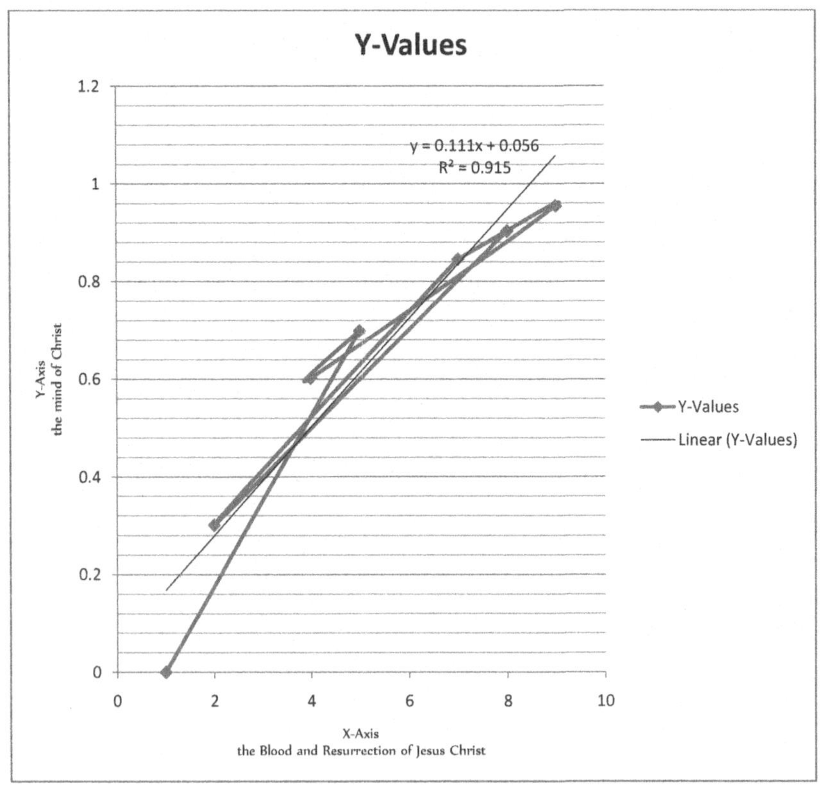

$10^{0}, 10^{0.6989}, 10^{0.6989}, 10^{0.6020}, 10^{0.9542}; 10^{0.8450}, 10^{0.8450}: 10^{0.3010}, 10^{0.9030}.$

Pilled Poplar, Hazel, and Chestnut bible rods 2

ABOUT THE AUTHOR

ABIOLA DEBORAH ADARAMOLA-ARIYEHUN, a Nigerian from Ekiti State in the western part of the country, the languages she speaks are Yoruba and English. She was born in Kano city and had both her primary and secondary education in Kano State, located in the northern part of the country. She attended the following tertiary institutions: University of Port-Harcourt, B.Sc Zoology; University of Calabar, PGD Education; University of Ibadan, M.Ed Exercise Physiology; Rutgers, The State University of New Jersey, U.S.A. BA Women and Gender Studies; University of Medicine and Dentistry, New Jersey. B Sc Nursing; Seton Hall University, New Jersey, MHA-(currently on-hold), she came back to Nigeria in 2012 to get married and founded Ellipsis-Lentiles Limited, a company that cater for the educational and health needs of the people.